DRAMA
CRITICISM

Guide to Gale Literary Criticism Series

For criticism on	Consult these Gale series
Authors now living or who died after December 31, 1999	*CONTEMPORARY LITERARY CRITICISM (CLC)*
Authors who died between 1900 and 1999	*TWENTIETH-CENTURY LITERARY CRITICISM (TCLC)*
Authors who died between 1800 and 1899	*NINETEENTH-CENTURY LITERATURE CRITICISM (NCLC)*
Authors who died between 1400 and 1799	*LITERATURE CRITICISM FROM 1400 TO 1800 (LC)* *SHAKESPEAREAN CRITICISM (SC)*
Authors who died before 1400	*CLASSICAL AND MEDIEVAL LITERATURE CRITICISM (CMLC)*
Authors of books for children and young adults	*CHILDREN'S LITERATURE REVIEW (CLR)*
Dramatists	*DRAMA CRITICISM (DC)*
Poets	*POETRY CRITICISM (PC)*
Short story writers	*SHORT STORY CRITICISM (SSC)*
Black writers of the past two hundred years	*BLACK LITERATURE CRITICISM (BLC)* *BLACK LITERATURE CRITICISM SUPPLEMENT (BLCS)*
Hispanic writers of the late nineteenth and twentieth centuries	*HISPANIC LITERATURE CRITICISM (HLC)* *HISPANIC LITERATURE CRITICISM SUPPLEMENT (HLCS)*
Native North American writers and orators of the eighteenth, nineteenth, and twentieth centuries	*NATIVE NORTH AMERICAN LITERATURE (NNAL)*
Major authors from the Renaissance to the present	*WORLD LITERATURE CRITICISM, 1500 TO THE PRESENT (WLC)* *WORLD LITERATURE CRITICISM SUPPLEMENT (WLCS)*

ISSN 1056-4349

DRAMA
CRITICISM

Criticism of the Most Significant and Widely Studied
Dramatic Works from all the World's Literatures

VOLUME 12

Linda Pavlovski, Editor

GALE GROUP

Detroit
New York
San Francisco
London
Boston
Woodbridge, CT

Library of Congress Catalog Card Number 92-648805
ISBN 0-7876-3140-X
ISSN 1056-4349
Printed in the United States of America

10 9 8 7 6 5 4 3 2 1

Contents

Preface

*D*rama Criticism (*DC*) is principally intended for beginning students of literature and theater as well as the average playgoer. The series is therefore designed to introduce readers to the most frequently studied playwrights of all time periods and nationalities and to present discerning commentary on dramatic works of enduring interest. Furthermore, *DC* seeks to acquaint the reader with the uses and functions of criticism itself. Selected from a diverse body of commentary, the essays in *DC* offer insights into the authors and their works but do not require that the reader possess a wide background in literary studies. Where appropriate, reviews of important productions of the plays discussed are also included to give students a heightened awareness of drama as a dynamic art form, one that many claim is fully realized only in performance.

DC was created in response to suggestions by the staffs of high school, college, and public libraries. These librarians observed a need for a series that assembles critical commentary on the world's most renowned dramatists in the same manner as Gale's *Short Story Criticism* (*SSC*) and *Poetry Criticism* (*PC*), which present material on writers of short fiction and poetry. Although playwrights are covered in such Gale literary criticism series as *Contemporary Literary Criticism* (*CLC*), *Twentieth-Century Literary Criticism* (*TCLC*), *Nineteenth-Century Literature Criticism* (*NCLC*), *Literature Criticism from 1400 to 1800* (*LC*), and *Classical and Medieval Literature Criticism* (*CMLC*), *DC* directs more concentrated attention on individual dramatists than is possible in the broader, survey-oriented entries in these Gale series. Commentary on the works of William Shakespeare may be found in *Shakespearean Criticism* (*SC*).

Scope of the Series

By collecting and organizing commentary on dramatists, *DC* assists students in their efforts to gain insight into literature, achieve better understanding of the texts, and formulate ideas for papers and assignments. A variety of interpretations and assessments is offered, allowing students to pursue their own interests and promoting awareness that literature is dynamic and responsive to many different opinions.

Approximately five to ten authors are included in each volume, and each entry presents a historical survey of the critical response to that playwright's work. The length of an entry is intended to reflect the amount of critical attention the author has received from critics writing in English and from foreign critics in translation. Every attempt has been made to identify and include the most significant essays on each author's work. In order to provide these important critical pieces, the editors sometimes reprint essays that have appeared elsewhere in Gale's literary criticism series. Such duplication, however, never exceeds twenty percent of a *DC* volume.

Organization of the Book

A *DC* entry consists of the following elements:

- The **Author Heading** consists of the playwright's most commonly used name, followed by birth and death dates. If an author consistently wrote under a pseudonym, the pseudonym is listed in the author heading and the real name given in parentheses on the first line of the introduction. Also located at the beginning of the introduction are any name variations under which the dramatist wrote, including transliterated forms of the names of authors whose languages use nonroman alphabets.

- The **Introduction** contains background information that introduces the reader to the author and the critical debates surrounding his or her work.

- A **Portrait of the Author** is included when available.

- The list of **Principal Works** is divided into two sections. The first section contains the author's dramatic pieces and is organized chronologically by date of first performance. If this has not been conclusively determined, the composition or publication date is used. The second section provides information on the author's major works in other genres.

- Essays offering **overviews and general studies of the dramatist's entire literary career** give the student broad perspectives on the writer's artistic development, themes, and concerns that recur in several of his or her works, the author's place in literary history, and other wide-ranging topics.

- **Criticism** of individual plays offers the reader in-depth discussions of a select number of the author's most important works. In some cases, the criticism is divided into two sections, each arranged chronologically. When a significant performance of a play can be identified (typically, the premier of a twentieth-century work), the first section of criticism will feature **production reviews** of this staging. Most entries include sections devoted to **critical commentary** that assesses the literary merit of the selected plays. When necessary, essays are carefully excerpted to focus on the work under consideration; often, however, essays and reviews are reprinted in their entirety. Footnotes are reprinted at the end of each essay or excerpt. In the case of excerpted criticism, only those footnotes that pertain to the excerpted texts are included.

- Critical essays are prefaced by brief **Annotations** explicating each piece.

- A complete **Bibliographic Citation,** designed to help the interested reader locate the original essay or book, precedes each piece of criticism.

- An annotated bibliography of **Further Reading** appears at the end of each entry and suggests resources for additional study. In some cases, significant essays for which the editors could not obtain reprint rights are included here. Boxed material following the further reading list provides references to other biographical and critical sources on the author in series published by Gale.

Cumulative Indexes

A **Cumulative Author Index** lists all of the authors that appear in a wide variety of reference sources published by the Gale Group, including *DC*. A complete list of these sources is found facing the first page of the Author Index. The index also includes birth and death dates and cross references between pseudonyms and actual names.

A **Cumulative Nationality Index** lists all authors featured in *DC* by nationality, followed by the number of the *DC* volume in which their entry appears.

A **Cumulative Title Index** lists in alphabetical order the individual plays discussed in the criticism contained in *DC*. Each title is followed by the author's last name and corresponding volume and page numbers where commentary on the work is located. English-language translations of original foreign-language titles are cross-referenced to the foreign titles so that all references to discussion of a work are combined in one listing.

Citing *Drama Criticism*

When writing papers, students who quote directly from any volume in *Drama Criticism* may use the following general formats to footnote reprinted criticism. The first example pertains to material drawn from periodicals, the second to materials reprinted from books.

Susan Sontag, "Going to the Theater, Etc.," *Partisan Review* XXXI, no. 3 (Summer 1964), 389-94; excerpted and reprinted in *Drama Criticism,* vol. 1, ed. Lawrence J. Trudeau (Detroit: Gale Research, 1991), 17-20.

Eugene M. Waith, *The Herculean Hero in Marlowe, Chapman, Shakespeare and Dryden* (Chatto & Windus, 1962); excerpted and reprinted in *Drama Criticism,* vol. 1, ed. Lawrence J. Trudeau (Detroit: Gale Research, 1991), 237-47.

Suggestions are Welcome

Readers who wish to suggest new features, topics, or authors to appear in future volumes, or who have other suggestions or comments are cordially invited to call, write, or fax the Managing Editor:

Managing Editor, Literary Criticism Series

The Gale Group

27500 Drake Road

Farmington Hills, MI 48331-3535

1-800-347-4253 (GALE)

Fax: 248-699-8054

Acknowledgments

The editors wish to thank the copyright holders of the excerpted criticism included in this volume and the permissions managers of many book and magazine publishing companies for assisting us in securing reproduction rights. We are also grateful to the staffs of the Detroit Public Library, the Library of Congress, the University of Detroit Mercy Library, Wayne State University Purdy/Kresge Library Complex, and the University of Michigan Libraries for making their resources available to us. Following is a list of the copyright holders who have granted us permission to reproduce material in this volume of *DC*. Every effort has been made to trace copyright, but if omissions have been made, please let us know.

COPYRIGHTED EXCERPTS IN *DC*, VOLUME 12, WERE REPRODUCED FROM THE FOLLOWING PERIODICALS:

COPYRIGHTED EXCERPTS IN *DC*, VOLUME 12, WERE REPRODUCED FROM THE FOLLOWING BOOKS:

Board of Regents of the State of Florida. Reproduced with the permission of the University Press of Florida..—Champion, Larry S. From *Thomas Dekker and the Traditions of English Drama.* Peter Lang, 1985. © Peter Lang Publishing, Inc., New York 1985. Reproduced by permission of the author.—Conover, James H. From *Thomas Dekker: An Analysis of Dramatic Struture.* Mouton, 1969. © Copyright 1969 in The Netherlands. Reproduced by permission of Mouton de Gruyter, a division of Walter de Gruyter & Co.—Cunard, Nancy. From *Negro: An Anthology.* Edited by Nancy Cunard and Hugh Ford. Frederick Ungar Publishing Company, 1970. Copyright © 1970 by Frederick Ungar Publishing Company, Inc. Reproduced by permission.—Gates, Jr., Henry Louis. From *Critical Essays on Zora Neale Hurston.* Edited by Gloria L. Cronin. G. K. Hall & Co., 1998. Copyright © 1998 by G. K. Hall & Co. Reproduced by permission.—Ionesco, Eugene. From *The Two Faces of Ionesco* by Rosette C. Lamont and Melvin J. Friedman. The Whitson Publishing Company, 1978. Copyright 1978 Rosette C. Lamont and Melvin J. Friedman. Reproduced by permission of the authors.—Kosok, Heinz. From *Irish Writers and The Theatre.* Edited by Masaru Sekine. Colin Smythe, 1986. Copyright © 1986 by Masaru Sekine and others. Reproduced by permission.—Krause, David. From an introduction to *Cock-A-Doodle Dandy.* By Sean O'Casey. The Catholic University of America Press, 1991. Copyright © 1991 The Catholic University of America Press. Reproduced by permission.—Krause, David. From *Cock-A-Doodle Dandy.* By Sean O'Casey. The Catholic University of America Press, 1991. Reproduced by permission.—Lamont, Rosette C. From *Inoesco's Imperatives: The Politics of Culture.* University of Michigan Press, 1993. Copyright © by the University of Michigan 1993. Reproduced by permission.—Langston, Hughes. From *Mule Bone: A Comedy of Negro Life.* Edited by George Houston Bass and Henry Louis Gates, Jr. HarperPerennial, 1991. Introductions copyright © 1991 by George Houston Bass and Henry Louis Gates, Jr. Reproduced by permission of HarperCollins Publishers.—Leidner, Alan C. From *Friedrich Von Schiller and The Drama of Human Existence.* Edited by Alexej Ugrinsky. Greenwood Press, 1988. Copyright © 1988 by Hofstra University. Reproduced by permission of Greenwood Publishing Group, Inc., Westport, CT.—Pacheco, Patrick. From *Critical Essays on Zora Neale Hurston.* Edited by Gloria L. Cronin. G. K. Hall & Co., 1998. Copyright © 1998 by G. K. Hall & Co. Reproduced by permission.—Price, George R. From *Thomas Dekker.* Twayne Publishers, Inc., 1969. Copyright © 1969 by Twayne Publishers, Inc. All rights reserved. Reproduced by permission.—Rich, Frank. From *Critical Essays on Zora Neale Hurston.* Edited by Gloria L. Cronin. G. K. Hall & Co., 1998. Copyright © 1998 by G. K. Hall & Co. Reproduced by permission.—Roberts, Patrick. From *The Psychology of Tragic Drama.* Routledge and Kegan Paul, 1975. © 1975 Patrick Roberts. Reproduced by permission.—Sharpe, Lesley. From *The World's Classics: Friedrich Schiller, Don Carlos and Mary Stuart.* Translated by Hilary Collier Sy-Quia. Oxford University Press, 1996. Translation copyright © Hilary Collier Sy-Quia and Peter Oswald 1996. Reproduced by permission.—Shirley, Peggy Faye. From *Serious and Tragic Elements In The Comedy of Thomas Dekker.* Institut Fur Englische Sprache Und Literatur Universitat Salzburg, 1975. Reproduced by permission.—Sontag, Susan. From *Against Interpretation and Other Essays.* Farrar, Straus & Giroux, 1966. Reproduced by permission of Farrar, Straus and Giroux, LLC. In the U.K. by the author.—Ungar, Frederick. From *Friedrich Schiller: An Anthology for Our Time.* Frederick Ungar Publishing Co., 1959. Copyright © 1959 by Frederick Ungar Publishing Co. Reproduced by permission.—Wells, G. A. From *Deutung und Bedeuntung: Studies in German and Comparative Literature Presented by Karl-Werner Mauer.* Edited by Brigitte Schludermann, Victor G. Doerksen, Robert J. Glendinning, and Evelyn Scherabon Firchow. © Copyright 1973 in The Netherlands Mouton & Co., N. V., Publishers, The Hague. Reproduced by permission of Mouton de Gruyter, a division of Walter de Gruyter & Co.—Witte, William. From *Schiller.* Basil Blackwell, 1949. Reproduced by permission.

PHOTOGRAPHS APPEARING IN *DC*, VOLUME 12, WERE RECEIVED FROM THE FOLLOWING SOURCES:

Dekker, Thomas, photograph. The Gamma Liaison Network. Reproduced by permission.—Hurston, Zora Neale, photograph. AP/Wide World Photos. Reproduced by permission.—Ionesco, Eugene, photograph. The Library of Congress.—O'Casey, Sean, photograph. The Library of Congress.—Schiller, Friedrich von (left arm resting on desk, holding a book), engraving. The German Information Center.

Thomas Dekker
1572-1632

English dramalist and essayist.

INTRODUCTION

A prolific author, Dekker wrote, alone or in collaboration, over forty plays, of which seventeen survive. His best-known dramas include *The Shoemaker's Holiday, Old Fortunatus, The Honest Whore,* and *The Witch of Edmonton.* He is also noted for having produced numerous pamphlets, such as *The Wonderful Yeare, The Belman of London, Lanthorne and Candle-Light,* and *A Rod for Run-Awayes,* which provide detailed pictures of the life of Elizabethan and Jacobean London. Admired in his own time for his writings in both comic and tragic veins, Dekker's reputation fell greatly during the eighteenth century but has been rehabilitated by a number of twentieth-century critics who praise Dekker for his romanticism, his ethical concerns, and his considerable, if sometimes uneven, craftsmanship in both drama and prose.

BIOGRAPHICAL INFORMATION

Dekker was born in London, possibly to a Dutch family, as scholars deduce from both his surname and his evident familiarity with Dutch language in *The Shoemaker's Holiday* and other works. Nothing is known of his life until the 1590s, when his name began appearing in theatrical documents. A 1594 entry in The Stationer's Register—a record of works licensed for publication—lists a "Tho: Decker" as the author of a drama entitled *The Jew of Venice,* a work that no longer survives. The next evidence of Dekker's activities dates from 1597, when theater manager Philip Henslowe recorded in his professional diary the hiring of Dekker to write and adapt plays for his company, the Lord Admiral's Men. Subsequent entries in Henslowe's diary indicate that during his tenure with the Lord Admiral's Men, Dekker had a hand in the composition or revision of dozens of plays, at times working with as many as three or four other writers. In the opening years of the seventeenth century, Dekker became involved in "the War of the Theaters," a literary quarrel in which Ben Jonson ridiculed both Dekker and John Marston in several plays, most notably *Poetaster* (1601). Dekker responded by mocking Jonson in *Satiro-Mastix. Or The Untrussing of the Humorous Poet.* Dekker wrote steadily for Henslowe until 1603, when the death of Elizabeth I, followed shortly by an outbreak of the plague, resulted in the closing of London's theaters. For the time deprived of the means to support himself by playwriting, Dekker turned to compos-

ing prose pamphlets. The epidemic prompted Dekker to publish *The Wonderful Yeare,* a collection of anecdotes, religious meditations, and lamentations for those who died. Surprisingly, in 1604 Dekker was jointly commissioned with Jonson to compose the pageant celebrating the coronation of James I. The two writers remained antipathetic to one another, however, and each published separately his share in the pageant, which was titled *The Magnificent Entertainment.* With the reopening of the theaters Dekker returned to drama, writing both parts of *The Honest Whore* in 1604-05. About two years later Dekker appears to have stopped writing for the stage, and for the next five years he concentrated exclusively on producing pamphlets. He returned to playwriting in 1611, but this activity was soon terminated as he was imprisoned for debt. He was, however, able to continue composing pamphlets, and he published several while in prison. After his release in 1619, Dekker worked with Samuel Rowley, John Ford, and others, creating such works as *The Virgin Martir* and *The Witch of Edmonton.* Dekker died sometime around 1632.

MAJOR WORKS

As a result of the varied conditions and diverse genres in which Dekker wrote, scholars find that his work as a whole is hard to characterize. One of his hallmarks, however, is comic, often raucous, banter. Even his religious play *The Virgin Martir* includes bawdy dialogue, which is given to the pagan antagonists of the title character Dorothea, contrasting their sensuality with her sanctity. Dekker is also often credited with a profound sensitivity to the plight of the poor, the laboring classes, and, particularly, the victims of persecution. Several critics have pointed out that the speeches of jailed prostitutes in Part Two of *The Honest Whore* indict society's indifference to poor women as a major cause of prostitution. In addition, Mother Sawyer, the eponymous witch of Edmonton, is sympathetically portrayed, making a pact with the devil only in response to her neighbors' cruel taunts regarding her ugliness and poverty. *The Shoemaker's Holiday,* perhaps Dekker's most popular work, is commonly regarded as a celebration of working-class life. This comedy depicting the rise of Simon Eyre to the position of Lord Mayor offers several portraits of honorable tradespeople and laborers. Dekker's compassion for the poor and suffering is also reflected in his pamphlets; for example, *The Wonderful Yeare* castigates those of his contemporaries who, fearing contagion, refused to nurse or comfort victims of the plague.

CRITICAL RECEPTION

Appraisals of Dekker's works have varied widely over the years. While in the seventeenth century Jonson satirized him as "Demetrius Fannius," an impoverished and incompetent "dresser of plays" in *Poetaster,* William Fennor praised Dekker as "the true heire of Appolo" in his *The Comptor's Commonwealth* (1617), and Edward Phillips lauded him as "a high-flier in wit" in his *Theatrum poetarum anglicanorum* (1675). In the eighteenth century Dekker was generally held in low esteem. For instance, Charles Dibdin, writing in 1795, censured the structure of Dekker's plays and maintained that it was "very probable that [Dekker] could not have been half so well respected as he was," were it not for his famous rivalry with Jonson. Subsequent critics frequently charged Dekker's plays with poor construction, though his reputation rose again in the early nineteenth century, when critics such as William Hazlitt and Charles Lamb praised him for the imaginative situations and believable characterizations in his dramas. Both Lamb and Hazlitt expressed admiration for Dekker's lyrical qualities, as did many later critics. In the Victorian period a number of writers lauded Dekker's compassion for the lower classes while condemning his coarse language and sexual humor. Early twentieth-century opinion continued to reproach Dekker's dramatic technique and considered the quality of his verse uneven and generally inferior to that of his prose.

Significantly, many critics now judge one of Dekker's greatest strengths to be his versatile prose style, which, as demonstrated in his pamphlets as well as his plays, is capable of both dignified formality and lively colloquialism. Recent commentary has increasingly examined Dekker's drama in the context of his overall literary output, with many critics finding a consistent moral view expressed throughout his work. Other modern scholars have challenged the notion that Dekker's plays are poorly integrated, citing thematic patterns, unified plots, consistency of characterization, and other evidence of Dekker's craftsmanship. With such studies has come a heightened appreciation of Dekker as an artist who, as Larry S. Champion has asserted, "genuinely deserves a considerably higher place in the development and maturation of Elizabethan-Jacobean-Caroline drama than most previous critics have been willing to acknowledge."

PRINCIPAL WORKS

Plays

The Jew of Venice 1594?
Black Bateman of the North, Part 1 [with Henry Chettle, Michael Drayton, and Robert Wilson] 1598
The Civil Wars of France 3 parts [with Drayton] 1598
Conan, Prince of Cornwall [with Drayton] 1598
Earle Godwin and His Sons 2 parts [with Chettle, Drayton, and Wilson] 1598
The Famous Wars of Henry I and the Prince of Wales [with Chettle and Drayton; also known as *The Welshman's Prize*] 1598
Hannibal and Hermes [with Chettle, Drayton, and Wilson] 1598
The Mad Man's Morris [with Drayton and Wilson] 1598
Phaeton 1598
Pierce of Winchester [with Drayton and Wilson] 1598
The Triangle (or Triplicity) of Cuckholds 1598
Worse Afeard than Hurt [with Drayton] 1598
Agamemnon [with Chettle; possibly the same play as *Orestes' Furies*] 1599
Page of Plymouth [with Ben Jonson] 1599
The Pleasant Comedie of Old Fortunatas 1599
The Shoemaker's Holiday. Or The Gentle Craft. With the Life of Simon Eyre, Shoomaker, and Lord Maior of London 1599
The Stepmother's Tragedy [with Chettle] 1599
The Tragedy of Robert II, King of Scots [with Chettle, Jonson, and Marston] 1599
Troilus and Cressida [with Chettle] 1599
Fair Constance of Rome, Part 1 [with Drayton, Wilson, Anthony Munday, and Richard Hathaway] 1600
Fortune's Tennis 1600
The Golden Ass, or Cupid and Psyche [with Chettle and John Day] 1600
Lust's Dominion, or The Lascivious Queen [with Marston, Day, and William Haughton; possibly the same play as *The Spanish Moor's Tragedy*] 1600

The Pleasant Comodie of Patient Grissill [with Chettle and Haughton] 1600

The Seven Wise Masters [with Chettle, Day, and Haughton] 1600

Satiro-Mastix. Or The Untrussing of the Humorous Poet 1601

Sebastian, King of Portugal [with Chettle] 1601

Blurt, Master Constable. Or The Spaniard's Night-Walke 1601-02

Ceasar's Fall [with Drayton, Munday, Middleton, and John Webster; also known as *Two Shapes*] 1602

Christmas Comes but Once a Year [with Chettle, Heywood, and Webster] 1602

Jephthah [with Munday] 1602

A Medicine for a Curst Wife 1602

The Famous History of Sir T. Wyat. With the Coronation of Queen Mary [with Webster, Chettle, Heywood, and Wentworth Smith; possibly the same play as *Lady Jane*] 1602

The Honest Whore, with, the Humours of the Patient Man, and the Longing Wife [with Thomas Middleton] 1604

West-ward Hoe [with Webster] 1604

The Second Part of The Honest Whore, With the Humours of the Patient Man, the Impatient Wife 1604-05

North-ward Hoe [with Webster] 1605

The Whore of Babylon 1605-06

The Roaring Girle, or Moll Cut-purse [with Middleton] 1611

If This Be Not a Good Play, the Devil Is in It 1611

Guy of Warwick [with Day] 1620

The Virgin Martir, A Tragedie [with Philip Massinger] 1620

A Tragi-Comedy: Called, Match Mee in London 1621?

The Witch of Edmonton, A known true Story. Composed into a Tragi-Comedy By divers well-esteemed Poets [with William Rowley and John Ford] 1621

The Noble Spanish Soldier. Or, A Contract Broken, Justly Reveng'd. A Tragedy. [with Day] c. 1622

The Wonder of a Kingdom [with Day] c. 1623

The Bristow Merchant [with Ford] 1624

The Fairy Knight [with Ford] 1624

The Late Murder of the Son upon the Mother [with Ford, Rowley, and Webster] 1624

The Sun's Darling: A Moral Masque [with Ford] 1624

Pageants

The Magnificent Entertainment: Given to King James upon His Passage through London 1604

Troia-Nova Triumphans. London Triumphing, or, The Solemne, Receiving of Sir J. Sinerton After Taking the Oath of Maioralty 1612

Lord Mayor's pageant 1627

Britannia's Honor: Brightly Shining in Severall Magnificent Shewes or Pageants, to Celebrate R. Deane, at His Inauguration into the Majoralty of London, October the 29th. 1628 1628

London's Tempe, or the Feild of Happines. To Celebrate J. Campebell, at His Inauguration into the Maioralty of London, the 29 of October, 1629 1629

Pamphlets

1603. The Wonderfull Yeare. Wherein Is Shewed the Picture of London, Lying Sicke of the Plague 1603

The Meeting of Gallants at an Ordinarie: or The Walkes in Powles, 1604

Newes from Graves-End: Sent to Nobody 1604

The Double PP. A Papist in Armes. Encountered by the Protestant. A Jesuite Marching before Them 1606

Jests to Make You Merie: With the Conjuring Up of Cock Watt [with George Wilkins] 1607

Newes from Hell; Brought by the Divells Carrier 1606; enlarged as *A Knights Conjuring. Done in Earnest: Discovered in Jest,* 1607

The Seven Deadly Sinnes of London: Drawne in Seven Severall Coaches, Through the Citie Bringing the Plague with Them 1606

The Belman of London: Bringing to Light the Most Notorious Villanies Now Practised in the Kingdome 1608

The Dead Tearme. Or Westminsters Complaint for Long Vacations and Short Termes 1608

Lanthorne and Candle-light. Or the Bell-mans Second Nights Walke 1608; amended edition, 1609; enlarged as *O per se o, or a new crier of Lanthorne and Candle-Light,* 1612; enlarged again as *Villanies Discovered by Lanthorne and Candle-Light,* 1616; enlarged again, 1620; enlarged again as *English Villanies,* 1632

Foure Birds of Noahs Arke 1609

The Guls Horne-Booke 1609

The Ravens Almanacke Foretelling of a Plague, Famine, and Civill Warre 1609

Worke for Armorours: or, The Peace Is Broken 1609

The Artillery Garden 1616

Dekker His Dreame. In Which, the Great Volumes of Heaven and Hell to Him Were Opened 1620

A Rod for Run-Awayes. Gods Tokens, of His Feareful Judgements, upon This City 1625

London Looke Backe, at That Yeare of Yeares 1625 1628

Warres, Warres, Warres 1628

The Blacke Rod: and the White Rod 1630

Penny-Wise Pound Foolish or, a Bristow Diamond, Set in Two Rings, and Both Crack'd 1631

OVERVIEWS AND GENERAL STUDIES

Normand Berlin (essay date 1966)

SOURCE: "Thomas Dekker: A Partial Reappraisal," in *Studies in English Literature 1500-1900,* Vol. VI, No. 2, Spring 1966, pp. 263-77.

[*In the following essay, Berlin contends that Dekker's works demonstrate that the playwright is "genuinely moral and often angry," adding: "When he can draw clear moral lines, solidified by a love for the class which originally drew these lines, he presents aesthetically satisfying drama."*]

Compared to other Elizabethan and Jacobean dramatists, Thomas Dekker has received little critical attention in recent years. It seems that the last word has been said about this profilic dramatist. All the clichés describing him are known and generally accepted by students of the drama. He has become a stereotype—the gentle, tolerant, lovable "moral sloven" who had his hand in too many plays, who occasionally sang a sweet song, who could at times present lively characters. Having been fixed in a formulated phrase, having been pinned, one can hardly see him wriggling on the critical wall. The purpose here is not to demonstrate the falsity of the stereotype, which often hits the truth, but to investigate Dekker's particular qualities of mind and art that produced such a stereotype, and to indicate that Dekker is more angry and more morally earnest than is commonly recognized. The fact is that the epithet "gentle" describes only one side of Dekker's character, and the condemnation of Dekker as a "moral sloven," although basically correct, needs discussion. For Dekker is essentially a stern moralist. Demonstrating this does not make him a better dramatist, but it will set the record straight.

Because M. C. Bradbrook accepts and forcefully transmits the Dekker stereotype in her *Growth and Structure of Elizabethan Comedy,* her clear views can represent the usual reaction to Dekker.[1] Bradbrook finds that Dekker's plays "have moments of tenderness, gleams of pathos, but the general effect is too often amorphous and blurred" (p. 121). She mentions his virtues of "sympathy, tolerance and spontaneity" (p. 122). She states that "Dekker writes at his best when he collaborates with someone who will stiffen the plot and provide him with clear outlines of character upon which he can impress his own lyric tenderness or gaiety" (p. 125). She alludes to his "incorrigible cheerfulness and unteachable simplicity" (p. 131). And she judges that "Dekker, in his easy pity and boundless tolerance, appears something of a moral sloven" (p. 125). Much of his writing, however, seems to belie each of these statements. The general effect of many of his plays, in and out of collaboration, is not blurred. His tolerance is not boundless, nor is his pity easy.

His three rogue pamphlets—*The Belman of London, Lanthorne and Candle-Light,* and *O per se O*—are perhaps the best place to begin a discussion of the "other" Dekker, for they not only display his anger but they also clearly present the clue to understanding Dekker's entire literary output. Most of the material in the rogue pamphlets is plagiarized from Thomas Harman and Robert Greene, but the pamphlets indicate an attitude toward the underworld which is far more condemnatory than any of his contemporaries. He emphasizes that the members of the underworld, whether they be wandering rogues or city sharpers, are "professed foes to the Republic, to honesty, to civility, and to all humanity." They are "savages," "monsters," "ugly

. . . in shape and divelish in conditions," "Wilde and Barbarous Rebels . . . in open armes against the Tranquility of the Weale publique." Their only cure is the gallows. To Dekker the underworld is a hell on earth, a source of disorder and confusion in the commonwealth. He is vehement in his denunciation of the underworld, strong in his hatred of the underworld—and always moral. No rogue in a Dekker pamphlet is allowed to repent, although repentance was a common practice in rogue literature. Dekker's anger and hatred stem from the important fact that thecitizens of London and England were the victims of the city and country thieves. It is his love for the citizens that puts him closer to the official enemies of the underworld than to the rogue pamphleteers. Whereas Greene, a Bohemian, can see the charm as well as the harm of the underworld, Dekker, a member of the bourgeoisie and a lover of the citizen class, can see only the harm. His love for the citizen world not only makes Dekker an angry man in behalf of the citizens, but is the most revealing focus for understanding his moral bias. His is the traditional strict morality of the middle-class which at times strongly suggests Puritan fervor.

The Shoemakers' Holiday is Dekker's most popular play and is the source for most of the epithets describing him. In it he displays in dramatic action his love for the citizens. Forgiveness and love and patriotism and pride in work are part of the play's atmosphere. Whether these qualities represent the citizen world as Dekker sees it or whether they are idealized—it is often difficult to make this kind of distinction in Dekker's plays—they still point to Dekker's moral seriousness. This play alone seems to justify the belief that the writer himself is "cheery, friendly, lovable."[2] "Nothing is purposed but mirth," says Dekker, and mirth is what he gives his audience. The joy in life is the keynote of the play, a joy only hinted at in Dekker's other plays. Dekker presents no elements to destroy this joy. The Ralph-Jane story is presented with a sweet kind of sadness, the audience knowing that Jane will always be true to her husband. Jane's display of loyalty for Ralph is unquestionably a Dekkerian ideal for citizen conduct, against which the behavior of citizens' wives of other plays must be measured. Once Lacy becomes an apprentice of Simon Eyre, the audience has no fear that Lacy will get his Rose. An apprentice of Simon Eyre must be happy! A reader of all of Dekker's plays can discern why this is the healthiest and liveliest—Dekker is portraying the people, the world, he loves most, and he is dealing with them exclusively. (The King is absorbed in the Eyre atmosphere and Lacy becomes a shoemaker's apprentice.) The air is clean. The characters are clean. The craftsman-citizen world is clean. But *Shoemakers' Holiday* is only one of seventeen plays that have survived from the forty-two that Dekker wrote. One should not derive all of a playwright's characteristics from a single play.

The Honest Whore[3] presents a less cheery Dekker whose tolerance displays specific bounds. The conversion of a whore, an Elizabethan commonplace in drama and pamphlet, is the play's main concern. Greene had successfully treated the subject in his "The Conversion of an English Courtezan," a first-person narrative about a girl turned wanton, her whorish affairs, and her final conversion. The conversion of this whore is caused by an honest clothier who reminds her that God is forever watching the world and that whores are eternally damned. She is affected by his talk, gives up whoredom, marries the clothier, and lives happily ever after. The conversion of Dekker's whore, Bellafront, is also caused by the speech of the man she loves, but the resemblance ends there, for Bellafront does not marry the man she loves and lives happily never after. Dekker's idea of conversion is far different from Greene's; it forcefully demonstrates Dekker's strong moral bias.

In the beginning of Act II, scene 1, Bellafront is a popular courtesan. At the end of the scene she has become the Honest Whore. That such a sudden conversion is believable is a credit to Dekker's ability to characterize. That the conversion occurs in the second act of a play that will discuss this conversion for eight more acts is an indication of Dekker's purpose. The converted harlots in other plays of the Elizabethan period and in Dekker's later plays announce their conversion in Act V; the play then ends and all's well. The conversion of Bellafront is the *beginning*—it sets off a chain of miseries which Bellafront must suffer. She must pay for the sins she committed in the underworld she rejects. Dekker is too stern a moralist, at least at the writing of this play, to allow for an easy conversion. Dekker, unlike the other rogue pamphleteers, never mentions conversion in his angry exposés of the underworld. This play, coming before the pamphlets, suggests why—the road to cleanliness and moral health is a treacherous one; only the most enduring can traverse it.

Bellafront is an experienced, witty prostitute, who is able to handle men with the assurance of a Meretrix. Her wordplay with her servant Roger, "a panderly Six-penny Rascall," her talk with the gallants who visit her, and her anger toward Matheo all display a woman set in the ways of harlotry. When she speaks with Hippolito, however, the soft side of her nature becomes evident. She sincerely desires to be loved by one man.

> O my Stars!
> Had I but met with one kind gentleman,
> That would have purchacde sin alone, to himselfe,
> For his owne private use, although scarce proper:
> Indifferent hansome: meetly legd and thyed:
> And my allowance reasonable—yfaith,
> According to my body—by my troth,
> I would have bin as true unto his pleasures,
> Yea, and as loyall to his afternoones,
> As ever a poore gentlewoman could be.
>
>   (II.i.267-76)[4]

She sees Hippolito as that potential lover. He, aided by his speech against harlotry, causes her to resolve to turn "pure honest." In Hippolito's tirade Dekker is able to present his own hatred for the whore. The speech is too long to quote in full; these excerpts will indicate the gentle Dekker's venom:

> You have no soule,
> That makes you wey so light: heavens treasure bought it,
> And halfe a crowne hath sold it; for your body,
> Its like the common shoare, that still receives
> All the townes filth. The sin of many men
> Is within you, and thus much I suppose,
> That if all your committers stood in ranke,
> Theide make a lane, (in which your shame might dwell)
> And with their spaces reach from hence to hell.
> Nay, shall I urge it more, there has bene knowne,
> As many by one harlot, maym'd and dismembered,
> As would ha stuft an Hospitall: this I might
> Apply to you, and perhaps do you right:
> O y'are as base as any beast that beares,
> Your body is ee'ne hirde, and so are theirs.
> Me thinks a toad is happier than a whore,
> That with one poison swells, with thousands more,
> The other stocks her veines: harlot? fie! fie,
> You are the miserablest Creatures breathing,
> The very slaves of nature.
>
> Oh you have damnation without pleasure for it!
> Such is the state of Harlots. To conclude,
> When you are old, and can well paynt no more,
> You turne Bawd, and are then worse then before:
> Make use of this: farewell.
>
>   (II.i.322-36, 360-64, 419-23)

The whore, for Dekker, is a damned filthy beast, with disease in every vein, and a menace to all who have contact with her. Despite the vehemence of this speech, Bellafront's first attempt at self-examination, when Hippolito leaves, brings forth this question:

> Yet why should sweet *Hipolito* shun mine eyes:
> For whose true love I would become pure-honest,
> Hate the worlds mixtures, and the smiles of gold:
> Am I not fayre? Why should he flye me then?
>
>   (II.i.430-433)

The harlot is not so affected by the subject matter and tone of the tirade as by Hippolito's reaction to her, personally. Bellafront, reviewing the words of Hippolito in her mind, seems to *discover* that her harlotry is the cause for Hippolito's disgust.

> *Hipolito* hath spyed some ugly blemish,
> Eclipsing all my beauties: I am foule:
> Harlot! I, that's the spot that taynts my soule.
>
>   (II.i.441-43)

Her vanity is a strong part of her nature and love is the impulse for her conversion. With this slight touch Dekker demonstrates his ability to present an essentially truthful depiction of character. Bellafront, now aware of her tainted soul, attempts to stab herself, but is stopped by Hippolito. She resolves to win love in some way, and ends the scene with these words: "Would all the Whores were as honest now, as I." The rest of Part I and all of Part II demonstrate the truth of this assertion.

From this point on Dekker is able to use Bellafront as his mouthpiece of morality. From her lips comes his invective against sin, whores, bawds, panders, and whoremongering gallants. This speech, chastising her bawd, Mistress Fingerlock, is typical of her new morality and emphasizes that she is a forceful enemy of sin.

> Hence, thou our sexes monster, poysonous Bawd,
> Lusts Factor, and damnations Orator,
> Gossip of hell, were all the Harlots sinnes
> Which the whole world conteynes, numbred together,
> Thine far exceeds them all; of all the creatures
> That ever were created, thou art basest:
> What serpent would beguile thee of thy Office?
> It is detestable: for thou liv'st
> Upon the dregs of Harlots, guard'st the dore,
> Whilst couples goe to dauncing: O course devill!
> Thou art the bastards curse, thou brandst his birth,
> The lechers French disease; for thou dry-suckst him:
> The Harlots poyson, and thine owne confusion.
>
> (III.ii.30-42)

Indeed, Bellafront has performed, as Matheo states, "one of *Hercules* labours"—a whore has turned honest.

Bellafront attempts by stratagems to win Hippolito, and when the play ends in Bethlem Monasterie, she even feigns madness, but to no avail. Hippolito has his Infelice; Bellafront accepts Matheo, the man that turned her whore, who claims that he has been "Cony-catcht, guld." Part I ends. Bellafront's conversion has not been too difficult—she is abused by the bawd, pander, gallants, and her future husband; she loses the one man she loves; she accepts the unscrupulous Matheo for her husband. Dekker must write another play to test the sincerity of her conversion.

In Part II Bellafront suffers with a worthless husband who dices, whores, and cheats. He forces Bellafront to beg for him. Her gown is taken from her back to be pawned. She is threatened with physical violence. Matheo even asks her to turn whore again because he needs the money. Bellafront, in misery, exclaims: "A thousand sorrowes strike / At one poore heart." Her situation is wretched. Orlando Friscobaldo's appearance causes her additional anguish, for she must keep her husband and father at peace with one another. Then a new temptation, the greatest of all, arises to test her honesty. Hippolito has become a "muttonmonger" and wishes to seduce Bellafront. He argues for harlotry, just as he argues against it in Part I. The man who caused her to convert, her savior, is now her tempter. But she resists and presents a speech against harlotry equal in moral fervor to his former speech. In short, Dekker makes her new way of life a continuous trial, a trial which ennobles her nature, a trial in many ways similar to the trial of the legendary whore, Thais, who also turned honest and had to suffer greatly before she gained Paradise. However, Dekker's whore remains, at the end of the play, with her worthless husband, and Dekker gives no indication that Matheo will ever change. No relief of her misery is in sight.

Dekker puts his main character through the miseries of a hell on earth. His treatment of Bellafront is influenced by his strict and severe morality. He makes the audience feel genuine sympathy for Bellafront's suffering, but the audience at the same time realizes that her being sinned against has been caused by her sinning. In the course of the two Parts of *The Honest Whore* Bellafront takes on the characteristics of a Jane. Her citizen virtues, especially her conjugal loyalty, make her a heroine, but her trials are not part of a holiday atmosphere. The misery of Bellafront seems everlasting.

Bellafront's acquisition of citizen virtues points to the importance of the play's subplot, which deals with the clean and healthy citizen world, represented by Candido and his circle. Candido is "a grave citizen" and the "mirror of patience." He is "so milde, so affable, so suffering, that nothing indeede can moove him." His wife Viola cannot endure his patience and tries in many ways to vex him—but she cannot. The gallants visit his shop, also attempting to vex him—but they cannot. Viola, as a last manuever, calls in officers to carry Candido to the madhouse—but even in the madhouse, where the complications of Part I are resolved, Candido remains patient. It is in the madhouse that Candido presents his famous speech, in which the sentiments expressed seem very close to Dekker's heart and which has helped to propagate the image of Dekker as the gentle man.

> Patience my Lord; why tis the soule of peace:
> Of all the vertues tis neerst kin to heaven.
> It makes men looke like Gods; the best of men
> That ere wore earth about him, was a sufferer,
> A soft, meeke, patient, humble, tranquill spirit,
> The first true Gentleman that ever breathd;
> The stock of *Patience* then cannot be poore,
> All it desires it has; what Monarch more?
>
> (Vi.ii.489-496)

The Duke, at the end of Part I, praises Candido's patience and says that Candido "shall teach our court to shine." In Part II Candido continues to display his patience. This time he has a new wife, who at first is strong-minded but learns to submit to her husband. The gallants again try to ruffle Candido, and again they are thwarted. When he goes to Matheo's house to see some pieces of lawn he finds that he is in the company of a bawd and pander and that the pieces of lawn are stolen goods. He is apprehended by officers and taken to Bridewell, where the plots of Part II are resolved. Candido again receives the praise of the Duke.

> Thou hast taught the Citty patience, now our Court
> Shall be thy Spheare, where from thy good report,
> Rumours this truth unto the world shall sing,
> A Patient man's a Pattern for a King.
>
> (V.ii.494-97)

The Candido story is the source of most of the play's humor. But it cannot be dismissed merely as a piece of merriment. Candido is, essentially, a Dekker hero. He is the representative of the citizen world, the world to which Dekker is most attached. He displays the qualities of industriousness, generosity, and patience. He is comically patient, to be sure, but Dekker forgets the comedy when Candido presents his speech on Patience and when the Duke considers him "a Patterne for a King." It is the very quality of patience that Bellafront displays in both parts of *The Honest Whore.* She, however, is heroic in her patience. Candido's comment that "the best of men . . . was a sufferer" applies to Bellafront almost as much as it does to Jesus. Jesus suffered for the sins of the world; Bellafront suffers for her own sins as a member of the underworld. *The Honest Whore* is basically a dramatic study of patience. To dismiss the Candido story with a chuckle is to neglect a significant element in this study.[5]

The Candido subplot clearly demonstrates how stern a moralist Dekker is, how important it is for his beloved citizen world to isolate itself from the corruption of the underworld. In Part I, the citizen world and the underworld make no contact. In Part II, they meet twice, with interesting results. Carolo, a courtier, gives the bawd and pander money to arrange a meeting between Candido's wife and himself. When the pander Bots presents Carolo's proposition to the bride, she emphatically scorns him, calls him "an arrant knave," and leaves his company. The virtuous wife of the citizen Candido utterly rejects the underworld's representative. Just as the play contains a parallel between the patience of Candido and the patience of Bellafront, so too it contains a parallel between the virtue of Candido's wife and the virtue of Bellafront—both cannot be seduced, both display conjugal loyalty, like Jane in *Shoemakers' Holiday.* Candido's bride and the honest whore are one in faithfulness, with Bellafront having the harder trial because she loved her seducer and because her husband is worthless. Bellafront, once a member of the underworld, in her moral recovery gathers to herself qualities of the citizen world.

The second meeting between the two worlds occurs when Candido goes to Matheo's house to see the pieces of lawn. The bawd and pander are there. Candido, not knowing Mistress Horseleech is a bawd, is introduced to her. She politely kisses him, which causes him to mutter, "Sh'as a breath stinkes worse then fifty Polecats. Sir, a word, is she a Lady?" He is able to smell her bawdiness. When he is told that she is a bawd he is ready to leave the house, but is forced to drink healths to her, which thoroughly disgusts him. The aversion of Dekker's citizen to a representative of the underworld is strikingly evident throughout the scene. The two worlds meet, but the citizen world is repelled.

The Honest Whore, Dekker's most conscientious effort, belies not only many of the clichés about Dekker's personality and moral fiber, but also many critical objections to his faulty dramaturgy.[6] He has complete control of his material. Bellafront's story directly affects the Hippolito-Infelice story. One need only mention that the courtier Matheo is married to the converted whore, that the gallants were customers of Bellafront, that Bellafront helps to resolve the Hippolito-Infelice plot. The play's un-

derplot, concerning the trials of the patient Candido, throws a revealing light on the main plot. In *The Honest Whore* the strictness of Dekker's morality seems to dictate a strictness in handling his material. Dekker acquired, at the writing of this play, Candido's patience.

When he put *The Honest Whore* behind him, Dekker left with it his strict adherence to a citizen morality. In *Westward Ho* and *Northward Ho,* both collaborations with Webster and both acted before private-theater audiences, the morality is easy. The plot of *Westward Ho,* like that of *Northward Ho,* deals with the intrigue between gallants and citizens' wives, helped along by the underworld. The underworld, represented by Birdlime, a disgusting bawd, and Luce, an experienced prostitute, provides Dekker with the moral norm for a mildly satiric attack on the citizens, which indicates nothing less than a changed concept of his much-loved bourgeoisie. The three citizens, Honeysuckle, Tenterhook, and Wafer, are customers of Luce, who runs a thriving trade with the help of Birdlime. That they are patrons of an underworld character, one who displays all of the traditional distasteful characteristics of the whore, indicates that Dekker is tampering with the citizen virtues he holds so high. Candido was repelled by the underworld; the citizens in this play wish to embrace it. The stern morality of *The Honest Whore* is slackening. In presenting the citizens' wives, Dekker neglects the moral values of *The Honest Whore.* Throughout the play there are surprising parallels between the bawd, the whore, and the citizens' wives. They all are coarse, but they will not endure coarseness in others. They all affect virtue. They all chastise tobacco-smoking and drunkenness. They all are immoral—the whore and bawd play with men for pay, the wives play with gallants for merriment. Whereas in *The Honest Whore* Bellafront took on the qualities of the play's citizen world, thereby demonstrating a true conversion, in this play the citizen world acquires the qualities of the underworld. This is seen even in the most fleeting lines. Mistress Wafer tells Mistress Tenterhook that she wishes her "the fortune to change thy name often." Her reason: "For theeves and widdowes love to shift many names, and make sweet use of it so." When Justiniano tells his wife that she was lucky to have received the jewels from the lecherous Earl, he exclaims: "Was it ever heard that such tyrings, were brought away from a Lord by any wench but thee *Moll,* without paying, unlesse the wench connycatcht him?" (IV.ii. 190-92). The methods of the underworld are not unknown or repugnant to these citizens.

That citizens visit the house of a whore and that the wives of citizens imitate whores and bawds indicates a decided slackening of the moral pattern found in *The Honest Whore.* It is true that at the play's end the wives display a change of attitude. They cheat the gallants—"They shall know that Cittizens wives have wit enough to out strip twenty such gulls." The wives are merry and wanton, but "pure about the heart." Dekker's love of the bourgeoisie still seems to emerge, but the stern moralist has been corrupted. His late plays, especially *Virgin Martyr* and *Match Me in London,* indicate that Dekker's *basic* citizen morality did not change. One must, therefore, look for other causes for his reversal of the traditional morality. Any or all of three causes are probable—the nature of the audience, Dekker's own hack tendencies, his collaboration with Webster.

Alfred Harbage has *The Honest Whore* and the *Ho* plays specifically in mind when he states that "the same authors who wrote amiably of commercialized vice for Paul's provide exposés and denunciations for the Fortune."[7] To please was Dekker's constant aim. His desire to entertain the audience at Paul's who would enjoy a satiric attack on the bourgeoisie and whose moral standards were less exacting than those of the middle class caused Dekker to compromise his moral position.

In addition, his collaboration with Webster may have affected his outlook in the *Ho* plays. Scholars dealing with this collaboration agree that Dekker was the "guiding spirit" in both *Westward Ho* and *Northward Ho.*[8] There is little doubt that Dekker wrote most of each play. But the exact nature of any collaboration cannot be demonstrated, even though a battery of valid tests can assign particular scenes to one dramatist or the other. Although it is logical to assume that Dekker, the older, more experienced, dramatist, influenced Webster, the apprentice, it is possible that the younger Webster gave the satiric impulse to a hack dramatist whose practice it was to compromise in matters of theater. This is in the realm of speculation, not specifically demonstrable, but it is useful in helping to explain Dekker's changed concept of the bourgeoisie. Dekker's attitude often depends upon his collaborator's attitude, as his later collaborations clearly indicate.

Northward Ho conforms to the new moral pattern set up in *Westward Ho.* In it the vociferous and experienced whore Doll Hornet is placed on the road of respectability. Dekker uses a typical Middleton trick of marrying his whore off to an unsympathetic character. He did this in *The Honest Whore* but the difference here indicates a shifting morality. Bellafront's marriage to Matheo was presented as a punishment for the whore, whereas Doll's marriage to Fetherstone is punishment for Fetherstone who marries her thinking she is a rich ward. Doll vows faithfulness to Fetherstone, who reconciles himself to his fate. Doll's conversion is easy. When one considers that the same dramatist who presented Bellafront presented Doll Hornet, only one conclusion can be drawn—Dekker's basically stern morality could be compromised under specific theatrical conditions.

Northward Ho, like *The Honest Whore,* has a scene in Bedlam, where a mad bawd is one of the inmates. She loves aqua vitae, swears by her virginity, and denies ever being in Bridewell. She is, in short, one of Dekker's traditionally disgusting bawds. Her appearance is very brief, but it serves to indicate a less healthy citizen class than appeared in *The Honest Whore* and *Shoemakers' Holiday,* for she voices her preference for "your London Prentice" and "taylors" as customers. The citizen-bawd

relationship sheds a disparaging light on the citizens, with the underworld once again providing the moral norm for a satiric thrust. The citizen world in *Northward Ho* has no "hero" like Candido and no outstanding virtues. The citizens still remain Dekker's favorites: "Sfoote ther's neare a Gentleman of them all shall gull a Citizen, and thinke to go scot-free." But his treatment of them has significantly changed. In the *Ho* plays one witnesses a clear breakdown of a traditional stern morality—a striking example of expediency undermining genuine belief.

The Honest Whore and the *Ho* plays present the two poles of Dekker's morality. His other plays find their places within this wide moral range. The morality of *The Roaring Girl* is close to the *Ho* plays. In it the character of Mary Frith, a notorious thief, is completely whitewashed.[9] Whereas in *The Honest Whore* the underworld was the object of Dekker's abuse, here it is romanticized. But many of his other plays, both early and late, are closer to the moral stance of *The Honest Whore.* In the romantic morality tale *Old Fortunatus* virtue and vice are clearly marked, as they are in *The Whore of Babylon,* in which Dekker ostensibly attacks Roman Catholicism. *Patient Grissil,*[10] where, as in *The Honest Whore,* the patience of a sympathetic character is tested, also clings to a strict citizen morality. *If This Be Not a Good Play, The Devil Is In It* clearly distinguishes between dark and light, between the hellish activities of a Barterville and the purity of the Sub-Prior, who Candido-like must hold his ears when whores sing. In the late tragicomedy *Match Me in London* Dekker deals with intrigue between court and citizens, as he did in the *Ho* plays, but here the citizens emerge completely clean. These plays testify to Dekker's basic moral bias, as does *The Virgin Martyr,* in which the severe morality of *The Honest Whore* is intesified— because, one must suspect, Dekker was working with Massinger, a collaborator whose moral position is close to his own. Forgiveness of sin was possible for a suffering Bellafront, and was implied in the easy conversion of a Doll Hornet, but Hircius and Spungius, a whoremonger and drunkard, are forcefully thrown outside the pale of Christianity.

A reading of all his plays indicates that Dekker was genuinely moral and often angry. When he displays his love for the citizen world, he is the gentle and tolerant Dekker—but he can also be the angry and intolerant Dekker of the rogue pamphlets, *The Honest Whore,* and *The Virgin Martyr.* When his morality is easy, as in the *Ho* plays, he may be called a "moral sloven"—but the phrase, although it points to a correct evaluation of the easily-corrupted Dekker, too strongly undermines a basically severe moralist. That this strict morality is, indeed, basic can be seen when one examines his dramaturgy. When his stern morality is translated directly into dramatic action Dekker presents his most effective drama. In *Shoemakers' Holiday,* where the citizen world is filled with merriment and moral health, one finds Dekker's most coherent plotting. *The Honest Whore,* where a converted harlot must suffer, where a Candido must avoid a bawd like the plague, presents his most carefully worked-out plot. When Dekker works against his geniune moral beliefs he becomes an awkward craftsman. When he can draw clear moral lines, solidified by a love for the class which originally drew these lines, he presents aesthetically satisfying drama. For Dekker a quality of mind seems to indicate a quality of dramaturgy.

The most valid cliché concerning Dekker is that he was a Henslowe hack. Discussing him in connection with his collaborators, confronting him in the light of scholarship concerning the nature of the audience, seeing him as a traditional middle-class moralist corrupted by the pressures of daily living, is a surer guide to Dekker's quality as man and artist than the epithets of gentle and cheery. Ben Jonson comes closest to the truth, perhaps, when in *Poetaster* he has Demetrius (Dekker) referred to as a "dresser of plays about the town."

Notes

1. Here are some similar reactions by other scholars. a) "Dekker loves them [his fellow men], and smiles at their foibles with a large tolerance of the true humanist," J. S. P. Tatlock and R. G. Martin, *Representative English Plays* (New York, 1938), p. 120. b) ". . . a romantic at heart, he tempered his comment on life with a kindly humor." T. M. Parrot and R. H. Ball, *A Short View of Elizabethan Drama* (New York, 1943), p. 114. c) "To the mental energy and literary facility of Defoe, he added the genial kindliness and the happy heart of Goldsmith." *Concise Cambridge History of English Literature* (Cambridge, 1944), p. 304. d) ". . . a sentimentally optimistic view of human nature." David Daiches, *A Critical History of English Literature* (New York, 1960), p. 327.

2. Tatlock and Martin, p. 121.

3. Part 1 of *The Honest Whore* is essentially Dekker's. Although Middleton may have written one or two scenes, his "part in the play seems to have been relatively minor" (Bowers, II, 14). Dekker's name alone appears on the title page. Part 2 is definitely Dekker's unassisted work.

4. *The Dramatic Works of Thomas Dekker*, ed. Fredson Bowers (Cambridge, 1955-1961). All quotations are taken from this edition.

5. Gamaliel Bradford would not even dismiss it with a chuckle; he considers the underplot "exceedingly dull." "The Women of Dekker," *Sewanee Review*, XXXIII (1925), 290.

6. A. H. Bullen asserts that Dekker "usually showed a reckless indifference in the management of his plot," *Elizabethans* (London, 1925), p. 77.

    Swinburne writes of Dekker's "besetting sin of laxity, his want of seriousness and steadiness, his idle, shambling, shifty way of writing," *Age of Shakespeare* (New York, 1908), p. 67.

    F. E. Pierce calls Dekker "one of the most careless writers of a careless age," *The Collaboration of Webster and Dekker* (New York, 1909), p. 3.

Ellis-Fermor says that he is "unconscious of art," *Jacobean Drama* (London, 1953), p. 118.

7. Alfred Harbage, *Shakespeare and The Rival Traditions* (New York, 1952), p. 196.

8. The quote is from Pierce, p. 131. Investigations by the following demonstrate that the *Ho* plays are essentially Dekker's.

    E. E. Stoll, *John Webster* (Boston, 1905).

    Mary Hunt, *Thomas Dekker* (New York, 1911).

    Rupert Brooke, *John Webster and the Elizabethan Drama* (London, 1917).

9. *The Roaring Girl* is a collaboration with Middleton. Which of the collaborators initially conceived the idea of making a heroine out of a famous cutpurse is, of course, difficult to ascertain and has produced differing scholarly opinions. Middleton's words in the Epistle to the Reader—"'tis the excellency of a Writer to leave things better than he finds 'em"—seem to indicate that the charitable view of Moll originated with him, but both dramatists obviously accept the new Moll and defend her throughout the play. Dekker's attitude seems once again to be caught from his collaborator.

10. Dekker wrote *Patient Grissil* in collaboration with Henry Chettle and William Haughton. The basic Grissil story and the subplot, dealing with Sir Owen apMeredith, are probably Dekker's.

George R. Price (essay date 1969)

SOURCE: "Dekker's Drama: Independent Work," in *Thomas Dekker*, Twayne Publishers, 1969, pp. 34-83.

[In the essay below, Price surveys the eight surviving plays that Dekker wrote without a collaborator. The critic argues that these were effective pieces that pleased their Elizabethan audiences.]

More than with most dramatists of the English Renaissance, it is necessary to begin a consideration of Dekker's plays with a reminder of how thoroughly this playwright is sustained by the native dramatic tradition. *The Shoemaker's Holiday* (1599), the most familiar of his works to twentieth-century readers, may be somewhat misleading in this respect; for, despite its romantic love-theme, this comedy is likely to be regarded as marking an advance in realism in its depiction of bourgeois life. Actually, the advance was being made, then and in the next decade, by Ben Jonson and such younger satiric dramatists as Marston and Middleton. In contrast, *The Shoemaker's Holiday* and Dekker's better plays continued throughout his career to rely on the conventions and devices which he had learned in the early 1590's; and these have little affinity with tragic or satiric realism. Although partitioning the English dramatic tradition into morality, romantic, comic, and chronicle elements may seem at first a needless, pedantic method (so closely are the conventions woven together), such division may nevertheless prove helpful as a preliminary analysis leading to a critical appraisal of the plays.

A word of caution, however, needs to be spoken. "Naïve and preposterous" is likely to be our judgment about any play such as *Patient Grissil* in which a medieval saint's legend and the taming-of-the-shrew theme are so oddly mingled. But so to dismiss the play is really to reveal our own unfamiliarity with the conventions Dekker has employed. Rather, our judgment should estimate primarily the truth inherent in the author's structure of values. Of course, the dramatist makes his statement by fusing story, verbal symbols and connotations, theatrical devices, and modes of acting; and his skill in combining these media determines the force of his utterance. However, in the Elizabethan age the media themselves had either originated in, or for generations been associated with, the philosophic and religious beliefs which the dramatist and his audience held in common. As readers, we must understand the full significance of the conventions if we are to gauge the playwright's success. An obvious example of traditional significance is the flat characterization, derived from morality plays and interludes, which Jonson, for instance, relied on to express moral truth in *Volpone*.

If this conception is true, and if Dekker seems to have handled the conventional elements effectively for the Elizabethan audience, our response to the archaic means he used is less important than the effect he produced. And this effect we must keep in mind. The stamina undoubtedly felt in many of Dekker's plays grows out of his command of conventions which are now foreign. The charge of "carelessness" too often laid on him by critics arises partly from their failing to recognize his full reliance on dramatic and histrionic tradition.

I ELIZABETHAN DRAMATIC CONVENTIONS

"'Tis out of Fashion to bring a Divell upon the Stage," Dekker remarked in his tract *News from Hell* (1606). But some two years later, in *If This Be Not a Good Play, the Devil Is in It,* he not only brought devils on stage, but represented damned souls tormented in Hell-fire. The explicit purpose of such a spectacle in *If This Be Not a Good Play* will be discussed later in this chapter; at this point we may pause only to note that Dekker did not exploit the mere fireworks of Medieval drama in other plays that have survived. But so consistently did he utilize elements of the mystery, morality, and interlude traditions that his plays demonstrate better than any other dramatist's the continuity of Medieval and Renaissance drama. What is more important, we are led to the conclusion that his fidelity to these conventions was caused not by his clinging to familiar ways indolently or unthinkingly, but by his conviction that the conventions most forcefully served to express the basic truths of life. The same belief prompted Thomas Heywood's complaint against the narrowed scope of Stuart drama.[1]

Therefore, in spite of the fact that Dekker's reliance on ancient conventions may sometimes appear routine and not very significant (as, for instance, his use of doggerel verse for a moralizing summary in Part II of *The Honest Whore*), we must keep in mind the original potency of the tradition. The audience in the public theaters of 1600 included a considerable number of people who had also, some years earlier, witnessed performances of mystery plays at Coventry, Chester, Kendal, or elsewhere; and, no doubt, nearly all of the audience had attended moralities and interludes.[2] To them, the conventions of religious drama were vital and significant, not amusing archaisms. The universally important contest of God with Satan for the soul of man gave to native dramatic tradition an impact we can scarcely imagine. Because Dekker, as man and as dramatist, grew up in what we may call "the last era of the Medieval drama" and believed the doctrine which that drama aimed to teach, he naturally utilized its resources as fully as possible. In doing so, of course, he also obeyed the Classical maxim to mingle the useful with the delightful.

As a result, Dekker's plays furnish the historian of drama with examples of more than twenty ancient conventions of theme, characterization, and theatrical devices.

I list the more important themes with the name of one play in which each theme occurs: the saint's legend (*The Virgin Martyr*); the testing of heroic virtue (*Patient Grissil*); the detection of evil counselors of the prince (*Patient Grissil*); the victory of patience over persecution (Part II of *The Honest Whore*); social satire in the Medieval tradition (*The Whore of Babylon*); and the peasantry used to voice justice and truth (*Sir Thomas Wyatt*).

Among conventions of characterization are the shrewish wife as comic figure (Part I of *The Honest Whore*); the Judas-like betrayer of his master (*Sir Thomas Wyatt*); personified ideas, such as Time, in conjunction with historical persons and events (*The Whore of Babylon*); personifications of moral forces, good or evil (*The Virgin Martyr*); persons who signify classes, not individuals (*If This Be Not a Good Play*); human persons who embody a single virtue or vice, each receiving his proper reward (*The Wonder of a Kingdom*); "depersonalization," that is, temporary abandonment of a character's individuality permitting him to voice a point of view more eloquently (*The Witch of Edmonton*); and the introduction of superhuman beings (*The Virgin Martyr*).

Finally, among theatrical and stage devices: formal debate between two moral points of view, with implicit appeal to the audience for decision (Part II of *The Honest Whore*); a scene of moral judgment to end the play, that is, a trial (*Old Fortunatus*); the formalizing of a motif, as in a dance of courtesans, for temptation (*If This Be Not a Good Play*); or as in a shift to contrasting expression, the use of archaic verse to utter forgiveness for the prodigal or to summarize the moral (Part II of *The Honest Whore*); showing executions on stage (*Old Fortunatus*); and the use of symbolic properties like the Mountain of Truth or the Tree of Vice (*The Whore of Babylon*).

The preceding features, which we may inclusively call "morality" conventions, have been named first because their moral implications were important to Dekker. However, it is clear that, both historically and in Dekker's drama, these conventions were adapted to general utility in chronicle play, comedy, and romance. An obvious example is the shrewish wife Viola, in Part I of *The Honest Whore*. No doubt she is a descendant of Noah's wife in the mystery plays. But Plautine comedy also presented the Elizabethans with the type of the tyrannical wife; and it is reasonable to suppose that sheer truth regarding actual English life helped to create the characters of the shrews in Elizabethan and Jacobean comedy. In summary, the "morality" conventions are to be understood as employed by Dekker whenever they are appropriate in any of the genres, and the following discussion does not repeat them.

Chronicles, or history plays, constitute a large proportion of the drama of the 1590's; and Henslowe's *Diary* indicates that Dekker wrote a good many of them. But of all this work we have only the garbled text of *Sir Thomas Wyatt* (1602?), said by its publisher to be a collaboration between Dekker and John Webster. *Wyatt* may be a combination of Parts I and II of *Lady Jane,* mentioned by Henslowe in 1602, or of parts of these plays. To the extent that it is by Dekker, as yet very hard to determine, it shows his use of a well-established theme of chronicle drama: a simplified, idealized, patriotic character opposed tragically by a group of ambitious, factious lords. The patriot is a staunch defender of Tudor ideas of sovereignty, including those of primogeniture and divine right. As defender of political truth, Wyatt is of the same type as Woodstock, hero of the anonymous play called by that name, and of Gaunt, in Shakespeare's *Richard II.*

As is often true in chronicles, the other characters in *Wyatt* fall into groups, chiefly the pair of ambitious nobles, Northumberland and Suffolk, supporters of Lady Jane as successor to Henry VIII, and the larger, rival faction which supports Princess Mary. In quality the members of the factions need not be, and are not, sharply distinguished from each other. Other political elements of the realm are represented by such groups of anonymous characters as soldiers and peasants. Like the gardeners in *Richard II,* the countrymen in *Wyatt,* when most significant (II.1), speak with the voice of *Res Publica* in the interludes; but they are otherwise just choric representatives of the masses, or "common conditions." Besides disorder, another aspect of the evil of civil conflict—the suffering visited on the whole nation—is expressed through choric laments by groups of noblewomen. Some of these conventions occur also in other Dekker plays.

In his handling of the comic elements of drama, Dekker is equally dependent on convention. Unquestionably he had a lively sense of the droll and ludicrous in human behavior. Yet with the possible exception of Thomas Heywood, no dramatist approaching Dekker's stature draws more often on the armory of standard comic types and devices which were familiar in the public theaters of the 1580's and 1590's. Five of these traditional resources may be grouped under the heading of stock characters: the loyal, but saucy, servingman, usually labelled the "Clown," a mischief-loving young fellow or a satiric old one, disrespectful to his master, but tolerated by him (*Match Me in London*); the absurd foreigner—vaunting, cowardly Spaniard, lewd Frenchman, crude Irish footman, avaricious Dutchman, or touchy Welshman—caricatured in temperament and manners, but ridiculous chiefly because of his dialect (*Satiromastix*); the female bawd who speaks lewd double entendres (*Match Me in London*); the pert page (*Match Me in London*); and the witty young lady-in-waiting (*Patient Grissil*).

Whether caricatures of fops, upstart gallants, and fantastic courtiers are cited as exemplifying stock characterization or satiric themes is unimportant; in any case, Dekker introduces these comic persons, frequently making them victims of the lady-in-waiting's repartee, which, it should be said, scores more points by well-tried puns and open ridicule than by wit (*Patient Grissil*). For more biting satire, however, Dekker also sets the impudent servingman against the fops (*Match Me in London*). All readers of *Shoemaker's Holiday* remember that Dekker relishes heavy repetition of absurd phrases ("prince am I none, yet am I nobly born"), a device that is the "humor" reduced to its simplest form. Occasionally, he also introduces the mock prophecy (*The Whore of Babylon*) and the dialogue with Echo (*If This Be Not a Good Play*).

Lastly, the conventions of romantic drama which Dekker uses are very numerous. He dramatizes folktale themes: the peasant girl and her royal lover (*Patient Grissil*); the persecuted but forgiving wife (*If This Be Not a Good Play*); long separation of parents and children (*Patient Grissil*); love at first sight (*Blurt, Master Constable*); the testing of lovers' faith in each other (*Satiromastix*); and the selfish ambition of fathers that destroys their children (*Sir Thomas Wyatt*). Among romantic characters we find the rejected lover who makes a vow of celibacy (*Shoemaker's Holiday*); in a different mood, the witty lady-in-waiting also does so (*Patient Grissil*). The villain in these plays, whether he is a revenger, a lustful king, or a tyrannical father, is converted to benevolence for the denouement (*Match Me in London*). His accomplice is also discovered to be a good man at the end (Part I of *The Honest Whore*). Characters are utilized for rather incongruous functions, becoming expositors, intriguers, or benefactors, according to the needs of major and minor plots (Part II of *The Honest Whore*). These manipulations of character might, of course, be properly placed in the category of devices.

There are many other conventional devices to be noted. Obviously, disguise is extremely common (*Shoemaker's Holiday*). For surprise or irony Dekker frequently relies on the administering of a sleeping potion (*Satiromastix*). Among the threats to the happiness of the lovers is *droit du seigneur* (*Satiromastix*). The happy ending of their trials is signalized by several marriages, a feast, and a dance

(*Satiromastix*). Magic appears in various forms (*If This Be Not a Good Play*), including witchcraft (*The Witch of Edmonton*). At times, mythical beings and spirits intervene in the action (*The Virgin Martyr*). Music is the cause or symbol of supernatural influence (*Old Fortunatus*) and also increases pathos (*Patient Grissil*). Passages of lyricism in the dialogue, written in the strains of Ovidian or Petrarchan verse, also heighten the sentiment (*Old Fortunatus*). On a lower level of dramaturgy, we find the familiar expedients of Elizabethan construction: great lapses of time (*Patient Grissil*); frequent shifts of scene (*Old Fortunatus*); and the use of the chorus—that is, prologue (*Old Fortunatus*) and the dumbshow (*The Whore of Babylon*), a device to which Dekker clings throughout his career.

The preceding lists are certainly incomplete. They will be supplemented by mention of Dekker's more artistic uses of traditional technique in the discussion of individual plays in this and in the next chapter. The intention of these analyses is to establish Dekker's major plays in their genres, then to evaluate them in broader critical fashion. The major independent plays I take to be these seven, in chronological order: *Old Fortunatus*; *The Shoemaker's Holiday*; *Satiromastix*; Part II of *The Honest Whore*; *The Whore of Babylon*; *If This Be Not a Good Play, the Devil Is in It*; and *Match Me in London.* Although Thomas Middleton collaborated with Dekker in Part I of *The Honest Whore,* Dekker's share is both large and characteristic; and Part II's development of the situations and characters of Part I practically requires that the earlier play be considered first.

II AN EXEMPLUM FOR THE COURT: *OLD FORTUNATUS* (1599)

Without question, *Old Fortunatus,* as we now have it, was written by Dekker as a parable for the moral instruction of the audience at Queen Elizabeth's court. The evidence leading to this conclusion lies in the dramatist's adaptation of the story, as well as in Henslowe's record of the steps in the composition of the play. But because the tale of Fortunatus is no longer so familiar as it once was, references to it will be more intelligible if we first review Dekker's version in the play.

The story is of the goddess Fortune's dealing with a poor man and his two sons, Ampedo and Andelocia. Finding Fortunatus asleep in a wood in Cyprus, the goddess awakens him and offers a choice of gifts—strength, health, beauty, long life, riches, or wisdom. When Fortunatus chooses riches, Fortune gives him a magic purse, always laden with ten gold pieces. Of course, it immediately enriches the father and his two sons, enabling Fortunatus to travel about the world. Meanwhile, we watch a scene in which Virtue and Vice plant trees while Fortune looks on, indifferent as to which tree flourishes. The fame of Fortunatus's wealth runs everywhere; in Babylon, the Sultan plots to discover the magic source of his visitor's gold. Fortunatus, who escapes this peril by pretending to be

unaware, innocently borrows the Suntan's magic wishing hat and wishes himself at home again.

When Fortune warns him of his imminent death, Fortunatus pleads with her to exchange the purse for the gift of wisdom for his sons; she refuses. The father leaves purse and hat to be used by both sons for their common benefit. He is scarcely cold, however, before the wastrel younger son, Andelocia, forces his brother to divide the use of the prizes year by year. Taking the purse, Andelocia goes to England with the Prince of Cyprus who intends to woo Agripyne, daughter of King Athelstane. The King, intrigued by Andelocia's flaunted riches, tells Agripyne to pretend love for Andelocia, then steal the purse. By giving the youth a sleeping potion, Agripyne succeeds. Andelocia returns to Cyprus, steals the wishing hat from Ampedo, cheats some Italian jewelers of their gems, and returns to England, disguised as a jewel merchant. While bargaining with Agripyne about his wares, he suddenly clasps her and takes her to a wilderness; there he threatens to abandon her unless she will promise to marry him. As she seems fainting from thirst, Andelocia climbs an apple tree (in reality, Vice's) to pick some luscious fruit. When Agripyne complains of the hot sun, he throws her his wishing hat. Unaware of its power, she wishes she were in England and is presently snatched away—with the hat.

Meantime, Vice's apples have grown horns on Andelocia's head. Fortune comes to him, bringing with her Vice and Virtue. The contending goddesses offer him the fruits of their trees; but having been enlightened by Fortune about the cause of his horns, Andelocia repents his bad life and chooses Virtue's apples. His horns fall off. During this time, King Athelstane in England promises to marry his daughter to the Prince of Cyprus. Now Andelocia, still lusting for the purse and hat, comes back disguised as an Irish costermonger and sells Vice's apples to Agripyne and to two foolish courtiers; they all grow horns after eating the fruit. The Prince of Cyprus renounces his claims to a horned princess. Disguised anew, this time as a French doctor, Andelocia gives the courtiers a pill to remove the horns; instead of helping Agripyne, he snatches up the wishing hat and carries the princess off to Ampedo's house in England. Ampedo has come there in hopes of turning Andelocia from his prodigal life. After Andelocia has finally obtained the magic purse from Agripyne he sends her, eating an apple of Virtue to remove her horns, to find her way back to court.

His malice unsatisfied, Andelocia returns to court, preparing to enjoy more trickery. Ampedo is meanwhile unable to dissuade him from his course and burns the wishing hat. Ampedo is seized by the de-horned courtiers who, in the belief that he has the magic purse, put him in the stocks in order to extort gold from him; there he dies of grief. When Andelocia falls into their hands, he loses his purse to them, is also stocked, and then is hanged. The play ends with a short trial scene in which Vice, Virtue, and Fortune claim sovereignty over Athelstane and his court. But Vice ultimately flees, and Fortune kneels to

Queen Elizabeth, the ruler of destiny, in whom Virtue finds the embodiment of herself.

This detailed summary enables us to see how Dekker shaped his source-material with a moral purpose; his play is not merely a naïve rehandling of a naïve folktale. A brief review of the relations of Dekker's plot to the work which was probably his immediate source[3]—the German *Volksbuch* "Of Fortunatus and His Purse and Wishing-Hat" (first published in 1509)—reveals some significant changes. The folktale moves slowly but clearly and presents the careers of the father and sons in sequence, so that a dramatist who planned to make two plays would have found a convenient dividing point at Fortunatus's death. However, Dekker produces a considerable overlap of the two parts; Fortunatus's death and bequeathing of the purse and hat come at the end of Act II. Contemporary readers of the *Volksbuch* probably enjoyed the story of Fortunatus's career chiefly because of the inserted episodes of murder, theft, and lust. Dekker has omitted nearly all of this material; in fact, he adapts only two events (both necessary to prepare for Andelocia's adventures): the father's encounter with the goddess Fortune and his theft of the Sultan's wishing hat. A chorus before Act II summarizes a few of Fortunatus's actions between these two episodes.

For the remaining three acts, Dekker adapts many, but not all, of Andelocia's exploits in relation to Agripyne; the chorus that precedes Act IV is an awkward device to weave in the omitted events necessary to understand the following scene. But more important than Dekker's struggle to dramatize the loose episodes in the *Volksbuch* is the change in tone at which he aimed. Partly through additional action, partly through lamentation, comment, and homily, Dekker emphasizes waste more than the other forms of vice in the careers of Fortunatus and Adelocia. The evil of prodigality, however, is a theme completely absent from the *Volksbuch*.

The process of Dekker's composition of the play could give further indications of his purpose. However, the obscurity in the theatrical origins of **Old Fortunatus** has caused problems for the historian of drama which are the most numerous among all Dekker's works. Certainly the play as we have it is Dekker's recasting and amplification of an older one, now lost, called by Henslowe *The First Part of Fortunatus* (February 3, 1596). But "First Part" implies a second part, either then existing or soon to be written, unless Henslowe's title, rather unusually, echoes the title of a lost book of the legend.[4] We know of no *Second Part*; for, when Henslowe first mentions Dekker's name in connection with the play on November 9, 1599, while recording a payment of forty shillings, he speaks of *The Whole History of Fortunatus*. Naturally, in the light of these two recorded titles, scholars have supposed that a *Second Part* may have been projected which was to deal with the adventures of Fortunatus's two sons, but that Dekker spontaneously, or at the actors' suggestion, decided to combine the father's and sons' adventures in one play, *The*

Whole History of Fortunatus. On the other hand, it has been denied that Dekker wrote *The First Part*, but it has been accepted without question that he wrote *The Whole History*.

Dekker obviously eliminated some episodes used in *The First Part of Fortunatus*, yet his recasting created an unusually long play. It was finally completed by November 30, 1599, when Dekker was paid six pounds for it.[5] The next day, however, Henslowe began a new series of payments to Dekker for the altering of *The Whole History of Fortunatus* "for the Court," as he says a few days later. The play was produced before Queen Elizabeth on December 27, 1599. There had hardly been time for a performance on the stage of the Rose Theater. And it is remarkable that the play is not mentioned again by Henslowe, and that *Old Fortunatus in His New Livery* was entered in the Stationers' Register on February 20, 1600, and published in that year "as it was played before the Queen's Majesty this Christmas."[6] In the quarto are printed two prologues by Dekker, one of them (like the epilogue) designed especially for the performance at court.

From the preceding data we can see that the play as we have it was in existence only about eight weeks before Dekker or the actors sold it to the publisher, the manuscript being probably in Dekker's own hand. This very early sale and the lack of further reference by Henslowe[7] do not prove conclusively that the play in its full length was not produced publicly again, but they definitely lead to that inference. If produced, **Old Fortunatus** was perhaps cut down to more normal length and made less expensive (in December the actors had borrowed ten pounds from Henslowe to buy "things" for the performance).

In spite of the many uncertainties in the history just given, the evidence surely justifies our conclusion that **Old Fortunatus** is one of Dekker's ambitious plays, one worked on seriously and intended for a sophisticated audience. The importance of this conclusion is not lessened by our uncertainty about whether Dekker wrote *The First Part of Fortunatus* in 1595, then four years later decided to amalgamate it and the remainder of the *Volksbuch* material in one play, or whether in 1599 he combined two existent plays. We are sure that in 1599 he joined certain episodes from *The First Part of Fortunatus* with some of Andelocia's adventures. And we can be almost equally sure that Henslowe's second series of large payments was for the composition of a substantial revision of the new play, specifically the incorporation into it of the morality element—the contest between Fortune, Vice, and Virtue—rather than simply for a contribution of a Prologue and an Epilogue for the court.[8] Then we make the valid inference that Dekker, having learned that *The Whole History of Fortunatus* was intended for performance at the court, deliberately attempted to add moral gravity to the fantastic story. He expected to have at court a more thoughtful and critical audience than that of the Rose Theater.

Although C. H. Herford's analysis of the changes that Dekker made in the fable of the *Volksbuch* is complete enough,⁹ his evaluation of the changes must be amended. He says that Dekker altered the character of Fortune from a fond, pampering mother (as in the source) to a stern, judicial goddess who disapproves and punishes Fortunatus's bad choice of riches. But it is not essentially the choice of riches that she condemns; it is his abuse of riches, his improvidence: "Thou hast eaten metals, and abusde my giftes, / Hast plaid the Ruffian, wasted that in ryots, / Which as a blessing I bestowed on thee" (II.2.235-37).

Second, Andelocia is displayed as the prodigal son, and his brother Ampedo, a virtuous, prudent youth, is the foil to him; whereas in the *Volksbuch,* Andelocia is envied as the lucky hero up to the last episode. Though Herford does not note the fact, the theme of evil prodigality is a favorite with Dekker throughout his life; he dwells on it in both plays and tracts. The contrast between Andelocia and Ampedo, therefore, is a parable; it is a quite definite moral preachment for Elizabeth's courtiers. Third, there is the rivalry of Fortune, Vice, and Virtue. Herford believes that, in the play as first planned, Fortune was shown as "the supreme arbiter of the world . . . in no hostile relation to moral good . . . at least tolerant of virtue."¹⁰ Yet for purposes of compliment to Queen Elizabeth, Virtue has been personified; and her supremacy over Fortune must be shown. Hence, says Herford, a seeming incoherence of ideas exists in the play.

We cannot deny that for the modern reader the Fortune-Virtue relation has an effect of incoherence; but it is likely that the Elizabethan audience saw little or no inconsistency. In the first place, the figure of Fortune is introduced as the capricious "Queene of chaunce" who thrusts pain or pleasure on men without regard to merit, seating base cowards in honor's chair, putting an idiot's cap on virtue's head. In this view of her actions, a man's vice or virtue is quite irrelevant, because her tumbling a prince from his throne is only a more spectacular instance of caprice and not really different from a beggar's finding money in the street. Now, it is important also to see that her enjoyment of her sport is increased by her awareness of the irony in her frustrating human expectations based on merit. As a dramatic person, Fortune must be satiric, or she is little more than an annoyance.

Dekker relies on this trait of her character (I.1.65-129) and then uses a development of it which is less obvious. Fortune's sportiveness is combined with scorn for the fools who think vice can bring them lasting pleasure, as she likewise shows her contempt for fools who think virtue will bring them protection. In Act IV (1.111-227) she is presiding over a contest between Virtue and Vice for the devotion of Andelocia. It is fully consistent with her satiric attitude ("Sing and amongst your Songs, mix bitter scorne" [117]) for her to identify Vice to Andelocia as the cause of the horns he now wears and of future evils, to identify Virtue in her fool's costume, to call Andelocia "fool," and to tell him how his trial will be continued. In no way does she control his choices, although she can alter his situation

in a moment. She remains entirely unpredictable, and the prodigal is entirely responsible for his moral decisions.

True, in the finale (V.2), Fortune seems momentarily severe and judicial, even angry (lines 206-223). But she performs, in fact, no judicial acts; she resigns the punishment of the evil courtiers, Longaville and Montrose, to Athelstane as she has resigned the punishment of Athelstane and Agripyne because Virtue pardoned them (224). Her acts, therefore, always remain devoid of moral quality. But as Fortune has been the major diety of the play, she is given a brief passage of solemn prophecy to speak about England's future wealth (259-60); then (her irony now being dropped) she relapses completely into the basic element of her character—blind capriciousness¹¹—and she stupidly supposes that Vice is more esteemed than Virtue. She tries to refer the decision of this question to the audience, but Virtue appeals to the Queen, her own embodiment. Vice flees, and Fortune makes herself the slave of Elizabeth.

For a Renaissance audience familiar with the abundant literature and iconography of the goddess, nothing in Dekker's representation of her is inconsistent with the final triumph of Virtue over Vice or with the traditional indifference of Fortune to moral quality in human beings. The only distinct change in her at any time is the omission of her satiric scorn in the last scene.

I have dwelt upon this aspect of the play as the most important, for it is the element most demonstrative of Dekker's serious theme, as it is also the most spectacular feature. Herford and others speak of the Fortune-Vice-Virtue episodes as masque elements, implying, perhaps, frivolity of purpose in them, a "frigid and artificial allegory."¹² But certainly in purpose and probably in dramatic effect the Fortune episodes exemplify what is essentially a surviving morality play, despite the exaggeration of spectacle and the omission of theological ideas. The episodes serve to introduce and deepen the evil of a specific vice, waste.

Indeed, as Dekker sees the legend, it provides two prodigals: old Fortunatus and Andelocia. We meet Fortunatus when he is old but still a fool (so Echo describes him), one who has lost his way in the forest of the world, but who yet wishes he had a little more virtue. Involuntary fasting has made him chaste, and poverty has made him patient—"marie[,] I haue praied little, and that makes mee [that] I still [*always*] daunce. . . ." (I.1.18-19). Rejecting wisdom and other good gifts, he chooses riches, and Fortune scorns him: "Farewel, vaine couetous foole, thou wilt repent" (I.1.308).

Likewise, Andelocia, the true son of his father, rants against the inequality in the world: "Art not thou mad, to see money on Goldsmithes stalles, and none in our purses?" Ampedo speaks the proper answer:

> But fooles haue alwaies this loose garment wore,
> Being poore themselues, they wish all others poore

. . .
Fie, brother *Andelocia,* hate this madnes,
Turne your eyes inward, and behold your soule,
That wants more than your body: burnish that
With glittering Vertue: and make Ideots grieue
To see your beautious mind in wisedome shine,
As you at their rich pouertie repine.

(I.2.99-100, 125-132)

But his remonstrance has no effect. After death, Fortunatus's body is carried away by satyrs, the slaves of Fortune, to a pagan burial; yet the warning given to his sons by his unhappy death is promptly flouted by Andelocia, who "in wildness tottre[s] out his youth" (IV.1.106). Dekker tries to focus the whole lesson where Fortune introduces Andelocia to Virtue and Vice in person (IV.1). Andelocia chooses Virtue. But he relapses at once into his former folly (V.2.50-61), and his end is hanging, though with time allowed for repentance:

Vertue, forgiue me, for I haue transgrest
Against thy lawes, my vowes are quite forgot . . .
Riches and knowledge are two gifts diuine.
They that abuse them both as I haue done,
To shame, to beggerie, to hell must runne.

(V.2.170-71, 173-75)

Although Andelocia's end is predictable, we are surprised to see Ampedo, so often the voice of caution, dying miserably in the stocks. However, Virtue explains that he also was a fool:

. . . Those that (like him) doe muffle
Vertue in clouds, and care not how shee shine,
Ile make their glorie like to his decline:
He made no vse of me, but like a miser,
Lockt vp his wealth in rustie barres of sloth . . .
So perish they that so keepe vertue poore.

(V.2.272-76, 279)

Indirectly addressing the noble audience, Virtue means that, possessed of the means to do good to the needy (the magic purse and hat), Ampedo did nothing. In short, his sin was sloth.

Old Fortunatus, then, is insistently a morality play. But it is the morality, or the interlude, in an awkward stage of change. Its elements are not fully harmonized. Charles Lamb eloquently praises the poetry of Orleans's romantic speeches; but this charm is too slight to count for much. What count are the moral preachments just analyzed, the scenes of spectacle (Fortune treading on kings as she mounts her throne; magical disappearances with the wishing hat), the intrigue at Athelstane's court, and the comedy. Irrespressible Shadow's clownage, Andelocia disguised as an Irish costermonger, the Soldan of Babylon being cozened of his wishing hat, Agripyne and her suitors wearing horns—these comic devices loudly compete with the morality play. The trouble is that they do not blend with it. Dekker's genuine earnestness in *Old Fortunatus* is partly frustrated by his employment of conventional elements of comedy and spectacle. However, the play has much more depth than has usually been found in it.

III A Ballad Theme: *The Shoemaker's Holiday* (1599)

The exuberant fun of **The Shoemaker's Holiday,** which has resulted in its distinction of being one of the few Elizabethan comedies—other than Shakespeare's or Jonson's—which are frequently revived in this century, leads some critics to the conclusion that it is Dekker's masterpiece. Acknowledging the play's vitality, we gain little by quibbling about the term "masterpiece"; but to label **The Shoemaker's Holiday** "Dekker's best romantic comedy" is certainly more exact. In none of his other surving plays does he mingle conventional comic and love-story elements so adroitly. However, to view the play as a masterpiece of realism or even as making a genuine innovation in any kind of realism is an error.

Before considering Dekker's use of romantic legend we should summarize the action of the comedy. When Rowland Lacy, prodigal nephew and heir of the Earl of Lincoln, finds himself penniless in Germany, he learns the trade of the shoemaker. After he has made his way back to London and has restored himself to his uncle's favor, he falls in love with Rose, daughter of a wealthy citizen, Sir Roger Otley, the Lord Mayor. Both his uncle and her father resolutely oppose the match as being against the interest of both families. A further complication is the English King's war against France (which king and which campaign Dekker leaves vague).[13] The Earl procures a colonelcy for Rowland; Sir Roger impresses certain tradesmen for the ranks, especially Ralph, journeyman to the master shoemaker, Simon Eyre. Ralph parts sadly from his wife Jane, the maidservant to Eyre's wife Margery.

Although the Lord Mayor has taken pains to sequester his daughter at his country home in Oldford, Rose is able to learn of Lacy's movements by sending her waiting-woman Sybil to the musters near London. Some weeks later, Lacy secretly returns from France, puts on the disguise of a Dutch shoemaker, and takes service with Eyre, replacing Ralph. Besides the fact that Lacy risks death for having deserted treasonably, Rose herself is imperilled by her father's decision to marry her to Hammon. Hammon, a citizen, has fallen in love with Rose when he encountered her near Oldford where he was hunting. However, she firmly refuses this match; Hammon, for his part, will not consent to Sir Roger's coercing his daughter into the marriage.

Meantime, Lacy helps Eyre, his master, to buy a cargo from a Dutch skipper and thus to profit greatly. Soon Eyre is elected Lord Mayor and is handsomely entertained by Otley at Oldford. Among Eyre's men on this occasion is Lacy, and Rose recognizes him. Later she summons Lacy to fit her with shoes, and thus they are able to plan elopement, with the aid of Sybil.

In the interim, the campaign in France has been suspended, and Ralph returns, crippled, to London. But he finds that

Jane has left Eyre's house, driven away by Mistress Eyre's scolding. Jane has opened her own seamstress shop (unknown to Ralph) where Hammon has discovered and wooed her. When he declares that Ralph is dead, she reluctantly agrees to marry Hammon. However, when Hammon's servant brings Ralph a loveknot shoe and orders him to make a new pair for a wedding, Ralph recognizes Jane's shoe. His fellows in Eyre's shop rally to help him intercept the procession on the way to church and to claim Jane for his wife.

Firke, one of Ralph's co-workers, delivers Rose's show at Oldford. There he is questioned by Sir Roger who has learned that Lacy is hiding in London. At this moment, word is brought that Rose has eloped with Hans the shoemaker; and the Earl of Lincoln, who has come to inquire about his nephew from Otley, surmises that it is Lacy in disguise. However, Firke misinforms the two old men about the church where the lovers are to be married. Lacy, who has revealed himself to Eyre and induced the master and his wife to be witnesses, is married to Rose at the Savoy while the two guardians are waiting for them at St. Faith's.

Although the Earl and Lord Mayor plead to the King for a separation of the lovers, Eyre's good humor and shrewdness win the day for Lacy and Rose. The King refuses to annul the marriage; instead, he restores Lacy's honor by knighting him (thus he also increases the Earl's honor). The guardians are reconciled to the marriage, and the play ends festively with the King's consent for his prentices to eat at Eyre's banquet.

In this well-written play Dekker has used imaginatively elements from three legends in Thomas Deloney's *The Gentle Craft*, Part I, a book published apparently at the end of 1597, though no copies of the first edition have survived. The three tales include two vulgarized Medieval saints' legends: that of St. Hugh's love for St. Winifred, perhaps to be called a tragedy because of their martyrdom, and that of St. Crispine's love for St. Ursula, which ends happily with their marriage. The third legend is the career of Simon Eyre, historically a woolen-draper but made a shoemaker by Deloney—a desirable change because both Hugh and Crispine disguised themselves as shoemakers, and because the book is addressed to the "Professors of the Gentle ['noble'] Craft; of what degree soeuer."

Actually, Dekker utilizes only three story elements from the saints' lives: that Hugh and Crispine are princes; that they disguise as shoemakers; and that Crispine courts Ursula while fitting her. But the dramatist makes frequent humorous allusion to other details of their legends. On the other hand, he appropriates most of Deloney's legend of Simon Eyre, omitting only a fabliau concerning Eyre's housemaid (not Jane); yet from that he borrows the name, but not the character, of Hans the Dutchman. It is noteworthy that in Deloney's account, Eyre, although he has a quiet sense of humor, is a much soberer and more dignified person than in the play. This difference fully

demonstrates Dekker's genius for characterization. He has kept the virtues of the original Eyre—industry and kindliness—and has rounded the character by adding tenderness for "my sweete lady *Madgy*," volubility, robustious humor, and, above all, an awareness of his own absurdities: ". . . Feare nothing *Rose*, let them al say what they can, [*sings*] dainty come thou to me: laughest thou?" (V.1.8-9). As a recent critic says, Eyre is a "shrewd exploiter of his own eccentricities."[14]

The careful structure of the play deserves a word of praise. As counterpoint to the evil of two ambitious old men's planning marriages of advantage for their children and thus thwarting the natural love between pure, devoted young folk, Dekker introduces the pathos of a young couple of the lower class separated by the crisis of war and reunited only after near tragedy. Besides these thematic parallels of love, youth, and fidelity, Dekker takes other pains to unify the two plots. The two male lovers are both shoemakers, one pretended, the other true; the French war threatens Lacy's love affair, but actually separates Ralph from Jane; and the same unwelcome wooer attempts to win, first Rose, then Jane. Firke, the journeyman shoemaker, a much transformed clever servant from Roman comedy, by a neat deception both frustrates the domineering fathers and simultaneously restores forlorn Jane to her faithful husband. And, very obviously, Simon Eyre assists this unification because his benevolence includes Lacy and Rose; his shop is a center of the action; and his shrewd exuberance wins his acceptance by all of society from King to prentices.

This structural unity is supported by deft transitions of feeling as episode follows episode, without the heavy exploitation of a particular theatrical scene by which Dekker sometimes offends us in other plays. Firke's and Sybil's coarse humor (half of it depending on by-play); the ironic vanity of Margery and the cunning of Simon; moments of pathetic separation and recognition; high hopes of lovers; exultation in successful disguise and deception; suspense for the outcome of a ruse or of the King's intervention; and songs, dances, and crowd scenes—all these are woven by Dekker into supremely good theater.

The realism of **Shoemaker's Holiday,** as I have said, is mainly of a traditional kind, like the romantic elements. It is true, of course, that the earlier popular comedy more often represents the absurdities, including the dialect, of rustic and village types like those in William Stevenson's *Gammer Gurton's Needle* (*circa* 1553), whereas the milieu in **Shoemaker's Holiday** is chiefly that of the city craftsmen. But the transition to London life was a natural one and may even be said to have been anticipated in *George a Greene, the Pinner of Wakefield* (possibly by Robert Greene, 1588), *The Weakest Goeth to the Wall,*[15] and probably in other plays. In *George a Greene* the pugnacious shoemakers of Bedford hob-nob and drink with King Edward; in *The Weakest Goeth to the Wall* a humorous botcher who carries his tools onto the stage (like Eyre's men) figures importantly in the play. Dekker's own advance upon earlier comic realism appears in only two aspects of **Shoemaker's Holiday.** He paints a single genre picture of the rising of a shopkeeper's household at dawn (I.4), a scene which dwells humorously on the master's futile efforts to get his wife, maids, and benchmen at work before seven. Dekker also shows us, perhaps more believably than ever before, the kind of shrewdness and independence of character, in both Eyre and Sir Roger Otley, which enabled the craftsmen to rise into the merchant class and then to enter the aristocracy. To recall the Dick Whittington legend and Deloney's stories helps to correct any misconception that Dekker was the first to record this breaking of social crust; much rather, we ought simply say that his depiction of its is quite plausible. He was far less interested than Deloney in the maneuvers by which Eyre founded his fortune; and, as for the values which usually motivate such men, if Jonson's and Massinger's plays are compared with **Shoemaker's Holiday,** Dekker reveals no important general truth. Instead, he merely shows us a very likable fellow who profits from a stroke of luck.

To find in **Shoemaker's Holiday** any deep social truth or vision of Elizabethan society is, I think, to see both the play and the society in a sentimental mood. The genuine realism present in the play (beyond that discussed above) is simply the psychological truth which Shakespeare and other masters have trained us to expect in nearly all drama. At times Dekker achieves it. Among such passages is the one[16] where Ralph returns from France to Eyre's shop and weeps from fatigue and grief while callous Mistress Eyre shamefacedly admits that she scolded Jane out of her service (III.2); and almost equally good is the one (IV.3) in which Hammon convinces Jane that Ralph has died in the war. These indeed do have universal appeal and show Dekker at his best. Such poignancy is not found in all scenes of *Shoemaker's Holiday;* but, where it is absent, Dekker is still the master showman and satisfies us with his skillful use of conventions.

IV FROM ROMANCE TO LAMPOON: *SATIROMASTIX* (1601)

In Chapter 1 a brief account was given of the War of the Theaters between Ben Jonson and the poetasters (as he described most of the other playwrights) and, in particular, John Marston and Dekker. Doubtless, Jonson labored hard to make *Poetaster* caustic enough to humiliate and frighten into silence all his enemies, including dramatists, actors, and critics. In fact, even today *Poetaster* raises laughter in many scenes and constantly draws admiration for its pungent style. In the days when all its allusions to personalities were clear, it must have been hilariously amusing to the audience at the Blackfriars. But while Jonson was still composing it—a process that took fifteen weeks, as the prologue tells—he learned that his enemies were preparing a counterblast. Jonson's reference to the fact in *Poetaster,* III. 4.352, indicates that he thought Marston was the leader.

However, the play that appeared alternately at the Globe and at the Paul's Boys' theater was **Satiromastix,** a work in which it is very difficult to find traces of Marston's style, but in which Dekker's style and technique are apparent almost everywhere. In the entry in the Stationers' Register and on the title page of the first edition only Dekker's name is mentioned. It is true that the epistle "To the World," which is unsigned but which Dekker certainly wrote, states, "Horace [Jonson] *hal'd his* Poetasters *to the Barre, the* Poetasters *untruss'd* Horace . . ." Yet nine lines below we find, "*I meete one* [critic who blames me] *. . . for that in untrussing* Horace, *I did onely whip his fortunes, and conditions of life, where the more noble* Reprehension *had bin of his mindes* Deformitie. . . ." Throughout the remaining thirty lines of the epistle the pronoun *I* is used in every line, with no mention of Marston. In other collaborations, however, Dekker usually gives credit quite carefully to his partner if there is opportunity to do so. Therefore, it is sensible to conclude that the mention of the untrussing quoted above simply refers to the *action in the play* (V.2.227-32), not to the composition of the play. Professor Bowers has shown that the manuscript which Dekker himself (as it seems) delivered to the publisher was a fair copy of Dekker's earlier draft and was possibly in his own hand, for his spellings are abundant throughout. Moreover, the dramatist read the quarto during or after the printing and furnished an errata list which was issued with the edition. From all this evidence we ought to infer that Marston's contribution to the play can hardly have been more than some general suggestions about the action as well as about the method of lampooning Horace most effectively.

Considering the result of Dekker's effort, Jonson would have been expected to say that Marston probably preferred to let Dekker take full credit. In fact, however, Jonson affected great disdain and withdrew from strife against "bare and beggarly conceits"; and Dekker's epistle "To the World" is written with the gaiety of complete triumph. It is appropriate to analyze those qualities of **Satiromastix** which discouraged Jonson from further combat, as well as those which aroused his contempt.

The main plot, set in the court of King William Rufus near the end of the eleventh century, is a very simple one, a tragic situation that is quickly resolved; it is easily completed in five scenes (I.1, II.1, III.2, V.1, and V.2) of only moderate length in a play that is longer than the average. Sir Walter Terrill, a courtier, marries Cælestine, daughter of Sir Quintilian Short-hose, apparently a rich merchant. The King, who has been invited to the wedding festivity, becomes infatuated with the bride's beauty and dares Sir Walter to show his faith in her purity by sending her to court that night, ostensibly to display her loveliness for a day or so to the nobility. Despite his anguish, Terrill is compelled by pride and honor to swear an oath that he will send her. After the King has gone, the young couple and the father lament this outcome, but Terrill cannot break his word. However, Sir Quintilian finds the ultimate preservative of his daughter's virtue—death by poison. Cælestine drinks the potion and seems to die at once, as Terrill agonizes. That night her body, seated in a chair, is brought by a group of maskers to the King's presence chamber. The King, who has been expecting treacherously to enjoy *droit du seigneur,* unmasks the bride and is aghast to find her dead. When Terrill denounces him as a tyrant, the King repents his evil and acknowledges his guilt. Thereupon, Cælestine revives from the sleeping potion, and the King restores her to Terrill.

It would be unjust to say that the handling of the conflict between love and honor, initiated by the King's dare, typically reveals Dekker's failure as a tragedian. We have too little of his tragedy left us by which to judge. His early tragedies, for which Francis Meres praised him, are lost, and the only surviving later one, **The Witch of Edmonton,** is a collaboration. But it is true that Dekker's handling of Terrill's dilemma is characteristic of his method in romance and tragicomedy. Although *Satiromastix* evolved into a lampoon, the Terrill-Cælestine plot was undoubtedly designed originally as tragicomedy.

Yet the situation consists of very tragic elements: the lovers, yearning for each other, are tortured by the code of honor which demands that Terrill manifest his trust in his bride and his King, thus delaying the consummation of their marriage and, far worse, threatening to desecrate their love and honor. Dekker does not falsify or obscure any of these elements; to do so would have been to frustrate his own intent by robbing his scenes of full impact. In order to control the audience's response to the tragic situation, however, he employs two conventions: First, the play begins and is maintained in the mood of broad comedy, with the result that the pseudo-tragic situation just escapes being submerged by farce and bawdy humor; second, the familiar device of a sleeping potion is signalled for the audience by Sir Quintilian's demeanor—he smiles as Terrill weeps over Cælestine's unconscious body:

> TERRILL. I had a constant wife, Ile tell the King;
> Vntill the King—what dost thou smile? art thou
> A Father?
>
> SIR QUINTILIAN. Yea, smiles on my cheekes arise,
> To see how sweetly a true virgin dyes.

Before Terrill can protest further, the maskers enter to carry Cælestine to court. It is notable that the resolution follows at once; there is no comic interruption. The rapidity of the action in these climactic scenes must also be credited to Dekker's tact in handling the theme. It should probably be added that the ceremonies which precede the unmasking of the dead Cælestine contribute to esthetic distancing of the lovers' ordeal and so obviate any tragic pain in the audience's feeling.

The worst charge that criticism can bring against **Satiromastix** is the painful artificiality of the dialogue among Terrill, Cælestine, and her father as they lament their disastrous situation (II.1, III.2). Their speeches are woven mostly of empty conceits, silly word-play, commonplace rhetorical patterns and figures; the rhymed couplets are

vapid. This inexcusable lapse in style was probably caused by Dekker's haste and by his shift of purpose from tragicomedy to satire.

Whether or not we credit Dekker with skill in the management of the main plot, it is surely plausible to think that he kept that plot to the brevity and simplicity of its original conception because of the overgrown comic actions which came to occupy about four-fifths of the play. Perhaps the comic plot was also planned more simply at first. It presents the farcical wooing of foolish Widow Miniver by two suitors: hairy Sir Vaughan ap Rees, a peppery Welsh knight with a ridiculous dialect, and bald Sir Adam Prickshaft, whose name contributes much bawdy allusion. Probably in Dekker's first plan a third suitor, a rascally soldier, rivaled the other two; and he may have been replaced by Captain Tucca, a boisterous, lewd bully with an amusing vocabulary. Tucca was first introduced by Jonson in *Poetaster;* Dekker has taken him over with no change except an increase of his villainy and fantastic scurrility. The rivalry of these three to win the widow proceeds through absurd trickery and a travesty of poetic contests to an undeserved success for Tucca.

More amusing than Tucca, however, are three other characters borrowed from *Poetaster;* Dekker keeps their original identities but changes the characters to sharpen his ridicule. Horace is Jonson; Crispinus, Marston; and Demetrius Fannius, Dekker himself. Naturally, Crispinus and Demetrius emerge fair-minded moderate men, poets concerned only with defending their reputations from Horace's persistent vilification. Dekker provides Horace with a moronic admirer, Asinius Bubo, whose historical identity has not been decided. These pseudo-Roman characters are intruded into the tragicomedy in several ways: Horace is employed by Terrill to furnish nuptial songs for the wedding festivity; Crispinus and Demetrius are included in Terrill's wedding party and have, between them, a total of three short lines in two scenes (probably the poets have been substituted for two Norman gentlemen of the court); Horace writes libels, for pay, against Sir Vaughan ap Rees's rivals and, for malice, bitter epigrams against Captain Tucca; Sir Vaughan hires Horace to write an ode in praise of hair, and Sir Adam employs Crispinus to recite a versified paradox in praise of baldness—all as strategy in wooing Widow Miniver.

Finally, Horace and Asinius are arraigned before the King in the last scene, as guilty of ". . . bitter *Satirisme,* of *Arrogance,* / Of *Selfe-loue,* of *Detraction,* of a blacke / And stinking *Insolence.* . . ." (V.2.220-222). The satyr suits which the two are wearing are untrussed and pulled off over their heads; then they are crowned with nettles. In *Poetaster,* Jonson provided an excellent satiric climax with the forcing of an emetic on Crispinus to make him vomit up his crudities of poetic diction. Dekker's scene of the untrussing, although less pungent satire, no doubt raised as loud a laughter.

It is not hard to see why Jonson gave up the contest after the production of **Satiromastix.** If the audiences at the private theaters had been polled, they would doubtless have voted *Poetaster* the better play, which it surely is. But Dekker had proved himself quite clever enough to defeat his adversary with the techniques of dramatic caricature—with Jonson's own weapons, in fact. Jonson's aggressive individualism made him a very broad target, and Dekker took full advantage of the fact. Jonson's physique—his red, pockmarked face, thin beard, staring eyes, hollow cheeks, shapeless nose, loud voice, "mountain belly"—are the constant objects of Tucca's malice; and they were probably simulated by the actor playing Horace. Jonson's picturesque history as bricklayer, homicide, jailbird, converted Papist, and itinerant actor dismissed from his company for lack of talent—all are flung at him repeatedly. (We should remember that Jonson's ridicule of Marston's red hair and Dekker's threadbare cloak partly explains and justifies Dekker's venom.) However, more important are Jonson's personality traits shown in action. Horace is exposed as a vain, short-tempered, repetitious, costive rhymester, a railer, a slanderer, a liar, and a coward. His toadyism toward noblemen and his cheating of gull-gallants are admitted even by himself.

Since all these traits had at least a semblance of truth, the remarkable fullness of the portrait must have been relished by many in the audience. Perhaps of equal enjoyment was Dekker's irony in using Jonson's own inventions, especially Horace and Tucca, in drawing the caricature. To relish the irony fully, one would first have to attend *Poetaster* at the Blackfriars and then, a few nights later, *Satiromastix* at Paul's. When Jonson learned that Tucca, whom he had created as a lampoon on an actual boisterous soldier, Captain Hannam, had been turned by Dekker into a lewd abuser of Jonson, he must have seen the futility of any more skirmishes against the poetasters.

Dekker's success in answering caricature with lampoon naturally invites a further comparison of the two plays in terms of their purpose and achievement. In *Poetaster,* Jonson strove for a characteristically high goal and by characteristically high means. We must agree with Professor Talbert that the play "is *primarily* a dramatic defense of poetry." More specifically, its discloses the evils that beset artists, the relations of princes and courtiers to poets, and the high functions of poets in human culture. Its method (not essentially a dramatic one) is "running the gamut of the barbarians," that is, ridiculing successively the various enemies of literary art.[17] Among these, of course, are poetasters; thus, incidentally, Marston and Dekker can be exposed to ridicule. (Doubtless, Jonson elaborated this feature of his plan beyond what strict proportion allowed.) Hence, *Poetaster* stands as an *ars poetica,* a work of literary doctrine, but one adapted for the stage. Its purpose is basically serious; its mode—satire—Jonson was striving with erudition and independence to adapt to theatrical form; its style is witty and eloquent. Despite these impressive claims, *Poetaster* has to be judged by the criterion of vitality in the theater. In this respect it is weaker, for it is thin in plot, though amusing in its episodes; and it is overly long in some speeches and in its totality.

Satiromastix obviously does not have equal merits as literature. A common—and stupid—criticism points out the violation of decorum in putting "Roman" characters into a Medieval story; in reality, Horace is no more a Roman than Sir Quintilian Shorthose is a Norman. Dekker has merely extended the principle used by Jonson in *Poetaster* (and by most other Elizabethan dramatists) of dramatizing contemporary manners and attitudes in an antique setting. If all the names in *Satiromastix* were clearly Norman, nothing in the play would be changed (except to weaken the effect of borrowing from *Poetaster*). Actually to be considered, rather, are the incongruities of tone or dramatic method that vitiate the play. From this point of view we must blame Dekker, in the first place, for the discord between the serious and the comic plots, which seem to be quite devoid of thematic relation to each other. Secondly, Dekker has elaborated the comic theme of Widow Miniver and her suitors to such a degree that the serious action ceases to count much in our imaginations or in the meaning of the play. Thirdly, in the comic plot Dekker has relied too heavily on conventionally crude dialect and farcically shallow characterization.

Yet, without regard to its success as a lampoon of Jonson, Dekker's portrait of Horace must be judged a remarkable comic characterization; and Tucca and Bubo are certainly comparable, if not equal, to Shakespeare's Pistol and Aguecheek. Perhaps no more can be claimed for the farce of Miniver's suitors than that it probably did not bore the audience at Paul's for whom it was written. In other words, like the rest of the play, it is good theater. We have to grant that *Satiromastix* is a potpourri not well blended; yet is not a contemptible work. And it served its original purpose extraordinarily well.

V Realism Merged with Romantic Convention: *The Honest Whore* (1604, 1605?)

Doubtless under the influence of Jonson's *Every Man in His Humour* and *Every Man Out of His Humour,* as well as of Marston's and Middleton's early "city comedies" and the vogue of formal satire from 1597 to 1600, Dekker, in two plays now called **The Honest Whore**,[18] tried to combine realistic depiction of London life with his accustomed morality and romance. Part I is, indeed, a collaboration with Middleton, a realist by temperament. His contribution (unusually limited in number of lines)[19] consists mainly of the shopkeeper scenes, in which the patience, or "humour," of Candido the linendraper is severely tested by his wife and by a crew of idle gallants. Despite the farcical humor of these episodes, Candido's triumphant virtue is eulogized and therefore truly constitutes part of Dekker's morality pattern, which is seen more plainly in the major action: the conversion of Bellafront from whoredom to chastity. Yet, as a dramatist trained in the practices of the early 1590's, Dekker could not let these morality elements compose the whole substance; accordingly, he frames them in a romantic love story. Characteristically, he subordinates realism of social manners to morality, humor, and romance.

The romantic plot has as its basis a familiar situation: the hostility of two noble families imperils the happiness of two lovers, their offspring. Gasparo, Duke of Milan, seeks to terminate the love affair of his daughter Infelice with Hippolito (whose family is not named); he arranges to have Dr. Benedict give the girl a sleeping potion; when it takes effect, the Duke announces that his daughter has died. After a public funeral procession which is interrupted by Hippolito's frantic demand for possession of the body and by his accusation of murder against the Duke, Infelice awakens in her bed chamber and is told that Hippolito is dead. She is taken to Bergamo for seclusion. The Duke now suggests to his accomplice that Hippolito should be poisoned; but although he seems to consent promptly (I.3.99), Dr. Benedict secretly initiates the moves that will frustrate the Duke by communicating the truth to the lovers, first, by a letter to Infelice and, secondly, by a talk with Hippolito.

The audience, however, cannot immediately see this apparent reversal of Dr. Benedict's character because three acts of the play intervene before his communications are made (IV.4). Meanwhile, the romance is suspended, and the other plots occupy the stage. When, at last, Hippolito learns from Dr. Benedict that Infelice is alive, the romance moves swiftly to its end. Aided by the physician, the lovers meet at Bethlehem Monastery, seven miles from Milan, where Friar Anselmo agrees to marry them in the evening; afterwards, they may escape under cover of darkness. But the gabbling tongue of Matheo, Hippolito's friend, has already given news of the plan to a courtier, who, in turn, has told it to the Duke. Another of Hippolito's friends brings word of the Duke's pursuit. The wedding is quickly performed. Although Bellafront does prevent the lovers from escaping in disguise as friars and does expose them, the Duke soon resigns himself to the marriage, for he has had no antipathy to Hippolito as a man.

The morality plot is more important than the romance, both in its very essence and in the amount of action given to it. Matheo, a dissolute gallant, has taken as his mistress the courtesan Bellafront; but she falls in love with Hippolito when Matheo brings his friend for a casual visit. Later, she privately avows her love to Hippolito, expecting his ready acquiescence in her passion; Hippolito, instead, replies with a lengthy diatribe about the odious character and fate of a whore. After he has gone, Bellafront is overcome with shame and love. She prepares to kill herself with the dagger which Hippolito accidentally left behind. But he returns for the weapon and prevents her suicide.

Repenting her evil life, Bellafront discharges her bawd and pimp and then rebuffs the group of gallants who frequent her lodging. However, her plea to Matheo that he marry her and restore her honor (he was her original seducer) is in vain. Although her renewed plea for Hippolito's love is equally fruitless, still her visit to his apartment enables her to overhear his appointment to meet Dr. Benedict. By some means, presumably from Matheo, Bel-lafront learns of the rendezvous at Bethlehem. There, after gaining entrance as a mad woman, she finds the Duke in a pliant mood and appeals to him for justice against Matheo. The Duke orders the wastrel to marry her, and the betrothal takes place as part of the play's resolution.

The comic plot exhibits the patience of the merchant Candido. The efforts of Viola, his perverse wife, to vex him seem to have no motive other than a sense of inferiority brought on by his self-control. Her envy is seconded by the mischief of a group of idle gallants. The action is dispersed throughout the play, mostly in Acts I, III, and IV, and consists of a series of tricks played on the imperturbable, but not stupid, merchant. Finally, soon after Viola has had him carried off to Bethlehem as a madman, she repents this trick and her envy. The Duke's sudden journey to the monastery causes her to follow in order to obtain Candido's release.

From these summaries it is apparent that the structure of Part I is less unified than that of *The Shoemaker's Holiday.* Two rather mechanical devices serve to tie the three actions together. The first of these is Hippolito's friendship with Matheo, which has no foundation in the men's qualities but is invented for economy: to allow Hippolito to function in both romantic and morality plots. Of course, this same function is performed by the group of gallants who serve as tormentors of Candido in the comic plot and as companions (in fact, one of them acts as informant) of the Duke in the love plot. The second device is Dekker's gathering of all the characters at Bethlehem Monastery, which, rather surprisingly, also houses Bedlam Hospital. Setting the denouement in Bedlam permits Dekker to entertain his audience with a show of madmen, which has but little relation to his drama. The gathering itself, however, once the lovers have circumvented the hostile father, facilitates the resolution. The Duke, in a rather sketchy judicial scene, deals out rewards to Bellafront and Candido.

Viewed as a structural device, Dr. Benedict's duplicity in his relations with Duke Gasparo is a little less mechanical. Benedict at first seems the ordinary tool-villain of Italianate melodrama (I.3); later scenes, however, lead to a different interpretation. We discover that he has always been the friend of the lovers; his offer to poison Hippolito (I.3.96-97) is only a ruse by which he may meet the young man, conceal him, and bring about the wedding. Far from acting the villain or the pretentious quack (conventional object of satire), Benedict functions like the kindly friar in other romantic comedies, especially Lawrence (in *Romeo and Juliet*) who is also learned in physic. In Act I, Benedict indicates by intonation and facial expression his secret horror of Gasparo's command to poison Hippolito; we note "although the fact ['deed'] be fowle" (I.3.99). Even before falsely reporting Hippolito's death to Gasparo, Benedict has written the whole truth to Infelice and summoned her to Bethlehem to meet her lover (IV.4.94-97). His long delay in revealing the truth to Hippolito has resulted from being "chambred vp, / To stop discouery"

(IV.4.82-83). His false report to the Duke of Hippolito's death has no plot function other than to revive the tension which has grown weak because of two and one-half acts devoted to the morality and comic actions. Gasparo is thus again shown to be a treacherous tyrant.

In summary, the audience's interpretation of the Physician's function in the play depends on the actor's skill in revealing his duplicity by conventional inflections, looks, and gestures more than on symbolism of costume or on the pattern of action, although the pattern is discernible after Benedict's introductory scene. After he has informed Hippolito of the plan for the secret wedding, Dr. Benedict disappears from the play. Friar Anselmo substitutes for him in Act V, and perhaps the same actor played both parts.

Although the artificiality of the plot devices used by Dekker in this play would be far less noticeable in the theater than it is to a reader, the dramatist is undeniably less skillful than in *The Shoemaker's Holiday* in applying technique to his purposes, particularly in the device of Hippolito's and Matheo's friendship. This tie seems especially implausible because the moral worlds of the romance and the morality plots are not assimilated (Part II is much better unified in this respect). Furthermore, if we take realism to mean the dramatist's representation of the drives and tensions of normal life and not just fidelity to language and social manners, we must say about Part I of *The Honest Whore,* as about *Shoemaker's Holiday,* that Dekker has subordinated realism to other purposes. When we look, for instance, at the only episode (II.1) which achieves notable satiric force—the scene where Bellafront makes her toilet and then entertains the gallants—we admire the vivid depiction in the first 230 lines and then its sequel—Hippolito's eloquent invective against whoredom. Jonson could not have improved either part. Underlying the whole scene, however, is a double motif that Jonson would have avoided: Bellafront instantaneously falls in love with Hippolito and, as a result of this emotional impetus, is changed at once from a frivolous, coarsened woman to a repentant sinner. Dekker's keen observation and brilliant style become the vehicles of familiar conventions of romance.

Although the scene displays great mastery of dramatic effects and truth to human feeling, at the end of it, beyond question, carnal love really dominates Bellafront: "Not speake to me! not looke! not bid farewell! / Hated! this must not be, some meanes Ile try. / Would all Whores were as honest now, as I" (II.1.454-56). Therefore, we have to deny Dekker credit for the deepest ethical feeling or psychological intuition. The same confusion of motives holds in Bellafront's remaining scenes and is even accentuated by less satisfactory theatrical conventions: the disguise of a page boy, the pretended madness, and the hackneyed recovery of Bellafront's virtue by a forced marriage to Matheo, her first seducer. She must be married, for this is a comedy.[20]

In spite of these reservations about the limited realism of Part I, the play is impressive for its scenes of pathos and poetry. Not much below Dekker's finest work, it apparently succeeded well on stage and was printed in four editions before 1616.

There is unanimity that Part II of **The Honest Whore** is wholly Dekker's, and the very general opinion is that this play is one of his best. Naturally seeking to repeat a successful formula, he offers the same principal characters—Bellafront, Hippolito, Matheo, and Infelice—as well as another testing of Candido, a fifth act enlivened by the humors of Bridewell (instead of Bedlam), and a reversal of the original moral situation. The reversal is the one to which Somerset Maugham devotes ponderous irony in *Rain*: the converted courtesan is pursued by the man who has won her back to virtue. But Dekker, never a cynic, has too deep a faith in human nature for an ironic ending. He is intent now on a domestic comedy (rather than a romantic one); but it must be moral. The action, however, is not simple but quite complicated.

After Matheo has been imprisoned for killing his opponent in a duel, Bellafront comes to Hippolito who is now happily married to Infelice. She brings Matheo's plea for help in getting a pardon. Hippolito, who promises to intercede with Duke Gasparo, is captivated by Bellafront's beauty. Later he meets her father, Orlando Friscobaldo, who has tried to cast her off and forget her because of her disgraceful life. Although Friscobaldo tells Hippolito that he will not help Bellafront, afterwards, disguised as a servant, he goes to Matheo's house. He arrives just after Matheo, released from jail by Hippolito's intervention, has been joyfully welcomed by Bellafront. She pleads with her husband to amend his life, but he is eager to return to his cronies. Friscobaldo, who offers to become Matheo's servant, is hired under the name of Pacheco.

Hippolito has tried to corrupt Bellafront's virtue with gifts; in particular, he bribes Pacheco to give her a purse full of gold. But Bellafront returns all the gifts to Hippolito through Friscobaldo. When Friscobaldo comes to Hippolito's house and delivers the gifts to Infelice, he thereby reveals that her husband is pursuing Bellafront. Later, Infelice cleverly draws from Hippolito a confession of his intended adultery. Ignoring his remorse, she indignantly denounces him. In his resentment he resolves to continue to woo Bellafront.

Matheo has meanwhile gambled away every penny he owns, even his sword and cloak. He comes home and urges Bellafront to go into the streets to sell her body. She refuses, and Matheo strips off her gown and sends Friscobaldo to pawn it, leaving Bellafront standing in her petticoat. When Matheo's friend, the courtier Lodovico, visits them, he gives Matheo one of his own suits. Friscobaldo's indignation has reached such a pitch that he goes home, puts on his own garments, and returns to Matheo's place as his father to berate the couple, especially Matheo. In Lodovico's fine clothing, Matheo has the effrontery to return Friscobaldo equal abuse. The father refuses to lend them money, leaves Matheo's house, resumes his servant's dress, and returns as Pacheco.

Matheo now tells him of a plan to rob old Friscobaldo. Left alone, Bellafront receives a visit from Hippolito, and the two engage in a formal argument on whoredom. Bellafront ends it by running away, but Hippolito continues in his determination to win her.

Friscobaldo reveals his identity to Duke Gasparo as well as a plan for arresting Matheo for robbery. The Duke supplements this plot by ordering the arrest of all prostitutes in Milan and their confinement in Bridewell. By this means he hopes to shame Hippolito out of his attachment to Bellafront. At a gathering of gallants and panders in Matheo's house (to which the innocent merchant Candido has also been invited), sergeants of the law arrest Matheo, Bellafront, Candido, and the panders and take them all to Bridewell. When the Duke, Infelice, Hippolito, and their retinue pay a visit to Bridewell, Bellafront pleads with the Duke for Matheo's pardon. Matheo admits to the robbery of Friscobaldo, but charges his wife with being both his accomplice and the whore of Hippolito. Infelice corroborates the second accusation. Hippolito furiously proclaims Bellafront's purity. At this point Pacheco-Friscobaldo removes his disguise. Matheo and Hippolito are overwhelmed with shame and confess their guilt. At Bellafront's renewed plea, Friscobaldo and the Duke pardon Matheo. Friscobaldo takes Matheo and Bellafront to live in his own house. Hippolito and Infelice are reconciled.

At the beginning of the minor plot we learn that the patient linen-draper, Candido, has lost his first wife and has just married for a second time. When his bride displays her temper at the wedding feast, the gallants, led by Lodovico, propose to teach Candido how to discipline a new wife. Disguised as a prentice, Lodovico induces Candido and his wife to duel with yardsticks; but she quickly submits to her husband. Thereafter, two other gullings of Candido follow; the second involves Candido's arrest for receiving stolen goods, a disgrace which he endures with patience and from which he is exonerated in Bridewell. The comic scenes are less ironically amusing than those in Part I.

Although Part II is crammed with intrigue, it is much more highly unified in theme than Part I. Part II is a successful blend of motifs from saints' legends and from Prodigal Son interludes of the earlier sixteenth century. Professor Michael Manheim's illuminating article on the themes of this play (see note 18 above) gives a persuasive demonstration of Dekker's artistry in the blending of all the elements of the work, including both the rather obscure one in which Hippolito dismisses the poor scholar (I.1) and the Bridewell scenes (V.2). Bellafront must resist Hippolito's seduction, patiently endure Matheo's cruelty, and strive to win him to an honest life by her devotion. Her ordeal is, in considerable part, a new version of the legend of Thais who, following her conversion from a life of lustfulness to one of purity, has to endure a severe test of her virtue.

Bellafront's tempter, Hippolito, parallels other representatives of the Prodigal Son in several plays of about the year

1600—Young Flowerdale, for example, in the anonymous *London Prodigal* (published 1605). However, Dekker has greatly modified the character-type by making Hippolito older and happily married; and his reform is not accomplished by the intervention of his own disguised father. Furthermore, there are no palliating circumstances for his lust. He is tested, and his vice is exposed, first by Infelice, then more decisively by Friscobaldo, who thereby reforms him. In fact, Friscobaldo is the agent, the disguised father, who puts Bellafront, Matheo, and Hippolito to the test and thereby both glorifies Bellafront's fortitude and reveals the corruption of the two men.

Purity and fortitude against temptation are not the same virtue as patience, which Bellafront also possesses to the highest degree, and which is Candido's strength. Bellafront is reminiscent, therefore, of Griselda as well as of Thais. In respect to patience, the other wronged wife, Infelice,[21] becomes a foil to Bellafront by her lack of sufferance. When, by a clever ruse, she has led Hippolito to confess his infidelity, her wrath simply provokes an answering anger in him and a fresh resolve to possess Bellafront. Thus Infelice's impatience is punished.

The moral lesson receives even more enforcement, however. The Candido plot, in two actions, dramatizes, first, the shopkeeper's very quick taming of his shrew, his new wife, who kneels and says submissively, ". . . I disdaine / The wife that is her husbands Soueraigne" (II.2.108-109). Secondly, his sublime patience is demonstrated in Bridewell through the trickery of the gallants. A medieval expression of the moral lesson of the Thais theme is a formal debate of over 130 lines (IV.1.256-394) between Bellafront and Hippolito on whoredom. Professor Manheim points out that this highly rhetorical argument is a reversal of the positions of the two contestants in Part I and gives the rhetorical victory to the woman. In Part I, Bellafront, in lustful passion, spoke the sophistries which truth, in Hippolito's person, refuted with indignant sincerity. In Part II, Hippolito, appealing directly to the audience for a verdict, states his case first and plays the role of lustful Fallacy; then Truth movingly confutes him.

Bellafront's virtue conquers at last, but does not triumph directly over Matheo's vice. As in life, virtue triumphs by drawing on the aid of friends—her father and the Duke. Friscobaldo's intrigue finally brings Matheo to shame and repentance.[22] By testing Bellafront's firmness, then, Friscobaldo plays a more important part in the dramatization of the theme than at first appears. Hazlitt and others have fervently praised the character of Friscobaldo as one of Dekker's best creations. Undoubtedly he is, but readers who are inclined to unsparing realism may consider the execrable Matheo a finer masterpiece of truth. After he has lost hat, cloak, and rapier at dice, Matheo returns home and tries to drive Bellafront into the streets to sell herself: "Must haue money, must haue some, must haue a Cloake, and Rapier, and things: will you goe set your limetwigs, and get me some birds, some money? . . . Must haue cash and pictures: doe ye heare, (frailty)?" (III.2.27-32). But when she refuses to go, Matheo begins to strip off her clothing in order to pawn it.

Unable to endure his daughter's degradation, Friscobaldo removes his disguise as servant, enters in his own person, and vilifies Matheo as a thief, cheater, and whoremonger, only to hear himself labeled an ass, churl, and mangy mule. In the course of this abusive exchange, Matheo asides to Bellafront: "Kneele, and get money of him. . . . Hang upon him . . . follow close . . . to him" (IV.1.120, 123-24). A little later, however, and strangely, Matheo's pride causes him to choke on learning that the roast of mutton he is relishing was given by a charitable neighbor! Scenes III.2 and IV.1 are genre pictures of sordid life unequalled in Elizabethan drama, not excepting Shakespeare's. The whole play shows signs of great care on Dekker's part. We can only wish he had sacrificed some of the didactic theatricalism of the Bridewell scenes for more of Matheo in action.

VI PATRIOTIC ALLEGORY: *THE WHORE OF BABYLON* (1606)

In publishing **The Whore of Babylon** in 1607, Dekker was clearly offering his politico-religious allegory with pride and confidence to his countrymen.[23] Although the theme of the play is the preservation of Elizabeth from assassination and of England from the Armada—events which had taken place more than nineteen years before—Dekker does not refer to any anachronism in the subject-matter for two probable reasons: His devotion to Elizabeth had not changed since his youth, and he was confident that the intense national emotion consequent on the discovery of the Gunpowder Plot was like his own and would applaud his patriotic poem. With respect to the Spenserian theme of England's destiny, Dekker is offering in drama a counterpart to *The Faerie Queene*. The opening sentence of *Lectori* has an obvious Spenserian phrasing: "The Generall scope of this Drammatical Poem, is to set forth (in Tropicall and shadowed collours) the Greatnes, Magnanimity, Constancy, Clemency, and the other incomparable Heroical vertues of our late Queene."

To be precise, the play is a political and religious allegory of England's former escape from peril, a figuring forth of the malignancy of England's secular enemies, Spain and Catholicism. For several reasons the Gunpowder Plot itself would not serve as a basis for a poem: its circumstances were too confused, and James I was not entirely English! But, from a perspective of seventeen years (to the time of the Plot), a Protestant Englishman could see infallibly the hand of Providence in the course of events in the 1580's. Dekker had probably long meditated on the dramatization of the theme. Spenser was above challenge in the epic, but a worthy poetic drama on England's greatest trial had never appeared.

Neither Dekker's aspiration nor its result is ridiculous. In 1606 the majority of Londoners, if not of all Englishmen, must have shared his belief that God had again intervened

directly to save England; he quite truly expressed their feelings about the dangers from Spain and Catholicism. Eighteen years later the failure of the negotiations for the marriage of Prince Charles to the Infanta provoked an outburst of the same feeling and force; and Middleton, borrowing here and there from Dekker's play, wrote for the King's Men one of the most successful political satires ever staged in England, *A Game at Chesse* (1624). Both the parallels and the contrasts between the two plays are interesting. We note in particular that Middleton boldly ventures to represent the events of recent months in Spain; Dekker's reference to the Gunpowder Plot is only by implication. His choice of the Armada-peril for his theme may have been a mistake because of the distance in time and the lack of correspondence of details with the events of the Plot. Whatever the reason, there is no record of any notable success for **The Whore of Babylon.** Dekker, perhaps rationalizing, complains of the "bad handling" which the Prince's Men gave his play at the Fortune Theater.[24]

In summary, the action of the play appears disjointed because the theme is exemplified in two dramatic modes: a pageant-like series of events which were rather remotely connected, historically and chronologically, and a number of interspersed imaginary and allegorical episodes. After a dumb show has represented the death of Queen Mary, the accession of Titania (Elizabeth), and the conversion of Fairie Land (England) to true religion, the Empress of Babylon (the Roman Church) incites her sons, the hierarchy, to send priests for the purpose of causing confusion in England. Moreover, the monarchs of Spain, France, and the Holy Roman Empire come to Fairie Land to propose marriage with Titania. She refuses them and jeers at their indignation.

Threatening vengeance, the King of France and the Emperor depart, but Satyrane, the King of Spain, stays in the hope of spreading poisonous doctrine, "suck[ing] allegiance from the common breast." Titania's wise counselors prepare for both insurrection within and invasion from without. Danger from within takes the form of two ambitious men, Paridel (Dr. Parry) and Campeius (Edmund Campion). But their malice meets with clemency, not death, from the Queen; they are banished. Appropriately, the Hollanders and the Prince of Portugal come to her for protection and receive it.

At a great council in Babylon (Spain), the Empress, the King of France, and the Emperor determine to assassinate Titania. For this purpose they employ Campeius and Dr. Ropus (Lopez), who have been seduced from their loyalty to Fairie Land by the King of Spain. The two renegades are sent to Fairie Land. Meantime, the council members agree to make an irresistible attack with Spain's immense sea power. Paridel, who has come under the sway of the Jesuits in Rome, is also despatched to Fairie Land.

Titania is unwillingly forced to condemn Mary, Queen of Scots, to death; but by words alone she overawes a lesser enemy, an assassin, and he flees from her unguarded presence. Dr. Ropus's poison plot and Paridell's dealing with Babylon are discovered, but Titania takes no vengeance. Meanwhile, the Armada has been launched from Babylon. When Paridel decides to kill the Queen one of his kinsmen reveals the plan to her courtiers, and before Paridel can muster courage to slay her, even though she is alone, he is apprehended.

Titania and her advisers make preparations for defense against the Armada. However, we learn of the disastrous defeat from the anguished cries of the three kings who witness it from afar (they are on stage). Titania is with her army in camp at Tilbury where Florimell (the Earl of Leicester) brings her news of the victory. Meanwhile, in Babylon, the Empress, hearing of the disaster, rages against the kings. The Emperor defies her, but France and Spain submit to her tyranny. Thus it ends.

The allegorical figures in *The Whore of Babylon* are Time (the father of Truth), Truth, Falsehood, and Plain Dealing. In addition to the initial dumbshow mentioned above, there are three others. In one we see the King of Spain's frustrated attempt to cast a fatal spell on Titania. In another the Empress of Babylon shows her satanic pride as she rides the seven-headed beast. In the last dumbshow Falsehood tries to penetrate Fairie Land with her crew of priests and traitors, such as Edmund Campion. Falsehood's disguise as Truth is exposed, and during this disclosure we learn that Plain Dealing has formerly (in the Middle Ages) mistaken Falsehood for Truth and has been her follower. Enlightened now, Plain Dealing follows Time and Truth as they pursue Falsehood with intent to denounce her. By this allegory Dekker wishes to transfer the medieval peasant, as spokesman of complaint or satire against social evils, into the contemporary world of Protestant England. Accordingly, Plain Dealing's most important dramatic function is to inform Titania of abuses which she is unable to observe because of her protected position—for instance, corruption among the clergy. The only characteristic element of comedy in this play appears in the contrast between Plain Dealing's blunt manner and Titania's gracious, serious bearing and language.

Dekker's intention—to manifest God's providential care for England and true religion through the creation and defense of Queen Elizabeth—is, of course, one of instruction. If that thesis and nothing more were demonstrated, the result might be simply reassurance or complacency for the audience. Although the play does not preach the moral conclusion, Dekker certainly intended that this moral be drawn: kings, lords, and commons, all alike, must hold God's favor by reforming abuses in the commonwealth and seeking justice and other virtues in Church and State. This theme is also present in one of his plague pamphlets which will be discussed in a later chapter.

Because the total import of the play is of such gravity, the dramatist was required to find the most direct, the clearest, and the most meaningful mode of instruction known to

him. Dekker accordingly turned back to the traditional genres of the chronicle play and the interlude, each recognized as charged with meaning, the one with patriotism, the other with moral truth. In post-Reformation days the genres had even been combined, as in the plays of John Bale and Sir David Lindsay. But there were no recent Elizabethan examples of such fusion for Dekker to imitate, and we should allow him the measure of originality he claims in his Prologue, that his "Muse / (Thats thus inspir'de) a Nouell path does tread. . . ." (22-23). Ignoring the "thin vailes" of poetic fiction which cover the identities of persons, we find that essentially *The Whore of Babylon* presents history with the freedom and forthright moral purpose of the chronicle-interlude.

The fiction, however, is an important component of the work, for it controls the tone of the play. Although Dekker does not use the term "allegory," his expression "Tropicall and shadowed collours" reveals his conception of his "Drammaticall Poem" (*Lectori*, 1-2). Transparent as the veil of the fiction was meant to be, the allegory makes more appropriate Dekker's use of such familiar medieval devices as long speeches of narrative and doctrine, groups of generalized characters to represent powers and forces (cardinals, kings, priests, and soldiers), and personified abstractions (Time, Truth, Plain Dealing). Although dumbshows were largely of Italian Renaissance origin, they and such theatrical spectacles as processions and councils were also appropriate to allegorical plays; and they have their counterparts in literary allegory from *Piers Plowman* to *The Faerie Queene*. Of course, Dekker actually borrows some details from Spenser's poem and attempts by doing so to increase the grandeur of his theme and style, to make his drama and Spenser's epic twin triumphs of English poetry and patriotism.

Among the borrowings are these: England imaged as a fairy land; the gathering of the knights at Titania's court; the frustrating of a conjuror's attempted enchantment of the Queen; Falsehood masquerading as Truth; and the names "Paridel" and "Satyrane," though the persons have nothing in common with Spenser's. (Incidentally, Dekker uses no archaism of language.) But the pervasive influence of Spenser is shown in Dekker's endeavor to idealize both Elizabeth's character and the glories of England in her reign. Undoubtedly his attitude was common; we find the philosophical courtier, Fulke Greville, expressing it in his life of Sir Philip Sidney (*circa* 1610). Therefore, Dekker was not naïve in his feeling, whatever may be our judgment of his accomplishment in *The Whore of Babylon.*

Despite the timely patriotic fervor of *The Whore of Babylon* and its eloquent verse, the audience may have found its dramaturgy too old-fashioned. Tastes in drama were changing, and the causes of change probably lay in both social and literary movements. Among the latter were the vogue of formal satire in verse and of melancholy in society and in literature, the revival of revenge tragedy and of character-writing, and especially the trend toward satiric realism which Jonson's experimental comedies had

launched in English drama. Whatever the relative importance of these developments, they either corresponded to
or caused changes which we can observe, around 1600, in
the plays written for the public theaters by such dramatists
as Thomas Heywood, John Webster, Shakespeare, and Dekker himself. A tendency was growing toward social realism, toward Italianate tragedy, and toward romance
dominated either by tragic feeling or by deeper psychological interest than had prevailed before. Accompanying a
sharpened concentration on human personality was a
gradual abandonment of didacticism by means of personified abstractions, overt conflict of good with evil, and
loose, episodic structure, as in **Old Fortunatus.** True, we
must guard against exaggerating the rapidity of the change,
for the era of the clown, the dumbshow, and the generalized character extended well beyond 1600, as Shakespeare's *Cymbeline* reminds us. However, the theme, and
especially the technique, of **The Whore of Babylon** must
have appeared somewhat archaic to the audience at the
Fortune.

In addition, a degree of ambiguity in the play's appeal
may have helped to dampen the audience's response. At
least to a twentieth-century reader, the alternation of two
feelings—indignation against the venality, ambition, and
disloyalty of wretches like Campion and Parry along with
contempt for their baseness—makes a rather incoherent
emotional pattern. Furthermore, since the virtue of Titania
and her counselors and warriors is unconquerable when
supported by Heaven's favor, then fear of Babylon is
superfluous.

To reason in this way, however, leads us to ignore the
anxiety created by the Gunpowder Plot, a fear for which
the play is meant as an antidote; and we overlook the
exultation generated by victory over the plotters and the
renewed interest in the subject of political assassination. It
should be noted also that **The Whore of Babylon,** through
Plain Dealing's words, attacks evils in contemporary
England: vices rampant in London; indolence among the
clergy; licentious satire in drama; avarice among lawyers;
and graft in the army. Hence, although the play capitalizes
to a degree on the public's emotion at the moment, the
dramatist does not fail to indicate the serious lessons to be
drawn from his picture of England protected by divine
intervention.

Certainly the poor reception of the play cannot be charged
to any lack of attention on Dekker's part. He has surely
used the techniques of earlier Elizabethan drama with as
much skill as Thomas Kyd or Robert Greene could have
shown at their best. And he has evidently devoted great
care to the eloquent verse; in fact, nothing that he has left
us is better than many of the poetic passages in **The Whore
of Babylon.** The Empress of Babylon begins an address to
her Council:

> When those Cælestial bodies that doe moue,
> Within the sacred Spheres of Princes bosomes
> Goe out of order, tis as if yon Regiment,

> Weare all in vp-roare; heauen should then be vext,
> Me thinkes such indignation should resemble,
> Dreadfull eclypses, that portend dire plagues
> To nations, fall to Empires, death to Kings,
> To Citties deuastation, to the world,
> That vniuersall hot calamitie
> Of the last horror.

(III.1.3-12)

(It seems that the young Milton may have included this
play in his reading.)

Again, in Act V, Scene 2, Florimel describes the preparations against the Armada in a style that may be compared
with familiar passages in Shakespeare's *Henry V*:

> Your goodly ships beare the most royall freight,
> That the world owes (true hearts:) their wombes are
> ful,
> Of noble spirits, each man in his face
> Shewes a Kings daunting looke, the souldiers stand
> So thickly on the decke, so brauely plum'd,
> (The Silken streamers wauing or'e their heades)
> That (seeing them) you would judge twere *Pentecost*
> And that the iollie youngsters of your townes,
> Had flockt togither in gay multitudes,
> For May-games, and for summer merriments,
> They looke so cheerely: In such little roome
> So many Faieries neuer dwelt at once,
> Neuer so many men were borne so soone. . . .

(168-180)

VII Social Satire: *If This Be Not a Good Play, the Devil Is in It* (1610?)

I have noted in Chapter 1 that an interval of about four
years, apparently devoted to writing tracts, falls between
1606 and 1610, when, to judge by topical allusions in it,
Dekker composed **If This Be Not a Good Play.**[25] After it
had been rejected by the Prince's Men at the Fortune, the
play was performed by the Queen's Men (formerly the
Earl of Worcester's Men, to whom Henslowe gave
financial aid). It played at the Red Bull where, traditionally, popular drama prevailed. The refusal by the Prince's
company, probably served to complete Dekker's embitter-
ment which began with what he felt was that company's
failure with **The Whore of Babylon.**

However, the old-fashioned theme and manner of the play
perhaps explain the rejection by the Prince's Men. Discarding altogether the technique developed by Jonson and
Middleton for depicting life and manners with pungent
realism, Dekker employs a folk tale not merely for explicit
moral purposes, but very much in the fashion of a moral
interlude of a half-century before; and once again he calls
on the traditional stage conventions and devices for
spectacle.

The Danish and German tale of Friar Ruus (or Rausch)
had been available in English since 1568, but in a form
crudely altered from the primitive version. However, as C.
H. Herford observes, Dekker returned "by sheer dramatic

instinct to the original legend, in the face of every version of it which he can possibly have known."[26] That is to say, Dekker rejected the picture of a corrupt monastery and restored the orderly house described in the primitive form of the legend in order to provide a greater challenge to the devil. In fact, although the friars are the object of much of the comedy, their superior, Clement, is a saint; the worst among them can be charged only with stupidity and callousness; and the portrayal of monasticism is free of the contemptuous malice that usually inspires such Elizabethan references to convents as those in the anonymous play *The Merry Devil of Edmonton* and in Middleton's *A Game at Chesse.* Compared to financier Bartervile, the friars in *If This Be Not a Good Play* appear virtuous.

Stated more precisely, Dekker's plan is to show three spheres of human life beset by the power of evil: the court; the Church; and the merchant class. Dekker intends a satire on contemporary life and if his view is not so wide as Jonathan Swift's, it is surely broad enough for a play. It is somewhat medieval in its method. After a superb first scene which presents a conclave in Hell, Satan despatches three devils, one to King Alphonso's court, a second to the priory, and a third to a financier. The success of these three tempters, of course, provides the fundamental satiric comment. At court, Bohor destroys Alphonso's idealism with no loss of time and with little trouble; in the priory, Rush has but limited success and corrupts only a few friars (the play reveals that religion suffers far more from men than from devils); but, in the counting house, Lurchall is at first overmatched by the ingenuity and unscrupulousness of a Machiavellian atheist who believes only in "nature." At the end Lurchall manages to trick the merchant into damnation. Because Dekker intends this drama to be a comedy, in the medieval as well as in the Elizabethan sense, its result must not be cynicism or utter pessimism. Corrupt King Alphonso is saved, therefore, by the humility, constancy, and love of his betrothed wife Ermenhild (still another patient Griselda); and the friary is preserved from destruction by Clement's courage and fortitude.[27]

Two great evils of contemporary England have been illustrated for a courtly or a general audience: the power of greedy counselors at court and the ruthless avarice among the merchant class. But the monarch (in the person of King Alphonso) has also been reproached. Instead of serving as the fountainhead of justice, he has protected the monopolists and has neglected soldiers, scholars, and sailors, the defenders of civilization. The nation may readily take a lesson from Dekker's moral poem, for so he regards it.[28]

Surely no play in the canon is more characteristic of Dekker's mind than this one. As Herford says:

> With no other help than his sound playwright's instincts, and without a suspicion of its immense potentialities, he had stumbled upon the very idea afterwards carried out in Goethe's *Faust*—the recasting of an old devil-story in terms of modern society. . . .

Unhappily, however, Decker was, after all, little more than a hack with ideas.[29]

Herford's conclusion, however, is quite unfair, whatever defects of art *If This Be Not a Good Play* possesses, for Dekker, could scarcely think otherwise than as a man of the sixteenth century. He was as incapable of Machiavelli's cynicism (in *Belphegor*) as of Goethe's egoism; for, as a Christian, he had to look at society as one who believes in sin, individual responsibility, and grace. In the tracts which he had been writing before *If This Be Not a Good Play*—such as *The Seven Deadly Sins of London, A Knight's Conjuring,* and *Work for Armorers*—he had exposed and satirized social evils of many kinds; and that concentration had been preparation for the play. Whereas our own tendency in this century has been to criticize Dekker for his blindness to society's responsibility for these evils, our more recent emphasis on the need for commitment now makes Dekker's attitude more acceptable.

The epilogue of this play (incorporated as V.4) may be regarded as an adequate summation of Dekker's view of the corruption in English society and, substantially, in all human society. When Dekker gives us his version of the *Inferno,* the walls of Hell open up. Seen in the flames are, first, Guy Faux and Ravaillac, traitors to their kings and countries, and themselves victims of Catholicism's malignancy; next appears a prodigal, a typical courtier who in one year "spent on whores, fooles and slaues, / An Armies maintenance"; then an extortionate merchant; finally, a Puritan, a black, shrunken soul, the betrayer of the English Church, the raiser of such a hellish uproar that Satan cannot make himself heard. Treason, waste, cruelty, and heresy are the cardinal sins. They are four, not seven; and the emphasis on treason as the most heinous shows a disappointing Elizabethan bias. Nevertheless, the scene and the whole play are rooted in medieval philosophy handed down through morality play, homily, and satire.

Compared with *Old Fortunatus,* Dekker's *If This Be Not a Good Play* would be difficult to revive today in the spirit in which it was written, not because it is more serious than his *Old Fortunatus,* but because its fundamental dramatic irony is a mode from which Dekker could never draw a flow of witty humor. A hasty reader may say that Dekker's use of the Belphegor theme degenerates into platitude or that its irony is lost in mere spectacle. Although unfair, that judgment would have some truth in it. Perhaps the only notable success of Dekker's irony is Lurchall's first frustration in handling Bartervile, the Machiavellian usurer. Dekker lacked the capacity to sustain the tone of that encounter, yet he had chosen a theme which required a strong gift for irony. To his credit, he refrained from supplying,[30] in place of ironic wit, buffoonery by Rush among the friars, as his source and as Christopher Marlowe's *Doctor Faustus* had prompted him to do. Even Scumbroth, the comic cook, is a restrained example of Dekker's usual clown. However, an unresolved tension between the expectations raised by the ironic situation and by Dekker's failure to satisfy them is the weakness of the play. The characters of devils impersonating men create but little satiric humor. At times the essential irony seems almost forgotten.

VIII THE FLETCHERIAN INFLUENCE: *MATCH ME IN LONDON* (1620?)

Although chronology has been of merely general relevance in our discussion thus far, the plays (except *Old Fortunatus*) have been considered in the order of their composition; and we have now arrived at about the year 1611. *Match Me in London,* the drama to which I now turn, was probably written between 1620 and 1623 soon after Dekker's release from debtors' prison.[31] This work also represents, no doubt, a number of lost plays composed during the period from 1610 to 1620 during which John Fletcher's prestige was growing in the London theaters. It is also true that out of approximately six surviving plays ascribed to Dekker and written after 1619, only *Match Me in London* is his alone, as the title page and the dedication reveal. Although some of the collaborations are better dramas, the inclusion of *Match Me in London* in this account is justified because it reveals Dekker's individual accommodation to the prevailing tendency in later Stuart drama.

Considering the variety of the plays that may reliably be attributed to Fletcher, it is rash to suggest by a formula the qualities that are common to all of them. However, Fletcher's constant use of piquant themes and his skillful technique hit the taste of the élite Jacobean audience so well that many of his competitors, including Philip Massinger, Thomas Middleton, and John Ford, were impelled to change their practice and imitate him, and so to enlighten us as to his originality. We may say, then, that Fletcherian tragicomedies commonly offer a complicated intrigue in the setting of a remote court; the motives of passionate love, devoted friendship, and sacred honor clash, and the conflict produces agonies among the courtiers and sovereigns who are the chief persons. The king is often a tyrant; yet absolute submission to his adulterous or jealous will is the law of his society, and it is usually rendered. The fascination of incest, seduction, or sadism may be strongly introduced in the play, but the action normally moves to a happy ending by means of discoveries at the denouement both of unknown relationships and of disguised persons, as well as by abrupt changes of character from evil to good.

Some of these elements can be seen in a résumé of *Match Me in London.* In Seville, the lustful King of Spain falls in love with Tormiella, a shopkeeper's wife. After he has failed to win her by secret intrigue, he forces her to come to court as a lady-in-waiting to his virtuous queen.[32] No persuasion or threats can shake Tormiella's devotion to her husband, Cordolente, however, and she remains chaste (although the audience is misled for a while on this point).[33] By a ruse, the queen tricks the king into revealing his love for Tormiella and then angrily rebukes him, but in vain. He furthers his tyrannical passion by plotting to have the queen charged with adultery. He succeeds, then orders a physician to kill both the queen and Tormiella's husband.

But Doctor Lupo is a disguised revenger named Luke Gazetto. A rejected suitor of Tormiella, he has followed her and Cordolente to Seville from Cordoba, whence they had fled after their elopement and secret marriage. Lupo, who has been biding his time, weaves an involved intrigue at the climax of which Cordolente, deprived of his wife, will be duped into stabbing Tormiella in the church while she is being married to the king. When this moment arrives, however, Cordolente recoils from desecrating the holy place with murder. Tormiella falls into his arms. A terrifying burst of thunder and lightning drives the royal party from the church before the marriage can take place. Following her talk with Cordolente, Tormiella is now able to inform the king of Lupo's villainy. From the doctor the king learns that the queen still lives; he repents and gladly reunites Tormiella and Cordolente.

Although the main plot is more complex than the preceding summary indicates, Dekker has added to it a political intrigue which is intended to stress the motif of personal honor clashing with loyalty to the sovereign. Valasco, the Admiral of Spain and the father of the wronged queen, has to repulse the treacherous maneuvers of Prince John, the king's ambitious brother and an enemy of Valasco as well. Valasco frustrates the Prince by threats, challenges, and shrewd countermoves. This minor plot is so devoid of action and relies so much on conventions of motive and situation that only careful reflection enables the modern reader to see its tensions. Nevertheless, both major and minor plots evidently dramatize the Fletcherian theme of a passion-ridden king who tyrannizes over subjects who may not resist his divinely given authority.

However, Dekker has modified many elements of his Jacobean play in an Elizabethan fashion. Tormiella, although of noble parentage, is a shopkeeper's wife and a faithful one; she resembles Jane, of *The Shoemaker's Holiday,* rather than the unnumbered lewd citizenesses of Jacobean comedy. Cordolente employs Bilbo, a voluble, comic servant of the same species as Shadow and Firke, though more subdued. Bilbo and a foolish courtier engage in a satirical debate on the vices of the court compared with those of the city. A number of scenes take place in Cordolente's shop, although it is true that they lack the realism introduced in *The Honest Whore.* After Tormiella has been carried off to the court, Cordolente, in disguise, identifies himself to his wife when he visits her to fit her with a pair of shoes—a device repeated from *The Shoemaker's Holiday.* Although the unhappy Queen of Spain is much more energetic than patient Grissil and Infelice, she is yet another example of the chaste, long-suffering wives whom Dekker admires. And, finally, the intricate plot, full of purposed seductions and murders, ends with only one death, that of one of the queen's servants. The king, Prince John, and Lupo repent; the queen, Valasco, Tormiella, and Cordolente forgive them. This conclusion in universal goodwill, appropriate for the romantic comedies of the 1590's, has not been well prepared for by humor of character or situation or by romantic sentiment. But, as we have said, the incongruity is usual in tragicomedy and is worth noting in **Match Me in London** only because the whole play lacks the geniality characteristic of Dekker.

Furthermore, **Match Me in London** lacks the strong moralism of Dekker's earlier plays as well as their implicit or expressed social criticism. It lacks also their patriotic feeling, warm sentiment, relish for absurdity of character, and passages of deep psychological realism. However, although this play may rightly be described as Dekker's attempt to please new tastes in drama which he did not really share, **Match Me,** like his earlier plays, displays his mastery of stagecraft. We may take for example an episode in Act II, Scene 4, which I have cited in a preceding paragraph—Tormiella's being taken to court. She enters the stage from Cordolente's house masked among a group of masked courtiers, men and women. She says only "Farewell!" to her husband who is standing aside with her father. Neither of them recognizes her. She goes off to court. When Cordolente and her father receive no response to their call for Tormiella, they enter the house and find her missing. The audience readily accepts this episode, including its brutal separation of young husband and wife, only because (1) it recognizes Tormiella when she detaches herself momentarily from the group for the farewell, though by convention her mask remains impenetrable for her husband and father; (2) the convention of drama is of absolute submission to the king's will, no matter how immoral; and (3) while the king, her would-be seducer, has already shown signs of remorse, Tormiella has shown signs of unyielding resistance to him. Her fidelity to Cordolente remains above question. Their separation, therefore, is not really tragic.

The frequent criticism that Dekker is weak in the construction of his plays may sometimes based on such scenes as the above from **Match Me in London** in which he relies quite successfuly on the conventions of his theater, although partly to the mystification of the modern reader. In fact, with regard to his technique, Professor Harbage suggests that Dekker's practiced hand was the constructive one in several collaborated plays of high merit, such as **The Witch of Edmonton.**[34] The present chapter, it is hoped, may have produced evidence to support that view against the older, too offhand judgment that Dekker was either ignorant of dramatic art or disgracefully negligent of it— "shiftless and careless" in Swinburne's words—or "haphazard," unable to "devise perspectives of artifice," as Miss Bradbrook says.[35] Although no one will claim great merit for **Match Me in London,** an imitative play contrived by a weary veteran, it does show, like its predecessors, Dekker's mastery of dramatic technique.

We have completed our survey of the seven plays which scholars are almost unanimous in believing to be entirely Dekker's. They are the survivors of a large output, perhaps thirty-five or forty plays; for the fragmentary state of dramatic records permits only a guess as to how many De-

kker wrote unaided. But we may probably assume, and validly, that these seven surviving plays are numerous and varied enough to represent Dekker's achievement fairly.

Notes

In 1630 was also published Part II of *The Honest Whore,* which in 1608 had been entered in the Register to Thomas Man, but without payment of fee, and which was now re-entered without transfer from Man to Nathaniel Butter, the publisher. Dekker's name is correctly spelled on the title page, but there is no Latin motto. The printer's copy appears to have been Dekker's autograph. It is doubtful whether Dekker sold two different manuscripts of the play to Man and to Butter or whether the actors sold the "foul papers" of the play to Butter.

1. "The Prologue," *A Challenge for Beauty, The Dramatic Works of Thomas Heywood,* V (London, 1874, 4-5.

2. Although papal excommunication of Queen Elizabeth in 1570 marks the beginning of suppression of the medieval cycles and other religious drama, Phillip Stubbes, in *The Anatomie of Abuses,* 1583, speaks of mysteries as still being produced. The passage is quoted in E.K. Chambers, *The Elizabethan Stage* (Oxford, 1923), IV, 222.

3. C. H. Herford, *Studies in the Literary Relations of England and Germany in the Sixteenth Century* (Cambridge, 1886), pp. 210, 405-06. The earliest Dutch translation held by the British Museum is dated 1631. Its title page says it is *De achte mael herdruckt,* but whether the seven previous printings were in Dutch is uncertain. Probably more German versions than Dutch translations had been published by 1596. [Mary L. Hunt, in *Thomas Dekker* (New York, 1911), p. 34, suggests] that Dekker went to the Netherlands in his youth and there read a German version.

4. But the *Volksbuch* of 1509, apparently the first edition, was not divided into parts, and I have not seen any record of later publication in parts. The first known English translation was entered in the Stationers' Register as *The History of Fortunatus* on June 22, 1615. Edward Arber, *A Transcript of the Registers of the Stationers of London; 1554-1640 A.D.,* III (London, 1876), 568.

5. The "31 of November," says Henslowe.

6. Professor Fredson Bowers has found a cancellation in the quarto which suggests that possibly two thirds of the edition had been sold by mid-February, 1601. "Essex's Rebellion and Dekker's *Old Fortunatus,*" *Review of English Studies,* III (1952), 365-366.

7. At the end of 1597 Henslowe stops recording the names of plays when entering his share of the proceeds from productions. But he refers to plays by name in other connections, for instance, payments to dramatists and purchases of costumes and properties.

8. This is also Professor Bowers's opinion, [*The Dramatic Works of Thomas Dekker,* I-IV (Cambridge, 1953-1961), I, 107]. Henslowe's phrases are "for the altering of the book" and "for the end of *Fortunatus* for the Court." [R. K. Foakes and R. T. Rickert, *Henslowe's Diary* (Cambridge, 1961), pp. 127, 128].

9. Herford, *Studies,* pp. 215-18.

10. Herford, *Studies,* p. 216.

11. She has to be told why Ampedo was punished (it was for sloth), lines 275-76.

12. Herford, *Studies,* pp. 217-18.

13. L. M. Manheim, "The King in *The Shoemaker's Holiday,*" *Notes and Queries,* CCII (1957), 432-33.

14. Alfred Harbage, "The Mystery of *Perkin Warbeck,*" in *Studies in the English Renaissance Drama,* ed. by Josephine W. Bennett, Oscar Cargill, and Vernon Hall (New York, 1959), p. 137.

15. Although *The Weakest* was published in 1600, other evidence suggests, without proving, a considerably earlier date of composition than that of *Shoemaker's Holiday.* In *The Weakest* I cannot find any real evidence of Dekker's authorship; but Miss Hunt thinks he revised it (pp. 42-5).

16. It is well praised by Una M. Ellis-Fermor, *The Jacobean Drama* (London, 1947), p. 124.

17. E. W. Talbert, "The Purpose and Technique of Jonson's *Poetaster,*" *Studies in Philology,* XLII (1945), 226, 251-252.

18. Dekker and Middleton's original title, judging by Henslowe's entry in his *Diary* before March 14, 1604, and by the entry in the Stationers' Register on November 9, 1604, was *The Humors of the Patient Man, the Longing Wife, and the Honest Whore.* Later Dekker decided to title the play *The Converted Courtesan,* which is the running title of the corrected edition. Meantime, however, the first edition had appeared as *The Honest Whore, with the Humors,* etc.; and, because of the popularity of Part I, this title was also used for Part II. On the appropriateness of *The Converted Courtesan* as the title, see Michael Manheim's excellent article, "The Thematic Structure of Dekker's *2 Honest Whore,*" *Studies in English Literature 1500-1900,* V (1965), 363-81.

19. After studying the texts of a number of Middleton's plays, and having twice made an analysis of the bibliographical and stylistic evidence both in Part I of *The Honest Whore* and in *The Roaring Girl,* I find that to the former play Middleton contributed between seven and eight hundred lines. His undoubted scenes are I.5, III.1, and III.3. Of very doubtful authorship are IV.2 and IV.3. However, it is apparent that Middleton is chiefly responsible for the scenes of the testing of Candido. Although Professor Bowers does not make a conjecture on the matter, I believe that the printer's copy was entirely in Dekker's handwriting; but if this is true, the fact would not preclude the presence of traces of Middleton's spelling and punctuation in the manuscript.

20. Furthermore, Middleton's contribution (especially I.5 and III.1), which is indeed more realistic than the rest of the play, is not impressively so, for it consists of ironic farce and attributes to Candido's wife a motive for her shrewishness (resentment) which is simpler than the perversity which Dekker suggested in I.4.

21. In the verse of Part I this quadrisyllable several times appears as "Infaeliche," presumably an Anglicized spelling of the Italian pronunciation.

22. The long show of Bridewell birds which follows Matheo's confession, "and I am now his Patient," V.2.192, allows ample time for him to show his change of heart by caressing Bellafront, though he does not speak.

23. The title page bears his name correctly spelled and a Latin motto, *Vexat Censura Columbas*; he supplies a full apparatus of *Drammatis Personae,* epistle *Lectori,* and theater *Prologue*; and the text of the play was in his own handwriting. He made some revisions for publication.

24. *Lectori,* line 39. See also Chapter 1.

25. The wording of the first clause in the title is that found in the head title and head lines of the quarto and is, therefore, probably Dekker's own. The title page has *If It Be Not Good,* etc., no doubt a printer's alteration.

26. Herford, *Studies,* p. 302.

27. The priory has been penetrated by avaricious Bartervile in disguise as a friar and has been handed over by corrupted Alphonso to a courtier. It surely represents ecclesiastical institutions or the English Church in general. "Woe to these dayes, / When to raise Vpstarts, the poor CHVRCH decays," III.3.122-123.

28. See the dedication to the Queen's Men and the Prologue, which proudly asks the audience, "Lend not [the poet] hands for *Pittie,* but for *Merit,*" 45. In the Epilogue, "Much Labour, Art, and Wit, make vp a Play," 7.

29. Herford, *Studies,* p. 317.

30. The Prologue to *If This Be Not* is Dekker's finest expression of his aims as a dramatist. I have discussed its chief ideas in the first section of Chapter 6.

31. *Match Me in London* was licensed for production by Sir Henry Herbert on August 21, 1623, as an "old play" formerly allowed by Sir George Buc. But the quoted phrase is one Herbert used for any play formerly licensed, whether recently or not; and Buc was still licensing in 1622. The title page of the first edition (1631) says the play was first produced at the Red Bull Theatre and later at the Phoenix. Dekker wrote for the Queen's Men about 1611 and for the Revels Company in 1619-1622—both of them occupants of the Red Bull. Professor G. E. Bentley favors the earlier date, *The Jacobean and Caroline Stage,* I (Oxford, 1941), 185, note 5. But Dekker's dedication to Carlell in 1631 says nothing of any revision, which one would expect for the Phoenix production of a play from 1611 (the Phoenix opened in 1617). Therefore, I believe that *Match Me* was originally played about 1620 by the Revels Company at the Red Bull and, after that company's extinction in 1622, by the Lady Elizabeth's at the Phoenix and by their successors, Queen Henrietta's Company. See Gerald Eades Bentley, *The Jacobean and Caroline Stage,* I (Oxford, 1956), pp. 165-69, 182-87, 219.

The difficulty in dating *Match Me* is typical of a number of Dekker's plays.

32. See IV.1.14-15; but the arrival of a party of ladies-in-waiting, II. 4.48, surely implies a royal command.

33. See III.3.44-47. The ambiguity is typical of tragicomedy.

34. Harbage, "Mystery of *Perkin Warbeck*," pp. 130-131, 137.

35. A. C. Swinburne, "Thomas Dekker," *The Nineteenth Century,* XXI (1887), 102; M. C. Bradbrook, *The Growth and Structure of Elizabethan Comedy* (London, 1955), p. 121.

Suzanne Blow (essay date 1972)

SOURCE: "Persuasion and Drama," in *Rhetoric in the Plays of Thomas Dekker,* Institut für Englishe Sprach und Literatur, 1972, pp. 28-65.

[*In the following chapter from her study of the elements of formal rhetoric in Dekker's works, Blow identifies the rhetorical devices used for persuasion and argumentation.*]

Except for prologues, aside, and the like, every speech in a play is directed at a dual audience: the theatre audience and the character or characters to whom it is addressed in dramatic context. When Dekker intended a speech to achieve a persuasive purpose within his story framework, he customarily exployed rhetorical figures and principles decorously selected to fit the character of the speaker and the dramatic situation. In regard to the theatre audience, he skillfully utilized the persuasive devices of rhetoric to move the spectators to sympathize with or react against certain characters or themes. In a very basic sense, Dekker used the techniques of the logic of probability—rhetoric—to establish dramatic probability.

Of course the principles of persuasion and the techniques of applying them, which were classified, analyzed, and illustrated in Renaissance handbooks of rhetoric, are principles that are still used and that still work. The traditional art of rhetoric, as Dekker and other Renaissance writers had learned it, merely put at their disposal more tested techniques and forms than anyone would be likely to work out on his own.

Examination of some of the persuasive figures that occur in Dekker's plays should yield some insight into his mode of creating the effects he sought. Henry Peacham's *Garden of Eloquence* serves as the principal source of rhetorical theory in defining and explaining the devices of persuasion, because it is the most inclusive and most readily applicable Renaissance figurative handbook. The material in stylistic manuals such as Peacham's is organized, . . . under the two main divisions of tropes and schemes. Peacham distinguished between them in this way: "The differ-ence between the Trope and the Scheme is this, that in the Trope there is a chaunge of signification, but not in the Scheme."[1] The category of schemes is again divided into two parts: patterns of words and patterns of thought; as Cicero explained, "The figure suggested by the words disappears if one alters the words, but that of the thoughts remains whatever words one chooses to employ."[2] The persuasive devices we are concerned with in Dekker's dramas find their expression in stylistic theory for the most part among the schemes of thought. Many of these schemes seem quite far removed from what is conceived of today as "figures of speech," for in the guise of figures they embody some of the same techniques of persuasion which Aristotle and Cicero taught in the non-stylistic parts of rhetoric.

To begin with, shall be considered Dekker's use of some figures that concern the defensive strategy of argumentation—countering or refuting an opponent's arguments and meeting his objections. Ancient rhetoricians had long insisted on the psychological truth that strict logic is not necessarily the most persuasive form of argument in most human situations;[3] consequently, we find that some of the well-known fallacies of logic were incorporated into rhetoric as devices of refutation because of their convincing effect.

The rhetorical counterpart of evading an issue, or answering irrelevantly, *Apoplanesis,* is one such figure. "The speaker leadeth away the mind of the hearer from the matter propounded or question in hand." Choice of this method, if detected, could reveal to an opponent the lack of a reply; but if *Apoplanesis* is successfully carried out, the hearer "shall quight forget the question, and think himself fully satisfyed, when in deede there is nothing answered."[4] Dekker employed this figure for comic effect in **The Shoemaker's Holiday.** In response to the questioning of Lincoln and the Lord Mayor about the whereabouts of Lacy and Rose, who had eloped, Firke (one of Simon Eyre's journeymen) attempted to distract their attention by giving irrelevant replies.

> LINC.
> Where is my Nephew married?
>
> FIRKE.
> Is he married? God give him joy, I am glad of it: they have a fine day, and the signe is in a good planet, Mars in Venus.
>
> L. MA.
> Villaine, thou toldst me that my daughter Rose, This morning should be married at Saint Faithes, We have watcht there these three houres at the least, Yet see we no such thing.
>
> FIRKE.
> Truly I am sorie for't, a Bride's a prettie thing.
>
> (V, ii, 102-109)

Since Firke and fellow-journeyman, Hodge, were only executing a delaying maneuver for the already safely married couple, the comic obviousness of the device served as humorous method of mocking Lincoln and the Lord Mayor.

Using an opponent's own accusations against him, which according to the rules of logic comprises the *ad hominem* or *tu quoque* fallacy, is nevertheless one of the most convincing defensive procedures in rhetoric, since it throws the attacker into personal confusion and can distract him from his strongest points. Peacham called this technique *Metastasis,* turning the objections on the objector.[5] Dekker exploited to the fullest extent the dramatic potential of *Metastasis* in **The Honest Whore, Part II** when Infaelice used this device to confront her husband Hippolito with evidence of his attempted affair with Bellafront. First she made a false confession that she had been unfaithful to him with his footman, thereby provoking from him an outburst of rage:

> A Harlot to my slave? the act is base,
> Common, but foule, so shall not thy disgrace:
> Could not I feed your appetite? Oh women
> You were created Angels, pure and faire;
> But since the first fell, tempting Devils you are,
> You ha been too much downe already, rise.
> Ile with no Strumpets breath be poysoned.
>
> (III, i, 159-168)

Then, displaying some intercepted love tokens intended for Bellafront, Infaelice paraphrased the very words of his condemnation.

> . . . the act is base
> Common, but foule, so shall not your disgrace:
> Could not I feed your appetite? Oh Men,
> You were created Angels, pure and faire,
> But since the first fell, worse than Devils you are.
> You should our shields be, but you prove our rods.
> Were there no Men, Women might live like gods.
> Guilty my Lord?
>
> (184-191)

Of course Hippolito had no alternative but to confess.

> Hip.
> Yes, guilty my good lady.
>
> Infae.
> Nay, you may laugh, but henceforth shun my bed,
> with no whores leavings Ile be poysoned.
>
> (191-193)

Hippolito would not have seemed nearly so deflated had his wife added only a flat accusation to her proof. Through her neat verbal trick Infaelice also managed to arouse his suspicion against his messenger and real ally, Bryan the Irish footman. Thus the plot was advanced, the lady's wit applauded, and an important aspect of her husband's basic character revealed in his quick acceptance of defeat. It was necessary for Dekker to present Hippolito as a not wholly unsympathetic character at this point in order to prepare

the audience to accept the sincerity of his change of heart at the end of the play, though of course primary sympathy goes to Infaelice in this scene.

Reductio ad absurdam, an effective and acceptable dialectical method of refuting objections, is achieved by demonstrating through cause and effect that the inevitable consequences of an act or idea will be ridiculous. The rhetorical arguments designed to produce the same effect, *Apodioxis* and *Diasyrmus,* do not depend on showing logical consequences; instead they make an opponent's objections seem absurd by scoffing, or as Peacham explains it "by some ridiculous example, to which the adversaries objection or argument is compared whereby it is either made ridiculous, or at least much disgraced."[6] Immediately following the death of Fortunatus, in **Old Fortunatus,** Andelocia met his brother Ampedo's objections about breaking their father's will with both scorn and a ridiculous example.

> Amped.
> Will you then violate our Fathers Will?
>
> Andel.
> A puritane? Keepe a dead mans Will? Indeed in the old time, when men were buried in soft Church-yardes, that their Ghosts might rise, it was good: but brother, now they are imprisoned in strong Brick and Marble, they are fast; feare not: away, away, these are fooleries, gulleries, trumperies.
>
> (*Old Fortunatus,* II, ii, 372-377)

Andelocia's willingness to use such a device on this occasion is a key to his reckless, headstrong character, and in terms of plot his impious attitude foreshadows his evil destiny.

Rhetoric taught that *Antipophora,* the defensive tactic of granting concessions and then minimizing their importance by the addition of some mitigating reason, was appropriate for countering an opponent's strongest arguments or objections.[7] Having made wealth his choice from among Dame Fortune's gifts, Fortunatus conceded that he might be vulnerable to an early death, but he rationalized,

> How quickly? If I die to morrow, ile be merrie today:
> if next day, ile be merrie to morrow. . . .
>
> (I, i, 315-316)

This *carpe diem* philosophy which he expressed as a compensation for short life established the frantic mood which pervaded all his succeeding actions. With the same device, but in a contrasting attitude, Bellafront conceded that she had been a whore, but on the strength of a long reformation, pleaded for the forgiveness of her father, Orlando.

> Those flames (like lightning flashes) are so spent
> The heate no more remaines, then where ships went,
> Or where birds cut the aire, the print remaines.
>
> (*The Honest Whore, Part II,* IV, i, 54-6)

Unknown to Bellafront, her father (who had been secretly helping her since early in the play, in the disguise of Matheo's servant Pachecho) had already forgiven her and was feigning his anger in this scene. Consequently, Bellafront's speech served only to reveal the calm self-possession and humility of her character in contrast to the hot-headed pride of Matheo, who within a few lines showed Orlando the door: "If you come to bark at her, because shee's a poore rogue; look you, here's a fine path, sir, and there, theres the doore" (75-6).

Antipophora is a disarmingly persuasive figure, since it impresses the hearer with the honesty and courage of the speaker. Fortunatus, faced with possible death, and Bellafront, faced with a disgraceful past, both conceded to a harsh reality and thus gained the admiration of the audience, which would then be favorably disposed to accept whatever extenuation was offered. It is a device Dekker used in both instances to make his audience sympathetic with something ordinarily undesirable: Fortunatus's motive for wanting riches above wisdom and Bellafront's history of prostitution.

The next group of figures is based on the persuasive device of implication, which Quintilian called *Emphasis*[8] and Peacham, *Collectio*.[9] Apparently these techniques arose from the assumption that the hearer is more likely to accept a conclusion or be impressed with an idea, regardless of inherent validity, if he has carried out part of the reasoning process himself. A logical step omitted by the speaker assumes a convincing and emphatic aspect when supplied by the audience; furthermore the speaker is relieved of the burden of any kind of proof. Besides its persuasive value, implication also yields the pleasure of discovery to the hearer.

Even an implication that is very readily grasped produces some of these effects, although it may be just a form of circumlocution or euphemism. In *The Shoemaker's Holiday,* Hodge's argument for releasing his fellow-journeyman Rafe from military draft is phrased to question Lacy's authority while avoiding open insult, "Why then you were as good be a corporall as a colonel, if you cannot discharge one good fellow" (I, i, 148-149). Fortunatus's euphemistic description of death, when he is debating between the gifts of power and wealth, betrays his own ominous dread, "And though mine arme should conquer twentie worlds, there's a leane fellow beates all conquerors" (*Old Fortunatus*, I, i, 269-270).

In the final prison scene of *The Honest Whore,* Part II, Candido, the patient linen draper, who has been accused of receiving stolen goods from Matheo, combined the techniques of concession and implication in his response to the Duke's charge.

> So they doe say, my Lord,
> Yet bought I them upon a Gentlemans word,
> And I imagine now, as I thought then,
> That there be Theeves, but no Theeves Gentlemen.

> (V, ii, 206-209)

The implied appeal to the Duke's prejudices was quite open; nevertheless it helped effect Candido's release. Dekker could not have picked a more appropriate appeal for Candido, whose shrewd tactfulness had been so frequently shown to contribute to his success as a merchant.

Noema is a type of *Collectio* said to require either long consideration or sharp wit on the part of the audience.[10] In the opening scene of **Satiromastix,** two ladies had beer strewing flowers about in preparation for Sir Walter Terrell's wedding, and the bride's father told them,

> O well done wenches, well done, well done, you have covered all the stony way to church with flowers, 'tis well, 'tis well, ther's an Embleame too, to be made out of these flowers and stones.

> (I, i, 60-63)

The theatre audience was expected to follow the implication, but, within the story framework, the two women were not. Thus Dekker adapted this persuasive device to the purpose of entertaining and flattering the minds of his spectators.

According to Peacham the use of *Noema* "serveth onely to conceale the sense from the common capacitie of the hearers: and to make it private to the wiser sort"; therefore he warned that it ought to be used "verie seldome, and then not without great cause, considering the deepe obscuritie of it."[11] Actually the emblem of the stony road to matrimony is not deeply obscure at all except to the hearers in the play. Because there is little time for long consideration of a specific figure by the audience during a performance, Peacham's caution about *Noema* particularly applied to drama, and Dekker rarely used the device.

But *Mycterismus,* a jest that depends upon implication and is "yet not so privy that it may not be well perceived,"[12] occurs more frequently in his plays, especially in witty exchanges between high-ranking persons. Beraldo, in **The Honest Whore, Part II,** was discussing with Lodovico, another courtier, the second marriage of Candido, who had gained his fame as "the patient man" for his endurance of his wife's fierce tongue.

> BER.
> I wonder, that being so stung with a Waspe before, he dares venture again to come about the eaves amongst Bees.

> LOD.
> Oh 'tis rare sucking a sweet Hony-combe.

Although Dekker generally employed this figure for wit, Peacham described its main function as a method of rebuke just short of sarcasm: "The use thereof differeth not much from the use of *Sarcasmus,* . . . The chiefe use of this figure serveth to represse pride, rebuke folly, and taunt vice: and may be likened to a blacke frost, which is wont to nip a man by the nose, before he can discerne it with his eye."[13] *Mycterismus* would seem to be the specific type of implication employed by Candido in his speech to the

Duke about "no Theeves Gentlemen." Peacham classified the device as a trope rather than a scheme; however it provokes the same type of mental response as other figures of implication. Of course hyperbole (including understatement) which we will consider later works on the same principle.

The contrary of implication, retraction of something already spoken, was another mode of persuasion taught by the rhetoricians. One commonly used device derived from this technique was called *Correctio*, "a figure which taketh away that that is said, and putteth a more meet word in the place . . . Paul to the Romans: By what law of workes, nay, by what law of faith." Peacham added the caution, "it behoveth that the latter wordes be mightier then the former."[14] By this figure Firke announced Simon Eyre's election to the office of sheriff: "My maister is chosen, my master is called, nay condemned by the crie of the countrie to be sheriffe of the Citie" (*The Shoemaker's Holiday,* III, ii, 106-108). In the prison scene of *The Honest Whore,* when Mistress Horsleach denied that she had ever been a procuress, "I am known for a motherly honest woman, and no Bawd" (V, ii, 371-372), one of her fellow prisoners, Catryne Bountinall, used *Correctio* in expressing indignant disbelief:

> Honest Mistris Horsleach, is this World, a World to keepe Bawds and Whores honest? How many times hast thou given Gentlemen a quart of wine in a gallon pot? how many twelve-penny Fees, nay two shilling Fees, nay, when any Embassadours ha been here, how many halfe crowne Fees hast thou taken?
>
> (V, ii, 376-381)

Essentially, *Correctio* was a method of emphasizing important words. Dekker seems to have used it here as a means, also, for directing a mounting emphasis in the actor's delivery of the lines.

Fallacious arguments, concession, implication, and retraction were some of the basic methods of rhetorical argumentation. Dekker employed them, as we have seen, in exactly the type of dramatic situation where formal proof was either unavailable, undesirable, or inadequate. Candido, for example, had no alternative but to rely on a verbal trick to persuade the Duke of his innocence, because Dekker had provided him with no witness or other material evidence. Although Infaelice had in her possession an intercepted letter and a jewel sent to Bellafront, her verbally turning the tables on Hippolito created a much more satisfying scene than simply confronting him would have, because his guilt was brought home to him in his own mind before he could have a chance to offer any extenuation.

An appeal to the hearer's wit is implicit in most of the foregoing modes of persuasion, and in figures derived from them, such as *Noema* and *Mycterismus*. Some of the persuasive devices of rhetoric, however, relied on moving an audience through dramatic or fictional techniques which attempted to convince the hearer directly through his emo-

tions or imagination without recourse to a reasoning process. Even in their original oratorical setting, these were rated by rhetoricians among the most effective methods of argumentative strategy.

Hypothetical dialogue and personification are two devices which require some degree of dramatic characterization by the speaker regardless of the type of discourse in which they occur. *Dialogue* or *Sermocinatio* is defined as assigning to some person language which conforms to his character;[15] if the speaker adds imitation of gesture and manner of speech the device is called *Mimesis*.[16] In an oration, hypothetical dialogue is essentially a short dramatic insert given for the purpose of gaining realism and vitality. Dekker used the figure in *The Honest Whore, Part II* to enliven Catryna Bountinall's denunciation of Mistress Horsleach's partner Bots as a pander. Bots had staked his claim to innocence on the gamble that none of the whores in Bridewell prison would reveal his identity, but when Catryna not only spoke to him but mimicked his typical utterances, his case was lost.

> How long is't since you held the doore for me, and cried too't agen, no body comes, yee Rogue you?
>
> (V, ii, 403-05)

Here *Dialogue* seems such a natural part of this speech that without further evidence one would hesitate to call it a conscious rhetorical device. However its function in convicting Bots and the previous use of *Collectio* by the same speaker seem to provide sufficient justification.

Ad Herennium defined personification as representing an absent person as present or making a mute or formless thing talk.[17] Fraunce's definition was similar,[18] but Peacham broadened the term, which the Elizabethans called *Prosopopoeia,* to include assigning life to dumb things in any way.[19] Like other images used in persuasion, it can convey a value judgment directly to the hearer's imagination with no pause necessary for justification or explanation; the hearer then accepts or rejects the judgment on an an intuitive rather than a rational basis. In *The Shoemaker's Holiday,* Lincoln's personification of Lacy's love for Rose conveys his evaluation of the whole affair:

> That old dog Love that fawnd upon him so,
> Love to that puling girle, his faire cheek't Rose
> . . . hath distracted him.
>
> (II, iv, 38-40)

The persuasive function of personification is especially prominent in *Old Fortunatus.* Fortunatus himself used the device in convincing his sons that traveling abroad would yield more pleasure than staying in their own country.

> When in the warmth of mine owne countries armes
> We yawn'd like sluggards, when this small Horizon
> Imprison'd up my body, then mine eyes
> Worshipt these clouds as brightest.
>
> (III, ii, 164-67)

In one of the scenes at the English court, Galloway tried by means of an image personifying derision to induce the love-melancholy Orleans to stop his foolish moping for Agripyne.

> ORLE.
> Ile gaze on heaven if Agripyne be there:
> If not: Fa, La, la, Sol, la, &c.
>
> GALL.
> O, call this madness in, see from the windows
> Of every eye Derision thrusts out cheekes,
> Wrinkled with Idiot laughter.
>
> (III, i, 28-30)

Both Fortunatus's image of sleeping in his country's arms and Galloway's of Derision's laughing, idiot face convey implicit value-judgments which demand intuitive or emotional rather than rational evaluation.

When Vice, in one of the play's Masque-like scenes, had planted a "faire tree of Gold with apples on it" to allure mortals; and Virtue, only a tree "with greene and withered leaves mingled together, and little fruit on it" (I, iii, stage directions), Fortune used a personification of autumn and another of the world in trying to sway Virtue to put up a better front.

> Poore Vertue, Fortune grieves to see thy lookes
> Want cunning to intice: Why hang these leaves,
> As loose as Autumnes haire (which every wind,
> In mockerie blowes from his rotten browes?) . . .
>
> On Crutches went this world but yester-day,
> Now it lies bed-rid, and is growne so old,
> That its growne young; for tis a child againe,
> A childish soule it hath, tis a meere foole:
> And fooles and children are well pleasde with toyes:
> Then Vertue, by a golden face like Vice.
>
> (I, iii, 46-69)

These two personifications are the key persuasive points of Fortune's speech: the first opens the argument; the second provides the basis of the plea for action—"buy a golden face." Here we see Dekker throwing his persuasive imagery on the side of wealth and pleasure in *Old Fortunatus;* Virtue's reply is only a truism, singularly lacking in eloquent appeal, "Virtue abhorres to weare a borrowed face" (I, iii,74).

On the side of Virtue, Ampedo does employ a personification of the "strumpet world" in defending his Puritanical ways to Andelocia:

> AMPED.
> I am not enamoured of this painted Idoll
> This strumpet world; for her most beautious lookes
> Are poysned baits, hung upon golden hookes.
> When fooles doe swim in wealth, her Cynthian beames
> Will wantonly daunce on the silver streames:
> But when this squinteide age sees vertue poore,
> And by a little sparke sits shivering,

> Begging at all, reliev'd at no mans doore,
> She smiles on her (as the Sunne shines on fire)
> To kill that little heate, and with her frowne
> Is proud, that she can treade poore vertue downe:
> Therefore her wrinckled brow makes not mine sowre,
> Her gifts are toyes, and I deride her power.
>
> (I, ii, 49-61)

But compared to Fortune's image, Ampedo's seems bombastic and long-winded, especially since Dekker has Andelocia and the servant Shadow thoroughly squelch his argument.

> SHAD.
> 'Tis not the crab-tree fac'd world neither that makes mine sowre.
>
> ANDEL.
> Her gifts toyes: wel brother vertue, we have let slip the ripe plucking of those toyes so long, that wee florish like Apple trees in September, (which having the falling sicknes) beare neither fruit nor leaves.
>
> (I, ii, 62-7)

Shadow, maintaining the figure, implies the potent argument of hunger, while Andelocia by the device of *Metastasis,* turns Ampedo's own words and image against him. In a final example, the personification of "wet eide Care" is the basis for Fortunatus's rationalization of the first part of Fortune's prophecy to him: "goe dwell with cares and quickly die" (I, i, 312).

> FORTUNAT. But now goe dwell with cares and quickly die? . . . Where dwels care. Hum ha, in what house dwels care, that I may choose an honester neighbor? In princes courts? No. Among faire Ladies, neither, theres no care dwels with them: but care how to be most gallant. Among gallants then? Fie, fie, no: care is afraid sure of a guilt Rapier, the sent of Muske is her poison, Tobacco choakes her, rich attire presseth her to death. Princes, faire Ladies and gallants, have amongst you then, for this wet eide wench Care dwelles with wretches: they are wretches that feele want, I shall feele none if I be never poore, therefore care I cashiere you my companie.
>
> (I, i, 314-25)

No one knows better than Fortunatus that care dwells with wretches; therefore the psychological validity of the fallacious argument is to him unassailable.

Peacham commented that *Prosopopoeia* was a figure common to oratory and poetry, and made special reference to its persuasive value: "This figure is an apt forme of speech to complaine, to accuse, to reprehend, to confirm, and to commend."[20] So frequent use of the figure for persuasion in *Old Fortunatus* implies that Dekker was consciously exploiting its rhetorical function. In other instances he seems to use it solely for the pleasure of the poetic effect. Agripyne personifies the Thames as a part of an epic simile describing her experience of being carried through the air by the power of the wishing hat:

> . . . for as I oft have seene
> (When angrie Thamesis hath curld her lockes,)

A whirle-wind come, and from her frizeld browes,
Snatch up a handful of those sweatie pearles,
That stoode upon her forehead, which awhile,
Being by the boystrous wind hung in the ayre,
At length hath flung them downe and raizd a storme.
Even with such furie was I wherryed up,
And by such force held prisoner in the cloudes,
And throwne by such a tempest downe againe.

(IV, ii, 8-17)

Firke's enthusiastic personification of the various foodstuffs with which Simon Eyre feasted the apprentices of London represents a comic adaptation of the figure:

O Hodge, O my brethren! theres cheere for the heavens, venson pasties walke up and down piping hot, like sergeants, beefe and brewesse comes marching in drie fattes, fritters and pancakes comes trowling in in wheele barrowes, hennes and orenges hopping in porters baskets, colloppes and egges in scuttles, and tartes and custardes comes quavering in in mault shovels.

(*The Shoemaker's Holiday*, V, ii, 188-194)

The variety of purposes and of imagery evident in Dekker's manipulation of this one figure provides impressive evidence of his imaginative and stylistic versatility.

As imitation of dialogue and personification require some dramatization on the part of a speaker, so the creation of a vivid descriptive passage belongs first of all to the realm of fiction. Cicero explained the oratorical function of description in his *De Inventione*.[21]

By a vivid verbal picture the event is brought before the eyes of the audience, so that they will think that they too would have done the same if they had been confronted with the same situation and the same cause for action at the same time.

By this definition we see that the persuasive purpose of *Descriptio* was to create a feeling of empathy for the speaker or his cause. The sub-division and ramification that the device underwent in Renaissance rhetoric books indicates that it held a position of considerable importance during Dekker's life-time. The general term *Descriptio* included word-portraits of a person, a thing, an event, a place, an imaginary place, and a particular time.[22] Examples of such set descriptions (essential to the repertoire of a dramatist writing for the bare Elizabethan stage) abound in Renaissance writing. Edgar's imaginary word picture of the cliffs of Dover in *King Lear* (IV, iv, 112-124) is one outstanding instance.

In Dekker's use of *Descriptio* its rhetorical function of creating empathy seems primary on many occasions. Fortunatus's account of the three days that he has wandered lost in the forest predisposes the audience to empathize with the speaker's fatigue and despair. It is one of Dekker's most effective portraits of time—*Chronographia*.

In this wood
With wearie sorrow have I wandered
And three times seene the sweating Sun take rest,

And three times franticke Cynthia naked ride,
About the rustie high-waies of the skies
Stucke full of burning Starres, which lent her light
To court her Negro paramour grim night.

(I, i, 152-58)

The creation of empathy for Fortunatus is essential at this point in the play, in order that the audience will be fully prepared to understand the old man's choice of wealth above all other gifts. Another vivid visualization of time occurs in Dekker's prologue to *The Whore of Babylon;* his intention is to arouse in the minds of his audience their memeries of the years of Elizabeth's reign and to establish a mutual nostalgic feeling for that period between himself and his spectators.

But as in Lantskip, Townes and Woods appeare
Small a farre off, yet to the Optick sence,
The mind shewes them as great as those more neere;
So, winged Time that long agoe flew hence
You must fetch back, with all those golden yeares
He stole, and here imagine still hee stands,
Thrusting his silver locke into your hands.
There hold it but two howres, it shall from Graves
Raise up the dead.

(9-17)

To be sure, both of these time portraits serve an expository purpose, but the creation of empathy seems an equally positive intention of the author. Bellafront's vivid description of how a prostitute feels upon meeting "a faire yong modest Damsell" in a public place comprises the final point upon which she rests her case in her defensive argument with Hippolito; it is one of the most decidedly persuasive uses of the figure in Dekker's plays.

Nothing did make me, when I loved them (Harlots) best
To loath them more then this: when in the street
A faire yong modest Damsell I did meet,
She seem'd to all a Dove (when I pass'd by)
And I (to all) a Raven: every eye
That followed her, went with a bashful glance:
At me, each bold and jeering countenance
Darted forth scorne. . . .
For (as if Heaven had set strange markes on Whores,
Because they should be pointing stocks to man)
Dress up in civilest shape a Curtizan,
Let her walke Saint-like, notelesse, and unknowne,
Yet she's betraid by some trick of her owne.

(IV, i, 369-85)

Just as Cicero instructed, Bellafront's purpose was to bring such a striking verbal picture before Hippolito's eyes that he could imaginatively experience for himself her former guilty feelings and would then be convinced that if he were confronted with the same situation his stand would be the same as hers.

Dekker's preface to the readers in *The Whore of Babylon* contains strong evidence that he thoroughly knew and consciously employed the standard rhetorical instructions concerning *Descriptio.* His analogy to painting—color, proportion, life-like representation—could have been taken directly from the *Garden of Eloquence.* Dekker describes his purpose,

> The Generall scope of this Dramaticall Poem, is to set forth (in Tropicall and shadowed collours) the Greatnes, Magnanimity, Constancy, Clemency, and the other incomparable Heroical vertues of our late Queene. . . . Wherein if according to the dignity of the Subject, I have not given it Lustre, and (to use the Painters rhetorick) doe so faile in my Depthes and Heightnings, that it is not to the life, let this excuse me. . . .
>
> (*Lectori,* 1-10)

Compare Peacham's analogy:

> By this exornation the Orator imitateth the cunning painter which doth not onely draw the true proportion of thinges, but also bestoweth naturall colours in their proper places . . . for hence it is, that by true proportion and due coloure, cunning and curious Images are made so like to the persons which they present, that they do not onely make a lively show of life, but also by outward countenance of the inward spirits and affection.[23]

The Honest Whore, Part II yields another direct reference to word painting in Orlando's description to Hippolito of a happy man:

> Ile give you (my lord) the true picture of a happy man; I was turning leaves over this morning, and found it, an excellent Italian Painter drew it. If I have it in the right colours, Ile bestow it on your Lordship . . .
>
> He that makes gold his wife, but not his whore, He that at noone-day walkes by a prison doore, He that 'ith Sunne is neither beame nor moate, He that's not mad after a Petticoate, . . . He that counts Youth his Sword, and Age his Staffe, He whose right hand carves his owne Epitaph, He that upon his death-bead is a Swan, And dead, no Crow, he is a happy man.
>
> (I, ii, 49-65)

In adapting this device to Bellafront's sententious old father, Dekker demonstrated again his skill in subordinating rhetorical forms to the need for consistency in characterization.

An abrupt shift in attitude or point of view—such as apostrophe, license of speech, and interrogation require—is, in an oratorical setting, a dramatic device designed to sway the audience with the element of surprise and to prevent monotony. Fraunce defined apostrophe as turning a speech away to someone for whom it was not first prepared,[24] and mentioned that the figure included poetic invocations. Dekker did not make extensive use of apostrophe for persuasion, although it was the device in *Old Fortunatus* with which Orleans concluded the debate with Galloway mentioned earlier; if Agripyne cannot be his he vows to love nothing but deformity,

> Now Agripyne's not mine, I vow to be
> In love with nothing but deformitie.
> O faire Deformitie, I muse all eyes

> Are not enamord of thee: thou didst never
> Murder mens hearts, or let them pine like wax,
> Melting against the Sunne of destinie.
>
> (III, i, 67-72)

In **The Honest Whore, Part II,** a moving and realistic use of apostrophe occurs in a soliloquy by Orlando Friscobaldo upon receiving from Hippolito news of Bellafront's poverty. After pretending a hard-hearted indifference to his disowned daughter while Hippolito was present, Orlando's true feelings burst out in a brief apostrophe to her as soon as he is alone.

> And fare you well sir, goe thy waies, we have few Lords of thy making, that love wenches for their honesty; Las my Girle! art thou poor? poverty dwells next doore to despaire, there's but a wall betweene them. . . . Ile to her, yet she shall not know me.
>
> (I, ii, 167-171)

Since this is the first knowledge the audience receives that Orlando is not the unforgiving ogre he seems, the sudden shift of speech, "Las my Girle! art thou poor?" creates, in relation to the development of the plot, very much the same effect of sharp dramatic surprise ideally sought as the rhetorical function of the figure in an oration.

Licentia, adopting an attitude of frankness of speech before those who should be reverenced or feared,[25] requires a sudden emotional shift on the part of the speaker. In the plot of **Satiromastix,** which revolves around the king's efforts to seduce Walter Terrell's bride Caelestine, the bridegroom's license of speech before the king shows a reversal of his previously weak character. Caelestine's father had given her a drug to make her appear dead so that she would not be dishonored by King William, who had bullied Terrell into bringing her untouched to court the first night of her marriage. Believing that the potion was deadly, Terrell finally spoke out.

> TER.
> I blush not King
> To call thee Tyrant: death hath set my face
> And made my bloud bold.
>
> (V, ii, 63-65)

The persuasive power of this speech, in addition to the fact of Caelestine's apparent death, is shown to be the cause of the King's recognition of his own guilt.

> KING.
> Doe not confound me quite; for mine owne guilt,
> Speakes more within me, then thy tongue containes;
> Thy sorrow is my shame.
>
> (V, ii, 84-86)

Licentia is one of several recurring devices Dekker uses to characterize Simon Eyre in **The Shoemaker's Holiday.** In his conversation with the king, who has come to dine with him, Eyre couteously asks permission to use license of speech.

EYRE.
I would be sory at my soule, that my boldness should
offend my king.

KING.
Nay, I pray thee good lord Mayor, be even as merry
As if thou wert among thy shoomakers.
It does me good to see thee in this humour.

(V, v, 10-14)

Permission granted, Eyre's mood shifts suddenly from
deference to familiar gaity.

EYRE. Saist thou me so my sweete Dioclesian? Then
hump, Prince am I none, yet am I princely borne, by
the Lord of Ludgate my Liege, Ile be as merrie as a
pie.

(V, v, 15-17)

Dekker, always consistent in his portrayal of the good-
natured shoemaker, applies here the suggestion from *Ad
Herennium* that the pungency of *Licentia* should perhaps
be mitigated by praise or pretense, that is by remonstrating
with the hearers as they wish to be remonstrated with.[26] It
is more than appropriate that in this play marked by a
democratic social philosophy Eyre, too, should be the
recipient of *Licentia* from a subordinate. On numerous occasions his journeyman Firke speaks out boldly and frankly
to him and to his wife, for example, in response to Eyre's
boisterous arousal of the household, cited earlier:

FIRKE. O master, ist you that speake bandog and bedlam
this morning, I was in a dreame, and muzed what
madde man was got into the street so earlie, have you
drunke this morning that your throate is so cleere?

(I, iv, 9-12)

In an oration, interrogation requires a dramatic shift to the
second person viewpoint: the speaker, abandoning an
impersonal tone, suddenly directs questions specifically to
the audience. Peacham classified and described five different kinds of interrogations: *Erotema*, strongly affirming or
denying something by asking a question; *Pysma*, using
many questions in one place to confuse an opponent; *Apo-
ria*, showing doubt about when to begin or what to say;
Hipophora, answering one's own question, and *Anacaenous*, asking counsel of adversaries or deliberating with
judges.[27]

Dekker wove a doubly comic twist into one occasion when
Erotema was used to affirm strongly the questioned truth
of an assertion made by Firke. Lincoln and the Lord
Mayor, suspecting Lacy's disguise as the Dutch shoemaker
Hans, had bribed Firke to tell when and where Rose and
Hans were to be married. With elaborate precautions of
secrecy and hesitation about taking the money, Firke
confided that the wedding was scheduled for the very next
morning. Asked if he was certain of his information, the
journeyman affirmed his knowledge with an indignant
outburst of questions.

FIRKE. Am I sure that Paules steeple is a handfull higher
then London stone? or that the pissing conduit leakes

nothing but pure mother Bunch? am I sure I am lustie
Firke, Gods nailes doe you thinke I am so base to gull
you?

(IV, iv, 109-12)

But his strong protests, which convinced the questioners,
affirmed a lie: he gulled them of their bribe money by
sending them to the wrong church to stop the wrong marriage.

Another use of interrogation in deception occurs in ***The
Honest Whore, Part II*** when, in response to Bellafront's
plea that she had no further acquaintance with prostitution,
her father Orlando concealed his true feelings by attempting to confuse the issue with many questions—*Pysma*.

ORL. No acquaintance with it? what maintains thee
then? any Rents coming in, any Stocke going, any
Plough jogging, any Ships sailing? Hast thou any Wares
to turne so much as to get a single penny by?

(IV, i, 62-5)

Then he answered the last question himself (*Hipophora*)
with an insinuation.

Yes, thou hast a Ware to sell.

(66)

In the final scene of the play, after Bellafront, in prison
and on trial before the Duke, had faced a nearly overwhelming accumulation of evidence against her, Dekker
assigned her the figure *Anacaenous,* asking counsel of her
adversaries. Her own husband had accused her of both being a whore and colluding with him in theft; Infaelice had
produced Hippolito's letter and jewel, and only Hippolito
had spoken in her defense:

HIP.
Against that black-mouthed Devill, against Letters and
Gold,
And against a jealous Wife I doe uphold
Thus farre her reputation, I could sooner
Shake the Appenines, and crumble Rockes to dust,
Then (tho Joves showre rayned downe) tempt her to
lust.

BELL.
What shall I say? (*Anacaenous*)

(V, ii, 173-77)

Hippolito's device is a persuasive comparison, a figure of
amplification to be discussed shortly. The simple pathos of
Bellafront's question moved her disguised father to reveal
himself immediately and repudiate the accusations against
her.

In the perennial debate between Andelocia and Ampedo in
Old Fortunatus is found another example of *Pysma*, the
attempt to overwhelm an opponent with many questions.
Andelocia, defending his pleasure goal, seems confident
that this interrogation will overcome his brother's objections.

ANDEL. Away with your purtie, brother, y'are an Asse, why doth this purse spit out gold but to be spent? why lives a man in this world, to dwell in the Suburbs of it, as you doe? Away forren simplicitie, away: are not eyes made to see faire Ladies? hearts to love them? tongues to court them, and hands to feele them? Out you Stocke, you stone, you log end: Are not legs made to daunce, and shall mine limp up and downe the world after your cloth-stockin-heeles?

> (V, ii, 50-7)

If Andelocia is really trying to convince Ampedo, he has violated the first principles of persuasion by alienating his audience. More likely, Dekker is presenting an internal conflict here: Andelocia's arguments are to reassure himself.

Of course these are only a few of the occasions when Dekker incorporated interrogation for persuasion into his plays. It is noteworthy that he did not ordinarily use it to convey strong arguments, but more frequently to multiply words when the audience would know that the speaker lacked reasons. We may infer that this is one of the figures which probably connoted insincerity to him and perhaps to his spectators.

According to the Ciceronian doctrine of invention *amplification,* arousing the sentiments and emotions of the hearers in connection with the human implications of the proof advanced, was the last step necessary for the persuasive presentation of any subject.[28] The devices based on dramatic emotional appeal, which we have been discussing, bear a close relation to this part of rhetoric. Quintilian stated these four modes of amplification: by overstatement as saying that a man who was beaten was murdered; by argumentation, reaching not only the highest point, but sometimes even beyond it through climactic arrangement; by comparison, seeking to elevate the subject by raising something lower; and by reasoning, through which "one thing is magnified in order that another may be corroborated."[29] It will be apparent that amplification is a very broad classification incorporating many figures from various categories; according to Peacham, "amplification is called by the name of a figure, yet as a generall of many specials."[30] The distinguishing characteristic of amplification is the purpose of making a thing seem greater or less than it is through emotional appeal. The emotional orientation of the figure is indicated by Peacham's description:

> For being well furnished with skill and habite of this figure, he the orator may prevaile much in drawing the minds of his hearers to his owne will and affection: he may winde them from their former opinions, and quite alter the former state of their mindes, he may move them to be of his side, to hold with him, to be led by him, as to mourne or to marvel, to love or to hate, to be pleased or to be angry, to favour, to desire or to be satisfied, to feare or to hope, to envy, to abhore, to pittie, to rejoyce, to be ashamed, to repent and finally to be subject to the power of his speech wither soever it tendeth.[31]

Taken in its broadest meaning amplification might include the whole art of rhetoric; therefore we shall consider it in its narrowest application and discuss here those figures which depend most directly on emotional appeal.

Amplification, by the way, is one of the rhetorical devices Dekker mentions specifically in his plays. The reference occurs in a speech by Shadow, the servant of Fortunatus and his sons, who like the shoemaker Firke is characterized by a delight in word play.

> FORTUNAT.
> . . . age is like love, it cannot be hid.
> SHAD.
> Or like Gun-powder a fire, or like a fool, or like a young novice new come to his lands; for all these will shew of what house they come: now sir, you may amplifie.

> (II, ii, 118-21)

Syngnome, by which the speaker grants pardon and forgiveness to an adversary who has done him much wrong, is an amplifying figure typical of those intended to evoke sympathy.[32] Dekker applies it extensively in ***The Honest Whore, Part II*** to move his audience to sympathize with his much wronged heroine, Bellafront. Her culminating speech of forgiveness comes after her husband, determined she will be executed with him, falsely accuses her of causing him to commit theft.

> MATH.
> She set the robbery, I perform'd it; she spur'd me on, I gallop'd away. . . .

> BELL.
> My Lords, (fellow give me speech) if my poore life
> May ransome thine, I yeeld it to the law.
> Thou hurt'st thy soul (yet wipest off no offense)
> By casting blots upon my Innocence.

> (V, ii, 122-28)

Dekker again uses *Syngnome* in ***Satiromastix*** to draw sympathy to the side of the poetasters. Speaking for them, Captain Tucca, having bitterly denounced Horace (Ben Jonson) for breaking oaths made in print to himself, to Crispinius (Marston), and to Demetrius Fannius (Dekker), suddenly demonstrates a forgiving spirit to Horace, "But come, lend mee thy hand, thou and I hance forth will be Alexander and Lodwicke, the Gemini, sworne brothers" (IV, ii, 106-08). Assigning to the poetasters rhetorical figures which are specifically designed to create an impression of benevolent rationality in contrast to the irrationally spiteful speeches given to Horace is one of Dekker's chief devices for accenting the theme of this satirical play.

His close familiarity with the rhetorical principles governing the use of *Philophronesis* (another quite open form of emotional appeal) can be observed in ***The Whore of Babylon.*** By this device a speaker facing powerful opposition resorts to "gentle speech, faire promises, and humble submission to mitigate the rage and cruelty of his adversary," but Peacham adds the warning, "the counterfeit submission of hypocrites is opposed to the true use of this figure."[33] Here is the speech in which the Empress of Babylon advises the kings of Spain, Italy, and France to employ *Philophronesis* in winning England back to Catholicism:

> EMPR. Draw all you faces sweetly, let your browes
> Be sleekd, your cheeks in dimples, give out smiles,
> Your voyces string with silver, wooe (like lovers)
> Sweare you have hils of pearle: shew her the world
> And say she shall have all, so shee will kneele
> And doe us reverence: but if she grow nice
> Dissemble, flatter, stoop to licke the dust
> She goes upon, and (like to serpents) creepe
> Upon your bellies in humilitie;
> And beg she would but with us joyne a league,
> To wed her land to ours.
>
> (I, i, 101-20)

Astonishingly, her advice follows the very same order as Peacham's: first, gentle speech, "your voices string with silver, wooe (like lovers)"; next, fair promises, "shew her the world / And say shee shall have all"; and finally, humble submission, "creepe upon your bellies in humilitie." Furthermore, it is obvious that this last is to be "the counterfeit submission of hypocrites" which Peacham warned against.

The figures of exclamation, even more numerous than those of interrogation, are among the means by which a speaker stirred by vehement emotion attempts to move his hearers to feel the same. These figures include outcries, curses, prayers, exhortations, commendations, thanks, blessings, complaints, predictions, oaths, laments, provocations, and expressions of joy or hatred.[34] Aristotle called exclamation the last refuge of argument: a method a speaker should resort to if he can defend his cause neither through equity ("Justice that goes beyond the written law") nor by excuse and extenuation.[35] This is only the familiar principle of trying to conceal a weak argument with a strong voice. Nevertheless, Peacham classified and described twenty-four different figures of exclamation in an attempt to include all the methods of uttering "vehement affections in vehement formes."[36]

Matheo, in **The Honest Whore, Part II,** is of all Dekker's characters the one who most frequently and typically used exclamations for persuasion. It is appropriate that he should employ this last resort in argument, since he is portrayed always in some stage of desperation and since most of his actions could hardly be rationally defended or even extenuated. In one memorable scene, Matheo, who had lost in a dice game all his own money, his cloak, his rapier, and twenty pounds given to him for safe-keeping by his servant Pachecho (Orlando in disguise), was reduced to taking off the very gown Bellafront was wearing in order to obtain some money by pawning it. Pachecho, hoping to produce some twinge of conscience, attempted to dissuade Matheo by suggesting that he use the twenty pounds instead; ironically, Matheo responded with a protest of constancy, an exclamation called *Eustathis.*

> ORL.
> Why, pray sir, employ some of that money you have of mine.

> MATH.
> Thine? Ile starve first, Ile beg first; when I touch a penny of that let these fingers ends rot.
>
> (III, ii, 46-8)

The illustration of *Eustathia* which Peacham cited from Tertullian will corroborate this identification of Matheo's protest.

> Let Lions clawes teare out our bowels, let the Gibbet hang us, let the fire consume us, let the sword cut us asunder, let wild beasts tread us under their feet: yet we Christians are by praier prepared to abide all paine and torments.[37]

The dramatic function of the figure in this scene is to provoke from the audience an outraged response to Matheo's unscrupulous villainy. Later Matheo employed the same kind of protest in refusing to listen to an accusation of theft.

> DUKE.
> Stand forth and heare your accusation.

> MATH.
> Ile heare none: I flie hie in that: rather than Kites shall seize upon me, and picke out mine eyes to my face, Ile strick my tallon thorow mine owne heart first, and spit my blood in theirs.
>
> (V, ii, 90-2)

"Imprecatio . . . a forme of speech by which the Orator detesteth and curseth some person or thing, for the evils which they bring with them"[38] was another type of exclamation favored by Matheo. Upon receiving the money for his wife's pawned dress, he pronounced a Dantean curse upon pawnbrokers: "An evill conscience gnaw them all, moths and plagues hang upon their lowsie wardrobs" (III, ii, 125-26). Bellafront's father, Orlando, was a favorite object of his imprecations: "Pox rot out his old stinking garbage" (II, i, 132); "This is your Father, your dam'd—confusion light upon all the generation of you" (IV, i, 156-57); "A plague choake him, and gnaw him to the bare bones" (IV, i, 179). These exclamations were of considerable importance in the revelation of Matheo's character, since they provided dramatic expression for his total lack of self-discipline and his envious, malcontented disposition.

As stated before, the persuasive function of the figures of amplification is to make a thing seem greater or less than it really is. The figure called *Incrementum* achieves this purpose through a climactic word arrangement "which by degrees ascendeth to the top of some thing or rather above the top."[39] Quintilian considered this technique as one of the four major modes of amplification; he suggested as an example: "it is an offence to bind a Roman citizen, a crime to scourge him, almost treason to put him to death, what to crucify him?"[40] *Incrementum* is another device which achieves its effectiveness through implication—that the thing being amplified is great or insignificant almost beyond the power of language to express. Paridell's kinsman, in **The Whore of Babylon,** met the learned doctor's arguments for killing the queen with a brief *Incrementum* condemning the baseness of the proposed assassination: "for what can be the close / But death, dishonour; yea damnation / To an act so base?" (V, i, 22-4). Simon Eyre employed the device to amplify his self-confidence in response to his wife's caution about the King's visit:

> Wife.
> Good my Lord have a care what you speake to his grace.
>
> Eyre.
> . . . Sim Eyre knowes how to speake to a Pope, to Sultan Soliman, to Tamburlaine and he were here: and shal I melt? Shal I droope before my Soveraigne?
>
> (V, iv, 51-4)

Earlier in the same scene, in Eyre's instructions to the shoemakers about serving the drinks at his feast for the London apprentices, we find him using the figure to amplify his bounteous hospitality, "let wine be plentiful as beer, and beere as water" (V, iv, 8).

Of all the rhetorical devices of persuasion found in his plays, Dekker seemed to consider the most potent the use of comparison to augment or diminish the value of a thing. The general figure for this kind of amplification was called, simply, *Comparatio,* which Peacham described as the comparison of less to greater in augmenting, greater to less in diminishing.[41] Like personification, comparison functions in persuasion by modifying the subjective evaluations of the hearer. In one way it can be the most subtle of persuasive techniques, since it operates largely outside the hearer's conscious judgment; in another, it depends on the most direct appeal, since the comparison works immediately on the emotions, prejudices, and sentimental associations of the hearer. On almost every occasion when Dekker used argumentation as a vital plot element, some type of comparison is found to be a key persuasive figure.

Although various other devices are used, comparisons form the body of both Hippolito's debate with Bellafront and her defense. Moving from less to greater, Hippolito compares a harlot's beauty to a peacock and her freedom to the sun:

> As Junoes proud bird spreads the fairest taile,
> So does a Strumpet hoist the loftiest saile.
> She's no mans slave; (men are her slaves) her eye
> Moves not on wheeles screwd up with Jealowsie.
> She (Horst, or Coacht) does merry journeys make,
> Free as the Sunne in his gilt Zodiake:
> As bravely does she shine, as fast she's driven,
> But staies not long in any house of Heaven,
> But shifts from Signe, to Signe: her amorous prizes
> More rich being when she's downe, then when she rizes.
>
> (IV, i, 275-284)

How is this strong persuasion? Hippolito had clearly said he intended to beat down her chastity "with the power of

Argument . . . By force of strong persuasion" (IV, i, 249-252), and here we have only argument by analogy, from a logical viewpoint one of the weakest and least valid kinds of proof. The strength of these comparisons is entirely psychological; the intention is to substitute the connotations of the color and beauty of the peacock and the gold grandeur of the sun for the cheap, tawdry associations Bellafront feels for her former profession. There is also, in the peacock and sun images, an inherent appeal to pride in order to combat any of her anxieties that degradation might accompany her yielding. Furthermore, the beauty, wealth, and pride Hippolito is trying to associate with the harlot's life is the exact opposite of the position of subservience, poverty, and abuse Bellafront holds as Matheo's faithful wife.

In combating his argument, Bellafront depends largely on a series of diminishing comparisons, from greater to less, designed to demolish the romantic aura Hippolito's language had cast around the prostitute.

> . . . nay she's common:
> Common? as spotted Leopard, whom for sport
> Men hunt, to get the flesh, but care not for't
> . . . so men love water,
> It serves to wash their hands, but (being once foule)
> The water downe is powred, cast out of doores,
> And even of such base use doe men make whores.
> A Harlot (like a Hen) more sweetnes reapes,
> To picke men one by one up, then in heapes:
> Yet all feeds but confounding. Say you should taste me,
>
> I serve but for the time, and when the day
> Of warre is done, am casheerd out of pay:
> If like lame Soldiers I could beg, that's all,
> And there's lusts Rendez-vous, an Hospitall.
>
> (IV, i, 310-28)

Dirty water, inedible meat, a lowly hen, an old lame soldier—all represent a reduction of Hippolito's glamorous imagery to the worthless and commonplace; and the noble Lord himself, by implication, is reduced to the value of a mere grain of chicken-feed! Later in the debate and nearer her conclusion, Bellafront attempts to convey her remembered uneasy associations of guilt and fear with her former trade through another series of comparisons.

> My bed seem'd like a Cabin hung in Hell,
> The Bawde Hells Porter, and the lickorish wine
> The Pander fetch'd was like an easie Fine,
> For which, me thought I leas'd away my soule,
> And oftentimes (even in my quaffing bowle)
> Thus said I to my selfe, I am a whore.
>
> (IV, i, 356-61)

Bellafront's emotions are the real battleground of this debate; the challenge to Hippolito is to cast a spell of words over her unpleasant memories. From a rhetorical point of view, we might say that he lost because he attacked the wrong emotional problem. In trying to substitute grandeur and pride for poverty and degradation, he overlooked the chief cause of her resolute stand, her feelings of guilty shame.

In *Satiromastix* augmenting and diminishing comparisons are the principal weapons in a quadrangle of persuasion involving King William, Sir Walter Terrell, Caelestine, and her father, Sir Quintilian. First, the king employs an augmenting comparison that appeals to Terrell's pride in persuading him to bring his bride to court.

> I wod but turne this spheare,
> Of Ladies eyes, and place it in the Court
> Where thy faire Bride should for the Zodiacke shine,
> And every Lady else sit for a signe.
> But all thy thoughts are yellow, thy sweet bloud
> Rebels, th'art jealous Wat; thus with proude revels
> To emmulate the masking firmament,
> Where Starres dance in the silver Hall of heaven.

> (II, i, 185-92)

King William conceals his true intentions by dazzling comparisons which delude Terrell and bring about his consent after other methods of persuasion have failed. Then Caelestine attempts to persuade Terrell to break his promise to the king by comparisons meant to diminish the value of oaths.

> CAEL.
> An oath? why, what's an oath? tis but the smoake,
> Of flame and bloud; the blister of the spirit,
> Which rizeth from the Steame of rage, the bubble
> That shootes up to the tongue, and scaldes the voice.

> (V, i, 32-5)

Intended to produce scorn for the worthlessness of his oath, Caelestine's comparisons imply, without her intending it, too much insult to Terrell's character to be persuasive. His self-esteem and judgment challenged, he simply counters with augmenting comparisons.

> TER.
> An oath? why tis the trafficke of the soule,
> 'Tis law within a man; the seale of faith,
> The bond of every conscience.

> (V, i, 40-2)

But Sir Quintilian manages by a very vivid diminishing comparison to convince Terrell it would be better for Caelestine to die than to lose her chastity, even to a king.

> SIR QUIN.
> Immagine her the cup of thy moist life
> What man would pledge a King in his owne wife?

> TER.
> She dyes: that sentence poisons her.

> (V, i, 129-31)

There are numerous other occasions in Dekker's plays when persuasion by this type of amplification is shown as the direct or indirect cause of action. In a final example, from *Match Me in London,* when the Queen, convinced

Tormiella has become her husband's mistress, locks the young girl in a room and threatens to kill her, Tormiella begins her dissuading speech with a comparison amplifying her own helplessness.

> Alas
> The Court to me is an inchanted tower
> Wherein I'me lockt by force, and bound by spels,
> A Heaven to some, to me ten thousand Hels.

> (III, iii, 25-8)

Although the potential murderess is not totally convinced by this figure alone, it does stop her immediate intention long enough for Tormiella to add enough other arguments to change the Queen's mind. The figure which finally persuades the jealous woman, by the way, is another emotional appeal which has already been pointed out as one of Matheo's favorite exclamations, *Eustathia,* the protestation of constancy.

> TORMI.
> If ever I have wrong'd your royall bed
> In act, in thought, nayle me for ever fast,
> To scape this Tyger of the Kings fierce lust
> I will doe any thing, I will speake treason
> Or Drinke a Cup of Poyson, which may blast
> My inticing face, and make it leprous foule:
> Ruine you all this, so you keepe up my Soule;
> That's all the wealth I care for.

> QUEEN.
> I have now
> No hart left to kill thee, rise.

> (III, iii, 44-52)

Tormiella's speeches here provide a classic example of rhetorical persuasion, which alters emotions (the queen is moved from wrath to sympathy) and produces, or, in this instance, prevents an act. That the queen did not reach intellectual certainty is demonstrated later in the play when her suspicions crop up again, but she is sufficiently moved to change her plan of action on the probability that Tormiella may be innocent.

Reviewing the occurrences of rhetorical persuasion in Dekker's plays, one finds some strong cumulative evidence to verify the thesis that he consciously adapted rhetorical figures to his dramatic purposes. Specifically, there are the direct references to amplification and word painting which have been noted, and the close parallel in *The Whore of Babylon* to Peacham's instructions about the use of *Philophronesis.*

One sees, also, Dekker's versatility and sense of dramatic fitness revealed in his successful adaptations of these persuasive devices to the purposes of plot development, comic effects, and characterization. He seems to have achieved particular mastery of their use in characterization through modifying them to suit the particular speaker, or typifying certain characters by recurring devices (Simon Eyre and Matheo, for example), or employing them as a method of bringing to expression the subjective feelings of a character (most clearly seen in the monologues of *Old Fortunatus*).

Notes

1. Henry Peacham, *The Garden of Eloquence* (London, 1577), D1^r.

2. *De Oratore* iii. 200.

3. Aristotle *Rh.* i. 1. 11-12.

4. Peacham, p. 117.

5. *Ibid.,* p. 181.

6. Peacham, pp. 39-40.

7. Peacham, p. 170.

8. *Inst.* ix. ii. 64.

9. Peacham, 1577, H2^r.

10. Peacham, p. 180.

11. Peacham, p. 181.

12. *Ibid.,* p. 38.

13. Peacham, p. 39.

14. *Ibid.,* p. 172.

15. *Ad Herennium* iv. 65, 66.

16. Peacham, p. 138.

17. iv. 66.

18. Abraham Fraunce, *The Arcadian Rhetorike* (London: Thomas Orwin, 1592), I, 31.

19. Peacham, p. 136.

20. Peacham, p. 137.

21. i, 26.

22. Peacham, pp. 134-43.

23. Peacham, p. 134.

24. Fraunce, *Arcadian Rhetorike,* I, 30.

25. *Ad Herennium,* iv. 48-50.

26. *Ad Herennium* iv. 48-50.

27. Peacham, pp. 105-110.

28. Howell, pp. 71-2.

29. *Inst.,* viii. 4. 1-15.

30. Peacham, p. 21.

31. Peacham, p. 21.

32. Peacham, p. 98.

33. Peacham, p. 96.

34. Peacham, pp. 62-84.

35. *Rh.* i. 13. 26,27.

36. Peacham, p. 62.

37. *Ibid.,* p. 69.

38. Peacham, p. 64.

39. *Ibid.,* p. 169.

40. *Inst.* viii, xxx. 4. 3-4.

41. Peacham, p. 156.

THE SHOEMAKER'S HOLIDAY

CRITICAL COMMENTARY

James H. Conover (essay date 1969)

SOURCE: *"The Shoemakers' Holiday, or the Gentle Craft,"* in *Thomas Dekker: An Analysis of Dramatic Structure,* Mouton, 1969, pp. 18-50.

[*In the essay below, Conover analyzes the various plots of* The Shoemaker's Holiday, *concluding that "the individual actions [of the play] are well articulated and . . . skillful devices have been employed to link the various actions and characters in a meaningful, coherent whole."*]

If a critic were attempting to develop the thesis that Dekker's skills and techniques gradually developed over a period of years that critic would face great difficulties with *The Shoemakers' Holiday, or The Gentle Craft.* Although it is the earliest of Dekker's extant plays, it is very nearly the best of the whole body of work. As will be seen, the playwright has taken three contrasting sets of incidents and has interwoven them to produce an almost inseparable whole.

This play, like *Old Fortunatus* and *If It Be Not Good,* is in part based upon a known source. It is a commonplace that Elizabethan dramatists—even the greatest—drew regularly upon both dramatic and non-dramatic literature for plot ideas. When such a source is known or suspected then it is profitable to investigate the playwright's use of the earlier work. It has been generally accepted that *Shoemaker's Holiday* is based upon Thomas Deloney's prose narrative, *The Gentle Craft,* which apparently was first registered in 1597,[1] although the earliest edition now in existence is dated 1637.[2] This work is made up of three tales concerning, respectively, Saint Hugh, Crispin and Crispianus, and Simon Eyre. The three tales all involve shoemakers but are not related in any other way. For his play Dekker selected incidents and characters from the second and third stories, and recombined them to produce what is in all respects an entirely new work. The procedure was not that of translating a narrative work directly into dramatic form, but of selection, combination, and expansion or compression. Only a few incidents, for example, are taken from the second tale, and those used are divided among several characters in the Dekker play. In the Deloney story two brothers who are princes are forced to hide, disguising themselves as shoemakers. One meets, woos, and secretly marries a princess. The other is called into the army and so distinguishes himself that eventually he can reveal his and his brother's identity. Dekker uses the disguise situation and the war context; he transforms the warrior prince into Rafe, a real, not pretended, shoemaker who is impressed and wounded in battle. In the Deloney story the disguises are assumed to save the lives of the princes, and the prince meets his wife-to-be after assuming the disguise; in the play, however, the disguise is employed by Lacy in order to further a love affair already in progress. Deloney's tale about Simon Eyre begins with Eyre as a youth and goes into considerable detail regarding the device by which the shoemaker makes his fortune. The story also includes a fairly elaborate minor action concerning a competition for the hand of a servant girl in the Eyre household. Dekker's play begins quite late in Eyre's career and only sketchily recounts the shoemaker's rise to fame. The servant girl in the narrative becomes Jane in the play and the competition for her hand is between a lowly shoemaker and a man of rank. As will be seen, Dekker's changes are extensive. Most significant is the way in which Deloney's entirely separate tales are fused into one play. The changes in social rank are also significant. Deloney's two young princes become in the play a noble and a shoemaker who are contrasted. The lower-class suitors for the maid become in the play a noble suitor and a shoemaker suitor. The importance of these competitions and contrasts between social rank will become more apparent in the detailed discussion of the play.

THE LACY-ROSE ACTION

I.i The Earl of Lincoln and Sir Otley, Lord Mayor of London, discuss the romance between the Earl's nephew, Lacy, and Otley's daughter, Rose. The two men voice to one another their mutual objections to the union, and reveal in asides other objections not so mutual. To separate the couple, Otley has sent Rose out of London to his country estate where Lacy cannot visit undetected, and Lincoln has secured from the King an army command for Lacy in the wars in France. Lacy and his cousin enter, and the older men wish them good fortune in the wars and exit. Lacy, however, arranges to have his cousin take over the army command until he, Lacy, can once more meet with Rose.

I.ii Rose, in the country, sends her servant to London for news of Lacy.

I.iii Lacy has discovered that Otley has "secrety conueyd my *Rose* from *London*" (I.iii.15), and he has disguised himself as a shoemaker to hide the fact that he is not with the army. In a soliloquy he expresses his hope to be employed in the shop of Simon Eyre.

I.iv These hopes are fulfilled in this scene when Lacy, now known as Hans, is hired as a journeyman shoemaker.[3]

II.i Hammon, a gentleman hunter, is told that the deer he is chasing has entered Otley's estate.

II.ii Instead of the deer, however, Hammon encounters Rose. He is immediately smitten with her, and Otley welcomes the hunter as a possible rival for the absent Lacy. Although the indications are that Rose will remain faithful to Lacy, this new complication—a Paris for Juliet—is left unresolved at the end of the scene, providing a small amount of suspense.

II.iv Up to this point Lincoln, Lacy's uncle, and Otley, Rose's father, have assumed that Lacy is in France, but

Lincoln's spy (introduced as such in the first scene of the play) returns with news of Lacy's absence from the army. Lincoln now begins a search for Lacy.

III.i The plot then returns to the Hammon complication. Rose, in her father's presence, refuses Hammon's suit. According to custom, however, Otley has the power to force his daughter to marry, but Hammon, a gentle gentleman, refuses Otley's offer, and this complication is removed from the plot. But Otley's anger and suspicions make him include Rose in the party to celebrate Eyre's appointment as Sheriff.

III.iii As his contribution to the celebration, Simon Eyre brings his journeymen shoemakers who perform a dance. Among the group is the disguised Lacy. He is spied out by Rose (but not, of course, by Otley) who then schemes with her maid to arrange a private meeting with Lacy.

IV.i The scheme becomes apparent in this scene. Sybil, the maid, appears in Eyre's shop and specifically designates Hans (Lacy) to be sent to fit Rose with shoes.

IV.iii Alone together at last Rose and Lacy plan to elope that night, but two elements of suspense are introduced into the scene: Otley enters, and Lacy's disguise is consequently put to a close test; and, Lincoln's imminent arrival is announced. As Otley goes to meet Lincoln the two lovers decide to run off immediately.

IV.iv As Otley and Lincoln confer they are brought the news that Rose has run off with Hans, the shoemaker. Lincoln quickly deduces that Hans and Lacy are one person, but the threat to find the couple and prohibit the marriage is forestalled by a fellow shoemaker who gives Lincoln and Otley false information concerning the time and whereabouts of the wedding.[4]

V.i Rose and Lacy are next seen in Eyre's shop as he sends them off to be married. They fear some kind of danger but Eyre, now Lord Mayor of London, promises his protection. Although not stated, the fear is of the King's anger over Lacy's desertion from the French wars.

V.ii The two disapproving relatives arrive at the wrong wedding, and after discovering the ruse, they set out to tell the King that Lacy has been a traitor so that the King will punish Lacy and divorce the couple.

V.iv Successfully wedded, Lacy and Rose return once more to Simon Eyre, who is preparing to entertain the King, and Lacy specifically asks him to intercede with the King on their behalf.

V.v Soon after the King pardons Lacy, Lincoln and Otley arrive and accuse Lacy of traitorous desertion, but the King has already pardoned that. Otley, however, demands as a father's right that the couple be separated. The King complies by divorcing them, but immediately declares them remarried. He stops Lincoln's objection to differences in social rank by reminding him that Lacy "stooped" to be a shoemaker, and quiets Otley's ambitions by knighting Lacy.

This first plot to make an appearance in the play involves a fairly simple and traditional situation in which a hoped-for marriage is temporarily thwarted. The point of attack is rather late, in that the couple has already met, fallen in love, apparently resolved to marry, and been faced with some complications. In a sense Dekker here departs from traditional Elizabethan practices. Madeleine Doran summarizes the differences of point of attack in classical and Elizabethan drama:

> The plot of a classical play typically begins *in media res* and follows the "artificial" order; the plot of an Elizabethan play normally follows the "natural" or historical order of events.[5]

She goes on to say.

> Elizabethan drama . . . generally begins at the beginning and proceeds straight through in chronological order until the end. This means that the motivation of action is within rather than precedent to the action of the play.[6]

Because here these events have taken place prior to the opening of the play, Dekker can emphasize the effect of separation of the lovers by keeping them apart for much of the play. They do not see one another, in fact, until the play is half completed. The audience first sees, not one of the lovers, but the uncle and the father, who represent the primary obstacle the lovers must overcome in order to marry. Rose and Lacy have, in a sense, three objectives: they must meet once more to plan an elopement; they must marry; and, finally, they must secure approval of their marriage. The approval is necessary both for custom's sake and in order to gain their rightful inheritances. These elements of approval are not developed to any great extent in the play but they are implicit in the situation.

All of the necessary exposition is handled in this first scene: the two young people love one another and wish to marry; their elders have taken action to prevent the union; and Lacy has been a shoemaker on the continent, a fact introduced by Lacy's uncle as an example of his wasteful and irresponsible nature, Lincoln's ostensible objection to the marriage.

Since the point of attack is late, the plot moves forward quickly at the outset as Lacy easily disposes of the first bar to their marriage, his service in France. This action, however, is the basis for the later complication, potential trouble with the King. Otley's action of hiding Rose outside of London puts her in the path of Hammon and a new complication is thus introduced. To a certain extent this breaks up what could be an overly-regular and too-smooth plot action, but it is disposed of through Rose's refusal and Hammon's gentlemanly unwillingness to force himself on Rose. Ironically, Otley's reaction to Rose's refusal serves to bring the two lovers together.

The scene (III.iii) in which Rose and Lacy are brought together for the first time in the play, is the crisis or turning point in the action of the plot. Crisis is used here to refer to Bradley's "critical point".

> There is therefore felt to be a critical point in the action which proves also to be a turning point. It is critical sometimes in the sense that until it is reached, the conflict is not, so to speak, clenched; one of the two sets of forces might subside, or a reconciliation might somehow be effected; while, as soon as it is reached, we feel this can no longer be.[7]

The later scene when the lovers meet alone, are almost discovered by Otley and Lincoln, and run away together is exciting and dramatically effective, but it provides ironic incident rather than complication or change, and follows inevitably from the earlier scene. The attempt by Otley and Lincoln to stop the wedding itself is defeated from the outset, and thus is neither critical nor suspenseful, because they possess false information. The lovers' central problem has been to overcome the hindrances put in the way of their reunion, and, once they manage to meet, the rest must follow.

The incidents or choices made by characters at the crisis produce or cause what Bradley as well as Freytag called the "catastrophe", referring to the final situation, the circumstances to which the action resolves at the end. Freytag described catastrophe as "the closing action . . . [that] the ancient stage called the exodus". He later noted that it "contains . . . the necessary consequences of the action and the characters [and that] the whole construction points toward the end. . . ."[8] Since both writers were primarily concerned with tragic drama the word catastrophe was particularly appropriate, but it is less so for non-tragic plays. Consequently, the word *climax* is here employed to refer to the final situation in a play or action of a play.

The climax of this plot, the scene with the four principals and the King, brings all together for the first time. The King functions obviously in the role of a *deus ex machina,* who answers all objections and solves all problems. Although his presence and actions are fairly well motivated by Simon Eyre, the King is not as adroit an example of the *deus ex machina* device as those to be found in **Honest Whore II** and **If It Be Not Good.** The audience is prepared for his presence, but he is something of an intrusion at the end of the play, and he is by no means so thoroughly involved with the action as are his counterparts in the plays mentioned. He is—God-like—above the action. The King, as knotcutter, goes a bit beyond his traditional role; he could have merely made pronouncements and ended it there, but the scene is made more effective by his maneuverings. He allows the charges of "traitor" to begin and Lacy to be seized even though pardon has been given. Instead of refusing to divorce the couple, he first does so, then remarries them, and finally skillfully answers the objections of both Lincoln and Otley. All of these actions in the scene produced a kind of artificial, though effective, suspense and complication.

Artificial, that is, in the sense that a serious ending would completely deny the mood and expectations so thoroughly established. And the King does at the end what he had planned to do throughout the scene.

Actually, it is Simon Eyre's presence that promises a happy resolution. If there was ever a character in drama with whom it would be impossible to associate tragic or serious outcomes, it is Simon. As will be seen, everything he touches turns to success and laughter. His promise of protection for Rose and Lacy is certain to be upheld. His function here, as will be demonstrated, is similar to that of Orlando Friscobaldo in **Honest Whore II.**

Other than the *deus ex machina* device which resolves it, the plot is tightly knit and well motivated in a cause and effect pattern. Fortuitous events play no part in the working out of the problems, and since the motivation for each scene is to be found in the action of earlier scenes the events appear to be in a necessary and natural order. The only situation not prepared for in the play is the appearance of Firk, Lacy's clownish fellow shoemaker, in IV.iv at Otley's home, shortly after Rose and Lacy flee. His story and false account of the time and place of the wedding permits the ceremony to take place unmolested. He says that he has come to fit Rose with some shoes, but that was the reason Lacy had been summoned. Obviously Lacy has sent him to put them off the scent and that is the meaning of Firk's aside, "It is that *Hauns* [Lacy], Ile so gull these diggers" (IV.iv.82-3), and his later statement that "I came hither of purpose with shooes to sir *Rogers* worship, whilst *Rose* his daughter be coniecatcht by *Hauns*" (IV.iv.145-46).

The final area of investigation concerning this action involves potential, but undramatized situations implicit in the story. The potential does not refer to the source; it has already been noted that Dekker has made radical departures from the source, omitting a number of incidents to be found there.[9] Potential here refers to situations which are either implied by the action of the play or are related but not dramatized.

Most of the potential events of the story are dramatized, excepting those which occurred before the play opened— the initial meetings of Rose and Lacy, Otley's decision to separate the pair by sending Rose out of London, and Lincoln's similar decision concerning the army command for Lacy. From that point to the end little is omitted; perhaps the only incidents not dramatized are Lacy's discovery of Rose's absence, described by Lacy in I.iii, the wedding that takes place "off-stage" between V.i and V.ii, and the appeal to the King by Lacy and Eyre that precedes the last scene of the play. Otley revealed the fact that Rose had been sent out of London in his first conversation with Lincoln, so there would be little to gain by dramatizing Lacy's discovery of the fact. The wedding ceremony would require at least one new character, and the dramatization of it might produce a stronger climactic effect than is desirable prior to the true climax in the last

scene. If it were a strong scene it would symbolize a culmination of the lovers' quest, an effect better saved for the last scene. The third omitted situation—the pleas to the King—would necessarily involve a recapitulation of many of the events known to the audience. Though such summaries at the end of a play have been effective at times, the practice is perhaps best avoided.

The Rafe-Jane Action

This plot also concerns a relatively simple love story; only five scenes of the play are devoted to it. A married couple is separated by war and eventually reunited after some near-tragic occurrences. The forces at work here are not so traditional as those of the first plot, and the couple themselves are unconventional. The standard complication of parental disapproval is an important element in the Lacy-Rose plot; the elders' objections to youths' desires and the son's and daughter's successful struggle with the father have been dramatic staples since the Greek drama. These conflicts within the family unit have provided much of the material for both serious and comic literature. In this second plot, however, the lovers are in effect separated by social forces, first war and then class distinctions. The two people are, moreover, both members of the working class, and shoemakers and seamstresses had not often been the principals in a dramatic tale, much less a romantic and serious love story.

I.i Unlike Rose and Lacy, Rafe and Jane are first seen together, and are then not united until the last scene concerned with their action. Prior to the opening of the play the newly married Rafe has been impressed for the army. Simon Eyre Rafe's employer, asks the commanding officer (Lacy) to discharge Rafe instead of taking him to France. The grounds are, as a fellow shoemaker says, "you doe more than you can answere, to press a man within a yeare and a day of his marriage" (I.i.149-50). Lacy regretfully refuses, however, and Rafe, in a very touching speech, asks Simon to be Jane's protector. As a parting gift, Rafe presents Jane with a pair of shoes he has made for her.

II.ii Some time later Rafe returns to Eyre's shop, apparently released from the army because of an injured leg; but he is met with the news that Jane has disappeared after some disagreement with Dame Eyre. Nothing explicit has prepared for this eventuality, unless the forbodings of the first scene and Dame Eyre's character can be made to account for it. So the situation is now reversed; Rafe has returned, but Jane is gone.

III.iv Jane, now working as a seamstress, is being courted by a gentleman, Hammon. She is touched by his sincerity, and when her refusal because of Rafe is countered by Hammon's information that Rafe is dead she tells him, "If euer I wed man it shall be you" (III.iv. 122). The complication here is two-fold; Jane believes Rafe is dead, and her suitor is a man of much higher social position with its consequent power and influence.

IV.ii The shoes which Rafe left with Jane provide the solution to a least part of the problem. Jane has apparently accepted Hammon's proposal. Hammond sends the old shoes to Eyre's shop so that a new pair of their size can be made for the wedding. The classical tokens of recognition reveal to Rafe the whereabouts of his Cinderella, and he plans to claim his wife from Hammon with the aid of his fellow shoemakers.

V.ii This scene dramatizes the rescue of Jane by Rafe and the shoemakers. After a verbal skirmish between the shoemakers and Hammon's supporters Jane is given a choice between the two men, and Hammon offers Rafe twenty pounds to give up his claim; but neither answer is really in doubt and Hammon magnanimously makes a gift of the money.

Like the Rose-Lacy action this plot begins at a critical point, the imminent separation of husband and wife. There is no leisurely development of character or earlier events; the couple is immediately thrust into the problem, and they begin to attempt its solution. While the army complication was immediately solved, apparently, in the other plot, here it prevails. Nor is it ever solved by the characters themselves, but runs its own course, outside the play, until Rafe is wounded.

Although there is considerable action in this brief plot, the two central characters are for the most part passive, somewhat at the mercy of the social forces mentioned above and of other characters. Most of the pleading for Rafe in the first scene comes from Eyre and the other shoemakers; Jane is put out of the household; Rafe does plan the shoemakers' interference with the wedding, but the other shoemakers actually conduct the affair.

The action has its crisis in Hammon's revelation to Jane that Rafe has been killed. It is ironic in the sense that while this news "frees" Jane for Hammon, and thus would seem to separate the couple, it also provides the means for their ultimate reunion. Conceivably the lame Rafe might not have found Jane had she continued as a seamstress, but the imminent wedding provides the occasion for the recognition of the pair of shoes.

The climax, of course, is in the decisions by Jane and Rafe to remain together despite Hammon's blandishments. As mentioned above neither answer is really in doubt, but the conflict between the shoemakers and the servants provides excitement. Rafe's last words on the matter—

> Sirrah *Hammon, Hammon,* dost thou thinke a Shoemaker is so base, to bee a bawde to his owne wife for commoditie, take thy golde, choake with it, were I not lame, I would make thee eate thy words.
>
> (V.iii.82-5)

—could bring cheers from an audience of 'prentices. As Simon Eyre and the King were agents who contributed to the climax of the Rose-Lacy plot, the shoemakers, particularly Hodge and Firk, are instrumental in the climax

of this plot. Their force, indeed almost a mob, provides the necessary support for Rafe's claim. They, in fact, voice his claim for him, functioning as junior editions of Simon Eyre. If this plot can be in part interpreted in social terms, this opposition of the mob of shoemakers to the group of the gentleman's household effectively presents the social conflict visually. The shoemakers triumph here, then again in opposition to Otley and Lincoln, and finally, gathering forces all along, they march off to their celebration to the sound of the pancake bell.

The degree to which the events of the plot are effectively articulated has already been touched upon. The least skillful link has to do with the surprising information that Jane no longer lives with the Eyres; most skillful is the Rafe's "death"-Jane's wedding-Jane's shoes-Jane's rescue sequence. Chance, however, plays a large, if not unreasonable, part in the plot, particularly in two instances: Hammon's possession of a casualty list and the fact that Jane's shoes are brought to Rafe himself. That Rafe is mistakenly listed among those considered dead is not in itself surprising since he was seriously wounded, and in a positive sense these elements of chance emphasize the passivity of the two characters, part of this plot's contribution to the total play to be discussed below. At one point Dekker seems to be aware of the amount of chance involved. After Rafe has been given the order to make shoes for the bride-to-be he says, "By this shoe said he, how am I amasde / At this strange accident?" (IV.ii.30-1).

The arrangement of the incidents seems to be purposeful, and not overly complex. The sequence employs a cause and effect pattern, with a single exception—scenes III.ii and III.iv could be reversed. That is, with slight modifications to explain her absence from the shoemaker's household, Jane's scene with Hammon could precede Rafe's homecoming. This change would lessen the present weakness noted above of lack of preparation for Dame Eyre's statement to Rafe that Jane is gone. But it would have several negative effects; first, and least important, it would break up the rather neat arrangement of scenes whereby the two are together in the first and last scenes and alternate—Rafe, Jane, Rafe—in the middle three scenes. More significant, however, would be the change in the emotional tone in the scene in which Jane is told that Rafe has been killed. The scene would be at once highly pathetic, since the viewer would take the casualty list as fact, and melodramatic, since the basis for the emotional reactions would later prove to be false. The intensity of emotions would not be in keeping with the comic tone of the play as a whole. With Rafe's lameness Dekker already skirts the line, and an apparently real death would indeed violate the balance of the play. Since, by the arrangement of the scenes, the audience knows the report to be untrue, it can react sympathetically to Jane's sorrow, but continue to hope for their eventual meeting. Moreover, the charges of chance brought above would pale in the face of such another element of surprise as suggested. To first kill off Rafe and then explain his death away as a battlefield mistake would be a much less desirable arrangement of scenes. Dekker has made the wise choice of suspense over surprise.

The plot is simple and straightforward, progressing from separation to reunion. If it had been more fully dramatized, showing Rafe's attempts to get home, for example, it would have had the effect of two parts; that is, his success in reaching London would have been an early and false climax, since the return to Eyre's shop and reunion with Jane appear to be synonymous.

Certainly, more could have been made of the plot; in addition to the scenes in France suggested above, two others are specifically described in the play itself. Jane and Dame Eyre, at some point between I.i and III.ii, argued and Jane was either put out of the house or left. Halstead notes the omission of this scene with apparent regret and suggests that it might have been a way to break the long hiatus in the plot.[10] Its inclusion would have eliminated the gap, but it would have had a negative effect on the characters of Eyre and his wife. Rafe had asked Simon Eyre in I.i to care for Jane in his absence, and his failure to do so cannot be emphasized without seriously undercutting audience regard for Eyre. This, for example, is why Dame Eyre, rather than Simon, gives the bad news to Rafe, who is then packed off to eat and rest so that he is not allowed (by the playwright) to confront Simon Eyre as he enters. Furthermore, the omitted scene must have put most of the blame on Dame Eyre, if dramatized, in order to support Jane's character. Jane, as part of a romantic and pathetic story, cannot appear in the role of a scolding fishwife without considerable harm to our later sympathy for her. Dame Eyre's snobbish and social climbing ways are seen in the play only in comic terms. If the other side of the coin is displayed in a scene in which she lords it over poor Jane, a change of tone is introduced that must affect the whole Simon Eyre story, and as her husband, Simon Eyre himself. The fact that the scene is related rather than dramatized gives it much less emphasis and impact, and permits Dame Eyre to put at least part of the blame on Jane, still without hurting Jane's character. The viewer can smilingly say to himself, "Oh, yes, Dame Eyre, I'm sure you suffered terribly from wicked Jane." But he must smile.

The other scene referred to, but omitted in the play, is one in which Rafe fits Jane with the new shoes ordered by Hammon's servant. Rafe describes this situation at some length, and it is used to confirm the fact that it is indeed Jane who is about to marry Hammon. It is easy to understand why Dekker did not include the scene, but difficult to know why it is mentioned at all. Showing the couple together before the rescue would make the rescue itself anti-climactic, and would unnecessarily emphasize the unlikely fact that Jane does not recognize her husband. The latter would not, to be sure, be surprising in Elizabethan drama. But there is no need for the reference; the shoes are sufficient identification. The description does provide another element of pathos, and perhaps it was for this reason that it was included.

One incident is implied by the general situation but not specifically described in the dialogue. That is, at the end of III.iv Jane sends Hammon off with the promise that, "If euer I wed man it shall be you" (III.iv.122). But Dekker omits the scene in which Jane actually accepts Hammon's proposal. The reasons for the omission are perhaps obvious. The speech quoted gives sufficient indication of what is to happen, and Jane is not subjected to a direct acceptance of a proposal so soon after her husband's death. Such a scene would also be something of a repetition of the original proposal scene, and thus extraneous.

Such a "fleshing out" would not be consistent with what might be considered an important and meritorius characteristic of the plot—its economy. The five scenes simply and quickly tell the whole story: departure for war, return from war and loss of wife; news of "death"; discovery of the shoes; and rescue and reunion. The effect is of speed and intensity; nothing is wasted. Each scene depicts an important and necessary incident. Alone this method for this plot would probably be too abrupt; its function within the complete play will be discussed later.

THE SIMON EYRE ACTION

The plot to be considered finally is that concerned with Simon Eyre, if a plot it can be called in any traditional sense of that term. Simply stated, the scenes depict history's easiest success story, a rise from craftsman to Lord Mayor of London, with a related increase of personal wealth and influence.

There are no true complications in the path of this progress, and very little of what is normally termed dramatic action, although a number of scenes in the total play are devoted to Eyre and his shop. Describing romantic comedy, C. F. T. Brooke notes that this type of play frequently lacks "the fundamental dramatic conflict which forms regularly the backbone both of comedy and tragedy. . . ."[11] Harbage points to this lack when he expresses his amazement that **Shoemakers' Holiday** has the "power to sustain interest with a pennyworth of evil for a pound of good".[12]

Since Simon Eyre is something of an historical character it can be argued that his ultimate achievement was known from the outset to the original London audiences, and that this expectation softens the surprise, or rather astonishment, at his meteoric rise. The character in the play certainly has not stated or implied ambitions. On the other hand, that he feels no limitations is apparent in the refrain that he repeats with variations, "prince am I none, yet am I noblie born" (II.iii.42).

The small amount of exposition needed for this plot is actually established in the first scene of the Rafe-Jane plot. Dekker simply and naturally has Simon introduce himself, family, and journeymen to Lacy in preparation for asking for Rafe's release from impressment. Enough is said in the scene to establish firmly Eyre's character.

I.iv The first scene actually devoted to Simon Eyre himself is the one in which the shoemaker shop is established as a locale and in which Lacy (Hans) is hired. Although the action is a necessary part of the Lacy-Rose plot it is also functional here.[13]

II.iii Lacy introduces the "skipper" of a ship to Eyre and also loans Eyre enough money for a down-payment on the valuable cargo. The original proposals of the business deal have taken place prior to the scene, and only the closing of the deal is dramatized. Eyre has been made an alderman of London sometime prior to the scene. The two elements of Eyre's rise—financial and political—are not at this point related, but are jointed by proximity. Once again, after a disagreement with Dame Eyre, the journeymen threaten to quit but are pacified by Simon.

III.i The next brief scene concerned with this plot is interlaced with one that is primarily concerned with the Rose-Lacy plot. The two elements mentioned above are joined as Otley (current Lord Mayor) reveals himself as Eyre's partner in the ship's cargo transaction which has yielded considerable profit. As a kind of reward he tells Eyre that he hopes to have him made Sheriff that very day.

III.ii The shoemakers and Simon's wife await the news of the hoped-for appointment, and Dekker indulges in some mild satire on Dame Eyre as a bourgeois nouveau riche. Eyre enters with the chain of office, and all prepare to dine with Otley to celebrate the new position.

III.iii Nothing happens in this scene to further the action. Otley and the Eyres dine together and are entertained with a dance by the shoemakers. Although this takes up most of the scene it should perhaps be considered part of the Rose-Lacy plot.

IV.i Scene III.ii anticipated the celebration, scene III.iii depicted it, and this scene is largely retrospect discussion of it by the journeymen. In passing, they mention the ill-health of several other aldermen, whose deaths would make Simon the Lord Mayor of London.

V.i Eyre next appears as Lord Mayor; and once again the action itself has taken place off-stage. Here he promises to protect Lacy and Rose, and begins preparation for the Shrove Tuesday pancake feast that is to occupy the rest of the play. At this point Eyre has achieved his complete personal success, and what follows could be considered anticlimactic if the plot is viewed solely as his success story.

V.iii The King is seen enroute to Eyre's celebration where he expects to be amused by Simon's "woonted merriment . . ." (V.iii.15).

V.iv Eyre directs the turmoil of the feast in which a "hundred tables wil not feast the fourth part of" the apprentices of London (V.iv.11-12). He reassures Lacy that he will intercede for him with the King.

V.v. Simon has done so, and this scene begins with the King pardoning Lacy. After the Rose-Lacy action is completed the celebration continues. "Mad Simon" entertains the King and persuades him to grant marketing privileges to shoemakers in the newly constructed Leadenhall.

Unlike the other two plots whose points of attack were relatively late in their actions, this one begins quite early, though not so early as the source. Each achievement—alderman, wealth, sheriff, mayor, and founder of the marketing customs and Pancake Day—is within the play. It is, as noted by Alexis Lange, almost epic in nature, certainly biographical.[14]

As a separate action it is highly episodic, and abrupt in its forward movement. It is even difficult to apply traditional plot-descriptive terms to the action. But part of the difficulty arises from the consideration of the plot as biographical, as being centrally concerned with a single man. In those terms the climax of the plot should be at the point at which Eyre becomes Lord Mayor, a scene not even dramatized. Actually the climax, though closely related to Simon Eyre, is in the establishment of the traditions of Shrove Tuesday and the use of Leadenhall, things Eyre did as Lord Mayor which had lasting public effect; the climax is not the personal achievement of an individual. The rank of Lord Mayor is, then, merely the final step toward the actual climax of the action.

Working backwards from this climax to the critical point in the action is somewhat easier. The only actions taken by Eyre which could be said to influence the outcome of this plot are the hiring of Lacy and the purchase of the ship's cargo. It is the second of these that actually provides the momentum which carries Eyre to the point at which he can institute the traditions.

Apart from the crisis-climax relationship, the arrangement of incidents is purely chronological. A chain reaction results in the outcome, but the later incidents all refer to the first two. Each event can come only after the preceding one, but it does not occur *because* of this preceding one; there is one cause and a series of related effects.

That is not to say that the plot consists of a series of surprises. The brief scene at Otley's house (III.i) prepares for the promotion to sheriff. Similarly, the journeymen shoemakers prepare us for the possibility that Eyre may become Lord Mayor by discussing the other aldermen, and Lacy tells Rose that Eyre can protect them because he is now Lord Mayor.

The opportune deaths of the senior aldermen, which permit Eyre to attain his highest rank, do seem to constitute a gross element of luck in the plot. Realistically the situation might have occurred, and indeed Simon Eyre probably did "work his way up" in this fashion. Actually the objections to this final movement in his progress are objections to the timing of the deaths rather than to the deaths themselves.

In studying this action apart from the total play there appears to be no realistic time lapse; now Eyre is Sheriff with seven aldermen between him and mayoralty, and instantly he is Lord Mayor and seven aldermen are dead. But the seven loom larger in analysis then they do in the context of the play. It must be remembered that none are characters in the play; they don't even have names. Their deaths are not mourned or regretted onstage or in the audience because in the context of the play they are not even human beings, but are nameless and actionless. The problem will be further softened when the plot is studied in relationship to the rest of the play.

Because of the wide span of the plot a few pertinent scenes have been omitted. It was noted earlier that Dekker has not dramatized the initial offer by Lacy to aid Eyre in the purchase of the ship's cargo. The scene (II.iii) begins after most of the arrangements have been made. A recent writer describes the business deal as a "sharp practice of which the modern equivalent would be obtaining credit by false trade references. . . ."[15] L. C. Knights comments on this description:

> Certainly the bargain by which Eyre gains 'full three thousand pound' is not very reputable, but there is no need to make much of it, or to connect it, as Dr. Robertson does, with 'the wave of speculation' which was then affecting all classes. Dekker merely intends to show that fortune is on the side of the good-hearted tradesman; it is characteristic that he slurs over the issues without thinking very hard about them.[16]

The prose source for the play does describe this business deal in more detail than the play, and includes an element of deception that can be described as "sharp practice". The simplest description of the situation in the play, however, is that Eyre borrows money from Lacy to make an investment that later turns out to be profitable. By eliminating the "shady" details Dekker has not slurred "over the issues", but has created a new and honorable situation. Knights's slighting remark would be justified if Dekker *had* included the deception and had continued to portray Eyre in a complimentary fashion. Thus Knights is guilty of judging both Dekker and Eyre in terms of the prose source rather than the play itself. It would seem, as a matter of fact, that Dekker did think about the issues involved. In the prose source Dame Eyre advises her husband:

> Be not known that you bargain for your own self, but tell him that you do it in behalf of one of the chief aldermen in the city.[17]

This subterfuge is to hide the fact that Eyre cannot pay the balance of the sale price until he sells part of the cargo. Later in the source Simon actually disguises himself as a rich man. Dekker not only eliminates all of the damning details, he also makes Eyre a genuine alderman, who quite rightfully dresses himself in his gown of office to receive the ship's captain. Dekker, then, consciously purifies the character of the man he is displaying as a model of the rising middle class.

A potential scene in which Eyre becomes Lord Mayor and tells his household of it or celebrates it is also absent from the play. There are several reasons for this omission. First, the scene would be a repetition in kind of the scenes concerning the promotion to Sheriff; secondly, occurring so late in the action, it would harm the effect of the last scenes of the play by providing two climaxes, one for his personal triumph and one for his public deeds.

All of these omissions, however, point to a rather peculiar aspect of the Simon Eyre action. There is a great deal of off-stage incident; there is also much amusing and energetic discussion onstage; but there is very little dramatized action directly related to the Eyre action. The great events in Simon's life—the acquisition of wealth, the attainment of the civic offices, and the construction of Leadenhall—are talked about, before and after the fact, but none are dramatized. Dekker very severely restricts the locale to the shoemaker shop where none of these incidents can take place, and whenever Simon leaves the shop he is accompanied by the troop of journeymen and apprentices. The effect of this technique is to emphasize the locale and the group. Simon is important as a character, but the whole group of shoemakers (including Simon, Rafe, and Lacy) is equally important to the meanings in the play.

RELATIONSHIP OF THE ACTIONS

The tendency of Elizabethan playwrights to compose plays with multiple plots has generated a good deal of critical comment. It is no longer fashionable to criticize a play solely on the grounds that it encompasses several actions, but a discussion and evaluation of the nature and effects of such richness is still valid. Bradbrook defends sub-plots as follows:

> It is true that the Elizabethans sometimes built a play from two quite unconnected stories, but this happens far less frequently than it is usual to suppose. For the subplot was contrasted and not interwoven with the main action: it reflected upon it, either as a criticism or a contrast, or a parallel illustration of the same moral worked out in another manner, a kind of echo or metaphor of the tragedy.[18]

She is, of course, speaking of tragedy here, and this fact no doubt explains the apparent disapproval of "interwoven" plots—that is, comedy or farce is not to be too closely related to the tragic action. It is assumed that Bradbook does not object to interwoven plots when they are of similar mood. The two actions in *King Lear,* for example, are interwoven in the sense that characters freely cross from one action to the other. In addition, the actions are interdependent; Edmund's early triumph over Edgar puts the bastard son in a position to later order Cordelia's death. Interdependent and interwoven actions may thus serve to unify a play. But the implied problem with tragedy is the effect of the mixture of moods within a play, and, as a matter of fact, Bradbrook goes on to discuss this problem in *The Changeling* and other plays. This problem can also present itself in essentially non-tragic dramas into which plots with serious moods are introduced.

When the three plots of *Shoemakers' Holiday* are combined to make the total play there are a variety of inter-reactions, which produce changes in the nature and effect of the individual plots. All three plots, for example, are alike in their simplicity, their concentration on skeletal story. But the result of their combination is one of richness, variety, and even complexity; so much so that a modern reviewer has complained of its "baffling complexities of plot and subplot. . . ."[19] The Eyre plot moves forward smoothly, without complication. The other two plots, with their minor turns and hesitancies, provide the necessary dramatic conflict. That is not to say that the other plots exist in the play merely to make the Simon Eyre story theatrical. As will be seen, they have a more important function as well.

One of the most important effects of the combination is in the play's time scheme. Mable Buland, in a study of Elizabethan playwrights' use of time, comments that in the play "Dekker has produced an effect of greater cohesion than properly belongs" to it.[20] The objection implied is that the three plots cannot begin at the same time and end together if any attention is paid to a realistic calendar of events. But they do seem to, and this is due to the way in which they are joined. The principal culprit is the Eyre plot. As noted above, the plot out of context seems abrupt, the rise too rapid—and on a calendar it is. When scenes from the other two plots are interlaced with it, however, it seems as if there is a sufficient time lapse. Note particularly the time between the promotion to Sheriff and Eyre's next appearance as Lord Mayor. Simon is last onstage at Otley's home in III.iii; although his shoemakers are seen and he is mentioned frequently, he as a character does not reappear again until the first scene of the last act. Dramatically he has been gone a long time—sufficient time, in fact, to make his new position as Lord Mayor acceptable despite the seven aldermen.

A similar effect appears in the Rafe-Jane plot. It was noted that the first two scenes of this plot concerned Rafe's departure and his return, an almost ludicrous juxtaposition. In the complete story, however, the two scenes are separated by eight scenes of the two other plots. So many scenes intrude that the character is practically forgotten and his return at this point gives the effect of a considerable time lapse, which serves its own and the Eyre plot purposes. If, of course, Rafe's character or the plot situation had been more complex, making greater demands on the memory, this break would cause confusion, but the only things the audience needs to recall are Rafe's marriage to Jane, his gift of the shoes, and the fact that he has been in the army.

Separated, the three stories seem to have quite different and sometimes conflicting emotional tones or atmospheres. Rafe and Jane's story—with its overtones of war, Rafe's wound, and apparent death—is pathetic and, alone, almost somber. That of Rose and Lacy is a mixture in itself; there are elements of the romance combined with intrigue comedy, in which disguise and mistaken identity are employed. Simon Eyre's plot is part history, part comedy in city manners, described by Hazelton Spencer as "depicted with a gusto so nearly Chaucerian that the combination is irresistible".[21] The atmosphere of this last plot permeates the play as a whole, but enough of the romantic and pathetic moods survive in combination with the robust earthiness to produce an impression of completeness or depth of view. As Shakespeare, in the three *Henry VI* plays, developed a composite picture of chaos on three levels of English society—the army, the nobility, and the commonalty—Dekker here succeeds in producing a realistic spectrum of emotional tone. The variety of tone, and more particularly the scope of society depicted in the play are characteristic of Dekker. As will be seen, the same effects are also present in such plays as **Honest Whore II** and **If It Be Not Good.** It is the shoemaker milieu that predominates here, however, and despite the fact that the Eyre plot comprises a minority of the total play, Simon "is the comic center and the realistic center of the play".[22] The Eyre action dominates first through the strength of the scenes themselves and the dynamism of Eyre's personality, and secondly through the fact that the two other plots with operate partly within the shoemaker locale.

Furthermore, both the Lacy-Rose and the Rafe-Jane actions are actually modified in tone through contact with the shoemakers. A certain coldness that results in part from the fact that Rose and Lacy are not allowed courtship scenes, and from the intrigue comedy elements, is lessened by Lacy's associations with the shoemakers. More particularly, one scene in the Rafe-Jane action is strongly affected. Alone, Rafe's return wounded from the wars and his loss of Jane are too pathetic in relation to the total tone of the play. But he returns to the vitality of Eyre's shop, and his scene is preceded by the light satire on Dame Eyre's vanity and followed by Simon's triumphant return as Sheriff. In the midst of this his sorrow cannot dominate. In this context fears of real tragedy are impossible.

UNIFYING DEVICES

Dekker employs a series of devices to achieve unity in the play. The first of these involves parallels or direct comparisons of characters in separate actions. The most comprehensive of these similarities comes in part from the source of the play—that is, the occupation of shoemaker. Within the general classification there are variations; Eyre is the shopowner, Rafe is a journeyman, and Lacy, of course, is only an imitation shoemaker. As will be seen in later chapters Dekker makes frequent use of disguise as a plot device. Bradbrook notes that "Disguises generally mean a drop in social status, . . ."[23] and here as elsewhere the playwright conforms to that pattern. The only exception in the plays to be studied is Gazetto in **Match Me in London.** As a shoemaker Lacy is protected from the spying eyes of his adversaries and he is free to move about in London. On this score the device is merely a plot expedient, but in this play there is something more than the easy assumption of another identity. Lacy did work as a shoemaker on the continent and he does so again here on Tower Street. His ability to pass as a craftsman is demonstrated among others of the craft; he is accepted by them and not just by Otley and Lincoln. This acceptance plays an important part in his action. He ultimately wins the King's pardon and intercession on two counts: as a lover, and as someone who has actually worked at this happy craft. His character has somehow improved through these associations. Even Otley, early in the play, considers this fact to be to Lacy's betterment. He says in an aside, "And yet your cosen *Rowland* might do well / Now he hath learn'd an occupation" (I.i.42-3). To work at a trade, in this play as well as in others written by Dekker, is a kind of virtue in itself, a mark of merit.

Rafe, too, benefits by his associations with the shoemakers. In his troubles with Hammon his fellows "rally round", demonstrating a comradery and a group loyalty. There is a clear consciousness of class, with attendant antagonisms to other groups. Firk, for example, takes a positive delight in gulling Otley and Lincoln as he sends them off to the wrong wedding. Firk functions here in a manner not unlike that of the intrigue slave in Roman comedy, enjoying every moment of his wit; but he aids a fellow artisan rather than a profligate young master. The scene is replete with references to the trade: ". . . my profession is the Gentle Craft" (IV.iv.90-1), "no, shal I proue *Iudas* to *Hans*? No, shall I crie treason to my corporation" (IV.iv.96-7), and "ha, ha, heres no craft in the Gentle Craft" (IV.iv,144-45). A similar group spirit appears in the scene in which the shoemakers rescue Jane from Hammon and his followers. Hodge opens the scene with a speech to his troop of journeymen:

> My masters, as we are the braue bloods of the shooe-
> makers, heires apparant to saint *Hugh,* and perpetuall
> benefactors to all good fellowes, thou shalt haue no
> wrong: were *Hammon* a king of spades he should not
> delue in thy close without thy sufferaunce. . . .
>
> (V.ii.1-5)

A few moments later he faces down Hammon's followers with, "My maisters and gentlemen, neuer draw your bird spittes, shoemakers are steele to the backe, men euery inch of them, al spirite" (V.ii.30-2).

A great part of this spirit emanates from Simon Eyre himself. In the first scene of the play, finding that the officers will not relent and cancel Rafe's impressment, he recommends Rafe to them with comparisons to Hector, Hercules, and Prince Arthur, among others, and urges Rafe to

> fight for the honour of the *Gentle Craft,* for the gentle-
> men Shoomakers, the couragious Cordwainers, the
> flower of saint *Martins,* the mad knaues of Bedlem,
> Fleetstreete, Towerstreete, and white Chappell, cracke
> me the crownes of the French knaues, a poxe on them,
> cracke them, fight, by the lord of Ludgate, fight my
> fine boy!
>
> (I.i. 211-16)

Throughout the play Eyre repeats his refrain, noted above, in which he distinguishes between nobility of rank and the true nobility of those born to be shoemakers.

Almost all of these references throughout the play refer specifically to the shoemaker trade, but at one point the idea is extended to include all tradespeople. When Otley complains that Rose is interested only in courtiers, Eyre advises her:

> a Courtier, wash, go by, stand not vppon pisherie pash-
> erie: those silken fellowes are but painted Images, out-
> sides, outsides *Rose,* their inner linings are torne: no
> my fine mouse, marry me with a Gentleman Grocer
> like my Lord Maior your Father, a Grocer is a sweet
> trade, Plums, Plums: had I a sonne or Daughter should
> marrie out of the generation and bloud of the shoe-
> makers, he should packe: what, the Gentle trade is a
> liuing for a man through Europe, through the world.
>
> (III.iii.40-7)

The second parallel between characters in separate plots unites Rafe and Lacy even more closely—that is, their secondary occupation as soldiers. They are both, in the fashion suitable to their social class, impressed for the army. Lacy, of course, is to be Rafe's superior officer, but the army duty produces similar problems for the two men—separation from wife or sweetheart. Incidentally, a further link is provided by the fact that the official who impressed Rafe and the other Londoners is the Lord Mayor, Rose's father and Lacy's antagonist. The war or soldier element is something more than a device to link plots, however. A definite contrast is set up by the playwright in the characters' reactions to the situation and the effect the situation has upon the two characters. Certainly it is not accidental that the incident in which Lacy is told he must assume his army command is immediately followed by that in which Rafe, too, is ordered in, ironically by Lacy. Lacy, the gentleman and officer, has made arrangements (at this point only temporary) to avoid his service in order to seek out his sweetheart, yet it is he who tells Rafe that he must serve and be separated from his wife. The juxtaposition of these two scenes from the two plots seems to be intended to comment upon the unwarranted advantages of the privileged class. Rafe is a passive element in the situation, while Lacy can manipulate events to his advantage. Rafe, too, is depicted later as suffering the real effects of war as he returns wounded, while Lacy is knighted to redeem the honor he lost in France by not being there. The foot soldier is maimed and the officer is titled.

The final common "occupation" to be found in the play is the Civic officer, the position of Lord Mayor of London which is held first by Otley and later, of course, by Simon Eyre. The only recognition of Otley's tenure of office, however, is in the statement mentioned above in which he is responsible for the impressment, and in the scene in which he tells Eyre he hopes to have him made sheriff.

A variation of this pattern of parallel occupations is the way in which Hodge and Firk act as minor Simon Eyres. When Eyre becomes sheriff he deeds his shop to Hodge, and Firk moves up to Hodge's position of foreman; success for Simon Eyre is reflected within the ranks of the shoemakers. More significantly, however, the shoemakers

(Eyre, Hodge, and Firk) function in similar ways in the two other plots of the play. Apart from the business transaction of the ship's cargo and his acceptance of the civic promotions, Eyre acts in the play primarily for others. He tries to aid Rafe at the outset, helps his employees, provides the feast for the apprentices, gains market advantages for shoemakers, builds Leadenhall, and contributes to the solution of Lacy's problems. In a limited fashion Firk and Hodge do the same thing. Firk tricks Otley and Lincoln, which allows Lacy and Rose to be married; and Firk and Hodge together are the principal agents in Jane's rescue from Hammon.

Perhaps the most important device by which Dekker unites the three plots is the participation of characters in several actions of the play. Several of these have already been noted. Simon Eyre acts in the Rafe-Jane plot at the outset and later becomes an important character in the Lacy-Rose plot. The action that Eyre takes in favor of Lacy in his problem with the King is motivated in part by the aid Lacy gave to Eyre in the ship's cargo transaction. In a sense Lacy's aid helped make Eyre sufficiently influential to aid Lacy. It is somewhat ironic that the money loaned by Lacy to Simon was originally given to Lacy by Lincoln and Otley. These "twenty Portugese" allow Eyre to make the down-payment on the cargo, which Otley later shares. Otley's investment is greater than his proportionate returns, and Simon Eyre is an early example of a businessman profiting with borrowed money.

Hammon also participates in two actions, functioning almost identically in both. As a suitor for Rose he threatens to make the separation of Rose and Lacy permanent. Later the planned wedding with Jane threatens to do the same thing to Jane and Rafe.

Finally there is Otley, who serves as an important character in the Rose-Lacy action as her father and a principal obstacle in the path of their marriage. In the Eyre plot he is the Lord Mayor and partner who promotes Simon Eyre to the position of Sheriff; and he is the Mayor who impresses Rafe and later mistakes Jane and Rafe for his own daughter and son-in-law.

These character cross-pollinations serve the play in a fashion besides the linking of one plot to another. They tend to give a broader view of all the characters because they are portrayed in a variety of activities. Otley is seen not only in his principal role as father-objector, but also as a business man, as host to the Eyre family. Fortunately for himself and the play, Lacy becomes something more than the young man who deserts his army to search for his sweetheart. He becomes a useful member of an admirable group of men, enjoying their beer and aiding a most likeable fellow, Simon Eyre, in his rise to fame and fortune. Hammon alone is merely functional; but perhaps more interest in him would produce concern for his successive failures in his search for a wife. As a matter of fact, Harbage says that Hammon "lingers in our minds as a plaintive and appealing figure; we hope that he found a heart-free maiden at last".[24] The character's forlorn exit is, however, immediately followed by the entrance of Lincoln and Otley, and audience sympathy for Hammon should be quickly changed to glee at the upsetting of these nobles.

Dekker also relates the separate actions by including incidents from two actions within one scene unit so that one plot blends into another. Partly because of the characters common to several plots, Dekker is able to present two actions simultaneously, or at least successively. This is a common practice for the last scene of a multiple plot play, but here the technique is brought near to a maximum effectiveness throughout the play. All in all eight scene units of the play include incidents of more than one plot. This number does not include those scenes (I.iii-iv; II.i-ii; IV.i-ii; and IV.iii-vi) between which the break appears to be primarily editorial rather than dramatic. A few examples will illustrate the technique.

The long, continuous, first scene includes incidents of two plots and introduces the characters of the third plot. Here the characters who appear in two actions link the incidents like a chain. Lincoln and Otley talk; Lacy and his cousin Askew join the discussion; the first two depart, and in a short while the Eyre group enters to talk to Lacy and Askew; finally these two leave and the Eyre group remains to bid farewell to Rafe.

Another scene, III.iii, employs a different technique. The party given by Otley is ostensibly to honor Simon Eyre as Sheriff, and as such contributes to Eyre's plot. But Eyre's contribution to the celebration, the dance of the shoemakers, provides the occasion for Lacy to find Rose, and for her to recognize him. One incident, then, contributes to two plots.

A final example of scenes with two actions is V.ii, in which yet another variation is employed. Here, the two actions are not simultaneous, but successive and parallel. The wedding party, consisting of Hammond and the masked Jane, is accosted by Rafe and the shoemakers. After the debate the "attackers" are triumphant and Hammon leaves the field, and the "new" couple, Rafe and Jane, remain. At this point another group of "attackers" arrives, Lincoln, Otley, and their supporters, who think the couple to be Rose and Lacy. After a short parody of the first discussion the couple is unmasked and these "attackers" are in a sense repulsed.

The cohesive devices discussed thus far might be subject to criticism because most of them are just that—devices. They display a high degree of skill in plotting, in manipulation of several intrigues, but they remain within the limited realm of technique. Unless a reason exists for uniting these apparently disparate actions the play is only an enjoyable exercise in technique. Reasons do exist, however, on a thematic level.

The Rafe-Jane story is essentially one of the triumph of love over social obstacles. The original separation is brought about by the wars with France, and although there seems to be some regulation prohibiting the impressment of a newly married man, Rafe, totally without influence or social position, is subject to the commands of those above him. That it is his position in society that forces him to serve is made quite clear in the play by the direct comparison of his plight with Lacy's solution of the same problem. Despite Lacy's promise to look after him—"Thou shalt not want, as I am a gentleman" (I.i.177)—Rafe's name appears on the casualty lists and he returns to London on crutches. Despite Simon Eyre's silent promise to care for Jane—"But gentle maister and my louing dame, / As you haue alwaies beene a friend to me, / So in my absence thinke vpon my wife" (I.i.199-201)—she is cast out of Eyre's household. Contrasted to the real pain they suffer are the more traditional romantic difficulties of Rose and Lacy, to whom they are linked by the simultaneously sympathetic and affluent Hammon. Jane, believing Rafe to be dead, is in no position to deny the urgings of Hammon. To refuse would be folly. Hammon specifically acknowledges their difference of position; "Thy wealth I know is little, my desires / Thirst not for gold" (III.iv.53-4), he says to Jane. Later he attempts to buy her from Rafe. But with the aid of the shoemakers Rafe overcomes these obstacles, and Jane, given a choice between the two men, states her feelings in very specific terms, "Thou art my husband and these humble weedes / Makes thee more beautiful than all his wealth" (V.ii.55-6).

Although Lacy serves as a social contrast to Rafe, he too has problems which stem from differences in social rank. Lincoln and Otley, again and again, state their objections in these terms. Lincoln is most to the point in the last scene of the play when he objects to the King, "Her bloud is too too base" (V.v.101-02). Otley is at once more ambiguous and more realistic. To Lincoln he says, "Too meane is my poore girle for his high birth" (I.i.11), but to Eyre he reveals a prejudice against courtiers and a preference for the moneyed middle class—"There came of late, / A proper Gentleman of faire reuenewes, / Whom gladly I would call sonne in law" (III.iii.32-4). Clearly, to be of the working class is not enough, for when he is told that Rose has eloped he responds, "A fleming butter boxe, a shoomaker / Will she forget her birth? Requite my care / With such ingratitude?" (IV.iv.42-4). But the two young people do succeed in marrying, and the King speaks the central idea of this action, "Dost thou not know, that loue repects no bloud? / Cares not for difference of birth or state" (V.v.104-05).

This theme is a sub-division of the theme of the play as a whole. It is not only love that does not respect birth or state, but also success in general. Achievement, promotion, advancement of all kinds are pictured in the play. For several of the characters in the play Simon Eyre is instrumental to success. At one point, when Dame Eyre herself scolds the journeymen, Simon reminds her, "haue not I tane you from selling tripes in Eastcheape, and set you in my shop, and made you haile fellowe with *Simon Eyre,* the shoomaker?" (II.iii.60-2). Her reactions to suc-

cess become a matter for satire. When Eyre sets out to buy the ship's cargo she has a premonition, "I do feele honour creepe vpon me, and which is more, a certaine rising in my flesh, but let that passe" (II.iii.133-35). And when Eyre becomes Sheriff her first concern is for suitable clothes—new shoes, farthingales, French hoods and periwigs. She takes on airs, asking Hans, "*Hans* pray thee tie my shooe" (III.ii.25), and passing out three penny gratuities to the workmen.

The shoemakers, too, rise up the social scale; Hodge takes over Eyre's shop and Firk becomes foreman. Eyre tells them that opportunity is open to all, that "you shall liue to be Sheriues of *London*" (III.ii.137-38). They take his counsel to heart, and after the celebration at Otley's home Hodge spurs his workmen with, "plie your worke to day, we loytred yesterday, to it pell mel, that we may liue to be Lord Maiors, or Aldermen at least" (IV.i.2-4).

Simon Eyre is, of course, the central example of the opportunities for success. As he rises from shoemaker to Alderman, rich man, Sheriff, and Lord Mayor he sings out his refrain "Prince am I none, yet am I princely born" on every occasion. Stoll, referring to the repeated description of "honest" Iago, says, "This various and appropriate repetition is both a simplifying and a unifying device. . . ."[25] Eyre's refrain performs a similar function in this play.

Although one writer, concerned perhaps by the lack of complication in the Eyre action, maintains that the "main plot has to do with the love of young Lacy and the mayor's daughter",[26] most critics consider the Eyre action to be central in the play.[27] Some have gone to far as to suggest that the other plots were added for mere variety's sake[28] or to strengthen an otherwise weak story. But if the Eyre action is indeed the main one, the structure of the play is not typical. Normally a play with several plots contains one plot that is obviously major and one or two others that are just as obviously subordinate to the first. To these plots the term "sub-plot" has been assigned. Sub-plots are usually physically subordinate as well. That is, less time and fewer lines are devoted to them than to the main plot. But here, the Lacy-Rose plot is developed in more detail than the Eyre plot, which in turn is not much "longer" than the action concerned with Rafe and Jane.[29] While the term sub-plot could be applied to the Rafe-Jane action, it does not seem suitable for the Lacy-Rose action. More important than these quantitative arguments is the tightly interwoven effect revealed by the description and discussion in the preceding pages. The play is, as Creizenach says, one in which the actions are woven "closely and artistically together"[30] They are woven so closely and are so mutually relevant that the structure is very nearly unique. The terms "main plot" and "sub-plot" just do not apply to this masterfully constructed drama.

Rather superficially, some critics have considered the play to have a number of structural weaknesses: the multiplicity of apparently diverse actions; the simplicity of forward movement of the individual actions; the lack of real complication or conflict; and the contradictory time scheme and opportune deaths of the seven aldermen.

It has been demonstrated here, however, that the individual actions are well articulated and that skillful devices have been employed to link the various actions and characters in a meaningful, coherent whole. In addition, the playwright seems to have been aware of the problems concerning the aldermen and time scheme, and has softened or disguised the problems somewhat. The other alleged weaknesses are in fact less weak than unique. Some of the structural procedures are unorthodox, outside of accepted practice, but they are both functional and highly effective in the play. Simplicity and multiplicity serve to further the basic meanings of the play—the exciting opportunities that were open to all irrespective of rank in this buoyant view of Elizabethan society. The result is a play that Fluchère properly calls "la comédie la plus entraînante de cette époque. . . ."[31]

Notes

1. *A Transcript of the Registers of the Company of Stationers of London; 1554-1640 A.D.,* ed. Edward Arber (London, 1876), III, 29.

2. Wilfrid J. Halliday (ed.), *Deloney's Gentle Craft* (Oxford, 1928), p. 7. This work is bound with separate pagination after *Dekker's Shoemaker's Holiday,* ed. J. R. Sutherland (Oxford, 1928).

3. Although the two scenes (I.iii and I.iv) are separated in Bowers' edition, the effect in the theatre would be one of conjunction. Lacy says "Here in Towerstreete, with *Ayre* the shooe-maker, / Meane I a while to worke. . . ." (I.iii.19-20). Four lines later he exits, and the stage is indeed empty, but Eyre immediately enters from his shop. The action, therefore, is continuous. Thirty-five lines later Lacy enters and is subsequently hired.

4. Once more two separate scenes (IV.iii and IV.iv) are indicated by Bowers, although the action is continuous. Otley leaves the "room" to go to receive Lincoln; Rose and Lacy decide and then run off; and Otley and Lincoln re-enter.

5. Madeleine Doran, *Endeavors of Art: A Study of Form in Elizabethan Drama* (Madison, 1954), p. 259.

6. *Ibid.,* p. 260.

7. Andrew Cecil Bradley, *Shakespearean Tragedy* (New York, 1949), p. 51.

8. Gustav Freytag, *Technique of the Drama,* trans. E. J. MacEwan (Chicago, 1904), pp. 137 and 139.

9. In Deloney's narrative, for example, the lovers are reconciled to the girl's father by means of their child, the result of their secret marriage.

10. William L. Halstead, "Thomas Dekker's Early Work for the Theatre" (unpublished Ph.D. dissertation, University of Southern California, 1937), pp. 102-04.

11. Charles Frederick Tucker Brooke, *The Tudor Drama* (Cambridge, Mass., 1911), p. 281.

12. Alfred Harbage, *Shakespeare and the Rival Traditions* (New York, 1952), p. 174.

13. Actually this is all that happens in the scene to serve the plot itself, but a certain amount of secondary complication is introduced that runs throughout the play. Both Eyre and his wife hesitate to hire the itinerant shoemaker, but the two journeymen insist, threatening to quit themselves if Eyre does not hire extra help. It is, perhaps, too much to suggest this as one of the earliest recorded instances of labor-management problems. The bickering between the journeymen and Dame Eyre occurs several times throughout the play as a minor conflict.

14. "Critical Essay", *The Later Contemporaries of Shakespeare,* Vol. III of *Representative English Comedies,* ed. Charles Mills Gayley (New York, 1914), 6.

15. Hector M. Robertson, *Aspects of the Rise of Economic Individualism* (Cambridge, Eng., 1933), pp. 190-191.

16. Lionel Charles Knights, *Drama and Society in the Age of Jonson* (New York, 1936), p. 237.

17. Halliday, p. 65.

18. Muriel C. Bradbrook, *Themes and Conventions of Elizabethan Tragedy* (Cambridge, Eng., 1957), p. 46.

19. John Mason Brown, *Two on the Aisle* (New York, 1938), p. 202.

20. Mable Buland, *The Presentation of Time in the Elizabethan Drama* (= *Yale Studies in English,* Vol. XLIV) (New York, 1912), 163.

21. *Elizabethan Plays* (Boston, 1933), p. 632.

22. John B. Moore, *The Comic and the Realistic in English Drama* (Chicago, 1925), p. 179.

23. Muriel Clara Bradbrook, "Shakespeare and the Use of Disguise", *Essays in Criticism,* II (April, 1952), 162.

24. *Rival Traditions,* p. 175.

25. Elmer Edgar Stoll, *Shakespeare and Other Masters* (Cambridge, Mass., 1940), p. 45.

26. Benjamin Brawley, *A Short History of the English Drama* (New York, 1921), p. 103.

27. Cf. Jones-Davies, I, 128; and Charles Frederick Tucker Brooke and Nathan Burton Paradise (eds.), *English Drama, 1580-1642* (New York, 1933), p. 264.

28. Thomas Marc Parrott and Robert Hamilton Ball, *A Short View of Elizabethan Drama* (New York, 1943), p. 108.

29. Gayley, p. 6.

30. Wilhelm Creizenach, *The English Drama in the Age of Shakespeare,* trans. Cecile Hugon (Philadelphia, 1916), p. 256.

31. Henri Fluchère, "Thomas Dekker et le Drame Bourgeois", *Cahiers du Sud,* XX (June, 1933), 195.

Peggy Faye Shirley (essay date 1975)

SOURCE: "Dekker's Use of Serious Elements in Comedy: *The Shoemakers' Holiday,*" in *Serious and Tragic Ele-*

ments in the Comedy of Thomas Dekker, Institut für Englishe Sprach und Literatur, 1975, pp. 12-36.

[*In the following essay, Shirley explores Dekker's mixture of gravity and levity in his depiction of situations and characters in* The Shoemaker's Holiday.]

Fredson Bowers notes in connection with *The Shoemakers' Holiday,* "On 15 July 1599 Henslowe had advanced £3 towards buying the book from Dekker, but the first recorded performance is that at court on 1 January 1600";[1] the first quarto, not listed in the Stationers' Register, is dated 1600. The quarto copy, Professor Bowers points out, did not carry the dramatist's name on the title-page; the Dekker critic feels, however, that the information from Henslowe's diary and internal evidence from the play itself form a sufficient basis for attributing the play solely to Dekker, and he draws from his own previous study[2] which concluded that an attempt to establish a theory of collaboration with Robert Wilson in the writing of this play was based on a forgery by J. Payne Collier.[3]

Professor Bowers' edition of Dekker's drama includes the short introductory piece addressed to all who follow the shoemaker's trade that refers to the presentation of the play before Elizabeth on New Year's Day in 1600. What is, perhaps, Dekker's first comment on the nature of comedy is contained in this foreword:

> . . . I present you here with a merrie conceited Comedie. . . . Take all in good worth that is well intended, for nothing is purposed but mirth, mirth lengthneth long life. . . .[4]

This purpose is, in fact, what Dekker ultimately achieves in *The Shoemakers's Holiday,* for the overall effect of the play is one of pleasure, good fun, a sense of well-being in seeing everything work out satisfactorily. This predominant tone is interrupted in a few places where Dekker, in order to remind his audience that reality involves moments of sensations other than pleasure, introduces scenes of sober weight. Even in these cases, however, Dekker makes his point and then uses some comic situations to return his spectators to the light-hearted mood he intends for them to enjoy.

The foreword of the play is succeeded by two songs presented in Professor Bowers' edition before the text of the play;[5] no evidence within the text itself points out the place in which each should properly appear.[6] Of these two, the first "Three-mans Song" presents the traditional picture of the young man who, even as he begs his love to listen while he tells of his love for her, suspects that she may prove unfaithful; the second song is a drinking song. The two are brought into this discussion because the use of such songs is often included in studies of the elements referred to as comic devices.[7]

After the central problem of the play—the love of Lacy and Rose for one another and the opposition of each one's family to the marriage—has been presented, the reader is introduced to a group of characters whose antics supply much of the play's buffoonery. Simon Eyre—the head of this group and the man whose promotions to sheriff and, finally, to Lord Mayor connect him with the characters of nobler rank in more than a proprietor-clientéle relationship—performs the necessary introduction of his cohorts. As he presents a petition to Lacy and Askew, he says

> . . . I am *Simon Eyre,* the mad Shoomaker of Towerstreete, this wench with the mealy mouth that will neuer tire, is my wife I can tel you, heres *Hodge* my man, and my foreman, heres *Firke* my fine firking iourneyman, and this is blubbered *Iane,* al we come to be suters for this honest *Rafe.* . . .[8]

These figures, although they sometimes serve as foils to draw attention to events among the gentry or to emphasize them, are individually important to the action of the play. The traits mentioned in the descriptive epithets of Eyre's introduction become more pronounced in the characters's personalities as the play advances; often it is the emphasis on or exaggeration of these very traits that makes the figures comical.

With the petition for his dismissal from military service denied, Rafe finds he must leave his newly wed Jane; the stage is, thus, prepared for their parting. The event should normally be a solemn affair—Jane may never see her husband again, and they have been married only a brief time. Yet Rafe's parting gift—not a ring, a jewel, or a kerchief, but a pair of shoes with Jane's name printed on them—is so out of order as far as romantic tradition is concerned that the scene is laughable rather than saddening. The audience is accustomed to a lover's farewell request that his beloved often take out the blade or jewel he has given her at parting and that she think about him as she turns over in her hands the object involved; to such an audience the request by Rafe that Jane think of him every morning as she pulls on the shoes he presents to her is indecorous enough to make the occasion considerably less than heart-rending. Dekker has, thus, taken a potentially grave situation and, by means of indecorum, caused his audience to accept it as a comic affair.

A new scene follows this incident, and it begins with the introduction of Rose, Lacy's beloved. She weaves a garland of flowers for him, lamenting her father's protective measures which have separated her from her sweetheart. The audience follows her speech, but before the despair of her situation can take effect on her listeners, her maid Sybil comes in and disrupts whatever empathy may have been building. Again, then, a potentially sober incident has been directed toward a comic resolution—in this case by means of the presentation of the flippant Sybil. This young woman is a carefree individual; she is interested in her mistress's welfare, but she is more interested in the prizes she gets as rewards for running errands. Somehow seriousness never touches Sybil; she continues to function on the surface, and her shallow attitude keeps the gravity of Rose's situation from touching the audience. This discussion of Sybil's frivolous manner, however, is not intended to imply that without her presence Rose's speech would work an Aristotelian catharsis of pity; Rose has a problem, yes, but her speech grows more and more hyperbolic until it becomes artificial. She ends with these lines springing from the recognized melancholic lover tradition:

. . . wretched I
Will sit and sigh for his [Lacy's] lost companie.

(I, ii, 63-4)

The audience realizes her grief is overdone and, thus, does not become caught up in the kind of vicarious despair that viewers of a tragic situation often, at least temporarily, experience during the unfolding of a drama. The prevailing comic mood therefore triumphs again, or at least it fails to yield to a real display of despair where Rose's plight is concerned.

Disguise is an agent frequently used in comedy, and it is responsible for a large number of the amusing situations in Dekker's **Shoemakers' Holiday.** Lacy cannot openly woo Rose for two reasons: (1) there is opposition to his courtship of a girl from a lower social class, and (2) he has been given a commission in the king's army and is, therefore, supposed to be in France. Not to be thwarted in his pursuit of Rose, however, the young nobleman dons the guise of a shoemaker and plans to become an apprentice to Simon Eyre. In explaining his disguise to the audience, Dekker's character finds an opportunity to employ the twofold purpose of comedy mentioned by Sir Philip Sidney[9] and reiterated later by John Dennis[10]—to "instruct" as well as to "delight." Lacy addresses love and expresses the following philosophical argument:

O loue, how powerfull art thou, that canst change
High birth to barenesse, and a noble mind,
To the meane semblance of a shooemaker?

(I, iii, 10-2)

This address is part of a speech similar to the one by Rose mentioned earlier. Lacy's distress over the opposition to his courting and marrying Rose is offset, too, by the entrance of blustering comic figures. This time it is the banter among Simon Eyre and his crew, following immediately upon Lacy's exit from stage, that keeps the audience from dwelling on any mournful tone connected with the injustice of Lacy's separation from Rose.

In the midst of the clamor that is supposedly the normal state around Eyre's shop, Lacy enters in his shoemaker's garb. He calls himself Hans and speaks a Dutch dialect that adds to the humor of his character for these reasons: (1) it is a garbled imitation of the dialect it represents; and (2) Simon's hands do not understand the foreign speech, and they comment on the language among themselves.[11]

The next incident that adds material to the comic structure of the play is found in a scene with Rose; Sybil; Hammon, ". . . a proper gentleman, a citizen by birth . . ." (II, ii,

58-59); and his brother-in-law Warner. The two men have come onto the grounds of Old Ford, the estate where Rose has been confined, to search for a deer they have sighted. The whole scene is line after line of witty repartée loaded with puns and fired back and forth as Hammon and Warner shift the object of their pursuit from the deer to Rose and Sybil. The men are serious in their attempts to woo the ladies, but Rose and Sybil thwart them at every turn with joking or sarcasm. The following lines of dialogue exemplify the verbal attack Hammon and Warner have to endure:

WAR.
Came not a bucke this way?
ROSE.
No, but two Does.

(II, ii, 13)

WAR.
Which way [did the deer flee] my sugar-candie, can you shew?
SYB.
Come vp good honnisops, vpon some, no.

(II, ii, 26-27)

HAM.
A deere, more deere is found within this place.
ROSE.
But not the deere (sir) which you had in chace.

(II, ii, 30-31)

SYB.
What kind of hart is that (deere hart) you seeke?
WAR.
A hart, deare hart.

(II, ii, 37-38)

ROSE.
To loose your heart, it's possible you can?
HAM.
My heart is lost.
ROSE.
Alacke good gentleman.
HAM.
This poore lost hart would I wish you might find.
ROSE.
You by such lucke might proue your hart a hind.
HAM.
Why Lucke had hornes, so haue I heard some say.
ROSE.
Now God and't be his wil send Luck into your way.

(II, ii, 39-44)

The audience here feels some sympathy for Hammon because he is ignorant of his position as the butt of Rose's pointed remarks. The sympathy, however, is not allowed to run to any depth because the listeners know that Rose belongs to Lacy. They know, therefore, that her apparently inhumanly apathetic treatment of Hammon does not make her a cold, scheming woman; she is capable of love, and she loyally bears that love for no one but Lacy. Hammon himself cannot be taken too seriously, either, because having failed to win Rose, he is going to turn his mind quickly toward the pursuit of Jane; later when he is faced with the fact that Jane has a live husband whom she loves, he will try to buy her from that husband. Members of the audience, then, having no sincerity of character before them that is worthy of their sympathy are able to join in the lightheartedness that is the prevailing quality of the drama.

Another reason for the audience's not dwelling on Hammon's plight is that immediately following the scene of the verbal battle, there is a scene at Eyre's shop involving the witty characters Firke and Hodge; these two, having been bested by their master's wife, are threatening to leave the business. They have used this threat before—to persuade Eyre to employ Hans as an apprentice—and the picture here, as in the first case, is almost that of two spoiled children who are going to run away from home unless their father does whatever is necessary to comfort them. Of course the spectators are going to enjoy this situation, particularly when the swaggering Eyre does take it upon himself to smooth out things for his apprentices.

Hammon, in the time lapse since he was last seen, has come to the point where he must declare his love for Rose openly. He tells her straightforwardly that he loves her—". . . dearer than my heart . . ." (III, i, 11)—but her reaction is the same verbal parrying to which he was subjected in their first encounter with each other. Rose's father offers to force his daughter to accept the proposal, but Hammon rejects the prospect of "enforced love" (III, i, 50). As previously mentioned, he announces that he will direct his attention in the future to another:

> There is a wench keepes shop in the old change,
> To her will I, it is not wealth I seeke,
> I haue enough, and wil preferre her loue
> Before the world. . . .
>
> (III, i, 51-54)

The next set of circumstances that allows the audience to enjoy the spirit of comedy is that connected with the preparation of the Eyre household to accept a change in social status—Simon is about to be appointed "Shiriffe," (III, ii, 15) and his wife especially is concerned about the adjustments she feels she must make in order to fill the position of an official's wife. When sophisticated terms such as *"compendious"* and *"tedious"* (III, ii, 8) creep into her previously vulgar—often bawdy—speech, the shoemakers are quick to note the change. Firke, for example, comments on the incongruity between her new speech pattern and her natural manner:

> O rare, your excellence is full of eloquence, how like a new carte wheele my dame speakes, and she lookes like an old musty ale-bottle going to scalding.
>
> (III, ii, 9-11)

In addition to her speech, her clothes and hair style become objects of conversation; she wants to be sure that these aspects of her appearance, too, suit her advanced social rank. Firke and Hodge continue to tease her, but she misses the point of the remarks leveled at her vanity. Some of these remarks are spoken in "Asides," but some of the

failure to comprehend is the result of ignorance on her part, a factor that adds to the humor.

The comic principle at work here is that which involves pretense, the act of assuming an appearance different from the one that belongs to the individual naturally. Spectators laugh as they watch Margery attempt to "be what she is not" because her pose is so strikingly artificial, so affected in its manner. The people around her know her so well that such marked deviation in her behavior lets them know what she is doing. They laugh because they realize that she is performing, acting out a role. The members of the audience laugh for two reasons: (1) they, too, see Margery acting and are amused at the incongruity of her behavior with her birth; and (2) they hear and understand the remarks of Firke and Hodge, and they laugh because the import of the wit does not touch Margery (because of her mental obtuseness or because of her desire to ignore the barbs which would point out the foolishness of her pretension).

In a later scene, a gathering at the Lord Mayor's estate, Margery approaches her husband with her philosophy of behavior dictated by social status. Simon's answer—a clear statement of his negative opinion regarding acting unnaturally among his associates—is included in the following passage from the scene:

> L. Ma.
> Now by my troth Ile tel thee maister *Eyre,*
> It does me good and al my breatheren,
> That such a madcap fellow as thy selfe
> Is entred into our societie.
> Wife.
> I but my Lord, hee must learne nowe to putte on grauitie.
> Eyre.
> Peace *Maggy,* a fig for grauitie, when I go to Guildhal in my scarlet gowne, Ile look as demurely as a saint, and speake as grauely as a Iustice of a peace, but now I am here at old Foord, at my good Lord Maiors house, let it go by, vanish *Maggy,* Ile be merrie, away with flip flap, these fooleries, these gulleries: what hunnie: prince am I none, yet am I princly borne. . . .
>
> (III, iii, 7-17)

Simon Eyre has some definite ideas about the manner in which he is to bear himself while he is performing the duties of his new office. He is not, however, going to allow the behavior thus defined to take the place of his normal patterns of conduct among his friends. Margery attempts to play the role of Lord Mayor's wife among her familiars, and she is made to look foolish because of her behavior. Simon Eyre wants to be no other when he is with those who expect him to be Simon Eyre; he reserves his official bearing for those situations in which he is expected to present a dignified appearance.

The entrance of Rafe, lamed from some military encounter, adds an element to the play that, considered in itself, is serious. Here Dekker is using one of the themes about which he personally seems to have had strong sentiments—the plight of the neglected soldier. Rafe comes in, and his crippled state becomes the object of various jokes and puns. The laughter is there, but it is not really the same kind of lighthearted, enjoyable laughter as that connected with the squabbles among Eyre's apprentices. From passages in some of Dekker's other plays,[12] it is apparent that Rafe is only one of many soldiers who were returning from war injured—in a number of cases too crippled to work. Rafe is fortunate; his wound, even compounded by the misery of finding that no one knows where his wife Jane has gone, will not lead him to have to beg for a living. Since he is a shoemaker by trade, he works with his hands; the leg wound that would cost many their jobs does not put Rafe out of work. The audience attending this play would be familiar with the many soldiers who depended on society for their existence. These spectators would laugh warmheartedly with the character in the play because he is the victor, not the object of despair in the situation; nevertheless, they would not fail to catch Dekker's reference to a condition that was a very real problem to many.

What the dramatist has done in this scene is to introduce into his comedy a sobering reminder of actuality; he handles the event in such a manner, however, that the confrontation with reality does not spoil the comic atmosphere that the play has created for the audience to enjoy.

In the time intervening since his last appearance, Hammon has sought Jane and has found her. Dekker reintroduces him in soliloquy, and Hammon tells the audience that he has wooed the seamstress three times and has been refused all three times. In the traditional pain of unsuccessful courtship, he mourns:

> . . . I am infortunate,
> I stil loue one, yet no body loues me, . . .

> (III, iv, 6-7)

Hammon then confronts Jane a fourth time and pleads again for her love. Their conversation is not a series of witty exchanges as was the dialogue between Hammon and Rose or Warner and Sybil. Jane is sincere in her speech with the ridiculously lovesick figure,[13] but love for her own husband keeps her from entertaining any thoughts of yielding to Hammon's plea.

On hearing that Jane's husband was among those sent to France, Hammon produces a letter which lists Rafe as one of those soldiers killed in military service there. Jane grieves realistically for her supposedly dead husband; except that the audience has already seen Rafe alive and back in Eyre's service, this scene would breed tragic feeling in the audience that would endanger the accomplishment of the play's purpose in which "nothing is purposed but mirth." Hammon, in determined pursuit, adds to her misery by continuing to plague her with protestations of his love. Actually, his proposals of marriage now become

even more pressing than they have been previously; believing Rafe dead, Hammon thinks that there is absolutely no reason why Jane should not marry him. Jane repeatedly begs Hammon to cease his continual proposals, but he does not give in until he gets what he considers at least a faint glimmer of acceptance. Jane remarks:

> Nay, for Gods loue peace,
> My sorrowes by your presence more increase,
> Not that you thus are present, but al griefe
> Desires to be alone, therefore in briefe
> Thus much I say, and saying bid adew,
> If euer I wed man it shall be you.

> (III, iv, 117-22)

When Jane does decide to marry Hammon, the prospective bridegroom sends a servant to Eyre's shop with one of Jane's shoes to be used as a measure in making her a new pair. The shoe falls, of course, into Rafe's hands, and he recognizes it as one of those he gave to his wife when he left her to go to France. The tradition mentioned in the discussion of their parting is, thus, picked up again as the parting token is used to identify and locate a lost lover. Here, as before, the use of the shoe to remind one of his beloved is amusing rather than touching. Somehow the picture of Rafe, clutching Jane's shoe and mourning over the fact that the wife he has lost is about to be married to someone else, is too outlandish to move the audience to pity. Thus Dekker once more uses a case of indecorum to turn a potentially sober situation into a comic scene.

Lacy, dressed as Hans the shoemaker, is able to see Rose on the pretense of fitting her with shoes. His disguise creates situations of comic irony, for his identity is known only to himself and to Rose; ignorance on the part of Rose's father, especially, makes possible some highly amusing speeches.

Firke, the apprentice whose clowning has been observed previously to some extent, is responsible for the comic turn taken by events which, otherwise, may have led to a tragic conclusion. A spy has revealed that Lacy is still in England rather than in France; as a result of his uncle's fervent search for him, Lacy and Rose make plans to be married as soon as possible. Firke implies that their marriage is forthcoming in the company of Lacy's uncle, Lincolne, and the Lord Mayor, but he purposely sends the searchers to the wrong church so that the wedding interrupted by them is that of Hammon and Jane rather than that of Lacy and Rose.

Before Lincolne and the Lord Mayor appear at the church where Hammon and Jane are to be married, Eyre's apprentices, intent on helping Rafe regain his wife, arrive there. Hodge reveals Rafe's presence to Jane, and she leaves Hammon's side immediately and goes to embrace her husband. At this point Hammon tries to buy Jane from Rafe, but Rafe tells Hammon in strong terms that gold will not separate him from his wife. Hammon, thwarted again in his pursuit of a wife, vows never to marry and leaves the stage.

The Lord Mayor and Lincolne, bent on stopping the wedding of Lacy and Rose, enter next. Thinking they have found the two for whom they have been searching, they approach Rafe and Jane, both of whom are masked. With the identities of these two characters concealed, Dekker allows Lincolne and the Lord Mayor to make fools of themselves; themselves the object of comic irony, they ignorantly make speeches about the blindness of those they assume are underneath the masks. As the realization that they have been made to look ridiculous by Firke's trick settles onto the Lord Mayor and Lincolne, a messenger brings word that the king is that day dining with Simon Eyre; the defeated but persistent pair head for the newly appointed Lord Mayor's house to plead with their ruler to dissolve the marriage of Lacy and Rose, for the news of that couple's wedding has been brought by the same messenger who has spoken of the king's whereabouts.

The king, a just man, does not want to separate Lacy and Rose. After some joking and sporting with Simon Eyre, he turns to the two young lovers; and, to please Lincolne and the former Lord Mayor, he declares the couple divorced. If the play had ended at this point, the comic atmosphere that has prevailed throughout the drama would have been strikingly disrupted. The king, however, decrees that the two whom he has separated are now rejoined as husband and wife. Tragedy has been averted—to the dismay of those characters who did not look for such an outcome.

With the marriages thus satisfactorily established, the play can be brought to a close. The king enjoys a banquet at Simon Eyre's home, but his eyes are on the upcoming war with France:

> Come Lordes, a while lets reuel it at home,
> When all our sports, and banquetings are done,
> Warres must right wrongs which Frenchmen haue begun.

> (V, v, 189-91)

The play ends, then, with marriages and a banquet, two of the devices which, according to Northrop Frye, are traditional ways of closing a comedy.[14] The subject of war mentioned in the last line of the play serves as a realistic touch, a reminder to the characters that their merrymaking is not all that there is to life.

In this review of the essential events and situations that comprise *The Shoemakers' Holiday,* the following elements have been seen to perpetrate comedy:

Indecorum

Unexpected substitution that violates the general nature of tradition keeps a potentially moving scene from being touching.

Incongruity

Closely related to indecorum, incongruity of speech, dress, manner, or action is comical to an audience who knows the true nature of the individual concerned and can see the discrepancy. Walter Kerr devotes an entire chapter of his book on dramatic theory to a discussion of elements that are funny because they violate the expected or natural pattern.[15]

Exaggeration

Speeches which contain extreme amplification of sentiment tend to amuse the audience rather than to stir them emotionally.

Ignorance

Lack of self-knowledge or knowledge of surrounding situations—in those cases where such a lack breeds no harm—causes spectators to smile indulgently from their "if-only-you-knew" stance. Henri Bergson brings out this idea in his statement, ". . . a comic character is generally comic in proportion to his ignorance of himself."[16] In tragedy this ignorance and the recognition that is its resolution[17] add to the tragic nature of the hero involved because of the regrettable acts that frequently spring from such lack of knowledge. In comedy, however, the greatest injuries suffered seem to be those that are concerned with wounded vanity.[18] Though this element is also common in tragedy—referred to then as *hubris*—there is a difference in its presentation in comedy. The comedy involves no malice, no irreversible misfortune, while the tragedy gives place to violence and incidents that bring irremediable harm—even death—to characters. This concept of the difference between the comic and tragic handling of pride is one possible amplification of Frye's statement, "Comedy is designed not to condemn evil, but to ridicule a lack of self-knowledge."[19] Comic ignorance does not give rise to serious injury; it does permit ridicule, but not to the point of being malicious. Most recognition that occurs in connection with a demonstration of ignorance in comedy brings a sheepish admission of a foolish position, not an awareness of guilt for some heinous act.

Disguise, Mask, Pretense

These three agents make possible comic irony or the comedy whose existence springs from situations whose characters and conditions are not what they seem to be. These various means of role-playing are inseparably related to some of the abstract elements already listed. Pretense, for example, tends to spawn some form of incongruity. Disguise always plays upon someone's ignorance; the result is generally irony, dramatic or verbal, amusing in a comic framework but often soberly pointed in tragedy.

Comic characters

The use of good-natured characters who are always finding subjects for sport—either among their peers or in another social group—keeps an audience in a comic mood. Dekker's play presents several successful comic characters, chief among whom is Simon Eyre.

In addition to these elements Thomas Dekker changes the course of potentially grave situations and shapes them into circumstances suitable to comedy. Northrop Frye, who sees all drama in terms of an ultimate resolution (a cycle of struggle, death, and rebirth)[20] would hail Dekker's work because it illustrates a principle important to Frye: ". . . comedy contains a potential tragedy within itself."[21] There are three major examples of this approach to tragedy and reversal from it in *The Shoemakers' Holiday:*

(1) The first of these is the return of Rafe, wounded, from his war experience. As the previous discussion of his

predicament has pointed out, Dekker uses Rafe to represent the wounded soldier of the era, a man frequently condemned to a life as a beggar. Rafe escapes that condemnation by assuming an air of acceptance regarding his lameness; rather than giving in to despair, he goes back to work as a shoemaker. Because he assumes mastery of the situation instead of allowing the situation to master him and dictate to him an existence of miserable self-pity, Rafe does not become a tragic figure. His potentially tragic circumstances work out happily under Dekker's hand; the result is that the members of the audience, through Rafe's lameness, are forced to stop in the midst of their hearty enjoyment long enough to remember that the darker aspect of reality is still a factor with which they must contend. Rafe's personal victory over the circumstances, however, makes the sobering moment fit acceptably within the comic framework. This incident is definitely the most notable of the serious elements involved in the play.

(2) Jane's sincere grief for her supposedly dead husband would give rise to a tragic turn of mind except for Dekker's arrangement of the scene. Although the news seems to be true to Jane, the audience know that Rafe is still alive; they have witnessed his return a few scenes earlier. Thus they can watch as Jane demonstrates her grief and yet not become involved, for they have knowledge of the situation that Jane does not have.

(3) The third situation with tones of potential tragedy is that of the love affair between Lacy and Rose. By means of Lacy's disguise and Firke's trickery, the couple manages to circumvent the family obstacles to their marriage. When the kinsmen find that they have been outwitted, they take the case to the king and ask him to dissolve the marriage. For a moment the audience is left open-mouthed; the play is a comedy, and the viewers expect it to end in marriage—yet before their eyes the sovereign humors the petitioners and decrees that the marriage between Lacy and Rose is dissolved. Dekker, however, does not leave his audience to wonder long; he has the king immediately declare the two lovers reunited in marriage. Whatever anxiety may have been developing is, thus, quickly dispelled; the potential tragedy of separation has been averted, and the comedy thus ends with the expected happy resolution.[22]

Notes

1. Fredson Bowers, "Textual Introduction" to Thomas Dekker's *The Shoemakers' Holiday,* in *The Dramatic Works of Thomas Dekker,* ed. by Fredson Bowers (4 vols. Cambridge: University Press, 1962), I, 9.

2. Fredson Bowers, "Thomas Dekker, Robert Wilson, and *The Shoemakers' Holiday,*" *Modern Language Notes,* LXIV (December, 1949), 517-19.

3. Bowers, "Textual Introduction," p. 9.

4. Thomas Dekker, foreword to his *Shoemakers' Holiday,* in *The Dramatic Works of Thomas Dekker,* ed. by Fredson Bowers (4 vols. Cambridge: University Press, 1962), I, 19.

5. Thomas Dekker, "The first Three-mans Song" and "The second Three-mans Song," in *The Dramatic Works of Thomas Dekker,* ed. by Fredson Bowers (4 vols. Cambridge: University Press, (1962), I, 20-1.

6. Bowers, "Textual Introduction," p. 9.

7. Kenneth Muir, ed., *Elizabethan Lyrics: A Critical Anthology* (New York: Barnes and Noble, Inc., 1958), pp. 31-2.

8. Thomas Dekker, *The Shoemakers' Holiday,* in *The Dramatic Works of Thomas Dekker,* ed. by Fredson Bowers, Vol. 1 (4 vols. Cambridge: University Press, 1962), I, i, 127-31. All further references to this work are from this edition and are cited in the text.

9. Sir Philip Sidney, *An Apologie for Poetrie,* ed. by J. Churton Collins (Oxford: Clarendon Press, 1924), p. 55.

10. John Dennis, "A Large Account of the Taste in Poetry, and the Causes of the Degeneracy of It," in *The Critical Works of John Dennis,* ed. by Edward Niles Hooker (2 vols. Baltimore: The Johns Hopkins Press, 1967), I, 284.

11. This same kind of play on dialect may be seen in Firke's conversation regarding the captain of the Dutch vessel (II, iii, 115-132).

12. Thomas Dekker, *If This Be Not a Good Play, the Devil Is In It* (I, ii, 123-136) and *The Pleasant Comedie of Old Fortunatus* (I, i, 116-119).

13. In the throes of lovers' melancholy, Hammon states his plea for Jane's love and makes the traditional declaration that his life depends on her acceptance of him:
Say, iudge, what is thy sentence, life, or death?
Mercie or crueltie lies in thy breath.

(III, iv, 56-7)

It is interesting to note the similarity of this plea to that addressed to Queen Elizabeth by Dekker regarding the importance of her favor toward the drama:
. . . your celestiall breath
Must send vs life, or sentence vs to death.

(Prologue, 17-8)

14. Northrop Frye, "The Argument of Comedy," in *Comedy: Plays, Theory, and Criticism,* ed. by Marvin Felheim (New York: Harcourt, Brace & World, Inc., 1962), p. 237.

15. Walter Kerr, "The Comic Incongruity," in *Tragedy and Comedy* (New York: Simon and Schuster, 1968), pp. 144-65.

16. Henri Bergson, *Laughter,* trans. by Cloudesley Brereton and Fred Rothwell (New York: The Macmillan Company, 1924), p. 29.

17. Aristotle, *The Poetics,* trans. by S. H. Batcher in *The Great Critics: An Anthology of Literary Criticism,* ed. by James Harry Smith and Edd Winfield Parks (New York: W. W. Norton and Company, Inc., 1967), p. 39.

18. Susanne K. Langer expresses an idea similar to this one in the following excerpt from her work *Feeling and Form:*

In comedy, therefore, there is a general trivialization of the human battle. Its dangers are not real disasters, but embarrassment and loss of face.

Susanne K. Langer, "The Great Dramatic Forms: The Comic Rhythm," from *Feeling and Form,* in *Comedy: Plays, Theory, and Criticism,* ed. by Marvin Felheim (New York: Harcourt, Brace & World, Inc., 1962), p. 252.

19. Frye, p. 237.

20. *Ibid.,* p. 238.

21. *Ibid.,* p. 239.

22. Robert Adger Law has written a study comparing Dekker's Lacy and Rose to Shakespeare's Romeo and Juliet. The critic omits one important parallel, however: the one that shows the two playwrights taking similar circumstances and working them out to suit their respective themes—Dekker comically and Shakespeare tragically.

Robert Adger Law, "*The Shoemakers' Holiday* and *Romeo and Juliet,*" *Studies in Philology,* XXI (April, 1924), 356-61.

David Scott Kastan (essay date 1987)

SOURCE: "Workshop and/as Playhouse: Comedy and Commerce in *The Shoemaker's Holiday,*" in *Studies in Philology*, Vol. LXXXIV, No. 3, Summer 1987, pp. 324-37.

[*In the essay below, Kastan maintains that* The Shoemaker's Holiday *is "a realistic portrait only of Elizabethan middle-class dreams—a fantasy of class fulfillment that would erase the tensions and contradictions created by the nascent capitalism of the late sixteenth-century."*]

Nothing is proposed but mirth," Thomas Dekker assures his readers in the dedicatory epistle to **The Shoemaker's Holiday.** "I present you here with a merry conceited comedy," he says, a play that had recently been acted before the Queen, that ever enthusiastic though hypersensitive theatre-goer, whose pleasure Dekker presents as evidence of the innocence of his offering: "the mirth and pleasant matter by her Highness graciously accepted, being indeed no way offensive."

Certainly critics have generally taken Dekker at his word. We are told again and again that the play is "indeed no way offensive," a triumph of middle-class vitality and generosity.[1] Its moral anomalies, if acknowledged at all, are subordinated to the genial energies of the exuberant Simon Eyre and his shoemakers. "In **The Shoemaker's Holiday,**" writes Joel Kaplan, "faith is encouraged in the energy of a madcap lord of mirth who can wonderfully and magically revitalize a commonwealth."[2]

But, of course, anomalies do exist: class antagonisms between Lincoln and the Lord Mayor frame the action; Rafe comes back wounded from the war in France, while the aristocratic Lacy deserts yet is eventually knighted; and Eyre's fortune is made in a sharp business practice in which at very least he is guilty of impersonating a city official. But we are never asked to dwell on these discords. The romantic logic of the plot overwhelms the social and economic tensions that are revealed: Rafe and Jane are reunited, Lacy and Rose are wed, and class conflicts dissolve in the harmonies celebrated and confirmed in the Shrove Tuesday banquet at Leadenhall.

Though critics have often mistaken its vitality for verisimilitude, certainly the play cannot be understood as a realistic portrait of Elizabethan middle-class life. It is a realistic portrait only of Elizabethan middle-class dreams—a fantasy of class fulfillment that would erase the tensions and contradictions created by the nascent capitalism of the late sixteenth-century. The comic form offers itself as an ideological resolution to the social problems the play engages. Social dislocations are rationalized and contained in a reassuring vision of coherence and community.

When, for example, Lacy enters disguised as Hans, looking for work as a shoemaker, Eyre dismisses him: "let him pass, let him vanish! We have a journeyman enow" (I.v.50-1). But the shoemakers themselves insist that he be taken on: "hire him, good master, that I may learn some gibble-gabble," says the irrepressible Firk, "'twill make us work the faster" (I.v.47-9); and Hodge threatens to quit: "if such a man as he cannot find work, Hodge is not for you" (I.v.60-1). In the face of the wishes of his men Eyre relents: "By the Lord of Ludgate, I love my men as my life. . . . Hodge, if he want work I'll hire him" (I.v.69-71).

In reality, relations between English craftsmen and immigrant workers were hardly so supportive. Early in the century, antagonism toward alien workers erupted in the Evil May Day riots of 1517. Later, a formal complaint was registered in 1571 against immigrants, asserting that "the custome of the citty, and Acts of Councell in the citty are that no man being a stranger to the liberties of the city shall use by handicraftes within the cittie." The complaint asked that existing legislation be enforced to enjoin alien workers from practicing "any manuall trade within this kingdome except they were brought uppe seven yeares apprentices to the trade according to that statute," and added smugly, "which none or very fewe of them have beene."[3] In 1593, officers of the Cordwainers' Company undertook unauthorized "searches" of the precinct of St. Martin's le Grand, where foreign workers had established themselves. The inhabitants protested to Lord Burghley; "Burghley's lawyers," however, as Valerie Pearl writes, "upheld the right of the Livery Company to enter the liberty 'and search alone,' but they replied in diplomatic tones: it would be convenient for the officer of the liberty to accompany the 'search' and this could be obtained by writing to the Lord Mayor."[4] In 1593 and 1595 there was rioting as anxieties about foreign workers worsened in the face of the disastrously sharp rise in rents and food prices which left perhaps half the population of urban laborers, according to one estimate, living "in direst poverty and squalor, on the edge of destitution and starvation."[5] Such economic conditions were unlikely to breed enthusiasm for the "new come in" Dutch shoemakers, whose number by 1599, the year of Dekker's play, had swelled to 131, well over a quarter of the total number paying the required quarterage to the Cordwainers' Company, and about the same number as the Company's 152 yeomen.[6]

Dekker, however, idealizes the actual atomization of the culture in a fantasy of social cohesion and respect. He knew the realities of urban poverty (having himself been jailed for debt in 1598) and the increasing inability of the city or state to conceive effective schemes of relief.[7] The guild structure that once served to unite craftsmen in a fraternity devoted to the welfare and security of its membership became increasingly hierarchical and entrepreneurial, converting work from a system of solidarity to a system of exchange. In *The Seven Deadly Sins of London* (1606), Dekker complains that the guilds "that were ordained to be communities, had lost their first privilege, and were now turned monopolies,"[8] structures no longer of communal association but of commercial advantage.

Historical tensions that did exist are effectively erased by the play, though the erasure cannot go unnoticed by an audience in 1599 who lived the social formations that Dekker idealizes. If this is a fantasy it knows itself as such, and therefore cannot help reveal the contradictions it apparently would repress, transforming its discontinuities into a fiction of social and economic harmony. For example, Eyre makes his fortune by buying the cargo of a ship owner who "dares not show his head" (II.iii.17) in London. Eyre exploits the disadvantage of the shipowner to become a "huge gainer" (II.iii.21) in a triumph of capitalist enterprise which permits enormous profit and negligible risk. It is the dream of the Renaissance profiteer, like Sir Lionel Cranfield who, in 1607, wrote to Sir Arthur Ingram: "One rule I desire may be observed between you and me, which is that neither of us seek to advance our estates by the other's loss, but that we may join faithfully to raise our fortunes by such casualties as this stirring age shall afford."[9] Eyre raises his fortune by one such casualty.

The play, however, refuses to engage any moral concern that the episode might elicit. Eyre's social ambitions (clear in Deloney's *Gentle Craft*, where Eyre says: "Beleeue me, wife . . . I was studying how to make my selfe Lord Maior and thee a Lady"[10]) are here successfully deflected onto Margery. Even Eyre's appearance to the captain dressed as an alderman, with "a seal ring" and in "a guarded gown and a damask cassock" (II.iii.103-04), is presented not as cunning hypocrisy but as proleptic propriety: as Hodge says, "now you look like yourself, master" (II.iii.112).

Dekker's strategy of idealization becomes stili clearer when we examine the purchase itself. Eyre obtains a cargo of "sugar, civet, almonds, cambric, and a towsand towsand tings" (II.iii.129-30), as the Dutch skipper says. These "tings," however, are precisely the luxuries that both English moralists and economists decried. The moralists were dismayed by "our present riot and luxury in diet and apparell,"[11] in the words of the Berkeley's historian, John Smyth; and the economists were disturbed by the outflow of capital, which might have revitalized the English economy, in the pursuit of unnecessary imports. Thus the Elizabethan merchant Gerrard de Malynes, in *The Canker of England's Commonwealth* (1601), lamented the "ouer-balancing of forraine commodities with our home commodities, which to supply or counteruaile draweth away our treasure and readie monie, to the great losse of the commonweale":

> our merchants, perceiuing a small gaine and sometimes none at all to be had vpon our home commodities, do buy and seek their gaines vpon forraine commodities . . . wherein although they may be gainers, yet the Realme generally beareth the losse, and they feed still vpon their mothers belly.[12]

"To export things of necessity," similarly complained Thomas Fuller some forty years later, "and to bring in foreign needless toys, makes a rich merchant and a poor kingdom."[13]

Dekker's play, however, offers us a rich merchant and a rich kingdom, joyfully dispelling whatever fears might attach themselves to Eyre's speculation. Firk immediately domesticates the purchase, defusing the moralists' worry about luxury: "O sweet master! O sweet wares: prunes, almonds, sugar-candy, carrot-roots, turnips!" (II.iii.132-33). And the improbably "good copen" (II.iii.5), the extraordinary bargain that Eyre achieves, minimizes the expenditure of "readie monie" that mercantilists feared. Dekker's audience is left free to enjoy Eyre's success, untroubled by the anxieties that actual speculation in 1599 might be expected to arouse in a society increasingly aware of its economic instability and its heterogeneous elements and interests.

Dekker confronts the increasingly complex social and economic organization of pre-industrialized England but converts it into a comforting fiction of reciprocity and respect. Even the availability of the Dutch cargo is determined by an emotional rather than an economic bond: Hodge reports that the Dutch skipper, "for the love he bears to Hans, offers my master a bargain in the commodities" (II.iii.18-9). The skipper's "love" is presented as the necessary precondition of Eyre's profit. Significantly, Hammon's unsuitability for success in the comic world is finally revealed as he reverses the terms of this exchange, conceiving of profit as predominant over love: "here in fair gold / Is twenty pounds," he tells Rafe; "I'll give it for thy Jane" (V.ii.78-9). His offer literalizes Jane's fear that "many . . . make it even a very trade to woo" (IV.i.64). But Rafe, of course, refuses: "dost thou think a Shoemaker is so base to be a bawd to his own wife for commodity?" (V.ii.84-5).

The reconfirmation of Rafe and Jane's marriage asserts the power of love over hostile social and economic forces that threaten to divide and degrade, and their love is affecting precisely because it succeeds in the face of such powerful threats. The blocking action is not primarily the suit of Hammon but a society in which Jane can actually be lost in the burgeoning urban density of London and Rafe apparently killed—though in fact only wounded—in a war in which the poor serve unwillingly and anonymously. The report of an English victory in France announces that

> Twelve thousand of the Frenchmen that day died,
> Four thousand English, and no man of name
> But Captain Hyam and young Ardington.

"Two gallant gentlemen," laments Lincoln; "I knew them well" (II.iv.8-11). But four thousand Englishmen without name, like Rafe, lie dead in France unremarked.

Impressment and casualty reports would not be matters of indifference to the Rose Theatre audience in 1599. For three years, beginning in 1596, the number of impressed soldiers had begun to increase dramatically as the Irish situation worsened demanding reinforcements and reports reached England of renewed Spanish invasion plans.[14] By the summer of 1599 the fear of an imminent Spanish attack grew acute. On August 1, John Chamberlain wrote from London to Dudley Carleton in Ostend:

> the alarme whereof begins to ringe in our eares here at home [is] as shrill as in your beseiged towne: for upon what groundes or goode intelligence I know not but we are all in a hurle as though the ennemie were at our doores. The Quenes shippes are all making redy, but this towne is commaunded to furnish 16 of theyre best ships to defend the river and 10000 men, whereof 6000 to be trayned presently and every man els to have his armes redy.[15]

But Rafe's safe return, after he has been reported dead, is a welcome fantasy of wish-fulfillment for a nation wearied and worried by war. Even his wound, if it testifies to the real dangers of combat, accommodates Dekker's strategy of idealization, for it serves to prove the ability of "the gentle craft" to protect and provide for its practitioners. "Now I want limbs to get wheron to feed," Rafe cries; but Hodge will have none of his self-pity: "Hast thou not hands, man? Thou shall never see a shoemaker want bread, though he have three fingers on a hand" (III.ii.78-80). Still able to function as a shoemaker, Rafe can make a living and make a life in a community of concern, and when Jane is found and recommits herself to him, her love confirms his place in the comic world and the irrelevance of his wound.

The reaffirmation of Rafe and Jane's marriage redeems the alienation of working-class lives, discharging the threats of social disintegration and neutralizing the temptations of materialism. Denying Hammon's suit, Jane turns to Rafe:

> Thou art my husband, and these humble weeds
> Makes thee more beautiful than all his wealth.
> Therefore I will but put off his attire,
> Returning it to the owner's hand.
>
> (V.ii.58-61)

But the play reveals an ambivalent fascination with money and property. The shoemakers insist that she not return what she has been given. "Not a rag, Jane," declares Hodge: "The law's on our side: he that sows in another man's ground forfeits his harvest" (V.ii.63-4). And similarly, after Rafe indignantly rejects Hammon's offer of money for Jane, Hammon presents it as a gift: "in lieu of that great wrong I offered thy Jane / To Jane and thee I give that twenty pound" (V.ii.91-2). Jane gets to keep the rich clothing Hammon gives her, and Rafe gets the twenty pounds he rejects; improbably, choice in this world does not involve loss.

Such denial is Dekker's characteristic strategy of "resolving" social contradiction. On two other occasions money is offered in exchange for the betrayal of loyalties: on each, integrity is powerfully asserted but again no one is forced to suffer its consequences. At the beginning of the play, Otley and his "brethren" give Lacy twenty pounds, nominally to "approve our loves / We bear unto my Lord, your uncle here" (I.i.67-8); Lincoln, however, understands the real function of the gift:

> To approve your loves to me? No, subtlety!
> Nephew, that twenty pound he doth bestow
> For joy to rid you from his daughter Rose.
>
> (I.i.71-3)

Like Hammon's offer, also of "twenty pound," Otley's assumes that emotions can be purchased or compensated in a commercial exchange. But in the wish-fulfilling logic of the play, Otley's challenge to the emotional authenticity of the relationship he opposes, like Hammon's, turns a would-be purchase price into a gift; and Lacy, like Rafe, gets to keep the twenty pound (which he gives to Askew) and stay with the woman he loves.

Again, in Act IV, Otley tries to buy a betrayal, offering Firk an angel to tell him where Lacy, disguised as Hans, has gone. Firk replies indignantly:

> No point! Shall I betray my brother? No! Shall I prove
> Judas to Hans? No! Shall I cry treason to my
> corporation? No! I shall be firked and yerked then.
> But
> give me your money: your angel shall tell you.
>
> (IV.v.97-100)

Firk takes the money, but does not betray either his "brother" or his "corporation"; he sends Otley to St. Faith's Church where Hammon hopes to wed Jane: "Sir Roger Otley will find my fellow lame Ralph's wife going to marry a gentleman, and then he'll stop her instead of his daughter. O brave, there will be fine tickling sport!" (IV.v.151-54).

In both plots, economic relations would distort and degrade human relationships. Dekker, however, resolves the love plots happily, overcoming the threatened alienation that money would effect—but not by repudiating it in a romantic fantasy of emotional authenticity existing beyond the reach of, and validated by its opposition to, economic realities, but even more improbably: in a romantic fantasy of emotional authenticity that need not repudiate it, indeed that need not address the issue of alienation at all. This is a world in which characters may have their cake and eat it too: they are permitted both to express their integrity and to enjoy that with which they have been tempted.

If the wish-fulfilling operations of the text validate this moral sleight-of-hand, they perform a similar operation in social terms. The formal ratification of the two marriages apparently at once repudiates and recuperates a social stratification whose moral inadequacy is revealed by its hostility to love. The love of Rafe and Jane succeeds in the face of a world which restricts working-class freedom and assails its integrity, and Lacy and Rose overcome class antagonisms and deficiencies, triumphing over aristocratic condescension and bourgeois acquisitiveness. But both relationships finally confirm traditional social hierarchy; the marriage of Rafe and Jane ratifies working-class commonality, and, while the marriage of Lacy and Rose presents itself as a successful adaptation to new social configurations, it too is revealed to be a more conservative gesture than at first appears. The King upbraids Lincoln who has opposed the marriage of his noble son with the middle-class Rose:

> Dost thou not know that love respects no blood,
> Cares not for difference of birth or state?
> The maid is young, well-born, fair, virtuous,
> A worthy bride for any gentleman.
>
> (V.v.108-11)

The King appeals to love and merit to counter Lincoln's corrosive class-consciousness. "The royal confirmation of the marriage of Rose and Lacy," signals, as the editors of the Revels edition assert, "the final overthrow of class division,"[16] but five lines later almost unnoticed the King firmly reestablishes the very social distinctions that he has just denied, as he knights Lacy:

> As for the honor which he lost in France,
> Thus I redeem it: Lacy, kneel thee down!
> Arise, Sir Rowland Lacy! Tell me now,
> Tell me in earnest, Otley, canst thou chide,
> Seeing thy Rose a lady and a bride.
>
> (V.v.116-20)

Love, perhaps, "cares not for difference of birth or state," but obviously the King, Lincoln, and Otley all do. The comic ending does not subvert social distinctions but reinforces them. Bourgeois desire is gratified by claiming rather than cancelling aristocratic privilege.

Again Dekker has it both ways: middle class desire for social mobility and aristocratic insistence upon social stratification are both accommodated, as when the King releases Eyre from obedience to courtly protocol: "good Lord Mayor, be even as merry / As if thou wert among thy shoemakers" (V.v.13-4). In the presence of the King, Eyre is free to behave as if he *were* among his shoemakers but

simultaneously reminded that he is not. The social and ideological contradiction thus becomes itself the term of its resolution, but such resolution can not be other than imaginary.

But the play, after all, is *The Shoemaker's Holiday,* and arguments about the placement of the title's apostrophe seem to miss the central point. The issue is not primarily whether the title refers to a holiday declared for the shoemakers (in which case the title is *The Shoemakers' Holiday*) or a holiday declared by Simon Eyre for all the apprentices of London (in which case the title is *The Shoemaker's Holiday*). Fredson Bowers, in the Cambridge *Dekker,* argues for the former, the Revels editors, Small-wood and Wells, for the latter, but the action of the play itself—and not merely the Shrove Tuesday feast that ends it—is, as I have been arguing, the holiday—a holiday from the historical world of social contradiction and consequence, as the tensions produced by the social realignments of the late sixteenth-century are wonderfully resolved in the communal, festive marketplace.

Indeed even the holiday is presented as holiday. The Shrove Tuesday celebration, which Hodge happily predicts "shall continue for ever" (V.ii.213), did continue but not always as a joyful celebration of social coherence and community. John Taylor, the water-poet, describes the Shrove Tuesday that Dekker's audience would have known: "in the morning, the whole kingdome is in quiet, but by that time the clocke strikes eleven, which (by the helpe of a knavish Sexton) is commonly before nine, then there is a bell rung, called The Pancake Bell, the sound whereof makes thousands of people distracted, and forget-full eyther of manners or humanitie."[17] The holiday was regularly marred by the riots of disgruntled apprentices, who, in 1617,

> to the number of 3 or 4000 committed extreame inso-lencies; part of this nomber, taking their course for Wapping, did there pull downe to the grownd 4 houses, spoiled all the goods therein, defaced many others, & a Justice of the Peace coming to appease them, while he was reading a Proclamacion, had his head broken with a brick batt. Th' other part, making for Drury Lane, where lately a newe playhouse is erected, they besett the house round, broke in, wounded divers of the play-ers, broke open their trunckes, & whatt apparrell, bookes, or other things they found, they burnt & cutt in peeces; & not content herewith, gott on the top of the house, & untiled it, & had not the Justices of Peace & Sherife levied an aide, & hindred their purpose, they would have laid that house likewise even with the grownd. In this skyrmishe one prentise was slaine, be-ing shott throughe the head with a pistoll, & many other of their fellowes were sore hurt, & such of them as are taken his Majestie hath commaunded shal be executed for example sake.[18]

In actuality, Shrove Tuesday became an occasion for the release of social tension, but in the play what is released is only fellowship and cheer.

As critical response to the play attests, Dekker has fashioned an almost irresistible image of social unity, successfully neutralizing the disintegrative threat of the emerging capitalism and civilizing its dynamism. History is turned into holiday, its tensions refused rather than refuted, recast into an ameliorative fantasy. The play's unnamed King, who should be the aloof and ineffective Henry VI who ruled in 1445 when the historical Simon Eyre was appointed Lord Mayor, is idealized as Henry V, who mingles comfortably with his subjects and promises victories in France.[19] But the impossibility of positively identifying Dekker's king points to the fact that he is less historical than romantic, a comforting portrait of royal benevolence to guarantee the middle-class energies that are articulated.

The play's prologue spoken before the Queen at court on New Year's Day in 1600, however, suggests a more problematic relation of subject and sovereign. The actors are the Queen's "meanest vassals" who stand before her as "wretches in a storm," fearful and impotent, dependent upon her favor:

> O grant, bright mirror of true chastity,
> From those life-breathing stars, your sun-like eyes,
> One gracious smile: for your celestial breath
> Must send us life, or sentence us to death.
>
> (Prologue.15-8)

If this is conventional flattery of Elizabeth, it is disturbing to discover its echo in Hammon's appeal to Jane: "Say, judge, what is thy sentence? Life or death? / Mercy or cruelty lies in thy breath" (III.iv.55-6). In Hammon's mouth the assertion of weakness blatantly functions as a strategy of manipulation; his conventional petrarchanism articulates and mediates the asymmetry of desire. In the players' prologue, Elizabeth's power is acknowledged and flattered, revealing anxieties produced by an asymmetry of power and belying the play's idealization of the relations betwen the monarch and his subjects.

In the play, the King's naming of Leadenhall ratifies Eyre's bourgeois energies and establishes the marketplace as both source and symbol of England's health and strength. Its potentially anarchic vitality is effectively contained by collective and patriotic loyalties. But Dekker's strategies of idealization are too blatant to function successfully as instruments of legitimation and social mystification. They declare themselves too openly as wish-fulfillments, and are at odds even with the conditions of their theatrical presentation.

Like the marketplace, the theatre was originally a space for the expression of communal energies but in the late sixteenth-century it too became an essentially commercial arena. "Man in business," wrote John Hall, lamenting the new, alienating commercial realities, "is but a Theatricall person"[20]; but the reality of the Renaissance stage was that theatrical persons were men in business. "The theatre is your poets' Royal Exchange," writes Dekker in *The Gull's Horn-Book,* "upon which their muses—that are now turned to merchants—meeting, barter away that light com-

modity of words for a lighter ware than words—plaudits and the breath of that great beast which like the threatenings of two cowards, vanish all into air."[21] Dekker's metaphor reflects the existing economic relation of the acting companies and their audiences. An actor might imagine himself an artist whose aristocratic patronage, however complex that relationship was, at least freed him from the commercial logic of exchange, but, as an observer noted in 1615, "howsoever hee pretends to have a royall Master or Mistress, his wages and dependance prove him to be the servant of the people."[22]

And the situation of the playwright was worse still, servant not merely of the audience but also of the acting company that purchased his script. Though praised by Francis Meres in 1598 as one of England's best playwrights, Dekker lived marginally in the London slums—at least when he was not in the London jails for debt, as he was for seven years. The enormous theatrical profits, that made Shakespeare, Alleyn, and Burbage rich, were made by sharers in the acting companies, not by their playwrights. "With mouthing words that better wits have framed," wrote the Cambridge authors of the *Parnassus* plays, "They purchase land, and now Esquiers are made" (2 *Return from Parnassus,* 1927-28). The playwrights, however, were poorly paid piece-workers. A play might command six pounds. Dekker received only three for *The Shoemaker's Holiday,* and in 1598 he was paid by Henslowe a total of thirty pounds for his work on sixteen plays. Art became a commodity to be bought cheap and resold for profits that never reached its maker.

The play—any play—was, then, part of a complex set of social and economic relations that exploited some and enriched (a few) others. The theatre might present itself as a green world of fantasy that audiences enter, like Rosalind and Orlando, to be free of the tensions of the real world, but in fact, like the green worlds of Shakespeare's comedies, the restraints and contradictions of the real world are merely disguised rather than discharged. "O happy work" (IV.i.14), Hammon gushes, watching Jane sew in the seamster's shop, but, though Dekker idealizes work in *The Shoemaker's Holiday,* the idealization takes place in a commercial theatrical environment that itself exposes the fantasy. The reality is that, for Dekker, the play is work, as for his characters work is play. *The Shoemaker's Holiday* presents commerce as comedy, converting the work place into a play space, but it does so in a playhouse that is fundamentally a workshop where such idealization can be no more and no less than a utopian compensation for the alienation and fragmentation of Dekker's London.[23]

Notes

1. See, for example, Patricia Thompson, "The Old Way and the New Way in Dekker and Massinger," *MLR* 51 (1956), 168-78; H. E. Toliver, "*The Shoemaker's Holiday:* Theme and Image," *Boston University Studies in English,* 5 (1961), 208-18; Joel H. Kaplan, "Virtue's Holiday: Thomas Dekker and

Simon Eyre," *Renaissance Drama* 2 (1969) 103-22. Peter Mortenson, "The Economics of Joy in *The Shoemakers' Holiday*," *SEL* 16 (1976), 241-52, has offered a counter-argument, focusing on the play's commercial ethos: "Dekker creates a grim world and encourages us to pretend that it is a green one" (252). See also the provocative essay of Lawrence Venuti, "Transformation of City Comedy: A Symptomatic Reading," *Assays* 3 (1985): 99-134, which recognizes the "darker side" of the comedy as well as the "implausible resolutions" that conclude it.

2. Kaplan, 117.

3. *Tudor Economic Documents,* eds. R. H. Tawney and Eileen Power (London: Longmans, Green and Co., 1924), 309-10.

4. Valerie Pearl, *London and the Outbreak of the Puritan Revolution* (London: Oxford University Press, 1961), 25.

5. Peter H. Ramsey, ed., *The Price Revolution in Sixteenth-Century England* (London: Methuen, 1971), 14-5.

6. George Unwin, *The Gilds and Companies of London* (1908; rpt. London: Frank Cass, 1963), 250.

7. See Penry Williams, *The Tudor Regime* (Oxford: Clarendon Press, 1979), 175-215; and Paul Slack, "Poverty and Social Regulation in Elizabethan England," *The Reign of Elizabeth I,* ed. Christopher Haigh (Athens, Georgia: The University of Georgia Press, 1985), 221-42.

8. *The Non-Dramatic Works of Thomas Dekker,* ed. Alexander B. Grosart (London: The Huth Library, 1889), 2, 174.

9. Quoted in E. Lipson, *The Economic History of England* (London: Adam and Charles Black, 1931), 3, 357.

10. *The Works of Thomas Deloney,* ed. Francis Oscar Mann (Oxford: Clarendon Press, 1912), 112.

11. Quoted in L. C. Knights, *Drama and Society in the Age of Jonson* (London: Chatto & Windus, 1937), 120.

12. In *Tudor Economic Documents,* 3, 395, 394.

13. Thomas Fuller, *The Holy State* (1642, facs. ed. New York: Columbia University Press, 1938), 2, 113.

14. Lindsay Boynton, *The Elizabethan Militia, 1558-1638* (London: Routledge and Kegan Paul, 1967), 198-206.

15. *The Letters of John Chamberlain,* ed. Norman Egbert McLure, (Philadelphia: The American Philosophical Society, 1939) 1, 78.

16. R. L. Smallwood and Stanley Wells (eds.), *The Shoemaker's Holiday* (Manchester: Manchester University Press, 1929), 42.

17. John Taylor, *Jack a Lent, His Beginning and Entertainment* (London, 1630), 12.

18. Quoted in G. E. Bentley, *The Jacobean and Caroline Stage* (Oxford: Clarendon Press, 1968), 6, 54.

19. See W. K. Chandler, "The Source of the Characters in *The Shoemaker's Holiday*," *MP* 27 (1929), 175-82; and Michael Manheim, "The King in Dekker's *The Shoemakers' Holiday*," *N & Q,* (new series) 4 (1957): 432.

20. John Hall, *The Advancement of Learning* (1649), ed. A. K. Croston (Liverpool: Liverpool University Press, 1953), 37.

21. *Thomas Dekker: Selected Prose Writings,* ed. E. D. Pendry, (London: Edward Arnold, 1968), 98.

22. Quoted in *The Elizabethan Stage,* ed. E. K. Chambers (Oxford: Clarendon Press, 1923), 4, 256.

23. I would like to thank various friends and colleagues who have contributed to the development of this essay, especially Daniel Karlin, Claire McEachern, Peter Stallybrass, and Albert Wertheim, who allowed me to present a version of the essay at a session arranged by the Drama Division of the MLA in December of 1985.

Martha Straznicky (essay date 1996)

SOURCE: "The End(s) of Discord in *The Shoemaker's Holiday*," in *Studies in English Literature 1500-1900,* Vol. 36, No. 2, Spring 1996, pp. 357-72.

[*In this essay, Straznicky asserts that* The Shoemaker's Holiday *"enacts an imaginary appropriation of civic authority and commercial wealth by a group of industrial laborers for whom both privileges were largely a matter of fantasy."*]

The Shoemaker's Holiday (1599) is one of only three Elizabethan comedies named after specific festive occasions.[1] While most critics have duly noted the importance of the festival to the play's structural and thematic design, their accounts employ a vague and moralistic vocabulary that is strangely out of keeping with the concrete, even materialistic language of the play itself. Michael Manheim, for example, sees the Guildhall feast as a "victory for the forces of humility and good will," and Arthur Kinney calls it "the still centre where passion and reason are themselves advanced, but made one and inseparable."[2] Even critics such as Peter Mortenson and David Scott Kastan, who have usefully situated the play within the complex network of social, political, and economic conditions in which it was written and performed, view the play's holiday as a simple generic trick, a shrewd deployment of the ideology of comedy to resolve the discordant labor relations and commercial practices of Elizabethan London that lie behind the play. Kastan, for example, describes "a holiday from the historical world of social contradiction and consequence, as the tensions produced by the social realignments of the late sixteenth-century are wonderfully resolved in the communal, festive marketplace."[3] Viewing the play's festivity as nothing more than the properly triumphant conclusion to economic discord, however, obscures the way in which the holiday itself is vitally engaged in the delineation and management of political and economic tensions. In other words, the end or resolution of discord in *The Shoemaker's Holiday* may embody rather than eliminate the conflicts that shape the play. By bringing to bear on Thomas Dekker's mythical feast the social function of corresponding Elizabethan festivals and thus reinvesting it with a historical register, the following discussion aims to show that *The Shoemaker's Holiday* purposely conserves a state of discord, and that the ends of such discord are in fact vital to the artisans' ideological, albeit imaginary, victory.

The Shoemaker's Holiday conflates two annual celebrations that would have been deeply familiar to Dekker's London audiences: Shrove Tuesday and Accession Day. Observed on the Tuesday immediately preceding Lent, Shrove Tuesday was a day of feasting and carousing during which legal strictures were loosened and normative social relations suspended. The privileges of festivity on Shrove Tuesday, however, were not equally distributed: the surviving records of Shrove Tuesday customs reveal that youth groups, specifically apprentices, were singularly empowered on this holiday.[4] Enacting a mock jurisdiction over what appear to be traditional morals, London apprentices raided brothels and carted prostitutes through the streets, stormed and vandalized theaters, carried out skimmingtons, and tortured performing animals. In François Laroque's view, the holiday's discriminatory customs seem to have a "penitential, sacrificial character," and Keith Thomas has suggested that they performed a "safety-valve" function for a segment of the population that was actively oppressed throughout the early modern period.[5] The inversion of normative age/youth relations on Shrove Tuesday, and the enforcement by the rioting youth of what are essentially conservative community values, render these festivities fundamentally double-edged: they cement a potentially rebellious group solidarity at the same time as they reinforce communally defined boundaries of acceptable personal behavior and professional occupation. Dekker's version of Shrove Tuesday, I will go on to argue, appropriates this very duality to inscribe moral boundaries between a variety of competing commercial practices, and, in so doing, to reinforce the collective identities of his audiences.

While explicit allusions to Shrove Tuesday dominate the concluding scene of *The Shoemaker's Holiday,* Dekker also expands the festival mood into a nationalist celebration of the monarch: the day is identified as "Saint Hugh's Holiday," and the king is assured that "Sim Eyre and my brethren the Gentlemen Shoemakers shall set your sweet Majesty's image cheek by jowl by Saint Hugh."[6] L. D. Timms has recently suggested that for an Elizabethan audience this additional layer of festivity would have been understood as an allusion to Elizabeth's Accession Day (17 November), an annual celebration of monarch, state, and religion which, by 1599, was a familiar feature of the urban festive calendar.[7] Although its precise origins are recorded only in anecdote and conjecture, Accession Day eventually became a crucial component of Elizabethan national political culture, commemorating as it did the

divinely ordained conquest of Protestantism over papacy and replacing the coincident Catholic feast of Saint Hugh of Lincoln in the old ecclesiastical calendar.[8] While the court glittered with spectacular tilts and entertainments, London's streets filled with bell-ringing, parishioners dutifully attended propagandist sermons, then celebrated with feasting, dance, torch-lit processions, and bonfires.[9] Unlike Shrove Tuesday, Accession Day was primarily a political festival, imposed from the top down, and designed to evoke in English subjects a sense of unique national and religious identity. Like Shrove Tuesday, however, Accession Day had a prescribed target of derision at whose expense the celebrating took place: specifically the Pope and, more generally, Roman Catholicism. While a few Catholic polemicists were predictably outraged at what they perceived to be idolatrous festivities, the only sizable opposition to the Protestant supplanting came from radical reformers dismayed by the transformation of the monarch into a hagiographical icon.[10] In general Accession Day was remarkably successful as a propagandist instrument, most likely because it fulfilled the psychic needs of a population whose festive traditions had been eroded by the Reformation.[11] In *The Shoemaker's Holiday,* Accession Day is repeatedly called to mind in the many allusions to Saint Hugh (also, conveniently, the patron saint of shoemakers), in addition to the explicit celebration of the monarch in the final scene. The politics and cultural conflicts embodied in Accession Day, however, are not nearly as close to the surface of the play as are those of Shrove Tuesday, perhaps because the cultural meaning of Accession Day is secure enough for Dekker's audiences to serve as bedrock upon which the play's more contentious commercial relations could be framed.[12]

The adjustment Dekker makes in representing Shrove Tuesday and Accession Day festivities points up the inherent ambiguity that anthropologists and literary critics have ascribed to festival, and particularly to the forms of symbolic inversion that characteristically appear in Elizabethan comedy.[13] As Peter Stallybrass rightly claims, "The *meaning* of such inversions is not, of course, a given. If they could, indeed, be read as *impossibilia,* farcical and implausible aberrations which reaffirm through antithesis the norm, they could equally be mobilized within a revolutionary iconography."[14] Furthermore, as Stallybrass also goes on to show, the familiar dichotomy of dominant/oppressed, which frequently serves as the basis for analyzing the politics of festivity, fails to account for the appropriation of festivity by groups that are neither strictly ruling nor strictly ruled, and whose members do not define themselves in specifically political or class terms. Festivity, then, is neither the sanctioned and ultimately harmless rite proposed by the "safety-valve" theory, nor the populist, antiauthoritarian liberation suggested by Mikhail Bakhtin.[15] Nor is it somewhere between the two, for a dualistic framework fails to capture the range of functions festivity performs within and among social groups. Festivity, however entrenched it may appear to be in a particular cultural tradition, is always available for appropriation to any group capable of mobilizing its resources.

One such mobilization is dramatized in **The Shoemaker's Holiday.** As in the contemporary historical analogues to Dekker's holiday, the shoemakers' celebration of group solidarity is concomitantly a triumph over persons and practices that have been positioned beyond what may be called the "festive boundary," a permeable yet clearly demarcated line separating that which is being celebrated from that which threatens the celebration. While critics usually commend the space within Dekker's festive boundary for being remarkably capacious and democratic, there are three clearly marked outsiders—Hammon, Oatley, and Lincoln—whose interests are not so much excluded as assimilated by the celebrants. The terms in which this boundary is framed, the precise criteria for inclusion and exclusion, and the seeming transformation of pre-festive discord into harmonious celebration reveal more about the play's stake in contemporary cultural conflicts than previous criticism has allowed.

The outsider whose role in the play's moral economy is both best and worst understood is Sir Hugh Lacy, Earl of Lincoln. Because he so obviously represents the conventional paternal opposition to youth and love, and because his opposition is fueled by clear-cut classist principles, Lincoln has received unduly brief critical notice. Most often, he is paired with Oatley as the embodiment of a class prejudice that Simon Eyre's new social order is committed to eliminating. For Joel H. Kaplan, Lincoln represents "false politeness" and "quiet hypocrisy"; for Manheim, he is "concerned only with 'outsides,' little with what a person really is," and for Kastan, he is an emblem of "aristocratic condescension."[16] Useful as these views are in revealing the importance of class struggle in the play, their terms of reference fail to explain the reestablishment of social hierarchy under the aegis of the new Lord Mayor. Put differently, while Lincoln is demonized for insisting on class difference as a reasonable criterion of suitability for marriage, that very same class difference organizes social relations during the play's holiday: the king tries to stave off Lincoln's objections to an interclass marriage by pointing out that Rose is "well born"; Lacy is knighted to make the marriage more palatable to Oatley; and the king briefly withdraws into a private conversation not with the artisanal Lord Mayor but with the peer Lincoln. What the play's festival seems to celebrate, then, is not the eradication of class difference but the inclusion of socially and politically disadvantaged groups within a newly expanded notion of nobility. Progressive as this might be, it is not the conclusion one might anticipate in view of the different successes of Lincoln and the coalition of his opponents.

There may be a more compelling reason why Lincoln is so comfortably positioned beyond the festive boundary. Dekker's allusions to Accession Day in the play's final scene remind us that there is at least some anti-Catholic strain to the celebrations, and for his first audiences "Sir *Hugh* Lacy, Earl of *Lincoln*" would almost certainly have called to mind the Catholic saint whose feast day had been supplanted by the Protestant queen. In churchwardens' records for local observances of Accession Day, "Saint Hugh's

Day" appears to have been used as a tag for the new holiday throughout the Elizabethan period, and Lincoln College, Oxford, a known Catholic stronghold early in Elizabeth's reign, reportedly inaugurated the Accession Day bell-ringing custom.[17] Furthermore, as Julia Gasper argues, for an Elizabethan audience the war in the play would most likely have called to mind Essex's Irish campaign of the previous year, and perhaps even the earlier English expedition of 1591-92 against the Catholic League in France, both contemporary campaigns on behalf of the Protestant cause.[18] Insofar, then, as the names "Hugh" and "Lincoln" may have been associated with Catholicism, the earl's defeat at play's end may be not so much a matter of class prejudice as a piece of subtle politico-religious propaganda reflecting a militant Protestantism, a position consistent with Dekker's other surviving work.[19]

The festive boundary in the play, however, is not as firm on this point as one might expect. First, Lincoln's association with Saint Hugh is not nearly as prominent a reminder of the old hagiographical material as are the constant allusions to the patron saint of shoemakers, something that is almost inevitable, given Dekker's choice of source.[20] In writing about a shoemaker, Dekker is able to grace the material success of a master craftsman (and budding commercial entrepreneur) with the divine sanction ascribed to the old saint's martyrdom at the hands of religious persecutors. This appropriation of Catholic hagiography is most evident in the career of Lacy, whose resemblance to his uncle in both nomenclature and status is the second seeming permutation of the play's festive boundary.[21] Well before Lacy has transformed himself into the Dutch immigrant worker Hans, we learn from his bemused uncle that the spendthrift's grand tour of the Continent culminated in apprenticeship to a shoemaker in Wittenberg, a geographical invention of Dekker's that once again points to a religio-political subtext in the play. As a shoemaker, Lacy/Hans is under the protection of Saint Hugh; however, as a Dutch shoemaker trained in the cradle of the Reformation, and as a shoemaker persecuted by a "papist" uncle, Lacy/Hans is a Protestant revision of Catholic hagiographical material. In terms of the play's religio-political slant, then, the festive boundary separating Lacy and the shoemakers from Lincoln appears permeable enough to allow certain of the powers of Catholic hagiography to be redefined as properly Protestant at the same time as Catholicism itself is successfully othered.[22]

Such a complex textual maneuver, however, would seem to be unwarranted by the social and economic status of Catholics in Dekker's London, who were by all accounts demographically insignificant and in no way a segregated group. Like other urban centers in Reformation Europe, London turned Protestant quickly, largely because governmental controls were both more visible and more powerful in the country's capital, and together with East Anglia it consequently posts the smallest Catholic populations in the country.[23] And while committees were set up to investigate Catholic prisoners, and searches of Catholic properties were carried out on a regular basis throughout the 1580s and 1590s, Catholics were never deemed a serious political threat.[24] In fact, the government appears to have found periodic imprisonment and economic controls to be sufficient means of restraining potential subversiveness. The economic controls in particular also impoverished many wealthy Catholics, so that by the late-Elizabethan period the economic status of even the most affluent among them was minor. In short, Catholics in late-Elizabethan London were an "insignificant minority."[25]

The cultural work of the anti-Catholic dimension of Dekker's festive boundary would thus seem to be more in the manner of simple reinforcement, perhaps even intensification, of the audience's firmly held views than an active negotiation of current social conflicts. It is also true, however, that the Catholic-Protestant conflict in the play is inextricable from the commercial and class conflicts with which the play is most importantly engaged. Lacy not only outwits his uncle, but he also and simultaneously outwits his future father-in-law, Oatley, whose economic position as a commercial capitalist also plants him, albeit less firmly, beyond Dekker's festive boundary. By placing Lincoln and Oatley in allied opposition to the play's dominant comic drive, Dekker appears to be cementing anti-Catholic and anti-commercial sentiments. It may be, then, that the uncontested anti-Catholicism of the play's festival mood provides a foundation for the more pressing controversy surrounding commercial activity.

That controversy is represented most unproblematically in the eventual defeat of Oatley's preferred son-in-law, Hammon—importantly, the only character who does not participate in the Shoemaker's Holiday. Hammon's dramatic function appears to be little more than to provide an ethical contrast to the play's romantic figures, but the terms in which he operates and in which he is described clearly mark him as a contrast also to the industrial laborers in the play. Although we first meet him hunting, a sport Dekker's audiences would see as aristocratic leisure,[26] and although he initially plays Petrarchan lover to Rose, he soon settles into the commercial discourse with which he claims to be most comfortable and which is his dominant register throughout the play, wooing as he does the impoverished and distraught Jane in absurd monetary terms. Significantly, Hammon tries to lure Jane away from her shop, and when she objects that "I cannot live by keeping holiday" (xii.31), he promises to pay her for the day's lost income. This incident is in keeping with the play's many other characterizations of Hammon: although Oatley favors him because he is a "citizen by birth" and "fairly allied" (vi.61), it is clear that "fair revenues" are Hammon's major recommendation (xi.34). We also learn that he lives in Watling Street, an area of London noted by Stow for its concentration of wealthy drapers.[27] And Hammon's spirits are buoyed throughout the play, even when faced with the successive losses of Rose and Jane, by confidence in his independent wealth. However ill-defined Hammon's finances may be, and however nebulous the source of his wealth, he is unequivocally marked as a rich citizen whose manners and habits are entirely alien to the world of manual labor.

On both counts, Hammon is fair prey for the shoemakers in the play, and it is fitting that he is the chief target of the Shrove Tuesday rioting at play's end. In Elizabethan London, Shrove Tuesday celebrations frequently bordered on the violent, as the numerous records of vandalism and physical assault on these occasions attest, and in a number of cases they actually broke out into full-scale riot.[28] Dekker's apprentices are similarly aggressive: they are equipped "all with cudgels, or such weapons" as they prepare to reclaim Jane for Ralph, and Hodge's repeated attempts to restrain them hint at their underlying brutality (xviii.s.d.). Although the incident never breaks out into physical fighting, the continual presence of a group of armed and hyped-up young men does imbue the scene with the violence characteristic of contemporary Shrove Tuesday festivities. Rather than using their power against prostitutes or actors, however, these apprentices target Hammon, and they appear to do so strictly on account of his conspicuous wealth.[29] In effect, this Shrove Tuesday attack punishes the nonlaboring commercial or mercantile capitalist and restores to his proper social position the injured and disadvantaged laborer. It is an exchange Hammon himself sportively notes: "Farewell, good fellows of the Gentle Trade, / Your morning's mirth my mourning day hath made." The "mirth" in this scene, then, is doing more than celebrating the solidarity of apprentices or reuniting a married couple; it more importantly firms up— and moralizes—a distinction between occupational practices that in fact constituted the chief industrial controversy in early modern London.[30]

One sign of an emerging capitalist economy in Dekker's time was the increasing importance of a new capitalist function: the commercial trader.[31] The commercial trader, or entrepreneurial middleman, was not directly involved in the production of goods but took on the distributive aspect of manufacture, buying completed goods from the craftsmen and selling them at a profit to a variety of markets. The success of the commercial trader in disrupting the traditional operation of the trade guilds is clear in the number of economic disputes that arose between the distributive and productive sectors, a far larger proportion of conflicts than any that arose among members of individual guilds or among the guilds themselves.[32] As George Unwin explains, all these disputes arose from the fact "that the craftsman was no longer in direct contact with the consumer, but was dependent on the capital of the middleman, whether as trader or as a direct employer, to find a market for his wares or his work."[33] This new economic division between production and trade was also reflected in the urban geography, with merchants making up about 28% of occupations within the city walls, particularly in the wealthy central parishes, and only 8% in extramural suburbs.[34] Similarly, the production of goods was concentrated in the eastern and southern neighborhoods of London, accounting in those districts for some 70% of occupations, with a much smaller proportion of manufacturing employment within the city center, roughly 53%.[35] What these figures indicate is that while about three-fifths of London's occupations continued to be in the production of goods, the wealth—judging by the distribution of occupations in the city's more affluent neighborhoods—was restricted to a minority mercantile class.[36] This unequal distribution of power and affluence predictably created occupational rivalries.

The triumph of the laboring shoemakers over Hammon in *The Shoemaker's Holiday* may well be an imaginary resolution of one such rivalry. A related case is the outwitting of Sir Roger Oatley, but in this instance Dekker's festival humor participates in political as well as economic controversy. Although Oatley's chief narrative role in the play is simply to obstruct his daughter's romance, Dekker's changes to his source material suggest that he had more in mind when he created Oatley than fulfilling a generic requirement. Oatley's counterpart in Deloney is an emperor, and the change in political status to Lord Mayor renders Oatley's otherwise conventional family troubles decidedly topical. The year before Dekker's play was staged, a former Lord Mayor of London, the fabulously wealthy Sir John Spencer, found himself in circumstances closely resembling those represented in the play.[37] His daughter Elizabeth—who reputedly carried a £40,000 dowry—was being sought in marriage by William, second Lord Compton, one of the most improvident courtiers of the time.[38] Spencer was strongly opposed to the match, evidently on the grounds of Compton's desperate financial straits, but Compton's court connections proved literally to out-class the power of Spencer's money. Elizabeth was removed from her father's care following allegations that he had abused her, and in 1599 Spencer was briefly imprisoned in the Fleet.[39] At the time Dekker was writing his play, the affair was yet unsettled, but the terms of the conflict were evidently timely enough for dramatic service.

What is at issue in both fictional and historical accounts is the social mobility that was occasioned, among other things, by the development of a capitalist economy. While successful commercial entrepreneurs such as Spencer, who had amassed an estimated fortune of between £500,000 and £800,000 in overseas and domestic trade,[40] were able to buy their way into the upper orders, many members of the landed aristocracy were forced by their own lack of capital funds to sell off ancestral estates or borrow heavily from London's money merchants, thus conspicuously sliding down the social ladder. A customary way of avoiding the embarrassment of debt was, in Lawrence Stone's terms, for the aristocracy periodically to arrange a "transfusion of mercantile blood—and mercantile money" through marriage.[41] Compton's suit for Elizabeth appears to be a case in point, although Dekker's revision of the incident diplomatically under-plays the issue of Lacy's dire finances.

Oatley's opposition to his daughter's marriage to Lacy is, in historical context, perfectly legitimate: there is every reason to believe that Lacy is nothing more than a spendthrift fortune-hunting prodigal. What is interesting, however, is that Dekker chooses to align the audience's sympathy not with the soon-to-be-robbed citizen but rather with the improvident aristocrat. In order to understand this particular piece of poetic justice, it is important to recall that Spencer was quite likely the most unpopular Lord Mayor in living memory. Both during and after his tenure, Spencer was known for three things: spectacular wealth, stinginess, and harassment of apprentices. His term in office appears to have been a particularly difficult one, coinciding with a severe food shortage and the notorious food riots of 1595. It was in other respects also a time of popular unrest, and Spencer's attempts to curb the instigators, largely the city's apprentices, were met with outright defiance and an attempted assassination.[42] Further to his discredit for the Rose audience, Spencer was one of the more vocal of antitheatrical civic authorities. He wrote at least two lengthy letters to Lord Burghley and the Privy Council insisting that the public performance of plays be suppressed.[43] In both letters, his campaign against the city's youth resurfaces in his charge that dramatic representations of "profane fables, Lascivious matters, cozonning devizes, & other vnseemly & scurrilous behaviours" are the chief cause of the "disorders & lewd demeanors wch appeer of late in young people of all degrees," and that the venue itself provides a dangerous opportunity for their unsupervised congregation. More specifically, Spencer actually insists that "the late stirr & mutinous attempt of those fiew apprentices and other servants" was directly "infected" by the theaters.[44] If Dekker's Rose audience did recognize Spencer in the habit of Oatley, then his defeat at the hands of the young Lacy and the apprentice shoemakers would have been a moment of communal triumph indeed.

And yet *The Shoemaker's Holiday* seems more to preserve than to dissolve the discordant political and economic conditions that pit apprentices against civic authorities and artisans against commercial capitalists: just as the defeat of Lincoln is the precondition for an imaginary assimilation of nobility and hagiography by the shoemakers, so the defeat of Oatley facilitates the transfer of his two key qualities, civic authority and wealth, to the shoemaker Simon Eyre. The making of Eyre's fortune has elicited a considerable amount of commentary. For most critics, Eyre's capitalist venture is one of the play's more cynical moments in which the otherwise sympathetic master craftsman resorts to deceit and debt in order to take advantage of a massive commercial opportunity.[45] There is no way to exonerate Eyre from these charges. What this incident reveals, surprisingly, is that the making of wealth by duplicitous means, and by means of commercial rather than industrial capital, is not unequivocally a moral perversion. What the play appears to be doing is condemning some and condoning other commercial enterprises, and making the distinction in terms of generosity since the main difference between Spencer and Eyre is in the disposal of their wealth: "Let your fellow prentices want no cheer. Let wine be plentiful as beer, and beer as water. Hang these penny-pinching fathers, that cram wealth in innocent lamb-skins" (xx.8-11).[46] There is also a large measure of reciprocity associated with Eyre's new wealth: his ability to capitalize on the Dutch cargo is made possible only by Hans's loan, and that loan is clearly figured as a reward for hiring the alien laborer.[47] Similarly, Eyre's acquisition of wealth and rise in social status include—rather than exclude—his fellow craftsmen (as the perpetually ill-provided Hodge rejoices in "Let's feed and be fat with my lord's bounty" (xviii.205), and it is clear that the apprentices in particular view their new holiday and the privileges it grants them as direct legacies of Eyre's commercial success. In other words, while Eyre's mercantile venture bears an uncomfortable resemblance to Spencer's financial dealings, the new Lord Mayor's unhesitating extension of the benefits of his wealth to all shoemakers renders the manner of acquisition not only acceptable but worthy of celebration.[48] The festival in *The Shoemaker's Holiday* thus enacts an imaginary appropriation of civic authority and commercial wealth by a group of industrial laborers for whom both privileges were largely a matter of fantasy.

That the play's concluding festival may have worked as fantasy for Dekker's first audiences leads to the question of how play text and performance context intersect. Because the historical record for the early modern period is notoriously thin on matters of theatrical reception, critics interested in the cultural work of drama rely primarily on textual and intertextual evidence alone. But the little information we do have about the make up of audiences at the various theaters and the stage success of particular plays can certainly provide us with some understanding of a play's engagement with contemporary controversies, particularly if the play is local and topical in orientation and if its generic structure prompts the dramatist to distinguish in some way between rewards and punishments. *The Shoemaker's Holiday* is a particularly rich case in point: its festive conclusion invites the audience to share in the shoemakers' triumphant appropriation of commercial and political power, thus not only reinforcing but also reinventing the interests of the apprentices and industrial capitalists among them.[49] Interestingly, following its Rose debut, *The Shoemaker's Holiday* was also performed and apparently well received at court on New Year's Day, 1600. Even though the court spectators differed radically from those who saw the play in Southwark, the end of discord represented in the festival also served as a redefinition of contemporary economic controversies in favor of the audience. The queen and courtiers who applauded *The Shoemaker's Holiday* likely did so because its resolution affirmed their own anti-commercial sentiment at the same time as it renewed the viability of nobilitas.[50] What this alignment of apparently dichotomous class sympathies reveals is the social and economic pressure being exerted by commercial capitalists in early modern London. Dekker's *The Shoemaker's Holiday,* both in text and performance context, may accordingly be understood as a mobilization of the power of traditional festivals to conduct controversy in such a way as to reinforce the shared economic and political interests of an industry and court that were slowly being displaced by new capitalist practices. The king's confident claim that "love ends all discord" is thus little more than a romantic mask for the economic and political terms in which the ends of discord in *The Shoemaker's Holiday* are in fact defined and achieved.

Notes

1. The other two plays are William Shakespeare's *Twelfth Night* (1600-02) and George Chapman's *May-Day* (1602-04).

2. Michael Manheim, "The Construction of *The Shoemakers' Holiday,*" *SEL* 10, 2 (Spring 1970): 315-23, 323; Arthur Kinney, "Thomas Dekker's Twelfth Night," *UTQ* 41, 1 (1971): 63-73, 64.

3. David Scott Kastan, "Workshop and/as Playhouse: Comedy and Commerce in *The Shoemaker's Holiday,*" *SP* 84, 3 (1987): 324-37, 333. See also Peter Mortenson, "The Economics of Joy in *The Shoemakers' Holiday,*" *SEL* 16, 2 (Spring 1976): 241-52, 248.

4. For a description of Shrove Tuesday customs in Elizabethan London, see François Laroque, *Shakespeare's Festive World: Elizabethan Seasonal Entertainment and the Professional Stage,* trans. Janet Lloyd (Cambridge: Cambridge Univ. Press, 1991), pp. 96-103, and David Cressy, *Bonfires and Bells: National Memory and the Protestant Calendar in Elizabethan and Stuart England* (London: Weidenfeld and Nicolson, 1989), pp. 18-9.

5. Laroque, p. 101; Keith Thomas, "Age and Authority in Early Modern England," *PBA* 62 (1976): 205-48, 219.

6. Thomas Dekker, *The Shoemaker's Holiday,* ed. R. L. Smallwood and Stanley Wells (Manchester: Manchester Univ. Press, 1979), xviii.225 and xxi.6-8. All subsequent references to Dekker are to this Revels edition.

7. L. D. Timms, "Dekker's *The Shoemaker's Holiday* and Elizabeth's Accession Day," *N&Q* n.s. 32, 1 (1985): 58.

8. Cressy gives an account of the alternative explanations for the origin of Accession Day on pp. 51-3; see also Roy Strong, "The Popular Celebration of the Accession Day of Queen Elizabeth I," *JWCI* 21, 1-2 (1958): 86-103, 87-8.

9. Strong, pp. 91-100.

10. Strong, p. 100.

11. Cressy, p. 50; Strong, p. 91.

12. The conflation in the play of holidays celebrating the power of both state and local community would seem to suggest that at least some festive forms of plebeian culture in early modern England were not structured, as Michael Bristol has argued, in opposition to the "dominant and privileged elites" (*Carnival and Theater: Plebeian Culture and the Structure of Authority in Renaissance England* [New York: Routledge, 1985], p. 72). Rather, *The Shoemaker's Holiday* reveals a unification of political interests between apparently dichotomous social groups when a newly empowered sector—the commercial elite—begins to threaten traditional communal life. For Bristol's views on the agonistic nature of plebeian festivals, see pp. 72-88 and 197-213.

13. For studies of symbolic inversion in *The Shoemaker's Holiday* see Kinney and Eril Barnett Hughes, "The Tradition of the Fool in Thomas Dekker's *The Shoemaker's Holiday,*" *Arkansas Philological Association Publications* 8, 2 (1982): 6-10.

14. Peter Stallybrass, "The World Turned Upside Down: Inversion, Gender and the State," in *The Matter of Difference: Materialist Feminist Criticism of Shakespeare,* ed. Valerie Wayne (New York: Harvester Wheatsheaf, 1991), pp. 201-20, 204.

15. The safety-valve theory of inversion, in which temporary inversion of norms is permitted by a society's dominant group in order to release social tensions, was proposed by Max Gluckman, *Custom and Conflict in Africa* (Oxford: Blackwell, 1966) in contrast, Mikhail Bakhtin's *Rabelais and His World,* trans. Helene Iswolsky (Cambridge MA: MIT Press, 1968), argues that symbolic inversion is essentially a transgressive unsettling of norms and regulations. A general overview of theories of festivity may be found in Bristol, pp. 26-39.

16. Joel H. Kaplan, "Virtue's Holiday: Thomas Dekker and Simon Eyre," *RenD* n.s. 2 (1969): 103-22, 110; Manheim, p. 317; Kastan, p. 332.

17. A particularly good example of the conflation of the two feasts is an entry for bell-ringing at Bishop's Stortford in Hertfordshire, where expenses are recorded in 1575 for "bred, drinck, and cheese for Ringing on St. Hewes daye in reioysing of the queenes prosperous Ragne" (quoted by Strong, p. 89; for other examples, see Strong, pp. 89-91). Strong also relates this anecdote: "Annually on the 17 November the college inmates enjoyed a 'gaudy day' in honour of their patron St. Hugh. It so happened about the year 1570 that some of the revellers went to the church of All Hallows to ring the bells for exercise. This resulted in the descent of the mayor, who charged them with popery for ringing a dirge for Queen Mary, to which one had the wit to reply that on the contrary it was for joy at the present Queen's accession. At this the mayor departed and ordered as many of the city's bells as possible to be rung in the Queen's honour" (p. 88).

18. Julia Gasper, *The Dragon and the Dove: The Plays of Thomas Dekker* (Oxford: Clarendon Press, 1990), p. 16. In this context, it may be fitting that Lincoln's commitment to the war effort is little more than a smoke screen for his desire to protect the Lacy family name from contamination by the citizen class.

19. Gasper, pp. 16-43.

20. Dekker's principal source is Thomas Deloney's *The Gentle Craft,* particularly the second and third stories of part 1. For a discussion of the relationship between the two works, see Smallwood and Wells, pp. 17-26.

21. Lacy's fortunes are, of course, modeled in large part on the legend of St. Hugh found in the first four chapters of *The Gentle Craft.* See Francis Oscar Mann, ed., *The Works of Thomas Deloney* (Oxford: Clarendon Press, 1912), pp. 73-89.

22. Significantly, much of the late 1590s repertoire of the Henslowe companies, for which Dekker wrote

23. William Raleigh Trimble, *The Catholic Laity in Elizabethan England 1559-1603* (Cambridge MA: Harvard Univ. Press, 1964), p. 214; Edward Norman, *Roman Catholicism in England from the Elizabethan Accession to the Second Vatican Council* (Oxford: Oxford Univ. Press, 1985), p. 32. At the same time, however, the wealthiest Catholics were also to be found in these areas. See Trimble, p. 180.

24. Trimble, p. 150.

25. Quoted in Jeremy Boulton, *Neighbourhood and Society: A London Suburb in the Seventeenth Century* (Cambridge: Cambridge Univ. Press, 1987), p. 284.

26. Keith Thomas, "Work and Leisure in Pre-Industrial Society," *Past and Present* 29 (1964): 50-66, 57.

27. Smallwood and Wells, xiv.23-4 n.

28. Laroque, p. 101.

29. Julia Gasper usefully suggests that the name Hammon could be meant to recall "Mammon," although she interprets the character's commercialism in religious rather than economic terms. See pp. 32-5.

30. The less than innocent "mirth" of this scene may also caution us not to take at face value Dekker's claim in the dedicatory epistle that "nothing is purposed but mirth" (Epistle, line 20).

31. George Unwin, *Industrial Organization in the Sixteenth and Seventeenth Centuries* (Oxford: Clarendon Press, 1904), p. 73.

32. Unwin, *Industrial Organization,* p. 122; George Unwin, *The Gilds and Companies of London* (1908; rprt. London: Frank Cass, 1963), p. 251.

33. Unwin, *Gilds and Companies,* p. 251.

34. A. L. Beier, "Engine of Manufacture: The Trades of London," in *London, 1500-1700: The Making of the Metropolis,* ed. A. L. Beier and Roger Finlay (London: Longman, 1986), pp. 141-67, 153.

35. Ibid.

36. For a graphic representation of this distribution, see Figure 3, "London commerce and industry described by Stow," in M. J. Power, "John Stow and His London," *Journal of Historical Geography* 11, 1 (1985): 1-20, 9.

37. This connection was first suggested by David Novarr, "Dekker's Gentle Craft and the Lord Mayor of London," *MP* 57, 4 (1960): 233-9.

38. Lawrence Stone, "The Peer and the Alderman's Daughter," *History Today* 11, 1 (1961): 48-55, 51.

39. Stone, p. 51; DNB, s.v. "Spencer, John."

40. DNB.

41. Stone, p. 48.

The Shoemaker's Holiday, reveals the political influence of Lord Howard of Effingham, the Lord Admiral, in its expressly Protestant values. See Andrew Gurr, *Playgoing in Shakespeare's London* (Cambridge: Cambridge Univ. Press, 1987), p. 148.

42. For a socio-historical analysis of these events, see Ian Archer, *The Pursuit of Stability: Social Relations in Elizabethan London* (Cambridge: Cambridge Univ. Press, 1991), pp. 1-9.

43. Both letters are printed in E. K. Chambers and W. W. Greg, eds., "Dramatic Records of the City of London: The Remembrancia," in The Malone Society's *Collections, Part I* (Oxford: Oxford Univ. Press, 1907), pp. 74-8.

44. Chambers and Greg, p. 77.

45. See for example Kaplan, p. 104; Kinney, p. 68; and Mortenson, p. 247.

46. Bristol discusses a related example of the way that ideals of traditional hospitality served to unite civic and plebeian interests in the policies developed around the celebration of Lent (pp. 80-5).

47. This is one of the play's most obvious bits of fictionalizing. Dutch immigrant laborers were in historical fact the target of allegations and attacks by Elizabethan tradesmen, although their numbers in no way rendered them a serious threat to the English labor force (Unwin, *Gilds and Companies,* pp. 246-51; see also Kaplan who discusses the matter of immigrant laborers in his reading of the play, pp. 325-6). Julia Gasper has recently suggested that Dekker's fairly easy positioning of the Dutch immigrant within an English household indicates that the play is more pro-Protestant than anti-immigrant (pp. 18-20).

48. Elizabethan ideals of civic office appear to inform this revision of the Lord Mayor's function. Ian Archer quotes Recorder Croke on the benefits of having the government of London run by its own freemen: it is "an incouragement to the one to governe well, a provocation to the other to obey well, the bond of love & societie knitting both together, banishing discord, the poison of all commen weales" (pp. 50-1). In reality, artisans and city elites were bound only by a rhetoric of reciprocal rights and obligations. On occasion, however, the outright violation of this nonverbal contract did incite popular unrest, as in the riots of 1595. Archer ascribes these riots specifically to "the personal failings of Mayor Spencer [who] was criticized for corruption in allowing the sale of offices, for failing to consult with his colleagues, for keeping too loose a rein on city administration, and for insatiable avarice" (p. 56). With respect to both generosity and reciprocity, Simon Eyre rightly supersedes Oatley/Spencer. The more general conflict between guild values and bourgeois values that is characteristic of the moral landscape of early industrial societies may also lie behind this fictional succession. On the moral culture of the guilds, see Antony Black, *Guilds and Civil Society in European Political Thought from the Twelfth Century to the Present* (Ithaca: Cornell Univ. Press, 1984). I thank an anonymous *SEL* reader for this reference.

49. The play's occupational and political sympathies appear to favor the interests of only one segment of the audience generally thought to have attended the Rose theater: "Courtiers, the 'clamorous fry' of law students, citizens, whores, porters and menservants all went to the Rose, Theatre and Curtain" (Gurr, p. 133). On the other hand, very few of these groups—with the possible exception of some citizens—would have objected strenuously to the subject matter and poetic justice of *The Shoemaker's Holiday.* As Gurr speculates, some playgoers were clearly excluded from the amphitheater repertoirs of the late 1590s, for the reopening of the hall playhouses in 1599 and 1600 was evidently intended to serve a new clientele of affluent merchants and professionals who would come to dominate this venue in the early seventeenth century. One has a difficult time imagining that *The Shoemaker's Holiday* would be well received by these audiences.

50. By 1599 both monarch and courtiers were well aware of their own increasing dependence on London's commercial capitalists. According to Robert Ashton, John Spencer was "[p]erhaps the most prominent of all lenders to the courtly world of fashion of his day" (*The City and the Court, 1603-1643* [Cambridge: Cambridge Univ. Press, 1979], p. 40). On the financial relationship between the aristocracy and London's money merchants, see also Ashton's *The Crown and the Money Market, 1603-1640* (Oxford: Clarendon Press, 1960).

THE HONEST WHORE

CRITICAL COMMENTARY

George E. Thornton (essay date 1955)

SOURCE: "The Social and Moral Philosophy of Thomas Dekker," in *Emporia State Research Studies,* Vol. 4, No. 2, December 1955, pp. 1-36.

[*In the following excerpt, Thornton evaluates the relative virtue and integrity of the various strata of society depicted in* The Honest Whore.]

> But gentlemen, I must disarme you then,
> There are of mad-men, as there are of tame,
> All humourd not alike: we have here some,
> So apish and phantasticke, play with a feather,
> And tho twould grieve a soule to see Gods image
> So blemisht and defac'd, yet doe they act
> Such anticke and such pretty lunacies,
> That spite of Sorrow they will make you smile:
> Others agen we have like hungry Lions,
> Fierce as the wilde Bulls, untameable as flies,
> And these have oftentimes from strangers sides
> Snatcht rapiers suddenly, and done much harme,
> Whom if you'l see, you must be weaponlesse.
>
> *The Honest Whore, I* (1604)

In discussing the plots of [*The Honest Whore*], *I & II,*[1] it is expedient to combine the two as one drama, since one is, actually, the sequel to the other. The plots are succinctly put forth in the original titles accorded the two plays. The 1604 edition of *HW, I* is described as "A Booke called The humours of the patient man, The longinge wyfe and the honest whore."[2] The 1630 edition of *HW, II* is entitled: "The Second Part of the Honest Whore, with the Humours of the Patient Man, the Impatient Wife: the Honest Whore perswaded by strong Arguments to turne Curtizan againe: her braue refuting those Arguments. And, lastly, the Comicall Passages of an Italian Bridewell, where the Scaene ends."[3]

The first plot of importance to *HW, I & II* concerns the efforts to marry of the royal lovers, Infelice and Count Hippolito, in spite of the objections of the girl's father, Duke Gasparo Trebazzi, ruler of Milan. In a scene at once reminiscent of Shakespeare's *Romeo and Juliet,* the Duke drugs his daughter and convinces Hippolito that she is dead; however, with the assistance of the court physician and a priest from Bedlam, the two lovers successfully thwart the Duke.

The second major plot concerns Candido, a patient linen draper, whose wife, Viola, spends most of her time attempting to provoke him to impatience. In her efforts she receives assistance from her brother, Fustigo, and from the gallants, Castruchio, Sinezi, Pioratto, and Fluello. Candido, however, survives the many trials put upon him and is patiently triumphant at the conclusions to both plays.

The third plot is the main one. It is the story of Bellafront, the titular character herself, who is reviled by Count Hippolito for her immorality. Realizing her depravity, she tries to return to respectable womanhood and is successful. However, on all sides, her moral redemption is combatted by her former associates. She achieves her triumph single-handedly through much suffering, so that she is recognized as a truly moral person at the conclusion of *HW, II.*

The lowest social level in both dramas is represented by the prostitute, the pander, and the bawd. These people are Bellafront, the prostitute; Roger, her servant and pander; and Mistress Fingerlock, a bawd. At the conclusion to *HW, II,* Dekker takes them to Bridewell and tries them for social indiscretion. In addition, the Bridewell scene introduces a collection of prostitutes with whom Dekker has not been concerned in either drama prior to this time— Mistress Horseleech, Dorothea Target, Penelope Whorehound, and Catherine Bountinall. Although he certainly considered these individuals to be beyond the conventional code of social morality, he does represent them as highly respected members of their own chosen profession; *i.e.,* he permits them loyally to support professional standards of their own. For example, one may observe Roger, Bellafront's servant, pursuing his work as pander in much the same way as an honest merchant might display his merchandise. Roger is proud, indeed, to be a member of Bellafront's establishment, for he respects her as the most successful woman of her station in all Milan. When she chides him for his monetary interests, naming him a ". . . slaue to sixpence, base metalled villain . . ." he is very indignant, for he considers himself a pander only to qual-

ity: "Sixpence? nay, that's not so: I never tooke under two shillings four-pence: I hope I know my fee." Dekker shows that Roger is proud of his position, that he is a man who takes pride in conducting his affairs with a respect for the ethics of his profession. At the same time, it is made clear that Roger, like any "honest" merchant, feels free to cheat if it be to his advantage. Here, one is reminded of Dekker's criticism of business standards in *The Seuen Deadly Sinnes of London*: while tradesmen were seen to use false weights and measures, Roger is now seen to water down the ale for Bellafront's customers and to forget, frequently, to return their change. Bellafront knows him and accuses him of lying to gentlemen customers, but he has a ready reply to her accusations:

> If it be my vocation to swear, every man in vocation: I hope my betters swear and dam themselves, and why should not I?[4]

Dekker was intrigued by the theory that, on society's lowest level, there is an open imitation of the sins of those who reside on society's higher levels. It is clear that the prostitutes imitate their betters in dress. In the Bridewell scene, again, a jailer explains that the prostitute's custom of dressing elaborately rests in her attempt to pass herself off as one of her more respectable sisters. She may dress lavishly, in one instance, like the ladies of gallants, since extravagance in clothing is fashionable. Later, she may affect the dress of the more humble, respectable woman of the merchant class. It is obvious that the philosophical jailer understands this vanity:

> No, my good Lord, that's onely but the vaile
> To her loose body, I haue seene her here
> In gayer Masking Suits, as seuerall Sawces
> Giue one Dish seuerall Tastes, so change of Habits
> In Whores is a bewitching Art: to day
> She's all in colours to besot Gallants,
> Then in modest blacke, to catch the Cittizen,
> And this from their Examinations drawne,
> Now shall you see a Monster both in shape
> And nature quite from these, that sheds no teare,
> Nor yet is nice, 'tis a plaine ramping Beare,
> Many such Whales are cast vpon this Shore.[5]

Both the jailer and Dekker admit that the citizenry of Milan (London) is easily duped into believing that outward appearance suggests a genuine quality to things. On the other hand, if Penelope Whorehound can be believed, she does not have the vice of debts:

> LODOVICO:
> . . . art in for debt?
> PENELOPE:
> No—is my Iudge, sir, I am in for no debts, I payd my Taylor for this Gowne, the last fiue shillings a weeke that was behind, yesterday.[6]

Dekker, one remembers, had previously chastised London citizens in *The Seuen Deadly Sinnes of London* for purchasing frivolous things and thereby running into debt for vanity's sake; so that, actually, in the light of this knowledge, Mistress Whorehound shows a moral superiority to the gallants, for she believes in paying her way. She is an ethical member of an illicit profession! Dekker seems reluctant to suggest that this kind of a woman is ashamed of her profession; rather, he would permit her to think of herself as a member of a very essential institution. She seems instinctively to recognize that there is a double standard to her society, and she cannot be surprised, therefore, to learn that gallants who engage her services privately will castigate her publicly or even take pleasure in witnessing the cruel punishments which society metes out to those of her profession. Indeed, the gallants who had been engaging in friendly, if bawdy, conversation in Bellafront's establishment flock to Bridewell to watch the wretched prostitutes as they are humiliated and punished. Although Dekker strengthens this theory as he works his way through all three levels of his society, it is strongest in his treatment of the gallant. He extends his sympathy, however, to the prostitutes when they are caught up by justice. Catherine Bountinall, for example, chides a fellow sister who wishes to deny her trade to escape punishment:

> Mary foh, honest? burnt at fourteene, seuen times whipt, sixe times carted, nine times duck'd, search'd by some hundred and fifty Constables, and yet you are honest? Honest Mistris Horsleach, is this World, a World to keep Bawds and Whores honest? How many times hast thou giuen Gentlemen a quart of wine in a gallon pot? how many twelue-penny Fees, nay two shillings Fees, nay, when any Embassadours ha beene heere, how many halfe crowne Fees hast thou taken? how many Carriers hast thou bribed for Country Wenches? how often haue I rinst your lungs in *Aqua vitae,* and yet you are honest?[7]

Catherine's contempt for the society which punishes her is scathing, and Dekker admires the woman for her courage and honesty, even if her morals, from society's viewpoint, leave much to be desired. She respects no one, it is true; when she is told that the Duke is present and that she should modify her language, she is even contemptuous of him and faces her punishment with strong heart:

> If the Deuill were here, I care not: set forward, yee Rogues, and giue attendance to your places, let Bawds and Whore be sad, for Ile sing and the Deuill were a dying.[8]

At the conclusion to *HW, II,* these women are convicted and sent off to beat hemp, the Duke himself directing the force of the law against the profession, obviously hoping thereby to purge Milan of its ills:

> Panders and Whores
> Are Citty-plagues, which being kept aliue,
> Nothing that lookes like goodnes ere can thriue.[9]

To Dekker, the prostitute is a product of the social contradictions of her society. Her establishment is a haven wherein gallants repair to drink, smoke, and swagger to their heart's content. It is an establishment with an atmosphere which the gallant's more conventional realm does not provide, in return for which, however, the woman is rewarded with the contempt of her society and with a gallant's renunciation when brought to justice. Ironically,

this justice, while openly punishing her, secretly encourages her practice. Catherine Bountinall and Dekker are aware of the hypocrisy inherent in this social attitude, and neither is reticent to exclaim against it. The prostitute exists for man's candlelight hours (*The Seuen Deadly Sinnes of London*); she cannot be acknowledged by the light of day.

Dekker is next concerned with the servant-apprentice class. His major contention is that most of the servants and all of the apprentices are eager to improve themselves socially, yet are rarely interested in working diligently to achieve their ambitions. They, too, imitate the superficial qualities which they discern in their betters. Candido's apprentices, for example, appreciate him more for his material success than for his goodly patience. Indeed, they assist his wife and the fun-loving gallants to deprive their master of that one virtue which makes him distinctive and valuable to society. George, for instance, seems to exemplify the worst qualities of the entire apprentice class. He is lazy, rude, and familiar with his customers. Candido unmasks him in *HW, I* when he sees him serving three gallant customers:

> I pray come neare, y'are very welcome gallants,
> Pray pardon my mans rudeness, for I feare me
> He's talkt above a Prentise with you. . . . [10]

Hippolito's servant betrays a similar kind of rudeness to his superiors. Ushering Bellafront into Hippolito's study, he annoys the Count, who becomes remonstrative:

> HIPPOLITO:
> Thou slave, thou hast let in the devil.
> SERVANT:
> Lord blesse us, where? hee's not cloven my Lord that I can see: besides the divell goes more like a Gentleman than a Page, good my Lord *Boon couragio.*
> HIPPOLITO:
> Thou hast let in a woman, in mans shape. And thou art damn't for't.
> SERVANT:
> Not damn'd I hope for putting in a woman to a Lord.[11]

In addition to emphasizing the servant's rudeness to the master, these lines serve further to illustrate his contempt for the whole nobility. Servants were frequently made to act the pander to their masters; this servant, therefore, can not understand his being berated for performing an act that ordinarily falls to the lot of a member of his station. Thus, he is similar to Candido's George in his ability to exchange repartee with his master. One recalls that, when George was demonstrating his master's fabrics to three gallants, the ensuing conversation concerning the quality of the material in question was laced with *double entendre* of obscene overtones. Dekker makes it clear, however, that the gallants provoked this verbal duel, so that it becomes their example which George is following. Although the gallants are fingering a bolt of cloth (appropriately called *she*) which George has shown them, they are in reality looking upon Candido's wife during the entire conversation:

> CASTRUCHIO:

What, and is this she saist thou?
GEORGE:
I, and the purest she that ever you fingered since you
were a gentleman: looke how even she is, looke how
cleane she is, ha, as even as the brow of *Cinthia,* and
as cleane as your sonnes and heires when they ha
spent all.[12]

At the same time, George has a contempt for the gallants
similar to that of Hippolito's servant for the nobility.

A different breed of servant, however, is introduced in
HW, II, offering an interesting contrast to George and
Hippolito's man. Bryan, Hippolito's groom and the
character in question, is devoted to his master. Unfortunately, his lack of knowledge of the English language (he
is Irish) is forever plunging him into serious trouble.
Although he worships his master, his actions always end
unhappily. For example, Infelice falsely "confesses" to
Hippolito an affair with the unfortunate Bryan, when she
learns that Hippolito himself has made advances to Bellafront. The Count believes her and, in a rage, beats the hapless man, who, throughout the struggle, does not know
what he has done:

HIPPOLITO:
Prate not, but get thee gone, I shall send else.
BRYAN:
I, doe predy, I had rather haue thee make a scabbard
of my guts, and let out all de Irish puddings in my
poore belly, den to be a false knaue to de I faat, I will
neuer see dyne own sweet face more. *A mawhid deer
a gra,* fare de well, fare de well, I wil goe steale
Cowes agen in *Ireland.*[13]

Bryan is the only member of the serving-class to retain an
old-fashioned virtue of duty and loyalty to master. It is
curious that Dekker should have made this loyal servant
an Irishman, for it was customary in this time to express a
contempt for the Irish. Undoubtedly, there is some ridicule
intended. Perhaps, he was suggesting that the less
sophisticated country of Ireland still held reverence for
humble virtue. If so, Ireland can produce loyal but
incompetent servants, if nothing else. Bryan, too, is further
annoyed by gallants who make him the butt of their nefarious jokes. They are a strange breed to him, for he does not
understand them at all. Perhaps, it is for this reason that he
does not attempt to imitate them. Consequently, he has a
degree of virility that is lacking in Dekker's other servant-
apprentice characterizations.

Dekker has so far concluded that the serving-class in his
England possesses little humility. Like their superiors, they
are arrogant, crude, and irresponsible. They have little
respect for their masters, and all show a tendency to imitate
the superficial qualities of the gallant. The one exception
is Bryan, who is actually abused when he tries to perform
his duties. Though he is stupid and has none of George's
wit, he does have a few virtues of the true servant. He is
one of the ironies of the author's social world.

Dekker next investigates the merchant group. Candido, the
patient linen draper, is a personification of the author's

"virtuous people," and will be observed in greater detail
later. He should be dealt with at this time only as he affects others within his own class. Viola, Candido's wife,
however, represents Dekker's pattern for this class. As the
wife of the great patient man, she has reason to appreciate
him the most; yet she tries constantly to undermine that
virtue which makes him outstanding. She lays elaborate
plans to provoke his temper. She would have him to be
like other women's husbands, and she is frustrated when
his patience cannot be shaken:

. . . he loues no frets, and is so free from anger that
many times I am ready to bite off my tongue, because
it wants that vertue which all womens tongues have (to
anger their husbands) Brother mine can by no thunder,
turne him into a sharpnesse.[14]

Viola's "brother mine" is very much like her with respect
to his superficial qualities. Fustigo is without ambition to
achieve success through hard work, yet he wants success.
He is arrogant, vain, extravagant, and lethargic. His
personality is made up of the worst features of the gallants
whom he imitates. He has had, at one time in his life, a
slight education. He mentions Albertus Magnus and Aristotle upon occasion, but his basic stupidity is revealed at
every turn. Viola, of course, has no difficulty in enlisting
his aid. In return, she agrees to give him ". . . a great
horseman's French feather. He *knows* what is fashionable!
Viola, actually, affords one the most lucid description of
her brother when she offers him the feather:

O, by any means, to shew your light head, else your
hat will sit like a coxcombe: to be briefe, you must be
in all points a most terrible wide-mouth'd swaggerer.[15]

Obviously, the role she desires him to play demands that
he be *himself.*

Fustigo's pretentious behavior is patterned after that of the
gallants in whom he envies luxurious living and ease. In
all respects, Fustigo is the gull, or his prototype, the kind
of person whom Dekker feigns to advise in *The Gvls
Horn-Booke.* He is without virtue. He is superficially
personified. He wants to be a gentleman, but he is
convinced, at the same time, that to be a gentleman he
must have sufficient money to afford the best tailor. In his
simple thought, the proof of a gentleman lies in the cut of
a coat and the whiteness of linen. It is clear to him that the
gentleman's delicate comportment, his fastidious toilet,
and his clever repartee make him successful with the ladies
and the envy of all. Moreover, his gentleman does not toil,
yet he reaps abundantly. One can imagine his horror when
Viola once told him that he was brother-in-law to a linen
draper! Dekker makes a neat contrast of Fustigo and Candido. The latter is the epitome of that success which may
be attained to by a man of perseverance and industry. The
former represents the degree to which the virtues of the
middle class man can be perverted when he disregards
place and imitates the most foolish of his superiors.

In Matheo, Dekker proposes an intermediary between the
merchant and the gallant. Matheo, Bellafront's original

seducer, was a member of the merchant class; however, when he first appears early in *HW, I,* Dekker would seem to place him next to Hippolito in social importance. Nevertheless, one suspects that Matheo has not long been a member of this class, for the Duke tells him that he *plays* the gentleman well and engages him in the plot to subdue the distracted Hippolito. Matheo, as well, fears that his new, exalted position in society may be endangered if Hippolito persists in antagonizing the Duke. He agrees, therefore, to assist the Duke, and in the lines which follow his decision, Dekker clearly shows Matheo's social position as he expresses deep fear for his "new Blacke cloakes." Eventually, Dekker will reveal Matheo as the most depraved character in the drama, for he is one individual who is thoroughly without scruple. He will do anything to further his ambitions,—to live in ease and to bask in luxury. Nor can he understand Hippolito's grief for Infelice, thought dead, for it is his contention that one woman will serve as well as another. When Hippolito, overcome with tragedy speaks of sorrow, Matheo unburdens himself of a contempt for all womankind:

> . . . sfoote women when they are alive are but dead commodities, for you shall have one woman lie upon many mens hands.[16]

When Hippolito insists that he shall never again look upon another woman, Matheo, in turn, vows that he will take his friend to a brothel within the next few days:

> If you have this strange monster, Honestie, in your belly, why so Jigmakers and Chroniclers shall picke something out of you: but and I smell not you and a bawdy house out within these ten daies, let my nose be as big as an English bag-pudding: Ile follow your Lordship though it be to the place aforenamed.[17]

Consequently, when next seen, Matheo has been successful in bringing Hippolito to the house of Bellafront. Matheo is very much at home in this environment, and, true to his own pattern, he expresses friendly contempt for Bellafront, a contempt which he displays for all women. It must flatter his ego to think that he originally had discovered the most attractive courtesan in all Milan! Furthermore, he appears to have a sinister power which he exercises over people. He was successful, at first, in seducing Bellafront, taking her from a good home and a kind and loving father. And he was successful, secondly, in bringing Hippolito, against the latter's wishes, to Bellafront's establishment. Hippolito, however, is most uncomfortable in the company of Bellafront, and the riotous behavior of Matheo and his friends only intensifies his grief. But Matheo pays him no need, for he is not one to waste sympathy on his fellow man.

Later, when Bellafront decides to abandon prostitution and announces her intentions to Matheo in the presence of the gallants, he believes that she is amusing herself at the expense of all present; he feels that she has invented the story for the purpose of being alone with him. That a person might wish self-redemption is a thought which never occurs to him! When the gallants subsequently leave, he congratulates her for what he calls her "gulling" of them:

> Ha, ha, thou dost gull em so rarely, so naturally: if I did not thinke thou hadst beene in earnest: thou art a sweete Rogue for't yfaith.[18]

This deep, sadistic pleasure which Matheo derives from a manipulation of people causes him to appreciate what he believes to be a similar trait in Bellafront. He shows more appreciation, indeed, for her in this one scene than he has before or ever will, but his amusement is shortlived. When she tells him that she hates him worst of all—"you were the first to giue me money for my soul"—, his rage is uncontrollable, and he releases his venom: "Is't possible to be impossible! . . . for a harlot to turn honest is one of Hercules labours. . . ." When she demands that he marry her, he replies that he will be "burnt first!" Dekker says that Matheo depends upon the naivete and honesty of other men whose traits enable him to victimize them; however, in the Bedlam scene of *HW, I,* he completes this characterization in the episode in which the Duke orders Matheo to marry Bellafront, an action for which he had previously said he would rather be "burnt." Matheo, back against the wall, complains:

> Cony-catcht, guld . . .
> Plague found you for't, tis well.
> The Cockolds stampe goes currant in all nations.[19]

At last, the past master of the art of gulling falls victim to his own devices. He is now the gull gulled, as it were, another of Dekker's ironies.

Dekker's gallants in *HW, I & II* are superficialities. They possess the immorality of which he spoke so vehemently in *The Seuen Deadly Sinnes of London.* They are rich, idle, frivolous, lecherous, dissembling, and cruel. They have provided the pattern which directly influences every class beneath them, and they are one of the forces contributing to the innocuous behavior of most of the *dramatis personae.* The apprentices imitate their clever but immodest conceits. Almost all of the characters imitate their idle qualities, apprentices and serving-men even neglecting their work because they think the gallants' easy lives to be fashionable. They are cruel to the prostitute, as are all other "respectable" classes in the dramas. Their consummate selfishness is the pattern for Fustigo and Matheo. Fustigo, in fact, is made thoroughly useless to his society because of his aping of gallant mannerisms, and Matheo represents the values of the gallant when carried to a natural and pernicious conclusion. Although these gallants possess few individual qualities of distinction, they are people who are admired by the majority of the characters in Dekker's works. The gentle class, which has been the core of medieval society, is shown through the gallant to be on the threshold of a complete degeneration. In short, the gallant and his standards are society as Dekker conceives of it in these two plays.

The loftiest social class in *HW, I & II* is represented by Count Hippolito, Infelice, his wife, and her father, Gasparo Trebazzi, ruler of Milan. The whole of society in these two plays rises or falls with the royal class. Hence, this class and Dekker's understanding of it are most essential to the development of his social and moral philosophy. Infelice, daughter to the Duke and member of the royal family of Milan, is an egotistical, strong-minded young woman who will not permit her desires to be frustrated. To the modern reader, the fact that she disobeyed her father and married the man of her choice does not seem amiss. However, to the Elizabethan and to the conservative Elizabethan like Dekker, Infelice's action would seem to be that of a willful and spoiled child of an ever-indulgent father. Dekker is calling attention, undoubtedly, to the fact that one whose duty it was to rule Milan and to disseminate justice and equity to all could not control his own daughter. Indeed, Infelice was very much the daughter of Trebazzi. He, too, was self-willed, self-indulgent. He was a man enraged when his will was defied, and he could commit a murder with no moral compunction. But it was only natural, therefore, during this episode that the Duke put the affairs of state from his mind and concentrate wholly upon his pressing family problems. However, as head of state, he was supposed to be an example to all. Dekker calls specific attention to this neglect of duty, yet the Duke was no more neglectful of his duties than were the lowliest citizens of Milan. Certainly, his own gallants at court were the products of his inability to teach by precept and example. The Duke was not playing the part to which God elected him; Dekker was a staunch believer in the divine rights of kingship which emphasized the importance of good example to one's subjects. Consequently, when Infelice pleads with the Duke to save her marriage from the threat of Bellafront, he decides to purge Milan of prostitution. He was not actually concerned with the act of stamping out an evil; such an idea was entirely contrary to his pronouncements. He was, first and last, interested in resolving his daughter's marital problem. One need only observe his subsequent proclamation to discern a lack of sincerity. The core of the man's whole social and moral philosophy is contained in the expression, "Nothing that lookes like goodnes ere can thriue."[20] How it probably concerned him greatly that his son-in-law's interest in Bellafront's charms could not "look like goodnes" to the state! However, that Bellafront was a good and moral woman was proved to the satisfaction of Orlando Friscibaldo, a man whom the Duke admired and respected. It is pertinent to realize that the Duke eventually explains his son-in-law's aberration in this way:

> . . . for to turne a Harlot
> Honest, it must be by strong Antidots,
> 'Tis rare, as to see Panthers change their spots.
> And when she's once a Starre (fixed) and shines bright,
> Tho 'twere impiety then to dim her light,
> Because we see such Tapers seldome burne.
> Yet 'tis the pride and glory of some men,
> To change her to a blazing Starre agen,
> And it may be, *Hippolito* does no more.
> It cannot be, but y'are acquainted all
> With that same madnesse of our Sonne-in-law,
> That dotes so on a Curtizan.[21]

To Dekker, the Duke's statement must have smacked of sacrilege.

The madman who speaks in the Bedlam scene of *HW, I* analyzes the social conditions of Milan and seems to be Dekker's mouthpiece for warning to all England. The scene is the one in which the madman has confused the Duke with his own son. He holds the Duke's hand and notices that the fingernails are long:

> Such nailes had my second boy: kneele downe thou varlet, and aske thy father blessing: Such nailes had my middelmost son, and I made him a Promoter: and he scrapt, and scrapt, til he got the divel and all: but he scrapt thus and thus and thus and it went under his legs, till at length a companie of kites, taking him for carrion, swept up all, all, all, all, all, all, all. If you love your lives, looke to your selves: see, see, see, see, the Turkes Gallies are fighting with my ships, Bownce goes the guns: ooh! cry the men: romble, romble goe the waters: Alas, there; tis sunke, tis sunke: I am undone, I am undone, you are the damn'd Pirates have undone me: you are by the Lord, you are, you are, stop'em, you are.[22]

Dekker's meaning is unmistakable. The state is ruled by a fool who keeps company with "kites," and, as a result, the ship of state is unmanned when the enemy attacks. The Duke, upon deciding to rid the city of prostitutes, continues the image:

> Ile try all Phisicke, and this Med'cine first:
> I haue directed Warrants strong and peremptory
> (To purge our Citty *Millan*, and to cure
> The outward Parts, the Suburbes) for the attaching
> Of all those women, who (like gold) want waight,
> Cities (like Ships) should haue no idle fraight.[23]

Earlier in *The Seuen Deadly Sinnes of London* Dekker had expressed his opinion that the plague was a visitation from God—it was a divine warning. Here, again, he seems to be saying, through his ship image, that the state is in danger of a new divine intervention, since London is so wasted.

The lasting impression of *HW, I & II* is that of Dekker's concern for individual and social morality. He believes that state inferior whose inhabitants are not virtuous; therefore, a state which is not good must be made good, else a vengeful God will destroy it. He believes further that this God, because He knows that man is weak, has given man examples of strongly moral people to emulate and from whom to learn virtue for himself. The whole class structure of these plays shows an interdependency of one class upon another, a kind of social chain of being, crowned by the ruling classes with the ruler himself ordained by God. Dekker concludes that it is God's wish that this ruler be a good and virtuous man. If he be not so by nature, says Dekker, he can learn to be so through study of a virtuous man. Now, Dekker's philosophy permits of two kinds of virtue. One man is virtuous by nature. He has a natural affinity for goodness. It does not require much struggle for him to remain good. He merely has to defend his virtue from attacks of the stupid, who cannot recognize virtue when they see it and consequently try to destroy it. There is a second kind of virtue, however, which is probably the greater of the two in Dekker's thinking, since it is achieved only through great moral struggle. It achieves strength through sin; it suffers the agony of the tormented but receives a final purity only after moving dangerously near to eternal damnation. Candido possesses Dekker's first kind of virtue—a virtue which Milton would call *blank*. Bellafront possesses the second kind, a tested virtue. And there is a third person, Orlando Friscobaldo, who typifies that which can be learned from observation of the virtuous man. He is capable of learning, and, what is more, capable of accepting the truth, even when it contradicts the fashions of the times. True, he is motivated by love for his daughter, but when she tells him she is no longer a prostitute, he pretends not to believe her. He even denies her. Later, he resolves to test her, and when he muses aloud, one is permitted to understand his true character:

> Las my Girle! art thou poore? pouerty dwells next
> doore to despaire, there's but a wall betweene them;
> despaire is one of hells Catch-powles; and lest that
> Deuill arrest her, Ile to her. . . . Yes, I will victuall the
> Campe for her. . . . [24]

With Bellafront's moral redemption, Orlando Friscobaldo's life is complete.

Dekker's *HW, I & II* are experiments in the negative presentation of moral virtue, in which are depicted various levels of morality, or the lack of it, which exist in mankind from the lowest state of society to the highest. At the very bottom of the scale of being there is a complete amorality, a total lack of understanding for much which is moral. At the top of the scale, there exist three characters who typify moral qualities. Although these three possess virtue, they differ in their kinds of morality and in the ways they have succeeded in achieving it. It would seem, therefore, to be Dekker's theory that few people have a knowledge or appreciation of virtue, insofar as most of the action in these two dramas is concerned with the attempts of those who represent the ungainly majority to deprive those who represent the virtuous minority of their virtue. That many of the scenes dealing with attempted seduction are laden with crude humor does not lessen the very serious intent of Dekker, but only veils it. Dekker would seem to have one think that virtue is rare, that the vulgar, the stupid, and the shallow are either oblivious to it or work consciously against it. The clever character becomes vain and frivolous in close analysis; the dull one becomes ambitious, yet lethargic, highly desirous of that which is sham and ephemeral. Dekker's evaluation of mankind is not pleasant, necessitating that he conceal such human spiritual weakness in clever comic exterior; the arrangement of his acts, by which two seemingly dissimilar plots dovetail and compliment each other, prevents Dekker's message from having a very direct contact with the audience. Indeed, upon cursory reading, the continuity of these acts seems haphazard, even to the point of being unplanned. It is only later that one realizes that Dekker has, perhaps, *gulled* his reader. The true message of *HW, I & II* is a hidden one, although there are visible signposts everywhere along the way. Out of these dramas has come Dekker's picture of social degredation. Always the moralist, he is understandably shocked by conditions as he finds them. At the same time, fortunately, he is also enough of a realist, a trait possibly derived from his pamphleteering days, to face up strongly to the situation in the interests of faithful reproduction. Although *HW, I & II* do not sustain his annoyance with the new order as he has shown it in his pamphlets, the dramas do reveal, often with a surprising subtlety, the whole complex social order of the London which Dekker knew.

Notes

1. There is a textual problem of dates, here. Dekker's *HW, I* was published in 1604; his *HW, II*, in 1630. It has long been assumed that the first play was also written around 1604; however, there is still speculation concerning the date of composition for the sequel. Although a quarter of a century had lapsed between publications of these two plays, Hunt contends that there is sufficient evidence to indicate that the second play was written shortly after the first (Mary Leland Hunt, *Thomas Dekker*, p. 94). On the other hand, there is the theory that the second play shows a greater maturity than the first, a theory which immediately suggests that *HW, II* may have been written on or about the date of its accepted publication date (*Thomas Dekker*, edited by Ernest Rhys, p. xxix). Henslowe mentions having made payment for *HW, I* to Dekker and Middleton between 1 January 1604 and 14 March 1604 (E. K. Chambers, *The Elizabethan Stage*, III, p. 295), and he records its acting by the Prince's Men soon afterwards. Middleton's share in the composition of *HW, I* is also a matter for disagreement. There is no doubt, however, that Middleton collaborated with Dekker, but it is difficult to single out those portions of the drama which belong to Middleton and those which belong to Dekker. Some critics contend that Middleton's contribution was negligible, consigning the major portions of the drama to Dekker (*Thomas Dekker*, edited by Ernest Rhys, p. xxx). However, Hunt finds evidence of Middleton's hand in *HW, II* (*op. cit*, p. 94).

2. . . . . p. 294.

3. *Loc. cit.*

4. Thomas Dekker, *The Dramatic Works of Thomas Dekker*, II, p. 49.

5. *Ibid.*, p. 178.

6. *Ibid.*, p. 177.

7. *Ibid.*, p. 179.

8. *Ibid.*, p. 181.

9. *Ibid.*, pp. 181-82.

10. *Ibid.*, p. 19.

11. *Ibid.*, p. 58.

12. *Ibid.*, p. 18.

13. *Ibid.*, p. 132.

14. *Ibid.*, p. 10.

15. *Ibid.*, p. 11.

16. *Ibid.*, p. 6.

17. *Ibid.*, p. 7.

18. *Ibid.*, p. 53.

19. *Ibid.*, p. 159.

20. *Ibid.*, p. 182.

21. *Ibid.*, pp. 156-57.

22. *Ibid.*, pp. 81-82.

23. *Ibid.*, p. 158.

24. *Ibid.*, p. 107.

Larry S. Champion (essay date 1985)

SOURCE: "The Early Years—Romantic Comedy, Satire," in *Thomas Dekker and the Traditions of English Drama,* Peter Lang, 1985, pp. 11-53.

[*In the excerpt below, Champion analyzes the construction of the two parts of* The Honest Whore. *He judges Part II a masterpiece, comparing its structure to that of "Shakespeare's most effective comedies."*]

Whatever the critical complaints about parts of the canon, Dekker's work at its rare best ranks, as A. H. Bullen has observed, "with the masterpieces of the Elizabethan drama."[1] And in any description of those moments, the two parts of *The Honest Whore* invariably place high on the list.[2] Yet, a comparison of these plays—like that of *Westward Ho* and *Northward Ho*—reveals significantly different levels of craftsmanship and, at the same time, provides clear evidence why Part II is one of his greatest works.[3] In both plays the attempt (as in Shakespeare's problem comedies) is to create, not the stylized, one-dimensional puppet of situation comedy, but rather a more complex character who is forced to confront a viable force of evil and to make ethical and moral decisions and who—in the course of the action—experiences a credible and genuine development. In these stage worlds the power of evil is real; and the characters, struggling on the fringe of comedy, must cope with the actual consequences of crime and sin.[4]

Such characters obviously create problems for the dramatist who desires to maintain a firm comic perspective for the spectator rather than see his narrative turn to melodrama or tragicomedy. Since the spectators' involvement with physical action does not extend beyond the superficial laughter that a humorous situation arouses, the playwright—to the extent that he can maintain such a perspective—has no difficulty in achieving a comic tone for "flat" characters who make no ethical decisions. On the other hand, with greater character complexity, the spectator is easily provoked into emotional identification with character and situation, and his comic perspective is blurred. Regardless of how the Renaissance comic form took shape, whether primarily from "Saturnalian release" or from "Terentian intrigue," the dramatic experience which is to divert rather than to distress is possible only so long as the spectator is either emotionally detached from the characters or, if emotionally involved, in possession of such knowledge or provoked into such a mood as to be assured of a happy end accomplished by means which only temporarily appear unpleasant.

In Part I the structure is loose and the effect disorderly. With the spectators' perspective at times unguided and consequently blurred and with critical character inconsistencies, the action at several points degenerates into sheer melodrama. In Part II the structure is firm, the comic perspective carefully controlled throughout; the result is a stage world in which, from a position of knowledgeable security, the spectators observe the development of characters obsessed with greed and lust but ultimately purged and presumably restored to a richer life through the power and grace of selfless love.

In Part I, more specifically, the comic perspective is maintained with only partial success; it depends to a large extent on a farcical secondary plot that involves six of the twelve scenes in Acts I-IV, before the plots merge in the final act. These scenes (second, fourth, fifth, seventh, tenth, eleventh) Dekker interweaves presumably to block the spectators' emotional involvement with a main plot dealing with unrequited love and apparent death. Candido, a linen draper, is depicted as a veritable "(mirror of patience) . . . [in whom one may] sooner raise a spleene in an Angell, than rough humour" (I.iv.15, 23-4). Equally stylized is his wife Viola, who is convinced that her husband, unless he can be goaded into a fit of passion, "haz not all things belonging to a man" (I.ii.58-9). Her philosophy in a nutshell is that "[w]omen must haue their longings, or they die" (136).

This rather ingenious variation of the battle of the sexes, in effect, sets humor against humor.[5] Through mockery and ridicule (in I.v as rakish courtiers enter his shop demanding a "pennyworth of lawne" cut from the very center of a seventeen-yard piece), through apparent cuckoldry (in III.i as Viola encourages her brother to take outlandish liberties with her in order to rouse her husband's jealousy), through physical abuse (in IV.iii as Candido is mistaken for George, his apprentice, and soundly cuffed by two "bravos"), and through mental abuse (in IV.iii as his wife's charges of insanity precipitate his detention at Bedlam), Candido perseveres in his incredible patience. Viola, instead, is the one to crack, admitting her shrewishness and swearing to "vex [his] spirit no more" (V.ii.479) as she petitions the Duke to release her husband from the asylum. Obviously this entire action must be played broadly, else the spectators would understandably begin to question not only Viola's motivation in her determination to infuriate her husband but also Candido's willingness to be mocked and bludgeoned in the name of a patience that by any realistic standard smells either of cowardice or of stupidity. But, played farcically, the one-dimensional characters provide a degree of comic distancing for the main plot; the linen-draper, in fact, survives the role as comic butt to emerge at the end of the play as a kind of middle-class hero who delivers an encomium on the virtues of patience as the "soule of peace" (489), the "perpetuall prisoners liberty" (500), the "bond-slaues freedom" (501), the "beggers Musick" (504), the "sap of blisse" (506). Above all, he observes—in a line calculated to sharpen the comic perspective during the sentimental fifth-act reconciliations—it is the "hunny gainst a waspish wife" (509). The bemused Duke can only admit that "[s]o calme a spirit is worth a golden Mine," even as he quips that "Twere sinne all women should such husbands haue, / For euery man must then be his wiues slaue" (515, 512-13).

Along with the interlaced double-plot, the elaborate artifice of Act V is apparently devised to reinforce the comic perspective during the final moments of the play. This action is replete with madhouse scenes (comic at least to the seventeenth-century audience), disguise, mistaken identity, plots and counterplots: Hippolito's disguise as he steals forth to Bethlem Monastery to wed Infelice, the Duke's disguise as a country gentleman to prevent the nuptials, the discovery of the Duke's plans by the lovers, their posthaste wedding and disguise as friars, and the reconciliation of Trebatzi and his son-in-law effected by Friar Anselmo.

Despite these comic devices the spectator in Part I does not, for the great bulk of the plot, observe the action from a vantage of superior knowledgeability. He is not led to anticipate a pattern of action which provides the emotional assurance of comedy at the same time it sustains the absorbing interest of narrative, and consequently there are several points at which the comic perspective is blurred. Indeed, the dominant tone at the outset of the play is far from comic—a macabre funeral procession for the fair Infelice who has "died" suddenly and mysteriously, a distraught lover who bursts upon the mourners with charges that the father is a "murderer" who has "kill'd her by [his] crueltie" (I.i.35), and the sorrowing father who—lashing out with equal vehemence—commands that, if Hippolito "proceede to vexe vs, your swordes / Seeke out his bowells" (15-6). The imagery further underscores the tragic tone of the scene. Infelice is one whose cheeks are "roses Withered" (23), her eyes a "paire of starres . . . Darkened and dim" (24-5), the "riuers / That fed her veines with warme and crimson streames, / Frozen and dried vp" (25-7). "[B]eautie [is] but a coarse" (55); "Queenes bodies are but trunckes to put in wormes / That now must feast with her, were euen bespoke, / And solemnely inuited like strange guests" (103-05). All of this, the spectators must accept as straightforward exposition as they tend to develop a sympathetic rapport with the aggrieved young lover. Understandably, then, they feel themselves to be the victims of an emotional trick when, well into the action—*two full scenes later,* they discover to their amazement that Infelice, far from dead, is herself the victim of a family

fued and of her father's determination to bar her romantic interest in Hippolito. He swears to "starue her on the Appenine" (I.iii.25) before he will permit the marriage; and, informing her that Hippolito is dead, he sends her to Bergamo where "[i]n a most wholesome aire" (76) she shall "[c]ast off this sorrow" (81). Publicly lamenting his previous sharpness toward Hippolito and his family, he secretly commands Doctor Benedict to murder the innocent lad: "Performe it; Ile create thee halfe mine heire" (98).[6]

Even though the events of these two scenes (I.i; I.iii) have eroded a firm perspective, the viewers—once the truth is revealed—are now at least in possession of sufficient information to observe the near tragic events from a vantage of comedy. Yet, a few scenes later Dekker and Middleton employ another narrative trick which further confuses the audience. In IV.iv the doctor reports that Hippolito is dead (poisoned when drinking a "health . . . [t]o *Infaelices* sweete departed soule" [8]) and urges Duke Trebatzi "to bury deepe, / This bloudy act of mine" (30-1). Again, since the spectator has no reason whatsoever to assume that this event has not actually occurred, the comic perspective is destroyed. And, again, the spectator is understandably troubled and far from emotionally satisfied to learn later that Dr. Benedict has been lying, that Hippolito is alive and healthy, and that the doctor—now bitter at the peremptory treatment he has received from the Duke—will reveal all to the youth and will aid him in rescuing and wedding Infelice.

A further difficulty concerning the perspective of the main plot involves the title character Bellafront, a notorious woman of the behind-door trade. It is difficult not to view her "conversion" as stylized; her alteration in the scope of a single scene from a practicing prostitute, bandying words of the trade with her servant Roger and with several of her best customers, to a repentant ("honest") whore replete with sermonettes, tears, and a dagger with which to end her shame is so shockingly sudden as to be comic—much like Valentine's conversion to love in *The Two Gentlemen of Verona* or Berowne's shift from anti-lover to Petrarchan doter in *Love's Labor's Lost*.[7] As if to emphasize the stylized quality of the action, the playwrights make no attempt to dramatize any credible motivation; we simply view the whore in one line, the penitent in another and all for the sake of the heart—Bellafront's true love at first sight of Hippolito—a stock motif in English romantic comedy since the work of the University Wits.

Once the spectator has accepted Bellafront as a stylized character, however, and has in this fashion blocked himself from emotional involvement with her, he is confronted with three consecutive scenes (III.ii, III.iii, IV.i) which appear designed to convince him *post hoc* of the sincerity of her conversion. She is berated in succession by her servant Roger and her confidante Mistress Fingerlock, who comprehend only the money lost as a result of the sea change; by her customers, who take obvious delight in mocking her new posture; by Matheo, who first was responsible for her sexual promiscuity and who laughs outright at her suggestion that he marry her and make her honest ("How, marry with a Punck, a Cockatrice, a Harlot? mary foh, Ile be burnt thorow the nose first" [III.iii.116-17]); and by Hippolito, who spurns her for violating his devotional to Infelice and flatly rejects her proffered love. Apparently broken at this point, Bellafront moans in soliloquy that she

> must therefore fly,
> From this vndoing Cittie, and with teares,
> Wash off all anger from my fathers brow.
>
> (IV.i.192-94)

These scenes, apparently calculated to evoke sympathy for the long-suffering regenerate, result in a richer and more complex characterization than the spectator has been led to expect from the stylized conversion earlier.

For this very reason the inconsistency in Bellafront's remaining appearances is all the more disturbing. Since her father is never mentioned after the short reference cited above, it is possible that Dekker, already planning a sequel, was providing a connecting link. But, in any event, there is no reason to believe that she is lying in her pronouncement. Indeed, the convention of the soliloquy assumes just the reverse. Yet we see her next, not at her father's home, but as a patient in Bethlem, and only later do we realize that her insanity is merely a pose. Moreover, the audience is totally unaware of her decision to forget her passionate love for Hippolito and to pursue her honor above her romance in the stratagem by which she gains Matheo as a husband. No doubt the spectator must overcome a momentary tendency to sympathize with Matheo as a victim in a ploy from which there is no honorable escape, much like the momentary tendency to sympathize with Bertram against Helena in *All's Well That Ends Well.* Forced to admit the truth of the "lunatic's" claim that he has rifled her most precious jewel and forced by the Duke to agree to marry her if and when she ever recovers her wits, Matheo is astounded as she calmly announces:

> *Matheo* thou art mine,
> I am not mad, but put on this disguise,
> Onely for you my Lord.
>
> (V.ii.432-34)

Certainly, the spectator—provoked alternately to laughter, tears, and disdain for the "honest whore"—is justified in feeling some degree of emotional dislocation.

In short, the viewer is at times totally unprepared for the direction of the narrative; uninformed as on several occasions he faces what he can only presume to be tragic events of an irrevocable nature and confused at times by inconsistencies in character, he is practiced upon just as much as certain characters in the plot. The main plot, frankly melodramatic as a result of this lack of comic control, falls short of truly effective comedy.

In sharp contrast, the action of Part II, written entirely by Dekker, is firmly controlled, the structure similar to that of

Shakespeare's most effective comedies. Of primary significance is Orlando Friscobaldo, Bellafront's father, who functions directly as a comic pointer, visibly controlling the various complications and providing through his actions and his comments a sufficiently comic view for the spectator to rest secure that an impenetrable circle of wit has exorcised any dangers of permanent consequence. As a result, the audience achieves a knowledgeable perspective through which it can anticipate a solution to the serious problems of the narrative and an outcome mutually pleasant to each of the principals. In his benevolent practice upon Bellafront, Hippolito, and Matheo, Friscobaldo is joined by Duke Gasparo Trebatzi, whose power is responsible for the final solutions. Dekker introduces, as an additional comic device, Bryan, an Irish footman whose zany activities provide moments of boisterous physical action and whose fractured punctuation—like that of Dr. Caius in *The Merry Wives of Windsor*—produces numerous bawdy doubles entendres. Finally, Dekker sharpens the comic perspective through a subplot featuring the further experiences of Candido the patient linen-draper.

This subplot, more specifically, is made to serve directly the larger design of the drama. Instead of, as in Part I, a narrative strand which involves eight of the fourteen scenes (six exclusively)—to all intents and purposes a double plot with separate complications and resolutions—this material involves only five of thirteen scenes (four exclusively) and, without an independent line of action, assumes its importance from its relationship, both thematic and structural, to the major action.[8] Lodovico's disguise as Candido's apprentice, for example, and his practice upon the new bride parodically parallel the action of the main plot, in which a benevolent practicer will likewise control the action in order to bring correction, adjustment, and eventual reconciliation. The moment the wife kneels in willing submission to her husband, Lodovico (who has coached the patient man in the art of masculine supremacy) removes his disguise with the quip: "I taught him to take thee downe: I hope thou canst take him downe without teaching" (II.ii.126-27). This action (I.iii; II.ii) does, of course, provide broad physical comedy; but, more importantly, with the main plot disguise established in the immediately preceding scene in Act I, and with the first significant activities of the practicer as a servant in his daughter's household occurring between the two farcical scenes, Dekker has obviously constructed the incident as a broadly comic parallel to the more complex issues of the main plot.

The two remaining incidents of the subplot share a similar relationship to the principal action. In III.iii Carolo and Lodovico, determined to cuckold the "patient Linnen Draper" (19) and flout his "fine yong smug Mistris" (20), seek the services of Mistress Horseleech and Bots, who are themselves out to procure fresh ammunition for their behind-door trade. Acting as a pander, Bots whisks the bemused wife aside and prattles on about a "waiting Gentlewoman of my Ladies" who wishes to see her; rebuffed on those grounds he admits in the same breath that the "naked truth is: my Lady hath a yong Knight, her sonne, who loues you" (III.iii.53-4). Although he fails again to arouse either the wife's interest or lust, he maintains his dishonest poise as he informs Carolo to name the afternoon and "she'll meet him at her Garden house" (66). While nothing ever comes of this incident— except Bot's comic punishment in the final act—it is inserted between two moments in which Bellafront faces the temptation to revert to whoredom: in III.ii to satisfy her despairing husband and in III.iv to satisfy the passionate wooer on whom she herself earlier doted. Like the earlier scenes this subplot action is significant only in context as a boisterous parallel to bolster the spectator's comic perspective on the main plot.

Finally, Candido's arrest for possession of stolen goods parallels the arrests of Matheo and Bellafront. Innocently drawn to Matheo's house to purchase certain linens from Matheo, Candido finds himself in the middle of a wild party of gallants who plan to have a "good fit of mirth" (IV.iii.19) by forcing him to drink, dance, and sing bawdy songs. Appalled by the liquor which is forced upon him and by the kiss which Mistress Horseleech bestows (the bawd whose "breath stinkes worse than fifty Polecats" [79]), the flustered linen-draper can muster no defense when the Constable bursts upon the scene with a warrant to "search for such stolne Ware" (170) and proceeds to arrest him ("Why sir? what house I pray? . . . Is't so? thankes, sir: I'm gone. . . . Indeed! . . . Me, sir, for what? . . . Must I so? . . . Ile send for Bayle. . . . To Bridewell to?" [165 et passim]). He is then forgotten at Bridewell until Orlando's practice has been fully exploited upon the main characters, after which he is rescued by the Duke and praised for his patience:

> these greene yong wits
> (We see by Circumstance) this plot hath laid,
> Still to prouoke thy patience, which they finde
> A wall of Brasse, no Armour's like the minde. . . .
> A Patient man's a Patterne for a King.
>
> (V.ii.490-93, 497)

Through the farcical misfortunes of Candido, then, Dekker sharpens the comic tone and blocks the spectators' emotional involvement at a point when the imprisonment of the major characters and the subsequent general reconciliation might otherwise blur the comic perspective. As in the best of Shakespeare's subplots, this material consists of comically stylized characters and of anecdotal incidents arranged and developed to parallel the events of the main plot and thus to strengthen the perspective through which the spectators realize the fuller comic possibilities of the entire play.

The more important structural device, as we have noted, is the function of Orlando Friscobaldo as the major comic pointer.[9] Introduced as an Old Master Merrythought spawning words as he sketches the character of a happy and carefree man ("After this Picture (my Lord) doe I striue to haue my face drawne: For I am not couetous, am not in debt, sit neither at the Dukes side, nor lie at his feete" [I.ii.67-9]), Orlando publicly proclaims his total alienation from his daughter. He immediately informs the audience, however, in a brief soliloquy that his concern is real, that he will "to her, yet she shall not know me: she shall drinke of my wealth, as beggers doe of running water, freely, yet neuer know from what Fountaines head it flowes" (171-73). Presenting himself as Pacheco (who, he avers, last served Orlando Friscobaldo), he seeks service with Matheo, and by slanderous remarks against his previous master he ironically provokes Bellafront to defend her father. The spectator, realizing that each is sincerely concerned for the other, begins to anticipate that their reconciliation will form a part of the general resolution. In his new position Pacheco observes the purse, ring, and letter by which the Duke's son tempts his daughter, and in another soliloquy he expresses his delight that she refuses to receive the bribe:

> [H]old out still, wench.
> All are not Bawds (I see now) that keepe doores,
> Nor all good wenches that are markt for Whores.
>
> (II.i.263-65)

The disguised father begins his direct manipulation of the action Act III as he attempts to protect Bellafront from both Hippolito and Matheo. For one thing, he moves to block Hippolito's access to his daughter. Under the ploy that his mistress' lands are being encircled by a designing neighbor and that she needs the Duke's protection, he gains an audience with Infelice. When she requests a survey of the land, he gives her instead the letter, purse, and ring—evidence of her husband's infidelity. In this manner he hopes, though without success, to stifle Hippolito's lust through Infelice's indignation. For another, he offers money secretly to Bellafront, assuring the spectators a few moments later that, despite Matheo's treatment of his wife, no harm will come to her: "Ile giue him hooke and line, a little more for all this" (III.ii.160). In Act IV Orlando moves directly against the degenerate husband. First, the father (without disguise) visits Matheo and berates him fiercely for his profligacy. Mocking his request for funds when he is so stupid as to "flie high" in an expensive gown he cannot afford in order to "keep the fashion" (i.8) with the "best ranke of gallants" (9) and openly branding him a "Thiefe, . . . a Cheater, Whoremonger, a Pot-hunter, a Borrower, a Begger" (91-2), Orlando forces his son-in-law to hear the truth and warns him of his impending arrest for the robbery of two peddlers (actually Orlando's servants disguised and planted for this purpose). Second, returning in the disguise of Pacheco, he literally saves his daughter from being beaten by the infuriated husband, proclaiming, as the cowardly assailant raises a stool to strike her: "Zownds, doe but touch one haire of her, and Ile so quilt your cap with old iron, that your coxcombe shall ake the worse these seuen yeeres for't" (190-92). Feigning reconciliation a short time later, Pacheco agrees to help Matheo rob his father-in-law, thereby setting the stage for the trap to be sprung upon the young rake.

Since the moment for judgment upon Bellafront, Matheo, and Hippolito requires more authority than Orlando possesses as an ordinary citizen of Milan, his practice in the final stages of the action is combined with the Duke's power. Informed of the entire situation, Trebatzi agrees not to reveal the plot. He then orders the arrest of all prostitutes past and present (a stratagem to get Bellafront in prison and lure Hippolito there to "saue" her) and the arrest of Matheo (on the charge of the previously designed robbery of the two peddlers). At Bridewell each character will more fully reveal his true nature. The dastardly Matheo will refuse to accept the responsibility for his own degeneracy by claiming not only that his wife planned the robbery but also that he caught her in bed with Hippolito; the saintly Bellafront will offer to sacrifice herself for the sake of one who does not deserve her devotion; the repentant Hippolito, whose nobler nature is again stirred, will defend Bellafront's honesty even though to do so is to expose publicly the nature of his own previous lust.

Set in Bridewell (as Part I in Bedlam), the fifth act again creates a heightened fictional tone as the action operates on multiple levels of awareness, all of which the spectator views from a position of omniscience.[10] Orlando, still disguised as Pacheco, stands trial with Matheo for robbery of the two peddlers, actually his own servants. Meanwhile Infelice observes unseen as Hippolito, impelled by lust, rushes to Bellafront. Then, in rapid succession the disguises are peeled away: Infelice steps forward to accuse her guilty husband; Orlando removes his disguise and stands as irrefutable evidence before his guilty son-in-law and his innocent daughter; and Duke Trebatzi reveals the full extent of his role and in like fashion stands before his guilty son-in-law. Acknowledging that he is "here to saue right, and to driue wrong hence" (V.ii.202), the Duke suggests the therapeutic value of the entire ruse in proclaiming Orlando "the true Phisician" (191). Both Hippolito, who admits that his cheek blushes at the ill, and Matheo, who declares himself the "Phisician's" "Patient" (192), are presumably transformed as they face the inescapable truth and stand fully revealed both to themselves and to the surrounding characters.[11] Only the final judgments remain when Bellafront will plead again for her husband, Matheo will be forgiven his faults, and the father will be reconciled with both his "honest" daughter and her mate.

From first to last, then, Orlando's comic spirit hovers over the main plot. Moreover, more systematically than in Part I, minor characters are utilized to sharpen the comic tone throughout the play. Bryan, the Irish footman, for example, appears in three scenes. In I.i he contributes to the comic perspective through the doubles entendres resulting from his difficulties with pronunciation (15-6, 20-1, 179-81). In III.i he provides comic insurance as Infelice reveals to Hippolito her knowledge of his sexual improprieties. In and out of the action like a comically victimized jack-in-the-box, a scapegoat for both the husband and the wife, he helps to prevent the spectators from becoming emotionally involved in a scene with all the narrative earmarks of tragedy. Finally, in III.iii Bryan, playing the part of a gallant, is set upon Candido to tear his fabric and test his patience. Mistress Horseleech and Bots are similar characters. This unwholesome pair furnish further bawdry in III.iii (in which they describe the various "Dishes" offered in their establishment [9-18] and attempt to cuckold Candido) and in IV.iii (in which the befuddled Candido finds himself kissing the bawd and, at Bots' insistence, "pledg[ing] this health . . . to my Mistris, a whore" [93-4]). Finally, in V.ii Dekker—amidst the sensational exposures and reconciliations—maintains an effective comic tone through these "two dishes of stew'd prunes" who remain comic butts throughout the scene. Arrested and dragged on stage, Bots swears that he is no pander, but a soldier who has seen "hottest Seruices in the Low-countries" (227), who was wounded "at the *Groyne*" (228), at *Cleuland*" (cleft-land), and "in *Gelderland*" (231). His pose is shattered, however, as Mistress Horseleech (paraded across the stage with her associates Dorothea Target, Penelope Whorehound, and Catherina Bountinall—like the Bedlamites in Part I) exposes his guilt by recognizing his "sweet face" (400) even though his head is covered in an attempt to conceal his identity.

While Orlando dispenses grace and mercy to those whom he has shocked into repentance, the Duke pronounces sentence upon the pander as the "basest" of all offenders. This incident—in which Bots' corruption is revealed, despite his disguise—becomes a kind of comic inversion of the situation of the main plot—in which a disguise is employed to expose the corrupt and the hypocritical in Matheo and Hippolito.

In sum, the force of evil is viable and active in Part II, and the characters are involved in decisions and problems replete with tragic potential. Even so, through the major comic controller, an effectively contrived subplot, and minor farcical characters who bolster the perspective at potentially critical moments, the spectator is constantly reminded not only that a benevolent authority stands behind the action to prevent disaster from striking but also that this power is directing the action to a conclusion both pleasant and beneficial. The result, like *Northward Ho,* is one of those rare occasions on which a sequel surpasses the original in structural excellence and dramatic effectiveness. In effect, Dekker in Part II retains both the principal characters and the juxtaposition of the farcical with the serio-comic. But he abandons the loose intrigue structure and brings into comic focus a complex and powerful human relationship not unlike those of Shakespeare's later comedies. The evil in man's nature prompts a character to action by which he loses his self-respect and his public reputation. In time, however, such a character, exposed to love in its finest hour—a love which yearns to give and forgive while asking nothing in return—stands fully revealed both to himself and to others. Through this self-knowledge and his subsequent regeneration, he is resorbed into a normal society, and the spectators have reason to assume that he will lead a fuller life as a result of his experience.

Just what spurred Dekker to write the sequel we cannot, of course, precisely determine. Perhaps for some reason he was specifically commissioned to continue the story; perhaps the success of Part I provided economic stimulation; perhaps he was called upon to produce a play on short notice and grabbed at the material freshest in his mind; perhaps the narrative possibilities haunted him as he considered the abrupt conclusion in which Bellafront (quite out of character) tricked Matheo for the sake of an honor which could hardly be regained through a marriage in name only to the first of her many bed partners; perhaps he was struck by the likelihood of disharmony between two intense young lovers, who loved each other passionately despite the insurmountable barriers of family and fate and who now—marriage consummated—suddenly find all opposition gone and adventure past;[12] perhaps the dramatic possibilities haunted him as he envisioned the more effective comedy which could result from a plot firmly structured to maintain the comic perspective throughout.[13]

In any event, given the similarities between *Measure For Measure* and *2 The Honest Whore*,[14] one of the fascinating possibilities concerns the continuing artistic interaction between Dekker and Shakespeare. Both plays depict a young woman willing to strain the quality of mercy in begging for a man who has grossly wronged her. Both involve a young man of political position whose reputation is sorely tarnished by hypocrisy and moral degeneracy but who is ultimately regenerated through the forgiving grace of love. Both also involve a betrothal or marriage temporarily estranged by a man whose venture into crime threatens literally to destroy him. Even more significant are the structural similarities. Both comedies depict a benevolent figure of power and authority who in disguise manipulates the action, as a veritable deus ex machina, in order to send several individuals through a series of moral tests and thereby provide the therapy by which to nourish, in the woman, the forgiving grace of selfless love and, in the men, the shame and repentance that will save them from themselves as well as from the law. Both, moreover, utilize a subplot featuring a prostitute and pander which sardonically parodies the principal action.

Although many Elizabethan comic plots share at least some of these features, it strains probability to assume that this particular relationship is merely coincidental. Not one of the points of similarity concerning character, narrative, or structure is found in *1 The Honest Whore*. Certainly the evidence suggests that in writing Part II Dekker was directly influenced by Shakespeare's play, of which the first recorded performance is December 26, 1604. Dekker and Middleton completed Part I early in 1604, Dekker alone Part II in 1605.[15] Through *Measure For Measure* he apparently realized the greater comic possibilities in the material and was encouraged to create the sequel. Orlando, in fact, is a more firmly conceived comic pointer than Vincentio, though Shakespeare's character is admittedly more profound. In any case, Dekker in Part II has produced a play excellent in structure and firm in characterization;

more important, whether "in response to his own maturing genius,"[16] the fashion of the Jacobean age, or the hand of a master craftsman, he has achieved one of his finest and most substantial works through this comic vision of the transforming power of human love.

Notes

1. "Thomas Dekker," *DNB* (London: Oxford Univ. Press, 1917), V, 750.

2. The "exception to all the generalizations about Dekker's faulty craftsmanship" (Normand Berlin, *The Base String: The Underworld in Elizabethan Drama* [Cranberry, N.J.: Farleigh Dickinson Univ. Press, 1967], p. 12), *The Honest Whore* achieves a great "degree of unity and harmony in conception and construction" (A. C. Swinburne, *The Age of Shakespeare* [London: Chatto and Windus, 1908], p. 73). The two parts "form Dekker's most ambitious and sustained effort" (Mary Leland Hunt, *Thomas Dekker: A Study* [New York: Columbia Univ. Press, 1911], 94), his "most carefully worked out plot" and his most "aesthetically satisfying drama" (Berlin, "Thomas Dekker: A Partial Reappraisal," *SEL,* 6 [1966], 277).

3. *The Honest Whore,* Part II, is "Dekker's masterpiece" (Hazelton Spencer, ed., *Elizabethan Plays* [Boston: Heath, 1933], p. 668), his "finest achievement" (W. W. Greg, as cited without documentation by Peter Ure in "Patient Madmen and Honest Whore: The Middleton-Dekker Oxymoron," *Essays and Studies* [London: Arnold, 1966], p. 18), in which we see a "lightning-like revelation of the recesses of the human soul" (Gamaliel Bradford, "The Women of Dekker," *Sewanee Review,* 33 [1925], 290). A masterfully unified play (Michael Manheim, "The Thematic Structure of Dekker's *2 Honest Whore,*" *SEL,* 5 [1965], 372), it reveals a "great mastery of . . . truth to human feeling (George R. Price, *Thomas Dekker* [New York: Twayne, 1969], 64). treated with "high seriousness, . . . vigor of characterization, and . . . noble poetry" (Hunt, p. 92). It is the rare critic who asserts that "the Second Part falls below the first" (Thomas Marc Parrott and Robert H. Ball, *A Short View of Elizabethan Drama* [New York: Scribner's, 1943], 111) or that it adds little to our knowledge of Dekker" (Arthur Brown, "Citizen Comedy and Domestic Drama," in *Jacobean Theatre,* ed. J. R. Brown and B. Harris [London: Arnold, 1960], 72.

4. The general tone of both plays, "sexy, urban, problematical" (Ure, *Essays and Studies,* p. 18), was shaped in part from a group of plays popular in the first decade of the century, "comedies . . . concerned chiefly with contrasting seeming and actual virtue, chiefly in sexual matters" (Manheim, *SEL,* 372). See also Hunt, p. 92 ff.; and Sidney R. Homan, Jr., "Shakespeare and Dekker as Keys to Ford's *'Tis Pity She's a Whore,*" *SEL,* 7 (1967), 269-76.

5. "A Patient Grizzle out of petticoats, or a Petruchio reversed" (William Hazlitt, *The Complete Works,* ed. P. P. Howe [London: Secker, 1931], VI, 239),

Candido provides the "farcical humor" (Price, p. 60). While Manheim (*SEL*, 372) sees no valid connection with the major action, Harry Keyishian ("Dekker's *Whore* and Marston's *Courtesan*," *ELN*, 4 [1967], 264) views the "advocates of self-control [Hippolito and Candido]" as the heroes of the play; and, to Ure (*Essays and Studies*, p. 27), the converted shrew of the Candido scenes matches the converted courtesan of the Bellafront scenes. Ronald J. Palumbo points out that the parallel between the two is developed early in *1 The Honest Whore* as a contrast between a trade leading to social order with one leading to social disorder ("Trade and Custom in *1 The Honest Whore*," *AN&Q*, 15 [1976], 34-5).

6. Certainly Price (p. 63) assumes more than the context of the scene will allow in his assertion that the spectator would receive assurance and comfort from the "intonation and facial expression" by which Benedict would signal "his secret horror of Gasparo's command to poison Hippolito." For an altogether different view, see A. L. Kistner and M. K. Kistner, "*1 Honest Whore*: A Comedy of Blood," *HAB*, 23, No. 4 (1972), 23-7.

7. Brown (pp. 70-1) notes that Dekker's tongue may have been straying to the middle of his cheek when, in the heat of Bellafront's "tear-jerker confession," he has her refer to Hippolito (her new love) as "meetly legd and thyed" (II.i.271).

8. Ure (*Essays and Studies*, pp. 29-30) deplores the change in Candido as botch-work. To the contrary, Manheim (*SEL*, p. 372) argues strongly for a close unity between main plot and subplot; Candido's taming his shrewish wife is the comic reversal of the Matheo-Bellafront action; so also the humiliation that Candido endures parallels that which Bellafront endures. Berlin (*SEL*, p. 271) suggests further a parallel between Bellafront's virtue and that of Candido's wife when propositioned by Bots.

9. Various critics, while not concerned with structure as such, have noted Friscobaldo's essential function. A "Simon Eyre grown old" (Parrott and Ball, p. 111), he is "the disguised father, who puts Bellafront, Matheo, and Hippolito to the test and thereby glorifies Bellafront's fortitude and reveals the corruption of the two men" (Price, pp. 67-8). "Among the great characters of English comedy" (Hunt, p. 98), "unforgettable" (Hazlitt, p.235), a "protector" and "perpetrator of tests" (Manheim (*SEL*, p. 366), he "controls the action and creates the emergency that enlightens Hippolito" (Keyishian, p. 265).

10. While Hunt (pp. 100-01) describes the Bridewell scene as merely "an appeal to the gallery," both Price and Manheim see a more significant purpose. "The long show of Bridewell birds which follows Matheo's confession . . . allows ample time for him to show his change of heart by caressing Bellafront, though he does not speak" (Price, p. 164 n). The scenes, according to Manheim (*SEL*, p. 381), serve—especially through Dorothea Target—to "recall Bellafront as she first appeared in Part I and thereby to contrast with Bellafront as she now appears." See also Charlotte Spivack, "Bedlam and Bridewell: Ironic Design in *The Honest Whore*," *Komos*, 3 (1973), 10-6.

11. "Matheo and Hippolito are overwhelmed with shame and guilt" (Price, p. 66). Nimitz (p. 129) sees Matheo as a figure of "noteworthy" development, and Hunt (p. 99) quite correctly observes that Dekker does not disturb the integrity of the character with a long and maudlin repentance.

12. Berlin (*SEL*, p. 269) conjectures that Dekker had to write another play "to test the sincerity of her [Bellafront's] conversion."

13. Part II is conceded to be Dekker's unassisted work, whereas Part I is a product of collaboration, however slight Middleton's contributions (See Fredson Bowers, *The Dramatic Works of Thomas Dekker*, 4 Vols. [Cambridge: Cambridge Univ. Press, 1953-1961], III, 133). Schoenbaum's argument that Middleton had no hand in Part I ("Middleton's Share in *The Honest Whore*," *N&Q*, 197 [1952], 3-4) is not generally accepted.

14. F. C. Fleay first noted s similarity in the plays in his observation that both *Measure For Measure* and *2 The Honest Whore* employ a contemporaneous statute "closing the suburb houses" (*A Biographical Chronicle of the English Drama* [London: Reeves and Turner, 1891], I, 132). More recently, Ure (*Essays and Studies*, pp. 36-7) has written that Friscobaldo "conducts an experiment, not always an openly benevolent one, much like the Duke in *Measure For Measure*."

15. Part I can be dated with certainty, and it is generally assumed that Part II followed soon thereafter, probably in 1605. See Jones-Davies, II, 369-71; Bowers, II, 3, 133; G. E. Bentley, *The Jacobean and Caroline Stage* (Oxford: Clarendon, 1956), III, 243; W. Bridges-Adams, *The Irresistible Theatre* (Cleveland: World Publishing Co., 1957), p. 248.

16. Spencer, p. 668.

Viviana Comensoli (essay date 1989)

SOURCE: "Gender and Eloquence in Dekker's *The Honest Whore, Part II*," in *English Studies in Canada*, Vol. XV, No. 3, September 1989, pp. 249-62.

[*In this essay, Comensoli argues that in the second part of* The Honest Whore, "*Dekker has included women in the Renaissance dictum that the practice of eloquence is 'the practice of power'.*"]

In Part I of *The Honest Whore* (1604), which Dekker co-authored with Middleton, the courtesan Bellafront tries to seduce the Count Hippolito, whose oration on the evils of her trade converts her to virtue (II.i.321-456).[1] Hardin Craig has noted that Hippolito's formal diatribe, which effects Bellafront's conversion, "is in the form of the forensic declamations" written by young men "in schools and universities" during the sixteenth century: "The force of persuasion establishes remorse of conscience in her [Bellafront's] heart by presenting to her a true picture of her trade, and her conversion follows as a matter of necessity."[2] Taking Craig's observation one step further, we note that Hippolito's declamation contains three elements which are traditionally associated with forensic rhetoric: the first is persuasion through judgement of former action, in this case the evil of Bellafront's trade (lines 326-423); the second is epideictic function, or the praise of virtue and the blame of vice, which informs all invective; and the third is deliberative function, or the consideration of a future course of action, namely Bellafront's perseverance in virtue (lines 425-56).[3] Ostensibly, at least, the play supports the traditional psychological function of rhetoric as "reformative or reclamatory."[4] Caxton, for one, in his translation of *Miroir du Monde* (1480) ascribes to the orator the ethical duty to "knowe the right and the wronge; ffor to doo wronge to another, who so doth it is loste and dampned, and for to doo right and reson to euery man, he is saued and geteth the loue of God his creatour."[5] Lawrence Andrewe's expanded version of Caxton's translation further defines rhetoric as "a scyence to cause another man by speche or by wrytynge to beleue or to do that thynge whyche thou woldest haue hym for to do."[6] Henry Peacham, writing in 1593, praises in similar fashion the figures of rhetoric as "martiall instruments both of defence & invasion" which permit us to "defend ourselves-,invade our enemies, revenge our wrongs, ayd the weake, deliver the simple from dangers, conserve true religion, & confute idolatry."[7] A warning sounded in many sixteenth- and seventeenth-century treatises on rhetorical and ethical practice "is that men will fall into vice without the good offices of the orator."[8]

Harry Keyishian, who finds the conversion scene in *The Honest Whore, Part I* strongly "sentimental," voices a common response when he writes that in the success of "the earnest, rational, puritanical Hippolito" who "not only resists temptation but converts his tempter . . . Dekker gives victory to traditional morality."[9] Yet, while Hippolito himself claims his intention has been to persuade Bellafront "mildly" and "not without sense or reason" (II.i.317), a number of ambiguities suggest the dramatists' uneasiness with forensic oratory as a universal form of persuasion. Throughout the play, Hippolito is frequently subject to sudden fits of melancholy as he mourns over the supposed death of his lover. Hippolito, observes a courtier moments prior to Bellafront's conversion, "betraies his youth too grosly to that tyrant melancholy" (II,i.204), a "disease" which Hippolito himself admits has made him "sicke" of love (IV.iv.103-04). At other times Hippolito is portrayed in a hot distemper, a condition which affects him as he enters Bellafront's home (II.i.244-48). The sensation of heat, according to medieval and Renaissance physiology, if caused by humoral imbalance, was a symptom of madness, which in turn was considered a "punishment for moral corruption."[10] Indeed, Hippolito's diatribe attests to a corrupt rational faculty. His invective is based on Christian ascetic morality, but it is expressed with a new virulence. The prostitute's body is compared to a sewer that "receiues / All the townes filth" (II.i.325-26), and to a plague that has "maym'd and dismembred" as many men "As would ha stuft an Hospitall" (lines 332-33). The images of excrement and mutilation combine with a bewildering array of images of voluptuousness, disease, and death, in keeping with the extreme cynicism and fearfulness associated with melancholia:

> O y'are as base as any beast that beares,
> Your body is ee'ne hirde, and so are theirs.
> . . . . .
> A harlot is like *Dunkirke,* true to none,
> Swallowes both English, Spanish, fulsome Dutch,
> Blacke-beard Italian, last of all the French,
> And he sticks to you faith: giues you your diet,
> Brings you acquainted, first with monsier Doctor,
> And then you know what followes. . . .
> Me thinks a toad is happier then a whore,
> That with one poison swells, with thousands more
> The other stocks her veines. . . .

>   (II.i.335-62)

Hippolito's invective overstrains the epideictic function of praise and blame; his language debases and degrades its objects, stripping Bellafront of her humanity.

Another major complication surrounding Bellafront's conversion is that her transition to virtue has been incited by an erotic attraction to her reformer. This ironic twist, together with Bellafront's highly stylized repentance-speech, renders suspect her reformation:

>   Eyther loue me,
> Or cleaue my bosome on thy Rapiers poynt:
> Yet doe not neyther; for thou then destroyst
> That which I loue thee for (thy vertues) here, here,
> Th'art crueller, and kilst me with disdayne:
> To die so, sheds no bloud, yet tis worse payne.
> *Exit* Hipolito.
>
> Not speake to me! not looke! not bid farewell
> Hated! this must not be, some means Ile try.
> Would all Whores were as honest now, as I.

>   (II.i.448-56)

The contradictory messages the spectator receives in *Part I* of the play give way to a more controlled comic plot in *Part II* (c. 1605-07), where Hippolito's moral backsliding and rhetorical limitations are confirmed, and where Dekker more forcefully and consistently questions the power of purely persuasive rhetoric to influence behaviour. Concomitant with this critique is the challenge at the heart of the play to another traditional assumption, namely that the practice of eloquence is the exclusive province of male virtue.

I

In *Part II* Bellafront is the patient wife of the spendthrift Matheo, who urges her to return to prostitution to cadge money. To intensify Bellafront's misery, Hippolito (who is married to the Duke's daughter Infelice) is now clearly lusting after Bellafront. A Jacobean audience familiar with the popular motif of the wife's temptation in domestic comedy would expect Bellafront to reject her suitor with piety and humility, and to follow up the rejection with a series of platitudes on the need for constancy in marriage and on the wife's duty to submit to her husband's will. Dekker, however, avoids the stock speeches of the patient wife, subjecting Hippolito both to Bellafront's eloquent resistance of the Count's advances and to Infelice's trenchant critique of the myth of the male's natural superiority. Both women defeat Hippolito in debate, even though his formal training in forensic oratory gives him a clear advantage.[11]

The play's analogues are a group of domestic comedies which were performed in the public theatres between 1600 and 1608. The chief dramatic paradigm is the testing of the wife's patience within a turbulent marriage. Michael Manheim observes that "a number of these comedies are built around a juxtaposition of tests, in which hypocrisy and deceit are revealed and condemned while virtue and patience are glorified."[12] The testing motif is a major structure in Thomas Heywood's *How a man May Choose a Good Wife from a Bad* (c. 1601-02) and in the anonymous *Fair Maid of Bristow* (c. 1603-04) and *The London Prodigal* (1604). The heroine is always an abused and patient wife whose trials move the plot forward. The husband-hero is a wastrel and a profligate whose backsliding precipitates his near-demise. Sometimes another principal character is a young man who is lusting after the heroine: "All three of these character types are tested: the youth by his lust, the husband by his bad luck, and the wife by the abuses of her husband on the one hand and the advances of the youth on the other."[13] Only the heroine is morally equipped to pass the trials. In the dénouement, following the husband's and the youth's repentance, she meekly receives public commendation, and the play ends with a series of hortatory speeches on the necessity of wifely patience and modesty. Thus in *How a Man May Choose a Good Wife from a Bad* Mistress Arthur is subjected to the cruelty of her husband, who poisons her in order to please his whore. After being rescued by Anselm, the lusty but sympathetic youth who offers to marry her and alleviate her suffering, the wife modestly rejects his advances with mundane speeches in praise of fortitude and perseverance. She never relies on eloquence as a weapon. In all of these comedies, characterization is subordinated to the didacticism of the conductbooks and other writings on domestic behaviour. As Peter Ure suggests, the "ethical basis" of most domestic comedies is "the doctrine, reiterated everywhere in the treatises, that the wife should win her mate with mildness."[14] Once the husband's reformation is secured, he must learn to command his household wisely and mercifully, although his success depends largely on his wife's virtue. *How a Man May Choose,* for example, ends with the reformed prodigal's advice to would-be husbands on how to choose between a good and a bad wife: "A good wife," we learn, will quietly "do her husband's will" endure provocation, and "conceal / Her husband's dangers," whereas "a bad wife" will neglect her "home" and be "cross, spiteful and madding."[15]

The homiletic basis of the genre is the conventional Renaissance notion that man perfects his virtue through command and eloquence, whereas woman perfects hers through obedience and silence. The notion evolved out of two major traditions: the Greek, which considered women naturally passive, and the patristic, which urged that women be silent as a consequence of Eve's glibness, which was responsible for the fall. "You are the one who opened the door to the Devil," wrote Tertullian of woman, "you are the one who persuaded him whom the Devil was not strong enough to attack"; "unable to remain silent," Eve made Adam "the carrier of that which she had imbibed from the Evil One."[16] From the Middle Ages to the seventeenth century the resistance to women practising eloquence was widespread. Francis Barbaro, for one, claimed that "By silence, indeed, women achieve the fame of eloquence."[17] The Aristotelian philosopher Francesco Robortello urged woman to submit her will to that of her husband on the basis of her moral weakness, which stemmed from faulty reasoning powers.[18] Virtue, we are frequently reminded in philosophical discourses, originally meant the quality of manliness, *vir* meaning man. For the traveller Thomas Coryat, who in 1608 warned his fellow-Englishmen of the dangers of the "elegant . . . Rhetoricall tongue" of Venetian courtesans,[19] men's virtue is threatened by female eloquence, for "to encounter a 'public woman' is to risk the casuistries of a previously masculine discourse."[20] As Margaret King, Ian Maclean, and Lisa Jardine have demonstrated, English and continental humanists also upheld social demarcations between men and women, despite their recommendations that women, who were considered morally equal to men, should be learned.[21] Moral philosophers such as Erasmus, Agrippa, and Vives, while viewing male and female virtue as identical, and while allowing for women to be educated, nevertheless affirmed the orthodox view of woman's natural tendency toward silence and humility, and of man's duty to command eloquently. The educator Leonardo Bruni urged women to study the liberal arts, but warned that "Rhetoric in all its forms,—public discussion, forensic argument, logical fence, . . .—lies absolutely outside the province of woman."[22] Similarly, Neoplatonic works such as Castiglione's *Book of the Courtier* (1528) and Nicholas Faret's *L'honnête homme* (1630), which propose identical capacities for virtue in men and women, insist that women's domestic function requires them to practise certain virtues not required in men, that is, modesty and silence, releasing them from the need to cultivate virtues which relate especially to men's role in the household, namely courage and eloquence. "This strategy of argument," suggests Maclean, "may reflect . . . no more than lip-service to the enhancement of the status of woman, and conservatism for its own sake, perhaps justified by a fear of the effects of social change."[23]

Dekker's rescue of the patient wife from a reductive dramatic tradition is the major achievement of *The Honest Whore, Part II.* Although the main plot, like its analogues, focuses on the plight of the wife, and ultimately upholds the virtue of patience—"Women," declares Bellafront at the end of the play, "shall learne of me, / To loue their husbands in greatest misery" (v.ii.468-69)—the action builds on a series of complications that displace orthodox structures and themes. In the Hippolito-Infelice action, marital conflict is resolved not through the wife's meekness but through the boldness of her language. In the Bellafront plot, the tests of the wife become the trials of a converted whore, who passes them with the aid of eloquence and courage as she struggles against economic destitution and social mistrust.

II

The issue of the wife's behaviour is thrown into relief in the confrontation scene between Hippolito and Infelice, who has learned of the count's desire for the former courtesan. Throughout the episode, Infelice capably directs the subject-matter and tenor of the conversation. Relying on reason and rhetorical virtuosity, she ultimately succeeds in exposing Hippolito's transgression by means of a riddle. "Expressing conflict between poser and solver," writes Linda Woodbridge, "riddles are often associated with women as with other classes not in authority—riddlers have power to make even an authority-figure look foolish."[24] As "a natural tool for combat between the sexes," the riddle frequently "occurs as a marriage test."[25] Infelice's verbal weapon is a complex form of the riddle known as emblematic vision, a type of metaphor which depends on "descriptive containment . . . [whereby] the subject is not described but circumscribed . . . [through] a circle of words drawn around it," and which is "closely related to . . . the parable."[26] The central image in Infelice's riddle is the clock, through which Hippolito is gradually forced to equate the absence of synchronism with discord in marriage (III.i.107-15). As the riddle increases in subtlety, Infelice displays an agile and inventive mind:

Hip. Why, *Infelice,* what should make you sad?

Inf. Nothing my lord, but my false watch, pray tell me,
You see, my clocke, or yours is out of frame,
Must we vpon the Workeman lay the blame,
Or on our selues that keep them?

(III.i.121-25)

Refusing to yield to her husband's blandishments, and to the socially sanctioned role of silence, Infelice startles Hippolito with a bold parody of his former diatribe against women as the downfall of men. Hippolito's apostrophe

oh women
You were created Angels, pure and faire;
But since the first fell, tempting Deuils you are,
You should be mens blisse, but you proue their rods:
Were there no Women, men might liue like gods . . .

(III.i.161-65)

is matched by Infelice's equally forceful injunction, through which she exposes his bombast and secures his admission of guilt:

Inf.   Oh Men,
You were created Angels, pure and faire,

But since the first fell, worse then Deuils you are.
You should our shields be, but you proue our rods.
Were there no Men, Women might liue like gods.
Guilty my Lord?

Hip. Yes, guilty my good Lady.

(III.i.186-92)

Rather than forgive her husband, Infelice commands him from her—"Nay, you may laugh, but henceforth shun my bed" (III.i.193)—challenging both his intellectual and sexual dominance.

Infelice's exhortations, her parody of Hippolito's language, and her complaint about the treachery of men render her outspoken and wilful. Dekker, moreover, never subordinates Infelice's behaviour to a more conventional ideal.[27] Throughout the play she insists on her need for self-expression in marriage, firmly rejecting the role of passive suffering. The latitude Dekker allows the aristocrat Infelice, whose rhetorical skills contrast sharply with the pious verse expected of patient wives in domestic comedies, can be partly attributed to verisimilitude with respect to class. A few women, notably rulers and others of aristocratic descent, were in principle allowed to cultivate eloquence in the public theatres, particularly in tragedy. Cinthio Giraldi, the sixteenth-century critic and playwright, observed that it was common theatrical practice for young ladies to be humble and for matrons to be not only decorous but servile as well: no woman of humble birth should exhibit wit, but aristocratic women, who were considered more knowledgeable and not strictly bound by domestic duties, were permitted to show more intelligence than their less sophisticated counterparts.[28] In order to find other female characters on the English stage who unequivocally challenge the dictum of silence we must therefore go beyond the confines of domestic comedy, although most of these plays are written after *The Honest Whore, Part II.* Normally, with the exception of Webster's Vittoria Corombona and to a lesser extent the Duchess of Malfi, such characters are not, as Infelice is not, the central figures of the play. Their function, like Infelice's, is to expose the transgressions of a male who is usually central to the action: cases in point are Tamyra and Charlotte in *The Revenge of Bussy D'Ambois,* Castabella in *The Atheist's Tragedy,* Marina in *Pericles,* and Hermione in *The Winter's Tale.*[29] Even in an earlier play such as *As You Like It,* where an assertive female has the leading role, a strong ambiguity surrounds Rosalind's verbal dexterity, which she practises in male disguise. Dekker's portrayal of female sagacity therefore breaks completely with the general rule of decorum when he makes Bellafront, a former prostitute from the ranks of the Jacobean underworld and the main character in the play, Infelice's intellectual equal. Dekker's interest in portraying intelligent, articulate females seems to have influenced later domestic plays, among them Nathan Field's *Amends for Ladies* (1610) and John Ford's *The Broken Heart* (1633), both of which include strong female leads. This interest is also sustained in the collaborations in which Dekker's was likely the controlling hand, namely the *Ho* plays (1605-07), **The Roaring Girl** (c. 1608-11), and **The Witch of Edmonton** (1621).

III

On the one hand, the Bellafront-Hippolito debate is rhetorically familiar in that it defends the ethical value of constancy in marriage. Michael Manheim has noted that through Hippolito's "specious" attempts to corrupt Bellafront, Dekker "is showing that lust and adultery cannot logically be defended"; Manheim's claim, however, that "Bellafront's victory is not surprising"[30] is not borne out by the dramatic and philosophical traditions which the play modifies. The unconventional appeal of the verbal conflict lies in the tension between Hippolito's rhetorical initiative, which is opportunistic and exploitative because it is ill-motivated,[31] and Bellafront's, which, although it does not rely on specialist knowledge, is rational, imaginative, and well-motivated.

Appealing to the support of the men in the audience (IV.i.256-59), Hippolito vainly asserts that he will seduce Bellafront "with the power of Argument" (line 249). While his proposal that prostitutes have more freedom than other women is rhetorically embellished through figures and hypotheses, it is nevertheless based on faulty logic,[32] as Bellafront's taunt implies:

> If all the threds
> Of Harlots lyues be fine as you would make them,
> Why doe not you perswade your wife turne whore,
> And all Dames else to fall before that sin?
>
> (IV.i.347-50)

Hippolito's unsuccessful strategy in conquering Bellafront "By force of strong perswasion" (line 252) confirms Dekker's doubts about persuasion as a moral construct in itself, a view consistent with his treatment of rhetoric in his prose pamphlets. These rely substantially on the method of Peter Ramus, for whom logic alone is capable of discovering truth, while persuasion "belong[s] to rhetoric and [is] merely decorative and ornamental."[33] Persuasion, according to a late sixteenth-century Ramian treatise, is the "arte of speaking finely,"[34] and can be employed only after a premise has been logically proposed. For the Spanish logician Juan Huarte, who like Dekker supports natural ability in learning and speaking, refinement of speech does not in itself promote true eloquence, which is governed by understanding.[35] Dekker's portrayal of an orator's use of persuasion to exploit and manipulate behaviour links him to a small group of English-Renaissance writers and commentators, including Shakespeare and Sidney, who could admit that if rhetoric could move the will to virtue it could also "enforce an evil cause, and impugne a good one."[36]

Hippolito's faulty reasoning thus cannot win over his opponent. But while Bellafront is not permitted to yield to her suitor, Dekker does not restrict her intellectual horizon. Bellafront's rejection of Hippolito is dramatically unorthodox not only because it claims for her a heretofore male

prerogative, but also because it lends psychological depth to her character, an element conspicuously lacking in the play's analogues. The first half of her argument conforms in tone to a forensic oration. Bellafront's language is formal and logical as she marshals evidence from Biblical history and Common Law to uphold the sanctity of monogamy (IV.i.301-08). Her claim that in the city of London "one woman" is now "shared betweene three hundred" (309-10) leads to a lengthy deliberation on the evils of prostitution, only ostensibly imitating Hippolito's declamation in **Part I**:

> Common? as spotted Leopards, whom for sport
> Men hunt, to get the flesh, but care not for't.
> So spread they Nets of gold, and tune their Calls,
> To inchaunt silly women to take falls:
>
> . . . . .
> men loue water,
> It serues to wash their hands, but (being once foule)
> The water downe is powred, cast out of doores,
> And euen of such base vse doe men make whores.
>
> (IV.i.311-21)

Like Hippolito's invective, Bellafront's relies on "mundane imagery—animals and sewage disposal,"[37] however, a significant shift in focus renders Bellafront's oration more vital. Whereas Hippolito portrayed men as completely at the mercy of the whore's "prettie Art" and "cunning net" (*Part I,* II.i.279), her "tycing" charms (282) "hook[ing] in a kind gentleman" only to leave him pox-ridden (305-08), Bellafront offers a more authentic picture of her former trade in which poor and naïve young women are easy prey to a depraved libertine attitude. As she calmly and logically develops her points, the argument becomes a strategic indictment of a money economy which exploits women and sex:

> Say you should taste me,
> I serue but for the time, and when the day
> Of warre is done, am casheerd out of pay:
> If like lame Soldiers I could beg, that's all,
> And there's lusts Rendez-vous, an Hospitall.
> Who then would be a mans slaue, a mans woman?
> She's halfe staru'd the first day that feeds in Common.
>
> (IV.i.324-30)

In the second half of the argument Bellafront unifies the disputation with subjective content, appealing to the spectator's understanding. Here Bellafront achieves eloquence through natural ability, highlighting the complexity of her experience.

> Like an ill husband (tho I knew the same,
> To be my vndoing) followed I that game.
> Oh when the worke of Lust had earn'd my bread,
> To taste it, how I trembled, lest each bit,
> Ere it went downe, should choake me (chewing it).
> My bed seem'd like a Cabin hung in Hell,
> The Bawde Hells Porter, and the lickorish wine
> The Pander fetch'd, was like an easie Fine,
> For which, me thought I leas'd away my soule,

And oftentimes (euen in my quaffing bowle)
Thus said I to my selfe, I am a whore,
And haue drunke downe thus much confusion more.

                                              (IV.i.351-62)

The exemplum is an evocative description of the psycho-logical effects of prostitution. In isolation these twelve lines, with their terse phrasing and gnomic tone, constitute an epigram. "What distinguishes, not simply the epigram, but profundity itself from platitude," observes Northrop Frye, "is very frequently rhetorical wit" employed in a verbal strategy which, unlike purely "persuasive rhetoric," seeks the fusion of "emotion and intellect."[38] In the final couplet there is a powerful moment of self-confrontation as Bellafront's burdened spirit is revealed in the spondaic rhythms of her verse: "And háue drúnke dówne th˘s múch c˘nfús˘on móre." The term "confusion" signifies both moral and psychological stasis: its ethical denotation is the discomfiture of moral purpose; in Renaissance psychology, the term also refers to "mental perturbation or agitation such as prevents the full command of the faculties" (OED), a predisposition to madness.[39]

Bellafront's reformation, moreover, has not been portrayed schematically. A number of critics have noted that during another trial of Bellafront's patience, in which her husband orders her to pawn everything, including her gown, Bella-front's rebuke of Matheo flouts the convention urging wives to submit humbly and serenely to their husbands' will:[40]

Thou art a Gamester, prethee throw at all,
Set all vpon one cast, we kneele and pray,
And struggle for life, yet must be cast away.
Meet misery quickly then, split all, sell all,
And when thou hast sold all, spend it, but I beseech thee
Build not thy mind on me to coyne thee more. . . .

                                              (III.ii.65-70)

While Bellafront's suffering is consistent with the human-ist view of patience and endurance as the area where female virtue equalled that of men, she shares with Infe-lice a bold disregard for the ethic of silent submission, altering the paradigm of eloquence and courage as male virtues.

IV

In the subplot, orthodox schemes are further undermined through parody and farce. The hero of the subplot is Can-dido, the patient linendraper who in *The Honest Whore, Part I* was married to the shrew Viola. In *Part II* Viola has died, and we meet the linendraper on the day of his wedding to a new wife whom Dekker never names (she is merely called "Bride" throughout the play). The wedding scene is interposed between Act I, scene i, which establishes the Hippolito-Infelice conflict, and Act II, scene i, which introduces the Bellafront-Matheo action. The wed-ding is celebrated amid abundant food and drink, contrast-ing sharply with the abject poverty of Bellafront's household and the domestic conflicts of the main plot. However, the festivity is suddenly interrupted when the Bride cuffs a servant for serving her sack instead of claret. Candido hurriedly makes excuses for her, and she leaves the celebration in anger. Candido's marital difficulties serve throughout as "a broadly comic parallel to the more complex issues of the main plot."[41] The testing pattern in the subplot, for instance, directly echoes the testing of patience in the main plot; more importantly, it parodies conventional formulas for a happy marriage. The courtier Lodovico, who secretly sets out to cuckold the linendrap-er's wife, pretends to be a concerned friend who desires to coach Candido in taming his rebellious wife.

LOD. This wench (your new wife) will take you downe
in your wedding shooes, vnlesse you hang her vp in
her wedding garters.

CAN. How, hang her in her garters?

LOD. Will you be a tame Pidgeon still? shall your backe
be like a Tortoys shell, to let Carts goe ouer it, yet not
to breake? This Shee-cat will haue more liues then
your last Pusse had, and will scratch worse, and mouze
you worse: looke toot.

                                              (I.iii.100-07)

Lodovico's barnyard imagery—"the Hen shall not ouer-crow the Cocke" (120-21)—and his advice to the linen-draper to "Sweare, swagger, brawle, fling; for fighting it's no matter, we ha had knocking Pusses enow already" (109-11) underscore a primitive attitude toward sexual conflict, which is never disputed by the linendraper. Lodovico's crude invectives against women and his claim that wives must be forcefully commanded by their husbands because "a woman was made of the rib of a man, and that rib was crooked" (111-12) mimic the traditional theological and scholastic view of woman's imperfection, a view severely undercut by the qualifications in the main plot.

Because Candido must uphold his reputation as a model of patience, he agrees to be coached by Lodovico "In any thing that's ciuill, honest, and iust" (I.iii.116). Convinced by Lodovico's promise that the coaching will be in jest, Candido agrees to master his wife, although his eagerness for the game undermines his concern with civility: "A curst Cowes milke I ha drunke once before, / And 'twas so ranke in taste, Ile drinke no more. / Wife, Ile tame you" (II.ii.72-4). Alexander Leggatt has observed that the battle between Candido and his wife "is conducted on the level of slapstick, with symbolic overtones: they prepare to fence, he with a yard and she with an ell. 'Yard' being a common term for the male sex organ, its use here suggests an elemental sexual conflict."[42] The comic theatricality of the testing leads to an equally absurd conclusion in which the couple is reconciled when the wife kneels in willing submission to her husband, promising to be forever patient and silent only if he will master her (II.ii.104-15). Only after the Bride has learned the lesson of humility does Candido reveal to her Lodovico's true identity, admitting his anger was in jest. Ironically, aggression, not patience, has brought about the reconciliation. Candido has learned that women desire their husbands to exert their dominance, but farce and parody have exposed the folly of the platitude.

The farcical behaviour of husband and wife in the subplot is thus counter-pointed by the resolutions of the main plot, where Bellafront's eloquence and frankness are as admirable as her patience, and where Infelice's virtues include a strong will and independence of mind. Through these complications Dekker has included women in the Renaissance dictum that the practice of eloquence is "the practice of power."[43]

Notes

1. *The Dramatic Works of Thomas Dekker*, ed. Fredson Bowers, 4 vols. (Cambridge: Cambridge Univ. Press, 1953-61), 2. Further references to Parts I and II of the play will be to this edition.

2. Hardin Craig, *The Enchanted Glass: The Renaissance Mind in Literature* (1935; rpt. Oxford: Basil Blackwell, 1952), p. 175.

3. For a comprehensive account of the features of forensic rhetoric and its development in England, see Richard J. Schoeck, "Lawyers and Rhetoric in Sixteenth-Century England," in *Renaissance Eloquence: Studies in the Theory and Practice of Renaissance Rhetoric*, ed. James J. Murphy (Berkeley, Los Angeles, and London: Univ. of California Press, 1983), pp. 274-91.

4. Brian Vickers, "'The Power of Persuasion': Images of the Orator, Elyot to Shakespeare," in *Renaissance Eloquence*, pp. 411-35; p. 420.

5. *Caxton's Mirrour of the World*, ed. O. L. Prior, EETS, OS 90 (London: Oxford Univ. Press, 1913), p. 36.

6. *The Arte or Crafte of Rhethoryke* (1524), ed. F. I. Carpenter (Chicago: Univ. of Chicago Press, 1899), p. 26.

7. *The Garden of Eloquence*, ed. W. G. Crane (Gainesville, Fla.: Scholars' Facsimiles and Reprints, 1954), sig. ABiv[r].

8. Vickers, p. 420.

9. Harry Keyishian, "Dekker's *Whore* and Marston's *Courtesan*," *English Language Notes*, 4 (1967), 262, 264. Mary Leland Hunt, in *Thomas Dekker: A Study* (New York: Columbia Univ. Press, 1911), p. 97, praises the dramatic impact of Bellafront's conversion as "a slow process involving the horror of past vileness, the anguish of rejected love, and continued hunger, blows, and abuse." Similarly, for Anne M. Haselkorn, in *Prostitution in Elizabethan and Jacobean Comedy* (New York: Whitson, 1983), the conversion is "very gradual and realistic" (p. 118), Dekker's "Puritan morality" requiring "that the sinner must suffer in order to achieve purification and true redemption" (p. 125). Alfred Harbage, in *Shakespeare and the Rival Traditions* (New York: Macmillan, 1952), considers the play "a tract against prostitution" (p. 197).

10. Lillian Feder, *Madness in Literature* (Princeton: Princeton Univ. Press, 1980), p. 101. See also Michael MacDonald, *Mystical Bedlam: Madness, Anxiety and Healing in Seventeenth-Century England* (Cambridge: Cambridge Univ. Press, 1981), pp. 182-83.

11. Dekker's accomplishment in portraying Bellafront's defeat of Hippolito in debate has been noted by Madeleine Doran, in *Endeavors of Art: A Study of Form in Elizabethan Drama* (Madison, Wis.: Univ. of Wisconsin Press, 1954), p. 222; M.-T. Jones-Davies, in *Un Peintre de la Vie Londonienne: Thomas Dekker*, 2 vols. (Paris: Didier, 1958), 2, 198-99; Michael Manheim, in "The Thematic Structure of Dekker's *2 Honest Whore*," *Studies in English Literature*, 5 (1965), 378; and Anne M. Haselkorn, *Prostitution in Elizabethan and Jacobean Comedy*, pp. 126-27. However, none of these critics locates the play's rhetorical innovations within the broader philosophical context of classical or Renaissance notions of male and female eloquence.

12. Manheim, "The Thematic Structure of Dekker's *2 Honest Whore*," 365.

13. Manheim, 365.

14. "Marriage and the Domestic Drama in Heywood and Ford," *English Studies*, 32 (1951), 202. See also Andrew Clark, *Domestic Drama: A Survey of the Origins, Antecedents and Nature of the Domestic Play in England, 1500-1640*, 2 vols. (Salzburg: Universität Salzburg, 1975), 2, 251.

15. Thomas Heywood, *How a Man May Choose a Good Wife from a Bad*, in Robert Dodsley, *A Select Collection of Old English Plays*, 4th edn., ed. W. Carew Hazlitt, 14 vols. (1874-1876; rpt. New York and London: Blom, 1964), 9, 96.

16. *Disciplinary, Moral and Ascetical Works*, trans. Rudolph Arbesmann, Sister Emily Joseph Daly, and Edwin A. Quain (New York: Fathers of the Church, Inc., 1959), pp. 118, 200. For a detailed discussion of misogyny in patristic teachings see Marina Warner, "Second Eve," in her *Alone of All Her Sex: The Myth and Cult of the Virgin Mary* (New York: Knopf, 1976), ch. 4.

17. "On Wifely Duties," in *The Earthly Republic*, ed. B. Kohl and R. Witt (Philadelphia: Univ. of Pennsylvania Press, 1978), p. 206.

18. *In libro politicos. Aristotelis disputatio* (Venice, 1552), p. 175.

19. *Coryat's Crudities* (1611; rpt. Glasgow: James MacLehose, 1905), 1, 405; cited in Ann Rosalind Jones, "City Women and Their Audiences: Louise Labe and Veronica Franco," in *Rewriting the Renaissance: The Discourses of Sexual Difference in Early Modern Europe*, ed. Margaret W. Ferguson, Maureen Quilligan, and Nancy J. Vickers (Chicago and London: Univ. of Chicago Press, 1986), p. 304.

20. Ann Rosalind Jones, p. 304.

21. Margaret L. King, "Book-Lined Cells: Women and Humanism in the Early Italian Renaissance," in *Beyond Their Sex: Learned Women of the European Past*, ed. Patricia H. Labalme (New York and London: New York Univ. Press, 1980), pp. 66-90; Ian Maclean, *The Renaissance Notion of Woman: A*

Study in the Fortunes of Scholasticism and Medical Science in European Intellectual Life (Cambridge: Cambridge Univ. Press, 1980), ch. 4; Lisa Jardine, "'O decus Italiae virgo' or, The Myth of the Learned Lady in the Renaissance," *The Historical Journal*, 28 (1985), 799-819.

22. *De Studiis et Literis,* in William Harrison Woodward, *Vittorino da Feltre and Other Humanist Educators: Essays and Versions* (1897; rpt., ed. Eugene F. Rice, Jr., New York: Teachers College, Columbia Univ., 1963), pp. 119-33; p. 126.

23. *The Renaissance Notion of Woman,* p. 56.

24. Linda Woodbridge, "Black and White and Red All Over: The Sonnet Mistress Amongst the Ndembu," *Renaissance Quarterly,* 40 (Summer, 1987), 285.

25. Woodbridge, 285.

26. Northrop Frye, *Anatomy of Criticism* (1957; rpt. Princeton: Princeton Univ. Press, 1971), p. 300.

27. Dekker's "feminist statement," writes Anne Parten of Infelice's speech in III.i.186-90, "is allowed to stand uncorrected" ("Masculine Adultery and Feminine Rejoinders in Shakespeare, Dekker and Sharpham," *Mosaic,* 17, I [Winter 1984], 13).

28. Cinthio Giraldi, *Discorsi intorno al comporre de i romanzi, delle comedie, e delle tragedie* (Venice, 1549), pp. 259-63; 271-76; cited in Doran, *Endeavors of Art,* p. 221.

29. Simon Shepherd, in *Amazons and Warrior Women: Varieties of Feminism in Seventeenth-Century Drama* (Brighton: Harvester Press, 1981), p. 112, notes that "in the case of female avengers" the women express "doctrines that were supposedly anathema to the assumed orthodoxy of patience," but the reason the dramatists do not temper these characters' outspokenness is that "they are not in the central focus" of the action.

30. "The Thematic Structure of Dekker's *2 Honest Whore,*" 378.

31. On the problem of rhetorical presentation which is opportunistic and which therefore subverts the ideal ethical function of rhetoric as the unveiling of truth, see Lisa Jardine, *Francis Bacon: Discovery and the Art of Discourse* (London and New York: Cambridge Univ. Press, 1974), pp. 15-6.

32. Manheim, 377.

33. Peter C. Schwartz, "Ramus and Dekker: The Influence of Ramian Logic and Method on the Form and Content of Seventeenth-Century Pamphlet Literature," diss., Bowling Green, 1978, p. 38.

34. Dudley Fenner, *The Artes of Logike and Rhethorike* (Middleburg, 1584), sig. Dl^v; cited in Schwartz, p. 38.

35. *Examen de Ingenios: The Examination of Men's Wits* (1594), trans. Richard Carew, ed. Carmen Rodgers (Gainesville, Fla.: Scholars Facsimiles and Reprints, 1959), p. 13; cited in Don Abbott, "La Retórica y el Renacimiento: An Overview of Spanish Theory," in James J. Murphy, ed., *Renaissance Eloquence,* pp. 95-104; pp. 98-9.

36. Vickers, "'The Power of Persuasion': Images of the Orator, Elyot to Shakespeare," p. 421. "Where the theorists stress the power of rhetoric to reclaim men from evil to good," writes Vickers (p. 423), they are silent about "its relation to, or propensity to be used by, evil" (p. 421).

37. Manheim, 378.

38. *Anatomy of Criticism,* p. 329.

39. See Lillian Feder, *Madness in Literature,* p. 103.

40. See Manheim, 369-70; M.-T. Jones-Davies, *Un Peintre de la Vie Londonienne,* 2, 198-99; and G. Nageswara Rao, *The Domestic Drama* (Tirupati: Sri Venkateswara Univ. Press [1978?]), ch. 1.

41. Larry S. Champion, *Thomas Dekker and the Traditions of English Drama* (New York: Peter Lang, 1985), p. 47. Like many commentators, Champion considers the Candido action dramatically significant only insofar as it "sharpens the comic tone" of the play: "this material consists of comically stylized characters and of anecdotal incidents arranged and developed to parallel the events of the main plot and thus to strengthen the perspective through which the spectators realize the fuller comic possibilities of the entire play" (p. 48). For Manheim, Candido's role as "the 'patient husband' who finally subdues a shrewish wife . . . is little more than a comic reversal of the Matheo-Bellafront action" (p. 372, n. 5).

42. Alexander Leggatt, *Citizen Comedy in the Age of Shakespeare* (Toronto and Buffalo: Univ. of Toronto Press, 1973), p. 92.

43. Nancy Struever, "Lorenzo Valla: Humanist Rhetoric and the Critique of the Classical Languages of Morality," in James J. Murphy, ed., *Renaissance Eloquence,* pp. 191-206; p. 204.

THE ROARING GIRL

CRITICAL COMMENTARY

Mary Beth Rose (essay date 1984)

SOURCE: "Women in Men's Clothing: Apparel and Social Stability in *The Roaring Girl*," in *English Literary Renaissance, Vol. 14, No. 3, Autumn 1984, pp. 367-91.*

[*In the essay below, Rose argues that* The Roaring Girl, *with its depiction of the cross-dressing Moll Frith, presents "an image of Jacobean society as unable to absorb one of its most vital and complex creations into the existing social and sexual hierarchies."*]

The central figure in Thomas Middleton and Thomas Dekker's city comedy ***The Roaring Girl*** (c. 1608-1611) is a woman named Moll Frith, whose distinguishing feature is that she walks around Jacobean London dressed in male clothing.[1] It should be stressed that Moll is not in disguise: she is neither a disguised player, a man pretending to be a woman; nor is she a disguised character, whose role requires a woman pretending to be a man. Unlike the disguised heroines of romantic comedy, Moll seeks not to conceal her sexual identity, but rather to display it. Although certain of the *Dramatis Personae* in *The Roaring Girl* occasionally fail to recognize her immediately, the fact that Moll is a woman is well known to every character in the play. She simply presents herself in society as a woman wearing men's clothes. Demanding merely by her presence that people reconcile her apparent sexual contradictions, she arouses unspeakable social and sexual anxieties in the established society of the play. Indeed Middleton and Dekker create Moll as the fulcrum of *The Roaring Girl,* and the other characters' reactions to her tend to define them as social and moral beings. As a result, society's effort to assess the identity of this female figure in male attire becomes the central dramatic and symbolic issue of the play.

Recognizing the title figure's assumption of male attire as the symbolic focus of social and moral concern in *The Roaring Girl* allows us to connect the play with the intense, often bitterly funny debate about women wearing men's clothes that was taking place in contemporary moral and religious writing, and which came to a head in 1620 with a pair of pamphlets entitled, respectively, *Hic Mulier: Or, The Man-Woman,* and *Haec-Vir: Or The Womanish-Man.*[2] Indeed the figure of the female in male apparel emerges from the documents of this controversy much as Moll Frith does from the text of *The Roaring Girl*: an embodiment of female independence boldly challenging established social and sexual values and, by the fact of her existence, requiring evaluation and response. Although historians of Renaissance conduct literature as well as more recent literary critics have discussed the *Hic Mulier / Haec-Vir* controversy,[3] no attempt has been made to view *The Roaring Girl,* with its "man-woman" heroine, in the context of this debate. Both because the controversial issue involved has an ongoing importance in Renaissance England and because I am not seeking to establish a direct influence between documents and play, the small chronological discrepancy between the performance and publication of *The Roaring Girl* (c. 1608-1611) and the high point of the debate (1620) is not relevant to my purposes here; rather I am interested in exploring the fact that the figure of the female in male attire is portrayed in both dramatic and social contexts with simultaneous admiration, desire, abhorrence, and fear. The following essay attempts to demonstrate the ways in which parallel treatments of women in men's clothing in the drama and the debate illuminate this phenomenon of fashion as the focus of considerable moral and social anxiety aroused by changing sexual values in Jacobean England; and to show that, taken together, artistic representation and social commentary suggest a deep cultural ambivalence in the British Renaissance about female independence and equality between the sexes.

I

Elizabethan and Jacobean sermons and conduct books continually castigate the fickleness of fashion and the vanity of sumptuous apparel. To cite one very typical example, the writer of the sermon "Against Excess of Apparel" in *Homilies Appointed to be Read in the Time of Queen Elizabeth* sees the English preoccupation with the novelties of fashion as a futile expenditure of energy, indicating an endlessly detrimental spiritual restlessness: "We are never contented, and therefore we prosper not."[4] Furthermore the conservative spirit frequently links propriety of dress with the coherence of society and views as a threat to social stability the tendency of the pretentious or the newly prosperous to dress so elegantly that it was becoming increasingly difficult to distinguish among social classes by the varied attire of their members.[5] Along with the upwardly mobile and the fop, women were singled out as creators of chaos for seeking to seduce men other than their husbands by wearing enticing clothes and for being generally disobedient, disrespectful, shallow, demonic, and extravagant in their preoccupation with fashion.[6]

From these characteristic themes the phenomenon of women dressing in male clothing begins gradually to assume a distinct identity as a separate issue; or, more accurately, as an issue that, in its symbolic significance, articulates a variety of social and moral concerns. The few available references to the phenomenon in the 1500s are largely parenthetical. In the early part of the sixteenth century, the idea of women wearing men's clothes apparently seemed too appalling even to be feared. Ever zealous of female virtue, John Louis Vives, for example, issues an ultimatum on the subject in *Instruction of a Christian Woman* (c. 1529) only as a last line in his chapter on feminine dress, a mere after-thought to the more important prohibitions against brazenness and extravagance in female attire. Citing Deuteronomy 22.5, he writes, "A woman shall use no mannes raymente, elles lette hir thinke she hath the mans stomacke, but take hede to the woordes of our Lorde: sayinge, a woman shall not put on mans apparell: for so to do is abhominable afore God. But I truste no woman will do it, excepte she be paste both honestee and shame."[7] Vives' confidence in womanly docility was, however, misplaced. In George Gascoigne's satire *The Steele Glas* (1576), complaints about women in male attire, although still relegated to the status of an epilogue, are nevertheless becoming decidedly more pointed and vociferous:

"What be they? women? masking in mens weedes?
With dutchkin dublets, . . . and with Jerkins jaggde?
With high copt hattes and fethers flaunt a flaunt?
They be so sure even *Wo* to *Men* in dede."[8]

The astonished despair of female modesty expressed in Gascoigne's mournful pun takes the form of accusations of sexual and, by clear inference, social, moral, and cosmic perversion in the rhetoric of Phillip Stubbes. Writing in 1583, in the midst of a general denunciation of the apparel of both sexes, Stubbes mentions women with "dublets and Jerkins as men have heer, buttoned up the brest, and made with wings, welts, and pinions on the shoulder points, as mans apparel is."[9] Stubbes lucidly states his indignant alarm at the possibility of not being able to distinguish between the sexes: "Our Apparell was given us as a signe distinctive to discern betwixt sex and sex, and therefore one to weare the Apparel of another sex is to . . . adulterate the veritie of his owne kinde. Wherefore these Women may not improperly be called *Hermaphroditi,* that is, Monsters of bothe kindes, half women, half men."[10]

While Stubbes' rhetoric is always colorfully extravagant, the topic of women in male attire continued to elicit highly emotional reactions at a growing rate, particularly in the second decade of the seventeenth century when, amidst a marked increase in satiric attacks upon women in general, references to the "monstrous . . . *Woman* of the *Masculine Gender*" multiplied notably.[11] As Louis B. Wright has demonstrated, this expansion in both the volume and hostility of satire against women represented the misogynistic, ultra-conservative voice in the lively debate about woman's nature, behavior, and role that was taking place in the moral and religious writing of the early decades of the century.[12] According to Wright and other critics, the content of this conduct literature can be distinguished roughly along class lines: where "learned and courtly" works tended to discuss women in the abstract and spiritualized terms of neoplatonic philosophy, middle-class tracts disputed more practical and social issues, such as the appropriateness of female apparel.[13] While the documents in the controversy surrounding women in male attire indicate that both upper- and middle-class females followed the fashion, they are much too partisan and factually imprecise to convey the actual extent to which the style was adopted.[14]

Nevertheless by 1620 the phenomenon of women in men's clothing had become prominent enough to evoke an outraged protest from King James, recorded in a letter of J. Chamberlain to Sir D. Carleton, dated January 15, 1620:

> Yesterday the bishop of London called together all his clergie about this towne, and told them he had expressed commandment from the King to will them to inveigh vehemently against the insolencie of our women, and theyre wearing of brode brimed hats, pointed dublets, theyre haire cut short or shorne, and some of them stilettoes or poinards, and such other trinckets of like moment; adding that if pulpit admonitions will not reform them he would proceed by another course; the truth is the world is very much out of order.

On February 12, Chamberlain adds the following: "Our pulpits ring continually of the insolence and impudence of women, and to help the matter forward the players have likewise taken them to taske, and so to the ballades and ballad-singers, so that they can come nowhere but theyre eares tingle; and if all this will not serve, the King threatens to fall upon theyre husbands, parents, or frends that have or shold have power over them, and make them pay for it."[15] The King's protest amounted to a declaration

of war. While undoubtedly resulting in part from James' considerable misogyny,[16] the actions following his protest also revealed that, among all the satiric targets on the subject of female fashion, women in men's clothing had assumed threatening enough proportions in the conservative mind to be singled out in a conscientious and thorough attempt to eliminate the style from social life. In February, 1620 the pamphlets *Hic Mulier,* which represented the conservative viewpoint, and *Haec-Vir,* which defended the practice of women wearing male attire, appeared. Because the pamphlets are anonymous, it is impossible to link their opinions to the gender of their author or authors. More importantly, the subject of the unconventional "man-woman" had evolved into a full-fledged debate, in which conservative and liberal positions are clearly and elaborately defined.

Wright believes the hostile conservative response to women in men's clothing was a defensive reaction against an increasingly successful demand both for moral and spiritual equality between the sexes and for greater social freedom for women: freedom, for example, from confinement to the home, from the double standard of sexual morality, from wife-beating and from forced marriage. "The average [i.e., middle-class] woman," Wright concludes, "was becoming articulate in her own defense and . . . was demanding social independence unknown in previous generations."[17] According to Wright, the female adoption of male apparel aggressively and visibly dramatized a bid for social independence, which comprised a largely successful and coherent challenge to existing sexual values that is reflected in *Haec-Vir,* a pamphlet Wright believes to be "the *Areopagitica* of the London woman, a woman who had attained greater freedom than any of her predecessors or than any of her European contemporaries."[18] It is true that the challenge that women in male attire presented to the existing imbalance of power between the sexes can be discerned in the vindictive bitterness of the opposition to the androgynous style. Yet Linda T. Fitz has recently provided a useful and fascinating corrective to the hopeful interpretation of the extent and coherence of Jacobean feminism advanced by Wright and critics like Juliet Dusinberre by stressing the restrictiveness, rather than the liberating potential, of middle-class conduct literature. In her discussion of the controversy surrounding women in men's clothing, Fitz points out some serious oversights in Wright's optimistic view of the *Hic Mulier/Haec-Vir* debate; nevertheless Fitz ends by conceding that "Wright is quite justified in his . . . assessment" of a resounding victory for female freedom articulated in this controversy.[19] My own analysis of the debate suggests an attitude toward the *Hic Mulier* phenomenon and the sexual freedom it represented which is more complex than either Wright perceives or Fitz explores, an attitude that both acknowledges injustice and fears change, that wants sexual freedom yet perceives its attainment as conflicting with an equally desirable social stability.

II

After an introductory lament that "since the daies of *Adam* women were never so Masculine" (sig. A3), the pamphlet *Hic Mulier* or *The Man-Woman* begins by propounding a familiar Renaissance ideal of woman as chaste, maternal, compassionate, discreet, and obedient, a model of behavior and sentiment from which the notorious "man-woman" is believed to depart "with a deformitie never before dream'd of" (sig. A3v).[20] In contrast to this modestly attired paragon, the *Hic Mulier* figure, sporting a "cloudy Ruffianly broad-brim'd Hatte, and wanton Feather . . . the loose, lascivious civill embracement of a French doublet . . . most ruffianly short lockes . . . for Needles, Swords . . . and for Prayer bookes, bawdy Jigs" is "not halfe man, halfe woman . . . but all Odyous, all Divell" (sigs. A4-A4v). In elaborating the polemical intention of this pamphlet—to eliminate the heinous fashion by demonizing its proponents—the author builds a case around two major arguments.

As might be expected, the first group of arguments centers on the dangerous sexual chaos which the author assumes will result from the breakdown of rigid gender distinctions symbolized by the "man-woman's" attire. The writer perceives in *Hic Mulier*'s choice of male clothes unconventional sexual behavior; therefore she automatically becomes a whore, who inspires by her lewd example a pernicious illicit sexuality in others. As implied in the description of her "loose, lascivious civil embracement of a French doublet, being all unbutton'd to entice" (sig. A4v), she will allow, even invite, "a shameless libertie to every loose passion" (sig. C2). Despite—indeed because of—her mannishness, then, *Hic Mulier* displays and encourages a free-floating sexuality, a possibility which the author views as socially destabilizing and therefore disastrous, "most pernicious to the common-wealth" (sig. C2). As we will see, this interesting association between socially threatening female sexiness and the breakdown of polarized gender identities and sexual roles becomes very important in **The Roaring Girl.** The fear seems to be that without rigidly assigned, gender-linked roles and behavior, legitimate, faithful erotic relations between the sexes will become impossible and the integrity of the family will consequently disintegrate: "they [i.e., the "men-women"] are neither men, nor women, but just good for nothing . . . they care not into what dangers they plunge either their Fortunes or Reputations, the disgrace of the whole Sexe, or the blot and obloquy of their private Families" (sigs. B2, C2).

However ominous, the unleashing of Eros and the breakdown of sexual polarization do not preoccupy the author as much as do questions of social status and hierarchy. The implied norm behind the satire in the pamphlet is a stable society which derives its coherence from the strict preservation of such essential distinctions as class, fortune, and rank. Not only do women in men's clothing come from various classes in society; they also have the unfortunate habit of dressing alike, obscuring not only the clarity of their gender, but the badge of their social status as well, and thereby endangering critically the predictable orderliness of social relations. To convey the seriousness of this offense, the author employs the rhetorical device of associating the hated style by turns with decaying aristocrats and gentry ("the adulterate branches of rich stocks" [sig. B1]), women of base birth ("stinking vapours drawne from dunghils" [sig. B1]), females of the upper classes "knowne great" ("no more shall their greatness or wealth save them from one particle of disgrace" [sigs. B1v, B2v]), and middle-class wives (tailors have "metamorphosed more modest old garments . . . for the use of Freemens wives than hath been worne in Court, Suburbs, or Countrey" [sig. C1v]), all of which leads to the indignant outburst: "It is an infection that emulates the plague, and throwes itselfe amongst women of all degrees . . . Shall we all be co-heires of one honor, one estate, and one habit?" (sigs. B1v, B4v). Like death and disease, then, the female in male attire serves as a leveler; and, just as such issues as the inflated sale of honors by the Crown seemed to the conservative mind to be undermining social coherence by threatening the traditional prestige of inherited nobility, so the phenomenon of women of different social positions dressing in similar male clothing appeared intolerably chaotic. As Fitz has shown, English Renaissance women, particularly in the middle classes, used their apparel as a showpiece to advertise the prosperity of their fathers and husbands.[21] That women should perversely refuse, by donning look-alike male clothes, to serve their crucial function as bearers of social class status and distinction is the issue that arouses the author's most vindictive antipathy: "Let . . . the powerfull Statute of apparell but lift up his Battle-Axe, so as every one may bee knowne by the true badge of their bloud, or Fortune: and then these *Chymera's* of deformitie will bee sent backe to hell, and there burne to Cynders in the flames of their owne malice" (sig. C1v).

The pamphlet *Hic Mulier* ends with an invective against all social change (sig. C3). Given the hectic violence of this author's conservatism, it is not surprising that the rebuttal in the pamphlet *Haec-Vir: Or The Womanish-Man,* which appeared seven days later, would dwell on the folly of thoughtlessly adhering to social custom. Interestingly, the *Haec-Vir* pamphlet ignores the issue of whether women of different social categories dressing alike as men disrupt the alignment of social classes; instead the second pamphlet argues solely in terms of gender and sexual roles. Rather than appearing as the product of a single mind, *Haec-Vir* is presented as a dialogue between two characters, the *Hic Mulier* and the *Haec-Vir* figures, suggesting by its very form and by the introduction of a new figure, the womanish man, to whom I will return, a greater openness to discussion and to cooperation between the sexes. The irrationality of the author of the first pamphlet is also clarified and undercut at the beginning of the second when the two figures conduct a witty exchange about their mutual inability to identify one another's gender. Thus a tolerant and urbane tone is set in which *Hic Mulier* (now a sympathetic figure) can defend her behavior.

Hic Mulier's defense elaborates in positive terms the fact that her attire symbolizes a demand for recognition of spiritual and moral equality between the sexes, a recognition which she regards as her birthright: "We are free-borne as Men, have as free election, and as free spirits, we are compounded of like parts, and may with like liberty make benefit of our Creations" (sig. B3). Consequently she counters *Haec-Vir's* charge that assuming male apparel makes her a mere slave to the novelties of fashion both by defining her outfit as symbolizing her freedom of choice and by redefining slavery as *Haec-Vir's* mindless submission to the tyranny of pointless custom, "for then custome, nothing is more absurd, nothing more foolish" (sig. B2). The customs she resents as most false and destructive to female freedom and equality are those gender-linked stereotypes which constrain female behavior to compliance, subordination, pathos, and passivity:

> But you say wee are barbarous and shameless and cast off all softness, to runne wilde through a wildernesse of opinions. In this you expresse more cruelty then in all the rest, because I stand not with my hands on my belly like a baby at *Bartholomew Fayre* . . . that am not dumbe when wantons court mee, as if Asse-like I were ready for all burthens, or because I weepe not when injury gripes me, like a woorried Deere in the fangs of many Curres: am I therefore barbarous or shamelesse?
>
> (sig. B3)

"*I stand not with my hands on my belly like a baby at* Bartholomew Fayre . . . *as if Asse-like I were ready for all burthens.*" *Hic Mulier* argues that to reduce woman to the position of static icon, allegedly "so much better in that she is something purer" (sig. B1v) than man, is actually to infantilize and dehumanize her by denying her full participation in adult reality, which she optimistically defines as a world of creative movement and change, in which man can "alter, frame, and fashion, according as his will and delight shall rule him" (sig. B1v). This conception, which locates adult reality in the creative opportunities provided by public life, recognizes that women are unjustly confined by tradition to perpetual fantasy and immaturity. It therefore forms the most strikingly modern of *Hic Mulier*'s arguments.

The eloquence and clarity with which these convictions are expressed make the retrenchment that occurs in the pamphlet's conclusion all the more startling. Having established herself as the rational contender in the debate, the "man-woman" suddenly withdraws before the irrational onslaught of *Haec-Vir*, the womanish man who ignores her arguments, rather than systematically rebutting them. Suddenly the focus shifts to the way that *Haec-Vir* (who, it has been suggested, represents the homosexuality of the Jacobean court)[22] has relinquished his manhood and become a fop, aberrant male behavior which is now viewed as the sole reason for the existence of the notorious "man-woman." In an astonishing abandonment of her considerable powers of logic, *Hic Mulier* nostalgically evokes chivalric gallantry, recalling the bygone days when men were men:

> Hence we have preserved (though to our owne shames) those manly things which you have forsaken, which would you againe accept, and restore to us the Blushes we lay'd by, when first wee put on your Masculine garments; doubt not but chaste thoughts and bashfulnesse will againe dwell in us . . . then will we love and serve you; then will we heare and obey you; then will wee like rich Jewels hang at your eares to take our Instructions.
>
> (sigs. C2v, C3v)

It is a bargain, an offer he can't refuse; the dialogue concludes with *Haec-Vir* having the last word, just as he had had the first, and the entire phenomenon of women in men's clothing is rationalized, not as an attempt to achieve unrealized social freedom for women, but rather to return society to the idealized sexual norm of gender polarization and male dominance. As in King James' protest and the end of the *Hic Mulier* pamphlet, responsibility for the unconventional style of female dress, now recognized by all as deformed, is seen to rest with men because power does.[23]

Although the concluding section of the *Haec-Vir* pamphlet articulates this drastic shift in perspective, it is nevertheless short, and it fails to cancel or even to qualify the dominant logic of *Hic Mulier*'s stirring defense of her freedom, a speech which remains the focus of the second pamphlet. We are therefore left with a disjunction between the stubbornly rebellious, salient content of the second pamphlet and the conservative structure of the debate as a whole. On the one hand, the dominant content of the *Haec-Vir* pamphlet convincingly challenges the justice and reality of the existing sexual power structure by enumerating the illusory, sentimental, and destructive premises on which it is based. On the other, the form of the debate as a whole perpetuates the status quo by attempting to absorb this cogent demand for change into a larger movement of re-aligning the established society into conformity with an old ideal, a rhetorical endeavor that does not, however, entirely succeed in quelling the vigor of the opposition. As a result of this disjunction between content and form, female independence and equality between the sexes are depicted in the debate as desirable and just, but also as impossible for a hierarchical society to absorb without unacceptable disruption.

III

A pronounced ambivalence toward sexual equality as represented by the *Hic Mulier* figure is discernible in the *Hic Mulier/Haec-Vir* debate, then, and this attitude can be viewed in aesthetic terms as a disjunction between content and form. In **The Roaring Girl** a similar dislocation between thematic content and dramatic form can be perceived in the representation of the title character, Moll Frith, a point to which I will return. Middleton and Dekker modeled their unusual central figure after a real-life "roaring girl," popularly known in Jacobean London as "Moll Cutpurse." As this name implies, the real Moll was an underworld figure, notorious as a thief, whore, brawler, and bawd. Much of the reliable evidence we have about her exists in the court records made after her several arrests for offenses that included a scandalous appearance at the Fortune Theater, where she "sat there upon the stage in the publique viewe of all the people there p[rese]nte in mans apparrell & playd upon her lute & sange a songe."[24] Most of the existing criticism of *The Roaring Girl* attempts to date the play with reference to this incident.[25]

Whatever the precise connections between the events in the life of the actual Mary Frith and the performance and publication of *The Roaring Girl,* the court records show that the playwrights drew heavily on the habits and physical appearance of the real-life Moll, with her brawling, singing, and smoking, her lute, her boots, her sword, and, above all, her breeches; as has been suggested, it is also probable that Middleton and Dekker were attempting to benefit from the *au courant* notoriety of the actual Moll in the timing of their play.[26] Nevertheless in his address to the reader attached to the 1611 quarto, Middleton takes pains to distinguish the created character from the real person, hinting that the play will present an idealized interpretation of this odd figure: "'Tis the excellency of a writer to leave things better than he finds 'em."[27] In fact the playwrights maintain an ambivalent attitude toward the outlaw status of their central character, in whom courageous moral and sexual principles combine with a marginal social identity, both of which are symbolized in the play by her male attire.

The address to the reader and ensuing prologue clarify the controversial nature of the title character and emphasize the importance of assessing her identity:

> Thus her character lies—
> Yet what need characters, when to give a guess
> Is better than the person to express?
> But would you know who 'tis? Would you hear her name?
> She's called mad Moll; her life our acts proclaim.
>
> (Prologue, 26-30)

In their introduction of Moll Frith, the playwrights evoke themes identical to those surrounding the *Hic Mulier* figure in the *Hic Mulier/Haec-Vir* debate. First, they associate Moll's male apparel with erotic appeal and illicit sexuality.

> For venery, you shall find enough for sixpence, but well couched and you mark it; for Venus being a woman passes through the play in doublet and breeches; a brave disguise and a safe one, if the statute untie not her codpiece point.
>
> ("To the Comic Play-Readers")

Secondly, as in the debate, erotic questions are less preoccupying than social ones: the entire prologue attempts to assign Moll a specific class and rank, "to know what girl this roaring girl should be / For of that tribe are many" (Prologue, 15-6). While the dramatists assure us that their Moll is neither criminal, brawler, whore, nor city wife, the question of her actual social status is left unanswered. As the action unfolds, the playwrights' vision of the controver-

sial "roaring girl's" exact position in the Jacobean social hierarchy gradually assumes its distinct and complicated shape; and other characters are defined as social and moral beings according to their responses to her.

The play has a traditional New Comedy plot in which a young man, Sebastian Wengrave, outwits his snobbish, greedy father, Sir Alexander Wengrave, who has threatened to disinherit Sebastian if he marries the woman he loves, all because of her relatively meager dowry. The subplot involves a theme equally characteristic of the Jacobean dramatic satirist: the attempt of lazy, poor, arrogant, upper-class "gallants" to cheat and seduce the wives of middle-class shopkeepers. Like the prologue and the *Hic Mulier/ Haec-Vir* debate, the main plot stresses social issues while the secondary plot focuses on erotic complications. The conservative faction in the play is most strikingly represented by the father, Sir Alexander, and the lecherous, misogynistic gallant, Laxton, both of whose negative attitudes toward Moll resemble those of the author of the *Hic Mulier* pamphlet toward women in men's clothing.

Moll enters the play for the first time during the subplot, as Laxton and his cohorts are busily seeking to form illicit liaisons with shopkeepers' wives, chuckling privately over their erotic cunning and prowess. In this Renaissance equivalent of the locker room, Moll, who will smoke and swear, is greeted enthusiastically by the men, although with considerably less relish by the women, one of whom screams, "Get you from my shop!" (2.1.248). Both men and women, however, associate her mannishness with deformed and illicit sexuality:

> MRS. G.Some will not stick to say she is a man, and some, both man and woman.
> LAX.That were excellent: she might first cuckold the husband, and then make him do as much for the wife.
>
> (2.1.219-22)

Like the author of the *Hic Mulier* pamphlet, Laxton finds this mannish woman sexy ("Heart, I would give but too much money to be nibbling with that wench") (2.1.193-94); he also automatically assumes from her unconventional sexual behavior that she is a whore: "I'll lay hard siege to her; money is that aqua fortis that eats into many a maidenhead; where the walls are flesh and blood, I'll ever pierce through with a golden augur" (2.1.203-05). Complacently, Laxton secures an assignation with Moll, to which he travels overcome with self-pleasure and a thrilling sense of his own power in arranging a forbidden encounter.

Laxton is unpleasantly surprised. In his confrontation with Moll, which takes the appropriate form of a duel, Moll emerges as a defiant champion of female freedom from male sexual dominion, a role symbolized by her male attire. When Laxton arrives on the scene searching for a woman in a "shag ruff, a frieze jerkin, a short sword, and a safeguard [i.e., a petticoat]" (3.1.34-35), Moll appears instead in male clothes, the significance of which she underscores: when Laxton, who takes a few moments to recognize her, remarks, "I'll swear I knew thee not," Moll replies meaningfully, "I'll swear you did not; but you shall know me now." Laxton, who is not at all clever, mistakes this response for an erotic overture: "No, not here; we shall be spied" (3.1.58-61). Discarding subtlety as hopeless, Moll beats up Laxton while delivering a stirring oration on the sexual injustices suffered by women at the hands of arrogant, slanderous men:

> Thou'rt one of those
> That thinks each woman thy fond flexible whore . . .
> How many of our sex, by such as thou,
> Have their good thoughts paid with a blasted name
> That never deserved loosely . . .
> There is no mercy in't.
>
> (3.1.77-93)

Furthermore, Moll attributes female sexual vulnerability specifically to the superior social power of male seducers, which she defies:

> In thee I defy all men, their worst hates
> And their best flatteries, all their golden witchcrafts,
> With which they entangle the poor spirits of fools,
> Distressed needle-women and tradefallen wives;
> Fish that must needs bite, or themselves be bitten.
> Such hungry things as these may soon be took
> With a worm fastened on a golden hook.
> Those are the lecher's food, his prey; he watches
> For quarreling wedlocks and poor shifting sisters.
>
> (3.1.97-105)

Finally, she does not simply dwell on female victimization, but asserts positively the capacity of women for full sexual responsibility, authority, and independence:

> I scorn to prostitute myself to a man,
> I that can prostitute a man to me . . .
> She that has wit and spirit,
> May scorn to live beholding to her body for meat;
> Or for apparel, like your common dame,
> That makes shame get her clothes to cover shame.
>
> (3.1.116-46)

Like the sympathetic *Hic Mulier* figure in the debate, Moll takes upon herself the defense of all women. Indeed Laxton's attempted violation of Moll's chastity connects her with, rather than distinguishes her from, the shopkeepers' wives, most of whom are willingly engaged in sexual collusion with the gallants when the play begins. As a result, we perceive that the "man-clothed" Moll,[28] the notorious roaring girl and *Hic Mulier*, is actually a sexual innocent compared to the conventional middle-class wives. More important than the wives' hypocrisy, however, is their eventual reform; at the end of the play they see through the schemes of their would-be seducers and choose to reject them in favor of their husbands just as Moll's defeat of Laxton has portended that they would. The seducing gallants who represent illicit sexuality therefore turn out

not to constitute a real threat to the social order at all. Moll herself recognizes this fact immediately: "Oh, the gallants of these times are shallow lechers . . . 'Tis impossible to know what woman is throughly honest, because she's ne'er throughly tried" (2.1.336-40).

As Moll's defeat of Laxton makes clear, free-floating, amoral eros is stripped of its socially destructive power when women decide to take responsibility for themselves. The aborted sexual encounter between Moll and Laxton also dramatizes the specious logic involved in connecting Moll's unconventional male attire automatically with whorish behavior. In their depiction of Laxton's complacence, the playwrights clearly associate lechery and misogyny with obtuse, unobservant social conformity.[29] As we have seen, the idea of mindlessly adhering to social custom is the principal target of the sympathetic *Hic Mulier* figure when she defends her freedom in the debate. In ***The Roaring Girl*** this theme is amplified in the main plot through the representation of the censorious attitudes and actions which Sir Alexander Wengrave takes toward Moll Frith.

In his self-righteousness, self-deception, and self-pity, Sir Alexander is all self, incapable of distinguishing his emotional attachments from virtue. Proud of what he thinks is his shrewd observation of social life, trying to conform to a preconceived ideal, he continually misapprehends the realities which confront him. Sebastian recognizes that his father's vulnerability to the opinion of others exceeds even his greed, and he forms a plan to gain both his inheritance and his true love, Mary Fitzallard, by telling his father that he plans to marry Moll Frith, the outrageous roaring girl who fights, smokes, swears, and wears men's clothes. Like Laxton, Sir Alexander assumes from Moll's masculine attire that she is both a whore and a thief, who can be entrapped into stealing money, exposed, and safely removed from the proximity of his son. Like Laxton, he fails repeatedly in his assaults on her integrity.

Sir Alexander inveighs against Moll as a monster (1.2.130-36; 2.2.81-83), a siren (2.1.219-20), a thief (1.2.175; 4.1.201-06; 2.2.139), and a whore (1.2.137; 2.2.160). One funny scene shows him spying on her, appalled as her tailor fits her for breeches. Like the conservative author of the *Hic Mulier* pamphlet, Sir Alexander perceives in Moll's male clothing a symbol not only of perverse sexuality, but also of the inevitable disintegration of stable marital relations: "Hoyda, breeches? What, will he marry a monster with two trinkets [i.e., testicles]? What age is this? If the wife go in breeches, the man must wear long coats, like a fool." (2.2.81-84). At the end of the play, before a nearly-reformed Sir Alexander has discovered his son's true marital intentions, Moll's urbane teasing exposes his desire to maintain rigid gender roles as a regressive anxiety:

> MOLL: (referring to herself) Methinks you should be proud of such a daughter,
> As good a man as your son . . .
> You do not know what benefits I bring with me;
> No cheat dares work upon you with thumb or knife,
> While you've a roaring girl to your son's wife.
>
> (5.2.153-62)

More than any of the specific evils he attributes to her, Sir Alexander fears Moll's conspicuousness, her unconventionality, her social aberrance; the sheer embarrassment of having such a daughter-in-law is equivalent to ruin. "Why wouldst thou fain marry to be pointed at?" he asks his son. "Why, as good marry a beacon on a hill, / Which all the country fix their eyes upon, / As her thy folly dotes on" (2.2.142-46). It is Sir Alexander's shallow, malicious willingness to accept received opinion without observing for himself, his bourgeois horror of nonconformity, that moves Sebastian to a rousing defense of Moll, the clearest articulation of her honesty in the play:

> He hates unworthily that by rote contemns . . .
>   Here's her worst,
> Sh'as a bold spirit that mingles with mankind,
> But nothing else comes near it; and often times
> Through her apparel somewhat shames her birth;
> But she is loose in nothing but in mirth.
> Would all Molls were no worse!
>
>   (2.2.176-86)

And it is precisely this thoughtless social conformity, dramatized by his malignant intolerance of Moll, that Sir Alexander abjures at the end, thereby making possible the formation of a new comic society which will be both flexible and just:

> Forgive me; now I cast the world's eyes from me,
> And look upon thee [i.e., Moll] freely with mine own
> . . .
> I'll never more
> Condemn by common voice, for that's the whore,
> That deceives man's opinion, mocks his trust,
> Cozens his love, and makes his heart unjust.
>
>   (5.2.244-51)

In "The Place of Laughter in Tudor and Stuart England," Keith Thomas analyzes the ways in which comedy conservatively affirms the status quo by revealing, mocking, and containing social tensions; yet, Thomas points out, "There was also a current of radical, critical laughter which, instead of reinforcing accepted norms, sought to give the world a nudge in a new direction."[30] Given the heavy emphasis which the majority of English Renaissance society placed on gender-polarized sexual decorum and subdued, modest female behavior, it is evident that, with their idealized comic portrait of the *Hic Mulier* figure Moll Frith, Dekker and Middleton were joining those who, like the author of the *Haec-Vir* pamphlet, were beginning to call for greater freedom for women and equality between the sexes. As we have seen, serious opposition to Moll is represented in the play as mindless conformity. Not only do the playwrights decline to link Moll's freewheeling, immodest habits and appearance with perverse or dishonest behavior, but they also give her ample opportunity to acquit herself from her reputation as a criminal (5.1.323-73). Furthermore, Dekker and Middleton portray as noble Moll's integrity in refusing Sebastian Wengrave's proposal of marriage, made before she knows it is only a sham to deceive his father. Like the sympathetic, eloquent *Hic*

Mulier figure, Moll refuses the conventional subordination required of a wife:

> I have no humor to marry . . . I have the head now of
> myself, and am man enough for a woman. Marriage is
> but a chopping and changing, where a maiden loses
> one head, and has a worse i' th' place.
>
>   (2.2.38-48)

Moll's virginity represents the particular condition of independence which Carolyn Heilbrun defines as "that fierce autonomy which separates the individual from the literal history of his sexual acts":[31] "Base is that mind that kneels unto her body . . . / My spirit shall be mistress of this house / As long as I have time in't" (3.1.149-52).

How far does *The Roaring Girl* go in its sympathetic imaginative vision of sexual nonconformity, female independence, and equality between the sexes, all conditions embodied in the title character? Clearly Laxton's humorous stupidity and Sir Alexander's petty malice are no match for Moll's integrity, vitality, intelligence, and courage. Yet a more subtle counter-movement in the play resists the absorption of Moll into the tolerant new society which forms in the final scene.

Far from direct disapproval, this strand of qualified feeling can be discerned as an ambiguous undercurrent in the primarily positive attitude with which Moll is regarded by Sebastian and his fiancée, Mary Fitzallard, the couple whose relationship and opinions represent the desirable social norm in the play. For example, when Sebastian reveals to Mary his scheme of pretending to court Moll, he describes the roaring girl as "a creature / so strange in quality" (1.1.100-01) that Mary could not possibly doubt his love. As noted, Sebastian provides the major defense of Moll in the play; but the defense, while eloquent and just, is delivered to his father in the course of a deception and is couched entirely in terms of existing standards of sexual decorum, the basis of which Sebastian never questions: "and oftentimes / Through her apparel [she] somewhat shames her birth; / But she is loose in nothing but in mirth" (2.2.183-85). Is Sebastian referring to Moll's gender, social status, or both in his reference to her birth? This point is never clarified, nor is the rather odd remark which Mary makes when Sebastian introduces her to Moll:

> SEB. This is the roaring wench must do us good.
> MARY. No poison, sir, but serves us for some use;
> Which is confirmed in her.
>
>   (4.1.148-50)

Furthermore, Moll herself seems to acquiesce in the view which regards her as aberrant, thereby indirectly affirming existing sexual values: when Sebastian proposes to her she responds, "A wife you know ought to be obedient, but I fear me I am too headstrong to obey . . . You see sir, I speak against myself" (2.2.40-41, 62). These and similar remarks are too infrequent and undeveloped to undercut the predominant theme of approval and admiration which surrounds Moll in the play; but they do qualify the potential for any radical change in sexual values implicit in the full social acceptance of Moll Frith.

The play makes clear that, if the stifling, malignant conformity which unjustly opposes Moll is one thing, incorporation of her into society is quite another. Full social acceptance is no more the destiny of the *Hic Mulier* figure in this play, no matter how benevolent, than it is the fate of the sympathetic *Hic Mulier* in the debate, no matter how reasonable, eloquent, or bold. Earlier I observed that the playwrights' ambivalence toward Moll can be discerned as a disjunction between thematic content and dramatic form. While the dominant content of **The Roaring Girl** elicits but does not clarify this issue, formal analysis makes its subtlety more readily perceptible. A brief discussion of the function of disguise in the play should help to clarify the point.

Although Moll Frith wears male clothing, she makes no attempt to conceal her identity and all the other characters know she is a woman: in short, she is not in disguise. When used simply to denote a costume, worn in a play or festival for example, "disguise" could be used as a morally neutral term in Jacobean England. But discussions of apparel in the moral and religious literature more often use "disguise" as an inclusive censorious term meaning, roughly, "deformity of nature" and comprehending in the range of disapproval not only the player, but the fop, dandy, overdressed woman and, of course, the *Hic Mulier*.[32] According to this conservative mentality, the roaring girl would be in "disguise"; but, as we have seen, the play rejects precisely this negative interpretation of Moll's apparel. More illuminating for present purposes is a brief comparison between Moll and the disguised heroines of Shakespearean romantic comedy.

In contrast to Moll, who insists on being recognized as a woman, heroines like Rosalind and Viola seek to conceal their identities and to protect themselves by masquerading as men. Modern criticism has been particularly adept at recognizing the symbolic, structural, and psychological functions of these romantic disguises. On the psychological level, the male disguise allows the Shakespearean heroine the social freedom to extend her personality and expand her identity by exploring the possibilities inherent in male sexual roles.[33] This opportunity for heightened awareness and personal growth incorporates into the desirable comic society formed at the end of the play an androgynous vision, recently defined as "a psychic striving for an ideal state of personal wholeness, a microcosmic attempt to imitate a mythic macrocosm," in which "being a human being entails more than one's sex identification and attendant gender development"[34]

The romantic comic form, however, represents neither a mythical nor a revolutionary society, but a renewed traditional society, whose stability and coherence is symbolized by marriage and is based on the maintenance of traditional sexual roles.[35] It is the temporary nature of the heroine's male disguise which contains the formal solution to the potential psychological and social problems it raises: that is, the heroine gladly sheds her disguise with its accompanying freedoms at the end of the play, in order to accept the customary social role of wife, thereby allowing the play's androgynous vision to remain spiritual and symbolic without awakening the audience's dissatisfaction or desire for social change.[36] Northrop Frye has shown that the resolution of comedy, which is usually erotic, is often brought about by a bisexual Eros figure who, like Puck, "is in himself sexually self-contained, being in a sense both male and female, and needing no expression of love beyond himself." In Shakespeare's later comedies, this structural role is taken over by the disguised female; but when the Eros figure is no longer supernatural, "his" character must break down, as Viola's does into Viola and Sebastian in *Twelfth Night,* or be superseded, as Rosalind's is, by the figure of Hymen in *As You Like It.*[37] As another critic puts it, "The temporary nature of the male disguise is of course essential, since the very nature of Shakespearean comedy is to affirm that disruption is temporary, that what has been turned topsy-turvy will be restored."[38]

Like Shakespearean comedy, **The Roaring Girl** concludes festively with the re-formation of a flexible and tolerant society, whose stability and integration are symbolized in marriage. But in **The Roaring Girl** the functions performed by the disguised heroine in Shakespeare are structurally divided and displaced. Moll clearly answers to much of Frye's analysis of the comic Eros figure: first, with her self-imposed virginity, refusal to marry, and men's clothes, she is "in a sense both male and female" and needs "no expression of love beyond [her]self"; secondly, it is she who brings about the benevolent and satisfactory resolution of the action when she actively helps Sebastian to gain Mary. Sebastian recognizes her function as the play's Eros figure when he says, "Twixt lovers' hearts she's a fit instrument / And has the art to help them to their own" (2.2.204-05). In Frye's terms, Moll is a figure in whom Eros "is a condition, not a desire."[39] But unlike Puck, Moll is not supernatural; she is human and will not disappear from social life. She is neither on an odyssey toward sexual and social integration, as Rosalind and Viola are, nor can she be said to grow psychologically, happily internalizing the discovery of love and freedom in the way that they do. She has no intention of marrying, no intention of relinquishing either her outfit or the unconventional principles and behavior it represents. She therefore assumes the social and psychological freedom of the traditional disguised heroine without providing the corresponding reassurance implicit in that heroine's eventual erotic transformation. These functions are instead displaced onto Mary Fitzallard, who, disguised as a page, joyously sheds the disguise to take her place as Sebastian's wife in the final scene. Moll, on the other hand, having served as the instrument who brings about the happy ending, is nevertheless excluded from the renewed comic society of married couples which forms on the stage at the end of the play. Sir Alexander makes this clear when he defines the new society by addressing "You kind gentlewomen, whose sparkling presence / Are glories set in marriage, beams of society / For all your loves give luster to my joys" (5.2.260-62). The playwrights conclude *The Roaring Girl* with an epilogue in which they emphasize the strangeness of the fictional, and the criminality of the real, Moll Frith.

In a sense the dramatists call attention to both a structural and social ambiguity in the world of the play by refusing to conflate Moll and Mary into a single figure.[40] By excluding Moll from the traditional, rejuvenated society demanded by the comic form, Middleton and Dekker never quite succeed in separating her from her outlaw status, despite the approval and admiration with which her integrity, courage, and freedom are depicted in the play. It is true that Moll herself displays nothing but a benign indifference toward acceptance by established society: "I pursue no pity; / Follow the law and you can cuck me, spare not; / Hang up my viol by me, and I care not." (5.2.253-55). Moll's good-natured indifference allows the predominant tone of the ending of the play to remain festive. Yet her definition of herself as anti-social (5.1.362-63) and her exclusion by others combine to render unsettling the fact that her sexual independence has left her isolated from the very social structure which her courage and vitality have done so much to enliven and renew. The question of her social identity, raised at the beginning of the play, therefore remains unresolved at the end. It is because she has helped to create a society from which she is both excluded and excludes herself that Moll's status remains unclear; insofar as it is ambiguous, marginal, and problematic, Moll's social identity can be seen as a metaphor for the changing condition of women in early modern England.

IV

Both *The Roaring Girl* and the *Hic Mulier/Haec-Vir* debate represent the figure of the woman in men's clothing as the symbolic focus of concern about sexual freedom and equality in Jacobean society. Each text depicts this unconventional figure as attractive and virtuous, while those who regard her as socially and sexually disruptive are represented in contrast as hostile, anxious, and self-deceived. When confronting the irrationality of her enemies, the *Hic Mulier* figure emerges as the voice of reason and common sense. In both play and debate it is she who possesses imagination, insight, and courage; it is she who embodies the promise of freedom and even of happiness. Nevertheless this hopeful, likeable figure fails in each context to gain full social acceptance; not only is she excluded by others, but she herself acquiesces in her own defeat: in the debate she retreats completely, surrendering to the very values she had arisen to oppose; in the play she remains pleasantly isolated from society, a loveable outlaw whose eccentricity insures that she will not constitute a social threat. But while these formal resolutions of debate and play are both agreeably festive in tone, neither effort to adhere to the comic purpose of reconciling social tensions is entirely convincing. The powerfully rendered figure of *Hic Mulier* continues in each case to tower over the less compelling society that

endeavors unsuccessfully to absorb her; viewed in terms of aesthetic logic, the *Hic Mulier* figure becomes content that cannot (illogically) be contained by form.

With their similarly ambivalent visions of *Hic Mulier* and Moll Frith as necessary but disruptive, benevolent but anti-social, both the debate and the play present an image of Jacobean society as unable to absorb one of its most vital and complex creations into the existing social and sexual hierarchies. The mixed approval and exclusion of the *Hic Mulier* figure evident in artistic representation and social commentary indicate a simultaneous search for and rejection of greater flexibility in sexual values. The parallel treatments of the controversy surrounding women in men's clothing in the dramatic and moral literature therefore combine to illuminate a particularly heightened time of groping for resolutions: in both *The Roaring Girl* and the *Hic Mulier/Haec-Vir* debate, the moral ambiguity and social challenge of sexual identity and equality as they were perceived in Renaissance England stand sharply before us.

Notes

1. I would like to acknowledge my gratitude to the Monticello College Foundation and The Newberry Library, whose generous support made possible the research for this essay.

2. The full names of these colorful pamphlets are as follows: *Hic Mulier: Or, The Man-Woman: Being a Medicine to cure the Coltish Disease of the Staggers in the Masculine-Feminines of our Times* and *Haec-Vir: Or The Womanish-Man: Being an Answer to a late Booke intituled Hic-Mulier.* All citations from the pamphlets are taken from the edition published by *The Rota* at the University of Exeter, 1973.

3. See Louis B. Wright, *Middle-Class Culture in Elizabethan England* (Chapel Hill, N.C., 1935), pp. 494-97; Carroll Camden, *The Elizabethan Woman* (New York, 1952), pp. 263-67; Juliet Dusinberre, *Shakespeare and the Nature of Women* (London, 1975), pp. 231-71; Linda T. Fitz, "What Says the Married Woman: Marriage Theory and Feminism in the English Renaissance," *Mosaic*, 13 (Winter, 1980), 1-22; and Linda Woodbridge, *Women and the English Renaissance: Literature and the Nature of Womankind, 1540-1620* (Urbana, 1984), pp. 139-51.

4. Quoted from *Certain Sermons or Homilies Appointed to be Read in Churches in the Time of Queen Elizabeth* (London: Society for Promoting Christian Knowledge, 1908), p. 327.

5. See, for example, "Against Excess of Apparel" in *Homilies;* Thomas Nashe, *Christs Teares over Jerusalem,* 1593, in John Dover Wilson, *Life in Shakespeare's England* (Cambridge, 1920), p. 125; and Phillip Stubbes, *Anatomy of Abuses,* 1583, ed. Frederick J. Furnivall, The New Shakespeare Society (London, 1877-1879), pp. 33-4.

6. See, for example, William Harrison, *Description of England, 1587* in Wilson, pp. 124-25. Cf. Wright, p. 493; Camden, pp. 257-67; and Fitz.

7. John Louis Vives, "Of raiments," in *Instruction of a Christian Woman,* trans. Richard Hyrde (1557), Book II, Chap. VIII. Deuteronomy 22.5 reads: "The Woman shall not wear that which pertaineth unto a man, neither shall a man put on a woman's garment: for all that do so *are* abomination unto the Lord thy God."

8. George Gascoigne, *The Steele Glas,* 1576, in ed. Edward Arber, *English Reprints,* V (London, 1868), pp. 82-3.

9. Stubbes, p. 73.

10. Stubbes, p. 73. Cf. Harrison, in Wilson, pp. 124-25.

11. Henry Fitzgeffrey, *Notes from Black-fryers,* 1617. Cited by Wright, p. 492. See Wright, pp. 483-94 for other references to the "man-woman," including Barnabe Rich, in *The Honestie of this Age* (1614); Alexander Niccoles, in *A Discourse of Marriage And Wiving* (ed. of 1620); and Thomas Adams, in *Mystical Bedlam* (1615).

12. Wright, p. 490. Anger against women reached its zenith in Joseph Swetnam's misogynistic tract, *The Araignment of Lewd, Idle, Froward, and unconstant Women* (1615), which had ten printings by 1634 and inspired several responses (see Wright, pp. 486-93), including a stage-play, *Swetnam, the Woman-hater, Arraigned by Women,* (1620).

13. Wright, p. 507 and Fitz, pp. 2-3.

14. Along with the numerous isolated references to the *Hic Mulier* phenomenon cited in Wright, these documents include the *Hic Mulier* and *Haec-Vir* pamphlets, noted above, and another pamphlet, *Mulde Sacke: Or The Apologie of Hic Mulier: To the late Declamation against her* (1620). By referring to the *Hic Mulier* phenomenon as a "transvestite movement," or even as a "rough-and-ready unisex movement" (p. 15), Fitz implies more coherence and range to the fashion than these pamphlets can document. Cf. Woodbridge, pp. 139-51.

15. Edward Phillips Statham, *A Jacobean Letter-Writer: The Life and Times of John Chamberlain* (London, 1920), pp. 182-83.

16. We should not, I think, take for granted that misogynistic and feminist attitudes can be aligned neatly with gender in the Renaissance. The relative paucity of literature in the early 1600s in which women are clearly speaking for themselves makes specifically female attitudes extremely difficult to distinguish and assess. Resolving the problem of the correlation between gender and attitude is not, however, prerequisite to the present analysis, which seeks to compare the sexual values clearly articulated in the *Hic Mulier/Haec-Vir* debate with the artistic conception of a *Hic Mulier* figure in *The Roaring Girl.*

17. Wright, p. 490.

18. Wright, p. 497.

19. Fitz, pp. 16-17. Fitz, for example, sees as unfortunate the argument in *Haec-Vir* (sig. C2v) that it is a law of nature that differences between the sexes be preserved by designated dress and behavior. She also remarks that "Renaissance women so far accepted the masculine rules of the game that they felt they had to adopt the clothing and external attributes of the male sex in order to be 'free.' This was true in drama as in life: witness the transvestite heroines of Shakespeare's romantic comedies." See also Woodbridge, pp. 148-49.

20. See Suzanne W. Hull, *Chaste Silent & Obedient: English Books for Women 1475-1640* (San Marino, Cal, 1982). Hull provides an ample bibliography of documents that articulate the Renaissance ideal of womanhood.

21. Fitz, pp. 9-10. Also see Wright, pp. 490-91. See also Dusinberre, pp. 234-35.

22. Dusinberre, pp. 234-35, 239.

23. See *Hic Mulier* (sig. C2v): "To you . . . that are Fathers, Husbands, or Sustainers of these new *Hermaphrodites,* belongs the cure of this Impostume; it is you that give fuell to the flames of their wilde indiscretion." Cf. J. Chamberlain, in Statham, pp. 182-83: "A tax upon unruly female relatives! . . . the King threatens to fall upon theyre husbands, parents or frends that have or shold have power over them, and make them pay for it."

24. Cited in P.A. Mulholland, "The Date of The Roaring Girl," *Review of English Studies,* 28 (1977), 22, 30-31. See also Andor Gomme, Introd., *The Roaring Girl,* by Thomas Middleton and Thomas Dekker, (London, 1976), pp. xiii-xix, and Margaret Dowling, "A Note on Moll Cutpurse—'The Roaring Girl,'" *Review of English Studies,* 10 (1934), 67-71. There is a pamphlet called *The Life and Death of Mrs. Mary Frith,* published in 1662, but it is not thought to be reliable. For a review of the play's dramatic and non-dramatic sources, as well as references to the real Moll Frith, see Gomme, pp. xiii-xix, and Mulholland, pp. 18-31.

25. Mulholland, pp. 18-31, is the most recent example. Gomme, pp. xiii-xix, also sums up the attempts to date the play.

26. Mulholland, 18-9. As Mulholland observes (pp. 20-1), the *Consistory of London Correction Book* record concerning Mary Frith, which he cites at length on pp. 30-1, provides an extraordinary account both of the actual Moll and of the vehement opposition in Jacobean society to women wearing male attire, which is one offense of hers that is reiterated in the *Correction Book* entry.

27. Thomas Middleton, "To the Comic Play-Readers, Venery and Laughter," in Thomas Dekker and Thomas Middleton, *The Roaring Girl.* All citations from the play are taken from *Drama of the English Renaissance,* eds. Russell A. Fraser and Norman Rabkin (New York, 1976), II, 334-38.

28. The phrase is from Fitz, p. 16.

29. Laxton expresses his general view of women in 3.2.266-69: "That wile / By which the serpent did the first woman beguile / Did ever since all women's bosoms fill; / You're apple-eaters all, deceivers still."

30. Keith Thomas, "The Place of Laughter in Tudor and Stuart England," *Times Literary Supplement* (January 21, 1977), 78.

31. Carolyn G. Heilbrun, *Toward a Recognition of Androgyny* (New York, 1973), p. 39.

32. See, for example, *Hic Mulier*, sig. C3: "Doe you make it the utter losse of your favour and bounty to have brought into your Family, any new fashion or disguise, that might either deforme Nature, or bee an injury to modestie." Cf. Harrison, in Wilson, p. 123: "You shall not see any so disguised as are my countrymen of England," and Nashe, in Wilson, p. 125: "England, the players' stage of gorgeous attire, the ape of all nations' superfluities, the continual masquer in outlandish habiliments, great plenty-scanting calamities art thou to await, for wanton disguising thyself against kind; and digressing from the plainness of thy ancestors."

33. See Alexander Leggatt, *Shakespeare's Comedy of Love* (London, 1974), p. 202; Helen Gardner, *"As You Like It,"* in *Modern Shakespearean Criticism,* ed. Alvin B. Kernan (New York, 1970), pp. 199, 202; Helene Moglen, "Disguise and Development: The Self and Society in *Twelfth Night,"* *Literature and Psychology,* 23 (1973), 13-9; and Dusinberre, p. 257.

34. Robert Kimbrough, "Androgyny Seen Through Shakespeare's Disguise," *Shakespeare Quarterly,* 33 (Spring, 1982), 20, 19. Cf. Margaret Boerner Beckman, "The Figure of Rosalind in *As You Like It,"* *Shakespeare Quarterly,* 29 (Winter, 1978), 44-51.

35. Cf. Gardner, pp. 190-203 and Northrop Frye, "The Argument of Comedy," in ed. Kernan, pp. 165-73.

36. Cf. C.L. Barber, *Shakespeare's Festive Comedy: A Study of Dramatic Form and its Relation to Social Custom* (Princeton, N.J., 1959), pp. 245-47; Leggatt, p. 211; F. H. Mares, "Viola and other Transvestist Heroines in Shakespeare's Comedies," in ed. B. A. W. Jackson, *Stratford Papers on Shakespeare* (McMaster University Library Press, 1969 for 1965-1967), pp. 96-109; and Nancy K. Hayles, "Sexual Disguise in *As You Like It* and *Twelfth Night,"* *Shakespeare Survey,* 32 (1979), 63-72.

37. Northrop Frye, *A Natural Perspective* (New York, 1965), pp. 82-83.

38. Clara Claiborne Park, "As We Like It: How a Girl Can be Smart and Still Popular," in *The Woman's Part,* eds. Carolyn Ruth Swift Lenz, Gayle Greene, and Carol Thomas Neely (Urbana, Ill., 1980), p. 108.

39. Frye, p. 83.

40. See Gomme, p. xxiii, who points out that Mary and Moll have the same name, and that Moll "impersonates" Mary in the final scene "in order to complete the trick which secures Mary's happiness."

Viviana Comensoli (essay date 1987)

SOURCE: "Play-making, Domestic Conduct, and the Multiple Plot in *The Roaring Girl,"* in *Studies in English Literature 1500-1900,* Vol. 27, No. 2, Spring 1987, pp. 249-66.

[*In the following essay, Comensoli contends that the three plots of* The Roaring Girl *together "convey the concern at the heart of the play with the degeneration of marriage and the family, a tension sustained in the antithesis between the household (consistently portrayed as the seat of spiritual and emotional stasis and confinement) and the city (the hub of multifariousness and freedom)."*]

I

Moll Cutpurse, the central character of Dekker and Middleton's ***The Roaring Girl*** (c. 1608-1611), is based on the notorious roarerMary Frith who frequented the Fortune Theater in man's apparel. Mary was described by a contemporary as "a very Tomrig or Rumpscuttle" who "sported only in boys' play and pastime," scorned girlish endeavors such as "sewing or stitching," and showed "rude inclinations."[1] While Moll Cutpurse does many of the things her real-life counterpart did—she wears men's clothes, carries a weapon, and mixes in taverns with members of the underworld—she also punishes lecherous gallants through her skillful sword-fighting and promotes the love-marriage of Mary Fitzallard and Sebastian Wengrave. T. S. Eliot was the first to praise ***The Roaring Girl*** as "one comedy which more than any other Elizabethan comedy realizes a free and noble womanhood," an achievement compensating for the play's rough plotting: "we read with toil through a mass of cheap conventional intrigue, and suddenly realize that we are . . . observing a real and unique human being."[2] Since Eliot's assessment the citizen-plot, with its commonplace motif of lusty gallants chasing citizen wives, has been largely viewed as a ponderous distraction from Moll's fascinating duality. Cyrus Hoy, for one, expresses a common sentiment when he laments the conventional comedy in the play, "with its seemingly compliant citizens' wives and the impecunious gallants who would like to seduce or live off them," but praises "the bold and often brilliantly original" portrait of Moll.[3] The Royal Shakespeare Company's 1983 production of the play, the first major production since the play's première at the Fortune,[4] portrayed Moll as a commendable virago but tampered considerably with the other plots in order to bring Moll's role into sharp focus.[5]

The few critics who have commented on the play's structural merits have stressed the orthodox design of the comic action and its progression toward a society renewed by married love. In 1970 David Holmes referred to the play as a "nexus of plots with a common motif," namely "the dignity of marriage."[6] More recently, some attention has been paid to the Sebastian Wengrave-Mary Fitzallard action in connection with Moll's role in bringing about the young lovers' marriage. Patrick Cheney, analyzing Moll's dual identity, links the marriage to Moll's symbolic function: because Moll "combines in her person both feminine and masculine traits, and uses her remarkable powers to unite other couples in love," she is suggestive of Renaissance representations of the hermaphrodite-figure, "a supreme symbol of two souls becoming one—particularly within the context of married love."[7] For Larry Champion, the play is "a complex pattern of schemes and counter-schemes" set in motion by Sebastian, whose feigned passion for Moll Cutpurse prompts his father to agree to his son's marriage to Mary Fitzallard, just as in the citizen-plot the gallants "set their practice upon the citizen-wives."[8] The plots are "effectively interwoven" to sustain a comic perspective and "a continuing assurance of the ultimate success of love and right reason" leading to "a happy ending."[9] Mary Beth Rose, in her analysis of the play in the context of the *Hic Mulier/Haec-Vir* controversy, acknowledges a certain amount of ambiguity in the dramatic portrayal of Moll, but also stresses the conventional nature of the comic ending.[10] Despite the pamphlet's late date, Moll is considered a direct dramatic parallel of the transvestite in *Hic Mulier,* where "the figure of the female in male attire" inspires "simultaneous admiration, desire, abhorrence, and fear."[11] While we detect authorial sympathy with "sexual non-conformity, female independence, and equality between the sexes," the play, argues Rose, ultimately resists Moll's integration into society: "having served as the instrument who brings about the happy ending," Moll "is nevertheless excluded from the renewed comic society of married couples which forms on the stage at the end of the play."[12] The "desirable social norm in the play" is thus not Moll's transvestism but the conservative "relationship and opinions" of Sebastian and Mary.[13] A full evaluation of Moll's relation to the multiple plot, I propose, must accommodate two significant qualifications: 1) while Moll does assist in ushering in the typical comic ending, she unequivocally renounces *for herself* the conventional values embodied by Mary and Sebastian, a choice which the audience is invited to condone; 2) although Moll and her roarer-companions reject conventional behavior, they are never excluded from the reformed society sketched in the denouement; instead, their presence during the final two scenes provides a compelling alternative to the ideal marriage. Moreover, the idealistic conclusion of the Sebastian-Mary action must be considered in relation to the dramatists' cynical treatment of marriage in the citizen-plot and its realistic treatment of conjugal malaise. Both Moll's misogamy and the citizens' domestic conflicts counterpoint the Sebastian-Mary action, indicating that the ideal marriage is a possibility not wholly realized, even in a transformed society.

Taken together, the three plots convey the concern at the heart of the play with the degeneration of marriage and the family, a tension sustained in the antithesis between the household (consistently portrayed as the seat of spiritual and emotional stasis and confinement) and the city (the hub of multifariousness and freedom). The multiple-plot structure is thus loosely unified through the careful arrangement of setting, so that altogether six scenes are set within various households and five in the city streets and fields around London. The world of the money-hungry social climbers and of the sycophantic gallants and self-satisfied citizens is ruled by the single pursuit of materialistic values. These characters are invariably either in their shops (notably architectural extensions of their homes) where they accumulate wealth, or at home where decep-

tion and bawdy innuendo underscore the deterioration of domestic life. The younger generation, represented by Sebastian Wengrave and Mary Fitzallard on the one hand, and by Moll Cutpurse and her roarer-companion Jack Dapper on the other, is removed from the world of the elders. Prior to their marriage, Mary and Sebastian are associated neither with the domestic sphere nor with the city, but stand apart in their idealism. For Moll and Jack, both the world of the elders and the idealism of Mary and Sebastian represent denial and limitation. Neither Moll nor Jack has or wants a home; their space is the street, the world of thieves, beggars, and drifters. Moll's contradictory behavior attests to the play's central paradox in that the resolution upholds both the ritualized cleansing of the *domus* through Mary and Sebastian's love-marriage and the roarers' rejection of that sphere in favor of the polymorphism of the city.

In the shift from one perspective to another, the spectator participates in a process of creating a multifaceted society as varied and paradoxical as the play. The tension agrees with the dramatists' idea of playmaking as a protean activity. Fashionable plays, argues Middleton in his address "To the Comicke Play-readers, Venery, and Laughter"[14] which prefaces the quarto, cater to popular taste: likening "The fashion of play-making" to "the alteration in apparell" (lines 1-2), Middleton observes that the time now being one "of sprucenes," plays are fashioned after the folly of "our Garments, single plots, quaint conceits, letcherous iests, drest vp in hanging sleeues" (lines 6-8). Middleton advises the audience that the play he and Dekker have written goes beyond popular fashion in denying easy solutions, a sentiment echoed in the Prologue, where we are cautioned against coming to the theater expecting to view a polished work, "a booke, / Compos'd to all perfections" (lines 2-3), which will gratify our preconceived notions of experience:

> each one comes
> And brings a play in's head with him: vp he summes,
> What he would of a Roaring Girle haue writ;
> If that he findes not here, he mewes at it.

> (lines 3-6)

Whereas fashionable plays are neatly packaged, closed systems, **The Roaring Girl** is methectic and open-ended, its emphasis on multiplicity and variability challenging the audience's complacency.

II

The play opens upon a typical conflict in city comedy; the father, Sir Alexander Wengrave, is determined to impede his son's marriage for reasons which are purely materialistic and self-serving. A recently-dubbed knight, Wengrave scorns Sebastian's love for Mary Fitzallard, whose dowry of five thousand marks renders her "but a beggars heire" (I.i.82). While the expository details are set forth Wengrave's house forms an obtrusive setting. The direct alignment of the two scenes comprising Act I draws our attention to the house's subdivisions, a fairly recent architectural phenomenon. During the late sixteenth and early seventeenth centuries, subdivided homes became indicative of status among the gentry and yeomanry.[15] This development corresponded to the increase in domestic comfort, as evidenced by improved methods of construction favoring well-lit open spaces and terraces[16] and generating a variety of household effects including upholstered furniture, chairs, draw tables, and beds with decorated frames. The new emphasis on domestic comfort represented "an important move towards the notion of individuality and sexual privacy."[17] The design of the Wengrave household confirms Wengrave's successful climb to the landed gentry, while his status-seeking is the focus of the play's sharpest satirical attack. Scene i, where the disguised Mary Fitzallard secretly visits Sebastian, is set in the foyer, situated near the "hall" or servants' quarter (I.i.16) and the "buttry" (line 21). In scene ii we enter "Th'inner roome" (I.ii.6) of the house where Wengrave is hosting a dinner party. Proud of his possessions, Wengrave subjects his guests (and the audience) to an extensive and disquieting tour of each room. We are led from the separate dining area which, ironically, is "too close" (line 6), to the cooler "Parlour" (line 7). From there, we proceed to the "galleries" in the center of the house (line 14) where a grotesque mosaic covers the walls, intensifying the claustrophobic atmosphere—"Within one square a thousand heads are laid / So close, that all of heads, the roome seems made" (I.ii.19-20)—and where the *trompe-l'oeil* effect of the floor waving "to and fro, / . . . like a floating Iland" (lines 30-31) projects an image of a world distorted by illusion.

As the dinner-party scene unfolds, the household is depicted essentially as an extension of a money economy. The adulteration of the once sacred bond between host and guest, for instance, is underscored by Wengrave's calculating advice to Greenwit upon learning of the young man's desire to leave sooner than decorum permits: "Your loue sir, has already giuen me some time, / And if you please to trust my age with more, / It shall pay double interest: Good sir stay" (I.ii.36-8). Wengrave's metaphor from commerce is a signal to the young man of the ethic that now rules the host-guest relationship, the guest's function being to defer to the host's pride and social status in exchange for patronage. As Wengrave dispenses wine during post-dinner formalities and grandly displays the furniture, which "Cost many a faire gray groat ere it came here" (line 12), his makeshift hospitality and the guests' hypocrisy are revealed through a series of double-entendres and vicious sexual innuendoes:

> ALEX. Pray make that stoole your pearch, good
> Maister *Goshawke*.
> GOSH. I stoope to your lure sir.
>   . . . . .
> ALEX.furnish maister *Laxton*
> With what he wants (a stone) a stoole I would say,
> A stoole.
> LAX. I had rather stand sir.
>
>   (I.ii.54-60)

The image of the household as the center of concupiscence links the Wengrave action and the citizen-plot where feeding, bawdy word-play, and sexual inadequacy form a complex configuration. Wengrave's feast is directly mirrored by the citizens' equally disquieting dinner party (III.ii). The scene opens upon a domestic squabble between the hosts, Prudence and Master Gallipot, disrupting the festive mood. Prudence enters "as from supper, her husband after her" (s.d.), and inveighs against Gallipot's uxorious behavior. On the surface the exchange is farcical, but broad comedy is restrained by the urgency of the language which alerts us to the couple's emotional and sexual dissatisfaction. Prudence is angry because her husband dotes on her as an infant dotes on its mother: "I thinke the baby would haue a teate it kyes so, pray be not so fond of me, . . . I'me vext at you to see how like a calfe you come bleating after me" (III.ii.2-5). The source of Prudence's frustration is Gallipot's refusal to "vp and ride" (line 9), provoking her lusty pursuit of the gallant Laxton.[18] The couple's conjugal problems are coherently sketched through an extended pattern of food imagery. Gallipot, whose virility is dubious—"Vp and ride, nay my pretty Pru, thats farre from my thought, ducke" (lines 10-1)—importunes his termagant wife to behave more decorously toward their guests, and attempts to appease her through proverbial food lore: "thy minde is nibbling at something, whats ist, what lyes vpon thy Stomach?" (lines 11-2). Suspecting that Prudence may have a lover, Gallipot articulates his suspicion through another barrage of food imagery: "I smel a goose, a couple of capons, and a gammon of bacon from her mother out of the country" (lines 70-1). Throughout the exchange Gallipot's need for oral gratification is strongly implied.[19] His inability to distinguish between feeding and love, his persistent whining—"the baby would haue a teate it kyes so"[20]—and his dependence on non-sexual contact are the source of Prudence's strongest reproach: "your loue is all words; giue mee deeds, I cannot abide a man thats too fond ouer me, so cookish; thou dost not know how to handle a woman in her kind" (lines 22-4).

The scene culminates in Prudence and Laxton's jest, whereby the gallant poses as the wife's original suitor who has come to reclaim her. Gallipot's uneasiness over having to relinquish his source of gratification to a rival, a prospect which he equates with being deprived of a choice dish of food, is an aggressive, infantile response—"Haue you [Laxton] so beggarly an appetite / When I vpon a dainty dish haue fed / To dine vpon my scraps, my leauings? ha sir?" (III.ii.229-31). When alone with Prudence, Gallipot is passive and obsequious, but to his rival and to society at large he appears sexually potent, a lie which he fosters through bawdy metaphors: "pray sir [Laxton] weare not her, for shee's a garment / So fitting for my body, I'me loath / Another should put it on, you will vndoe both" (lines 234-36). The uneasy tone is sustained in the reconciliation scene (IV.ii) where Gallipot forgives Laxton because the gallant has not actually seduced the wife, but does not offer to forgive Prudence (IV.ii.318-20). Audiences at the Fortune Theater could compare Gallipot's behavior with that of Master Frankford, the husband-hero of Heywood's domestic tragedy *A Woman Killed With Kindness* (c. 1603), which Christianized the revenge ethic in its sympathetic portrayal of a husband who forgives rather than condemns his wife's adultery. Whereas Frankford's sacrifice preserves the conjugal ideal, Gallipot's bombast during the reconciliation scene points not only to moral lassitude but also to the continuation of conjugal strife. That the marriage will never be free of conflict is confirmed by Gallipot's bold invitation of the gallant to dinner, in which he chastises Prudence with a derogatory epithet, masking once again his sexual inadequacy: "Wee'll crowne our table with it [Laxton's jest]: wife brag no more, / Of holding out: who most brags is most whore" (lines 323-24).

The unsettling tone of the Prudence-Gallipot action is only partly attenuated by the more whitewashed marriage of Master and Mistress Openwork. The central concern in the Openwork action is the husband's exposure of Goshawk's lechery: Openwork dupes the gallant by pretending that Mistress Openwork's shrewishness has led him to keep a whore in the suburbs (II.i.272-76). Openwork's test of his wife's fidelity, which she in turn requites with a feigned desire for Goshawk, is therefore only a pretense to dupe the gallant and to teach him to "deale vpon mens wiues no more" (IV.ii.216). Once the gallant has learned the valuable lesson, the action concludes with Openwork's invitation of Goshawk to dinner, paralleling Gallipot's forgiveness of Laxton:

> MAIST. OPEN. Make my house yours sir still.
> GOSH. No.
> MAIST. OPEN. I say you shall:
> Seeing (thus besieg'd) it holds out, 'twill neuer fall.
>
> (lines 217-19)

Ostensibly preserved is the general rule of decorum in the public theaters requiring gallants who attempt the seduction of citizen-wives to "come off badly."[21] That Gallipot's "virtue" remains questionable, however, has been established by his response to Laxton's and Prudence's jest. A moral ambiguity also qualifies Openwork's behavior. Goshawk's admission of guilt prompts Openwork to muse on the world's imperfection—"On fairest cheeks, wife nothing is perfect borne. / . . . What's this whole world but a gilt rotten pill?" / . . . The world can hardly yeeld a perfect friend" (IV.ii.204-13). The remark undercuts not only the confident tone of Openwork's offer of his house to the gallant, but also the promise of social stability brought about by his hospitality.[22]

From the point of view of citizen comedy, perhaps the most disturbing element of the resolution of the citizen-plot concerns the problem of Prudence Gallipot's lascivious behavior. Unlike Mistress Openwork's feigned passion for Goshawk, Prudence's desire for Laxton is never uncovered as a pretense. In Act II we learn that the affair is not consummated because the gallant has no intention of seducing the wife (II.i.114-23); he merely desires Galli-

pot's money, which he lavishes on other women. While Mistress Openwork comes to appreciate her husband's virtue, Prudence merely informs us that she is "ridd" of Laxton (IV.ii.40). We are given no firm indication that she unequivocally yields to Gallipot's apparent virtue.[23] Prudence's unrepentant desire is a rare occurrence in a comedy performed in the public theater where citizen-wives were not portrayed as adulterous.[24]

III

The disturbed, unregenerate world of the citizens and the landed gentry is juxtaposed with the stable, more innocent world of the young lovers, Mary and Sebastian. Their world is suffused with an aura of sacredness manifested chiefly in their dialogue which teems with devotional imagery. The couple's secret betrothal is not a grotesque extension of eating, nor is it founded on sexual appetite; instead, it is, in Mary's words, a union sanctioned by heaven: "in one knot / Haue both our hands byt'h hands of heauen bene tyed" (I.i.68-9). For Mary, matrimony is "a bond fast sealed, with solemne oathes, / Subscribed vnto . . . with your soule: / Deliuered as your deed in sight of heauen" (lines 51-3). Mary distinguishes between love which is "wouen sleightly" (line 29) and a nobler love which is "truely bred ith the soule" (line 31). The denouement, where Mary and Sebastian reiterate their marriage vows with the blessing of their elders and of society at large, reinforces the idea of marriage as the field where one ought to practise virtue. Indeed, the language in this scene is so transformed that it becomes epideictic. In tone and structure the final one hundred lines of the play recall the celebration of marriage in epithalamic verse. Mary, dressed as a "Bride," is brought in "twixt two noble friends" (V.ii.168), and the wedding is celebrated by all of society: the guests include lords, gentlemen, ladies, citizens and their wives, and the roarers Moll Cutpurse and Trapdoor. Having abandoned his "wilfull rashnesse" (line 193) the reformed Wengrave, like the epithalamist, "call[s] into being the ideal event which the wedding must be, the ideal as defined partly by the convention, partly by the particular society, partly by the poet."[25] Repenting his former blindness, Wengrave extols the wedding as a sacred occasion (lines 173-74) and invokes heaven's blessing of the couple (line 202). He also articulates the epithalamist's conventional praise of the bride's virtue and beauty (lines 189-95), and the familiar wish for offspring and material prosperity: "the best ioyes, / That can in worldly shapes to man betide, / Are fertill lands, and a faire fruitfull Bride" (lines 202-04). The scene ends with Wengrave's injunction, "as I am, so all goe pleas'd away" (line 266), echoing the epithalamist's command to break off the revelry so that the bedding of the couple may take place.

The stylized epithalamic cadences of the final scene enhance the conventional nature of Mary and Sebastian's union which represents the renewal, typical of New-Comic endings, of a society made barren by its obsession with mercantile values. However, before he can enjoy the benefits of his new life, Sebastian, like the prodigals of

New Comedy, asks and receives his father's forgiveness
for the sorrow he has caused him (V.ii.170-73).[26] Paradoxically, the strongly idealistic nature of Mary and Sebastian's marriage is tempered by the Moll Cutpurse-Jack
Dapper action, where language creates a radically different
kind of personal and social transformation.

IV

The central ambiguity of the multiple plot hinges on the
contradictions embodied in Moll Cutpurse, who aids Sebastian in securing his father's approval of his marriage
while asserting that she herself would never agree to marry
(V.ii.214). Moll's rejection of marriage derives in part
from the Christian ascetic tradition. In her refusal to submit
not only to men but to her own physical nature, Moll associates independence with physical denial:

> shee that has wit, and spirit,
> May scorne to liue beholding to her body for meate,
> Or for apparell like your common dame,
> That makes shame get her cloathes, to couer shame.

> (III.i.133-36)

Moll expresses the traditional dichotomy between body
and spirit, rejecting altogether the world of desire where
identity is governed by "apparell" and where marriage is
not the union of opposites but the handmaiden of lust:

> Base is that minde, that kneels vnto her body,
> As if a husband stood in awe on's wife,
> My spirit shall be Mistresse of this house,
> As long as I haue time in't.

> (lines 137-40)

Elsewhere, however, Moll confesses to Sebastian that she
has renounced marriage and the pleasures of the flesh for
more practical, self-serving reasons: "I haue no humor to
marry, I loue to lye aboth sides ath bed my selfe; and
againe ath'other side; a wife you know ought to be obedient, but I feare me I am too headstrong to obey, therefore
Ile nere go about it" (II.ii.35-8). Moll rejects marriage
because it denies a woman freedom to act as she pleases
in the world: "I haue the head now of my selfe, and am
man enough for a woman, marriage is but a chopping and
changing, where a maiden looses one head, and has a
worse ith place" (lines 40-3). Moll, whose sense of self is
highly individualized, views marriage as a threat to a
woman's identity, marriage being the exchange of one
"head" for another in that a wife replaces her maidenhead
(a symbol, to Moll, of independence) with the sovereignty
of her husband.

At the same time that Moll chooses independence for
herself, she is aware of the loss which her renunciation
necessitates. As she plays on the viol for Sebastian, Moll
sings of her dream at the core of which is a subtle tension
between denial and desire. The first part of the dream
concerns a woman who delights in "unwomanly" pastimes
such as squandering money and mixing with vulgar
company:

> *I dreame there is a Mistresse,*
> . . . . .
> *Shee sayes shee went to'th Bursse for patternes,*
>   *You shall finde her at* Saint Katherns,
> *And comes home with neuer a penny.*

> (IV.i.99-105)

The woman in the dream, like Moll herself, does not buy
"patternes" to sew dresses, sewing being the quintessential
stereotypical occupation of women; instead, she prefers to
carouse in "Saint Katherns," the dockside district in
London's east end, which was "notorious for its brew-
houses and taverns."[27] In the second part of the dream
Moll describes the sexual adventures of an adulterous
woman (lines 109-19), a fantasy which gives Moll
pleasure, although she is careful to distinguish between
her dream-life and reality: "Hang vp the viall now sir: all
this while I was in a dreame; one shall lie rudely then, but
being awake, I keepe my legges together" (lines 122-24).
Moll's dream suggests we are viewing neither a symbol of
virtue nor the two-dimensional virago of the *Hic Mulier*
pamphlet, but a complex individual whose dream/song
embodies the self's ambiguous relationship to the world.
Through her transvestism, Moll has adopted the more
forceful male role in order to escape subordination,
although she has done so by sacrificing her sexual longing,
a compromise which her dream brings into relief.[28] Yet the
loss for Moll is preferable to a life of wifely submission.
Proud of her independence, Moll cannot tolerate the
subjugation which marriage entails, a loss which, by
implication, will follow even Mary Fitzallard's entrance
into the *domus*.

Moll's fullness and complexity are expressed through her
adaptability: she is at home both in the world of "the
Temple" (III.i.164) and amid thieves and prostitutes in
Chicke Lane (line 167). Her duality encompasses both her
proficiency as a musician (an accomplishment which a
Renaissance audience would appreciate as indicative of
harmony, refinement, and felicity) and her mastery of a
different kind of "music," namely thieves' cant (V.i).
Throughout the play the dramatists underscore Moll's
protean nature, which cannot be understood by those
whose understanding is weak or who conceive of the world
two-dimensionally. Moll's strangeness is disturbing and
everywhere draws mistrust. To those who fear her, she is
"madde Moll" (Prologue, line 30; I.i.94), a despised "flesh
fly," a "scuruy woman" (I.ii.127-28), and "some Monster"
(line 138). To Moll's fellow-roarer, Trapdoor, Moll's
identity is confusing and unpredictable: "I like you the
worse because you shift your lodging so often" (III.i.168).
Even the truth-obsessed Mistress Openwork denies Moll
her "house and shop" (II.i.211) on the basis of Moll's
outrageous appearance.

Moll's boldly unconventional nature corresponds to the
play's identity as a work of art. Just as in Moll's world
clothes often make the person, play-making, we noted in
Middleton's address to the audience, is frequently only a
matter of catering to the current fashion. *The Roaring Girl*

counters the popular trend not only because the play frustrates expectation but also because it is subject to censorship for defying a law which upholds the sanctity of appearance: "For Venus being a woman passes through the play in doublet and breeches, a braue disguise and a safe one, if the Statute vnty not her cod-peice point" ("To the Comicke Play-readers," lines 13-5). The statute in question is the law forbidding women to wear male dress, which arose from "the controversy then raging over women's role and rights, their wearing men's hats or masculine dress . . . be[ing] one of the signs of moral degeneration."[29] The purpose of art, argues Middleton, is to expose truth, even if it might not always be "fit for the Times, and the Tearmers" (line 8). Moll is never forced to renounce her choices in order to gratify what Middleton considers the unreasonable expectations of certain spectators among the large citizen audiences who frequented the Fortune playhouse. At the same time, the play's favorable portrayal of a strongly independent woman points to the dramatists' awareness of an increasingly assertive audience of city women who, as the *hic mulier* controversy attests, were demanding and gradually "getting more freedom."[30]

In the final scene Moll indirectly flouts Mary and Sebastian's wedding by prophesying she will marry only when society undergoes a seemingly impossible reformation that would see, among other things, "Honesty and truth vnslandred, / Woman man'd, but neuer pandred," and "Cheaters booted, but not coacht" (V.ii.219-21). Lord Noland's alarmed reply—"This sounds like domes-day" (line 225)—is countered by Moll with a disturbing quip: "Then were marriage best, / For if I should repent, I were soone at rest" (lines 126-27). Moll's misogamy provides a powerful alternative to the veneration of marriage and procreation that informs the epithalamic ending.

V

Dekker and Middleton's provocation of the audience, together with their opposition to unjust authority, is underscored by Moll's participation in the Jack Dapper action. That Jack functions dramatically as Moll's double is suggested by Moll's street name, "Iack" (V.ii.97-98; lines 212, 215). A profligate and a spendthrift who lives on credit, Jack Dapper lavishes his money on tobacco and wine, and associates with prostitutes and catamites (III.iii.55-64). His father Davy Dapper, who is resolved to punish Jack's profligate ways, orders his arrest and detention in Bridewell, the notorious house of correction. The farcical overtones of the arrest, however, block the audience's sympathy for the father. The search for Jack is carried out amid absurd hunting cries and references to the quest for game (lines 158-91), and is headed by Sergeant Curtilax, a blusterer whose primitive understanding renders him a disturbing defender of the law: "all that liue in the world, are but great fish and little fish, and feede vpon one another" (lines 134-35). Moll's intervention prevents the arrest. Moll forcibly rescues Jack from the sergeant's custody (lines 200-10), an offense which under Jacobean

law was "very serious"[31] in that it could lead to a long imprisonment. In the aftermath, neither Moll nor Jack repents the crime; instead, Moll describes her part as her "perfect one good worke to day" (line 212). The next time we see Moll and Jack together is during the long canting episode in the final act where they mingle freely among cutpurses and delight in their knowledge of the underworld.[32]

The canting scene, which is interposed between the resolution of the citizen-plot (IV.ii) and the glorious epithalamic ending (V.ii), is crucial to the play's thematic and structural design.[33] As a prelude to the canting, Moll and her fellow-roarers join with Jack Dapper in deriding his father's unsuccessful attempt to have him imprisoned. In direct counterpoint to Sebastian's request for his own father's forgiveness (V.ii.170-72), Jack renounces repentance, declaring that not even prison would reform him: "as though a Counter, which is a parke, in which all the wilde beasts of the Citty run head by head could tame mee" (V.i.40-1). The rowdy tone of the celebration also contrasts sharply with that of the wedding feast that transpires in Wengrave's household. The roarers will celebrate Jack's freedom by carousing in the London streets and taverns, and by feasting at "Pimlico . . . that nappy land of spice-cakes" (lines 49-50), described elsewhere in Dekker as a mad world frequented by revellers and crammed with "Bawdy houses."[34] The audience, moreover, is coaxed into assenting to the roarers' adventure through Lord Noland's participation in the action. A strictly sympathetic character from the upper ranks of society, Lord Noland eagerly follows the roarers, inviting his friends to join in the celebration: "Heeres such a merry ging, I could find in my heart to saile to the worlds end with such company, come Gentlemen let's on" (V.i.51-2). After the roarers flaunt their skills in the obscurities of thieves' cant, Moll engages Tearcat in a boisterous drinking song for which they receive "two shillings six pence" (line 220) from Lord Noland and his friends:

> MOLL. Come you rogue sing with me.
> A gage of ben Rom-house
> In a bousing ken of Rom-vile.
> T. CAT. Is Benar then a Caster,
> Pecke, penman, lap or popler,
> Which we mill in deuse a vile.
> BOTH. Oh I wud lib all the lightmans.
> Oh I woud lib all the darkemans,
> By the sollamon, vnder the Ruffemans.
> By the sollamon in the Hartmans.
> T. CAT. And scoure the Quire cramp ring,
> And couch till a pallyard docked my dell,
> So my bousy nab might skew rome bouse well.
>
> (V.i.194-207)

The final refrain, "Auast to the pad, let vs bing, / Auast to the pad, let vs bing" (lines 208-209), which translates "Away to the highway, let us go,"[35] asserts Moll and Tearcat's loyalty to the open streets. In Moll's subsequent paraphrase of the song (lines 235-40), which amounts to "let's drink and be merry," we learn that we have been listening to an ode to freedom. The inscrutable nature of the argot, together with its rough and spirited cadences, balances the stylized verse in the epithalamic conclusion, bestowing on the roarers' language a similar power to please the audience.

The Moll Cutpurse-Jack Dapper action is never subordinated to the Mary-Sebastian plot. Instead, the play interweaves a pattern of divergent meanings, suspending and resuspending a firm resolution until all the characters are reunited in the final scene where society is recreated as a network of disparate structures. Central to the process of renewal is the sympathetic presentation, in the popular theater, of a heroine's desire for self-realization. *The Roaring Girl* exposes the folly of popular opinion, including in this case secular law, by demonstrating that Moll's disguise is a "safe one" ("To the Comic Play-Readers," line 14), that is, "morally sound and mentally sane" (OED). Thus by the end of the play, both Alexander Wengrave and the audience are capable of judging Moll according to her worth, realizing that the "common voyce" is the real "whore," in that it "deceiues mans opinion; mockes his trust, / Cozens his loue, and makes his heart vniust" (V.ii.248-50). While the play's epithalamic ending calls attention to the possibility of regeneration through marriage, Moll and the roarers' affirmation of another "order" upholds a strikingly different set of values, fulfilling the play's promise of complexity and multiplicity.

Notes

1. Letter from John Chamberlain to Dudley Carleton, 11 February 1612; quoted in A. H. Bullen, ed., *The Works of Thomas Middleton*, 8 vols. (London: J.C. Nimmo, 1885), 4:4.

2. T. S. Eliot, *Elizabethan Essays* (New York: Haskell House, 1964), pp. 100, 89.

3. Cyrus Hoy, *Introductions, Notes, and Commentaries to texts in "The Dramatic Works of Thomas Dekker," Edited by Fredson Bowers*, 4 vols. (Cambridge: Cambridge Univ. Press, 1980), 3:9. Norman A. Brittin also praises Moll as "an upright, goodhearted girl of great size and strength who, like a questing knight, helps her friends and whose bad reputation is undeserved," but ignores the function of the citizen-plot (*Thomas Middleton* [New York: Twayne, 1972], p. 77).

4. The play has been performed infrequently. P. Mulholland, in "Let her roar again: *The Roaring Girl* Revived," *RORD* 18 (1985):15-27, notes that since 1951, the date of "the earliest modern production on record" (p. 15), there have been six stage productions, of which the Royal Shakespeare Company's is the "most important" (p. 19), and one radio adaptation. See also Marilyn Roberts, "A Preliminary Check-List of Productions of Thomas Middleton's Plays," *RORD* 18 (1985):37-61; 52-3.

5. To "make the play 'slightly more deft,'" the director Barry Kyle "altered the order of some scenes in Act 1 and shifted the last half of Act 4 to the middle of Act 5" (Francesca Simon, "The Honest Cutpurse at the Play: Francesca Simon talks to Barry Kyle about the RSC's *Roaring Girl* starring Helen Mirren," *The Sunday Times*, 24 April 1983, p. 42e). The "effect," wrote one reviewer, was a strong emphasis on Moll, while the rest of the action tended toward "vertical tourism" (Irving Wardle, "Distant Echo of Jacobean Mirth," *The London Times*, 27 April 1983, p. 14). Another reviewer praised Helen Mirren's spirited portrayal of Moll, but complained of loss of "audience involvement" as a result of Kyle's "cut[ting] and patch[ing]," which made for "three or four plots awkwardly interwined" (Russell Taylor, in *Drama: The Quarterly Theatre Review* [Autumn 1983]:40-1; 40).

6. David M. Holmes, *The Art of Thomas Middleton: A Critical Study* (Oxford: Clarendon Press, 1970), pp. 102, 107.

7. Patrick Cheney, "Moll Cutpurse as Hermaphrodite in Dekker and Middleton's *The Roaring Girl*," *Ren&R* n.s. 7 (May 1983):124, 125.

8. Larry S. Champion, *Thomas Dekker and the Traditions of English Drama* (New York: Peter Lang, 1985), p. 82.

9. Champion, p. 85.

10. Mary Beth Rose, "Women in Men's Clothing: Apparel and Social Stability in *The Roaring Girl*," *ELR* 14 (Autumn 1984): 367-91. The literary and social contexts of the controversy over the issue of women in men's apparel, which "came to a head in 1620 with a pair of pamphlets entitled, respectively, *Hic Mulier: Or, The Man-Woman*, and *Haec-Vir: Or the Womanish-Man*" (Rose, pp. 367-88), are fully explored in Linda Woodbridge, *Women and the English Renaissance: Literature and the Nature of Womankind, 1540-1620* (Urbana and Chicago: Univ. of Illinois Press, 1984), passim. For my argument concerning the dramatic complexity and attractiveness of the central character of *The Roaring Girl*, I am indebted to Woodbridge's observation that the play not only "gives favorable treatment to a man-clothed virago" (p. 250), but also "paints an intriguing portrait of modern assertive women" (p. 262).

11. Rose, p. 368.

12. Rose, p. 389.

13. Rose, p. 385.

14. *The Dramatic Works of Thomas Dekker*, ed. Fredson Bowers, 4 vols. (Cambridge: Cambridge Univ. Press, 1953-1961), 3:11. Subsequent references to the play will be to this edition.

15. Sheila Rowbotham, *Hidden from History: 300 Years of Women's Oppression and the Fight Against It*, 2nd edn. (London: Pluto Press, 1974), p. 3.

16. Michel Grivelet, *Thomas Heywood et le Drame Domestique Elizabéthain* (Paris: Librairie Marcel Didier, 1957), pp. 19-20. See also Marjorie Quennell and C. H. B. Quennell, *A History of Everyday Things in England: 1500-1799*, 5th edn., vol. 2 of *A History of Everyday Things in England*, 4 vols. (London: Batsford, 1960), chs. 1 and 2; and W. G. Hoskins, "The Rebuilding of Rural England, 1570-1640," in *Provincial England: Essays in Social*

and Economic History (London and New York: Macmillan and St. Martin's Press, 1963), pp. 131-48.

17. Rowbotham, p. 3.

18. Andor Gomme, ed., *The Roaring Girl* (London and New York: Benn and Norton, 1976), p. 64, n. 9, observes that "'Ride' was Standard English for sexual intercourse," and suggests that Mistress Gallipot might be "picking up a sexual suggestion in her husband's last word ['come'] and possibly 'hony'."

19. Understood psychoanalytically, Gallipot's excessive passivity, his dependence on non-sexual affection, and his delight in infantile behavior are manifestations of an oral compulsion. "Because the oral phase occupies the earliest period when self and object are still not clearly differentiated," writes Norman N. Holland, the phase "establish[es] . . . our abilities to do nothing, to be passive" (*The Dynamics of Literary Response* [New York: Oxford Univ. Press], 1968, p. 36).

20. The term "kyes," as used by Prudence Gallipot, indicates "baby-talk": in talking to her husband, she uses the language of nursemaids (Gomme, p. 63, n. 3). In this case, notes Gomme, "Master Gallipot is the baby."

21. Alexander Leggatt, *Citizen Comedy in the Age of Shakespeare* (Toronto and Buffalo: Univ. of Toronto Press, 1973), p. 135.

22. Critics tend to ignore the ambiguities of the reconciliation scene in the citizen-plot. For Larry Champion, "The feast that follows is . . . a commonplace symbol of reconciliation and social harmony throughout Renaissance comedy" (*Thomas Dekker and the Traditions of English Drama*, p. 84). Andor Gomme views the reconciliation as part of the play's broader message that "deception and scheming" are "found everywhere and can always be unmasked by plain dealing" ("Introduction," *The Roaring Girl*, p. xxiv). Patrick Cheney writes that "the primary aim" of the citizen-plot "is to reunite the wives with their husbands; and the secondary aim is to expose the gallants for men of lust, and then to incorporate them as friends to the married couples" ("Moll Cutpurse as Hermaphrodite in Dekker and Middleton's *The Roaring Girl*," p. 128). Similarly, Mary Beth Rose suggests that the scene restores marital harmony, mitigating the "illicit sexuality" represented by "the seducing gallants, who . . . herefore turn out not to constitute a real threat to the social order at all" ("Women in Men's Clothing: Apparel and Social Stability in *The Roaring Girl*," p. 382). A very different view is put forth by Simon Shepherd, in *Amazons and Warrior Women: Varieties of Feminism in Seventeenth-Century Drama* (Brighton: Harvester Press, 1981): Prudence and Mistress Gallipot are pawns in "the male world" which exploits women by relegating them to "the emotional and sexual sphere" (p. 49). The citizen-plot reconciles the husbands with the gallants "to the exclusion of the women, who remain used and dissatisfied" (p. 80). Shepherd's interpretation is not entirely borne out by the text, where the women are never passive in their dealings with the men, and where the reconciliation between Openwork and Goshawk is tenuous.

23. David Holmes notes that "Mistress Gallipot's deficiencies, deceitfulness, and proneness to corruption, contrast with Mistress Openwork's plain dealing and moral hardihood" (*The Art Of Thomas Middleton*, p. 107), but he does not substantiate the claim. The Royal Shakespeare Company's production also differentiated between the citizen-couples: "At their appearance in the final scene of the play some unease still attended the Gallipots, though balanced by the firmer relationship of the Openworks" (P. Mulholland, "Let her roar again: *The Roaring Girl* Revived," p. 23). Gomme, on the other hand, echoes a prevalent view in his suggestion that both wives "realize how much more solidly worthwhile their husbands are than the gallants whom they can, it seems, trap so easily," although he acknowledges that "the innuendoes" in the dialogue between the two women (IV.ii.40ff.) "are so broad that one cannot believe they have altogether given up the search for new delights" ("Introduction," *The Roaring Girl,* p. xxx).

24. Alfred Harbage, *Shakespeare and the Rival Traditions* (New York: Macmillan, 1952), p. 249. Harbage notes that the "single exception" is Chapman's *Blind Beggar of Alexandria* (1598).

25. Thomas M. Greene, "Spenser and the Epithalamic Convention," in *Edmund Spenser: Epithalamion,* ed. R. Beum (Columbus, Ohio: Charles E. Merrill, 1968), pp. 37-52; p. 43. For a comprehensive analysis of the literary conventions of epithalamic verse in European literature see Virginia Tufte, *The Poetry of Marriage: The Epithalamium in Europe and Its Development in England* (Los Angeles: Tinnon-Brown, 1970).

26. Although George E. Rowe, Jr., in *Thomas Middleton & the New Comedy Tradition* (Lincoln and London: Univ. of Nebraska Press, 1977) does not analyze *The Roaring Girl,* attributing the play largely to Dekker (p. 23), he offers a valuable discussion of the structures of New Comedy and of Middleton's sustained critique of traditional comic values: "Middleton does not revise tradition in order to create new syntheses. . . . He revises it in order to reject it" (p. 17). I concur with Rowe's suggestion that *The Roaring Girl* harbors a comic vision that is closer to Dekker's; by upholding a synthesis of discordant elements, I believe, the play modifies Middleton's otherwise cynical treatment of comic themes. For an account of the debate surrounding the play's authorship see Gomme, pp. xxxii-xxxv, and Champion, *Thomas Dekker and the Traditions of English Drama*, p. 173, n. 52.

27. Cyrus Hoy, 3:46, n. 104.

28. "Moll must dress as a man," notes Caroline L. Cherry, "to make people respect her and take her seriously" and "to express herself fully" (*The Most Unvaluedst Purchase: Women in the Plays of Thomas Middleton* [Salzburg: Universität Salzburg, 1973], pp. 104-05). Simon Shepherd observes that Moll "connects . . . chastity and . . . freedom" (*Amazons and Warrior Women,* p. 78).

29. Margot Heinemann, *Puritanism and Theatre: Thomas Middleton and Opposition Drama Under the Early Stuarts* (Cambridge and New York: Cambridge Univ. Press, 1980), p. 100. See also Louis B. Wright, *Middle-Class Culture in Elizabethan England* (1935; rpt. Ithaca: Cornell Univ. Press, 1958), pp. 494ff.

30. Linda Woodbridge, *Women and the English Renaissance,* p. 263.

31. Gomme, p. 87, n. 211.

32. In his review of the 1983 production, Irving Wardle notes that although roarers, "from Ancient Pistol and Jonson's Kastril to the roaring academy in *A Fair Quarrel,* were the much-ridiculed skinheads of their time," in *The Roaring Girl* "the sympathy is entirely on the roarer's side" ("Distant Echo of Jacobean Mirth," p. 14).

33. Critics unanimously attribute this scene to Dekker. The canting, however, is usually considered "an almost complete irrelevance to the remainder of the play" (Gomme, p. xxx). Champion, on the other hand, argues that the canting episode "serves through its linguistic hilarity to prevent a tone of heavy sentimentality in the reconciliation scenes that both precede . . . and follow" (*Thomas Dekker and the Traditions of English Drama,* p. 85).

34. Thomas Dekker, *Worke for Armorours* (1609), Biv; quoted in Hoy, 3:49, n. 12.

35. Gomme, p. 126, n. 194.

Jane Baston (essay date 1997)

SOURCE: "Rehabilitating Moll's Subversion in *The Roaring Girl,*" in *Studies in English Literature 1500-1900,* Vol. 37, No. 2, Spring 1997, pp. 317-35.

[*In this essay, Baston insists that "Moll's defiance is reinvented in* The Roaring Girl *in order to be contained, enervated, and eventually incorporated into the prevailing social apparatus."*]

On 12 February 1612 in a letter to Sir Dudley Carleton, John Chamberlain included an account of the punishments of three women. Of the first two he writes: "The Lady of Shrewsberie is still in the Towre rather upon wilfulnes, then upon any great matter she is charged withall: only the King is resolute that she shall aunswer to certain interrogatories, and she is as obstinate to make none, nor to be examined. The other weeke a younge mignon of Sir Pexall Brockas did penance at Paules Crosse, whom he had entertained and abused since she was twelve years old."[1]

But what do we learn from this account? Certainly something about the subjugation of women at this time—a subjugation that seems to recognize no class boundaries. Lady Shrewsbury's refusal to answer certain questions amounts to "wilfulnes" for which she is imprisoned. Although in this case she is refusing to answer the king, willfulness in a woman was tantamount to a crime.[2] The

second unfortunate, the unnamed "young mignon" of Sir Pexall Brockas, was made to submit to public penance in what seems to be public shaming of the victim of sexual abuse. Thus we have a woman imprisoned for refusing to submit to a man's will, and a woman punished for submitting to a man's will. Finally, Chamberlain writes of a third woman, Moll Cutpurse, who achieved a curious reversal of the expected order:

> and this last Sonday Mall Cut-purse a notorious baggage (that used to go in mans apparell and challenged the feild of divers gallants) was brought to the same place, where she wept bitterly and seemed very penitent, but yt is since doubted she was maudelin druncke, beeing discovered to have tipled of three quarts of sacke before she came to her penaunce: she had the daintiest preacher or ghostly father that ever I saw in pulpit, one Ratcliffe of Brazen Nose in Oxford, a likelier man to have led the revells in some ynne of court then to be where he was, but the best is he did extreem badly, and so wearied the audience that the best part went away, and the rest taried rather to heare Mall Cutpurse then him.[3]

By adopting at least the external signs of conformity—"she wept bitterly and seemed very penitent"—and exploiting the ineptness of the authority figure—the preacher Ratcliffe who "so wearied the audience"—Moll Cutpurse subverts the intended display. Ironically, it is for subversion of the power structure for which Moll was being punished in the first place.

Records show that Moll was known as a thief. Mark Eccles gives details of three records of Mary Frith in the Middlesex Sessions Court rolls between 1600 and 1608, where she is accused of stealing purses.[4] My own search of the Calendar of Assize Records has turned up another reference to Mary Frith. The Southwark Assizes of 26 March 1610 indict Mary Frythe for burglary, stating that, "On 8th September, 1609, she burgled the house of Alice Bayly at St Olave and stole £7 7s in money, 2 gold angels, a gold 20 shilling piece, 2 gold half-crowns, a gold ring (6s) and 2 crystal stones set in silver (20d)." The record also shows that she was found not guilty.[5]

But it was Moll's metaphorical and physical challenge to patriarchy that Chamberlain comments on, "a notorious baggage that used to go in man's apparell and challenged the feild of divers gallants."[6] Through her apparent acquiescence to the ritual humiliation of public shaming, Moll subverts the dominant power mechanisms of the community with an individual charisma. She effects her move from dissenter to maverick, and turns the spectacle of public shaming into a theatrical extravaganza. This is no small achievement when female intrusion into male codes could be very harshly punished, even or especially by the disempowered mob—as shown by the fate of one seventeenth-century woman, Ann Morrow, "who had been found guilty of disguising herself as a man for the purpose of marrying three different women, was blinded by stones flung at her by an exceptionally violent crowd."[7]

This paper examines women's "transgressions" within the prevailing patriarchy to show how such threats were countered and largely suppressed. After placing my argument within recent criticism on *The Roaring Girl,* a play which treats Moll, I will examine the "transgression" of cross-dressing as it appears in seventeenth-century pamphlets and church records, and finally in the dramatic representation of Moll. Specifically, I will show how Moll's defiance is reinvented in *The Roaring Girl* in order to be contained, enervated, and eventually incorporated into the prevailing social apparatus.

II

Until recent years criticism of *The Roaring Girl* was sparse.[8] But Mary Beth Rose's important essay, "Women in Men's Clothing: Apparel and Social Stability in *The Roaring Girl,*" initiated new cultural readings of the play.[9] Rose links *The Roaring Girl* with the pamphlets *Hic Mulier* and *Haec Vir,* and locates all these texts in the context of the "moral and social anxiety aroused by changing sexual values in Jacobean England" (p. 368). Documenting Moll's defiance of conventional social and sexual behavior, Rose suggests that the figure of Moll calls for a "greater freedom for women and equality between the sexes" (p. 385). Rose concludes, however, that such freedoms are eventually undercut because "the play resists the absorption of Moll into the tolerant new society which forms in the final scene" (p. 385). In "Crossdressing, the Theatre, and Gender Struggle in Early Modern England," Jean Howard extends Rose's argument as she sees Moll there to "protest injustices"; in an even more recent essay Howard similarly "appropriate[s] Moll for radical purposes" to show "how she lodges a critique of the specific material institutions and circumstances which oppressed women in early modern England."[10] Although neither Rose nor Howard sees Moll as totally successful in challenging conventional gender roles, they do both stress Moll's role as a radical, critiquing patriarchal society and calling for greater freedom and equality for women.

Two other critics who have contributed to this debate are Jonathan Dollimore and Stephen Orgel. While Jonathan Dollimore's recent essay, "Subjectivity, Sexuality, and Transgression: The Jacobean Connection," would seem to take greater account of Moll's containment, he too ends up seeing the play as largely subversive. Dollimore disrupts the binary opposition of subversion and containment and suggests that we see the latter as a "potentially productive process."[11] Thus "the very process of repressing one kind of subversive knowledge, actually produces another."[12] However, I would argue that although this political model may be viable, it is not manifested in *The Roaring Girl.* The specifics of the play, as I illustrate later, do not ultimately suggest anything beyond Moll's circumscription.[13] Stephen Orgel in "The Subtexts of *The Roaring Girl,*" questions the "relation between the construction of gender and its performance."[14] Although he recognizes that Moll's portrayal in the play as an "honorable, comic, sentimental peacemaker" is very different from the "dangerous scoundrel" of the documents, he does not identify this as a containment of Moll.[15] Rather, Orgel

argues that by the end of the play "Moll is acknowledged to be an attractive and powerful figure, both on stage and off it."[16]

In contrast with these critics, I suggest that the vision of the play is far more reactionary than radical. I argue that *The Roaring Girl* subtly but thoroughly stages Moll's recuperation. In my view, the play rewrites Moll's subversion through seeming acquiescence (as observed by Chamberlain) into a mere gesture towards subversion which is ultimately recuperated. Although in the early part of the play Moll does appear to challenge and subvert gender and class norms, a close examination of the final acts reveals that she is gradually contained and incorporated into the prevailing social apparatus of the play. Whereas Rose interprets Moll in the final scene as outside the "tolerant new society," I argue that Moll has become rehabilitated into a society which is neither new nor tolerant.

III

Early seventeenth-century English accounts of cross-dressing make clear that a woman dressing up as a man posed a considerable threat. The overt signs of sexuality which previously proclaimed 'femaleness' were now hidden. The challenge to established norms becomes more potent in its very covertness.

Although there is a long history of women taking on male garb, from Joan of Arc to the American jazz musician Billie Tipton,[17] evidence suggests that there was a rise in female-to-male cross-dressing during the early seventeenth century.[18] Linda Woodbridge notes that female transvestism came to the fore again around 1606 with the publication of "*Henry Parrot* in *The Movs Trap* (epigram 24), 1606, and Richard Niccols in *The Cuckow* (Sig. C2v), 1607. Both satirize women in male attire. From then on, the movement gained momentum, public and literary interest in it climaxing between 1615 and 1620."[19]

Of course a woman dressing as a man was not always intended as a challenge to patriarchy. In many cases women who adopted male clothing were doing so for a particular practical purpose such as escaping poverty, becoming soldiers to follow their lovers to war, or as erotic stimulation. Indeed, many of the women apprehended at this time were accused of prostitution.[20] However, when necessity did not dictate the wearing of male styles, women's adoption of them was particularly threatening. Instances of women wearing male garb to church are of particular interest. My own search of the records of the Archdeaconry of Essex Acts found that a Joan Towler of Downham "came into church in mannes apparell upon the sabath daie in the servyce time."[21] There appears to be no practical reason for appearing in church in male clothing, and the fact that Joan Towler appeared in her own parish church would suggest that she was deliberately challenging the authority of the church and the village.[22] Joan Towler was not an isolated case. Indeed, the preacher John

Williams in *A Sermon of Apparell,* 1619, rails against women for distracting the congregation by coming into church "halfe male, and halfe female . . . lifting vp towards his throne *two plaister'd eies* and a *polled head* . . . In *Sattin* (I warrant you) in stead of sackecloath."[23]

Undoubtedly women's cross-dressing did cause social anxiety. It struck at the base of hierarchies based on gender, and, in the light of preacher Williams's indignation at the women wearing satin rather than sackcloth, it also undermined hierarchies based on rank. Such concern with controlling women who transgressed is not surprising at a time when fear over the "crisis of order" abounded.[24] As David Underdown has observed, "[b]etween 1560 and 1640 local court records show an intense concern about unruly women."[25] The particular concern with cross-dressing peaked around 1620 with the publication of *Hic Mulier* and *Haec Vir*—an attack and counterattack on women's cross-dressing; and, although these were published after *The Roaring Girl,* we can see some of the same strategies used to demonize women who stepped out of line.

The pamphlet *Hic Mulier; or, The Man-Woman: Being a Medicine to Cure the Coltish Disease of the Staggers in the Masculine-Feminines of Our Times,* 1620, attacks the "masculine-feminine" woman who adopts not only "masculine" dress but also masculine behaviors, "from bold speech, to impudent action . . . and will be still most Masculine, most mankind, and most monstrous."[26] Such demonizing of the woman is common in the misogynistic diatribes of this time.[27] This mechanism of separation is used throughout *Hic Mulier.* The masculine woman is separated from good women, social standing, and ultimately the whole of humankind.

In order to separate the masculine woman from the "good" woman, the speaker in this pamphlet suggests that the adoption of masculine dress signifies sexual promiscuity: "exchanging the modest attire of the comely Hood, Cawle, Coyfe, handsome Dresse or Kerchiefe, to the cloudy Ruffianly broad-brim'd Hatte, and wanton feather, the modest upper parts of a concealing straight gowne, to the loose, lascivious civil embracement of the French doublet, being all unbutton'd to entice all of one shape to hide deformitie, and extreme short wasted to give a most easy way to every luxurious action."[28]

Here then, women are accused of dressing in male styles in order to give quick and easy access to their bodies—the dress of the whore. Women really are in a "no-win" situation since the speaker criticizes women for not wearing the "straight gowne" with its "concealing upper parts," while at the same time he condemns the looseness of the French doublet as lascivious. Masculine women are also denied the possibility of social standing for they are all "but ragges of Gentry, torne from better pieces for their foule staines, or else the adulterate branches of rich Stocks."[29] The final step expels the masculine woman from the human community. They will be "so much like a man

in all things, that they are neither men, nor women, but just good for nothing."[30] Here the woman's transgression effectively excludes her from existence; she becomes "nothing."

The British Crown promoted this tactic of separating cross-dressing women from the community. In a letter dated 25 January 1620, Chamberlain reports that King James had instructed the clergy to "inveigh vehemently and bitterly in theyre sermons against the insolencie of our women."[31] Less than a month later, on 12 February 1620, Chamberlain's entry identifies yet other channels for controlling the "impudence of women." The authorities recruit the forces of popular culture—players and ballad singers, and in case their influence proves ineffective, "the King threatens to fall upon theyre [the transgressors'] husbands, parents, or frends that have or shold have powre over them and make them pay for yt."[32]

In summary, the practices of control included separation from, and ostracization by, the community—a curious blend of solitary confinement and public shaming.

IV

Thomas Middleton's and Thomas Dekker's play, *The Roaring Girl,* addresses these mechanisms of control, but also goes beyond the strategies of separation and shaming to "rehabilitate" the roaring girl—Moll Cutpurse. Rehabilitation seeks to reform and normalize deviant behavior; thus, it not only effaces the original threat, but strengthens and extends the authority structures that the deviant undermined. What appears as Moll's "victory" in Middleton and Dekker's play is subtle recuperation. Moll cannot achieve on the stage the defiance she contrived in real life. In Chamberlain's account of Moll's "penance," she adopts the external signs of conformity in order to subvert and undermine the status quo; she produces her own "stage," on which she fashions herself into a spectacle. But the play inverts that construction. Her stage representation, which on the surface seems empowering, is in fact conforming.[33] The play fashions Moll into an eccentric pantomime character—a spirited principal boy—rather than a spokeswoman for a new world order, transforming her into a matchmaker, mediator, and conciliator, all in the service of venery, not radical feminism.

Even the title page of the 1611 quarto of *The Roaring Girl* illustrates Moll's recuperation when compared with the frontispiece to *The Life and Death of Mrs Mary Frith,* an anonymous document first published in 1622.[34] In the illustration for the play, although wearing full male dress, Moll looks like a woman dressed as a man. The small features and round body proclaim her gender, while the self-conscious pose holding her "props" (the pipe and sword), and the flowers in the hat and shoes make clear her function to amuse. Whereas the later illustration, which appears in a document purporting to be at least part autobiographical, shows a more masculine figure even though we cannot see the breeches. The stance of the figure is more natural and authoritative, the gaze more direct, and the effect more threatening.

Thomas Middleton's address "To The Comic Play Readers" sets out many of the mechanisms that fashion the fictional Moll.[35] His extended metaphorical juxtaposition of play making and alterations in apparel introduces a central issue in the play, Moll's adoption of male clothes. But Middleton suggests that such cross-dressing is a disguise: "for Venus being a woman, passes through the play in doublet and breeches; a brave disguise and a safe one" (Address, lines 15-9). Here Moll is seen as playing a role—her "disguise" is "brave" and "safe," rather than subversive. More importantly, her role as Venus presents "Venery and Laughter to The Readers" in a manner that allows Middleton to assure the reader that the play will defuse any potential threat. Moll's eventual reformation is adumbrated by Middleton's belief that "'Tis excellency of a writer to leave things better than he finds 'em" (line 23), in the sense that "worse things . . . the world has taxed [Moll] for than has been written of her" (lines 21-33).

But how does Middleton leave things better? For whom is Moll's reformation better? She is no longer deviant and therefore she is better for society; she is better in upholding the status quo. Even before we see the unveiling of Moll's reform, we are dealing with a sanitized Moll. The Prologue assures us that of the many types of Roaring Girls that exist, "our" Roaring Girl is a cut above a "suburb roarer" who "roars at midnight in deep tavern bowls," and neither is she a "civil city-roaring girl, whose pride, feasting, and riding, shakes her husband's state" (lines 23-4). The Prologue presents Moll the fiction—"she flies / With wings more lofty" (line 25)—while making a claim of truth for the play "her life our acts proclaim" (line 30). But such acts do not proclaim Moll's life. They institutionalize her; they reduce her to stereotype; they subtly undercut her political potency. They fashion a socially acceptable Moll contained not only in their words but literally on their stage as Mary Frith (aka Moll Cutpurse) sits on the stage playing her viol.[36]

Moll's eventual rehabilitation is made more effective by her demonization early in the play. Here some direct comparisons with Hic Mulier are useful. Both Hic Mulier and Moll are identified as the Other—one outside the norm—a deviant. In both cases they reveal a social practice of demonization of women. Both *The Roaring Girl* and *Hic Mulier* place the "man woman" against a picture of a "good woman." The speaker in *Hic Mulier* rejoices that there are still women who "are in the fulnesse of perfection, you that are the crowne of nature's worke, the complements of mens excellencies, and the Seminaries of propagation; you that maintaine the world, support mankinde, and give life to societies; you, that armed with the infinite power of Vertue, are Castles impregnable, Rivers unsailable, Seas immoveable."[37]

In *The Roaring Girl,* Neatfoot, Sir Alexander's serving man, takes up similar themes in his opening addresses to Mary Fitzallard, the "good woman." He refers to her as "emblem of fragility" (I.i.3), "fairest tree of generation" (I.i.8). He praises her "chastity" and "modesty." Although we have to recognize the sexual innuendo and ridiculously elaborate diction in Neatfoot's language as a part of the comic tradition, Mary's refusal to be drawn into this establishes her as the model woman, embodying the traditional traits of femininity—modesty and chastity.

After establishing this paradigm of woman, both texts go on to study the Other—the bad woman. Like Hic Mulier, Moll is shown as strange and monstrous. In the first act of the play Sebastian observes:

> There's a wench
> Called Moll, mad Moll, or merry Moll; a creature
> So strange in quality, a whole city takes
> Note of her name and person.
>
> (I.i.99-102)

As Sebastian continues to describe Moll, the "strange" quality turns to something more sinister. He explains that his father believes him to be "bewitched" (I.i.107), and that in loving Moll he follows a "crooked way" (I.i.108). This progression toward Moll's demonization culminates in Sir Alexander's description of Moll:

> It is a thing
> One knows not how to name; her birth began
> Ere she was all made; 'tis woman more than man,
> Man more than woman; and, which to none can hap,
> The sun gives two shadows in one shape;
> Nay, more, let this strange thing walk, stand, or sit
> No blazing star draws more eyes after it.
> *Sir Davy.* A monster! 'Tis some monster.
>
> (I.ii.130-7)

Sir Alex's final line encapsulates the potential problem that Moll poses. The real-life Moll on the public stage of St. Paul's draws all eyes to her, and therein lies her power.

Yet while act I builds up her demonization, act II is something of an anticlimax. Ostensibly concerned with the subplot of the merchants, their wives, the local "gallants," and the sexual subterfuge going on between the latter two groups, act II presents certain female stereotypes. Mistress Gallipot is the unfaithful wife who swindles money from her husband to give to her lover; Mistress Openwork is a scold who controls her husband. In relation to these women, Moll presents us with nothing more shocking than her sharing a pipe with the assembled gallants. She is not even sporting her male apparel; she enters in a frieze jerkin and a black safeguard.[38] Moreover, Laxton renders Moll's strength into sexual vivaciousness: "Heart, I would give but too much money to be nibbling with that wench; life, sh'as the spirit of four great parishes, and a voice that will drown all the city. Methinks a brave captain might get all his soldiers upon her" (II.i.194-8).

Even though later Moll clearly rejects Laxton's treatment of her as a sexual object, such a response subverts her potential authority and replaces it with mere spirited caprice. Indeed, Goshawk's remark, "'Tis the maddest fantasticalist girl" (II.i.213), lessens Moll's threat from that of devil to daredevil—from a mad creature to a madcap—enervating her power and reducing her to an acceptable stereotype.

Moll's discussion of marriage with Sebastian (precipitated by his proposal to her) reveals some interesting conflicts in her attitude and role. Although her words appear to reflect a free spirit—a reference to bisexuality—"I have no humour to marry; I love to lie o' both sides o' th' bed myself" (II.ii.38), she still reinforces the dominant view of marriage—"a wife, you know, ought to be obedient, but I fear me I am too headstrong to obey" (II.ii.35-40). Here Moll is fitting into the traditional requirements of marriage rather than seeking to change them. Her use of the word "headstrong" suggests the willfulness of a naughty girl rather than a credible critique of marriage. A few lines later she even seems to be perpetuating the demonizing of women, when she suggests that women trick men into marriage: "if every woman would deal with their suitor so honestly, poor younger brothers would not be so often gulled with old cozening widows, that turn o'er all their wealth in a trust to some kinsman, and make the poor gentleman work hard for a pension" (II.ii.62-7).

Such misogynistic stereotypes are more suited to the mouth of that arch-conservative, Sir Alex. At this point Moll seems to have taken on not only the apparel of men but also many of their prejudices! By the end of act II, Moll moves from being a monster to a matchmaker, from a virago to Venus. Sebastian resolves to get Moll's help in his plan to marry Mary, for

> 'Twixt lovers' hearts she's fit instrument,
> And has the art to help them to their own.
> By her advice, for in that craft she's wise,
> My love and I may meet, spite all spies.

(II.ii.205-8)

However, before Moll effects the meeting and marriage between Sebastian and Mary, she deals with Laxton. Act III marks the peak of Moll's resistance; subsequently her threat becomes enervated. Moll's confrontation with Laxton in III.i indicates a degree of resistance. She rejects his advances, lectures him on behalf of "fallen women," and eventually physically fights and wounds him. Moll rebuffs Laxton's treatment of her as a whore:

> What durst move you Sir
> To think me whorish? A name which I'd tear out
> From the high German's throat, if it lay ledger there
> To dispatch privy slanders against me.

(III.i.93-6)

But, more significantly, she also decries the system represented by Laxton which forces women into prostitution:

> In thee I defy all men, their worst hates
> And their best flatteries, all their golden witchcrafts,

> With which they entangle the poor spirits of fools,
> Distressed needle-women and trade-fallen wives;
> Fish that must needs bite, or themselves be bitten;
> Such hungry things as these may soon be took
> With a worm fastened on a golden hook:
> Those are the lecher's food, his prey; he watches
> For quarrelling wedlocks and poor shifting sisters;
> 'Tis the best fish he takes.

(III.i.97-106)

Here she suggests that women are forced into prostitution by economic necessity and she locates the "blame" and "slur" of prostitution with male exploiters. Thus Moll opposes the system which usually treats women as sexual enchantresses intent on corrupting men. Undoubtedly Moll shows resistance, but in the context of her eventual rehabilitation this resistance ultimately reinscribes and eventually extends existing power. Moll's final containment and silence adds credibility to the status quo.

Acts IV and V restore harmony through Moll. Her roles as conciliator, matchmaker, and translator demonstrate the extent of her rehabilitation. Act IV presents a depoliticized, domesticated version of earlier threats. Mary Fitzallard adopts a page's clothing, not to demonstrate her commitment to Hic Mulier, but as a disguise to enable her to meet her lover. Thus Moll now devitalizes her main strategy of resistance (the donning of male clothing). She comments to Sebastian, "My tailor fitted her well; How like you his work?" (IV.i.71).

Similarly a good natured banter replaces Moll's earlier pattern of fighting; Sebastian gives the viol to Moll telling her to "end thy quarrel singing" (IV.i.81). And she not only accepts but initiates sexual innuendo in her reply to him: "I'll play my part as well as I can; it shall ne'er be said I came into a gentleman's chamber, and let his instrument hang by the walls" (IV.i.86-8). Such bawdy punning as continues throughout act IV is typical of the double entendre present in much Jacobean drama, but it also undermines some of our earlier impressions of Moll.

Specifically this scene presents the interchange between Moll, Sebastian, and Sir Alex, in which Sir Alex (knowing she is not the "musician" that Sebastian claims) consistently places Moll in the role of whore. The double entendres of "fingering," "the most delicate stroke," and "pricksongs," objectify Moll in sexual terms. These puns and Sir Alex's asides invite the audience to laugh, and through that laughter to recognize that Moll is no threat to order. She is just a "fit instrument," serving at best the plot, and at worst patricians such as Sir Alex.

This scene ends with Sebastian and Moll reveling in their supposed deception of Sebastian's father. But since the audience knows that Sir Alex is not deceived, Moll's final line, "He that can take me for a male musician, I can't choose but make him my instrument, and play upon him" (IV.i.214-6), invites the following inversion: that Moll cannot disguise herself—and that that self is a "fit instrument" to be played upon. Although Moll can defend herself against the direct assault by Laxton, when he thinks her his "fond flexible whore" (III.i.78), she is defenseless against Sir Alex's asides and innuendo which become the subtext that ultimately contains her.

Finally, Moll's role as translator in act V shows her capitulation to the dominant practices of class and gender. Throughout V.i she takes up an appropriately obsequious stand in relation to the gentry. First, she "saves" Sir Beauteous from giving money to Teardrop and Trapdoor, exposing them as "base rogues." And yet only a few lines later she is part of a "canting" duet with Trapdoor that reduces her to thief and whore. Moreover, she adopts this role for the entertainment of the assembled gentry, and at the expense of her own dignity. For example, Trapdoor's song in which he suggests to Moll that they "wap" and "niggle" under the "ruffman's" (i.e., copulate under the hedge) contains Moll in the same way as Sir Alex's asides and innuendo in the previous scene. That is, although Moll is supposedly playing a role ("musician" in the first example, "canting partner" in the latter), the implication is clear. Moll's credibility as an independent force is belittled. Her one show of anger during the duet is dismissed by Sir Beauteous: "This is excellent! One fit more, good Moll" (V.i.219). Her earlier articulate voice is effaced by the argot of thieves and whores.

Moll's songs in the final two acts incorporate her into the group of manageable, controllable, and even lovable rogues. This culminates at the end of her duet with Tearcat when all the others present exclaim: "Fine knaves, i'faith!" (V.i.235). The "omnes" are, of course, the male gentry of the play who can now comfortably incorporate Moll into the London underworld where her idiosyncrasies can be contained.

Moll's final rejection of marriage, unlike her earlier speech on prostitution, is not threatening. Its ambiguous content and riddling form make it a theatrical set piece rather than a serious rejection of marriage. Compared to her earlier critique of a system that forces women into prostitution, which was complex, eloquent, and authoritative, this latter piece—her final speech of any length—is clichéd and seems to be there, for entertainment value alone. Certainly the response it elicits from Sir Alexander, "In troth thou'art a good wench" (line 228), suggests that Moll's rejection of marriage is not to be taken as radical critique.

There has been no radical shift in terms of gender or class: Sir Alex's magnanimity toward Moll is obviously a result of his relief that she will not be his future daughter-in-law. The play ends with the strengthening of the ruling class through the union of Sebastian and Mary. The last words of the play go to Sir Alex as he supposedly makes "amends" to Moll. Those amends are, of course, in the form of angels—an economic gesture by the patrician class to avoid moral investment in the real issues.

By the close of the play, then, Moll's actions, words, and appearance are no longer threatening. Her function of matchmaker allows her to bask in the benevolence of Sir Alexander Wengrave and his cronies. Her incisive speeches have been dulled into comic misrule. And her appearance, her "trademark"—that for which she was best known—has been "redressed." For in her last appearance in the play Moll is dressed in female clothing.[39] Her *rehabilitation* in every sense of the word is complete.[40]

As the title page presages, the play ***The Roaring Girl*** recuperates Moll's defiance. She is reinvented to become a mere translator rather than an interpreter; a singer harmonizing inequalities rather than a roarer protesting them; and finally a riddling rhymster rather than an articulate spokeswoman. By the end of the play Moll has been recuperated into the network of social relations. She can now be dismissed as a "good wench" (V.ii.225)—a description that subsumes Moll into existing class and gender hierarchies and so ensures her rehabilitation into the existing patriarchy.[41]

Notes

1. Norman Egbert McClure, ed., *The Letters of John Chamberlain,* vol. 1 (Philadelphia: The American Philosophical Society, 1939), p. 334.

2. As McClure tells us, this was Mary, wife of the seventh earl of Shrewsbury. She was imprisoned for acquiescing in the marriage of her niece, the Lady Arabella Stuart (p. 334 n. 13).

3. McClure, p. 334.

4. Mark Eccles, "Mary Frith, The Roaring Girl," *N&Q* n.s. 32, 1 (March 1985): 65-6.

5. Public Records Office, London, Calendar of Assize Records, Surrey Indictments, James I. Southwark Assizes, 26 March 1610 (#336).

6. Here Chamberlain impugns Moll sexually by calling her a "notorious baggage" (a common epithet for a whore). Chamberlain's choice of language reveals the connection, at least in the minds of many commentators of the time, between female cross-dressing and female promiscuity.

7. Christopher Hibbert, *The Roots of Evil: A Social History of Crime and Punishment* (London: Weidenfeld and Nicolson, 1963), p. 29.

8. Early criticism of the play concentrated on Moll's character. T. S. Eliot in *Elizabethan Essays* (New York: Haskell House, 1964) saw Moll as embodying a "free and noble womanhood" (p. 100). The dating and stage history of the play are dealt with in two articles by P. A. Mulholland: "The Date of *The Roaring Girl,*" *RES* n.s. 28, 109 (February 1977): 18-31; and "Let her roar again: The Roaring Girl Revived," *RORD* 18 (1985): 15-27. Patrick Cheney, in "Moll Cutpurse as Hermaphrodite in Dekker and Middleton's *The Roaring Girl,*" *Ren&R* n.s. 7, 2 (May 1983): 120-34, sees Moll as a traditional Renaissance hermaphrodite figure, "a supreme symbol of two souls becoming one," who brings about a society renewed by married love (p. 124). Viviana Comensoli, in "Play-making, Domestic Conduct, and the Multiple Plot in *The Roaring Girl,*" *SEL* 27, 2 (Spring 1987): 249-66, analyzes

the multiple plot of the play to show that "Moll's misogamy and the citizens' domestic conflicts counterpoint the Sebastian-Mary action" indicating the central concern of the play—"the degeneration of marriage and the Family" (p. 251).

9. Mary Beth Rose, "Women in Men's Clothing: Apparel and Social Stability in *The Roaring Girl*," *ELR* 14, 3 (Autumn 1984): 367-91. Subsequent references will appear parenthetically in the text.

10. Jean E. Howard, "Crossdressing, the Theatre, and Gender Struggle in Early Modern England," *SQ* 39, 4 (Winter 1988): 418-40, 436; and "Sex and Social Conflict: The Erotics of *The Roaring Girl*," in *Erotic Politics: Desire on the Renaissance Stage,* ed. Susan Zimmerman (New York: Routledge, 1992), pp. 170-90, 180. Deborah Jacobs in "Critical Imperialism and Renaissance Drama: The Case of *The Roaring Girl*," in *Feminism, Bakhtin, and the Dialogic,* ed. Dale M. Bauer and Susan Jaret McKinstry (Albany: State Univ. of New York Press, 1991), criticizes such "feminist" readings for their transhistorical assumptions and suggests that "we have to admit to a past in which gender might be less central or radically different" (p. 76). Although caution is needed when using anachronistic terms, it is still necessary and indeed enlightening to talk about *The Roaring Girl* as challenging and being recuperated by patriarchal authority, since even a brief examination of sermons, ballads, church records, and polemics of the time makes clear the subordination of women and the attendant controls and mechanisms designed to ensure its continuation.

11. Jonathan Dollimore, "Subjectivity, Sexuality, and Transgression: The Jacobean Connection," *RenD* n.s. 17 (1986): 53-81, 71.

12. Dollimore, p. 72.

13. In his essay Dollimore does not illustrate how this "potentially productive process" works in *The Roaring Girl* (p. 71), but rather turns to Fletcher's *Love's Cure.* Marjorie Garber, in "The Logic of the Transvestite," in *Staging the Renaissance,* ed. David Scott Kastan and Peter Stallybrass (New York and London: Routledge, 1991), pp. 221-34, also disrupts "materialist and historicist feminist" readings which view the play as about "the economic injustices of the sex gender system." Garber recognizes the "anxiety about sexuality" present in the play, but locates it with the "sexual inadequacies of men" (p. 221). Moll, through constant references to castration, emasculation, and penises, becomes "phallicized" (p. 227).

14. Stephen Orgel, "The Subtexts of *The Roaring Girl*," in *Erotic Politics: Desire on the Renaissance Stage,* pp. 12-26, 13.

15. Orgel, p. 22.

16. Orgel, p. 25.

17. In January 1989, when Billie Tipton died, it was revealed that "he" was a woman. Tipton's wife, Kitty Oakes, explained that Tipton thought becoming a man was the only way to join a swing band in the 1930s.

18. Rudolf M. Dekker and Lotte C. van de Pol, in *The Tradition of Female Transvestism in Early Modern*

Europe (London: Macmillan, 1989), document 119 "women living as men" in the Netherlands between 1550 and 1839.

19. Linda Woodbridge, *Women and the English Renaissance: Literature and the Nature of Womankind, 1540-1620* (Urbana and Chicago: Univ. of Illinois Press, 1984), p. 141.

20. Jean E. Howard in "Crossdressing" quotes research by R. Mark Benbow of records of the Repertories of the Alderman's Court in the London City Record Office and from the Bridewell Court Minute Books between 1565 and 1605. These show that many of the women apprehended were accused of prostitution (p. 420).

21. Public Records Office, Chelmsford, Essex D/AEA 17 (1596) folio 149.

22. David Underdown, in *Revel, Riot, and Rebellion: Popular Politics and Culture in England, 1603-1660* (Oxford: Clarendon Press, 1985), talks about the importance of the parish as an institution: "The parish church was automatically the site of the formal gatherings in which the unity of the village and its hierarchical order were symbolically affirmed" (p. 14). Acts such as Joan Towler's may also be seen in relation to other instances of female resistance to church practices such as "churching," in which new mothers participated in a ritual "cleansing" before they could take communion again. Phyllis Mack, in her study of female prophets, *Visionary Women: Ecstatic Prophecy in Seventeenth-Century England* (Berkeley: Univ. of California Press, 1992), gives details of such resistance, pp. 36, 53.

23. Quoted in Woodbridge, pp. 142-3.

24. For a full discussion on order and disorder in the early seventeenth century, see Underdown.

25. Underdown, p. 39.

26. *Hic Mulier; or, The Man-Woman: Being a Medicine to Cure the Coltish Disease of the Staggers in the Masculine-Feminines of Our Times,* 1620 (Exeter, England: Rota Press, 1973), sig. A3.

27. Joseph Swetnam's *The Arraignment of Lewd, Idle, Froward, and Unconstant Women,* 1615, repeated the traditional arguments about women's flawed natures and dangerous tongues.

28. *Hic Mulier,* sigs. A4r-A4v.

29. *Hic Mulier,* sig. B1.

30. *Hic Mulier,* sig. B2.

31. Chamberlain, p. 286.

32. Chamberlain, p. 289.

33. On this point I disagree with Jean E. Howard, who suggests in "Cross-dressing" that "one of the most transgressive acts the real Moll Frith performed was to sit, in her masculine attire, on the stage of the Fortune and to sing a song upon the lute" (p. 440). In my view, by so doing Moll is validating her own recuperation. Her presence on the stage is a visible containment—an "emasculation"—of her transgression.

34. *The Life and Death of Mrs Mary Frith, Commonly called Moll Cutpurse,* ed. Randall S. Nakayama (1662; rprt. New York and London: Garland, 1993). This work is divided into three parts: the preface, an introduction relating Moll's early life, and a third section entitled "Moll Frith's Diary." The three animals in the illustration draw on specific elements of seventeenth-century iconography. An initial reading could see the monkey as Lust, the lion as Masculine Strength, and the parrot as Imitation.

35. *The Roaring Girl* in *Drama in the English Renaissance II, The Stuart Period,* ed. Russell A. Fraser and Norman Rabkin (New York and London: Macmillan, 1976). All references to the play are to this edition and will be cited parenthetically in the text by act, scene, and line numbers.

36. For a full account of Moll's appearance on the stage at the Fortune Theater see Mulholland, "The Date of *The Roaring Girl.*"

37. *Hic Mulier,* sigs. A3r-A3v.

38. Although a jerkin is a male garment usually worn over a doublet, on the important part, i.e., her lower half, she is wearing a petticoat.

39. At the beginning of V.ii, Moll enters dressed as a man. She then disappears and comes back on "masked," but she must now be in female garb for Sir Alexander Wengrave to believe that she is Sebastian's bride.

40. According to the OED, the stem "habilitate" from the Latin *habilitare* can mean to establish character or reputation as well as to fit or to clothe.

41. I am grateful to Laura Knoppers for her helpful comments and suggestions on earlier drafts of this essay.

FURTHER READING

Bibliography

Adler, Doris Ray. *Thomas Dekker: A Reference Guide.* Boston: G. K. Hall, 1983.
Annotated bibliography of primary and secondary works relating to Dekker.

Criticism

Brown, Arthur. "Citizen Comedy and Domestic Drama." In *Jacobean Theatre,* edited by John Russell Brown and Bernard Harris, pp. 63-83. Stratford-upon-Avon Studies 1. London: Edward Arnold, 1960.
Argues that Dekker "wrote in a popular and romantic vein" which was more concerned with plot than was the rhetorical and intellectual drama of such playwrights as Ben Jonson.

Gasper, Julia. *The Dragon and the Dove: The Plays of Thomas Dekker.* Oxford: Clarendon Press, 1990, 241 p.
Focuses on the religious and political aspects of Dekker's plays.

Gregg, Kate L. *Thomas Dekker: A Study in Economic and Social Backgrounds.* Seattle: University of Washington Press, 1924, 112 p.
Considers the evidently contradictory judgments of mercantile capitalism expressed in Dekker's works, which generally laud commerce as the source of many blessings, yet condemn hardships brought about by the inequalities it produced.

Hoy, Cyrus. *Introductions, Notes, and Commentaries to texts in "The Dramatic Works of Thomas Dekker"* Edited by Fredson Bowers. 4 vols. Cambridge: Cambridge University Press, 1980.
Useful critical introductions and comments to accompany Bowers's 1953-61 collection of *The Dramatic Works of Thomas Dekker.*

McLuskie, Kathleen E. *Dekker and Heywood: Professional Dramatists.* New York: St. Martin's Press, 1994, 200 p.
Emphasizes the stagecraft of Dekker's and Heywood's works.

Ross, Gordon N. "Dekker's *The Shoemakers' Holiday.*" *The Explicator* 44, no. 3 (Spring 1988): 7-9.
Considers Margery Eyre "[o]ne of the most entertaining and carefully drawn minor characters in Elizabethan comedy."

Additional coverage of Dekker's life and career is contained in the following sources published by the Gale Group: *Dictionary of Literary Biography,* **Vols. 62, 172;** *DISCovering Authors Modules: Dramatists Module, Literature Criticism from 1400 to 1800,* **Vol. 22.**

Zora Neale Hurston
1891-1960

American novelist, folklorist, short story writer, autobiographer, essayist, dramatist, librettist, and anthropologist.

INTRODUCTION

Hurston is considered among the foremost writers of the Harlem Renaissance, an era of unprecedented achievement in African-American art and literature during the 1920s and 1930s. Although her drama and fiction, which depicts the common black folk of her native Southern Florida, was largely unconcerned with racial injustices of the time, Hurston's long-neglected works have undergone substantial critical reevaluation, particularly since the advent of the black protest novel and the rise to prominence during the 1950s of Richard Wright, Ralph Ellison, and James Baldwin. In addition to publishing novels and plays, three nonfiction works and numerous short stories and essays, Hurston is acknowledged as an influential collector and reteller of black American folklore. Lillie P. Howard stated: "[Hurston's] works are important because they affirm blackness (while not denying whiteness) in a black-denying society. They present characters who are not all lovable but who are undeniably and realistically human. They record the history, the life, of a place and time which are remarkably like other places and times, though perhaps a bit more honest in the rendering."

BIOGRAPHICAL INFORMATION

Hurston was born in Eatonville, Florida, the first incorporated black township in the United States and the setting for most of her writing. At the age of fourteen, she left home to work as a maid with a traveling Gilbert and Sullivan theatrical troupe. In 1923, Hurston entered Howard University, a black college in Washington, D.C., where she published short stories in *Stylus,* the university literary magazine, and attracted the attention of noted sociologist Charles S. Johnson. With Johnson's encouragement, Hurston moved to New York City in 1925 and subsequently secured a scholarship to Barnard College. While at Barnard, and later at Columbia University, Hurston studied anthropology under Franz Boas, a renowned anthropologist of the era. During this period, Hurston continued to publish short stories and began establishing friendships with many important black writers. In 1927, together with Langston Hughes and other artists, Hurston founded *Fire!,* a short-lived literary magazine devoted to African-American culture. Hurston's collaboration with Hughes continued on the drama *Mule Bone: A Comedy of Negro*

Life (1991), the source of which was the Hurston short story "The Bone of Contention." Apparently displeased with Hughes's additions to the story, Hurston later maintained that she was the sole author of *Mule Bone* and attempted to copyright the work in her name only in October of 1930, thus alienating Hughes. In the 1930s and 1940s Hurston's reputation steadily grew, based upon the success of her novels and folklore collections. By 1948, after the publication of *Seraph on the Suwanee* and its dismal reception by critics and audiences, however, Hurston's career went into steady decline. Bordering on destitution throughout the 1950s, she suffered a stroke in October of 1959, and died at the Saint Lucie County Welfare Home on January 28, 1960.

MAJOR WORKS

Hurston's first published play,*Color Struck: A Play in Four Scenes* (1925) concerns a black woman's obsession with skin color. Jealous and embittered by what she perceives as John's preference for light-skinned blacks, Emmaline leaves him. Some twenty years later, John locates Emma and asks her to marry him. As she considers his proposal, she notices his well-meaning attention to her ailing, light-skinned daughter. Enraged, she condemns him for his supposed colorism. The disappointed John departs. Shortly thereafter Emma's neglected daughter dies. *The First One: A Play in One Act* (1927) visits the biblical theme of Noah's curse on his wayward son Ham: "His skin shall be black. . . . He shall serve his brothers and they shall rule over him." Hurston uses the theme ironically in the play; Ham's skin is changed to black and he is forced into exile, but he maintains his sense of pleasure in life. The 1931 black musical revue *Fast and Furious* contains several sketches by Hurston, which depart from the norms of the minstrel show in that they endeavor to present blacks without the trappings of stage stereotypes. This trend continued in *The Great Day* (1932). Representative of Hurston's solo musical revues, *The Great Day* reflects her efforts to portray an authentic black voice on the American stage, and contains portions of what Hurston would later publish in the folktale-inspired stories of her *Mules and Men* (1935). The musical drama *Polk County: A Comedy of Negro Life on a Sawmill Camp* (1944) concerns a mulatto woman, Leafy Lee, as she travels south from New York in an effort to master blues music. Once she enters a Florida camp, Leafy Lee wins the friendship of Big Sweet who becomes a protector and teacher to her and marries the guitar-playing, My Honey. *Mule Bone,* set in Eatonville, Florida, recounts the rivalry of Jim Weston and Dave Carter over a woman, Daisy Taylor. Their conflict reaches a climax as both men claim to have killed a turkey for Taylor. A fight ensues, and Weston attacks Carter with a mule bone. The subsequent trial sees Jim Weston exiled from town, only to be joined by a now-reconciled Carter, who has since learned that the woman they were pursuing requires that he get a job.

CRITICAL RECEPTION

Throughout her career, Hurston struggled to see her dramatic works realized on the stage. Despite achieving some recognition during her lifetime, including several prizes afforded by the periodical *Opportunity*, Hurston's plays were largely neglected by producers and critics. Since her death, Hurston's reputation and popularity have significantly grown, as evidenced by the reissuing of several of her works, including *Their Eyes Were Watching God*, in the late 1980s. By the 1990s the process of rediscovering Hurston's work has led to a more substantial regard for her plays, particularly her collaborative drama *Mule Bone*. Still, most critical studies of Hurston have focused extensively on her private life, such as her well-publicized falling out with the co-author of *Mule Bone*, Langston Hughes. Nevertheless, as critical interest in her dramas increases, assessments of the cultural and thematic importance of her dramatic work have begun to appear. By the end of the twentieth century, most critics concur that what exists are only preliminary investigations of the plays, works that demand further, substantive analysis. Overall, Hurston's dramas, like her fiction, are deemed significant

for the insights they provide into the human condition. In a dedication to *I Love Myself When I Am Laughing . . . and Then Again When I Am Looking Mean and Impressive: A Zora Neale Hurston Reader*, Alice Walker summarized Hurston's achievements: "We love Zora Neale Hurston for her work, first, and then again (as she and all Eatonville would say) we love her for herself. For the humor and courage with which she encountered a life she infrequently designed, for her absolute disinterest in becoming either white or bourgeois, and for her *devoted* appreciation of her own culture, which is an inspiration to us all."

PRINCIPAL WORKS

Plays

Color Struck: A Play in Four Scenes 1925
The First One: A Play in One Act 1927
Fast and Furious [with Clinton Fletcher and Tim Moore] 1931
The Great Day 1932
The Fiery Chariot 1935
Polk County: A Comedy of Negro Life on a Sawmill Camp [with Dorothy Waring] 1944
**Mule Bone: A Comedy of Negro Life* [with Langston Hughes] 1991

Other Major Works

Jonah's Gourd Vine (novel) 1934
Mules and Men (short stories) 1935
Their Eyes Were Watching God (novel) 1937
Tell My Horse [also published as *Voodoo Gods: An Inquiry into Native Myths and Magic in Jamaica and Haiti*] (nonfiction) 1938
Moses, Man of the Mountain [also published as *The Man of the Mountain*] (novel) 1939
Dust Tracks on a Road (autobiography) 1942
Seraph on the Suwanee (novel) 1948
I Love Myself When I Am Laughing . . . and Then Again When I am Looking Mean and Impressive: A Zora Neale Hurston Reader (fiction and nonfiction) 1979
The Sanctified Church (essays) 1981
Spunk: The Selected Stories of Zora Neale Hurston (short stories) 1985

*This one-act play, based on "Ole Massa and John Who Wanted To Go to Heaven" from *Mules and Men,* survives in typescript only.

**This comedy, completed by Hughes and Hurston in 1930, was first staged in 1991 with a prologue and epilogue by George Houston Bass.

AUTHOR COMMENTARY

Zora Neale Hurston (essay date 1931)

SOURCE: "Characteristics of Negro Expression," in *Ne-*

gro: An Anthology, edited by Nancy Cunard, Frederick Ungar Publishing Co., 1970, pp. 24-31.

[In the following excerpt, originally published in 1931, Hurston explains the view of African-American expression that informs her works, observing the drama, originality, and dialect of black communication.]

DRAMA

The Negro's universal mimicry is not so much a thing in itself as an evidence of something that permeates his entire self. And that thing is drama.

His very words are action words. His interpretation of the English language is in terms of pictures. One act described in terms of another. Hence the rich metaphor and simile.

The metaphor is of course very primitive. It is easier to illustrate than it is to explain because action came before speech. Let us make a parallel. Language is like money. In primitive communities actual goods, however bulky, are bartered for what one wants. This finally evolves into coin, the coin being not real wealth but a symbol of wealth. Still later even coin is abandoned for legal tender, and still later for cheques in certain usages.

Every phase of Negro life is highly dramatised. No matter how joyful or how sad the case there is sufficient poise for drama. Everything is acted out. Unconsciously for the most part of course. There is an impromptu ceremony always ready for every hour of life. No little moment passes unadorned.

Now the people with highly developed languages have words for detached ideas. That is legal tender. "That-which-we-squat-on" has become "chair." "Groan-causer" has evolved into "spear," and soon. Some individuals even conceive of the equivalent of cheque words, like "ideation" and "pleonastic." Perhaps we might say that *Paradise Lost* and *Sartor Resartus* are written in cheque words.

The primitive man exchanges descriptive words. His terms are all close fitting. Frequently the Negro, even with detached words in his vocabulary—not evolved in him but transplanted on his tongue by contact—must add action to it to make it do. So we have "chop-axe," "sitting-chair," "cook-pot" and the like because the speaker has in his mind the picture of the object in use. Action. Everything illustrated. So we can say the white man thinks in a written language and the Negro thinks in hieroglyphics.

A bit of Negro drama familiar to all is the frequent meeting of two opponents who threaten to do atrocious murder one upon the other.

Who has not observed a robust young Negro chap posing upon a street corner, possessed of nothing but his clothing, his strength and his youth? Does he bear himself like a pauper? No, Louis XIV could be no more insolent in his assurance. His eyes say plainly "Female, halt!" His posture exults "Ah, female, I am the eternal male, the giver of life. Behold in my hot flesh all the delights of this world. Salute me, I am strength." All this with a languid posture, there is no mistaking his meaning.

A Negro girl strolls past the corner lounger. Her whole body panging and posing. A slight shoulder movement that calls attention to her bust, that is all of a dare. A hippy undulation below the waist that is a sheaf of promises tied with conscious power. She is acting out "I'm a darned sweet woman and you know it."

These little plays by strolling players are acted out daily in a dozen streets in a thousand cities, and no one ever mistakes the meaning.

WILL TO ADORN

The will to adorn is the second most notable characteristic in Negro expression. Perhaps his idea of ornament does not attempt to meet conventional standards, but it satisfies the soul of its creator.

In this respect the American Negro has done wonders to the English language. It has often been but it is equally true that he has made over a great part of the tongue to his liking and has had his revision accepted by the ruling class. No one listening to a Southern white man talk could deny this. Not only has he softened and toned down strongly consonanted words like "aren't" to "aint" and the like, he has made new force words out of old feeble elements. Examples of this are "ham-shanked," "battle-hammed," "double-teen," "bodaciously," "muffle-jawed."

But the Negro's greatest contribution to the language is: (1) the use of metaphor and simile; (2) the use of the double descriptive; (3) the use of verbal nouns.

1. METAPHOR AND SIMILE
One at a time, like lawyers going to heaven.
You sho is propaganda.
Sobbing hearted.
I'll beat you till: (*a*) rope like okra, (*b*) slack like lime, (*c*) smell like onions.
Fatal for naked.
Kyting along.
That's a lynch.
That's a rope.
Cloakers—deceivers.
Regular as pig-tracks.
Mule blood—black molasses.
Syndicating—gossiping.
Flambeaux—cheap café (lighted by flambeaux).
To put yo'self on de ladder.
2. THE DOUBLE DESCRIPTIVE
High-tall.
Little-tee-ninchy (tiny).
Low-down.
Top-superior.
Sham-polish.
Lady-people.
Kill-dead.
Hot-boiling.

Chop-axe.
Sitting-chairs.
De watch wall.
Speedy-hurry.
More great and more better.
3. VERBAL NOUNS
She features somebody I know.
Funeralize.
Sense me into it.
Puts the shamery on him.
'Taint everybody you kin confidence.
I wouldn't friend with her.
Jooking—playing piano or guitar as it is done in Jook-
houses (houses of ill-fame).
Uglying away.
I wouldn't scorn my name all up on you.
Bookooing (beaucoup) around—showing off.

NOUNS FROM VERBS
Won't stand a broke.
She won't take a listen.
He won't stand straightening.
That is such a compelment.
That's a lynch.

The stark, trimmed phrases of the Occident seem too bare
for the voluptuous child of the sun, hence the adornment.
It arises out of the same impulse as the wearing of jewelry
and the making of sculpture—the urge to adorn.

On the walls of the homes of the average Negro one
always finds a glut of gaudy calendars, wall pockets and
advertising lithographs. The sophisticated white man or
Negro would tolerate none of these, even if they bore a
likeness to the Mona Lisa. No commercial art for decoration. Nor the calendar nor the advertisement spoils the
picture for this lowly man. He sees the beauty in spite of
the declaration of the Portland Cement Works or the
butcher's announcement. I saw in Mobile a room in which
there was an over-stuffed mohair living-room suite, an
imitation mahogany bed and chifferobe, a console victrola.
The walls were gaily papered with Sunday supplements of
the *Mobile Register*. There were seven calendars and three
wall pockets. One of them was decorated with a lace doily.
The mantel-shelf was covered with a scarf of deep home-
made lace, looped up with a huge bow of pink crêpe paper.
Over the door was a huge lithograph showing the Treaty
of Versailles being signed with a Waterman fountain pen.

It was grotesque, yes. But it indicated the desire for beauty.
And decorating a decoration, as in the case of the doily on
the gaudy wall pocket, did not seem out of place to the
hostess. The feeling back of such an act is that there can
never be enough of beauty, let alone too much. Perhaps
she is right. We each have our standards of art, and thus
are we all interested parties and so unfit to pass judgment
upon the art concepts of others.

Whatever the Negro does of his own volition he embel-
lishes. His religious service is for the greater part excellent
prose poetry. Both prayers and sermons are tooled and
polished until they are true works of art. The supplication

is forgotten in the frenzy of creation. The prayer of the
white man is considered humorous in its bleakness. The
beauty of the Old Testament does not exceed that of a
Negro prayer.

ANGULARITY

After adornment the next most striking manifestation of
the Negro is Angularity. Everything that he touches
becomes angular. In all African sculpture and doctrine of
any sort we find the same thing.

Anyone watching Negro dancers will be struck by the
same phenomenon. Every posture is another angle. Pleas-
ing, yes. But an effect achieved by the very means which
an European strives to avoid.

The pictures on the walls are hung at deep angles.
Furniture is always set at an angle. I have instances of a
piece of furniture in the *middle* of a wall being set with
one end nearer the wall than the other to avoid the simple
straight line.

ASYMMETRY

Asymmetry is a definite feature of Negro art. I have no
samples of true Negro painting unless we count the African
shields, but the sculpture and carvings are full of this
beauty and lack of symmetry.

It is present in the literature, both prose and verse. I offer
an example of this quality in verse from Langston Hughes:

> I aint gonna mistreat ma good gal any more,
> I'm just gonna kill her next time she makes me sore.
>
>   . . . . .
>
> I treats her kind but she don't do me right,
> She fights and quarrels most ever' night.
>
>   . . . . .
>
> I can't have no woman's got such low-down ways
> Cause de blue gum woman aint de style now'days.
>
>   . . . . .
>
> I brought her from the South and she's goin on back,
> Else I'll use her head for a carpet track.

It is the lack of symmetry which makes Negro dancing so
difficult for white dancers to learn. The abrupt and
unexpected changes. The frequent change of key and time
are evidences of this quality in music. (Note the St. Louis
Blues.)

The dancing of the justly famous Bo-Jangles and Snake
Hips are excellent examples.

The presence of rhythm and lack of symmetry are
paradoxical, but there they are. Both are present to a
marked degree. There is always rhythm, but it is the
rhythm of segments. Each unit has a rhythm of its own,
but when the whole is assembled it is lacking in sym-

metry. But easily workable to a Negro who is accustomed to the break in going from one part to another, so that he adjusts himself to the new tempo.

. . . . .

Negro Folklore

Negro folklore is not a thing of the past. It is still in the making. Its great variety shows the adaptability of the black man: nothing is too old or too new, domestic or foreign, high or low, for his use. God and the Devil are paired, and are treated no more reverently than Rockefeller and Ford. Both of these men are prominent in folklore, Ford being particularly strong, and they talk and act like good-natured stevedores or mill-hands. Ole Massa is sometimes a smart man and often a fool. The automobile is ranged alongside of the oxcart. The angels and the apostles walk and talk like section hands. And through it all walks Jack, the greatest culture hero of the South; Jack beats them all—even the Devil, who is often smarter than God.

Culture Heroes

The Devil is next after Jack as a culture hero. He can out-smart everyone but Jack. God is absolutely no match for him. He is good-natured and full of humour. The sort of person one may count on to help out in any difficulty.

Peter the Apostle is the third in importance. One need not look far for the explanation. The Negro is not a Christian really. The primitive gods are not deities of too subtle inner reflection; they are hard-working bodies who serve their devotees just as laboriously as the suppliant serves them. Gods of physical violence, stopping at nothing to serve their followers. Now of all the apostles Peter is the most active. When the other ten fell back trembling in the garden, Peter wielded the blade on the posse. Peter first and foremost in all action. The gods of no peoples have been philosophic until the people themselves have approached that state.

The rabbit, the bear, the lion, the buzzard, the fox are culture heroes from the animal world. The rabbit is far in the lead of all the others and is blood brother to Jack. In short, the trickster-hero of West Africa has been transplanted to America.

John Henry is a culture hero in song, but no more so than Stacker Lee, Smokey Joe or Bad Lazarus. There are many, many Negroes who have never heard of any of the song heroes, but none who do not know John (Jack) and the rabbit.

Examples of Folklore and the Modern Culture Hero

why de porpoise's tail is on crosswise

Now, I want to tell you 'bout de porpoise. God had done made de world and everything. He set de moon and de stars in de sky. He got de fishes of de sea, and de fowls of de air completed.

He made de sun and hung it up. Then He made a nice gold track for it to run on. Then He said, "Now, Sun, I got everything made but Time. That's up to you. I want you to start out and go round de world on dis track just as fast as you kin make it. And de time it takes you to go and come, I'm going to call day and night." De Sun went zoonin' on cross de elements. Now, de porpoise was hanging round there and heard God what he tole de Sun, so he decided he'd take dat trip round de world hisself. He looked up and saw de Sun kytin' along, so he lit out too, him and dat Sun!

So de porpoise beat de Sun round de world by one hour and three minutes. So God said, "Aw naw, this aint gointer do! I didn't mean for nothin' to be faster than de Sun!" So God run dat porpoise for three days before he run him down and caught him, and took his tail off and put it on crossways to slow him up. Still he's de fastest thing in de water.

And dat's why de porpoise got his tail on crossways.

rockefeller and ford

Once John D. Rockefeller and Henry Ford was woofing at each other. Rockefeller told Henry Ford he could build a solid gold road round the world. Henry Ford told him if he would he would look at it and see if he liked it, and if he did he would buy it and put one of his tin lizzies on it.

Originality

It has been said so often that the Negro is lacking in originality that it has almost become a gospel. Outward signs seem to bear this out. But if one looks closely its falsity is immediately evident.

It is obvious that to get back to original sources is much too difficult for any group to claim very much as a certainty. What we really mean by originality is the modification of ideas. The most ardent admirer of the great Shakespeare cannot claim first source even for him. It is his treatment of the borrowed material.

So if we look at it squarely, the Negro is a very original being. While he lives and moves in the midst of a white civilisation, everything that he touches is re-interpreted for his own use. He has modified the language, mode of food preparation, practice of medicine, and most certainly the religion of his new country, just as he adapted to suit himself the Sheik hair-cut made famous by Rudolph Valentino.

Everyone is familiar with the Negro's modification of the whites' musical instruments, so that his interpretation has been adopted by the white man himself and then re-interpreted. In so many words, Paul Whiteman is giving an imitation of a Negro orchestra making use of white-invented musical instruments in a Negro way. Thus has arisen a new art in the civilised world, and thus has our so-called civilisation come. The exchange and re-exchange of ideas between groups.

Imitation

The Negro, the world over, is famous as a mimic. But this in no way damages his standing as an original. Mimicry is an art in itself. If it is not, then all art must fall by the same blow that strikes it down. When sculpture, painting, acting, dancing, literature neither reflect nor suggest anything in nature or human experience we turn away with a dull wonder in our hearts at why the thing was done. Moreover, the contention that the Negro imitates from a feeling of inferiority is incorrect. He mimics for the love of it. The group of Negroes who slavishly imitate is small. The average Negro glories in his ways. The highly educated Negro the same. The self-despisement lies in a middle class who scorns to do or be anything Negro. "That's just like a Nigger" is the most terrible rebuke one can lay upon this kind. He wears drab clothing, sits through a boresome church service, pretends to have no interest in the community, holds beauty contests, and otherwise apes all the mediocrities of the white brother. The truly cultured Negro scorns him, and the Negro "farthest down" is too busy "spreading his junk" in his own way to see or care. He likes his own things best. Even the group who are not Negroes but belong to the "sixth race," buy such records as "Shake dat thing" and "Tight lak dat." They really enjoy hearing a good bible-beater preach, but wild horses could drag no such admission from them. Their ready-made expression is: "We done got away from all that now." Some refuse to countenance Negro music on the grounds that it is niggerism, and for that reason should be done away with. Roland Hayes was thoroughly denounced for singing spirituals until he was accepted by white audiences. Langston Hughes is not considered a poet by this group because he writes of the man in the ditch, who is more numerous and real among us than any other.

But, this group aside, let us say that the art of mimicry is better developed in the Negro than in other racial groups. He does it as the mocking-bird does it, for the love of it, and not because he wishes to be like the one imitated. I saw a group of small Negro boys imitating a cat defecating and the subsequent toilet of the cat. It was very realistic, and they enjoyed it as much as if they had been imitating a coronation ceremony. The dances are full of imitations of various animals. The buzzard lope, walking the dog, the pig's hind legs, holding the mule, elephant squat, pigeon's wing, falling off the log, seabord (imitation of an engine starting), and the like.

ABSENCE OF THE CONCEPT OF PRIVACY

It is said that Negroes keep nothing secret, that they have no reserve. This ought not to seem strange when one considers that we are an outdoor people accustomed to communal life. Add this to all-permeating drama and you have the explanation.

There is no privacy in an African village. Loves, fights, possessions are, to misquote Woodrow Wilson, "Open disagreements openly arrived at." The community is given the benefit of a good fight as well as a good wedding. An audience is a necessary part of any drama. We merely go with nature rather than against it.

Discord is more natural than accord. If we accept the doctrine of the survival of the fittest there are more fight-

ing honors than there are honors for other achievements. Humanity places premiums on all things necessary to its well-being, and a valiant and good fighter is valuable in any community. So why hide the light under a bushel? Moreover, intimidation is a recognised part of warfare the world over, and threats certainly must be listed under that head. So that a great threatener must certainly be considered an aid to the fighting machine. . . . There is nothing so exhilarating as watching well-matched opponents go into action. The entire world likes action, for that matter. Hence prize-fighters become millionaires.

Likewise love-making is a biological necessity the world over and an art among Negroes. So that a man or woman who is proficient sees no reason why the fact should not be moot. He swaggers. She struts hippily about. Songs are built on the power to charm beneath the bed-clothes. Here again we have individuals striving to excel in what the community considers an art. Then if all of his world is seeking a great lover, why should he not speak right out loud?

It is all in a view-point. Love-making and fighting in all their branches are high arts, other things are arts among other groups where they brag about their proficiency just as brazenly as we do about these things that others consider matters for conversation behind closed doors. At any rate, the white man is despised by Negroes as a very poor fighter individually, and a very poor lover. One Negro, speaking of white men, said, "White folks is alright when dey gits in de bank and on de law bench, but dey sho' kin lie about wimmen folks."

I pressed him to explain. "Well you see, white mens makes out they marries wimmen to look at they eyes, and they know they gits em for just what us gits em for. 'Nother thing, white mens say they goes clear round de world and wins all de wimmen folks way from they men folks. Dat's a lie too. They don't win nothin, they buys em. Now de way I figgers it, if a woman don't want me enough to be wid me, 'thout I got to pay her, she kin rock right on, but these here white men don't know what to do wid a woman when they gits her—dat's how come they gives they wimmen so much. They got to. Us wimmen works jus as hard as us does an come home an sleep wid us every night. They own wouldn't do it and its de mens fault. Dese white men done fooled theyself bout dese wimmen.

"Now me, I keeps me some wimmens all de time. Dat's whut dey wuz put here for—us mens to use. Dat's right now, Miss. Y'all wuz put here so us mens could have some pleasure. Course I don't run round like heap uh men folks. But if my ole lady go way from me and stay more'n two weeks, I got to git me somebody, aint I?"

THE JOOK

Jook is the word for a Negro pleasure house. It may mean a bawdy house. It may mean the house set apart on public works where the men and women dance, drink and gamble. Often it is a combination of all these.

In past generations the music was furnished by "boxes," another word for guitars. One guitar was enough for a dance; to have two was considered excellent. Where two were playing one man played the lead and the other seconded him. The first player was "picking" and the second was "framming," that is, playing chords while the lead carried the melody by dexterous finger work. Sometimes a third player was added, and he played a tom-tom effect on the low strings. Believe it or not, this is excellent dance music.

Pianos soon came to take the place of the boxes, and now player-pianos and victrolas are in all of the Jooks.

Musically speaking, the Jook is the most important place in America. For in its smelly, shoddy confines has been born the secular music known as blues, and on blues has been founded jazz. The singing and playing in the true Negro style is called "jooking."

The songs grow by incremental repetition as they travel from mouth to mouth and from Jook to Jook for years before they reach outside ears. Hence the great variety of subject-matter in each song.

The Negro dances circulated over the world were also conceived inside the Jooks. They too make the round of Jooks and public works before going into the outside world.

In this respect it is interesting to mention the Black Bottom. I have read several false accounts of its origin and name. One writer claimed that it got its name from the black sticky mud on the bottom of the Mississippi river. Other equally absurd statements gummed the press. Now the dance really originated in the Jook section of Nashville, Tennessee, around Fourth Avenue. This is a tough neighbourhood known as Black Bottom—hence the name.

The Charleston is perhaps forty years old, and was danced up and down the Atlantic seaboard from North Carolina to Key West, Florida.

The Negro social dance is slow and sensuous. The idea in the Jook is to gain sensation, and not so much exercise. So that just enough foot movement is added to keep the dancers on the floor. A tremendous sex stimulation is gained from this. But who is trying to avoid it? The man, the woman, the time and the place have met. Rather, little intimate names are indulged in to heap fire on fire.

These too have spread to all the world.

The Negro theatre, as built up by the Negro, is based on Jook situations, with women, gambling, fighting, drinking. Shows like "Dixie to Broadway" are only Negro in cast, and could just as well have come from pre-Soviet Russia.

Another interesting thing—Negro shows before being tampered with did not specialise in octoroon chorus girls. The girl who could hoist a Jook song from her belly and lam it against the front door of the theatre was the lead, even if she were as black as the hinges of hell. The question was "Can she jook?" She must also have a good belly wobble, and her hips must, to quote a popular work song, "Shake like jelly all over and be so broad, Lawd, Lawd, and be so broad." So that the bleached chorus is the result of a white demand and not the Negro's.

The woman in the Jook may be nappy headed and black, but if she is a good lover she gets there just the same. A favorite Jook song of the past has this to say:

> *Singer:* It aint good looks dat takes you through dis world.
> *Audience:* What is it, good mama?
> *Singer:* Elgin movements in your hips
>   Twenty years guarantee.

And it always brought down the house too.

> Oh de white gal rides in a Cadillac,
> De yaller gal rides de same,
> Black gal rides in a rusty Ford
> But she gits dere just de same.

The sort of woman her men idealise is the type that is put forth in the theatre. The art-creating Negro prefers a not too thin woman who can shake like jelly all over as she dances and sings, and that is the type he put forth on the stage. She has been banished by the white producer and the Negro who takes his cue from the white.

Of course a black woman is never the wife of the upper class Negro in the North. This state of affairs does not obtain in the South, however. I have noted numerous cases where the wife was considerably darker than the husband. People of some substance, too.

This scornful attitude towards black women receives mouth sanction by the mud-sills.

Even on the works and in the Jooks the black man sings disparagingly of black women. They say that she is evil. That she sleeps with her fists doubled up and ready for action. All over they are making a little drama of waking up a yaller wife and a black one.

A man is lying beside his yaller wife and wakes her up. She says to him, "Darling, do you know what I was dreaming when you woke me up?" He says, "No honey, what was you dreaming?" She says, "I dreamt I had done cooked you a big, fine dinner and we was setting down to eat out de same plate and I was setting on yo' lap jus huggin you and kissin you and you was so sweet."

Wake up a black woman, and before you kin git any sense into her she be done up and lammed you over the head four or five times. When you git her quiet she'll say, "Nigger, know whut I was dreamin when you woke me up?"

You say, "No honey, what was you dreamin?" She says, "I dreamt you shook yo' rusty fist under my nose and I split yo' head open wid a axe."

But in spite of disparaging fictitious drama, in real life the black girl is drawing on his account at the commissary. Down in the Cypress Swamp as he swings his axe he chants:

> Dat ole black gal, she keep on grumblin,
> New pair shoes, new pair shoes,
> I'm goint to buy her shoes and stockings
> Slippers too, slippers too.

Then adds aside: "Blacker de berry, sweeter de juice."

To be sure the black gal is still in power, men are still cutting and shooting their way to her pillow. To the queen of the Jook!

Speaking of the influence of the Jook, I noted that Mae West in "Sex" had much more flavor of the turpentine quarters than she did of the white bawd. I know that the piece she played on the piano is a very old Jook composition. "Honey let yo' drawers hang low" had been played and sung in every Jook in the South for at least thirty-five years. It has always puzzled me why she thought it likely to be played in a Canadian bawdy house.

Speaking of the use of Negro material by white performers, it is astonishing that so many are trying it, and I have never seen one yet entirely realistic. They often have all the elements of the song, dance, or expression, but they are misplaced or distorted by the accent falling on the wrong element. Every one seems to think that the Negro is easily imitated when nothing is further from the truth. Without exception I wonder why the black-face comedians *are* black-face; it is a puzzle—good comedians, but darn poor niggers. Gershwin and the other "Negro" rhapsodists come under this same axe. Just about as Negro as caviar or Ann Pennington's athletic Black Bottom. When the Negroes who knew the Black Bottom in its cradle saw the Broadway version they asked each other, "Is you learnt dat *new* Black Bottom yet?" Proof that it was not *their* dance.

And God only knows what the world has suffered from the white damsels who try to sing Blues.

The Negroes themselves have sinned also in this respect. In spite of the goings up and down on the earth, from the original Fisk Jubilee Singers down to the present, there has been no genuine presentation of Negro songs to white audiences. The spirituals that have been sung around the world are Negroid to be sure, but so full of musicians' tricks that Negro congregations are highly entertained when they hear their old songs so changed. They never use the new style songs, and these are never heard unless perchance some daughter or son has been off to college and returns with one of the old songs with its face lifted, so to speak.

I am of the opinion that this trick style of delivery was originated by the Fisk Singers; Tuskeegee and Hampton followed suit and have helped spread this misconception

of Negro spirituals. This Glee Club style has gone on so long and become so fixed among concert singers that it is considered quite authentic. But I say again, that not one concert singer in the world is singing the songs as the Negro song-makers sing them.

If anyone wishes to prove the truth of this let him step into some unfashionable Negro church and hear for himself.

To those who want to institute the Negro theatre, let me say it is already established. It is lacking in wealth, so it is not seen in the high places. A creature with a white head and Negro feet struts the Metropolitan boards. The real Negro theatre is in the Jooks and the cabarets. Self-conscious individuals may turn away the eye and say, "Let us search elsewhere for our dramatic art." Let 'em search. They certainly won's find it. Butter Beans and Susie, Bo-Jangles and Snake Hips are the only performers of the real Negro school it has ever been my pleasure to behold in New York.

DIALECT

If we are to believe the majority of writers of Negro dialect and the burnt-cork artists, Negro speech is a weird thing, full of "ams" and "Ises." Fortunately we don't have to believe them. We may go directly to the Negro and let him speak for himself.

I know that I run the risk of being damned as an infidel for declaring that nowhere can be found the Negro who asks "am it?" nor yet his brother who announces "Ise uh gwinter." He exists only for a certain type of writers and performers.

Very few Negroes, educated or not, use a clear clipped "I." It verges more or less upon "Ah." I think the lip form is responsible for this to a great extent. By experiment the reader will find that a sharp "I" is very much easier with a thin taut lip than with a full soft lip. Like tightening violin strings.

If one listens closely one will note too that a word is slurred in one position in the sentence but clearly pronounced in another. This is particularly true of the pronouns. A pronoun as a subject is likely to be clearly enunciated, but slurred as an object. For example: "You better not let me ketch yuh."

There is a tendency in some localities to add the "h" to "it" and pronounce it "hit." Probably a vestige of old English. In some localities "if" is "ef."

In story telling "so" is universally the connective. It is used even as an introductory word, at the very beginning of a story. In religious expression "and" is used. The trend in stories is to state conclusions; in religion, to enumerate.

I am mentioning only the most general rules in dialect because there are so many quirks that belong only to certain localities that nothing less than a volume would be adequate.

OVERVIEWS AND GENERAL STUDIES

Warren J. Carson (essay date 1991)

SOURCE: "Hurston as Dramatist: The Florida Connection," in *Zora in Florida*, University of Central Florida Press, 1991, pp. 121-29.

[*In the following essay, Carson discusses Hurston's early "Florida" plays:* Color Struck, The First One, *and* The Fiery Chariot.]

While a considerable amount of scholarly work exists on the writing career of Zora Neale Hurston, the bulk of it concerns her novels, in particular *Their Eyes Were Watching God* (1937), which is considered by most to be her finest literary achievement. Her other works, including short stories, folklore studies, and the autobiography, *Dust Tracks on a Road* (1942), occasionally attract some critical attention, especially in the last decade. Other dimensions of Hurston's long career, which spanned nearly forty years, have largely been ignored altogether or at best afforded only a passing mention. This is true of her several early poems, her journalistic work, and especially her plays. That Hurston's plays have not triggered any critical interest to speak of is interesting enough in itself, particularly when we consider that it was a play that brought her to the attention of Harlem Renaissance circles, and when we consider her lifelong interest in drama and the stage. The purpose of this chapter, then, is twofold: to examine, briefly, Hurston's career as a dramatist, and to point out the Florida aspects of her few plays.

Hurston's entry into the Harlem Renaissance circle was marked by the publication of several short stories and the 1925 prize-winning play *Color Struck.* The play marked the beginning of a strong interest in writing and producing dramatic art that was to stay with Hurston throughout the remainder of her career. Shortly after *Color Struck* won second prize in the drama division of the 1925 literary contest sponsored by *Opportunity,* the official magazine of the National Urban League, a second play, *The First One,* was entered in the 1926 *Opportunity* contest and "later printed in Charles S. Johnson's collectanea of Renaissance writing, *Ebony and Topaz* (1927)" (Hemenway, 68). Actually, Hurston had submitted another play in 1925 along with *Color Struck.* Nothing is known about it except its title—*Spears*—because, according to Robert Hemenway, it was lost (74).

In subsequent years Hurston—in addition to writing novels and compiling folklore collections—produced shows that included drama, native dance, and music gathered during her folklore expeditions. More important, Hurston was involved in several collaborative efforts: Her 1930 collaboration with Langston Hughes produced the play *Mule Bone* and resulted in a major dispute between the two collaborators. In 1939-40, Hurston worked with noted North Carolina playwright Paul Green. And in 1944 Hurston's collaboration with Dorothy Waring produced *Polk County: A Comedy of Negro Life in a Sawmill Camp, with Authentic Negro Music.* Sadly enough, neither of the plays written with Hughes or Waring has been published or widely produced, and the intended collaboration with Green never came to fruition, although Hemenway reports that "she and Green toyed with the idea of collaborating on a play called 'John de Conquerer'" (255).

The account of *Mule Bone* is certainly an interesting one, not so much from the standpoint of the play itself as from the controversy that it sparked between Hurston and Hughes. According to Hemenway, "Hughes claimed that he was to do the construction, plot, characterization and some dialogue, and that Hurston was to provide the authentic Florida color, give the dialogue a true southern flavor, and insert turns of phrase and 'highly amusing details' from her collecting trips" (137). However, exactly who did just what is not known. What is known is that Hughes and Hurston each claimed that he or she did the greater portion of the work on the play and went about claiming it as his or her own. There were numerous disputes over a proposed production, and the whole episode eventually ended with Hurston and Hughes actively avoiding each other for the rest of their lives. The play itself remains in manuscript form, although "[a]fter Hurston's death he [Hughes] permitted the third act to be published in *Drama Critique*" (145).

A study of this act will certainly verify Hurston's obvious presence at work in *Mule Bone,* whatever the nature of her role. The Florida setting—this time "near a Negro village in the Florida backwoods" (Hughes and Hurston, [1930] 1964, 103)—is just as colorfully drawn and as intricately detailed as the Florida settings of Hurston's major works. Furthermore, the scene, which takes place on "a high stretch of railroad track through a luxurious Florida forest" (103), is drawn with the care, fondness, and empathy that only one familiar with it could recount. Most important, however, is the language, the dialogue with "true southern flavor," which Hurston adds with her firsthand knowledge of its flair and cadences. This colorful language abounds in *Mule Bone,* suggesting a plethora of amusing images, from "box-ankled" and "ugly-rump" Negroes to "half-pint Baptists" and "gator-faced jigs." Moreover, the very importance of oral skills in the black community is addressed when a verbal contest ensues between Jim and Dave as they try to convince Daisy of the superiority of their individual affections. For example, when Jim assures Daisy that "I love you like God loves Gabriel—an' dat's His best angel," Dave counters with "Daisy, I love you harder than de thunder can bump a stump—if I don't, God's a gopher" (104). This generally good-natured bantering between friends (although they have had a fight over Daisy and Jim has attacked Dave with the bone of a dead mule) can be recognized as yet another aspect of the rich oral tradition that includes the dozens (a verbal contest that often consists of trading insults), the work song, the blues, the Negro spiritual, and rap, to mention a few of its popular manifestations.

The other interesting point about **Mule Bone** is that its subject matter did not die for Hurston. Parts of the original story continued to show up in subsequent works, particularly in *Their Eyes Were Watching God* and *Polk County.* It is also interesting to note that portions of her proposed collaboration with Paul Green also showed up in **Polk County.**

Rather than being a fully developed drama, **Polk County,** set in a sawmill camp in central Florida some fifty miles from Hurston's hometown of Eatonville, is more akin to the "revues" for which she became a popular producer in the late 1920s and early 1930s. These revues, which included **"The Great Day"** (1932) and **"From Sun to Sun"** (1933), both depicting life at Florida railroad camps, combined dialogue with native music and dance and were designed, from Hurston's point of view, to advance her philosophy of a *real* Negro American drama. In a letter to Langston Hughes dated April 12, 1928, Hurston wrote, "The Negro's outstanding characteristic is drama. That is why he appears so imitative. Drama is mimicry . . ." (quoted in Hemenway, 114). Hurston was primarily concerned with authenticity in drama, a concern no doubt made more urgent by her training as an anthropologist. She felt, according to Hemenway, that while white playwrights like Eugene O'Neill, Paul Green, and Dubose Heyward were well meaning, their re-creations of black life were not as realistic or as actual as they ought to be (115). In the letter quoted above, Hurston writes, "Did I tell you before I left about the new, the *real* Negro art theater I plan? Well, I shall, or rather we shall act out the folk tales, however short, with the abrupt angularity and naivete of the primitive 'bama Nigger. Quote that with naive [*sic*] settings" (115). It is clear, then, as we shall see, that Hurston indeed tried wherever possible to present the real, the pure essence of black life in her work.

Hurston's first play, **Color Struck,** is subtitled "A Play in Four Scenes." Actually, it consists of four sketches strung together in a rather loose fashion, and certainly it does not show Hurston at her best. Indeed, it is the work of a young and immature writer, for the scenes are not sufficiently developed and the characters, for the most part, are not convincingly delineated. Furthermore, from a technical standpoint, the play is probably too brief to justify the difficulty that would be incurred in staging it.

The story line is a simple one. Aboard a train, a group of blacks are bound for central Florida to participate in the statewide cakewalk (a dance contest with cakes as prizes for the most accomplished walking steps), which is probably an annual event. Among the group are the principal characters, John Turner and Emma Beazeby, an attractive couple from Jacksonville who are expected to win the cakewalk. During the trip and all during the festivities, Emma hounds John about looking at the light-skinned ladies; in fact, she becomes so upset by her obsessive jealousy that she cannot participate in the grand finale, even though she and John have been named the winners of the semifinal round. The final scene takes place twenty years later when John returns from the North to seek Emma's hand in marriage, but finds that Emma, who during the course of those years has given birth to an extremely light-complexioned child, is just as obsessed with color as ever. Emma, having misinterpreted John's attempt to comfort her sick daughter, accuses him of still being "color struck." Stung by the unfair accusation, John leaves; Emma is left alone with her daughter.

John, the protagonist, is by far the most fully developed of the characters in **Color Struck.** Hurston portrays him as fun-loving, but not to the point of being unfaithful or dishonorable; sensitive, but not to the point of being indecisive. John loves Emma: that much is clear; and that he occasionally looks at another woman in no way detracts from his feelings for her. When Emma refuses to "walk the cake" with him—for which he has practiced almost a year—John promptly, though reluctantly, seeks out another partner, who just happens to be the mulatto Effie Jones, so as not to have spent his time practicing in vain and to relish his status as the most popular cakewalker in the state. When we see John some twenty years later, he is still loving and compassionate, yet he knows when he has been beaten. He leaves Emma as he finds her—still obsessively jealous over what she perceives as John's obsession with light skin. John finally realizes that Emma will never change: "So this is the woman I've been wearing over my heart like a rose for twenty years! She so despises her own skin that she can't believe any one else could love it" ([1925], 1926, 14).

On the other hand, Hurston portrays Emma as an unsympathetic character. She is flat and shallow. Her major trait is jealousy, which leads to self-pity, something that Hurston obviously cannot abide. Emma is described in the *dramatis personae* as "a black woman." When we first see Emma she is berating John for daring to look at a light-skinned woman: "You wuz grinning at her and she wuz grinning back jes lake a ole chessy cat!" (8); and several lines later: "Jes the same every time you sees a yaller face, you *takes* a chance" (8). In the last scene, twenty years later, Emma is more obsessed than ever and continues to hurl the same accusations at John: "I knowed it! A half white skin" (14). Emma indulges in self-pity to the point that she can neither enjoy the pleasantries of life nor accept any love from John. The extent of her self-pity is characterized by such statements as "Oh—them yaller wenches! How I hates 'em! They gets everything, they gets everything everybody else wants! The men, the jobs—everything! The whole world is got a sign on it. Wanted: Light colored. Us blacks was made for cobblestones" (11). Hurston clearly objects to such self-indulgence by showing the debilitating power that such jealousy and self-pity have on an individual, for even after twenty years, Emma is still "unable to accept the love of a good man" (Hemenway, 47). Moreover, she continues to wallow in jealousy and self-pity. Ironically, Emma has fallen prey to the very thing she has continued to accuse John of: she has given birth out of wedlock, fathered by a near-white man (or perhaps white), which makes all the more poignant and pathetic her earlier lamentation, "Oh, them half whites, they gets everything, they gets everything everybody else wants!"

As mentioned previously, none of the four scenes are well developed. Hemenway concludes, and rightly so, that the play's "only memorable scene is the cakewalk" (47). The cakewalk is indeed a colorful, rather elegant affair. The participants have come from points all across Florida for fellowship and to compete. The ladies and gentlemen are resplendent in their finery, including "plug" hats for the men. The air is one of joviality; the Jacksonville delegation certainly has a good time en route to the cakewalk, and, except for Emma, all appear to enjoy themselves while there, and we may assume they will on the return trip home, especially since John and Effie won the cake in a unanimous decision. The only other scene that bears some mention is the opening scene aboard the train. While it does not generate any excitement, it can be juxtaposed against another train scene that Hurston was to use more than twenty years later in her autobiography. In *Color Struck*, ladies and gentlemen of a rather bourgeois background occupy the coach. While there are baskets of food, they are neatly deposited in the overhead compartments; and while "There is a little friendly pushing and shoving" (7), the riders are mostly orderly and well behaved. This contrasts directly with the picture drawn in "My People! My People!" from *Dust Tracks on a Road*, where some of the coach occupants are characterized as coarse, loud, boisterous, rude, uncouth, and certainly not the kinds of persons that the more refined blacks would want to sit down with. This is but one example of Hurston's tendency to use and reuse material until all its dimensions have been examined and exhausted, or at least until she has discovered the dimension she was looking for.

Finally, scene 3 must be mentioned as the most technically problematic of all the scenes. One supposes, of course, that it is designed as an interlude. While this is certainly acceptable in drama, it is seldom done with so little dialogue—there are two announcements by the master of ceremonies, nothing else—or with a curtain in the middle of a single scene. In today's technologically advanced theater, what Hurston intended could certainly be achieved by lighting. As this was not the case in 1925, however, it seems that she might have adopted a smoother, less obtrusive technique for marking the change of the moment; perhaps it would have been easiest to rewrite the scene, for its action could have been incorporated in scene 2 without great difficulty. Whatever the remedy, something should have been done to eliminate, or at least minimize, the structural fragmentation the scene poses.

One very wonderful feature of the play is the language. Hurston demonstrates very early in her career her knack for capturing the vernacular of southern speech, especially that of black Floridians. Her use of language also shows her fondness for folk speech. *Color Struck* is rich not only in dialect, but more important, in cleverly disguised insults such as "mullethead Jacksonville Coon" (9), referring to

the scavenger fish with the large, ugly, monstrous, protruding forehead; and "She calls herself a big cigar, but *I* kin smoke her" (10), meaning that if all else fails, one can assert a superior physical prowess over another. Hurston continued using dialect and other folk elements of speech throughout her career. Sometimes it is used to evoke humor or sympathy, or to command respect; but as with its use in *Color Struck*, it is never used condescendingly. Rather, Hurston recognizes dialect's worth and employs it to its fullest in presenting reality as she saw it. Her ability with regard to language is certainly a mark of her genius.

By far the most outstanding feature of the play is its theme—color struck. As used in black communities, "color struck" is an ambiguous term, although Hemenway sees it only as "the intraracial color consciousness addressed by the bourgeoisie . . . [which] addresses those who envy whites biologically and intellectually" (47). This assessment identifies only one aspect of being "color struck." Lighter-hued blacks can be color struck by thinking they are superior to darker-skinned blacks because their skin color more closely approximates that of whites; dark-complexioned blacks can be color struck by thinking likewise, that lighter skin and straighter hair would somehow make them better and more acceptable. This dimension can manifest itself in three ways: (1) dark-skinned persons may abuse blacks with light skin; (2) they may try to make themselves lighter through the use of chemical skin lighteners and hair straighteners; or (3) they may resign themselves to an obsessive self-indulgence and self-pity. Emma certainly embodies each of these manifestations.

An old maxim that used to be popular in certain black circles, and that still surfaces occasionally today, states:

If you're light, you're all right;
If you're brown, stick around;
If you're black, get back!

This is obviously how Emma Beazeby perceives her own situation vis-à-vis Effie Jones. Her obsession with color is clear from the beginning, as she accuses John of gawking at and ogling every light-skinned woman he sees. Emma then resorts to pouting, verbal abuse of Effie, threats of physical violence, and finally, self-pity. Emma's jealous love for John is compounded by her inferiority complex regarding her own dark skin. She ruins her chances for any happiness by alienating John; even when asked to marry him twenty years later, Emma is still not able to forget her obsession with color. Once again she alienates John, and in the end is left alone. Moreover, as mentioned, Emma has conceived a near-white child out of wedlock, which adds an ironic twist to her constant accusations of John. In Emma, we find Hurston challenging not only the ridiculous uselessness of the notion of color but of obsession of any kind. It is John, the protagonist, who speaks Hurston's philosophy of affirmation when he says "Dancing is dancing no matter who is doing it" (*Color Struck*, 8). In other words, life is for the full enjoyment of everyone.

It is interesting, and, I think, important, to note the timing of the play. In the harlem of the mid 1920s, Marcus Garvey's Universal Negro Improvement Association was in its heyday, with its motto "Africa for Africans at Home and Abroad." Garvey believed in the purity of the black race and overtly attacked products of miscegenated bloodlines as being "devils" like their pure-white ancestors. Knowing Hurston's disdain of race prejudice and her impatience with extremity of any sort, we may conjecture that this is her answer to what she considered the incredible foolishness of intraracial prejudice. Whatever the motivation, *Color Struck* does, for all its faults, show that Hurston is not afraid to meet challenges head on, even when they involve the touchy, almost taboo, subject of being color struck; furthermore, the play is indeed a sensitive and realistic portrayal of an important social event in the black communities of the South.

Color is also the central theme of Hurston's second play, *The First One* (1927), which won first place in the drama division of the 1927 *Opportunity* contest and was published that same year in Charles S. Johnson's collection of Harlem Renaissance writing, *Ebony and Topaz*. This short one-act play is actually a dramatization of the biblical story of Noah's curse on his youngest son, Ham, which resulted in Ham and his descendants being accursed with black skin and destined to be servants of mankind forever. The brief account is found in Genesis 10: 21-27. Hurston expands this account in an effort to explore the age-old preoccupation with skin color, and she goes even further to establish the negative emotions that continue to be associated with the color black. For example, after Noah, who is still in a drunken stupor, utters his curse, the others shrink back in horror, and one character exclaims, "Black! He could not mean *black*" (*The First One* [1927], 1971, 56). Later, when Ham becomes aware of the curse and examines himself, he "gaz[es] horrified at his hands" and exclaims, "Black! . . . Why Noah, my father and lord of the Earth, why?" (57). As the other family members withdraw from Ham, as if his diabolical color will perhaps contaminate them, Noah seals Ham's banishment with the following pronouncement: "Thou are black. Arise and go out from among us that we may see thy face no more" (57), which serves, in Hurston's estimation, as a precursor to "If you're black, get back."

While *The First One* offers nothing by way of a Florida connection as such, the play itself is far more skillfully wrought than its predecessor, *Color Struck*. For example, because *The First One* is limited to only one scene within the one act—unlike *Color Struck*—Hurston achieves far more unity; in other words, *The First One* does not suffer from an overpowering sense of fragmentation as does the earlier play. In addition to her technical improvement as a playwright, Hurston evinces in *The First One* her early interest in African-American folklore, which, of course, becomes more pronounced in *Mules and Men* (1935) and *Tell My Horse* (1938), and her interest in an Afrocentric interpretation of the Bible, which receives wider attention in *Moses, Man of the Mountain* (1939) and the novel about Herod Hurston was writing just prior to her death.

Hurston's *The Fiery Chariot*, another one-act play based on "Ole Massa and John Who Wanted To Go to Heaven" from *Mules and Men,* also has a Florida setting. The play version survives only in typescript, but its story is essentially the same as the folktale, give or take a few details. *The Fiery Chariot* is set on a plantation in Florida prior to the end of the Civil War. The central characters are Ike, his wife, Dinah, and the white "Massa" of the plantation, and the story is a humorous portrayal of "getting what you pray for." Ike prays insistently for Jesus to come and rescue him from the evils of plantation life and take him to heaven aboard a fiery chariot. Dinah has warned Ike repeatedly that one day he might just get what he asks for. One day the "Ole Massa" overhears Ike's lamentations and his pleading for comfort, and decides to "spook" Ike; thus, "Ole Massa" dons a white sheet and informs Ike that he has heard his pleas and has come to take him to heaven. What follows is a hilariously funny account of Ike's continued stalling and excuse making, even his trying to get Dinah to go in his place, and finally his asking this would be God to step back: "Yessuh, Jesus. Oh Lawd, the radiance of yo' countenance is so bright, Ah can't come out by yuh. Stand back jes' a lil' bit please" (6). After repeating this request several times and finally being accommodated, "Ike leaps past him out of the door" (6). In her study of *The Fiery Chariot,* Adele Newson observes that this play "supports both the well known motif of John the trickster and the stereotypical image of black men possessing superior physical speed" (36). The humor of the play, however, remains its most salient and important feature, deeply rooted as it is in African-American folklore. Furthermore, Dinah wryly notes that "God ain't got no time wid yo' pappy and him barefooted too" (7), which Newson rightly observes as adding "humor both to the motif and the stereotype" (36).

Clearly, the study of Hurston's few plays reinforces her insistence that black drama should be a sincere, realistic reflection of black life. The strong sense of place, the powerful imagery, the incorporation of music, dance, and spectacle, and the dramatic use of language are tributes not only to Hurston's immense and versatile talent, but underscore her philosophy regarding the ingenuity of black culture.

Works Cited

Hemenway, Robert. *Zora Neale Hurston: A Literary Biography.* Urbana: University of Illinois Press, 1977.

Hughes, Langston, and Hurston, Zora Neale (1930). "*Mule Bone: A Comedy of Negro Life,* Act III." *Drama Critique* (Spring 1964): 103-7.

Hurston, Zora Neale. *Color Struck* (1925). In *Fire* 1 (1926). Facsimile reprint by the Negro Universities Press, 1970, 7-14.

———. *Dust Tracks on a Road.* 1942. Reprint, with introduction by Robert Hemenway. Urbana: University of Illinois Press, 1984.

———. *The Fiery Chariot* (1935). Typescript. James Weldon Johnson Collection, Yale University Library, New Haven, CT.

———. *The First One* (1927). In *Ebony and Topaz,* edited by Charles S. Johnson, 53-57. Facsimile reprint by Books for Libraries Press, 1971.

———. *Polk County: A Comedy of Negro Life in a Sawmill Camp, with Authentic Negro Music* (1944). James Weldon Johnson Collection, Yale University, New Haven, CT.

———. *Their Eyes Were Watching God.* Philadelphia: Lippincott, 1937.

Newson, Adele S. "The Fiery Chariot." *Zora Neale Hurston Forum* 1, no. 1 (Fall 1986): 32-7.

John Lowe (essay date 1995)

SOURCE: "From Mule Bones to Funny Bones: The Plays of Zora Neale Hurston," in *The Southern Quarterly*, Vol. XXXIII, Nos. 2-3, Winter-Spring, 1995, pp. 65-78.

[*In the following essay, Lowe studies Hurston's dramatic works and the difficulties she experienced getting them into production.*]

Zora Neale Hurston has recently been rescued from literary oblivion and installed as a major figure in the American literary canon. Her stature thus far, however, has stemmed from her success as a novelist, especially in her masterwork, *Their Eyes Were Watching God* (1937). Some Hurston aficionados were therefore surprised when the play she coauthored with Langston Hughes, *Mule Bone*, had its Broadway debut in 1991. Did Hurston write plays as well? Indeed she did. In fact, one of her first publications was a play, and she never gave up trying to mount a successful production.

As a preacher's daughter, Hurston came by her dramatic gifts naturally. John Hurston, born a slave, overcame his humble origins by marrying Lucy Potts, the daughter of a well-to-do farmer and by heeding a call from God. A strapping man, he was a commanding figure in the pulpit and made the most of his booming voice and musical gifts. Zora Neale was born on either 7 January or 15 January 1891 in Notasulga, Alabama, not far from Booker T. Washington's Tuskegee Institute. She was the sixth of John and Lucy's children. One son, Isaac, died in childhood, and three more sons were born after the family relocated in Eatonville, an all-black town in central Florida, in the early 1890s. In her autobiography, Hurston vividly recalls learning the dynamics of African American performance style from the men swapping lies on the porch of Joe Clarke's general store.

Hurston's apparently happy life fell apart in 1904 when her mother died. She did not get along with her stepmother and eventually left Florida as a lady's maid for a traveling Gilbert and Sullivan company, thus inaugurating her theatrical experiences. After a series of jobs and a sequence of college courses at Morgan State and Howard University, Hurston won a scholarship to Barnard College, where she studied with Ruth Benedict and Franz Boas, the founders of American anthropology. While in New York she also met the leading figures of the New Negro literary movement and soon became one of the leading "niggerati," a she called them, herself. One of her several contributions to the Harlem Renaissance, as it has become known, was a play, *Color Struck*, which she published in a short-lived magazine, *Fire!!* She also submitted a play, "Spears" (since lost), to *Opportunity*'s writing contest in 1925; the piece was awarded an honorable mention.

Aside from the material surrounding *Mule Bone*'s publication and premiere, some brief commentary by her biographer, Robert E. Hemenway, and articles by Adele Newsome on **"The Fiery Chariot"** and Lynda Hill on plays that dramatize Hurston's life and work, virtually nothing has been written on Hurston as dramatist. One finds some insight into her dramatic program, however, by examining the nature of her few published and several unpublished plays, a sequence initiated with *Color Struck*.

This four-scene play initially depicts a group of laughing, animated friends boarding the Jim Crow railway car in Jacksonville enroute to a cakewalk contest in St. Augustine in 1900. The crowd predicts that John and Emma will win: "They's the bestest cakewalkers in dis state" (7). When these two appear, however, they argue because the dark Emma thinks brown-skinned John has been flirting with the mulatto Effie. Throughout the play, Emma's jealousy and morbid self-hatred keep her from accepting John's love. Her tragedy, however, is played out in the early scenes against the boisterous comedy enacted by her friends, and the lovingly detailed cakewalk contest in scenes 2 and 3. Joe Clarke, mayor of Eatonville, who plays a prominent role in much of Hurston's fiction, appears for the first time here. Emma, jealous again, refuses to perform with John, who goes on anyway, partnering Effie. As Emma watches, they win the contest.

The fourth and final scene takes place twenty years later. Emma is revealed nursing her light-skinned, invalid daughter when John enters. Although he has not seen her since the cakewalk and has since been married and widowed, he still loves Emma. She supposes he married a light-skinned woman, but John says he chose a dark wife because he longed for Emma. He teases her when he discovers her invalid teenage daughter is nearly white. He tells her he will stay with the girl while Emma goes for the white doctor she insists on. Instead of going for the doctor, however, Emma doubles back and accuses John of lust for her daughter. Disgusted, John leaves. The doctor arrives, but he is too late to save Emma's daughter and tells her that she might have lived had she sent for him sooner. The play's melodrama makes it top heavy, but it succeeds in suggesting the creativity and exuberance of African American culture and in sketching in the parameters of color prejudice within the African American community.

Hurston was asked to contribute a piece to Charles S. Johnson's *Ebony and Topaz: A Collectanea*, an anthology of black writing that appeared in 1927, and she chose a play. *The First One: A Play in One Act* is set in the Valley of Ararat three years after the flood and features Noah, his wife, their three sons Shem, Japeth and Ham, Eve, Ham's wife and the sons' wives and children. This was the first of several pieces that Hurston would set in biblical times, frequently in black dialect. Here, however, Hurston uses standard speech. As the play opens, Noah and everyone else stand fuming because Ham, the wayward son, is once again late for the annual commemoration of the delivery from the flood. Ham comes in playing a harp, dressed in a goat-skin and a green wreath, obviously linking him with both Orpheus and Bacchus. Shem's wife criticizes Ham because he doesn't bring an offering and because, unlike his brothers who toil in the fields, he merely tends flocks and sings. After a brief ceremony, the characters recall the flood and the deliverance in dramatic language. Noah calls upon Ham to play and sing to help them forget. Noah gets drunk to forget the images of the dead faces that floated by the ark. When Ham, also inebriated, laughingly reports on his father's nakedness in the tent—"The old Ram . . . he has had no spring for years." Shem's jealous wife seizes the opportunity and wakes Noah, reporting the deed but not the identity of the perpetrator. Noah, enraged, roars that "His skin shall be black . . . He and his seed forever. He shall serve his brothers and they shall rule over him" (55). Later, all involved are appalled and try to reverse the curse, but Ham comes in laughing, unaware that he has been turned black. His son has changed color as well. Noah banishes them, fearing that blackness is contagious. Ham, rather than show dismay, laughs cynically, saying "Oh, remain with your flocks and fields and vineyards, to covet, to sweat, to die and to know no peace, I go to the sun" (57).

Two things are worth noting about this play. First is that the origin of a race is in its founding father's joke. Second, the ending suggests that "The First [Black] One," a being who knows the true value of life, is superior to whites. Thus Hurston's playlet both embraces and inverts the traditional interpretation of the biblical passage upon which it is based.

In the meantime, Hurston continued her education at Columbia. Encouraged by Boas, she began a series of trips to Florida to gather folklore materials. This work was facilitated for years by the sponsorship of a wealthy white woman, Mrs. Osgood Mason, who also supported the careers of Hurston's gifted friends, the writers Langston Hughes and Alain Locke, as well as the musician Hall Johnson, who was active in the Broadway theater. All of them called Mrs. Mason "Godmother."

Even during the years of this patron's largesse, Hurston had to scramble to make ends meet. In 1931 she was hired to write some sketches for *Fast and Furious,* a black musical review produced by Forbes Randolph. She also appeared as a pom-pom girl in a football sketch and helped direct the show, which folded after a week. Her next theatrical adventure was writing sketches for the revue

Jungle Scandals, which also closed quickly. Hurston had nothing but scorn for both of these shows and saw an opportunity to correct their errors with a musical of her own. Accordingly, she sought out Hall Johnson, who had directed the chorus of the wildly successful *Green Pastures* in 1931. Hurston thought that the play, written by a white man, Marc Connelly, was a dreadful hash of black culture, but she knew Johnson was master of his craft. She decided to set a single day in a railroad work camp to music. At first she thought of calling it *Spunk* but settled on *The Great Day*. Johnson worked on the project desultorily, but finally withdrew, only to filch some of Hurston's material for his production *Run Little Chillun,* which opened to favorable reviews in 1931.

In spite of these early disappointments, Hurston peservered. By pawning some of her possessions to raise funds and wheedling the final backing from Godmother, *The Great Day* was presented at New York's John Golden Theater on 10 January 1932. It used a concert format, and Alain Locke wrote the program notes. In the first part of the program, the audience saw workers arising and going to the job, singing songs as they laid track, returning to their homes where their children played folk games, and listening to a preacher's sermons accompanied by spirituals. Part 2 presented an evening's entertainment at the local "jook" (nightclub), consisting mainly of blues songs, ending with half the cast doing a blues song, half singing *Deep River*. No theatrical producer came forward to offer an extended run and the show lost money, even though it attracted a good crowd and favorable reviews. Godmother refused to let Hurston ever again put on the play as written and also forbade the theatrical use of other portions of *Mules and Men*. Hurston did succeed in mounting an edited version of *The Great Day* at Manhattan's New School on 29 March 1932. A program of this production survives, and *Theatre Arts* published a photo of the cast.

The next year, back home in Florida, Hurston and her friend Robert Wunsch of the Rollins College English department produced a January performance of the revised *The Great Day* to great acclaim, using a new title, *From Sun to Sun*. A second performance was given in February. In this form, the musical was mounted in a number of other cities in Florida, including Eatonville. Two years later, Hurston repeated the show in abbreviated concert form at Fisk University in Nashville and followed with a performance in Chicago, using still another title, *Singing Steel,* casting it with aspiring singers from the YWCA. Once again the show received good reviews, but, more importantly, officials from the Rosenwald Foundation, impressed by Hurston's research, offered to sponsor her return to Columbia to work on a PhD in anthropology.

We have no script for these musicals, but the Library of Congress owns tapes of many of the musical numbers. A version was pieced together for a performance at the 1993 Zora Neale Hurston Festival of the Arts in Eatonville.

Hurston did write down a one-act play that was part of the Rollins *From Sun to Sun* performance in 1933. The unpublished version, now in the Hurston Collection of the University of Florida, **"The Fiery Chariot,"** creates a seven-page drama out of an old folktale. The play takes place in Dinah and Ike's slave cabin. Initially Ike comically wars with his little son over a baked sweet potato but soon switches to a comic duel with Dinah, who criticizes Ike in lively vernacular for praying every night to God to come get him in his fiery chariot. "Ah betcher God gits so tired uh yo' noise dat when He sees you gittin' down, he gwan in his privy house and slam de door." Ole Massa hears Ike praying and appears before the door wearing a sheet, claiming to be the Lord come in his chariot. Ike hides under the bed and tells Dinah to tell him he isn't there. Ole Massa says Dinah will do, and Ike urges her to go. When Dinah reveals Ike, he comes out and quivers at the sight of the Lord in his white sheet and stalls by saying he needs to put his Sunday shirt on. Then it's his Sunday pants. Finally, he persuades Ole Massa to step back some and bolts out the door and away. When Ike's son asks if God will catch him, Dinah answers, "You know God aint got no time wid yo' pappy and him barefooted too." Although the play builds on an old comic tradition, it has serious undertones. Ike prays for death because Ole Massa works him so hard; Ole Massa's decision to take Dinah instead verges toward the habit actual owners had of appropriating the bodies of their female slaves. Finally, Ike's clever method of escaping Ole Massa/God links him with the heroics of the legendary trickster slave, High John de Conquer.

The most important Hurston play is a collaboration with Langston Hughes, *Mule Bone,* which they wrote in 1930 but never produced, as the authors had a "falling out" right after it was written and never reconciled. In 1985 Henry Louis Gates, Jr. read the play at Yale and began a campaign to have it produced, but the revival almost did not come about. A staged reading before one hundred prominent black writers and theater people in 1988 led over half of them to urge the project be shelved, partly because its humor seemed stereotypical—it made extensive use of vernacular and racial humor, including the word "nigger." Changes were duly made, and *Mule Bone* was finally brought to the New York stage in March 1991, edited and revised by George Houston Bass, Ann Cattaneo, Henry Louis Gates, Jr., Arnold Rampersad and the director, Michael Schultz. Taj Mahal provided the musical numbers, which included lyrics drawn from some poems by Hughes. Bass wrote a "frame" story involving Hurston herself, who pronounced to the audience that the evening's event was a result of her scientific folklore expeditions.

In both the original and revised versions, the plot is based on Hurston's short story "The Bone of Contention," which detailed the falling out of two friends who quarrel over a turkey one of them has shot. In the three-act version, the two men, Jim Weston, a musician, and Dave Carter, a dancer, form a musical team. They quarrel over a flirtatious local domestic worker, Daisy Taylor, who skillfully plays them off against each other. The real voice in the play, however, belongs to the community. The men on Joe

Clarke's porch and the women who stroll by offer a continual stream of commentary on the triangle, tell jokes and stories, and play local card games and checkers. A political parallel emerges in the Reverend Simms's public campaign to unseat Joe Clarke as mayor. Even children contribute, playing out classic African American folk games for the audience. The community takes sides according to religious denominations after Jim (a Methodist) knocks Dave (a Baptist) out with a mule bone. Act 2 largely consists of the "trial," held at the Macedonia Baptist Church, presided over by Mayor Clarke. But his leadership is challenged by Reverend Simms, who later spars with Reverend Childers. Their rivalry is matched by the wickedly comic duel between the Methodist Sister Lewis and the Baptist Sister Taylor, who signify to each other to beat the band, seemingly setting off various other quarrels. A continuing joke is the general ineffectiveness of the town marshall, Lum Boger, to coerce anyone, of any denomination. The latter proves that the mule bone is indeed a dangerous weapon by quoting Samson's story from the Bible. Clarke rules that Dave be banished for two years.

The brief third act focuses on the romantic triangle. After toying with the rivals, Daisy chooses Jim and demands that he take a good job as the white folks' yardman. When Jim refuses, she sidles up to Dave, but he too rejects her. The play ends with the two men back together, determined to make the town accept them both.

Mule Bone enjoyed limited success at the box office. It closed on 14 April 1991 after twenty-seven previews and sixty-seven performances. Although a few critics found it funny and historic (Kissel), an "exuberant" theatrical event (Beaufort) and a "wonderful piece of black theater" (Barnes), it was deemed "an amiable curiosity" (Winer), "one of the American theater's more tantalizing might-have-beens" (Rich), "pleasant but uneventful" (Wilson) and a "theatrical curio" (Watt)" by other critics, who found it charming but dramatically deficient.

During the thirties, Hurston spent most of her time in Florida writing her novels, two books of folklore and working for the Federal Writers' Project. In October 1934 she wrote from Chicago to her friend James Weldon Johnson about a visit she had just made to Fisk University. There, President Jones asked Hurston to consider attending Yale Drama School for a year to study directing and the allied dramatic arts as preparation for establishing an experimental theater at Fisk. The idea, Hurston wrote, was "to create the Negro drama out of the Negro himself" (Yale, James Weldon Johnson Collection). Despite this and other ambitious but ultimately unrealized plans to create a new and authentic "negro drama," Hurston wrote mostly nonfiction afterward, but did publish an autobiography in 1942 and a final novel in 1948.

Hurston's only other full-length play, *Polk Country: A Comedy of Negro Life on a Sawmill Camp with Authentic Negro Music in Three Acts* was written in collaboration with Dorothy Waring and copyrighted in 1944, but it has never been published or produced. Although like *Mule Bone* it lacks a compelling story line, it demonstrates that Hurston never gave up trying to achieve her dream of the "real Negro theater" she had outlined to Hughes in 1928: "We shall act out the folk tales, however short, with the abrupt angularity and naivete of the primitive 'bama Nigger" (Yale, James Weldon Johnson Collection). *Polk County* attempts to meet this goal with a combination of humor, folklore and music. It clearly comes mainly from Hurston's own work as folklore collector in the real Polk County, and whatever the mysterious Dorothy Waring contributed must have been marginal.

Mule Bone has recently been published, and the debate still rages about Hughes's role in composing it. Conversely, *Polk County* is little known and, in some ways, represents a more intriguing turn in Hurston's dramatic career. Accordingly, I will treat it here more exhaustively than *Mule Bone*, which, in any case, demands a more complicated analysis than I can provide here.

The subtitle of *Polk County*, "A Comedy of Negro Life on a Sawmill Camp with Authentic Negro Music," speaks to Hurston's longstanding disdain for adulterated forms of African American music. The "scene and setting" section that introduces the piece describes the lush Florida landscape, replete with Spanish moss, cypress, scrubby palmettoes and bull alligators. The workers' quarters are described in some detail, too. The impermanence of the scene dominates:

> No fenced in yards, few flowers, and those poorly tended. Few attempts at any kind of decoration or relief of ugliness. Everyone lives temporary. They go from job to job, or from job to jail and from jail to job. Working, loving temporarily and often without thought of permanence in anything, wearing their switch-blade knives and guns as a habit like the men of the Old West, fighting, cutting and being cut, such a camp where there is little law, and the peace officers of state and county barred by the management, these refugees from life see nothing unlovely in the sordid camp. They love it and when they leave there, will seek another place like it.

Hurston underlines the importance of this seemingly casual tableau:

> Such a place is the cradle of the Blues and work songs.

Accordingly, the scenarios she foregrounds often center on love, anguish, jealousy and betrayal—and skew the traditional notions of gender roles to do so. The women, for instance, are said to be

> misfits . . . seldom good looking, intelligent, or adjustable. . . . They too pack knives. No stigma attaches to them for prison terms. In fact, their prestige is increased if they have made time for a serious cutting. It passes for bravery—something to give themselves a rating in their small world, where no intellectual activities exist. Hence the boastful song: I'm going to make me a graveyard of my own, etc.

The story line is simple. A mulatto, Leafy Lee, has wandered down from New York hoping to learn the blues. This device runs throughout the play and provides the rationale for the insertion of most of the musical numbers. Leafy is befriended by the dominant personality in the camp, Big Sweet, who uses her fists and knife to protect Leafy and to maintain order when the white Bossman isn't around. Clearly, Leafy represents a fictional equivalent of Hurston herself, whose attempt to collect folklore under the protection of the real Big Sweet is detailed in *Mules and Men. Polk County*, however, makes more out of Big Sweet's role as *teacher.* As she tells Leafy, "I aim to put *my* wisdom tooth in your head. I mean to be your forerunner like John the Baptist." And in many ways, Big Sweet seems like Hurston, too, especially in her declaration "It matters a difference where I go, just so I go laughing."

Big Sweet's man Lonnie is friends with My Honey, a guitar player, who is sought after by Dicey, a sour, scheming, dark-complexioned woman. Significantly, Dicey's plans to break up Big Sweet and Lonnie find temporary success only when she can involve the white Quarters Boss. In the course of the play, Dicey's strategy of setting the other characters against each other fails, and Leafy and My Honey marry, setting a new "civilizing" standard the other characters intend to follow.

Despite its many grimly realistic and naturalistic aspects, the play is by no means intent on slice-of-life theatrics. *Polk County* might more properly be termed a musical comedy with surreal touches, in that the opening page lists twenty-seven "Vocal and Instrumental Numbers. The play opens with Lonnie waking the quarters up with a ritual comic chant, as he raps on the porches with a stick. The work song obviously has elements of the spirituals in it, for it begins with "Wake up, Jacob! Get on the rock / Taint quite day, but it's five o'clock!" After this religious opening, however, he shifts to a reference to quotidian toil: "Wake up bullies! Day's a'breaking / Get your hoecake a'baking, and your shirt-tail shaking!" Then the social order weighs in: "It know you feel blue / I don't want you, but the Bossman do!" This is followed by a comic reference to the natural world: "What did the rooster say to the hen? / Aint had no loving in the lord knows when." In fact, the stage directions indicate that at this point a rooster and his hens should cross the stage, and they have *lines* to say. Clearly we are in the world of magic realism, 1940s style. The animals parody the humans: When the rooster dances around a hen, coaxing "How about a lil' kiss?" she replies, evasively "I want some shoes," a motif Hurston frequently uses with "roundheeled" women, most notably with Ora, the vixen who appears at the end of *Jonah's Gourd Vine* and in the story of Aunt Ca'line in "The Eatonville Anthology." The comic interplay between the chickens is quite intricate and leads up to the rooster complaining "You Polk County hens always hollering for shoes! Why I have to buy you shoes to love you? You get just as much out of it as I do. Aw, cutta-cut cut!" The rooster's suggestion that one hen represents all those in Polk County mirrors a hen's earlier, parallel suggestion: "These Polk County roosters! They want plenty loving, but they don't buy you no shoes." Moreover, the "chicken theme" reappears in more human form later, when Big Sweet says of her rival "Ella Wall aint no big hen's biddy, if she do lay gobbler's eggs."

The anthropomorphic play here creates an interesting affinity with the animal cast of Janacek's opera *The Cunning Little Vixen* (1924), while the several descriptions of lights slowly going on, breakfast sounds and so on from the morning sequence might stem from a similar scene in Gershwin's *Porgy and Bess* (1935). The surreal quality of these moments in **Polk County** relate to those (quite a few) devoted to Lonnie's readings of his extravagant dreams and visions. In one, he tells us, he rode to heaven on a crow, "diamond-shining black. One wing rests on the morning and the other brushes off the sundown." Throughout the play, Lonnie compares himself to High John the Conquer, the mythic folk hero who similarly looms larger than life and enjoys magical powers in the natural world. All these "magic realism" touches appear only to be submerged by the play's basically realistic veneer, but the play ends, as we shall see, with an expressionistically surreal display.

Whatever the mode at work at any given moment, however, the play ultimately stands or falls on the strength of its many striking characters. Like **Mule Bone, Polk County**'s cast is large: sixteen named characters and many others play parts. Hurston, obviously profiting from her experiences with **From Sun to Sun**, included twenty-seven vocal and instrumental numbers. Virtually all of the human characters reprise roles they played in Hurston's book of folklore, *Mules and Men* and thus are presumably based in fact.

The Hurston we see here is franker than she was in earlier works, especially about both racial attitudes and sexuality. Dicey, for instance, is described in the cast list as a

> homely narrow-contracted little black woman, who has been slighted by Nature and feels "evil" about it. Suffers from the "black ass." Her strongest emotion is envy. . . . Yearns to gain a reputation as "bad" (the fame of a sawmill camp) to compensate for her lack of success with men. . . . Being short, scrawny and black, a pretty yellow girl arouses violent envy in her.

Throughout the play, Leafy and My Honey's courtship has a communal dimension, affording much commentary from the cast on the nature of love. Leafy up to this point plays out a parallel to the role Hurston herself played in Polk County in *Mules and Men.*

Interestingly, Lonnie's "visions" involve African retentions and dreams of liberation and glory. The community attends to these visions eagerly, and they look forward to Lonnie's cheering music. As one character claims, everyone would leave the place if Lonnie wasn't there, suggesting that he parallels the role Tea Cake plays on the Muck in Hurston's novel *Their Eyes Were Watching God,*

but also pointing to the key role African American cultural traditions have played in making harsh work bearable.

On the other hand, Hurston signals that dreams can be dangerous. One manifestation of Big Sweet's violent power emerges when we learn she regularly "lams" Lonnie to bring him back to reality:

> I just sort of taps him once in a while. You see, Lonnie got his mind way up in the air, and I taps him to make him know that the ground is here right on, and that there's minks on it trying to take advantage of him all the time. They cant fool *me.* Lonnie dreams pretty things. Thats what make I love him so.

Furthermore, her "lamming" Lonnie finds exponential expansion in her general role as disciplinarian for the community. As Sop-the-Bottom asserts, "More men makes time [work] now than they used to cause Big Sweet keeps a lot of 'em from cutting the fool and going to jail." This thematic device, especially as it focuses on Lonnie's dreams/madness, recalls that used in Hemingway's powerful story "The Battler" (1925), and the similar situation in Steinbeck's *Of Mice and Men* (1937). In both of these tales, violence on the part of a loving "caretaker" becomes necessary to still a dreaming and disturbed personality.

Another echo of an earlier Hurston work is heard in the name of Leafy Lee. Janie's mother in *Their Eyes,* also a mulatto, is named Leafy. Here this gentle ingenue yearns to be a blues singer and much of the second act is devoted to using her "lessons" as occasions for song.

Another character who has a counterpart in *Their Eyes* is Sop-the-Bottom. Here he appears as one with a "big appetite, a rather good gambler at Georgia Skin but not above being sharp with less efficient players. Not really wicked, but considers himself smart." Sop plays a more sinister role in *Their Eyes;* conversely, Ella Wall, a figure recycled from *Mules and Men,* becomes far more menacing in **Polk County.** The cast list presents her as "primitive and pagan," yet one who "has the air of a conqueror. She is strutting and self-assured and accustomed to the favors of men which she in return grants freely. She practices Voodoo and feels she leads a charmed life."

As in **Mules**, the real dynamo of the comedy is Ella's nemesis, Big Sweet, who is "two whole women and a gang of men." Although she can physically dispatch any enemy, it is her arsenal of verbal taunts that makes her truly formidable and entertaining. Kicking Nunkie, she emphasizes her actions with words:

> You multiplied cockroach! I'll teach you to die next time I hit you. . . . Beating my Lonnie out of his money. Gimmie! If you don't, and that quick, they going to tote you through three yards—this yard, the churchyard, and the graveyard.

Here, as in many other scenes, Big Sweet appropriates traditionally male modes of action, talk and stance. When she finally gets caught in the meshes of Dicey's scheme, she fights her way out after finding inspiration in the example of the legendary hero, High John de Conquer. Like him, she possesses an arsenal of comic one-liners: "If God send me a pistol, I'll send him a man!" or "Pulling after a man that dont want you, is just like peeping in a jug with one eye; you can't see a thing but darkness." But then, even minor characters are blessed with pithy expressions: Laura tells Lonnie, "You got a grin on you like a dead dog in the sunshine."

The richly metaphoric humor of the backwoods community is not unique to the black workers. The white Quarters Boss, who in some ways is sympathetically drawn, can signify with the best of them. Mocking the community's defense of Big Sweet, he declares,

> Thats all I can hear from most of you. Big Sweet aint never done a thing but praise the Lord. Her mouth is a prayer-book and her lips flap just like a Bible. But where do all these head-lumps come from that the Company Doctor is always greasing? . . . How can I keep order like that?

This comic passage underlines, however, the way in which Big Sweet has operated within the community *precisely* to keep order, which obviates the need for white interference and dominance. Hurston thus uses comic exchanges to illustrate quite serious points.

Despite her role as villain, Dicey is portrayed somewhat sympathetically, in that she resembles the despairing Emma of *Color-Struck* in her bitterness over color: "I know I aint yellow, and aint got no long straight hair, but I got feelings just like anybody else." She tries to gain revenge with her knife and through association with the rough and ready Ella Wall, who is brought in toward the end of the play for a dramatic show-down with Big Sweet. Ella also presides over a compelling hoodoo scene in the woods, providing more exotica.

Big Sweet plays a more complex role here than in *Mules and Men*. For instance, she wistfully explains to maidenly Leafy just how she lost her virginity and how she became accustomed to "careless love." She also claims that God directed her to kick the "behinds" of people who try to take advantage of folks. Nor is this introspective moment atypical, despite the overwhelming comedy of the play. A minor character, Laura B., comments at one point "Everybody is by themselves a heap of times, even when they's in company." Later, Lonnie sings movingly of the dangers and hardships of sawmill work: "keep on like that until you die. . . . Just moving around in the cage."

The dangers of Polk County are not confined to the machinery. Still another name repeated from *Their Eyes* is Nunkie. In the earlier book she is a woman; here Nunkie is a man, a "no-good gambler—shifty and irresponsible. His soul is as black as his face and his face is as black as the sins he commits," a description that partakes of the stereotypical concepts of blackness. As many of these descriptions suggest, throughout these opening pages, Hurston emphasizes the danger and violence of the scene and

even claims that "at least one person is killed every pay night." Polk County clearly represents a "backwoods" counterpart to the more refined community of Eatonville and seems equivalent to many other fictional backwoods communities created by other southern writers, such as those in the books of Hurston's sometime friend and fellow chronicler of Florida, Marjorie Kinnan Rawlings (especially in *South Moon Under*, 1933), or the Frenchmen's Bend tales of William Faulkner. In these types of narratives, the frontier ethos provides a sharper edge to the dramatic action, an exotic and legendary setting and more possibilities for violence, conflict and, ultimately, "civilizing" redemption.

One should not, however, assume that these "backwoods" people come off as barbarians; far from it. Hurston wants us to perceive tht they have a vivid culture and works out various stratagems to *make* us see it. As in *Mule Bone*, children play typical African American games as part of the display of everyday life in the Quarters. Also as in *Mule Bone,* the central scenes are communal. In the latter play, the key conflict is the quarrel between the Methodists and Baptists that accompanies Jim's "trial." Here the chief battles take place in the Quarters jook, which is elaborately described, and in the woods, where Ella and her partisans' hoodoo fails to conjure Leafy and My Honey's marriage. A feast follows, along with Lonnie's pronouncement "You can git what you want if you go about things the right way."

The pattern of the play—order, chaos, order, concluding with a marriage—is that of the traditional stage comedy, but Hurston reinvents it with her transposition of the genre into the register of a dialect-driven, black backwoods culture, one rich in linguistic, cultural and dramatic nuance. As in virtually all of her works, the folk humor generates the dynamism, which buoys and amplifies every page and scene. A few examples will suffice. Hurston mines the "I'm so . . . that . . ." of African American jokes here, after Sop-the-Bottom signs his "I'm going to make me a graveyard of my own." Do-Dirty starts it by saying "I'm so mean till I'll kill a baby just born this morning," followed by Few Clothes's escalation "Man, I'm mean! I have to tote a pistol with me when I go to the well, to keep from gitting in a fight with my ownself. I got Indian blood in me. Reckon that's how come I'm so mean," and all the other men say that they have some in them too. This sequence relates to others in the African American comic repertory that Hurston used tirelessly, such as the "so ugly that . . ." or "so black that . . ." comic sequences. Interestingly, she radically transforms one version of the tradition. She always deplored the "Black Black woman" jokes that focused on the supposed evil of darker women. Here she subtracts the color component, but leaves the rest. When Sop-the-Bottom brags, "I shacked up with a woman once that was so contrary she used to sleep humped up in bed so you couldnt find no way to stretch out comfortable to sleep," Lonnie ups the ante by claiming "I done seen 'em dreaming. They dont never dream about roses and scenery and sunshine like a sweet woman do. Naw, they dreams about hatchets and knives and pistols, and ice-picks and splitting open people's heads."

A second example, also centered in communal comic exchange, appears when the men talk about how Lonnie was ripped off by the dirty dealing of Nunkie the night before, using comic proverbs and folk sayings to connote a serious sequence of events. They saw it happening, but didn't tell Lonnie. As Few Clothes says, "I aint no bet-straightener. Its more folks in the graveyard right now from straightening bets than anything else. Blind me aint got no business at the show." They prophesy that Big Sweet will take care of Nunkie.

> FEW CLOTHES: [S]he bound to find it out. My woman done found it out and she wouldnt let her shirt-tail touch her till she run tell Big Sweet all she know.
>
> SOP: He [Nunkie] claim that his knife going to back Big Sweet off him. Claim he aint scared, but I know better. He's talking at the big gate.
>
> DO-DIRTY: "Before she turn him loose she'll make him tell her that she is Lord Jesus, and besides her there is no other.

Amazingly, despite the relatively naturalistic presentation of most of the play, it ends expressionistically. After the feast and the commitment of the previously lawless community to marriage and stability, a huge rainbow descends and all get on board, plates in hand, with Lonnie singing "I ride the rainbow, when I see Jesus," the song he sang as he made his entrance at the beginning of the play. With the presence of his fellow "riders" on the rainbow, his individual song becomes communal. The curtain falls as the rainbow ascends.

Hurston never found the rainbow herself. In the fifties she drifted from job to job, while working on various manuscripts. When she died in 1960, she was living in a county charity facility. She never achieved the dream of founding a new "Negro" dramatic movement. Her life, however, had been highly dramatic and despite its end, fulfilling.

As these brief descriptions of her plays suggest, Hurston devised some inventive dramatizations of African American folk life and customs. White theatrical producers of her time, however, wanted the tried and true formulas when they dared present plays with predominantly black casts. They had no interest in experimenting with Hurston's authentic modes.

To be fair, however, it should be borne in mind that Hurston's emphasis on group culture and interaction led her to sacrifice a focus on strongly individual central plots, the basic staple of mainstage American theater. Moreover, although she sought to provide an alternative to contemporary, often racist, stereotypes of blacks, today's audiences are likely to find even *her* versions embarrassing throwbacks to an earlier time, when African Americans themselves used forms of address and metaphor that have

now been discarded. The fact that **Mule Bone** had to be edited prior to production and then failed to attract an audience offers illustration of this point.

Hurston's fiction has taken a central place in the American literary canon, but it seems unlikely that her plays will be produced in the near future, largely because, for many readers, they seem to move uncomfortably close to stereotypes, even though Hurston felt she was doing just the opposite in her own day and time. In the more expansive mode of her fiction she was able to burst through into fully-fleshed characterizations, something that eluded her as dramatist. Finally, for many, the plays' small-town settings, situations and language simply seem dated when placed next to those of contemporary African American dramas and comedies. Thus despite their many charms and innovations, Hurston's work for the theater appears headed for the "historical curiosity shelf." It seems likely, however, that her fiction and her own lively autobiography will continue to furnish subjects for the American stage.

This condition could change, however, if there were published editions of all of Hurston's plays, and directors and producers who were capable of meeting the challenges that Hurston's scripts present. Literary critics could hasten this project by moving beyond *Their Eyes* and *Dust Tracks* into a wide-ranging discussion of the totality of Hurston's work, including the dramas. Ultimately, however, we will never know now effective her "genuine Negro drama" is unless producers come forward. Only then, with her words quickened into theatrical life, will we really be able to judge the success of dramatist Zora Neale Hurston's attempt to "let the people sing."

Barbara Speisman (essay date 1998)

SOURCE: "From 'Spears' to *The Great Day*: Zora Neale Hurston's Vision of a Real Negro Theater," in *The Southern Quarterly*, Vol. XXXVI, No. 3, Spring, 1998, pp. 34-46.

[*In the following essay, Speisman surveys Hurston's career as a dramatist and her influence on American theater.*]

On 12 April 1926, in a letter to Langston Hughes, Zora Neale Hurston asked Hughes a question: "Did I tell you before I left about the new, the REAL Negro art theater I Plan? Well I shall, or rather we shall act out the folk tales, however short with the abrupt angularity and naivete of the primitive 'bama Nigger. . . . What do you think?" (Hemenway 115). From 1927 to 1930 Hurston had the opportunity to interpret what "had gone unseen for three hundred years" (113), and she shared many of her discoveries with Hughes, her colleague and friend. Traveling to isolated, rural African American communities, such as Magazine Point, Alabama, as well as her home village of Eatonville, Florida, Hurston came to realize that the folktales and songs she heard during her travels were not creations of the past, but of the everchanging present.

Pretending to be a gangster's girlfriend on the run in a Loughman, Florida, turpentine camp, she had become friends with Big Sweet, a "jook" woman who could out-talk, out-fight, and out-love her male counterparts in the camp. Big Sweet had been instrumental in teaching Hurston the importance of the jook in the development of the "real Negro theater," the theater of "the people farthest down." Hurston came to believe that the real Negro theater was in the "jooks" of the South "where women, like Big Sweet, could hoist a jook song from her belly and lam it against the front door of the theater" ("Characteristics" 254). Hurston was persuaded that only theater could truly convey the mercurial nature, as well as cultural richness, of the folklife, tales, and songs she learned. She wanted to share not only her subject matter with Langston Hughes, but also her vision of a script that would not follow the standard two or three-act format. Hurston also advanced the concept that the real Negro play should be angular in structure, which was similar to African dance ("Characteristics" 247). Thus, at the beginning of her professional career as a folklorist, Hurston was forming a totally different concept of the type of play that she hoped to write; one that would be radically different, not only in theme and subject matter, but in structure as well.

Hughes shared Hurston's enthusiasm for an authentic folk theater in which African Americans would write, direct, and perform their own material. Like Hurston, Hughes believed that "The Negro outstanding characteristic is drama" ("Characteristics" 247), and he proposed to coauthor a folk play with Hurston that would be a real departure in the drama. Hurston's dream of a "real Negro art theater" (Hemenway 115) was one that she would hold onto for much of her creative life. It was, however, one that brought her great frustration and disappointment and even caused her to be alienated from Hughes, a sharer of her dream.

Although Hurston's published work has received much critical attention, her role as a playwright still needs more investigation. Perhaps one of the chief reasons her plays have not received the attention they deserve is that so few of her manuscripts are in published form. Lynda Marion Hill points out in her ground-breaking study *Social Rituals and the Verbal Art of Zora Neale Hurston:*

> Hurston's theatrical career is virtually a lost segment of Hurston's work, and that having available documenta-tion of her staged productions is essential not only to be able to write a thorough historical account but to reproduce the play, in writing or on stage. (201)

During the spring and summer of 1997, however, several of Hurston's play manuscripts have surfaced. Wyatt Hour-ston Day, an African American manuscript collector, discovered "Spears" which was first published in Hurst-on's sorority yearbook, the Zeta Phi Beta *X RAY* for 1925. Alice L. Birney, historian of American literature at the Library of Congress, has discovered three full-length plays and several dramatic skits copyrighted by Hurston from 1925 to 1944. The plays include "Meet the Mamma," a

musical play, copyrighted 12 July 1925, less than three months after the *Opportunity* Award Banquet at which Hurston won second prize for her play **Color Struck** and an honorable mention for "Spears." "Cold Keener," a musi-cal revue, and "De Turkey and de Law," a comedy in three acts, were both copyrighted 29 October 1930, shortly before an argument between Hurston and Langston Hughes over authorship of **Mule Bone**. On 21 July 1931, Hurston copyrighted four comical sketches: "Poker," "Lawing and Jawing," "Woolfing," and "Forty Yards." Hurston did not copyright another play until 15 June 1935, when she copyrighted "Spunk." With Hurston's permission, Jose-phine Van Dolzen Pease copyrighted, on 7 April 1936, "Three Authentic Folk Dances from the Deep South," which are dances to be performed by children. These dances consist of "Rabbit Dance," "Chick-Ma Chick, Ma," Cranney Crow," and "Sissie in the Barn." The final play, and one familiar to Hurston scholars, was "Polk County" which Hurston coauthored with Dorothy Waring; its copyright date was 9 December 1944.[1]

Collectively these manuscripts are over three hundred pages in length, and provide the reader a rich selection with which to analyze Hurston's conviction that the folk-life material she had collected in the South would best reach a greater audience "as the product of folk perfor-mance" (Abrahams and Kalcik 229). Hurston came to her definition of a real Negro art theater after the three years she spent researching in the South, but her odyssey as a playwright began several years earlier.

Hurston's first association with drama probably came in 1915 to 1916 while she was employed as a maid in the Gilbert and Sullivan troupe which introduced her to profes-sional actors and musicians. Although she did not actively participate in any of the performances, she certainly had the opportunity to explore the structure of plays, acting, and directing techniques Later, from 1916 to 1919, Hur-ston moved to Baltimore where her sister Sarah had a rooming house near Pennsylvania Avenue[2] which was renowned for its theaters. Here well-known African American performers, like Ethel Waters, often performed. Hurston, therefore, had ample opportunity to observe the then current African American stage drama and musical entertainment. In 1919 Hurston graduated from Morgan Academy and was encouraged by Mae Miller, a young Washington playwright and poet, to enter Howard University's drama department (Perkins 77). This fact sug-gests Hurston's early interest in the theater.

Her formal study of drama and, in particular, African American drama was at Howard University. Hurston's initial concept of theater was formed under the tutelage of Thomas Montgomery Gregory who had organized the Howard Players to perform plays about Negro life. Gregory had been a member of Professor Baker's famous English 47 Workshop at Harvard University that had served as the dramatic training ground for Thomas Woolf and Eugene O'Neill. Gregory was friends with O'Neill, and O'Neill visited Howard's drama department in 1923 while Hurston was a student. O'Neill and his Provinceton Players took an active interest in the Howard Players and Gregory's hope of developing a national Negro theater.[3] Gregory was also unique in that he believed that African American women were capable of writing plays, and encouraged his women students to become playwrights (Perkins 78). Although Hurston wrote *Color Struck*, "Spears," and "Meet the Mamma" while studying with Gregory, no record has been located that would indicate whether or not Hurston had any of her plays produced while a member of the Howard Players. Gregory kept excellent files, but Hurston's only mention is as a violinist for the Howard orchestra.

However, Gregory was one of the judges for the *Opportunity* Award Banquet, held on 1 May 1925, which formally ushered in the Harlem Renaissance. There Hurston won second prize for her play *Color Struck* and honorable mention for "Spears." These plays, African American in content, followed the traditional one and two-act structure. No mention was made of "Meet the Mamma," her blues musical. Not long after the *Opportunity* presentation, the Negro Art Theater of Harlem opened with her play, *Color Struck*.[4] With this formal production, Hurston began to make a name for herself as a playwright.

Color Struck, a play about miscegenation, has received much critical attention, but "Spears" has yet to be examined. It appears that in writing "Spears" Hurston was influenced by the Tarzan craze that was sweeping the country at the time—her characters are dressed in lion skins and loin cloths, with bone jewelry and rings in their noses and ears. Hurston was gambling that she could capitalize on the myth of Africa popular in white America's imagination. Although the characters in the play are unbelievable, the plot contrived, and the ending expected, Hurston's sense of humor and satirical style are evident. "Spears" was not part of Hurston's efforts to establish an authentic American Negro theater, but was rather an attempt to satirize the white concept of what they thought African primitivism to be,[5] and perhaps to produce a commercial success.

The play centers on the Luallaba tribe who have been unable to find food and are starving, making them vulnerable to their enemies, the Wahehes. Monanga, King of the Luallabas, meets with Bombay, his old counselor, to debate their predicament. Bombay, like Polonius in Shakespeare's *Hamlet,* provides bombastic, silly advice. Bombay tells his chief that their problem may be solved by "selling our young women to the Wahehes for good." Zaida, the King's beautiful daughter, appears on the scene to announce that she and the other women are hungry, and to ask what her father means to do about it. Uledi, a warrior in love with her, has hidden food and provides Zaida with something to eat. As Zaida eats, the rest of the tribe follows each morsel of meat from the girl's hand to her mouth with their eyes and mimic swallowing when she does. Act 1 ends when the King demands that his medicine man "make medicine

for rain" which will solve their problem. The Medicine Man and his accomplices, the Witch Woman and a chicken, participate in a rain dance and, as the drums beat furiously, the dancing grows wilder and Hurston's stage directions are "that this will continue for nine minutes."

In act 2, a Wahehe warrior accuses Uledi of stealing food and, as a result, Uledi must die or the tribe will fight the Luallabas. When presented with this decision, Monanga quickly agrees that Ulede must perish in order that the tribe may be preserved. However, in Pocohantas style, Saida begs her father to save Ulede's life. Monanga's answer is "that women were not made to counsel men but to serve them." Zaida's reply is that "we women have no minds at all. We know nothing . . . what we saw yesterday is today forgotten." She then cleverly reminds her father of Uledi's many heroic adventures, how he saved her life, and "How he is first to hear your voice always. If Uledi has done wrong let me be killed in his place. Your slave has spoken." The play ends with the Luallaba tribe overcoming their enemies and Uledi and Saida in each other's arms. Although "Spears" was published, we do not know if Hurston ever managed to have it performed.

From 1926 to 1930, Hurston may not have written plays, but she was developing ideas about what should constitute the real Negro art theater, and shared with Hughes much of the folk material she had collected. For financial reasons, both Hurston and Hughes had entered into an agreement with Charlotte Osgood Mason, a wealthy patron of the arts, which allowed her to have a great measure of control over their lives and writings. In particular, Hurston had signed a contract with Mason on 8 December 1927 which gave Mason complete ownership of Hurston's collected material and the methods by which it would be presented and published (Hemenway 109). Although Mason informed Hurston that she should not consider using her folk material for theatrical purposes, Hurston persevered in her desire for the "glorious . . . departure in the drama" (Hemenway 115).

Upon her return to New York in the winter of 1930, Mason insisted that Hurston complete the manuscript that would become *Mules and Men*. At the same time, Hughes lived nearby and was finishing his novel *Not Without Laughter.* During the spring of 1930, the two friends were finally able to begin writing a play which they believed would change the course of African American theater. Hurston wisely selected "The Bone of Contention," a story she had written while a student at Howard, to avoid Mason's wrath if she found out about the project.

The folktale tells the story of Dave Carter, the best hunter in Eatonville, who, after capturing a wild turkey, is hit over the head with a mule bone by Jim Weston, the town's bully. Dave wants Jim arrested and complains to Mayor Joe Clark: "He can't lam me over mah head wid no mule bone and steal mah turkey and go braggin' about it!" The community divides into Baptists who support Carter, and Methodists who support Weston. The Baptists win and Jim is banished from Eatonville for two years.

Hurston wanted to shape "The Bone of Contention" into a new form that would eliminate the minstrel concept of the African American theater which, even in plays such as *Shuffle Along,* still controlled white audiences' attention. A common form of the minstrel show had two male characters fighting over a girl with the comedy generated through short or even one liners. Hurston wanted to present a full theatrical environment in which the isolated "punch lines" would be produced in a natural manner.[6] Hurston became alarmed, however, when Hughes replaced the turkey as the central figure of conflict and instead, in a stereotypical manner, has Dave and Jim fight over a girl (Hemenway 138). Hurston had not intended her tale to be that of two men fighting over their sexual prowess, but rather that they would prove who was the better hunter and man. Dave and Jim's conflict over a woman is closer to the minstrel theme and jokes which Hurston wanted to avoid. In Hughes's version the two men are the best of friends; whereas, in Hurston's folktale, Jim is disliked by Dave, as well as the majority of Eatonville's people.

The structure of Hurston's folktale is simple with few characters, but in adapting the folktale into a play, Hughes included nineteen major characters and twenty-two minor ones. Undoubtedly, Hurston came to believe that Hughes's additions were contrary to her original folktale and that he was changing her story to such an extent that it no longer seemed her own. Hughes was later to say that at the time Hurston appeared to be happy with their joint authorship of **Mule Bone**, and he was totally surprised when she claimed complete ownership (Hemenway 138).

In May 1930, still supported by Mason, Hurston left Hughes to return to the South supposedly to complete the trial scene of act 2. However, during that time Hurston not only rewrote the play so that it more closely resembled "The Bone of Contention" in its original form, but it appears that she also completed "Cold Keener."

Hurston's first major change from the jointly written play was to alter the title from "Mule Bone" to "De Turkey and De Law," so that there would be no doubt that the fight over the turkey was the main conflict in the play and that Dave and Jim were enemies. By emphasizing Dave's superior hunting abilities, he becomes more a folk hero than a stereotypical minstrel character. We do not know whose idea it was to structure Hurston's folktale into a three-act play, but it was a form that she used only once more, that we know of, and that was in **"Polk County,"** another cooperative effort with a coauthor. Although Hurston did retain the three-act form in "De Turkey and De Law," she simplified and changed much of the structure of the first act.

In **Mule Bone** the play begins with several Eatonville natives gathering on the front porch of Joe Clark's store. Several of the characters whom Hurston included in her *Eatonville Anthology* (1926) are introduced, for example, Mrs. Roberts, the begging woman who pleads for food for her hungry children. Hurston begins "De Turkey and De Law," however, with a group of Eatonville children playing "Chicka-Ma Chick" in which a young girl pretends to be a mother hen protecting her children from a hawk. One of the children, "Big Girl," a tomboy, leads the group and seems to resemble Hurston as a child in Eatonville. Like young Hurston, she flaunts grown-up authority, and when a voice offstage calls, "If you don't come here wid dat soap you better!", the child tearfully replies, "Soons I git grown I'm gointer run away. Every time a person gits to havin' fun, it's come here." A page later Hurston changes Big Girl's name to Bessie and one of the men on Joe Clark's store porch refers to her as a "sassy lil binch who needs her guts stomped out." It appears that Hurston was becoming an active participant in the action of the play, a technique she would later use in *Mules and Men.*

Hurston retained Hughes's addition of Daisy as a central character in the play. But, where Hughes interjected Daisy as the major source of conflict between the two rivals, Hurston's Daisy chooses the man who is the better hunter and consequently the better provider. Thus, in Hurston's version, Daisy's character is truer to the folk quality that she intended, rather than to Hughes's minstrel concept.

Hurston returned to Florida to write the second scene of the second act in which the Baptists and the Methodists have the trial which will determine whether Jim or Dave is at fault, and she is sole author of this part of the play.

Act 3 in both **Mule Bone** and "De Turkey and De Law" are the same except that Hurston includes the turkey episode as the central conflict. Daisy informs Jim that she knows Dave is the better shot and killed the turkey to give to her and that Jim "couldn't hit de side of a barn wid uh bass fiddle." Dave answers, "Course I kilt it, and it for you." The resolution of both plays is with Daisy insisting that the man of her choice must work for a living. Jim and Dave agree, however, that no woman is worth working for; they become friends and decide to return to Eatonville together. Only the stage directions at the end of the plays differ. In **Mule Bone** the stage directions are: "They start back together towards the town, Jim picking a dance tune on his guitar, and Dave cutting back on the ties besides him, singing, prancing, and happily they exist." After the final line of dialogue in "De Turkey and De Law," Hurston's stage direction is simply "Curtain."

We do not know if Hughes ever read a copy of "De Turkey and De Law," nor why after Hurston copyrighted it as sole author, she never attempted to have it produced or published. Whatever the personal relations between the two authors and their competition for Mason's support, Zora Neale Hurston and Langston Hughes lost not only their friendship, but the chance to have either version of their coauthored plays produced. In Hughes's autobiography, *The Big Sea,* he admits that "the story was her story, the dialogue her dialogue, and the play her play—even if I had put it together" (158).

In a letter to Mason dated 17 May 1932, Hurston was still bitter about Hughes's claim of authorship. She writes: "I have a most ungracious letter from Langston Hughes in which he renounces his claim upon the play. His manner of doing so is one of the most unworthy things he ever did." Hurston and Hughes gave up any attempt for a stage production of either "De Turkey and De Law" or **Mule Bone**. However, the question remains as to why Hurston did not then focus her attention on "Cold Keener," the musical revue that she had copyrighted on the same day as "De Turkey and De Law."

In "Cold Keener" she experimented with a concept of a real Negro theater as being built upon the folktales, music, and dances of the "primitive Negroes" whose daily lives had so inspired her. "Cold Keener" is possibly Hurston's first attempt at dramatizing some of the material that would later be more fully developed in her fiction, *Mules and Men,* and later in the successful musical revue, **The Great Day.** Before this, Hurston's correspondence had not mentioned "Cold Keener" or her hopes for its success. As Kathy A. Perkins in her study of *Black Female Playwrights Before 1950* noted, "Between 1930 and 1935, Hurston became preoccupied with making a name for herself in the theater. She wrote over twelve plays during this period" (77).

Hurston's legal agreement with Mason may have been the reason that she never actively attempted to interest theatrical producers in producing "Cold Keener." Since it is the only complete manuscript of one of Hurston's revues, however, it deserves particular attention.

"Cold Keener" consists of nine skits that have no relationship to one another either in character, theme, or setting. Thus, the sharp "primitive" angularity that Hurston desired as her ideal dramatic form is obtained. The skits have no dramatic thread, such as a narrator or music, to relate to one another, but are linked mainly by their very differences. Even the unusual grammatical forms seem to stress the sharp contrasts of the folktales. The title appears to be another way of portraying the links of orality that bound the folktales and folklife she had researched in the South to their relationship to her research in Harlem and the Bahamas. The daily life of a "pimp" on Lenox Avenue might be totally different from that of Joe Wiley who lives in Magazine Point, Alabama, but their verbal skills unite them. Although blacks in the Bahamas were exposed to a completely different daily environment, they, like southern African Americans, used song as a common thread of communication. Thus, the structure of "Cold Keener" offered Hurston a chance to present the variety of her folk experience in the South, Harlem, and the Bahamas.

Facing the title page of the script of "Cold Keener," Hurston lists the nine skits which make up the revue: "Filling Station," "Cock Robin," "Heaven," "Mr. Frog," "Lenox Avenue," "House that Jack Built," "Bahamas," "Railroad Camp," and "Jook." A summary of the individual skits will help to appreciate Hurston's "journey structure" and her knowledge of the orality that united the different communities.

"Filling Station" begins "Time: Present." "Place: A Point on the Alabama-Georgia line." "Setting: A filling station upstage center." Named "The State Line Filling Station," it stretches nearly across the stage. The road passes before and through it. A line down the center of the stage to the footlights divides the left side, "Alabama State Line," from the right, "Georgia State Line." A Model T Ford rattles up and wakes the proprietor:

PROPRIETOR (Sleepily). How many?

FORD DRIVER. Two.

PROPRIETOR. Two what?

(The Proprietor gets a quart cup and measures the gas and rings the hose to be sure to get it all, then he pours it in the tank.)

FORD DRIVER. You better look at my water and air, too.

(He has a very expensive and ornate cap on the radiator, but otherwise the car is most dilapidated. As the Proprietor pours the water into the radiator, the driver gets out of the car and stands off from it looking it over.)

FORD DRIVER. Say, Jimpson, they tells me you got a new mechanic 'round here that's just too tight.

PROPRIETOR. That's right. He kin do more wid 'em than the man that made 'em.

FORD DRIVER. Well, looka here. My car kinda needs overhauling and maybe a little paint. Look her over and tell me just what you could do to make her look like a brand new car for.

(Proprietor lifts the hood and looks. Walks around and studies the car from all angles. Then stops at the front and examines the radiator cap.)

PROPRIETOR. Well, I tell yo. You see it's like this. This car needs a whole heap of things done to it. But being as you're a friend of mine—tell you what I'll do. I'll just jack that radiator cap up and run a brand new Ford under it for four hundred and ninety-five dollars.

FORD DRIVER. (Indignantly). Whut de hen-fire you think I'm goin' tuh let you rob me of my car? That's a GOOD car.

The skit continues as a good looking girl who has had a flat tire drives up to the filling station and says, "I had a flat down the road and I changed it, but it's not fixed. Do you vulcanize?" The Proprietor answers, "We do everything but the buzzard lope—and that's gone outa style." When both the Proprietor and the Ford Driver fail in correctly placing the tire back on the car, the girl kicks it into place herself. The Proprietor and Ford Driver are impressed:

PROPRIETOR. That's a tight little slice of pig-meat! Damned if I don't believe I'll go to Georgia!

FORD DRIVER. She ain't no pig-meat! That's a married 'oman.

PROPRIETOR. You know her?

FORD DRIVER. Nope, never seen her before.

PROPRIETOR. Well, how can you tell she's married?

FORD DRIVER. Didn't you see that kick? A woman that can kick like that done had some man to practice on.

Soon after this exchange, a new, elegant Chevrolet arrives and the rest of the skit involves a bragging contest between the Ford driver and the Chevrolet driver about which has the greater car.

Hurston would later rewrite and publish "Cock Robin," the next skit, as "Cock Robin, Beale Street" in the *Southern Literary Messenger* for July 1941 (Hemenway 290). The major difference between the skit and the short story is that in the skit Hurston eliminates Uncle July, the narrator, who has witnessed Cock Robin's death. Unlike the story, the skit begins with Cock Robin staggering into the "shimmy shack" with three arrows sticking in him as he falls dead. The birds inquire about the identity of the murderer and why he would kill Cock Robin. The sparrow admits that he did the dirty deed because he caught Cock Robin "shacking up" with his wife.

> SPARROW. Well, I'll tell you. When me and my wife first started to nestin, she never laid nothin' but plain white eggs. But since Cock Robin been hangin' round our place—every time I go out on a worm hunt, when I come back, she's done laid another blue egg.

As in the story, the skit has the birds discuss the arrangements for Cock Robin's funeral. In the story, the birds decide "to leave de white folks bury him! Dey always loves to take charge." In the skit, however, the owl says, "Well, whoever pays de bill can have de body. Who go-inter pay de bills?" Since no one wants to pay for Cock Robin's funeral, the birds exit to attend Sister Speckled Hen's "grand barbecue and fish fry." With the orchestra playing, the birds strut off the stage. This is the first mention of an orchestra, but it is prominent in "Heaven," the third skit.

As the curtain rises on "Heaven," the audience sees a flight of golden stairs ascending from the orchestra pit at mid-stage. The sound of a mouth organ being played in a blues mood way is heard. Jim, a survivor of the Johnstown flood, appears before St. Peter and attempts to impress him with the power of the flood. Jim begins to describe the horrors of the flood to an old man.

> JIM. Hello, old folks, how long you been here?
>
> OLD MAN. Oh, a long time.
>
> JIM. I just got here from de Johnstown flood. Man, dat waz some water! Chickens floatin, folks floatin, horses floatin, houses floatin. Man, dat wuz water.
>
> (Starting away in disgust) Aw, shucks, you ain't seen no water. (He exits right.) Jim looks hurt and puzzled for a moment, then calls out to St. Peter.
>
> JIM. Say Peter, thought you said everybody here was nice and sociable. See how dat ole man treated me when I tryin to show him manners and politeness by tellin him bout de flood?
>
> PETER. You can't tell that man bout no flood—that's NOAH.

At the end of the skit Jim has received his wings and against the angel's wishes, decides to fly, but crashes. However, Jim seems happy enough playing his harp, and the curtain quickly descends as he "plays and sings." Hurston does not provide any instruction as to what Jim is singing.

In the skit, "Mr. Frog," Hurston emphasizes movement and rhythm. The time is "when animals talked," and the place is "a Florida swamp." Hurston's stage directions call for a "girl dancer" to impersonate a "pine tree":

> As the curtain rises, the sun is setting. The tree is motionless. With the music it begins to sway slightly, but increases its motion all the time. Enter down stage left, the South Wind dances with the tree for about a minute. Enter West Wind upstage right and both dance with tree. . . . The tempo increases with the entrance of each wind. . . . When all four winds are on, there is a violent wind dance for a minute till the sun finally sets and the winds take their places at their entrances and sink to the ground and remain there.

Actors costumed as frogs, an alligator, birds, bettles, flies, and a snake "all enter from different points and take places among the trees and bushes." As the frogs chorus croaks, "a big frog" enters from "upstage center," hops on a toadstool and sings the old child's ballad, "Mister Frog Went Courtin." At the climax of the skit "the Lover Frog" marries "Miss Mousie," and Mrs. Snake passes "all around dat wedding cake decorated with fireflies." The skit concludes when "the groom loads his wife on a tortoise and they start off. The bride and groom exit to a slow curtain, and as they leave the chorus dances and sings 'unhunh, unhunh, unhunh, unhunh.'"

Although Hurston portrays the scene with a child's whimsical imagination, "Mr. Frog" could not possibly be staged in a practical way. The animal characters might be at home in a Walt Disney film, but a director would have a difficult challenge staging the skit. However, the skit does work as a child's story and might be adapted to that genre.

Following the naiveté of "Mr. Frog," "Lenox Avenue" comes as a shock, an example of what Hurston means by "cold keener," an abrupt change of setting, mood, and language. The stage is set to resemble a busy New York street corner by having a "back drop showing intersections and houses." The autos keep whirling past on a scenic band. The action begins when "a very effeminate young man enters with a large cretonne sewing bag on his wrist." The young man is approached by a police officer who inquires what is in the bag; his knitting, he replies, and he is taking it to the army because "the boys must have their sox, you know." As he waves "a fluffy goodbye," he says, "Toodle-oo, old cabbage, I must try to get the boys out of the trenches before Christmas."

The young man exits, and a married couple, who are loudly arguing over the husband's philandering, enter. The woman holds her own, and when the husband says, "Bye, bye, Mamma, you can't snore in my ear no more," the wife answers, "You might as well stop dat wringing and twisting, cause I know you want me some again, cause I'm a damn sweet woman and you know it." They exit and a newly married couple enter who are also arguing over the husband's promiscuity. When the husband threatens to beat his wife, she answers:

WIFE. You better not hit me, nigger.

MAN. I'll hit you just as sure as Jesus rode a jackass.

WIFE. Turn go of me, fool. I dare you to hit me! If you stick your rusty foot in my face, you going to jail.

MAN. How come I'm going to jail?

WIFE. Cause there a cop right there on the corner and I'm going to holler like a pretty white woman.

The skit seems to be an early version of Hurston's short story, "Story in Harlem Slang," which appeared in the *American Mercury* in 1942 (Hemenway 290). In the story two pimps accost a young woman and attempt to hustle her for money and sex, but she verbally outwits them. At the end of the story, the young woman's final retort is the same as that in the skit.

The "House that Jack Built" is similar to "Mr. Frog Went Courtin" in that Hurston again structures a skit on a familiar child's story. The setting is an "old-fashioned schoolhouse" in the "deep south," but the children "are large" and the "girls are pretty." The main character, De Otis Blunt, is poorly dressed and the dunce of the class whom the teacher constantly picks on. Because it is Friday, recitation day, the teacher warns the students that "anybody don't know a speech today will get a good whipping and be kept after school." Many of the students fail to perform and provide the usual excuses of "I didn't learn none or I forgot mine." When it is De Otis's turn everyone expects him to excuse himself, but he surprises the class by providing a ten-minute recitation of the "House That Jack Built." As De Otis recites he begins to dance, and the teacher and students dance in chorus with him. "De Otis dances till he shudders down to the floor and lies there shivering in rhythm." In the chants and dances De Otis approximates the present day musical form of rap.[7]

In both "Mr. Frog" and "House That Jack Built" Hurston uses two well-known English children's stories instead of African American folktales. She is, perhaps, attempting to show that certain stories have become part of the literary lore of both white and black cultures and that African American children interpret the stories in their own way and bring the uniqueness of their interpretation to the stories.

Hurston's script of "Bahamas," the seventh skit, has several penciled slash marks across it as though she were uncertain as to whether to retain certain parts. The skit opens in Harlem with the arrival of Joe Wiley, a character also of *Mules and Men,* who has been invited to the Bahamas and then to Africa by the Emperor Jones—the main character in Eugene O'Neill's play. With the sound of the "ship's sirens and the sounds of anchors and chains," the setting quickly changes to Prince George's Wharf in the Bahamas, with the singing of "Caesar Riley" as background. The Emperor Jones enters and welcomes Joe Wiley with the statement:

To Africa! When I get there with my conquering black legions I am not going to ask Great Britain what they are doing there. I'm just going to say get out! . . . Board the fleet, let us sail for Africa and freedom. . . . And ninety days from now, I shall have a Black House, side by side with the White House in Washington!

Apparently, Hurston is using the character of the Emperor Jones to satirize Marcus Garvey and his back-to-Africa movement.

In the main part of the skit Hurston employs the songs and dances she had observed while researching folk material in the Bahamas. This is obviously a rough draft of "Bahamas," however. Hurston would later eliminate the character of the Emperor Jones, but retain the Bahamian dances and songs which she uses in the conclusion of *The Great Day*. For example, at the conclusion of "Bahamas," Hurston includes a ring dance with drummers playing and actors singing. As "drums flourish" the actors sing:

Bimini gal is a hell of a trouble
Never get licking till you go down to Bimini.

In the last two skits, "Railroad Camp" and "Jook," Hurston returns to the Florida setting. These two would also later appear in a version of *The Great Day*. As the curtain rises on "Railroad Camp," there is "a length of railroad track on an embankment" and "ten men are spiking rails with sledge hammers." The water boy leads the singing:

Dat ol' (wham) black gal (wham)!
She keep on grumblin' (wham)!
New pair shoes (wham), new pair shoes (wham)!

During the entire skit the men sing lining songs and conclude with "Shove it over! Hey, hey can't you line it, can't you move it."

In "Jook," which concludes "Cold Keener," Hurston returns to her original dramatic premise that the real Negro theater originated in the "jooks" of the South. As Hurston includes Joe Wiley, a real person, in "Bahamas," she now introduces Big Sweet who befriended her in the Loughman Turpentine Camp, and who would later play an important role in *Mules and Men,* as well as in **"Polk County."** In "Jook" Hurston's folks act out the classic blues motif of drinking, gambling, fighting, and singing about the fickleness of love.

The setting is a sawmill jook house with a dilapidated piano in one corner. When the curtain goes up, Nunkie is at the piano playing and singing as three couples "slow-drag" and sing "John Barton." Black-Boy, Stack of Dollars, Blue-Front, and Muttsy stroll into the jook and start to play cards. Big Sweet enters and interrupts the game by asking Stack "to read de deck for me." Stack refuses and accuses Big Sweet of "shackin up" with another man. Sexual tension increases with the arrival of Ella Ward, Hurston's actual rival at the Loughman Turpentine Camp. Ella enters and tries to pick a fight with Big Sweet. Instead of fighting, however, Ella grabs a guitar from beside the piano, walks to the center of the stage, puts one foot up on the chair, and sings "John Henry."

Hurston's main purpose in "Jook" appears to be to include as many jook songs and dances as possible in a short period of time. The typescript shows that she probably hurried the composition for there are some grammatical errors and names of characters are spelled differently; for example, the final spelling of Ella Ward is Willa Ward.

After rewriting "De Turkey and De Law," writing "Cold Keener," and copyrighting the two plays, Hurston, during the fall of 1931, continued to actively pursue a theatrical production. However, she was still supported by Mason who believed that a theatrical presentation would corrupt the material that would be published as *Mules and Men*. Still, Hurston persisted and wrote three sketches for *Fast and Furious*." a colored revue in thirty-seven scenes" (Hemenway 175). After *Fast and Furious* failed at the box office, she wrote several sketches for "Jungle Scandals," which was also a commercial failure. Hurston admitted that the writing for the two revues was stereotyped and she was not pleased with her work (177). The four skits Hurston copyrighted in July 1931 may well be some of the material that she wrote for the two revues. "Forty Yards," one of the skits, is about a football game between Howard and Lincoln and may be the skit in which Hurston, playing a cheerleader, made her first dramatic appearance (Hemenway 175).

In September 1932, Hurston completed the manuscript of *Mules and Men*, thus formally ending her contract with Mason. However, she still needed Mason's financial support so that she could adapt the folk materials in *Mules and Men* into a dramatic script. On 10 January 1932, Hurston finally achieved her dream of producing "real Negro theater." *The Great Day*, a Negro Folk Concert, opened at the John Golden Theater in New York.

> I saw the Negro music and musicians were getting lost in the betting ring. I just wanted people to know what real Negro music sounded like. Not only did I want the singing very natural, I wanted to display West Indian folk dancing. I had witnessed the dynamic fire Dance . . . I had to admit to myself that we had nothing in America to equal it. (Appendix 804)

Hurston's production of *The Great Day* changed the course of American musical theater because for the first time the "real voice," "the rich black juice" of the songs she had heard at turpentine camps, prison camps, railroad camps, and jooks were presented as she had conceived them (Appendix 807). Ironically, however, because Mason had provided funds for only the one night's presentation, Hurston was once again frustrated in her attempts to become a successful playwright. With no money to pay

the actors and the loss of Mason's patronage, Hurston decided to "go home to Florida, and try to write the book I had in mind" (Appendix 808). Nevertheless, she continued to believe that dramatic presentation was the primary form through which to present African American folklife, songs, and tales.

No completed manuscript of *The Great Day* exists and apparently Hurston did not copyright it. In addition to working on *The Great Day*, Hurston wrote "Spunk," a musical revue in which she believed she had at last accomplished her goal of realistically presenting African American tales, songs, and dances. She wrote about her hopes for "Spunk" to Mason. In the writing of "Spunk," she believed "the public will see growth rather than decline" (Hemenway 177). Hurston copyrighted "Spunk," but a typescript has not been found. But, even without the completed manuscript of *The Great Day* or even a portion of "Spunk," Hurston scholars and admirers may be able to more fully comprehend Hurston's theatrical vision now that some newly located materials are available for study.

Though Hurston was something of a rebel while a student of Montgomery Gregory at Howard University, she still wrote her plays in the conventional forms. Returning to the South during the years 1927 to 1930 as a trained anthropologist, she came to understand the uniqueness of the folk material she had gathered and its fragility. With revolutionary zeal, she determined not only to preserve the folklore, tales, songs, and dances, but to recreate them in a structure that would best bring them to life—and that was drama. Most of her attempts at playwriting, however, were thwarted, whether through disagreements about theme and structure when she coauthored plays with Langston Hughes or Dorothy Waring, or through lack of financial backing.

Perhaps if Mason had provided her more freedom in the use of her material, Hurston might have had greater success. But by the time *Mules and Men* was finally published, and Mason no longer part of her life and work, the Depression had ended and white America's interest in African American theatrical themes had waned.

For most of her creative life, Hurston continued to rewrite and produce versions of *The Great Day*. According to RoseMary Barnes,[8] who knew Hurston in Eau Gallie during the fifties when Hurston was her baby-sitter, Hurston arranged a production of *The Great Day*, acted by African American students, for the local Women's Club. Barnes attended the performance and recalls that the mainly white audience was thoroughly entertained. She and her parents, however, were Hurston's employers and knew the physical effort that Hurston had expended in attempts to produce her play. Working as a maid, broke, sick, with her books out of print, Hurston still believed that drama and music represented the soul of her people. She was still determined that while there was life in her body she would continue to see that white and black Americans heard not only her voice, but the voice of the "people farthest down."

Notes

1. Most of the new Hurston manuscripts are located in the Manuscript Division of the Library of Congress. "Meet the Mamma" is in custody of the Music Division and "Polk County" in the Rare Book and Manuscript Division.

2. Sarah Mack is listed in the 1916 *Baltimore City Directory for Colored Americans* as having an eating establishment at 1507 Laurens Street which was adjacent to Pennsylvania Avenue. At the time this was one of the most segregated areas in the country.

3. Not only was O'Neill a speaker at Howard, but he also helped to bring his play "The Emperor Jones" to campus with the renowned Charles Gilpin in the lead role. Cleon Throckmorton, technical director of the Provinceton Players, made weekly trips to Howard to teach a class in scenic design. Information about Eugene O'Neill's Howard connection may be found in the Montgomery Gregory papers at Howard University.

4. Information about Hurston's early interest in the theater may be found in correspondence between Hurston and Annie Nathan Meyer during the years 1925 to 1926 when Hurston was a student at Barnard and under Meyer's sponsorship. Meyer was also a playwright, and so the two had much in common. Myrna Goldenberg has researched the letters, and information used in this paper is taken from her essay, "The Barnard Connection: Zora Neale Hurston and Annie Nathan Meyer," which was presented at the First Zora Neale Hurston Conference held in Eatonville, FL, in January 1990.

5. For more information about the importance of primitivism during this period, see Ann Douglas's *Terrible Honesty, Mongrel Manhattan in the 1920.*

6. For information about the history of African American popular music from 1895 to 1930, see *From Cakewalks to Concert Halls* (Washington: Elliott and Clark, 1992) by Thomas L. Morgan and William Barlow.

7. "A History of the Blues." Lecture by Robert B. Jones on 3 October 1997 at Myth, Memory, and Migration in the Black South Conference, U of Alabama, Tuscaloosa. In his lecture Jones demonstrated the close relationship of the blues form to that of present day rap.

8. Interview with RoseMary Barnes held in Macon, GA, 16 July 1996.

Works Cited

Abrahams, Roger, and Susan Kalcik. "Folklore and Cultural Pluralism." *Frontiers of Folklore in the Modern World.* Ed. Richard M. Dorson. The Hague: Mouton P, 1978. 46.

Day, Wyatt Houston. "Some Newly Discovered Works by Zora Neale Hurston." *Eighth Annual Program for the Zora Neale Hurston Festival of the Arts and Humanities.* Eatonville, FL: Assoc. to Preserve the Eatonville Community, 1997.

Douglas, Ann. *Terrible Honesty, Mongrel Manhattan in the 1920* (New York: Farrar, 1995).

Goldenberg, Myrna. "The Barnard Connection: Zora Neale Hurston and Annie Nathan Myers." *All About Zora.* Winter Park, FL: Four-G P, 1991.

Hemenway, Robert E. *Zora Neale Hurston: A Literary Biography.* Urbana: U of Illinois P, 1977.

Hill, Lynda Marion. *Social Rituals and the Verbal Art of Zora Neale Hurston.* Washington: Howard UP, 1996.

Hughes, Langston. *The Big Sea.* New York: Hill and Wang, 1940.

Hughes, Langston, and Zora Neale Hurston. *Mule Bone, A Comedy of Negro Life.* Ed. George Houston Bass and Henry Louis Gates, Jr. New York: Harper/Perennial, 1991.

Hurston, Zora Neale. "Characteristics of Negro Expression." *Social Rituals and the Verbal Art of Zora Neale Hurston.* Lynda Marion Hill Washington: Howard UP, 1996. 201, 243-57.

Hurston, Zora Neale. Appendix. 1942. *Dust Tracks On a Road.* Library of America, 1995.

———. "Cold Keener." Unpublished. Washington: Library of Congress.

———. "De Turkey and de Law." Unpublished. Washington: Library of Congress.

———. "Spears." Zeta Phi Beta *X Ray,* 1925.

Perkins, Kathy A. *Black Female Playwrights.* Bloomington: Indiana UP, 1989.

MULE BONE

PRODUCTION REVIEWS

Henry Louis Gates Jr. (review date 1991)

SOURCE: "Why the *Mule Bone* Debate Goes On," in *Critical Essays on Zora Neale Hurston,* edited by Gloria L. Cronin, G. K. Hall & Co., 1998, pp. 225-28.

[*In the following review, originally published in the* New York Times *on February 10, 1991, Gates considers Hurston's desire to portray authentic black culture in* Mule Bone.]

Controversy over the play *Mule Bone* has existed ever since it was written by Langston Hughes and Zora Neale Hurston in 1930. Not only did an authors' quarrel prevent the play from being produced, but its exclusive use of black folk vernacular has also provoked debate. In 1984, when the play became part of the publishing project of Dr. Henry Louis Gates Jr., the editor of Hurston's complete works, he sent a copy of it to Gregory Mosher, then the artistic director of the Goodman Theater in Chicago. When

Mr. Mosher moved to the Lincoln Center Theater in New York, he brought the play with him, and eventually the theater decided to mount it. Dr. Gates and George Houston Bass, the literary executor of the Hughes estate, edited the play and served as consultants to the production. *Mule Bone* is being published this month to coincide with its world premiere Thursday at the Ethel Barrymore Theater on Broadway. Dr. Gates, the John Spencer Bassett Professor of English at Duke University, was elected to the board of Lincoln Center Theater last spring.

For a people who seem to care so much about their public image, you would think blacks would spend more energy creating the conditions for the sort of theater and art they want, rather than worrying about how they are perceived by the larger society. But many black people still seem to believe that the images of themselves projected on television, film and stage must be policed and monitored from within. Such convictions are difficult—even painful—to change. And never more so than in the case of *Mule Bone*, the controversial 1930 Langston Hughes-Zora Neale Hurston play that is only now being produced for the first time, almost 60 years to the day after it was originally scheduled to open.

Why should a folk comedy about the residents of a small Florida town in the 1920's cause such anxiety? Because of its exclusive use of black vernacular as the language of drama.

In analyzing the discomfort *Mule Bone* has aroused over the decades, the playwright Ntozake Shange has said that Hurston's language "always made black people nervous because it reflects rural diction and syntax—the creation of a different kind of English."

"Are we still trying to figure out what is real about ourselves that we know about that makes it too dangerous to say it in public?" she asked.

Ms. Shange was speaking at a 1988 forum at Lincoln Center at which the play was read and the merits of staging it debated—"in a post-Tawana Brawley decade," as the theater's artistic director, Gregory Mosher, put it. Few occasions have brought together more prominent black actors, directors, writers and critics than that November reading: the actors Ruby Dee, Paul Winfield, Giancarlo Esposito and Joe Morton, and the playwrights Ed Bullins and Ron Milner were among the nearly 100 people present, along with Hughes's biographer, Arnold Rampersad, the literary executor of the Hughes estate, George Houston Bass, who died last September, and myself.

As each speaker commented, often passionately, it seemed incredible that the debate was occurring in the first place. Why would anyone believe there are still aspects of black culture that should be hidden because they are somehow "embarrassing"?

Mule Bone is a revelation of life "behind the veil," in the words of W. E. B. DuBois. It portrays what black people

say and think and feel—when no white people are around—in a highly metaphorical and densely lyrical language that is as far removed from minstrelsy as a Margaux is from Ripple. It was startling to hear the play read aloud and enjoyed by actors who weren't even alive when it was written. The experience called to mind sitting in a black barbershop, or a church meeting—any one of a number of ritualized or communal settings. A sign of the boldness of Hughes (1902-1967) and Hurston (1891-1960) was that they dared to unveil one of these ritual settings and hoped to base a new idea of theater on it. Would the actors and writers in the late 1980's find poetry and music in this language, or would it call to mind minstrelsy, vaudeville and Amos 'n' Andy? Was it Sambo and Aunt Jemima, or was it art?

Sixty years after *Mule Bone* was written, many black Americans still feel that their precarious political and social condition within American society warrants a guarded attitude toward the way images of their culture are projected. Even a work by two of the greatest writers in the tradition cannot escape these concerns, concerns that would lead some to censorship, presumably because of "what white people might think," as if white racists attend black plays or read black literature to justify their prejudices. While the causes of racism are legion, literature hardly looms large among them.

Yet much of the motivation for the creation of what is now called the Harlem Renaissance—that remarkable flowering of black literature and the visual arts that occurred during the 20's, when *Mule Bone* was conceived—was implicitly political. Through the demonstration of sublime artistic capacity, black Americans—merely 60 years "up from slavery," as Booker T. Washington described it—could dispel forever the nagging doubts that white Americans might have about their innate intellectual potential. Then, the argument went, blacks could easily traverse the long and bumpy road toward civil rights and social equality.

Given this burdensome role of black art, it was inevitable that debates about the nature of that art—about what today we call its "political correctness"—would be heated in black artistic circles.

These debates have proved to be rancorous, from that 20's renaissance through the battles between social realism and symbolism in the 30's to the militant black arts movement in the 60's. More recently, there have been bitter arguments about sexism, misogyny and the depiction of black women and men in the works of Alice Walker, Toni Morrison, Michele Wallace and Ms. Shange, as well as controversies about the writings of such social critics as Shelby Steele and Stanley Crouch. "The Negro in Art: How Shall He Be Portrayed?"—the subject of a forum published by DuBois in *The Crisis* magazine in the mid-20's—can be identified as the dominant concern of black artists and their critics for the last 70 years.

Black art in the 20th century, then, is a pivotal arena in which to chart worries about "political correctness." The burden of representing "the race" in accordance with explicitly political programs can have a devastating impact on black creativity. Perhaps only black musicians and their music, until rap arose, have escaped this problem, because so much of what they composed was in nonverbal forms and because historically black music existed primarily for a black market. Categorized that way, it escaped the gaze of white Americans who, paradoxically, are the principal concern of those who would police the political effects of black art.

But such fears were not for the likes of Zora Neale Hurston. In April 1928 she wrote Hughes about her interest in a culturally authentic African-American theater, one constructed on a foundation of black vernacular: "Did I tell you about the new, the real Negro theater I plan? Well, I shall, or rather we shall act out the folk tales, however short, with the abrupt angularity and naivete of the primitive 'bama Nigger." It would be, she assured him, "a really new departure in the drama."

Hurston and Hughes did more than share the dream of a vernacular theater. They also established themselves as creative writers and critics by underscoring the value of black folk culture, both in itself and as the basis for formal artistic traditions. But the enormous potential of this collaborative effort was never realized, because, as Hughes wrote on his manuscript copy of the play's text, "the authors fell out."

Exactly why they "fell out" has never been clear, but the story of this abortive collaboration is one of the most curious in American literary history. For whatever reason, Hurston would copyright **Mule Bone** in her own name and deny Hughes's role in its writing.

The action of their play turns on a triangle of desire between a guitarist, Jim Weston (played by Kenny Neal), and an unnamed dancer (Dave Carter Eric Ware), who are best friends as well as a musical duo, and their growing rivalry for the affections of Daisy Taylor (Akosua Busia). Directed by Michael Schultz, **Mule Bone** has a score by Taj Mahal, who has set five Langston Hughes poems to music and composed four songs for the Lincoln Center production.

Eventually, the two friends quarrel and Weston strikes Carter with the hock bone of an "ole yaller mule." He is arrested and his trial forms the heart of the play. The trial, and most of the second act, takes place in the Macedonia Baptist Church, converted into a courthouse for the occasion, with Mayor Joe Clark (Samuel E. Wright) presiding. The resolution of the case turns upon an amusing biblical exegesis: Can a mule bone be a criminal weapon? If so, then Weston is guilty; if not, he is innocent.

Using Judges 18:18, Carter's "attorney" (his minister, played by Arthur French) proves that since a donkey is the father of a mule, and since Samson slew 3,000 Philistines with the jawbone of an ass, and since "de further back you

gits on uh mule de more dangerous he gits, an' if de jawbone slewed 3,000 people, by de time you gits back tuh his hocks it's pizen enough tuh kill 10,000." Therefore, "I ask y'all, whut kin be mo' dangerous dan uh mule bone?" Weston is banished from the town, which was based on Hurston's own Eatonville, Fla. The final scene depicts the two friends' reconciliation after both reject Daisy's demand that her husband get a proper job.

What is so controversial about all this? Hughes and Hurston develop their drama by imitating and repeating historical black folk rituals. Black folklore and Southern rural black vernacular English served as the foundation for what they hoped would be a truly new art form. It would refute the long racist tradition, in minstrelsy and vaudeville, of black characters as ignorant buffoons and black vernacular English as the language of idiots, of those "darkies" who had peopled the American stage for a full century before **Mule Bone**.

This explains why they subtitled their play *A Comedy of Negro Life* and why they claimed that it was "the first real Negro folk comedy." By using the vernacular tradition as the basis of their play—indeed, as the basis of a new theory of black drama—Hurston and Hughes sought to create a work that would undo a century of racist representations of black people.

It is clear that Hurston and Hughes believed the time had come to lift the veil that separates black culture from white, allowing black art to speak in its own voice, without prior restraint. Had they not fallen out, one can only wonder at the effect that a successful Broadway production of **Mule Bone** in the early 1930's might have had on the development of black theater.

Patrick Pacheco (review date 1991)

SOURCE: "A Discovery Worth the Wait," in *Critical Essays on Zora Neale Hurston,* edited by Gloria L. Cronin, G. K. Hall & Co., 1998, pp. 232-36.

[*In the following review, originally published in the* Los Angeles Times *on February 24, 1991, Pacheco acknowledges the dramatic limitations of* Mule Bone *but favorably assesses its first production in 1991.*]

In the Broadway production of **Mule Bone,** the characters gathered on the teeming porch of Joe Clark's general store in Eatonville, Fla., tease and cajole each other, laughing at the small-town follies at the heart of this 1930 comedy written by Langston Hughes and Zora Neale Hurston.

Given the familiarity with which the all-black cast of 30 inhabit their roles, it seems as though these folks have been sitting on that porch forever. But **Mule Bone** is coming to the stage 60 years after writer Hurston and poet Hughes, the royal couple of the Harlem Renaissance in the 1920's, collaborated on the project. Featuring a half-dozen songs added by blues composer Taj Mahal, *Mule Bone,* subtitled *A Comedy of Negro Life,* opened earlier this month for a limited run. While some critics found the material thin, others acknowledged its place in America's cultural history.

Indeed, *Mule Bone* is one of the curiosities of this Broadway season—a Rip Van Winkle awakened to entertain audiences in a Spike Lee era. Based on a Hurston short story, the play was intended to liberate the stage of its time of the black stereotypes which were then popular—the cavorting "darkies" of minstrel shows, vaudeville and musical revues. In April of 1928, Hurston described her concept to Hughes as "real Negro theater . . . we shall act out the folk tales, however short, with the abrupt angularity and naivete of the primitive "bama Nigger.'"

After sketching a couple of drafts of the three-act play, the collaborators had what has been called a "mysterious falling-out" and the production was canceled. The play lay neglected in a drawer until 1983, when Henry Louis Gates Jr., the noted Duke University English professor, brought the unfinished manuscript to Gregory Mosher, then the artistic director at the Goodman Theater in Chicago, who, intrigued, brought the script with him when he moved to Lincoln Center in 1985.

However, in the decades since the play was written, playwrights from Lorraine Hansberry (*Raisin in the Sun*) to August Wilson (*Fences*) had liberated the "stage darkie" far beyond the scope of the *Mule Bone* creators' intent—so much so that Hurston's "primitive" figure might now appear offensive to blacks and whites alike. In a "post-Tawana Brawley decade," as Mosher describes it, what could be gained from a play in which blacks insulted each other in a rural dialect? Was *Mule Bone* simply a socially regressive museum piece better left dormant? The caricatures of Deacon Hambo, Old Man Brazzle, Lum Boger, Teets and Bootsie, among others, appeared, verbally at least, akin to characters in white-written works such as "Song of the South," which had raised questions of their own.

Lincoln Center Theater undertook the current production only after the play was hotly debated at a 1988 reading, a discussion that revealed the sensitivity heightened by racial tensions. Some argued that hewing to "political correctness" could be devastating to black creativity, whether one was talking about *Mule Bone* or the portrayal of male characters in Alice Walker's *The Color Purple.*

Prof. Gates later stated in a *New York Times* essay that "60 years after *Mule Bone*, many black Americans still feel that their precarious political and social condition within American society warrants a guarded attitude toward the way images of their culture are projected. Even a work by two of the greatest writers in the tradition cannot escape these concerns, concerns that would lead some to censorship, presumably because of 'what white people might think.' . . ."

The producers felt confident enough that the authenticity of the material would override these concerns. Michael Schultz, who after a distinguished tenure with the Negro Ensemble Company, had worked in television and film (*Cooley High, Car Wash*), was enlisted as director; writer George Houston Bass provided a new prologue and epilogue; and Taj Mahal set Langston Hughes' poems to music to fill in the slots where the creators had indicated there should be traditional folk songs.

Still, there were concessions to "what white people might think" in the editing of the play. The word "nigger" was deleted from the dialogue, as were all sexist allusions to women as chattel.

Other more troubling issues of "political correctness" remained. Was the play worthy of a production simply because the title page featured the names, as Gates noted, of "two of the greatest writers" of the black tradition, despite its limitations as theater? Might it not be historically important but theatrically feeble?

After all, these townfolk were in service to a leisurely driven plot, the rivalry between Jim and Dave, a song-and-dance team, for the affection of the coquettish Daisy. When guitar-twanging Jim whacks his best friend over the head with "de hock bone of an old yaller mule," his trial divides the town's Baptists and Methodists who argue whether a mule bone can be considered, a weapon, according to the Bible. In the play's vernacular, the minister's argument clinches Jim's conviction: "Since de further back on a mule you goes, do mo' dangerous he gits, by de time you gits clear back tuh his hocks he's rankpizen (poison)." This was hardly compelling material for a Broadway audience familiar with playwrights like Wilson whose emotionally rich *Piano Lesson* is set in the same decade as *Mule Bone*.

Mosher says that he was not bothered by the skimpiness of the script Gates sent to him. Apart from the importance of producing a "lost work" of the Harlem Renaissance, he says that he was captivated by the "richness of detail and uniqueness of spirit" of the story-telling—the first instance of African-Americans themselves turning a light on a world which was merely a shadow in most dramas written up to that time.

Though the play is about a people "60 years up from slavery," racial conflicts happen beyond the railroad tracks of Eatonville. Because Hurston's hometown was the first incorporated black municipality in the United States, the play's comic spirit could emerge untained by the victimization occurring in other communities. The central social structure of *Mule Bone* is determined not by color but by divisions between rich and poor, the powerful and the powerless, Baptists and Methodists.

"But the point of the play is not social work," Mosher adds. "What Hughes and Hurston did was to come along and tap into an entire people's dream life. It addresses the subconscious of an entire community. It brings us no nearer to an understanding of problems of racism, but its effect on the imagination can be joyous."

At 39, Hurston had by then mastered in her numerous short stories the colorful dialogue of a small-town existence and embroidered it with humor. A decade younger, Hughes is credited with giving the play dramatic structure, most specifically in changing the plot so that the boys come to blows over a pretty girl rather than over a turkey, as happened in the original story. This was merely a vehicle which the authors then used to elaborate their cultural legacy. In this regard, *Mule Bone* might be considered as representative of a community's "dream life" as Thornton Wilder's *Our Town*—which captured the archetypes and vernacular of New England, even as it transcended them.

"And nothing happened in the first act of *Our Town* either!" says Mosher, who directed a revival of it on Broadway a few years ago. "It used to drive me crazy. Why would anybody want to come back for the second act? I wondered. And yet, like in *Mule Bone,* they're saying these things for the first time, unraveling this tapestry of life which, at least for me, is thrilling to behold and absorb."

While *Mule Bone* might strike some whites as an entertaining dip into African-Americana, the play appears to viscerally engage the blacks in the audience, attesting to its familiarity and authenticity. The enjoyment stems at least in part from the simplicity of a show in which the biggest crisis is whether or not to build a municipal jail—this before a multi-racial audience that has seen a frightening crime wave in their hometown.

"There are more burning issues out there," says director Michael Schultz, "but this wasn't meant to address those. I've always thought of this as 'a black valentine' to revel in. To say to both whites and to blacks, but blacks especially, 'this is part of your heritage, too.'"

Rousing the dream life concocted by Hughes and Hurston was no easy task, he adds. "And those guys were dead, they couldn't help." The burden fell mostly to the cast to flesh out the broadly comic, sketchily written characters and to add whatever resonance the play might have for a 1991 audience. The difficulty of casting was exacerbated by the fact that many actors simply couldn't handle the rural dialect. Says Schultz, "It had to do with how much in touch with their roots they were."

Theresa Merritt had no problem filling out the ample Katie Pitts, who sassily sings "Shake That Thing" in the show. "My people were from Emory, Ala., and there were Katie Pittses around there," she says. "You know, those women who [are a] little more worldly because they've been up to the sinful North and come back home."

Meritt herself journeyed up to the "sinful North" in the early '40's to pursue a singing career birthed in the Alabama Baptist camp meetings where, as a child, she learned to express herself singing before the congregation. The arc of the actress's career—from her Broadway debut in *Carmen Jones* (1943), to her featured role in August Wilson's *Ma Rainey's Black Bottom,* for which she was nominated for a Tony Award in 1985—reflects the transformation black theater has undergone as it has explored and refined the process begun by Hurston and Hughes.

For Merritt, as well as for other veterans, *Mule Bone* signifies a "comin' around again," as the actress puts it. "My early life was a lot like in *Mule Bone*, people sittin' around telling tall tales about ghosts in graveyards and who's sleeping around with whom. During the day, we'd sing hymns and then on Saturday night, the grown-ups listened to the jazz records they'd put on the Victrola. Jazz was sin music, not fit for children, so we'd have to sneak down. Years later, when I was asked to play Ma Rainey, I knew she'd sung 'Shake That Thing.' I didn't get to sing it then so I was delighted when they asked me to sing it in this show."

Unlike Merritt, 25-year-old Eric Ware had no memories of his own to draw upon in creating suave Dave Carter, who seduces Daisy with his hip-rolling shuffle. But he used certain historical references his grandmother from Greene, Ala., gave him—"She said they used to call a guy like Dave 'a jelly.'" But Ware says he drew inspiration from rides on the uptown IRT subway as well.

"Dave is fast-paced, nonchalant and cocky," he says, "and you can see that on the subway. There's that same physicality in a group of boys together and one of them is talking about what he did last night, and it's 'Hey!' or 'Ya-cha-cha!' It's that same enjoyment of telling the stories and the effect the words have on people." What anchors the show for a contemporary audience is the score played by an off-stage combo complementing the work of Kenny Neal, who plays the guitar-picking Jim.

Once Taj Mahal started reading the poems, he says, the music leaped from the page to his guitar. "I was shocked at how well versed Langston was in the blues," says Mahal. "My parents were always saying Langston this and Langston that, but I thought he was bourgeois, all that search for connectedness. The blues didn't care whether you were listening to it or not. It just had to sing its song."

His songs for *Mule Bone*, says Mahal, were intended to take the audience back to a certain period but also to give them the feeling that they were moving forward. "If you listen carefully," he says, "you can hear cultural relatives of the blues: r&b, soul, gospel, even a little bit of jazz and calypso. There's a certain crying blues you could put out there, but once I started reading through the poems, I started rocking."

Mahal says he saw the fusion between African-American storytelling and the blues in both Hughes' poetry and the play. The art of laughter was one of the black folk's gift to American culture. But, "it's the art of laughing to keep from crying. That's what the blues is about too."

Frank Rich (review date 1991)

SOURCE: "A Difficult Birth for *Mule Bone,*" in *Critical Essays on Zora Neale Hurston*, edited by Gloria L. Cronin, G. K. Hall & Co., 1998, pp. 229-31.

[*In the following review, originally published in the* New York Times *on February 15, 1991, Rich enumerates several flaws in the Lincoln Center Theater production of* Mule Bone, *and observes that the play "feels like a rough draft in which two competing voices are trying to reach a compromise."*]

If ever there was a promising idea for a play, it is the enigmatic story of what went on when two giants of the Harlem Renaissance briefly collided in 1930 to collaborate on "a comedy of Negro life" they titled *Mule Bone.*

The writers were the poet Langston Hughes and the anthropologist, folklorist and novelist Zora Neale Hurston. Both were in their late 20's, and both had the same dream of a new truly African-American theater. Their goal was Broadway, which they hoped to liberate from the stereotypical minstrel musicals (the many progeny of *Shuffle Along*) and sentimental problem dramas (*Green Pastures, Porgy*) that then distorted the black experience on the mainstream stage. Yet *Mule Bone* was never finished and never produced because, as Hughes put it, "the authors fell out."

What went wrong? No one knows for sure, despite the fascinating and painstaking efforts of both writers' authoritative biographers, Arnold Rampersad (Hughes) and Robert E. Hemenway (Hurston), to piece the events together. Everyone agrees, as Henry Louis Gates Jr. has written, that the fight was "an extremely ugly affair" that at the very least involved a battle over authorial credit and the neurotic machinations of a wealthy white patron. Hurston's present-day publisher, Harper Perennial, has just brought out a first edition of the uncompleted text of *Mule Bone* in which all the relevant biographical accounts and documentary evidence have been assembled, and the volume leaves no doubt that whatever the provocation, the Hughes-Hurston conflict was the stuff of high drama.

The same, sad to say, cannot be said of *Mule Bone* itself, at least as mounted by Lincoln Center Theater at the Barrymore Theater on Broadway, six full decades after Hurston and Hughes set their sights on the Great White Way. This is an evening that can most kindly be described as innocuous—not an adjective usually attached to either of its authors—and it is not even a scrupulously authentic representation of what Hughes and Hurston wrote, fragmented and problematic as their aborted collaboration was. Indeed, there's something disturbingly disingenuous about the entire production. This *Mule Bone* is at once so watered down and bloated by various emendations that one can never be entirely sure if Lincoln Center Theater is conscientiously trying to complete and resuscitate a lost, unfinished work or is merely picking its carcass to confer a classy literary pedigree on a broad, often bland quasi-musical seemingly pitched to a contemporary Broadway audience.

On occasion—rare occasion—this rendition does make clear what Hurston and Hughes had in mind, which was to bring to the stage, unfiltered by white sensibilities, the genuine language, culture and lives of black people who had been shaped by both a rich African heritage and the oppression of American racism. The play was adapted from an unpublished Hurston story recounting one of the many folk tales she had collected during her anthropological exploration of Eatonville, Fla., the black town where she was born. In the story, two male friends come to blows over a turkey, with one knocking out the other with a mule bone and ending up in a trial that turns on an issue of biblical interpretation. In the play, the object of dispute is a woman named Daisy, not a turkey—the change is believed to have been Hughes's—but the anecdote remains in any case an excuse for an explosion of vernacular speech, blues poetry and extravagantly ritualized storytelling.

Perhaps if the writers had had the chance to finish *Mule Bone* and to see it with an audience, they would have tightened or rethought what was a work in progress. Perhaps even if they had completed their mission, *Mule Bone* would still seem as dated today as other ambitious American plays of its exact vintage, such as Eugene O'Neill's "Mourning Becomes Electra." We'll never know. As the text stands, it often feels like a rough draft in which two competing voices were trying to reach a compromise. Among the more arresting sections are a boisterous trial scene featuring dueling Baptist and Methodist congregations and a late-evening confrontation in which the antagonists compete for their woman's hand with hyperbolic metaphors. When the men try to court Daisy by bragging about how long a chain-gang sentence they would serve to win her over, *Mule Bone* surely succeeds in creating startling, linguistically lush folk comedy that nonetheless reflects the tragic legacy of slavery.

Those scattered passages, as well as sporadic well-turned lines, make the Barrymore vibrate, but they are surrounded by slack sequences and contemporary interpolations. *Mule Bone* opens with an embarrassing prologue by George Houston Bass, the literary executor of the Hughes estate until his death last year, in which Hurston herself awkwardly appears as a character on stage and gives the audience a primer on her career. At other isolated junctures five Hughes poems have been set to music by Taj Mahal, and sweet as the music and words are, the songs are not particularly well sung and always bring a flaccidly constructed show to a self-defeating halt. Dianne McIntyre's rudimentary, thigh-and-knee-slapping choreography lends only perfunctory animation.

As staged by Michael Schultz, who is certainly capable of tougher work, the whole enterprise has a candied Disneyesque tone, more folksy than folk. **Mule Bone** entirely lacks the striking visual style and gut-deep acting with which George C. Wolfe and his collaborators so precisely distilled the toughminded voice of Hurston and the passions of her characters in "Spunk" last year. ("Spunk" also dramatized three Hurston stories in less time than **Mule Bone** takes to dramatize one.) Here the production design is mostly hokey, the performances often aspire to be cute, and even the fisticuffs are not played for keeps. While the authors intended **Mule Bone** to be funny, this production confuses corny affability with folk humor.

No wonder, then, that a number of precocious children roam the stage. The company is also profusely stocked with distinguished actors who have a lot of time on their hands while waiting for an occasional cue: Reggie Montgomery, Frances Foster, Robert Earl Jones, Arthur French. Though the three principal performers—Eric Ware, Kenny Neal, Akosua Busia—are at best likeably amateurish, their efforts are balanced by the assured center-stage turns of such old pros as Leonard Jackson, as a fuming man of the cloth, and Theresa Merritt, who gets to shimmy to a traditional blues recalling her Broadway performance as August Wilson's Ma Rainey. But it is all too typical of the evening that Ms. Merritt's song, the sole rousing musical interlude, is abruptly truncated before it can reach a soaring conclusion. It's almost as if this maiden production were determined to make **Mule Bone** prove on stage what it has always been in literary legend—a false start that remains one of the American theater's more tantalizing might-have-beens.

CRITICAL COMMENTARY

Henry Louis Gates Jr. (essay date 1991)

SOURCE: "A Tragedy of Negro Life," in *Mule Bone: A Comedy of Negro Life by Langston Hughes and Zora Neale Hurston,* Harper Perennial, 1991, pp. 5-24.

[*In the following essay, Gates details the collaboration of Langston Hughes and Hurston on the play* Mule Bone, *and describes the plot and historical influence of the drama.*]

> *This play was never done because the authors fell out.*
> —Langston Hughes, 1931

And fall out, unfortunately, they did, thereby creating the most notorious literary quarrel in African-American cultural history, and one of the most thoroughly documented collaborations in black American literature. Langston Hughes published an account entitled "Literary Quarrel" as the penultimate chapter—indeed, almost as a coda or an afterthought—in his autobiography, *The Big Sea*

(1940). Robert Hemenway, Zora Neale Hurston's biographer, published a chapter in his biography entitled "Mule Bone," and Arnold Rampersad, Hughes's biographer, presents an equally detailed account in volume one of his *The Life of Langston Hughes.* Only Zora Neale Hurston, of the two principals, did not make public her views of the episode. But she did leave several letters (as did Hughes) in which she explains some of her behavior and feelings. In addition, Hurston left the manuscript of the short story, "The Bone of Contention," upon which the play was based. These documents—letters, the short story, Hughes's account, and two accounts from careful and judicious scholars—as well as a draft of the text of the play, **Mule Bone: A Comedy of Negro Life**, comprise the full record of the curious history of this brilliant collaboration between two extraordinarily talented African-American writers. We have assembled this archival and published data here to provide contemporary readers with the fullest possible account of a complex and bizarre incident that will forever remain impossible to understand completely, beclouded in inexplicable motivation.

In a sense, this is a casebook of a crucial—and ugly—chapter in the history of the Harlem Renaissance, that extraordinarily rich period in American cultural history that witnessed the birth of jazz, the coming to fruition of the classic blues, and the first systematic attempt to generate an entire literary and cultural movement by black Americans. The Harlem Renaissance, also called "The New Negro Renaissance," is generally thought to have begun in the early 1920s and ended early on in the Great Depression, about the time when Hughes and Hurston had their dispute. The origins of the Renaissance are, of course, complex and have been written about extensively. It is clear, however, that the production of a rich and various black art, especially the written arts and the theatre, could very well help to reshape the public image of black people within American society and facilitate thereby their long struggle for civil rights, a struggle that commenced almost as soon as the last battle of the Civil War ended. As James Weldon Johnson put it in the "Preface" to his *Book of American Negro Poetry* (1922):

> A people may be great through many means, but there is one by which its greatness is recognized and acknowledged. The final measure of the greatness of all peoples is the amount and standard of the literature and art they produced. The world does not know that a people is great until that people produces great literature and art. No people that has produced great literature and art has ever been looked upon by the world as distinctly inferior.

If, then, African-Americans created a recognizable and valued canon of literature, its effect would have enormous political ramifications: "The status of the Negro in the United States," Johnson concluded, "is more a question of national mental attitude toward the race than of actual conditions. And nothing will do more to change that mental attitude and raise his status than a demonstration of intellectual parity by the Negro through the production of literature and art."

Johnson, by 1922 one of the venerable figures of the black literary and theatrical traditions, effectively issued a call to arms for the creation of a literary movement. Soon, political organizations such as the National Association for the Advancement of Colored People (NAACP) and the National Urban League, through their magazines, *The Crisis* and *Opportunity,* began to sponsor literary competitions, judged by prominent members of the American literati, with the winners receiving cash prizes, publication in the journals, and often book contracts. At the prompting of Charles Johnson, the editor of *Opportunity,* Hurston submitted two short stories—"Spunk" and "Black Death"—and two plays—*Color Struck* and *Spears*—for consideration in *Opportunity*'s annual literary contests in 1925 and 1926. While "Spunk" and *Color Struck* won second-place prizes, *Spears* and "Black Death" won honorable mention. Two other short stories, "Drenched in Light" and "Muttsy" would be published in *Opportunity,* along with "Spunk." It was at the 1925 annual awards dinner that she met another award winner, Langston Hughes, who took third prize jointly with Countee Cullen and first prize for his great poem, "The Weary Blues." It was a momentous occasion, attended by "the greatest gathering of black and white literati ever assembled in one room," as Arnold Rampersad notes, and included among its judges Eugene O'Neill, John Farrar, Witter Bynner, Alexander Woolcott, and Robert Benchley. Hughes was quite taken with Hurston, Rampersad tells us: She "'is a clever girl, isn't she?' he soon wrote to a friend; 'I would like to know her.'" Eventually, he would know her all too well.

II

Between 1925 and their collaboration on the writing of *Mule Bone* between March and June 1930, Hughes and Hurston came to know each other well. As Rampersad reports, by mid-summer of 1926, the two were planning a black jazz and blues opera. Hemenway calls it "an opera that would be the first authentic rendering of black folk-life, presenting folk songs, dances, and tales that Hurston would collect." By the end of that summer, the two (along with Wallace Thurman, John P. Davis, Gwen Bennett, Bruce Nugent, and Aaron Douglass, all members of what was jokingly called "The Niggerati") decided to found a magazine, called *Fire!!,* the title taken from a Hughes poem. The following year, in July 1927, Hughes and Hurston met quite by accident in Mobile, Alabama, and decided to drive together to Manhattan in her car, "Sassy Susie." "I knew it would be fun travelling with her," Rampersad reports Hughes writing. "It was." The trip lasted about a month, with the two sharing notes on hoodoo, folktales, and the blues along the way, and even meeting Bessie Smith, the great classic blues singer. Shortly after this trip, Hughes introduced Hurston to his patron, Charlotte van der Veer Quick Mason, who would contribute about $75,000 to Harlem Renaissance writers, including $15,000 to Hurston. While Hughes received $150 per month, Hurston received $200. Ironically, their subsidies would end just about the time of their feud over *Mule Bone*; although Hurston's contract ended March 30, 1931, she received "irregular" payments until September 1932;

Hughes and she fell out late in 1930, just before his confrontation with Hurston in Cleveland.

A more natural combination for a collaboration among the writers of the Harlem Renaissance, one can scarcely imagine—especially in the theatre! Hurston wrote to Hughes often during the early period of her research in the South, collecting black folklore as part of her doctoral research in anthropology at Columbia under Franz Boas; Hemenway describes her correspondence as "frequent and conspiratorial," providing "an unintentional documentary of the expedition." In April 1928, she shared with Hughes her plans for a culturally authentic African-American theatre, one constructed upon a foundation of the black vernacular: "Did I tell you before I left about the new, the *real* Negro theatre I plan? Well, I shall, or rather we shall act out the folk tales, however short, with the abrupt angularity and naivete of the primitive 'bama Nigger. Quote that with native settings. What do you think?" They would share the burdens and the glory: "Of course, you know I didn't dream of that theatre as a one man stunt. I had you helping 50-50 from the start. In fact, I am perfectly willing to be 40 to your 60 since you are always so much more practical than I. But I know it is going to be *glorious!* A really new departure in the drama." Despite their enthusiasm for this idea, however, Mrs. Mason ("Godmother") disapproved; as Hurston wrote to Alain Locke, the veritable dean of the Harlem Renaissance and another beneficiary of Mrs. Mason's patronage: "Godmother was very anxious that I should say to you that the plans—rather the hazy dreams of the theatre I talked to you about should never be mentioned again. She trusts her three children [Hurston, Hughes, and Locke] to never let those words pass their lips again until the gods decree that they shall materialize."

Not only did the two share the dream of a vernacular theatre and opera, but both had established themselves as creative writers and critics by underscoring the value of black folk culture, both of itself and as the basis for formal artistic traditions. By 1930, when, at last, the two would write *Mule Bone*, Hughes had published two brilliant, widely acclaimed, experimental books of poetry that utilized the blues and jazz as both form and content. And Hurston, though yet to publish a novel, had published sixteen short stories, plays, and essays, in prestigious journals such as *Opportunity, Messenger,* and the *Journal of Negro History,* and was pursuing a Ph.D. thesis in anthropology which was to be built around her extensive collection of Afro-American myths. With Hurston's mastery of the vernacular and compelling sense of story, and Hughes's impressive sense of poetic and theatrical structure, it would have been difficult to imagine a more ideal team to construct "a real Negro theatre." For, at ages twenty-eight and twenty-nine respectively, [Hurston, the scholar Cheryl Wall discovered, shaved ten years from her age. Actually, in 1930, she would have been thirty-nine, not twenty-nine, as she claimed.] Hughes and Hurston bore every promise of reshaping completely the direction of the development of African-American literature away from the blind imitation of American literature and toward a bold and vibrant synthesis of formal American literature and African-American vernacular.

III

The enormous potential of this collaborative effort was never realized, we know, because, as Hughes wrote on his manuscript copy of the text, "the authors fell out." Exactly *why* they "fell out" is not completely clear, despite the valiant attempts of Hemenway and Rampersad to reconstruct the curious series of events that led to such disastrous consequences. While we do know that Hughes and Hurston wrote acts one and three together, and, as Hemenway reports, "at least one scene of the second act," it is impossible to ascertain who wrote what. Hurston had conceived the plot, based as it was on her short story, "The Bone of Contention" (published here for the first time). Hughes would write that he "plotted out and typed the play based on her story," and that Hurston "authenticated and flavored the dialogue and added highly humorous details." Rampersad's estimate is probably the most accurate: "Hurston's contribution was almost certainly the greater to a play set in an all-black town in the backwoods South (she drew here on her childhood memories), with an abundance of tall tales, wicked quips, and farcical styles of which she was absolute master and Langston not much more than a sometimes student. . . . Whatever dramatic distinction the play would have, Hurston certainly brought to it." But, just as surely, it was Hughes who shaped the material into a play, into comic drama, with a plot, a dramatic structure, and a beginning, middle, and end. While Hurston had published a play, and Hughes had not yet completed his first play, Hughes was the superior dramatist. Neither, however, would ever achieve the results that they did, in close collaboration, with *Mule Bone.*

While we cannot explain Hurston's motivation for denying Hughes's collaboration, which caused the dispute and the ending of their friendship, we can re-create the strange series of events through the following chronology, which is based on the accounts of Hemenway and Rampersad, printed in this book:

Late February-early March 1930: Hughes meets Theresa Helburn of the Dramatists Guild at a party; Helburn complains about the lack of real comedies about blacks.

April-May 1930: Hughes and Hurston write the first draft of "Mule Bone" in Westfield, New Jersey. Complete acts one and three and at least scene one of act two, dictating to Louise Thompson.

May 1930: Hughes's relation with patron, Mrs. Mason, begins to collapse.

June 1930: Hurston returns to the South, ostensibly to complete the trial scene of act two.

September 1930: Hurston returns, apparently without the scene completed.

October 1930: Hurston files for copyright of *Mule Bone* as sole author.

December 1930-January 1931: Hughes ends relationship with "Godmother," Mrs. Mason.

January 1931: Hughes returns to his mother's home in Cleveland, has tonsillectomy.

Winter 1930-31: Hurston gives Carl Van Vechten copy of play. Van Vechten sends it to Barrett Clark, reader for the Theatre Guild. Clark, an employee of Samuel French, the theatrical producer, contacts Rowena Jelliffe and sends script.

January 15, 1931: Hughes visits Rowena and Alexander Jelliffe, directors of the settlement playhouse "Karamu House," home of the black theatre troupe the Gilpin Players. Rowena Jelliffe explains that she has obtained the rights to a play entitled *Mule Bone* by Zora Neale Hurston.

January 16, 1931: Hughes phones Hurston to protest her action. Hurston denies knowledge of play being sent to French or to Jelliffe. Hughes incredulous.

January 16, 1931: Hughes writes to Carl Van Vechten asking for his advice.

January 17, 1931: Louise Thompson arrives in Cleveland, in her capacity as official of the American Interracial Seminar.

January 18, 1931: Hurston visits Van Vechten, and "cried and carried on no end."

January 19, 1931: Hughes mails copy of play to U.S. copyright office, in name of Hurston and himself. Received January 22.

January 20, 1931: Hughes receives Hurston's letter denying joint authorship and complaining about Louise Thompson's compensation.

January 20, 1931: French's company wires Jelliffe refusing Hurston's permission to authorize production. Demands return of script.

January 20-21, 1931: Hurston sends three telegrams reversing her decision; authorizes the production and agrees to collaborate with Hughes.

January 21, 1931: Hughes receives Hurston letter of January 18, denying Hughes's collaboration and revealing resentment over Hughes's friendship with Louise Thompson.

January 21-26, 1931: Hurston agrees to come to Cleveland to collaborate with Hughes on rewrites; first performance scheduled for February 15.

February 1, 1931: Hughes's twenty-ninth birthday. Hurston arrives in Cleveland, meets with Hughes, resolves differences, misses scheduled meeting with Gilpin Players. That evening, the Gilpin Players meet and vote to cancel play, but reconsider. All seems set for a Cleveland opening and a Broadway run.

February 2, 1931: Hurston learns that Louise Thompson has visited Cleveland and seen Hughes. Hurston berates Mrs. Jelliffe.

February 3, 1931: Hurston visits Hughes at his home and rudely cancels production.

August 1931: Wallace Thurman (estranged husband of Louise Thompson) hired to revise *Mule Bone.* Hughes writes to Dramatists Guild declaring joint authorship.

1940: Hughes publishes account in *The Big Sea.*

1964: Hughes publishes act three in *Drama Critique.*

This, in barest outline, is an account of the bizarre events of an extremely ugly affair. As Hemenway and Rampersad make clear, Hurston justified her denial of Hughes's collaboration by claiming anger over Hughes's apparent proposal that Louise Thompson be given a share of all royalties, and that she be made the business manager of any Broadway production that might evolve. In Hurston's words:

> In the beginning, Langston, I was very eager to do the play with you. ANYthing you said would go over big with me. But scarcely had we gotten underway before you made three propositions that shook me to the foundation of myself. First: that three way split with Louise. Now Langston, nobody has in the history of the world given a typist an interest in a work for typing it. Nobody would think of it unless they were prejudiced in favor of the typist.

If this seems scant reason, sixty years later, for Hurston's protest over Thompson's financial role to assume such an extreme form, her behavior was no doubt also motivated, as Hemenway and Rampersad argue, by Hughes's deteriorating relationship with Mrs. Mason and Hurston's desire to continue hers, even if at Hughes's expense. Hurston kept Mrs. Mason abreast of these developments over the play, and even sent her copies of Hughes's letters to her, all the while denying his claims to Mason. What seems clear, however, is that Hurston's behavior was not justified by her anger over Hughes's friendship with Thompson, and that her claim of sole authorship should not have been made. As Hughes concluded, "our art was broken," as was both their friendship and the promise of a new and bold direction in black theatre.

IV

Certainly one tragic aspect of the failure of Hughes and Hurston to produce and publish **Mule Bone** was the interruption of the impact that it might have had on the shape and direction of Afro-American theatre. Among all of the black arts, greater expectations were held for none more than for black theatre. As early as 1918, W. E. B. Du Bois, writing in *The Crisis,* argued that "the value of [a sustained Afro-American theatre] for Negro art can scarcely be overestimated." In 1925, Du Bois would help to found Krigwa, a black theatre group in Harlem, dedicated to drama that is "by," "for," "about," and "near *us,*" a self-contained and self-sustaining Afro-American theatre. Du Bois was just one of many critics who felt that the drama was the most crucial form of all of the arts for the future of black artistic development, and that it was precisely in this area that blacks had most signally failed. As Alain Locke put it, "Despite the fact that Negro life is somehow felt to be particularly rich in dramatic values, both as folk experience and as a folk temperament, its actual yield, so far as worthwhile drama goes, has been very inconsiderable." And, in another essay published in 1927, Locke wrote:

> In the appraisal of the possible contribution of the Negro to the American theatre, there are those who find the greatest promise in the rising drama of Negro life.

Others see possibilities of a deeper, though subtler influence upon what is after all more vital, the technical aspects of the arts of the theatre. Until very recently the Negro influence upon American drama has been negligible, whereas even under the handicaps of second-hand exploitation and restriction to the popular amusement stage, the Negro actor has already considerably influenced our stage and its arts. One would do well to imagine what might happen if the art of the Negro actor should really become artistically lifted and liberated. Transpose the possible resources of Negro song and dance and pantomime to the serious stage, envisage an American drama under the galvanizing stimulus of a rich transfusion of essential folk-arts and you may anticipate what I mean. ("The Negro and the American Theatre")

There can be little doubt that Locke here voices the theory of black drama that Hurston and Hughes sought to embody in their unwritten black opera and in **Mule Bone**. (Hurston had, by the way, once described the relationship among the three as that of a triangle, with Hughes and her forming the base, and Locke the apex.)

There are many reasons for the supposed primacy of the theatre among the arts of the Harlem Renaissance. Many scholars date the commencement of the Renaissance itself to the phenomenal and unprecedented success of Eubie Blake's and Noble Sissle's all-black Broadway musical, *Shuffle Along,* which opened in 1921. (Blake and Sissle did the score, and Aubrey Lyles and Flournoy Miller did the book.) As Bruce Kellner informs us, "Often the week's first run business was so heavy that the street on which it was playing had to be designated for one-way traffic only." Josephine Baker, Florence Mills, and Paul Robeson were just a few of the performers who played in this musical.

Predictably, the success of *Shuffle Along* spawned a whole host of imitators, including *Alabama Bound, Bandana Land, Black Bottom Revue, Black Scandals, Blackbirds, Chocolate Blondes, Chocolate Browns, Chocolate Dandies, Darktown Scandals, Darktown Strutters, Goin' White, Lucky Sambo, North Ain't South, Raisin' Cane, Strut Miss Lizzie, Seven-Eleven, Dixie to Broadway,* and *Runnin' Wild* (which introduced "The Charleston"), to list just a few. Jazz, the dance, acting, and an extraordinarily large white and sympathetic audience made the theatre an enormously promising venue for a black art that would transform the public image of the Negro. Its effect was both broad and immediate; there was not the sort of mediation necessary between artist and audience as is the case with a printed book. What's more, theatre as a combination of several arts—poetry, narrative, music, the dance, acting, the visual arts—allowed blacks to bring together the full range of their traditions, vernacular and formal, rather than just one. The great potential of the theatre was hard to resist.

Resistance, however, arose from tradition itself. The roots of black theatre in the twenties were buried in the soil of minstrelsy and vaudeville. Musicals such as *Shuffle Along* did indeed reach tens of thousands more Americans than would any book before *Native Son* (1940). But what image did they represent, and at what cost? Reviews of *Shuffle Along* often turned on phrases such as "extreme energy," "the sun of their good humor." Especially notable were the dancers' "jiggling," "prancing," "wiggling," and "cavorting." In other words, what this sort of black theatre did was to reinforce the stereotype of black people as happy-go-lucky, overly sensual bodies. And while it was (and remains) difficult to disrupt the integrity of jazz and Afro-American dance, even in association with quasi-minstrel forms, it is difficult to imagine how the *intelligence* of these artistic traditions could shine through the raucous humor of this kind of theatre. Broadway, in other words, stood as the counterpoint to the sort of written art that Hughes and Hurston were determined to create, even if they envied Broadway's potential and actual market. Accordingly, they decided to intervene, to do for the drama what Hughes had done for poetry and what Hurston would do (in *Jonah's Gourd Vine* [1934] and *Their Eyes Were Watching God* [1937]) for the novel, which was to shape a formal written art out of the vast and untapped black vernacular tradition.

Mule Bone was based on a Hurston short story, "The Bone of Contention," which Hurston never published. For the Hurston scholar, it is particularly fascinating as a glimpse into Hurston's manner of revising or transforming the oral tradition (she had collected the story in her folklore research) and because of its representation of various characters (such as Eatonville, an all-black town where Hurston was born, Joe Clarke and his store, the yellow mule and his mock burial) who would recur in subsequent works, such as *Mule Bone* and *Their Eyes Were Watching God*.

The story's plot unfolds as follows: Dave Carter and Jim Weston are hunting turkeys one evening. Carter claims to have shot a turkey, while Weston is loading his gun. Weston claims that it is his shot that killed the turkey. They struggle. Jim Weston strikes Dave Carter on the head with "de hockbone" of a mule, Carter alleges, and steals his turkey.

The remainder of the plot depicts the trial, held at the Baptist Church and presided over by Mayor Joe Clarke. Weston is a Methodist while Clarke is a Baptist, and the townspeople are equally divided between the two denominations. They are also fiercely competitive, bringing a religious significance to the quarrel. In fact, Carter and Weston would be represented in court by their ministers, Rev. Simms (Methodist) and Elder Long (Baptist). "The respective congregations were lined up behind their leaders," the text tells us.

The resolution of the dilemma turns on traditional African-American biblical exegesis: can a mule-bone be a weapon? If it can, then it follows that its use could constitute a criminal act. Using Judges 15:16, Elder Long proves that since a donkey is the father of a mule, and since Samson slew one thousand Philistines with the jaw-bone of an ass, and since "de further back on a mule you goes, do mo'

dangerous he gits," then "by de time you gits clear back tuh his hocks hes rank pizen." Jim Weston is banished from town.

The plot of *Mule Bone* is very similar. The play consists of three acts, and includes Jim Weston and Dave Carter (best friends), Joe Clarke, but now Daisy Taylor, over whom Weston and Clarke will, inevitably, quarrel. Weston will strike Carter with the hock-bone of "Brazzle's ole yaller mule," during an argument over Daisy on the front porch of Clarke's store. Weston is arrested, Carter is rushed off to be treated, leaving Daisy alone wondering who's going to walk her home.

Act Two consists of two scenes. The first reveals the subtext of the trial—the struggle between Joe Clarke and Elder Simms for mayor, and the class tension between the Baptists and the Methodists. Scene Two occurs mostly in the Macedonia Baptist Church, newly transformed into a courthouse, with Joe Clarke presiding. As in the short story, the Methodists and Baptists seat themselves on opposite sides, even singing competing hymns (Baptists, "Onward Christian Soldiers" and the Methodists, "All Hail the Power of Jesus's Name") when the mayor asks that the proceedings commence with a hymn. Act Two proceeds as does the short story, with Judges 18:18 coming to bear in exactly the same manner as had Judges 15:16. Jim Weston, found guilty, is banished from town for two years.

Act Three depicts the reconciliation of Jim and Dave, and Jim's return to Eatonville, following their joint rejection of Daisy, who as it turns out, wants her husband to "work for her white folks." What is most interesting about this scene is that the tension between Dave and Jim is resolved in a witty and sustained verbal dual, in which the two trade cleverly improvised hyperbolic claims of their love for Daisy, in an elaborate ritual of courtship. As Hemenway puts it:

> When Dave asks Jim how much time he would do for Daisy on the chain gang, Jim answers, "Twenty years and like it." Dave exults, "See dat, Daisy, Dat nigger ain't willin to do no time for you. I'd beg de judge to gimme life."

> Again a significant stage direction interrupts the dialogue. By telling us that "both Jim and Dave laugh," Hurston and Hughes were trying to show the sense of verbal play and rhetorical improvisation characteristic of Eatonville generally, and Joe Clark's store-front porch specifically. . . . The contest is a ritual, designed to defuse the violence implicit in the conflict, to channel the aggression into mental rather than physical terms. The manner in which the courting contest ends suggests its ritualistic nature: Dave says to Daisy, "Don't you be skeered, baby. Papa kin take keer o you [To Jim: suiting the action to the word] Countin from de finger back to de thumb. . . . Start anything, I got you some." Jim is taken aback: "Aw, I don't want no more fight wid you, Dave." Dave replies, "Who said anything about fighting? We just provin who love Daisy de best."

This courtship ritual, like so much of the verbal "signifying" rituals in which the characters engage throughout the play, are both reflections of historical folk rituals practiced by African Americans as well as their extensions or elaborations. As Hemenway shows so carefully in his essay appended to this volume, often the characters' dialogues are taken directly from the black vernacular tradition. As often, however, Hughes and Hurston are *imitating* that tradition, improvising upon a historical foundation of ritualized oral discourse, which Hurston had been collecting as part of her graduate research in anthropology with Franz Boas. Hughes and Hurston, in other words, were drawing upon the black vernacular tradition both to "ground" their drama in that discourse but also to "extend" the vernacular itself.

Mule Bone, then, was not a mere vehicle for black folklore, rather, black folklore, served as the basis, the foundation, for what they hoped would be a truly new art form: an art form that would stand in relation to traditional American drama in the way that Hughes's "blues poetry" stood to American poetry and Hurston's vernacular fictions stood to the American novel. *Mule Bone,* in other words, was meant to be the dramatic embodiment of James Weldon Johnson's demand that "the colored poet in the United States needs to do . . . something like what Synge did for the Irish; he needs to find a form that will express the racial spirit by symbols from within rather than by symbols from without, such as the mere mutilation of English spelling and pronunciation. He needs a form that is freer and larger than dialect, but which will still hold the racial flavor; a form expressing the imagery, the idioms, the peculiar turns of thought, and the distinctive humor and pathos, too, of the Negro, but which will also be capable of voicing the deepest and highest emotions and aspirations, and allow of the widest range of subjects and the widest scope of treatment." Dialect, Johnson continued, was doomed by its racist textual heritage:

> Negro dialect is at present a medium that is not capable of giving expression to the varied conditions of Negro life in America, and much less is it capable of giving the fullest interpretation of Negro character and psychology. This is no indictment against the dialect as dialect, but against the mould of convention in which Negro dialect in the United States has been set.

Mule Bone was also a refutation of Johnson's claim that "Negro dialect" "is an instrument with but two full stops, humor and pathos," because of the racist minstrel and vaudeville representations of black characters and their language. This is what they meant when they subtitled their play "A Comedy of Negro Life" and when they claimed that *Mule Bone* was "the first real Negro folk comedy."

By using the vernacular tradition as the foundation for their drama—indeed, as the basis for a new *theory* of black drama—Hughes and Hurston succeeded quite impressively in creating a play that implicitly *critiqued* and explicitly *reversed* the racist stereotypes of the ignorant dialect-speaking darky that had populated the stages of the minstrel and vaudeville traditions. Indeed, we can only

wonder at the effect that a successful Broadway production of *Mule Bone* might have had on the subsequent development of black theatre, given the play's sheer novelty and freshness of language.

With their turn to the vernacular, however, Hurston and Hughes also seem at times to reinscribe the explicit sexism of that tradition, through the discussions of physical abuse and wife-beatings as agents of control, which the male characters on Joe Clarke's store-front porch seem to take for granted as a "natural" part of sexual relations. These exchanges are quite disturbing for our generation of readers, demanding as they do a forceful critique by the reader. Daisy's representation in a triangle of desire as the *object* of her lovers' verbal dueling rather than as one who duels herself, a mode of dueling that demands great intelligence, is also a concern, even if this concern is tempered somewhat by the fact that it is she who controls their complex relationship all along, as demonstrated when she dismisses them both when they will not accede to her demands that they get jobs and provide support for her own efforts at self-sufficiency: "Both of you niggers can git yo' hat on yo' heads and git on down de road. Neither one of y'all don't have to have me. I got a good job and plenty men beggin' for yo' change." Despite this, however, the depiction of female characters and sexual relations in *Mule Bone* almost never escapes the limitation of the social realities that the vernacular tradition reflects.

Mule Bone was never completed. Hurston, in a frantic attempt to demonstrate to Hughes's lawyer, Arthur Spingarn, that she had indeed been the play's sole author, sent him more handwritten revisions of large sections of the play, creating still another version. We have reprinted here, however, the last version on which Hughes and Hurston collaborated. Despite its limitations as a work-in-progress, it stands as a daring attempt to resurrect black poetic language from the burial grounds of racist stereotypes. Had it been performed, the power of its poetic language could very well have altered forever the evolution of African-American drama enabling the theatre to fulfill its great—and still unfulfilled—potential among the African-American arts.

Selected Bibliography

Baker, Houston A., Jr. *Modernism and the Harlem Renaissance.* Chicago: University of Chicago Press, 1987.

Du Bois, W. E. B. "Can the Negro Save the Drama?" *Theatre Magazine* XXXVIII (July 1923): 12, 68.

Du Bois, W. E. B. "The Krigwa Players Little Negro Theatre." *Amsterdam News* (October 5, 1927) and *Crisis* XXXII, No. 3 (July 1926): 134-36.

Du Bois, W. E. B. "The Negro and the American Stage." *Crisis* XXVIII, No. 2 (June 1924): 55-60.

Du Bois, W. E. B. "The Negro Theatre." *Crisis* XV (February 1918): 165.

Fabre, Geneviève. *Drumbeats, Masks, and Metaphors: Contemporary Afro-American Theatre.* Cambridge, Mass.: Harvard University Press, 1983.

Hemenway, Robert. *Zora Neale Hurston: A Literary Biography.* Urbana, Ill.: University of Illinios, 1977.

Huggins, Nathan Irvin. *Harlem Renaissance.* New York: Oxford University Press, 1971.

Johnson, James Weldon. "Preface." In *The Book of American Negro Poetry.* New York: Harcourt, Brace, Jovanovich, 1931.

Kellner, Bruce. *The Harlem Renaissance: A Historical Dictionary of the Era.* New York: Methuen, 1987.

Lewis, David Levering. *When Harlem Was in Vogue.* New York: Alfred A. Knopf, 1981.

Locke, Alain. "The Drama of Negro Life." *Theatre Arts Monthly* 10 (October 1926): 701-06.

Locke, Alain. "The Negro and the American Stage." *Theatre Arts Monthly* 10 (February 1926): 112-20.

Rampersad, Arnold. *The Life of Langston Hughes. Vol. 1: 1902-1941: I, Too, Sing America.* New York: Oxford University Press, 1986.

Lisa Boyd (essay date 1994-1995)

SOURCE: "The Folk, the Blues, and the Problems of *Mule Bone*," in *The Langston Hughes Review*, Vol. XIII, No. 1, Fall-Spring, 1994-1995, pp. 33-44.

[*In the following essay, Boyd offers an initial evaluation of* Mule Bone, *a plays she suggests requires further critical study. She examines the famous literary quarrel of its authors, Hurston and Langston Hughes, and maintains that although the play presents stereotyped characters and a weak plot, it features a tragic sensibility beneath its comic surface.*]

> Dream-singers
> Story-tellers
> Dancers
> Loud laughters in the hands of Fate—My people
>
>   Langston Hughes, "My People"
>
> "big picture talkers were using
> a side of the world for a canvas"
>
>   Zora Neale Hurston, *Their Eyes Were Watching God*
> We
> Who have nothing to lose
> Must laugh and dance
> Lest our laugher
> Goes from
> Us.
>
>   Langston Hughes, "Black Dancers"

Greatly anticipated as one of the most important recoveries in Black American literature, *Mule Bone: A Comedy of Negro Life*, written by Langston Hughes and Zora Neale Hurston in 1930, was finally published and produced in 1991. Yet, despite the talent of the authors and hopes for the success of a black vernacular theater which Hurston and Hughes envisioned, *Mule Bone* was received as little

more than an interesting Black American literary artifact. Three years after its publication and production, this work has yet to stimulate serious critical discussion.

Instead of critically analyzing the play itself, scholars have focused on Hurston and Hughes's quarrel which resulted in the burying of *Mule Bone* in 1931 and in the end of the authors' friendship the same year. Critics continue to search through the letters and autobiographical writings of Hurston and Hughes while hoping to find explanations for their falling out over *Mule Bone,* but none of the explanations found there has proved satisfactory. I propose that critics have been looking at the wrong texts for answers, for Hurston and Hughes, themselves, were most likely unaware of the real reasons for their dispute over *Mule Bone*. The answers lie in the text of *Mule Bone* itself; there we can find evidence of the conflicting aesthetics of Hurston and Hughes that explain the controversy over *Mule Bone* and its poor critical reception.

The complicated nature of the dispute surrounding *Mule Bone* demands a complex critical approach to the study of the play. Therefore, my critical method to *Mule Bone* will combine literary history, formalism, and intertextuality. I will examine the play by placing the authors and the text in their historical context, by examining the critical reception of the production of the play, by formally analyzing the text, and by observing the play in relation to other works by the authors.

Left unfinished by the authors after their well-documented quarrel over the play, *Mule Bone* was edited for the 1991 Harper Collins publication, yet despite careful editing, the play remains unpolished[1] The three acts of the play are not balanced and are not well integrated.[2] Act one introduces us to the major characters and the major themes of the play. Action begins on the porch on Saturday afternoon in the midst of community activities. Men are playing checkers and cards, telling tales, and commenting on all that occurs around them. Gendered relationships and the political and religious dynamics of the town are central to act one and to the rest of the play. The love triangle of Daisy, Jim, and Dave takes center stage two-thirds of the way through the act, and act one ends with the arrest of Jim for hitting Dave in the head with a mule bone.

Act two is divided into two scenes, and the first one focuses almost solely on the women and children of the town discussing the imminent trial of Jim—which has quickly become a political platform from which Elder Simms attacks Joe Clarke's position as mayor. Scene two takes place inside the Baptist church where the Methodists and Baptists have chosen sides, with the Baptists championing Dave and the Methodists defending Jim. The discussion of law is important as is the religious reasoning used to defend each side of the dispute. It is clear that Jim and Dave's fight is simply a catalyst for the community split foreshadowed in act one. The Baptist Rev. Childers's eloquent argument based on the interpretation of Samson's slaying of the Philistines with the jaw bone of an ass leads to a sentence of banishment for Jim.

The community that dominated act two is absent from act three, which takes place on the railroad tracks just outside of town. Jim, having been banished, is contemplating his future when Daisy enters. She quickly reels him in again just before Dave enters. Both confess their love for Daisy, and a lying contest ensues. Jim wins the contest, and Daisy asks him to marry her. She rethinks, however, when she learns that he won't work for "her white folks" in order to support her, and she turns to Dave who also refuses to work. At the end of the play, Daisy leaves them both, and Dave and Jim return to town together in tempting anyone to try to enforce the banishment.

When *Mule Bone: A Comedy of Negro Life* was finally produced in 1991 at the Lincoln Center Theater, sixty years after it was written, it received reviews which were more negative than positive. To these reviewers, the modern audience was so far removed from the experience of the play itself that it was little more than an interesting page from the history books of Black American literature. The producers seem to have been aware from the beginning that *Mule Bone* would be problematic for modern audiences. When the play was first discussed by leading Black American literary critics, actors, playwrights, and scholars in 1988, even these experts in the field of Black literature, theater, and culture were uncomfortable with many aspects of the play. The drama was, therefore, revamped, toned down, and made more innocuous for the 1991 production. George Houston Bass, writer and executor of the Hughes estate, provided a new prologue and epilogue; Taj Mahal set Hughes' poems to blues music as a substitute for the traditional folk songs indicated by the authors; "the word 'nigger' was deleted from the dialogue as were all sexist allusions to women as chattel" (Pacheco 78); and Zora Neale Hurston appears as a character in the prologue assuring the audience that "the town is being observed through the 'spyglass of anthropology.' The play is folklore, not fact. So be it" (David Richards, 29).

In his *New York Times* review of the production, Frank Rich calls it "not even a scrupulously authentic representation of what Hughes and Hurston wrote, fragmented and problematic as their aborted collaboration was" (C1). Using images that call to mind the descriptions of "Brazzle's old yaller mule" itself (*Mule Bone* 53), Rich goes on to question the very intentions of the producers:

> This "Mule Bone" is at once so watered down and bloated by various emendations that one can never be entirely sure if Lincoln Center Theater is conscientiously trying to complete and resuscitate a lost, unfinished work or is merely picking its carcass to confer a classy literary pedigree on a broad, often bland quasi-musical seemingly pitched to a contemporary Broadway audience. (C1)

For this reason, Rich questions the relevance of *Mule Bone* for a modern audience. He says that "Perhaps even if [Hughes and Hurston] had completed their mission, *Mule Bone* would still seem as dated today as other ambitious American plays of its exact vintage" (C24.) David Richards, following the same lines, says, "Although it has

been fitted with a new prologue and epilogue by George Houston Bass and music by Taj Mahal and given an energetic staging by Michael Schultz, it remains very much a dramatic artifact-more viable today as sociology than as entertainment" (29). If, then, *Mule Bone* is simply a "dramatic artifact," why resurrect it for the Broadway audience of 1991?

The answer may lie not in the field of theater, but in the field of literary scholarship itself. The resurrection of *Mule Bone* has been the project of scholar Henry Louis Gates, Jr.,[3] who got help from writer George Houston Bass—the aim being not merely to make a lost text available for modern audiences (both literary and dramatic), but to help redefine the literary movement out of which this play comes. We can easily see this redefinition materializing as Patrick Pacheco, in his review "A Discovery Worth the Wait?", calls Hurston and Hughes the "royal couple of the Harlem Renaissance" (4). During the historical period of the Harlem Renaissance—roughly the 1920s and 1930s—Hurston and Hughes were certainly not the "royal couple." They were most often misunderstood and rebuked for their fascination with the "low" elements of Black American culture. Both received acclaim early in their careers but were pushed to the edge of the Harlem Renaissance inner circle during its height as they delved deeper into the folk. Hurston's "minstrelsy" use of folklore and Hughes's blues poetry made them outsiders in a movement which at the time was defined by Alain Locke, Jessie Fauset, Countee Cullen, and others of the "Talented Tenth."

Current literary scholarship, however, has redefined the Harlem Renaissance—privileging the folk of Hurston and Hughes over the "racial uplift" of the Talented Tenth. Yet, despite this reprivileging, it is the folk of *Mule Bone* which continues to make it a problematic work for critics and audiences.

It seems that the perplexing nature of *Mule Bone* has caused literary critics conveniently to avoid the play itself and its folk elements by focusing on the quarrel between Hurston and Hughes over the authorship and production of the play. This dispute is well-documented in the 1991 edition of *Mule Bone* edited by Bass and Gates, and therefore I will not discuss the specifics of it here. But the conflict is important for my discussion not in itself but in what it has become. In her brief review of the resurrected text and the various material published with it, Janet Ingraham points out that the "bitter authorship dispute which kept this important collaboration unpublished and unproduced for 60 years provides a sobering *context* for this spirited black Southern folk story" (emphasis mine).

For most critics, however, the dispute between Hurston and Hughes has not been merely a context for the play; it has become the dominant text, overshadowing that of *Mule Bone*. It seems that students and critics of Black American literature know much more about the controversy that surrounds the play than they do about the play itself. This point may be partially explained in that a text of the play was not available for the general public until very recently though a few historical accounts of the dispute were. The text was available to certain scholars, however, and while many of these scholars read manuscripts of the play, they still chose to focus their discussions on the quarrel instead of the play.[4] Hurston's biographer Robert Hemenway devotes a whole chapter of *Zora Neale Hurston: A Literary Biography* to "Mule Bone," beginning his discussion with and spending over half the chapter on the Hurston-Hughes collaboration and dispute. When he finally turns to the play itself, it is with the sigh, "The play is the thing, however" (176). But by paying at least partial attention to the play itself, Hemenway does what few other critics have done.[5]

From existing letters and accounts of various aspects of the quarrel, literary critics have pieced together the events and have hypothesized as to the reasons for the falling out of Hurston and Hughes over *Mule Bone*. The motivations behind the controversy are intertwined and complicated (Hemenway calls them "tangled, filled with bad behavior, shrill voices, and feigned innocence" [162]), but among the explanations given for the dispute are various mutual misunderstandings about the events that occurred, petty jealousy on the part of Hurston over typist Louise Thompson, and loyalty or lack thereof to shared patron, Mrs. Osgood Mason, better known as "Godmother"—none of which are very compelling or satisfying reasons[6] What is most interesting is that none of these conjectures places any reponsibility for the dispute in the play itself. It is important, then, to move from the *Mule Bone* controversy to the dreams and plans which Hughes and Hurston had for the work.

Literary and theater critics alike assign a shared motive to Hughes and Hurston in the creation and production of *Mule Bone*. They had wishfully discussed the ideal of a new Black theater for a while, and the complaint by Theresa Halburn of the Dramatists Guild to Hughes in early 1930 that all the plays about black people which the guild received were serious problem dramas—"Why didn't someone write a comedy—not a minstrel show, but a real comedy?" (Hemenway 162)—was the catalyst for their collaboration that became *Mule Bone: A Comedy of Negro Life*. In a blurb on the Lincoln Center production, *U.S. News & World Reports* says that Mule Bone is "a play that [Hughes and Hurston] hoped would hit Broadway and radically alter theatrical depictions of the ways black Americans lived and spoke"; Henry Louis Gates, Jr., in his discussion of the play in *The New York Times*, says that "Black folklore and Southern rural black vernacular English served as the foundation for what they hoped would be a truly new art form" (8).

Yet despite their shared general intentions for the play and for Black American theater itself, there is a fundamental difference in the way Hughes and Hurston conceptualize the folk, and this difference is evident in an examination of *Mule Bone* itself and its relation to other works by the authors. Because of the nature in which Hurston and

Hughes worked on *Mule Bone* together, mostly by dictating to typist Louise Thompson, it is impossible to assign credit for specific elements of the play to one or the other of them. There do appear to be two conflicting strains running through *Mule Bone*, however, and this more fundamental conflict may offer yet another explanation for the Mule Bone controversy and for the problematic nature of the play.[7]

In his manifesto "The Negro Artist and the Racial Mountain," Langston Hughes and makes clear what he believes the path of Black American literature and art should be. Lamenting what he sees as a desire for whiteness in Black American art, Hughes praises the masses:

> But then there are the low-down folks, the so-called common element, and they are the majority—may the Lord be praised! The people who have their nip of gin on Saturday nights and are not too important to themselves or the community, or too well fed, or too learned to watch the lazy world go round. They live on Seventh Street in Washington or State Street in Chicago and they do not particularly care whether they are like white folks or anybody else. Their joy runs, bang into ecstasy. Their religion soars to a shout. Work maybe a little today, rest a little tomorrow. Play awhile. Sing awhile. O, let's dance! These common people are not afraid of spirituals, as for a long time their more intellectual brethen were, and jazz is their child. They furnish a wealth of colorful, distinctive material for any artist because they still hold their own individuality in the face of American standardization. And perhaps these common people will give to the world its truly great Negro artist, the one who is not afraid to be himself. (259)

In his romantic description of the folk here, it is apparent that Hughes sees himself as an outsider in the world of the folk. Folk culture, then, is material to be used in art; it is a medium for artistic production.

In contrast, Zora Neale Hurston comes from the "common people," and per Hughes's definition, she may be the "truly great Negro artist." Hurston's experience of and her relationship with the folk are, therefore, very different from Hughes's. For Hurston, then, the folk is not merely a medium for art; it is art itself especially drama. In her essay "Characteristics of Negro Expression," written for Nancy Cunard's *Negro: An Anthology,* Hurston makes this clear. She begins the piece by declaring that the "Negro's universal mimicry is not so much a thing in itself as an evidence of something that permeates his entire self. And that thing is drama" (24). Drama is not simply an element of folk life it is folk life. To Hurston, "Every phase of Negro life is highly dramatized. No matter how joyful or how sad the case there is sufficient poise for drama. Everything is acted out. Unconsciously for the most part of course. There is an impromptu ceremony always ready for every hour of life. No little moment passes unadorned" (24). Her new Black American theater, therefore, would not utilize folk culture; it would be folk culture.[8]

It is the distinction between Hurston and Hughes's visions of how to use folk culture that becomes evident when we examine the critical reception of the 1991 Lincoln Center production of *Mule Bone*—particularly in the discussion of plot and stereotyping. Addressing what he sees as a lack of plot and an excessive amount of storytelling, David Richards says that the play "checks in at more than two hours, when 30 minutes would do just fine" (5).[9] He believes that "it's just not a very good play" and seems to base his argument on what he sees as the problematics of the plot.[10] Richards concludes by saying that

> Simple as it is, the plot is left unattended for great stretches at a time, while the townsfolk devote themselves to gossip and neighborly insult. Any 15 minutes of this rural slice of life tells you as much as the whole. Fussing and feuding is, after all, fussing and feuding. The characters—henpecked husband, domineering spouse, sanctimonious preacher, dim-witted sheriff—are overly familiar types by now. (29)

Richards's remarks are founded on a traditional definition of theater, as one might expect, and he, therefore, defines the plot very specifically as the love triangle of Daisy, Jim, and Dave. For him, then, the community activities of storytelling, lying, and feuding are simply reduced to a rural slice of life" of which a small taste will do just as well as a whole piece. He fails to see the subtlety of what is occurring on the porch and in the church as a plot in itself.

Long before Daisy, Jim, and Dave appear in Act one, the major themes of *Mule Bone* have been introduced. The people sitting on and around the porch—men, women, and children—discuss the relationships of men and women, the religious dispute of the Methodists and the Baptists, and the political rivalry of Mayor Clarke and Elder Simms. Simms criticizes the way in which Clarke has been running the town and makes his ambitions clear by saying, "Well, there ain't no sense in no one man stayin' Mayor all the time." Clarke replies, "Well it's my town and I can be mayor jus' as long as I want to. It was me that put this town on the map" (77). Later during the trial, Jim realizes that the dispute is no longer about his hitting Dave; it has become a religious and political war, and they are simply pawns. Exasperated, he laments, "You niggers just tryin to get us messed up on some kind o' mess" (119). Clarke, a Methodist like Simms, establishes the Baptist chuch as the court site and sides with the Baptists in the community fight in order to protect his position. Similarly, in "The Bone of Contention," the short story on which *Mule Bone* is based, the narrator explains that Jim and Dave and their dispute were unimportant: "It was evident to the simplest person in the village long before three o'clock that this was to be a religious and political fight" (33).

Turning again to the original story on which the play was based, we see that Daisy, the "plump, dark and sexy, . . . fickle" (*Mule Bone* 45) woman of *Mule Bone*, does not exist. The dispute between Jim and Dave in "The Bone of Contention" is over a turkey, which each man claims to have shot. We learn from various sources that the addition of Daisy as "the bone of contention" was the invention of Hughes and was not a welcome addition in the eyes of Hurston.[11] Ruthe Sheffey emphasizes the importance of

this aspect of the play by pointing out that when Hurston submitted the play for copyright in her own name, "she had reinserted the turkey as an object of contention instead of the girl, a matter of great moment to her" (219).

The precarious place of Daisy in *Mule Bone* is central to Sheffey's argument, and she makes much more of Hurston's resistance to Daisy than other critics have. To Sheffey, Daisy and what she represents is a viable explanation for the dispute between Hughes and Hurston over the play. She champions Hurston's cause, declaring that

> by insisting on dropping the fight for Daisy's favor as the mainspring of the play, Hurston attempted heroically to resist the subtle mythology which placed Black women in the mold of Madonna or whore and which cast her in a position of powerlessness. The debates about the play show Hurston's insistence on female personhood, only later to be strongly affirmed in Janie Crawford in *Their Eyes Were Watching God*. (222-23)

Although her argument is interesting, it perhaps and too easily uses Hughes as a scapegoat for the play's failure.[12]

Sheffey's argument based on Hurston's strong dislike for Daisy and the stereotypes she perpetuates is undercut when we realize that Hurston returned to Daisy later in her writing career. In *Their Eyes Were Watching God*, Daisy Blunt[13] is a central figure in the courtship ritual which is performed on the porch of Jody Stark's store. Her entrance onto the scene is remarkably similar in kind to her entrance in *Mule Bone* both emphasizing her sexuality. In *Mule Bone* she enters assertively, knowing she will be the center of attention and putting Mayor Clarke "in de mind of . . . a great big mango . . . a sweet smell, you know, with a strong flavor, but not something you could mash up like a strawberry. Something with a body to it" (60). Similarly, in *Their Eyes Were Watching God*,

> Daisy is walking a drum tune. You can almost hear it by looking at the way she walks. She is black and she knows that white clothes look good on her, so she wears them for dress up. She's got those big black eyes with plenty shiny white in them that makes them shine like brand new money and she knows what God gave women eyelashes for, too. Her hair is not what you might call straight. It's negro hair, but it's got a kind of white flavor. Like the piece of string out of a ham. It's not ham at all, but it's been around ham and got the flavor. It was spread down thick and heavy over her shoulders and looked just right under a big white hat. (63-4)

I agree with Sheffey that Hurston's resistance to making Daisy the center of Jim and Dave's dispute is vitally important, although I disagree with her about the grounds on which Hurston so vehemently objected to Daisy. Hurston may well have objected to the stereotypical image of black womanhood manifested in Daisy, but that concern was secondary to her concern about the folk. The introduction of a love plot with Daisy at the center forces the folk community into the background[14]—an addition which alters the entire nature of the play and of the new Black American theater envisioned by Hurston. For Hughes the creation of Daisy and the love triangle is not problematic; it is a way of utilizing the folk in producing Black American drama. Hurston's conceptualization of plot, as I have described it, is much freer; Hughes's more conventional.[15]

When Hurston and Hughes fell out and *Mule Bone* was not produced, Hurston rewrote the courship scene from the play into her novel *Their Eyes Were Watching God.* As it appears she would have rather done in the play, she subordinates the courtship ritual to the interaction of the community on the porch. Just as in the play the argument is "over Daisy . . . over somethin' or nother o' no importance . . ." (127), in the short story, "the assault and the gobbler were unimportant" (33). Like the turkey, the love plot is only a device through which the community can play. She makes it clear in *Their Eyes* that "They know it's not courtship. It's acting-out courtship and everybody is in the play" (63). The community as a whole is central. Daisy, Jim, and Dave are at the same time center and not-center; they are the means to the plot but not the plot itself.[16]

Running through *Mule Bone*, then, there are two plots or levels of action. This can be easily seen in the alternating nature of scenes and actors. Act one begins on the porch in the midst of the Saturday afternoon lying sessions. Although Daisy appears relatively early in the act so that the men on the porch can discuss her and prepare for the entry of Jim and David, these rivals for her affection do not appear until two-thirds of the way through the first act. Daisy does not play a role in act two at all—except to be an object of discussion. Jim and Dave actually appear as little more than props during the trial—what began as their quarrel has become the battle of the community, and as a result, Jim and Dave are ignored for the most part. Act three, reversing what has occurred in act two, focuses solely on the love triangle, although the community has a role as a strong and silent (actually not so silent at the very beginning of the act as they chase Jim out of town) force. It is this alternating and intertwined plot—Hughes's love plot and Hurston's community plot—which causes confusion and becomes problematic for audiences and critics. Because the authors could not reconcile this important issue in the play, readers and viewers are left to struggle through it.

As attention in the play is directed away from the interaction of the members of the Eatonville community toward Daisy and the love plot, subversive and challenging elements of *Mule Bone* are dismissed, without a second glance, as stereotypes. It is interesting that a work which was originally planned in an attempt to "liberate the stage of its time of the black stereotypes which were then popular—the cavorting 'darkies' of minstrel shows, vaudeville and musical reviews (Pacheco 4) would be labeled as a play that perpetuates stereotypes of Black Americans. In his review, David Richards says that "Because of the unabashed country dialect and the broad characterizations, *Mule Bone* has long been viewed in

some quarters as perpetuating noxious stereotypes" (29). The changes which were made in the play for its 1991 production—deletion of certain words and references, the disclaimer of the Zora character, etc.—speak to this very issue. There was a real fear on the part of the producers that some aspects of the play "might now appear offensive to blacks and whites alike" (Pacheco 4).[17]

In a *New York Times* article, Henry Louis Gates, Jr., asks, "Why would anyone believe there are still aspects of black culture that should be hidden because they are somehow 'embarrassing'?" He says that "sixty years after *Mule Bone* was written, many black Americans still feel that their precarious political and social condition within American society warrants a guarded attitude toward the way images of their culture are projected" (5). Instead of a stereotype, Gates believes that "*Mule Bone* is a revelation of life 'behind the veil' . . . It portays what black people say and think and feel—when no white people are around—in a highly metaphorical and densely lyrical language" (5).

If Hurston and Hughes were in conflict over certain aspects of *Mule Bone,* it was certainly not in what I shall call the blues elements of the play. It is in these blues moments that *Mule Bone* invokes stereotypical images deliberately in order to subvert them. In a deviation from the original folk music planned for the play, Taj Mahal was asked to write the score for the 1991 production of *Mule Bone,* and he chose to set Hughes' poetry to the blues. Patrick Pacheco reports that Mahal "saw the fusion between African-American storytelling and the blues in both Hughes' poetry and the play." For Mahal, "the art of laughter was one of the black folk's gifts to American culture. But, it's the art of laughing to keep from crying. That's what the blues is about too" (79).

It is the art of the blues that gets lost in the confusion over plot in *Mule Bone*. In his poem "Minstrel Man," Langston Hughes juxtaposes the image of the happy minstrel with the subversion of the blues in a manner that is reminiscent of Paul Laurence Dunbar's "We Wear the Mask":

> Because my mouth
> Is wide with laughter
> You do not hear
> My inner cry.
> Because my feet
> Are gay with dancing
> You do not know
> I die.

If we care to listen, we are made painfully aware throughout *Mule Bone* of the tragedy and despair that the laughter and comedy of the store front wards off.[18]

In establishing the setting for Act one, Hughes and Hurston take pains to describe the mood of the Saturday afternoon around the store. Although Saturday is a special day of relaxation in American society generally, the relaxation takes on added dimensions for the rural Black

American community. Saturday afternoon is a day away from work, away from white bosses; it is, as Gates suggests, a time to reveal what is "behind the veil." Despite the comfortable nature of the porch, however, reminders of "reality" intrude.[19] One of the first images we are confronted with is a scene which reappears almost identically in *Their Eyes Were Watching God.* Mrs. Jake Roberts comes into the store with *"her professional whine"* and begs mayor and store owner Joe Clarke for food for herself and her children. While she could be dismissed as a source of laughter for the porch with her ritualistic begging, she needs to be seen as a reminder of a pressing problem in the rural community—hunger. While she is a source of entertainment, she also suggests the reality which looms just off the porch steps.

While whites are notably absent from the cast of *Mule Bone*, their oppressive presence in the lives of Eatonville's all-black community is apparent throughout the play. Jim and Dave play for the white folks in Maitland, and Daisy is a domestic servant for a white family that has taken her to the North for a period of time. For Jim and Dave Saturday away from the white folks is especially important. Their song and dance is particularly exuberant because, as Jim tells Daisy, we'se been playin' for the white folks all week. We'se playin' for the colored now" (85).[20]

Most sobering of all of the images of white folks in the play is the brief mention of the lynching of Jim's father. Hambo interrupts the interesting and amusing discussion of "law" with the statement, "We never drove off his pappy. De white folks took an' hung him for killin' dat man in Kissimmee for nothin'" (133). This interjection serves not only as a shocking reality check, but as commentary on the whole debate over the white folks' law. Just as the argument between Mayor Clarke and Rev. Simms over building a jail forces us to question the nature of crime and punishment, the mention of the lynching awakens us to the lawlessness of the law. Yet the controlling image of subversion in *Mule Bone* is work itself—connecting "Brazzle's old yaller mule," the Saturday afteroon lying sessions, the women's household responsibilities, and the hard labor of slavery. These images of work are tied most closely to the characters Jim and Dave.[21]

Although critics have consistently defined Daisy as a stereotypical figure, few have said the same about dancer Dave Carter and Guitarist Jim Weston, the two-man song and dance team vying for Daisy's affections. Dave is described in the list of characters as a "soft, happy-go-lucky character, slightly dumb and unable to talk rapidly and wittily," Jim as "slightly arrogant, aggressive, somewhat self-important, ready with his tongue" (45). From these descriptions it would appear that they would be just as open to the criticism of stereotypes, but possibly because they appear in more of the play than she does, and because Daisy is the object of their gaze, they have avoided such criticism.

Jim and Dave refuse to work jobs of traditional menial labor, not because they are "shiftless and lazy," but because

of the implications of that work. Shortly after they begin playing for the folks on the store porch and are castigated for never working, Jim declares, "Some folks think you ain't workin' lessen you smellin' a mule. Think you gotta be beatin' a man to his barn every mornin'" (85). As we know the mule, especially for Hurston, is a complicated image, but in this case, we can certainly relate it to the manual labor and abuse of slavery. Taking the white folks' money for playing and dancing for them is a way for Dave and Jim to resist the existing power structures. Daisy's demand that the man who marries her must come to work for "her white folks" as a yard man is completely unacceptable to Jim and Dave. She unwittingly brings the rivals back together and returns them to the community as she returns to "her white folks" alone.[22]

Despite—and maybe because of—these blues elements of the play, *Mule Bone* is a divided work confusing and complicated for audiences, readers, and scholars. In describing the tragicomic elements of Hughes' work, R. Baxter Miller has said that "the veneer of humor . . . has deceived the reader again and again, for comedy almost invariably coexists with the deeper pathos that threatens and ennobles it" (100). This certainly applies to *Mule Bone,* for in subtitling their play *A Comedy of Negro Life,* Hurston and Hughes deceived their audience and left them unprepared for what they would face in the play. The tragedy which waits just off the front steps of the general store and which constantly threatens to invade the comic world transforms *Mule Bone* into "A Tragicomedy of Negro Life."

The misnaming of *Mule Bone* by Hurston and Hughes is important for it speaks directly to the inability of audiences to connect with what is happening on stage, to which reviews of the 1991 production have drawn attention. In "Black Drama and Its Audience," Helene Keyssar points out that "the critic's goal must be to reveal not only the dramatic situation described but also the dramatic situation that occurs between the play and the audience. At the core of what a play means is not simply what it is about or what it says, but also what it does" (14). For it Keyssar, what a play can do is dependent upon the personal investment of the audience in what is happening on the stage-a play "demands a recognition in public of the worlds it presents" (2) The choice of the Lincoln Center Theatre producers of *Mule Bone* to create a Zora character and have her declare that the play is simply an anthropological study of folkflore does exactly what Keyssar warns against; it distances the audience from what occurs on stage, destroying "the dramatic situation that occurs between the play and the audience." The play becomes simply the recovery of an historical moment which will not and can not have any real influence on the audience; the members of the audience are allowed to be observers who can remain comfortably detached. They are not made to feel the tragedy just under the surface of the comedy of *Mule Bone*.

From collaboration to production, then, *Mule Bone* continues to be a problematic play. The separate visions of

Hughes and Hurston do not cease to wage war on each other, forcing the play to operate on different levels, causing confusion and misunderstanding. The folk and the blues cannot save it. *Mule Bone* will remain as Hurston and Hughes left it, an interesting work to study for all its possibilities but a difficult work to stage in all its realities.

Notes

1. The unpolished nature of the play is most clearly evident in the inconsistent naming of characters throughout *Mule Bone*. Daisy Taylor is called Daisy Blunt at certain points, and her mother is Mrs. Blunt throughout the play. She is apparently unrelated to Mrs. Taylor. When Hurston reused some of the elements from *Mule Bone* for *Their Eyes Were Watching God,* she renamed Daisy Taylor as Daisy Blunt, thus clearing up the inconsistency.

2. This may be explained by the way in which Hurston and Hughes worked on the play together. It is clear that they wrote most of acts one and three together but that Hurston may have written the majority of act two by herself.

3. In one of the only positive reviews of the Lincoln Center production of *Mule Bone,* which begins "Exuberance is busting out all over the stage," John Beaufort says that "Mr. Gates has performed a signal service to the cause of African-American theater and, more immediately, for the delight of Broadway audiences." Seeing the play as a quaint artifact, it seems, Beaufort praises *Mule Bone* not for its dramatic merits but because it "occupies a unique place in the history of African-American theater."

4. In his discussion of Hurston as a dramatist, Warren Carson makes it clear that the play is simply not as interesting as the dispute which surrounds it: "The account of *Mule Bone* is certainly an interesting one, not so much from the standpoint of the play itself as from the controversy that it sparked between Hurston and Hughes" (122).

5. Hemenway's colleague, Arnold Rampersad, the Hughes biographer, undertakes no such project. He discusses only the *Mule Bone* dispute as it relates to Hughes's life.

6. Maybe it is the unsatisfactory nature of these explanations for the dispute which cause critics to return again and again to the quarrel instead of the play.

7. Ruthe T. Sheffey is one of the only other scholars to discuss the different visions of the authors. She polarizes the perspectives of Hughes and Hurston along the lines of gender representation, and as we would expect from the founder of the Zora Neale Hurston Society and the editor of the *Zora Neale Hurston Forum,* she champions Hurston's cause, basically denouncing Hughes as a sexist. I will return to Sheffey and the issue of gender stereotyping later.

8. In his introduction to *Mule Bone,* Henry Louis Gates, Jr., states that "[i]n April 1928, [Hurston] shared with Hughes her plans for a culturally authentic African-American theatre, one constructed upon a foundation of the black vernacular: 'Did I tell you before I left about the new, the *real* Negro theatre I plan? Well, I shall, or rather we shall act out the folk tales, however short, with the abrupt angularity and naivete of the primitive 'bama Nigger. Quote that with native settings. What do you think? . . . I know it is going to be *glorious!* A really new departure in the drama" ' (9).

9. Similarly, Edith Oliver, who is pleased with the folk elements of the play but confused about the plot, complains that "much as I enjoyed the talk and the goings on, I couldn't track any play at all" (82).

10. Richards prefaces his synopsis of the play with the comment. "The plot—when 'Mule Bone' gets around to it—. . ." (29)

11. Hemenway tells us that "the turkey was dropped (over Hurston's objections) and a girl made the root of the argument" (163).

12. Sheffey polarizes Hurston and Hughes as writers and as woman and man, placing blame squarely on the shoulders of Hughes. She says, "The separate revisions of 'Mule Bone' done by Zora reveal her stubbornly resisting putting yet another black sensuous woman on stage as a vaudeville curiosity whose sexual favors are easily dispensed. On the contrary, Hughes' revisions in the character of Daisy Blunt and in the addition of Bootsie Putts reinforce the erotic/exotic fantasies about Black women, the lust and sensuality added as obvious thrill-seeking dramatic devices" (220).

13. She is Daisy Taylor in *Mule Bone.*

14. This point is made quite evident when we consider the reviews of the 1991 production I have previously mentioned which subordinate the community to the love triangle of Daisy, Jim, and Dave and thus are upset when the "plot" is not attended to as it should be.

15. In "Crayon Enlargements of Life," Robert Hemenway makes clear the centrality of community life in Hurston's work. He says, "When Hurston writes of Eatonville, the store porch is all-important. It is the center of the community, the totem representing black cultural tradition; it is where the values of the group are manifested in verbal behavior. The store porch, in Zora's language, is 'the center of the world.' To describe the porch's activities she often uses the phrase 'crayon enlargments of life'—When the people sat around on the porch and passed around the pictures of their thoughts for the others to look at and see, it was nice. The fact that the thought pictures were always crayon enlargements of life made it even nicer to listen to'" (78).

16. The place of the love plot as center and not center is most clearly seen in Daisy's role in the play. As the central cause of Jim and Dave's fight, Daisy is the center of the love plot, and her place (and the place of the love plot) is obvious in the stage directions at the end of act one: *"DAISY stands alone, unnoticed in the center of the stage"* (99).

17. This is interesting in that Ruthe Sheffey sees the inclusion of Daisy and the primitive sexualism

which surrounds her as a deliberate move on Hughes's part to include "enough white fantasies about Afro-Americans to make the play a commercial success" (224). Commenting on Hurston's "The Guilded Six-Bits," Gayl Jones makes an observation which is particularly important to the discussion of the audience. In this story, "we are inside rather than outside the black community and there is not the same double-conscious concern with an exclusive white audience" (147). By extension, we could say the same thing about "The Bone of Contention" and could hypothesize about the possibilities of a more unified *Mule Bone*.

18. Eleanor Traylor defines this as "the double blade of humor which in Afro-American tradition carves the smile as it spears the tear" (57).

19. As Darwin Turner described another of Hughes's plays, "shadows of a troubled world appear at the edge of the gay and the comic" (142)

20. Oceola Jones, the main character in Hughes' "The Blues I'm Playing," experiences a similar relief when she returns to playing jazz for Harlem house parties after studying classical piano and playing for her white patron, Mrs. Ellsworth.

21. Eleanor Traylor would define Jim and Dave as blues heroes—"We know that the blues hero puts on a particular vestment. While the tragic hero dresses in the blood-stained cloak of nobility, destined for certain defeat, and while the comic hero wears the mantle of ordinary humanity, muddling in pedestrian concerns, the blues hero puts on the cloak of irony which shields him not from the wound of nobility nor from the foibles of the ordinary, but prepares him for the task of endurance which is his ordeal" (60).

22. Ruthe Sheffey takes issue with this problematic ending, describing the final scene as one of "joyous male bonding and female exclusion, the two men starting their music up, singing together as friends, and starting happily back to town" (227). Yet, Daisy seems to be excluded not because she is a woman but because she aligns herself with "her white folks"—choosing stability over resistance.

Works Cited

Beaufort, John. "'Mule Bone' Debuts After 60 Years." *The Christian Science Monitor* 26 Feb. 1991: 13.

Gates, Henry Louis, Jr., Introduction. "A Tragedy of Negro Life." *Mule Bone: A Comedy of Negro Life.* Eds. George Houston Bass and Hentry Louis Gates, Jr., New York: Harper Collins, 1991. 5-24.

————."Why the 'Mule Bone' Debate Goes On." *The New York Times* 10 Feb. 1991, sec. 2: 5,8.

Hemenway, Robert E. *Zora Neale Hurston: A Literary Biography.* 1977.

Hughes, Langston. "Black Dancers." *The Crisis* 40.5 (Sept 1930): 110.

————."The Blues I'm Playing." *The Ways of White Folks.* New York: Knopf, 1933. 96-120.

————".Minstrel Man." *The Crisis* 31.2 (Dec. 1925): 66-67.

————".My People." *The Crisis* 24.2 (June 1922): 72.

————".The Negro Artist and the Racial Mountain." *Black Expression: Essays by and About Black Americans in the Creative Arts.* Eds. Houston A. Baker, Jr., and Patricia Redmond. Chicago: U of Chicago Press, 1989. 258-63.

Hughes, Langston and Zora Neale Hurston. *Mule Bone: A Comedy of Negro Life.* 1931. Eds. George Houston Bass and Henry Louis Gates, Jr., New York: Harper Collins, 1991. 161-84; 189-209.

Hurston, Zora Neale. "The Bone of Contention." *Mule Bone: A Comedy of Negro Life.* Eds. George Houston Bass and Henry Louis Gates, Jr., New York: Harper Collins, 1991. 25-39.

————."Characteristics of Negro Expression." *Negro: An Anthology.* Ed. and coll. Nancy Cunard. 1934. Ed. and abr. Hugh Ford. New York: Frederick Ungar. 1970. 24-37.

————.*Their Eyes Were Watching God.* 1937. New York: Harper & Row, 1990.

Ingraham, Janet. Rev. of *Mule Bone: A Comedy of Negro Life,* by Langston Hughes and Zora Hurston. *Library Journal* 116.2 (Feb. 1, 1991): 78.

Jones, Gayl. "Breaking Out of the Conventions of Dialect." *Zora Neale Hurston: Critical Perspectives Past and Present.* Eds. Henry Louis Gates, Jr., and K. A. Appiah. New York: Amistad, 1993. 141-53.

Keyssar, Helene. "Black Drama and Its Audience: Evolutions and Revolutions." *The Curtain and the Veil: Strategies in Black Drama.* New York: Burt Franklin & Co., 1981. 1-18.

Miller, R. Baxter. "'I Heard Ma Rainey': The Tragicomic Imagination." *The Art and Imagination of Langston Hughes.* Lexington: University Press of Kentucky, 1989. 99-118.

Oliver, Edith. Rev. of *Mule Bone: A Comedy of Negro Life,* by Langston Hughes and Zora Neale Hurston. *The New Yorker* 67.1 (Feb. 25, 1991): 82.

Pacheco, Patrick. "A Discovery Worth the Wait?" *Los Angeles Times* 24 Feb. 1991, Calendar: 4, 78-9.

Rampersad, Arnold. *The Life of Langston Hughes.* Vol 1. 1986.

Rich, Frank. "A Difficult Birth for 'Mule Bone.'" *The New York Times* 15 Feb. 1991: C1, 24.

Richards, David. "An English Tea and a Folk Tale." *The New York Times* 24 Feb. 1991, sec. 2: 5, 29.

Sheffey, Ruthe T. "Zora Hurston and Langston Hughes's 'Mule Bone': An Authentic Folk Comedy and the Compromised Tradition." *Trajectory: Fueling the Future and Preserving the African-American Literary Past.* Baltimore: Morgan State University Press, 1989. 211-31.

Traylor, Eleanor W. "Two Afro-American Contributions to Dramatic Form." *The Theater of Black Americans: A Collection of Critical Essays.* Ed. Errol Hill. Vol. 1. Englewood Cliffs, NJ: Prentice-Hall, Inc., 1980. 45-60.

Turner, Darwin T. "Langston Hughes as Playwright." *The Theater of Black Americans: A Collection of Critical Essays.* Ed. Errol Hill. Vol. 1 Englewood Cliffs, NJ: Prentice-Hall, Inc., 1980. 136-47.

COLOR STRUCK

CRITICAL COMMENTARY

H. Lin Classon (essay date 1997)

SOURCE: "Re-evaluating *Color Struck:* Zora Neale Hurston and the Issue of Colorism," in *Theatre Studies*, Vol. 42, 1997, pp. 5-18.

[*In the following essay, Classon probes* Color Struck *as a work of social criticism and as the "tragedy of a dark-skinned woman." Additionally, Classon emphasizes the importance of this relatively neglected play to an understanding of Hurston's life and work.*]

Zora Neale Hurston was born in Eatonville, Florida, an all-Black community, in 1891.[1] While in New York attending Barnard College and studying anthropology under Franz Boas, she made significant contributions to the Harlem Renaissance. "From the 1930s through the 1960s, Hurston was the most prolific and accomplished black woman writer in America."[2] In spite of her historic accomplishments, Hurston spent her last years unnoticed and died in obscurity in 1960. It was not until the 1970s, when writers such as Alice Walker made a conscious effort to restore Hurston's status as the 'foremother' of African American literature, that Hurston was awarded the attention she deserved.[3] Since then Hurston's work has inspired many African American writers and feminist thinkers. Presently, she is best known to the general public as the author of the novel, *Their Eyes Were Watching God* (1937). In recent years, there seems to be a "Zora fever," as manifested in the journals, conferences, and festivals devoted to her. Yet, despite the enthusiasm for rediscovering everything written by Hurston, one of her earlier works, the play *Color Struck*, remains neglected.

In 1925, Hurston wrote *Color Struck* for *Opportunity*'s Literary Contest. Both the play and Hurston's short story, *Spunk,* were awarded second prize. These awards brought Hurston to the attention of the most important and promising Black literary talents of the Harlem Renaissance. She seized the opportunity and "jump(ed) at the sun" as her mother had encouraged her. Eager to remind people of her accomplishment, she walked into the party following the *Opportunity* Award Dinner, flung her "long, bright-colored scarf" around her neck, and dramatically called out, "Ca-laaaah struuuck."[4] However, despite this flamboyant entrance and Alice Walker's subsequent retelling of this antic of Hurston's, *Color Struck,* has never gained much

of Hurston's biographers' or critics' attention. Until today, references to the play in the bibliographies and biographies of Hurston amount to little more than this anecdote of her eccentricity. For example, Robert Hemenway, discusses *Color Struck* in only one paragraph; he labels it "an apprentice work" and then devotes his attention to her other literary works.[5] Warren J. Carson, one of the few scholars who has written about *Color Struck*, argues that her plays have not generated enough critical attention, "particularly when we consider that it was a play that brought her to the attention of Harlem Renaissance circles, and when we consider her life-long interest in drama and the stage."[6] As a theatrical debut, *Color Struck* has been judged amateurish in comparison to Hurston's short story, *Sweat,* written at approximately the same time. Hemenway hails *Sweat* as "remarkable," and "her best fiction of the period."[7] Yet the play deserves greater scholarly scrutiny if one seeks to reconstruct a more complete image of Hurston. I intend to re-evaluate *Color Struck* through a study of the content and structure of the play, the techniques employed by the dramatist, and the social and cultural significance of the play itself. I also wish to unravel some of the mystifying contradictions in Hurston's personalities by looking at Hurston's choice of topic, colorism, against the background of 1920s' Harlem, and her use of "camouflage" as a survival tactic in the male-dominated Harlem Renaissance.[8] Lastly, by restoring *Color Struck* to our memory of Hurston, I wish to argue for Hurston's place as a pioneer in African American drama of social commentary.

Color Struck: A Play in Four Scenes, is set in the first decade of this century. It opens with a boisterous scene on a Jim Crow coach in which a group of black people gaily board the train bound for St. Augustine for a cakewalk contest. Within this group are John and Emmaline, the most promising contestants. On their journey Emma accuses John of paying 'unwarranted' attention to every light-skinned girl he meets, especially Effie, who is also on the train. In Scene Two Hurston transports the audience to the anteroom to the dance hall where the contestants are feasting on home-made pies and fried chicken and amusing themselves before the contest. Emma's jealousy and suspicion strike again when she sees John with Effie. Emma asks John to quit the contest and go home with her. John adamantly refuses and enters the dance hall alone, leaving Emma behind. In the next scene (the cakewalk scene), John and his new partner, Effie, win the contest. Emma remains alone on stage after the crowd carries John and Effie away in triumph. Scene Three, the final scene, takes place twenty years later. John finally finds Emma again and asks her to marry him. In the course of their reunion Emma misconstrues John's efforts to comfort her ill, light-skinned daughter and rebukes him. Frustrated and angered by Emma's obsession with skin color, John leaves. During the delay resulting from this misunderstanding, Emma's daughter dies for lack of medical care.

On the surface, the play is divided into two parts: the comic and festive drama of the first two scenes, in which Hurston emphasizes "authentic" dialects and portrayals of the folk, and the last scene which has greater similarities to the style of genteel writers, such as Angelina Grimke and Georgia Douglas Johnson. The episodic structure was a novel practice at a time when most one-act plays followed a straight plot line from the beginning to the end. The resulting montage-like effect of *Color Struck* may have resulted from Hurston's inexperience as a playwright, but it may well have been a deliberate choice. Regardless, she should receive credit for experimenting with a new form and attempting to offer American theatre something untraditional. In addition, the juxtaposition of the comic and tragic elements of this play can be viewed as an attempt to unite folk drama and social protest plays. Hurston depicted the social phenomenon of color consciousness together with folk music and dance. This amalgamation may have been a covert challenge to the limited function of art advocated by prominent leaders of the Harlem Renaissance.

Hurston's attention to social issues has been overlooked by scholars who depict *Color Struck* "not a very effective drama" or criticize the play for its loosely connected structure.[9] These scholars are only partially correct. The play appears loosely connected and ineffective when it is only read. But we have every reason to believe that Hurston did not write this play merely for the pleasure of reading; she expected the play to be produced. Hurston was introduced to theatre at an early age; while a teenager, she worked as a wardrobe girl in a Gilbert and Sullivan repertory company. Moreover, she attended Howard University when the Howard Players was flourishing. Alain Locke, who was responsible for introducing Hurston to the chief editor of *Opportunity* in 1925, was one of the Players most enthusiastic supporters. Later, she was admitted into *Stylus,* the campus literary club formed by Locke and Montgomery Gregory, organizer and director of the Howard Players.[10] Throughout her life, she showed great interest in having her plays produced,[11] and even thought of "redoing the railroad coach scene from her play *Color Struck*.[12] In theatrical production, music, light, choreographic movement, and scenery would help to to integrate the themes of the play into a single entity. *Color Struck* was already composed with the music and dance elements needed to integrate the first three scenes and compensate for the lack of dialogue in Scene Three. The greatest challenge is the ending, which seems to be of a different style than the previous scenes. Critics have ultimately argued that the mixture of comic and tragic elements seems to bring confusion, hinder a full development of the scenes, and thus weaken the force of the play.[13]

If the reader avoids the initial temptation to type this work as a hybrid folk drama, the play actually displays great dramatic effect. In every scene Hurston skillfully mixes the earthy festival spirit with the journey toward Emma's tragic downfall. The first scene opens with witty wordplay between the passengers on board. The excitement this generates is further heightened by the music and dancing. The argument between John and Emma is soon resolved and a moment of intimacy is shared between them. But by the curtain's fall Emma and John are alone on stage, and the scene ends on Emma's ominous line, "Just for myself alone is the only way I know how to love."[14] The next scene also starts with a festival atmosphere. People around John and Emma are enjoying themselves, but against the background of the jubilant dance hall, Emma and John have another vehement quarrel. Hurston creates an atmosphere in which, in the midst of a bright and joyful space, a cloud of darkness encompasses the two of them. Again, the scene ends when everyone leaves for the party; only this time Emma, bitter and sorrowful, is left alone on stage. Scene Three is the stunning cakewalk scene. The atmosphere is gay, boisterous, and almost frantic. Lynda Marion Hill describes a cakewalk dance as "a precursor to chorus-line dancing in musical theatre. A high-kicking movement, half strolling, half prancing . . . [in which] the spotlight is on music . . . and the spectacular bowing, petticoat flinging, silk hat-tipping, graceful gesturing, precision strutting and parading, singing hand-clapping accompaniment."[15] Emma, in contrast to the public celebration, is rendered wordless. The first part of the play then ends in a note of frenzied excitement when Effie and John are carried away in triumph by the cheering crowd, which obscures Emma from the view of the audience. Yet the silent figure of Emma still looms over the dance hall, foreshadowing a fall after this climactic moment. With the sounds of exhilaration still ringing in the ears of the audience, the fate of Emma and John remains unresolved. In Scene Four, the audience discovers Emma sitting alone in a gloomy shack. According to the stage directions, the stage is dark (98); the foreboding darkness from previous scenes has accumulated and is now materialized on stage. The scene presents an astonishing contrast to the festivity of the previous moment, and at the same time an inevitable denouement following the crescendo of Emma's sorrow, anger and frustration. Instead of indicating an ineffective drama, this ending, with thoughtful direction, can impress upon the audience the destructive force of colorism and racism.

Moreover, as I have stated previously, Hurston's effort to combine a representation of the "authentic" folk and an implicit critique of colorism may have been a covert challenge to the heated debates between leaders of the Harlem Renaissance over the function of art. The two literary giants of the Harlem Renaissance, W. E. B. Du Bois and Alain Locke, pointed to two distinct directions for the artistic output of the New Negro. Alain Locke advocated "Art for Art's Sake." He rejected "overt propaganda and 'racial rhetoric' for the most part as obstacles to literary excellence and universal acceptance."[16] By contrast, Du Bois made clear his objection to Locke's proposal when he proclaimed, "I stand in utter shamelessness and say that whatever art I have for writing has been used always for propaganda for gaining the right of black folk to love and enjoy. I do not care a damn for any art that is not used for propaganda."[17] Although the two men seldom acknowledged the similarities in their philosophies, Locke included Du Bois' article of social protest, "The Negro Mind Reaches Out," in his era-defining anthology, *The New*

Negro, and Du Bois also sided with Locke in the promotion of Negro folk art, especially in theatre. Hurston accepted their guidance and their rhetoric with some suspicion. She recognized the barrier between the two views to be superficial, while many scholars of the Harlem Renaissance still fail to do so. The artificial divisions between colors in *Color Struck* physicalizes and reflects the superficiality of this barrier. Furthermore, I contend that, when read with an awareness of *marasa* consciousness, Hurston's work can be seen as a challenge to the artificial binaries between art and politics. Vèvè A. Clark has argued that this *marasa* consciousness can be used to interpret diasporic African literature. According to Clark, "*Marasa* is a mythical theory of textual relationships based on the Haitian Vodoun sign for the Divine Twins, the *marasa.* . . . *Marasa* states the oppositions and invites participation in the formation of another principle entirely. . . . *marasa* consciousness invites us to imagine beyond the binary."[18] The play illustrates that the two ends can be brought together not only through the two-part structure but also through recognition of Hurston's ability to embed social protest in a genuine folk drama. By doing this, Hurston created something new and vivacious.

The story of Hurston's project takes an ironic turn when it is noted that one of the three judges for the drama section in the *Opportunity*'s Literary Contest was Montgomery Gregory. He and Alain Locke generally shared the same view of the New Negro art. With Locke's assistance, Gregory founded the Howard Players. The ostensibly nonpolitical purpose of the organization was, according to Gregory, "to fashion a drama that shall merit the respect and win the admiration of the world."[19] Because of Hurston's international camouflage, the aspect of social criticism in *Color Struck* had been overlooked. Hence Gregory, by awarding *Color Struck* a prize, presumably considered it a work engaged more in folk art than in social protest. This interpretation of *Color Struck* as a work of pure art rather than of social consciousness is further manifested by the fact that the play was published for the first time in *Fire!!* in 1926.

Fire!! was an ambitious enterprise taken up by the younger writers of the Harlem Renaissance including Langston Hughes, Aaron Douglas, and Hurston. They aspired to "create a magazine which would be unconcerned 'with sociological problems or propaganda.' *Fire!!* was to be a 'non-commercial product interested only in the arts.'" What was more central in these young artists' aesthetics was the demand to go to the "proletariat rather than to the bourgeoisie for characters and material, . . . to people who still retained some individual race qualities and who were not totally white American in every respect save color of skin."[20] That *Color Struck* was included in a magazine that repudiated any art with a social message is somewhat puzzling. But Hemenway's interpretation of the play may demonstrate one way to read *Color Struck* according to the literary criteria of *Fire!!:*

> Its subject is the intraracial color-consciousness exercised by the bourgeoisie, and it addresses *those*

who envy whites biologically or intellectually. It is an account of a *poor woman* so self-conscious about her dark skin that she is unable to accept the love of a *good man.* . . . [I]t comes to life only when the folk of north-central Florida engage their wit in friendly verbal competition. . . . but its theme is consistent with *Fire!!*'s aims. It celebrated the proletariat, and it condemned a common bourgeois attitude.[21]

In this type of reading, *Color Struck* becomes a play that recounts a personal tragedy that Emma has brought upon herself. It attacks the Black middle-class and all those who accept their values; it thus glorifies the proletariat and those who reject the bourgeois ideology. Instead of commanding the reader's sympathy, Emma is viewed unsympathetically, and John, ironically, is identified as the victim of her jealousy. According to this interpretation, Hurston, by dramatizing Emma's tragic ending, condemned the self-pity and self-indulgence that result from accepting the bourgeois color-complex.[22] The preconception of Hurston as a folklorist who lacked concern for the social plight of her people is held by many of Hurston's critics and has been the foundation for attacks against Hurston's character and works alike. In their eagerness to criticize Hurston for being "more interested in folklore and dialect than in social criticism" and for neglecting "racial tensions,"[23] these critics overlook the social problem raised by the play. It is disturbing to think that a play such as *Color Struck* can be interpreted as a criticism of the victims of colorism, instead of a criticism of colorism itself.

Such a misreading implies a forgetfulness of history. Unquestionably, John is depicted as a kind and faithful man throughout the play, and his frustration with Emma's paranoia warrants the audience's sympathy. However, the play is not about a good man rejected by an unworthy woman obsessed with her own skin color. Rather, the influence colorism exerts upon Emma is the unifying force of the whole play. The folk scene, the cakewalk, the dance, and the music all are the background for the tragedy of a dark-skinned woman. Amid the play's colorful events, songs, and humor, the plot is propelled by Emma's growing jealousy, obsession, rage, fear, and desperation. And finally, only when the stage is stripped bare of color and excitement in the last scene is the pathos felt most forcefully. Emma's desolation is materialized on stage through the darkness, the sound of the rocking chair, her "monotonous gait," and "a dry sob now and then" as the curtain falls (102). To see Emma in a sympathetic light, to understand her obsession, one needs to acknowledge the existence of colorism. Hurston assumed her audience would know this form of prejudice, and at the same time, challenged her audience to face its ramifications. The unspoken history of prejudice and paranoia is embedded in Emma's own prejudice and paranoia. The invisible scar on the Black soul is shown through Emma's brutal denial of her self-worth.[24]

The seeds of Emma's colorism had been sown even before the first shipment of African slaves arrived in the New World, when women were raped on slave ships. The history of colorism is entrenched in the history of slavery.

Rapes, sexual exploitation, and, though relatively rare in the earliest periods, legal and illegal interracial marriages, resulted in a wide spectrum of skin tones among African Americans. In the beginning, the color caste system was created and propagated by white racists who believed that white skin represented advanced civilization, intelligence, and morals. The light-skinned slaves were then used as house servants since they were considered to be closer to the White race. The situation was complicated by the high proportion of female house servants raped or sexually exploited by the men in the house. Even after the Civil War, it was still much easier for lighter-skinned ex-slaves to find employment or education with Whites. Because from the beginning, the light-skinned Black Americans had a better chance to improve their lives socially and economically than people of darker skin, and also because the imprinting of the dominant ideology carries with it the idea of the color caste, intraracial color discrimination developed.[25] Emma's anger towards light-skinned women and her self-hatred burst forth in violent tirades:

> Oh—them yaller wenches! How I hate 'em! They gets everything they wants—. . . . Oh, them half whites, they gets everything, they gets everything everybody else wants! The men, the jobs—everything! The whole world is got a sign on it. Wanted: Light Colored. Us blacks was made for cobble stones (96-7).

To argue that Emma here is being irrational or that she is merely carried away by her jealousy denies the genuine injustice she experiences; she is expressing the historical anguish suffered by dark-skinned Blacks.[26]

In order to further understand the criticism embedded in the play and to surmise the reason behind Hurston's creation of as "unsympathetic" a character as Emma, one must understand the social and cultural context of the 1920s. By the 1920s, although interracial marriages were still illegal in the South and in many northern states, "marriages between black men and white women had increased significantly."[27] In the 1930s, in an article entitled "America's Changing Color Line," Heba Jannath went so far as to claim that America was becoming Black through a steady increase of the mixed population.[28] Nevertheless, the myth of the "tragic mulatto" did not disappear with the increased number of mulattoes. Instead, the ability of many to pass as white allowed them to disappear from the Black population. The "vanishing mulatto" became, by 1925, what editorials referred to as "one of the most important, the most enigmatic, and romantic small groups on earth."[29] Through the 1920s mulattoes remained one of the favorite inspirations of aspiring writers.[30] "Let us train ourselves to see beauty in black," Du Bois called out in 1920.[31] Yet, despite the praise of Blacks' innate beauty by leaders such as Locke, Du Bois, and Marcus Garvey, the public perception of beauty had been molded by the dominant, white values. The theatrical practice during the era, the "Roaring Twenties," clearly reveals the adoption of the dominant aesthetic standard. Encouraged by the raving success of the all Black musical *Shuffle Along* in 1921, Black musicals became a sensation for both Black and white audiences.

Unfortunately, the success of musicals, instead of affirming Black beauty, only furthered the color caste system. In order to be accepted into the mainstream culture and attract more clientele, most of the imitative musicals and revues employed exclusively light-skinned actresses. Donald Bogle points out that "the black chorus line was . . . distinguished by the fact that its members were almost cafe-au-lait cuties. . . . In photographs of the old chorus lines, occasionally a brown face appears, but there is never a dark one."[32] In addition to the theatrical reinscription of the color caste system, the film industry developed its own color "casting" system for Black actresses. Similar to the trend in literature, the tragic mulatto had been "a movie maker's darling" since the silent period of motion pictures. The popularity enjoyed by movies only highlighted the appearances of light-skinned Black actresses as the romantic interest, and, the darker-skinned actresses, in contrast, as maids or other minor roles. Even in the more than twenty films of the most famous Black film maker, Oscar Micheaux, only light-skinned Black performers could be found.[33]

On the one hand, Hurston, writing in 1924 and 1925, was reflecting these cultural and aesthetic trends. On the other hand, *Color Struck* also anticipated the series of light-skinned movie stars who were about to appear on the silver screen with the emergence of sound motion pictures. They would play an important role in defining the meaning of Black beauty up until the 1950s. By the 1960s Black Americans would directly attack the bleaching of the Black beauty standard and reaffirm the "Black is Beautiful" credo. Curiously, despite such an obviously provocative title, with few exceptions, discussions of Hurston's play did not address the sociopolitical issues raised by the term "color struck." The play is still seen as the personal tragedy of a color-struck woman rather than an allegory about the community.[34] In the face of blatant interracial racism, discussions of intraracial colorism have been silenced. Especially in a time when White racism was being collectively attacked, and Black pride was fiercely asserted, Black audiences neither expected nor welcomed criticism from within the community.[35] Moreover, during periods of race consolidation, such as the Harlem Renaissance, outspoken people who engaged in self-criticism were often denounced as traitors who washed their dirty linen in front of Whites. With a theme such as colorism, a suspicious and also embarrassing subject for Black leaders as well as the Black public, *Color Struck* would not win approval without the disguise of a play celebrating the folk spirit. As Hurston was usually determined to have her works published and plays produced, she naturally used the tactics of camouflage—presenting (and seeing) this play as a story with a Southern folk flavor—when writing and promoting *Color Struck*.

Hurston constantly subverted the traditional and dominant ideology behind a facade of conformity. Since Alice Walker rediscovered Hurston, the ambiguities of Hurston's personalities and politics have been explained as a means of survival in the white-centered and male-dominant literary world. "If the Renaissance had a gender, it was male," argues Erlene Stetson.[36] Ralph D. Story also emphasizes Hurston's role as a "southern black woman challenging the traditional position of women and exceeding the aesthetic space they had been traditionally provided."[37] In order to have *Color Struck* published, Hurston chose not to flaunt the social criticism in the play or to explicitly contradict the editorial criteria of *Fire!!*. She thus avoided discussing any deeper intentions for writing *Color Struck*. In this context, the play serves to defend Hurston against critics who criticize her as "a woman predisposed to identify more with whites (and whose) parents had large quantities of white blood in their veins,"[38] or accuse her of being a colorist simply because Janie in *Their Eyes Were Watching God* is light-skinned.[39] Walker suggests that Hurston chose a light-skinned woman as the protagonist for her novel not because she was a colorist, but "because Hurston was not blind and therefore saw that black men (and black women) have been, and are, colorist to an embarrassing degree."[40] By using a light-skinned mulatto heroine, she improved her chances of obtaining patronage, having her work published, and surviving as an artist. But unlike Jessie Fauset's mulatto heroines who are cultured and fragile in the tradition of the tragic mulatto, Hurston's Janie marries three times, kills her abusive third husband, and faces life on her own. Janie is indeed an "anti-romantic symbol of the mulatto 'type'."[41] I contend that Hurston used the strategy of camouflage—seemingly saying (or showing) something, while signifying (or pointing towards) another.[42] This act of camouflage enabled Hurston to challenge the status quo, even inside the Harlem community, and to compete against her male contemporaries.

To counteract the traditional devaluation of Hurston's works based on her personal behavior and statements Alice Walker and other scholars advocate an aesthetic approach to appreciating Hurston's art. They succeed in reestablishing an image of Hurston so confident and triumphant in her ability to be who she was, that she was able to declare, "I love myself when I am laughing . . . and then again when I am looking mean and impressive," and to wonder, "How *can* any deny themselves the pleasure of my company? It's beyond me."[43] Nevertheless, Hurston's behavior and a number of her statements belied this image of self-confidence. As an adolescent, Hurston "grew self-conscious about her looks, feeling that no man could really care for her."[44] The willful subterfuge regarding her age also shows that Hurston cared about how she was seen by others, especially as a woman.[45] In addition, she seemed to be quite self-conscious about her skin color. When commenting on the novelist Fannie Hurst's desire to be seen with Hurston in public, she claimed "It was because Hurst liked the way [my] dark skin highlighted her own lily-like complexion."[46] Hurston's physical appearance is a matter of some dispute. According to some sources, Hurston was "reddish light brown," "big-boned, with freckles and high cheek bones."[47] Regardless of her genuine skin color, judging from Hurston's own words and obsession with her own skin color, she thought of herself as a dark-skinned woman. Supported by these ac-

counts of Hurston, a conclusion can be justly drawn that Hurston did not write *Color Struck* with only folk art in mind, nor did she write it from a completely objective perspective. She likely wrote the play out of her personal experience, and the writing became an outlet for her angst as a "dark-skinned" woman.

Having been raised in an all-Black community, Hurston naturally experienced 'culture shock' when she arrived in a city that judged her by her skin color. In her essay, "How It Feels To Be Colored Me," Hurston recollected the day she became "colored":

> I was sent to school in Jacksonville. I left Eatonville . . . as Zora. When I disembarked from the river-boat at Jacksonville, she was no more. It seemed that I had suffered a sea change. I was not Zora of Orange County any more, I was now a little colored girl. I found it out in certain ways. In my heart as well as in the mirror, I became a fast brown—warranted not to rub nor run.[48]

Given the psychological significance of the contradiction between the childhood affirmation of her Black self and her experience in the world outside Eatonville, it is not surprising that Hurston's persona is rich with contradictions for her contemporaries and later generations. Hemenway summarizes the complexity of Hurston's personality by claiming that Hurston appeared to be "a woman who rejoiced in print about the beauty of being black. . . . [Though] she retreated into a privacy that protected her sense of self; publicly, she avoided confrontation by announcing that she didn't look at a person's color, only one's worth."[49] Therefore, when Hurston lamented bourgeois colorism and praised the beauty of being Black, she could at the same time show compassion towards the self-deprecatory Emma, a fellow victim of dark skin and racism.

In 1926, Du Bois wrote to Hurston, "No black people ever considered their color unusual or unbeautiful [*sic*] until they were taught to through others and then could only be taught this through physical force."[50] Intraracial prejudice is caused by interracial discrimination; the reality of colorism always carries with it the invisible presence of racism. Acknowledging this reality allows us to see operating in *Color Struck* Sandra Richards' notion of the absent potential. Richards argument can be applied to *Color Struck* once we understand that "[t]he unwritten, or an absence from the script, is a potential presence implicit in performance."[51] In the opening scene of *Color Struck*, without the presence of a single white person, the stigma of racism is poignantly felt in the Jim Crow railroad car. Emma's near white daughter also suggests a white or half-white male presence. Because she is not married, Emma may have been raped by a white or near-white man, or she may have deliberately sought out a white heritage for her offspring in order to save her child from the "curse" of dark skin. The entrance of the white doctor, the only white character in the play, is stunning and alarming. Earlier, when John suggests that Emma go and find a "colored" doctor, reasoning that "There must be some good colored ones around here now," Emma responds with disgust, "I wouldn't let one of 'em tend my cat if I had one!" (101) The appearance of the white doctor again illustrates the disdain Emma has for everything Black, herself included. Ironically, even though she trusts white doctors more than she trusts Black ones, the white doctor is ultimately unable to save her daughter. The presence of the white doctor utterly destroys the illusion of a homogeneous, all-Black world. From the absent white presence in the Jim Crow car in the first scene, to the authority assumed by the white doctor, even though he is unable to save Emma's daughter, Hurston brings the formerly invisible yet substantial white oppression into the view of the audience. According to Sandra Richards, "[the previous] frivolity is happening within a circumscribed space of racism. Implicit behind the laughter is a painful reality that these characters have chosen to ignore temporarily."[52] Confined to a racist environment, the tragic ending of *Color Struck*, far from being a stylistic incongruity, has lurked from the beginning in the midst of the characters' laughter.

Raised in a Southern rural all-Black community, Hurston was deeply rooted in the folk culture that was being celebrated in the Harlem Renaissance. Unlike other literary figures from a mostly middle-class background, who served and praised the folk from an elevated and detached position, Hurston spoke from the depth of her heart. She came from the folk. For most of her contemporaries, Hurston represented the folk. Undoubtedly, when she wrote *Color Struck*, she was speaking for Emma and her people. They could be striving to live up to the bourgeois standard, but they still retained their customs and traditions, despised or, at best, pitied by the very people they tried to emulate. By using a dark-skinned heroine, Hurston defied the bourgeois sensibility and also the convention of the tragic mulatto. The characterization of Emma works against the usual depictions of dark-skinned women. Instead of being a desexualized "mammie," Emma is flirtatious, sexy, and, to John at least, physically attractive. She is capable of all human emotions: love, hate, tenderness, passion and jealousy. The impact of the internalized color consciousness is so devastating that Emma is unable to trust John with her own light-skinned daughter, and this mistrust eventually causes her daughter's death. With the death of this child, Hurston dramatized the ferocity of institutionalized colorism. Likewise, through *Color Struck*, Hurston addressed the contradictions between the efforts of the aspiring Black genteel class to gain recognition within the dominant society and the implicit self-hatred manifested in the media and the public attitude toward assimilation. The play implicitly attacks the "politics of respectability" advocated by middle-class Black women, as an effort to integrate at the risk of losing respect for whatever is Black. The obvious class differences between these elite bourgeois women, or "Club women"—so named for their involvement in social or religious "clubs" designed to organize Black communities and to seek the acceptance and assimilation of Black people by the dominant society—and those they meant to convert werereflected in the differences between John, who is light-skinned, and Emma,

after an interval of twenty years. Emma's view of herself: "Ah aint got a whole lot lak you. Nobody don't git rich in no white-folks' kitchen, nor in de washtub. You know Ah aint no school-teacher an' nothin' lak dat" (100), sets her economically and socially apart from John and the educated middle class. The movement of the "politics of respectability" sought to uplift the lower class to meet the standards of the dominant society, but its advocates overlooked the price the poor and the uneducated had to pay to achieve this form of "racial uplift." They were instructed by the educated to abandon their old values and to conform to those of the dominant culture, and that was easily interpreted to mean that whatever was black was improper and unwanted.[53] The price could be as high as, in the case of Emma's family, one's happiness and even one's life.

At a time when the "race problem" was the most popular theme for writers, and when solidarity among Blacks was enthusiastically demanded, it took honesty and courage to criticize internalized racism so harshly. Even today, few people have addressed the question as openly in their literary works as Hurston. In her novels *Quicksand* and *Passing* Nella Larsen attempted to subvert the "popular and traditional genteel image of the near-white female," but her criticism of color consciousness comes from the point of view of light-skinned women who have been suffocated by "upper class Black gentility" and exploited by whites as "exotic primitives."[54] In the end, Larsen's heroines are still presented as tragic, and the miseries of their dark-skinned counterparts are overshadowed by their own tragedies. Few other plays have shown the effect of the internal color complex in such a grim and harsh light as *Color Struck*. It can be seen as the forerunner of plays that question the self-affirmation of a Black identity or the definition of beauty in the Black community, such as Adrienne Kennedy's *Funny House of a Negro* (1964), Elaine Jackson's *Paper Dolls* (1983), and George Wolfe's *The Colored Museum* (1986). To date, the play has not been given the attention and evaluation it deserves. Devoting greater attention to the structure, content, and background of *Color Struck* not only helps us understand Hurston's work and life more thoroughly but also repudiates the charge against Hurston of nonchalance towards racism. Furthermore, such an effort shows Hurston to be a groundbreaking dramatist who intentionally combined aesthetics and social protest, courageously raised issues once silenced, and openly challenged the status quo from inside the Harlem Renaissance, a movement to which she made a profound contribution.

Notes

1. I am grateful for Professor Sandra Richards' comments and her class, African American Women Playwrights, which initiated my interest in Zora Neale Hurston and *Color Struck*. Any omissions or errors are, of course, my own.

2. Lillie P. Howard, "Zora Neale Hurston," in *Afro-American Writers from the Harlem Renaissance to 1940,* vol. 51 of *Dictionary of Literary*

Biography, ed. Trudier Harris (Detroit, Mich.: Bruccoli Clark Layman, 1987), 133. Many other biographical works on Hurston listed the year of her birth as 1901. According to Howard, Hurston "kept the exact year of her birth such a secret that it was only until recently that a conclusive date, 1891, was uncovered" (134).

3. Lately, there has been also an effort to re-evaluate Hurston's ethnographic works in the American South, and to re-interpret her fictions as ethnography. For example, Kamala Visweswaran resurrects Hurston's ethnography as one of the forerunners of feminist ethnography in *Fictions of Feminist Ethnography* (Minneapolis, Minn.: University of Minnesota Press, 1994).

4. Robert E. Hemenway, *Zora Neale Hurston: A Literary Biography* (Urbana, Ill.: University of Illinois Press, 1977), 60.

5. Ibid., 47.

6. Warren J. Carson, "Hurston as Dramatist: The Florida Connection," in *Zora in Florida,* eds. Steve Glassman and Kathryn Lee Seidel (Orlando, Fla.: University of Florida Press, 1991), 121. Carson may have exaggerated the role of *Color Struck* in Hurston's life. Her short story *Spunk* alone could have brought her to the *Opportunity* Award Dinner and made her immediately famous. It was, in fact, *Spunk* that drew novelists Annie Nathan Meyer's and Fannie Hurst's attention to Hurston's genius. Meyer, one of the founders of Barnard College, then obtained a scholarship for Hurston at Barnard; Hurst employed Hurston for more than a year. See Hemenway, 20-1. Sandra L. Richards in "Writing the Absent Potential: Drama, Performance, and the Canon of African-American Literature," in *Performativity and Performance,* eds. Eve Kosofsky Sedgwick and Andrew Parker (New York: Routledge, 1995), also discusses *Color Struck.* Richards's article concentrates on the "absent potential," that is, the potential meanings and readings that can be embodied and signified simply by the actual presence of the actors on stage, and uses *Color Struck* and *Ma Rainey's Black Bottom* to demonstrate her point. In her new book, *Social Rituals and the Verbal Art of Zora Neale Hurston,* Lynda Marion Hill devotes a short section to *Color Struck.* She uses this play as a means to study Hurston's participation in the "authenticity debate." See Lynda Marion Hill, "Authenticity and the Convergence of Color, 'Race,' and Class," in *Social Rituals and the Verbal Art of Zora Neale Hurston* (Washington, D.C.: Howard University Press, 1996), 103-13.

7. Hemenway, 60.

8. This gender-informed use of camouflage can be likened to historian Darlene Clark Hine's explanation of African American women's "culture of dissemblance." Hine claims "[B]lack women adopted a 'culture of dissemblance'—a self-imposed secrecy and invisibility—in order to shield themselves emotionally and physically." (In Evelyn Brooks Higginbotham, *The Righteous Discontent: The Women's Movement in the Black Baptist Church 1880-1920* [Cambridge: Howard University Press,

1993], 193-94). Although Hine is talking about African American women's fear of rape, I believe that the idea of a "culture of dissemblance" may be seen as a survival tactic adopted by people who face oppression in different ways.

9. Hemenway, 47; Carson, 123-26.

10. Hemenway, 19.

11. Kathy A. Perkins, introduction to *Color Struck,* in *Black Female Playwrights,* ed. Kathy A. Perkins (Bloomington, Ind.: Indiana University Press, 1989), 77-8.

12. Hemenway, 127.

13. Carson and Hemenway find the juxtaposition of the two apparently incompatible theatrical forms dissatisfactory. Both agree that the "only memorable scene is the cake walk." See Hemenway, 47; Carson, 125.

14. Zora Neale Hurston, *Color Struck,* in Perkins, 93. Hereafter, only text citations of page numbers will be given for references to the play.

15. Hill, 109-10.

16. Robert Hayden, preface to *The New Negro,* ed. Alain Locke (1925; reprint, New York: Atheneum, 1969), xii.

17. W. E. B. Du Bois, "Criteria of Negro Art," in *Selections from* The Crisis, ed. Herbert Aptheker (Millwood, N.Y.: Kraus-Thomson, 1983), 2:448. First published in *The Crisis* 32, no. 6 (October 1926): 296

18. Vèvè A. Clark, "Developing Diaspora Literacy and *Marasa* Consciousness," in *Comparative American Identities: Race, Sex, and Nationality in the Modern Text,* ed. Hortense J. Spillers (London: Routledge, 1991), 43.

19. Montgomery Gregory, "A Chronology of the Negro Theatre," in *Plays of Negro Life,* ed. Alain Locke (New York: Harper & Brothers, 1927), 417.

20. Hemenway, 44-45.

21. Ibid., 47. Emphasis added.

22. See Carson, 127.

23. Daryl C. Dance, "Zora Neale Hurston," in *American Women Writers: Bibliographical Essays,* eds. Maurice Duke, Jackson R. Bryer, and M. Thomas Inge (London: Greenwood, 1983), 343.

24. By pointing a finger at intraracial prejudice, I do not mean to dismiss interracial racism, nor do I attempt to blame the victim. It is important to keep in mind that colorism has developed alongside and because of racism.

25. For a comprehensive discussion of Black color consciousness, see Kathy Russell, Midge Wilson, and Ronald Hall, *The Color Complex* (New York: Harcourt Brace Jovanovich, 1992).

26. Because sexist practices teach women to please men and to judge themselves by how others see them, it is undeniable that colorism exerts a stronger pressure on African American women. For a discussion of the double bind of sexism and

colorism, see Margo Okazawa-Rey, Tracy Robinson, and Janie Victoria Ward, "Black Women and the Politics of Skin Color and Hair," *Women's Studies Quarterly* 14, nos. 1,2 (spring/summer 1986): 13-14.

27. Vashti Crutcher Lewis, "Nella Larsen's Use of the Near-White Female in *Quicksand* and *Passing*," *Perspectives of Black Popular Culture,* ed. Harry B. Shaw (Bowling Green, Oh.: Bowling Green State University Press, 1990), 37.

28. Heba Jannath, "America's Changing Color Line," in *Negro Anthology 1931-1933,* ed. Nancy Cunard (New York: Negro University Press, 1969).

29. *Opportunity* 3, no. 34 (October 1925), 291.

30. One of the first literary works featuring a mulatto with light skin and straight hair was William Wells Brown's *Clotel* (1853). Other early works featuring light-skinned Black women include Frances E. White Harper's *Iola Leroy* (1865), Nella Larsen's *Quick Sand* (1928) and *Passing* (1929), and Jessie Fauset's *Plumb Bun* (1929). For a discussion of mulattoes in films, see Donald Bogle's *Toms, Coons, Mulattoes, Mammies, and Bucks: An Interpretive History of Blacks in American Films* (New York: Viking Press, 1973). According to Bogle, "The third figure of the black pantheon and the one that proved itself a moviemaker's darlin is the tragic mulatto" (9). He also states, sarcastically, that the mulatto's tragedy lies not in that she can or wants to pass as white but that "she wants to be white" (60). In the theatre history of the dominant (Euro-American) culture, there are many dramatizations of this desire, notably Dion Boucicault's *The Octoroon* (1959) in which Zoe, the Octoroon, commits suicide because of that drop of Black blood.

31. Du Bois, "In Black," in *Selections from* The Crisis, 1: 278. First published in *The Crisis* 20, no. 6 (October 1920): 263-66.

32. Donald Bogle, *Brown Sugar* (New York: Harmony Books, 1980), 38. The phenomenal Josephine Baker was first turned down after she auditioned for *Shuffle Along* because she was too dark. She then put on the lightest face powder available and was hired only as a dresser. Eventually she became popular after her accidental appearance in the show, but she continued to appear as a comic pickaninny character. Ironically, Baker's ultimate success resulted from her recognition of her unfavorable stance as a brown woman, who can "never get attention on her looks alone, being neither "the white [nor] black ideal of beauty or appeal." She understood this disadvantage and was determined to make use of her "effervescence." Later, in 1925, she showed up on the Parisian stage almost naked, dazzled post-war Europe, and became a star overnight (Bogle, 43-51).

33. See Bogle, *Toms, Coons, Mulattos, Mammies, and Bucks,* 9, 113-14. Also Kathy Russell, Midge Wilson, and Ronald Hall, *The Color Complex* (New York: Harcourt Brace Jovanovich, 1992), 146. These texts and Bogle's *Brown Sugar* offer useful discussions of near white Black actresses in the movie industry

34. Two exceptions are Hill's book and Richards' article. See note 7.

35. At the time when *Color Struck* was written, the generally hostile sentiment of Black audiences towards self-critical elements in Black plays was readily apparent. For examples, see the editorial in *Crisis* 27 (June 1924) and the correspondence in *Opportunity* 3, no. 28 (April 1925). There remains a fear of talking about intraracial prejudice openly for fear that the dominant culture may use it as an excuse to blame the victim or to dismiss its own racism. For example, Ntozake Shange's *for colored girls who have considered suicide/when the rainbow is enuf* has been attacked by some in the African American community because the play, instead of exclusively attacking racism in the larger society, touches upon sexism and domestic violence inside the community.

36. Ann Allen Shockley, "Afro-American Women Writers: *The New Negro Movement 1924-1933*," in *Rereading Modernism: New Directions in Feminist Criticism,* ed. Lisa Rado (New York: Garland Publishing, 1994), 127.

37. Ralph D. Story, "Gender and Ambition: Zora Neale Hurston in the Harlem Renaissance," in *The Black Scholar* 20 (summer/fall 1989): 27.

38. Chidi Ikonne, *From Du Bois to Van Vechten: The Early New Negro Literature, 1903-1926* (Westport, Conn.: Greenwood, 1981), 183, quoted in Story, 25.

39. Lynda Hill states that Hurston "seems to prefer darker skinned performers, rather than 'mulattoes,' to appear in her concerts and musical revues" (112).

40. Alice Walker, dedication to *I Love Myself When I Am Laughing . . . And Then Again When I Am Looking Mean and Impressive,* ed. Alice Walker (New York: The Feminist Press, 1979), 2.

41. Erlene Stetson, "*Their Eyes Were Watching God:* A Woman's Story," *Regionalism And the Female Imagination* 4, no. 1 (1979): 30-36, quoted in Dance, 339.

42. In *The Signifying Monkey: A Theory of African-American Literary Criticism* (New York: Oxford University Press, 1988), Henry Louis Gates, Jr. points out that "signifyin(g) . . . depends on the success of the signifier at invoking an absent meaning ambiguously 'present' in a carefully wrought statement" (86).

43. Hurston, "How It Feels to be Colored Me," in *I Love Myself When I Am Laughing,* 155.

44. Hemenway, 17.

45. Though the contention between Hurston and Langston Hughes during the writing of *Mule Bone* may have resulted from more complicated causes, that a younger woman was involved in the triangular partnership has not been completely ruled out. For a thorough discussion of the controversy of *Mule Bone,* see *Mule Bone: A Comedy of Negro Life and the Complete Story of the Mule Bone Controversy.* eds. George Houston Bass and Henry Louis Gates, Jr. (New York: Harper Perennial, 1991).

46. Hemenway, 21. Hurston was quick to point out the contrast between their skin tones. She stated that

Hurst "knows exactly what goes with her very white skin, black hair and sloe eyes, and she wears it." *Dust Tracks On a Road* (New York: Harper Perennial, 1991), 176.

47. See Hemenway 9. See also Mary Helen Washington, introduction to *I Love Myself When I Am Laughing,* 7. There are three different accounts concerning Hurston's complexion. Fannie Hurst described Hurston as "light yellow;" another reference claimed that she was "black as coal;" yet another said "she was reddish light brown." Washington concludes that the last description is the closest to photographs of Hurston and reports of other eyewitnesses (24).

48. Hurston, "How It Feels to Be Colored Me," in *I Love Myself When I Am Laughing*, 153.

49. Hemenway, 6.

50. W. E. B. DuBois to Zora Neale Hurston, 23 June 1926, *The World of W. E. B. Du Bois: A Quotation Sourcebook,* ed. Meyer Weinberg (London: Greenwood, 1992), 80.

51. Richards, 83. See note 7.

52. Ibid., 74-75.

53. For a thorough discussion of "the politics of respectability," see Evelyn Brooks Higginbotham, "The Politics of Respectability," in *The Righteous Discontent: The Woman's Movement in the Black Baptist Church 1880-1920* (Cambridge: Howard University Press, 1933).

54. Lewis, 36. For a further discussion of Nella Larsen, see Cheryl A. Wall, "Nella Larsen: Passing for What?" in *Women of the Harlem Renaissance* (Bloomington, Ind.: Indiana University Press, 1995).

FURTHER READING

Criticism

Hemenway, Robert E. *"Mule Bone."* In *Zora Neale Hurston: A Literary Biography*, pp. 136-58. Urbana: University of Illinois Press, 1977.

Details the collaborative writing of *Mule Bone* by Hurston and Langston Hughes, and their later falling out. Hemenway goes on to describe the play itself, calling it "an interesting attempt to transcend black dramatic stereotypes."

Hill, Lynda M. "Staging Hurston's Life and Work." In *Acting Out: Feminist Performances*, edited by Lynda Hart and Peggy Phelan, pp. 295-313. Ann Arbor: University of Michigan Press, 1993.

Considers Hurston as an interpreter of black culture, viewing her dramatic work in relation to that of her peers and estimating the influence of her aesthetic on subsequent stage performances. Hill concludes that Hurston "is a progenitor, indeed and archetype, for theater artists who recognize that her life and work has empowered a new generation. . . ."

Perkins, Kathy A. "Zora Neale Hurston." In *Black Female Playwrights: An Anthology of Plays before 1950*, pp. 75-9. Bloomington: Indiana University Press, 1989.

Brief survey of Hurston's life and career as a dramatist.

Eugène Ionesco
1909-1994

Romanian-born French playwright, essayist, novelist, autobiographer, and critic.

INTRODUCTION

One of the major figures in modern European experimental drama, Ionesco is best known for his innovative techniques using things and words in the theater and his association with the movement of the 1950s and 1960s known as the "Theater of the Absurd." His "anti-plays," which push both speech and action past the limits of rationality, cast doubt on traditional, naturalistic theatrical conventions and established assumptions about language and human nature, stressing the absurdity of life, humans' ever-present awareness of death, and the impossibility of communication. These and the related themes of human alienation and the destructive forces of modern society are presented in his plays with a surface humor that comments upon and serves to counterpoint the horror and anguish of human life that lies beneath. Like his contemporary and fellow "absurdist" Samuel Beckett, Ionesco replaces customary plots, structure, and language with fragmentary, contradictory, and often nonsensical dialogue and surreal images in order to present a world of chaos that mocks established institutions and conformity. His revolutionary approach to theater and his darkly comic vision reveal his distrust of all forms of ideology, as he urges his audiences to explore their own imaginations and awaken themselves to the potentialities of their own existence. Although Ionesco spent his dramatic career deriding the establishment, in 1971 he was elected to the conservative Académie Française, a sign not that the playwright had changed his earlier radical views to conform to the mainstream, but rather that his unique approach had altered the institution of theater in France and the world.

BIOGRAPHICAL INFORMATION

Ionesco was born in Slatina, Romania, to a French mother and a Romanian father. He spent his happy, early childhood years in France, returning to Romania after his parents' divorce in 1925. In 1929 he enrolled at the University of Bucharest, where he specialized in French literature. After taking his degree he lived in Bucharest, where he taught French and began writing poetry and literary criticism. In 1936 he married a philosophy student, Rodica Burlieano, and two years later the couple moved to France after Ionesco accepted a scholarship to prepare a dissertation on the subject of death in modern French

poetry. He spent the next ten years in Paris working as a journalist, teacher, and proofreader, deliberately avoiding the theater, which he dismissed as a complete waste of time and energy.

In 1948, at age thirty-nine, Ionesco began his career in the theater—quite by accident. He had undertaken to learn English by using a popular self-teaching method, and while reciting the seemingly random phrases used in the instruction manual found the task to make less and less sense. At the same time he found the phrases full of humorous possibilities and felt that they had a surreal existence of their own that was quite separate from their ordinary meaning. He soon abandoned the idea of learning English and conceived the idea of writing his first play by jotting down words and rearranging sentences. He showed the finished product (written in French) to a director and then to an editor at a major publishing house, both of whom dismissed the work. However, a friend showed it to Nicholas Bataille, a young director with a small company who immediately recognized its originality and produced it for the stage. *The Bald Soprano,* so named after an actor in the company, while rehearsing, uttered the phrase "bald prima donna" instead of "blond prima donna," was a failure when it opened in 1950, with the audience shouting out rude comments throughout the performance. However, Ionesco found his vocation and continued to write plays, developing further the antilogical ideas of his first work. His prolific output from 1950 to 1955 included some of his best-known plays: *The Lesson, The Chairs, Victims of Duty, Amédée, or How to Get Rid of it,* and *Jack, or The Submission.* After 1951 his work began to attract critical attention, and by 1955 his reputation was firmly established in France. He also found himself at the forefront of a revolutionary new theater, which included such established names as Beckett and Arthur Adamov, that broke ties with realist forms, emphasized experimental methods, and stressed the irrationality in human life.

Ionesco continued to write for the stage until the early 1970s, enjoying a growing international reputation, earning awards for his work, and seeing many of his plays adapted as ballets. From the late 1960s through the 1980s his creativity became increasingly directed at experiments with other genres, including autobiography, criticism, and fiction. In the last decade of his life Ionesco gave up writing and devoted himself to painting and exhibiting his works. He died in Paris in 1994.

MAJOR WORKS

Ionesco's early plays, those written before 1956, are still considered among his best, as they present with startling originality and immediacy his recurrent themes of the difficulty of communication, the impotence of reason, and self-estrangement. In *The Bald Soprano,* about a couple who stumble upon the fact that they are indeed man and wife in the course of their meaningless conversation, and *The Lesson,* in which a professor and student find it increasingly difficult to communicate in words, Ionesco uses nonsensical dialogue in the form of familiar clichés and slogans to mock commonplace notions about the world. In plays such as *The Chairs, The Future is in Eggs, Victims of Duty, The New Tenant,* and *Amédée,* Ionesco populates his stage with meaningless physical objects to emphasize his theme of unreason and convey a nightmarish sense of inanity.

Although Ionesco's reputation as a serious dramatist began to flourish in the mid-1950s, in 1958 he was criticized by one of his early champions, the British critic Kenneth Tynan, for producing "nonsense theater" and not living up to the social role expected of a writer. The charge leveled at Ionesco was that his work was politically indifferent and therefore irrelevant. The "London Controversy," as it was called, had Ionesco defending himself against promoting in his theater the ill-conceived "solutions" to social and political questions advocated by left-wing and right-wing thinkers alike. But many commentators, including the director Orson Welles, continued to feel that Ionesco was shunning his appropriate function by not engaging in

political debate in his work. It seems that Ionesco was affected by this criticism, because beginning in the late 1950s he began to produce work that seemed to strive for political relevance. In his cycle of plays *The Killers, Rhinoceros, Exit the King,* and *A Stroll in the Air,* in which appear his "Everyman" Bérenger, a brave and idealistic man who has heroic qualities but always loses, Ionesco overtly criticizes totalitarianism and presents deeper analyses of the complexity of human aspirations than in his earlier works. His retelling of Shakespeare's *Macbeth,* written in 1973, is also a study of political tyranny.

Ionesco's dramatic works in the late 1960s and early 1970s returned to the more fragmented construction of his earlier efforts. The theme of death also becomes an overriding concern during this period, as seen in *Hunger and Thirst* and *The Killing Game.* The works of the 1970s, including *Journey Among the Dead* and *Man With Bags,* are notable for their use of dream elements, the fantastic, and the blurred line between humans' conscious and subconscious states.

In addition to his plays, Ionesco has written a novel, *The Hermit,* a collection of short stories, children's stories, criticism, and autobiography. In his several collections of essays and his autobiographical works, such as *Notes and Counter-notes* and *Fragments of a Journal,* Ionesco develops many of the ideas presented in his plays and comments on his dramas and critics' reactions to them. Like his dramatic works, his non-fiction is marked with a vehement opposition to political programs, oppression, and the constraints placed on the individual's imagination.

CRITICAL RECEPTION

Early reviewers and audiences found Ionesco's plays obscure and inaccessible, largely because they broke all the rules of naturalistic theater. Today critics agree that one of Ionesco's great achievements is in making nonrepresentational and surrealistic techniques acceptable to viewers and allowing them to think beyond the bounds of conventional experience and language. As he became established as an important new voice that was invigorating modern theater, Ionesco was praised in left-wing circles and reviled by the right because of his iconoclastic approach. However, those on the left soon rejected him because of his refusal to accept any ideology and his seemingly apolitical stance. Ionesco himself complained that reviewers were too quick to judge his work based on their own ideological bias rather than a thorough understanding or appreciation of his method or literary merit. Contemporary commentators have begun to recognize that even in his early, so-called "nonsense" work there is a clear sociopolitical stance in his passionate defense of individual freedoms, even if Ionesco himself always refused to classify it as such.

While Ionesco continued to have detractors throughout his career, and not only for his seeming anti-leftist positions—at least one critic has faulted his plays for being unduly negative and containing elements of misanthropy—his reputation today is as one of the masters of a provocative performance style that engages audiences directly and urges them to think by giving bizarre embodiment to the commonplace. Some commentators have tried to capture the "meaning" behind the apparently meaninglessness of the language and situations Ionesco presents, while others claim that viewers and readers should look beyond meaning and concentrate on the "manner" rather than the "matter" of his works. For the most part, assessment of the plays has concerned Ionesco's use of proliferating objects to represent external forces that dominate the human spirit; his assault on empty forms of language; the use of the irrational to liberate the imagination; an existential view of life as both tragic and comic; and the longing for freedom that is distinctive of his characters. Many of these appraisals share a recognition that although the worlds Ionesco creates are bizarre, chaotic, and frightening, he holds out the hope that the human imagination, if freed, can marvel at the astonishing fact of human existence in a fleeting world.

PRINCIPAL WORKS

Plays

La cantatrice chauve [*The Bald Soprano*] 1950
La leçon [*The Lesson*] 1951
Les chaises [*The Chairs*] 1952
Victimes du devoir [*Victims of Duty*] 1953
Amédée; ou, comment s'en débarraser [*Amédée; or, How to Get Rid of It*] 1954
Jacques; ou, la soumission [*Jack; or, The Submission*] 1955
L'Avenir est dans les oeufs [*The Future is in Eggs*] 1957
Le nouveau locataire [*The New Tenant*] 1957
Tueur sans gages [*The Killer*] 1958
Rhinocéros [*Rhinoceros*] 1959
Le piéton de l'air [*A Stroll in the Air*] 1962
Le roi se meurt [*Exit the King*] 1962
La soif et la faim [*Hunger and Thirst*] 1964
Jeux de massacre [*The Killing Game*] 1970
Macbett [*Macbeth*] 1972
Ce formidable bordel! [*A Hell of a Mess*] 1975
L'homme aux valises [*Man with Bags*] 1975
Voyages chex les morts: Thèmes et variations [*Journeys among the Dead*] 1980
Théâtre complet 1992

Other Major Works

Non [*No*] (criticism) 1934
Notes et contre-notes [*Notes and Counter-notes*] (essays, addresses, lectures) 1962

La photo du colonel [*The Colonel's Photographs*] (narratives, short stories) 1962
Seven Capital Sins (screenplay) 1962
Journal en miettes (journal/autobiography) 1967
Présent passé, passé présent (autobiography) 1968
Contes no.1-4 (children's stories) 1969-70
Le solitaire [*The Hermit*] (novel) 1972
Antidotes (essays) 1979
Un homme en question (essays) 1979
Viata grotesca si tragica a lui Victor Hugo: Hugoliade [*Hugoliad: The Grotesque and Tragic Life of Victor Hugo*] (criticism) 1982
La quête intermittente (autobiography) 1988

AUTHOR COMMENTARY

Richard Schechner (interview date 1963)

SOURCE: "An Interview with Ionesco," in *Tulane Drama Review,* Volume 7, No. 3, Spring, 1963, pp. 163-68.

[*In the following conversation, Ionesco is characteristically reluctant to classify his plays and ideas, and reveals his annoyance at the tendency for "literary specialists" to ask irrelevant questions about the artist's work.*]

Schechner: *If there is a central theme to your work, it seems to be the search for the self. Your characters either don't know who they are (the Smiths, the Martins), or they are forced to abandon their identity (Jack, the Pupil), or else they are tortured in their effort to find themselves (Choubert). Yet, with Berenger, you have created a character who is himself. Could you discuss this aspect of your theatre's development?*

Ionesco: That is only one of my themes. The others, it seems to me, are: death, evil, political and social ills, old age, nothingness or absence. If "Berenger is himself," that's fine. I, however, cannot discuss this "development," nor the essential reality of the character. It's up to you to do that. Forgetting, if you please, everything that the critics have said about it. Commentaries become oppressive. Or rather, they constitute a screen which is placed between the reader and the work itself. Act as though you had read none of what the critics, favorable or unfavorable, have said. It's the work that we should read first; and it's to the work itself that we must constantly return.

Schechner: *What effect, if any, have Sartre and his analysis of the self in* Being and Nothingness *had upon your work? Has* Nausea *influenced your work?*

Ionesco: Not at all. Besides, I don't think much of Sartre. I believe also that my fundamental reaction is the very opposite of his. Consciousness, the awareness of existence provokes in me an astonishment which is a source of joy. This astonishment is like a state of grace. I am depressed when it forsakes me, when I am not astonished, when existence becomes routine because of exhaustion, lack of awareness, or distraction. This is what happens most of the time.

Schechner: *You have stated that the archetype is hidden within the stereotype. Is this one of the reasons why you, while making fun of clichés, continue to use them? Does the cliché hide a vacuum in the individual at the same time that it reveals a universal truth, especially in* **The Killer** *and* **Rhinoceros?**

Ionesco: An archetype is universal, of course. It is essential truth, a source. A stereotype is routine. Routine and cliché separate man from himself, hide him from himself, separate him from his deepest truth. In *The Killer* and *Rhinoceros,* Berenger destroys his own clichés as he speaks. And so, he sees beyond them. His questions no longer have easy answers. Perhaps he arrives in this way at fundamental questions which lie beyond false answers, that is to say ready-made answers (made by others, of course) which are not real answers. After all, to have no answer is better than to have a false one.

Schechner: *Would you say that the Berenger plays are written in a more classical style than the plays which preceded them?*

Ionesco: Perhaps. I don't know. It's a secondary problem, a problem of literary technique.

Schechner: *Is Berenger an everyman, an archetype? Is he a bourgeois hero?*

Ionesco: What is a hero? What is a bourgeois? What is a non-bourgeois hero? You're falling into clichés. The Marxist double talk is lying in wait for you! Communist conformity is as bourgeois as bourgeois conformity.

Schechner: *You write that the inner and outer worlds correspond just as do your personal world and the world of others. Is this identity the source of what you call classicism? What do you mean by "inner world" in such plays as* **Bald Soprano** *and* **The Maid to Marry?**

Ionesco: You're giving me a headache! Decidedly, you are a literary specialist. Let's say that *The Bald Soprano* is the expression of my personal feeling of the astonishing (*insolite*). A state of astonishment that breaks through clichés, which bursts clichés, by stressing those very clichés. The universe surprises me. The universe of clichés surprises me also. In *The Maid to Marry,* it seems to me that I am dealing chiefly with the impersonal world of clichés. The two characters are lost in their clichés. Lost. The illogic of the ending should shake up the spectators.

Schechner: *Was there a turning pont in your life, or in your idea of the theatre, between* **Amédée** *and* **The Killer?** *Your theatre seems to find a new existence with* **The Killer.**

Ionesco: I have no ideas about the theatre. Or at the most, about technical problems. With each play, everytime I begin to write, I ask myself how I can best express what I want to say. May I repeat, this is of minor importance. A turning point? There are always turning points. Everything is transition. We turn, and turn. But what can my "life" matter to you? My life in the final analysis is only the time that I have been able to write my works, to see, to listen, to write. What is written counts. I've lived for my work. It is my work which expresses, it is *my* life, or life in general. It is in my works that you must look for my life.

Schechner: *Also, you seem to abandon the theme of the couple in your Berenger plays. Before* **The Killer,** *your plays were constructed around the man-woman relationship, or about the family.*

Ionesco: Woman, or the members of the family, are also others. As well as being another aspect of oneself. Others are everywhere, and oneself is also in others. I abandon the couple, I take it up again, I abandon it, I take it up again, I abandon it, and so on. Whether I speak of, or express, the reality of another, of one or of several, it's about the same thing: the same "world" is manifested. A single person can represent others; a person alone also "bathes" in his epoch, speaks for others or for me.

Schechner: *Are you concerned by the political situation in France? If such concern exists, does it find expression in your work?*

Ionesco: Like all my countrymen, I feel concerned. But I don't feel concerned alone by the immediate current events. Current events are always the reflection of something more profound. Today's current events may or may not appear in my work. Perhaps they already do appear? I need distance to perceive it.

Schechner: *What relationship is there between words and objects in your work? Are the disarticulation of language and the proliferation of objects two phases of the same phenomenon?*

Ionesco: Perhaps. I believe so. What do you think? They aren't phases; they are simultaneous processes.

Schechner: *What influence, if any, has Artaud had on you?*

Ionesco: I read him recently. It may be a case of the meeting of minds.

Schechner: *What influence has the cinema had on you?*

Ionesco: I think it must have had one, since I've been going to the movies for years and years. You figure it out. That's your work.

Schechner: *You've said yourself, that you are not a "man of the theatre." Yet, your work is by far among the most* *theatrical of our day. How did you learn stage language without ever having worked on the stage?*

Ionesco: That proves that I'm a man of the theatre anyway. How did you learn to breathe from the first second of your life without anyone ever teaching you? The theatre is a natural function also.

Schechner: *What authors and directors are closest to you? What young writers do you prefer?*

Ionesco: Shakespeare, Calderon, Kleist, Chekhov, and others. Dubillard, Weingarten, and others.

Schechner: *You have said that once a form of art is accepted, it is outmoded. How do you look upon your early works today? Where is the avant-garde?*

Ionesco: That's true. Acceptance of an art form outmodes it. I don't know what to think of my early works today. To find the avant-garde all you must do is look around you. Besides, the avant-garde doesn't exist, or else it always exists. Everything is the avant-garde of something; there's no stopping.

Schechner: *Would you like to see your plays performed in a theatre like the TNP or on the Boulevard?*

Ionesco: Why not? It's all the same to me. But the TNP has already congealed into a set form of Masses, ceremonies; its politico-ideological inhibitions, its obsessions.

Schechner: *Has Camus influenced you? Particularly his* Myth of Sisyphus *and* The Stranger? *And Kafka?*

Ionesco: Camus? Perhaps. I esteem him very highly. Kafka has certainly influenced me.

* * *

Ionesco's P. S.—History and Literary Criticism. A man speaks to you. Instead of listening to the profound meaning of his words, instead of realizing what he wants to tell you, for he is speaking to you (or he is speaking alone, out loud, but his speech has a certain coherence; or else he is building a world, a structure appears), you do not receive this world, you only listen to the sounds. You say: how strangely he pronounces his "r," his "e," his "o"; say, where does that archaic expression come from? Or: where is his accent from? South of the Loire? Or: say, someone already told me the same thing he's saying; I wonder if he agrees with the other fellow?

Eugène Ionesco (essay date 1978)

SOURCE: "Why Do I Write? A Summing Up," in *The Two Faces of Ionesco*, The Whitson Publishing Company, 1978, pp. 5-19.

[*In the following essay, Ionesco sums up his reasons for writing, which include trying to recapture the paradisiacal light of his childhood and reveal it to others; communicating what he considers to be the dazzling miracle of existence, complete with its joys and horrors; and affirming through the creative act his presence in the universe.*]

I am still asking myself this question. I've been writing for a long time. When I was thirteen, I wrote my first play, at about eleven or twelve I was writing poems, and I was all of eleven when I started my memoirs: two pages of a school notebook. It isn't as though there was a lack of things to say. I know that at that time I still had a clear recollection of my early childhood, when I was two or three years old, a time which has now become the memory of a memory of a memory. Seven or eight was the awakening of love; I was deeply attracted by a little girl of the same age. Then, when I was nine, there was another, Agnes. She lived eight kilometers from the Mill of the Chapelle-Anthenaise where I spent my childhood, a farm at St-Jean-sur-Mayenne. I made faces to make her laugh, and laugh she did, closing her eyes, revealing dimples, and tossing her blond hair. What has become of her? If she is still alive, she must be a fat peasant woman, perhaps a grandmother. There would also be other things to tell: the discovery of the cinema, or the magic lantern; my arrival in the country, the barn, the hearth, and old man Baptiste with his missing thumb on the right hand. Many other things: the school, the teacher, old man Guéné, the priest, Durand, the tippler, who returned dead drunk from his rounds of the farms of the *commune*. Everywhere he went they'd give him cider, or pear brandy.

Then there was my first confession when I said yes to all the priest's questions because I couldn't make out what he was saying—he was muttering under his breath—and it seemed better to take upon myself imaginary sins rather than to let any slip by. I could have spoken of my little friends, Raymond, Maurice, Simone, and of the games we played. But all this required training which one acquires later. We speak of our childhood when we're no longer in it, when we no longer understand it very well. Of course, we also fail to understand what we are when we are children, but, at any rate, I was conscious of being alive when I lived in the Mayenne, I lived in happiness, joy, knowing somehow that each moment was fullness without knowing the word fullness. I lived in a kind of dazzlement. The first rift occured when I had to leave the Chapelle-Anthenaise. But with time the light dimmed, and now I realize I was not suited to being a farmer, ungifted as I am for manual labor. Some of my school pals from the *école communale*, Lucien, Auguste, have become wealthy farmers. To me, however, it seems that they lead quite a hard life, and that there's little play left in their daily existence. They cast an indifferent eye on frolicking children. Perhaps I might have been the village teacher but my only vacations would have been school holidays which are not real holidays for adults.

One of the real reasons for which I write must be to find once again the marvellous element of childhood beyond daily life, joy beyond drama, freshness beyond hardship. Palm Sunday, when the tiny village streets were strewn with flowers and branches, was a transfiguration under the April sun. On religious feast days, I would climb the narrow, rocky path, guided by the church bells, and the church itself would appear little by little, first the top of the bell tower with its weathercock, then the whole steeple outlined against the blue sky. The world was beautiful, and I was conscious of it, everything was fresh and pure. I repeat: it is to find this beauty again, intact in the mud, that I write literary works. All my books, all my plays are a call, the expression of nostalgia, a search for a treasure buried in the ocean, lost in the tragedy of history. Or, if you prefer, what I am looking for and seem to find from time to time, is light. This is my basic reason for writing literature, and for having nourished myself by it. Always in search of this light, its presence beyond the shadows a certainty. I write in the night, in anguish, by the brief flicker of humor. But this is not the light I'm seeking, not that lighting. I want a play of intimate confession, or a novel to remain shadowy until one issues into the light. In my novel, *Le Solitaire* (*The Loner*), as one comes out of a long moral tunnel, one is greeted finally by a dazzling landscape with the morning sun shining on a flowering tree, a green bush. In **Hunger and Thirst,** Jean, the wanderer, sees a silver ladder rising from the earth into the azure of the heavens, and in *Amédée or How to Get Rid of It,* the hero flies up in the direction of the Milky Way. In **The Chairs,** however, the characters have but a dim recollection of a church standing in a luminous garden, then the light fades and the play opens into the void. And so on.

Most of the time these images of light, quickly fading, or, on the contrary seeming to arise naturally at the end of a lengthy journey, have not been willed into existence but found. Or, if they appear in the conscious mind, it is because they first came to me in dreams. I mean by this that in my plays, or my written meditations, I have the feeling of embarking on a voyage of exploration, of groping my way through a dark forest, in the middle of the night. I do not know whether I will ever reach my goal, or even if a goal exists. I proceed without a clear outline, and the end comes of its own accord. It can be an awareness of failure, as in my last play, **L'Homme aux valises,** or of success providing that the end resembles a new beginning.

I am in fact seeking a world which has recovered its virginity; I would like to repossess the paradisiacal light of my childhood, the glory of the first day, an untarnished glory, and of an intact universe which would appear before me as though it were new born. It is as though I wanted to witness the event of creation before the Fall, looking for it within myself, as if attempting to swim up the stream of History, or within my characters who are other incarnations of my self, or who are like those others who resemble me in their quest, conscious or not, of an absolute light. It is because they have not mapped out a road to follow that my characters wander in the dark, the absurd, in incomprehension and anguish. It has often been suggested that I speak a great deal of my anxieties. I rather think that I

refer to those of human beings caught in the grayishness of daily existence, or in misfortune, people who mistakenly believe that they are prisoners of the impasses of history and politics, but who, as a result, become ready victims of exploitation, repression and wars. To return to what I way saying, I would like to stress that the state of childhood, and a certain intensity of light are indissolubly fused in my mind. All that is not light is anguish, sinister shadows. I write to find anew this light and communicate it to others. This light is at the outer edge of the absolute which I lose, and find again. It is also astonishment. I see myself in my childhood photos, eyes wide open, amazed by the very fact of existence. I haven't changed. The primordial wonder is still part of me. I am here, I've been put here, surrounded with all of this and all of that. I still don't know what happened to me. I've always been deeply touched by the beauty of the world. When I was eight, and then nine, I lived two months of April, and two months of May I will never forget. I ran along a path edged with primrose, gamboled through fresh green meadows, full of an indescribable joy of being. These colors, this dazzling light, haunt my mind so that when I say that the world is a prison I am not being truthful. In the Spring, I recognized the colors, the beauty, the light of a paradise whose memory I have kept. Even now, in order to escape from my anguish, I place myself marginally, peering with profound attention at the world, as though I were seeing it all for the first time, on the very first day of consciousness. Standing back, away from the world, I contemplate it as though I were not part of it. Then it may still happen that I will feel transports of joy. Wonder having reached its zenith, I no longer doubt anything. I feel certain that I was born for eternity, that death does not exist, that all is miraculous. A glorious presence. I am grateful then to witness this Manifestation and participate in it. And since I participate in this particular Manifestation, I will take part in all the Manifestations of the divinity, for all eternity. It is at such moments, beyond the tragedy and anguish of the world, that I am certain of being fully, truly conscious. I recover the age when I would walk, hazel stick in hand, among primroses and violets, and the sweet smells permeating the light of spring. The world and I were just beginning. Yes, it is to speak of my wonder that I write. But joy is not always part of wonder, or rather I am rarely sufficiently astonished to reach this kind of joy, this ecstasy. Most of the time the sky is dark, most of the time I live in anguish, used to feeling anguish, habituated to the habitual. The click which illumines everything happens with increasing rarity. I try to remember, I attempt to hold on to the miracle of light, and at times I succeed, but with age it becomes increasingly difficult. The passing years of personal history are like the stormy, tragic, demoniacal centuries of universal History. A tumultuous past, thick as memories, or as the collective memory of the world separates me, and all of us, from the beginning. We live inured to anguish and misfortune, and if on occasion I perceive that the world is a celebration, I also know, as all of you do, that it is misery.

There was to begin with the initial amazement: the conscious awareness of existence, an astonishment which I might call metaphysical, a pure surprise experienced in joy and light, free of any judgment brought to bear on the universe, the kind of astonishment which I recover only at moments of grace, in themselves extremely rare. Then a second type of amazement was grafted onto the first, the ascertainment that evil exists, or perhaps more simply that things are bad. This discovery that evil is among us, that at this moment it gnaws away at us, destroying us, preventing that we take cognizance of the miraculous, as though it were not part and parcel of the miracle of existence, is a frightful knowledge. Thus, the joy of being is strangled, submerged by misfortune which is as inexplicable as existence, tied to existence. Misfortune is a profound enigma. This theme has been debated by countless philosophers, theologians, sociologists. I myself will not dwell on this insoluble problem. I simply want to state that as a writer universal misfortune is my intimate, personal business. I must transcend evil in order to reach, beyond evil, not happiness, but a transient joy. In a naive, awkward way, my works are inspired by evil and anguish. Evil has squelched my joy. It is my circumambient atmosphere, and yet it continues to amaze me as does the light. It weighs more heavily than the light. I feel its weight upon my shoulders. In my plays I did not seek to discuss it, but to show it. The fact that it is inexplicable renders all our plans, all our acts absurd. This is what I feel as an artist. I found the existential enigma acceptable, but not the mystery of evil. And what is all the more unacceptable is the fact that evil is law, and that human beings are not responsible for its existence. But of course it suffices to look at a drop of water under a microscope to see that cells, that microscopic organisms, fight among themselves, kill and devour one another. What takes place on the level of the infinitely small, happens at every level of universal greatness. War is indeed the law of life. That's all it is. All of us know this, but we no longer pay attention. If only we were to be conscious of it, to even give it some thought, we would realize that this is not the way things should be, that life is impossible. It is already puzzling to be squeezed between birth and death, but to be forced to kill and be killed is inadmissible. The existential condition is inadmissible. We live in a closed economy; nothing comes to us from outside, and we are forced to devour one another. Go in peace and eat each other. I have the feeling that creatures are not in complete agreement with this state of things. We make one small gesture and precipitate the catastrophic end of protozoan worlds, dig in our shovels and destroy a nation of ants. Every gesture, every movement, be they insignificant, provoke disasters, catastrophes. I walk through this meadow without thinking that all the plants in it struggle for vital space, and that the roots of these magnificent trees, by reaching deeper in the earth, bring about suffering, tragedies, kill. Every step I take also kills. And so I say to myself that the beauty of the world is a deception.

Later in life, at about fifteen or sixteen, when we are all disciples of Pascal, without necessarily having read Pascal,

but simply by looking at the stars, I was seized by the vertigo of infinite spaces. The infinitely small is even more vertiginous than the infinitely large. To be unable to conceive a limitless world, to be unable to imagine the infinite, is our fundamental infirmity. Nor do we really understand what we are doing. We are made to do things we do not understand, of which we are not responsible. For a superior intelligence, we are all ridiculous wild beasts, tamed to perform meaningless acts in a circus, performing them with no understanding of what they are. We are being mocked; we are someone's plaything. If at least we could know. we are plunged in darkest ignorance, doing the opposite of what we think we're doing, not masters of ourselves. Everything eludes our control. We make revolutions to institute justice and freedom. We institute injustice and tyranny. We are dupes. Everything turns against us. I have no idea if there is meaning or not, if the world is absurd or not, for us it is absurd, we are absurd, we live in the absurd. We were born deceived.

Condemned to know nothing, except that tragedy is universal, we are now being told that death is a natural phenomenon, that suffering is natural, that we must accept it because it is natural. This is no solution. Why is it natural, and what does natural mean? The natural is the incurable, something I refuse to accept; it is a law I deny, but there is nothing one can do, and I am in the trap of what appears to be the beauty of this world. Still, there is one thing we can be conscious of: all is tragedy. To explain this by original sin is no explanation. Why was there original sin, and did such a thing really exist? What is far more extraordinary is that finally each and every one of us is conscious of universal tragedy. Also that each of us is the center of the universe, each human being lives in a state of anguish he cannot share with billions of other human beings who nevertheless experience the same anguish. Each one of us is like Atlas who bears alone the full weight of the world. And yet, they tell me, I can discuss this with a friend who will not necessarily murder me, I can go this evening to a concert, or a play. To hear what, see what? The same insoluble tragedy. I can go on to a good restaurant for a fine meal, and I will eat animals they have killed for it, and vegetables whose life span I interrupted. What I can do is not think of it. But let's watch out, for the same menacing force weighs upon our lives. We will be killed by other men, or germs, or on account of a psychic imbalance. There are moments of respite, short recesses at the expense of others. I realize of course that I am proferring the most banal of statements. At least one calls them banalities, when they are fundamental truths which people try to push aside in order not to think of them and go on living. We are told that we musn't be obsessed by things, that it is abnormal that things should obsess us. It seems to me that what is abnormal is that things should not obsess us, and that a thirst for life, a desire to live put our consciousness to sleep. We are all metaphysically alienated. Unconsciousness is added on to our alienation.

In these conditions, a man I call conscious, a man for whom these elementary truths are present, can he accept to go on living? I have a friend, a philosopher of despair, not at all insensitive, who lives in pessimism as in his natural element. He speaks a great deal, is a brilliant conversationalist and a jolly person. "Modern man," he likes to state, "fiddles with the incurable." That's exactly what he does. Let's do likewise. We live on various levels of consciousness. Since there is nothing we can do, since we are all doomed to die, let's be merry. But let's not be duped. We ought to keep, in the background of our consciousness, what we know. And we must also come out with it to set people on the right path. First, let's try to kill as little as possible. Ideologies do nothing but prompt us to murder. Let's demystify. It is now obvious that colonial empires have been erected, and massacres perpetrated in the name of Christianity and love. Other colonial empires are being formed at the price of even greater slaughter perpetrated in the name of justice and human fraternity. It is essential to come to the realization that so called ideologies are nothing but convenient masks used by those who yield to the explosion of the irrational or extrarational forces of crime inscribed in the very fibers of our nature. If there is a battle to wage, let it be against criminal instincts which find alibis in ideologies. If we cannot avoid massacring plants and animals, let us at least stop killing human beings. Neither philosophies, nor theology, nor Marxism have been able to solve the problem of evil, nor to explain its presence. No human society, above all not the communist one, has succeeded in averting or even diminishing it. Wrath is everywhere. Justice is not equity, it is vengeance and punishment. If the evil perpetrated by men upon one another undergoes a change of aspect, it remains fundamentally the same in its deepest nature.

Thus, I have written also to ask myself this particular question, to probe this mystery. It is the theme of my play, *The Killer,* in which the hero questions the assassin to ask him, in vain, what are the reasons for his hatred. Hatred must have excuses; it has no reasons. A murderer kills because he cannot help himself, without motive, with a kind of candor and purity. By killing others, we murder ourselves. To live beyond good and evil, to consider a thing to be beyond good and evil, as Nietzsche wished, is not possible. He himself went mad with pity when he saw an old horse slump down and die. There is pity then, not Eros but Agape. But charity is grace, a gift.

There is perhaps one way out still; it is contemplation, the wonder in the face of the existential fact as I said earlier. This might be, after all, a way of being beyond good and evil. I know it is difficult to live in the state of astonished wonder when one is serving a life sentence, undergoing forced labor with machine guns turned upon you, or simply having a toothache. Still, let us live in that state of wonder to the extent that it is possible. The richness of creation is infinite. No man resembles another, no signature is alike. One can never find two men with the same fingerprints; no one is anyone other than himself. This fact can also plunge you into amazement. It is also a miracle. In America, modern men of science have transcended atheism. Physicists, mathematicians, researchers in the natural sci-

ences believe they know that creation has a finality, a plan, that it is the grand design of a conscience which directs it. No individual can be born for nothing. If there is a final plan to the universe, then there must also be some kind of plan for the individual, and for every particle of matter. We must keep faith. This too will pass. The world may be merely a gigantic joke played by God on man. That's what the protagonist of my play, *A Hell of a Mess,* comes to realize at the end of it when he bursts out laughing; his whole life has been spent questioning himself and the mystery of creation, and all at once he sees that it's all been a terrible gag. I have no doubt been inspired by the story of a Zen monk who, in old age, having spent his whole life in search of a key, the seed of an explanation as to the meaning of it all, receives an illumination. Looking about himself with new eyes, he exclaims: "What deception!" and cannot stop laughing. I'm also thinking of an Italian film whose title I have forgotten along with the name of the director. I saw the film long ago, right after the Second World War. It showed German soldiers occupying a convent. Italian partisans attack the convent and the Germans leave, except one, more absent minded. He wears glasses, must be an intellectual. Alone in the convent, he is chased by a knife-wielding partisan who pursues him into the very chapel. This place will not prove to be a sanctuary. In his precipitous flight, the German knocks down a statue of the Virgin, then a cross bearing a tormented, bloody Christ. The Italian catches up with the soldier, and knifes him in the back. He falls. He looks about him, as though seeing the world for the first time in all its horror, takes off his glasses, and asks out loud: "Why, but why?" and dies. Here also there's a kind of illumination, and this ultimate question is in fact an ascertainment. This is the first and the last time that this man has thought about the world, and he has come to the realization of existential horror. Why this horror, why the absurdity of horror? This question can be posited from the very birth of consciousness, as it can also at the end of our existence. But throughout our life we are all plunged in horror as though it were the understood state of affairs, without ever questioning it. We are so used to things as they are that it is the act of questioning which seems absurd, when, in reality, what is senseless is not to question. Thus, to posit this fundamental question is already an illumination. It is at least the full realization of the basic problem: why horror?

I repeat that I don't have the feeling that I have said things that are new, but rather that I experienced intensely two contradictory apprehensions: the world is at once marvelous and atrocious, a miracle and hell, and these antithetical feelings, these two obvious truths, constitute the backdrop of my personal existence and my oeuvre. I said at the beginning of this lecture that I was wondering why I wrote. When I analyze myself I come up with a temporary yet substantial answer. I write to give account of these fundamental truths, these absolute questions: why existence, or rather how, and also how is evil possible, and how does it fit in with the existential miracle. I write to remind people of these problems, to make them aware of them so that they watch out and never forget. It is enough if they remember it from time to time. Why not forget, but, on the other hand, why not remember? We must be conscious of our destiny in order to know how to situate ourselves in relation to others, and to ourselves. Our social awareness flows out of our metaphysical consciousness, out of our existential intuition. By not forgetting who we are, where we're at, we will understand ourselves better. A human fraternity based on the metaphysical condition is more secure than one grounded in politics. A questioning without a metaphysical answer is far more authentic, and in the end useful than all the false and partial answers given by politics. Knowing that each individual among billions is a whole, a center, and that all the others are ourselves, we will be more accepting of ourselves, that is to say, for it is the same thing, of others. We must consider that each one of us, paradoxically, is the world's navel. Thus, every individual will be able to acquire a greater importance, we, ourselves, a lesser one, with the greater one being accorded to the others. We are, at one and the same time, unimportant and very important, and our destiny is identical. New human relationships can spring from this awareness. It is the feeling of amazement and wonder in the face of the world we contemplate, tied to the intuition that everything is at the same time suffering, which can constitute the fundamental basis of human fraternity, and of a metaphysical humanism. As Jean Paul Sartre wrote in *No Exit,* hell is other people. The others are us, we could answer. If we cannot make our common existence a paradise, we can nevertheless transform it into a less thorny, disagreeable passage.

The theatre that some of us have written since 1950 is radically different from *boulevard* theatre. In fact, it is its opposite. Contrary to *boulevard* theatre which is free of problems and questions, and is entertainment, ours, despite its humor, its derisive snicker, is a theatre which puts in question the totality of human destiny, of our existential condition. Whereas popular theatre puts consciousness to sleep since it neither disturbs nor reassures, we have been told that we are disquieting, and that since there is good dose of disquiet in the world already, it would be nice not to increase our problems, at least for a time. But this time passes quickly and we find ourselves face to face with our anguish. Personally, *boulevard* theatre increases my anguish more than anguish. It is unbearable, so empty and useless does it seem. But as to us, we do not want to chase anguish away. We try to make it familiar so that it can be surmounted. The world can be comical, or derisory, it can also seem tragic, in any case it isn't funny. Nothing is funny.

Nor do we write political theatre, or, at least, not purely political. Politics seem to me to be also entertainment, a horrifying kind of entertainment, but entertainment nevertheless. That is to say that politics cannot be detached from metaphysics. Without metaphysics, politics do not express a fundamental human problem. They constitute in such case a limited, secondary activity, stripped of ultimate implications. Two centuries of politics and revolutions

have instituted neither liberty, nor justice, nor fraternity. Politics offer no answer to the fundamental questions: who are we, where do we come from, where are we going? They are maintained within strict limits, cut away from transcendental roots. Metaphysics have also been unable to offer definitive answers, and such is the case of science, and the philosophy of sciences. The only possible answer is the question itself. It reactualizes within our consciousness the certainty of our fraternity in ignorance, beyond social class, beyond the barriers of our fundamental identity, beyond the differences between human beings. This consciousness cannot cancel out anguish, but it is able, as politics are not, to stop provoking wars and massacres. Politics are alienation, and can be experienced only as the analyzable, or unanalyzable reflection of the passions which direct them, dominate them, making us into puppets. Political theatre can bring only a very limited illumination. Ideological theatre is inferior to the ideology it wishes to illustrate, and of which it is the tool. Since political theatre reflects ideologies familiar to us, it is tautological. For a century, and above all in the last fifty years, it has rehashed the same themes. Thus, political theatre makes us as unconscious metaphysically as *boulevard* theatre. We must depoliticize theatre. Political theatre can teach us nothing new.

I would not be telling the whole truth if I were to affirm that the reasons I have just given are the only ones which impelled me to write. Many of the latter came to me in stages, as I progressed in my career in the theatre and found myself confronted by the diverse theatre guides, masters of the mind, directors of human conscience who came forward to give me proper orientation. I also met along the way recruiters of committed art and theatre. Some twenty years ago, or more, Jean Vauthier and I were summoned by a Mr. Panigel whom we did not know. After slight hesitation, we accepted his invitation. Mr. Panigel was a member of the Communist party, at that time extremely pro-Stalin. He addressed us in the following terms: "Boys, you have a bit of talent, but no ideas. You can't write theatre without ideas. I'll instruct you. It is I who will provide you with ideas. We'll meet periodically, and I will teach you how to write." Obviously, we never returned to see this gentleman. At about the same time, or perhaps a year later, Bernard Dort wrote a lengthy article, a whole page in *L'Express* on Adamov and on me. Our two photographs illustrated the text in the paper. What did Dort say in his article? It appeared that, as he saw it, both of us had done until then good negative work: we had criticized bourgeois or petty bourgeois society, which was fine but not sufficient.—Of course, this sort of criticism was the least of my own concerns, but this was not clear from the piece.—The latter went on to say that Adamov and I had a good deal of talent, and that we could become the two greatest men of contemporary theatre. One condition had to be fulfilled. No more negative criticism, from now on we had to make positive statements or we would suffer the consequences of having nothing to say. To renew ourselves, to become adult writers who have reached their majority, there was only one possibility: become committed writers. One spoke a lot of commitment at that time. It was essential to take part in the social, political struggle. We had to create a revolutionary theatre, not only in form, but in content, and in underlying intent, for this was commitment. To become committed did not mean to opt for the cause you were interested in, but simply to become a card carrying, militant member of the Communist party. Only this was commitment and nothing else. Our theatre had to become one of Marxist instruction. Such was the new definition of popular theatre: to educate the masses in this particular way, not even solely in Marxism, but rather train them to follow the orders of the day. The latter, issued by the governments of the countries of Eastern Europe to the intellectuals of these countries, from which independent thinkers wish to escape, and do so, at the price of enormous personal sacrifice, are the very one the occidental ideologues wanted to impose on us. In France, as in England and Germany, the opposition, or rather the ideological fashion brought to bear, or attempted to exercise a veritable form of censorship. I felt that I belonged to a minority, crushed between bourgeois convention and the new ideological convention. I was alone, in disagreement with everyone, ill at ease, deprived of a spiritual family. Of course, I did not give in. Adamov did not resist; he accepted commitment, converted to an elementary kind of Marxism and Brechtianism and was applauded by the ideological critics. But he did not receive the plaudits of the public. A minority of bourgeois thinkers, who thought of themselves as revolutionary, people with no contacts with humanity at large, were his only supporters. Arthur Adamov denied his early plays and lost himself as a writer and an artist. I know that at the end of his life he regretted this action.

The young bourgeois, reactionary by nature, now no longer young but still intent on indulging in literary criticism, believed they were getting "close to the masses," to the will of the masses, and that they would teach the proletariat what the proletariat is supposed to be. But we know that for them, "the masses" and "the proletariat" were nothing but abstract ideas. They never worked in factories, nor in the fields; all they knew were society's *salons.*

I myself wrote committed plays. Such a one is **Rhinoceros,** as is **The Killer,** and a number of others, in spots. Only, I did not commit myself in the direction desired by the ideologues. I pointed out the existence of evil in a thousand different societies, in thousands of different aspects. The ideologues held this against me. From that time on they began to write both in newspapers and in literary reviews that my works were worthless, that I had been untrue to myself whereas in reality I was listening to myself alone. Because I was not in agreement with them, because I had not obeyed them, they decreed that I had no talent, and that they were bitterly sorry to have mistakenly attributed some to me earlier on. They went so far as to attempt to take back what they had published about me, declaring, as Bernard Dort did in the course of a lecture delivered on a trip through Europe, that I had been given "too much importance" when, in actual fact, it was he who had at

first lavished this attention upon me. But let us leave for some other time these personal polemics despite their curious insight into what goes on behind the curtain not of a theatre, but of literary criticism in general, and dramatic criticism in particular, at least that of contemporary critics who are never objective being much too passionately involved. One can make mistakes when one is passionate about objectivity, but one makes conscious mistakes, or lies to oneself, when the passions have ideological orientation. Thus, it must be said that if one accords "too much importance" to anything these days, it is to contemporary criticism.

I would like to return to the first impulses which propelled me to write. I have said that I wanted to communicate my dazzlement by the very fact of existence, then, after the apprehension of the existential miracle, that of horror and evil, and finally, as I explored existence in detail, I had ideas to express. But, in order not to withhold anything, I must add the gratuitous joy of writing, of inventing, the delight of imagining, and telling things which never happened to me. In short, the joy of creation, that is to add to the universe things which were not there before, to add on a small universe, or universes, to the universe. Isn't it true that each writer, each artist, each poet wishes to imitate God, doesn't he wish to be a little God who can create gratuitously, without reason, in sport, because he is free and in a way that is totally free?

When I went to the *école communale,* the older children of the next class would tell me about the strange and difficult homework they had to do: composition. They had to write stories, or improvise upon a theme. I was impressed, and I decided that it must be very hard indeed, but very beautiful. I couldn't wait to try it myself. For most of my school friends this was the worst of chores. For me it held a mystery. Finally, the following year, as I graduated from one class to the next, I was put to the test of composition. We had just had a village fair. We were asked to write about it. I described an imaginary fair, with bits of dialogue. I got the highest mark, and the teacher read my composition out loud in the classroom. What seemed to impress him most was that the story was in dialogue form, contrary to all the others. The teacher congratulated me for inventing dialogue, which, he said to me, had been invented long ago. I went on writing more compositions, always with the same sense of joy. Since we were not assigned enough compositions in class I began to write stories, just for myself. I can say that I've been a writer since the age of nine, that is to say since forever. A born writer. I've never been able to do anything but literature. Literature gave me great pleasure, my own and that of others. I also began to love paintings, those that tell stories, like Breughel for example where there are country fairs with lots of people, or Canaletto where you can see unreal looking people walking through the unreal town of Venice, a whole life, a universe taken from reality but become imaginary, and then Dutch interiors, ancient portraits where the quality of the art work is deepened by the documentary, human quality. Yes, there's a whole world which may be real or not, a world which used to fill me with nostalgia for things which could have been, or had existed once but were no longer there, worlds offered yet defunct. And I wrote to offer worlds in turn, possible worlds, other possible worlds. So, it was in childhood that I experienced the purest pleasure of writing, and that my vocation came to the fore. The miracle of the world was such that I was not only dazzled by it, as I have just said, but that I wanted to imitate this miracle by making miracles of my own. Creation.

Thus, it is in this dazzlement before the world, in this astonishment at the thought of the marvel of the world, and in the joy of invention that I find the fundamental, conscious or semi-conscious, or subconscious reasons for writing, for artistic creation. The other reasons, more adult, therefore less pure, less naive, came later. When I entered the ring of polemics, I began to answer, to explain, to explain myself, to deliver messages and anti-messages, but always I went on questioning, for it is this interrogation above all things which is closest to the impulses of childhood.

There is one more reason which you must guess since it is not only that of artists but of each and everyone of us: to do everything so that the world I have seen, the people I have known, the landscape of my childhood and other landscapes I saw later, would never be forgotten, lost in nothingness. One writes to perpetuate all this, to perpetuate oneself, to triumph over death. We are here with our paintings, our music, our poems, our books, in search of a kind of immortality. One writes in order not to die completely, not to die at once, since everything perishes in the end. And I believe that among all these reasons, the two strongest are the following: to allow others to share in the astonishment, the dazzlement of existing, in the miracle of this world of ours, and to shout to God and to other men our anguish, letting it be known that we existed. All the rest is secondary.

OVERVIEWS AND GENERAL STUDIES

Leonard C. Pronko (essay date 1959)

SOURCE: "The Anti-Spiritual Victory in the Theater of Ionesco," in *Modern Drama,* Vol. 2, No. 2, May 1959, pp. 29-35.

[*In the following essay, Pronko argues that in Ionesco's theater impersonal, anti-spiritual forces, symbolized in physical objects, dominate and conquer humankind, and that dead things are victorious over that which is alive.*]

THE FRENCH DRAMATISTS who began writing about 1950, baptized by M. Jean Duvignaud the "School of Paris,"

have sometimes been called "anti-theatrical," for they employ dramatic methods which are frequently opposed to those of the conventional theater. Writers like Ionesco, Beckett, and the early Adamov wish to return to what might be called "pure theater," that is to say a type of theater employing means which are strictly theatrical and do not belong to the realms of philosophy, psychology, sociology or politics. One of the favorite devices of such a theater is the presentation of the author's views in a visual way, using space and movement rather than language. In *Waiting for Godot,* for example, the moral suffering of mankind is depicted physically by shoes which do not fit, hats which scratch, servants visibly attached to masters, and watches which do not run. In a play like Adamov's *The Parody,* the solitude and bewilderment of modern man are represented by a decor (including a clock without hands) which remains the same, but is constantly foreign because seen from different angles. In *The Big and the Little Manoeuvre,* a man's destruction by incomprehensible and impersonal forces is made more palpable by his loss of one limb after the other.

The theater of Ionesco is rich in examples of this phenomenon. In the essays he has published in various French periodicals, Ionesco has described quite explicitly the feeling he is attempting to evoke by giving such undue importance to the physical aspects of his theater. There are two fundamental states of consciousness at the root of his plays, he tells us in "The Point of Departure" (*Cahier des Quatre Saisons,* August, 1955). One is that of evanescence, and the other that of heaviness or opacity. The latter feeling most often dominates, and we feel the universe crushing in upon us:

> Matter fills everything, takes up all space, annihilates all liberty under its weight; the horizon shrinks, and the world becomes a stifling dungeon. Speech crumbles, but in another way, words fall like stones, like corpses; I feel myself overcome by heavy forces against which I wage a losing battle.

Such a "victory of anti-spiritual forces," of the dead *thing* over that which is alive, is expressed on many levels in the theater of Ionesco. Setting and properties, language, characters, and structure, each contributes in a slightly different way to the impression of heaviness or opacity.

The first and most obvious level, that of physical objects, plays a particularly large role in the later comedies. In the earlier plays, **The Bald Soprano** (1950?), **The Lesson** (1950), and **Jack or the Submission** (1950), the stage is encumbered not with an oppressive amount of matter, but with fantastic characters and what one might call solidified language. In **The Chairs** (1951) the characters are more realistic, the language less absurd, and the accumulation of objects as a means of expressing solitude, uselessness and loss of liberty makes its appearance. The Old Man and the Old Woman, living in a dilapidated apartment on a lonely island, await the arrival of their guests to whom the Man will reveal his "Message" before the two leap to their deaths. The guests arrive and a chair is brought for each.

The guests are, however, invisible, and soon the stage is cluttered with chairs, suggesting that even when people are present there is an absence of humanity and an overabundance of the object. The physical universe and society, in the form of the chairs, gradually accumulate between the two old people so that at the end of the play, as they leap from their respective windows at either side of the stage, there is no opportunity for them to meet again. The last guest to arrive is "His Majesty," and in spite of strenuous efforts to reach him, neither of the characters is able to get through the mass of chairs. The setting of the play also suggests the futility of life, and a lack of meaning, for there are ten doors in this small apartment, and the characters go in and out all and any, aware that they all lead to the same place.

In *Victims of Duty* (1952) the crushing force of life, and of an inimical world, is manifested by a huge crust of bread which the Inspector forces Choubert to chew and swallow with great difficulty. At the same time, Choubert's wife is preparing coffee for her guest, and brings out dozens of teacups which she piles upon a buffet.

In *Amédée or How to Get Rid of It* (1953), the dead love of Amédée and Madeleine, their bitter and quarrelsome relationship, is represented by a cadaver which they discovered in their bedroom some fifteen years ago. It is stricken with "geometric progression," and has been growing ever since. Moreover large mushrooms have been sprouting in the bedroom where the fascinating body is kept. Suddenly the body starts growing at a vertiginous rate, and huge toadstools spring up in the living room as well. By the end of the second act the corpse stretches across the entire stage, ready to knock a hole in the front door by the force of its ever-growing feet. Amédée and Madeleine have been forced to make space by piling the furniture in a corner of the room, and are scarcely visible any longer, so much are they dominated by the deadweight of their meaningless life together, crowded out of house and home by cabinets and corpses. Amédée finally succeeds in pulling the huge body out a window, and drags it through the streets down to the Seine, but he is discovered by the police, and escapes by simply flying into the air. The ending is weak and somewhat obscure, although Ionesco may wish to suggest by Amédée's buoyancy the elation and complete liberation he experiences upon freeing himself from this burden.

The New Tenant (1954) reminds us of the second act of *Amédée,* but without the body. A man comes to take possession of his new apartment. The movers arrive with the furniture, and carry it into the room, until every inch of space is covered, the windows blocked, and the doors obstructed. The stairway, we learn, is still full of furniture, the streets are crowded, traffic has stopped, and the subway system is paralyzed. Here we are in a universe which has been overcome entirely by matter, and there is nothing to do but follow the example of the New Tenant who, invisible behind tall screens and cupboards, asks the movers to turn out the lights as they leave.

In the early plays, dead matter is suggested not so much by visible objects (although they are present too in the worn out clothing and shabby settings) as by language which is treated not as a living instrument of communication, but as something solidified and lifeless. Words are used for themselves, for their sounds rather than their meanings, and an order of suggestion rather than logic is frequently followed. Ionesco has called *The Bald Soprano* "the tragedy of language," and it is in this play that we witness a total breakdown of communication on the linguistic level. Words are used which have apparent meaning, but in the context in which they are placed they lose their significance and appear absurd and empty. The process begins in the stage directions as the set is described: "English middle-class living room, with English armchairs. An English evening. Mr. Smith, an Englishman, in his English armchair and slippers, etc." The adjective "English" is used to a point where it becomes empty of meaning, ending with the senseless seventeen English strokes on the English clock.

As the play opens Mr. and Mrs. Smith are spending a quiet evening at home. Mrs. Smith, in language strangely reminiscent of conversation manuals (which Ionesco has admittedly used in constructing the dialogue of this play), outlines the meal they have just had, describes the members of the family, and in general indulges in a delightful parody of the inane chit-chat which forms so large a part of daily conversation. Fatuous phrases, trite proverbs which are not at all à propos, and absurd word associations constantly crop up: Roumanian folklorique yogurt, which is good for appendicitis and apotheosis. Mr. Smith emerges from his newspaper to wonder why the ages of the deceased are always given, but never those of the newborn. In the discussion of Bobby Watson, who died two years ago, we see a complete confusion of time, character and meaning, and yet within each sentence there is sense. It is only when set side by side with the others that the absurdity is apparent. "He died two years ago," says Mr. Smith. "You remember, we went to his funeral a year and a half ago." And later he points out, "People were talking about his death already three years ago." To which Mrs. Smith adds, "Poor Bobby, he had been dead for four years and his body was still warm."

Bobby Watson's wife, it turns out, is also called Bobby Watson, as are his son, daughter, and all the other people to whom he is related. Language has broken down completely, and we are lost in a world where there are no longer any distinguishing tags.

Guests arrive, the Martins and the Captain of the Fire Department. An argument ensues, followed by the usual chit-chat strewn with such original observations as, "The truth lies between the two," "The heart is ageless," "Truth is not found in books, but in life." The guests begin to tell stories, each one more pointless than the other, ending up in the masterly tale told by the Fireman, entitled "The Cold": "My brother-in-law had, on his father's side, a blood cousin whose maternal uncle had a father-in-law whose paternal grandfather had married as a second wife a young native whose brother had met, on one of his voyages a girl with whom he fell in love and by whom he had a son who married . . . etc., etc." This continues for a full page. It is the victory of language over logic, of empty conversation over meaningful discourse, of dead phrases over a living content.

The play ends at a high pitch as the language disintegrates into complete nonsense and unintelligible repetition of syllables, the characters shouting at one another in their anger at not understanding. And as the curtain falls we are back at the beginning of the play, with the Martins occupying the places originally occupied by the Smiths, and Mrs. Martin reciting the same empty phrases that Mrs. Smith had uttered.

In *The Lesson* a professor, at first humble and meek, gives a private lesson to a young girl eager to take her "Total Doctorate." He so dominates her by his "learning" and personality that at the end she is reduced to a somnambulistic state, and he kills her. The knowledge of the young student is dead knowledge, so to speak, for it is not a thing which she really knows, but only something which she has memorized. There is a significant commentary on language in the professor's lecture on philology, which is at the same time a parody of pedantry. In absurd terms, he discusses the "Neo-Spanish" tongues: Spanish, Latin, Italian, Portuguese, Roumanian, Sardanapolous, Spanish and Neo-Spanish. The differences between these related languages, we learn, are imperceptible, since all the words of all the languages are the same. As an example he employs the sentence, "The roses of my grandmother are as yellow as my grandfather who was Asiatic." In all languages it is identical, and yet when the girl repeats the sentence, it is never correct according to the professor. The only really safe words, it is suggested, are nonsense syllables, for words which are heavy with meaning, always end up succumbing, crumbling, or bursting like balloons.

In *Jack* a nonsense phrase, "I like potatoes with bacon," stands for an acceptance of society and all that it imposes upon us. Jack at first refuses to utter a word, a rebel against his family who want to marry him to Roberte. The family overwhelms him with invective: he is a *mononstre, vilenain,* an *actographe.* His sister Jacqueline cries, "Je te déteste, de t'exertre," while his mother reminds him how she taught him to "progresser, transgresser, grasseyer," for she has been all things to him, "une amie, un mari, un marin." As in *The Bald Soprano,* words are no longer used as counters, but simply stand for themselves, meaningless blobs, suggested by other words. Trite phrases are again thrown in for no apparent reason. Jacques finally gives in and accepts, not the original fiancée, but her sister, who has three noses, and nine fingers on one hand. She tells Jacques that in the basement of her chateau all things are called "cat." Again language has broken down completely, and serves absolutely no meaningful purpose. Cats are called cats; insects, cats; chairs, cats; one, cat; two, cat; etc. So whether one wishes to say, "I'm tired,

let's go to sleep," or "Bring me some cold noodles, warm lemonade and no coffee," one says, "Cat, cat, cat, cat, cat, etc." "Oh," concludes Jacques, "how easy it is to speak! It's not even worth the trouble." This is also the conclusion of the New Tenant, who, expressing himself in terms of light and dark, simply says good night, turns out the light, and remains in his wordless solitude.

The same techniques are employed in *The Chairs* where "Drink your tea, Semiramis," and "You might have been a general chief, etc.," return with the monotony of a hey-nonny-nonny refrain, and with just about as much meaning. Words suggest other words because of sound, regardless of meaning, and the absurd physical presence of the word is before us once again rather than any reality of which it is a symbol. "Were you sure to invite everyone," asks the Old Woman, "Le Pape, les papillons, et les papiers?" (The Pope, the butterflies and the papers). Several times words are repeated so frequently that they become only a sound, totally emptied of their meaning, as when one repeats one's own name so long that it becomes simply an object in itself. Will the Orator come to reveal the Old Man's message? "Il viendra," (he will come) says the Old Man confidently. And the word is repeated ten times, then changed to the present tense, and repeated five more times.

The ultimate irony is that life itself, even a rich and successful life which contributes something to society (which is certainly not the case with the two old ruins on the stage before us), is finally reduced to nothing but a word, to a street name. "Let's die and enter into legend," says the Old Woman, "At least we'll have our street." And the old couple plunge to their death repeating ecstatically, "Nous aurons notre rue!"

The Chairs seems to be a transitional play in the career of Ionesco. In it we may see the gross exaggeration of language, and the grotesque characters so typical of the first plays. At the same time, these elements are not so prominent, and there is a certain realism in the presentation of the Old Man and Woman. This realistic presentation of the characters is seen again in *Victims of Duty, Amédée* and *The New Tenant,* however fantastic the situations may be. It is in these more "realistic" plays that the visible objects play an important role, and one suspects that this is a sort of compensation for the lack of dead language presented as such and the lack of puppet-like characters who are exaggeratedly mechanical, and therefore representative, once again, of that which is dead and cumbersome rather than vital and potentially spiritual.

For Ionesco's characters are dead, all of them entombed within his restricting universe with walls closing in upon them, and buried also within their own solitude, each one separated from all others in a world where communication is absolutely impossible. The huge cadaver on stage in *Amédée* is not the only dead body in the play, and Amédée is fortunate if he is resurrected at the end, for he is the only resurrected character in Ionesco's theater, the only one to escape from this world. He does so only at his wife's expense, for as he ascends he drops upon her head the gigantic hat and beard belonging to the body he has finally gotten rid of.

Even the more realistic characters in the later plays perform meaningless and mechanical activities. Amédée is caught up in the senseless repetition of the play he is writing, and of which he never gets beyond the third speech. Madeleine is tangled in the wires of her job as telephone receptionist. And both of them have accepted mechanically, without thinking, the presence of the body in their apartment. In fact, they no longer can remember who it is, or where it came from. The mechanical rhythm of the movers in *The New Tenant* is obvious, as they bring in the furniture. The concierge in the same play speaks in a vacuum, never waits for the answers, but gives them herself.

The Old Woman in *The Chairs* becomes a grotesque automaton as she rushes from door to door bringing in chairs, and when the room is crowded she automatically takes on the role of usher and begins selling programs and candy.

The lack of any individual existence of the characters in *Jack* is underlined by the fact that all the members of one family are called Jacques, and all those of the other, Robert. The same technique is used in *The Bald Soprano* when Bobby Watson is mentioned. The Martins, in the same play, are so lost in their individual solitude that after years of married life they do not recognize each other. Their life together has been one of mechanical repetition. People are so interchangeable, so anonymous, that at the end of the play the Martins may take the roles assumed at the beginning by the Smiths.

The structure of these plays is frequently circular, and we find ourselves at the end at exactly the same point from which we started out. This is true of *The Bald Soprano;* of *The Lesson,* where the professor kills his student, the bell rings and another student is about to enter as the curtain falls; and of *Victims of Duty,* where everyone is conquered by the inhuman force of duty and the curtain falls on all the characters masticating the hard crust of bread imposed by society, and seeing to it that all the others are doing the same.

Those plays which are not constructed along these lines, usually follow a descending line, beginning with something resembling life, and ending, after absurd repetitions of one kind or another, in absolute silence. *The Chairs* and *The New Tenant* both end on a note of silence and emptiness. The world, dominated by substance, has become a graveyard.

This unhappy outlook on life is, surprisingly enough, presented by Ionesco in a way that is extremely amusing. One reason for this is that he employs the very technique of comedy—reduction of the living to the mechanical, exaggerated repetition—to express his particular view. The

heaviness and opacity of life's atmosphere, the overabundance of matter is at least partially relieved by the element of humor, which Ionesco considers a "happy symptom of the other presence," evanescence or lightness. There is a profound unity, then, in this theater, where the very humor which is a symptom of lightness, at the same time makes patent the victory of the anti-spiritual forces in life.

One might be tempted to argue with the author over the paradox which lies at the base of his theatrical conception. But Ionesco is after all a dramatist, and makes (even less than other playwrights) no claims as a thinker. He stands for "pure theater," and we can only be grateful that this paradox has produced plays which are amusing, suggestive, and refreshingly original.

Bernard F. Dukore (essay date 1961)

SOURCE: "The Theater of Ionesco: A Union of Form and Substance," in *Educational Theatre Journal*, Vol. XIII, No. 3, October 1961, pp. 174-81.

[*In the following essay, Dukore analyzes* The Bald Soprano *and* The Lesson *to show that, contrary to Ionesco's critics, his plays are not formless or meaningless, and explains that while his works are unorthodox and not concerned with psychological realism or political ideology, in Ionesco's drama form is a direct outgrowth of subject matter.*]

The plays of Eugene Ionesco have inspired both violent condemnation and rhapsodic adulation. When an off-Broadway theatre recently produced *The Bald Soprano* and *Jack,* their advertisements featured a "For-and-Against" column of critical judgments, and urged the public to decide for itself. The public decided not to decide for itself, but accepted the "Against" verdict. Yet the statements on the "Against" side were not the sole reason that the production did not succeed, for Ionesco's supporters often have a habit of alienating his potential public. In a characteristically enthusiastic article, William Saroyan declared that Ionesco's plays "bewilder, delight, annoy, astonish, amaze and amuse" him.[1] Jacques Lemarchand, an ardent supporter of Ionesco, stated that Ionesco's theatre "is not a psychological theatre, it is not a symbolist theatre, it is not a social theatre, nor is it a poetic or a surrealistic one. . . . The Theatre of Eugene Ionesco is certainly the strangest . . . to have emerged from the post-war period."[2] These statements have helped create an image of Ionesco as the incomprehensible poet of the obscure. Until very recently, Ionesco himself has not done much to create a different impression. Such statements as "reality is unreal . . . words are just noises"[3] have fostered the legend that Ionesco writes little more than fascinating double-talk.

Lately, however, Ionesco has become more articulate, and in his recent writings and speeches about the theatre, we can see a logical aesthetic credo. A new style of art is usually unpopular, he reminds us, chiefly because its technique is unfamiliar. To illustrate this, he compares Proust and Sue.

> Eugène Sue was extremely popular. Proust was not. He was not understood. He did not speak to everyone. . . . Today it is Proust who offers a wealth of truth, it is Eugène Sue who seems empty. How fortunate that the authorities did not forbid Proust to write in a Proustian language![4]

The type of theatre against which Ionesco usually inveighs is the ideological theatre, the theatre which claims social usefulness as its main function. This, he says, is nonsense, for when the theatre "tries to become the vehicle of ideologies, it can only become their popularizer. It simplifies them dangerously. . . . An ideological theatre is insufficiently philosophical."[5] And it is more illuminating to read a psychological treatise than to visit a psychological theatre, for the latter is insufficiently psychological. Pirandello, he says, is now outdated,

> since his theatre is founded upon theories of personality or of many-faceted truth, theories which since psychoanalysis and depth psychology seem clear as day. By confirming the correctness of Pirandello's theories, modern psychology, necessarily going further in the exploration of the human psyche, gives him a certain validity, but at the same time renders him insufficient and useless: since it says more completely and more scientifically that which Pirandello has said.[6]

But although Ionesco harangues against the ideological theatre, he does not maintain, as Terrence Rattigan did in his debate with Bernard Shaw, that ideas have no place in the theatre. Ionesco draws a line between ideas and ideology: "A work of art is not devoid of ideas. Since it is life or the expression of life, ideas are emanated from it: the work of art does not emanate from an ideology."[7] He makes a distinction between ideas which are universal in character and those which are local and specific, such as political ideas.

Ionesco remembers that as a child he was held spellbound by the puppet shows in the Luxembourg Gardens, and in fact his plays are descendants of these puppet plays. His theatre is a *guignol*, a theatre of caricature and of the grotesque, a theatre that exaggerates life and that becomes larger than life. Ionesco finds the realistic theatre insufficient and unsatisfying. It is necessary, he says,

> to go all the way in the grotesque, in caricature, beyond the pale irony of witty drawing room comedies. Not drawing room comedies, but farce, an extreme burlesque exaggeration. Humor, yes, but with the methods of burlesque. A hard comedy, without finesse, excessive. . . . Theatre is an extreme exaggeration of feelings, an exaggeration which disjoints the real[8]

Ionesco is not a crank writing meaningless absurdities or colorful vagaries. His plays are different from the conventional types of plays. He writes neither from the viewpoint of psychological realism nor from the viewpoint of a political ideology. Because of this, the form of his plays is neither the form of the well-made play nor of epic

theatre. But his plays are not formless. Artistic unity, he maintains, "satisfies an inner need and does not answer the logic of some structural order imposed from without."[9] To understand the form of his plays, one must go to the plays themselves, and not to some preconceived notion of play construction. Ionesco's plays are neither formless nor meaningless. To prove this, I would like to take *The Bald Soprano* and *The Lesson*—two plays dissimilar in form, both plays different from the type of theatre we usually encounter—and to analyze their meaning, and how the form of each reflects that meaning.

Both *The Bald Soprano* and *The Lesson* begin with recognizable theatrical conventions, and promptly turn them upside down. In *The Lesson,* the Maid admits the Pupil into the house, and the latter meets the Professor for the first time. This is a conventional means of giving exposition. Characters meet for the first time and discuss their backgrounds. In *The Bald Soprano,* a husband and wife are relaxing after dinner: she knits, and he reads the newspaper. What could be more familiar? In both plays, the opening situations are familiar. The audience has seen them in the realistic theatre. What happens later is not familiar.

The Bald Soprano seems to be formless because it does not use the plot structure of the realistic play. But is not this lack of plot, this apparent lack of form, this willful lack of meaningful forward motion—is it not exactly the right form for a play that reveals lives which are formless and which lack meaningful forward motion?

Note the opening stage direction:

> SCENE: *A middle-class English interior, with English armchairs. An English evening. Mr. Smith, an Englishman, seated in his English armchair and wearing English slippers, is smoking his English pipe and reading an English newspaper, near an English fire. He is wearing English spectacles and a small gray English moustache. Beside him, in another English armchair, Mrs. Smith, an English-woman, is darning some English socks. A long moment of English silence. The English silence. The English clock strikes 17 English strokes.*[10]

Except for the clock striking seventeen times, this is a stunning picture of bourgeois conventionality. And this image of bourgeois conventionality is developed throughout the course of the play.

No sooner have the chimes struck seventeen times than Mrs. Smith announces that it is nine o'clock. A joke? Of course it is a joke. But it also reveals that the specific time of day is meaningless, because from hour to hour and day to day, their lives are essentially the same. It is also noteworthy that the couple is named Smith: a perfectly conventional, nondescript, middle-class name for conventional, nondescript, middle-class people.

Mrs. Smith continues: "We've drunk the soup, and eaten the fish and chips, and the English salad. The children have drunk English water. We've eaten well this evening. That's because we live in the suburbs of London and because our name is Smith." The complacency and smug self-satisfaction of the bourgeois is established at the very start of the play.

The uniformity, as well as the lack of vital life in the lives of the members of the bourgeoisie is revealed when the Smiths discuss Bobby Watson, whom Mr. Smith describes as a "veritable living corpse." Bobby Watson has a wife, also named Bobby Watson.

> Since they both had the same name, you could never tell one from the other when you saw them together. It was only after his death that you could really tell which was which. And there are still people today who confuse her with the deceased and offer their condolences to him.

There is no difference in the pattern of existence between one bourgeois and another, difference in sex notwithstanding. That people still confuse the dead man with the living woman indicates further the lifelessness of bourgeois existence, for quick or dead the bourgeois Bobby is a corpse. When asked to describe Mrs. Bobby Watson, Mr. Smith first states that she is not pretty, then that she is pretty; first that she is big and stout, then that she is small and thin. The outward appearance of the bourgeois does not matter: since their lives are exactly the same, their peculiar physical characteristics are unimportant. To reinforce this point, Ionesco informs us that the Watsons have a son and a daughter, named Bobby and Bobby, an uncle named Bobby Watson, and an aunt named Bobby Watson. Every bourgeois is a Bobby Watson.

Ionesco frequently employs a grotesque reversal of the usual. He accomplishes this by taking a familiar situation, injecting into that situation a single element which renders it completely improbable, and then writing the scene as though the improbable element were not there. Such a scene occurs when Mr. and Mrs. Martin enter. Each thinks the other looks familiar. They discover that they are originally from Manchester, that they came to London on the same train, that they sat in the same compartment, and that they now live in the same house. A man and a woman are attracted by each other, and discover that they have seen each other before. So far, there is nothing unusual— except that we know their names are Mr. and Mrs. Martin. Then they discover that they live in the same room, sleep in the same bed, and are parents of the same child. Bourgeois love is revealed as not only formalized and standardized, but as something which has become a series of clichés. Bourgeois lovers neither really see nor really know each other. That passion has disappeared, and that excitement has become boredom is clearly indicated in the opening stage directions of the scene: *The dialogue which follows must be spoken in voices that are drawling, monotonous, a little singsong, without nuances.* And at what would normally be the high point of passion, *They sit together in the same armchair, their arms around each other, and fall asleep.* Upon awakening, Mr. Martin is-

sues the following declaration of love: "Darling, let's forget all that has not passed between us . . . and live as before." Mrs. Martin passionlessly agrees. The lack of passion and vitality will continue; they will go on as before.

The Smiths return, the party begins, and Ionesco presents not only a brilliant satire on cocktail party conversation, but—and more to the point—on the bourgeois preoccupation with inconsequentials. At first, each of the characters gropes for something profound with which to impress the others. The result is a plethora of banalities. When Mr. Martin states, "We all have colds," Mr. Smith adds the penetrating observation, "Nevertheless, it's not chilly." The group then discusses interesting and important events. For example:

> MRS. MARTIN (*graciously*): Oh well, today I witnessed something extraordinary. Something really incredible. . . . In the street, near a café, I saw a man, properly dressed, about fifty years old, or not even that. . . . Well, I'm sure you'll say that I'm making it up—he was down on one knee and he was bent over.
>
> MR. MARTIN, MR. SMITH, MRS. SMITH: Oh!
>
> MRS. MARTIN: Yes, bent over. . . . I went near him to see what he was doing. . . .
>
> MR. SMITH: And?
>
> MRS. MARTIN: He was tying his shoe lace which had come undone.
>
> MR. MARTIN, MR. SMITH, MRS. SMITH: Fantastic!
>
> MR. SMITH: If someone else had told me this, I'd not believe it.

By having these people regard this incident as extraordinary, Ionesco emphasizes the triviality of their lives.

The doorbell rings. Mrs. Smith goes to the door to answer it. She returns with the announcement that no one was there. This occurs twice more. When the doorbell rings a fourth time, she refuses to go. Mr. Smith goes to the door and returns with the Fire Chief, who rang the doorbell the fourth time. He admits that he rang it the third time, and then hid himself as a joke. But he tells them that no one had rung the doorbell when it rang the first two times. The women maintain, "Experience teaches us that when one hears the doorbell ring it is because there is never anyone there," and the men the reverse. When the argument gets heated, the Fire Chief intervenes and extinguishes the "fire": "You are both partly right. When the doorbell rings, sometimes there is someone, other times there is no one." This satisfies all concerned, for it is the classic bourgeois manner of settling controversies: choosing the middle path between two extremes.

It is appropriate that the visitor is a Fire Chief, for what a fireman does is what the bourgeois does. He puts out fires, extinguishes the flames of human passion. And since the Fire Chief is under orders to extinguish all the fires in the city, he goes around looking for fires (sparks of vital life) to extinguish. He will not find such fires in middle-class homes, and when he asks if there is a fire for him to put out, the Smiths and Martins answer that there is not even a smell of anything burning.

The lives of these people are not only passionless, but pointless. What is of vital importance to them is actually trivial. What promises to be highly exciting turns out to be dull, and a tempest in a teapot is greeted with the significance of a cosmic catastrophe. The characters tell each other pointless stories based on commonplace incidents. Finally, the Fire Chief goes through an absurdly long and involved genealogy ("My brother-in-law had, on the paternal side, a first cousin whose maternal uncle had a father-in-law whose paternal grandfather had married as his second wife a young native whose brother . . ." etc.) as preface to a story whose "point" (amazing revelation of the extraordinary!) is that one of these people caught a cold in the winter.

At this point, enter the Maid, who turns out to be the Fire Chief's sweet-heart. Here, too, passion is extinct, for, as the Fire Chief declares, "It was she who extinguished my first fires." Not kindled, but extinguished. This is the ideal of young love: passion extinguished.

The Maid wants to read a poem to the guests (i.e., join them on an equal footing) but the Smiths are shocked at this effrontery. Although she manages to frighten them into letting her recite a poem, they push her offstage as soon as they can. The sanctity of the middle-class must be protected from lower-class upstarts.

When the Fire Chief leaves, Ionesco presents another illustration of the dull routine of these people's lives. The party conversation becomes a series of clichés. "To each his own," "An Englishman's home is truly his castle," "Charity begins at home"—these clichés follow each other with no logical continuity. The words gradually become nonsense syllables, and the nonsense syllables solitary vowels and consonants, as one character yells, "A, e, i, o, u" and another screeches, "B, c, d, f, g." The meaninglessness of their lives is conveyed by the manner in which they express themselves: meaningless sentences and phrases which degenerate into more meaningless syllables and letters.

Finally, to reinforce the point that these people are not individualized characters but are prototypes of the bourgeois man and woman, the lights that descend on the "final" scene come up to discover Mr. and Mrs. Martin seated in exactly the same positions as Mr. and Mrs. Smith in the beginning of the play, and saying the same words that the Smiths had said. The play ends exactly where it began.

The Bald Soprano is a satire on bourgeois life, which, the play shows us, is horrible in its dull conventionality, its rigidity, its lack of vital life. Since the lives of these people lack purpose and direction, Ionesco has removed from the play the conventional dramatic structure which would have given them purpose and direction. The play is deliberately static. Ionesco purposely avoids a forward motion of plot, choosing instead a succession of scenes, each of which is connected to the other by theme, each revealing the banality of these people's lives, and culminating in a screaming mass of clichés.

The title is explained when the Fire Chief inquires of the bald soprano, and is told, "She always wears her hair in the same style." And so it is with the bourgeoisie. Each lives daily the same life as the previous day, and the day of each is like the day of the other.

The opening of *The Lesson* is not as bizarre as that of *The Bald Soprano.* There is nothing comparable to a clock striking seventeen times and an announcement that it is nine o'clock. On the contrary, the opening of *The Lesson* is as conventional as any admirer of the realistic theatre could desire. A doorbell rings. A Maid admits a Pupil to the house, and asks her to wait for the Professor, who will arrive shortly to give her a lesson. What follows when the Professor arrives is far from conventional.

Having named—with difficulty—the four seasons, the Pupil announces, to the Professor's satisfaction, that she wants to study for a doctorate. When the Pupil answers that one and one are two, the Professor marvels at her knowledge, tells her that she is very advanced in her studies, and that she will easily get a doctorate. A few moments later, our doctoral candidate is unable to subtract three from four. Nevertheless, she is able to multiply—in a split second—3,755,998,251 by 5,162,303,508. Soon, the Professor explains that the difference between two languages is their striking resemblance to each other, and that they are different despite their identical characteristics.

Although *The Lesson* may be regarded as a satire on the educational process—which it is—I do not think that this is either its sole or even its chief meaning.

Let us begin by examining what happens.

The Maid admits the Pupil for a lesson. The Professor arrives, and gets acquainted with the Pupil. The Maid warns him not to teach arithmetic, but he ignores her warning. He begins the lesson by trying to find out what the Pupil already knows, and gives her a simple test in addition, which she passes easily. Next, he gives her a simple test in subtraction, which she fails. He then tries to teach her subtraction, but fails. He introduces the subject of linguistics and comparative philology, also against the Maid's advice, and fails again. Finally, he murders the Pupil. The Maid comes in and discovers the crime. He tries to kill her, but does not succeed. She helps him to get rid of the evidence, and to prepare for the next pupil, to whom, presumably, he will do the same thing.

The Lesson is a tightly organized play, with a recognizable plot. A teacher tries to teach a lesson to a pupil. He is increasingly frustrated at his inability to do so. These failures gradually assume the shape of a nightmare as he becomes less and less able to make her understand what he is talking about.

A lesson is essentially a form of communication, an attempt to pass on information from one person to another. In this play, the attempt is unsuccessful. And Ionesco's theme emerges from this: people cannot effectively communicate with each other. The Professor tries to teach the Pupil the two basic elements of communication, words and numbers. But he cannot do so. To the communicator, everything is clear and logical, and in the first half of the play, we see the lesson through the eyes of the communicator, the Professor. His attempts to explain subtraction are perfectly clear to us: we know exactly what he is talking about. But by the time he gets into linguistics and philology, we see the lesson through the eyes of the Pupil. What the Professor says is unintelligible. That which distinguishes Spanish from neo-Spanish, he explains, "is their striking resemblance which makes it so hard to distinguish them from each other." These languages are "diverse in spite of the fact that they present wholly identical characteristics." Each successive attempt to communicate fails, and each failure causes frustration, which creates a frenzy that results in murder. The inability to communicate translates itself into frustration on the part of the teacher, pain (toothache) on the part of the pupil, and finally murder, the culmination of the frustration and the pain. Nor will it end this time. The process will repeat itself with each new pupil. Communication will not be achieved.

The function of each character is directly related to this theme. The Professor's major objective is to teach, to communicate meaning; the Pupil's is to learn, to understand his meaning. And the Maid is one of those souls who is not concerned with communication or meaning; she is concerned only with her job. She keeps the place in order and cleans up her employer's mess.

Running beneath all of this, as a constant counterpoint to the theme of non-communication, is a strong sexual motif. This is apparent from the very entrance of the Professor, and is stressed by Ionesco in his opening description of him:

> *He rubs his hands together constantly: occasionally a lewd gleam comes into his eyes and is quickly repressed.*

> *During the course of the play . . . the lewd gleam in his eyes will become a steady devouring flame.*

As soon as he enters, he notices that the Pupil is well developed for her age. When she says, referring to the test that he will give her, that she is ready for him, he is taken aback. "Ready for me? . . . (*A gleam in the eye, quickly dispelled, a gesture immediately checked.*) It is I who am ready for you, Mademoiselle. I am at your service." Throughout the play, there are sex symbols. The Professor refers to the arithmetic lesson as "arithmetical knitting." In trying to teach her subtraction, he talks about biting her ears. The chief sexual element, however, is the fact that in

the middle of the lesson, the Pupil gets a toothache. Ionesco could have chosen a crick in the neck, or writer's cramp but he chose a toothache. A toothache is internal. And the moment the Pupil first gets this toothache is significant. In a speech filled with an insistent, caressing rhythm, the Professor discusses words. These words, which are "charged with significance" and heavy with meaning, dive downwards and "burst like balloons." At this point, the Pupil gets a toothache. At this point, the hymen is ruptured. From here until the murder, we have a subtle rhythm of speech and action increasing in force as the Professor makes deeper insertion, until he reaches orgasm: murder. The rhythm of the speech is smoothly, then more violently, caressing:

> pass delicately, caressingly, over the vocal cords, which, like harps or leaves in the wind, will suddenly shake, agitate, vibrate, vibrate, vibrate or uvulate, or fricate or jostle against each other, or sibilate, sibilate, placing everything in movement, the uvula, the tongue, the palate, the teeth . . . the lips. . . . Finally the words come out through the nose, the mouth, the ears, the pores, drawing along with them all the organs that we have named, torn up by the roots, in a powerful, majestic flight . . .

The rhythm becomes strongly fricative:

> farrago instead of farrago, fee fi fo fum instead of fee fi fo fum, Philip instead of Philip, fictory instead of fictory, February instead of February . . .

From the tantalizing fricatives, the rhythm of the scene, completely linked to the continuing cycles of the action (effort, failure, frustration, renewed effort, etc.) builds steadily in intensity until it reaches a dramatic and sexual climax in the murder.

> PROFESSOR: Repeat, repeat: knife . . . knife . . . knife . . .
>
> PUPIL: I've got a pain . . . my throat, neck . . . oh, my shoulders . . . my breast . . . knife . . .
>
> PROFESSOR: Knife . . . knife . . . knife . . .
>
> PUPIL: My hips . . . knife . . . my thighs . . . kni . . .
>
> PROFESSOR: Pronounce it carefully . . . knife . . . knife . . .
>
> PUPIL: Knife . . . my throat . . .
>
> PROFESSOR: Knife . . . knife . . .
>
> PUPIL: Knife . . . my shoulders . . . my arms, my breast, my hips . . . knife . . . knife . . .
>
> PROFESSOR: That's right . . . Now, you're pronouncing it well . . .
>
> PUPIL: Knife . . . my breast . . . my stomach . . .

He stabs her. Ejaculation occurs at precisely the same moment as the murder. In addition, the manner in which he kills her is important. He does not strangle her: he uses a knife—a phallic knife.

The sex motif is developed as an undertone that reinforces the basic theme of the play, the inability to communicate.

In the sex act, we have the most basic form of human communication. It is ironic that despite this basic way in which two people unite, they are more apart than ever; that despite the apparent communication, there is really no communication. This irony not only reinforces the theme, but reinforces the nightmare quality of the play.

The functions of the chief characters attain new significance when seen in the light of the sex motif. The Professor, in attempting to teach and to communicate meaning, is trying to penetrate. The Pupil, in attempting to learn and to understand meaning, is trying to receive.

The form of each of these plays is, as we have seen, a direct outgrowth of its subject matter. The lack of meaningful forward motion in **The Bald Soprano** and the nightmare intensity of **The Lesson** spring from the inner worlds of these plays. Ionesco does not begin with a theatrical form (such as the well-made-play) which he uses to develop his subject. Instead, he begins with a subject, and from that subject derives his form. Form and content are so interrelated, that these highly unorthodox plays possess an artistic unity which would hardly have been attained had Ionesco poured his subject matter into an orthodox form.

Notes

1. William Saroyan, "Ionesco," *Theatre Arts,* XLII (July, 1958), 25.

2. Jacques Lemarchand, "Le Théâtre d'Eugène Ionesco," in Eugène Ionesco, *Théâtre* (Paris, 1954), I, 11-12. My translation.

3. Quoted in Muriel Reed, "Ionesco," *Réalités* (December, 1957), p. 50.

4. Eugene Ionesco, "The Avant-Garde Theatre," *World Theatre,* VIII (Autumn, 1959), 184.

5. Eugene Ionesco, "Discovering the Theatre," trans. Leonard C. Pronko, *The Tulane Drama Review,* IV (September, 1959), 9.

6. Ibid., p. 8.

7. Ionesco, "The Avant-Garde Theatre," p. 194.

8. Ionesco, "Discovering the Theatre," pp. 10-11.

9. Eugene Ionesco, "The Starting Point," in Eugene Ionesco, *Plays,* trans. Donald Watson (London, 1958), I, ix.

10. This and subsequent quotations from *The Bald Soprano* and *The Lesson* are from Eugene Ionesco, *Four Plays,* trans. Donald M. Allen (New York, 1958). Another English translation is available: Eugene Ionesco, *Plays,* trans. Donald Watson (London, 1958), Vol. I. The reader is invited to compare these with the French edition: Eugène Ionesco, *Thèdtre* (Paris, 1954), Vol. I. Ionesco's plays present language problems that are sometimes insurmountable. In *The Bald Soprano,* for example, Ionesco has Mr. Martin announce that he took a train from Manchester at *"une demie après huit"* and arrived in London at *"un quart avant cinq."* The grammatical construction is English. Although the correct French would be *"huit heures et demie"* and *"cinq heures moins le quart,"* he has made the English Mr. Martin say—in French—"a half after eight" and "a quarter before five," which is a general equivalent of "half past eight" and "a quarter before five," which joke his French audience would certainly understand. The only way to give the flavor of the original would be to make the characters French rather than English, and to have them say, "eight hours and a half" and "five hours less the quarter."

George G. Strem (essay date 1962)

SOURCE: "Ritual and Poetry in Eugène Ionesco's Theatre," in *The Texas Quarterly,* Vol. V, No. 4, Winter 1962, pp. 149-58.

[*In the following essay, Strem asserts that Ionesco creates a personal, poetical theater by using his inner voices rather than his rational faculties to produce his work, and says that by bringing the ritual of daily life onto his stage the playwright returns to the origins of dramatic expression.*]

As a playwright Eugene Ionesco has a feeling of uneasiness, to say the least, about the contemporary theatre, especially about the contemporary French theatre. He accuses the latter of being too doctrinary. Too many writers are using the stage as a pulpit to expose and impose their philosophies.

His own convictions in the matter of theatrical art he summarized in his play **Improvisation.** Here Ionesco stages himself under his own name, demonstrating the way in which he works, or rather, how his works arise by spontaneous generation. The accent is on *impromptu:* in the beginning there is the creative urge. The playwright, vehicle of creation, patiently waits until the first impulse is followed by another, a first word evokes a sequence, a question its reply, until finally the dialogue falls into a pattern according to its own law. However, even while his play is still in gestation, philosophers of the market place urge him to elaborate a plot which should conform to their own individual and contradictory doctrines. One of them wants to convert him to the epic theatre à la Brecht, another to essentialism (existentialism), a third to another fashionable philosophy. For a while he endures the swell of pompous clichès, but he eventually manages to state his own profession of faith regarding the art of playwriting:

> "Le théâtre est, pour moi, la projection sur scène du monde du dedans: c'est dans mes rêves, dans mes angoisses, dans mes désirs obscurs, dans mes contradictions intérieures que, pour ma part, je me réserve le droit de prendre cette matière thêâtrale."[1]

These lines reveal the nature of the quarrel between Ionesco and the conventional theatre. Ionesco does not seek theatrical substance in dialectics brought in from the outside; rather, he finds the conflict within himself and uses the stage to exteriorize it. In the strict sense of the drama his theatre is therefore undramatic; nonetheless, it makes excellent theatre. Since he admits that his plays aim at self-expression, he must turn away from the conventional techniques of playwriting to achieve this aim. He rejects the categorical imperative of a plot—conceived as a prearranged concatenation of events—for he is not interested in telling a dramatized story. In **Victims of Duty** he takes issue with this conventional requirement of plotmaking. To think out a plot, he says, is not different from writing a suspense story; in fact, he contends, all playwriting has been since antiquity the writing of suspense stories. Where there is a plot, there is a solution found in advance; it is held in reserve to produce it at the right moment. It is the *deus ex machina* to save author and spectator from embarrassment; it is reassuring, its existence is known in advance, it therefore perverts the basic law of life which is unpredictability.

> "On cherche, on trouve. Autant tout révéler dès le début."

Essentially, the reproach Ionesco levels against the traditional theatre is that it does not take into account the powerful drive of modern art to enrich itself from nonrational sources that bathe all existence. Already Jean Cocteau had declared in 1936 in his preface to *Renaud et Armide*:

> "L'epoque allait venir où, loin de contredire la sottise, il s'agirait de contredire l'intelligence. Mais on ne peut contredire l'intelligence que par l'emploi lyrique des sentiments."

We shall see that Ionesco does just that: he creates a personal, that is to say poetical theatre in order to dispute the right of reason to serve as unique guide and mirror of man's world. He relies on what he terms "le mecanisme createur," to write his plays. We have already explained what this means as to the creative process; his work is not the product of his brain but the dictation of inner voices. His writing technique consists of resorting to sound effects, puns, and apparently nonsensical phrases to produce a certain magic like that of the witch doctors among primitive peoples. Thus, he creates an atmosphere charged with emotion; it appeals not to the reasoning faculties but to the feelings and sensitivity of the spectator. Moreover there is no "imitation of action" in Ionesco's theater in the Aristotelian sense; his dialogues are no mere conversation to illustrate and explain the action, as it is the case in many of the so-called "well-made plays"; rather, they constitute the very tissue and fabric of the drama, forming what Francis Ferguson calls "the plot as the soul of the play."[2]

In addition to harking back to his inner voices Ionesco also allows outside influences to shape his plays. The title of **The Bald Soprano** is due, for example, to a slip of the tongue of one of the tired actors during a rehearsal. Ionesco, present at the rehearsal, found the accidental encounter of the words "cantatrice" and "chauve" extremely propitious to express the satirical intent of his play; he therefore changed the original title "English without Tears," which had in its turn been borrowed from an advertisement of a language-teaching method. Undoubtedly Ionesco believes that works of art are the concern of the entire universe, which brings them about through manifold influences as it would create a planet or a mountain. His theatre, as he puts it, is not written; it writes itself.

His medium, the words of the human language, fascinates him. This Rumanian-born author is a great master and juggler of the French language in which he writes. In this respect he is the direct heir and continuator of Rabelais, also a disciple of Rimbaud, Mallarmé, Baudelaire, and others. Words he realizes, participate in the universal duality as much as anything else. They are valid as keys to conventional understanding but also in their own right as musical entities. As such they possess a certain evocative quality.

Deprived of their rational connotation, words in **The Bald Soprano** produce a sound-pattern characteristic of the social contacts of Western man, epitomized in the British middle class. The chatter of nonsensical or silly phrases symbolizes the inability of man to communicate with his fellow men. By giving up all pretense of meaning, the author shows that our conversations have no regard for true communication. He gets his point across by reproducing the ritual of daily family life in its innumerable manifestations. The comical effect achieved by the nonsense of the words, accompanied by that of the gestures, has deep tragic implications. The play conforms to Ionesco's own definition of the theater, for it is the expression of his anguish about the nonsensical character of our daily lives, and on a higher plane also about the meaning of our existence. The same will hold for all of Ionesco's productions; from one end to the other of his theatre he presents the manifold aspects of the Human Comedy, the force and satire of which surpass Balzac's interpretation.

Let us take, for example, another of his popular plays, **The Lesson.** Gibberish produced in imitation of the sound pattern of modern life again constitutes its theme, this time between a professor and his pupil at their lesson. The rational being, the professor, is overcome by the power of words. The endless repetitions of certain formulae intoxicate him; their magic unleashes deep-seated, murderous instincts in him. The fact that such magic ceremonial always results in the same ritualistic sacrifice of a human being is announced in form of a warning, uttered by the maid: "La philologie mene au pire." The student too begins to succumb to this word magic: through increasingly involved, increasingly nonsensical periods, circumlocutions, and repetitions, she is brought into a state of torpor, accompanied by a physical sensation that feels like toothache. Tension is on the rise, comparable to that produced by a savage beating of drums. Several times the professor repeats the word *couteau*—it refers to the glittering blade that he has taken out of its cache and is now holding in his hands. The word is decomposed: cou-teau. The first syllable alludes suggestively, alluringly, danger-ously to the neck of the student that beacons to the frenzied man handling the glittering object; the second syllable "teau" is very close to "tue," the lethal verb that brings the ritual to the culminating point. "Le couteau tue," the knife strikes the girl with enormous force as the High Priest im-molates the sacrificial victim. The result was not calculated, though it could be foreseen; the professor acted in an intoxicated state as if under the effect of a drug. The ritual has certain prescribed forms and gestures but it is never exactly the same—just as was the case at the Dionysian festivals.

Like **The Bald Soprano,** this second play transcends the individual plane and attains a collective meaning. **The Lesson** suggests that people are swayed not by reason but by their passions. The learned man who turns murderer when he is intoxicated by words is the so-called civilized man who has been brought into a state of frenzy in which he is capable of wholesale massacre of his fellow men. The magic of nonsensical phrases proclaims the inanity of our whole civilization, Ionesco's condemnation of the misuse of erudition.

The creative mechanism that produced **The Lesson** is the unfolding of a ritual, comparable to the production of primitive dances and a ritualistic act in which they culminate. There is no dramatic conflict brought in from the outside; the play is a journey back into the jungle of the human soul. And again, as in **Soprano,** the end of the play shows that the same ritual is about to start all over again, that it will renew itself while repeating itself. The dead girl is carried out, a new student will take her place, the performers will perform, sinister forces will recom-mence their action; the deeply hidden sense or the shock-ing nonsense of human sacrifice, of life and death, of hu-man striving and failure will be once more hinted at, the same ritual arriving at the same results—*da capo al fine.*

Magic and ritual produce the theme of a third play, **Jack, or The Submission.** As in **Soprano,** the characters are interchangeable. This is indicated by the ingenious artifice of calling all the relatives of the male protagonist Jack, all of those of his female counterpart Roberta. The various members of the same clan are differentiated by numbers only. Both tribes gang up on Jack No. 1, whose tragedy and crime is that he is an individual. The pathos of the play, underlining the futile struggle of the individual against the all-submerging forces of our mass civilization, the "submision" of the title, is enhanced by nonconven-tional techniques based once more upon the performance of certain ritualistic acts and the magic of sound effects. At first, Jack No. 1 boldly faces the hostile armies of his enemies. He proclaims that he dares dislike the universally adopted dish of potatoes with bacon. Then all the pressure, clamor, and hatred of public opinion weigh down upon him. He must conform; with the dish he must accept all the paraphernalia of the mass man, must choose a bride not according to his own taste but according to the needs

of the community. Once defeated on the score of the insipid nourishment, our sad hero turns his former defi-ance into a negative one by going all the way on the road toward his debasement. Not only will he espouse an ugly bride but he will choose the most repulsive of the Rober-tas, the one with three noses and nine fingers on each of her hands. The ritual that consecrates this immolation of the individual on the altar of public opinion is most expres-sive and depressive. The bride is a sorceress who promises to Jack a one-syllable language. This syllable is "cha" which is, as pronounced in French, the sound of kissing, that is of sensual pleasure. The multiplication of this sound in the combinations of *cha-armant, château, chameau, chaminadour, charrue, chagrin, chabot, chaloupe, cha-land, chalet, chatouille, chapître, chahut, chamarré, cha-peau,* and finally *chat* (cat) represents the insistent, recur-rent, irresistible lure of the Flesh to which Jack abandons himself. The verbal magic is further strengthened by the ritual of gestures. The members of the two tribes, witness-ing the embrace of the defeated rebel and his cat of a bride, execute a savage dance around the lovers; they make all kinds of grotesque gestures, they utter animal cries. The obscurity of the night and the passion of their senses make the lovers unaware of the crawling, crouching, moan-ing, and heavy breathing around them, of the squatting teeming mankind that celebrates their downfall. Finally everything dissipates; only the Woman, with the nine long, grabbing fingers on her hands, agitating like snakes, remains visible.[3]

Ionesco is, like his contemporary and fellow playwright Jean Anouilh, an author of but a few basic themes which recur throughout his theatre. Thus we retrieve the theme of the impossibility of a breakthrough in human communica-tion in **The Bald Soprano, The Lesson,** and **Jack;** and the question of the absurdity of the human condition in view of the inevitability of death in most of the plays. All these motives are intertwined in **The Killer,** one of Ionesco's most forceful plays, a three-acter. In the first two acts the protagonist is faced with the brutal, sly, maliciously destructive work of a Killer who is out to deter man from creating, from persevering in the ways of Life. Our hero's first reaction is that of indignation rather than of horror; it is the reaction of the social man who invokes the help of society against an enemy of society. He finds nothing but indifference and incomprehension; stupidity reigns supreme. Finally, in the last, magnificent monologues of the third act, the revolt of the protagonist against the Killer transcends society to rise to the metaphysical plane. Death is presented here in an actual exteriorization of the dreaded monster. The "monologue interieur" of the hero is converted into an imaginary dialogue, to make it percep-tible on the stage.[4] The grinning killer is the projection of the hero's, that is of Man's, inner vision. It is to this embodiment of his vision that he addresses his questions, but they are answered by the hero himself, for the Killer remains speechless though terribly present throughout the scene. The questions are those man eternally asks in the face of death. Man wants to understand the reason for his inevitable destruction. All he gets for an answer is a cynical grin from the Killer. The latter, represented as a puny fellow to make the dread he inspires all the more ridiculous, will nevertheless overwhelm and slaughter the human hero. Man implores but the other remains implacable. Man would like to combat the Killer and perhaps he has the means of doing it (Bérenger, our protagonist, has two guns which he once aims at his enemy), but he is so fascinated by him that he finally kneels down, disarmed, to receive the deathly blow. The ritual of killing is performed according to varying and yet eternally the same laws. Again, as in *The Lesson,* the knife of the High Priest is raised to immolate the victim. The inability of the hero to oppose the killer means perhaps that deep down man knows that death is good, death is wise, and that the living do not understand death. One almost has the impression that our hero has been at all times on the side of Death against Life which he finds senseless. If we apply the same conclusion to the author himself—for he admittedly expresses his own anguish and his own feelings in his theatre—we find that, indeed, death is an obsession with Ionesco. He fears and desires it at the same time; as he puts it, he fears his desire for Death.[5]

Death lurking upon Man, ambushing him in the midst of life's preoccupations, is the subject of still another play, *The New Tenant.* The ritual of death is staged here through the moving-in and installation of the personified Death, the new tenant, into the house of life. All around us the paraphernalia of death encumber our horizon. The furniture of the new tenant keeps coming; it takes up all the space in the apartment, in the hall, in the street. The dark-clothed gentleman who sits down in his chair and puts out the light, to wait in the darkness, is a strong and obvious symbol. One is reminded of the ephemeral character of life, one becomes painfully aware of the ever present possibility of one's own, sudden end. In the midst of this stern symphony, comic elements appear, the comic being produced, as usual, though reversal of the normal attitudes of people or the normal attributes of things. Heavy pieces of furniture are handled with the greatest ease by the movers while small vases weigh them down. One can interpret such theatrical tricks any way one wishes, but the light and graceful vases clearly seem to have more weight, that is more importance from the perspective of the play than the massive pieces of furniture.

Since Ionesco conceives of the theatre as the projection of his inner world, as we saw in his declaration of faith above, and since he is an artist, it follows that he endeavors to create a poetic theatre. That does not mean that he will write his plays in verse but, rather, he will give them poetical content. Of him can be said what had been asserted about the writers of the twenties and early thirties centered in Paris, namely that they "tried to substitute the poetry of the theatre for poetry in the theatre." (Fergusson, Chapter Seven). It is in the name of poetic reality, which he holds superior to the materialistic representation of our universe, that he protests against the monopoly of the rational, Racinian tradition of the French stage. This poetic reality, he creates by the same sound effects that he employs to reproduce ritual on the stage, also by the settings and by leading us into the realm of the subconscious and superconscious. In *The Killer,* for example, the loneliness of man in the face of Death is suggested by the dazzling whiteness of the décor, while in *The New Tenant* the conventional black clothes of the New Tenant makes Death a respectable and acceptable figure. The final scene of the former play is a poem on the horror of death, the latter on the frailness of human life. The hero's monologue in *The Killer* is a long lament, while the entire ritual of the moving in of Death in the second play forms an elegy.

Ionesco believes in the liberating action of poetry; he could say with Jean Cocteau that "the poet disintoxicates the world." Indeed, this is the theme of his three-act play, *Amédée, or How to Get Rid of It,* also, indirectly, of *Victims of Duty.* The first two acts of *Amédée* make us participate in the hero's growing anguish about his wasted life, his feeling of guilt, his desperate attempt to escape the prison of everyday reality by trying to create a work of art, his daily renewed failure; we also participate in his efforts to lead his wife back to the world of beauty and poetry which had been theirs at the beginning of their love. There is much telling symbolism in the play: a dead man whom Amédée might or might not have killed—that is, his own higher self—lives with him ever more demandingly, keeps growing, taking up an increasingly large part of his apartment; then there are the poisonous mushrooms, symbols of his gnawing, ever growing anguish. All this is extremely powerful. The tension in Amédée's soul—the tension in the play—steadily increases; we witness the struggle between his humdrum preoccupations and his strong yearning to extricate himself, between his higher visions and the petty thoughts of his wife, until the situation matures to a point of explosion. The third act comes as *détente,* in contrast to the tense last act of *The Killer.* Now Amédée's inner world is projected into the outer world through a street scene. With superhuman efforts our protagonist has succeeded in ejecting his phantoms; the dead man is dragged out into the open and so begins Amédée's liberation. Finally he will soar above this material world and disappear into higher regions.

Poetry is very much present even in such a pessimistic play as *Jack, or the Submission.* For a second Jack retrieves something of his former self when he dreams aloud of a fountain of light, of glowing water, of a fire of ice, of fiery snows. Also the dialogue between him and his bride is a poem of great fantasy, reminiscent of the encounter between Ibsen's *Peer Gynt* and the Green-Clad Woman; indeed the entire scene of their final union recalls the one in the Royal Hall of the King of the Dovre-Trolls. Jack, like Peer Gynt, succumbs to sensual temptation; he ceases to be himself, that is a human who aspires ever higher, but will become like a troll who is sufficient to himself. The hero of *Victims of Duty* is the negative counterpart of *Amédée.* With the same materials the author created two works, one with a positive, the other with a negative hero, as Ibsen did in *Brandt* and *Peer Gynt* or Sartre in *The Flies* and *No Exit,* respectively. The dead man becomes, in *Victims of Duty,* a detective, symbol of a self-searching spirit. Again a playwright reflects on his art and yearns to know himself better in order to be able to create. Once more his wife is called Madeleine, and once more she drags him down instead of helping him; she enslaves him by means of sensual temptation and persuades him to stay in this world of material reality. Thus the protagonist's efforts to escape end with dismal failure; a modern Icarus, incapable of taking off, his wings drop and he ends up with his rear end in the wastepaper basket. From then on society takes him back with a vengeance. He is fed on insipid food; they make a child, that is a conventional man, of him.

Perhaps the most poetic, most moving of Ionesco's plays is *The Chairs,* called by the author a "tragic farce." The word "tragic" applies to man's inability to communicate with his fellow men, a theme recurrent in Ionesco's theatre. This theme is expressed here more emphatically, unmixed with other themes; it is the theme of man's loneliness, which, according to Lemarchand, constitutes the key to Ionesco's theatrical production.

The protagonist, again flanked by his wife, is this time Old Man who has arrived at the extreme limit of age allowed to humans. His horizon is limited by a waste of waters; he is on an island of hopelessness, of finality. On the threshold of his death his dead friends return to him. He and his wife scurry about to provide chairs, scores of chairs, for the guests. These invisible visitors are wonderfully alive. To them, through them, our pitiful hero tries to vindicate his wasted existence; his wife echoes his boastful words— she wants to believe him and wants him to believe what he cannot believe; both know that they are lying. Before the eyes of the dying man the theatre of life with its tragicomic and usual incidents, its chaotic sounds, its spectacle-like remoteness and unremoteness and unreality, is unfolding itself.

Each visitor is supposed to have come to honor him; each is a witness for the defense at this pre-trial of man's soul, a soul ready to appear before the Eternal. In this world of make-believe, these ghosts are all that remain to him. And the visitors who have come to discharge our hero become more and more numerous; they must sit close to each other on their chairs. The most illustrious of them is the Emperor, who, by the splendor of his rank, has come to support the defense; he is Greatness for which Old Man has always aspired and which has always eluded him. This time our hero wants to shake hands with the Emperor, to thank him for the honor he has done him by coming; but the crowd is so dense that he is unable to push his way through to him. The Emperor is sitting on a rostrum where he is joined by the Orator, the only visitor of flesh and blood among the many invisible ones. The Orator's role is to present all the world-shaking thoughts which had accumulated in the hero's mind during his lifetime but which he himself had been incapable of expounding. Now, at this supreme hour, he will summarize them and redeem the world, redeem the author of the message at the same time.

All are waiting, intent upon the message. The cacophony of vulgar and trivial sounds in the theatre forms an ironic contrast between the lofty expectations of the audience on the stage and that in the auditorium. The Orator opens his mouth to speak but can only utter some inarticulate, guttural sounds. And so the great message of Man is lost forever.

In this atmosphere of dream, the Orator turns out to be the most hypothetical of all characters, though he be of actual flesh and blood.

By bringing the ritual of daily life into the theatre Ionesco returns to the origins of dramatic expression as it was done in pre-Aeschylean tragedy, also in Christian liturgy and liturgistic representations. In his use of symbolistic, impressionistic, and surrealistic techniques he was influenced by the early one-acters of Maurice Maeterlinck, also by the stage tricks of Jean Cocteau with whom he shares the belief that all truly artistic creation is poetry. He has learned some of the reversal techniques of Pirandello, also the simplifying and reducing methods of Beckett. Like Beckett, Ionesco strips man of his veneer of civilization to point to his savagery, his greed and selfishnes, his inability to love, also his helplessness in an uncomprehending and incomprehensible universe. Nevertheless in his criticism and portraying of man Ionesco never descends to the limit of utter despair which characterizes Beckett. One can say that Ionesco has not lost sympathy and solidarity with his heroes. This is natural, for he portrays his own solitude, he writes subjective theatre.

In addition to other forerunners, it is almost sure that Kafka has left his mark upon Ionesco, though this cannot be proven by any direct reference to that author in Ionesco's writings. Indeed such plays as *Jack, or The Submission* and *Victims of Duty* strongly remind us of the hallucinating short stories of Kafka, *The Hunger Artist* and *The Metamorphosis.* Also, Ionesco's repeated presentation of the woman who degrades man is reminiscent of some of the feminine figures around the hero of *The Castle.*

Ionesco's revolt against the rational theatre is understandable. Too often the theatre is mistaken for a lecture hall in France. Racine, the omnipotence of logic, the well-coordinated play have not lost their prestige there. Yet France and the rest of the world no longer live in a powerful monarchy, in a universe where all stars revolve around a central Sun. Our present world is one of kaleidoscopic images which blend and change too fast to be fully intelligible. Modern man, especially the modern artist, tries to break out of the prison of man's limited intelligence and aspires to grasp things that are outside the domain of his reason. The theatre should mirror this bewildering world of ours.

Ionesco's revolt repeats, at a distance of about one hundred and thirty years, that of the French Romantics which began with the battle of *Hermani.* However, instead of a rebellious new poetry and unruly scenes he uses satire to signify his revolt. His mockery of our society never impairs the poetical content and spirit of his plays by which he affirms his belief in a new, higher reality. His word consciousness, his poetical spirit relate him in direct line to Shakespeare whom he considers his spiritual liege lord; at the same time, he recognizes Molière as one of his masters. He tries to continue Molière's tradition by presenting human situations, the human frailness that prevails at all times, also by striving for some guiding light that will allow the individual to assert himself against the levelling and stultifying forces of our society, as he depicted them so vividly in the recent **Rhinoceros.** In view of Ionesco's horror of mass civilization he naturally heaps scorn and sarcasm on all totalitarian ideologies which insult man's reason, which resort to any means to inveigle or browbeat him into thoughtless obedience. It would be erroneous to believe that by revolting against the monopoly of reason in the presentation of human situations Ionesco abdicates reason. On the contrary, he believes that reason is man's precious equipment to maintain his moral integrity.

Ionesco is an innovator in the best tradition of modern art, fighting the encroachment of reason on man's emotional world, and at the same time fighting conformity, a force that threatens art itself. Essentially he frees the theatre from its many shackles, restores and enlarges its freedom.

Notes

1. *L'Impromptu de l'Alma,* E. I. Theatre, Gallimard, 16-eme edition. I will refer to this edition in all of the following quotations from Ionesco's works.

2. *The Idea of a Theatre.* See the chapter "Two Aspects of the Plot: Form and Purpose."

3. The Woman, dragging Man down into the mire of sensuous pleasures occurs in other Ionesco plays.

4. The stage instructions given by the author leave it up to the producer either to make the Killer invisible, in order to signify, as it were, that he exists only within the mind and soul of the protagonist, or—and this is the more theatrical solution—to make him appear as a frail man, an outcast who, by his very appearance, emphasizes his hostility to society. The appearance of the Killer on the stage is necessary to foster the illusion of a dialogue.

5. "J'ai peur de mourir, sans doute, parce que, sans le savoir, je désire mourir. J'ai peur donc du désir que j'ai de mourir."

Susan Sontag (essay date 1964)

SOURCE: "Ionesco" in *Against Interpretation and Other Essays,* Anchor Books, 1966, pp. 115-23.

[*In the following essay, Sontag notes that Ionesco's early work, in which he discovers and uses theatrically the poetry of clichés and language-as-thing, is interesting and original. However, she finds his later work infused with a crude, simplistic negativity that is extracted from his* earlier artistic discovery, and considers his attitudes a *"type of misanthropy covered over with fashionable clichés of cultural diagnosis."*]

It is fitting that a playwright whose best works apotheosize the platitude has compiled a book on the theater crammed with platitudes.[1] I quote, at random:

> *Didacticism is above all an attitude of mind and an expression of the will to dominate.*
>
> *A work of art really is above all an adventure of the mind.*
>
> *Some have said that Boris Vian's* The Empire Builders *was inspired by my own* Amédée. *Actually, no one is inspired by anyone except by his own self and his own anguish.*
>
> *I detect a crisis of thought, which is manifested by a crisis of language; words no longer meaning anything.*
>
> *No society has even been able to abolish human sadness; no political system can deliver us from the pain of living, from our fear of death, our thirst for the absolute.*

What is one to make of a view at once so lofty and so banal? As if this were not enough, Ionesco's essays are laden with superfluous self-explication and unctuous vanity. Again, at random:

> *I can affirm that neither the public nor the critics have influenced me.*
>
> *Perhaps I am socially minded in spite of myself.*
>
> *With me every play springs from a kind of self-analysis.*
>
> *I am not an ideologue, for I am straightforward and objective.*
>
> *The world ought not to interest me so much. In reality, I am obsessed with it.*

Etcetera, etcetera. Ionesco's essays on the theater offer a good deal of such, presumably unconscious, humor.

There are, to be sure, some ideas in *Notes and Counter Notes* worth taking seriously, none of them original with Ionesco. One is the idea of the theater as an instrument which, by dislocating the real, freshens the sense of reality. Such a function for the theater plainly calls not only for a new dramaturgy, but for a new body of plays. "No more masterpieces," Artaud demanded in *The Theatre and Its Double,* the most daring and profound manifesto of the modern theater. Like Artaud, Ionesco scorns the "literary" theater of the past: he likes to read Shakespeare and Kleist but not to see them performed, while Corneille, Molière, Ibsen, Strindberg, Pirandello, Giraudoux and company bore him either way. If the old-fashioned theater pieces must be done at all, Ionesco suggests (as did Artaud) a certain trick. One should play "against" the text: by grafting a serious, formal production onto a text that is absurd, wild, comic, or by treating a solemn text in the spirit of buffoonery. Along with the rejection of the literary theater—the theater of plot and individual character— Ionesco calls for the scrupulous avoidance of all psychology, for psychology means "realism," and realism is dull and confines the imagination. His rejection of psychology permits the revival of a device common to all non-realistic theatrical traditions (it is equivalent to frontality in naïve painting), in which the characters turn to face the audience (rather than each other), stating their names, identities, habits, tastes, acts . . . All this, of course, is very familiar: the canonical modern style in the theater. Most of the interesting ideas in *Notes and Counter Notes* are watered-down Artaud; or rather Artaud spruced up and made charming, ingratiating; Artaud without his hatreds, Artaud without his madness. Ionesco comes closest to being original in certain remarks about humor, which he understands as poor mad Artaud did not at all. Artaud's notion of a Theater of Cruelty emphasized the darker registers of fantasy: frenzied spectacle, melodramatic deeds, bloody apparitions, screams, transports. Ionesco, noting that any tragedy becomes comic simply if it is speeded up, has devoted himself to the violently comic. Instead of the cave or the palace or the temple or the heath, he sets most of his plays in the living room. His comic terrain is the banality and oppressiveness of the "home"—be it the bachelor's furnished room, the scholar's study, the married couple's parlor. Underneath the forms of conventional life, Ionesco would demonstrate, lies madness, the obliteration of personality.

But Ionesco's plays, it seems to me, need little explanation. If an account of his work is desired, Richard N. Coe's excellent short book on Ionesco, published in 1961 in the English *Writers and Critics* series, offers a far more coherent and compact defense of the plays than anything in *Notes and Counter Notes*. The interest of Ionesco on Ionesco is not for its author's theory of theater, but for what the book suggests about the puzzling thinness—puzzling considering their richness of theme—of Ionesco's plays. The tone of the book tells a great deal. For behind the relentless egotism of Ionesco's writings on the theater— the allusions to unending battles with obtuse critics and a bovine public—is an insistent, plaintive uneasiness. Ionesco protests, incessantly, that he has been misunderstood. Therefore, everything he says at one point in *Notes and Counter Notes*, he takes back on another page. (Though these writings span the years 1951-61, there is no development in the argument.) His plays are avant-garde theater; there is no such thing as avant-garde theater. He is writing social criticism; he is not writing social criticism. He is a humanist; he is morally and emotionally estranged from humanity. Throughout, he writes as a man sure—whatever you say of him, whatever he says of himself—that his true gifts are misunderstood.

What is Ionesco's accomplishment? Judging by the most exacting standards, he has written one really remarkable and beautiful play, *Jack, or the Submission* (1950); one brilliant lesser work, *The Bald Soprano,* his first play (written 1948-49); and several effective short plays which are pungent reprises of the same material, *The Lesson* (1950), *The Chairs* (1951), and *The New Tenant* (1953). All these plays—Ionesco is a prolific writer—are "early"

Ionesco. The later works are marred by a diffuseness in the dramatic purpose and an increasing, unwieldly self-consciousness. The diffuseness can be clearly seen in *Victims of Duty* (1952), a work with some powerful sections but unhappily overexplicit. Or one can compare his best play, *Jack,* with a short sequel using the same characters, *The Future Is in Eggs* (1951). *Jack* abounds with splendid harsh fantasy, ingenious and logical; it alone, of all Ionesco's plays, gives us something up to the standard of Artaud: the Theater of Cruelty as Comedy. But in *The Future Is in Eggs,* Ionesco has embarked upon the disastrous course of his later writings, railing against "views" and tediously attributing to his characters a concern with the state of the theater, the nature of language, and so forth. Ionesco is an artist of considerable gifts who has been victimized by "ideas." His work has become water-logged with them; his talents have coarsened. In *Notes and Counter Notes* we have a chunk of that endless labor of self-explication and self-vindication as a playwright and thinker which occupies the whole of his play, *Improvisation,* which dictates the intrusive remarks on playwriting in *Victims of Duty* and *Amédée,* which inspires the oversimplified critique of modern society in *The Killer* and *Rhinoceros.*

Ionesco's original artistic impulse was his discovery of the poetry of banality. His first play, *The Bald Soprano,* was written almost by accident, he says, after he discovered the Smiths and the Martins *en famille* in the Assimil phrase book he bought when he decided to study English. And all the subsequent plays of Ionesco continued at least to open with a volleying back and forth of clichés. By extension, the discovery of the poetry of cliché led to the discovery of the poetry of meaninglessness—the convertibility of all words into one another. (Thus, the litany of *"chat"* at the end of *Jack.*) It has been said that Ionesco's early plays are "about" meaninglessness, or "about" non-communication. But this misses the important fact that in much of modern art one can no longer really speak of subject-matter in the old sense. Rather, the subject-matter is the technique. What Ionesco did—no mean feat—was to appropriate for the theater one of the great technical discoveries of modern poetry: that all language can be considered from the outside, as by a stranger. Ionesco disclosed the *dramatic* resources of this attitude, long known but hitherto confined to modern poetry. His early plays are not "about" meaninglessness. They are attempts to use meaninglessness theatrically.

Ionesco's discovery of the cliché meant that he declined to see language as an instrument of communication or self-expression, but rather as an exotic substance secreted—in a sort of trance—by interchangeable persons. His next discovery, also long familiar in modern poetry, was that he could treat language as a palpable thing. (Thus, the teacher kills the student in *The Lesson* with the word "knife.") The key device for making language into a thing is repetition. This verbal repetition is dramatized further by another persistent motif of Ionesco's plays: the cancerous, irrational multiplication of material things. (Thus: the egg in *The*

Future Is in Eggs; the chairs in *The Chairs;* the furniture in *The New Tenant;* the boxes in *The Killer;* the cups in *Victims of Duty;* the noses and fingers of Roberta II in *Jack;* the corpse in *Amédée, or How to Get Rid of It.*) These repeating words, these demonically proliferating things, can only be exorcised as in a dream, by being obliterated. Logically, poetically—and *not* because of any "ideas" Ionesco has about the nature of individual and society—his plays must end either in a *da capo* repetition, or in incredible violence. Some typical endings are: massacre of the audience (the proposed end of *The Bald Soprano*), suicide (*The Chairs*), entombment and silence (*The New Tenant*), unintelligibility and animal moans (*Jack*), monstrous physical coercion (*Victims of Duty*), the collapse of the stage (*The Future Is in Eggs*). In Ionesco's plays, the recurrent nightmare is of a wholly clogged, overrun world. (The nightmare is explicit with respect to the furniture in *The New Tenant,* the rhinoceroses in *Rhinoceros.*) The plays therefore must end in either chaos or non-being, destruction or silence.

These discoveries of the poetry of cliché and of language-as-thing gave Ionesco some remarkable theatrical material. But then ideas were born, a theory about the meaning of this theater of meaninglessness took up residence in Ionesco's work. The most fashionable modern experiences were invoked. Ionesco and his defenders claimed that he had begun with his experience of the meaninglessness of contemporary existence, and developed his theater of cliché to express this. It seems more likely that he began with the discovery of the poetry of banality, and then, alas, called on a theory to bulwark it. This theory amounts to the hardiest clichés of the criticism of "mass society," all scrambled together—alienation, standardization, dehumanization. To sum up this dreadfully familiar discontent, Ionesco's favorite word of abuse is "bourgeois," or sometimes "petty bourgeois." Ionesco's bourgeois has little in common with that favorite target of Leftist rhetoric, although perhaps he has adopted it from that source. For Ionesco, "bourgeois" means everything he doesn't like: it means "realism" in the theater (something like the way Brecht used "Aristotelian"); it means ideology; it means conformism. Of course, none of this would have mattered were it merely a question of Ionesco's pronouncements on his work. What mattered is that increasingly it began to infect his work. More and more, Ionesco tended to "indicate" shamelessly what he was doing. (One cringes when, at the end of *The Lesson,* the professor dons a swastika armband as he prepares to dispose of the corpse of his student.) Ionesco began with a fantasy, the vision of a world inhabited by language puppets. He was not criticizing anything, much less discovering what in an early essay he called "The Tragedy of Language." He was just discovering one way in which language could be used. Only afterward was a set of crude, simplistic attitudes extracted from this artistic discovery—attitudes about the contemporary standardization and dehumanization of man, all laid at the feet of a stuffed ogre called the "bourgeois," "Society," etc. The time then came for the affirmation of individual man against this ogre. Thus Ionesco's work passed through an unfortunate and familiar double phase: first, works of anti-theater, parody; then, the socially constructive plays. These later plays are thin stuff. And the weakest in all his oeuvre are the Bérenger plays—*The Killer* (1957), *Rhinoceros* (1960), and *The Pedestrian of the Air* (1962)—where Ionesco (as he said) created in Bérenger an alter ego, an Everyman, a beleaguered hero, a character "to rejoin humanity." The difficulty is that affirmation of man cannot simply be willed, either in morals or in art. If it is merely willed, the result is always unconvincing, and usually pretentious.

In this, Ionesco's development is just the reverse of Brecht's. Brecht's early works—*Baal, In the Jungle of Cities*—give way to the "positive" plays which are his masterpieces: *The Good Woman of Setzuan, The Caucasian Chalk Circle, Mother Courage.* But then—quite apart from the theories they espouse—Brecht is simply a much greater writer than Ionesco. To Ionesco, of course, he represents the arch-villain, the arch-bourgeois. He is political. But Ionesco's attacks on Brecht and the Brechtians—and on the idea of a politically committed art—are trivial. Brecht's political attitudes are, at best, the occasion for his humanism. They allow him to focus and expand his drama. The choice Ionesco insists on, between political affirmation and affirmation of man, is spurious, and dangerous besides.

Compared with Brecht, Genet, and Beckett, Ionesco is a minor writer even at his best. His work does not have the same weight, the same full-bloodedness, the same grandeur and relevance. Ionesco's plays, especially the shorter ones (the form for which his gifts are most suited), have their considerable virtues: charm, wit, a nice feeling for the macabre; above all, theatricality. But the recurrent themes—identities slipping out of gear, the monstrous proliferation of things, the gruesomeness of togetherness—are rarely so moving, so appalling, as they might be. Perhaps it is because—with the exception of *Jack,* where Ionesco lets his fantasy have its head—the terrible is always, somehow, circumscribed by the cute. Ionesco's morbid farces are the boulevard comedies of the avant-grade sensibility; as one English critic has pointed out, little really separates Ionesco's whimsy of conformity from Feydeau's whimsy of adultery. Both are skillful, cold, self-referring.

To be sure, Ionesco's plays—and writings about the theater—pay strenuous lip service to the emotions. Of *The Bald Soprano,* for instance, Ionesco says that it is about "talking and saying nothing because [of] the absence of any inner life." The Smiths and the Martins represent man totally absorbed in his social context, they "have forgotten the meaning of emotion." But what of the numerous descriptions which Ionesco gives in *Notes and Counter Notes* of his own inability to feel—an inability which he regards as rescuing him from being, rather than turning him into, a mass man? It is not protest against passionlessness which moves Ionesco, but a kind of misanthropy, which he has covered over with fashionable clichés of cultural diagnosis. The sensibility behind this theater is tight, defensive, and riddled with sexual disgust. Disgust is the powerful motor in Ionesco's plays: out of disgust, he makes comedies of the distasteful.

Disgust with the human condition is perfectly valid material for art. But disgust for ideas, expressed by a man with little talent for ideas, is another matter. This is what mars many of Ionesco's plays and makes his collection of writings on the theater irritating rather than amusing. Disgusted with ideas as one more foul human excrescence, Ionesco flails about in this repetitious book, at once assuming and disavowing all positions. The unifying theme of *Notes and Counter Notes* is his desire to maintain a position that is not a position, a view that is no view—in a word, to be intellectually invulnerable. But this is impossible, since initially he experiences an idea only as a cliché: "systems of thought on all sides are nothing more than alibis, something to hide reality (another cliché word) from us." By a sickening glide in the argument, ideas somehow become identified with politics, and all politics identified with a fascistic nightmare world. When Ionesco says, "I believe that what separates us all from one another is simply society itself, or, if you like, politics," he is expressing his anti-intellectualism rather than a position about politics. This can be seen with special clarity in the most interesting section in the book (pp. 87-108), the so-called London Controversy, an exchange of essays and letters with Kenneth Tynan, representing ostensibly a Brechtian point of view, which first appeared in the English weekly *The Observer* in 1958. The high moment of this controversy is a noble and eloquent letter from Orson Welles, who points out that the separation between art and politics cannot emerge, much less prosper, except in a certain kind of society. As Welles wrote, "Whatever is valuable is likely to have a rather shopsoiled name," and all freedoms—including Ionesco's privilege to shrug his shoulders at politics—"were, at one time or another, political achievements." It is not "politics which is the arch-enemy of art; it is neutrality . . . [which is] a political position like any other. . . . If we are doomed indeed, let M. Ionesco go down fighting with the rest of us. He should have the courage of our platitudes."

What is disconcerting about Ionesco's work is, then, the intellectual complacency it sponsors. I have no quarrel with works of art that contain no ideas at all; on the contrary, much of the greatest art is of this kind. Think of the films of Ozu, Jarry's *Ubu Roi,* Nabokov's *Lolita,* Genet's *Our Lady of the Flowers*—to take four modern examples. But the intellectual blankness is one (often very salutary) thing, intellectual surrender is another. In Ionesco's case, the intellect that has surrendered is not interesting, relying as it does on a view of the world that sets up an opposition between the wholly monstrous and the wholly banal. At first we may take pleasure in the monstrousness of the monstrous, but finally we are left with the banality of banality.

Notes

1. *Notes and Counter Notes: Writings on the Theatre* by Eugène Ionesco, Translated by Donald Watson. New York, Grove.

Peter Thomson (essay date 1970)

SOURCE: "Games and Plays: An Approach to Ionesco," in *Educational Theatre Journal,* Vol. XXII, No. 1, March 1970, pp. 60-70.

[*In the following essay, Thomson argues against critics who appraise Ionesco in terms of his plays' meaning, and calls for a reassertion of interest in the playwright's work based on his "manner" rather than his "matter." He goes on to discuss the use of games as they operate in Ionesco's absurd world.*]

I have in front of me Donald Watson's seventh admirably translated volume of Ionesco's plays, and I am puzzled. Reading the main and most recent piece, *Hunger and Thirst (Le Soif et La Faim),* was a struggle almost uninterrupted by delight. Has Ionesco changed? Has the climate? Have I? The three shorter pieces in Volume 7 were first published in 1963, in Paris. *The Picture (Le Tableau)* is a one-act piece with a thrusting theatricality reminiscent of *The Lesson,* and a conclusion that is merely silly. *Anger (La Colère)* is a scenario that formed one of the sections of the film *The Seven Deadly Sins.* It is witty, sudden, and obvious. *Salutations (Les Salutations)* is an adverbial exercise that could not reasonably have been expected to get into print had it not been preceded by its author's reputation. It may prove no more than Ionesco's mischievous willingness to write juvenilia at the wrong end of his career. *Hunger and Thrust* was first published in 1966. Donald Watson makes no reference to any performance of the play—"Three Episodes" is Ionesco's description, and one which ought, perhaps, to be adhered to—and, writing in England at the end of 1969, I can think of no immediate reason for any performance to take place. It is, in structural outline, a quest-play; and if the knight-errant (or anti-knight-errant) is not specifically Bérenger, he shares with the Bérenger of *Exit the King (Le Roi se meurt)* a solicitous wife Marie (here Marie-Madeleine) and with the Bérenger of *A Stroll in the Air (Le Piéton de l'air)* a gentle daughter Marthe. Episode One begins with Jean resentfully ready, with Sartrean "bad faith," to accept his "destiny," but dreaming of alternatives:

> A house perched up in the mountains. There are such things, you know. Or even on some river. Not right *in* the river, but built out over the water, with flower-faces at the windows, flowers with their roots and stalks out of sight, just the top of them showing, flowers you can stretch out and touch. There are flowers that weep, of course, but also some that laugh. Why not choose flowers that shoot up in the world and smile?
>
> MARIE: Gardens and houses like that are beyond our means, not within *our* reach. (p. 12)

It was with an implausible hope of gardens that Marthe brought down the final curtain of *A Stroll in the Air:*

> Perhaps it will all come right in the end . . . Perhaps the flames will die down, perhaps the ice will melt, perhaps the depths will rise. Perhaps the . . . the gardens . . . the gardens . . . (*They go out*)
>
> (*VI*, 77)[1]

And it is by an insistence on the unattainability of the garden that Marie-Madeleine tries to deter Jean from his quest in *Hunger and Thirst:*

> What garden it is you hope to find? You can't really go. You know *we're* here, you know *I'm* here. You're joking aren't you, you're staying aren't you, pretending aren't you? From your heart you cannot tear out love, the wrench would be too great, no-one could heal that wound. You can't pull up the roots of love, you can't tear love from your heart, the love in your heart, from your heart. It's a game you're playing, isn't it?
>
> (*VII*, 30-31)

It is a speech, and indeed a play, lacking in Ionesco's usual linguistic confidence, the clumsy prelude to an actual rather than a metaphorical game. By creeping off-stage to hide behind the back wall, Jean initiates a game of hide-and-seek in which Marie-Madeleine becomes an unwilling participant. On Ionesco's plastic stage, hide-and-seek is a game of unpredictable scope, but it is handled in this play with strident literalism:

> MARIE: Jean, you can't have gone out, can you? You can't have gone away, can you? You'd have told me, wouldn't you? Answer! Cooee! I can hear him. No. I can't hear him. This is a cruel game. Much too cruel! (*She goes on looking for him automatically, with less and less conviction, not looking too hard, slowing the pace down.*) No, he can't tear this love from his heart. (*She goes out for a few seconds and while she is chanting this sort of refrain, Jean appears. He violently tears from his heart a branch of briar rose, his face screwed up with pain, wipes the drops of blood from his fingers on his shirt; puts the branch down on the table, carefully buttons his jacket and then tiptoes out.*)
>
> (*VII*, 34-35)

Jean escapes, and almost immediately, by one of those transformation-scenes Ionesco might just as well have borrowed from nineteenth-century pantomime, the garden appears:

> *The back wall . . . vanishes. You can see a garden: trees in blossom, tall green grass, a very blue sky. . . . Then, on the left of this landscape, which is also on the audience's left, you can see a silver ladder appear, hanging in the air, the top of it out of sight.*
>
> (*VII*, 36)

There is, of course, a melancholy irony in the timing of the garden-revelation. Jean has already embarked on his quest. In Episode Two, having failed to meet a woman he cannot accurately describe, he spells out his limited existentialism to the two keepers of an empty, mountain-top museum:

Oh, my friends, my keepers, I was so comfortable in my discomfort! Listen: and I'll tell you. I wanted to escape old age, keep out of the rut. It's life I'm looking for! Joy I'm after! I've longed for fulfilment and all I find is torment. I had to choose between peace and passion. I chose passion, fool that I was! Yet I was safe enough in my hide-out, firmly locked in gloom and nostalgia, remorse and anguish, fears and responsibilities, like so many walls all round me. The fear of death was my truest shield. Now the walls have collapsed. And here I am, defenceless, exposed to the blazing inferno of life, and in the freezing grip of despair. I wanted life and life has hurled itself at me. It's crippling me, killing me. Why didn't I have the sense to welcome resignation? All my old scars have opened, my wounds are bleeding again. Thousands of knives are driving into my flesh.

> (*VII*, 46-47)

The mental state is Faustian, and Jean achieves even less by his new freedom than Marlowe's Faustus. Episode Three brings him to a monastery-prison-barracks where he witnesses a masque-cum-torture illustrative of man's enslavement to the means of life. When the garden of Episode One reappears, Marie-Madeleine and Marthe are standing in it, but Jean and the audience glimpse it through the iron bars of the monastery-prison. Jean is in debt to his sinister hosts; he owes them *time*. They demand as repayment that he should serve as a waiter, satisfying their physical hunger and thirst, and the play ends in a chorus of counting that accompanies Jean's increasingly frantic distribution of soup. Behind this rhythmic action is the garden, the reminder of the spiritual hunger and thirst that initiated Jean's quest, and Marie-Madeleine promising (or threatening?):

> We'll wait! We'll wait! No matter how long, I'll wait for you, I'll wait for you forever!
>
> (*VII*, 106)

That the coupling of Marie-Madeleine and Marthe gives to the garden a Lazarus-like acquaintance with death[2] seems to me to possess a necessary significance which does nothing to increase my interest in the play. *Hunger and Thirst* is closer to being a pièce a thèse than a writer of Ionesco's stated views ought ever to have come. Its atavism—the whole of Volume 7 is depressingly atavistic—ought to be apparent even in so sketchy an account as this. I have to ask myself what claim Ionesco has to continued critical attention.

The approach recommended by so many critics, the explanatory method typified with well-meaning thoroughness by George E. Wellwarth,[3] is of surprisingly small service in a re-appraisal of the dramatist who had so incalculable an effect on theatre in the west in the fifties. The response to any explication of an Ionesco play is not an excited, "Is *that* what it means?" but a disgruntled, "Is that *all* it means?" It is no longer news that eschatology takes a curious turn in a world that has lost its God. The critical attempt to direct our attention to Ionesco's meaning exposes him increasingly to our ridicule. The theatrical symbols have lost their effectiveness as they have lost their "surprise"; but Ionesco's frequent denials of any polemic intention in his writing ought to make us wary of giving the *meaning* of his plays primacy over their *conduct*. Words like "commentary" and "allegory" do little to explain Ionesco's peculiar impact, yet they can both be found in Wellwarth:

> *Rhinoceros,* like *The Lesson,* is an obvious commentary on the disintegration of reason and morality under a totalitarian state. Only those unfamiliar with the history of Nazism will be at all puzzled by its allegory.[4]

Ionesco has denied the deliberateness that Wellwarth here ascribes to him:

> I have no ideas before I write a play. I have them after I have written a play, or when I am not writing at all. I believe that artistic creation is spontaneous. At least it is for me. . . . Only spontaneity can guarantee a direct knowledge of reality. All ideology ends up with indirect knowledge which is only secondary, oblique and falsified.[5]

The "guarantee" proposed here is alarmingly sanguine, but we should surely grant to Ionesco a greater concern for the knowledge of reality than for its interpretation. His particular attractiveness, at the outset of his career, was his brave refusal to provide audiences with such traditional incentives to attention as are implied in Wellwarth's exegesis. These incentives have now been provided by critics, and the atavism of his recent work *may* be the result of a critical backlash, of Ionesco's writing, for the first time consciously, what he is told he has always written. It is time to reassert an interest in Ionesco that is based on his manner rather than his matter, to apply to his own work the kind of sympathetic scrutiny he applied to Pirandello's:

> It is no longer the discovery of the antagonisms of personality which interests us in Pirandello, but what he does with it, dramatically speaking. Its purely theatrical interest is extra-scientific; it is beyond his ideology. What remains of Pirandello is the mechanism of his theatre, its movement (*jeu*)[6]

It is with this in mind that I propose an analogy with games as a useful tool in the appreciation of Ionesco's conduct of his plays.

The interest of many modern dramatists in games as structural or textural devices must be obvious. Adamov tells us that *Le Ping Pong* sprang from a single image of two old men playing ping-pong, the finished play's final scene.[7] Ping-pong, objectively observed and perhaps largely because of the noise it makes and the banality of the equipment it requires, is already closer to absurdity than most games. As an image of life it is devastatingly reductive. (In *The Tea Party* Pinter seems to be using the same game as a reductive sexual image.) Like *Le Ping Pong, Endgame* incorporates the idea of a game in its title, though denying us a determinate game as absolutely as it denies us a determinate end. Genet's characters play charades that are like rituals, and perform rituals that are like charades. Jarry's Père Ubu organises an on-stage race.

Through the game of hopscotch in *The Happy Haven,* Arden expounds and exposes two of the geriatric inmates. The game of cricket played on stage in Edward Bond's *The Pope's Wedding* is the prelude to Scopey's self-discovery. Pinter makes explicit use of games (in *The Tea Party* and *The Basement*), of party games (in *The Tea Party* and *The Birthday Party*), and charades (in *The Lover,* where the Lover/Mistress charade carries an aura of pretence into the "real" marriage); but he is also a consistent exploiter of the related psychological games recently expounded by Eric Berne.[8] All Pinter's plays might, I suspect, provide lucid illustrations of Berne's thesis. In *The Homecoming,* for example, Ruth, whilst generally playing "Let's you and him fight," does at one point present her leg for scrutiny in a literal version of "The Stocking Game."

Ionesco is overtly less interested in games than many of his contemporaries. The hide-and-seek of **Hunger and Thirst** is a rare example of an announced game played according to its own rules. But there is, as Ionesco has observed,[9] a "progressive heightening" of the action in his plays that seems to owe more to the gathering of tension when a result is anticipated than to any thrust from the plot; and there is, more significantly, an analogy with games in the theory of spontaneous creation. The combative dialogue of his plays is, according to this theory, self-propelling, the second "stroke" conditioned by the first, the third by the second and so on, as in a rally at tennis. The parallel with Pirandello breaks down here, for Pirandello's "ideology," whatever may be one's view of it, provides a reason for the ordering of dialogue that is more architectonic than any Ionesco admits to. It was, I suggest, the removal of any apparent pre-conditioning of the dialogue by the total meaning of the play that most confused Ionesco's first audiences. Certainly it was the combative, rally-like composition of the dialogue that James Saunders imitated in *Alas Poor Fred* (Scarborough, 1959), which he calls "a duologue in the style of Ionesco" and which claims a place among the masterpieces of theatrical parody. There is an amusing example of the effect on Ionesco's life-style of his dramatic method in a recently republished interview.[10] It seems to have occurred to Ionesco about half-way through his meeting with Professor Rosette Lamont in 1960 that she would take seriously, or at least unresistingly, almost anything he cared to say. For a while the interview reads like a segment of absurdist dialogue, where Ionesco's responses are less *answers* than *counters* to the questions: The failure of answers to measure up to questions is an essential feature of Ionesco's style. Clearly there are philosophical implications, but the more immediate effect is to augment the unpredictable, game-like tone of the dialogue. In the placing of a particular speech, the dramatist's eye is not, evidently, on what must succeed it, but on what has in fact immediately preceded it.

LAMONT: Who are the great 'pataphysicians?

IONESCO: Raymond Queneau, Jacques Prévert, and Boris Vian before he died, were among them, but I believe that the actual rulers of 'Pataphysics are secret. Queneau, Dubuffet, René Clair and myself—we're a front. We're there for glory. The real head of the Collège de 'Pataphysique is a gentleman by the name of Salmon, who died recently and was reincarnated under the name of Latisane. I believe it's the same one.

LAMONT: And who is Latisane?

IONESCO: It's Salmon.

LAMONT: And this Latisane, what does he do in life?

IONESCO: He has a double who is a teacher.

It is, then, in the first place texturally that the analogy with games may be of some service in a re-appraisal of Ionesco. A discussion of the larger structural analogy requires some preface.

Lord Justice Birkett, in a speech of welcome to, I think, the touring Australian cricketers, made an observation which I quote as accurately as I can from memory: "The English, being naturally an unspiritual people, invented cricket to give them a concept of eternity." Despite its pungency the remark has no descriptive validity. Cricket, like all games, is directly opposed to open-ended concepts like eternity and infinity. Games take place in a prescribed area, and their end in time is implicit in their beginning. The duration of a game is normally determined in either of two ways.[11] In the first, as in football in its various national forms, a time-limit is pre-established, and the score on the completion of this *set time* is declared the result of the game. (Ionesco is on the way to exploiting the resources of set time in **Exit the King** when Marguerite warns Berenger: "You're going to die in an hour and a half, you're going to die at the end of the show" [V, 26].) In the second, as in tennis, the game continues according to its own internal logic until a result is reached, and the clock has no direct bearing on it. Whatever may be the temporal strategy of individual scenes,[12] plays as a whole normally use *result time,* which is to say that it is the completion of the story rather than the running out of time that brings them to an end.[13]

There are, of course, exceptions to the strict alternatives. If **Exit the King** may be said to exploit both set time and result time, so many certain games. In boxing, for example, the spectator is held in tension by the possible imposition of result time on set time. The same is true of cricket, though the imposition there is never as sudden as it may be in boxing. A five-day Test Match may end on the first, second, third, or fourth day. Often a large part of the game is played without any likelihood of a determinate result, though with the guarantee inherent in set time that it must end. No game has been more subject to experiments with time, the most interesting for our purpose being the notorious "Timeless Test." In a five-match series played in South Africa between England and South Africa the first four matches were drawn. It was agreed to play the last to a finish, so cricket abandoned the normal constraint of set time and committed itself to the alternative discipline of result time. It was a disaster. After eleven days there was still no immediate prospect of a result, and the game was

called off to allow the English players to catch the return boat. The fiasco was not, perhaps, inevitable, nor was it unlikely. A change in the form of a game is also a change in its content.[14]

Where a play may be said to employ both set time and result time, it normally does so in a way directly opposed to that of boxing and cricket. A scarcely perceptible initial restlessness in the auditorium is the first sign that, for a part of the audience at least, set time is up and a quick result is hoped for. The application to the play of these external concepts of time is already evidence that the playwright has failed to draw the audience away from "real" time into the symbolic time-sequence of his play. But to some modern dramatists the set time and result time of games offer exciting alternatives to the symbolic time that has traditionally kept the play at an acceptable distance from life.[15] I once failed to persuade a theatre director to stage a play of mine in which the result of a game with rolling balls, played in the round by actors, determined whether the game itself should be the beginning or the end of the action. Now, five years later, I might persuade him.

My concern here is with games rather than with time, but the two are not easily separable. Both operate in the *meaningful* world[16] to reassure us of the link between beginnings and ends, cause and effect, becoming and being, and both can be made to operate in an *absurd* world precisely to deny the existence of any such link. To be late for an appointment is bad. To be on time and yet to meet no one is worse. But to be unable to make an appointment at all, ever—the clocks have no hands (Adamov), the seasons change without warning (*Waiting for Godot*)—that is terrifying. And that is the plight of Jean in Episode Two ("The Rendezvous") of **Hunger and Thirst** when he tries to establish the chance of his meeting the woman of his mirages:

JEAN: What's the time?

1ST KEEPER: Midday.

JEAN: What's the time?

2ND KEEPER: One o'clock.

JEAN: What's the time?

1ST KEEPER: Late afternoon.

(*VII*, 45)

The use of games is not, of course, new to drama. The duel in *Hamlet* is played through to a significant end under the inset discipline of result time, and a student has drawn my attention to twenty plays written between 1603 and 1633 in which games take place on stage.[17] There are doubtless many more. The English public schools have no monopoly on the recognition that the playing of games brings people into significant relationships with each other. Party games are generally designed to do the same thing more forcibly, and the analogous psychological games have always been played by competitive man, eager for whatever reason to be victorious or to be defeated. To approach what may be different in the use of game-structure in the absurdist theatre, and in Ionesco in particular, we need to look again at the idea of results. There are at least four ways of turning game-structures into absurdist attacks on the reassuring connection of cause and effect.

(1) *Play the game right through according to the rules, but announce an entirely unrelated result.*—Spectators who have just watched Manchester United score five goals against West Ham United's two will be required to accept a declared result that makes West Ham the winners by two goals to nil. Something like this happens in Ionesco's short piece, **Maid to Marry.** The play begins with the Lady's reference to her daughter—"My daughter, let me tell you, was quite brilliant in her studies"—and returns to the theme after the Gentleman's long domination of the conversation:

> LADY: She's gone a long way with her studies. I've always longed for her to be a typist. So has she. She's just got her diploma. She's going to join a firm that deals in fraudulent transactions. . . .
>
> GENTLEMAN: She must be very proud and happy.
>
> LADY: She's dancing for joy from morning to night. She's worked so hard, poor little soul!
>
> GENTLEMAN: Now she's won the reward for her labours.
>
> LADY: It only remains for me now to find her a good husband.
>
> GENTLEMAN: She's a fine girl.
>
> LADY: (*looking out into the wings*) Well now, there *is* my daughter just coming. I'll introduce you to her.
>
> (*The LADY's daughter comes in. She is a man, about thirty years old, robust and virile, with a bushy black moustache, wearing a grey suit.*)
>
> (*III*, 158)

The effect is predominantly comic, but the unruffled acceptance by the actors of a non sequitur so extreme belongs to a world in which the state of being has no recognisable relationship with the state of becoming. In *Maid to Marry* the shock-result technique is all on the surface, but it is of the kind suggested by the game analogy. If this is the result, what has the game been about? If the adolescent girl is a mature man, what has the conversation been about? The same quizzical dislocation of game and result, of process and conclusion extends over the whole conduct of **The Lesson,** and is the single structural principle of **The Future Is in Eggs.** This play opens with Jacques and Roberta in the same coital embrace they had held at the end of **Jacques.** They have been there for three years, and the surrounding families are now crying out for results:

> My son, if you want me to be proud of you, try and instigate, instigate production. . . .
>
> (*IV*, 132)

The result is eggs, a great profusion of eggs, a startling effect which immediately follows their separation, but for

which there is no discernible cause. A game has been visibly played, but the announced result is not related to it.

(2) *Don't bother to play the game at all, just announce the result.*—England's February snow has produced a disturbing example of this absurd idea. On two consecutive Saturdays in February 1969, so many football matches were postponed that the big-money business of the Football Pools could not be normally conducted. Instead a committee, calling itself a Pools Panel, was formed to discuss the likely outcome of the postponed matches. At the end of the afternoon the results of the games that had *not* been played were announced along with the results of those that had. Transferred to the theatre, such a concern for the curtain line has bizarre possibilities, but, as Tardieu suggests in his spoof 'whodunnit' *The Crowd up at the Monor,*[18] it is a logical extension of most detective plays. Ionesco goes further. It is his reiterated view that a disproportionate emphasis on results is a characteristic of all drama previous to his own. Choubert in **Victims of Duty,** for example, tells his inattentive wife:

> All the plays that have ever been written, from Ancient Greece to the present day, have never really been anything but thrillers. Drama's always been realistic and there's always been a detective about. Every play's an investigation brought to a successful conclusion. There's a riddle, and it's solved in the final scene. Sometimes earlier. You seek, and then you find. Might as well give the game away at the start.
>
> (*II*, 269)

With the entry of the Detective, **Victims of Duty** becomes an aggressive parody of conventional dramaturgy. The whole subsequent action, Choubert's ordeal of duty, is directed towards the discovery of an answer to the Detective's question, "Where is Mallot?" The single-minded pursuit of results is always subject to Ionesco's mockery. Results belong in a world that has fixed points of reference, a world that can be "held still," but Ionesco's world is constantly moving, constantly being transformed. The parodic twist in **Victims of Duty** is that there can be no result. Choubert has no idea where, or even who, Mallot is. The play is written in direct opposition to "All the plays that have ever been written." It cannot be "brought to a successful conclusion." The misplaced human concern for the result above the game/play is acknowledged by Choubert in order that it may be exposed and mocked by Ionesco.

(3) *Play the game with complete seriousness in obedience to ridiculous rules, accepting as conclusive the necessarily inconclusive result.*—Games of this sort are a feature of the international competitions televised on the Eurovision network under the suggestive title, *Jeux sans Frontières.* Competitors carry buckets of water along slippery poles, burst balloons in a variety of improbable ways, joust with pillows on narrow planks poised over pools of cold water etc. The whole thing is taken with the utmost seriousness by the players, and by a large section of the television audience. A satirical purpose is likely to underlie this sort

of game in literature. The great egg controversy that divides the Lilliputians is Swift's application of the technique. In his novel, *The Incomparable Atuk,*[19] Mordecai Richler exaggerates the absurdity of the television "quiz-game"—not an easy thing to exaggerate—in order to demonstrate the extremity of his Eskimo hero's corruption by materialistic values. Atuk must answer the million-dollar question in the programme "Stick Out Your Neck" with his neck in the groove of a guillotine. When he gives the wrong answer the blade descends.

The game analogy suggested here has some application to a large part of Ionesco's work. The eccentric rules of conduct invented by the players of **The Chairs** and **The Bald Prima Donna,** together with the absoluteness of their obedience to them, are an obvious example. The comic line of **Amédée** is dependent on the disparity between the grotesqueness of the 'game' and the seriousness of the players. What Ionesco most commonly exposes in the plays that employ this technique is man's collaboration in the curtailment of his own aspirations, his willingness to settle for the contingencies, his tendency to mistake quantity for quality. Ionesco has, in my own view, been too often seduced by the theatricality of the ridiculous into betraying the absurd, and it is in this, the least important of the four game-structures, that the betrayal is most readily apparent to his hostile critics. A jeu d'esprit like **The Motor Show** (V), a short sketch in which two people take seriously what is manifestly ludicrous, is either too marginal to need defence or too puerile to deserve it.

(4) *Play the game according to the rules, under the gradually dawning and desperate realisation that there is no possibility of a result.*—This is the most philosophically significant of the game analogies that can be used to illustrate the theatre of the absurd. It is the kind of game played in *Waiting for Godot.* It is a game in which goals can be scored, but can never accumulate because they can never be linked to each other. There is no end, and so no beginning, no effect and therefore no cause, no state of being to confirm the condition of becoming.

There can, of course, be no parallel in actual games. However indolent the participation, games are played purposively towards a result. The games of *Waiting for Godot* are aimless, not increasingly but consistently aimless. The classic absurdist game is the one in which players form a circle and pass a clock round it from hand to hand.

"What are you doing?"

"Passing the time."

Ionesco's awareness of the applicability to his world of this kind of game is evident in **Victims of Duty, A Stroll in the Air, Frenzy for Two** (VI) and elsewhere, but the heightening of the action as the play progresses gives a contrary impression of movement towards an end. It is, perhaps, partly as a result of this that he does not achieve that precise and terrifying point of balance, between agony

and laughter, that is so outstanding a feature of Beckett's writing. Ionesco defines less clearly than Beckett the actual comedy and latent tragedy of playing towards nothing—of playing, that is, towards neither the final whistle nor the end of the game. But no dramatist has been more determined to deny his audience a "solution." His plays are not ends in themselves, but part of a continuing endlessness; and to those who defy him in their demand for ends he offers a cheerless message:

> For you see, my dear chap, art and logic are two different things, and if you have to call on logic to understand art, art in other words life, vanishes; only logic, in other words death, remains.
>
> (*The Picture, VII,* 131)

The modern audience member, I have already suggested, is being increasingly invited to carry over his understanding of tension from his experience as a spectator of a game. The implications are generally discomforting. The dramatists have pre-judged the competition and found it futile, but the players act in ignorance of this. Absurdist plays constantly exploit the disparity between the levels of awareness, not of the characters simply, but of the characters and their creator. Games are an excellent image of the faith in a reliable connection between cause and effect. The player of a game strives towards a determinable end, using only those means that are allowed by the rules of the game. These rules impose on him at every moment certain necessities of decision and conduct, and the concept of necessity has a crucial place in absurdist irony. Beckett describes Watt's response to Mr. Knott's modus vivendi:

> But he had hardly felt the absurdity of those things, on the one hand, and the necessity of those others, on the other (for it is rare that the feeling of absurdity is not followed by the feeling of necessity), when he felt the absurdity of those things of which he had just felt the necessity (for it is rare that the feeling of necessity is not followed by the feeling of absurdity).[20]

The player of games must go on obeying the necessities of the game, even after the purpose of obedience has gone, and is therefore constantly in the presence of the absurdity which is consequent on necessity. We use words, we accumulate wealth, we tell the time, but we know that words and wealth can be emptied of significance, and that time is a fiction as soon as it has been divided. The lucid dénouement of the well-made play is foreign to the game-structure of absurdist drama. The most that can be offered to the players is a powerful illusion of significance, and the lukewarm hand of Avery Brundage on their shoulder to remind them that the taking part and not the winning is the real incentive.[21]

Notes

1. All quotations from Ionesco are from *Plays,* trans. Donald Watson, 7 vols. (London, 1957-68).

2. The easiest reference is to The Gospel According to St. John xi.

3. George E. Wellwarth, *The Theater of Protest and Paradox* (New York, 1964).

4. Wellwarth, p. 67.

5. From "Discovering the Theatre," originally published in *Tulane Drama Review,* but quoted here from *Theatre in the Twentieth Century,* ed. R. W. Corrigan (New York, 1963), p. 92.

6. *Ibid.,* p. 83.

7. Arthur Adamov, *Théâtre II* (Paris, 1955), p. 15.

8. Eric Berne, *Games People Play* (New York, 1964). The two games referred to are described in Part II under the general heading, "Sexual Games."

9. Cited in Martin Esslin, *The Theatre of the Absurd* (New York, 1961), p. 131. Ionesco is referring to his technique in *The Lesson,* but, as Esslin suggests, the observation has a more general accuracy.

10. *The Playwrights Speak,* ed. Walter Wager (London, 1969). The American edition appeared two years earlier. In the English edition the passage quoted can be found on p. 129.

11. For an illuminating application of game theory to the drama cf. Richard Schechner, "Approaches to Theory/Criticism," *Tulane Drama Review,* X (Summer 1966), 20-53. Schechner lists three kinds of time: Event (here "Result"), Set, and Symbolic.

12. Henry Livings, for instance, explains the method of *Stop It, Whoever You Are* in terms of roughly worked out set time: "I broke down the story into 'units' of about ten minutes each—about as long, I reckoned, as you can hold a new situation clearly and totally in mind." The comment is quoted in John Russell Taylor, *Anger and After* (London, 1963), p. 262.

13. This understates the operation in the theatre of a kind of *set time.* Plays can be denied performance because they are "too long" or "too short." The understood *right length* is still proximate to the "two hours' traffic" of Shakespeare's stage. In television drama, set time operates more aggressively.

14. Match-play golf is an intriguing example of game-structure. The game can finish on any green from the tenth onwards, but the result has to take the idea of the eighteenth hole into account. A victory on the tenth green is nominated a victory by 10 (or 9) and 8, ten up and eight to play. There is no set time in golf, so that match-play offers a structure in which the ideal result time can be anticipated or exceeded by the actual result time. (The abandonment of snooker when only the black ball remains and one player has an invincible lead is a minor parallel which could be the cause of extreme frustration if extended to the theatre!)

15. For a description of Symbolic Time in this context, cf. Schechner, p. 29.

16. My choice of words is suggested by a sentence in Arnold P. Hinchliffe's lucid short book, *The Absurd* (London, 1969), p. 56: "Ionesco himself has tended to suggest that the opposite of Absurd is Meaningful."

17. R. J. Millington, "The Use of Stage Properties on the Elizabethan stage," unpublished M. A. thesis, University of Manchester, 1970.

18. Jean Tardieu, *The Underground Lovers and Other Experimental Plays,* trans. Colin Duckworth (London, 1968).

19. Mordecai Richler, *The Incomparable Atuk* (London, 1963).

20. Samuel Beckett, *Watt* (Paris, 1958), p. 146.

21. In his interview with Professor Lamont, Ionesco gives this account of Bérenger: "He has the feeling that he is struggling against the whole world, that he alone can save the world. Of course he knows all along that it isn't so, but he acts as though it were" (Wager, p. 125). Whether or not I am right in sensing something of the Olympic spirit in this Bérenger—the Bérenger that is, of *The Killer* and *Rhinoceros*—I am confident of Ionesco's agreement that the benign sportsmanship of Avery Brundage, millionaire Chairman of the Olympic Committee, had an absurdity all its own in the fraught Mexico Games of 1968.

In the context of this paper, it is intriguing to note the title of Ionesco's latest play—*Jeu de Massacre.* Ionesco explained to an interviewer, "that's the name of a game you play at funfairs when you have to knock out all the figures in a shy" (*The Guardian,* 6 Feb. 1970). *Jeu de Massacre* is scheduled to receive its world première in Düsseldorf in 1970.

Mary Ann Witt (essay date 1972)

SOURCE: " Eugène Ionesco and the Dialectic of Space," in *Modern Language Quarterly,* Vol. 33, No. 3, September 1972, pp. 312-26.

[*In the following essay, Witt discusses the polar states such as evanescence and heaviness, lightness and darkness, open space and restriction, that are evident in Ionesco's plays; notes his use of the arrangement of spatial images; and asserts that Ionesco's characters are hemmed in, lonely creatures longing for liberation.*]

Throughout his journals and in his notes on the theater, Eugène Ionesco refers to the two basic states of consciousness which, he claims, are at the origin of all his plays. One is represented as a sensation of levity, evanescence, luminosity: "Chacun de nous a pu sentir, à certains moments, que le monde a une substance de rêve, que les murs n'ont plus d'épaisseur, qu'il nous semble voir à travers tout, dans un univers sans espace, uniquement fait de clartés et de couleurs. . . ."[1] The physical sensations are translated emotionally either as an experience of euphoria and marvel or as *vertige*—a Pascalian anguish before infinite space. The opposite state, far more frequent, is the sensation of being closed in and weighted down. It is sometimes described in terms reminiscent of Baudelaire's *Spleen:* "Un rideau, un mur infranchissable s'interpose entre moi et le monde, entre moi et moi-même, la matière remplit tout, prend toute la place, anéantit toute liberté sous son poids, l'horizon se rétrécit, le monde devient un cachot étouffant."[2] Images or dreams of walls and prisons haunt Ionesco's private writings and are most often associated with fear of death, metaphysical ignorance, the anguish of solitude, regret and remorse over past life, or, in another context, the pressures of society and "sinking" into domesticity. Yet imprisonment is sometimes seen as a form of protection, a haven of solitude.

Polar states such as evanescence and heaviness, light and darkness, the feeling of being closed in and that of flying through space are also evident throughout Ionesco's plays and stories after *La Cantatrice chauve* and *La Leçon,* which are primarily concerned with language. Rosette Lamont has analyzed the images of air and matter in *Le Piéton de l'air* and *Victimes du devoir* and has discussed the proliferation of matter in other plays.[3] Simone Benmussa's comprehensive study demonstrates that Ionesco's theater is based on the interplay of poetic images rather than on conventional dramatic elements such as plot and character.[4] At one point she states that the physical opposites of evanescence and heaviness are at the basis of the construction of Ionesco's plays,[5] but since her efforts are directed toward listing and interpreting *all* of Ionesco's dramatic imagery, she does not develop this important notion. By isolating the polar images of closed and open space I hope to be able to define more clearly the workings of certain fundamental structures and themes in Ionesco's work.

The anti-Brechtian Ionesco has led a long and consistent polemic against a theater of commitment. For him great drama is extratemporal, and the most profound communication in any art form takes place between one solitude and another. "En exprimant mes obsessions fondamentales, j'exprime ma plus profonde humanité. . . ."[6] Ionesco's most fundamental obsession is with death. In his argument for the primacy of universal situations he particularly emphasizes two examples of great theater. Both are concerned with the realization of an impending death, and both are set in a prison. Richard II's soliloquy in the dungeon of Pomfret castle in Shakespeare's tragedy is a "theatrical archetype" for man's fundamental, solitary condition.[7] The prison in Brendan Behan's *The Quare Fellow,* where prisoners and guards become united in awaiting the death of the unseen protagonist, stands for all societies, for the human condition.[8]

If imprisonment is both a personal experience and a universal situation, it is particularly suited for representation on stage. In Ionesco's plays there are no dungeons or cells with iron bars: these have been replaced by the petty bourgeois living room. It is primarily in this, his most prevalent décor, that Ionesco works out his "archetypes." The opposite image of open or infinite space is more difficult to suggest on stage, but it may be done through language or with lighting and the absence of décor. Other images, both scenic and verbal, such as mud, wetness, heaviness or fire, light and dryness, may accompany the two poles, but the spatial images, in the theater particularly, are primary. They serve not only as poetic metaphors but also as means of advancing the plot. Nearly all of Ionesco's

plays can be seen structurally in terms of what I shall call a dialectic of space.

In their arrangement of spatial images, Ionesco's major works (after *La Cantatrice chauve* and *La Leçon*) fall more or less into four categories. In the first, the scene is set in a closed-in, shabby interior which becomes progressively confining, usually because of the invasion of material objects. When confinement of the major characters reaches what seems to be its utmost limit (a parallel to the Sartrean *situation-limite*), a decision of some sort is forced on them; but it is accompanied by an interlude in which action stops completely and gives way to lyricism, often a meditation on the past and a fusion of images of enclosure and infinity. *Amédée ou Comment s'en débarrasser, Les Chaises, Le Roi se meurt,* and Ionesco's only short story which did not become a play, "La Vase," belong here. In the plays of the second category—*Le Nouveau Locataire, Délire à deux, Jacques ou La Soumission, L'Aventr est dans les œufs, Rhinocéros,* and *Victimes du devoir*—the movement is also one of progressive confinement, but the resolution is a burial within. Here too the action, at the point of greatest confinement, will often give way to a lyricism in which the two contrasting images appear. The suggestion of a cosmic holocaust, of which the situation represented on the stage is only a small part or a reflection, is also characteristic of these plays. *Le Piéton de l'air,* in which Ionesco concentrates on a development of the open-space image, constitutes a third category by itself. The fourth, comprised of the two long plays *Tueur sans gages* and *La Soif et la faim,* is characterized by an alternation between "open" and "closed" scenes. I shall attempt to deal with these four types by concentrating on one play from each with brief mention of the others.[9]

The dull interior that constitutes the principal décor of *Amédée ou Comment s'en débarrasser* is remarkable only for its multiple functions as living room, study, and telephone office. We learn in the first act that since the death or murder of Madeleine's former lover, fifteen years previous, Amédée and his wife have been imprisoned in their apartment. The corpse that occupies their bedroom acts as both judge and jailer for them.

By the end of the first act the corpse has caught its incurable disease, "geometric progression." Space on stage becomes increasingly restricted, not only because of the corpse's rapid growth, but also because of the furniture brought out of the bedroom. Madeleine and Amédée are caught in a very literal *situation-limite.* Once they make the decision to get rid of the corpse, the action stops and gives way to a dream sequence in which the husband and wife are represented by their *sosies* Amédée II and Madeleine II.

The dialogue in the second act gives some clue to the nature of the corpse which has held the couple prisoner. Originally, it may have been the cadaver of their dead love, as Leonard Pronko has suggested,[10] but through the years it has progressed into more than that. Listening to

Madeleine review the past, Amédée comments on her habits: "Des reproches, toujours des reproches, ce qui est fait est fait, inutile les remords . . ." (I, 261).[11] A pluperfect clause followed by a conditional is perhaps Madeleine's favorite construction ("Si tu avais déclaré son décès à temps, on aurait la prescription maintenant . . . nous ne vivrions pas comme des prisonniers, comme des coupables . . ." (I, 264-65) and of course expresses regret over an unchangeable situation. If Madeleine is trapped by regret, Amédée is trapped by remorse. Vague guilt feelings nag him, but he is unable to do anything about them. In the end the lost years add their contribution to the trap.

The Madeleine II-Amédée II interlude is like a duet in which Ionesco's favorite contrasting images are pitted against one another. While Madeleine II sings ugliness, darkness, heaviness, unhappiness, imprisonment, Amédée II sings beauty, light, weightlessness, joy, liberty. The duet ends with a rhymed battle between "maison de fer" and "maison de verre" (I, 281).

The counterpoint between the *sosies* (who represent the young Madeleine and Amédée) is echoed in the scene in which the corpse is pushed out the window. It is first stated in the décor itself. In his stage directions Ionesco insists that a striking contrast must be felt between the beauty of the night, the moonlight entering the window, and the "macabre" look of the room (I, 289). One should bear in mind that at this point the window is opened for the first time in fifteen years. The entrance of moonlight and starlight into the room seems to reawaken the lyricism and the expectations which the spectator has just seen to be dormant in Amédée. The first breath of outside air evokes his yearning to escape from enclosure to its opposite. Amédée's ecstatic description of the night culminates with "Et de l'espace, de l'espace, un espace infini!" (I, 290).

Unlike most of Ionesco's characters, Amédée will fulfill his desire for infinite space. The corpse which has imprisoned him for fifteen years, suddenly transformed into a parachute, becomes the instrument of his deliverance. In the highly comic ending (there are two versions) Ionesco seems to be making a statement on art and the artist. We are reminded in the last scene that Amédée is supposed to be a writer. Dangling in the air, he makes a rather pathetic profession of faith: "Je suis confus, je m'excuse, Messieurs, Mesdames, je m'excuse . . . Je voudrais bien rester . . . Rester les pieds sur terre . . . Je suis pour le progrès, je désire être utile à mes semblables . . . Je suis pour le réalisme social . . ." (I, 307). Madeleine's final plea with her husband is "Ta carrière dramatique!" Imprisoned by dead love, guilt, remorse and regret, Amédée's career was, to say the least, nonproductive. But those very obsessions which limit and oppress in daily life can become, if given a free outlet (unrestricted by the dictates of usefulness), the stuff of creation. As much as Amédée might consciously wish to be a good and useful citizen, his obsessions, in league with his fantasies, were determined to make of him an artist.

Amédée's joyful flight is exceptional in Ionesco's work. More frequently, a leap into space or an escape from imprisonment is associated with annihilation, with death. This is the case in "La Vase," **Les Chaises**, and **Le Roi se meurt**, all of which follow to some extent the pattern of **Amédée**. The combination of the polar images of open space and restriction is particularly striking in "La Vase." It is the account in the first person of a sickness, culminating in the description of a consciousness that observes the death and disintegration of its own body. The transformation from health to sickness, from optimism to pessimism, is accompanied by a shift from open space to closed room, from mobility to immobility. As in *Amédée,* the point of greatest immobility concurs with a duet of opposing images, but here the sole protagonist plays two parts. In a state of near paralysis, the dying man shut in his room envisions the dissolution of the material objects which surround him and a merging of his prison with limitless space: "Au crépuscule, enveloppés par les ombres moites, les meubles perdaient peu à peu leurs formes et, la nuit venue, s'effaçaient entièrement, silencieusement engloutis, avec la chambre, avec le monde même, comme dans un océan de ténèbres, sans limites."[12]

As Amédée is forced to a decision by the growing corpse, the narrator of "La Vase" is forced into action by the "dead weight" of his own body. Like Amédée he breaks out of a sealed prison, ventures into the open, and disposes of a body—his own. Rather than rising into the air, however, the body here is allowed to sink into a marsh while the bodiless "I" merges with an infinite blue sky. Although some sort of dualistic separation has taken place, there is nothing that suggests a Platonic or Christian immortal soul being liberated from the body. The final words "je partis" can only mean "I ceased to exist." The merging of the closing eye with the clear sky is in the end as suggestive of utter annihilation as is the sinking of the body in the mire.

Les Chaises, like **Amédée,** portrays on stage claustration by geometric progression. Here too, at the most crowded moment, Ionesco introduces a contrasting image—a powerful light which invades the old couple's island home through the door and windows and suggests at once a new hope and an opening out. Yet Sémiramis and her husband end their lives meaninglessly. They escape from a trap to die in a dark void.

Le Roi se meurt is, like "La Vase," the story of a growing sickness and approaching death and, like **Les Chaises**, a kind of endgame. The stage is not filled with matter in this play, but imprisonment is suggested in the language and by the eventual closing of doors around the king. The king is "trapped" by the inevitability of his death. Queen Marie offers him what would seem to be the only possible way out: "Plonge dans l'étonnement et la stupéfaction sans limites, ainsi tu peux être sans limites, ainsi tu peux être infiniment. Sois étonné, sois ébloui, tout est étrange, indéfinissable. Écarte les barreaux de la prison, enfonce ses murs, évade-toi des définitions. Tu respireras" (IV, 41-42). This state of *étonnement,* of a fresh, poetic wonder before the world, is described recurrently by Ionesco in his journals and essays. Always associated with light and space, sometimes with childhood and sometimes with creativity, it is a form of mystical deliverance available to every human being, a way of transcending time, evading determinism.[13] It cannot, however, stave off death. At least King Bérenger is unable to take this escape. On the contrary, he is closed into his throne room with Queen Marguerite, who will teach him to die. In the end, the king on his throne is swallowed up by a foggy gray light.

Le Roi se meurt differs from *Les Chaises* in that the illusion of a void is created on stage. It shares with this play the suggestion of death and destruction beyond the limits of the scene portrayed. This type of suggestion is prevalent in the plays of the second category which end, not with emptiness, but with total imprisonment or encumbrance. In *Délire à deux,* for example, a war raging in the street seems only an enlargement of the domestic battle of two aging lovers trapped with and by each other in another of Ionesco's grim petty bourgeois rooms. The plight of the couple is objectified and framed by the absurd debate on the tortoise and the snail which opens and closes the dialogue. Whether or not the two are the same animal as she contends and he contests, both are creatures with protective shells like the room in which the man and woman barricade themselves. But protection against the outside world forces them to live with each other in an ongoing battle. Like the dialogue between Madeleine and Amédée and between the old man and woman in *Les Chaises,* the words exchanged in *Délire* are full of regrets and remorse. Here the past conditional dominates: each character blames the other for what he or she has become in contrast to what "might have been."

As the war comes closer to them, the reaction of these human turtles is to withdraw as far as possible into their shelter. They shut the windows, the shutters, the door, and then begin to barricade themselves with furniture. Their final position, which indeed resembles that of a tortoise or snail, is under the bed. Here again action, in the most confined position, gives way to nostalgia and lyricism. In the case of the two middle-aged lovers the lyricism is somewhat truncated, but each experiences an evocation of a lost childhood paradise, of a past without the conditional. The images are of fish in the water and of rainbows.

This scene states in a comic, distorted way one of Ionesco's most profound themes. In his deepest solitude, in his encirclement by death, man communicates with others more than in the course of normal life or in any group involvement. But this moment is a brief one in *Délire à deux.* Ionesco goes on to show that resolutions on a social or political level do not necessarily have any effect on the private hell of individuals. If "she" and "he" saw their own obsessions reflected in the war, they return to their private battle once the danger is past and peace has come. They also rebuild their falling house, barricading the doors and windows even more than before as if to construct a protection from death itself, in any form. "Il y a des courants d'air. Il y a la grippe, il y a les microbes et puis il faut prévoir" (III, 224), she explains. The last words—"Tortue!" "Limace!"—bring the play to a circular conclusion.

The process of barricading oneself within a room is almost the sole subject of *Le Nouveau Locataire.* Here the world is solipsistic to a point well beyond *Délire à deux.* Disaster in the outside world is not merely reflected in the private world; it is created by it. The new tenant fills up the outside world and stops its normal movement with his *own* possessions. Thus an inner, individual state of being is made visible on stage. The active part of the mind gradually becomes inactive and inhibited by its own "furniture"—obsessions, desires, fears, and other subconscious rumblings. In this play, escape is not even suggested. No image of space or light interrupts the methodical, self-imposed burial of the new tenant.

The other plays in this group (ending in confinement) deal with several characters, and in these it is the social, rather than the inner, world which engulfs and imprisons its victims on stage. The imagery in *Jacques ou La Soumission,* an early play, is created more by language than by use of stage material. Yet its structure parallels that of *Délire à deux* and *Le Nouveau Locataire.* At the climax of the play the couple, Jacques and Roberte, are closed in alone. Jacques understands that he has been trapped and confesses as much to Roberte: "Ils m'ont trompé . . . Et comment sortir? Ils ont bouché les portes, les fenêtres avec du rien, ils ont enlevé les escaliers . . . Je veux absolument m'en aller. Si on ne peut pas passer par le grenier, il reste la cave . . . Il vaut mieux passer par en bas que d'être là" (I, 116-17). Roberte will offer him precisely this exit, but first, characteristically at the point of greatest confinement, she creates a poem of open space, dryness, and light. The same movement takes place in *L'Avenir est dans les œufs,* in which, as Pronko describes it, Jacques is "slowly swallowed up by animalism and materialism."[14] He is allowed a small rebellion and an outcry of protest—"Je veux une fontaine de lumière, de l'eau incandescente" (II, 230)—but production, matter, the family, and the white race win out.

In *Victimes du devoir* Choubert is also finally engulfed by matter and the forces of order, but not before he almost flies away and escapes. The imprisonment of Bérenger in his own room at the end of *Rhinocéros* is of a different oder. Unlike the new tenant's, Bérenger's inner space is free; it is the world outside that is encumbered with rhinoceroses. When Daisy goes to join the herd, Bérenger retains his humanity in what for Ionesco is the only possible way—by preserving his solitude.

Le Piéton de l'air (the play of the third category) might be called "The Liberation of Bérenger." It is the only work in which Ionesco attempts to deal almost entirely with images of free space and evanescene rather than with their opposites. Bérenger's flight seems to be for Ionesco a kind of laboratory experiment to test what would happen if the dream of transcending human limits were realized. It is in a sense a sequel to *Amédée*—and this Bérenger is the only other character in Ionesco's work who is a writer. The flight follows a kind of curve. Bérenger is at first literally uplifted by joy, full of confidence and pride.[15] During his departure the tone changes. His wife Joséphine experiences an acute anguish, and all of the characters become distorted as in a dream. One of the dream sequences is particularly significant for the development of the spatial imagery. It is a confrontation between John Bull ("le gros personnage") and a little boy. The boy runs toward a wall which he attempts to climb, is caught by the man, pleads that he wants to walk in the sky and light and that he does not want to return to his cell. The fat man then gives him a lesson: "Petit imbécile, tu apprendras que la lumière est bien plus belle quand on la regarde du fond d'un trou noir et que le ciel est bien plus pur quand on le voit à travers la grille de la lucarne" (III, 181-82). Bérenger's return seems to confirm John Bull's harsh common sense. The surrealistic visions he describes from the other side of the wall are of death and destruction. Bérenger's perceptions of light and space are no longer accompanied by joy but by terror. It is the Pascalian terror before infinite nothingness: "Après, il n'y a plus rien, plus rien que les abîmes illimités . . . que les abîmes" (III, 198). The experiment with liberation has failed, and Bérenger remains as if dangling between finitude and infinity.

A dialectic of space is at the basis of the structure of Ionesco's two long plays, *Tueur sans gages* and *La Soif et la faim.* The three acts of *Tueur* can be described as open-closed-open, those of *Soif* as closed-open-closed. Both plays follow the destiny of a character through the extremes of closed and open space like a swinging pendulum—an equilibrium between the two is never reached. *Tueur sans gages* opens with a décor made entirely of lights in which Berenger seems to find the outward realization of his deepest longings. Yet as soon as he hears of the work of a killer in the "radiant" city, the lighting changes to gray and objects being to come on stage. The setting of the second act, in Bérenger's apartment (which must correspond to his most frequent state of mind), is characterized by an oppressive low roof, darkness, and heaviness. The menace of death is present here too in the sickly Edouard. Yet Bérenger leaves this situation in a burst of optimism and action, and the third act finds him in the open again. In the last part of this act Ionesco uses a décor that in a way synthesizes the open and closed spaces in acts 1 and 2. Space on the stage is first enlarged to suggest solitude and emptiness. Then walls are to be moved to form a corridor around Bérenger "afin de donner l'impression que Bérenger va être pris dans un guet-apens . . . il aura l'air, finalement, de vouloir s'enfuir" (II, 158). The corridor can suggest both limitlessness and imprisonment. At the very end of the play the two images merge in another way. When Bérenger meets the killer, the corridor disappears; there remain only a wall and the sensation of "le vide de la plaine" (II, 161). The emptiness suggests Bérenger's solitude and the meaninglessness of his endeavor, and the wall corresponds to the impassibility of the killer.[16] Closed and open or limited and

vacant encounter each other here on mutual ground. Absurdity, anguish, and death are met at either extreme.

Ionesco's two fundamental images and the themes that accompany them are most fully developed in *La Soif et la faim.* A reversal of the acts of *Tueur,* the movement here is closed-open-closed, with a juxtaposition rather than a synthesis at the end. A counterpoint between the two images runs throughout the play and has its source in the character of Jean, who can never be content with either condition but is constantly searching for one or the other. His wife, Marie-Madeleine, describes his predicament neatly: "Si ce n'est pas l'agoraphobie, c'est la claustrophobie" (IV, 77). Jean spends most of the first act complaining about their present dwelling, a sordid basement, contrasting it with their previous spacious, luminous apartment. Repressed remorse, objectified in the figure of Aunt Adelaide, "weighs" on him. Yet the family had lived in the basement before moving to the other house, and Marie-Madeleine claims that Jean made the decision to return. Thus a pattern of perpetual alternation is established.

For Marie-Madeleine, as for Queen Marie in *Le Roi se meurt,* it is possible to find happiness within imprisonment, to destroy the sense of confinement by a mere shift in attitude. After Jean has left her, she is thus able to "free" herself. At the end of the first act, the back wall of the house has disappeared, and Marie-Madeleine stands before a luminous garden in an attitude of *étonnement.*

The second episode follows Jean in his quest for liberty. In the décor here height has replaced the underground; clear horizons, the walls. Yet Jean is far from free. His agoraphobia does not take long to manifest itself. Growing impatient with waiting for a mythical woman to appear at a museum on the mountain, he begins to speak nostalgically to the only other characters present, the two museum guardians, of the shelter he left behind.

> Pourtant, j'étais à l'abri, bien enfermé dans ma tristesse, dans ma nostalgie, dans ma peur, dans mes remords, dans mon angoisse, dans ma responsabilité, à l'abri. C'était autant de murs qui m'entouraient. La crainte de la mort était mon bouclier le plus solide. Les murs se sont écroulés et me voici, vulnérable. Les murs se sont écroulés et me voici dans le feu torride de la vie, dans le lucide désespoir de la détresses. (IV, 114)

In open space, with absolute freedom of choice before him, Jean is in a state of anguish. The despair of limitlessness necessitates action as much as the pressure of limits. Once Jean has discovered for himself a banal but fundamental truth, "il n'y a aucune raison de vivre" (IV, 117), he must continue his wandering, hoping, acting as if he will be given a reason to live.

It is not difficult to imagine that Jean would seek out another enclosure. The décor of the third episode is more than that—it represents the main room of "une sorte de monastère-caserne-prison" (IV, 121). Downstage is a barred door behind which one sees first a gray, foggy landscape (corresponding to the "morne plaine" which is the recurrent theme in Jean's description of his travels), then, at the end of the play, the luminous garden of act 1 with Jean's wife and daughter.

The episode of Brechtoll and Tripp, the "education-re-education" show put on for Jean's benefit, is not only a play within a play, but also a prison within a prison. The atheist and the believer come on stage in cages, and the "play" consists of tantalizing them with freedom (opening the cage door) and soup. One of the tasks which Frère Tarabas proposes to accomplish in his re-education procedure is the "demystification" of liberty. His assumption is that imprisonment of some sort is the natural condition of man in society. "Réfléchissez" (he addresses the prisoners who demand their liberty): "les prisons vides, les rues pleines de gens qui errent, qui errent . . . Ce serait le monde à l'envers" (IV, 139). Here, he argues, the prisoners are safe, protected; outside they might be "free" to die of cold. What the two men now call "liberty" or "imprisonment" is merely a result of habit or prejudice—it can be changed. The argument is a familiar one.

The "establishment" (the proper word for the place, according to Frère Tarabas) in act 3 represents a collective or social form of confinement in contrast to the personal or familial form in act 1. Frère Tarabas explains to Jean that they suspected he would come: "C'est la maison où l'on vient d'habitude" (IV, 123). This is perhaps a way of stating that a quest, if it has an end, ends with an answer, thus with an ideology, thus with an organized system. Whether "la bonne auberge" represents a religious monastery, the realization of the socialist utopia,[17] or a psychiatric clinic,[18] it is an institution characterized by both security and oppression. For Ionesco, who could write, "le camp de concentration est la société telle qu'elle est dans son essence, quintessenciée,"[19] it is surely a model for all varieties of social organization. Every society has its ruling class, and the ruling class will oppress those who are not with them. There is no more real outlet for individual assertion within an institutional framework than in a concentration camp.

After the play, Frère Tarabas uses comparable techniques on Jean. In adding up the hours (days, months, years?) of service he owes the "establishment," he presents the obligation as if it were a natural expression of human solidarity.

> Nous nous devons des services les uns aux autres. Nous sommes des humains. Nous avons des obligations les uns vis-à-vis des autres, à moins de préférer la cage de la solitude. Mais cela n'est pas un endroit confortable. Vous ne pouvez y tenir ni tout à fait debout, ni tout à fait assis. (IV, 164)[20]

The natural outcome of the play of Brechtoll and Tripp (there are twenty-nine more episodes!) would be the "freeing" of the prisoners from their cages to become willing and docile members of the community. Solitude, individuality, or the expression of deviant ideas is made into an uncomfortable cage by a society that wants conformity

and harmony. The brothers now set about making Jean into a member of the community. He is given a monk's habit and a duty to perform.

The end of act 3 is a reversal of the situation at the end of act 1: Jean is imprisoned, Marie-Madeleine and Marthe are outside. Once again eternity or timelessness is associated with open space, and the rapid passing of time with closed space. Marie-Madeleine in the garden seems forever young while the brothers count out the passing minutes and hours in Jean's prison. Jean's vision of his wife and daughter is through bars. The play ends on this poignant note of separation and with the impression that Jean will never be able to liberate himself to join those he loves. If he did, would his vacillation not recur?

The spatial images in Ionesco's work which serve the dramatist in constructing his plot act as symbols for the poet and the recorder of dreams. The feeling of being enclosed or cut off and the simultaneous desire for liberation emerge as two of the strongest themes in Ionesco's journals and essays as well as in his creative works. The two states are indeed, in his view, at the basis of the history of civilizations. All religions, all ideologies, he claims, have been founded on the assumption that life in the present is a prison or an "alienation" and on the corresponding nostalgia for liberty, happiness, the "true" life or paradise.[21] Ionesco's own dreams and fantasies are filled with the same images, and occasionally he attempts to interpret them. The recurrent dream of a wall, which appears throughout *Journal en miettes,* is seen to contain multiple meanings:

> Le mur est donc le mur d'une prison, de ma prison; il est la mort puisqu'il semble être un cimetière vu de très loin; ce mur est le mur d'une église, il me sépare d'une communauté: il est donc l'expression de ma solitude, de la non-interpénétration. . . . Il est en même temps l'obstacle à la connaissance, il est ce qui cache la vie, la vérité. En somme c'est le mystère de la vie et de la mort que je veux percer; ni plus ni moins. (pp. 102-103)

All of Ionesco's characters are hemmed-in, lonely creatures longing, however obscurely, for some sort of liberating answer, a resolution that will free them from their limitations. For many of them—Amédée and Madeleine, the old couple in *Les Chaises,* the couple in *Délire à deux,* Jean and Marie-Madeleine—imprisonment is a way of life. Couples, in particular, tend to keep each other trapped in the quagmire of domesticity or in "remorse" and "regrets." For others—the narrator of "La Vase," the new tenant, King Bérenger, and the Bérenger of *Tueur sans gages*—being enclosed is a way of death, a stifling of the self by the self, or an encounter with the ultimate absurdity. For the Bérenger of *Rhinocéros,* confinement means separation from a community, but in spite of Ionesco's statement in his journal, the community is never seen as something desirable. More often, it is itself the cause of the claustration and suffocation of an individual. This is the case in *Jacques ou La Soumission, L'Avenir est dans les œufs, Victimes du devoir,* and *La Soif et la faim.* If one ventures out of the cage of solitude, one is more than likely to end up in a concentration camp.

The prisoners' dream of liberation takes the form of a yearning for open, unencumbered space, usually bathed in light. It is sometimes characterized by dryness, sometimes by vegetation, and is associated with feelings of buoyancy, giddiness, exhilaration, joy. Amédée and the Bérenger of **Piéton** represent the feeling quite literally in being lifted off the earth. The narrator of "La Vase" experiences the lightness of a kite and a vision of infinity when rid of his body. Marie-Madeleine is able to perceive an idyllic landscape through her capacity for *étonnement*. Images of light and space appear in the dreams and fantasies of such prisoners as Jacques, Choubert, Sémiramis and her husband, the Bérenger of **Tueur**, and Jean. For a while the latter two think that they have found their inner vision realized in an actual setting. Yet the realization inevitably fails.

Another type of open-space image, characterized by gray light or darkness, is more likely to be found in "reality" by Ionesco's characters. It is "la morne plaine" in Jean's account of his journey, "le vide de la plaine" at the end of **Tueur sans gages,** the gray light at the end of *Le Roi se meurt,* the dark void around the island in **Les Chaises.** This may be associated with limitless, anxiety-producing freedom or with meaningless, universal death. Hoping for the deliverance represented by space and light (as do the old couple in **Les Chaises**), Ionesco's characters are more apt to encounter the dark, limitless void.

Absurdity, the non-answer behind the mystery of existence, or death seems to be what is encountered at the extremes of imprisonment or open space. Liberation is something never achieved, only glimpsed. True freedom would mean a transcendence of the dialectic of space.

> Est libre celui qui ne sait même pas qu'il est libre, ni qu'il y a la liberté, ni qu'il y a l'emprisonnement. Est libre non pas celui qui est au-delà du bien et du mal, mais en dehors des obsessions de la liberté et de la prison. . . . Libre . . . celui . . . pour qui mourir et vivre c'est la même chose.[22]

Such freedom is beyond Ionesco and the creatures of his imagination. Impeded and frustrated by both the restrictions of the human condition and the intuition of an infinite universe devoid of unity or meaning, they can, at best, envision momentarily images that suggest liberation. Paradoxically, such visions are most intense at the point of greatest confinement and solitude. Yet the dreams of the solitary individual remain unfulfilled in reality; at most they can partially be brought forth by artistic creation which can shed "une petite lueur grisâtre, un tout petit début d'illumination"[23] on the opacity of things. Imprisonment, in its various forms, is a reality. One does what one can from within.

Notes

1. *Notes et contre-notes* (Paris, 1962), p. 140.

2. *Ibid.,* p. 141.

3. See "The Proliferation of Matter in Ionesco's Plays," *ECr,* 2 (1962), 189-97, and "Air and Matter: Ionesco's 'Le Piéton de l'air' and 'Victimes du devoir.' " *FR,* 38 (1965). 349-61.

4. *Ionesco* (Paris, 1966).

5. *Ibid.,* p. 67.

6. *Notes et contre-notes,* p. 34.

7. *Ibid.,* p. 18.

8. *Ibid.,* p. 34.

9. Because of limited space I have not included Ionesco's latest play. *Jeux de massacre* (1970), in this study. Though the play does not fit into any of the four categories, the confinement imagery that dominates it would merit a separate, lengthy treatment.

10. *Avant-Garde: The Experimental Theater in France* (Berkeley and Los Angeles, 1962), p. 94.

11. All quotations from Ionesco's plays are from *Théâtre,* 4 vols. (Paris, 1954-66), and are cited by volume and page number. In his *Journal en miettes* (Paris, 1967), p. 149. Ionesco speaks of remorse and regret as "the prison" for him.

12. *La Photo du colonel: Récits* (Paris, 1962). p. 145.

13. Ionesco claims to have attained such states himself: "J'ai eu l'expérience, j'ai su ce qu'est être en dehors de l'Histoire. On peut y arriver. Cet état d'étonnement premier, de stupéfaction est propre à la condition humaine et peut illuminer quiconque au-delà de sa condition sociale, de son temps historique, du conditionnement économique" (*Journal en miettes,* p. 70). The understanding that he seeks is both mystical and Platonic: "Détruire les murs du réel qui nous sépare de la réalité, participer à l'être pour vivre comme au premier jour de la naissance du monde . . ." (*Présent passé passé présent* [Paris, 1968], p. 215).

14. *Avant-Garde,* p. 74.

15. In *Présent passé passé présent* (pp. 223-24) Ionesco recounts an experience of elation, a feeling of almost being able to fly, which must have been the impetus for writing *Le Piéton de l'air.* The sensation of joy and wonder is associated with light, which is in turn equated with expansion of space or destruction of limits: "La stupéfaction surgit, éclata, déborda, faisant dissoudre les frontières des choses, désarticulant les définitions . . . comme la lumière semblait faire disparaître les murs. . . ."

16. A "blind force" or "incomprehensible destiny" is associated with the vision of both an "impenetrable" soldier and a wall in *Journal en miettes* (p. 197).

17. Ionesco has explained that the prison episode in *La Soif et la faim* was partially a reference to the trial of Siniavsky and Daniel and that the setting of the third act could represent the prison which the socialist utopia had become in Soviet Russia (*Arts et loisirs,* March 9-15, 1966, p. 19).

18. Ionesco compares the psychiatric clinic in Switzerland in which he spent some time to a caserne, prison, and concentration camp (*Journal en miettes,* pp. 151. 213-14). Frère Tarabas's language

occasionally suggests that of a psychiatrist with a patient, and he tells Jean that their institution was once a clinic (IV, 132).

19. *Journal en miettes,* p. 156.

20. This would seem to refer to the medieval prison cell called the "little ease" or *malconfort*—an important image in Camus's *La Chute.*

21. See *Présent passé passé présent,* pp. 227-28.

22. *Journal en miettes,* p. 100.

23. *Ibid.,* p. 120.

George E. Craddock, Jr. (essay date 1971)

SOURCE: "Escape and Fulfillment in the Theatre of Eugène Ionesco," in *The Southern Quarterly,* Vol. X, No. 1, October 1971, pp. 15-22.

[*In the following essay, Craddock argues that a major concern in Ionesco's work is the breaking out of confining social structures and awakening of the individual to the full potentialities of existence. According to Ionesco this can be done through exercising the imagination and creativity, those innate capacities that are best developed in solitude, which is where humans find their true selves.*]

In Ionesco's theatre two major themes stand out: alienation and fulfillment. The first of these is one which Ionesco has in common with the other major playwrights of the theatre of the absurd. The theme of fulfillment, however, is less typical of the works of the other contemporary playwrights, but it is a vital part of Ionesco's theatre.

Ionesco's major concern about the human condition revolves around his belief that the important goals of life are lost in the maze of routine daily actions. Social living channels the individual's physical and mental activities to such an extent that he becomes a kind of conditioned human being. By giving most of his attention to the exterior world, the individual fails to give sufficient attention to his inner life. Thus he starves his higher self of artistic or creative activity, and he loses an important dimension of his identity.

In an article in *Notes et contre-notes* Ionesco states that people who have become prisoners of social reality are "appauvris, aliénés, vidés."[1] Their ability to marvel at the many facets of existence has been killed, and in its place they find fatigue and boredom. This is the sickness which Ionesco feels is prevalent in modern society and which is caused by the opposition of man's nature and his condition. A symptom of this sickness is a malaise, a sensation of being weighted down by the forces of life, of being without energy or enthusiasm. This gives the individual the feeling of not belonging to the world and of longing to be elsewhere.

In expressing such a mental state in his theatre, Ionesco frankly admits that he is using his own feelings and that his plays are exorcisms of his own anxieties. He writes of two basic states which he goes through: heaviness and lightness. The latter state gives him a feeling of euphoria and of refound liberty, but this happy state is very rare. More often he feels crushed by the universe and longs for something to take him away from what he calls his "prison quotidienne."[2] He has a vague nostalgia of some other world ("un ailleurs"), from which he feels separated and which he misses. This state of being ill at ease in life he has expressed as follows:

> Je ne me sens pas tout à fait appartenir au monde. . . . J'ai plutôt l'impression que je suis d'ailleurs. Si je savais quel est cet ailleurs, ça irait bien mieux. . . . Le fait d'être habité par une nostalgie incompréhensible serait tout de même le signe qu'il y a un ailleurs. Cet ailleurs est, peut-être, si je puis dire, un "ici" que je ne retrouve pas; peut-être ce que je cherche n'est pas ici. . . . Je constate donc tout simplement que je suis là, ce "je" difficile à définir, et c'est bien pour exprimer, pour faire part de mon étonnement et de ma nostalgie que j'écris.[3]

Ionesco endows some of his characters with his own malaise. These are the exceptional ones, however, for he sees most people as being too insensitive to be aware of any malaise. Most of his characters are resigned to the world as it is. They make no complaint; they are, like the Smiths and the Martins, quite at home in their routine world, where they believe themselves fulfilled. Not all, however. There are some who realize that there is a lost dimension to their lives, and they look for it in their memories, dreams, and imagination.

The earliest appearance of such a character is the protagonist of ***Jacques ou la soumission,***[4] who reveals in a long expressive monologue how disappointed he is with life and why he would like to escape: He was more perceptive than most people, and he realized early in life what the world was all about. He did not like the things he saw and he complained about them openly. Whenever he complained, people told him that everything would be remedied. To make up for all this, they promised him decorations, awards, and other trivialities. But he was not pleased with these, for they did not touch upon the real problem. He insisted that the situation be changed. Everyone swore to give him satisfaction, even gave him official promises with many legal seals. To pacify him, as well as to divert his mind to other things, they took him on voyages, and at first he let himself fall into this trap. But eventually he realized that all this was faked, that they had changed nothing, that the world was as bad as ever. He wanted to protest, but there was no one who would hear him. He wanted to escape, but all the exits were blocked. He was told that there were exits, but he could not find them. But there was still the cellar door of sensual pleasure. If he could not escape from above, he could at least escape from below. His baser instincts win out, as he lets himself be lured into marriage; and he is trapped into the restricted and limited atmosphere of domestic life.

Jacques reappears in a sequel, *L'Avenir est dans les oeufs,*[5] in which he is controlled further by the family and by society—so much so, that he is not even consulted when the family decides on the careers for his many offspring. When he does try to offer his views, they call him down. They claim that he has lost his faith, and they ask him what he really wants. He replies in a poetic outburst: "Je veux une fontaine de lumière, de l'eau incandescente, un feu de glace, des neiges de feu."[6] This sudden outburst represents his real nature trying to break out of his bondage to middle-class life—the heart of the poet, longing for beauty, but stifled by the chores of daily life. He is brought back to reality, as his family insists that he must do his social duty. If he needs any beauty in his life, he can always go to displays of fireworks, or perhaps take in a chateau from time to time.

In *Amédée ou Comment s'en débarrasser*[7] we again see the killing effect upon the individual as a result of domestic life. Amédée is a writer, but he cannot get past the first line of his work. His wife constantly ridicules and criticizes him. In the next room a body keeps growing until it crowds out both Amédée and his wife. This body could be taken to represent Amédée's own higher self, killed by the cares and duties of domestic and social life. The more Amédée settles down into bourgeois routine, the bigger the body grows. It is his lost dimension—that part of his life representing his individuality and creativity.

Ionesco's most famous treatment of social duty as a killing force on the individual is *Victimes du devoir,*[8] in which he shows that society's control over the individual is so thorough that even his inner life is in danger of being controlled by exterior forces. Choubert, the protagonist of the play, tries to escape his social identity and look for his true self. He does this by means of going back into his memory and his imagination, where the outer world cannot penetrate, but where—in this instance—there is a detective who tries to enter even into that most private domain of one's life. In the most famous scene of the play, Choubert—in his imagination—climbs a mountain and attempts to fly away. The detective and the wife, in collaboration, do all they can to call him back to his social life. Finally, his wife ridicules him until he loses his confidence and falls. He has failed to escape; he is then watched even more closely, as he is ordered to fulfill his social duty.

Jacques, Amédée, and Choubert are all embryonic forms of Bérenger, a later creation, who has been called Ionesco's finest. Ionesco uses Bérenger in three of his major plays: *Tueur sans gages, Le Rhinocéros,* and *Le Piéton de l'air.*[9] Bérenger is essentially an Everyman, and might also be taken to represent Ionesco's own views. He has learned from experience that we are not living in a golden age. He has given up his illusions and has done his best to adjust to his mediocre existence. But he is dissatisfied with his life, and he yearns for another. He speaks of a warmth which once pervaded his life—an "élan vital," which he has lost through the years. He is aware that something is wrong, even though he cannot grasp exactly what it is. The character Jean in *La Soif et la Faim*[10] is of the same race as Bérenger. He longs for a world of beauty even though he lives in the midst of ugliness, and he tries to attain it, to struggle against the forces which try to hold him down.

It is through such protagonists that Ionesco shows us the major symptoms of that most discussed modern malady, alienation. But Ionesco not only exposes the malady, he also proposes a cure: to recapture that part of one's nature from which he has been alienated. This idea he expresses in his theatre, on the metaphorical level, and in his articles, on the polemical level. Even as early as *Amédée,* Ionesco has presented this form of fulfillment, as Amédée recaptures the lost dimension of his basic self. This happens in a very strange way, but one which is perfectly comprehensible, if one understands the dead body as representing Amédée's lost self. Amédée takes the body from his apartment (where the atmosphere is so stifling and dead that there are mushrooms growing) and drags it out into the street, where a surprising thing happens. The body becomes very light and goes upward, carrying Amédée with it. He becomes intoxicated with joy; he has become reunited with his lost self, and he goes off into outer space, completely happy, as the play ends.

This same idea Ionesco develops more fully in *Le Piéton de l'air,* in which he shows us a Bérenger who has a rare moment of lightness which frees him from the heaviness of life. He is filled with such joy that he first walks above the ground, then really flies, saying that he has found again the forgotten means to do this. The onlookers—the conditioned human beings—tell him that this is not natural. He assures them that it is, claiming that flying is an indispensable need and an innate faculty which everyone has forgotten. When we do not fly, he says, it is worse than when we have been deprived of nourishment. He is told that it is too late to relearn it, but he replies that one must try if he is to become a more complete being. After all, he warns, if we are not careful, we might even forget how to walk. Bérenger insists that he will remain a pedestrian, both of the earth and of the air.

Ionesco uses the act of flying in *Le Piéton de l'air* to express a breaking out of the confines of one's limited social existence into the limitless opportunity which life offers. He wishes to awaken people's minds to the full potentialities of life, and he calls for total liberty of thought and a new awareness of reality. In *Le Piéton de l'air* he implies that one refinds his basic self—this lost dimension—on exercising his full capabilities.

This idea is also expressed in Ionesco's articles, in which he suggests creation (especially artistic creation), dreaming, and imagination as some of the means of breaking away from life's limitations. He sees imagination as more important than "la réalité concrète, matérielle, appauvrie, vidée, limitée."[11] He believes that it is not by a limited notion of reality that the authentic nature of things is discovered: "La nature authentique des choses, la vérité ne peut nous être révélée que par la fantaisie plus réaliste que tous les réalismes."[12] Dreaming, likewise, can reveal to the mind many things which are not noticed when one is awake. Ionesco writes: "Lorsque je rêve je n'ai pas le sentiment d'abdiquer la pensée. J'ai au contraire l'impression que je vois, en rêvant, des vérités, qui m'apparaissent, des évidences, dans une lumière plus éclatante, avec une acuité plus impitoyable qu'à l'état de veille."[13]

Ionesco sees imagination as a kind of power; it is "la force vivante et créatrice de l'esprit humain."[14] Imagination is a source of the joy of existence; it is part of man's true nature. The world that is within needs further exploration: "L'espace est immense à l'intérieur de nous-mêmes. Qui ose s'y aventurer? Il nous faut des explorateurs, des découvreurs de mondes inconnus qui sont en nous, qui sont à découvrir en nous."[15] Using our power to think is one way to deliver ourselves from our condition. Ionesco wonders if art might not be the means to this deliverance:

> Je me demande si l'art ne pourrait pas être la libération, le réapprentissage d'une liberté dont nous sommes déshabitués, que nous avons oubliée, dont l'absence fait souffrir aussi bien ceux qui se croient libres que ceux qui pensent ne pas pouvoir l'être; mais un apprentissage 'indirect.'[16]

Ionesco writes that there is innate in man a creative instinct, which must be given an outlet: "La création est une nécessité instinctive, extra-consciente; parce que imaginer, inventer, découvrir, créer, est une fonction aussi naturelle que la respiration."[17] This need to invent, to express oneself by creating, is what raises man above the animals. He observes that all of us, at one time or another, have written, or at least tried to write, or else have tried to paint, to act, to compose music, or to build something, if only a rabbit cage. There is not always any practical utility to this, or, if so, it is only a pretext to let our creative nature express itself.[18] The act of creating is for Ionesco this "passage vers autre chose" which man longs for. It is an attempt to satisfy what he calls "notre soif de l'absolu." It is a way to call into play the undeveloped faculties which have been given up to the demands of social life.

This type of fulfillment requires solitude, which Ionesco defends against those who think of it as anti-social behavior: "La solitude n'est pas séparation mais recueillement, alors que les groupements, les sociétés ne sont, le plus souvent, comme on l'a déjà dit, que des solitaires réunis."[19] It is in our solitude, he claims, that we find our real selves. He feels that he is more truly himself when he is alone and that often society alienates him from himself and from others. His social self does not fully reveal him: "Lorsque je suis à la surface sociale de moi-même je suis impersonnel. Ou je suis très peu moi-même."[20]

Ionesco claims that his plays try to show that man is more than just a social animal who is a prisoner of his time. He refers to a "communauté extra-historique," which he says is a more fundamental one than the society of any one time.

Si je peux m'exprimer en paradoxe, je dirai que la société véritable, l'authentique communauté humaine, est extra-sociale,—c'est une société plus vaste et plus profonde, celle qui se révèle par des angoisses communes, des désirs, des nostalgies secrètes qui sont le fait de tous.[21]

He wonders what the term "social" really means, and he believes that there are many misunderstandings in connection with this word. Too often, he feels, things which are said to have a social interest in reality have more of a political or practical value. He finds that man in general is truer to himself than the man who is limited to his own epoch, and he tries in his plays to penetrate the complex structure of society to rediscover the basic man. Man's nature is not to be found entirely in his social self, but also in his inner life, which can be as rich as the exterior one: "Le monde intérieur peut être aussi riche que le monde du dehors. L'un et l'autre ne sont, d'ailleurs, que les deux aspects d'une même réalité."[22] It is by returning to the interior life that man in society can recapture his equilibrium and find his fulfillment.

Notes

1. *Notes et contre-notes* (Paris: Gallimard, 1962), 74.

2. *Ibid.,* 140-41.

3. "L'auteur et ses problèmes," *Revue de Métaphysique et de morale,* LXVIII (October-December, 1963), 411.

4. Théâtre (Paris: Gallimard, 1954-1966), I, 95-127.

5. *Ibid.,* II, 203-29.

6. *Ibid.,* 228.

7. *Ibid.,* I, 237-333.

8. *Ibid.,* 181-235.

9. *Ibid.,* II, 59-172; III, 7-117; III, 119-98.

10. *Ibid.,* IV, 75-180.

11. *Notes et contre-notes,* 4-5.

12. *Ibid.,* 123.

13. *Ibid.,* 93.

14. *Ibid.,* 130.

15. *Ibid.,* 207.

16. "Depuis dix ans je me bats contre l'esprit bourgeois et les tyrannies politiques," *Arts,* No. 758 (January, 1960), 26.

17. "L'auteur et ses problèmes," 409.

18. *Notes et contre-notes,* 103-04.

19. *Ibid.,* 129.

20. *Ibid.,* 95.

21. *Ibid.,* 73.

22. *Ibid.,* 111.

J. K. Newberry (essay date 1975)

SOURCE: "The Evolution of the Dramatic Technique of Eugène Ionesco," in *Nottingham French Studies,* Vol. XIV, No. 1, May 1975, pp. 31-41.

[*In the following essay, Newberry examines the development of Ionesco's dramatic technique, especially in* La Cantatrice Chauve, Les Chaises, *and* Le Roi se meurt, *all of which, the critic considers, share a common element: "the indivisible mixture of tragedy and comedy."*]

It is now almost twenty-five years since Eugène Ionesco first made his appearance in the French theatre with his explosive play *La Cantatrice Chauve* of 1950. Since that date Ionesco has built up a considerable "œuvre" of both one-act and longer plays. From almost complete obscurity he has now become established as one of the major contributors to the French theatre of the twentieth century and his fame has stretched far beyond the shores of France itself. In 1971 he was elected to the Académie Française, something one would not have dared to forecast after the initial failure of *La Cantatrice Chauve.* How has his dramatic technique evolved during his career?

In an article of this nature it is impossible to give a complete picture of the evolution of Ionesco's dramatic technique.[1] I shall therefore limit myself to marking out the major developments and to saying whether such changes as are evident have been beneficial to Ionesco's art.

It is first of all necessary to define what is meant by the word "technique". For the purpose of this study technique will be studied under the headings of structure, language, plot, character, the types of plays, and enactment, that is to say how Ionesco himself visualizes their being performed.

Ionesco's dramatic career can be conveniently divided into three sections. The first is concerned exclusively with the one-act play and, with one or two exceptions, is confined to the years 1950-1956. The second contains his first plays of more than one act, namely *Amédée* (1954) and the four plays which have Bérenger as their central character. These plays were written between 1957 and 1962 and are *Tueur sans gages, Rhinocéros, Le Piéton de l'air* and *Le Roi se meurt.* The third section is also concerned with longer plays and stretches from 1966 to 1973. These plays are *La Soif et la Faim, Jeux de massacre, Macbett* and *Ce formidable bordel.*

It is my contention that the outstanding one-act plays are *La Cantatrice Chauve* and *Les Chaises.* I propose to look at these two plays in some detail.

La Cantatrice Chauve is the play which first brought about the realization that the French stage was seeing the arrival of an unusual and original writer. It was, and still is, in the correct sense, a shocking play. Its structure is essentially circular. By that I mean that there is no end to the play, other than through the act of the curtain being drawn. The words which open the play are those which end it, the same thing will be repeated *ad infinitum.* This is because Ionesco wishes us to know that what happens during the play will go on happening in the same way again and again, the only real change being that the characters will change places. What Monsieur and Madame Smith say at the beginning will be said by Monsieur and Madame Martin at the end. They are stuck in their humdrum, petit-bourgeois existence, and are incapable of breaking out of it.

Les Chaises (1951) has a more complex structure. There is no presentation of an argument which is then developed and finally concluded neatly, giving one the opportunity to experience a sense of satisfaction at the end of the play. This would be impossible for a dramatist who has consistently argued that a work of art asks questions and does not dare to try to give answers. *Les Chaises* builds up slowly but surely towards its climax when the Old Man, supported by his wife, is to deliver his message to an expectant audience through the lips of an Orator. Guests, all of them invisible, (are they, or are they not, present?) are introduced into the room. More and more chairs are brought on stage, all to be occupied by invisible people. The pace of the action increases. The invisible Emperor arrives, thus crowning the importance of the occasion. Finally, the Orator appears but he is visible, effecting a feeling of surprise in the audience which has become accustomed to the emptiness of the stage. The old couple commit suicide, leaving the delivery of their message to this Orator. This is the climax, but the Orator is a deaf-mute, he can utter only incomprehensible grunts. Thus the climax becomes a huge anti-climax. At the end of the play the stage is left empty, except for the chairs, but we do hear, for the first time, the human noises of the invisible crowd, which leave us with the uncomfortable feeling that perhaps these people have been present all the time. A huge question mark hangs over the end of the play, as befits the aim of the author. The mystery is not unravelled for us, there is no dénouement. There cannot be, since we must be left to draw our own conclusions to the questions, "What is life all about? Can we communicate to others our own basic philosophy? Do we understand our own personal lives? Even if we do, is language a suitable vehicle of communication?" So what is left at the end? Nothing, a void, a "néant". Thus the play ends with nothing to be seen: but for the chairs, the stage is empty. *Les Chaises* is a masterpiece of dramatic architecture.

The problem of language is important in Ionesco's one-act plays, especially in the earliest ones. He is very concerned with the questions of communication and the disintegration of language.

The language of *La Cantatrice Chauve* was drawn from a course designed to teach English to French people. Ionesco was struck by the uselessness of the phrases which purported to be fundamental to the learning of a language and built his play around such phrases to show how empty, how devoid of meaning language had really become. The characters speak for the sake of speaking and do not really communicate with one another. Their speech is riddled with clichés, and gradually the language disintegrates to the extent of becoming a collection of meaningless, rhythmical sounds which are, however, just as meaningful as the words and phrases which have gone before. Words are empty, they have become depersonalized, so, at the end of the play, Ionesco strings them together just because they have a similarity in sound. It is like a party-game: a word is spoken and then one follws it with the first word which comes to mind.

> M. Martin: Sully!
>
> M. Smith: Prudhomme.
>
> Mme. Martin: François!
>
> M. Smith: François!
>
> Mme. Smith: Coppée.
>
> M. Martin: Coppée.
>
> Mme. Martin: Coppée Sully.[2]
>
> M. Smith: Coppée Sully.[3]

However, there is something beyond a mere stringing together of sounds. The words chosen tell us something about the characters. The authors they mention are as dull and out-dated as they themselves in their bourgeois existence. The play ends with the entire cast rhythmically chanting the phrases "C'est pas par là, c'est par ici!"

La Cantatrice Chauve is a negative play. It says what language is not and does not suggest what it might be. However, from his very first play, Ionesco makes us aware of an area of major concern to him, the misuse of language and its possible disintegration. In *Les Chaises* we see a development of the inability to communicate, or rather the problem is put on an even more serious level. The old man and his wife are decrepit, so is the language they use. She insists upon his re-telling a favourite story. This is akin to a child demanding the same story time after time. For a child familiarity provides a sense of security, a feeling that here is something which he knows. For the old couple it is quite different. They are in their second childhood and, sadly, there is only one story they know, the sum total of a long life. She laughs in order to fortify her husband. The story goes on, reaches its end, and the language collapses into meaningless, infantile phrases. They are pathetic, so is their story. Their life has been worthless, so is the story. Their existence is disintegrating, so does the language of the story. There is no logical progression to the language which the couple use. He has a message to deliver to posterity, but has not the power to deliver it. Language is inadequate for such a task, one can speak only for oneself. The old man needs an orator, a professional speaker, to deliver his message. He and his wife commit suicide, content that their life has not been wasted. In Ionesco's world, of course, where words are treacherous, the professional user of them is the arch-traitor. The Orator is dumb and makes only ugly grunts and groans:

> He, Mme, mm, mm,
>
> Ju, gou, hou, hou,
>
> Heu, heu, gu, gou, gueue. (I, 179).

He cannot even write an intelligible phrase on the blackboard:

> ANGEPAIN
>
> puis
>
> NNAA NNM NW NW NW. (I, 179).

There is no means of communication. At the end we are left to contemplate the rows of empty chairs, we are confronted by Ionesco's, by the dramatist's dilemma. How can he make himself understood, since he has shown that language disintegrates? So, with this play, Ionesco's questioning of the use of language becomes more serious. In fact, if language is absurd, so is the creative art of writing. To a certain extent Ionesco solved the problem by giving great importance in his plays to the use of visual effects. A visual image is more readily understood than an oral one.

The plot of *La Cantatrice Chauve* is arranged in such a way as to show the irrational resulting from the rational. The events in the life of the Smith family are presented, a family which has lost the joy of living. They are surprised by nothing: even the appearance of a fireman in their living room does not disturb their equilibrium. As for the fireman, he knows where and when a fire is to take place—the tragedies of life are all down on the time-table. The whole pattern of existence, as depicted in the play, is predictable. People are all alike, thinking and acting like robots. Thus the plot of the play is designed to achieve the effect of boredom, in a world which is so well-ordered and imperturbable that it results in chaos. One cannot distinguish one person or event from another. The rational has resulted in the chaotic, as is shown by the disintegration of language at the end of the play. Even more tragic is the fact that this pattern of events will go on repeating itself, as we saw when dealing with the structure of the play.

In *Les Chaises* the plot leads towards a climax via a series of smaller climaxes. The first is the arrival of the first guest resulting in astonishment at his being invisible. The old couple become more and more excited as guests arrive, the ultimate glory being the appearance of the invisible Emperor. This is superseded by the appearance of the visible Orator. With the Emperor and Orator present, the couple see the realization of their dreams and commit suicide, gaining more dignity in death than they ever possessed in life. This is the real moment of climax; tension has been mounting and we are now ready to hear the message. However, what happens is a huge anti-climax, for the Orator is deaf and dumb. The play ends on a quieter, but nonetheless menacing tone, with the stage empty except for the rows of chairs. The plot is very powerful, the events being skilfully manipulated by Ionesco to achieve the required effect. More things happen in *Les Chaises* than in any other of his one-act plays, so that the plot is easier to pick out and more traditional in the terms normally accepted. Not only is there a use of narrative, but this narrative is also arranged in a deliberate way, the incidents taking on meaning through the way in which Ionesco interrelates them.

In Ionesco's one-act plays we find no fresh and original studies of individual character. What we do find are ready-to-hand characterizations or, more exactly, caricatures. We meet types, rather than individuals, and faceless types into the bargain. The individual has been swallowed up in society and much of the tragedy of Ionesco's plays is to be found in the absence of ever-new, living contact between people. They are devoid of all verve and humanity, playing out their roles in a robot-like world. They are anonymous, for the most part indistinguishable one from another.

These characters are all drawn from the petit-bourgeois class of society, the group according to Ionesco most concerned with its petty prejudices, most comfortable in its existence, most devoid of any joy in living. Also, a fact which is extremely important, it is for him the class which predominates in modern society and personifies stupidity and lack of culture, whilst claiming to possess all these virtues. In dealing with people, Ionesco is not really concerned with the social injustices such as poverty, hunger, inequality, but more with their metaphysical deficiencies.

The characters of *La Cantatrice Chauve* are puppets, sub-human beings, who are all alike. Outside the Smiths' drawing-room is a townful of Bobby Watsons, both male and female! Inside, the Smiths and Martins move more like marionettes than real people.

The main characters of *Les Chaises* are more human, but they still have no real identify. The old man and his wife cannot discover their role in life, probably because they have not got one. They long to be important, or rather she longs for him to be important. The only positive act they accomplish in life is suicide, one positive act at the end of a life filled with tentative attempts to do something meaningful. In death they are happier than in life. It matters little that we see the absurdity of the suicide. They may be deluded in their happiness, but at least they are released from the trauma of living.

It must be said that the important characters in *Les Chaises* are, for the most part, invisible. They are made uncomfortably concrete as the play progresses. In fact they seem more real than the ludicrous figure of the Orator. The grotesque manner in which he is dressed gives him an air of unreality. He cannot even do what he is supposed to do. Most of the characters may be invisible, but they have more dignity in a disintegrating world than any of the visible characters. The overall impression which we gain from this play is that of people unable to achieve anything of value in life.

When looking at Ionesco's one-act plays it is not unreasonable to start from the basic premise that they are amusing, often hilarious. On what does this comedy depend for its effect? The simple answer is that it comes from the use of the unexpected, both linguistically and visually. Nicolas Bataille, producer of *La Cantatrice Chauve,* said, when I talked to him, that there are phrases in the play: . . . qui vous sautent à la figure.[4] This is the most comic of all Ionesco's plays. Its comedy springs from its surprising use of language. In order that the full effect may be realized, the characters must deliver every line seriously. For example, there is the maid who, quite calmly, announces:

> Mon vrai nom est Sherlock Holmès. (I, 32).

That the characters take themselves so very seriously adds to the comedy. The humour is maintained throughout the work, which is not always the case in Ionesco's one-act plays. However, the basic problems of inability to communicate and the anonymity of people leave an overall air of tragedy achieved through derisive comedy.

In *Les Chaises* comedy is always close to the surface without ever being dominant. The ridiculous situation of the old couple becomes less ridiculous as the play develops. Their language is, at first, amusing, until we realize that this is the only way they can speak. Similarly the invisibility of the "guests" ceases to be amusing as we grow accustomed to it. The visibility of the Orator is, likewise, comic, but he soon becomes far more tragic in his significance. However, tragedy generally overrides comedy. The self-deception of the old couple is tragic, as is their pointless suicide. The eerie macabre ending takes the comedy away from the invisibility of the guests.

It seems right to call Ionesco's one-act plays tragi-comedies, in the sense that they are comedies with an unhappy ending, taking ending to mean the final impression they leave with the spectator. Ionesco does make his audiences laugh, but he is basically concerned with serious, disturbing problems. The laughter is one of derision, not of release or sympathy. Ionesco laughs at life because it is absurd and he holds it in scorn, at least in his one-act plays. His genius is for intermingling the comic and the tragic, as in *La Cantatrice Chauve* and *Les Chaises.* Where this mixture is not evident he becomes less effective.

Within his plays Ionesco displays an acute sense of the way in which they should be performed. His printed texts contain numerous stage directions. In *La Cantatrice Chauve* he makes effective use of the clock which: frappe dix-sept coups anglais. (I, 19). When this clock strikes seventeen times, Mme Smith observes:

> Tiens, il est neuf heures. (I, 19).

As the characters lose control of their language and thought, the clock is used to emphasize this loss of control.

> On se sent qu'il y a un certain énervement. Les coups que frappe la pendule sont plus nerveux aussi. (I, 53).

Thus an inanimate object is used most effectively to contribute to the progression from the extraordinary to the final, wild degradation. However, the major impact in the play is through a highly unusual use of language.

This is not so with *Les Chaises,* where visual effects are of paramount importance, as can be seen from a quick glance at the text with its numerous stage directions. The chairs themselves, and how they are brought in, are very important. Their very presence on-stage, and their emptiness, is a powerful means of giving concrete reality to the abstract void. There is nothing in the world of the old couple, therefore no-one can be seen on the many chairs. The room is empty except for these same chairs. We literally see nothing on stage.

The role of lighting becomes important. At the beginning it is subdued, in order to show the essential dullness of the old couple's life. As "guests" arrive the room has to appear huge and this is done through lighting, building up to a dazzling brightness at the "appearance" of the Emperor. At the end of the play we return to the subdued lighting of the opening. Thus the general movement of the play is served by the lighting—a dull beginning changing to excitement at the arrival of the Emperor and a return to depressing dullness when the whole exercise is seen to have been futile.

Les Chaises is the most evocative of all Ionesco's plays. Much is suggested rather than clearly exposed. He demands much of the actors, who must make us feel the presence of the void. They have to give the impression of being amongst a crowd of people. Long periods of silence are used, during which the actors, rushing about, bringing in more chairs, getting more and more exhausted, make the invisible guests' presence seem more real. The ending of the play is very evocative. We are meant to feel uneasy, to reflect upon the nothingness we have seen.

> Tout cela doit durer assez longtemps pour que le public—le vrai et le visible—s'en aille avec cette fin bien gravée dans l'esprit. (I, 180).

The greatness of *Les Chaises* lies in its many intangible qualities which become uncannily tangible and make a deep impression upon the audience. Its many nuances are thought-provoking.

That the next play to concern us is *Le Roi se meurt,* written, and first performed, in 1962, does not mean that everything Ionesco wrote between 1951 and 1962 is being dismissed as irrelevant. However, when he moved from writing short, one-act plays to longer pieces, he did seem to be aiming for a particular goal, which he reached in *Le Roi se meurt,* the last of the four "Bérenger plays".

The structure of the play is very simple. We are told early on that King Bérenger I is dying. Only he does not believe the fact, being unwilling to recognize what is happening. He has two wives, Marguerite and Marie. The former is intent upon making him face up to the truth, the latter is more intent upon hiding it from him. It is Marguerite who starts a sort of countdown by saying to Bérenger: Tu vas

mourir à la fin du spectacle. (IV, 22); and even more explicitly: Tu vas mourir dans une heure vingt-cinq minutes. (IV, 29). After a reign of 277 years 3 months (!) Bérenger is coming to the same end as everyone else. At last he realizes what is happening and is gripped by fear. No-one can help and he is forced to sit down, a posture which he sees as indicating the approach of death. He is wearing out physically and mentally, and complains about not having had enough time to live. Marguerite is penetrating his defences more and more, but fear still prevents his seeing clearly, fear plus the brake in the persons of Marie and Juliette (infirmière et femme de ménage) who try to hold back the inevitable.

We now reach a major turning point in the play, where Jacques Mauclair,[5] producer at the play's création, inserted an interval. The King says he is dying, albeit without fully understanding what he is saying. As Marguerite's arguments begin to outweigh those of Marie, the play becomes a soliloquy by the King, as he goes over the things in life which have given him pleasure. These pleasures, most of them very simple, are of the past. Life no longer concerns him. The one phrase which dominates his vocabulary is "je meurs". He and his whole world are crumbling. His retinue leaves one by one, insincere to the last, deceiving him, in his now physical blindness, by saying that they will stay by his side. The last to leave is Marguerite, but she, too, has to leave, just before his death, since he must die alone. So finally he remains isolated on his throne, which is swallowed up in a sort of mist. The King is dead. The ending is neither a climax nor an anti-climax, it is simply inevitable, realistic rather than pessimistic.

The structure of *Le Roi se meurt* is superb. A central theme is developed. There are no unnecessary divergences, just a slow, steady progression to an inevitable end. There is no suspense, the end always being kept before us. The structure is simple, the effect powerful. We are spectators at the death of a person, here a King; death spares no-one, and we are in fact watching our own death. King Bérenger is humanity which has to face up to the ultimate absurdity in life, which is death.

It is in the realm of language where *Le Roi se meurt* shows the greatest change in Ionesco's technique from that of the one-act plays. No longer is he concerned with the problems of language disintegrating, of impossibility of communication. In this play he produces a text of considerable literary value. The language of the Guard is wonderfully absurd. In a formal manner, always tinged with comedy, he conveys an atmosphere of lassitude:

> Le ciel est couvert, les nuages n'ont pas l'air de vouloir se dissiper facilement. Le soleil est en retard. J'ai pourtant entendu le Roi lui donner l'ordre d'apparaître. (IV, 11).

Bérenger's doctor insists upon using very learned phrases to explain the obvious. Also, in a situation where Bérenger needs to be given firm encouragement, Marie can only indulge in sentimentality and pointless flattery. She sees not only an illustrious past for Bérenger but also a present and a future, and this for a dying man. However Marguerite, in some superb speeches, provides the much-needed voice of harsh reality. A wonderful simile describes the state of the Kingdom:

> . . . le royaume est plein de trous comme un immense gruyère. (IV, 15).

She counteracts the sentimentality of Marie with cold logic and makes Bérenger realize that his life is of the past, and of the past alone.

The speech of Bérenger himself moves from sheer refusal to believe that he will die, to fear, and finally to resignation. The most poignant factor within the play is hearing this helpless man being forced to admit:

> Je suis plein, mais de trous. On me ronge. Les trous s'élargissent, ils n'ont pas de fond. J'ai le vertige quand je me penche sur mes propres trous, je finis. (IV, 54).

In this grave situation, the dialogue is often sharp and witty. For example, when Bérenger refers to life, Marguerite skilfully turns the remark towards death:

> Le Roi: J'aimerais redoubler.
>
> Marguerite: Tu passeras l'examen. Il n'y a pas de redoublants. (IV, 33).

Within the play is a mock litany, its tone entirely in keeping with the pseudoritualistic atmosphere, since the play is essentially a death rite. Finally, the closing section of the play contains some of the most moving, tragic language Ionesco has ever written.

The greatness of *Le Roi se meurt* is to be found in the greatness of its text. There is no verbosity, there are many ringing phrases rising to a level of poetry, of tragic poignancy which is, however, tinged with the comic. This is always typical of Ionesco at his best.

The plot of this play is beautifully controlled. It is a study of the psychological awareness of death within the mind of one human being. It is very simple, with no diversions from the linear development. There is no climax, no dénouement, because the end is inevitable. The plot is concerned with how, rather than whether, this end will be reached. It is worth noting that Bérenger is in a "privileged" position. He knows when he will die. All most of us know is that we shall die.

In Ionesco's longer plays we find not only caricatures but also full characters. Anonymity of people is not a major problem. What does concern the characters is how the individual can find self-fulfilment in a society which restricts his movements and where the absurdity of death is always threatening life.

The Guard in *Le Roi se meurt* is a magnificent character. He is grotesquely funny, his every utterance being totally out of keeping with the solemnity of the occasion. Yet,

through him, the absurdity of death is shown. Without any sign of emotion he announces the various steps along the road to Bérenger's death. He has no effect upon the King, but, in a way which borders on ghoulish humour, he echoes the progress towards death. The Doctor is a mocking portrayal of the inability of medicine and scientific knowledge to cope with the phenomenon of death. Juliette is the biggest nonentity in the play. She is redundant. Having totally depended on the King, with his death she will be useless. She is well-meaning but has no reserves to call upon in adversity. Similarly Marie is to be pitied more than despised. She is no more than a flatterer and is unequipped to deal with the harsh factors in life. Metaphysical problems are beyond her terms of reference. These are much more the prerogative of Marguerite, Bérenger's first wife. She is the most formidable character of all Ionesco's plays. She has an unswerving honesty and is incredibly cool in a situation charged with emotion. Marguerite is the high-priestess in the ceremonial rite preparing the sacrificial offering, Bérenger, for the moment of consecration, death. Despite the title of the play, it is she who dominates it, having the strength of character to deal with the certainty of death.

Through his major male characters Ionesco more or less puts himself on stage. He speaks through them. In *Le Roi se meurt* we meet Bérenger for the fourth, and last, time. It is important to say that he is not the same man in each play. He is more different aspects of Ionesco himself. King Bérenger embodies the dramatist's fears about death, which become something of an obsession in his later plays, but here it has great dramatic value. Reconciliation to the idea of death would be impossible for a writer with no fixed religious beliefs. Therefore acceptance is the highest state to which Ionesco, the man, can aspire. The ability to face up to such a problem does perhaps suggest that Ionesco is much more at ease with life than in many of his earlier plays.

Le Roi se meurt is the nearest Ionesco comes to great tragedy. He seems to be searching for it in his longer plays and at last achieves his aim. However, this is not tragedy without a comic element. Black comedy is provided by the character of the Guard and, to a lesser extent, of the Doctor. The tragedy of the play is not of the classical mould. We do not observe a character arguing out in his own mind the demands of reason against the temptations of love and passion. Ionesco displays his own brand of tragicomedy, the indivisible liaison of two genres. This tragedy of the absurd reaches heights which he has never reached before in his longer plays and which he has never reached since.

When we come to look at the enactment of *Le Roi se meurt* we find confirmation of Ionesco's movement away from the powerful visual imagery of *Les Chaises.* The text stands by itself. Stage directions are cut down to a basic minimum. As the use of the visual becomes less important this play can be seen as Ionesco's ultimate goal.

The plays of Eugène Ionesco which mark him as a major contributor to the French theatre of the past twenty years are *La Cantatrice Chauve, Les Chaises* and *Le Roi se meurt.* Each is his first dramatic statement on an area of particular concern. The first is concerned with the use, or misuse, of language and the anonymity of people. The second is about the impossibility of communicating one's own "message" to others and the void in life. The last reveals Ionesco's fear at the absurd, but inevitable, prospect of death.

So these plays are of differing themes, but they have one element in common, namely the indivisible mixture of tragedy and comedy. It is Ionesco's genius to make audiences laugh whilst confronting them with grave problems. There is no pathos in his tragedy, no attempt to make us pity the characters involved. Through laughter the tragedy becomes one of derision.

In each play Ionesco achieves his desired effect in differing ways. *La Cantatrice Chauve* is filled with banal phrases used at unexpected moments. They explode in the faces of the audience. *Les Chaises* is a play of visual imagery showing the nothingness of existence. *Le Roi se meurt* is above all a great text, the most rhetorical of Ionesco's plays which never deteriorates into verbosity.

For these three plays alone Ionesco must at least be considered one of the greatest French dramatists of the post-war years. He has changed a great deal, especially during the past ten years when his plays have become more traditional and certainly less comic. He no longer provides the kind of drama which shatters cherished theatrical prejudices. The revolutionary dramatist of 1950 is now a figure of the literary Establishment. Nonetheless, as I have tried to show, his theatre does contain unique qualities which should be able to weather the test of time. That I have ignored his work after the year of 1962 may be taken as an indication that these unique qualities do not show themselves so effectively in the plays of this period. As Nicolas Bataille said to me, somewhat sadly:

> . . . ce qui est extraordinaire, c'est un révolutionnaire qui se sert du comique pour faire sa révolution. . . . Il est en train de supprimer le rire de ses pièces. C'est ça qui est dommage.

Notes

1. For a detailed treatment of the subject see J. K. Newberry, *An evaluation of the plays of Eugène Ionesco with special reference to dramatic technique,* M.Phil. thesis, Nottingham University, 1974.

2. Eugène Ionesco, *Théâtre* (Paris, Gallimard, 1954-1966), 4 volumes, Volume I, p. 55. All subsequent references to Ionesco texts found in this edition will be indicated solely by the volume and page number.

3. Eugène Ionesco, *Théâtre* (Paris, Gallimard, 1954-1966), 4 volumes, Volume I, p. 55. All subsequent references to Ionesco texts found in this edition will be indicated solely by the volume and page number.

4. See Newberry, *op. cit.,* for full text of interview.

5. See Newberry, *op. cit.,* for full text of interview with Mauclair.

Patrick Roberts (essay date 1975)

SOURCE: "Ionesco: Paroxysm and Proliferation," in *The Psychology of Tragic Drama,* Routledge and Kegan Paul, 1975, pp. 102-26.

[*In the following essay, Roberts explores the intensification of plot, incongruity, and parodistic fantasy that are characteristic of Ionesco's plays, and asserts that his dramas display "the insight of a veritable master of the irrational."*]

Eugene Ionesco, writing of his own theatrical ambitions, argues as follows:[1]

> What was needed . . . was to go right down to the very basis of the grotesque, the realm of caricature . . . to push everything to paroxysm, to the point where the sources of the tragic lie. To create a theatre of violence—violently comic, violently dramatic.

The path to the 'basis of the grotesque' lay through introspection, an examination of the inner life: defending himself in the *Observer* against Kenneth Tynan's attack on his subjectivism, he wrote:[2]

> To discover the fundamental problem common to all mankind I must ask myself what *my* fundamental problem is, what my most ineradicable fear is. I am certain then to find the problems and fears of literally everyone. That is the true road into my own darkness, our darkness, which I try to bring to the light of day. . . .

This darkness lies in the common inheritance of the primitive and irrational, a perception of which conditions the structure as well as the meaning of Ionesco's plays. Two aspects of the 'fundamental problem', as illustrated in his theatre, are of especial relevance to my theme. First, there is an element of paroxysm and intensification; the characteristic movement of the plays is one of acceleration, of instinctual urges ever more frenziedly and maniacally released. As Ionesco's comment on the grotesque shows, this makes for comedy; in place of Pinter's enigmatic slow-burning menace, Ionesco offers us a feverish dance of incongruity, in which the contrary elements of anarchic protest against order on the one hand, and the fear of chaos and nothingness on the other, are held in dramatic balance. Something that can properly be called comedy, in spite of powerful tragic overtones, is also ensured by a certain lightness of tone and temperament which distinguishes Ionesco from other major practitioners of 'Absurd' drama; the amiably helpless hero is in a well-established comic tradition, as is the taste for parodistic fantasy.

Intensification is of the essence of Ionesco's plots. *The Lesson* develops feverishly from a conventional beginning—the small change of talk between hesitant Professor and eager pupil—to rape and murder; in *The Chairs,* more and more chairs fill the scene as the old couple welcome invisible guests; in *Amédée,* the corpse in the next room gets bigger and bigger as the play proceeds. In these two plays the second aspect of the 'fundamental problem' is even more prominent: proliferation. 'The horror of proliferation', in Esslin's words, 'is one of the most characteristic images we find in Ionesco's plays.'[3] Ionesco himself calls it 'the point of departure', along with its opposite and complement, a feeling of emptiness and unreality:[4]

> Two fundamental states of consciousness are at the root of all my plays. These two basic feelings are those of . . . emptiness and of an overabundance of presence; of the unreal transparency of the world, and of its opaqueness. . . . The sensation of evanescence results in a feeling of anguish, a sort of dizziness. But all of this can just as well become euphoric; anguish is suddenly transformed into liberty. . . . This state of consciousness is very rare, to be sure. . . . I am most often under the dominion of the opposite feeling: lightness changes to heaviness, transparency to thickness; the world weighs heavily; the universe crushes me. . . . Matter fills everything, takes up all space. . . . Speech crumbles. . . .

This is a very revealing statement of Ionesco. We are certainly made more aware in the plays of the proliferating tyranny of matter than of any sense of liberation: the growing corpse in *Amédée* which is beginning to sprout mushrooms; the bread and coffee cups that fill the stage in *Victims of Duty;* the encirclement of Bérenger by rhinoceros heads in *Rhinocéros;* the ever-increasing flood of furniture which pours into the room of *The New Tenant.* Moreover, the persecutory threat represented by the oppressive density of matter is liable to be intensified, not relieved, by its alternating aspect of unreality; the sensation of the 'unreal transparency' of the world causes vertigo, dizziness. Ionesco describes his sensations while writing his first play, *The Bald Prima Donna,* apparently almost by accident while learning English by the Assimil method:[5]

> While writing the play . . . I felt sick, dizzy, nauseated. I had to interrupt my work . . . and, wondering all the time what demon was prodding me on, lie down on my couch for fear of seeing my work sink into nothingness, and me with it.

However, 'anguish is suddenly transformed into liberty'; it is important to see that the lightness and euphoria which this sense of evanescence occasionally induces may themselves be associated with proliferation. Thus the writing of *The Bald Prima Donna* was at first experienced by Ionesco as an unexpected and extraordinary proliferation of original words and characters out of the bare clichés of the Assimil primer. Words began to behave like the spreading objects that were to fill the plays:[6]

> The very simple, luminously clear statements I had copied diligently into my . . . notebook, left to themselves, fermented after a while, lost their original identity, expanded and overflowed.

The experience, though disconcerting in the way described, was also stimulating; Ionesco conveys vividly the excitement he felt at seeing, for the first time, his word-creations coming to life through the interpretation of actors and the response of an audience:[7]

> To incarnate phantasms, to give them life, is a prodigious irreplaceable adventure, to such an extent that I myself was overcome when, during rehearsals of my first play, I suddenly saw characters move on the stage who had come out of myself. I was frightened. By what right had I been able to do this? Was this allowed? . . . It was almost diabolical.

He seems to be describing here a kind of creative proliferation of the self, successful perhaps in counteracting the destructive proliferation of matter; its similarity to the persecutory experience makes it ambivalent, at once exciting and appalling. The end of *Amédée,* where the anonymous hero floats off into the air, drawn up out of reach of his oppressors by the oppressing corpse itself which now 'seems to have opened out like a sail or huge parachute' seems to symbolize this ambivalent feeling of the author; the source of persecution, the growing corpse, becomes itself the means of liberation. Though Amédée claims he is being carried off involuntarily, there is a lightness of spirit and euphoric excitement about the conclusion: 'Forgive me, Ladies and Gentlemen, I'm terribly sorry! Forgive me! Oh, dear! But I feel so frisky, so frisky. (He disappears.)'[8] His disappearance is signalized by brilliant lights and flashes in the sky, 'comets, shooting stars, etc.'; he is deaf to his wife's plea that he can 'come home, the mushrooms have bloomed'.[9] The blooming mushrooms recall the grotesquely blossoming corpse (both travesties of true growth); in contrast to these oppressive presences, the lights in the sky are liberating, celebratory of Amédée's triumphant release from earthbound matter. The contrasting images seem clearly to represent the opposite poles of Ionesco's 'fundamental states of consciousness', of heaviness and lightness, overabundance and transparency.

Paroxysm, or intensification; fullness, with its inevitable complement of emptiness. These two aspects of Ionesco's inner drama exemplify in a striking manner part of the basic structure of infantile fantasy as explored by psychoanalysis. Ionesco's account, quoted above, of how he came to write his first play, shows clearly how close he has kept to unconscious sources of feeling; he emphasizes both the semi-voluntary nature of the activity—as though his conscious self were being taken over by something deeper—and the powerful physical reaction, of dizziness and nausea, that suggests an involvement of the personality at a deep level. Like Pinter, he does not write from an abstract idea, but because he is possessed by an image, the pictorial or fictional representation of a feeling:[10]

> I have no ideas before I write a play. I have them when I have written the play or while I am not writing at all. I believe that artistic creation is spontaneous. It certainly is so for me.

In discussing *The Bacchae* I sought to show how easily greed may produce anxiety in the infant. First, there is anxiety springing from the realization that the breast can be withdrawn; even though he may be receiving ample food, the greedy baby's gratification may be so short-lived that this anxiety, basically a fear of starvation, is very readily activated. Second, there is anxiety over what his greed in its excess may do to the mother, in emptying her breast and so rendering her incapable of feeding him. The greed is itself likely to be stimulated by anxiety, so that a vicious circle is set up, the greed producing anxiety and the anxiety in its turn further increasing the greed. This situation may cause the baby to seek to get rid of the unwanted feelings by putting them into the mother, projecting his greed and anxiety into the person who represents to him, in the very earliest stage of life, the greater part if not the whole of the external world. The more successful this mechanism the more dangerous and disturbing it is likely to prove. Just as by introjection the outer world may be taken into the self, and so experienced as part of the inner life, so by projection that outer world may be experienced as actually endowed with those parts of the self that are put into it. Thus the mother is now felt to contain the baby's greedy and anxious impulses; not only may she then be believed incapable of feeding him adequately, but through the identification or confusion of child with mother which is an essential part of the mechanism of projection she may now be experienced as a restless devouring creature who threatens to stifle the child with his own greed. If it be accepted that the mother represents, at this early stage, the greater part of the external world to the child, then the later fear of invasion by proliferating objects can be seen as an extension of this original experience.

Proliferation may thus be taken to represent, at one level, the invasiveness of the infantile self experienced, through projective identification, as a hostile external force attacking and persecuting its victims. Ionesco shows an intuitive understanding of the vital part played by identification in this process; the victims appear as in some way responsible for, or at any rate very closely related to, the proliferating objects. A stage direction in *Amédée* makes the point with peculiar precision. As Amédée succeeds, with a 'superhuman effort', in pulling the now vastly extended body up on to the window-sill, at the moment it yields to him 'the impression should be given that . . . it is dragging the whole house with it and tugging at the entrails of the two principal characters'.[11] A typical confusion of identity between mother and child, represented here by the corpse and the two characters, has occurred. Moreover, the intimate relationship of mother to child makes the situation profoundly claustrophobic. The child may attempt in fantasy to project the whole of himself into the mother in order to restore the prenatal organic unity between them and so put an end to the damaging attacks brought about by subsequent separation. Again, the more this fantasy succeeds the more dangerous it will prove to be; finally separate now, the child cannot re-enter the safe place without the risk of suffocation. It is thus right that we should have the impression that Ionesco's characters are in danger of being actually swallowed up by the monstrous

proliferation of matter that surrounds them. ('Matter fills everything, takes up all space.') The child's greedy and invasive projections have already made of the mother a monster who will envelop, suffocate, and finally absorb him.

It will be recalled that Ionesco sees, as the contrasting and complementary 'fundamental state of consciousness' to over-abundance of presence, emptiness: a condition both agonizing and, more rarely, exhilarating. Emptiness again suggests greed: if the 'overabundance of presence' suggests the greedy child who projects his greed into the mother, the emptiness suggests the child who for the same reason is no longer able to receive nourishment from her. The painfulness of this very common experience of emptiness and unreality, in the self and the external world, is explicable in psychoanalytical terms as the result of a projection of too great a part of the self, leading inevitably to a sense of impoverishment. Unreality is experienced because a great part of the self has been temporarily lost; the anxiety over identity inherent in this condition (am I a real person?) may well be exacerbated by the suppressed awareness that the 'real' self that has been projected is hostile and invasive, a threat to peace. Ionesco gives a moving and penetrating account of having experienced this state of consciousness in childhood:[12]

> When I was a child I lived near the Square de Vaugiraud. I remember—it was so long ago!—the badly lit street on an autumn or winter evening. My mother held me by the hand; I was afraid, as children are afraid; we were out shopping, for the evening meal. On the sidewalks sombre silhouettes in agitated movement . . . phantomlike, hallucinatory shadows. When that image of that street comes to life again in my memory, when I think that almost all those people are now dead, everything seems a shadow, evanescence. I am seized by a vertigo of anxiety. . . .

The contrasting state of exhilaration, in which 'anguish is suddenly transformed into liberty', may be thought to signalize a counteracting fantasy of omnipotence. In place of the experience of impoverishment and loss, the self, free of its hostile and invasive parts, enjoys an exhilarating if dangerous sense of liberation that may be felt to transcend normal physical limits. It will be recalled that in the third and final act of *Amédée,* matter, that had threatened to fill everything, is left behind altogether as the hero soars triumphantly into the upper air; that this is a child's dream of freedom is emphasized by the language of the watching crowd:[13]

> *Madeleine* (to the sky) Come along now, Amédée, won't you ever be serious?
>
> *Second Policeman* (looking up at the sky and wagging his finger at Amédée as one would at a child) You little rascal, you!
>
> *Soldier* Why Junior, you bad boy!

Under the spell of this feeling happiness seems unqualified, absolute. In another play, *The Killer,* Bérenger, the typical Ionesco hero, describes it as 'a blazing fire inside me . . . youthfulness, a spring no autumn could touch; a source of light, glowing wells of joy that seemed inexhaustible'.[14] Later—he is describing a landscape so beautiful it makes him forget everything else—he speaks significantly of 'that deep sky and that sun, which seemed to be coming nearer, within my grasp, in a world that was made for me'.[15] Not only does the world exist for his gratification but he fills the world with himself: 'My own peace and light spread in their turn throughout the world, I was filling the universe with a kind of ethereal energy.'[16] The image is surely that of an identification with the mother as source of all goodness and nourishment. In place of emptiness and unreality, there is a superabundance of reality; all other experiences, and even existence, are validated by the fantasy fulfilment of this first and most profound wish: 'I walked and ran and cried I *am*, I *am*, *everything* is, everything *is.* . . .'[17] The experience is comparable to the ecstasy of union celebrated by the Bacchants; the reforging of the physical link with the mother that is so often described, as Bérenger describes it here, as both familiar and new. The description is apt, for it is the buried life that is being rediscovered: 'Everything was virgin, purified, discovered anew. I had a feeling of inexpressible surprise, yet at the same time it was all quite familiar to me.'[18] As these quotations show, the experience possesses a perhaps unique value as the rediscovery of the deepest and most real happiness known to the self; but it is the urge to maintain this happiness pure and undiluted that stimulates the omnipotence, the denial of pain and loss that is ultimately damaging. Death itself is denied—inevitably, for the magic reunion with the mother has been substituted for the separation and growing away from her that is the condition of health and maturity, but must end finally in death: 'A song of triumph rose from the depths of my being: I *was,* I realized I had always *been,* that I was no longer going to die.'[19] It is also worth noting that in the imagery expressive of this mood there is a sexual colouring; the triumphant union with the mother may be experienced, it is implied, as a sexual possession of her. The fireworks and shooting stars of **Amédée** which accompany the hero's apotheosis suggest orgasm, while the language of **The Killer,** though still metaphorical, is more direct; Bérenger speaks of 'glowing wells of joy' and of 'filling the Universe with an ethereal energy'.[20] The sense of omnipotence is complete.

Alternating with liberty, anguish; an accurate recognition of the price to be paid for the fantasy of omnipotence is enacted in the plays. There is the Icarus-like fall into dizziness and emptiness, as the reality of the infant's helplessness and hunger breaks through the fantasy. There is also the pain of separation, part of a recognition that in the process of rapturous identification with and possession of the mother in fantasy, the real mother is lost. Bérenger in **The Killer** describes both aspects of the feeling, in a passage that follows immediately the long evocation of ecstasy from which I have already quoted. There is a change of mood:[21]

> And suddenly, or rather gradually . . . no, it was all at once, I don't know, I only know that everything went grey and pale and neutral again. Not really, of course, the sky was still pure, but it wasn't the same purity. . . . It was like a conjuring trick.

Fantasies of omnipotence do indeed partake of the nature of conjuring tricks. Bérenger continues:[22]

> There was a kind of chaotic vacuum inside me, I was overcome with the immense sadness you feel at a moment of tragic and intolerable separation . . . I felt lost among all those people, all those *things.* . . .

As soon as the sense of omnipotence fades, objects begin to threaten again. The play ends with Bérenger's submission to the knife of the 'Tueur sans Gages',[23] the gratuitous killer, in appearance a shambling one-eyed dwarf, giggling and imbecile; the murderous dwarf here suggests the death-dealing aspects of the omnipotent child. Movingly and tragically, the finale presents the inevitability of death, in contrast to the fantasy of freedom and happiness; in the words of the short story, 'La Photo du Colonel', from which the play was later elaborated:[24]

> No words, friendly or authoritative, could have convinced him; all the promise of happiness, all the love in the world, could not have reached him; beauty would not have made him relent, nor irony have shamed him. . . .

Death is the more intolerable and absurd, not because the happiness had been so real, but because there had been a certain unreality about it. To argue, as Esslin does, that **The Killer** portrays not only the inevitability and unacceptability of death but the absurdity of human existence itself—'No argument of morality or expediency can prevail against the half-witted, idiotic futility of the human condition. . . .'[25] is surely to impose an alien philosophy of despair on Ionesco's subtle, poetic presentation of experience. Esslin makes a similar point when he argues that even in the radiant city of the first act (seemingly a representation in objective terms of Bérenger's private happiness) 'the presence of death makes life futile and absurd'.[26] It is rather the unreality of the radiant city that produces this effect—the unreality of a world where all human needs are catered for by perfect planning, where 'it's all calculated, all intentional. Nothing . . . left to chance', not even the weather; the climate is of everlasting spring sunshine, 'in this district it never rains at all'.[27] It is appropriate that the killer should walk in this city whose inhabitants have deserted it or, if unable to leave, stay hidden within their beautiful flats (Bérenger is puzzled by the city's abandoned air); in its unreal perfection it is already empty, a place of fantasy not reality, a place of the dead. Bérenger fails to see this, in his rapturous acclamation of the city in the first act, just as he fails to see the elements of omnipotent yearning and denial of loss in his own memories of transcendent happiness. Ionesco's heroes are so sympathetic that the extent of their surrender to overmastering fantasy may well be missed; this surrender is surely the central preoccupation of a writer who has described his theatre as 'the projection on to the stage of the world within—my dreams, my anguish, my dark desires, my inner contradictions. . . .'[28] **The Killer** is a more powerful play than *Amédée* not because it testifies to the supposed meaninglessness of existence but because it suggests a fuller recognition of the truth about fantasy. The dissatisfaction expressed by critics about the third act of *Amédée*—that there is a decline of tension, that the transition from heaviness to lightness cannot be adequately realized in dramatic terms—may be symptomatic of an uneasiness about the hero's apotheosis at the end of the play, with its implications of an uninhibited triumph of fantasy. The ambivalence conveyed by Amédée's guilt at abandoning his earth-bound companions, and by the crucial role played by the corpse in his escape, does little to offset the euphoria. The euphoria is very appealing, but it does not altogether ring true. However, if there is an element of indulgence in the finale of *Amédée,* for the most part Ionesco displays a penetrating and lucid understanding of the crucial role played by unconscious fantasy in normal life, as 'an activity of the mind that accompanies every impulse . . .';[29] without such understanding he could not evoke so well the darker and more damaging aspects of its mastery over us. (The darkness is usually relieved by a certain instinctive human sympathy and, often, an infectious gaiety; love and affection always exist as a possibility, however remote, in the relationships of Ionesco's characters.) He recognizes, notably in *The Killer* and *The Chairs,* how fantasy embodies our daydreams of happiness and our longing for peace and security as well as our invasive and destructive wishes; above all, he sees the tragic link that may be forged between the two.

It is in such ways as this that the feeling of emptiness and evanescence is experienced as profoundly ambivalent, Janus faced in its contrasting anguish and euphoria. It will be recalled that the act of artistic creation itself and its consequences are described by Ionesco as partaking of this ambivalence; to see 'characters move on the stage who had come out of myself' is both frightening and exhilarating, 'a prodigious, irreplaceable adventure'.[30] The adventure is rightly felt to be dangerous; polarized between fulfilment (fulfilled achievement) and omnipotence (omnipotent fantasy), what I have called the creative proliferation of writing seems to Ionesco to partake of a Faustian bargain—'Was this allowed? . . . It was almost diabolical.'[31] (Images of procreation often occur in Ionesco in the context of fantasies of proliferation: the corpse in *Amédée* which produces blossoming mushrooms, the unceasing basketsful of eggs hatched by Roberte at the end of another play, *The Future is in Eggs*.) In thus conceiving of art as an extension of the self, its material the artist's own fantasies and conflicts, Ionesco is firmly in the Romantic tradition; he makes the large claim that, as Professor Sutherland notes, is implicit in the attitude of the early Romantic poets—'This was important to me; it must therefore be so to all men.'[32] At the same time, the justification of the claim lies in the Romantic artist's perception of the universal revealed through the experience of a single consciousness:[33]

> For me, the theatre is the projection on to the stage of the world within—it is in my dreams, my anguish, my dark desires, my inner contradictions that I reserve the right to find the stuff of my plays. As I am not alone in the world—as each one of us, in the depths of his being, is at the same time everyone else—my dreams and desires, my anguish and my obsessions do not belong to myself alone; they are part of the heritage of my ancestors, a very ancient deposit to which all mankind may lay claim.

The response to Ionesco's plays shows that his judgment here is right; he speaks to us so effectively through his profound understanding of the inner life, supported by the ability to find compelling dramatic images in which to express it. In a defence of the free employment of fantastic or magical effects on the stage he writes:[34]

> I personally would like to bring a tortoise on to the stage, turn it into a race horse, then into a hat, a song, a dragon, and a fountain of water. One can dare anything in the theatre. . . . Let the playwright be accused of being arbitrary. Yes, the theatre is the place where one *can* be arbitrary. As a matter of fact, it *is not arbitrary. The imagination is not arbitrary, it is revealing. . . .* [my italics]

The apparent chaos of the inner life of fantasy is found to possess an inner meaning and coherence. This discovery, the truth of which Ionesco expresses in the cogent final sentence of this passage, is central to psychoanalytical thinking; his own theatre bears it out.

One of Ionesco's subtlest treatments of the 'two fundamental states of consciousness', of overabundance and emptiness, is *The Chairs*. Here the emptiness lies at the heart of the overabundance, for the ever increasing number of chairs are set out by the old couple for non-existent guests, while the stream of polite conversation is addressed to the ears of the audience alone. The central theme of the play, as Ionesco defines it, in a letter to the director of the first production, Sylvain Dhomme, is emptiness and unreality; it is unusually close to Beckett in mood:[35]

> The subject of the play is not the message, nor the failure of life, nor the moral disaster of the two old people, but the chairs themselves; that is to say, the absence of people . . . the unreality of the world, metaphysical emptiness. The theme of the play is nothingness. . . .

Ionesco also calls it a 'tragic farce'. It will be remembered that Bérenger in *The Killer* experiences a 'chaotic vacuum' of loss and unreality: 'I felt lost among all those people, all those things'. In *The Chairs* the unreality that, in certain states of consciousness, seems to be a property of the external world as well as of the self, is conveyed through an image of great power—'the chairs themselves'.[36] By means of this image the experience of unreality is embodied directly in the drama; in place of the hero being unable to communicate his feelings and needs to other characters who exist independently of him, as in *Amédée* or *The Killer*—the normal way of expressing this situation—the two chief figures people the stage with characters with whom they communicate freely but who exist only in their imagination. In terms of psychological symbolism, it may be said that the external world has been reduced to their own projections into it. There is always a possibility that the infant through his projective and omnipotent fantasies may experience a loss both of self and real mother so complete that a sense of total isolation results, his need for love and understanding completely frustrated. Such an early situation seems to be represented in the predicament of the old couple, which Ionesco interestingly refers to in the passage quoted above as a 'moral disaster'[37] though they do retain a certain reality to each other. It is noteworthy that the maternal aspect of the old woman's attitude to her husband is emphasized: 'Mummy's with you, what are you afraid of?'[38] she declares when he is distressed at the thought of having wrecked his career. He for his part sobs for his mother 'with his mouth wide open, like a baby',[39] in the accents of a child who has broken a toy; she rocks him backwards and forwards on her knee to comfort him, but at first he sulkily refuses to accept her in the maternal role—'you're not my real Mummy'.[40] However, their relationship is very much that of spoiled child and indulgent mother, he looking to her for continuous consolation and support; towards the end of the play she echoes, exactly, his speeches, and he remarks to an old flame of his, a Mrs Lovely, one of the imaginary guests, 'My worthy spouse, Semiramis, has taken the place of my mother.'[41] The dialogue at various points impresses on us that the old man is also a child; thus, he describes how the revelation he is about to dispense to his guests came to him when, at the age of forty, he was sitting on his father's lap before going to bed. (Some visitors laugh at him and tell him he's a man, but he thinks 'But I'm not married yet. So I must still be a child.') In another passage, evocative of the tragedy of the parent/child relationship, the old woman informs one of the guests that they had had a child who abandoned his grief-stricken parents because 'they killed all the birds' and whom they never saw again; simultaneously, the old man tells another guest that they never had a child, but that *he* had abandoned *his* mother, leaving her to die in a ditch. The confusion of identities here suggests that it is the child part of the old man who is the hero of both these incidents: a child whose guilt over his fantasied cruelty to the parents is assuaged by a projection of that cruelty into them—'Daddy, mummy, you're wicked, wicked! . . . The streets are full of the birds you've killed and the little children dying.'[42]

A sense of frustrated omnipotence, again reminiscent of an early infantile situation, is also prominent in the old man's talk. He feels that he is singled out from the mass of men by the achievements that might have been his 'if he had had a little ambition in Life', by the extent of his humiliation and sufferings—he describes himself as having been 'a lightning conductor for catastrophe'—and above all by his role as a saviour:[43]

> And then, no one ever took any notice of me . . . and yet it was I, I tell you, it was I and I alone who could have saved mankind, suffering, sick mankind . . . I haven't given up hope of saving mankind, there is still time, and my plan is ready.

This conviction is actually responsible for the drama presented to us: the guests have been summoned in order that they may listen to the old man's message, the fruit of a lifetime's experience. He has hired a professional orator to deliver the message 'who'll answer for me, who'll explain to you exactly how we feel about everything . . . he'll make it all clear. . . . rsquo;[44] The arrival of the Orator is the consummation of the old couple's lives; he 'really exists. In flesh and blood. . . . It's not a dream.'[45] As they now have nothing more to ask of life, they leap out of the window to their deaths in the sea. Their disappearance is the signal for the hitherto silent and impassive Orator to face the rows of empty chairs and attempt to speak. However, he is deaf and dumb; his desperate efforts to make himself understood only produce 'moans and groans and the sort of guttural sounds made by deaf mutes'. The resourceful idea occurs to him of writing his message on the blackboard, but the result is likewise gibberish, along with the single word 'Angepain' (Angelbread). Thus the message the old man could not speak himself remains unspoken. There is a hint, in the fact that he disappears as soon as the Orator appears, that he is to recover his lost identity in the identity of the Orator; but the sense of unreality remains undimmed. Indeed, finally it is only the unreal that has reality; a magnificent final image conveys this to us when, at the Orator's departure, 'for the first time human noises seem to be coming from the invisible crowd; snatches of laughter, whisperings . . . little sarcastic coughs'.[46] As Ionesco recognizes, it is a familiar theatrical paradox—the baseless fabric of the stage's vision—presented in a new context:[47]

> The invisible elements must be more and more clearly present, more and more real (to give unreality to reality one must give reality to the unreal) until the point is reached . . . when the unreal elements speak and move . . . and nothingness can be heard, is made concrete. . . .

The paradox is pushed to the point where the author succeeds in communicating to the audience his conviction of incommunicability and nothingness. The non-existent 'human noises', the stage direction continues, 'should last just long enough for the real and visible public to go away with this ending firmly fixed in their minds'.[48] The empty chairs, as has been pointed out, do of themselves suggest a theatre, and the Orator's inability to deliver the precious message hints at the difficulties and discouragement the artist may experience in the effort to reach his public if, like Ionesco, he 'projects on to the stage the world within'. There is no doubt that he has succeeded in reaching them in *The Chairs.*

In the opening paragraph of this section I suggested that there were two features of Ionesco's drama of especial relevance to my subject: first, proliferation and all that is associated with it; second, intensification. *The Lesson,* the play of Ionesco which provides an exceptionally concentrated and powerful example of this second feature, also embodies in an unusually direct form the content of an infantile fantasy. There are three characters: The Professor, aged between fifty and sixty, the Girl Pupil of eighteen, and the Maid of forty-five to fifty. The pattern of the play is a reversal of roles by Professor and Pupil. At the outset the Professor is 'excessively polite, very shy, a voice subdued by its timidity', while the Pupil is described as 'vivacious, dynamic, and of a cheerful disposition'. As the play proceeds, however, '[he] will grow more and more sure of himself, excitable, aggressive, domineering', while 'she will become more and more passive, until she is nothing more than object, limp and inert . . . in the hands of the Professor'. Ionesco explains carefully, in this long stage direction with which he introduces his characters to us, how every feature of appearance and behaviour is to correspond to this change; thus the Professor's voice should change 'from thin and piping at the start . . . to an extremely powerful, braying, sonorous instrument at the end; whereas the Pupil's voice, after being very clear and resonant . . . will fade almost into inaudibility'. The 'prurient gleam' that at first 'now and again . . . quickly dismissed, lights up his eyes . . . will end by blazing into an insistent, lecherous, devouring flame'.[49]

It is characteristic of infantile sadistic fantasies that while under their spell the infant should lose to a great extent his sense of the mother as a person and retain only the sense of her as an object, receptacle for the spoiling sadistic attacks. Indeed this sense of the woman as merely object, present for the gratification of own's own needs but without needs of her own, remains the single most typical feature of adult male sadism. I have previously tried to show how sadism, in Melanie Klein's view, has its origins in infantile envy.[50] The envy is experienced as a result of the infant's awareness of his own helplessness and dependence in contrast to the mother's independence and freedom:[51]

> whenever he is hungry or feels neglected, the child's frustration leads to the phantasy that the milk and love are deliberately withheld from him, or kept by the mother for her own benefit.

Envy is essentially spoiling in nature; the urge to possess the loved object, normally the breast, is characterized by powerful feelings of frustration and resentment. I have already mentioned how the projection of bad parts of the child into the mother may lead to a persecutory situation. In a context of sadistic fantasy, projection is likely to play its part in the denigration of the coveted object, the mother's body or breast. Containing the bad envious parts of the child, the breast is experienced as a bad as well as a good object and can thus be attacked with the less guilt. However, the sadistic fantasy at its most intense may try to avoid the persecutory consequences of projection by experiencing the mother's body as exclusively object, to be freely used for the satisfaction and containment of envious impulses; the infant is thus defended against the potentially threatening and persecutory aspects of the mother as a person into whom such feelings have been projected.

It is this extreme situation, pathological if acted out but very common in fantasy, that Ionesco presents in *The Lesson*. The reversal of rules by which the vivacious and charming girl pupil is transformed into an inert and limp object suggests both the root of sadism in envy and the compulsive nature of the urge to spoil and destroy. The climax is of a simultaneous rape and murder, confirmation that the sadistic fantasy is at its purest and most intense; as the Professor 'kills the Pupil with a spectacular thrust of the knife' he first cries out in satisfaction, then[52]

> She too cries out, then falls, crumpling into an immodest position on the chair . . . they both cry out, murderer and victim, at the same moment.

It is an accurately rendered parody of sexual intercourse, the woman's body being used simply as receptacle for the knife, or penis. Even at the climax of a sadistic fantasy some sense of the real function of the woman's body must be retained, as provider first of food and subsequently of mutual sexual satisfaction, if it is to continue to be desired and coveted. It is thus appropriate that the murderous act should be experienced as orgasm: 'after the first blow, he gives the dead Pupil a second thrust of the knife, with an upward movement; and then he starts visibly and his whole body shudders'.[53] His next words—the first he speaks after the act of rape—show the mechanism of projection at work; the projection has resulted in a denigration of the envied object, so that a retrospective justification is available for the sadistic attack and the welcome release of tension enjoyed, at first, without guilt:[54]

> *Professor* (out of breath, stammering) Trollop. . . . She asked for it. . . . Now I feel better. . . . Ah! . . . I'm tired. . . .

I mentioned that sadistic fantasies at their most intense may lose sight of the woman as a person, as the Professor virtually loses sight of the Girl Pupil except as a vehicle for his sadism. However, *The Lesson* is greatly strengthened by the introduction of a different, and less pathological, relationship between the man and another woman. In the person of the Maid Ionesco has given us the kind of disapproving but indulgent mother figure who might be expected to support and encourage the child's sadistic fantasies. The relationship between her and the Professor, deployed in the epilogue that, after the climax of the murder, closes the play, is demonstrably that of mother and child. At the climax itself there is a subtle anticipation of the Professor's child self; as Professor and Pupil approach the moment of truth, he enjoins her to repeat after him the word 'Knife': 'Say it again, watch it. (Like a child) Knifey . . . Knifey.'[55] After the murder, the Professor, in a reaction of horror at finding the body of a pupil on his hands, calls in panic for the Maid. She is at first severe and unsympathetic: 'Aren't you ashamed of yourself, at your age too!'[56] Vexed at her reproaches, he defends himself by accusing the dead girl of being 'a bad pupil'; Professor and Maid then enact with remarkable precision the parts of a nasty child turning on its mother and the mother responding with interest:[57]

> *Professor* (approaching the maid slyly, his knife behind his back) It's none of your business! (He tries to strike

her a terrific blow, but she seizes his wrist and twists it; the Professor drops his knife). . . . Forgive me!

(The Maid strikes the Professor twice, forcibly and noisily, so that he falls to the ground on his behind, snivelling.)

Maid You little murderer! Revolting little swine! Wanted to do that to me, did you! I'm not one of your blessed pupils!

(She hauls him up by the back of his collar. . . . He is afraid of being hit again and protects himself with his elbow, like a child.)

Having thus established her ascendancy, she relents. It is already clear from an earlier scene that she has known all the time what is going to happen and has allowed it to happen; she warns the Professor not to go too far— 'Philology is the worst of all . . . you won't say I didn't warn you![58] Later, however, although she recognizes that with the toothache induced in the Pupil by the philology lesson 'the worst symptom'[59] has arrived, she leaves the two alone together. Now, with the body of the Pupil between them, she responds to the Professor's sobs and protestations with something like sympathy, as soon as he has admitted he is sorry:

Maid At least you're sorry you did it?

Professor Oh yes, Marie, I swear I am.

Maid I can't help feeling for you. Come now! You're not a bad boy after all! . . .

She exacts a promise that he won't do it again, significantly because it might be bad for him ('it would give you heart trouble . . .'); she then helps him to plan the funeral and advises him how best to protect himself, finally assisting him to carry the body off stage.[60]

This fine scene suggests in almost every particular the mother who overlooks the murderous pranks of the child because she is too big to be seriously threatened by them; the initial violence of her response combines with the absence of any real disapproval on her part to stimulate his sadism, which is effectively displaced on to the more vulnerable target of the girl pupil. Structurally the scene is integral to the meaning of the play, which presents us both with the roots of sadism in infantile fantasy and with a cogent example of a later, indirect manifestation of the impulse in the exploitation of language for the purposes of sadistic domination. The adult teacher who forces a parody of learning down the pupil's throat and the child caught out by its mother in a nasty sadistic game are linked by the enacted fantasy of the rape cum murder. Ionesco is careful to preserve a sense of fantasy throughout the grotesque climax; the knife with which the Professor kills the Pupil, and with which he later threatens the Maid, is invisible. Moreover, when the Professor asks, of the coffins which the Maid is to order for him 'What if anyone asks us what's inside?' she replies, '. . . We'll say they're empty. Besides, no one will ask any questions. *They're used to it*'[61] [my italics].

We are, indeed, all used to it, although it is not often recognized for what it is. *The Lesson* is not a morality play, but none the less it embodies a valuable and neglected truth: that primitive sadistic instincts do not only, or indeed normally, find gross physical expression, but find effective release in many less obvious and more subtle ways. Ionesco's choice of the teaching situation is an apt one for this purpose. The educative process can degenerate into an exercise of power at the expense of the pupil, a power that is sadistic in origin in that it reflects in displaced form an early sadistic impulse. *The Lesson* shows how the urge to dominate and control may at first take the milder form of a metaphorical seduction and if this proves unsuccessful develop into metaphorical rape. (It must be remembered that the design of the play requires that the seduction remain metaphorical while the rape is presented as literal and actual.) Both processes concern themselves with the needs of the teacher and not with those of the taught. The student may be seduced into believing that he is learning when he is really serving the teacher's ego, whether by acting as willing receptacle for an exhibitionist display on the teacher's part or by himself making such a display of prowess in response to flattery and encouragement by the teacher; both processes are a substitute for the mutual effort of learning. In terms of early experience, a narcissistic and exhibitionistic activity, involving masturbatory fantasies or at a later state fantasies of intercourse with the mother, has been substituted for feeding. Rape, in terms of the metaphor, suggests the bludgeoning of the pupil into an acceptance of what is arbitrarily prescribed by the teacher; it is a penetration by force—the psychological force at the disposal of superior age, experience, knowledge. Neither process can be regarded as uncommon in the teaching relationship.

Seduction is certainly present in *The Lesson.* At first the Professor flatters and conciliates his Pupil:[62]

Pupil One and one make two.

Professor (astonished by his pupil's erudition) But that's very good indeed! You're extremely advanced in your studies. You'll have very little difficulty in passing all your Doctorate examinations.

Later he displays his own prowess in the field of comparative philology, in a long nonsensical declamation about the neo-Spanish languages; the Pupil is at first delighted and fascinated. However, as the Professor becomes more insistent and aggressive in his self-display, refusing to permit any interruption, the Pupil suddenly announces that she has toothache. From this point onwards she defies the Professor by means of her toothache, rejecting and even mocking his instruction; he only succeeds in overcoming her defiance by an increasing, and increasingly violent, pressure. The toothache may perhaps indicate loss of the power of speech and so of language; the parody of the whole learning process is an important element in the play. Just as, positively speaking, language is seen as an instrument of power, so negatively the communication of knowledge is mocked in the nonsense games played by the pair in language and arithmetic:[63]

Pupil I can count up to . . . infinity.

Professor That's impossible.

Pupil Up to sixteen, then.

Professor That's quite far enough. We must all recognize our limitations.

It is worth noting here, in the context of the parody of learning, a comic device by which Ionesco reinforces the 'progressive heightening and intensification' he is seeking: the Pupil can do complex sums of addition with miraculous ease, but she cannot subtract, arguing, for example, that three from four makes seven.

The toothache has perhaps an additional significance: the persistent but feeble resistance to instruction offered by this means is seen to act as provocation to the Professor, whose tone and manner, already assertive, are transformed into open sadism:[64]

Professor . . . And so on and so on. . . .

Pupil That's enough! That's enough! I've got . . .

Professor The toothache! The toothache! . . . Teeth, teeth, teeth, teeth! . . . I'll have them all out for you in a minute. . . .

There is even a hint, in the obsessive nature of the Pupil's complaints of toothache, that to her teaching in itself is experienced as a violation, a painful penetration of her body by the voice of the Professor:[65]

Pupil That's enough! I've had enough! Besides, my teeth ache and my feet ache and my head aches. . . . You make my ears ache, too. What a voice you've got! How piercing it is!

Professor Say Knife. . . . Kni . . . Fff. . . .

Her fantasies may be thought to play a part in the situation, operating in collusion with the Professor's fantasies to bring about the fatal conclusion; this is certainly in keeping with the general impression made on us by the play. Admittedly, at this point the Professor is already threatening her with sadistic violence; as we know from the opening stage direction, by now his voice has grown more powerful and piercing. However, the passage is reminiscent of one in *Amédée*, where Amédée's loving enthusiasm is experienced by Madeleine, his wife, as a sadistic attack: 'Your voice is so piercing! You are deafening me! Hurting me! Don't rend my darkness! S-a-dist! . . .'[66] As Martin Esslin comments: 'The situation is that of an ardent lover and a girl who regards all advances as acts of violence and rape.'[67]

I suggested earlier that Ionesco understands how ubiquitously a primitive, infantile sadism operates in normal adult human affairs in a concealed and displaced form. By a bold paradox, this point is made by a reversal—by the presentation of a normal activity, teaching, that develops rapidly into a grotesquely sadistic situation. A final touch reinforces our sense of the operation of a basic aggressive drive in a form unrecognized, and so socially and morally

acceptable. We learn from the Maid—she is speaking of the Professor's crime—that 'it's the fortieth time today! And every day it's the same story! Every day! . . .'[68] Clearly she is used to it, just as people in general are used to the sight of the coffins of his victims. The extravagance, by being pushed so far, succeeds brilliantly since 'one can dare anything in the theatre',[69] in the author's words. *The Lesson* points the moral, in its own essentially comic terms, that sadism is not merely a psychopathic perversion but a universal, even commonplace, illness, affecting respectable professors and their bright pupils. Ionesco calls *The Lesson* a comic drama; whatever the wider implications, it is certainly comic in its preoccupation with incongruity and also in a certain emotional detachment. There is none of the plangency of feeling or poetic suggestiveness to be found in *The Killer* or *The Chairs;* I suspect that for Ionesco there is little or no poetry in sadism. This is greatly to his credit—a refreshing contrast to writers whose only source of poetry seems to lie in the sadomasochistic areas of experience. If *The Lesson* has less depth for this reason, it has a compensating concentration of effect. More importantly, it displays, in common with the other plays of Ionesco I have discussed, the power and insight of a veritable master of the irrational, one who follows 'the true road into my own darkness, our darkness, which I try to bring to the light of day'.[70]

Notes

1. E. Ionesco, 'Expérience du Théâtre', *Nouvelle Revue Française,* (Paris, 1 February 1958), pp. 258-9. I owe this and other quotations from Ionesco's writings on the drama to Martin Esslin, *The Theatre of the Absurd* (New York, 1961), ch. 3.

2. Ionesco, 'The Playwright's Role', *Observer* (6 July 1958). Tynan's criticism appeared in the previous number of the paper.

3. Esslin, op. cit., ch. 3, p. 99.

4. Ionesco, 'The Point of Departure', *Cahiers des Quatre Saisons,* no. 1 (Paris).

5. Ionesco, 'La Tragédie du Langage', *Spectacles,* no. 2 (Paris, July 1958).

6. Ibid.

7. 'Expérience du Théâtre', p. 258.

8. Ionesco, *Amédée,* trans. Donald Watson, *Plays II* (London, 1958), p. 226.

9. Ibid.

10. 'Expérience du Théâtre', p. 268.

11. *Amédée,* ed. cit., p. 62.

12. Ionesco, 'Lorsque j'écris . . .', *Cahiers des Quatre Saisons,* no. 15.

13. *Amédée,* ed. cit., p. 227.

14. Ionesco, *The Killer,* trans. Donald Watson (London, 1958), p. 77.

15. Ibid., pp. 80-1.

16. Ibid.

17. Ibid., p. 82.

18. Ibid., p. 81.

19. Ibid.

20. See above.

21. *The Killer,* ed. cit., p. 82.

22. Ibid., p. 83.

23. The French title of the play.

24. *Evergreen Review,* March 1957 (trans. Stanley Reed).

25. Esslin, op. cit., pp. 122-3.

26. *The Killer,* ed. cit., pp. 68-9.

27. Ibid.

28. Ionesco, *Improvisation,* trans. Donald Watson, *Plays III* (London: Calder; New York: Grove Press, 1960), pp. 112-13.

29. Melanie Klein, *Our Adult World and its Roots in Infancy* (London, 1960), p.6.

30. See above, p. 104.

31. Ibid.

32. J. R. Sutherland, *A Preface to Eighteenth Century Poetry* (Oxford, 1948), p. 161.

33. *Improvisation,* pp. 112-13.

34. 'Eugène Ionesco ouvre le feu', *World Theatre,* VIII, 3, Autumn 1959.

35. Letter from Ionesco to Sylvain Dhomme, quoted by F. Towarnicki, 'Des Chaises vides . . . à Broadway', *Spectacles,* no. 2 (Paris, July 1958).

36. Letter from Ionesco to Dhomme.

37. See above, p. 113.

38. Ionesco, *The Chairs,* trans. Donald Watson (London, 1968), p. 13.

39. Ibid., p. 13.

40. Ibid.

41. Ibid., p. 30.

42. Ibid., pp. 31-2.

43. Ibid., p. 50.

44. Ibid., p. 44.

45. Ibid., p. 53.

46. Ibid., final stage directions, pp. 59-60.

47. Letter from Ionesco to Dhomme.

48. *The Chairs,* final stage directions, ed. cit., pp. 59-60.

49. Ionesco, *The Lesson,* trans. Donald Watson (London, 1958), Penguin edition, pp. 182-83.

50. See above, p. 17.

51. Klein, op. cit., p. 8.

52. *The Lesson,* ed. cit., p. 214.

53. Ibid.

54. Ibid.

55. Ibid., p. 213.

56. Ibid., pp. 215-16.

57. Ibid., p. 198.

58. Ibid., p. 198.

59. Ibid., p. 211.

60. Ibid., pp. 216-17.

61. Ibid., p. 217. I discuss the point of the plurality of coffins later in this chapter (see p. 123).

62. Ibid., p. 189.

63. Ibid., pp. 190-91.

64. Ibid., p. 208.

65. Ibid., p. 212.

66. *Amédée,* ed. cit., p. 48.

67. Esslin, op. cit., p. 108.

68. *The Lesson,* ed. cit., p. 215.

69. See above, p. 113.

70. See above, p. 102.

Germaine Brée (essay date 1978)

SOURCE: "Ionesco's Later Plays: Experiments in Dramatic Form," in *The Two Faces of Ionesco*, edited by Rosette C. Lamont and Melvin J. Friedman, The Whitson Publishing Company, 1978, pp. 101-18.

[*In the following essay, Brée studies three Ionesco plays from the 1960s,* A Stroll in the Air, Exit the King, *and* Hunger and Thirst, *in relation to his essays of the same period, and argues that the dramas constitute an effort on the part of the playwright to communicate, via the state, a view of life as "provisional, sincere, problematic, yet positive."*]

Découvertes (Discoveries), one of Ionesco's more recent essays, came out in 1969 in the semi-de-luxe series entitled "The paths of creation" published by Skira. The over-all title of the series is self-explanatory. Writers—Aragon, Butor, Prévert—and critics—Barthes, Caillois, Starobinski, Picon—approach the topic from various, personal angles. Ionesco's contribution is disarming, partly because it is unpretentious and obviously genuine and partly because it is vividly illustrated by Ionesco himself.

A dozen brightly colored plates, full page or spread over a double page, and a few small marginal sketches, cherry-trees or childishly simplified figures—accompany the text. Dominant is the figure of "the king," plastic in shape and diversely colored, a humorous, appealing and something disturbing projection of his creator's self-image in various situations and moods. Then there is the eye, detached and immobile, contemplating with obvious stupefaction brightly colored shapes moving across the page; or sometimes carried along in their flow. There are, besides a couple of picture stories done in a child-like—but vigorous—idiom: a walk in the country for example, one of Ionesco's familiar methaphors for happiness.

A double of Ionesco is present in these illustrations, a self-projection, whether as king, eye, or participating figure, a visual record of the manner in which Ionesco perceives himself in what he calls his "encounters with the world." That these illustrations are closely connected with both Ionesco's personal and his stage world it is easy to see at a glance; they are proof of how visual, spatial, and idiosyncratic are the forms of expression that come naturally to him. The self-images of *Découvertes,* the verbal images Ionesco uses to describe his "paths" to creation, are related to his sense of the stage. Ionesco perceives himself as situated in space; and it is in spatial terms that he defines a range of intense emotions through which he responds to the world. Let me give just one example, linked to the initial perception of the self as "eye."[1] In *Découvertes* Ionesco describes the child in the pram as enthralled spectator to the flow of shapes and colors flowing past him in the light. These are analogous to the brightly colored shapes moving across the page of the book and they recall the "apparitions," Ionesco describes in *Notes* . . . "fruits of the void, flowers of nothingness . . . ovements, configurations, colors" that float before his eyes at those moments of exhilaration when he happens to "love the world" and in it "discovers beauty."[2] But a gigantic unknown object moves across the space—the shadow of a tree sensed by the child as a personal menace and deliberate aggression, causing an inner shrinkage of his world, and terror. The incident is revealing and fundamental and its patterning of a shrinking space as the shape of fear is a constant in Ionesco's stage world. The "I-eye" watches a world that deploys its changing colors and configurations harmlessly "like a carpet," harmlessly and boundlessly. "The seasons seemed to spread out in space. The world was a decorative background, with its colors now dark and now bright with its flowers and grass appearing, then disappearing, coming towards us, moving away from us, unfolding before our eyes, while we ourselves stayed in the same place, watching time pass, ourselves being out of time . . . rdquo;[3] The image denotes a contemplative state of non-involvement and delight, which one might call aesthetic. Disturbance comes when the "monstrous shadow" invades the space of both contemplator and contemplated, veiling the light. The darkening is a threat, an aggression, a terrifying "apparition," accompanied by the contraction of the spectacle, the shrinkage of the boundless space.Fear as we have seen is a contraction of free space and the disruption of the spectacle. It is a premonition of the "fall" which Ionesco describes again in spatial terms: "Then all of a sudden there came a kind of terrible reversal; it was as though a centrifugal force had projected me out of my immutability into the midst of things that go and come back and go away for good . . . At sixteen it was all over. I was in time, in flight, in finiteness."[4] The monstrous shadow then is death. Ionesco's perception of himself, as he describes it in these very early schemas, contains one highly dramatic element: his sense of discomfort in a closed or contracting space. For him the "room" or "house" will never be the habitual intimate self-contained space in which the self is at home in a protective shell. It cuts the "I-eye" out of its rightful realm. Nothing in Ionesco's language refers us to a "place within," and the hastily

improvised refuges in which Ionesco withdraws are always flimsy and temporary: "I settle down in the moment, I surround myself with the walls of the moment. I shelter under the roof of the moment . . . rdquo; but the moment passes.[5]

Subjective, emotionally charged, and spatially organized, Ionesco's world is not introverted. And when Ionesco speaks of his stage-world as an "architecture" he certainly refers to something other than the merely verbal patternings of the plays themselves. The stage, after all, is the locus of a spectacle and it is closely akin too to the limiting, self-defensive, temporary room, thereby to the two basic though antithetical images Ionesco has of his relation to the outer world, his "encounters with the world." It is not surprising then that when in *Découvertes* he goes back to his childhood, what he refers to first of all are his perceptions of that world. In their freshness they seem singularly absent from the greater number of his plays, at least until the sixties. The child Ionesco moves in the vast space of a countryside that furnishes the elements of a privileged spatial imagery, a language of the emotions, quite simple in its elements: delight is a "fête," a spectacle of "changing perspectives" where sky, color, fruits, fields deploy ever fascinating configurations under the play of light; boredom is a dreary sky over a vast grey endless steppe; mystery is a threshold, when, stepping through a breach in the ramparts the boy saw a field of corn, golden in the sun, the emblem of a world "beyond the gates." Fear is the giant shadow of a tree thrown across the sunlit path. The visual and spatial elements are strong, and the emotions intense. But not the conflicts. In fact conflicts are singularly absent from these images. One could readily surmise wha Ionesco suggests that it is as a protest against the absence of that world that he created its obverse: the enclosed Ionesco stage. It is form of exorcism.

Ionesco's essays *Notes and Counter-notes, Fragments of a Journal* and *Découvertes* show the simplicity of the metaphors that underly Ionesco's stage worlds, and how closely connected they are to his own modes of perception. Abstraction is not his forte. He is temporamentally adverse to theoretical reasoning as his polemical exchanges—with Kenneth Tynan for example—have shown. His violent dislike for ideologically "committed" writers among his contemporaries is visceral; his reactions to Brecht, Sartre and even Camus are notorious. Even in debate, his language, sometimes confusedly, tends to become visual and spatialized: "Les Sartrismes nous engluent, nous figent dans les cachots et fers de cet engagement." (Sartrisms glue us, gell us into the prison cells and irons of commitment.) It matters little to Ionesco that the spatial metaphor of the prison cell and the solidity of the irons are incompatible with the borrowed Sartrean image of engulfment in a viscous substance like glue. What matters is the sense of fear and physical discomfort the words convey. On the whole, Ionesco is not sensitive to the full implications of the words he sets on the page but rather to their cumulative value as signs rather than expressions of his feeling. Thence a certain poverty and haphazardness in the linguistic texture of his plays, particularly striking if one compares it to the rich tonalities of a Beckett text. What compensates for the lack of resonance is the mobility of the verbal patternings—so often and so extensively analyzed—that give his theater its baroque flavor. Here again the language develops on a single plane, flatly.

The only work Ionesco recognizes as having influenced his approach to art is Croce's *Aesthetic.* He often seems to be merely echoing the *Aesthetic,* to which he refers specifically in *Découvertes,* but here again in a rather haphazarad way. Art, as he conceives it, is "intuitive knowledge," "lyrical intuition," the objectification of subjective perceptions. An autonomous free activity, it transmits a concrete individual "vision," born of emotion that freely shapes a "whole" imaginary situation. One can readily identify Croce's language: "aesthetic intuition"; art as an "individual expressive fact"; "expression" as "free inspiration."[6] Ionesco has vehemently reiterated, too, Croce's contention that "the search for the end of art is ridiculous" and his injunction to "leave the artist is peace." In a rather broad sense one might say that Ionesco's theater as a whole is a long and vehement injunction to the society of men to leave him in peace. But beyond this, there is nothing systematic about his ideas. Hence his frustration when his concept of art as "the expressive elaboration of impressions," to use Croce's words, is challenged. This aesthetic would hardly in itself, however, account for the stage-world he has set up, although as we have seen, it does correspond to his natural inclination. What remains unexplained is the connection of those impressions to the forms of drama he has elaborated.

It may come as a surprise that Ionesco considers "wonder" as the most fundamental of those emotions that opened up his way toward creation. In *Découvertes* he designates wonder as the "deepest reaction" of his consciousness. He describes it as the physical state, of elation or euphoria in the presence of light which he considers the fundamental experience of his childhood. "It is in order to speak of that light, to speak of that wonder, of a light, a sky, a wonder stronger than anguish, dominating anguish, that I turned to literature" (60). Wonder or, as Ionesco also notes "stupefaction" in the presence of the everyday spectacle of the world is connected to an immediacy of apprehension that can inform—as Gide would say—both the absurdist's and the mystic's illumination. Ionesco, in a recent interview, seemed to designate the first when he spoke of the "negative illuminating" of his childhood concerning death and annihilation.[7] Their obsessive role in the shaping of his theatrical idiom has been abundantly discussed. But no one, to my knowledge, before Ionesco himself has stressed the "positive" illuminations which appears in *Découvertes* as dominant in his work. This is certainly paradoxical.

The assertion, it is true, has come late. Ionesco himself had heretofore stressed rather his state of "conflict with the universe" as the only "capital" faction in his psychic make-up. The more affirmative statement seems to coincide with a recent cast of mind and to have accompanied Ionesco's desire, as play-wright, to transcend certain limitations in his work.

Since the sixties, notably, Ionesco has become an ever more active participant and in fact protagonist in his own plays. Whereas the Béranger of **Rhinoceros** is hardly more than a state of mind, King Bérenger I in **Exit the King,**[8] Herbert Bérénger, the "stroller in the air" and Jean, the central character in **Hunger and Thirst** are far more obvious projections of the author. And in the last two plays he has included not only himself, but the family trio, himself, his wife and daughter. Ionesco has recently carried this development into film. He appears as actor, for the first time, in a film entitled *La Vase (Slime);* and as sole actor portraying his own disintegration and absorption into the slime of a river-bed.

In the three plays, all produced in the sixties, Ionesco does seem to me to have conceived his stage-space and sets in a new fashion although in some aspects it is anticipated in the early **Chairs** and **The Killer.** Herbert Bérenger may well be very close to his creator when he declares "literary activity is no longer a game, can no longer be a game for me. It should be a passage toward something else" and adds that he seeks "inner renewal." One might suspect of course that Ionesco is mocking some "serious" theory of art; but in the light of *Découvertes* it does not seem so: he speaks in quiet earnestness. With all due caution passing from the ambiguous stage experience of Herbert Bérenger to the autobiographical *Découvertes* one notes that Ionesco, speaking of the "light" and "wonder" that flooded his childhood, also speaks of himself as moving at present, along "an upward slope": "Perhaps even today, after tens of years, it is still that light which nourishes me, which keeps me alive, which has proved stronger than my bouts of distress and my depressions, has guided me through abysses and allowed me to find the path, if not to the top at least to the upward slope" (61).

In spite of the simplicity of its language, *Découvertes* presents rather startling assertions. Several times Ionesco refers to what he calls "the Manifestation," capitalizing the word, relating it to those moments of wonder that are flooded by light: "We do not know the essence of things or of the Manifestation, but we can use things or compose with them" (28). "Thought expresses itself in or through language, language being the reflection of the universal Manifestation which expresses the pre-existent thought of God" (44). "In the immobility of the recaptured plenitude of awareness, I mean of an awareness in which I recover myself, it is the essential event only that I recover, the primordial event, the Manifestation, like a luminous veil through which I glimpse the shadow of what is manifested. In the immobility of my attentive gaze, it is not time that flows past, it is the Manifestation which unfolds as in a space outside time, without time" (83). And again, after describing moments of depression, Ionesco returns to his image: "There will be, there are new dawns, the fête. Yes all can change, suddenly. I can recover childhood.[9] And the world can be made to fit me. Tomorrow, tomorrow there will perhaps be a different universal Manifestation, another Creation and I shall be dazzled by it once again, absorbed in contemplation, vainly trying to orient myself in it . . . Tomorrow, a completely new world, more astonishing than ever, with another or other suns, in another sky" (126). The illumination of the world from some unknown source unfolding before the immobile contemplative "I-eye" situated somewhere within it now as spectator sends us back to the child in the pram, to the child-spectator of the puppet-show, to God's thought immanent in his creation.

Most individuals inclined, to contemplation have experienced comparable moments of stillness and harmony; but not perhaps with the same intensity of "illumination." Clearly Ionesco here has borrowed the esoteric language of the initiates to transmit what he sees as a recurrent quasi-physical and essential relationship with the world, lost and found and lost again, but nonetheless always there "beyond the gates." I am not suggesting that Ionesco ever immersed himself in Sufism for instance or other forms of oriental cults. But the vocabulary is indicative: path, light, immobility, plenitude, vision, veil, timelessness, strangeness, Manifestation. Whatever the origin of the vocabulary the experience it relates seems genuine enough and seems to be connected with Ionesco's renewal of his dramatic idiom in the sixties. His attempt to express the transcendent on the stage does not seem to have proved satisfactory to Ionesco himself: "I have never been able to say this adequately," he notes of those moments of recovery, "What I say is never true enough, the words are not right enough, I have not yet found the appropriate language for these thoughts, feelings, emotions, for the unsayable truth that I keep trying to express which is stronger than all anxiety" (75). Somewhat self-consciously, Ionesco seems here to be combatting the negative image of himself as the destructive playwright of the absurd. But Jean, the protagonist of **Hunger and Thirst,** when urged to give an account of his extensive travels, proves as inarticulate as his creator. "Illumination" is not easy to translate into words. There seems to be a further admission of defeat in *Découvertes.* Ionesco will, he says, henceforward "write no more dramas" remaining content to "construct small make-believe worlds" just to amuse himself. It is a fact of course that of those three plays of the sixties so intimately connected with his own tête-à-tête with himself, the only one to enjoy success was *Exit the King* (1962). French audiences and critics reacted coldly to the spectacular fantasy of *A Stroll in the Air* (1963), while the most ambitious of all Ionesco's plays to date, **Hunger and Thirst** (1966), was an unmitigated failure.

The year 1972 opened with a production of Macbett,[10] the first major Ionesco play since that failure. It could hardly be described as a success. Ionesco's description of the play suggested that he was trying for something beyond parody, but yet more removed from his own universe. While still struggling with the theme of death, though in a more detached frame of mind, Ionesco proposed to dramatize the "problem of power, ambition and nefarious action." Reversing a current cliché, as he so likes to do, Ionesco proposed as a solution to man's inhumanity to man, a society governed by a computer, carefully programmed by

a few sages whose distributive justice—social and economic—would be free from men's propensity to exploit and enslave other men. From that standpoint what better remedy than the "dehumanization" of the computer? The play, whatever its merits or demerits, seems closer in type to **Rhinoceros** than to the three more subjective and introspective plays of the sixties. A phase perhaps in Ionesco's development is over.

I propose to examine briefly the three plays of the sixties from the point of view of and in relation to the essays of the same period. The articles collected in *Notes . . .* (1962) go back to the fifties. Consequently, I shall refer primarily as I have already done to *Fragments of a Journal* (1967) and *Découvertes* which with the three plays comprise the bulk of Ionesco's work between the popular **Rhinoceros** and the dubious **Macbett.**

The first and most striking feature of the three plays is the manner in which Ionesco makes use of the stage space. In the stage direction to **Stroller in the air,** Ionesco refers to "primitive" painting which he distinguishes from the "surrealistic." He was pointing to the use medieval artists make of the flat space of the picture to suggest other dimensions of the story depicted. In his three plays, he clearly wanted to give the sense of different spheres of consciousness co-existing within the same space. The basic action in the three plays is that of "passage." The departure, journey, or "stroll" are fundamental metaphors in all three and, in fact, constitute the action. In **Exit the King** the king must pass from his rapidly disintegrating habitat into a limitless space. In **Stroller in the air,** the "anti-world" impinges upon Herbert Bérenger's given world, and a visible bridge entices him into the vast reaches of that world. In **Hunger and Thirst** each episode takes place in its own compartment, each connected to the other by Jean's long journeying. At the end, beyond the walls and bars that hold him prisoner, Jean sees, as in a medieval painting, the idyllic garden with his wife and child, out of reach but co-existent and self-contained within its own space. Obviously Ionesco was attempting to overcome the spatial limitations of the stage. Ionesco has always used the stage, like the expressionists, as a metaphor to objectify an inner ambience. But in no sense did his stage suggest the presence of a quasi-metaphysical dimension in the character's existence; this is surely what the new "architecture" of the three plays of the sixties conveys. Ionesco seems to have wanted to project his doubles onto a cosmic plane, "a space outside time," suggestive of a destiny beyond. The new dimensions are awesome and inhuman, it is the "universal landscape" to which he alludes in *Découvertes.* Herbert Bérenger leaps lightheartedly into the world beyond, but he returns a sobered man bearing tales of devastation and a terrifying void. As to Jean, he measured his own solitude in the rarefied atmosphere and "pure light" of a terrace suspended in the void of the "kingdom of light." The "grand route" and the circle are recurrent images, but the journey to the center of the circumference remains inconclusive. The necessary passage can be made only in solitude. King Béranger's palace, like his kingdom, crumbles and decays; Jean runs away from the disintegrating basement apartment into which he has just moved with his wife and child and in *A Stroll in the Air* as the play starts, a bomb destroys Bérenger's pleasant English house. What matters in a writer's work, says Ionesco, are the questions he asks and he defines his work as an "architecture of question"—disposed as it were in three layers—"What is all this here?" "Who am I?" "Why am I here, surrounded by all that?" For Ionesco the metaphor of the voyage is linked to the metaphysical why: it is "only by travelling from one why to the next as far as the why that is unanswerable; that man attains the level of the creative principle." (*Fragments . . . 26*) Thus the theme of the solitary journey seems intentionally connected with the attempt of the play-wright to transcend the former limits of his stage. And yet the "architecture of questions" is not quite clear. For *Exit the King* seems rather a statement on how to die than on "Why do I die?" and Bérenger's adventures bear more on confrontation with the unanswerable than on the questioning of it. In these plays Ionesco attempted to situate his protagonist beyond the way and in relation to the unanswerable: death, the immense spaces of the "anti-world," the solitary heights of Jean's journey towards the light. If it is not always very clear on stage in what terms he is asking the why, it seems certain that it is not in rational terms. The three plays attempt to create moods, hence situations, in which the rational underpinning of everday life is no longer operative; the structure of the plays is thereby affected. This "leaving behind" of the world of the real and ordinary has always been characteristic of Ionesco's stage. But not until the sixties did he attempt to do more, through the interplay of setting and the distortion of language, than use the stage in parodic fasion, somewhat like one of the Surrealists' autodestructive machines.

It might be surmised that it was in part the growing success of Brecht in France, from 1954, when the Berliner ensemble took Paris by storm, into the sixties, that moved Ionesco both to the kind of self-analysis evident in the essays and to a deeper concern with the structure of his own stage-world. In this perspective *Rhinoceros* might well be considered as a transitional play, a ferocious attack upon the Brechtian ideological stage. *Exit the King, A Stroll in the Air, Hunger and Thirst* use and reverse Brechtian patterns: the insatiable appetite of Jean recalls the craving for food or drink of many Brechtian characters from Schweik's friend Baloun on; as does King Bérenger's obligation to consent to his own death. Above all, it is Jean's confrontation with and his imprisonment by the burlesque and sinister monastic order which provide a bitter comment on Brecht's call to the individual to accept social discipline in the interests of a higher cause. Ionesco seems furthermore to have confronted somewhat the same problems as a playwright: how to connect the inner world of feeling to outer reality so as to establish it concretely on stage. His problem, however, was the obverse of Brecht's since the French dramatist's theater has consistently been founded on feeling, on a visceral distrust of all formalized social

compartments. His own sensibility then is the only ground he trusted for the foundation of his stage world. The shift from the negative and gleeful parodic destruction of everyday reality to the sense of the play as communication to the audience of the positive feeling for existence that justified the destruction of illusory reflections posed the question of a new theatrical language. How could a playwright project concretely on the stage the inarticulated and ambivalent perceptions which he describes in *Découvertes?* The statement could only be metaphoric and individual—thence the open use of the autobiographical "double" as protagonist.

In a quite different way from Brecht's, Ionesco turned to a narrative form of drama, transferring feeling into fantasy. Whereas in his first plays he manipulated language itself to estrange the spectator while ruthlessly gearing him to the destructive mechanisms of the play, in these later plays the fantasy could come alive only through the emotional power of the character's situation as revealed in his language. The main difficulty for Ionesco seems clearly to lie in the initial metaphor that establishes the character's world, the stage world of the play. He had to turn his former stage world inside out and obtain the identification of his public with the protagonist—himself—rather than bring about a shared estrangement. Bérenger in *Rhinoceros* is a typical example of this turnabout, although it is already adumbrated in *The Killer.* But in both of these plays the protagonist's posture is refusal. And, it may be inferred, useless refusal. He is destroyed along with the situation with which he enters into conflict.

There is no doubt at all that the Crocean conception of the intuited form seems to apply to Ionesco. He has amply documented the wholly emotional quasi-physiological origin of the basic, and complex, metaphors that put so personal a stamp upon his plays. His dilemma is that the strongest of these psychic moods or "climates" coincide with a loss of the sense of reality. The sense of reality for Ionesco coincides with immobility, with himself as "eye" and center to the world: "The earth and the stars moved around me who stood still at the center of everything. The earth and its fields and its snow and rain all moved around me." (*Fragments . . . 22*) This creates a positive view of the world as spectacle, and is hardly dramatic. What is dramatic is a loss of the equilibrium. Ionesco has repeatedly described the two forms of disequilibrium that plague him: one is elation, that sense of "taking off" physically from an imponderable world, which furnished the end metaphor of *How to get rid of it,* (Amédée's exit in a balloon) and the whole movement of *A Stroll in the Air;* the other, the sense of slow suffocation and dissolution in slowly rising mud, Ionesco's metaphor for routine and habit.[11] This is the more predominant of his stage building blocks.

For Ionesco, the room, peculiarly well suited for transferral to the stage-set, is no symbol of refuge; it is charged with a sinister metaphoric meaning. The house sinks "into the ground like a basement, with damp walls and slits for windows . . . always on the point of sinking in . . . of being flooded, of falling to pieces . . ." The earth on which it rests is not a refuge either: "For me, earth is not a foster mother, it means mud . . . decomposition . . . death which terrifies me . . . tombs." But the dangerous and disquieting element is water: "Water for me does not mean abundance, nor calm, nor purity; it generally appears to me as dirty, anguish." The primarily concrete terms in which Ionesco's fears and obsessions beset him are clearly symbolic. "When I dream of the inside of a house, it is always sinking down into the damp earth." And the house can be a transparent subterfuge to ward off the reality of time: "I settle down in the moment, I surround myself with the walls of the moment, I shelter under the roof of the moment."[12]

The "good-evil" duality in this dramatic system is ambivalent both physically and conceptually. The stage world itself is a temporary structure set up in a spatialized, boundless continuity, within which outer and inner spaces operate, interpenetrate, exclude one another or coincide. These are the spheres out of which Ionesco has sought to fashion his plays, not out of events or ideas: "What I want to concretize," he stated, "is the expression of origins. Not what comes to pass, but what does not come to pass or does not pass." (89) The spatialization of mood and the synthesis into a single image are characteristic: the rising mud is both fear and time; the act of levitation is ecstasy and freedom to view a world "deployed" outside time. But it shuts Ionesco out of the world. "I could not hear nor see anything that took place. They no longer heard me from the world which had become for me a forbidden space . . . a closed world . . . wrinkled as it were, fissured, metallic, infinitely hostile . . . in a light without light." (*Découvertes,* 104).

If the intimate, the familiar, the customary become potentially dangerous and disastrous, so does the alluring unknown, new and untried. A double movement animates Ionesco's perception of himself in regard to reality and it fashions the spatial images through which he projects himself. His stage world is in fact a physical extension of that perception, an attempted exorcism of inner danger via the stage. Only occasionally does Ionesco "become again the spectator of the whole spectacle." And, if he started to write plays, it was, in order to "surround himself with a world, to speak from out of that world, from that stage-world to the world." (Découvertes 91).

The personal concerns of Ionesco are clearly stated through the metaphors that shaped the stage-world of the three later plays: the disintegrating palace and kingdom are correlatives for the decay of a body, and of the whole system of relations of which it is the center; Bérenger's "Stroll in the air" leads him, via the magic bridge into hostile cold spaces where he is "shut out" from human warmth. Jean's escape from the mud-invaded family basement lifts him to the exalted but solitary peaks, thence into a prison for those who hunger and thirst for certainty, an illusory refuge whose symbolism I shall explore later. Ionesco has taken

pains to emphasize the personal and emotive source of the play: "I had written the work so that I might learn to die. It was to be a lesson, a sort of physical exercise, a gradual progress, stage by stage towards the ineluctable end, which I tried to make accessible to other people" (*Fragments* . . . 88), he says of *Exit the King.* When discovering *A Stroll in the Air,* he notes that it was born of a long-time dream of an English holiday and his biographical allusions to *Hunger and Thirst* are innumerable: "I have travelled in search of an intact world over which time would have no power. The food I hunger for, the drink for which I thirst are not an infant's food or drink. Knowledge is what I hunger and thirst for. If I really knew what I hunger and thirst for I should feel easier . . . The man who gives everything becomes like someone dying of hunger and thirst, lying on the grond, pale, gasping, begging for a glass of water. It is going to be an endless business feeding him. The man who has given everything takes everything back. He is insatiable." (*Fragments* 11, 60, 89) In this context, the pseudomonastery of the play, with its suave brainwashing techniques and ruthless apparatus of coercion and constraint, is Ionesco's symbolisation of totalitarian attempts to control and exploit that inner craving, itself expressed in the vision of the garden just out of reach—the garden enclosing the loved wife and child, removed from the trivialities of everyday living.

These three plays unquestionably reveal an aspect of Ionesco which has heretofore remained elusive, but they are also a key to his limitations. They develop through initial metaphors that cannot evolve dramatically; it seems plausible to surmise that the cinema would prove a more satisfactory medium. The most successful of these plays is *Exit the King,* where the situation, the stage metaphor and the personal emotion at its source are particularly well integrated. But the difficulty with which Ionesco must contend is nonetheless obvious. Once the image of the disintegrating world has been posed in terms of the physical environment of the king, only through reports can its step-by-step progress be registered in the play until it actually reaches the body of the king. In other words, the metaphor can only be reiterated and diversified, not greatly extended. A baroque verbal inventiveness alone reflects the struggle between the king's failing hold on life and the final relinquishment of life in death. The baroque and rather lugubriously comic visions of the king's real decrepitude visible in the physical space around him function a surface diversions rather than as expressions of a growing inner awareness. Much in the same way the fantasy world of *Stroller in the Air* is presented visually rather than dramatically; it is episodic in structure. Although, in my eyes at least, the fairy-tale quality is real and both theme and techniques valid and innovative, the actual stage display overshadows the personal communication Ionesco intended: levitation in space, like physical disintegration, does not harbour many dramatic possibilities. In other words, since in these plays the essential theme is visually expressed, language is in fact accessory. This is disconcerting for the audience at a loss to relate the visual to the commentary it elicits. What Ionesco seems to have tried to do is paradoxical. An "inventive or creative" language, he notes in *Découvertes,* is the attempt to "seize, state, integrate and communicate something incommunicable to still uncommunicated"; and in order to make his statement the writer must "disarticulate" language, make it transparent so that the world can appear "through it in its original strangeness." But in fact, as he "organizes his phantasms"—to use his terms—on stage in *A Stroll in the Air,* the actual language through which the "world," Ionesco's world, appears is largely hieroglyphic. The central theme is the physical "take off" of Bérenger into the spaces beyond, his disappearance and return and his unwelcome attempt to communicate the emptiness and void he has encountered. The idea is simple and the stage metaphor through which it is enacted is simple too, an adaptation to the stage of circus acrobatics. But the ambience within which Bérenger's exploit takes place is intricate, involving criss-cross patterns of situation and mood, in pure Ionesco style, developing one out of the other through the interplay of language. One may fully enjoy the "fête" as Ionesco calls it of changing perspectives, as language effectively disrupts rigid patterns of behavior to display mood—a mood of delight in things, and harmony with them. It is possible too to follow the development of the situation as Bérenger's elation turns into vision, and the "anti-world" begins to invade the real. But from there on any creative use of language is lost as the significance of the situation is polarized in the concrete image of Bérenger's acrobatics in space. The stage image, is not strong enough or rich enough to give the play a continuing impetus, and it weakens what appears to be Ionesco's intent: to communicate his own sense of a man's immense curiosity for and confrontation with the unknowable. *Hunger and Thirst* seems to have been Ionesco's attempt at a total objective statement of the contradictory inner experience born of his "encounters with the world." He seems to have sensed the limitations put upon the development of the play by the metaphoric extension of mood to a physical outer stage space. *Hunger and Thirst* seems to evidence his desire to move out of the one-act single situation pattern prevalent in his theater. It certainly suggests a cyclical pattern: in the first act Jean's sense of the familiar world of wife and child as intolerable routine and limitation is symbolized in the disintegrating basement of the stage set and the conflict between his love for his wife and his revolt ends with his disappearance; the emergence of Jean on the high mountain summit outside a museum in pure and dazzling light is the locus of the second act, a dead end where Jean's expected rendez-vous with "her" does not take place. In the third act Jean, worn out and starved, arrives at the ambiguous innmonastery where he is held. Through the bars he glimpses his goal, the ideal garden in which the wife and child he left fourteen years before dwell in harmony. The metaphor of the voyage links the three main scenes. But again they themselves are static. And the drama seems to reside in their immutability, and one might infer, in their co-existence. It would of course be necessary to study in greater detail the play of language within each unit so established, but this would go well beyond the limits of this paper.

What I have attempted to establish is that the three plays in question constitute an earnest and deliberate effort on the part of Ionesco to communicate, via the stage, a view of life as provisional, sincere, problematic, yet positive. It is an attempt to transcend the closed world of the individual ego. If the dramatist did not fully succeed, I have suggested that it is largely because his initial awareness of existence is essentially contemplative and passive, embodied in the spatial metaphors by which his characters are bounded and which elicits their reactions. The drama in the three plays of the sixties arises from the central character's obligation in *Exit the King* or, in the other two plays, his impulse to "pass beyond," a passage only realized in death.

Ionesco has been reproached for his foray into metaphysics. Yet, in terms of the playwright himself it corresponded to a need; and though as a result, these plays except for *Exit the King* have been less successful than the earlier ones, they are undoubtedly far more interesting as a key to the man's sensibility, and perhaps to his limitations. For Ionesco a play is essentially a "projection of the self into that substance which is the world . . . that is to say a pattern, a shape, an architecture." (*Fragments,* 129) It would be idle to attempt to differentiate between the three words as applied to his work. But all three point to an overall static design rather than to any dynamics within the structure. In the last analysis one is tempted to conclude that, in a very real sense, Ionesco's language was used in his first plays as a form of collage, a sonorous outer substance. The last plays are attempts at regaining conscious control of one's emotions; they present mature forms of structuring that seem uneasily poised between the episodic fable, personal and didactic, and the lyrical quest with its episodes of departure, alienation, return and reconciliation. But in neither case is the basic "pattern", "shape", or "architecture" dramatic, except insofar as it is a spectacle wherein Ionesco as playwright re-establishes himself as "eye" confronting, first through the malleable stuff of language, then through his mythical doubles, his disturbing "encounters" with the world.

Notes

1. "I was eyes, wide open in stupefaction and incomprehension." *Découvertes* (Geneva: Editions Albert Skira, 1969), p. 28.
2. *Notes et Contre-notes,* Gallimard. Collection "Idées" 1962 (295-96). I shall refer to the volume as *Notes . . .* "Apparitions" and disappearances whether of people and things have been a constant, sometimes refreshing, sometimes tiresome feature of Ionesco's stage-craft. They are obviously connected with his perception of reality as gratuitous spectacle and transferred to his stage via the mediation of puppet show techniques; the puppet show in itself, as Ionesco has often said, was one of the most memorable "apparitions" in his childhood world.

3. *Fragments of a Journal* (New York: Grove Press, 1969), p. 11.

4. *Ibid.*

5. *Ibid.,* p. 147.

6. Croce's clear-cut distinction of the intuitive-aesthetic and logical-demonstrative, his attack upon "historical intellectualism," his insistence upon the "non-logical, non-historical character of the aesthetic fact" are all echoed in Ionesco's essays. One might summarize Ionesco's fundamental point of view by quoting Croce as follows: "The aesthetic fact is altogether completed in the expressive elaboration of impressions. When we have achieved the word within us, conceived definitely and vividly a figure or statue, or found a musical motive, expression is born and is complete; there is no need for anything else" (*Aesthetic* translated by Douglas Ainslee [New York, The Noonday Press, 1960]. p. 50).

7. *Le Figaro littéraire,* January 7, 1972.

8. He identifies himself as King, not only in his illustrations but in *Fragments* of a Journal: "I am the principal figure, the center of the cosmos (that developed over the years)" p. 109.

9. Ionesco specifically connects the Manifestation with childhood, with a world from which "the shadows disappear" and in which "wonder" enlarges his eyes once more as the world opens up again.

10. "Never have I written with so much pleasure on a theme or themes that are rather sinister," said Ionesco of *Macbett.* "In spite of all that is going on around me I was seized as I progressed, in spite of Pakistan, Ireland, India, Africa, Asia, America, Europe, by a happiness I don't understand myself." *Op. cit.*

11. He links it with his childhood terror at the flooding of his house by the rising water of the Seine.

12. *Fragments of a Journal,* pp. 117, 134, 147.

Nancy Lane (essay date 1983)

SOURCE: "Human/Non-human Relationships in Ionesco's Theatre: Conflict and Collaboration," in *Kentucky Romance Quarterly,* Vol. 30, No. 3, Summer 1983, pp. 240-50.

[*In the following essay, Lane examines the role of décor in Ionesco's plays, asserting that the external surroundings interact with other "characters" on stage in a wide range of relationships, for example as antagonists and collaborators.*]

One of the most striking features of Eugène Ionesco's theatre is the prominent role accorded to décor. In fact, so many critics have commented upon this subject that there might appear to be little or nothing left to add to the volumes already written. Nearly all critics (relying perhaps too much on Ionesco's own extraordinarily verbose commentary on his motives and personal obsessions[1]) have viewed the role of décor as metaphorical, without defining

exactly what a theatrical metaphor might be, or distinguishing such a figure from metaphors found in poetry, prose fiction, or essays. The proliferation of objects, for example, has been interpreted as a metaphor translating Ionesco's metaphysical anguish when confronted by the "trop plein" of the material world and the ontological "vide" of human existence. Rosette Lamont compares the proliferation of matter in Ionesco's plays to Sartrian nausea, summoning up a "private nightmare of all men, of Man, in fact, when he becomes aware of his human situation in the oppressive, heavy world of material presences."[2] Similar is Dubrovsky's well-known analysis of the same phenomenon in what he calls an "ontological" theatre: "Cette croissance géométrique et incontrôlable d'objects pour la plupart de fabrication humaine et qui finissent par chasser l'homme traduit à la fois le vain effort de l'homme pour se donner par une production matérielle insensée l'être qui lui manque et la victoire ontologique inévitable de l'en-soi sur le pour-soi. Les choses sont le cauchemar de la conscience."[3] References to dreams abound in Ionesco criticism, even as above in critics who see Ionesco's work as basically metaphysical in its orientation, and a number of critics (including Ionesco himself) analyze the role of décor in psychological terms; décor becomes the objective correlative of oneiric, Jungian archetypes. For Paul Vernois, as for many others, it is axiomatic that Ionesco's theatre is oneiric, originating in images and symbols associated with personal as well as archetypal myths. Referring to recurring objects, Vernois states: "Eléments essentiels d'une technique onirique, ils poussent au délire les pulsions et les répulsions des personnages: à travers eux se renforce jusqu'à l'absurde le caractère insolite de la mise en scène."[4] Closely linked to such analyses are those which take as their point of departure Ionesco's widely-quoted pronouncement that at the origin of his theatre is the opposition between "evanescence" and "lourdeur."[5] Richard Coe's analysis follows this line of inquiry, for example: "La vision, chez Ionesco, d'un univers instable entre le diaphane et l'impénétrable, la volatilité de l'esprit et la lourdeur du plomb . . . trouve son expression dramatique dans des effets de lumière et de décors. D'un côté, la fluorescence verte triste et nue de *Jacques* et des *Chaises,* le rayonnement froid de *Tueur sans gages* ou du scénario de ballet *Apprendre â marcher;* de l'autre côté, l'annihilation progressive de l'esprit et de la vie de l'être humain par la prolifération des objects."[6]

All of these critics, whether they view décor as metaphysical metaphor or psychological projection, have provided valuable insights into Ionesco's theatre, but they have also sometimes given the mistaken impression that the relationships between the human and non-human domains in these plays is a personal phenomenon arising from the playwright's inner visions. Furthermore, such analyses often fail to take into account the unique semiotic system of the theatre, ignoring differences as fundamental as those between plays and other types of discourse, or between dramatic characters and human beings.[7]

Rather than being an exclusively personal characteristic of Ionesco's theatre, the elevation of the status of décor arises from a recognition and exploitation of theatre as a *performed* genre distinguishing much of 20th-century French theatre from traditional "realistic" theatre. Strictly speaking, the play itself exists only on the level of the performed. Elements of the performance (lighting, props, sound effects, etc.) which are clearly non-human in the world of the performance are equally capable of performing a character in the play as is a human actor. In fact, the blurring or elimination of boundaries separating the human and non-human codes is one of the hallmarks of the work of playwrights as diverse as Apollinaire, Cocteau, Ribemont-Dessaignes, Ivan Goll, Ghelderode, Tardieu, Adamov, Arrabal, Weingarten, Vian, Vauthier, and Beckett. In such plays, non-human elements of décor are no longer servile accessories in the world of the play; neither are they metaphors, signifiers limited to a role of psychological projection. Rather, they are true actors, performing characters involved in dynamic relationships with other characters, who may or may not be performed by human actors.[8]

Such dynamic relationships between human and non-human elements fall into one of two very general categories. In the first category are instances where human characters interact with a vivified non-human domain which remains separate from the human characters. In plays such as Beckett's *Comédie* (in which a spotlight interrogates the human characters) or Vian's *Les Bâtisseurs d'empire* (where a mysterious noise and its ally—le Schmürz—terrorize and finally murder the human family), for example, each character (human or non-human) is a discrete entity, and these characters relate to each other as antagonists. A second type of relationship exists when there is interpenetration of the two codes, so that a human character is not just at odds with a vivified environment, but is, to some degree, indistinguishable from it. That is, some of the signs which constitute a given dramatic character may be dispersed throughout the environment of the play, creating dynamic relationships of a sort different from those which operate between two separate characters.

Generally, most of Ionesco's early plays fall into the first category outlined above. The clock in *La Cantatrice chauve,* the piles of furniture in *Le Nouveau locataire,* the eggs of *L'Avenir est dans les oeufs,* the teacups in *Victimes du devoir,* the cadaver/balloon of *Amédée,* or the chairs in *Les Chaises* are all examples of non-human performers which are hostile to the human characters. With the last two plays mentioned, however, the distinction between separate characters begins to blur; one frequent interpretation of the cadaver and mushrooms of *Amédée* is that they are symbolic exteriorizations of the human characters' guilt and remorse.[9] Such an interpretation is strongly seconded by Ionesco himself: "J'ai essayé, par exemple, d'extérioriser l'angoisse . . . de mes personnages dans les objets, de faire parler les décors, . . . de donner des images concrètes de la frayeur, ou du regret, du remords, de l'aliénation, . . ."[10]

As Ionesco's craft matured, the relationship of human to non-human became the sort described in the second category. The proliferating object either disappeared or assumed a role less dominant than in the early plays,[11] and other elements of décor (particularly lighting) began to perform, creating dynamics more sophisticated and complex than simple antagonism between separate human and non-human characters. An early example of this use of décor appears in *Les Chaises,* where the lighting at the end of the play brightens as the old couple's emotions reach their peak, and fades to gloomy somberness with their death. Thus, there is collaboration between the light and the human characters. Even more than collaboration, however, there is a certain degree of identity between character and environment; the characters' joy and death are exteriorized in an environment which participates with the human actors in performing the two aged characters. A similar use of décor appears much later in Scene 10 of *Ce Formidable bordel!* The main character's sudden euphoria caused by a single ray of light is exteriorized in a complete transformation of the atmosphere of the bistro where he is seated: the light is bright and cheerful, the orders of the other customers are nearly sung rather than spoken, movements become dance-like, and even the sound of rattling dishes becomes melodious. This last example represents, however, more the exception than the rule in Ionesco's most recent dramaturgy, where the role of décor has either become more clearly "spectacular" (as in *La Soif et la Faim,* for example) or has faded into relative insignificance alongside the increasingly verbal, stridently polemic, or specifically oneiric concerns of plays such as *Ce Formidable bordel!, Jeux de massacre,* or *L'Homme aux valises.*

While the role of the non-human domain is apparent in those plays filled with invading objects, it is in the complex, humanized plays of the "Bérenger" cycle that the role of décor, though perhaps less obvious, is dramatically richest, translating into dramatic signs man's ambiguous relationship to his environment and even to himself. This essay will explore how the non-human elements of décor interact with the human domain in patterns of conflict and collaboration in two of these plays.

The role of lighting in *Tueur sans gages*[12] has been remarked by nearly every critic of the play and by Ionesco himself; it is nearly universally accepted to be the recreation of the euphoric feeling experienced by the playwright during his childhood at La Chapelle-Anthenaise.[13] Not only is it the single most important element of décor, not only is it a potent symbol—it is, in fact, an active character in the play, both the accomplice and the enemy of Bérenger, the principal human character. From the moment the curtain rises on a nearly-empty stage, light is to play a major role. As Ionesco's lengthy stage directions clearly indicate, apart from the human actors, light alone serves to establish the calm atmosphere and tone of the first act. Although lighting is practically the only décor, the "cité radieuse" in the world of the play is full of houses, trees, and flowers. Thus, the "cité" is unseen only for the spectator and not for the characters in the play.

This visit to a heretofore unknown part of the city is an overwhelming revelation for Bérenger. In the first place, it represents an absolute contrast to his everyday life in another part of the city. The bleak, grayish light of the very beginning of the play (before the appearance of the "cité") had reflected the atmosphere which reigns throughout the rest of the city, where "le ciel est gris comme les cheveux d'une vieille femme" (p. 67). The contrast between the gray light in the rest of the city and the brilliance of the "cité radieuse" signifies far more than a simple difference in weather, however. In the play, the light—and all the rest of Bérenger's surroundings—are inextricably linked to his emotions and desires. In his neighborhood, and, more specifically, in his apartment, "tout est humide: le charbon, le pain, le vent, le vin, les murs, l'air, et même le feu" (p. 67). As the Architect indicates, this state of affairs is not coincidental, but is rather the concrete manifestation of the mood of the inhabitants: "Je vois, c'est moral" (p. 66). By contrast, the light of the "cité" has the power to dissipate both meteorological and emotional gloom.

It would perhaps seem, at first glance, that the effect of the light on Bérenger's emotional state is nothing more than the normal reaction good weather produces in one's mood. In this play, however, the significance of the light is far greater; it is, in fact, a vitally important extension of Bérenger himself. The true significance of the light's impact on Bérenger is quite clear in his lengthy explanation of his new-found joy, which is worth citing in its entirety:

> Un décor, cela n'est que superficiel, de l'esthétisme, s'il ne s'agit pas, comment dire, d'un décor, d'une ambiance qui correspondrait à une nécessité intérieure, qui serait, en quelque sorte . . . le jaillissement, le prolongement de l'univers du dedans. Seulement, pour qu'il puisse jaillir, cet univers du dedans, il lui faut le secours extérieur d'une certaine lumière existante, physique, d'un monde objectivement nouveau. Des jardins, du ciel bleu, un printemps qui correspondent à l'univers intérieur, dans lequel celui-ci puisse se reconnaître, qui soit comme sa traduction ou comme son anticipation, ou ses miroirs dans lesquels son sourire pourrait se réfléchir . . . dans lesquels il puisse se reconnaître, dire: voilà ce que je suis en vérité et que j'avais oublié, un être souriant dans un monde souriant . . . *En somme, monde intérieur, monde ext*érieur, ce sont des expressions impropres, il n'y a pas de véritables frontières entre ces soi-disant deux mondes; il y a une impulsion première, évidemment, qui vient de nous, et lorsqu'elle ne peut se réaliser objectivement, lorsqu'il n'y a pas accord total entre moi du dedans et moi du dehors c'est la catastrophe, la contradiction universelle, la cassure. (p. 73; emphasis added)

Bérenger thus establishes an identity between "monde intérieur" and "monde extérieur," an identity which serves as the basis for dramatic tension in the play. The light in the "cité" is the "objective" exteriorization of the energy and "élan vital" which Bérenger had thought lost long ago; "ce foyer puissant de chaleur intérieure," "une lumière rayonnante, des sources lumineuses de joie" (p. 74)—the very terms which he uses to describe this energy demonstrate the identity of internal and external worlds.

The whole play is based upon a dichotomy between light and darkness, both interior and exterior. In a very concrete sense, light equals energy and life, while darkness equals fatigue and death. From the moment he enters the "cité radieuse," Bérenger's very existence is dependent upon his making of his environment an accomplice in his search for self-realization. In the internal and external radiance which he discovers here, Bérenger believes that he has finally found "un accord total entre moi du dedans et moi du dehors."

This "accord total" is soon shattered, however, with Bérenger's discovery that a mysterious assassin is decimating the population of the "cité." The killer drowns two or three victims a day in a pool which appears suddenly on stage. (It is appropriate that this discordant note in the "cité" should appear to the audience, probably by means of projection. With the rest of the décor in the "cité" consisting solely of lighting, the sudden appearance of the pool is all the more shocking and sinister.) With the introduction of this jarring element, harmony—or collaboration—between character and environment is destroyed, and, as Bérenger had said, without harmony, "c'est la catastrophe, la contradiction universelle, la cassure." The environment which Bérenger had thought was his accomplice has become his enemy, and he is plunged again into darkness and fatigue, now all the more intolerable because he has just experienced light and energy. Thus, Bérenger is compelled to begin his search for the killer, who seems to be immune from detection and capture. This search is no ordinary manhunt, but rather Bérenger's desperate attempt to end conflict between the internal and external worlds, i.e., between the character and a hostile environment. This killer is a creature of darkness; by removing him, Bérenger hopes to reestablish harmony, to make an accomplice rather than an enemy of his environment.

In contrast to the stark brilliance of the first act, the décor of the second act is gloomy, "lourd, laid, et contraste fortement avec l'absence de décor ou le décor uniquement de lumière du premier acte" (p. 100). The setting is Bérenger's apartment, the scenic exteriorization of the gray, damp, chilly existence which his visit to the "cité" has made intolerable. Armed with physical evidence supplied by a friend, Bérenger sets out to enlist the aid of the police in capturing the killer. As the spectator must suspect, and as the final act will reveal, the nature of the killer is such that he is invulnerable to anything so mundane as arrest by the police.

The final confrontation scene between Bérenger and the killer stands in symmetrical contrast to the beginning of the play. As in the beginning, light is almost the only element of décor, the rest of the set having faded into obscurity to leave Bérenger alone in the dim light of dusk. Just as the brilliant light of the "cité" was the exteriorization of confident energy and hope, this "lumière blafarde" is the exteriorization of Bérenger's vulnerable, discouraged fatigue.

In the stage directions, Ionesco offers two alternative suggestions of how the character of the killer should be performed. The killer may either be performed by an actor or: "Une autre possibilité: pas du Tueur. On n'entend que son ricanement. Bérenger parle seul dans l'ombre." (p. 162.) In our opinion, the second alternative is by far the better choice. In the first place, an unseen killer establishes or reinforces the symmetry of the play. The "cité radieuse" was a city of light, and the killer is a creature of darkness; the absence of a human actor to perform the killer thus corresponds to the absence of a detailed set in the "cité." A human actor in this role might even detract from the killer's impact, for the somber lighting and Bérenger's own fear make the killer's presence just as palpable and, perhaps, even more threatening than would be the case if a human actor were to perform this role. With an "invisible" killer, the light-darkness dichotomy upon which the play is based is maintained. The gloom of the play's ending balances the radiance of the beginning; the radiance, which was Bérenger's accomplice in his quest for life, is finally vanquished by darkness. Bérenger finds an enemy rather than a benevolent collaborator in his environment, and the triumph of darkness over light is the triumph of death over life—the catastrophe which Bérenger had earlier feared.

An unseen killer is thus indicated by the opposition of light and darkness in the play. There is, however, an even more compelling reason why the killer should not be performed by a human actor. Bérenger's search for the killer was based on his assumption that his relationship to the killer is one of simple conflict with a being separate from himself. By eliminating the killer, he hopes to reestablish harmony with his environment. With a human actor in the role of the killer, this assumption would tend to be confirmed, and Bérenger's death would be the result of conflict with a hostile alien force. As Bérenger has said, however, there are no barriers between the internal and external worlds, and we have hypothesized an identity between these two worlds as being of fundamental importance in this play. Viewed from this perspective, the killer is the exteriorization of Bérenger's own fear to the same degree that the "cité" was the exteriorization of his hopes, and what seems at first to be conflict between character and environment becomes collaboration or complicity instead. First, as Ionesco indicates at the beginning of the final scene, the killer's presence is a function of Bérenger's fear: "On devra sentir la proximité de sa présence par la montée même de l'angoisse de Bérenger" (pp. 158-59). Then, Bérenger attempts to enter into dialogue with the killer, trying to find out what motivates him and what might placate him, but the killer's only response is an occasional chuckle. In fact, it is Bérenger himself who supplies all of the killer's responses.[14] With an "invisible" killer, this scene is more clearly monologue than dialogue, in spite of Bérenger's assumption to the contrary. Ultimately, Bérenger's failure to elicit any answer from the killer stems from the fact that Bérenger is, finally, the killer's accomplice; as the stage directions indicate: "Bérenger trouve en lui-même, malgré lui-même, contre lui-même, des arguments en faveur du Tueur" (p. 62).

With all attempts to enter into dialogue necessarily proving fruitless, Bérenger makes one last desperate effort to vanquish the killer by shooting him, but this last spasm of life asserted against death is doomed to failure.[15] Once again, the absence of a human actor in this role would be effective here, underscoring the futility of Bérenger's struggle. As the play ends, he drops the pistols with which he would have shot the killer, assumes a position of complete submission, and gives up the struggle.

In spite of Bérenger's assertions to the contrary, the relationship between this character and the killer is one of collaboration rather than conflict. Since the interior and exterior worlds are inextricably linked with each other, the conflict between light and darkness—between the "cité radieuse" and the killer—is the exteriorization of the conflict between life and death within Bérenger himself, and the character's death is not so much a murder as it is suicide. Schematically, the tensions in the play may be represented as shown in the diagram.

By the projection of conflicting aspects of Bérenger's personality into his surroundings, *Tueur sans gages* illustrates interpenetration of character and environment. *Le Roi se meurt,* on the other hand, presents collaboration between character and environment in its most extreme form.

In an article entitled "Ionesco and the Phantom," Kenneth Tynan criticized Ionesco in the following terms: "M. Ionesco, I fear, is on the brink of believing that his distortions are more valid and important than the external world it is their proper function to interpret. To adapt Johnson, I am not yet so lost in drama criticism as to forget that plays are the daughters of earth, and that things are the sons of heaven. But M. Ionesco is in danger of forgetting; of locking himself up in that hall of mirrors which in philosophy is known as solipsism."[16] It is not our concern here to debate whether or not Ionesco is "guilty" of solipsism; in any case, we do not agree that the "proper function" of a play is to "interpret the external world." The word "solipsism" is, however, particularly appropriate when applied to certain characters in some of Ionesco's plays; collaboration between a character and his surroundings ultimately implies a certain degree of solipsism. In *Le Roi se meurt*[17] the world of the play is, in fact, completely solipsistic with regard to its central character, King Bérenger I.

As the title indicates, the play is concerned with the last few hours in the life of Bérenger. It is not about death so much as it is about the process of dying: when Bérenger finally dies, the play is over. Bérenger's first wife Marguerite clearly establishes this identity between the play and Bérenger's final agony when she tells him: "Tu vas mourir dans une heure et demie, tu vas mourir à la fin du spectacle" (p. 22). The ending of the play is thus fixed from the beginning; the question is not whether the king will die, but rather how he will die.

Tension is established between opposing forces which try to pull Bérenger in opposite directions. Marguerite and his doctor tell Bérenger that he must abdicate "moralement, administrativement," and "physiquement" (p. 23). Defying these forces which advocate acquiescence is Marie, the king's young second wife, who urges him to refuse to give his consent to death. In the middle is Bérenger, who begins by refusing to accept Marguerite's assertion: "Je mourrai quand je voudrai, je suis le Roi, c'est moi qui décide" (p. 23). The progression (or "plot") of the play consists of Bérenger's moving from this position to one of acquiescence.[18]

A second source of dramatic interest in the play is the collaboration of the "exterior" world in Bérenger's death. As was the case in *Tueur sans gages,* there are no boundaries separating "monde intérieur" from "monde extérieur" in King Bérenger's solipsistic world. At one point, he even echoes Tynan's remark about the "hall of mirrors" in which Ionesco is allegedly trapped: "Je me vois. Derrière toute chose, je suis. . . . Je suis la terre, je suis le ciel, je suis le vent, je suis le feu. Suis-je dans tous les miroirs, ou bien suis-je le miroir de tout?" (p. 67.)

As the play progresses, it becomes increasingly apparent that the entire world of the play exists totally as a function of Bérenger's will, an exteriorization of the character himself. Before the character even appears, his imminent death is reflected in the state of disrepair into which the palace is falling. The Guard tries to heat up the room, to no avail: "Chauffage allume-toi. Rien à faire, ça ne marche pas. Chauffage, allume-toi. Le radiateur reste froid. Ce n'est pas ma faute. Il ne m'a pas dit qu'il me retirait la délégation du feu!" (p. 10.) The floor is covered with dust and cigarette butts; during the night, a crack has appeared in the wall, and Marguerite announces that it is "irreversible." Toward the end of the play, it is the widening of this fissure which signals the imminence of the character's death. After the king's kidneys stop functioning the loud beating of his heart literally shakes the palace, causing the walls to tremble and fall.[19]

It is not only the on-stage world, but also the off-stage world of the play which is falling into ruin and chaos. As his two wives remark, Bérenger and his kingdom grew up together, and they are disappearing together (p. 62). The cow in the stable can no longer give milk, and the only children left in the kingdom are "quelques enfants goitreux, débiles mentaux congénitaux, des mongoliens, des hydrocéphales" (p. 22). The country's borders and mountains are shrinking, and the whole kingdom is dying.[20] Ruin extends even beyond the kingdom into the cosmos itself. Mars and Saturn have collided, the Sun has lost most of its energy, snow is falling on the Sun's north pole, the Milky Way is congealing, and the comet, exhausted and moribund, has curled up with its tail around it, like a dying dog (p. 17). As Juliette the maid observes: "La terre s'efface avec lui. Les astres s'évanouissent. L'eau disparaît. Disparaissent le feu, l'air, un univers, tant d'univers. . . . Il emporte tout cela dans son gouffre." (p. 62.)

Bérenger's surroundings thus reflect and collaborate in his death; the world of the play is indeed an extension of the character. It is during Bérenger's final dying moments, however, that the solipsism of the world of the play becomes absolute. First of all, the other characters disappear one by one; when the king is no longer able to see or remember them, they cease to exist. First Marie, then the Guard, Juliette, and the Doctor disappear, until Bérenger is left alone with Marguerite to guide him through the final steps toward death. Bérenger dies, and the stage directions show clearly that the world of the play dies with him.[21] Ionesco's emphasis on the importance of this final "jeu de décor" underlines the vital role décor must play in any production of *Le Roi se meurt.* By capitalizing on the capacity of non-human elements to *perform,* just as the human actors perform, the play powerfully presents the process of dying viewed from the perspective of a character whose whole world disappears along with him. Solipsism is no defect here, but rather the primary source of the play's considerable impact.

The theoretical framework offered here, because it is based on appreciation of performance rather than on texts alone, will provide a useful analytical model for dealing with the role of décor, not only in Ionesco, but in the many other plays which exploit human/non-human relationships. This does not contradict interpretations based on literary, metaphysical, or psychological grounds; rather, it complements them, providing a specifically theatrical field to which such grids may be applied. Once décor is accorded the status of actor, the character it performs becomes capable of interacting with other characters in a wide range of relationships, only two of which—antagonist and collaborator—are studied here.

Notes

1. The most illuminating of Ionesco's remarks on theatre remain those in the collection of essays *Notes et contre-notes* (Paris: Gallimard, 1962), in the journal extracts published in *Journal en miettes* (Paris: Mercure de France, 1967) and *Présent passé passé présent* (Paris: Mercure de France, 1968), and in the *Entretiens avec Eugène Ionesco* (Paris: Pierre Belfond, 1966), a series of interviews done by Claude Bonnefoy. Although they contain some important texts, the more recent collections—*Antidotes* (Paris: Gallimard, 1977) and *Un Homme en question* (Paris: Gallimard, 1979)—are less useful in providing insight into Ionesco's work, since they are repetitive and devoted in large part to denunciations of political tyranny.

2. Rosette C. Lamont, "The Proliferation of Matter in Ionesco's Plays," *Esprit Créateur* 2 (1962), 193.

3. J. Serge Dubrovsky, "Le Rire de Ionesco," *Nouvelle Revue Française* (Feb., 1960), p. 317. This article appeared first in English under the title "Eugène Ionesco and the Comedy of the Absurd" in *Yale French Studies* 23 (1959), 3-10. For similar discussions of the proliferating object, see Claude Abastado, *Eugène Ionesco* (Paris: Bordas, 1971), p. 244, and Jacques Guicharnaud, *Modern French Theatre from Giraudoux to Genet* (New Haven: Yale University Press, 1967), pp. 221-28.

4. Paul Vernois, *La Dynamique théâtrale d'Eugène Ionesco* (Paris: Klincksieck, 1972), p. 167. Several other critics have used a Jungian or psychoanalytical approach to this question, often with fascinating results. In the chapter on Ionesco ("Ionesco: Paroxysm and Proliferation") in his book *The Psychology of Tragic Drama* (London and Boston: Routledge and Kegan Paul, 1975), Patrick Roberts associates proliferation (of words as well as objects) with infantile anxieties. In "La Proliferation dans le théâtre d'Eugène Ionesco," published in Paul Vernois, ed., *L'Onirisme et l'insolite dans le théâtre français contemporain* (Paris: Klincksieck, 1974), Michel Lioure calls proliferating objects "métaphores obsédantes" deriving from a 'mythe personnel" (p. 135), and also finds that proliferation of matter is but a sub-category of proliferation of all kinds: verbosity, procreation, contagion, and death, extending to the plot and structure of the plays. Ionesco has written at length about his own dreams. See especially *Journal en miettes* (pp. 35-37, 44-45, 54-55, 81-143), which contains many accounts of dreams as well as Ionesco's thoughts on Jung and Freud; also, *Entretiens. . . .* pp. 10-11, 38-41, 74-75.

5. See, for example, *Entretiens . . .* p. 41: "Vous dites qu'il y a dans mon théâtre beaucoup de boue, d'enlisement. Cela correspond à l'un de mes deux états. Je me sens ou bien lourd ou bien léger, ou bien trop lourd ou bien trop léger. La légèreté c'est l'évanescence euphorique qui peut devenir tragique ou douleureuse quand il y a angoisse."

6. Richard Coe, "La Farce tragique," *Cahiers Renaud-Barrault* 42 (1963), 48. See also Leonard Pronko, "The Anti-Spiritual Victory in the Theatre of Ionesco," *Modern Drama* 2 (1959), 29-35; and Rosette C. Lamont, "Air and Matter: Ionesco's *Le Piéton de l'Air* and *Victimes du devoir*," *French Review* 38 (1965), 349-361.

7. Unlike a human being, a dramatic character neither lives nor dies, but only appears; a dramatic character is seen and heard, but only during a dramatic performance, and can never be touched. A dramatic character is a set of gestures, "une entité psychologique sans physiologie" (Robert Champigny, *Le Genre dramatique* [Monte Carlo: Regain, 1965], p. 139).

8. Several critics have emphasized the use of object as actor. Simone Benmussa, in "Les Ensevelis dans le théâtre d'Eugène Ionesco," *Cahiers Renaud-Barrault* 22-23 (1958), 197-207, states that "l'objet posséde une vie propre" and says that Ionesco's work differs from contemporary realism because "l'objet y joue un rôle indépendant" (p. 201). In his *Le Théâtre de dérision* (Paris: Gallimard, 1974), Emmanuel Jacquart speaks of what he calls "le langage scénique" in a fashion quite reminiscent of Artaud: "Décors, costumes, accessoires, éclairages, bruitages et dialogues [and, one might add, the body and voice of the human actor] n'ont plus d'existence propre. C'est par leur convergence, leur complémentarité ou leur contradiction qu'ils donnent le jour au sens." (p. 150.) For Jacques Poliéri, "L'objet dans le théâtre de Ionesco . . . est considéré comme un personnage parmi d'autres"

("Notes sur le texte, le décor et le geste dans le théâtre de Jean Tardieu," *Cahiers Renaud-Barrault* 22-3 [1958], 208-210).

9. Robert Tener, in "These Places, This Private Landscape: First Suggestions for a Topological Approach to Ionesco's Bérenger Plays," *Papers on Language and Literature* 13 (1977), 391-400, discusses the intimate relationship of inner and outer realities in Ionesco's theatre: "The sense that a human being is spatially analagous to an inner and outer world and reflects a similar binary configuration in the universe permeates Ionesco's thought." Richard Schechner finds, in "The Inner and the Outer Reality," *Tulane Drama Review* 7 (1963), 187-217, that dialectical tension between inner and outer reality—never in harmony with each other—replaces plot, and that proliferation of objects is symbolic of characters' alienation from themselves and from the world. Both of these analyses are similar, in part, to the approach I will use below in explicating two Bérenger plays.

10. *Notes et contre-notes,* p. 86.

11. According to Schechner, in the article cited above, this is because the characters in the later plays are no longer alienated, are no longer ontologically insecure. As for the proliferation of suitcases at the end of *L'Homme aux valises,* these objects do not engulf or dominate the human characters as is the case in the early plays.

12. Eugène Ionesco, *Théâtre,* 5 vols. (Paris: Gallimard, 1954-74), II, 59-171. References to this play will be documented parenthetically in the text.

13. See, for example, *Journal . . .* pp. 68-70; *Entretiens . . .* pp. 14-15.

14. "Elle est trop loin, la Préfecture? Ou est-ce moi qui ai parlé? (Ricanement du Tueur.) Vous vous moquez de moil! J'appelle la police, on va vous arrêter. (Ricanement du Tueur.) Vous dites que c'est inutile, on ne m'entendrait pas d'ici?" (p. 162.)

15. "Oh—que ma force est faible contre ta froide détermination, contre ta cruauté sans merci! . . . Et que peuvent les balles elles-mêmes contre l'énergie infinie de ton obstination?" (p. 171.)

16. Kenneth Tynan, "Ionesco and the Phantom," *The Observer* (6 July 1958), p. 15.

17. *Théâtre,* IV, 7-74. References to this play will be given parenthetically in the text.

18. Ionesco's obsession with the whole matter of death and dying is well-known; most critics have viewed this play as a ritualized apprenticeship, inspired by Ionesco's readings in non-Western mystical or religious writings, and providing an optimistic alternative to nihilism. Rosette Lamont, in "The Double Apprenticeship: Life and the Process of Dying," in *The Phenomenon of Death: Faces of Mortality,* ed. Edith Wyschogrod (New York: Harper and Row, 1973), pp. 198-224, sees the king's death as metamorphosis into Bodhisattva. M.S. Barranger follows in the same direction, using Tibetan Yoga as the basis for seeing the end of the play as a triumph rather than a tragedy ("Death as Initiation in *Exit the King,*" *Educational Theater Journal* 27 [1975],

504-07). Warren Tucker, in *"Le Roi se meurt"* et les *Upanishads,"* *French Review* 49 (1976), 397-400, uses Hindu mythology as the basis for his equally positive interpretation of the play. Although Tucker never mentions Dr. Elisabeth Kubler-Ross's study of terminally-ill patients *On Death and Dying* (New York: Macmillan, 1969), he mentions that the king passes through exactly those five stages experienced by terminally-ill patients: denial and isolation, anger, bargaining, depression, and acceptance. It is my opinion that it is Ionesco's profound insight into the psychology of dying which explains the stages through which Bérenger passes, rather than an optimistic belief in the achieving of some sort of serenity after death. All of Ionesco's self-described moments of euphoria are accompanied by intense light, brilliance, and evanescence. The ending of this play is somber and dark in the extreme, which would seem to undermine an interpretation of the play as a serene acceptance of death as metamorphosis.

19. " . . . Un coeur fou. Vous entendez? (On entend les battements affolés du coeur du Roi:) Ça part, ça va trés vite, ça ralentit, ça part de nouveau à toute allure. (Les battements de coeur du Roi ébranlent la maison. La fissure s'élargit au mur, d'autres apparaissent. Un pan peut s'écrouler ou s'effacer)." (p. 63; it is the doctor who is speaking.)

20. "Le printemps qui était encore là hier soir nous a quittés il y a deux heures trente. Voici novembre. Audelà des frontières, l'herbe s'est mise à pousser. . . . Chez nous, les feuilles se sont desséchées. Elles se décrochent. Les arbres soupirent et meurent. La terre se fend encore plus que d'habitude." (p. 17.)

21. "Le Roi est assis sur son trône. On aura vu, pendant cette dernière scène, disparaître progressivement les portes, les fenêtres, les murs de la salle du trône. Ce jeu de décor est très important.

"Maintenant, il n'y a plus rien sur le plateau sauf le Roi sur son trône dans une lumière grise. Puis, le Roi et son trône disparaissent également.

"Enfin, il n'y a plus que cette lumière grise.

"La disparition des fenêtres, portes, murs, Roi et trône doit se faire lentement, progressivement, très nettement. Le Roi assis sur son trône doit rester visible quelque temps avant de sombrer dans une sorte de brume." (p. 74.)

Lynne Retford (essay date 1987)

SOURCE: "Irony in Ionesco," in *French Literature Series,* Vol. XIV, 1987, pp. 174-77.

[*In the following essay, Retford explores four categories of irony in* The Lesson, The Bald Soprano, The Killer, *and* Victims of Duty, *and asserts that Ionesco uses irony to reflect and world in flux and as a statement of his metaphysical sentiments that life is both tragic and comic.*]

Eugene Ionesco transmits an extreme awareness of the plight of contemporary man through an artistic act of defiance at the absurdity of existence. This note, using the four plays *La Leçon. La Cantatrice Chauve, Tueur sans gages* and *Victimes du devoir,* explores four categories of irony: Cosmic Irony, Personal Irony, the Irony of Systems, and Artistic Irony.

COSMIC IRONY

Cosmic irony is a given in the Ionescian world. There is a metaphysical conflict which is productive of irony: on one hand, the endeavor of man to judge the universe in terms of an ultimate ideal or goal, and on the other, the perception of non-rationality and lack of purpose which constitute that universe.

This is the key theme of cosmic irony, but Ionesco works more specifically with other manifestations. For him, because death is inescapable, life is absurd. Life is constantly in a state of breaking down:

Le Professeur: Il ne faut pas uniquement intégrer. Il faut aussi désintégrer. C'est ça la vie. . . .[1]

In *Tueur sans gages* we see death as being everywhere, affecting men, women and children without discrimination, and knowing everything: to Ionesco, it is this fact which makes life so unreal. He shows, however, that death does not work in a vacuum, for the victims and the killer in *Tueur sans gages* are accomplices. Outside of literature, in this day of terrorism and hostage-taking, this collusion is commonly known as the "Stockholm Syndrome."

PERSONAL IRONY

Ionesco's view of man is pessimistic, and indeed, derisory. His characters are not so much persons as they are *personnages.* Their lives are banal and their most trivial experiences merit the word *fantastique.* Characters have become automatons, which leads to comic results, and also tragic irony.

They refuse to take personal responsibility for their actions. Both *Victimes du devoir* and *Tueur sans gages* are plays about the rupture between private and public lives. We know what this attitude leads to: Madeleine allies herself with the policeman in torturing her husband, and does it in the name of hospitality. Other Ionesco plays also reveal this theme: in *La Leçon,* the maid is an accomplice to the professor's crime, and in *Tueur sans gages,* we are led to fault Edouard for the murders as we do the Killer. Fear of assuming risks only leads to ugliness and destruction. People even refuse to accept the responsibility for finding meaning in their own lives. In *Victimes du devoir,* Choubert's father states: "Tu naquis, mon fils, juste au moment où j'allais dynamiter la planète. C'est ta naissance qui la sauva. Tu m'empêchas, du moins, de tuer le monde dans mon coeur . . ." (p. 205).

They cannot and/or will not think for themselves. Madeleine suggests that Choubert speak with some "authorized person" before he decides on the validity of his artistic theories, and in the same play the policeman calls himself a soldier who does not think, but only carries out the orders he receives. What Ionesco does is show us the essence of humans (care, acceptance of responsibilities, thought) broken down. People kill in order to live: "La mort n'a pas à être appuyée par une idéologie. Vivre c'est mourir et c'est tuer: chaque créature se défend en tuant, tue pour vivre."[2]

IRONY OF SYSTEMS

Ionesco's pessimistic world view finds yet another expression in the ridigity of systems. His condemnation of systems is enormous in scope, covering educational, psychological, political, philosophical and artistic systems in the four plays. The idea of causation is mocked, first in *La Cantatrice Chauve,* and then in *Tueur sans gages,* when the concierge explains to the mailman: "Ça c'est trop fort! Il peut pas être sorti. Peut-être qu'il dort, mais c'est pas dans ses habitudes! Frappez plus fort. Moi, je vais voir!"[3] (p. 114).

Bérenger's argument with the Killer at the end of *Tueur sans gages* is useless for two reasons: first, because Death is inescapable, and second, because no system can hope to convince because they are all impractical and unworkable. The characters, nonetheless, continue to believe in the various systems although they have been proved not to work.

In his *Notes et contre-notes,* Ionesco makes these observations about political and social systems: "Aucune société n'a pu abolir la tristesse humaine, aucun système politique ne peut nous libérer de la douleur de vivre, de la peur de mourir, de notre soif de l'absolu. C'est la condition humaine qui gouverne la condition sociale, non le contraire . . ." (p. 143). In many instances, man is defined through his social utility, and not through his "human" attributes, an attitude which creates the rupture between personal and public life. Ironically, the people who make the most sense in the Ionescian world are those who are not involved in a formal, organized system. These are the members of the lower classes (the concierge who has read Marcus Aurelius and other philosophers, but who finds philosophical systems not suitable for everyday living), and the outcasts.

Ionesco's burlesque of theatrical conventions is also based on the charge of rigidity. He faults them for turning what could be exciting and alive into something static and inert, that is, another system. It is here that we enter into creative irony.

ARTISTIC IRONY

André Malraux has stated that an artist creates a work of art as a revenge against a meaningless world, and Ionesco corroborates with "écrire c'est agir."[4] Artistic irony occurs in many forms: intervention of the artist in his own work, characters discussing the playwright and his works, discussion in the work itself of methods of presentation,

interspersed hints which are not cleared up until the end, manipulating the reader. Ionesco uses many of these techniques.

He has often been called an author who believes that words are meaningless; the irony resides here in the use of words by someone who so obviously distrusts them. There is a distrust because there is a duplicity inherent in language, and because language gives a false sense of security. In *La Leçon* and *La Cantatrice Chauve,* there is a complete breakdown in language, where language becomes an instrument of aggression, pain and even death. Language manipulates people, who are not able to use it to serve themselves.

In *Victimes du devoir,* Ionesco develops a technique already used in embryo in *La Cantatrice Chauve,* the discussion of an experimental fable at the beginning of the play. The main artistic theme of the play is the validity of Aristotelian versus non-Aristotelian drama, and Ionesco undermines traditional drama by presenting a non-Aristotelian play. He succeeds in many ways, by destroying the unities of time, place, character and genre (the play moves from detective to psychological to literary to domestic types), and by confusing the spectators with the actors. Despite Ionesco's attempts, the play still contains a certain sequence of action, a certain structure. In addition, the murder of Nicolas is a fine example of a *deus ex machina!*

Ionesco presents traditional characters to us, whose appearance contradicts their actions: one would never expect a professor to be a murderer, nor a mild-mannered common man like Bérenger to be a man of action. He plays on our sense of sound and language. He throws us a sentence such as "J'aime mieux pondre un oeuf que voler un boeuf" from *La Cantatrice Chauve,* and we almost let it go: it looks and sounds like a sentence, its rhyme scheme makes it sound like a proverb, it has all the grammatical necessities of a sentence, but it doesn't have the intentionality of a sentence.

Irony is always double-edged, and one of the reasons it is used by Ionesco is to reflect a world in flux, an unsure world, a world of multiple perspectives, free of rigidity. It is in addition a statement of his metaphysical sentiments, his view that life is both tragic and comic.

Notes

1. *La Leçon,* in Eugène Ionesco, *Théâtre I,* (Gallimard, 1954), p. 69. All further parenthetical references to Ionesco's plays are to this edition.

2. Eugène Ionesco, *Notes et contre-notes,* (Paris: Gallimard, 1966), p. 221.

3. *Théâtre II,* p. 114.

4. *Notes . . .* p. 16.

Robert L. Tener (essay date 1987)

SOURCE: "Scenic Metaphors: A Study of Ionesco's Geometrical Vision of Human Relationships in the Bérenger

Plays," in *Papers on Language and Literature,* Vol. 23, No. 2, Spring 1987, pp. 175-91.

[*In the following essay, Tener treats the use of décor and other visual and aural theatrical metaphors as the dramatic expression of internal and external forces that surround the protagonist in Ionesco's Bérenger plays.*]

An important characteristic of drama closely related to characters and plot is the scenic space wherein the actions take place. For Anne Ubersfeld, "l'espace scénique peut aussi apparaître comme un vaste champ psychique où s'affrontent des forces qui sont les forces psychiques du moi. La scène est alors assimilable à un champ clos où s'affrontent les éléments du moi divisé, clivé" [the scenic space may also appear like a broad, psychic field where forces face each other which are the psychic forces of the self. The stage is then similar to a medieval list where the elements of the divided, cloven self face each other].[1] While some playwrights seem unaware of the importance of the scenic space (most seem to view drama not as an art form but as a representational slice of life), others, such as Eugene O'Neill, Henrik Ibsen, Anton Chekhov, and Eugène Ionesco tie the psychological implications of inside and outside, up and down, closed or open, repetitive or non-repetitive, circular or linear actions closely to the themes of their plays. Scenic space for Nancy Lane appears to be part of the semiotic system Ionesco uses, evident especially in the *décors* which she says are not "servile accessories." Playing down the poetic importance of visual as well as aural images, she finds in Ionesco's early plays that the non-human characters are hostile to the human ones.[2] Other critics interpret décor or scenic space in metaphorical, psychological, or even oneiric terms. For Paul Vernois, for example, the basis of Ionesco's work is oneiric, drawing on images and symbols associated with personal and archetypal myths. His book-length study, indebted to Leo Spitzer's principles of linguistic criticism and illustrated with various schemata, discusses the elements of polarization and modalities of knowledge. Closely linked to such analyses is the work of Mary A. Witt. More restricted than my own approach, despite some overlapping, she narrows her study to a primary discussion of evanescence and heaviness, light and darkness, the feeling of being closed in and that of flying through space. In this study I treat the décor and other theatrical metaphors (both visual and aural—taking metaphor to mean the implicit and explicit images suggested by what one sees and hears) as the dramatic expression of forces both external and internal that surround or affect Bérenger. At the heart of the Bérenger plays the scenic metaphors suggest Ionesco's mistrust of rational models of reality as solutions or approaches to life's problems. Vernois sees the source of these metaphors in Ionesco's oneiric vision; I see it in his habit of viewing the world through images much as a poet perceives experiences. For Ionesco especially the dramatic vision of life manifests itself through spatial metaphors, geometrical patterns as it were, that lend themselves to analogic descriptions of life

processes and forces in which human beings are involved, much as the sine wave can be used to describe the variations in a writer's career.

One of the earliest critics to see this characteristic in Ionesco's plays, Georges Matoré, asserts

> Fréquemment, dans son théâtre, l'espace scénique se rétrécit suivant un tracé qu'on pourrait assimiler à une spirale ou à des cercles concentriques:les objects envahissant peu à peu la scène (*les Chaises, la Nouveau locataire*) de manière à ne plus laisser au personnage principal que l'espace exiger d'une cellule de condamné à mort. Ce lent rétrécissement physique est lié à un encerclement moral, à un ensevelissement. L'espace de Ionesco est une peau de chagrin.[3]
>
> [Frequently, in his theater, the scenic space shrinks according to a pattern that one might liken to a spiral or to concentric circles: little by little objects invade the scene (*Les Chaises, La Nouveau locataire*) so as to allow the main character no more than the space demands of a cell for those condemned to death. This slow material shrinking is bound to a moral encircling, to a shrouding. Ionesco's space is a wild animal's skin that expands or contracts according to passion expended.]

This geometrical vision of human relationships and processes, while evident in all of Ionesco's plays, appears as a dominant element in the dramas written from 1952 through 1959 when he was exploring the dramatic and artistic possibilities of space and language. As Paul Vernois has pointed out, the plays written between those years have a to-and-fro or an up-and-down movement, a "mouvement scénique primordial destiné à être repris et orchestré dans les grandes pièces" [a primordial scenic movement intended to be revived and orchestrated in the major plays].[4] In addition most of the plays written during this period, which includes the Bérenger series, have a visual and aural contracting action moving from a wide, loose perspective to a small, private world. Each also presents an intimate living area as an entrapping spatial form polarized in terms of the oneiric house opposed by an apartment or throne room. And each reveals that life or its representations tend to invade or contaminate not only the rational models but also the intuitive or idealized dreams mankind creates in an attempt to give life meaning by stopping its chaotic movement. Nancy Lane finds that the role of the "non-human domain," which involves the décor, in the Bérenger cycle translates "into dramatic signs man's ambiguous relationship to his environment and even to himself."[5]

Not only the to-and-fro but also the up-and-down movements are realized metaphorically in *Tueur sans gages.*[6] Within its three-act form, Ionesco places Bérenger at the center of visual and aural images which suggest forces of harmony and content or those of logic and rationality. In other instances they reflect Bérenger's internal state. The connotations of the stage images are then altered through a falling or descending action as in *Les Chaises* and *Amédée.* The total effect suggests the generalized destructive impact of life on dreams of harmony or rationality. As a consequence Bérenger cannot remain in the scenic center and be restored to his emotional, intellectual, and physical well being. The action begins in the first act with the description of the radiant city as an architectural utopia. Logically it is the ideal city. But logic is not life in Ionesco's dramatic world. Because it models an abstraction, like the ideal group gathering to hear the ideal speech, we cannot see it directly, being told about it by Bérenger, who intrudes by chance into this ideal region. The radiant city is characterized by a cluster of images which suggest its rationality and obsessive systemization rather than any organic fullness of a garden of paradise. Unlike a harmonizing image poised between physical reality and the abstract cultural world, it stands neither as a place for life nor as a work of art. According to Nancy Lane, Bérenger tries to make the city his accomplice to end conflict between him and the environment.[7]

Once Ionesco has established these characteristics, however, he informs us that Dany, the architect's secretary, wants to resign from the civil service and that stones are often thrown in the city although the inhabitants are not injured by them. The first event suggests a movement out from the city's center, the second a downward pattern. The psychological nature of the scene changes with the sound of a falling stone, acquiring negative and destructive overtones. To emphasize this new direction, Ionesco informs us that the inhabitants are leaving this city, which fragments man just as it has its designer, who had divided his two ears and eyes between Bérenger and the borough. The images suggest that the city has fallen morally, acquired a defect, as though its life-supporting qualities have been contaminated by intruders with no feeling for logic and order.

The second act presents Bérenger's apartment as a closed area cut off from harmonious relationships with the physical reality around it. Although as his home it is supposed to be a source of strength, a variety of intrusions have actually contaminated its power. Just before Bérenger reaches his apartment, Ionesco provides a scene filled with loud, clichéd talk from a variety of people about the cost of living, sickness, and their dog's life. In the background are heard the intrusive metallic sounds of hammers, motorcycles, sirens. The entire scene forms a cluster of contaminating sense impressions engulfing the apartment. Every element suggests that the apartment is isolated from the social world and that its door helps shut out what Bérenger dislikes, the emotional chaos of a society that does not function logically.

Bérenger's apartment offers no place of repose to reorganize his thoughts and to integrate his experience with his childhood memories. Instead the place seems to hold ugly, old, and comically askew elements which lack a warm revitalizing touch. Nor can it keep out all of the exterior comic ugliness. The scenic image focuses on Édouard sitting in the middle of the room, a position that dominates the scene visually. His description suggests that he is a contaminating intruder. He has a thin body, a withered right arm, lung trouble, a bad cough, a temperature, and a

pale face. The scenic image of Bérenger's apartment-home is conceived as a repository of qualities that could constrict or destroy him, presenting an aura of tense irony and fragmented existence. What once reinforced life now seems not only old fashioned but also slightly dangerous.

A new action is precipitated by a falling movement indirectly associated with the killer. As Édouard picks up the briefcase which contains the killer's plans, its contents spill out onto the table. Feeling now that he has evidence of the killer's timetable and pattern of operation, Bérenger wants Édouard to accompany him to report the matter to the police.

The action of the last act starts with a conceptual image, adds intruders, then changes through a falling movement, and ends with an enclosing metaphor. The visual image is conceived in terms of surrealistic elements associated with a public bench, a street in far perspective, a setting sun, and a raised pavement section like a wall in back hiding a street leading far in the distance toward the buildings of the Préfecture, the symbol of law and order. Thus two separate visual areas are immediately established by the presence of the wall. The drift of the psychological action is to move from one area (a rational or ideal place contaminated by chaos) through or past a barrier to another area (a place of logic or order), a movement reflected in Bérenger's unsuccessful attempts to persuade others to adopt his views or to let him pass. Mother Peep's campaign actions, Édouard's need to rest, the discovery that the briefcase had been forgotten, and the appearance of the unusually tall policeman function as barriers preventing Bérenger from reaching the Préfecture. Soon other barriers fill the scene. A second policeman on stilts and army trucks appear. Then a traffic jam develops. In comparison with the barriers which seem gigantic or overpowering, Bérenger (the symbol of confused life?) appears quite small. Inexplicably, politics, physical tiredness, the ineffectual bureaucracy of the police and the army, metallic and mechanical objects, and ordinary things like a bench seem to exert a force that prevents or inhibits the horizontal movement of the action.

Suddenly the scenic image alters in preparation for the dominant downward flow of the psychological action. Its negative elements suggest visually the gradual loss of vitality in Bérenger. The stage becomes empty; the avenue is deserted. The stage directions emphasize Bérenger's isolation. So far in the distance rises the Préfecture toward which Bérenger moves, that the perspective creates the impression of a long passageway leading into "un guet-apens" (159) [a trap]. All at once the killer appears, standing on the bench or wall. His description reinforces the sense of loneliness as well as the absence of harmonious and restorative qualities. He jumps down to ground level, not in an act of submission to Bérenger (though he is quite small), but in a manner visually echoing the falling stones, the dropped photographs, the movement down from the abstract regions of thought to earth, the pattern by which chaos and the irrational conquer life's idealism and energy.

Similarly at the end, Bérenger repeats the dominant visual image of the play when he kneels to beg the killer. The image is re-emphasized when he lowers his "deux vieux pistolets démodés" (172) [two, old, outmoded pistols], bends his head, and waits. From this final event there exists no exit. The blazing fire in Bérenger, his source of light, wells of joy and enormous energy have been overcome. Ironically the irrational and inexplicable, man's primal fear, remain uninfluenced by the rational and the dream, both of which are impotent in the end.

In his analysis of **Rhinocéros**[8] Paul Vernois commented that,

> La hantise de la verticalité diminue apparemment dans **Rhinocéros** mais elle n'est pas tout à fait éliminée de la structure de la pièce. Pendant la moitié de l'action, à l'acte II en particulier, l'intrigue se déroule sur deux plans: le bureau de Bérenger après la destruction de l'escalier est devenu une sorte de mirador pour la chasse aux fauves. . . . Rejoindre les rhinocéros, c'est faire une chute jusqu'au moment où ceux-ci ont envahi. Le mythe est si bien ourdi que la notion même de culpabilité ou de valeurs (esthétiques en particulier) disparaît quand la dénivellation des humains et des rhinocéros est abolie.[9]

> [The haunting sense of verticality diminishes apparently in **Rhinocéros** but it is not entirely eliminated from the structure of the play. During half of the action, in act 2 particularly, the plot unwinds in two schemes: the office of Bérenger after the destruction of the stairs has become a kind of watch tower for the hunting of wild animals. . . . To join the rhinoceroses is to fall until only those predominate. The myth is so well woven that the very notion of guilt or values (aesthetic in particular) vanishes when the difference in kind between human beings and rhinoceroses is abolished.]

Despite Paul Vernois's response, the verticality of **Rhinocéros** does not seem diminished to me. Rather, it seems emphasized more as the general direction of the scenic images, unlike that in **Tueur sans gages,** is gradually upward. The action moves from an exterior, public, ground-level social center in a small French village through an area of rationality located visually on the upper levels in a printing office, into two interior, private, intimate second-floor apartments. In the first meeting between Jean and Bérenger, set on a Sunday in the center of a small village, Jean is identified with a sense of logic, order, self-discipline, and present time, while Bérenger is associated with disorder, feeling, irrationality, and past time. Into this innocuously pleasant setting comes a series of intrusions or invasions which contaminate the effect and expand the natural oppositions between order and disorder, public and private, already evident. The first invasion is the sound of a rhinoceros. Next Le Logicien and his friend intrude on the scene; soon Daisy comes by; and sounds of a rhinoceros are repeated.

But the cluster of social images with its impressions of pleasant soporific order and little physical activity has altered with many characters entering and leaving the area. Their frenzied activities provide a horizontal thrust to the general stage image. At the end of the act, all the characters except Bérenger leave so that in effect he remains isolated. Instead of feeling refreshed and given a new view on life, he is quite upset and drinks brandy to escape reality. For him the center of socializing influences has changed into a place of isolation.

Emphasizing verticality, Ionesco moves the scenic image from ground level into the upper regions suggestive of abstract activities as in **Le Piéton de L'air** or **Les Chaises.**[10] The setting is the second-floor legal printing offices of M. Papillon, an obvious ironical focus of order, logic, rationality as the repository of mankind's rules for governing. Again there is a series of intrusions and invasions. The impact of the rhinoceros is felt through the highly disorganized and often irrational discussion taking place about the cause and nature of the happening. Bérenger's coming to work late revives the disordered argument. Other intrusions follow: Madame Boeuf comes with mistruths; a trumpeting rhinoceros is heard; and the stairs collapse.

With the destruction of the stairs, the major physical link between this center of rationality and the outside lower world has been removed. But the exterior ground world, rapidly being inhabited by giant animals, has ceased to have any positive correlation with the inner models Bérenger has of his known world. The public, social area has turned into a center of animality removed from the power of rationality to invest it with meaning. There is apparently no escape for these characters from the centers of rationality except through some other rational model such as a metaphor (an ironical, even satirical, escape). Thus with the aid of the firemen, the employees leave through the window, an ironical action suggesting metaphorically that they float out on their own line of sight. Their sanctuary of rationality and order has been turned into a trap, the first major visual image to suggest the play's dominant state of consciousness, the "sensation of being closed in" as in **Amédée.**[11]

The location of the action continues on the upper level for the remainder of the play, emphasizing its negative relationships to mental models and especially to personal, intimate space. The last scene of act 2 focuses on Jean's apartment; all of act 3 occurs in Bérenger's place. What is important spatially is that in Jean's home there are two centers of action, the bedroom where Jean talks with Bérenger and the bathroom where he becomes a rhinoceros. In the sequence developed through these two areas, the thrust of the action is horizontal in a to-and-fro manner, reflecting the rhythm of the first act. Paul Vernois suggests encirclement.[12] Jean goes back and forth between the two rooms, each time becoming more rhinoceros-like. Thus, in his home, supposed to have a stabilizing effect through its associations with logic and rationality, Jean metamorphoses into a rhinoceros.

From this area of metamorphosis which has trapped Jean, as though rationality and logic are the real enemy from which mankind cannot flee, Bérenger has no immediate escape. At each of the exits, doors and window, he sees only the huge animals. Finally he throws himself against the back wall, as though to deny physical reality, and as it crashes down, flees from the horror of a home that has failed its inhabitant. Beyond a logical reality, the scene is surrealistic. Ionesco does not explain how Bérenger keeps from falling down to ground level.

In exploring his idea of encirclement, Paul Vernois provides a valuable comment in understanding what has happened to Jean and Bérenger:

> À l'encerclement par la matière répond l'encerclement par l'idéologie dans ***Rhinocéros***. . . . Bien vite les occupants, de moins en moins nombreux, vont comprendre leur situation critique car les rhinocéros qui se sont rendus maîtres de la ville vont tout envahir. . . . Les têtes des rhinocéros encombreront non seulement la coulisse, mais les fenêtres, côté cour et côté jardin et la fosse d'orchestre. La salle sera malicieusement assimilée au troupeau d'animaux et de ce fait l'encerclement du plateau deviendra complet et provocant.[13]

> [The encircling by the ideology in ***Rhinocéros*** corresponds to the encircling by the material. . . . Quite quickly the inhabitants, less and less numerous, will understand their critical situation because the rhinoceroses which have made themselves masters of the city are going to spread everywhere. . . . The heads of the rhinoceroses will congest not only the wings, but the windows, the court side and the garden side and the orchestra pit. The room will be slyly likened to a herd of animals and for that reason the encirclement of the stage will become complete and provocative.]

The major focus, however, has always been on Bérenger, the center of disorder, feeling, irrationality, and nostalgia. As all places identified with the power of the mind to impose order have become areas of animality, Ionesco shows that Bérenger's home, which is supposed to help him keep his human shape and identity, no longer functions as an emotionally unifying source.[14] Despite intrusions from the lower world—rhinoceros's sounds, Dudard, and Daisy—Bérenger remains isolated, as at the end of act 1, in the midst of what cannot restore him to harmonious feelings and from which he cannot escape. He is like a fixture in the human past, trapped in an intimate space without even a surrealistic exit and isolated from physical reality by a matrix of fear.

Indeed the play seems to show that the basic models of man's rationality have failed to give Bérenger meaning. All that is left is the irrational dream. Pictures of old men and a huge worm have become ugly in contrast to all the beautiful rhinoceroses' heads lining the walls, door, and footlights. His room has become a gallery. Uncertain of himself and his human condition, he finds the rhinoceroses beautiful, dull green colors wonderful, and their song charming. The characteristics that define the human condition seem meaningless. Smooth brows are now ugly.

Fixed conceptually in time and space and artistically in the play, he alone represents immobility and loss of relationships (an ambivalent stubbornness of the human will?), becoming, as he says, "un monstre" (117) [a monster]. G. Richard Danner finds little in Bérenger's life "worth defending."[15] Ironically the only way Bérenger can resist rhinoceritis is by denying a fundamental characteristic of life, the ability to change and adapt. His behavior illustrates the dilemma of modern man, who is often blinded to the pattern of life by his species's centeredness. While on one level he clearly represents the solitary individual who resists the power of political movements, on another level the events of the play suggest that rational as well as emotional and intuitive models of reality are just that, models. Before the Pirandellian flux and irrationality of life, such models during crisis periods offer little help and direction to human beings. G. Richard Danner suggests that rhinoceritis is "an alternate life-style well worth trying."[16]

The irrationality of life and its chaotic power seem also to be the theme of *Le Roi se meurt*.[17] But in this play, instead of establishing a physical symbol like the oneiric house to stand in a harmonizing relationship with King Bérenger, Ionesco has created a cluster of metaphors and spiraling movements which seem to constrict and delimit King Bérenger until he is squeezed into nothingness. Mary A. Witt finds this play has the quality of imprisonment suggested by its language, revealing the "eventual closing of doors around the king."[18] For Paul Vernois, the central characteristic is reflected in a circle image:

> Cette impression angoissante de cercle qui se referme commande la dramaturgie du ***Roi se Meurt*** où l'on retrouve à tout instant l'image obsédante de la peau de chagrin. Sans doute le royaume rapetisse de jour en jour comme l'entourage des familiers du roi, mais il y a plus grave: le domane qu'embrassent les sens du mourant rétrécit lui aussi.[19]

> [This distressing impression of a circle which closes again orders the dramaturgy of *Le Roi se Meurt* where one rediscovers at the same instant the haunting image of the wild animal's skin that expands or contracts according to passion expended. Without a doubt the kingdom shrinks from day to day like the king's intimate entourage, but there is something more serious: the domain which feels the senses of dying shrinks also.]

At the most obvious level, the metaphor is theatrical space and time, that is, King Bérenger's world is the play in which he appears as a character. Because the entire play takes only an hour and a half to produce, Marguerite says to Bérenger, "Tu vas mourir dans une heure et demie, tu vas mourir à la fin du spectacle" (22). [You are going to die in a hour and a half, you are going to die at the end of the play.] Every event in Bérenger's kingdom has a cyclical external life limited by this fact (as though Life is limited by Art), to be repeated at every performance. While the play is an abstract fictive work, having been written and printed, it has also become a part of the physical world to be experienced. Thus it has a line of action carefully programmed for the activities of its characters and other elements, like a map providing the exact coordinates for the lineal and temporal progress of a journey. Marguerite even says that Bérenger is like a man on a journey. Nor can this plot or journey be reversed. It runs with its own entropy downward in one direction to the fall of the curtain, its theatrical end. As if to emphasize this point, Ionesco has Marguerite say that "Elle est irréversible" (11) [It is irreversible].

Embedded within this old theatrical metaphor that all the world's a stage is the metaphor that the King is the universe; the universe is the King. Because the movement is from a general to a more specific metaphor, the action of the play starts to spiral down and inward. He apparently has had the power of gods in whom all things reside and take their being. He has been able to command the sun, to cause trees to germinate, to make rain fall and thunderbolts to occur. He even has the power to decide when he wants to die, providing that he has the time and can make up his mind. King Bérenger and the universe form a closed system limited, however, by the duration of the primary metaphor, the play's production. But he is aging rapidly and losing power; his universe has clouded over, has cracks in the walls, and its mountains are sinking.

Indeed everything is quickly shrinking to a third metaphorical level wherein the King is the state and the state the King, all implying that the state of the King is that of his country. In this metaphorical relationship his palace is falling down, his country's boundaries are diminishing, and his people are aging. Even his army, like his guard, cannot move. His crown drops off, his scepter falls down, and the law for the first time seems to limit him. Everywhere one looks, the sources of life and experience are losing their vitality.

The action now moves to a fourth metaphor: Bérenger presented as an ordinary person with memories, loves, and other personal relationships, qualities needed to help him stand and be himself. As his desire for Marie rapidly weakens, his recollections fade. In the midst of these delimiting events a minor vertical pattern temporarily emerges: when Bérenger stands there is a sense of life, and when he falls there is a suggestion of death. But like the other concepts and feelings, love finally goes as Marie vanishes. All the other people continue to disappear until only Bérenger and Marguerite are left. Perhaps she is the last to remain because she is the projection of his power of habit or will-to-be, which has provided heretofore a core of meaning for Bérenger, like the stubborn resistance of Bérenger in *Rhinocéros*. But she goes too. Everything now collapses into the final center of nothingness as even Bérenger and his throne disappear, leaving only a "lumière grise" (74) [gray light] in the neutral space of the stage.

The metaphorical movement in the play is downward with a simultaneous inward horizontal thrust. Both of these suggest that the playing area is a crossing where some quality of mankind's perceptions of reality stops. Thus King Bérenger enters and immediately leaves, his action capturing the essence of the play. Before long all the characters cross the audience's visual and aural fields and

exit. Then the play settles down and Ionesco allows us to see the spiraling collapse of this theatrical metaphor. Nancy Lane says that the play "presents collaboration between character and environment in its most extreme form," finding "no boundaries separating 'monde interieur' from 'monde exterieur' in King Bérenger's solipsistic world."[20] All the time, however, Ionesco keeps us aware that the entire play as a dramatic construction is set within the real world of the audience and that the mysterious "they" which Bérenger insists had promised him that he could choose the time when he would die is, in the audience's world, Ionesco the playwright and the audience. If they like the play, it will repeat itself in every performance; if they do not, it will die on the boards.

While the metaphorical movement in *Le Roi se meurt* is a descending spiral, the dynamics of *Le Piéton de l'air* shifts from horizontal to dominant vertical scenic images with an overpowering sense of enclosure. It is as though Ionesco creates a landscape suggestive of a container from which there is no exit for its dramatis personae, just as an element of a painting cannot escape from its frame, or a character in a novel from its pages (both forms of art being, like language, ways to fix and delimit events). In this play Mary A. Witt finds a concentration on the open space image related to the "dream of transcending human limits," the latter being expressed metaphorically as a flight that "follows a kind of curve." But because "the experiment with liberation has failed . . . Bérenger remains as if dangling between finitude and infinity."[21] On the other hand Paul Vernois sees the play's quality as a spiral:

> *Le Piéton de l'Air* matérialise sur scène l'hélice géométrique d'une façon spectaculaire si l'on s'en rapporte à la disposition des praticables décrite par l'auteur dans son texte de l'édition Gallimard. . . . Si le mouvement hélicoidal est un jeu scénique de cirque, il peut prendre la forme beaucoup plus angoissante d'un maelström, d'un tourbillon, c'est-à-dire d'une spirale dans l'espace qui engendre vertige et désarroi.[22]
>
> [*Le Piéton de l'Air* objectifies on stage the geometrical spiral in a spectacular manner if one relies on the arrangement of the moveable stage props described by the author in his text from the Gallimard edition. . . . If the helical movement is a scenic circus game, it can take the more distressing form of a maelstrom, of a whirlwind, that is to say of a spiral space which creates vertigo and confusion.]

The scenic image presents an artistic stereotype of spring, one probably based on Ionesco's memories of his transcendental childhood experiences.[23] But it is also an abstract utopia-like world whose surrealism is constantly emphasized through the sudden appearance of flowers, a ladder, John Bull, dead people, a German war bomber, and a visitor from an anti-world. What we see, instead of the traditional form of a play, is Ionesco's dramatic model of a fictive reality with its own qualities and laws; it is not a reflection or a map of the spectator's reality in any one to one sense.

The quality that is finally achieved, or the statement the play seems to make, is that the spatial condition seen on the stage is a trap. Life itself is a dead end. But the limits which define the cul-de-sac are not part of the scene. As with a framed picture, the inhabitants cannot escape the confines of the art form. The act of inclusion restricts the definition of life and its qualities. Even though Bérenger can fly, he cannot soar out of the scenic image.

The spatial sense of the plot as a container that traps rather than unifies is closely associated with verticality. Seeing nothing but walls around her, the First Lady feels like a prisoner. When the visitor from the anti-world appears, Bérenger explains that it is as if the man had fallen from the blue, "est passé du l'autre côté du mur" (145) [has passed to the other side of the wall]. The image becomes obvious when Bérenger says that the cosmos is "une sorte de boîte" (152) [a kind of box] and that when he flies he reaches the ridge of a "toit invisible" (196) [invisible roof]. The scenic image depresses and delimits the self instead of restoring it to harmonious relationships; nor does it present an account of reality. Indeed, as we have seen in the other plays, reality for Ionesco cannot be grasped either by fictional, that is artistic, models or by other paradigms of the conscious mind.

Not even language can reveal reality. Rather, as Loren Eiseley has noted, "language implies boundaries." Through language man "has created an unnatural world of his own, which he calls the cultural world, and in which he feels at home. It defines his needs and allows him to lay a small immobilizing spell upon the nearer portions of his universe." But "it transforms that universe into a cosmic prison house which is no sooner mapped than man feels its inadequacy and his own."[24] In effect what Bérenger seems to be implying in the interview with the journalist, when he says that literature cannot account fully for reality, is that his mental models have no correspondence with reality, are no longer positive unifying forms like the oneiric house poised between reality and the world of the mind able to fix memories and dreams into a satisfying whole.

After the interview scene Ionesco subtly changes the scenic image to suggest a model of the brain's memory and thought. Dead and fictional characters appear and behave like real people. Madame Joséphine is surprised to learn that her father is as young looking as he was at twenty-five. The entire sequence represents an intrusive and ironic projection of Joséphine's memory and thoughts which, instead of creating harmonizing relationships, can only continue to fragment meaning. The quality repeatedly revealed through these scenic images is that everything is a terrible trap: setting, characters, language, thought, memory. Even the sounds of music seem to come from "les sirènes" (141) [the sirens].

Having established the visual and aural impression of an overpowering enclosure, Ionesco presents a different sensory cluster. A visitor from the anti-world appears and a flowered column rises. The new scenic image suggests that this sequence occurs at the boundary between two worlds of abstraction: the play which is a form of art consciously visualized and the anti-world, a form of the Ideal not consciously seen but which the mind wishes could transcend rational limitations. Rosette C. Lamont has much the same interpretation in her view that "Bérenger's apocalyptic vision reveals that the green meadow of Gloucestershire provides a kind of truce between the uncreated void and Non-Being."[25] While elements from the anti-world can appear in both universes, the inhabitants of the world of the landscape play cannot leave theirs. Because their world is a metaphorical conception, it can only fragment them.

With this much established, Ionesco begins the dominant vertical images. Bérenger says that he feels "si léger" (155) [so light]. Other things occur to suggest that the anti-world has some effect on Bérenger's universe. A bridge appears, and time seems to Bérenger as if the years were empty sacks. Amidst this fusion of time and entrapment, Bérenger loses corporality and floats or flies away. He is able to move into the far reaches of the sky paralleling metaphorically those of the imagination. As he explains, to fly is to recover an innate but long lost ability. But he cannot ascend to a harmonizing center able to integrate experience for him, despite his transcendental efforts to unify space and time.

The confining characteristic of the play, which suggests that the processes of the brain, its concepts, memories, and dreams are cul-de-sacs, is now more clearly determined by the scenic images. Joséphine says that her friends are "des objects vides dans le désert . . . enfermés dans leur carapace" (180) [empty objects in the desert . . . enclosed in their shell]. She herself feels "minuscule dans ce monde énorme" (180) [tiny in this enormous world]. John Bull appears as a fat man chasing a little boy who does not want to be put back in his cell, and a hangman dressed in white appears with a gibbet. Everything seems to reflect metaphorically the nothingness of the mind that, box-like, encloses one. To reinforce this effect, Ionesco has the stage darken as though it too were a container. Then it is filled with "lueurs rouges et sanglantes; grands bruits de tonnerre ou de bombardements" (190) [red and bloody flashes; loud noises of thunder or of shellings]. As the voice of the descending Bérenger is heard, stage, lighting, and sounds theatrically reflect the delimiting aspects of man's imagination.

Such scenic images reveal the loss of home and other basic concepts which relate man harmoniously to reality.[26] Berenger's description of what he saw on his flight is like a series of details from a Hieronymous Bosch painting, filled with overlapping and inconsistent naturalized images causing fear: "des hommes qui avaient des têtes d'oies," "des hommes qui léchaient les culs des guenons, buvaient la pisse des truies," "des colonnes de guillotinés marchant sans têtes," and "des sauterelles géantes, des anges déchus, des archanges vaincus" (195) [some men who had heads of geese, some who licked the asses of monkeys, drank the piss of sows, several columns of guillotined people marching without heads, some giant grasshoppers, some fallen angels, some defeated archangels]. None of these images acts as a model of reality with any unifying and restorative power. Instead they create further impressions of the delimitation of life and the threat of being confronted by a continual enclosing process. For example, Bérenger says that he reached "l'arête du toit invisible . . . où se rejoignent l'espace et le temps" [ridge of the invisible roof . . . where space and time are joined together] and gives a prophetic vision of the destruction of everything, of infinite pits and millions of universes "qui s'évanouissent" (196-7) [which vanish]. His description suggests that the concept of space as a product of the mind has limits or boundaries that can be touched but not penetrated.

The movement of the play has been affected by the horizontal and vertical qualities in the scenic images, which have emphasized the nature of the limitations implicit in the mind's concepts. Although Ionesco places his dramatic projections and images at the boundary between the outer and inner worlds as Pinter did in *No Man's Land,* he suggests that ideas have lost their harmonizing and imaginative power to fix memory, dream, and experience into a satisfying whole. In one sense Ionesco has developed his Bérenger plays through a dialectic of images to communicate more vividly than words his feeling for man's inability to escape the concepts which the brain by necessity has to create and which often turn out to be alienating or fragmenting models of reality. Thus the oneiric home and its related representations of thought have lost their humanistic function in Ionesco's plays and remain as part of his personal nostalgic investment in his boyhood past.

For Ionesco the mind apparently creates its own worlds, transcends them, and then annihilates everything, reducing thought to an empty neutral grey. Yet ironically the Bérenger plays, as plays *per se,* artistic products of Ionesco's mind, tend to deny the conclusion that all thought is reductive or that Ionesco preaches a personal form of nihilism, as Kenneth Tynan fears.[27] As dramas they survive for others to discuss and provide subtle ideological models which tend to act as limited oneiric forms for Ionesco. They enable him to externalize his thoughts and feelings. Clearly they are not mental traps for him, as literature seems to be for Bérenger. Instead they offer the possibility that Ionesco's stage has its own concrete language and that the dramatic world of his plays is its own organization, a thing as separate from those who occupy it as it is from being a map of physical reality. Indeed, for Ionesco the play appears to replace the oneiric house.

Notes

1. Anne Ubersfeld, *Lire Le Théâtre* (Paris: Éditions Sociales, 1977) 170. See also the following: Robert L. Tener, " 'These Places, This Private Landscape': First Suggestions for a Topological Approach to Ionesco's Bérenger Plays," *Papers on Language and Literature* 13 (1977): 391-400; Paul Vernois, *La Dynamique Théâtrale D'Eugène Ionesco* (Paris: Éditions Klincksieck, 1972) 5, 26-8; Mary A. Witt, "Eugène Ionesco and the Dialectic of Space," *Modern Language Quarterly* 33 (1972): 312-26; Eugène Ionesco, *Présent passé Passé présent* (Paris: Mercure de France, 1968) 43-4, 80-1, 210-11. For an excellent discussion of space and drama see the following: Etienne Souriau, "Le Cube et La Sphere," *Architecture et Dramaturgie,* ed. Ernest Flammarion (Paris: Bibliotheque D'Esthetique, 1950) 63-83; Yi-Fu Yuan, *Space and Place: The Perspective of Experience* (Minneapolis: U of Minnesota P, 1977); Diana Agrest, "Design versus Non-Design," *Oppositions* 6 (Fall 1976): 45-68. Note: I am responsible for all translations.

2. Nancy Lane, "Human/Non-human Relationship in Ionesco's Theatre: Conflict and Collaboration," *Kentucky Romance Quarterly* 30.3 (1983): 240-41. For further comments on this idea see the following: Rosette C. Lamont, "Air and Matter: Ionesco's 'Le Piéton de l'air' and 'Victimes du devoir,' " *French Review* 38.3 (1965): 349-61; Eugène Ionesco, "Experience du théâtre," *Le Nouvelle Revue Française* 62 (1958): 247-70. In "Experience du théâtre," Ionesco says 'Le théâtre est autant visuel qu'auditif. Il n'est pas une suite d'images, comme le cinéma, mais une construction, une architecture mouvante d'images scénique. . . . Il est donc non seulment permis, mais recommandé de faire jouer les accessoires, vivre les objects, d'animer les décors, de concrétiser les symboles" (262). [The theater is as much visual as auditory. It is not a sequence of images, like the cinema, but an edifice, a moving architecture of scenic images. . . . It is then not only permissible, but adviseable to set the properties into action, to cause things to come alive, to animate the scenery, to make the symbols concrete.]

3. George Matoré, *L'Espace Humain,* Sciences et Techniques humanies 2 (Paris: La Colombe, 1962) 210.

4. Vernois 60. His comment applies to the plays between 1952 and 1959.

5. Lane 241-42.

6. All references to *Tueur sans gages* are from Eugène Ionesco, *Théâtre* (Paris: Éditions Gallimard, 1958) 2: 59-172, and are cited parenthetically by page number in the text.

7. Lane 243-44.

8. All references to *Rhinocéros* are from Eugène Ionesco, *Théâtre* (Paris: Éditions Gallimard, 1963) 3: 7-117, and are cited parenthetically by page number in the text. See also Vernois 60.

9. Vernois 65.

10. All references to *Le Piéton de l'air* are from Eugène Ionesco, *Théâtre* (Paris: Éditions Gallimard, 1963) 3:119-98, and are cited parenthetically by page number in the text.

11. Witt 312.

12. Vernois 79.

13. Vernois 79-80.

14. In her discussion of Ionesco's use of space, Mary A. Witt says that "imprisonment is both a personal experience and a universal situation" and suggests it is the quality of the petty bourgeois living room for Ionesco (313).

15. G. Richard Danner, "Bérenger's Dubious Defense of Humanity in *Rhinocéros*," *French Review* 53.2 (1979): 210.

16. Danner 213.

17. All references to *Le Roi se meurt* are from Eugène Ionesco, *Théâtre* (Paris: Éditions Gallimard, 1963) 4: 7-74, and are cited parenthetically by page number in the text.

18. Witt 317.

19. Vernois 80.

20. Lane 246-47.

21. Witt 320.

22. Vernois 96-7.

23. See Ionesco, *Présent passé Passé présent* 35-6, 218-19, 269-70.

24. Loren Eiseley, *The Invisible Pyramid* (New York: Scribners, 1970) 31-32.

25. Lamont 358.

26. See Pat Burnett, "Behavior Geography and the Philosophy of Mind," *Spatial Choice and Spatial Behavior*, ed. Reginald G. Golledge and Gerard Rushton (Columbus: Ohio State UP, 1976) 25. Burnett indicates that it is generally "held that human beings employ mental models of the world to organize their spatial behavior, that is, 'the mind mediates between the environment and behavior in it.'" Ionesco has interesting ideas about this in *Notes et contre-notes* (Paris: Éditions Gallimard, 1962) 32, 33, 85.

27. Kenneth Tynan, "Ionesco: homme du destin?," in Eugène Ionesco, *Notes et contre-notes* 70-71.

Rosette C. Lamont (essay date 1993)

SOURCE: "Ionescoland " in *Ionesco's Imperatives: The Politics of Culture*, University of Michigan Press, 1993, pp. 13-20.

[*In the following essay, an earlier version of which appeared in her volume,* Ionesco: A Collection of Critical Essays *published by Prentice Hall in 1973, Lamont explores the bizarre world of Ionesco's dramas, where the protagonists are in search of perfection as they live in dreariness; where objects seem to be endowed with independent existence; where a feeling of heaviness hangs over people; where relief from drudgery is usually fleeting; where the absurdities of existence are expressed in a dislocated language of clichés; and which looks familiar but is disturbingly other and leaves visitors feeling stimulated and estranged.*]

Marcel Proust once stated that every artist is the citizen of a foreign country whose topography, moral landscape, climate, and customs he or she interprets in his or her works. This land, governed by its own laws, exists within each artist as his or her private universe.

Eugène Ionesco takes Proust's assertion a step further when he claims that every writer creates an autonomous world parallel to the one we believe is "real." For Ionesco, the writer must not hold a mirror up to nature, as nineteenth-century realists proclaimed, but represent the life of those who inhabit the space on the other side of the looking glass. Yet, Ionesco considers himself a modern realist since the suprareality he crystallizes on the stage is a complete kind of reality that comprises both the conscious and the subconscious worlds.

How do we, readers and viewers of his plays, approach this bizarre world? Proust might have advised us to become travelers, open-minded tourists. Certainly we must be ready to wander and wonder, to proceed like people who enter an unfamiliar house. We go from room to room, floor to floor, often in the dark. Gradually, we discover where the hallway leads, what lies behind each door. If the house is sensibly constructed, the novelty of its architecture shall not prevent us from dwelling in this habitation. In fact, its peculiar charm will grow on us, make us feel that this intriguing house is a home.

If, like Lewis Carroll's Alice, we step through the looking glass into Ionescoland, we will find a gray, muddy soil, an overcast sky. Everywhere there are fissures in the ground, treacherous crevices, holes that open upon the void. Marshes await the unwary traveler. Occasionally, one happens upon an isolated village, one of those untouched rural communities bypassed by so-called technological progress. There, the daily round of activities is dictated by traditional occupations: farming, cooking, religious holidays. These rare outposts are oases in the wasteland, mirages, places out of time, crystallizations of things past.

More often than not, Ionesco's characters are city dwellers. They inhabit basement apartments that slowly sink into the slimy soil beneath. Rain falls steadily with no sun breaking through the low clouds. And, in the winter, the snow turns sooty. However, once in a while, an amazing illumination occurs, an epiphany: a wall of one of these dank lodgings grows transparent, revealing a hidden garden. The flowers, shining brightly in the grass like scattered precious stones, the single tree at the center, are magical. But, like those of the Cluny tapestry depicting the Unicorn and the Maid, these mystical apparitions are doomed to fade.

Haunted by this momentary lifting of the veil, Ionesco's protagonists set out in search of perfection. Sometimes, after climbing to great heights, they catch a glimpse of a dazzling sky, its unblemished azure teasingly out of reach. At other times, the wanderer reaches an orderly city neighborhood, a technological paradise. The light created by the engineer of this utopia is reminiscent of the glow experienced on the solitary heights, yet there is nothing spiritual about it; it is an ersatz, machine-controlled illumination. This urban marvel may be free of the vagaries of climatic alterations but not of evil, crime, and death. In fact, it is in these very places that killers tend to go on a rampage, as though this perfect setting elicits the surfacing of the monsters of the subconscious. In Ionescoland, the utopian dream is synonymous with dehumanization. Like Dostoyevsky's jaundiced "underground man," Ionesco harbors a strong dislike of Crystal Palaces.

The citizens of Ionescoland tend to be middle-aged, or even very old. Their careworn faces are deeply lined; their hair is the gray of the sooty snow covering the pavement of city sidewalks. More often than not, couples are childless, staying together out of habit, or an anguished, tender pity for their life companions. The wives slowly become mothers of their childlike husbands. Together they wait for death that comes inexorably, entrapping and crushing them. In the meantime, they huddle in tiny rooms crowded with heavy pieces of furniture. Outside these paltry havens there is nothing but silence and darkness.

In this peculiar country people are objects, while things seem endowed with a kind of independent existence, a will of their own. Mushrooms proliferate on the floor of a damp room under the growing legs of a corpse who has mysteriously taken over the couple's bedroom, and the conjugal bed. The rhythm of disaster is marked by the hysteria of matter. Objects multiply, like the cells of a cancerous growth, overwhelming, entombing the frantic protagonists: empty chairs carried in at a dizzying pace by the Old Woman *(The Chairs),* who must keep up with the delirious expansion of the imaginings she and her husband share; pieces of furniture piling up to form a kind of Egyptian pyramid around "the new tenant" trapped by his possessions; coffee cups brought in at breakneck speed by the over-hospitable wife of a man cross-examined in his own home by an unexpected detective *(Victims of Duty);* monstrous eggs hatched by a young husband who watches with amazement a progeny of things and people, chaotic matter doomed by future wars to become a mass of scrambled eggs *(The Future Is in Eggs).* Thus, we are made to witness the triumph of a brutal technology crowned by the looming of the atomic mushroom.

According to Ionesco, the Enlightenment's vision of limitless progress was a dangerous illusion. He recognizes within himself two fundamental states of consciousness that make up the polar principles of a personal dialectic: a feeling of heaviness due to the oppressive presence of matter, and a sense of airiness, lightness, freedom. The drudgery of daily existence weighs upon human beings, plunging them into opaque, viscous matter. At rare moments of grace everything seems easy, light, transparent. When this occurs, Ionesco's protagonist experiences a miraculous recovery of the state of childhood. The dazzling glow he espies is not of this world; it is similar to the light into which Dante, led by Beatrice, ascends when

they scale the sublime region of Paradise. Most of the time, however, Ionescoland is overcast by the somber shadows that characterize our all too solid and sullied world.

There are some avenues of escape. The protagonist might discover that he possesses the wondrous gift of levitation. Bursts of optimism propel him upward to the level of tree tops, then still higher, into the galaxy. Encapsulated in his longing for freedom, this self-sufficient astronaut, whose envelope of flesh is his only flying machine, is able to explore space by walking through the skies around the planet earth. The character's short triumph, however, proves illusory since, as he looks down upon the universe, he sees hellish regions where biological life cannot endure. How does one continue living with such dreadful knowledge? Ionesco believes that laughter, a sense of humor—the distinguishing human characteristic—may tame anguish. Wit and lucidity are powerful weapons in the struggle against all-devouring time, power-hungry tyrants, and even the forces of our subconscious. In the hands of an artist and a poet, wit becomes a rapier, humor a shield.

Ionescoland rises from the moist, intimate, sexual substratum, the watery principle associated with the female. It is a difficult birth. Once expelled from the visceral crib of the womb in which humans would like to linger, the inhabitants of Ionesco's country dream of escaping to ethereal regions. However, they are unable to forget that they issued from the depths. Descent is the attraction of the abyss, a longing to be unborn, uncreated, a desire for annihilation. The opposite dream of flight, of a positive escape, is associated, as Gaston Bachelard points out in *L'Air et les songes,* with a philosophy of the will. Therefore, the protagonists of Ionesco's plays are driven simultaneously in two polar directions, attracted to God and Satan at once. This is what Baudelaire calls in one of his essays "the simultaneous pull" downward and upward.

Ionesco was deeply influenced by Baudelaire's fundamental duality. The future playwright, who returned to France from Romania on the eve of World War II, owed his escape from fascism to a fellowship granted him for a projected doctoral dissertation on Baudelaire's treatment of the theme of death. Both in Ionesco's plays and in his private journals one hears echoes from the nineteenth-century poet's ironic, unfinished, moral autobiography, *My Heart Laid Bare.* Baudelaire and Ionesco are equally aware of the ascensional/descensional human impulse. Although double-edged, it stems from the psychic need of transcendence. One of Baudelaire's finest prose poems bears the English title "Anywhere Out of this World." The text presents a speaker and a listener. The first offers his friend various remote places where he might find peace of mind and discover amazing sights. The second does not react in any fashion to these suggestions, until, at the very end, he bursts out with the desperate, bitter exclamation: "Anywhere out of this world." Ionesco's antiheroes share this sentiment.

Ionesco is a poet of the four elements, a cosmic visionary. For him, as for many of the poets he admires, earth is the most alien of the four elements, a place of exile. Below the thin crust of our globe burns the fire that threatens to consume the universe. Fire, air, and water haunt the poet-dramatist's imagination while he must sojourn on this earth.

Fire is intimately tied to an apocalyptic vision. In **The Bald Soprano,** a universal fire is prophesied by the maid. In fact, she recites a comic poem announcing the end of the world; it is written in honor of her lover, the Fire Chief. At the end of **Killing Game** flames spread through the plague-ridden city, destroying those few people spared by the epidemic that ravaged the community. Although this tragicomedy follows closely Daniel Defoe's *A Journal of the Plague Year,* culminating in events that evoke the great fire of London, the conflagration engulfing the unnamed city acquires cosmic dimensions since the flames spread from town to country, engulfing the entire planet.

Fire in Ionescoland is akin to the unearthly illumination that breaks into the life of the mystics that the dramatist studied and continues to read: St. John of the Cross, the Neoplatonists, Plotinus, the Hesychasts, the Hassidic story tellers. In his first published volume of memoirs, *Fragments of a Journal,* Ionesco tells the following story culled from Martin Buber's *Tales of the Hassidim:* "Rabbi Dov Baer, the maggid of Mezritch, once begged Heaven to show him a man whose every limb and every fibre was holy. Then they showed him the form of the Baal Shem Tov, and it was all fire. There was no shred of substance in it. It was nothing but flame."[1]

In his essay "Eugène Ionesco and 'La Nostalgie du Paradis,' "[2] Mircea Eliade detects an influence on the dramatist of the Byzantine mystics. Eliade explains that like many Romanian writers of his generation Ionesco was attracted by the Byzantine spirituality of the Eastern Orthodox tradition. In the Balkans, as in Russia, there has always been a pull in two geographic and cultural directions: the West, particularly French culture, and the Orient. Ionesco attempts to fuse the philosophies of East and West, but his aversion to Cartesianism, to classical logic, reinforces the mystical influences of Buddhism, Neoplatonism, and Gnosticism.

Ionescoland may be a kind of no man's land because it is situated at the crossroads of various cultures. It is a place where people of the most varied backgrounds live side by side, where one expects to hear seven or eight languages, or perhaps a composite tongue made up of all of these. "I'm just a peasant from the Danube!" Ionesco likes to quip. He comes from a part of Europe where there are Turks, Sephardic Jews (what's left of them), Greeks, Albanians, Armenians, Gypsies. Ionesco, a French Romanian, is what the American painter R. B. Kitaj calls, when describing himself, "a Diasporist." As such, he is a man with a hundred eyes, half of them behind his head.

What the eyes see the tongue must express. For Ionesco, the absurdity of being can still be put into words, although language itself has become fractured, and discourse deconstructed. Ionesco claims that he writes and speaks in order to find out what he thinks. Perhaps because the dramatist divided the first part of his life between France and Romania, he never took either one of his two native languages for granted. In fact, he harbors a tender feeling for his mother tongue, which was indeed his mother's tongue. The French he writes is characterized by classical purity, even when his word games betray his multilingualism, which brings him closer to James Joyce, and to a number of his contemporaries: Samuel Beckett, Arthur Adamov, Fernando Arrabal—an Irishman, a Russian, and a Spaniard, all writing in French. Like the prophet Abraham, they are "strangers and sojourners."

The language of Ionescoland is intentionally made up of clichés. Like proverbs, the latter reflect popular wisdom, but, as they pass from mouth to mouth, they lose their initial pungency. The trite expressions used and misused by the concierges and the petty bourgeois of Ionesco's plays weave an aural tapestry, the monotonous music of popular culture. The protagonists of the plays are surrounded by these flat utterances. Although they themselves do not use clichés, they are being used by them, manipulated by ambient platitudes. The subsidiary characters who come in contact with the protagonists are embodiments of hackneyed thoughts. Yet this language, "weary, stale, flat, and unprofitable,"[3] has nevertheless terrifying power. Events seem shaped by words. As Richard Schechner states: "Words are no longer the vehicles of thoughts and feelings; they are themselves actions—the initiators of dramatic events."[4]

In Ionescoland, linear discourse becomes dislocated. No inner logic governs the sequence of words; the rules of syntax have evaporated. Words float like bits of wreckage, coming together as though magnetized by sound alone. Signifier and signified fall apart, broken asunder. Some of these techniques stem from surrealist free association, but Ionesco's intentions are not playful. As Leo Spitzer demonstrated, neologisms may be rooted in the known, but they journey toward the new, the unknown, perhaps the unknowable.[5]

Ionesco intends to shake our faith in what lies behind the word, what is hidden at the core of so-called civilized discourse. He mounts a concerted attack on language because he intends to shake his reader, his audience, out of a natural propensity to lethargy, to the unquestioning acceptance of certain values or premises. The dramatist's fantastic isomorphisms, grotesque onomatopoeias, enumerations, numerologies, pseudo-Pythagorean calculations, mock-logical constructs and syllogisms constitute an intellectual circus act of great elegance and daring. It is a verbal walk on a tight rope stretched over the Void. As he peers down, he exclaims:

> What a flood of images, words, characters . . .
> symbolic figures, signs, all at the same time and meaning more or less the same thing, though never exactly the same, a chaotic jumble of messages that I may

perhaps in the end understand but which tells me no more about the fundamental problem: what is this world?[6]

Ionesco created Ionescoland to question that "chaotic jumble." His "country" may look familiar at first, but it is actually teasingly, disturbingly *other*. The untranslatable French word the dramatist favors is *insolite* (the dictionary offers the translation *unwonted*). What Ionesco means to suggest is his desire to introduce the reader, or audience, into a strange universe, to create a positive, stimulating sense of estrangement. He wishes to lure us into his diasporic state by flipping open his refugee's suitcase full of trinkets from various epochs and cultures. Like Kitaj, this "man with bags" refuses to be caught in amber. In fact, he welcomes a creative misreading, for the gathering he envisions is that of the dispersed.

For Ionesco, the literary artist is the sum of his or her dreams, and of the expression these dreams are given in the work. By creating a new literary form, the writer attempts to race against time. For time will uncreate the artist since death is unavoidable; but, in the brief interim passage between birth and the ultimate dissolution, one is able to shape a world in one's own image. Thus, by degrees, the disappearing human being, Ionesco, becomes absorbed in his creation, Ionescoland.

Notes

1. Ionesco, *Fragments of a Journal,* trans. Jean Stewart (New York: Grove Press, 1969), 70.

2. Mircea Eliade, "Eugene Ionesco and 'La Nostalgie du Paradis,' " in *The Two Faces of Ionesco,* ed. Rosette C. Lamont and Melvin J. Friedman (Troy, NY: The Whitston Publishing Company, 1978), 22.

3. William Shakespeare, *Hamlet* (I.ii.133).

4. Richard Schechner, "*The Bald Soprano* and *The Lesson:* An Inquiry into Play Structure," in *Ionesco,* ed. Rosette C. Lamont (Englewood Cliffs, NJ: Prentice Hall, 1973), 25.

5. In his *Essays in Historical Semantics* (New York: S. F. Vanni, 1948), Spitzer states: "Not to deal with the meaning of learned words means simply to shy away from the whole semantic content of our civilization" (5).

6. Ionesco, *Fragments of a Journal,* 119.

Michael Holland (essay date 1996)

SOURCE: "Ionesco and Tradition," in *Nottingham French Studies,* Vol. 35, No 1, Spring 1996, pp. 53-66.

[*In the following essay, Holland argues that Ionesco, the radical innovator, restored Tradition to theater with his discovery of the inherent theatricality of language, as he moved away from the defeatist and fatalist attitudes of other modernists and brought theater back to the stage in the form of original work.*]

In a lecture given in Helsinki in 1959 and subsequently published under the title 'Discours sur l'avant-garde', Eugène Ionesco claims that his theatre originates in '[un] refus du traditionnalisme pour retrouver la tradition'[1] Because an original author seeks to say something radically new, he might appear, by virtue of his originality, to be in conflict with tradition. But according to Ionesco the opposite is in fact the case:

> dans la mesure où le poète a le sentiment que le language ne cerne plus le réel, n'exprime plus une vérité, son effort est justement de cerner ce réel, de le mieux exprimer, d'une façon plus violente, plus éloquente, plus nette, plus précise, plus adéquate. En cela il essaie de rejoindre, en la modernisant, une tradition vivante, qui s'est perdue.[2]

On the surface, it would seem difficult to apply Ionesco's words to his own career. Initially, he made his name through forcefully rejecting everything that was traditional about the theatre; then, once his name was established, he became associated with the sort of traditionalism that has become synonymous with political and social conservatism. What then is the 'tradition vivante' to which he refers?

Traditions abound, but there is only one Tradition. For a given age, it is the true legacy of the past. In the modern age, it became a dubious gift: a poisoned chalice. Rather than being enfolded comfortably in its mantle, an heir to Tradition was singled out and left alone to bear a burden that previous ages had failed to lighten: the burden of change. That burden had now become unbearable. Tradition turns time into history through the medium of changing forms. An age in history emerges when a change takes place in this relation to changing form. The age derives its historical identity and its character from the reflection on change to which it gives rise, and from the particular emotional attitude which accompanies that reflection. In a given age, to be a true traditionalist is thus not to be a guardian of inherited forms; it is to be aware of what Tradition truly signifies: the demand placed upon human beings by historical consciousness of time to change their relationship to change with time. Historically, the traditionalist is therefore always a potential revolutionary. In an article entitled 'Toujours sur l'avant-garde', published the year before his Helsinki lecture, Ionesco explicitly links tradition and revolution to a common attitude towards history:

> [l']expérience révolutionnaire de l'avant-garde [. . . apparaît nécessairement, pour ainsi dire d'elle-même, au moment où certains systèmes d'expression se sont fatigués, usés; lorsqu'ils se sont corrompus; lorsqu'ils se sont éloignés d'un modèle oublié. [. . . Et cette redécouverte, nécessitée par l'histoire artistique dans laquelle les modèles et les formes se sont détériorés—s'est faite grâce à un art, un *language* tirant sa source d'une réalité extra-historique.[3]

To be an heir to Tradition is thus to reflect historically on change from outside of history, constantly to scrutinise the changeability of change with reference to a timeless model of perfection, towards which changing form tends through time. But for the age into which Ionesco was born, this awareness of Tradition took the form of an anguished paralysis. Modernity was installed as an age of profound negativity, since it seemed that the only change that could henceforth be made to the way forms change was a stop to change. The modern age thus received Tradition as a sign of defeat. Hence the fatalism of its political and social 'traditionalists'. In art and culture, that defeat was experienced more acutely than in any other domain. At the same time, as in no other domain, defeat provided the conditions for a renewal and a continuation of what, as Tradition, seemed at an end, announcing a radical change of age (of epoch) whose threshold still remains to be crossed. If only *in passing,* Ionesco's theatre plays a significant role in this revival of Tradition.

The age whose inheritance Ionesco shares is a profoundly negative one because it is characterised by a generalised encounter with the limits of existing forms of expression. As Post-Romanticism declined into Decadence, writers found themselves confronted ever more insistently with the fact that there was nothing more to be said. What Mario Praz acknowledged to be the essence of Romanticism, name 'that which cannot be described',[4] came to the fore in the last years of the nineteenth century. If 'it is romantic to consider concrete expression as a decadence, a contamination',[5] by that stage the trappings of Romanticism had fallen away, leaving only a core of paralysed mutism. For Maupassant, 'tout est rengaine';[6] for Vallès, 'tout est copié'.[7] Huysmans describes in retrospect how the Naturalism he fled 'était condamné à se rabâcher, en piétinant sur place', so that it had become an 'impasse,' a 'cul-de-sac';[8] while the hero of Barrès's *Sous l'oeil des barbares* declares: 'Peu à peu, jour sombre, on se l'avoue: tout est dit, redit: aucune idée qu'il ne soit honteux d'exprimer (. . . rien ne vaut que par la forme du dire'.[9]

The discovery of the limits of existing form at the end of the nineteenth century is certainly the most powerful blow to Tradition there has ever been. Something had gone fundamentally wrong with the historical process of transmitting and receiving forms through time, something which exposed the very *movement* of Tradition to doubt. Tradition lives through change. Forms succeed forms, tending ever closer to a model of perfection. The artist of Tradition, plunged into history as he changes the forms he inherits from the past, also stands outside of history as he scrutinises the gradual fulfilment through formal change of a perfection which is neither past nor future, since it is beyond time. With the modern age, the harmony and balance of this process were definitively disrupted. In itself, the discovery that no more could be said was nothing new: it is an integral moment in Tradition considered as change to forms through time. What made it decisive was the resignation that accompanied it, the disillusioned lucidity expressed by Jacques Vaché when he wrote of 'l'inutilité théâtrale (et sans joie) de tout. *Quand on sait*'.[10] Yet such lucidity in its turn had always had its place in developing Tradition, as that scrutiny of change which is the mark of

the true traditionalist. If living forms had become 'uselessly theatrical', the *knowledge* that this was the case ought just as well to have been an insight that change must go on. Tradition has come to a halt yet forms remain imperfect. Since Tradition must continue, change must change.

Yet the process did come to a halt. Dissatisfaction with existing form became dissatisfaction with form itself. History therefore stopped, but stopped short. What Auerbach called the 'living historicity' of 'figure',[11] that productive difference between timeless model and historically changing form, collapsed and as it were died. The model had become debased. No difference existed any more between perfection and perfectibility. Form was simply form, and as such, inadequate. The lucidity with which the traditionalist had always scrutinised the process of change from without now became the disillusioned contemplation of a catastrophic sham. Meanwhile all the human energy invested, as desire, in the process of perfectibility which Tradition had inspired, deprived of an outlet, remained pent up yet uncontainable. Exiled from form, adrift in what Rimbaud called *l'informe,*[12] it had no way of externalising its own now radical changeability in the form of new modes of expression ('trouver une langue').

In short there occurred, in modernity, what may be termed a radical *polarisation* of experience in the domain of art and culture. Tradition had always required of the traditionalist that he be both inside and outside of history. Now, not only had that extra-historical perspective opened on to nothing (since form as such could no longer be discerned outside the limits of existing form); there was no longer any field of exercise within the domain of existing form for the passions and energies which provided the source of change. These too therefore found themselves somehow 'outside', as a pure excess of raw emotion, defined and characterised by nothing save its essential changeability. It is thus that the Subject of modernity found himself defined as an absolute 'outsider': his reason and his emotions thrust together in a stifling yet horizonless claustrum. This situation—a plenitude of lifeless form, outside of which, in a formless dimension of negative lucidity, emotion without object or direction expended its energy in a state of absolute instability—is, I would argue, the ultimate legacy of Western Tradition, handed down to the modern age and bringing History considered as progress and perfectibility to a halt. As such, it is therefore the end of Tradition. Though it is not possible to examine it further here, the polarised, paralysed stance into which it locks the modern Self underlies all artistic and cultural awareness from the later nineteenth century onwards. It presents an extraordinary combination of fixity and instability, out of which a whole range of responses to the limits of existing form emerged, from the backward-looking resignation of *l'art pour l'art* and its ultimate expression: Decadence, to the innovative search for a language of *l'informe* going from Rimbaud through to Dada. It is from within this stance that Ionesco emerges as an original writer for the theatre.

Ionesco's accounts of his outlook and experience prior to his turn to the theatre when he was nearing forty, mark him out unmistakably as a modernist. As early as 1941 he wrote:

> être libre, être hors de l'Histoire, ne pas être dans l'ordre du monde, ne pas être un instrument de l'orchestre ou une note de la symphonie. Ne pas être sur la scène. Tout voir et entendre de la salle. Comme hors de l'univers. Si on est sur la scène, si on fait partie de l'orchestre, nous n'entendons que le tumulte, nous ne saisissons que les dissonances.[13]

The stability provided here by the dualism of the theatre metaphor (*scène / salle*) will subsequently disappear from his retrospective accounts of the state he was in before he discovered the reality of theatre. Time and again he will emphasise the *instability* of the 'outside' to which he found himself exiled, once the paradise of childhood was left behind, and from which he would never escape. As he said to Claude Bonnefoy in 1966: 'toute réjouissance avait comme un trou à l'intérieur d'elle-même qui la dévorait'.[14] In 'L'auteur et ses problèmes' (1963) he writes:

> Tout à fait au fond du moi-même c'est la nuit que je trouve . . . la nuit, ou plutôt une lumière aveuglante.[15]

While later in his conversation with Bonnefoy he observes:

> Vous dites qu'il y a dans mon théâtre beaucoup de boue, d'enlisement. Cela correspond justement à l'un de mes deux états. Je me sens ou bien lourd ou bien léger. La légèreté c'est l'évanescence euphorique qui peut devenir tragique ou douloureuse quand il y a angoisse. Quand il n'y a pas angoisse, c'est la facilité d'être. (p. 41)

There is thus, Bonnefoy observes, a sort of incoherence or disequilibrium at the origin of Ionesco's theatre, to which Ionesco replies:

> Oui. A un moment donné les choses me paraissent claires. Je peux discourir plus facilement mais je n'écris pas. A d'autres moments, c'est comme s'il y avait un tremblement de terre dans mon microcosme, comme si tout s'effondrait, et c'est une sorte de nuit, ou plutôt un mélange de lumière et d'ombre, un monde chaotique. (p. 79)

It is between what he calls his 'deux états', made up of opposing visions and conflicting emotions, that he swung painfully and uncontrollably throughout his life. Excluded from the domain of forms, unable to write, his was an exemplary experience of the polarisation of existence which is the defining characteristic of all modernity. Until, that is, the theatre provided him with an equilibrium. To understand the complex nature of that equilibrium, which, it must be noted, does not enable Ionesco immediately to write, it is necessary to examine carefully the ways in which modernity sought to emerge from the crisis which defined it.

Ionesco was a latecomer to the modern condition. Well before he found himself the heir to a Tradition that had died, others had sought a way of disengaging culture from the impasse constituted by the paralysed, polarised stance which was the ultimate legacy handed down by Tradition. Extremes such as suicide (Vaché) or renunciation (Rimbaud) were less frequent than attempts at channeling the energies that had been deprived of an outlet in form, into a new temporal relation with form. Vallès's political activism, Barrès's nationalism, Huysmans' mysticism (and Péguy's choice of all three options) have in common the emotional and practical espousal of forms existing, or called on to exist, in an a-temporal present, either metaphysical or ideological. Their responses seek, each in its way, to convert the collapse of model into form which had expelled the present from History, into an attempt at *establishing* the model *in* the present, either metaphysically or ideologically, as form, and so redeeming History, harnessing the energy of human desire and reviving Tradition.

However, though these responses and others like them provide much of the history of modernity and its response to Tradition, the true heirs to what Tradition hands down to the modern age are neither those who simply succumbed to paralysis, nor those who sought to convert it into the paradox of active conservatism, but those who were willing to sustain the lucid insight into the changing nature of forms which is the mark of the true traditionalist. In revealing, at the end of the nineteenth century, that the changeability of forms was at an end, so that they could only endure or else decay, this insight imposed upon art and culture as never before a demand for *silence* in response to Tradition.

Music and painting, which are arts of silence from the standpoint of language, took the lead in searching for a way beyond the end to change of form. Paradoxically, their revolutions permitted the arts of language (in particular the novel) to hang back from making the move that they had made, by providing them with a *metaphor* for formal change which they would not themselves undergo until considerably later. For its part, however, theatre appeared incapable of change. As Ionesco wrote more than once, it remained squarely 'en retard': 'L'avant-garde a été stoppé au théâtre, sinon dans la littérature'.[16] Ionesco blames this rather cursorily on the wars and tyrannies that arose in the first half of the twentieth century. Frantisek Deak has recently offered a more probing sociological explanation, arguing that the decline in theatre can be attributed to a decline in the theatricality of social life, the replacement of court by street.[17] Given the unique social function of drama, a sociological interpretation of the crisis of theatre at this time is inevitable. Yet the apparent homology between *stage* and *world* should not encourage a simplified understanding of that crisis. Once theatre is drawn into the generalised collapse of form which occurs with the dawn of modernity, it separates out to display two *distinct* formal levels, each of which 'represents' the world as a whole: the level of mimetic reflection (human beings in a situation) and the level of language. Though these two levels of form are also present in the novel, the nature of theatrical performance separates them from each other absolutely, since each calls on a different means of representation in order to fulfil its social role. For each, however, the illusion of presentness achieved through representation relies on real presence: that of objects, light and sound on the one hand, that of language itself in its spoken form (voice) on the other. With the terminal crisis of form that occurred at the end of the nineteenth century, that illusion of presentness was discredited. Yet theatre seemed to offer nothing else. It therefore appeared impervious to the breakdown of form affecting modernity, and hence no more than a crude illusion. It is from this perspective that theatre came to be seen as 'en retard'.

Nevertheless, within the retarded frame provided by real presence, changes were happening at the level of language, which now began to assert its autonomy from the mimetic forms which had hitherto determined its role. Peter Szondi has shown how theatre as Drama played a key role in defining the modern, 'interpersonal' world which emerged at the Renaissance, through being essentially an art of dialogue.[18] Hence theatre could not accommodate the breakdown in communication occasioned by the discovery that 'tout est dit'. In an attempt at doing so, dialogue in the theatre gave way to monologue. According to Jean-Pierre Sarrazac:

> L'intrusion dévastatrice du monologue sur le territoire du dialogue dramatique—on pouvait suivre depuis Ibsen, Tchékhov et Strindberg les péripéties de la guerre de mouvement que se livraient ces deux principes contradictories—témoigne que la lutte est engagée contre le *trop homogène* de la langue du théâtre.[19]

For Sarrazac, however, this response to the limits of form (their 'homogeneity') leads *directly* to new forms of theatrical language:

> il s'agit moins, en fait, de consacrer le monologue comme forme hégémonique du texte moderne que d'instituer l'hétérogénéité dans les formes du language. [. . . A l'organicité du dialogue, les textes théatraux d'aujourd'hui répondent par le choc des blocs de language étrangers voire réfractaires les uns aux autres. Par la lutte des langues. (p. 136)

In his view, this development, which he calls a *hybridisation* (p. 137), is traceable back through the history of the monologue (hence via the pre-modern age which Szondi evokes) to 'un partage dialectique du sujet' found in the philosophical soliloquies of Antiquity (p. 129). However, Sarrazac is reaching too far back and too far forward in this explanation of the rise of modern theatre. He thus ignores the precise nature of the *present* in which, faced historically with the collapse of Tradition and the end of change, modernity sought to respond. At that moment, monologue in the theatre was neither dialectical nor heterogeneous (part of a 'polylogue' as Sarrazac also puts it (p. 134)): it was the voice of solitary individualism confronting the unsayable from without, the form given to language by a mind exiled beyond the limits of form. Ultimately, monologue under such conditions could lead only to silence. Theatre thus became, in its turn, an art of silence like music and painting, and Maeterlinck was its author.

Yet the *status* of theatre as an art of silence, compared to either music or painting, was profoundly ambivalent. Like them, it began to provide a wealth of those metaphors for silence thanks to which the arts of language kept silence at bay. Unlike music or painting, however, it remained bound up with the language it had reduced to silence. Its *retard* must therefore be examined very carefully, if its true import is to be grasped. The theory of a simple trajectory, in the evolution of theatre towards its modern or 'avantgarde' incarnation, misses out the key phase constituted by that *retard*. In fact it is precisely thanks to its enduring backwardness that the art of theatre acquired a key role in the development of modern art forms at the turn of the century.

Everything hinges on the emergence of two distinct levels of form in the theatre which I have referred to. At the level of social representation, theatre's *retard* amounted to the persistence of forms which were henceforth inadequate. Such backwardness could only inspire a flight from the theatre. But at the level of language, the *retard* took a form which on the contrary delayed that flight. The Symbolist theatre of silence, which was an attempt at overcoming the *retard* at the level of representation by disengaging language from it, finally achieved the opposite goal. As dialogue tended towards monologue, and monologue towards silence, the mutism of its figures and the emptiness of its stage became a *mirror* for the paralysed, polarised stance which was the final legacy of Tradition. Hence, left behind in so far as it could do no more than hold up an imperfect mirror to modernity, theatre nevertheless clung on by offering, as an alternative, the consolation of fascinated Narcissism to the subject of modernity. With nothing to offer except silence, it continued to provide a silent reflection of that silence.[20]

In one way, therefore, the dual nature of its *retard* locked theatre more decisively than any other art into the paralysis affecting change of form in the late nineteenth century, by turning it into a paralysing phantasm of the modern condition. Yet precisely for this reason, it also offered greater potential for a renewal of change than any other art. But between the moment when Tradition ground to a halt with the advent of modernity, and the working-out of a 'postmodern' response to its end, what the term 'theatre' refers to underwent total change. Notwithstanding the perennial nature of its old forms, there is, strictly speaking, no *direct* relation between what theatre was up until the end of the nineteenth century, and what it is today. This is because, having become thanks to its theatricality what no other art of language could be without ceasing to exist: an art of silence, theatre was taken over, in its pure theatricality, by that purest of the arts of language, poetry. What poetry discovered in theatre was not just an art-form *en retard*, but one with the capacity to *retard* the reduction of the arts of language to silence with the discovery that 'tout est dit', by containing that moment of silence *within* the limits of its own empty form. Theatre had become the site of a highly unstable paradox: what lay *beyond* the capacity of the human mind to express it was nevertheless located *within* the most elementary expressive frame there is: that of representation by means of real presence. Presence with nothing to represent had become the signifier of language with nothing to say. Such was the instability of this 'degree zero' situation that theatre itself could do no more than refine upon it: no evolution could possibly occur without theatre, in its turn, succumbing totally to silence and ceasing to exist. The paralysis at that level was as total as it was at the level of modernist subjectivity, whose fixation the theatre sustained. As the modern age took stock of the collapse of Tradition that had brought it about, the theatre (*la scène*) began to provide poets in their turn with a metaphor for their condition, just as music and painting had. More often than not, however, this was once again a means of warding off the challenge posed by the crisis of form. Thanks to one man, however, a relation developed between theatre and poetry at this time which went much further, amounting to an absolute transformation of each of them. Not only did he abolish the existing distinction between the two by subsuming them both within language; in so doing he displaced the distinction, in language, between imagination and thought, literature and philosophy, to produce what may be called a 'theatricalisation' of language which has since become the identifying mark of all 'post-modernity'.[21] That man was Stéphane Mallarmé. Though he never wrote for the theatre, he transformed its identity decisively. No understanding of what Ionesco achieved in the theatre is possible without taking account of how Mallarmé revolutionised Tradition.

Much has been written about theatricality in Mallarmé's work. Yet time and again, writers stop short of acknowledging what nevertheless seems undeniable: Mallarmé married the arts of poetry and theatre by introducing into language as poetry what theatre alone had hitherto been capable of placing there: namely a silence which, though a reflection of the limits of language, did not amount to an extinction of language, but rather a *step back* which offered a perspective upon language at its limit. Mallarmé, who lived the experience of the limits of form more acutely and more painfully than almost any other writer, saw in the theatre of silence not so much a mirror-image of his own sterile paralysis (which he dramatises repeatedly in his earlier verse), as a hitherto ignored or unused dimension to language itself. A dimension whose substance is silence, in that it lies beyond the limits of expressive form; but one whose silence lies, at the same time, within the bounds of expression, as theatre had shown. The theatre of silence had put an end to the living presence of language in its changing forms. The enduring presence of the physical stage, deprived of its mimetic function, had then become the asemantic signifier of silence: the meaningless support for the meaningless it signified. Theatre, in its raw physicality, thus provided a perspective on language in the totality of its forms. What Mallarmé saw in this was a means of *representing* or *staging* language in a way which had never hitherto been possible.

There thus occurs, in Mallarmé's writing, a theatricalisation of language for which the physical theatre provides, at the very most, a means of access, no more (what Mary Lewis Shaw has recently termed 'an aperture onto metaphysical truth').[22] The outer stage, in its empty visibility, is henceforth merely a crude projection of what he terms *la scène intérieure*, the inner stage of the mind, which, in a reference to *Hamlet*, he calls '[le] prototype du reste',[23] and whose existence is not determined by vision. His repeated reference back to *Hamlet*, 'la pièce que je crois celle par excellence', is also significant for the way it allows him to distance himself from the contemporary theatre of silence, and break its hold over the silent theatricality of the inner stage. In 'Planches et feuillets', he decisively contrasts the latent *drame* to be found even in a reading of Shakespeare with its absence in Maeterlinck's work:

> Lear, Hamlet lui-même, Cordélie, Ophélie, je cite des héros reculés très avant dans la légende ou leur lointain spécial, agissent en toute vie, tangibles, intenses: lus, ils froissent la page, pour surgir, corporels. Différente j'envisageai la *Princesse Maleine,* une après-midi de lecture restée l'ingénue et étrange que je sache; où domina l'abandon, au contraire, d'un milieu à quoi, pour une cause, rien de simplement humain ne convenait.[24]

There is thus more to this move from outer to inner stage on Mallarmé's part than mere disaffection. Unlike Maeterlinck, he wishes to *carry over* from theatre into language something much more basically physical than even the crudest of staging could ever be, since it is always present at a distance. To read *La Princesse Maleine* is merely to be aware of the physicality of the visible stage *in absentia*. To read Shakespeare, on the contrary, is to experience the upsurge of a physicality present in everyone: the intense and even violent physicality of the body in its invisible immediacy. Far from *spiritualising* the function of the stage, as Haskell M. Block has claimed,[25] Mallarmé is seeking rather to *theatricalise* the mind, and hence allow it to accommodate for the first time what is its absolute antithesis: the body. Mallarmé's aim is to introduce into the sphere of language, considered as limited form ('tout est dit') that exorbitant moment of silence to which modernity has been reduced, and which it dramatises as a polarisation separating a mute self and a closed world of forms. That silence, captured in the theatre by means of the 'retarded' materiality of the outer stage, already exists *within* each person, as the raw immediacy of sentiment and sensation which Mallarmé sought from the outset to introduce into the language of his poetry.[26] Mallarmé discovers that the paralysed stance in which modernity is caught is no more than a reaction of horror to what has been revealed beyond the limits of form with the collapse of Tradition: not the negativity of a pure absence, but the unstable, impure presence of the body in its inconceivable but all too imaginable immediacy. At the absolute crisis-point arising from the collapse of Tradition, the *retard* by which theatre lived on (as Symbolism), beyond the encounter with its own limits (its Naturalism), allowed a poet caught outside the limits of language to see a chance of overcoming the paralysis affecting *all* forms of expression at the time, by opening up the language, by way of its own physicality, to the formlessness and changeability which characterise its real 'outside': the body.

Language henceforth offered a 'perspective' upon itself by becoming its own 'stage'. Once discovered, that 'inner stage' offered what modernity despaired of: a mode of changeability which took account of the fact that forms themselves could not change. By extinguishing vision, it transformed the perspective on nothing which the collapse of Tradition had opened up (the 'terrifying obviousness' of an 'unthinkable blankness . . . beyond' to which Malcolm Bowie refers in relation to *Un Coup de dés*)[27] from being a source of horrified polarisation into a mobile presence within the sphere of language: displacing it, interrupting it and undoing it in response to the unstable quantum of bodily subjectivity (sentiment and sensation) that lies simultaneously outside and inside the bounds of expression. In so *translating* what the polarisation of experience had rendered chaotic into a new poetic order, Mallarmé brought about a revolution in Tradition with implications for all art, and in particular the theatre. He was the first to distinguish, within the polarisation of the modernist stance, a dynamic duality unaffected by the paralysis it displayed. He thus opened up the modernist 'outside' in which subjectivity was exiled, and, by making it accessible to language, established a new site on which to explore the relationship between mind and body. In so doing, he collapsed the illusory poles between which subjectivity in the modern age was caught, and so eliminated the stance by which the age defined itself. He thereby dispelled at a stroke the emotional form taken by the *pathos* of modernist experience: that nihilistic anguish which he himself endured for much of his creative life, and whose only 'language' was silence. In both of these respects, his revolution rendered the theatre in its existing form defunct: neither its mimetic frame not its modes of language (whether dialogue or monologue) could accommodate the serene exorbitancy of expression allowed by the theatricalisation of language which he proposed. In the wake of this revolution, if the theatre were to discover new forms, these could only be derived from the theatricalisation of language and the shift from outer to inner stage which were accomplished in Mallarmé's work. Theatre could only *return* to the stage by way of language. For any playwright finding himself an heir to Tradition, the revolution by which Tradition moved on, thanks to Mallarmé, beyond the discovery of the limits of form, overturned the traditional hierarchy of forms in the theatre irrevocably. If the outer stage had hitherto provided a *container* for the language of a play, henceforth the theatricality of language would dictate the nature of theatre performance: the outer stage would be at the service of the inner stage of language.

A proper appreciation of Ionesco's theatre requires that it be seen as just such a *return,* using the outer stage in relation to the theatricality of language in order to overcome the breakdown of form and the collapse of Tradition. As he himself said: 'tout est language au théâtre (. . . . Tout n'est que language. Un language essayant de révéler

l'ahistoire, peut-être même d'intégrer celle-ci dans l'histoire'.[28] I have already indicated to what extent Ionesco's experience confined him within a modernist stance. The challenge presented by his turn to the theatre with *La Cantatrice chauve* is to see how, like Mallarmé, he found a way of translating that experience into a relationship with form, while sustaining and promoting the perspective on form opened up by the collapse of Tradition. When he states, in his Helsinki lecture, that 'une chose dite est déjà morte, la réalité est au-delà d'elle',[29] he is unmistakably reaffirming that 'traditionalist' perspective. On the surface, however, *La Cantatrice chauve* appears to offer a response of a very un-Mallarmean nature. There can be no doubt that it introduces into the domain of limited form—demoted to the status of banal cliché— an ordering principle which these forms themselves cannot accommodate. But the new 'order' thus created ultimately seems indistinguishable from total disorder. It does not so much recall the serene deconstructions of Mallarmé as the jubilant destructiveness of Dada. As with Dada, the fact that the *scene* of such destruction is the stage appears coincidental.

This is where Ionesco's now classic account of how he came to write for the theatre offers up its true lesson.[30] On one level, his experience of learning English brought to a head the situation in which he had long found himself. Sentences such as 'il y a sept jours dans la semaine' or 'le plancher est en bas, le plafond est en haut' are, as Ionesco observed, 'indiscutablement vraie[s]' (p. 248). They are thus instances of language at its limits. What he calls '[leur] caractère indubitable, parfaitement axiomatique' (p. 249) means that, in each case, no more can be said in the form in which it has been said. Confronted with these 'vérités fondamentales', these 'constatations profondes' (p. 248), Ionesco found that words had suddenly lost their sense and become 'des écorces sonores' (p. 252). In response, he found himself 'pris d'un véritable malaise, des vertiges, des nausées', and obliged to lie down on the sofa, 'avec la crainte de le voir sombrer dans le néant; et moi avec' (p. 252). Language experienced as living form had collapsed for Ionesco, opening up a dizzying perspective on a void to which he henceforth felt exiled, mind and body.

Already, however, the changes which allowed him to break out of this stance had begun to occur: left to themselves, the perfect but useless sentences in his notebook had begun to alter in shape from within. Something was going on inside them which would transform them directly, by Ionesco's account, into the work of theatre known as *La Cantatrice chauve.* But although, by that account, the play begins to sound like latter-day Dada (the verbs Ionesco uses to describe the changes are all negative: 'se corrompirent', 'se dénaturèrent', 'se déréglèrent'), something is present in both his experience and his play which orients his response decisively away from Dada. At the level of his experience, this is provided by the fact that the language in which it occurs is not his own: it is a foreign language. The speaker of a foreign language occupies an ambivalent position: both 'inside' it in so far as it expresses what he or she has to say, but at the same time at a distance from it, since the true forms of that expression are to be found in another language. That distance is never entirely suppressed, for as long as the foreign speaker remains a foreign speaker. Ionesco's experience with the sentences in his notebook was thus very different from what it would have been, had they been in French (his mother tongue). Because what would have been lacking, in that case, is some vantage-point from which to observe the whole process while enduring it at the same time. What the stance offered to the speaker of a foreign language ensures is that, at all times, he appears to himself to be both inside the language and outside of it: both speaker and listener, in a relation of simultaneous alternation which differs absolutely from any to be found within his own, since he listens from what, in relation to the foreign language, appears as an absolute outside. This is, of course, a total illusion. The detachment we have as speakers of a foreign language is one provided by language: any 'outside' nevertheless lies *within* language. Significantly, it is the very same illusion which determines the late nineteenth-century response to the collapse of Tradition: the stance according to which subjectivity was felt to lie *outside* of the confines of language. If certain writers saw a way beyond the paralysis imposed by this inhibiting phantasm, it was simply because, in a variety of ways, they saw through the illusion. Their task, as artists, was then to seek ways of expressing, through language, what it is to find oneself outside of language; to discover in language a dimension of exteriority: in Mallarmé's terms, to prise open an inner stage and bring about a *theatricalisation* of language.

In the process, as Ionesco has said, theatre itself remained *en retard.* If the experience of language he describes led him to the theatre, therefore, it is not because theatre appeared as a convenient container for that experience. On the contrary, he felt nothing but distaste for the theatre as it existed. It was rather that he became aware, with an acuteness arising from the *Verfremdung* of speaking a foreign language, of the theatricality of language itself, that inner margin of silence lying beyond the limits of its ability to give form to experience through expression, but passing within those limits in such a way that to occupy it and give expression to its silence opens upon an entirely new relation in and to language.

In itself, therefore, Ionesco's *expérience du théâtre* was neither original nor strictly theatrical: it was the discovery of what writers had been exploring since the end of the nineteenth century, namely the inherent theatricality of language. So profound was that experience in his case that it thrust Ionesco dizzily into the writerly disposition he had for so long lacked, and provided him with an original project for the theatre. His nausea and astonishment were the signs of an absolute awakening to what Tradition had become. But what ensures Ionesco's true originality is that the theatricality he had awoken to was not just theatrical: it required the theatre to give it expression. Whereas Mal-

larmé could say of 'L'Après-midi d'un faune' that it was 'non possible au théâtre, mais exigeant le théâtre', for Ionesco the theatricality of language demanded the theatre and to be possible as theatre.

In what was and remains the most decisive theatrical gesture in the twentieth century, Ionesco did no less than restore theatre to the stage in the form of original works. Eschewing the doctrinal efforts of Artaud, he transformed his experience of theatre (which could only be an experience of language and hence non-theatrical) directly into theatre. The illusion created in the speaker of a foreign language that he is both inside and outside language allowed Ionesco to break free of the illusion, shared with the entire modern age, that experience lies outside the limits of language's ability to express it. But what allowed him to escape the corresponding illusion: that the alternative to that polarisation can only be chaos and cacophony, was his recognition of a dimension in language which could be explored using the illusory outside provided by the material stage.

From *La Cantatrice chauve* to *Les Chaises* but no further (hence only *in passing*), Ionesco returned to what, in his Helsinki lecture, he called 'un modèle intérieur de théâtre',[31] where what he calls 'les schèmes permanents, profonds, de la théâtralité', and elsewhere 'les schèmes mentaux permanents du théâtre'[32] are to be found. Then if only then, Ionesco can justifiably be said to be a writer of Tradition.

Notes

1. *Ibid.,* p. 87.

2. *Ibid.,* pp. 85-6.

3. *Ibid.,* pp. 85-6.

4. Mario Praz, *The Romantic Agony* (Oxford: Oxford University Press, 1970 [1951]), p. 14.

5. *Ibid.,* p. 15.

6. Guy de Maupassant, letter to Marie Bashkirtsef, April 1884, cited in Marie-Claire Bancquart, *Maupassant conteur fantastique* (Paris: Ardires des Lettres Modernes, 1976), p.14.

7. Jules Vallès, 'Victimes du livre', in *Œuvres Complètes,* edited by L. Scheler (Paris: Editeurs Français Réunis, 1950-), vol. 7, p. 143.

8. J-K Huysmans, 'Préface écrite vingt ans après le roman' [1903], in *A Rebours* (Paris: Fasquelle, 1955 [1884]). pp. 7-26 (pp. 7, 10, 11).

9. Maurice Barrès, *Sous l'oeil des barbares* (1888), in *Le Culte du moi,* préface de Hubert Juin (Paris: U. G. E., 1986), p. 46.

10. Jacques Vaché, letter to André Breton dated 29 April 1917, in André Breton, *Anthologie de l'humour noir* (Paris: Jean-Jacques Pauvert, 1966 [Livre de Poche]), p. 380.

11. Erich Auerbach, 'Figura', in *Scenes from the Drama of European Literature* (Gloucs: Massachusets, Peter Smith, 1973 [1959]), p. 56.

12. Arthur Rimbaud, letter to Paul Demeny (the so-called 'Lettre du Voyant'), 15 May 1871, in *Œuvres,* edited by Suzanne Bernard (Paris: Editions Garnier, 1960), pp. 344-50 (p. 347).

13. Eugène Ionesco, *Passé présent, présent passé* (Paris: Mercure de France, 1968), pp. 74-5.

14. Claude Bonnefoy, *Entretiens avec Eugène Ionesco* (Paris: Editions Pierre Belfond, 1966), p. 13.

15. *Notes et contre-notes,* p. 22.

16. 'Discours sur l'avant-garde', *op. cit.,* p. 89.

17. Frantisek Deak, *Symbolist Theatre* (Baltimore and London: Johns Hopkins University Press, 1993), p. 14

18. Peter Szondi, *Theorie des modernen Dramas* (Frankfurt-am-Main: Suhrkamp Verlag, 1963), p. 15.

19. Jean-Pierre Sarrazac, *L'Avenir du drame* (Lausanne: Editions de l'Aire, 1981), pp. 135-6.

20. In the fourth of Rilke's *Duineser Elegien* (11. 52-6) this stance is represented as an attitude of intense waiting before an empty stage.

21. See Jean-François Lyotard, 'The unconscious as mise-èn-scène', in *Performance in Post-Modern Culture,* ed. Michel Benamou and Charles Caramello (Madison: Wisconsin, Coda Press, 1977), pp. 87-98: '[T]he most simple utterance carries with it a primitive rhetoric. Its being uttered, its arrangement have already made it a diminutive stage' (p. 90).

22. Mary Lewis Shaw, *Performance in the Texts of Mallarmé* (University Park PA, Pennsylvania University Press, 1993), p. 68. As her use of the term 'metaphysical' might suggest, however, Shaw in her turn remains reluctant to envisage Mallarmé's theatricalisation of language in its full implications.

23. Stéphane Mallarmé, 'Hamlet', in 'Crayonné au théŒatre', (*Euvres Complètes* (Paris: Gallimard, Bibliotheque de la Pléiade, 1945), pp. 299-302 (p. 300).

24. *Op. cit.,* pp. 328-30 (p. 329).

25. Haskell M. Block, 'Mallarmé and the materialisation of the abstract in modern drama', in *Aux Sources de la vérité du théâtre moderne,* ed. James B. Sanders (Paris: Editions Minard, 1977), pp. 41-51 (p. 43).

26. Of 'Renouveau' he wrote to Cazalis in 1862: 'C'est un genre assez nouveau que cette poésie où les effets matériels du sang, des nerfs sont analysés et mêlés aux effets moraux, de l'esprit, de l'âme.' Cited in *Œuvres Complètes, op. cit.,* p. 1425.

27. Malcolm Bowie, *Mallarmé or the Art of Being Difficult* (Cambridge: Cambridge University Press, 1978), p. 116.

28. *Notes et contre-notes,* p. 197.

29. *Notes et contre-notes,* p. 77.

30. See 'La Tragédie du language', in *Notes et contre-notes,* pp. 247-54.

31. *Notes et contre-notes,* p. 86.

32. *Notes et contre-notes,* p. 190.

FURTHER READING

Criticism

Barranger, M. S. "Death as Initiation in *Exit the King.*" *Educational Theater Journal* 27 (August 1975): 504-07.
Examines *Exit the King* in the context of Tibetan philosophy, seeing the end of the play as a triumph rather than a tragedy.

Coe, Richard. *Ionesco: A Study of His Plays.* New York: Grove Press, 1961. 120 p.
Comprehensive, analytic survey of Ionesco's work that includes photographs, bibliography, and a translation of the play *The Niece-Wife.*

Cohn, Ruby. "Berenger, Protagonist of an Anti-Playwright." *Modern Drama* 8 (1965): 127-33.
Examines the development of Ionesco's Everyman, Bérenger, in the four plays in which he appears.

Coleman, Ingrid. "The Professor's Dilemma: The Absurd Comic Principle in Ionesco's *La Leçon.*" *Perspectives on Contemporary Literature* 7 (1981): 44-53.
Assesses the absurdist comic humor in the play that is set off by the mutual misunderstanding of the two main characters.

———. "Memory into 'Message'": The Forgetting of the Myth of Origins in Ionesco's *Les Chaises. Perspectives on Contemporary Literature* Vol. 9 (1983): 60-8.
Views the old couple in the play as the sole survivors of a world destroyed by a flood who suffer from a senile loss of memory.

DeFuria, Richard. "At the Intersection of Freud and Ionesco." *Modern Language Notes* 87 (1972): 971-76.
Compares the notion of the joke in Freud's thought and its use in Ionesco's dramas.

Esslin, Martin. *The Theatre of the Absurd.* New York: Doubleday, 1961. 364 p.
Important work that introduced the notion of the theater of the absurd; contains an essay on Ionesco.

Gaensbauer, Deborah B. *Eugène Ionesco Revisited.* New York: Twayne Publishers, 1996. 364 p.
Survey of Ionesco's career, emphasizing that much of his work is autobiographical; includes an extensive bibliography of primary and secondary literature.

Hayman, Ronald. *Eugène Ionesco.* London: Heinemann, 1972; rev. ed. New York: Ungar, 1976. 214 p.
Important critical study with chapters analyzing individual plays; includes an interview with Ionesco.

Ionesco, Eugène. *Notes and Counter-Notes: Writings on the Theatre.* Translated by Donald Watson. New York: Grove Press, 1964, 271 p.

Collections of essays, addresses, and lectures on drama largely written in response to what other people have said about Ionesco's theater.

————. *Fragments of a Journal.* Translated by Jean Stewart. New York: Grove Press, 1968, 271 p.

What Ionesco calls an "exploration in the tangled impenetrable forest in search of myself."

Jacobsen, Josephine, and William R. Mueller. *Ionesco and Genet: An Early Comparative Study.* New York: Hill and Wang, 1968. 242 p.

Comparative study of the plays of Jean Genet and Ionesco in the absurdist context.

Klaver, Elizabeth. "The Play of Language in Ionesco's *Play of Chairs*." *Modern Drama* 32 (1989): 521-31.

Argues that the Ionesco's words in *The Lesson* "go beyond discourse, performing dramatic action."

Kyle, Linda Davis. "The Grotesque in *Amédée, or How to Get Rid of It*." *Modern Drama* 19 (1976): 281-89.

Examines the elements of the grotesque in the play, including the central symbol of the corpse.

Lamont, Rosette C. "The Proliferation of Matter in Ionesco's Plays." *French Review* 32, No. 4 (February 1959): 319-28.

Asserts that the proliferation of objects in Ionesco's plays emphasizes the anguish of the human being in the oppressive world of material presences.

————. "The Hero in Spite of Himself." *Yale French Studies* 29 (1962): 73-81.

Examines the character of Bérenger, protagonist of *Rhinoceros,* who is seen as an unlikely champion, an anti-hero who is a true hero, and emblem of our troubled epoch.

————. "From *Macbeth* to *Macbett*." *Modern Drama* 15 (1972): 231-53.

Compares Ionesco's work to Shakespeare's tragedy, noting similarities and differences and characterizing the former as an angry, witty, and serious examination of political tyranny.

————, editor. *Ionesco: A Collection of Critical Essays.* Twentieth Century Views. Englewood Cliffs, NJ: Prentice-Hall, 1973. 188 p.

Includes essays by some of the foremost Ionesco scholars: J. S. Doubrovsky, Richard Schechner, Richard N. Coe, and Lamont.

————, and Friedman, Melvin J., eds. *The Two Faces of Ionesco.* 283 p. Troy, NY: Whitson, 1978.

Volume of criticism including important essays by Mircea Eliade, Robert Champigny, and Lamont; includes a bibliography of secondary literature organized by year of publication.

————. *Ionesco's Imperatives.* Ann Arbor: University of Michigan Press, 1993. 328 p.

Detailed study by the foremost scholar of Ionesco's writing; emphasizes the political and historical background that informs the playwright's work.

Lane, Nancy. "Expressing the Inexpressible: Ionesco and the Struggle with Language." *Postscript* (1991): 1-7.

Maintains that Ionesco's career represents his lifelong struggle against words, and that it is through language that his characters try to recover the lost paradise that preceded language, or to "express the inexpressible."

————. *Understanding Eugène Ionesco.* Columbia: University of South Carolina Press, 1994. 242 p.

Comprehensive survey of Ionesco's work divided up into discussions of particular themes or plays; includes biographical material and an extensive bibliography of secondary sources.

Lazar, Moshe, editor. *The Dream and the Play: Ionesco's Theatrical Quest.* Malibu, Calif.: Undena, 1982. 176 p.

Published proceedings of the 1980 symposium on Ionesco's work held at the University of Southern California; includes important pieces by leading scholars and an essay by Ionesco.

Martin, George. "Berenger and His Counterpart in 'La Photo du colonel.'" *Modern Drama* 17 (1974): 189-97.

Compares the dramatic character Bérenger to the protagonist of one of Ionesco's short stories.

Messenger, Theodore. "Who was that lady. . . ? The Problem of Identity in *The Bald Soprano*." *North Dakota Quarterly.* Vol. 36, No. 2 (1968): 5-20.

Analyzes a recurring problem in the play—of how one identifies himself or anyone else.

Purdy, Strother B. "A Reading of Ionesco's *The Killer*." *Modern Drama* 10 (1968): 416-23.

Attempts to bring together the various "symbolic correspondences" in the play to show that they make sense, or "order," together.

Schechner, Richard. "The Inner and the Outer Reality." *Tulane Drama Review* 7 (1963): 187-217.

Argues that the dialectical tension between the inner and outer reality replaces plot in Ionesco's plays, and that the many objects that appear in the drama are symbolic of characters' alienation from themselves and the world.

Tener, Robert L. "These Places. This Private Landscape. First Suggestions for a Topological Approach to Ionesco's Berenger Plays." *Papers on Language and Literature* 13 (1977): 319-40.

Discusses the intimate relationship of inner and outer realities in Ionesco's theater.

Additional coverage of Ionesco's life and career is contained in the following sources published by the Gale Group: *Contemporary Authors New Revision Series,* **Vol. 55;** *Contemporary Literary Criticism,* **Vols. 1, 4, 6, 9,11, 15, 41, 86;** *DISCovering Authors; DISCovering Authors: British;DISCovering Authors: Canadian; DISCovering Authors: Dramatists Module; DISCovering Authors: Most-studied Authors Module; Major 20th-Century Writers,* **Eds. 1, 2;** *Something about the Author,* **Vol. 7;** *Something about the Author,* **Obit 79;** *World Literature Criticism.*

Sean O'Casey
1880-1964

Irish dramatist and essayist.

INTRODUCTION

Widely recognized as one of the most original and accomplished dramatists of the twentieth century, O'Casey wrote formally innovative and aggressively iconoclastic plays which condemn war, satirize the follies of the Irish people, and celebrate the perseverance of the working class. A highly controversial figure in life as in the theatre, O'Casey openly expressed his Irish nationalist sympathies and defiantly embraced communism throughout his career. Hailed for his early set of naturalistic tragicomedies generally known as "the Dublin trilogy," which have been regularly performed since their premieres, O'Casey gradually developed a dramaturgical style marked by expressionistic aesthetics and socialist doctrines, to which critics and audiences alike have responded less enthusiastically—sometimes in anger and even violence.

BIOGRAPHICAL INFORMATION

Christened John Casey, O'Casey was the son of Protestant, working-class parents in predominantly Catholic Dublin. His father died when O'Casey was six years old, which worsened the family's already precarious economic situation. Consequently, O'Casey received little formal education and no medical treatment for a congenital eye disease, which affected his vision for the rest of his life. Despite these disadvantages, O'Casey extensively read Shakespeare and other classics of English literature as a teenager, while he supported himself with a series of clerical and manual labor jobs. About 1906 he left the Protestant church, became an agnostic, and gradually cultivated zealous nationalist sympathies as a member of the Gaelic League, in which he taught himself the Gaelic language and studied its literature. O'Casey later joined the Irish Republican Brotherhood, a radical group responsible for plotting the 1916 Easter Rising. Although O'Casey did not participate in the actual rebellion, the event and its aftermath deeply influenced him, inspiring the action of his most famous plays. After publishing several lyrical ballads and poems under the Gaelic pseudonym Sean O'Cathasaigh, as well as *The Story of the Irish Citizen Army* (1919), he started writing plays and submitted them for production to the renowned Abbey Theatre in Dublin. Despite rejecting his first four submissions, the directors eventually accepted his next effort, *The Shadow of a Gunman,* which premiered early in 1923 to critical acclaim

and reopened later that year, playing to SRO houses. The following spring the Abbey Theatre produced *Juno & the Paycock,* which also proved popular at the box office and with the critics. O'Casey's theatrical successes usually are credited with saving the Abbey from near bankruptcy. In 1926, during the fourth performance at the Abbey of his next play, *The Plough and the Stars,* a riot ensued, which temporarily stopped the show as police were called in to restore order. No further disturbances occurred during the rest of its run, but ticket sales boomed, as its controversial subject matter was debated in Irish newspapers. Meanwhile, O'Casey went to England to receive the Hawthornden Prize for *Juno & the Paycock* and to participate in the London productions of his plays. Despite the commercial and popular success of O'Casey's first three plays, the directors at the Abbey Theatre publicly rejected his experimental play, *The Silver Tassie* (1929), an action that effectively ended his affiliation with the theatre and forced him into self-imposed exile in England until his death. Soon after *The Silver Tassie* opened in London, the Great

Depression began, which severely limited attendance at live theatrical events. Consequently, O'Casey completed only two plays during the 1930s—*Within the Gates* (1934) and the one-act *The End of the Beginning* (1937)—working instead on his six-volume autobiography, which he published intermittently between 1939 and 1954. Throughout the 1940s and 1950s O'Casey continued the dramatic experimentation that he had pursued since *The Silver Tassie,* abandoning realistic conventions in favor of a rhetorical formalism that emphasized his poetic and ideological sympathies. Notable productions of this period include a series of plays sometimes called his "colored" plays as well as *Cock-a-Doodle Dandy* (1949), *The Bishop's Bonfire* (1955), and *The Drums of Father Ned* (1957). These plays, however, generally failed to attract as much widespread popular or critical acclaim as his early dramas had, especially among Irish audiences and critics who tended to disparage O'Casey's theatrical works. In the 1960s O'Casey's plays experienced a brief revival of scholarly interest, particularly in the United States, which prompted various American university productions of such late plays as *Behind the Green Curtains* (1962) and *Figuro in the Night* (1962). O'Casey died in 1964.

MAJOR WORKS

Collectively referred to as "the Dublin trilogy," O'Casey's first three plays dramatize the plight of Irish slum-dwellers during the political and social upheaval that surrounded the Easter Rising as well as the subsequent Irish civil war of the early 1920s, though not in chronological order. Set in Dublin's tenements in the wake of the Easter Rising, *The Shadow of a Gunman* portrays the tragic consequences of the guerilla warfare—historically known as "the troubles"—waged by the Irish Republican Army (IRA) and British soldiers for several inhabitants who get caught up in the political violence. The action of *Juno & the Paycock* occurs during the hostilities of the civil war, when neighbor killed neighbor. The play chronicles the troubles of an impoverished Dublin family whose dissension and strife mirror the national situation and delineate the nobility and foibles that compose the character of the Irish people. *The Plough and the Stars* follows the intertwined destinies of Dublin Catholics and Protestants who live in the same tenement during the violence of the Easter Rising. Similarly, *The Silver Tassie* concerns the brutality and absurdity of war— specifically, the effects of World War I on Irish and British soldiers—but this play also marks a change in O'Casey's dramatic style. Here, the action relies on expressionistic techniques, particularly evident in the second act, which incorporates colloquial speech and plainsong chant with an apocalyptic staging of the front lines at Flanders. Subsequent plays reveal O'Casey's penchant for expressionistic devices and stylized dialogue, including *Within the Gates,* which symbolically dramatizes the situation of the modern world through the personal interactions in a crowded urban park, and the series of plays usually referred to as "the colored plays." Comprising *The Star Turns Red* (1940), *Purple Dust* (1943), *Red Roses for Me* (1943), and *Oak Leaves and Lavender*

(1946), these plays explicitly reinforce O'Casey's socialist ideals, and for this reason, many critics dismiss them as propaganda pieces and technically inferior dramas. His later plays, including *Cock-a-Doodle Dandy* (his personal favorite), *The Bishop's Bonfire, Drums for Father Ned,* and *Behind the Green Curtains,* represent a blend of fantasy, ritual, and farcical satire that challenge deeply ingrained Irish attitudes toward politics, religion, sex, and art, which O'Casey portrayed as intellectually repressed and cowed into submission by a hypocritical clergy.

CRITICAL RECEPTION

A common critical response to O'Casey's body of dramatic works has asserted that his "Dublin trilogy" represents his highest achievement, and many critics have acknowledged that these tragicomedies almost single handedly reinvigorated the Irish-Anglo theater with their gritty portraits of industrial, urban life. At the same time, however, critics generally have maintained that O'Casey's plays after *The Plough and the Stars* fail to attain a similar level of artistic vision, claiming that they are marred by overt didacticism and ideological propaganda. Furthermore, most critics have perceived a noticeable break in his dramaturgical style, beginning with *The Silver Tassie,* denying any resemblance between the conventions of his early drama and that of his later plays. Despite the widespread acceptance of such views, some recent scholars have characterized O'Casey's dramatic art as a precursor of the "total theater" experience, citing the presence of such diverse elements as vaudeville, melodrama, sentimentality, literary and historical allusions, and alternately poetic and polemical language. While many scholars have hesitantly granted accord with this perspective, they also have been reluctant to deal with O'Casey's ideological commitments in similar fashion, frequently isolating them from his technical accomplishments in the theatre.

PRINCIPAL WORKS

Plays

The Shadow of a Gunman 1923
Cathleen Listens In 1923
Juno and the Paycock 1924
Nannie's Night Out 1924
The Plough and the Stars 1926
The Silver Tassie 1929
Within the Gates 1934
The End of the Beginning 1937
A Pound on Demand 1939
The Star Turns Red 1940
Purple Dust 1943
Red Roses for Me 1943

Oak Leaves and Lavender 1946
Cock-a-Doodle Dandy 1949
Bedtime Story 1952
Hall of Healing 1952
Time to Go 1952
The Bishop's Bonfire 1955
The Drums of Father Ned 1959
Figuro in the Night 1962
The Moon Shines on Kylenamoe 1962
Behind the Green Curtains 1962
*Feathers from a Green Crow 1962
The Harvest Festival 1980

Other Major Works

The Story of the Irish Citizen Army (nonfiction) 1919
I Knock at the Door (autobiography) 1939
Pictures in the Hallway (autobiography) 1942
Drums under the Windows (autobiography) 1945
Inishfallen, Fare Thee Well (autobiography) 1949
Rose and Crown (autobiography) 1952
Sunset and the Evening Star (autobiography) 1954
The Green Crow (essays and short stories) 1956
Blasts and Benedictions (essays) (1967)

*These dates indicate the first publication of *Feathers from a Green Crow* and *The Harvest Festival*, which was was originally written between 1918 and 1919. Neither has been performed to date.

AUTHOR COMMENTARY

Sean O'Casey (essay date 1953)

SOURCE: "The Power of Laughter: Weapon Against Evil," in *The Green Crow,* George Braziller, Inc., 1956, pp. 226-32.

[*In the following essay, which was originally published in 1953, O'Casey addresses the role and significance of a sense of humor in both literature and life.*]

Laughter is wine for the soul—laughter soft, or loud and deep, tinged through with seriousness Comedy and tragedy step through life together, arm in arm, all along, out along, down along lea. A laugh is the loud echo of a sigh; a sigh the faint echo of a laugh. A laugh is a great natural stimulator, a pushful entry into life; and once we can laugh, we can live. It is the hilarious declaration made by man that life is worth living. Man is always hopeful of, always pushing towards, better things; and to bring this about, a change must be made in the actual way of life; so laughter is brought in to mock at things as they are so that they may topple down, and make room for better things to come.

People are somewhat afraid of laughing. Many times, when laughter abounded, I have heard the warning remark, "Oh, give it a rest, or it'll end in a cry." It is odd how many seem to be curiously envious of laughter, never of grief. You can have more than your fill of grief, and nobody minds: they never grudge your grief to you. You are given the world to grieve in; laughter is more often confined to a corner. We are more afraid of laughter than we are of grief. The saying is all wrong—it should be "Grieve, and the world grieves with you; laugh, and you laugh alone." Laughter may be a bad thing; grief is invariably a good or a harmless one.

Laughter tends to mock the pompous and the pretentious; all man's boastful gadding about, all his pretty pomps, his hoary customs, his wornout creeds, changing the glitter of them into the dullest hue of lead. The bigger the subject, the sharper the laugh. No one can escape it: not the grave judge in his robe and threatening wig; the parson and his saw; the general full of his sword and his medals; the palled prelate, tripping about, a blessing in one hand, a curse in the other; the politician carrying his magic wand of Wendy windy words; they all fear laughter, for the quiet laugh or the loud one upends them, strips them of pretense, and leaves them naked to enemy and friend.

Laughter is allowed when it laughs at the foibles of ordinary men, but frowned on and thought unseemly when it makes fun of superstitions, creeds, customs, and the blown-up importance of brief authority of those going in velvet and fine linen. The ban on laughter stretches back to the day when man wore skins and defended himself with the stone hammer. Many enemies have always surrounded laughter, have tried to banish it from life; and many have perished on the high gallows tree because they laughed at those who had been given power over them. Hell-fire tried to burn it, and the weeping for sins committed did all that was possible to drown it; but laughter came safely through the ordeals of fire and water; came smiling through. The people clung to laughter, and held it safe, holding both its sides, in their midst; out in the field, at home in the mud hovel, under the castle wall, at the very gateway of the Abbey.

Every chance of leisure the medieval peasant and worker snatched from his fearsome and fiery labor was spent in low revelry, banned by the church, deprecated by the grandees; the hodden gray put on gay and colorful ribbons, and the hours went in making love, listening to and singing ditties mocking spiritual pastor and master, and whirling rapturously and riotously round the beribboned maypole. The bawl of the ballad came into the Abbey or Priory Church, and poured through the open windows of the Castle Hall, irritating and distracting the lord and his lady poring over the pictured book of hours. In story whispered from ear to ear, in song sung at peasant gatherings, they saw themselves as they were seen by their people, and they didn't like it; they weren't amused, for these things ate into their dignity, made them nearer to the common stature of common men, who learned that the grand and the distant ones were but a hand's span away from themselves.

Nothing could kill or stay laughter, or hold it fast in one place. It spread itself out all over the world, for, though men show their thoughts in many different manners and modes, they all laugh the same way.

When Christianity became a power, and took the place of the Roman Empire, they closed the theaters, deeming them places of surly rioting and brazen infamy, destroying souls, displeasing God, and hindering holiness on its dismal way. Bang, bang went the doors, shutting poor Satan in with the shadows. The dispersed actors became wandering minstrels, and whereas before they had been thorns in the Church's fingers, now, in songs of laughter, satire, and ridicule, they shot arrows into her breast and into her two things. A lot of the minor clergy joined them, and added their songs, too, to the ballads of the minstrels, ridiculing and damaging the rulers of both Church and State. Footsore, tired, hungry, and ragged, they laughed their way along the highway of lord and bishop; they put a laughable ban on everything they knew, all they had heard of, laughing on, though the end of many was a drear death in a ditch, with the curse of the Church as a hard pillow for a stiffening head.

Nothing seems too high or low for the humorist; he is above honor, above faith, preserving sense in religion and sanity in life. The minstrels thought (as we should think, too) that "The most completely lost of all days is that on which one hasn't laughed." So, if you get a chance in the hurry and complexity of life, laugh when the sun shines, when the rain falls, or even when the frost bites the skin or touches the heart with a chill.

Laughter has always been a puzzle to the thinker, a kind of a monkey-puzzle, a tree that doesn't look like a tree at all, but is as much a tree as any other one. Philosophers and sages have stopped up many and many a night, seeking an explanation, trying out a definition of comedy; but have gone to bed no wiser, and dead tired, while man kept on laughing, content to enjoy it, and never bothering his head as to what it was. Crowds of thinkers have set down big theories about laughter and comedy, among them the great Aristotle, Plato, Socrates, Jamblichus, and Kant; but though all of them were often blue in the face thinking it out, none of them got to the bottom of its mystery.

One American writer has connected laughter with Salvation; and maybe he isn't far wrong. He says: "The Church will prosper not through diminishing its requirements upon its members, nor in punishing them too severely for their delinquencies, but in showing mercy and kindness. Mercy is a flexible connective between the ideal and the real; it is a proper manifestation of the comic spirit. God, too, has a sense of humor: is He not revealed unto us as full of compassion, long-suffering, and merciful?" That is Dudley Zuver's opinion, and a new and odd one it will be to many. Not to David Lyndsay, the Scottish poet of the sixteenth

century, who saw God near breaking his sides laughing at a rogue of an old woman who got past the indignant St. Peter by the use of her ready and tricky tongue.

It is high time and low time that we made a sense of humor an attribute of whatever God there may be. Why, at times, the whole earth must present a comic picture to whatever deity may be watching its antics. There's the United Nations, for instance, never more divided than now in conference, sub-conference, committee, sub-committee, this council and that council, trying out one question, and making a thousand more questions out of their discussions. What fools these mortals be!

It is odd—significant, too—that in any litany whatsoever, Catholic or Protestant, Methodist or Baptist, there isn't a single petition for a sense of humor. There are petitions for everything, ideal conditions and real conditions; for everything except a sense of humor. If they petitioned for this, and got it, then the other petitions wouldn't be so many, for they would understand themselves more clearly, and cease to pester God to do things for them that they could do in an easier and better way for themselves. They would become more tolerant, would priest and parson, more understanding, more sociable, and, in many ways, more worthy of heaven and of earth. So let all who pray ask for what most of them need badly, a sense of humor to lighten their way through life, making it merrier for themselves and easier for others. Then there will be something in the carol's greeting—God rest you merry, gentlemen!

Even Shakespeare seems to be somewhat shy of laughter; even he. He rarely—save in the play, *Troilus and Cressida*—goes all out for the mockery of the heroic and the nobility. He often dismisses his clowns with a scornful gesture, as if half apologizing for their existence. He gives a semi-comic and partly-pathetic touch to the death of Falstaff, his supreme comic character, and makes poor Bardolph swing by the neck from the end of a rope for stealing a silver pyx out of a church during the campaign in France. Mistress Quickly and Doll Tearsheet suddenly become shadows; so does Poins. Only the ranting Pistol is left to eat the leek, and then creep away from life forever. Shakespeare kept ridicule warm for the lower class, recognizing in his middle-class way that to criticize the nobility by comic characterization might be dangerous, by letting the peasant and poor worker know what they really looked like. Yet, by and large, we can warmly feel how Shakespeare loved his rascals, a love so deep that, in their drawing, he made them live forever.

Where was laughter born, and when was it first heard? No one seems to know. We don't even know what it is. A baby knows how to cry before it learns to laugh. Its first smile is regarded as a miracle. So it is—the greatest and most valuable miracle born amongst men, though one thinker, Vico, says that "laughter is an attribute of second-rate minds." Let it be, then, for it is a lovely humor. It is so intensely human: however we may differ in color, in thought, in manners, in ideologies, we all laugh the same way; it is a golden chain binding us all together. The human mind will always be second-rate in the sense of still having to learn. To rise above humor is to rise above partiality, and no human being can do this; we are all partial, one way or another. We do not seek to be gods; we are content to be good men and good women; useful, neighborly, and fond of life, rounding it off with a big laugh and a little sleep.

The conscious humorist, said Vico, is a very low fellow. We're all very low fellows, for all of us, some time or another, are conscious humorists. And well we are, for our souls' sake, and for the sake of man's sanity. We couldn't live without comedy. Let us pray: Oh, Lord, give us a sense of humor with courage to manifest it forth, so that we may laugh to shame the pomps, the vanities, the sense of self-importance of the Big Fellows that the world sometimes sends among us, and who try to take our peace away. Amen.

Sean O'Casey (essay date 1956)

SOURCE: "Tender Tears for Poor O'Casey," in *The Green Crow*, George Braziller, Inc., 1956, pp. 177-90.

[*In the following essay, O'Casey responds to the animosity expressed by Dublin critics towards his plays, particularly their relentless berating of* The Bishop's Bonfire.]

It touches the heart to think of the deep and lasting affection in which the critics of Dublin hold O'Casey tight, and the big, round tears they shed so sadly over his present irresponsible playwrighting. He is lost! they cry, and will be utterly so, if he doesn't amend his ways, and turn back to first principles. He refuses; he won't: weep on, weep on, his hour is past! Tinkling their one-stringed harps, they sit them down by the waters of Anna Livia Plurabelle, and weep for the lone, lost bard. They want him to go back to the writing of another *Juno and the Paycock;* to the period of the first three "great" or "fine" or "grand"—they always give an uplifting adjective to the noun when they mention them—plays; and, because, so far, he has declined, they are about to build a wailing wall in Dublin to commemorate the poor playwright who took the wrong turning. Am I exaggerating now, or what? I don't think so. Listen; and let us take these critics in the order of their disappearance.

In an issue of the *Irish Times* in 1940, a critic, whose name doesn't appear on his comments, moans dolefully (though I imagine I feel a thrill-thread of joy through the moaning) in a review of *The Star Turns Red,* saying: "This play drives us to the thought that in *The Plough and the Stars* O'Casey's star saw the last moment of its proper brightness. These early plays were loved for the fresh fun they made in the theater [evidently a fellow fond of a loud guffaw at anything], and for their vivid version

of already 'familiar characters.' We liked these plays because they said things about our serio-comic warfare, which, all the time we had been enduring them, we wanted so fiercely to say ourselves, but just couldn't, because we were afraid. [See? This critic liked these plays, not because they were fine plays, but because they said things he was afraid to say—and that, in his opinion, goes for drama criticism.] Then Mr. O'Casey, blown sky-high above his audiences, began to write 'great' plays. The first was *The Silver Tassie,* which the Abbey Theater at first refused—in Mr. O'Casey's artistic interest only. The latter history of that play is linked closely with the decline of his star." That's Duine gan ainm for you.

A critic signing himself "K" quotes a critic named A. E. Malone as writing in 1929 in *The Irish Drama:* "For the moment the future of O'Casey is artistically a problem upon which no decided opinion can be given [and he giving a decided opinion all the time!]. It may be suggested that his basis [his basis!] is definitely localized and except his talent be greater than it at present appears to be, his future will be as much a part of Dublin as was his past." And "K" adds for himself, "How triumphantly true!" There is nothing true in it, for there is nothing decided in it. The man was afraid to decide anything. Every man is localized insofar as he can only be himself. I can tell "K" definitely, without the slightest reservation, that however "great" O'Casey's talent may be or may become, his "future" will be as much a part of Dublin as was his past; just as Joyce carried the city to the end of his life in his heart and in his soul. In the last play written the identity is as clear and unmistakable as it is in the first one.

T. C. Murray, the dramatist *de facto,* and critic *de jure,* is also very hot and bothered about O'Casey's way of playwrighting. Says he, "O'Casey took a strange twist after he had written his earlier plays, a lamentable thing to most of us. To discern the lamentable thing that has happened, we have only to recall those earlier masterpieces of his. One hears again and again, What's wrong with O'Casey? This is the question his best friends have long been asking." That's the question, Joxer; that's the question. His best friends! And doesn't he know them well!

> One early mornin' as I roved out,
> I heard a man singin' with grreat llaamentaation!

Valentin Iremonger, a writer himself, commenting in the *Irish Times,* says, with hand on his troubled heart and a tear in his poetic eye, "I am still young enough to feel sorry—and a little angry—watching genius being squandered away and frittered away upon ephemeral concepts such as Mr. O'Casey has elected to promulgate." Imagine "electing to promulgate ephemeral concepts"! Still there's dignity and sorrow in the sentence. But comicality too. As if Father O'Flynn, putting his blackthorn in his pocket, said, suddenly, "Th' time for jokin's past—we must be serious now." Mr. Iremonger is, presumably, a young fellow, so here's a bit of advice from an old one: Let him think a little longer before he writes some of his sentences. He is young enough to learn to write more clearly. I will give one instance of his thoughtless commenting as a critic of the drama: He is nearly distraught because of the difference between the way in which Feelim in one play receives news of the death of his son and that in which Juno, in another play, receives news of the death of hers. Treating the play with the mind of a pacifist, rather than with that of a critic, he fails to see the different circumstances, the different environment, the different psychological influences of friends and neighbors in the two plays, or the enormous effect they have on those who live among them. Mr. Iremonger—to give another instance of sleepy drama criticism—resents the fact that **Oakleaves and Lavender** doesn't follow the pattern of realism woven into "the early plays, that made O'Casey so secure"; yet when Feelim, the character in the play mentioned, reacts realistically to the killing of his son, and vows vengeance on the heads of those who did it, and their comrades who helped them to do it, Iremonger goes all white, and moans out a pacifistic sermon, reminding O'Casey that "two can play at that game," which O'Casey knows quite well—and more than two for that matter; but all this is beside the point, for here Iremonger is judging a play, not as a drama critic, but as a pacifist. This critic heads his commentary with the title of "Rude Mechanicals." What are "mechanicals," and when do they become "rude"? Conversely, what are gentle and good-natured mechanicals? No mechanicals are ruder than those of Shakespeare, but they are delightful, lasting, incensing the woes of life with immortal laughter. "Ghost Dancers," he says again, "are devices long since popular with amateur dramatists everywhere." Everywhere? What is an amateur dramatist? And where's the "everywhere" where these and their ghostly dancers are to be found? When a statement like this is made, the critic should give instances of the numerous plays by amateur dramatists in which these ghostly dancers have appeared.

A Mr. Gabriel Fallon, drama critic of the *Standard* (a weekly journal whose editorial office is in the porchway of heaven's doorway), listens to this tale of woe, and adds the tears of middle age to the virgin ones of Mr. Iremonger. Ay, indeed: "Even middle age may drown an eye [why only one; why not the two?] unused to flow on being compelled to witness the incandescence of genius doused in an overflow of its own willfulness." Another dignified sentence. He isn't done yet: "Unless there is a return to first principles, we shall all be forced to join our young poet in his anger and tears." Tears, tidal tears! What, all of you to be forced to anger and tears? Unless O'Casey goes back to first principles. Really? All Eire in tears! Over O'Casey. That's too bad to be true. "How is it," Mr. Fallon asks, "that a number of English critics described **Red Roses For Me** as a magnificent piece of dramatic poetry?" O'Casey doesn't know, and isn't concerned very much about it. While reminding Mr. Fallon that all the English critics aren't English (Ivor Brown is a Scotsman; Mr. Trewin is a Cornishman; and Desmond MacCarthy must have come from somewhere out of Spain), it isn't the question of the goodness or badness of a play that is the more important thing; it is the going back on the idea that

the drama must change and develop a new outlook, a broader scope, and a fresh style, if it is to live as an art alongside the art of architecture, of painting, and of music. In my opinion, the time has passed for a drama to devote its expression to one aspect of life alone, and to consider that aspect of life as dominant for the time the play takes to unfold itself; that in one play one aspect of life must be the beginning, the middle, and the end of it. Consistency of mood and of manner isn't always, indeed, not even often, found in life, and why should it then be demanded in a play? This new aspect of playwrighting which puzzled audiences here in 1929—and some of the critics too—is now puzzling the Dublin critics in 1947, and provoking them to anger and tears. What angers most of them, however, is that it hasn't been altogether a failure. A jewel moved about in the hand shows many flashes of light and color; and the human life, moved about by circumstances of tragedy and comedy, shows more than many flashes of diversity in the unity of its many-sided human nature. Of course, a great play may be written around one aspect of life, but it doesn't follow that this must be the one way forever in which dramatists are to show life on the stage to those interested in the theater. Not of course that a fine play, or even a great play, may not again be written by a newer dramatist in the "realistic" manner; but it will need to be a fine one to lift itself from the sameness of the tens of thousands of realistic or naturalistic plays that have gone before it. They are as numerous as the shadowy, silvery pictures painted by Corot—hundreds of them, with additional hundreds of perfect imitations, so beloved of so many, especially by Æ; though few words of praise were given to the portraits he painted, the loveliest things Corot did. Why? Because the portraits were what only Corot could do, while the silvery landscapes could be done by a hand holding a brush with a little craft and trickery to aid it. Dramatists cannot go on imitating themselves, and, when they get tired of that, imitating others. They must change, must experiment, must develop their power, or try to, if the drama is to live.

But are those earlier plays of O'Casey the "great works" they are said to be by O'Casey's "best friends"? And is the tear at this moment shed the genuine tear it is said to be? When these "early masterpieces" appeared first on the stage, did they get the applause they deserved from the eminent Irish critics of the day? Were these plays, when they appeared, "loved for the fresh fun they made in the theater"? Did the then lower lights and the higher lights of Dublin think that these plays made O'Casey "secure" in the high-light of the drama? Let us see.

Here's what A. E. Malone (then considered an authority on the drama), Malone with his pert mustache on his little, frightened face, here's what he said: "**The Plough and the Stars** isn't as good a play as **Juno**. It is a series of *tableaux vivants*. O'Casey is a photographic artist. In the **Plough** O'Casey strives after a literary quality of speech which is alien to Dublin slum dwellers. The play has the structure of the cinema and the revenue. The Prostitute, Rosie Redmond, has no significance whatever [a touch of humor here]. The career of O'Casey induces fear for his future." As if afraid his readers might forget what he had said, he comes out again, a little stronger: "Is O'Casey a dramatist? Is he but a combination of the cinema and the dictaphone? His plays are phases of Dublin life under conditions as abnormal as they are transient. His humor is the humor of the music-hall without its skill, or the sharpened point of its wit." Well, O'Casey is in no way ashamed for anything of a music-hall nature appearing in his plays. Well, here's a lad who wrote a big, big book, a "book of great authority," on the Irish Theater, who couldn't, wouldn't make up his mind about poor O'Casey, and gave most of his criticisms in a series of questions because the thought was father to the wish.

Most people will remember the tremendous opposition the plays met from the Plain People; but was this worse than that of Liam O'Flaherty, who, in a letter denouncing Yeats's defense of the play, tersely informed Yeats and the world that "in my opinion, *The Plough and the Stars* is a bad play." At the same time, in the *Irish Statesman,* F. R. Higgins, the poet, came out with the revelation that "A new political quality, approved by the arrogance of the Gall, is the only quality for which O'Casey is offered applause. His is a technique based on the revue structure, in the quintessence of an all-Abbey burlesque, intensified by 'diversions' and Handy Andy incidents, with somewhat more original settings. His plays are but a laborious bowing on a one-string fiddle, and 'Fluther' is but the successor of Boyle's more lively ragtime. O'Casey in his new play entirely lacks the sincerity of an artist."

Well, there's the stern, quiet testimony of a poet, doing away with all the praise and good report of the Iremongers, the Fallons, and the Murrays. But there's another—Austin Clarke, a poet, too. He said, with the same poise and quietness, that "Several writers of the new Irish school [himself included of course] believe that Mr. O'Casey's work is a crude exploitation of our poorer people in the Anglo-Irish tradition that is now moribund."

O'Casey exploiting the poor! And now they want him to go on with this nefarious practice. Pilfer the lot of them; take the last penny from them, then leave them to God! I wonder is it really O'Casey who does this bad thing? I shouldn't put anything past him, for he carries the Red Star in the lapel of his coat, emblazoned with those dangerous weapons—the hammer and the sickle.

But we haven't come to the end of the list yet. There are a few left still. There's Professor Daniel Corkery, the man who found the hidden Ireland. In an article praising Clifford Odets' *Golden Boy* he shows how this play far surpasses the "realistic" plays of O'Casey. And since *Golden Boy* is but a third-rate play, then O'Casey's realistic plays must be low down, deep, among the dead men. One more from others: R. M. Fox of Dublin, a writer, in the *New Statesman* in an issue of August, 1928, calls these plays "The Drama of the Dregs." He says, "Peasant drama in Ireland has been succeeded by slum drama,

though such an authority as W. B. Yeats tells us that the peasant drama is done, and slum drama will have a very short reign. As entertainment, this kind of drama is permissible. Neither the peasant nor the slum play deals in any direct fashion with typical problems of a group of people. But group problems may not lend themselves to drama, certainly not to melodrama, and so on the stage they are neglected. Besides entertainment we need truth." Well, there's R. M. Fox for you, telling you and me about the drama; all about the drama. He seems to think truth should be entertaining, though I know an Irish proverb that says truth is always bitter.

It wouldn't be fair to forget the recent roar of Brinsley Macnamara about "the vulgarity of O'Casey's worthless plays that have always been given far too much honor and attention by the Abbey Theater." So there is heard a pretty fine chorus against these "masterpieces" that have made "O'Casey so secure in the theater," from the sparrow-like chirrup of Mr. Austin Clarke to the ready and heady roar of Brinsley Macnamara.

Now these who said these things are just as intelligent, just as important, as those who have come after them. Their criticism is as likely to be right as the criticism of the present-day complainers; so what is the playwright to do? Here we have a vociferous assembly, men of gifts, some of them intellectuals, declaiming against these early "masterpieces" as bad plays, bad art, exploitation of Eire's poorer people, and decisively declaring that O'Casey was equipped only with the technique of the revue, the quick eye of the camera, and the ready pickup mind of the dictaphone; having nothing at all of the dramatist in either heart or head. And yet the critics of today implore O'Casey, with tears in their eyes, to go back to "first principles." All this shows how stupid these Irish critics are; that they fear O'Casey only a little less than they fear themselves; it tells O'Casey that he mustn't pay any attention to these chiming bells of St. Mary's ordering him back to the land of beginning again.

It shows, too, that Eire needs critics more than she needs playwrights. She has had good plays, good actors, good producers, but always weak, timid, frustrated, and damned bad critics. We have had no drama critic since Yeats, who, with his hazel wand and the red berry tied to an end, tried to exorcise inanity and commercialism out of the Theater of his day. But Yeats was a critic only in his spare time, and then only of the theater insubstantial. He tried to change the Theater of the world through the few things done on the Abbey stage, and, though he failed, he gave Ireland a great beginning.

The Irish Theater needs a critic who will set down the comments of the chronicles of the stage with precision, knowledge, and above all, with courage; refusing to condemn the new because he does not understand it (like the later pictures of Picasso), or dislikes it; a critic able to enter all her halls with confidence, from the highest thing the Theater has ever done to the dialogue and diversions of a Jimmy O'Dea on the Olympia stage. A critic who will never be influenced by his paper's policy or profit; who will be unafraid of clique or cleric; who, in his criticism, will separate himself from the seduction of a friend, or from animosity towards an enemy; who will know the theater of the Continent as well as he knows his own, far back, and present achievement; a critic who will look upon a play as a play, indifferent to whether it hurts or heals. Where is there a critic like that in Eire? Is there one of them who isn't afraid of his paper boss; afraid of his clique of friends; afraid of his clerical consorts; half afraid of his own thoughts? Nowhere; not yet, anyhow.

Now look, young dramatists, you have a theater to develop and to defend, and it is for this reason that I appeal to the younger (and so braver) writers in Ireland today who still go in half fear of clerical and clique; a theater of which we can be proud and of which others who know speak in high praise. Now, this isn't mere rhetorical bounce on the part of O'Casey. Listen to what George Jean Nathan, the famous American drama critic, says of the Irish Theater: "I take it there is small critical question, save alone in the lands of dictated appraisal, that the modern Irish drama leads what is left of the European theater. Our own theater is quick and alive and in many ways admirable, but its plays come mainly out of galvanic impulse rather than deep meditation. And only out of deep meditation is true drama born. Surely in searching the stage of the world theater of the later years it is difficult to find a body possessed of the Celtic poetic pulse. Surely, except in sporadic instances, that quality which insinuates into the mind and emotion its peculiarly lingering after-image is rare in the plays of men nurtured in other soils. It isn't, certainly, that all the plays that are coming out of Eire soil are masterpieces. Very, very far from that. But, as I have written in the past, in even the poorest of them, one finds a probity, a passionate undertone, a brave resolve, and a hint of spiritual music that one all too infrequently encounters in the present dramaturgy of other peoples. And in the finer plays there is a poetic sweep, a surge of human emotions, and a warm, golden glow that even the best drama of other countries most often lacks." This quotation forms part of a preface to a book published by Random House, New York; it is titled *Five Great Modern Irish Plays* and costs ninety-five cents. The sale of this book may run into many thousands of copies; so one can see how many will come to regard the Irish Theater as something to be held in honor, and spoken of with respect. Readers will accept the statement on the flap of the jacket which tells the buyer that "No nation has made a richer contribution to the recent literature of the Theater than Ireland." Than Ireland.

This is a big heraldry of Ireland's theatrical fame. It would be a shame to let the colors fade or the gold tarnish. We should try to keep the colors bright, or even make them brighter. It is an expansive shield, with room for many new designs and waxing symbols; and we can't afford to let any slinking, shrinking critic push a hand aside, eager to put a new one there.

In everything but politics, perhaps even in politics, Ireland is lagging behind—dragging her feet after her like a half-nourished child. In the novel and short story, Ireland holds her own; but in music, in painting (imagine a Dublin art critic having to rush to the National Library to search out a thing or two about Picasso!), we are still in the age of infancy. Let us, at least, hold on to our place in Drama. Ireland won't hold it long if the present-day drama critics have their way; if destructive criticism takes the form of condemning any new thought, every new style used to try to widen the achievement of the living theater; or if constructive criticism takes the form of Brinsley Macnamara's purification, when he advises that audiences should "receive a play that had no appeal, or was simply boring, in stony silence—just no applause at the end, no calls [not even catcalls?], the merciful fall of the curtain putting a finish to the matter." Finis, the end. No applause, no calls—just the fall of the curtain, and stony silence. Was there ever before such an example of telepathic regimentation suggested to save the Irish Theater? Never, and, let us hope, there never will be again; for the thing is impossible.

To O'Casey, these are but *saecula saeculorum* critics. What they said thirty years ago about *Juno* and the *Plough,* they say today about whatever play he may chance to write. Not a single good berry from the bunches on the tree. Of the horde of Irish critics, one only stood out to say a word for the playwright as he murmured, "One longed in recent weeks for an angry Yeats to castigate the Irish critics for their behavior over Cyril Cusack's production of O'Casey's latest play"; one erudite critic, Donat O'Donnell, mixing a murmur with a heart-breaking sigh, called it "this sorry business"; all of them running, not for pens, but for pokers. One of the tearful lads, mentioned earlier on, not content with a first-night review, ran into a corner to write an "Open Letter to Sean O'Casey," starting with a doleful roar of "What in the name of fortune is the matter with you?" Oh, dear, what can the matter be; oh, dear, what can the matter be—Seaneen has gone to the fair! "I'll tell you," he goes on. "In the first place it is because your overweening vanity is severely hurt. You don't like criticism, Sean O'Casey; you only like praise." Musta been vanity fair O'Casey went to. Vanity of vanities, saith this preacher, all is vanity, and O'Casey is gorgeous with it.

So, young Irish dramatists, go ahead, and don't bother about the critics. They are no use to you. They don't know their own minds. The most of them are influenced by their jobs. Wait till a good critic appears, and then stop awhile to listen. You'll soon get to know him when he (or she) comes, though with Ireland as she is, there'll be but a poor chance for the poor man to live or write. While the dramatists wait for the coming of a pure and proper critic, there is nothing to be done but to go on doing their best to keep Eire in the forefront of the world's drama. Should the shadow of Censorship steal over that deep meditation, mentioned by George Jean Nathan, let the dramatists turn their faces to London and New York; for, if there be fullness of merit in what they create, their work will find there, sooner or later, the fulfillment of production. Take ye no thought for the contempt these places are held in by some of the critics.

So go ahead, my hearties of Irish dramatists, for Eire, and for New York and London. Remember that every Irish dramatist, the oul' ones as well as the young, longs in his heart—and not in a corner either, but in the core—to have his play's name shine in the red, yellow, and blue lights of Broadway and the streets of London's West End. And to quote Nathan again, let every dramatist be modest enough to be "a pilgrim on the road to a Mecca that is ever just over the skyline."

OVERVIEWS AND GENERAL STUDIES

John Jordan (essay date 1980)

SOURCE: "The Passionate Autodidact: The Importance of Litera Scripta for O'Casey," in *Irish University Review*, Vol. 10, No. 1, Spring, 1980, pp. 59-76.

[*In the essay below, Jordan examines the importance of literary allusions in O'Casey's dramaturgy.*]

He took the Reading Lesson-book out of his pocket, opened it, and recited:

> I chatther, chatther as I flow
> To join the brimming river,
> For men may come and men may go,
> But I go on for ever.

Well, he'd learned poethry and kissed a girl. If he hadn' gone to school, he'd met the scholars; if he hadn' gone into the house, he had knocked at the door.[1]

I

Sean O'Casey is the most bookish of all Irish dramatists.[2] From *The Shadow of a Gunman* (1923) to the last three plays, published together, *Behind the Green Curtains, Figuro in the Night* and *The Moon Shines on Kylenamoe* (1961), quotations from and references to the books he had read or at the least was aware of (and chiefly from his protracted incubatory period), play an important part in his dramaturgy. The importance of the Book, for that child who preened himself on being able to read Tennyson's "The Brook", is nowhere better attested than in certain passages from the third and fourth volumes of his autobiography, where something like moral judgment enters into his observations of the literary taste of others. Cultural snobbery is not uncommonly an acrid fruit of autodidacticism. Here is a magnificent passage from *Drums Under the Windows* (1946) which, while it has imaginative

truth, is yet wrong-headed about individuals, certainly about Thomas MacDonagh, Joseph Mary Plunkett and John Francis (later "Sean") MacEntee:

Pity, though, few of them cared a thraneen about art, literature, or science. In this respect, even, they weren't International. A few of them, one of the Plunkets, MacDonagh, and McEntee, paddled in the summertime in the dull waters of poor verse; but gave hardly any sign that they had ever plunged into the waters that kept the world green. No mention of art, science, or music appeared in *Sinn Fein* or *Irish Freedom*. To them, no book existed save ones like *The Resurrection of Hungary* or the *Sinn Fein Year Book*. None of them ever seemed to go to a play, bar one that made them crow in pain and anger. A great many of them were ignorant of the finest things of the mind, as the onslaught on Synge showed. Even Mangan was beyond them. All of them knew his Dark Rosaleen by heart; sang it so often that one got tired of her sighing and weeping, longing to hear her roar out vulgar words with the vigour of a Pegeen Mike. But Mangan's splendid Ode to The Maguire was known to hardly any of them, or, if known, never mentioned. In all the years of his sojourn in Irish Ireland, he never once heard it mentioned. Thomas Davis was their pattern and their pride. He sang for them every hour of the day, and, if he happened to tire, . . . William Rooney, Griffith's great butty, sang instead. In a literary sense, they could have chosen a king in Mitchel; instead they put a heavy gilded crown on the pauper Davis. Almost all of them feared the singing of Yeats, and many were openly hostile to him, though few of them could quote a line from a poem of his. All they treasured of him was the dream which fashioned the little play about Cathleen Ni Houlihan, a tiny bubble, iridescent with a green tinge . . . Apart from Pearse, Seumas Deakin, and Tom Clarke, few of the others showed any liking for book, play, poem, or picture. (*A*, I, 616-17)

But if O'Casey makes an almost blanket indictment of Irish Ireland's cultural poverty, he mades a comparable indictment of the impunity of Anglo-Irish Ireland's literary taste. Yeats, Lady Gregory, Oliver St John Gogarty and James Stephens are rapped on the knuckles with varying degrees of severity in *Inishfallen, Fare Thee Well* (1949). He tells of how, knowing from Lady Gregory that she had just given Yeats *The Idiot* and *The Brothers Karamazov*, the poet had had the effrontery to hail him, O'Casey, as "the Irish Dostoievsky".

Another Dostoievsky! An Irish one, this time! And Yeats only after reading the man's book for the first time the night before. . . . Yeats was trying to impress Sean with his knowledge of Dostoievsky. That was a weakness in the poet. But why hadn't Sean the courage to tell Yeats that he knew damn all about the Russian writer? That was a weakness in Sean. (*A*, II, 163)

Clearly Yeats's ignorance at sixty of Dostoievsky is as culpable for O'Casey as his attempt to conceal it. And he goes on to expose 'weakness' in other established figures in the Anglo-Irish Pantheon. At Coole, Lady Gregory read to him from Hardy's *The Dynasts, Moby Dick* and W.H. Hudson's *The Purple Land* (*A*, II, 115). But on the station at Athenry he came upon her "sitting on a bench, her head lovingly close to a book". He approached her and "Catching in her dulling ear a sound of his movement, she snapped her book shut but not before he had seen that the book was called *Peg o' My Heart*". Seeing "the look of bewilderment in his eye" she said 'Ah, dat book? I fordet who dave it to me. I just wanted to see what tort it was'.[3]

At A.E.'s house he catches Stephens out "suddenly and hurriedly asking A.E., author of the Homeward Songs, for a Blood-and-Thunder novel, and A.E. had fished one out from his books, without a search; he had plunged a hand in among the books and out came the Blood-and-Thunder novel" (*A*, II, 163). A.E.'s literary taste is further castigated in a stylized conversation between O'Casey, and two companions, in a Dublin pub: says O'Casey, "But then he couldn't stand Shakespeare's *Sonnets,* didn't like his plays and no wonder for Alexandre Dumas, Zane Grey, and others like them, were the literary nectar his gods gave him" (*A*, II, 178). This manifest injustice concerns me here less than O'Casey's insistence on the importance of the top-drawer Book. But perhaps the most telling evidence of O'Casey's absolutism in literary taste deals with Gogarty and, again, Yeats.

> Long afterwards, when Oliver Gogarty came on a visit to him in London, what he had known before was confirmed again. Gogarty had entered on a whirlwind of restlessness. He had flung down his suitcase, the impact had burst it open, and a book fell out on to the floor. Sean's wife and Oliver had made a dive together to get it, but Gogarty was a second too late; and Sean saw the title of one of Edgar Wallace's rich and rare inventions. (*A*, II, 166)

The spectacle of Gogarty and Eileen O'Casey 'diving' for the 'rich and rare' with its echoes from *The Tempest* (I.ii.399) and Thomas Moore, ("Rich and Rare Were the Gems She Wore") is mildly comic: more disturbing is the surprisingly sharp-eyed Sherlock O'Casey. Sherlock O'Casey goes on to recount a visit to Yeats when the poet was "busy with his last anthology of modern poetry". In the course of a wide-ranging conversation "Sean's eyes kept turning to glance at a disordered pile of books strewing the marble mantelshelf" Yeats noticed "and cocked one of his own eyes towards them—for the other was covered with a thick green shade—and remarked that they were Wild Western Tales and Detective Stories. Yeats made no bones about it" (*A*, II, 166). He turned "for shelter and rest to Zane Grey and Dorothy Sayers". O'Casey's reaction is decidedly a moral one. "Dope, thought Sean. He uses them as dope to lull the mind to sleep, just as the one-two, one-two mind of a Roman Catholic keeps awake by reading the tuppenny booklets of the Catholic Truth Society". He has referred to the 'weakness' of Yeats and also of Stephens (*A*, II, 163). The moral tone of his strictures on bad taste in literature is clinched in the following:

> Aye indeed; even the greater gods of Dublin had their frailties and their faults. They could sometimes build their little cocks of antic hay, and try to tumble about in them. The lordly ones weren't always quite so lordly with literature as they generally posed to be. (*A*, II, 166)

I should add that Aldous Huxley's novel *Antic Hay* was published in 1923, but Oliver St John Gogarty's autobiog-

raphy of his early days, *Tumbling in the Hay* did not appear until 1939, three years after Yeats's *Oxford Book of Modern Verse,* on which he was at work when O'Casey visited him at Lancaster Gate.

II

When his father, Michael Casey, was dying, "Johnny Casside", the *persona* O'Casey created for himself as a child, records "There was one comfort, that if he died, he would die in the midst of his books" (*A*, I, 27). There were, it seems, alongside "a regiment of theological controversial books" including Merle D'Aubigne's *History of the Reformation,* the Enblish Bible, the Latin Vulgate, the Douai Testament and Cruden's *Concordance* (a book essential, by the way, for all or most O'Casey exegesis), the novels of Dickens, Scott, George Eliot, Meredith and Thackeray, the poetry of Burns, Keats, Milton, Gray and Pope, *The Decline and Fall of the Roman Empire* and Locke's *Essay on the Human Understanding* (*A*, I, 27-8). It may be noticed that O'Casey's listing has no pedantic regard for chronology: e.g. Dickens before Scott, Burns and Keats before Milton. And of course there was Shakespeare. From the remnants of "her father's fine store" Ella [Isabella], O'Casey's married elder sister, unearthed some "unsaleable books, from which to give her brother some elementary education" (*A*, I, 172). Thus O'Casey learned to read "Poethry" as indicated above. It is possible to chart from the volumes after *I Knock at the Door* (1939) a laborious self-education and the effect it had on his life and the effect, as I hope to show further, on his dramatic canon.

O'Casey was scarcely into his teens when he became involved in rehearsals for a charity concert at the Coffee Palace in Townshend Street. "Johnny Casside" was to play Henry VI to his brother Archie's Gloucester in *Henry VI*, V.iii. (*A*, I, 191). He "learned the part from one of three volumes of the *Works of Shakespeare* won as a prize by Ella when she was a student in Marlborough House Teachers' Training College" (*A*, I, 192). But, at this stage "Johnny Casside" is more for Dion Boucicault than Shakespeare. "What a pity they hadn't chosen a bit outa *Conn the Shaughraun* instead of pouncin' on Shakespeare's stiff stuff. If they only knew, Boucicault was the boy to choose" (*A*, I, 195). He fancies himself as Father Dolan in Boucicault's *The Shaughraun* (1874). A passage from Act I, Scene 1, is quoted, I would say from memory, since it diverges slightly from the printed text.[4] Because of the death of the Duke of Clarence the Coffee House concert was cancelled, but at fifteen he did indeed play Father Dolan, at the Mechanics' Institute, later converted into the Abbey Theatre (*A*, I, 305-8). But before that he had acted for the Townshend Dramatic Society in scenes from *3 Henry VI, Julius Caesar* and *Henry VIII* as well as from Boucicault, including *The Octoroon* (1859) and "lots of others in Dick's little orange-coloured books of Standard Plays" (*A*, I, 298).

At the Mechanics' Institute he had free passes for the shows of a former Boucicault star Charlie Sullivan in whose company his brother Archie had small parts (*A,* I, 299). But this familiarity with a decidedly non-literary theatre was not enjoyed *in vacuo.* He was reading Shakespeare outside the range of the snippets provided by the Townshend Dramatic Society. He was buying books and reading them, as well as poring over what remained of his father's old books, including Merle d'Aubigné. He torments his mates, senior and junior, in the emporium where he works, with his superior general knowledge and especially his catechumen's knowledge of Shakespeare. "Settin' aside the Chronicle Plays, name ten of the others. No answer? Yous couldn't. What's th' name o' th' play containin' the quarrel between th' two celebrated families, an' what was the city where they lived called? No answer? Verona, Verona, th' city; Montague and Capulet, th' families." He baits his superior, Dyke, with allusions to "fiery Tybalt" and *Romeo and Juliet* I.i., lines 4, 50-57 (the dialogue between the servants of Capulet and Montague). I cannot trace "dismantled messengers" to which he refers (*A,* I, 276).

The books he was buying included novels by Balzac, Scott, Dickens, Hugo, Fenimore Cooper and Dumas (presumably, his respect for Dumas had diminished by the time he met A.E.) and, in poetry, "the works of Byron, Shelley, Keats, Goldsmith, Tennyson, Eliza Cook—a terrible waste of sixpence—Gray and the Golden Treasury, with the glorious Globe edition of Shakespeare falling to bits." (*A,* I, 289) In 1966, Jack Lindsay wrote: "I should like incidentally to stress the debt I feel he owed to Ruskin for helping him as a young man to gain a broad, subtle, and unsectarian sense of the issues."[5] Ruskin indeed bulked large in the young O'Casey's library. He had *The Seven Lamps of Architecture, Sesame and Lilies, Ethics of the Dust, Unto This Last* and *The Crown of Wild Olive* (*A,* I, 289). The last-named, being four lectures, on Work, War, Traffic and the Future of England, published in 1882, is of special importance. Literally, he burned the midnight oil over grammar, geography and history. "Whenever he got tired of these things, he read some bit from the *Deserted Village* or from Ruskin's *Crown of Wild Olives*" [sic]. His dwindling paraffin's "last few inches were giving a flickering salute to the glories of Goldsmith, Ruskin and Marlowe" (*A,* I, 348-9). When a zealous Nationalist friend, Ayamonn O'Farrel, calls on him, bringing *Speeches from the Dock* and the *Life of Wolfe Tone* (*A,* I, 354-7), Johnny Casside spouts *The Crown of Wild Olive* at him, and how far O'Casey was steeped in this book may be judged from the fact that in *Pictures in the Hallway* he appears to be writing from memory; the texts quoted (from "War" and "Traffic") vary significantly from Ruskin's. One of the more important variations is O'Casey's anticipation of Ruskin's "Goddess of Getting-On" which in fact occurs a page later in the original.[6]

O'Casey also makes much, writing of Johnny Casside's teens, of his adventures in the acquirement of a Collected Milton. In the context he quotes *Paradise Lost,* VI, 207-19, "from a book on Elocution, left behind by his father." (*A,* I, 286) In the event, he steals the Milton from Hanna's bookshop on Bachelor's Walk, thus giving ammunition to a self-righteous Dublin journalist who denounced him, as recently as 1975, as "a self-confessed thief and cheat."[7] But, clearly, "buyin' a book was a serious thing" for the young autodidact.

Untypically, *Drums Under the Windows* (1946) has a formal literary epigraph, but unacknowledged: "Study that house. / I think about its jokes and stories." This of course is from Yeats's second-last play.[8] There are many Yeats references in *Drums,* of which I cite the more important. At a Connolly meeting "Sean" (as "Johnny Casside" becomes as an adult) reflects in fantastic terms on Griffith who is present, and on varying attitudes to Yeats, specifically in relation to his receipt of a pension from the British Crown. (His name was put on the Civil List at the end of 1910[9])

> We have too few, too few such men to spare a one like Yeats the poet, and the Gaelic Leaguers who heard him grew silent. Devil a much you fellows do to keep a few shillings jingling in the poet's pocket. What about the Israelites who took gold, silver, and jewels from the Egyptians before they left them? If England pays the man's rent, then let it be counted unto righteousness for her. None of you know a single poem by Yeats, not even *The Ballad of Father Gilligan.* And the poor oul' gaum, Cardinal Logue, condemning *Countess Cathleen* though he hadn't read a line of it. We were paying a deep price for that sort of thing since Parnell went away from us. He himself had read the ballad only. (*A,* I, 416)

That last is an extraordinary admission if, in fact, it refers to 1911, when Yeats's pension became public knowledge. Elsewhere, we learn that in 1907 he had never seen *Cathleen Ni Houlihan,* "a shilling was too much for him to spare for a play" and wished he could see "this play by Singe or Sinje" (*A,* I, 519). (*The Playboy.*) He will tell us in *Inishfallen, Fare Thee Well* (1949) that when he began to submit plays to the Abbey in the 'twenties he had only twice been to the theatre: in December 1917 to see *Blight* by Gogarty (and, apparently, it was accompanied by Lady Gregory's *The Jackdaw*), and, most likely, in August 1920, to see Shaw's *Androcles and the Lion* accompanied by James Stephens's *The Wooing of Julia Elizabeth* (*A,* II, 96). Later, after his Abbey successes, when Lennox Robinson was entertaining him to dinner at the Thirteen Club, he discovered that he was ignorant of writers that "were common names in the mouths of those who sat beside him." He had never seen or read Andreiev or Giacosa or Maeterlinck or Benavente or Pirandello:

> . . . while Sean whispered the names of Shaw and Strindberg which they didn't seem to catch, though he instinctively kept firm silence about Dion Boucicault, whose work he knew as well as Shakespeare's; afterwards provoking an agonized My Gawd! from Mr. Robinson, when he stammered the names of Webster, Ford, and Massinger. (*A,* II, 105)

Here again, is the slightly priggish tone of the autodidact, who believes that he has acquired a gravamen of solid literary culture, as distinct from others with more formal education (neither Yeats nor Robinson had much of that) and a cosmopolitan background, but with a questionable enthusiasm for the exotic and modish. In fact before 1926 when O'Casey left Ireland, Robinson's Dublin Drama League had produced plays by Andreiev, Benavente and Pirandello, and indeed his beloved Shaw and Strindberg.[10] O'Casey must or should have known this. But for better or worse, he sniffed a gilded rat in the Thirteen Club.

III

Almost from the beginning of his career as a published writer, O'Casey tended to air his hard-won learning. The title-page of *The Story of Thomas Ashe* (1917) bore lines from Browning. The following year a second edition re-titled *The Sacrifice of Thomas Ashe* had lines from Pope on the cover, and on the title-page Shakespeare and Pope again.[11] Pope and Browning seem indecorous in the context of the hunger-striker Ashe and the great Glasnevin funeral in 1917. Antony's lines on the dead Brutus (*Julius Caesar* V.v. 73-5) are little more congruous.

In the first staged play *The Shadow of a Gunman* (1923) O'Casey left the hall-mark of his self-conscious literary culture on his hero (or anti-hero), the would-be poet and player gunman, Donal Davoren. In the stage directions we are told that he has "an *inherited and self-developed devotion to 'the might of design, the mystery of colour, and the belief in the redemption of all things by beauty everlasting'*."[12] Davoren echoes Dubedat, from whose dying speech in Shaw's *The Doctor's Dilemma* O'Casey's quotation is taken, when in Act II he attacks the People: "To them the might of design is a three-roomed house or a capacious bed" (*CP*, I, 127). But Davoren's chief contact with the more 'poetic' aspects of literature is through Shelley's great unactable verse-play *Prometheus Unbound,* from which three times in Act I and again towards the curtain he quotes Prometheus's refrain "Ah me! pain, pain ever, forever!"[13] As an index to character or type, the line is viable: Davoren's anguish, at least initially, is factitious and so requires for sustenance incommensurate statements. At the beginning of Act II he quotes ii. 281-84 from *Epipsychidion:*

> The cold chaste Moon, the Queen of Heaven's bright
> isles,
> Who makes all beautiful on which she smiles;
> That wandering shrine of soft yet icy flame,
> Which ever is transformed, but still the same.
>
> (*CP*, I, 125)

The full-stop is O'Casey's, for the line runs on in a half-line, "And warms not, but illumines." Should the Shelley quotations seem obtrusive, a case may be made for them as suggested above. I do not think that the same might be said for Davoren's reply to his room-mate Seumas Shield's query as to the time: "The village cock hath thrice done salutation to the morn". The pedlar Shields's quick response need not seem odd in a man of the kind who as a boy may have frequented the Mechanics' Institute: "Shakespeare, Richard the III, Act Five, Scene III. It was

Ratcliffe said that to Richard just before the battle of Bosworth" (*CP*, I, 131). What is odd is that while Shields's location of the line is exact Davoren's quotation is not. It should be "the early village cock", though "twice" instead of "thrice" may be Davoren's essay at a feeble donnish joke. Elsewhere (*CP*, I, 93) Davoren laces his conversation with familiar quotations from *The Rubai'yat of Omar Khayam* and Milton's Sonnet XIX ("When I consider how my light is spent"). But none of his quotations has the effect of his incorporation into his last speech of *Ecclesiastes* 12.6 in part: "Or ever the silver cord be loosed, or the golden bowl be broken" (*CP*, I, 156-7). In later plays O'Casey will be bolder in his use of the Old Testament.

In his first full-length play *Juno and the Paycock* (1924) O'Casey almost certainly used books as symbols. Mary Boyle is an enlightened Minnie Powell. She reads above her station. Her father "Jackie" Boyle, the Captain, has caught her reading a volume of Ibsen: "three stories, The Doll's House, Ghosts, an' The Wild Duck,—buks only fit for chiselurs"! To which, "Joxer" Daly rejoins "Didja ever rade *Elizabeth, or Th' Exile o' Sibayria?*"[14] This is not Joxer's only favourite book. He has also a stock of mediocre verse of which the following are two samples (I have de-Joxerised them.):

> And how can man die better
> Than facing fearful odds
> For the ashes of his fathers
> And the temples of his Gods?
>
> (*CP*, I, 27)

This is from Horatius, XXVIII, in Macaulay's *Lays of Ancient Rome* (1867). The provenance of the second on Joxer's lips is rather mysterious.

> Tender-hearted stroke a nettle
> And it stings you for your pains.
> Grasp it like a man of mettle
> And it soft as silk remains.
>
> (*CP*, I, 27)

The author of those sublimely trite lines was Aaron Hill (1685-1750), who wrote tragedies and farces, some for Drury Lane. Joxer has two other favourite books, whose titles are introduced at crucial moments. He observes of Father Farrell, "I wondher did he ever read the Story o' Irelan'." And Boyle replies "Be J.L. Sullivan? Don't you know he didn't" (*CP*, I, 38). It seems unlikely that the audiences of 1924 (or since) got the joke. *The Story of Ireland or a Narrative of Irish History written for Irish Youth* was written and published by Alexander Martin Sullivan (Dublin 1886). 'J.L. Sullivan' is Boyle's conflation of this Sullivan and the Irish-American boxer. At the end of the play the drunken Joxer has the penultimate speech: "D'jever rade Willie . . . Reilly . . . an' his own . . . Colleen . . . Bawn? It's a darlin' story, a daarlin' story!" (*CP*, I, 89). William Carleton's novel *Willy Reilly and His Dear Colleen Bawn* was published in 1850-51, and a revised version in 1855. Just eleven years before the historical time of **Juno** James Duffy of Dublin brought out an edition (1909). The novel, by the way, has nothing to do with Gerald Griffin's *The Collegians* (1829), from which Dion Boucicault took material for his play *The Colleen Bawn* (1860).[15]

If Mary Boyle and Ibsen represent an attempt to escape from a washed-out popular culture then Joxer with his "darlin stories", *Elizabeth or the Exiles of Siberia,* Sullivan's *The Story of Ireland* and Carleton's *Willy Reilly,* his snatches from Macaulay, Hill and others may be said to represent that culture at its nadir. And Boyle's reaction to the news of his daughter's pregnancy prefigures venonmous attacks on the Book in plays written many years later:

> Her an' her readin'! That's more o' th' blasted nonsense that has the house fallin' down on top of us! What did th' likes of her, born in a tenement house, want with readin'? Her readin's afther bringin' her to a nice pass—oh, it's madnin', madnin', madnin'! (*CP,* I, 75)

But there is a reference in **Juno** which goes further back than Mary Boyle's explorations of continental drama, which may be taken as a reflection of O'Casey's own. Curiously it occurs in a speech from "Captain" Boyle. "An', as it blowed an' blowed, I ofen looked up at the sky an' assed meself the question—what is the stars, what is the stars? . . . An' then, I'd have another look, an' I'd ass meself—what is the moon?" (*CP,* I, 26) This may be compared with this from *Pictures in the Hallway:* "Johnny glanced up at a sickle moon hanging in the sky among a throng of stars. What was it and what were they? He had looked in the pages of Ball's *Story of the Heavens* and at the pictures, but it was all too hard for him yet." (*A,* I, 256) Sir Robert Stawell Ball's *The Story of the Heavens* was published (London: Cassell) in 1885, and reissued in 1886 and 1891. The coincidence of the adolescent Johnny's and the middle-aged Boyle's reflections suggests, I submit, some investigation into how far O'Casey *distributed* his actual experience among his characters.

The Plough and the Stars (1926) is the first play in which O'Casey makes use of the Old Testament as a stroke in stageportraiture. This he can do without loss of verisimilitude, since Bessie Burgess is at least the remains of an Evangelical Protestant. O'Casey has her quote the Bible inexactly, as when she castigates Mrs. Gogan none too obliquely: ". . . a middle-aged married woman makin' herself th' centre of a circle of men is as a woman that is loud an' stubborn whose feet abideth not in her own house" (*CP,* I, 202). The verse, *Proverbs* 7.11., "She is loud and stubborn; her feet abide not in her house," is more insulting than it might appear to the non-Bible reader, for it is preceded in *Proverbs* by "And, behold, there met him a woman with the attire of a harlot, and subtil of heart" and succeeded by "Now she is without, now in the streets, and lieth in wait at every corner." O'Casey in 1926 may have enjoyed airing his knowledge of the Old Testament before a largely Roman Catholic audience. Few Catholics, I hazard, would have been able to place Bess-

ie's prayer at the end of Act III: "Oh, God, be Thou my help in time o' throuble. An' shelter me safely in th' shadow of Thy wings!" (*CP,* I, 238) In fact, Bessie, characteristically, garbles *Psalms* 36.7., 46.1., 61.4., and 63.7., to make her sublime appeal.

If O'Casey appeals to us through his use of Biblical language, so also does he through the rhetoric of P.H. Pearse which also, of course, is an integral in the structure of Act II. Pearse's writings had appeared in collected bookform 1917-1922 and so were easily available to O'Casey when he was writing **The Plough.** The extracts from Pearse's speech at the graveside of O'Donovan O'Rossa are not all that is heard of him in Act II (*CP,* I, 213). We also hear him quoting from an article he published in *Spark* in December 1915, "Peace and the Gael", an article which "went too far even for Connolly".[16] From it O'Casey culled the passage in which Pearse declares:

> The old heart of the earth needed to be warmed with the red wine of the battlefields. . . . Such august homage was never [before] offered to God as this: the homage of millions of lives given gladly for love of country. (*CP,* I, 196)

This statement by Pearse, derived from print, is more crucial to the significance of Act II than the passages from the Rossa oration, since it attempts to glorify *all* war, "for love of country" as "homage" to God. Act II in effect is, on one level, O'Casey's first major pacifist statement (he will exhibit a rather different stance towards the Second World War). We may with hindsight see that, having made that statement, it was not unlikely that he would go on to write a play like **The Silver Tassie** (1928).

Davoren quoted *Ecclesiastes,* Bessie Burgess quoted *Proverbs* and *Psalms,* The Croucher, who opens Act II of **Tassie,** paraphrases and adapts verses from *Ezekiel* 37, which, I would say, would be unfamiliar to the vast majority of audiences. But the provenance of The Croucher's speeches is crucial. Thus *Ezekiel* 37.9, runs "Prophesy unto the wind, prophesy, son of man, and say to the wind, Thus saith the Lord God, O breath, and breathe upon these slain, that they live", but becomes from The Croucher "And he said, prophesy, and say unto the wind, come from the four winds a breath and breathe upon these living that they may die." (*CP,* II, 36) The Croucher reverses the sense of the Lord's message to the preacher, just as the warlords have reversed the Gospels.

IV

The Silver Tassie, though rejected by the Abbey, had been intended for that theatre. **Within The Gates** (1933) was the first of eight full-length plays which were not (as well as two near full-length and four one-act[17] plays). The explicitly bookish content of this play is not great. The Atheist, adoptive father of The Young Woman, established her (after a fashion), in the line of Mary Boyle. He boasts to The Dreamer, "D'ye know, one time, the lass near knew the whole of Pine's [Paine's] *Age of Reason* off by 'eart!"

(*CP*, II, 124) That line is from the Stage Version which appeared in *Collected Plays;* it does not appear in the original printed text of 1933. But an amusing exchange, between the Bishop and the Bishop's Sister after he has made something of an ass of himself blessing babies in the park, is not carried over to the Stage Version from the text of 1933:

> *Bishop's Sister.* Shall we go somewhere dear, and read a little of Tennyson?
>
> *Bishop (snappily).* Oh, damn old Tennyson.[18]

The Star Turns Red (1940), O'Casey's apocalyptic version of Irish Labour's past and future, is remarkably pure from the bookishness one might expect from O'Casey's treatment of such a subject. There is perhaps an echo from the first lines of Yeats's "Sailing to Byzantium" in Jack's speech in Act III which begins "The young in each other's arms shall go on confirming the vigour of life." (*CP*, II, 319)

In **Purple Dust** (1940) O'Casey pillages well known English verse not to laud it, but to satirize the cultural pretentions of his two English refugees from the War: Basil Stoke and Cyril Poges. The fact that Stoke Poges is a village associated with the composition of Gray's "Elegy in a Country Churchyard" suggests that O'Casey, temporarily at least, has had his surfeit of official English culture. In the space of a few pages, Poges, romanticizing over his Irish mansion and the joys of country seclusion, hesitates over schoolbook lines from Wordsworth's "The Solitary Reaper"; attempts to paraphrase his Sonnet "The world is too much with us; late and soon"; misquotes Poe's "To Helen" ("the glory that was Rome and the grandeur that was Greece"), and maintains that "Shakespeare knew what he was talking about when he said that"; hits on [Wordsworth's] "the primrose by the river's brim, a yellow primrose was to him, but it was nothing more," as one of "the wild flowers that Shakespeare loved" (*CP*, III, 21-5). Clearly Poges is the product of a culture in which all other poets have been, as it were, strained through Wordsworth. Space considerations preclude full quotation of the stonemason O'Killigain's onslaught on "good old Wordsworth". It is inordinately vicious (*CP*, III, 21-2). In line with O'Killigain's perfervid deflation of Wordsworth in his description of Oxford, as, parodying James Thomson, "The city of dissolute might!" (*CP*, III, 103) When O'Killigain bids Avril, Poges's lady, be ready to leave when the river rises, Poges surpasses himself in trite quotations: "Come with me and be my love! Come into the garden Maud" (*CP*, III, 109). Marlowe of course he gets wrong. He closes the play, however, with his first *conscious* misquotations: from Browning's "Home Thoughts, From Abroad" he distils: "Would to God I were in England, now that winter's here!" (*CP*, III, 119)

If Poges (and Stoke) represent the superficies of public school culture Ayamonn Breydon in **Red Roses for Me** (1942) represents the genuineness of enlightened working-class culture. When the play opens we find him rehearsing

Gloucester in *3 Henry VI* V.vi. for a concern in the local Temperance Hall. Ayamonn says of the audiences: ". . . they're afraid of Shakespeare out of all that's been said of him. They think he's beyond them, while all the time he's part of the kingdom of heaven in the nature of everyman." (*CP*, III, 131) Later (p. 136) we hear that one Mullcanny will be bringing Ayamonn Haeckel's *The Riddle of the Universe.* Later again in Act I, Ayamonn offers to lend an Irish Irelander Ruskin's *The Crown of Wild Olive* and there follows a conversation that resembles Johnny Casside's with the tram conductor and includes the self same quotation from Ruskin.[19] In Act II Ayamonn reads out *Hamlet* 11.ii, 613-4 and cries, "Oh, Will, you were a boyo; a brave boyo, though, and a beautiful one!" (p. 163). In Act IV (p. 208), Ayamonn's friend, the Rev Mr Clinton, defends the young man's cross of daffodils for Easter, to his verger, with Shakespeare: *The Winter's Tale* IV.iv. 118-20. The verger's reply typifies the response already indicated by Ayamonn: "Altogether too high up for poor me, sir."

Ayamonn Breydon with his Shakespeare, his Ruskin, his Haeckel, his reproductions of Fra Angelico and Constable, is of course an idealized image of O'Casey himself. But he is something more: Everyman redeeming himself from the depths by the power of the Book, of *litera scripta.* The importance of *litera scripta* is seen even in his often jingoistic play about wartime England **Oak Leaves and Lavender** (1946). The ghostly Dancers who return to the blacked-out manorial house maintain that "Goldsmith, Berkeley, Boyle, Addison, Hone, Swift, and Sheridan still bear flaming torches through the streets of life" (*CP*, IV, 9). The Irish Leftist Drishogue bids his English friend Edgar fight and perhaps die for all the Englands: "For all of them in the greatness of England's mighty human soul set forth in what Shakespeare, Shelley, Keats, and Milton sang . . ." (*CP*, IV, 29). The Land Girl Jennie larks about with tags from Gray and Fitzgerald (p. 33). Drishogue's father, the butler Feelim, shows off to the pacifist Pobjoy about his knowledge of both the birth-place and grave of Milton (p. 95). Even in bouts of farcical comedy, we are never allowed to forget the mighty dead of literature.

The Book has an important place also in the last five plays to be discussed here. In **Cock-a-Doodle Dandy** (1949) Father Domineer come to exorcize the house of Michael Marthraun hears that Michael's daughter Loreleen has "evil books", gets into a frenzy not dissimilar from Jackie Boyle's in **Juno:** "Bring them out, bring them out! How often have I to warn you against books! Hell's bells tolling people away from th' truth!" (*CP*, IV, 200-1) Books are brought out for his inspection. They are "A book about Voltaire" which Father Domineer maintains has been banned[20] and "Ullisississies, or something" (p. 201). The books are sent to the Presbytery to be burned, another apparent victory for the pressure groups of anti-intellectualism. Loreleen, of course, is another variation on Minnie Powell-Mary Boyle. Robert Hogan has noted that "Of the late plays **The Drums of Father Ned** and **Behind the Green Curtains** are probably the most allusive, and

The Bishop's Bonfire is probably the least".[21] But possibly that gorgeous prop, the "buckineeno" later "bookneeno", a horn or cornet blown at inauspicious moments by the statue of the Bishop's patron, St. Tremolo, has its origins in O'Casey's literary experience. "St. Tremolo" we are told was "the fella . . . who played a buck, a buckineeno, in the old Roman Army."[22] O'Casey would have perhaps encountered "the bucina, the Roman war-trumpet" in Act I of Shaw's *Caesar and Cleopatra* where it is described as making a "terrible bellowing note".[23] If we see "St. Tremolo" as a commander-in-chief of Ballyoonagh's Roman legions, there is an added comic dimension to the fatuous gesture of the Bishop's Bonfire in which "piles of bad books an' evil pictures . . . are to go away in flames." (p. 29) A priest-writer who loved books is alluded to in the liberal young Father Boheroe's speech to Foorawn who has asked him if he is going to watch the Bishop's Bonfire: "my road goes in an opposite direction, where, though there be no cedars, at least, I shall walk under the stars." (p. 113) The allusion to Canon Sheehan,[24] I fear, is lost on most of those who read O'Casey.

The Drums of Father Ned (1960) gives us a development of Father Boheroe, but Father Ned does not appear. Under his influence Doonavale ("Shut his mouth") is waking up, and the young people are preparing a Boucicault-type play for An Tóstal.[25] In this springtime for Doonavale literary allusions are rife. Johnny Casside and Jackie Boyle creep into the mind when young Michael and Nora look at the stars (p. 82) and Nora completes Michael's quotation from Tennyson's "Locksley Hall" (ll. 9-10). The nouveaux riches Binningtons try to impress guests with a story about Yeats and Gogarty in Gogarty's *As I was Going Down Sackville Street,* but never get to tell it (p. 88). Michael scandalizes all by stating that God "may be but a shout in th' street" (p. 92) echoing Joyce.[26] Nora quotes Eliot in reverse when she says that the question of Red timber in Doonavale will be answered "not with a whimper, but with a bang!"[27] Binnington and McGilligan, in dishevelled mayoral robes, in feeble bravado quote (p. 101) from Blake's *Milton* inaccurately ("burnished gold" and "arras of desire"). The local allusions in **Behind the Green Curtains** (1961), a play set in Dublin and a town outside called Ballybeedhost ("Bally-Be-Quiet": compare Doonavale), are numerous but the purely literary allusions are thin on the ground. The enlightened industrialist Chatastray has Renan's *Life of Jesus* in his library: the journalist McGeelish takes it for "some cod book o' devotions".[28] The progressive worker, Beoman quotes Burns ("Wee, sleekit, cow'rin, tim'rous beastie") (p. 81), when Chatastray yields to ecclesiastical pressure (*Le chat* has become a mouse, perhaps).

Figuro in the Night (1961) bristles with an old man's literary jokes. It is an Old Woman who introduces Eliot's Sweeney Agonistes when she asks if Adam and Eve could sit forever "undher a breadfruit, undher a banyan, undher a bamboo tree, in a garden, eatin' grapes."[29] It is an Old Man who counters with Thomas Edward Brown's "A garden is a lovesome thing, God wot," and precipitates

lovely nonsense (p. 99). Another Old Man misquotes *The Ancient Mariner* (ll. 115-6) and is complemented by yet another greybeard (p. 106) misquoting ll. 117-8. The first of these two Old Men plays on *Hamlet* III.iv.103 (and possibly *The Mikado*) when he describes how his clothes have become "a thing o' shreds and patches" (p. 107). He also asks "Oh who'll call for th' robin an' th' wren" for protection against "all kinds of evil things" (p. 111), in the wake of the notorious Brussels "Figuro" set down overnight in Dublin, thus recalling Cornelia's lament for Marcello in Webster's *The White Devil* V.iv. This bookish joke is perhaps one of O'Casey's most bitter and effective: an echo from Renaissance tragedy in life and theatre introduced into the manic prurience of contemporary Ireland as he saw it.

I have by no means covered all the ground in this article which has attempted to establish not merely the weight of literary reference in O'Casey's plays, but also his life-long love and respect for books. He throve on them and often his imagination was fired by *litera scripta*. The autobiographies and the plays in a manner complement each other up to 1955 and provide one of many O'Casey portraits: the passionate autodidact.

Notes

1. *I Knock at the Door* (1939), in *Autobiographies* (2 vols., London: Macmillan, 1963), I, 175. *Autobiographies* is hereafter cited as A.

2. Denis Johnston runs him closely. See *The Dramatic Works of Denis Johnston* (3 vols., Gerrards Cross: Colin Smythe, 1977, 1979-).

3. A, II, 165. See J. Hartley Manners, *Peg o' My Heart* (New York: Grosset, 1912). The play was first produced in 1913.

4. A, I, 195-6. Cf. David Krause, ed., *The Dolmen Boucicault* (Dublin: The Dolmen Press, 1963), pp. 181-2.

5. Jack Lindsay, "Sean O'Casey as a Socialist Artist", in Ronald Ayling (ed.), *Sean O'Casey: Modern Judgements* (London: Macmillan, 1969), p. 202.

6. A, I, 356. See John Ruskin, *The Crown of Wild Olive* (Orpington, Kent: G. Allen, 1882), pp. 90-1.

7. A, I, 293. Cf. Anthony Butler, "Town Talk", *Evening Herald,* 22 July 1975.

8. *Purgatory,* in *Collected Plays* (London: Macmillan, second edition, 1963), p. 681.

9. Joseph Hone, *W.B. Yeats, 1865-1939* (London: Macmillan, second edition, 1962), p. 249.

10. Brenna Katz Clarke and Harold Ferrar, *The Dublin Drama League 1919-1941* (Dublin: The Dolmen Press, 1979), pp. 22-31. "Sean O'Casey attended, [Gabriel] Fallon estimates, about sixty per cent of the Drama League's plays" (p. 16).

11. Ronald Ayling and Michael J. Durkan, *Sean O'Casey: A Bibliography* (London and Basingstoke: The Macmillan Press, 1978), p. 7.

12. *Collected Plays* (4 vols., London: Macmillan, 1949-64), I, 93. Hereafter cited as *CP*.

13. *CP*, I, 96, 101, 105, 156.

14. *CP*, I, 23. *Elizabeth; or, the Exiles of Siberia*, a novel by Marie Cottin, was first published in Paris in 1806, the first Dublin edition (a translation) appearing in 1811. It went through many editions up to the 1890s. Maurice Harmon describes it as "that kind of sentimental novel in which heroines of extraordinary virtue undergo the most unlikely hazards and are then rewarded by marriage, money, happiness and position." See Harmon's article, "Didja ever rade Elizabeth, or Th' Exile o' Sibayria?" in *Era*, 3 (n.d.), 34-38. The quotation is from p. 34.

15. André Boné, *William Carleton, romancier irlandais (1794-1869)* (Paris: Publications de la Sorbonne, 1978), p. 129.

16. Ruth Dudley Edwards, *Patrick Pearse: The Triumph of Failure* (London: Faber, 1979), p. 245.

17. For space considerations I have omitted all the one-act plays, of which there are eight extant. See Ayling and Durkan, *A Bibliography*.

18. *Within the Gates* (London: Macmillan, 1933), p. 55.

19. *CP*, III, 157-8. Cf. *A*, I, 355-6.

20. Probably an allusion to Alfred Noyes's *Voltaire* (London: Sheed and Ward, 1936). Noyes, a convert to the Catholic church, displeased the Holy Office.

21. "The Haunted Inkbottle", in *The James Joyce Quarterly*, VIII (No. 1, Fall 1970), p. 86. See also Christopher Murray, "Two More Allusions in *Cock-a-Doodle Dandy*", in *The Sean O'Casey Review*, IV (No. 1, Fall 1977), 6-18.

22. *The Bishop's Bonfire* (London: Macmillan, 1955), p. 53.

23. *Complete Plays with Prefaces* (6 vols., New York: Dodd, Mead, 1963), III, p. 380.

24. See P.A. Sheehan, *Under the Cedars and the Stars* (Dublin: Browne and Nolan, 1903).

25. *The Drums of Father Ned* (London: Macmillan, 1960), p. 34.

26. Ibid., p. 92. Cf. James Joyce, *Ulysses* (London: Bodley Head, 1962), p. 42.

27. Ibid., p. 95. Cf. T.S. Eliot, "The Hollow Men", in *The Complete Poems and Plays* (New York: Harcourt, Brace and World, 1962), p. 59.

28. *Behind the Green Curtains, Figuro in the Night, The Moon Shines on Kylenamoe* (London: Macmillan, 1961), p. 28.

29. *Figuro*, p. 99. Cf. T.S. Eliot, *Collected Poems and Plays*, p. 81.

Heinz Kosok (essay date 1986)

SOURCE: "Juno and the Playwrights: The Influence of Sean O'Casey on Twentieth-Century Drama," in *Irish Writers and the Theatre,* edited by Masaru Sekine, Colin Smythe, 1986, pp. 71-86.

[*In the following essay, Kosok demonstrates that O'Casey's influence on contemporary dramatists was negligible beyond his work in the "Dublin trilogy."*]

> I come from the same area as Sean O'Casey about whom I don't intend to say anything for the simple reason that it would be like praising the Lakes of Killarney—a piece of impertinence. As far as I'm concerned, all I can say is that O'Casey's like champagne, one's wedding night, or the Aurora Borealis or whatever you call them—all them lights.[1]

This is how an Irish fellow dramatist, Brendan Behan, reacted to the plays of Sean O'Casey, whom he considered 'the greatest playwright living in my opinion',[2] and whom he defended vigorously against O'Casey's Irish critics:

> In the United States, O'Casey is studied and praised in schools and universities all over the country. In the U.S.S.R. he is a highly respected artist. O'Casey is one of the few remaining unifying influences in a divided world. Why the hell should he care about a few crawthumpers in Ireland?[3]

Behan's praise, even if worded somewhat exuberantly, is fairly typical of the reaction of many twentieth-century dramatists to the plays of Sean O'Casey. John Arden (to cite a few highly diverse playwrights) confessed: '. . . I have been continuously inspired and excited by his plays—from all periods of his work . . .' and he defended O'Casey as an experimental playwright and as a European rather than an Irishman.[4] Equally, Arnold Wesker stated: 'I can only say he was among my loves and influences'.[5] Arthur Adamov insisted on his attachment to the plays of O'Casey whose 'tenderness' he singled out for special praise as O'Casey's most exceptional merit;[6] and he even placed O'Casey on the same level as Brecht.[7] Bertolt Brecht more than once referred approvingly to the plays of O'Casey.[8] And Brian Friel stated quite simply: 'We all came out from under his overcoat.'[9]

Eugene O'Neill and Denis Johnston also spoke very highly of O'Casey's early plays, even if they were not prepared to accept his later departure from the realities of the Dublin slums. O'Neill grumbled after he had read ***The Star Turns Red***: '. . . O'Casey is an artist and the soap box is no place for his great talent. The hell of it seems to be, when an artist starts saving the world, he starts losing himself'.[10] And Johnston fired a whole barrage of articles against O'Casey's later plays while conferring upon his earlier ones the greatest honour a writer has to give, that of parodying them. Not only did he insist 'The consummate craftsman who could create the second Act of ***The Plough and the Stars*** clearly knows as much as need be known about the English language . . .',[11] he also called his own play about the Easter Rising *The Scythe and the Sunset,* and in *The Old Lady Says 'No!'* he even brought a worker playwright named O'Cooney on stage who is a replica of O'Casey at the time of his early fame.

Distinctly negative pronouncements are less easy to discover. The shrillest of them is that made by Brinsley MacNamara who, when he was a director of the Abbey

Theatre, denounced his fellow directors and the Dublin audience in 1935 for their 'wholly uncritical, and I might say, almost insane admiration for the vulgar and worthless plays of Mr. O'Casey'.[12]

If O'Casey found widespread acclaim among his fellow dramatists, the question remains whether their pronouncements are indicative of an influence that O'Casey may have exerted on their plays. Did he in any way shape the work of his contemporaries (as artists, if not in age) such as Brecht or O'Neill, or did a younger generation—Behan, Arden, Wesker and others—follow him as a model? And if such an influence is discovered, how does one measure it? It is of course highly dangerous to set down every superficial parallel as a possible influence; serious research into literary influences has often been discredited by source-hunting of this kind.

Literary critics have usually been just as vague on the subject of a possible O'Caseyan influence as O'Casey's fellow dramatists. If John Arden, for instance, is characterised as 'a writer whose theatrical genius is strangely similar to that of O'Casey',[13] it hardly helps to pinpoint concrete influences. Usually, critics have not taken the question any further than the following statement which is quite useless as criticism:

> . . . O'Casey extended his experiment by mixing realistic and non-realistic techniques in his plays—a mingled form which he was to use in all his later plays, and which has subsequently been used by most modern dramatists, to mention some representative examples, Obey's *Noah* (1931), Wilder's *Our Town* (1938), Giraudoux's *Madwoman of Chaillot* (1945), Williams's *The Glass Menagerie* (1944), Miller's *Death of a Salesman* (1949).[14]

What, if anything, one is inclined to ask, do these playwrights have in common with O'Casey; are they supposed to have consciously or subconsciously imitated him; and was there nobody given to 'mixing realistic and non-realistic techniques' (whatever these may be) *before* O'Casey? Even when his influence is seen as limited to one particular group of playwrights, it is still described in far from precise terms, as in the following statement:

> . . . his working-class origin, and apprenticeship as a labourer rather than an intellectual, made him a culture hero of the new English dramatists of 1956. Worthy on his record of the highest official honours, here was a world-famous man of the theatre who, even in old age, made no concessions to established authority. . . . You can read his influence most obviously, of course, in *The Quare Fellow* and *The Hostage* by Brendan Behan. But O'Casey's influence goes much further than that. It extends to Arden, Wesker, Delaney, Rudkin, Alun Owen and a dozen others, wherever in fact urban dialect is shaped, selected and built up to the purposes of serious drama, wherever the rejects of society, the soldiers in *Serjeant Musgrave's Dance* or the rustics in *Afore Night Come,* are put in the centre of the stage and given a voice. They copied his faults, too, whenever they cultivated a folksy togetherness or let feeble stereotypes put the case for the ruling classes.[15]

The question of literary influence is certainly a difficult one. It is difficult not only where the technical problem of detecting and documenting such influence is concerned. It also encompasses the question of evaluation. Does a writer's importance depend on the amount of influence he has exerted on others? Would it be possible to argue, in other words, that a writer's literary qualities could be measured in terms of his influence? Or could one say, conversely, that the truly great artist is so special that he cannot be copied or imitated or even taken as a model by others? In the field of twentieth-century drama, Strindberg, Ibsen, Chekhov, Wilder and Brecht can be seen as examples of the first case, while Hauptmann, O'Neill, Shaw and Anouilh illustrate the second. The influence of Brecht, to take an example, upon a host of other writers was perhaps even greater than the literary quality of his works would have warranted; it is not too much to say that the whole course of twentieth-century drama would have been different if it had not been for the model of Brecht—a model that often was not even realised as such. On the other hand, O'Neill remained a lonely giant without followers, whose greatness seems to stand out even more because he did not initiate any tradition whatsoever.

Where O'Casey is concerned, both arguments could be used with equal conviction. O'Casey wrote highly diverse plays, which renders it practically impossible to make general statements about his work. If one sub-divides his career as a playwright into five phases,[16] it is only the first one, with his great 'Dublin' plays like ***Juno and the Paycock*** and ***The Plough and the Stars,*** that can be shown to have been influential for other dramatists. In his later plays, especially in masterpieces like ***The Silver Tassie, Red Roses for Me*** and ***Cock-a-doodle Dandy,*** O'Casey was moving in a direction where apparently nobody wanted to, or was able to, follow him. As far as his plays written after 1926 are concerned, the question of his influence on other writers could be answered in one brief sentence: it was largely non-existent.

A variety of reasons can be cited to account for this statement. First, O'Casey's exceptional life history made it difficult for him to come into close contact with other writers. He was forty-three when his first play reached the stage; consequently he was always at least half a generation older than his 'contemporary' fellow dramatists. This is partly why he never had access to a larger circle of writers. In addition, his social status and his fragmentary, largely autodidactic education prevented him from being accepted as a 'man of letters'. When he settled down in Devon in 1938, he isolated himself in a geographic as well as a social sense from the literary scenes of London and Dublin. It was only during his sojourn of slightly more than ten years in or near London that he had a chance to make closer contact with other writers, but even then he seems not to have availed himself more than occasionally of this opportunity. Therefore younger playwrights had little chance of being closely acquainted with him; an influence on the immediate personal level was practically impossible.

Second, after 1926, when O'Casey had moved to England, he also lacked direct contact with a particular theatre that could have staged model productions of his plays, as did the Abbey Theatre with his early works. An influence like the one exerted by Brecht through the Theater am Schiffbauerdamm was impossible for him after 1926.

Third, again with the exception of his early plays, O'Casey's writings did not gain any great influence through the theatre, simply because they were not acted frequently enough. Most of his plays after **The Plough and the Stars** received only one or two productions during his life-time in the English-speaking world, and several of these took place in provincial or even amateur theatres, far removed from the beaten track of critics and the general public alike. Consequently, younger playwrights whom he might have induced to learn from him did not have a chance of seeing more than an accidental selection of his writings on stage.

Fourth, O'Casey did not develop any coherent dramatic theory. His various statements on the drama, the theatre, and on literary theory in general are highly relevant to an understanding of his own works; they are always interesting, often amusing and sometimes remarkably astute, but they do not add up to any organic system of critical insights.

And fifth, because he lacked any basic dramatic theory, his plays are markedly divergent, even more so perhaps than those of such fellow dramatists as Hauptmann or O'Neill. Few of them are based in any way on insights derived from the preceding work; in the second and third phases of his career especially, each play constitutes a new departure and tries to solve new problems. This variety makes O'Casey a truly experimental playwright, but it has certainly reduced his influence on others, and it makes it practically impossible to recognize any influence derived from the whole body of his work. Instead, one has to look for the influence of individual plays.

An example of such isolated influence by an individual play can perhaps be seen in T.S. Eliot's *The Family Reunion*, the choric technique of which may well have been modelled on O'Casey's **Within the Gates**. Eliot had seen the London production of **Within the Gates** in 1934, and had shown himself impressed by O'Casey's use of chants in his play; he later thought that he might have been unconsciously influenced by O'Casey.[17]

Such individual influences of O'Casey's later plays dwindle into insignificance however in comparison with the unmistakable impact of the early plays, especially **The Shadow of a Gunman, Juno and the Paycock,** and **The Plough and the Stars**. Not surprisingly, such influence makes itself felt most of all in Anglo-Irish drama. Here, his influence seems to have worked in two ways, not only in the form of direct imitation, which is, of course, predominant, but also as an impulse to be as different as possible from O'Casey, the desire not at any cost to be taken as a follower. O'Casey's importance as a model *and* also an anti-model for the whole of Anglo-Irish drama

since the twenties can be appreciated when one observes that the only history of drama to cover this field, Robert Hogan's *After the Irish Renaissance,* cites O'Casey on almost every page as a standard of evaluation for all other playwrights.

For a while it had looked as if the O'Caseyan influence would produce a flood of melodramatic plays about the Irish War of Independence and the Civil War. This is underlined by an amusing review of a long-forgotten play, Gerald Brosnan's *Before Midnight,* of 1928, written at a time when O'Casey had already turned away from this material:

> I do not suppose that the spiritual father of the Abbey gunmen, C.I.D. men and prostitutes who has recently forsaken his offspring will claim the literary paternity of Mr. Gerald Brosna, or that Mr. Brosnan will acknowledge any relationship with him. I do not suppose, either, that the Abbey audience will accept *Before Midnight* even as a drop of O'Casey war-substitute. But I do plead for a Kellog pact of dramatic disarmament and the blowing-up of dumps. In art there is no such thing as a successful school. O'Casey, as a man of genius, closed the door he opened. It makes a strong man blench to think of an O'Casey school, to think of the myriad of Mr. Brosnan's unproduced colleagues who are raiding Dublin tenement houses, stuffing their plays in vain with revolvers and prositutes and C.I.D. men.[18]

Fortunately the reviewer's misgivings did not come true. A few works only of this particular tradition have been preserved. The most remarkable among them is undoubtedly Brendan Behan's *The Hostage* which has been called 'a gaily subversive play in the O'Casey tradition'[19] and had the greatest success of all Irish works in that mould.

Behan's indebtedness to O'Casey can fully be gauged only when one considers the original Gaelic version, *An Giall,* in addition to Joan Littlewood's English adaptation. Here the action has not yet been broken up into 'alienating' music-hall acts, and the parallels to O'Casey are much more obvious. It is not, however, sufficient to speak simply of an influence on the part of O'Casey, for Behan in many respects went beyond his model, developing and sometimes exaggerating O'Caseyan motifs. As in **The Shadow of a Gunman, Juno and the Paycock** and parts of **The Plough and the Stars,** the scenery of *The Hostage* is a room in a tenement house; like O'Casey, Behan was thinking of a definite house in Dublin. Several of his characters are immediately reminiscent of O'Casey's figures; the humorous, sceptical, quarrelsome and nevertheless helpful Pat cannot be imagined without the model of Fluther Good, and Teresa, in her strange mixture of fairy-tale naiveté, shyness, healthy self-confidence, practical altruism, courage and affection is closely related to Minnie Powell. It is also tempting to see Monsewer, who in his ridiculous kilt haunts the play as a symbol of the dead past and is treated by everybody with mock respect, as a relation of the Man in the Kilts in **Kathleen Listen In;** yet it is unlikely that Behan knew O'Casey's early play, for it was not published until 1961. It is more certain, however, that he refers to

Rosie Redmond from *The Plough and the Stars,* the first and most famous prostitute on the Irish stage, when, in characteristic exaggeration of his model, he depicts a whole brothel whose inmates, prostitutes, pimps, homosexuals, are treated with the same humour, understanding and compassion as was Rosie.

The stage events in *The Hostage* are projected onto a politicomilitary background action that repeatedly erupts on the stage, immediately affecting the stage characters. Behan, however, is much critical of the historical process than his predecessor. The I.R.A. activities of the nineteen-fifties, as an anachronistic continuation of the struggle for independence, are not only, as in O'Casey, criticised by some of the stage-figures, but are disparaged by the action itself: the senseless and accidental death of young Leslie condemns those who are responsible for his kidnapping. In addition, the guerilla fighters are, in contrast to O'Casey, shown here in a decidedly negative light. On the other hand, the real struggel for independence which is constantly present in the conversation of the stage figures, is treated with a similar objectivity to that found in O'Casey. In both cases, however, it is not the politico-military action but its effects on individual, well-defined characters that is at the centre of the play. In his juxtaposition of serious and comic elements, Behan goes beyond O'Casey, although at the time of *Juno and the Paycock* this must have appeared hardly possible. There is no doubt that Behan could achieve this extreme blending of styles only after the path had been prepared for him by O'Casey.

The Hostage, as a late reaction to O'Casey's plays of the Revolution and the Civil War, takes up an exceptional position. In the meantime, O'Casey's early plays had been much more influential in another field of Irish drama. O'Casey was the first to introduce the world of the Dublin slums to world literature, and the specific tradition he created is that of the family play set in the slums. Once the tradition had been established, dozens of plays were set in the tenements around Mountjoy Square. Only a few of them have appeared in print; Seamus de Burca's *The Howards* (1960), Robert Collis's *Marrowbone Lane* (1939) and Brendan Behan's short-play *Moving Out* (1952) may be cited as examples. All three deal with family histories from the Dublin slums and belong to the O'Casey tradition in a wider sense, although they do not show any specific indebtedness to O'Casey.

Several plays, however, written under the influence of O'Casey's works derive more directly from *Juno and the Paycock.* Louis D'Alton's *The Mousetrap* (1938), for instance, depicts a family strongly reminiscent of *Juno and the Paycock,* with a sneering and domineering but unsuccessful father, a long-suffering mother, a son who through one rash action mars his whole future and is finally arrested for murder, and a daughter who is left pregnant by the intruder from the outside world. Like O'Casey's play, *The Mousetrap* is realistic in intention, with roughly sketched characters and nicely observed dialogue, but the plot is far too contrived, the disasters succeeding each

other with improbable rapidity because, unlike O'Casey, the author tries to confine his action within the classically acceptable 24 hours limit. At the time of its publication the author's obvious sympathy for the 'fallen' girl, and his understanding for the seducer, together with his contempt for the upholders of conventional morality, apparently made the play unacceptable for the Irish stage, while its model has become a staple of the Irish theatrical repertoire.

Walter Macken's *Mungo's Mansion* (1946) transfers O'Casey's characters from the Dublin tenements to the slums of Galway. The unemployed Mungo is another 'Captain' Boyle, seen slightly less critically, whose excitability is motivated at least in part by a previous accident. His love-hate relationship to the ragged Mowleogs is immediately reminiscent of Boyle and Joxer, a similarity underlined by the unexpected win in the sweep-stake. As in O'Casey, this play, under the rather repulsive surface of quarrels and egoism, hides a great deal of attachment, helpfulness and uncomplicated humanity. The chief differences are the absence of a character comparable to Juno and the absence of a politico-military background action.[20]

A Juno-like character is present, however, in a play that transfers the atmosphere of O'Casey's drama to yet another town, a poor area of Waterford: this is James Cheasty's *Francey* (1961). Again, as in *Mungo's Mansion,* the conflict between the care-worn, protective mother and her spendthrift husband is intensified by the presence of a parasitic character, a direct successor of Joxer, revealingly named Jock, who exploits the title character, a direct successor of 'Captain' Boyle, and turns against him when the source has fallen dry. There is also a hare-brained neighbour addicted to the lowest type of gossip, whose words could have come directly from O'Casey's Mrs. Madigan, without, however, taking on her thematic function in the play. Francey himself is another braggart who lives in a world of fantasy and cares nothing for his wife, senselessly spending the compensation money he has received after a road-accident, until his married life, as well as his children, are ruined. Unlike O'Casey's play the motif of unexpected, destructive wealth has become central, triggering off a melodramatic action that leads to an unmitigated catastrophe. The protective forces embodied in Juno are here not strong enough to counteract the destructive forces of 'Captain' Boyle. Obviously the author has taken over the individual ingredients of O'Casey's play without grasping their contextual, supra-individual meaning. It is, perhaps, the absence of a more general background action, more than anything else, that leads Cheasty into the double abyss of sentimentality and sensationalism.

Both the Juno-character and the general background action are present in a work that more than any other resembles the O'Casey play: Joseph Tomelty's *The End House* (1944). In this case it is sufficient to characterise Tomelty's work, without any explicit comparison, in order to draw attention to the obvious parallels with *Juno and the Paycock. The End House* is set in a poor, Catholic quarter of Belfast, the historical background being the Troubles of

1938. The central characters are the unemployed braggart and show-off MacAstocker, his wife Sar Alice, who throughout her life has been struggling for the survival of her family and does not expect any more from life than to provide enough to eat for her relations, her daughter Monica, who hopes to achieve a higher station in life and wants to leave the influence of the slums behind her, and her son Seamus, who has just been released from a prison sentence for his membership in the illegal I.R.A. The initial situation of the play concerns the death of a neighbour who has been shot by I.R.A. men because he had betrayed one of them to the police. The audience learns about his death when a newspaper article is read at the beginning of the play. This event is succeeded by a series of catastrophes: Sar Alice loses her insurance money, MacAstocker is injured in an accident, Monica falls in love with an English soldier who deserts with the money borrowed from her and leaves her helpless, possibly pregnant, Seamus is probably involved in the killing of the neighbour and is himself shot during a raid. Sar Alice and Monica remain as the victims, who are not even able to repay the money they borrowed from their neighbours and thus lose their good name.

In view of these parallels, which are supported by many minor details, it is necessary to emphasise the differences between the two plays in order to protect Tomelty from the accusation of straightforward plagiarism. The characters in *The End House* are seen less critically. MacAstocker is less depreciated by his actions than Boyle, and there is no character comparable to Joxer. In his place, Tomelty has introduced two 'positive' helpful neighbours, and the cornet player Stewartie is his most interesting innovation. Because of the absence of a Joxer-like character, *The End House* lacks a great deal of the humour of *Juno and the Paycock;* its emotional tone, therefore, is more homogeneous. It is stamped by the author's compassion for the victims of the political situation. Although there is no attempt to make the theme explicit, as O'Casey had in Juno's prayer, the author's purpose in the play is more obvious and more unified. Where all the stage characters are seen with sympathy, and are presented as innocent victims, the responsibility for such a situation must fall entirely on the existing political system, which is additionally criticised here in the brutality and despotism of the police.

A direct continuation of *The End House* may be seen in John Boyd's *The Flats* (1971), set in the Belfast of 1969. The 'end house' has here been replaced by the 'end flat', situated in a strategic position in a block of flats. It is commandeered both by the British Army and by the Civil Defence Committee, at a time when a Protestant mob threatens to attack the flats inhabited predominantly by Catholics. This situation gives rise to extended discussions of various political viewpoints: militant republicanism, moderate nationalism, pacifism, socialism, the self-styled neutrality of the British Army, and a wholly understandable individualism concerned only with personal survival. Whereas the political background events have thus been updated, the mechanism for projecting them onto the stage

is still that provided by O'Casey in *Juno and the Paycock.* The list of *dramatis personae* again reads like a description of O'Casey's play. There is the same constellation of the unemployed father who neglects his family, the care-worn mother untiring in her efforts to keep the family together, the outsider son who engages in subversive activities, and the disillusioned daughter who hopes for an escape from the slums through her fiancé who comes over from England. It is true that Boyd has omitted the time-worn motifs of seduction and unexpected riches, but the whole atmosphere of slum life under the pressure of a military conflict is closely reminiscent of *Juno and the Paycock,* and so is Boyd's use of test situations to distinguish between various attitudes to life, even to the point where a British soldier is to be given a cup of tea, and the characters react in various ways to this challenge, just as Johnny's demand for a glass of water in O'Casey's play had helped to distinguish between Juno and Mary. Even if Joe Donellan is not such a despicable good-for-nothing as 'Captain' Boyle, numerous details (including Kathleen's concluding prayer) point to the immense influence of O'Casey's work. It is a measure of O'Casey's success that his play is so much more convincing, unified, life-like, moving and universal than its successors and will be remembered when all the others are forgotten.

The literary reactions to *Juno and the Paycock,* however, were not limited to Anglo-Irish drama. In fact, the influence of this play could hardly have been more widespread geographically as well as chronologically. It was O'Casey's only work to have initiated a new and still living literary tradition, that of the family play set in the slums. This type of play undoubtedly owed something to the tradition of bourgeois tragedy, but it is precisely those traits that O'Casey added to the tradition, especially the transfer of the events into the squalid world of big-city slums, that were widely imitated. If *Juno and the Paycock* was not the first play with such a setting, it was the first that was internationally successful. Moreover, O'Casey provided a specific combination of characters, plot elements and motifs which reappeared in a number of plays, rendering a concrete influence in each case more than probable. Four examples may be briefly described to illustrate this point.

One of the best-known English plays between the two world wars, justly appreciated by audiences throughout Britain, was *Love on the Dole* (1934) by Ronald Gow and Walter Greenwood, a play set in the world of the unemployed, a working-class quarter of Salford, Lancashire. Its constellation of *dramatis personae,* however, is that of *Juno and the Paycock*: the unemployed father, the indefatigable mother who alone keeps the family together, the daughter striving for 'higher' values. As in *Juno and the Paycock* the action is determined by the dual motifs of seduction and of unexpected wealth that disappears as soon as it has been won, and it is interspersed with comic elements. As in O'Casey's play, the necessity of strikes and demonstrations is discussed. Although none of these elements alone would suffice to constitute an influence, their combination points quite clearly to O'Casey.

Clifford Odets's *Awake and Sing!* (1935) belongs to the same period as *Love on the Dole*. Of this play it has been said: 'Awake and Sing!, though not so great a play, is **Juno and the Paycock** transposed from the Dublin slums to the Jewish Bronx of New York. It has the same pattern of coarseness and sensibility, the quality that can send poetry, like a shaft of sunlight, through the squalor of a tenement'.[21] The specific Dublin milieu, unique in language and characters, has here been replaced by another, equally specific milieu. It is true that in O'Casey's Dublin the Berger family's standard of living would hardly qualify them as the inhabitants of a slum, but the higher material demands of the American way of life classify them as members of the lowest social class whose existence is constantly threatened by unemployment. It is significant that the descriptions of the *dramatis personae* with which Odets prefaces his play, could be transferred, with very slight modifications, to the characters in **Juno and the Paycock**. The relationship of Bessie to Juno, for instance, can hardly be overlooked:

> BESSIE BERGER, as she herself states, is not only the mother in this home but also the father. She is constantly arranging and taking care of her family. She loves life, likes to laugh, has great resourcefulness, and enjoys living from day to day. A high degree of energy accounts for her quick exasperation at ineptitude. She is a shrewd judge of realistic qualities in people in the sense of being able to gauge quickly their effectiveness. In her eyes all of the people in the house are equal. She is naive and quick in emotional response. She is afraid of utter poverty. She is proper according to her own standards, which are fairly close to those of most middle-class families. She knows that when one lives in the jungle one must look out for the wild life.[22]

She tyrannises her family because she is deeply concerned about their happiness. She asserts herself against her husband who has been defeated by life and lives in fruitless memories of the past, as well as against her son who rebels against a purely materialistic attitude, and she cares for her self-confident daughter who would like to dissociate herself from the family, when she expects an illegitimate child and finds that no other refuge is left to her. Like the motif of seduction, the motif of unexpected wealth (Jacob's insurance money when he kills himself), point to the model of O'Casey's play. Even more reminiscent of O'Casey is the fact that this family in the process of disintegration, shaken by various catastrophes, entirely cut off from the world outside and thrown upon itself, is nevertheless not presented as an image of hopelessness and despair. Small gestures of affection are still capable of fending off the apparently all-powerful fate of poverty, and the final victory of Juno's humanity is here paralleled in Ralph's defeat of resignation and material dependence, even though Odets's solution seems to be less organic than O'Casey's.

Arnold Wesker's early play *Chicken Soup with Barley* (1958) is set in a similar and equally well-defined social context as *Awake and Sing!*, the world of East European Jewish emigrants in London. Although it appeared more than twenty years later, it has its starting point in the same

historical situation, the thirties, a period overshadowed by economic crises and mass unemployment that seemed to predict an imminent end to the capitalist bourgeois way of life. In *Chicken Soup with Barley* the familiar constellation of *dramatis personae* from **Juno and the Paycock** is again clearly recognizable (in the other two plays of the *Chicken Soup Trilogy* it is still present, though less obvious).[23] The resolute and optimistic mother who fights for the material welfare of her family, the resigned, passive, egocentric father, the son who is engaged in political activities and his elder sister, initially equally active but later disillusioned, all owe their existence as much to the model of the Boyle family as to Wesker's personal experience. The relationship is sometimes underlined in conspicuous details. Ada, for instance, turns one of 'Captain' Boyle's favourite terms against her father, who is so closely related to Boyle: 'Daddy—you are the world's biggest procrastinator'. And Sarah's indefatigable care for her family's welfare is symbolised in the same action as Juno's motherliness: her never-tiring readiness to make tea as a spontaneous cure-all for problems, sorrows and disease:

> SARAH: Sit down, both of you; I'll get the kettle on [*Goes off to kitchen.*]
>
> MOUNTY: [*to Bessie*] Always put the kettle on—that was the first thing Sarah always did. Am I right, Harry? I'm right, aren't I? [*shouting to Sarah*] Remember, Sarah? It was always a cup of tea first.[24]

Juno reacts in an identical way:

> MRS. BOYLE: There, now; go back an' lie down again, an' Ill bring you in a nice cup o' tay.
>
> JOHNNY: Tay, tay, tay! You're always thinkin' o' tay. If a man was dyin' you'd thry to make him swally a cup o' tay![25]

Even more important is the fact that *Chicken Soup with Barley*, like **Juno and the Paycock**, is projected onto a historical background action which intensifies the stage events and raises them to a universal plane. The changing role of socialism in the England of the thirties, forties and fifties that dominates the discussions of the stage characters and is occasionally projected on stage when they take part in demonstrations and, like Johnny, are wounded, is depicted with the same sceptical objectivity as the civil war in **Juno and the Paycock**, the author refraining from restricting his characters' individuality by imposing any opinion of his own. *Chicken Soup with Barley* is the most remarkable example of the far-reaching influence that O'Casey exerted, without, however, in any way constraining his successors' originality of creation.

Another, not quite so conspicuous example is Errol John's *Moon on a Rainbow Shawl* (1958), of which Doris Lessing has said with some exaggeration: '. . . it is nearer to O'Casey than anything else in our language'.[26] O'Casey's Dublin tenement milieu has here undergone a more unusual transformation, and yet the ugly slums of Port of Spain, Trinidad, show surprising parallels to the world of 'Captain' Boyle, underlining the universality of O'Casey's play. The precise representation of a world of poverty characterised by its dialect, habits and types of persons is equally reminiscent of O'Casey, as is the unsentimental poetisation of this world. As in *Juno and the Paycock,* brutal egoism exists side by side with a most admirable altruism, and one finds the resigned adaptation to apparently unavoidable necessities as well as the attempt at revolt. The situation of Mary has been shared between two characters, Rosa who will be alone to care for her child, and Esther, who has not (yet?) given up the struggle against the repressive forces of her surroundings. The clearest O'Casey influence is, however, again to be found in the parents: Sophia has been made ruthless and angry by the responsibilities that have been forced upon her, but she takes her role as the protectress of the family as seriously as Juno, while Charlie in his resignation escapes from his duties into drunkenness and the reminiscences of his past as a cricket star.

The influence of Sean O'Casey on twentieth-century drama has, therefore, not been as extensive as that of some other playwrights, like Ibsen, Chekhov or Brecht. As a basically optimistic playwright he stood little chance of widespread imitation at a time when pessimism had become the vogue even in popular entertainment. As an experimental playwright he could not build up a tradition of O'Casey plays, because he tended to question the technique of each of his own plays in the following works. And as a playwright who combined highly diverse styles—the tragic and the farcical, the realistic and the fantastic, the poetic and the allegorical—he did not project a unified image that could be followed by less gifted writers.

He did, however, exert a strong influence in a few clearly circumscribed fields. He introduced the slums of Dublin to the stage and made them acceptable as a literary milieu. He encouraged Irish authors to write about the tenement dwellers, and to do so with the typical O'Caseyan mixture of humour, understanding and compassion. And most of all, he created in *Juno and the Paycock* a play that could be followed, in its over-all structure as well as in many details of characterisation, plot motifs, and theme, in many parts of the world, a play, moreover, that presents one of the most important links between traditional bourgeois tragedy and modern proletarian drama. In addition to his own plays, this basic pattern of *Juno and the Paycock* was O'Casey's most valuable gift to the world of literature.

Notes

1. *Brendan Behan's Island: An Irish Sketch-book.* London: Transworld Publishers, 1965, pp. 12-14.

2. *Confessions of an Irish Rebel.* London: Hutchinson, 1965, p.30.

3. Letter to the *Irish Times* (29 August 1961), quoted by John O'Riordan, 'O'Casey's Dublin Critics', *Library Review,* 21, ii (1967), 63.

4. Letter to the *Observer* (27 September 1964), quoted *ibid.*

5. Quoted in Bernard Leroy, 'Two Committed Playwrights: Wesker and O'Casey', in: Patrick Rafroidi, Raymonde Popot and William Parker (eds), *Aspects of the Irish Theatre.* Lille: Editions Universitaires, 1972, p.116.

6. 'J'ai souvent dit et répe´té mon attachement à l'oeuvre de Sean O'Casey, où l'ambiguité des situations et des personnages n'entrainent presque jamais confusions et équivoques, et où la sévérité, non plus, ne devient pas hargneuse. La tendresse d'O'Casey pour ses personnages me frappe à chaque nouvelle représentation, et c'est peut-être là que se trouve son plus exceptionnel mérite.' Arthur Adamov, 'La femme avenir de l'homme' dans l'oeuvre de Sean O'Casey', *Lettres Francaises,* no. 1028 (1964).

7. *Sinn und Form,* 13 (1961), 938-939.

8. See Beate Lahrmann-Hartung, *Sean O'Casey und das epische Theater Bertolt Brechts,* Neue Studien zur Anglistik und Amerikanistik, 28. Frankfurt: Lang, 1983, p.10.

9. *Sean O'Casey Review,* 4 (1978), 87.

10. Quoted in Arthur and Barbara Gelb, *O'Neill.* New York: Harper & Row, 2nd ed. 1973, p.830.

11. 'Joxer in Totnes: A Study in Sean O'Casey', *Irish Writing,* no. 13 (Dec. 1950), 52.

12. Quoted by Robert Hogan, *After the Irish Renaissance: A Critical History of the Irish Drama since 'The Plough and the Stars'.* London: Macmillan, 1968, p.32.

13. Kevin Casey, 'The Excitements and the Disappointments', in: Sean McCann (ed.) *The World of Sean O'Casey.* London: Four Square Books, 1966, p.218.

14. David Krause, *Sean O'Casey: The Man and His Work.* London: MacGibbon & Kee, 1960, p.99.

15. Laurence Kitchin, *Drama in the Sixties: Form and Interpretation.* London: Faber, 1966, pp.105-106.

16. For details of his career, see the present author's *O'Casey the Dramatist.* Gerrards Cross: Colin Smythe, 1985.

17. Ronald Ayling, 'The Poetic Drama of T.S. Eliot', *English Studies in Africa,* 2 (1959), 247-50.

18. C.P.C., 'Before Midnight', *Irish Statesman* (July 21, 1928), 392.

19. Kitchin, *Drama in the Sixties,* p. 98.

20. On the personal relationship between Macken and O'Casey, see Heinz Kosok, 'O'Casey and An Taibhdhearc', *O'Casey Annual,* 3 (1984), 115-23.

21. Audrey Williamson, *Theatre of Two Decades.* London: Rockliff, 1951, p.165.

22. Clifford Odets, *Golden Boy, Awake and Sing!, The Big Knife.* Harmondsworth: Penguin Books, 1963, p.117.

23. For comparisons between the two plays, see for instance, Margery M. Morgan, 'Arnold Wesker: The Celebrated Instinct', in: Hedwig Bock and Albert Wertheim (eds.), *Essays on Contemporary British Drama* (München: Hueber, 1981), p.34; and Robert Fricker, *Das moderne englische Drama* (Göttingen:

Vandenhoeck und Ruprecht, 2nd ed. 1964), pp.148-149, 153.

24. *The Wesker Trilogy.* Harmondsworth: Penguin Books, rev. ed. 1979, pp. 40, 58.

25. Sean O'Casey, *Collected Plays,* vol. I. London: Macmillan, 1957, p.7.

26. Quoted on the cover of Errol John, *Moon on a Rainbow Shawl.* London: Faber, 2nd ed. 1963.

Christopher Innes (essay date 1990)

SOURCE: "The Essential Continuity of Sean O'Casey," in *Modern Drama,* Vol. XXXIII, No. 3, September, 1990, pp. 419-33.

[*In the essay below, Innes argues that O'Casey's dramaturgical development exhibits a consistent pattern rather than a break in styles, as most critics maintain.*]

There is a general assumption behind almost all critical approaches to Sean O'Casey's work, which deserves examination, if only because it is so common. Despite Denis Johnston's assertion in 1926, the year of *The Plough and the Stars,* that O'Casey's first three plays are increasingly poetic in dialogue and expressionistic in form, the Dublin trilogy is almost invariably held up as an example of naturalism. Equally, all his theatrical output from the 1934 production of *Within the Gates,* whether labelled expressionist or fantasy, is seen as the stylistic antithesis of the early plays. Biographic reference is used to support this: O'Casey's move from Ireland to England after the *Plough* riots is taken as the sign of a radical departure in subject matter. To some critics his 1928 break with the Abbey theatre gave him the liberty to explore new dramatic forms. To others it shows limitations that come from writing without the practical discipline of stage production, resulting in flawed language and abstract characterization. In both cases, *The Silver Tassie,* as the immediate cause of O'Casey's break with the Abbey, is considered an amalgam of opposing styles, signalling the transition from one to another.

One recent critic at least has tried to redress the balance by emphasizing the realistic basis of the symbolism in his two most expressionistic works. But this argument for the unity of O'Casey's vision still accepts the unquestioned naturalism of his Dublin plays, and its premise is that throughout his career O'Casey employed a "basically realistic technique."[1] By contrast, the continuity of O'Casey's work should be seen as far more radical, since his early trilogy can be shown to be no less non-naturalistic beneath its apparent surface than his later recognizably symbolic plays. Even the shift in characterization, from seemingly individualized and rounded figures towards the typical and two-dimensional, is demonstrably part of a consistent development, instead of being evidence of a break between two different styles. Indeed, the critical

views that posit such division in O'Casey's career lead to inherently contradictory conclusions.

That O'Casey's post-war plays have had remarkably few performances is conventionally seen as being directly due to their poetic expressionism and overt political bias (the latter indeed being the reason for their adoption by the Berliner Ensemble). Conversely, the popularity of the early plays becomes evidence for the absence of specifically these qualities, leading to the type of judgement put most directly by Joseph Wood Krutch: "[O'Casey] offers no solution; he proposes no remedy; he suggests no hope." "His plays lack form, lack movement, and in the final analysis lack any informing purpose." More recently and more subtly this analysis has been used to align O'Casey with the existentialist vision of "life as farce with which tragic experience must come to terms" in depicting "a world whose structures will never live up to their promise."[2] Yet this line is highly problematic in the light of O'Casey's firmly held socialist principles, practically expressed in his association with the labour leader, Jim Larkin, and his involvement in founding the Irish Citizens' Army. Acknowledging that these form the background for the Dublin plays logically leads to the argument that they represent a repudiation of Marxism—a conclusion which can only be sustained by assuming there is no continuity with later works such as *The Star Turns Red* (1940) and *Red Roses for Me* (1943).

Another case in point is the influence of Bernard Shaw. Shaw, of course, intervened in defence of *The Silver Tassie,* and critics have generally followed Denis Johnston (who deplored the "damage done by the honeyed poison of G.B.S.") in seeing his influence as mainly limited to O'Casey's subsequent didactic work. Certainly the model of Shaw is most noticeable in *Purple Dust* (1940, first produced 1945), where the situation of a rich Englishman's attempt to impose his ethos on an Irish village, the major characters and the satiric contrast between neo-colonialism and the supposedly backward natives directly echo *John Bull's Other Island.*[3] In particular the major thematic motif of O'Casey's last trilogy of symbolic fantasies is a clear reworking of Shaw's Life Force—though simplified to liberating sexuality—the vital principle embodied in the emblematic title figure of *Cock-a-doodle Dandy* (1949, first professional performance 1958), "a gay bird. . . . A bit unruly at times" who both tricks the police into shooting holes in the top hat of bourgeois respectability and conjures up a storm that whirls the puritanical priest away through the air, "rousing up commotion among the young and the souls zealous for life" as well as affirming though his dancing "the right of the joy of life to live courageously in the hearts of men." Following Shaw, the carriers of this Life Force are female: Loreleen, explicitly associated with the "Red Cock" by her dress and in the dialogue, who is victimized and banished by the life-denying representatives of the repressive society; the Every-woman figure of Jannice in *Within the Gates,* who obeys the call of the Dreamer-poet to "Sing them silent, dance them still, and laugh them into an open shame!"—thus overcoming

Bishop, Atheist, dispossessed masses, all who "carry furl'd the fainting flag of a dead hope and a dead faith," and affirming the joyfulness of existence even as she dies.[4]

However, key lines from *The Doctor's Dilemma* are also quoted in the opening stage directions to O'Casey's first play, *The Shadow of a Gunman* 1923), and again in the dialogue of *Within the Gates,* while the subtitles of plays throughout his career echo Shaw's use of subtitles: *A Political Phantasy* (*Kathleen Listens In,* 1923), *A Wayward Comedy* (*Purple Dust*), *A Sincerious Comedy* (*Hall of Healing,* 1951, unperformed). Indeed, O'Casey, who was still quoting Shaw in support of his own views up to the year of his death in 1964, stressed it was Shaw's example that weaned him from the Gaelic League and first inspired him to write for the stage: "I abandoned the romantic cult of Nationalism sixty years ago, and saw the real Ireland when I read the cheap edition of Shaw's *John Bull's Other Island;* hating only poverty, hunger, and disease." The type of objectivity, particularly in the satiric perspective on his own revolutionary ideals, on which the definition of O'Casey's early drama as naturalistic is based, can be seen as deriving from Shaw. So too can his characteristic use of irony, as for instance in the juxtaposition of the red glare of the burning city under bombardment with the British soldier's chorus of "Keep the 'owme fires burning" that closes *The Plough and the Stars,* which exactly repeats the ending of *Heartbreak House* in a different context.[5]

This ironic objectivity gives his Dublin trilogy much of its dramatic power, and its qualities can be most clearly seen in relation to autobiographical material. In *The Shadow of a Gunman,* for instance, several characters are identifiable real life portraits and the poet-protagonist is in many ways a self-projection. Yet Davoren is explicitly an anti-hero, "on the run" (O'Casey's first title for the play) from the overcrowded poverty of the slums, political violence, and the "common people" for whom "beauty is for sale in a butcher's shop." A satiric representation of O'Casey's previous, pre-Shaw values, he stands for the sentimental idealism of the Gaelic League. His reference points are mythic heroes of Irish legend or the symbol of Kathleen ni Houlihan (which Yeats had made synonymous with the romantic image of Irish liberation, and which O'Casey tried to expropriate for his socialist vision in *Kathleen Listens In*—produced the same year). His poetry is used as an excuse for avoiding life; and a rhetorical line from Shelley substitutes for emotional involvement: "Ah me, alas! Pain, pain ever, for ever. Like thee, Prometheus, no change, no pause, no hope. Ah, life, life, life!"[6]

All the characters are equally subject to this kind of posturing, with the action turning on the gap between their illusions and reality. Just like the timid Grigson, recasting his encounter with the brutal Auxiliaries into the heroic mode after his wife has just given a graphic description of his humiliating self-abasement, so Davoren fosters the admiration of the tenement's inhabitants in mistaking his subjective escapism for the bravery of a gunman "on the run,"

only to finally recognize his guilt and cowardice. Even then, the inflated language of his self-condemnation as "poet and poltroon, poltroon and poet," together with his repeat of the Shelley theme-note from the beginning, imply that this is nothing more than an alternative form of escapism—the sorrowing outcast instead of the dangerous shadow of the man of action—and that this pasteboard Prometheus will never break his chains of illusion.

The only possible exception is the real gunman. But Maguire is no more than a *deus ex machina,* the actual shadow of the ironic title that Davoren applies to himself, and the disregard for the safety of the innocent whose freedom he is so ready to kill—and die—for, in leaving the bag of bombs behind, implies an equivalent romanticism in his Cause. As Davoren's peddler-companion, who frequently seems to voice O'Casey's views, describes it, "their Mass is a burnin' buildin'; their De Profundis is 'The Soldiers' Song . . . —an' it's all for 'the glory o' God an' the honour o' Ireland'."[7] Even Minnie, whose openness and self-sacrifice give her the status of a tragic heroine, is governed by illusion. When the Auxiliaries beat down the door to search the house, it is sentimental attraction to an imaginary gunman-poet that motivates her to take responsibility for the bombs. The bravado of her cry, "Up the Republic!," is an attempt to live up to the expectations of this non-existent figure as she is dragged down the stairs outside his room. And she is not shot for her action in concealing weapons, nor for her revolutionary sentiments, but by mistake—and possibly by the gunmen she believes she is supporting—when the Auxiliaries' truck is ambushed.

The tragedy of her death is that it is not only pointless, but unnecessary. It underlines the real cost of the escapism illustrated in different degrees by other characters in rather over-literal terms, since she is killed while trying to escape from the violence that is not only the defining fact of their environment, but the touchstone for their illusions. The fighting off-stage not only undercuts pretensions to bravery:

> GRIGSON If a man keeps a stiff upper front—Merciful God, there's an ambush! [*Explosions of two bursting bombs are heard on the street outside the house . . .*]

It dismisses philosophic detachment, poetic fervour, nationalist ideals, religious faith:

> SEAMUS . . . No man need be afraid with a crowd of angels round him; thanks to God for His Holy religion!
>
> DAVOREN You're welcome to your angels; philosophy is mine; philosophy that makes the coward brave; the sufferer defiant; the weak strong; the . . .
>
> [*A volley of shots is heard in a lane that runs parallel with the wall of the backyard. Religion and philosophy are forgotten in the violent fear of a nervous equality.*]

The boldness of the juxtapositions, the repetitions, and the presentation of all the characters as variations on the same theme, make O'Casey's use of irony crudely obvious in this early play. It is most effective when limited to the foreground situation, rather than based on contrasts between personal action and the historical background, as with the braces Seamus peddles:

> They're great value; I only hope I'll be able to get enough o' them. I'm wearing a pair of them meself—they'd do Cuchullian, they're so strong. *(Counting the spoons)* . . . And still we're looking for freedom—ye gods, it's a glorious country! *(He lets one fall, which he stoops to pick up.)* Oh, my God, there's the braces after breakin'.
>
> DAVOREN That doesn't look as if they were strong enough for Cuchullian.
>
> SEAMUS I put a heavy strain on them too sudden.[8]

This broad farce is taken directly from the Music Hall—it is not coincidental that exactly the same comic turn provides the anti-climax of *Waiting for Godot,* since there is a clear kinship between Beckett's clown-like tramps and O'Casey's shabby self-deceivers—and carries over into the other parts of the Dublin trilogy, as does the same use of irony to control the audience's critical perception. However, both Music Hall elements and the opposition of character against context become progressively subtler, as well as better integrated with the action in the two following plays. Boyle and Joxer, as classic drunkards convinced the earth is reeling because they can't stand straight, illustrate the actual situation at the end of ***Juno and the Paycock***: both their domestic circle and the society outside have indeed broken down "in a terr . . . ible state o' . . . chassis," but it is the failure of moral perception, not the existential nature of the world, that is responsible for the chaos. In the central scene of ***The Plough and the Stars*** the stock skit is more naturalistic, two disreputable women tearing each other's hair out over insults to their respectability, and barely indicated (the barman breaks up the fight before Mrs. Grogan and Bessie get their hands on one another), while the thematic reverberations are even wider. Set against the Republican rally outside the pub, it undercuts the orator's death-bound mysticism with its rhetoric of patriotic sacrifice and redemptive bloodshedding, reducing the coming battle for independence to a farcical squabble. Beyond that it points to the First World War—also a heroic analogue for the orator—undermining idealistic justifications for the slaughter in the trenches through the association of "poor little Catholic Belgium" with "poor little Catholic Ireland," which ironically puts the protestant loyalist in the position of her German enemies.[9]

It was this scene, of course, that sparked the riots at the Abbey's 1926 production of the play. Focussing on the flag of the title (degraded by its presence in a pub), the depiction of the men who fought in the Uprising as less than heroic (held back by their wives, fearful under fire, motivated by self preservation once the battle is lost), and the presence of a prostitute among the characters ("an abominable play. . . . There are no streetwalkers in Dublin!"), the public demonstration illustrated O'Casey's point exactly. As he pointed out in "A Reply to the Crit-

ics," which emphasized the realistic basis of his portrayal, the romantic idealism "about 'the Ireland that remembers with tear-dimmed eyes all that Easter Week stands for' makes me sick. Some of the men cannot even get a job."[10]

The Plough and the Stars is always cited as O'Casey's most developed naturalistic play. The multiple focus and interweaving strands of action replace the simplification of a dominant protagonist by a social panorama, without losing the human scale, and this form itself incorporates the thematic statement. It embodies an image of community, which is mirrored in the way the inhabitants of the slum tenement develop a sense of group responsibility under the pressure of external events that threaten the group's existence and destroy the narrower social unit of the family. Tenuous and contingent, in plot terms the actual community is always on the point of disruption through the deaths of its individual members; whether all too literally inflamed by delusive ideals (Jack Clitheroe, trapped in a burning building), a victim of circumstance (Bessie Burgess, shot in error by the British soldiers she supports), or a statistic of poverty (the young girl, Mollser, dying of consumption). On the stylistic level, however, comic dissension—the sword-waving chase around a kitchen table in Act I, the baby thrust into the arms of an unwilling man, and dumped on the pub floor, when the women square off in Act II—gives way to tragic unity. The positive social vision suggested in the structure, but not affirmed by the dramatic action, thus implicitly endorses the young socialist's response to the Republican ideal of independence: "Dope, dope. There's only one war worth havin': th' war for th' economic emancipation of th' proletariat."[11]

Typically for this stage in O'Casey's development, while his views may be presented, their spokesman is treated satirically. Derogatorily named "the Covey," and incongruously trying to attract a prostitute's attentions or impress a British Corporal with the pretentious catchphrase of "Did y'ever read, comrade, Jenersky's *Thesis on the Origin, Development, an' Consolidation of th' Evolutionary Idea of the Proletariat?,*" his political theorizing is contemptuously dismissed by all the other characters. Similarly, the first sign of solidarity among the tenement inhabitants is the anti-social activity of looting, which may create an unlikely team out of the former female antagonists, but discredits the socialist's ideological understanding—though not, as is often assumed, the political principles themselves—and shows materialistic greed banishing an appeal to common humanity in the other noncombatant men.

O'Casey's approach is exemplified in the treatment of Bessie Burgess; not only, as a pro-British Protestant and vocal anti-Republican, the outsider in the tenement group, but the least sympathetic character for the predominantly Catholic and Nationalist Dublin audience of the time. The sentimentally attractive Nora Clitheroe, retreating into an Ophelia-like madness when her husband rejects her for Republican ideals, offers a conventional (and deliberately illusory) tragic image. But the real heroine of the tragedy is Bessie, who becomes the human centre of the community, nursing the woman she had despised at the beginning of the play and sacrificing her own life for her safety. Bringing the Dublin spectators to identify with her forms a practical demonstration of the socialist's contention that "there's no such thing as an Irishman, or an Englishman, or a German or a Turk; we're all only human bein's." At the same time sympathy is not made easy. It is Bessie's insults that provoke Jack into returning to his death in the already hopeless battle, and her reaction when shot is to curse the helplessly terrified Nora as "you bitch."[12]

Once the riots had subsided, the play was praised for "the astonishing accuracy of . . . photographic detail," and indeed the basis for several scenes is documentary. For instance the orator's rhetoric is taken verbatim from Pearse's speeches, while O'Casey emphasized that "of these very words Jim Connolly himself said almost the same thing as the Covey." Yet this factual background is set against a highly patterned thematic structure, which approaches melodrama at points such as the oath to the flags:

> CAPT. BRENNAN *[catching up The Plough and the Stars].*
>
> Imprisonment for th' Independence of Ireland!
>
> LIEUT. LANGON *[catching up the Tri-colour].* Wounds for th' Independence of Ireland!
>
> CLITHEROE Death for th' Independence of Ireland!
>
> THE THREE *[together]* So help us God![13]

The melodramatic tone of the speeches might be simply a naturalistic response to the passion of the moment, if the fate of each character did not exactly correspond to his vow. As this indicates, even the characterization is less naturalistic than it appears. With their emblematic names and identifying catchphrases—the Covey's grandiose book-title, Fluther Good's reiterated "derogatory" and "vice versa"—these are the equivalent of the stock figures that Strindberg rejected in the classic definition of naturalism that prefaces *Miss Julie,* while one has a clearly literary genesis. Nora, like the Ibsen heroine from whom she takes her name, deceives her equally patronizing husband in order to save him, and has her doll's house destroyed by her inability to intercept a letter.

Thus even O'Casey's most naturalistic work contains the seeds of his later development, and the connections are clearest in *Juno and the Paycock.* The original centre of the play, "the tragedy of a crippled IRA man, one Johnny Boyle," is typically melodramatic in concept and treatment. The guilty betrayer is hounded by conscience to the brink of self-betrayal, with his life linked to a flickering crimson votive light, which goes out as his executioners approach (even if the classic formula of Boucicault—or Irving's *The Bells*—is reversed by transforming villain into victim). At the same time, the surrounding action, which not only parallels and extends this core, but dominates it through the vivid vitality of the characters, is openly allegorical.

The reference to Mrs. Boyle and her husband in the title may be ironic, Juno only a nickname—but as the schoolmaster points out, it is still intended to remind "one of Homer's glorious story of ancient gods and heroes." On the symbolic level of the play she can be seen as a countertype to the Yeatsian Kathleen Ni Houlihan, Ireland as the archetypal mother mourning the loss of her sons in place of the virginal siren welcoming the death of her lovers, a contrast parodistically encapsulated in her husband's linguistic confusion:

> BOYLE *(solemnly)* . . . Requiescat in pace . . . or, usin' our oul' tongue like St. Patrick or St. Bridget, Guh say-eree jeea ayera!
>
> MARY Oh, father, that's not Rest in Peace; that's God save Ireland.
>
> BOYLE U-u-ugh, it's all the same—isn't it a prayer?

Even the most naturalistic aspects of Juno's characterization have representative significance. O'Casey's description—*"twenty years ago* [ie. at the first performance of Yeats's *Kathleen Ni Houlihan,* 1902] *she must have been a pretty woman; but her face has now assumed . . . a look of listless monotony and harassed anxiety, blending with an expression of mechanical resistance"*[14]—measures the deterioration of Nationalist idealism in terms of its human cost and lack of material or political benefits for the working-classes.

This is the major motif of the play as a whole. Even more explicitly than in *The Plough and the Stars,* since here all the action takes place inside a single house, the tenement stands for the nation beneath its local specificity. Each of the women has a husband or son maimed or killed—with Johnny as a human calendar of revolutionary conflict: crippled by a bullet in the hip during Easter Week 1916 (a relatively minor wound analogous perhaps to the 15 rebels hanged by the British), losing an arm in the civil war period of *Shadow of a Gunman,* and finally his life (a progressive dismemberment mirroring the increasing bitterness of the fighting; in 1922 the Free State government executed 77 Republican leaders)—and the Boyle family fortunes are the vicissitudes of the Irish people in microcosm.

The legacy that provides an illusory windfall stands for the newly won national sovereignty. This is underlined for the audience by Boyle's assertion, significantly placed just after an unanswered knock of doom (in the shape of a trench-coated gunman) and immediately before the entry of Bentham to announce their unexpected good fortune, that "Today . . . there's goin' to be issued a proclamation be me, establishin' an independent Republic, an' Juno'll have to take an oath of allegiance." The Captain's characteristic confusion of constitutional terms and ironic misinterpretation of liberty as the evasion of social responsibility is a clear criticism of the false expectations engendered by nationhood, tangibly illustrated in the cheap and garishly vulgar furnishing the family buys on credit, the pretentious gramophone and the bourgeois suit that replaces Boyle's labouring trousers. The pompous schoolmaster's incompetence in drawing up the will, which deprives them of the promised riches, can be seen as O'Casey's comment on the politicians' drafting of the constitution, while the resulting material destitution offers a graphic image of moral bankruptcy in the state. The stage set itself is dismantled by the two removal men who repossess almost all the family's possessions to pay their debts, paralleled by the forcible removal of Johnny by his two executioners. Juno has learnt from the loss of her own son the compassion she so signally lacked with her neighbour's exactly comparable bereavement. But she leaves to work elsewhere for the future in the form of Mary's unborn child, abandoned by the Bentham / politicians who seduced her and rejected by the other contender for her favour, the socialist / Labour Movement, whose narrow morality makes him incapable of living up to his humanitarian ideals. Juno's heavily-weighted prayer to "take away our hearts o' stone, and give us hearts o' flesh" counterbalances the pair of comic drunkards, who incongruously point the moral that "The counthry'll have to steady itself . . . it's goin' . . . to hell. . . . No matther . . . what any one may . . . say . . . Irelan' sober . . . is Irelan' . . . free."[15] But the darkened and stripped stage is left to the inebriated forces of anarchy, O'Casey's most satiric version of the escape artists and "shadows" of sentimental patriotism, who form his major target from the title figure of the first play in the Dublin trilogy to the intoxicating silhouette of Pearse in *The Plough and the Stars.*

The discomforting irony of sharp juxtapositions at the end of *Juno,* may give an overwhelming impression of objectivity. However, as Samuel Beckett observed, reviewing *Windfalls:*

> Mr. O'Casey is a master of knockabout in this very serious and honourable sense—that he discerns the principle of disintegration in even the most complacent solidities, and activates it to their explosion. This is the energy of his theatre, the triumph of the principle of knockabout in situation, in all its elements and on all its planes, from the furniture to the higher centres.

This could be applied equally to *Juno:* practically none of the elements that combine in the final image are naturalistic. Despite O'Casey's vehement assertion that "I have nothing to do with Beckett. . . . his philosophy isn't my philosophy, for within him there is no hazard of hope," Beckett's approval of a specific play has sometimes been used to support a view of O'Casey in general as a proto-Absurdist, whose early plays express an existential nihilism.[16] Yet, leaving aside the completely unBeckettian social reference, the sequence of impressions that define the ending is clearly intended as a protest and a warning, while the solution is suggested by the structure of the following play in the series. Rather than resigning an audience to the pointlessness of human effort in the face of a recalcitrant universe, the bleakness of the comic closing moment calls for a value judgement, conditioned by the preceding balance between the continuing cycle of violence and the call for a wider humanity.

The positive message becomes increasingly open and direct in O'Casey's subsequent plays; and as explicit statement replaces oblique suggestion, the realistic surface disappears. Settings symbolize philosophical oppositions or emotional states, while ideological manipulation replaces personal motive in the characters. At its extreme this results in the Morality play psychomachia of *Within the Gates,* where good and evil "angels" (The Dreamer/ The Atheist) struggle for the protagonist's soul against a backdrop of war memorial and maypole. Similarly the conflict in *The Star Turns Red* is defined dialectically by the church spire and the foundry chimney seen through windows either side of the stage, the portraits of a Bishop and Lenin on the walls. The resolution is symbolized by the addition of *"a white cross on which a red hammer and sickle are imposed,"* and a single speech from Red Jim (an idealized projection of Jim Larkin) is sufficient to transform the grief of a weeping girl into triumphant affirmation:

> Up, young woman, and join in the glowing hour your lover died to fashion. He fought for life, for life is all; and death is nothing!
>
> *[Julia stands up with her right fist clenched. The playing and singing of "The Internationale" grow louder. Soldiers and sailors appear at the windows, and all join in the singing.]*

At the same time the language becomes poetic to reflect universal thematic intentions—all too often, as J.B. Priestley was the first to point out (reviewing *Oak Leaves and Lavender,* 1947), resulting in "windy rhetoric that obscures the characters and blunts the situations. . . . O'Casey in Dublin created literature, whereas O'Casey in Devon is merely being literary."[17]

Another factor frequently pointed to in critical discussions of *The Silver Tassie,* apart from O'Casey's isolation from both the society that provided the material for his early plays and the requirements of a specific theatre that shaped them, is the influence of German expressionism: in particular Toller's *Masse-Mensch,* performed by the Dublin Drama League under the title of *Masses and Man* in 1925, and *Transfiguration.* Given O'Casey's personal links to Denis Johnston, and Johnston's interest in Toller (which led him to direct *Hoppla!* for the League in 1929), it is certainly reasonable to suggest that O'Casey became exposed to the expressionist approach then. But at this point in O'Casey's career, the effect of Toller's example, even on the war sequence of Act II, seems rather general. It is only with *The Star Turns Red*—written for Unity Theatre, which was largely responsible for introducing Toller and Kaiser to the English stage, and to which O'Casey may have turned for precisely that reason as well as their shared Marxism—that the model of *Masses and Man* can be specifically traced. The expressionist combination of religious humanitarianism and left-wing politics, which made their radical dramatic form seem the proclamation of a new social order, corresponded with the views already implicit in the Dublin trilogy. But now, what before had remained on a thematic level, became embodied in the style. The decisive new element is the utopianism inherent in the expressionist approach. This is reflected in O'Casey's generic switch from the "Tragedy" of his early plays to "Comedy" for his subsequent work; and the nature of the change can be seen in the intermediate "Tragi-Comedy" of *The Silver Tassie.*

On the surface the opening has the characteristics of the previous plays: set in a Dublin tenement, with a pair of cowardly boasters, and focussing on group interaction. By itself the wedding bowl smashed by the physically dominating Teddy Foran is on the same level of significance as the red votive light in *Juno.* However, the parallel between the bowl and the *"silver cup joyously, rather than reverentially, elevated, as a priest would elevate a chalice"*[18] transforms both into obvious symbols, with the thematic connection being emphasized by the crushing of the silver cup that ends the play. In addition, the naturalistically depicted characters have a single line of thought that in conventional terms would seem obsessive. "Tambourine theology" is an accurate description of all the speeches of one, while both Mrs. Foran and Harry Heegan's mother have no other concern in sending their men off to the First World War trenches but the maintenance money from the government for dependents of soldiers of Active Service. In fact the characters have hardly more developed personalities than the openly expressionistic figures of Act II, being designed to serve a didactic pattern. The dominant males of the opening are defined purely in terms of physical vitality to provide the maximum contrast to the war-cripples they become, the soccer hero Harry being paralysed from the waist down, the blinded Teddy being subservient to the wife he had terrorized, while in place of being a hero-worshipper spurned by the girls, Barney throttles the helpless Harry and wins his former fiancée.

At first glance the war sequence seems a complete contrast, with its class-conscious caricatures, anonymous soldiers and chanted verse. The only named character, Barney, is pinioned to a gun-wheel in direct comparison and contrast to a life-size Christ-figure with one arm released from the crucifix, either side of a howitzer to which the soldiers pray when the enemy attack. The tone is set by antiphonal chanting: "Kyrie eleison" from within the ruined monastery and an inverted version of Ezekiel's prophecy of resurrection from a blood-covered death figure. Stage directions stress the distinction between these symbolic objects and reality, *"Every feature of the scene seems a little distorted from its original appearance,"* and when the guns fire *"Only flashes are seen, no noise is heard."* Yet in the first production Harry doubled as 1st Soldier without any noticeable incongruity.[19] Indeed, in the following hospital scene this surreal treatment coexists with the naturalistic surface—with the figures both interacting as individuals and reduced to numbers by the system, the same counterpoint between off-stage latin liturgy and human pain closing the episode—and the double image of reality is projected onto the final return to a Dublin setting. The bitter presence of the maimed makes the Football Club dance grotesque; conversational dialogue continually modulates into antiphonal patterns:

SYLVESTER . . . give him breath to sing his song an' play the ukelele.

MRS. HEEGAN Just as he used to do.

SYLVESTER Behind the trenches.

SIMON In the Rest Camps.

MRS. FORAN Out in France.

HARRY I can see, but I cannot dance.

TEDDY I can dance but I cannot see. . . .

HARRY There's something wrong with life when men can walk.

TEDDY There's something wrong with life when men can see.

We are challenged to look behind naturalistic surfaces. In retrospect the apparent normality of the tenement is as illusory as the balloons and coloured streamers of the dance hall. As Shaw commented in his defence of *The Silver Tassie,* "The first act is not a bit realistic; it is deliberately fantastic . . . poetry."[20]

In much the same way, the "dramatic dehiscence" noted by Beckett undermines the apparent naturalism of the Dublin trilogy. The combination of Music Hall turn with melodrama, as well as stock characterization and, above all, the strongly allegorical action, are precisely the qualities that form the dramaturgical basis for O'Casey's later works. The change of style is more a shift in emphasis than a new approach. The mythic dimension is already present in *Juno,* and even in *Shadow of a Gunman,* where Minnie is "A Helen of Troy come to live in a tenement!" Exactly the same allegory, on which the action of Juno is based, reappears in more didactic and openly symbolic plays. The O'Houlihan house of *Kathleen Listens In,* bought in exchange for the family cow of living standards and its door painted green, stands for national independence, with the subsequent political conflict represented by the demands of the Worker that the house be painted red versus the Republican extremist's "Yous'll grow shamrocks or yous'll grow nothin'!."[21] The decaying mansion of *Purple Dust* is Ireland again, with independence again embodied by the destruction of its interior. But there the terms are cultural rather than political, with the flood that drives out Stokes and Poges—the wealthy English neo-colonists, named after the village that inspired Gray's "Elegy," whose intention of reviving the feudal past is sabotaged by the down-to-earth vitality of the locals—symbolizing the sweeping away of cultural imperialism and capitalism by the river of time. Conversely, the celebration of the Life Force that finds its fullest expression in O'Casey's last fantasies is also present in *The Plough and the Stars,* with Rosie Redmond's song of sexual pleasure and procreation (censored in the original Abbey production) in counterpoint to the men marching off to their deaths in the Easter Uprising.

O'Casey's work, then, has a consistent unity. His early plays signal a move beyond the limits of dramatic naturalism as much as the later, more obviously experimental works. Though in different ways, both correspond to his concept of "The new form in drama [which] will take qualities found in classical, romantic and expressionistic plays, will blend them together, breathe the breath of life into the new form and create a new drama."[22] As such his search is a prototype for the various attempts to develop new forms of social realism which can be found in the contemporary generation of politically oriented dramatists from Osborne to Hare or Edgar. Yet, with the exception of Denis Johnston's counter-play to **The Plough and the Stars, The Scythe and the Sunset** (1958) and a general influence on the later, marginalized Irish work of John Arden, O'Casey's work has had no specific effect on subsequent British or Irish theatre.

The critical misreading of O'Casey, interpreting his development in terms of a radical change in style, is arguably the major reason for O'Casey's lack of influence. Yeats's attack on **The Silver Tassie** for its apparent abandonment of the earlier plays' dramatic principles, based on a purely naturalistic reading of the Dublin trilogy, is typical. O'Casey's withdrawal to England and his increasingly overt political bias may have been contributing factors in banishing his later plays from the stage. But Yeats's criticism not only initiated the break with the Abbey. It established the terms for discussion of O'Casey's work by exaggerating the realism of his early plays as much as by singling out the expressionistic elements of **The Silver Tassie.** As a result, whether seeking to promote O'Casey's post-1930 stylistic experimentation, commenting on its problematic language and characterization, or choosing to focus exclusively on the Abbey plays, subsequent criticism has emphasized a division that is more apparent than actual.

Notes

1. Carol Kleiman, *Sean O'Casey's Bridge of Vision: Four Essays on Structure and Perspective* (Toronto, 1982), cf. pp. 49, 51.

2. Joseph W. Krutch, *"Modernism" in Modern Drama: A Definition and an Estimate* (Ithaca, NY, 1953), p. 99 and in *The Nation,* 21 December 1927; Desmond E.S. Maxwell, *A Critical History of Modern Irish Drama 1891-1980* (Cambridge, 1984), pp. 112 and 98. A more extreme form of this interpretation is offered by Kleiman, who proposes O'Casey as not only a precursor of Beckett, but also of Ionesco, and as paralleling Artaud's Theatre of Cruelty (Kleiman, pp. 87ff).

3. *The Collected Plays of Sean O'Casey* Vol. 1, 4 (London, 1949, 1951), pp. 93 and 231, quoting Dubedat's dying speech: "I believe in . . . the might of design, the mystery of colour, the belief in the redemption of all things by beauty everlasting" and "I have . . . never denied my faith. . . . I've fought the good fight" (G.B. Shaw, *Doctor's Dilemma* [London, 1932], p. 163). For parallels between *Purple Dust* and *John Bull's Other Island,* cf. Saros Cowasjee, *Sean O'Casey: The Man Behind the Plays* (London, 1963), pp. 156-7, while R.B. Parker, "Bernard Shaw and Sean O'Casey," *Queen's*

Quarterly, 73 (1966), 13-34 offers a detailed analysis of the relationship.

4. *Collected Plays,* Vol. 4, p. 144; O'Casey, *Blasts and Benedictions: Articles and Stories* (London, 1967), p. 145; *Collected Plays,* Vol. 2, pp. 228, 196.

5. See Denis Johnston, "Sean O'Casey: A Biography and an Appraisal," *Modern Drama,* 4 (1961/62), 327; O'Casey, *Under a Colored Cap* (London, 1963), p. 263 (Cf. also *Autobiographies I* [London, 1963], p. 558); *Collected Plays,* Vol. 1, p. 261.

6. See William Armstrong, "History, Autobiography, and *The Shadow of a Gunman,*" *Modern Drama,* 2 (1959/60), 417ff; *Collected Plays,* Vol. 1, pp. 127, 105.

7. *Collected Plays,* Vol. 1, pp. 153, 157.

8. By contrast to Minnie, the woman arrested with her does not jump out of the truck and survives. *Collected Plays,* Vol. 1, pp. 153, 155, 133, 98.

9. *Collected Plays,* Vol. 1, pp. 89, 201.

10. Joseph Holloway, cit. *Lady Gregory's Journals 1916-30,* ed. Lennox Robinson (London, 1946), p. 99; *Blasts and Benedictions,* p. 91.

11. *Collected Plays,* Vol. 1, p. 203. For a fuller treatment of the structure in *The Plough and the Stars,* cf. Heinz Kosok, *O'Casey the Dramatist,* (Irish Literary Studies 19), trans. Kosok and Joseph T. Swann (Totowa, NJ, 1985), pp. 71ff.

12. *Collected Plays,* Vol. 1, pp. 249, 170, 258.

13. *Dublin Magazine,* 1 (1926), 64; *Blasts and Benedictions,* p. 93; *Collected Plays,* Vol. 1, p. 214.

14. Gabriel Fallon, *Sean O'Casey: The Man I Knew* (London, 1965), p. 17 (according to this memoir O'Casey "mentioned this play many times and always it was the tragedy of Johnny. I cannot recall that he once spoke about Juno or Joxer or the Captain"); *Collected Plays,* Vol. I, pp. 31, 33-4, 4.

15. *Collected Plays,* Vol. 1, pp. 27, 88.

16. Samuel Beckett, "The Essential and the Incidental," *The Bookman,* 86 (1934) (in *Sean O'Casey: A Collection of Critical Essays,* ed. Thomas Kilroy, [Englewood Cliffs, NJ, 1975], p. 167); *Blasts and Benedictions,* p. 51; Cf. Katharine J. Worth, "O'Casey's Dramatic Symbolism," *Modern Drama,* 4 (1961/62), 260-67 as well as Kleiman, pp. 87ff.

17. *Collected Plays,* Vol. 2, pp. 277 and 353-54; *Our Time,* 5 (1945/46), 238.

18. *Collected Plays,* Vol. 2, pp. 23-25.

19. *Collected Plays,* Vol. 2, pp. 36 and 56; for a detailed discussion of the way O'Casey unifies naturalistic and expressionistic elements in *The Silver Tassie* as well as *Red Roses for Me,* see Kleiman, pp. 49ff (though she argues that the doubling in Vincent Massey's production was inappropriate, and the correct parallel is between Heegan and the death-figure of The Croucher, p. 35).

20. *Collected Plays,* Vol. 2, pp. 93-4; Shaw, a letter to Lady Gregory, June 1928, cit. Peter Kavanagh, *The Story of the Abbey Theatre* (New York, 1950), p. 141.

21. *Complete Plays,* Vol. 5 (London, 1984), p. 475.

22. O'Casey, *New York Times,* 21 October 1934, Section 9, p. 3.

THE SHADOW OF A GUNMAN

PRODUCTION REVIEWS

Punch (review date 8 June 1927)

SOURCE: A review of *The Shadow of a Gunman,* in *Punch,* Vol. 172, June 8, 1927, p. 637.

[*In the following review of the London premiere of* The Shadow of a Gunman, *the critic focuses on O'Casey's dramatic technique, observing that the play's comedic overtones undermines its tragic dénouement.*]

One assumes that Mr. Sean O'Casey's method of setting his tragedy against a pattern of jokes is not due to ignorance of the difficulties involved but is a deliberate device to heighten the effect of the catastrophe. In *The Shadow of a Gunman* the tragic ending is effective enough when it arrives, but it is not sufficiently prepared, or perhaps too subtly, so that the audience has got itself into a thoroughly rollicking mood (sustained by Mr. Arthur Sinclair's broad diverting humour) and refuses to smile but must needs laugh aloud at everything. The discerning, who in the Second Act begin to see the drift of the playwright's plan, are necessarily grieved. However, I think Mr. O'Casey must share some of the blame for that.

Donal Davoren, a young poet—whether good or bad it was not easy to determine, as Mr. Harry Hutchinson persistently read his verses to the backcloth—is sharing a room in the distraught Dublin of 1920 with a vulgar feckless pedlar, *Seumas Shields.* The other denizens of the tenement have decided that *Donal* is a gunman on the run, which flatters the boy's vanity and helps him to retain the admiration of that sturdy patriot, pretty little *Minnie Powell.* When the house is raided by the "auxiliaries," *Minnie* takes the bag of bombs which some casual member of the I.R.A. has left under *Seumas'* bed to her own room, thinking they will be less likely to be looked for there, and, when they are found and the young girl is haled to the lorry by her brutal captors, the two room-fellows, whose brave pretences have given place to abject terror, let her go to her death, the poet cursing his cowardice, the huckster bawling that it was no affair of his annyway.

Irish dramatists of the candid school are not kind to their countrymen. Mr. O'Casey has indeed an almost in human detachment. The black-and-tanner who makes the search of *Seumas's* room is a bully and a ruffian, but he is a less contemptible figure than *Seumas* or *Donal* or *Tommy Owens,* the little boasting slum-rat, or the drink-sodden *Adolphus Grigson,* with his Bible and his law-abiding pose.

This play is a reminder of unhappy things that both Irishmen and Englishmen of sensibility would be glad to forget. Perhaps, then, there is something to be said for the laughter which is the standard English way of relief from disquieting reflection. I hope that was partly the explanation of it.

Mr. Arthur Sinclair, who plays most of the two Acts in his untidy bed, has a wonderful Sinclair part. A gross, lazy, peppery humbug of a man is *Seumas Shields.* Mr. Harry Hutchinson's *Donal* was skilfully and carefully played—a little too quietly for comfortable hearing. Mr. Sydney Morgan's *Adolphus* couldn't have been bettered, and Mr. Brian O'Dare's *Tommy Owens* was horribly effective. Miss Maire O'Neill and Miss Sara Allgood gave us two competent short studies of Irish women, and Miss Eileen Carey's charming little portrait of *Minnie* owed more perhaps to her natural gifts than to her technical accomplishment. I say "perhaps," because it isn't easy to be sure that her reticent method wasn't a deliberate choice and the best choice for the part. This company of players deserves the benefit of all doubts.

J. M. Synge's *Riders to the Sea,* with Miss Sara Allgood in her old part of the bereaved *Maurya,* did not move us as it was wont to do. Is this really no more than a too self-conscious literary drama which fails to wear?

Three ladies of the audience performed deeds of grace which deserve a chronicler. One (poordarling!) afflicted with a cough twice fled from the theatre to avoid spoiling her neighbours' pleasure; two others, coming late, stood through the first play. A tablet should be put up to them at the Court *in perpetuam rei memoriam.*

Richard Jennings (review date 18 June 1927)

SOURCE: A review of *The Shadow of a Gunman,* in *The Spectator,* Vol. 138, No. 5164, June 18, 1927, p. 1062.

[*In the following review of the Court Theatre production of* The Shadow of a Gunman, *Jennings perceives a problem with O'Casey's comedic timing and the play's tragic intent.*]

Mr. Sean O'Casey's *Shadow of a Gunman,* now running at the Court Theatre, has renewed the old controversy about ill-timed laughter in the theatre. Playgoers will not accept rebuke from dramatic crities, and, in spite of a strong denunciation in the *Times,* I found an audience, a few nights later, still laughing loudly at scenes that entangled everyday Dublin humours with tragic emergencies—the compound being characteristic of Mr. O'Casey's method. Have we, then, forgotten all about the horrors in Ireland? Do they mean nothing to us? Or was it, rather, that Mr. Arthur Sinclair, as the pedlar, having compelled mirth, from the depths of his bed, in the first act, could not repress it in the second, where, still in bed, he is beset by the Black-and Tans? For, obviously, Mr. Sinclair is too fine an artist to sentimentalize. He plays his part as it should be played; consistently he is the loud-tongued loafer. What happens to him, in his recumbent posture, or to those about him, isn't, so to speak, his affair: events do not remould middle-aged characters. But the audience, surely, should have discriminated. However, they had an excuse—Mr. O'Casey so closely mingles the tragic-satirical moods that some must laugh, while, perhaps, others weep. Only, tears don't make such a noise as merriment.

CRITICAL COMMENTARY

William A. Armstrong (essay date 1960)

SOURCE: "History, Autobiography, and *The Shadow of a Gunman,*" in *Modern Drama,* Vol. 2, No. 4, February, 1960, pp. 417-24.

[*In the following essay, Armstrong compares* The Shadow of Gunman *with certain parts of the fourth volume of O'Casey's autobiography, revealing the significance of the personal element that determines the play's formal features.*]

Sean O'Casey is said to prefer his first major work, *The Shadow of a Gunman,* to his next play, *Juno and the Paycock.* To many of his readers, however, *The Shadow of a Gunman* has seemed much more limited, local, and topical in appeal. Passing judgement on O'Casey's achievement in this play in *The Nineteenth Century and After* (April, 1925), Andrew E. Malone has declared that "his characters are taken from the slums of Dublin, and his theme is little more than a commentary upon the war-like conditions of the city during the year 1920." One purpose of this article is to suggest that this verdict is a deceptive half-truth. O'Casey certainly does provide a realistic cross-section of life in a Dublin slum in 1920, and, as will be shown, the play certainly acquires greater significance when it is related to the social and political history of that year. But even where O'Casey's representation is closest to social or historical fact it exhibits a distinctive tone and colouring imparted by his imagination in obedience to a dramatic design. Moreover, a comparison between the play and certain parts of his autobiography, *Inishfallen, Fare Thee Well* (1949) reveals that the personal element in the play is more important that the historical one because it helped to determine its form and the interpretation of life which that form was designed to emphasize.

O'Casey dates the period of his play as May, 1920. During this month the bitter struggle between the Crown and the Irish separatist movement known as Sinn Féin ("We

Ourselves") reached a critical stage. Before the end of 1919, Sinn Féin and its legislative assembly, Dáil Éireann, had been declared illegal, and Lloyd George had devised his "Bill for the Better Government of Ireland," which recommended separate parliaments for the six northeastern counties and for the other twenty-six counties of Ireland. This scheme for partition at once intensified the struggle between Sinn Féin and the British Executive in Ireland. After the shooting of a policeman in Dublin on February 20th, 1920, a curfew was imposed on the city, making it illegal for any persons other than members of the Crown forces to be in the streets between midnight and 5 a.m. Soon afterwards the curfew period was extended and began at 8 p.m. On March 24th, four days before the Second Reading of Lloyd George's Bill at Westminster, the power of the British Executive was reinforced by the first detachments of a special police force recruited from the toughest ex-servicemen of the First World War. These detachments wore khaki coats with black trousers and black caps and were promptly christened "the Black and Tans" after a well-known Tipperary pack of foxhounds. To combat these forces, the Irish Republican Army split into small groups of fifteen to thirty men who used guerilla tactics to keep their foes under constant strain. Many of its fighters lived on the run, moving continuously from place to place and seldom sleeping at home. By May, 1920, the forces of the Crown were being gradually forced back to their headquarters in Dublin and many Irish Protestants who had previously been strong supporters of the Union with England had become passive spectators of the struggle.

Most of these facts are vividly reflected in *The Shadow of a Gunman* which had an immense local appeal when it was first acted at the Abbey Theatre on April 12th, 1923. Its action hinges on the fact that a poet, Donal Davoren, who has recently come to share a Dublin tenement with Seumas Shields, allows himself to be regarded as a gunman "on the run." *On the Run,* indeed, was O'Casey's original title for the play and he abandoned it only because a drama of that name already existed. Another character, Maguire, is a real gunman on the run and is killed in a guerilla action not far from Dublin. A third character, Grigson, is an Orangeman and professes loyalty to the Crown, but he is politically passive and assures Davoren that "there never was a drop av informer's blood in the whole family av Grigson." While Grigson is out drinking during the curfew period, his wife is worried in case he may be shot by the Black and Tans. Soon after Grigson's safe return, shots are heard in the lane outside and Davoren and Shields are terrified at the prospect of a raid because Maguire has left a bag of bombs in their room. Shields prays that the raiders may be Tommies and not the dreaded Tans.

Discussing the behaviour of the Black and Tans in *The Revolution in Ireland* (1923), W. Alison Phillips primly remarks that "there is evidence that some of these men—by no means all—brought to Ireland the loose views as to the rights of property which had been current during the war at the front, and helped themselves to what they needed without in these requisitions always discriminating between the loyal and the disloyal." In the play, Mrs. Grigson's description of how the Black and Tans treat her husband puts flesh on the dry bones of this generalization. To prove his loyalty, Grigson puts a big *Bible* on his table, open at the First Epistle of St. Peter, with a pious text on obedience to the King marked in red ink. The representatives of the Crown are unimpressed, however; the Black and Tans fling Grigson's *Bible* on the floor, interpret his picture of King William crossing the Boyne as seditious propaganda, and force him to sing, "We shall meet in the Sweet Bye an' Bye" as they drink his whisky. After arresting Minnie Powell, who had bravely concealed Maguire's bombs in her room, the Black and Tans raid another house and immediately afterwards are caught in the ambush in which Minnie is killed.

The setting of the play reinforces the strong local interest of these events. The scene represents "A room in a tenement in Hilljoy Square, Dublin." There is no such place as "Hilljoy Square" in Dublin, but the significant combination of "hill," "joy," and "square" and some other details in the play made it pretty certain that O'Casey was representing a tenement in Mountjoy Square, which is situated in the northeastern part of the city and was built between 1792 and 1818 at a time when it was fashionable to live on the north side of the Liffey. By the end of the nineteenth century, however, the south side had again become the fashionable residential area, and many of the fine Georgian houses in Mountjoy Square and the surrounding district had been converted into tenements which were occupied by the poorest citizens. The Georgian architecture of Mountjoy Square and its surroundings no doubt explains why the scene of the play is described as a *Return Room*, in which two large windows *occupy practically the whole of the back wall space*, and why Mr. Gallogher and his family are described as the tenants of a "front drawing-room" and their obnoxious neighbours, the Dwyers, as the tenants of a "back drawing-room" in a house nearby.

In May, 1920, the tenements of Dublin were appallingly overcrowded. In 1913, a Local Government Board Commission recorded that 21,000 families were living in one-room tenements, of which 9,000 were occupied by four or more persons. In O'Casey's play, Mr. Gallogher's tenement falls into the latter category for it is occupied by his two children as well as his wife and himself. The complaint which Gallogher makes to Davoren, whom he regards as an important member of the Irish Republican Army, is due to over-crowded conditions of life. Despite his protests, Mrs. Dwyer has persisted in allowing her children to keep the hall door open and to use the hall as a playground. "The name calling and the language" of the Dwyers is "something abominable" and Mrs. Gallogher often has to lock her door to keep them from assaulting her. Gallogher fears that things will get worse when Mr. Dwyer, a seaman, comes home, and anxiously petitions the Irish Republican Army for protection.

The quaintly-worded petition which Gallogher brings to Davoren establishes yet another connection between the

play and the revolutionary situation in Ireland in May, 1920. Early in 1920, the Dáil Éireann began to organize its own police and its own law courts in opposition to those of the Crown. By June, Republican courts had been established in no less than twenty-one counties and the royal judges who went on circuit found no litigants awaiting them. In May and June the pressure of business in the Republican courts became so great that the Dáil was obliged to limit the cases to be heard to those licensed by its Minister for Home Affairs. Against this background, Gallogher's letter of May 21st to the "Gentlemen of the Irish Republican Army" acquires additional significance. The anomalous legal conditions of the time explain why he carefully excuses himself for having taken out a summons against the Dwyers because "there was no Republican Courts" at the time when he did so, and why he adds that he did not proceed with it because he has "a strong objection to foreign courts as such." He goes on to urge the Republicans to send "some of your army or police," preferably with guns, to his tenement, for he believes that he has "a Primmy Fashy Case against Mrs. Dwyer and all her heirs."

O'Casey certainly made abundant use of local geography and history when he wrote **The Shadow of a Gunman.** But his choice of material is selective and his treatment is consistently ironical. There is a visual irony in the very setting in which Shield's meagre, slovenly furnishings clutter a room in a Georgian mansion in a once-fashionable square. The dangers of the curfew period set Mrs. Grigson worrying about her absent husband, but they also produce the irony of her canny speculation: "Do the insurance companies pay if a man is shot after curfew?" In their treatment of Grigson, the Black and Tans are the unconscious agents of the irony of poetic justice because Grigson is a boastful tippler who treats his wife like a skivvy. The Republican Courts were established with the high purpose of saving Ireland from anarchy during a time of great emergency; Gallogher expects them to sort out a tenement squabble. If O'Casey had preserved his original title, *On the Run*, it would have combined irony with topicality since Davoren is an artist "on the run" in search of peaceful conditions of work, not the dedicated gunman he is taken for. In *The Playboy of the Western World*, the pose so artfully assumed by Christie Mahon stimulates both his imagination and that of his admirers; in **The Shadow of a Gunman,** Davoren's half-hearted pose illustrates only his vanity and evokes only vainglory or self-interest in such characters as Tommy Owens, Grigson, and Gallogher. The saddest of the many ironies in the play is that Minnie Powell sacrifices herself for a versifier whom she regards as a patriot as well as a poet.

II

Minnie Powell represents the most positive set of values in **The Shadow of a Gunman.** These values emerge chiefly from the interaction between Minnie, Davoren, and Shields. A comparison between the play and the third and fourth sections of *Inishfallen, Fare Thee Well* (1949) provides good reasons for believing that these three characters had their origins in certain experiences described by O'Casey in this autobiography and that he modified and intensified these experiences to create the contrast between Minnie, Davoren, and Shields which is the main theme of the play.

In his autobiography, O'Casey describes how the behavior of his brother made it impossible for him to carry on with his creative writing in their Dublin tenement and how he moved to another tenement in a different house. This parallels Davoren's move from one tenement to another so as to be able to work in peace. One night when O'Casey lay in bed in his new abode the house was raided by Black and Tans; in the play, Davoren finds himself in the same predicament. In his autobiography, O'Casey describes "a volley of battering blows on the obstinate wooden door, mingled with the crash of falling glass" which indicated that "the panels on each side of it had been shattered by hammer or rifle-butt." These details are closely paralleled by the stage-direction in the play: *There is heard at the street door a violent and continuous knocking, followed by the crash of glass and the beating of the door with rifle butts.* As O'Casey awaited the entry of the raiders, he thought of Whitman's lines, "Come lovely and soothing death, Undulate round the world, serenely arriving," and pondered the fact that "Death doesn't arrive serenely here. . . ." Correspondingly, Davoren recalls Shelley's description of "the cold chaste moon . . . Who makes all beautiful on which she smiles," and bitterly reflects that the moon "couldn't make this thrice accursed room beautiful."

At the back of the house described in the autobiography is a "large shed that was said to be used as a carpenter's shop" by O'Casey's neighbor, Mr. Ballynoy, a thin, delicate man who was reputed to care "for no manner of politics." A similar building appears in the play when Shields mentions that "There's a stable at the back of the house with an entrance from the yard; it's used as a carpenter's shop." Shields goes on to suggest that this shop is used for the manufacture of bombs, but whether this is so is never revealed, and in the play the passage about it is rather redundant. The carpenter's shop probably found its way into the play because the Black and Tans discovered that the shed described in the autobiography contained a large quantity of explosives. These had evidently been manufactured by Mr. Ballynoy, who was wounded when he tried to prevent the raiders from entering the shed. As he stands in the lorry after his arrest, Ballynoy's final gesture is one of patriotic defiance: "'Up th' Republic!' he shouted with the full force of his voice." This gesture is strikingly paralleled in the play; when Minnie Powell is thrust into a lorry after her arrest, she shouts "'Up the Republic!'" at the top of her voice.

Though O'Casey's sympathies were with the Republicans, there were moments when he grew weary of the fighting and contemplated both sides with a jaundiced eye: "Gun peals and slogan cries were things happy enough in a song, but they made misery in a busy street. . . . The sovereign people were having a tough time of it from enemies on the left and friends on the right. Going out for a stroll, or to purchase a necessary, no one knew when he'd have to fall flat on his belly, to wait for death to go by, in the midst of smoke and fire and horrifying noises. . . . Christian Protestant England and Christian Catholic Ireland were banging away at each other for God, for King, and Country." In the play Shields re-echoes these bitter sentiments when he exclaims, "It's the civilians that suffer; when there's an ambush, they don't know where to run. Shot in the back to save the British Empire, an' shot in the breast to save the soul of Ireland. I'm a Nationalist meself, right enough . . . but I draw the line when I hear the gunmen blowin' about dyin' for the people, when it's the people that are dyin' for the gunmen!"

III

In its modification of the personal experiences and feelings just described, O'Casey's imagination makes Davoren an embodiment of frustrated life, Shields an embodiment of life turned sour and superstitious, and Minnie Powell an embodiment of an ideal fullness of life, in order to create that intense contrast between masculine and feminine nature which is fundamental to his interpretation of human existence. The particular form of Davoren's frustration is that of an artist at odds with society; Shields is a nationalist who has degenerated into abysmal selfishness. The two characters are aptly symbolized by certain properties among the untidy furnishings of their tenement: the self-protective superstition of Shields by the crucifix and the statues of the Virgin and the Sacred Heart on the mantelpiece; the aesthetic aspirations of Davoren by the flowers, the books and the typewriter[1] on the table. Both have catchphrases expressive of their exaggerated discontents. Shields makes any annoyance, however trivial, an excuse for invective against the "Irish People" as a whole, and his misanthropy persistently finds vent in the refrain, "Oh, Kathleen ni Houlihan, your way's a thorny way." Whenever Davoren's attempts to write are interrupted, he echoes the words of Shelley's tormented Prometheus, "Ah me! alas, pain, pain, pain ever, for ever." Each of them proudly claims that his creed sets him above fear. According to Shields, "No man need be afraid with a crowd of angels round him; thanks to God for His Holy religion!" and Davoren retorts, "You're welcome to your angels; philosophy is mine; philosophy that makes the coward brave; the sufferer defiant; the weak strong. . . ." A second later a volley of shots outside reduces both of them to the same state of abject fear.

For all the mock-heroic effect of his Promethean pose, Davoren is not an unsympathetic character. Unlike Joyce's Stephen Dedalus, he is a portrait of the artist as a not-so-young man subject to the withering effects of poverty, the noise and interruptions of slum life, and the danger of sudden death in a time of revolution and war. Yet his aesthetic creed has much in common with that of Dedalus. It is described at the outset of the play as a devotion to *the might of design, the mystery of colour, and the belief in the redemption of all things by beauty everlasting.*" These phrases are borrowed from Dubedat's climactic speech in the fourth act of Shaw's *The Doctor's Dilemma.* They are repeated when Shields maliciously remarks that "a poet's claim to greatness depends upon his power to put passion in the common people," and Davoren bitterly replies, ". . . to the people there is no mystery of colour. . . . To them the might of design is a three-roomed house or a capacious bed. To them beauty is for sale in a butcher's shop. . . . The poet ever strives to save the people; the people ever strive to destroy the poet." This is a central issue in the play. It is put to the test by Davoren's reactions to Minnie Powell.

Characteristically, Davoren is reluctant to admit Minnie when she knocks gently on his door. But their conversation reveals that this daughter of the people is an unconscious devotee of all that Davoren values most; she loves beauty, design, and colour in the forms available to her—the poetry of Burns, the music of Tommy Owens's melodeon, and the flowers on Davoren's table. What is more, she has the courage and the feeling of community that Davoren lacks; "I don't know how you like to be by yourself," she tells him, "I couldn't stick it long." Davoren forgets his timidity as he joyfully realizes that Minnie embodies his ideals; "My soul within art thou, Minnie!" he exclaims, but after she has gone his exaltation gives way to uneasiness as he ponders the dangers of being "the shadow of a gunman" to please her.

Shield's reaction to Minnie exhibits his misanthropy at its worst. She is "an ignorant little bitch that thinks of nothing but jazz dances, foxtrots, picture theatres an' dress" and would "give the world an' all to be gaddin' about with a gunman" but would not grieve long if he were shot or hung. As for her courage, "She wouldn't sacrifice a jazz dance to save a man's life." Minnie gives the lie to this and to Davoren's assertion that "the people ever strive to destroy the poet" when she takes the bombs from their room and is killed after being arrested. Shields is unmoved by this sacrifice; he sees in it nothing more than a gratifying confirmation of his superstitious belief that the tapping on the wall was an ill omen. But for Davoren it is a tragic experience which leads him to know his own nature better; he recognizes that he is "poltroon and poet," and it is a measure of his development that in his final lament Shelley's words, "Ah me, alas! Pain, pain, pain ever, for ever!" no longer sound mock-heroic on his lips. In *A Portrait of the Artist as a Young Man*, Dedalus's aesthetic adventure ends with an inspiring epiphany of beauty; Davoren's ends with a revelation of the moral inadequacy of his creed.

The contrast between Davoren and Shields and Minnie Powell raises **The Shadow of a Gunman** to a tragic level. This major design is reinforced by several lesser but parallel contrasts. Like Davoren and Shields, most of the other men in the play are intent on vanity or self-preservation; only the women show themselves capable of courage and charity like Minnie Powell's. The pathetic Mr. Gallogher is under the wing of the immensely maternal Mrs. Hender-

son, who teases him out of his timidity and admires his fantastic prose. Grigson's drinking and boasting flourish at the expense of Mrs. Grigson, who lets him have most of their food, *getting just enough to give her strength to do the necessary work of the household.* In the face of danger and death, a moral paralysis afflicts the men, whereas the sympathies of the women expand; Mrs. Grigson mourns the death of Minnie and Mrs. Henderson is arrested for fighting the Black and Tans. **The Shadow of a Gunman** is skillfully constructed to create a contrast between the masculine and the feminine character as stern as that elaborated in **Juno and the Paycock.** The most significant difference between **The Shadow of a Gunman** and O'Casey's autobiography lies in the substitution of Minnie Powell for Mr. Ballynoy. No less than Yeats' Countess Cathleen and Synge's Deirdre, Minnie Powell treads the thorny way of Cathleen ni Houlihan; Shields' catch-phrase is more revelant than he will ever realize. It is this mythopoeic level of meaning which makes **The Shadow of a Gunman** much more than "a commentary upon the warlike conditions of the city during the year 1920" and brings it into contact with what Yeats called the *anima mundi,* the world of ideal passion, to which the tragic heroine aspires even at the cost of her physical destruction.

Notes

1. One is rather surprised to find that the impecunious Davoren owns a typewriter. Like the carpenter's shop, it may have found its way into the play *via* the experiences recounted in *Inishfallen, Fare Thee Well.* In the sixth section of this autobiography, O'Casey records how he managed to acquire a secondhand typewriter by hire-purchase just after the events already described.

JUNO & THE PAYCOCK

PRODUCTION REVIEWS

The Living Age (review date 3 May 1924)

SOURCE: A review of *Juno & the Paycock,* in *The Living Age,* Vol. 321, No. 4165, May 3, 1924, pp. 869-70.

[*In the following review of the world première of* Juno & the Paycock, *the critic praises the play's deft blend of comedy and tragedy, particularly the light touch at its end.*]

The Abbey Theatre in Dublin, which was the scene of the early triumphs of Lady Gregory, Yeats, and Synge, has come into its own again with a new play by Mr. Sean O'Casey, **Juno and the Paycock.** The play is an extraordinary mingling of light comedy which, from criticisms, appears to verge almost upon farce, with an undercurrent of the bitterest tragedy emerging emphatically at the end of the play, but yielding in the last few minutes of the action to the comic interest, so that the play ends—most unconventionally for a modern drama—in laughter.

Mr. O'Casey, like that other Irish dramatist, Mr. Shaw, is superior to the demands of the 'well-made play.' Analyzed—though nobody has any business to analyze a play—*Juno and the Paycock* seems to deal with a little bit of everything and to have no construction at all; but, having once safely broken all the rules, Mr. O'Casey contrives to produce a work which is universally praised, a few critics even venturing the adjective 'great.'

In Act I the audience sees the Doyle family living in a humble tenement and about to become public charges. Juno is the mother, the Paycock is her husband, who is out of work and given to the indigent habit of 'paycocking' around Dublin bars. There is a crippled son and a ne'er-do-well daughter. In the second act this dismal company suddenly learn, or at any rate believe they have learned, that the family is to receive a legacy. Their way of living changes instantly. The shabby room is filled with paper flowers, they buy a new phonograph, beer flows, the daughter becomes engaged to marry a young solicitor.

Then suddenly they find out that the legacy never existed. Their furniture is seized, the son is led out for execution at an oddly unprepared moment in the action, more like real life than the stage—real life, that is, as it was until recently in Ireland. Juno, the mother, after putting up with her worthless husband for thirty years, decides to leave him and devote herself to her daughter. The roaring comedy has become tragedy. Then, just at the end, the 'Captain' and his boon companion, Joxer, return to the room, both drunk, both quite unable to understand why it is deserted and why the furniture is gone.

It is a situation that requires careful handling and skillful writing on the part of the author. Mr. O'Casey's lines call up in the audience's mind what has gone before—not the tragedy but all the recent merrymaking. The two last characters on the stage are quite oblivious of tragedy, shrewd, beery, rather sodden. They settle down to talk a humorous, futile philosophy. The audience laughs.

The author of the play is a workingman who has written five other plays, only one of which has been produced. Yet of *Juno and the Paycock* a London critic says that 'the sooner it comes to London the better.' Mr. O'Casey earns his living by cleaning up a workingmen's club, and Liam O'Flaherty, writing in the London *Daily Herald,* describes him as 'so unused to congratulations that he nearly wrung my hand off.'

'As he dodged around the floor with his broom,' writes Mr. O'Flaherty, 'sweeping a piece of orange peel from under this form, knocking an empty packet of cigarettes off that form, he kept talking about Chekhov, the misery of the Irish workers, the origin of "Captain" Doyle, the greatest character in his play.

'His emaciated face, with the small eyes that seem to pierce one through and through and then wander off in another direction as if they were saying, "I've seen through him," makes one feel that after all it is worth one's while to suffer in order to feel that spirit of divine rebellion that makes great art possible.'

Edward Alden Jewell (review date 28 May 1924)

SOURCE: A review of *Juno & the Paycock,* in *The Nation,* Vol. 118, No. 3073, May 28, 1924, pp. 617-19.

[*In the following review of the debut of* Juno & the Paycock *at the Abbey Theatre, Jewell lauds O'Casey's "unique" interpretation of life in the Dublin slums, especially the authenticity of his characters that surpass cliches of the Irish peasantry.*]

The Abbey Theater, Dublin, is a somber little playhouse, rather bleak, and crude in equipment; yet it has brought to light some of the most notable works of modern dramatic art. The late John M. Synge, W. B. Yeats, Padraic Colum, Lady Gregory, Seumas O'Kelly, Lord Dunsany have sat in the stalls to watch their own premiers; while from it, a few seasons ago, issued the company which toured America with Lennox Robinson's "The Whiteheaded Boy." I doubt, however, whether any piece has been seen at the Abbey finer than "June[sic] and the Paycock." The week of its production literary Dublin talked of little else. Mr. Yeats, Lennox Robinson, Æ were in agreement as to its high and impartial fidelity; and Lady Gregory (who, being one of the directors of the theater, had read [*Juno and the Paycock*] in manuscript) journeyed all the way from her home in the west of Ireland to see it performed. James Stephens said of the play that "it is plumped like an orange, full of sap." One of the local dramatic critics gave as his opinion: "Mr. O'Casey is the nearest approach to a genius we have had in Irish literature for the stage in a very considerable time."

And this "genius" is a bricklayer's assistant, plying his trade from day to day. He could not attend a tea in the greenroom of the Abbey to which I was asked, because there wouldn't be time to wash the mortar off his hands and get into respectable garb. Sean O'Casey lives in a single room, furnished with a bed, a chair, a table, and a lamp. His passion is books. I learned what he did with his royalty receipts for the opening two weeks: got the cheque cashed immediately and went down to the second-hand bookshops along the quai, where he indulged in an orgy. As a child he begged in the streets for his food. Today he is able to eat only the plainest and most frugal fare, because his digestive organs have been ruined by starvation. Now that he is in the way of becoming famous, the attitude of his fellows in the bricklaying world has changed: they think him a snob. They do not know Sean O'Casey.

June [sic], far from being a Grecian goddess, is a woman of the Dublin slums, so nicknamed because she chanced to have been born in June; "paycock" is simply dialect for the bird of gorgeous tail plumage. The fact that this is a play about Dublin life makes it in a sense unique. With depictions of peasant character and manners, patrons of the Abbey have grown very familiar. It was left to a hod-carrier to give them the capital—not Dublin's gay and intellectual side, to be sure, but a cross-section, marvelously real, of its slums. Mr. O'Casey, who understands the people about whom he writes, knocks out a wall, and we behold the living apartment of a two-room tenement flat inhabited by the Boyle family.

It is a barren domicile—not so very different from his own, I fancy; just a few wooden chairs, a rough table, crazy curtains at the windows, and the walls presenting various strata of paper, tattered in spots, patched in others. A poor fire smolders on the hearth, where we see a kettle for tea and a pan containing a solitary sausage. On the mantelpiece an alarm clock reposes face downward, that being the only position in which it will function as a clock. Before a picture of the Virgin a small light burns.

The plot is simple. At times one feels it to be non-existent, and yet there is a plot. The play is expertly, if not in all respects flawlessly, put together. Its story is woven about the tragic figure of Johnny Boyle, the young son of the house, who in 1916 was a Republican, taking part in the Easter Week uprising where he lost an arm. Now he has become a Free Stater, and, shortly before the time in which the action begins (1922), has given some evidence against a former Republican comrade who, having failed to change his politics, is shot by soldiers of the Free State. Johnny cowers under an abject, disorganizing dread of the retribution he feels relentlessly closing in. The Republicans are on his track; he is a marked man. So long, he believes, as the little red flame is there before the Virgin's picture, harm cannot reach him. And in this superstition seems to reside a kind of terrible authenticity. The light burns on; but in the last act it flickers—it goes out. Two gunmen are at the door, their pistols leveled. Johnny Boyle is to go with them, no matter where or for what purpose. It is the end: another victim to the insatiate lust of civil warfare.

The author takes advantage, dramatically, of the death of the young Republican, for which Johnny is indirectly responsible, bringing the bereaved mother, in the second act, to the door of the Boyle flat, where she pauses on her way to the grave. "It's a sad journey we're goin' on," sobs a woman who is with her, "but God is good, an' the Republic won't be always down." Scant consolation this, however, proves.

MRS. TANCRED. Ah, what good is that to me now? Whether they're up or down won't bring me darlin' son back from the grave.

NEIGHBOR. Still an' all, he died a noble death, an' we'll bury him like a king.

MRS. TANCRED. Ah, what's the pains I suffered bringin' him into the world to carry him to his cradle, to the pains I'm sufferin' now, carryin' him out o' the world to bring him to his grave? . . . Mother o' God, Mother

o' God, have pity! O blessed Virgin, where were you when me darlin' son was riddled with bullets? . . . Sacred heart of the Crucified Jesus, take away our hearts o' stone . . . an' give us hearts o' flesh. . . . Take away this murtherin' hate . . . an' give us Thine own eternal love!

It is a note of anguish destined to repetition, even in phrase; for although June Boyle, watching the funeral procession from a window, can mutter: "Maybe it's nearly time we had a little less respect for the dead, an' a little more respect for the livin'," yet, when her son's turn arrives, in a frenzy she lifts her hands to heaven and voices the same prayer: "Take away this murtherin' hate . . . an' give us Thine own eternal love!" The words drop like burning tears of agony—an agony so awful that, sitting there in the desolate dark of the theater, the wind coldly shaking the exit doors, the witnesses' heart is torn with pain and compassion. The debacle, in its poignancy unbearable almost is yet keyed to the noble elevation of Greek tragedy which, throughout, visits Sean O'Casey's play with the distinguishing mark of greatness.

June[sic] is described, in the author's manuscript, as a woman of forty-five. "Her face has assumed that look which ultimately settles down upon the faces of the working class: a look of listless monotony and harassed anxiety, blending with an expression of mechanical resistance." It is she whose shoulders endure the weight of the household. Her son is shattered. Her husband will not work when he can possibly avoid it (though his mouth is full of brave talk). To Mary, the daughter, who has turned Socialist, June wearily replies:

Ah, wear whatever ribbon you like, girl, only don't be botherin' me. I don't know what a girl on strike wants to be wearin' a ribbon round her head for or silk stockin's on her legs either. It's wearin' them things that make the employers think they're givin' yous too much money.

Yes, life for June is neither smooth nor sweet. Yet there is a snatch of pseudo good-fortune ahead; for a "will," purporting to leave to her husband, "Captain" Boyle, a snug sum of money, suddenly drops into the family lap. The facts behind that document are these: A certain school-teacher and amateur theosophist named Charlie Bentham (a man much higher in the social scale than the Boyles), has looked upon Mary and found her worthy his desire. By way of wooing—for in the Dublin slums it is not considered good form for a girl sunk in poverty to be courted by a man of affluence or position—Bentham represents himself as a legal ambassador authorized to handle the will (which he has fabricated). The Boyles are to be well off as soon as it becomes operative. Mary succumbs at once, throwing over a lover of her stratum, Jerry Devine.

Old Man Boyle, flushed with the wine of this unexpected windfall, borrows right and left from his neighbors, so that no time may be lost in beginning to enjoy the legacy. He orders clothes from a tailor. New furnishings turn the flat into a gaudy abode: one with difficulty recognizes the tenement livingroom of former times when the curtain rises on the second act. Of course this eldorado lasts only long enough for Bentham to have his way with Mary and then, in the traditional fashion, to depart on other adventures, leaving her with child. Nemesis is fiendishly thorough. Creditors descend. The tailor confiscates "Captain" Boyle's prized new suit (not paid for). Movers denude the flat of its grandeur. Johnny is snatched by Republicans to his death—this once more emphasizing the background of political chaos: of murder, destruction, the violence of an age drunk and mad.

And yet, curiously enough, plentifully equipped, too, is this grim play with comedy, which in essence seems more heart-breaking than the outcome itself. "Captain" Boyle is at all times a tragi-comic figure, portrayed as

> a man of about sixty-five, stout, gray-haired. His neck is short, and his head looks like a stone ball such as one sometimes sees on top of a gate-post. His cheeks, reddish-purple, are puffed out, as if he were always repressing an almost irrepressible ejaculation. He carries himself with the upper part of his body slightly thrust forward. His walk is a slow inconsequential strut. His clothes are dingy, and he wears a faded seaman's cap with a glazed peak.

Boyle's title, "Captain," derives from his having once taken a trip in a collier from Dublin to Liverpool; but he likes to pose as a mighty man of the sea. We savor this legend in one of the dialogues between Boyle and his boon companion, "Joxer" Daly, whose face is "like a bundle of crinkled paper," whose eyes hold a cunning twinkle, and who has "a habit of constantly shrugging."

They sit together over the "Captain's" breakfast of sausage, while the voice of a coal vender is heard chanting outside in the street: "Blocks . . . coal blocks! Blocks . . . coal blocks!" This apparently starts a train of thought.

> BOYLE. Them was days, Joxer, them was days! Nothin' was too hot or too heavy for me then. Sailin' from the Gulf o' Mexico to the Antarctic Ocean. I seen things—I seen things, Joxer—that no mortal man should speak about that knows his Cathecism. Often an' often, when I was fixed to th' wheel with a marlinspike, an' the win's blowin' fierce, an' the waves lashin' till you'd think every minute was goin' to be your last, an' it blowed an' blowed—blow is the *right* word, Joxer, but blowed is what the sailors use—
>
> JOXER. Oh, it's a darlin' word, a daarlin' word!
>
> BOYLE. An' as it blowed an' blowed, I often looked up at the sky an' assed meself the question: What is the stars? What is the stars?
>
> VOICE OF COAL VENDER. Any blocks, coal blocks! Blocks, coal blocks!
>
> JOXER. Ah, that's the question, that's the question: What is the stars?
>
> BOYLE. An' then, I'd have another look, an' I'd ass meself: What is the moon?

A wonderful scene, annihilating in its futility, its maudlin talk of stars and moon, with a coal vender crying his wares. It even held a sort of eerie beauty.

Then there is the joust in the second act, to celebrate the Boyles's turn of fortune. Impromptu songs are sung. Never to be forgotten is the duet from "Il Trovatore," between mother and daughter: full of tremolos and uncertainties; full of a pride on June's part and of a shy girlish confusion on Mary's—for Bentham is present, and she must do herself justice. Finally, the gramophone is turned on. And it is this hilarious scene which is broken by Mrs. Tancred, with her prayer to the heart of the Crucified Jesus.

Light and shade are extraordinarily crocheted. The play is veritable growth of the soil: complete, unsparing, and true—like the performance. Sara Allgood as June, Barry Fitzgerald as the "Captain," and F. J. McCormick as "Joxer," lifted their roles to a plain of creation, with art that never once showed threadbare. The Johnny of Arthur Shields was a finely studied characterization; and I have never seen a more exquisite bit of work in the theater than Eileen Crowe's picture of Mary singing before her lover.

After the smash-up, "Captain" Boyle goes out with "Joxer" to drown his sorrows. It is these two unspeakable old cronies, returned at night to a room bereft of all save a smoky lamp, who conclude the piece:

> BOYLE. If th' worst comes to th' worst, I'll join . . . a flyin' column! I did me bit in Easther Week—had no business to be there . . . but Captain Boyle's Captain Boyle!
>
> JOXER. Breathes there a man with soul so de—ad . . . this me—ow—n . . . me native . . . land!
>
> BOYLE. Commandant Kelly . . . died in them arms, Joxer. "Tell me Volunteer butties," says he, "that I . . . died for . . . Ireland!"
>
> JOXER. D'jever read Willy Reilly an' his *Own Colleen Bawn?*
>
> BOYLE. I'm tellin' you, Joxer, th' whole worl's in a terrible state o' chassis!
>
> JOXER. Ah . . . it's a darlin' book! A daaarlin' . . . book!

The curtain mercifully intervenes; one could endure no more.

***The Spectator* (review date 21 November 1925)**

SOURCE: A review of *Juno & the Paycock,* in *The Spectator,* Vol. 135, No. 5082, November 21, 1925, pp. 923-24.

[*In the following review of the London debut of* Juno & the Paycock, *the critic focuses on the dramatic atmosphere, local color, and Irish idiom of the play.*]

What would an Irish play be if it were stripped of its atmosphere and "local colour" and native idiom?

An unfair, an impossible question; a test we need not impose upon a work of art in which form and matter (see Flaubert and Pater) emerge inseparable. We must not complain of Mr. Sean O'Casey's *Juno and the Paycock,* which deserves and has won such high praise in Dublin, and now in London at the Royalty Theatre, that its *donée,* its theme, its formula, are of the most familiar known to the modern stage. It is enough that the new dramatist's version of the thriftless work-shy Micawber is, in his dialogue and soliloquy, *noc* Micawber, but a very real re-creation of a very familiar type—the drunken drifting Jack Boyle, dryland sailor, who lives on a false nautical prestige and upon the devotion of a wife of the sharp-tongued yet endlessly enduring type, whom, as a type, we have seen so often; yet, now, as she is played by Miss Sara Allgood, seem never to have seen before. The daughter of these two, seduced, "betrayed," is also the daughter of a thousand unfortunates in like predicament. Yet, though Mr. O'Casey has not done so well with her as he has with her father and mother, he has set her, for a heightening of her plight, amongst the rigid unforgivingness of Catholics, in a tenement house where lights burn before the image of the Mother of God, upon whom the fear-crazed son, darkly involved in fierce Irish politics, relies for the protection that fails him when a couple of young gunmen come to hale him to death.

These children, these parents, are what they are because we are in Dublin in 1922, under the stress, between Free Stater and Republican Die-Hards, of that charming virtue, patriotism. You cannot de-localize them, and in this case the atmosphere *is* the play. "From the form the idea is born."

Thus you forget, under Mr. O'Casey's magic, how often before you have been invited to watch the effects of a suddenly promised legacy from a half-forgotten relative, not only upon a nearly penniless family, but also upon the neighbours and cronies who "come about" and drink and talk and sing—at rather unnecessary length, for there is a *longueur* in the middle of the second act—and then the counter-effects upon them of removal of this luck and of the coming of ruin in the daughter's disgrace and the son's death. *Splendeurs et Misères!* But here the splendours have a particular savour, as represented by plush sofas and chairs, rashly purchased on account; while the accent of prosperity is given in the incomparable lounging importance that Mr. Arthur Sinclair knows how to convey into every look and gesture of "Captain" Jack Boyle, the "peacock." The miseries and recovered poverty are gathered up and dignified by Miss Sara Allgood's beautiful picture of the mother upon whom alone, at the end, the weight of this burden falls. For the "Captain"—drunk again—returns to the denuded living-room only to maunder uselessly about the chaos of the world.

This play, indeed, owes an immense amount to the acting, which diminishes still recognisable awkwardnesses here and there: the delay already mentioned in the second act; the moralizing introduction of another afflicted mother, in one scene, in order that the mother-heroine may get a foretaste of her own coming disaster; the rather tedious humours and quotations-mania of drunkard No. 2, Captain

Boyle's companion, one "Joxer" Daly (Mr. Sydney Morgan). The admirable simplicity and reticence of the players helps to conceal a very promising beginner's lack of discrimination and selection in the wit of dialogue. Mr. O'Casey gives his characters some delightful things to say; others less delightful. The bogus "Captain" will object to being followed to one of his drinking haunts, as a man may object to "having the motions of his body watched, as an astronomer watches the stars." He will assert, when his wife finds theosophy a "curious" belief: "All religions are curious, for who would believe in them if they were not?" And also—less happily—he will, in the course of a reminiscence, revive the old joke about "each moment being his next." The audience, which laughs at all these things, will laugh louder than ever at the sound of a cork popping in the "Captain's" adjacent bedroom. Mr. O'Casey, in fact, has not—could not yet be expected to have—the exquisite unity of tone and style that enchanted us when we first listened to *The Well of the Saints* or to *The Playboy of the Western World.* But to discover one Synge is enough for one theatre. The Abbey Theatre did that; and now, in Mr. O'Casey, it has shown us how fruitful and lasting its influence is likely to be.

CRITICAL COMMENTARY

Leslie Thomson (essay date 1986)

SOURCE: "Opening the Eyes of the Audience: Visual and Verbal Imagery in *Juno & the Paycock,*" in *Modern Drama,* Vol. XXIX, No. 4, December, 1986, pp. 556-66.

[*In the following essay, Thomson outlines the delusions about Irish reality and the underlying causes that animate* Juno & the Paycock, *showing how visual and verbal imagery reinforces a pessimistic interpretation of the play's meaning.*]

Near the end of *Juno and the Paycock,* Mary says, "My poor little child that'll have no father!" Juno comforts her, saying, "It'll have what's far better—It'll have two mothers."[1] Given what we have seen of the men in the play, our initial inclination might be to agree with Juno; however, to do so would be to join the characters in their delusions and to ignore the realities with which O'Casey confronts us. To encourage his audience to see Ireland, and the world, realistically and dispassionately, O'Casey creates a complex pattern of verbal and visual imagery which should prompt our awareness of the sad truths his characters, even Juno, do not see. Through the play this imagery reinforces the message conveyed in the final tableau: that in a world where Boyles and Joxers prevail, two mothers may be relatively "better" but nothing has changed, nor will it, because the delusions and their causes remain.

This view goes against the more optimistic interpretations most critics put on the play. While the irony of Boyle's final appearance is usually acknowledged, it is often seen as being countered by, rather than countering, Juno's last words and departure. In general, the view is that, if the controlling mood of the play is bleak, Juno's "heroism" overcomes it and gives us cause to hope. William Armstrong sees a sharp contrast between the male and female characters, "from which the women emerge as far superior to the men because of their capacity for love, altruism, and wisdom. The men in the play are all deluded, self-centred, and hypocritical." Armstrong believes that "Unlike Boyle, Juno becomes a stronger and wiser character under the stress of tragic circumstances." For Errol Durbach, Juno is the "indomitable mother . . . Opposing the peacocks of the play, almost singlehandedly." In a somewhat ambiguous description, John O'Riordan asserts that "The dominance of Juno, in her moments of suffering and fixation of mothering tyranny, in her day-to-day existence of resisting and doing, instead of yielding and dreaming, is the play's fortitude and triumph." But while O'Riordan believes that Juno "leaves in tragic dignity," he acknowledges that she is "unable to offer any salvation." This less optimistic—and less sentimental—view of Juno is the one held by James Simmons, who says that Juno's need to care for her family "has placed blinkers of family interest over her vision of life." Of Juno's assertion that two mothers are better, Simmons observes: "This is very homely, and Juno is never more than a very limited woman . . . Mrs. Boyle still understands nothing about political freedom or social justice."[2] That Juno cannot and should not be seen as a heroic figure because of both her character and circumstances are conveyed to us by O'Casey through his use of visual and verbal imagery.

The juxtaposition of the departure of Juno and Mary with the arrival of Boyle and Joxer at the end of the play is the final instance of the method of ironic implication which is O'Casey's organizing principle. On the one hand, we see a mother and her daughter, who is soon to be a mother herself, facing a present necessity dictated by cruel reality; on the other, we have Boyle and his "son," Joxer, spouting drunken fantasies of heroic deeds in a dead past. Just when the audience believes the play to be ending on a hopeful note with the departure of Juno and Mary, it is brought up short by the unexpected re-entrance of Joxer and Boyle. Their drunken "epilogue" should prompt the audience to see that at the end of *Juno and the Paycock* the "world" is in the same "state o' chassis" it has been in since the play began, because nothing has happened to eliminate the causes of that chaos. Not even Juno has been able to change things, and it is important to be conscious of this and to ask why it is so. To convey the answer, O'Casey juxtaposes a series of ideas, actions, and symbols which form an ironic commentary that speaks for itself, as it were, making overt authorial intrusion unnecessary.[3] What it says is that Ireland's twin obsessions of politics and religion are at the heart of the chaos; more specifically, that Nationalism and Roman Catholicism are romantic illusions which permit, even encourage, an escape from reality very much the way alcohol—that symbol of Irish escapism—does.

O'Casey's actor friend, Gabriel Fallon, who played Bentham in the first production of *Juno and the Paycock,* tells us that "[O'Casey] had been telling me for some time about a play he had mapped out, a play which would deal with the tragedy of a crippled I.R.A. man, one Johnny Boyle. He mentioned this play many times and always it was the tragedy of Johnny. I cannot recall that he spoke about Juno or Joxer or the Captain, always Johnny."[4] This suggests a focus which bears study. Johnny, the son of Boyle and of Juno, is at once a product, a victim, and a perpetuator of the play's chaotic world. All the men in *Juno and the Paycock* are self-deluded escapists; none is able or willing to assume his responsibilities as a member of society. To dramatize this problem, its causes and consequences, O'Casey uses Johnny Boyle. Johnny Boyle is the son of Ireland who has betrayed his motherland and prays to the Mother of God for protection while actually being protected from harsh reality by his real mother, Juno. The ironic implications of these three conflicting mother-son relationships—Ireland, Virgin, Juno: Johnny— establish the foundation upon which O'Casey builds.[5] As the spectator becomes increasingly aware of the symbolism operative here, he is likely to become attuned to other related images—both verbal and visual—manifesting the same dichotomies.

The initial stage directions describe a physical, visual opposition, the symbolism of which will be worked through the action. On the back wall is the picture of the Virgin with the votive light burning beneath it. On the right side of the room is the fireplace. *"Johnny Boyle is sitting crouched by the fire."* The burning votive candle is the Virgin Mary's and the burning fire is Juno's. Juno's fire, which burns throughout the play, is both the source of warmth and the means of cooking the food that keeps the Boyles alive. O'Casey makes a point of having not only Johnny but also Boyle, Mary, and Juno herself call our attention to the significance of her fire as a symbol of safety and comfort. Just after Boyle enters for the first time, thinking Juno has left, he invites Joxer to "pull over to the fire, Joxer, an' we'll have a cup o' tay in a minute." Juno appears unexpectedly from behind the curtain and says, "(*with sweet irony—poking the fire, and turning her head to glare at Joxer*), Pull over to the fire, Joxer Daley, an' we'll have a cup o' tay in a minute!" When Joxer refuses, eager to escape, Juno repeats the invitation, giving it added emphasis: "Pull over to the fire, Joxer Daly; people is always far more comfortabler here than they are in their own place" (I, p. II). A few minutes later, during the argument between Jerry Devine and Mary, Boyle's ineffectuality is dramatized as his speech and actions develop the Juno-fire-food connection:

> Chiselurs don't care a damn now about their parents, they're bringin' their fathers' grey hairs down with sorra to the grave, an' laughin' at it, laughin' at it. Ah, I suppose it's just the same everywhere—the whole worl's in a state o' chassis! (*He sits by the fire*) Breakfast! Well, they can keep their breakfast for me. Not if they went down on their bended knees would I take it—I'll show them I've a little spirit left in me still! (*He goes over to the press, takes out a plate and*

looks at it) Sassige! Well, let her keep her sassige. (*He returns to the fire, takes up the teapot and gives it a gentle shake*) The tea's wet right enough. (I, pp. 18-19)

The significance of the fire is further developed in the second Act. When Johnny enters he "*sits down moodily at the fire.*" And shortly after when Bentham enters, Juno, "*in a flutter,*" invites him to "sit down Mr. Bentham . . . no, not there . . . in th' easy chair be the fire . . . there, that's betther." At the end of Act II everyone leaves except Johnny, who still "*sits moodily by the fire*" when the Mobilizer enters to tell him of the meeting he must attend to answer questions about the death of Robbie Tancred (pp. 34, 35, 50).

When they are troubled, the characters seek out the comforting fire. At the top of Act III we are told that "*a bright fire burns in the grate; Mary . . . is sitting on a chair by the fire, leaning forward, her hands under her chin, her elbows on her knees. A look of dejection, mingled with uncertain anxiety, is on her face . . . The votive light under the picture of the Virgin gleams more redly than ever*" (III, p. 51). Mary and Juno leave to go to the doctor's. When they return O'Casey tells us that "*it is apparent from the serious look on* [Juno's] *face that something has happened.*" After silently removing her hat and coat she "*sits down by the fire.*" Later, Mary comes in and again sits "*by the fire,*" only to be confronted by Johnny about her pregnancy. Finally, when the curtain rises following Johnny's departure with the two Irregulars, Mary and Juno, "*one on each side are sitting in a darkened room, by the fire*" (III, pp. 60, 65, 69).

Set against the association of Juno with the fire, and the implication that both are an ever-present source of stability and comfort taken for granted by the others, is the association of the votive light with the Virgin Mary. Early in Act I Johnny is afraid of being left alone and asks his mother to check the Virgin's "fire":

> JUNO Amn't I nicely handicapped with the whole o' yous! I don't known what any o' yous ud do without your ma. (*To* JOHNNY) Your father'll be here in a minute, an' if you want anythin,' he'll get it for you.

> JOHNNY I hate assin' him for anythin' . . . He hates to be assed to stir . . . Is the light lightin' before the picture o' the virgin?

> JUNO Yis, Yis! The wan inside to St. Anthony isn't enough, but he must have another wan to the Virgin here! (I, p. 9)[6]

This conflict between Virgin and Juno, illusion and reality, is the source of another of the juxtapositions controlling the action and the language of the play. As Durbach has observed, O'Casey creates stage business to prompt our awareness that whenever Johnny calls on the Mother of God it is Juno who responds.[7] When in Act II Johnny rushes out of the bedroom believing he has seen the ghost of Robbie Tancred, he cries: "Blessed Mother o' God, shelter me, shelther your son!" But it is Juno, "*catching him in her arms,*" who shelters him. "What's wrong with you? What ails you? Sit down, sit down, here, on the bed

. . . there now . . . there now." When Johnny describes what has frightened him, Juno tells Boyle to "get him a glass o' whisky." As elsewhere, O'Casey prolongs the moment in order to prompt the spectator to perceive the symbolic content of an outwardly realistic episode. Johnny begs Juno, "Sit here, sit here, mother . . . between me an' the door." Juno, the quintessential mother, shelters her grown child: "I'll sit beside you as long as you like." Johnny explains what he has seen, ending with a plea: "Mother o' God, keep him away from me!" But, once more, it is Juno who comforts him: "There, there, child, you've imagined it all . . . Here, drink more o' this—it'll do you good" (pp. 38-9). It is a small but significant point that even for Juno alcohol is the antidote to offer when prayer does not provide an escape from political realities.

Johnny's dependence on the Virgin Mother is emphasized in three related scenes. When the Irregulars pull Johnny offstage in Act III, as he prays to the Mother of God for protection against punishment for his betrayal of Mother Ireland, the two "religions" and the two symbolic "Mothers" of the play are brought together for the final time. Near the end of Act I, Johnny says to Juno, "Ireland only half free'll never be at peace while she has a son left to pull a trigger" (p. 27).[8] Act II concludes with the juxtaposition of Robbie Tancred's funeral and the visit of the Mobilizer. He warns Johnny: "remember your oath," to which Johnny replies: "Good God, haven't I done enough for Ireland?" The Mobilizer's response: "Boyle, no man can do enough for Ireland!" is spoken over the prayer of the mourners: "Hail, Mary, full of grace, the Lord is with Thee; Blessed art Thou amongst women, and blessed, etc." (p. 50).

When the Irregulars are dragging Johnny out in the final Act, they ask if he has his prayer beads. Johnny replies, "are yous goin' to do in a comrade?—look at me arm, I lost it for Ireland." The second Irregular replies; "Commandant Tancred lost his life for Ireland." Johnny, who has looked to the Virgin Mother for protection, is murdered because his real mother, who has always sheltered and defended him before, is not there to do so again as she is busy mothering her other child. Thus, while Juno's actions prompt our admiration, and her loss of Johnny elicits our sympathy, we should be wary of seeing as wholly positive her qualities as "goddess of the hearth." It is necessary to realize that Johnny's retreat into one room, where Juno protects him from the consequences of his betrayal, is of a piece with the avoidance of responsibility, the escape from reality, offered by prayer—or by alcohol

The uneasy co-existence of Ireland's twin "religions," Nationalism and Catholicism, is a central theme of *Juno and the Paycock.* O'Casey's treatment of this issue is consistently ironic; he provides the evidence but leaves it to us to make our own evaluations and come to our own conclusions. To achieve this end he capitalizes on the verbal element of his medium; for to say that each of the characters—including Juno—pays "lip-service" to the causes of both Nationalism and Catholicism is to go to the heart of the sad truth. Boyle is merely the most voluble practitioner of the art of mouthing platitudes and clichés as one would mouth prayers learned by rote. Through the play, whether the subject is politics or religion, the formula for observance is one of "bead-telling": the unthinking repetition of hypnotic phrases which, rather than acknowledging responsibility, permit the avoidance of it. Six times Boyle declares that the world or the country is in "a state o' chassis," but when confronted with the reality of Robbie Tancred's funeral he says: "We've nothin to do with these things, one way or t'other. That's the Government's business, an' let them do what we're payin' them for doin'" (II, p. 47).

During a performance the spectator should become conscious of a pattern of repetitions, both verbal and visual, conveying the combination of empty habit and self-preservation which governs the behaviour of all the characters. To encourage our awareness of this element and to control our responses to it, O'Casey gives us Joxer, the character who is virtually a caricature of those who mean nothing they say and say nothing they mean. In Joxer's verbal scrambling to keep pace with Boyle's changing opinions, O'Casey captures the art of avoiding commitment while seeming committed. Joxer's constant echoing of Boyle and his mouthing of empty platitudes form a comic undercurrent that runs through the play. But the Joxer-centred commentary is often more overt, and then the conflation of politics, religion, and alcohol becomes clear and telling. O'Casey uses Joxer, the parrot-parasite, to detach the audience and to make it aware of the dangerous reality below the amusing caricature.[9] In the first Act, when Joxer encourages Boyle to assert his rights with Juno, he recites an easy-to-memorize rhymed couplet expressing a platitude linking the two ideals romanticized by the Irish: "How can a man die bether than facin' fearful odds, For th' ashes of his fathers an' the temples of his gods?" (p. 24).

But it is in Act II that Joxer's thematic function is most subtly and deftly developed. During the celebration Boyle calls on Joxer to sing "wan of [his] shut-eyed wans," whereupon Joxer *takes a drink . . . solemnly closes his eyes,"* and fails miserably to perform, not once but twice, because he cannot remember the words of two love songs. In one colloquial phrase O'Casey encapsulates a central idea of the play: "shut-eyed ones," whether they be songs, prayers, or nationalistic slogans, are either remembered as a reflex action born of repetition, or not at all. And, like alcohol, they are effective "pain-killers," masking, however temporarily, the realities of factional hatred. "Shut-eyed" ones are implicitly contrasted with what might be called "open-eyed ones"—accurate perceptions of reality born of harsh experience—made apparent only by their virtual absence in the play.

The characters' inability to perceive both the relationship between words and their meanings, and the significance of oft-repeated slogans or prayers are important elements of the plot of *Juno and the Paycock*. Indeed, it is not by ac-

cident that Boyle's inheritance is lost because Bentham's wording of the will is imprecise. Upon learning that his dead cousin has left him some money Boyle mouths pieties about going into mourning. In Boyle's insincere prayer for his cousin O'Casey also brings the ironic conflation of Catholicism and Nationalism to the surface once more. After calling for "a wet—a jar—a boul" to celebrate, Boyle pompously intones:

> . . . Requiescat in pace . . . or, usin' our oul' tongue like St. Patrick or St. Bridget, Guh sayeree jeea ayera!
>
> MARY Oh, father, that's not Rest in Peace; that's God save Ireland.
>
> BOYLE U-u-ugh, it's all the same—isn't it a prayer? . . . (I, p. 29)

But it is especially Joxer whose clichés betray him and call our attention to the gap between what is and what should be in the spiritual, religious, and social worlds of the play. For example, in Act III Joxer steals Boyle's stout and feigns innocence, commiserating: "Oh, that's shocking; ah, man's inhumanity to man makes countless thousands mourn!" (p. 57). And in the final moments of the play, as Boyle and Joxer stumble drunkenly around the empty stage, Joxer inadvertently chooses a particularly apposite line of verse, becoming, in effect, O'Casey's spokesman:

> Breathes there a man with soul . . . so . . . de . . . ad . . . this . . . me . . . o . . . wn, me nat . . . ive l . . . an'! (p. 72)

While Joxer and Boyle are used by O'Casey to highlight the self-centred escapism expressed in the idea of "shut-eyed ones," each of the characters is blinded like Johnny by misplaced faith in illusions—even Juno. Certainly O'Casey's treatment of Juno is the most complex and troublesome, but if we follow the signals sent via Joxer, Boyle, and Johnny we will see that Juno too depends on slogans—those of prayer in her case—when reality overwhelms her. If we add to this the consequences of Juno's partisan mothering—itself an example of "shut-eyed" behaviour—the need to reconsider her "heroism" becomes apparent. Instances of O'Casey's questioning of what Juno represents occur throughout the play. For example, while Juno can acknowledge that "With all our churches an' religions, the worl's not a bit better," she also believes that, "if the people ud folley up their religion better there'd be a better chance for us—" (II, p. 36). In ironic commentary, O'Casey follows this simple hope with Bentham's exposition of his "religion" of Life-Breath and Prawna, rightly ridiculed by Boyle, whose only religion is the bottle.

However, it is Juno's repetition of Mrs. Tancred's prayer that should trouble the attentive spectator most, coming when it does at the main climax of the play after so many "shut-eyed ones," and being followed as it is by the unexpected entrance of the drunken Boyle and Joxer. Not surprisingly, many of those critics who see Juno as heroic also tend to put a positive interpretation on her echoing of

Mrs. Tancred, even when they perceive the ironies. Armstrong says that "Juno speaks for all mothers of her generation in Ireland" when she repeats the prayer, and for Heinz Kosok, she "takes on symbolic traits" thereby. O'Riordan believes that in her repetition of Mrs. Tancred's lament Juno "reiterates the final message of the play."[10] It is also usual to point to Juno's acknowledgement of her kinship with Mrs. Tancred as proof that Juno has learned something in the course of the play. This may be true, but what she has learned is to be more of a mother than ever, and to place even greater faith in the power of motherhood—real and symbolic—to counter the social and political realities of her world. The irony is that the very qualities which make Juno's nickname so apposite themselves permit the romantic delusions to exist and flourish. Thus, there is a danger of sentimentalizing Juno, of "shutting our eyes" to the reality that her repetition of the prayer is prompting us to see.

In Act II the pathos surrounding Mrs. Tancred will be felt by the audience; but it has little effect on the Boyles and their guests, who continue to celebrate after she has cried out her prayer to Mary and her Son:

> Mother o' God, Mother o' God, have pity on the pair of us . . . O Blessed Virgin, where were you when me darlin' son was riddled with bullets, when me darlin' son was riddled with bullets! . . . Sacred Heart of the Crucified Jesus, take away our hearts o' stone . . . an' give us hearts o' flesh! . . . Take away this murdherin' hate . . . an' give us Thine own eternal love! (II, p. 46)

To make the ineffectuality of this prayer even more poignant and telling, O'Casey has Juno herself personify the "hearts o' stone" when she says, in the complacency of an ignorance we do not share: "In wan way, she deserves all she got; for lately she let th' Die-hards make an open house of th' place" (p. 47). Had Juno known what we suspect of Johnny's involvment in Tancred's death she would not have spoken thus. And Juno's later acknowledgement of her hard-heartedness towards Mrs. Tancred is prompted by the realization that in death Robbie Tancred, like Johnny, is not "a Diehard or a Stater, but only a poor dead son!" (p. 71). It is certainly true that in repeating Mrs. Tancred's prayer to the paradigmatic Mother and Son, Juno joins all those mothers whose sons have died serving a romantic cause, whether religious, or political, or both. There is also the sad irony that both Mrs. Tancred and Juno pray for a solution to a conflict born of religious differences in a country which has itself become a religion with opposing factions. Equally, the play's conflation of three mothers—Ireland, Virgin, and Juno—suggests how each fosters the worship of the other, thus perpetuating the chaos we see.

The end of **Juno and the Paycock** is made up of three separate but related climaxes, the effects of which combine to impress us. First the audience watches as Johnny Boyle—the embodiment of the destructive coexistence of Catholicism and Nationalism in the Irish psyche—goes to his death at the hands of the Die-hards, praying to the Virgin Mary to save him. What follows should prompt the attentive spectator to perceive the reasons why the situation will not change. In Johnny's parents, Juno and her Paycock, O'Casey personifies and dramatizes the inextricable, conflicting obsessions at the heart of Ireland's "troubles." Defeated by reality, Juno falls back on the ineffectual prayers of Catholicism, while the drunken Boyle retreats into his alcoholic delusions of Nationalist heroism. The concluding sequence—Johnny, Juno, Boyle—speaks for itself: when the Boyles of the world prevail, chaos is inevitable.

If, as the son of Juno and Boyle, Johnny combines and is destroyed by the two perverted ideals they represent, this is also true of their daughter Mary. Some of O'Casey's most subtle imagery is used in his development of Mary's role. Repeatedly he focuses on Mary to illuminate a point made elsewhere, creating moments which form nuggets of meaning through effective juxtaposition. Early in the play Juno is waiting impatiently for Boyle to return and lamenting his lack of a job, while Mary is preoccupied with her appearance. Juno's speech concludes:

> An' constantly singin', no less, when he ought always to be on his knees offerin' up a Novena for a job!
>
> MARY (*trying a ribbon fillet-wise around her head*) I don't like this ribbon, ma; I think I'll wear the green—it looks bether than the blue.
>
> JUNO Ah, wear whatever ribbon you like, girl, only don't be botherin' me. (p. 7)

It is as difficult to believe that Mary's name is without ironic implications as it is to ignore the suggestiveness of the green and blue ribbons. Juno suggests a Novena—a prayer to the Virgin Mary—as a solution for unemployment. In choosing between two ribbons, Mary rejects the blue—the Virgin's colour—in favour of the green—the colour of Ireland. Juno's reaction is one of indifference; in her single-minded battle to protect her home and family the reasons for conflict represented by this ironic symbolism are unimportant, but she ignores them at her peril.

If colour imagery seems intentional in this early scene, a second instance confirms O'Casey's purpose. In the second Act, Bentham enters, is invited to sit by the fire by a fawning Juno, and is listening to Boyle reflect pompously on the "chassis" of the country.[11] A flirtatious Mary enters and is greeted by Bentham.[12] The episode continues:

> BOYLE We were just talkin' when you kem in, Mary; I was tellin' Mr. Bentham that the whole counthry's in a state o' chassis.
>
> MARY (*to* BENTHAM) Would you prefer the green or the blue ribbon around me hair, Charlie?
>
> JUNO Mary, your father's speakin'.
>
> BOYLE (*rapidly*) I was jus' tellin' Mr. Bentham that the whole counthry's in a state o' chassis.
>
> MARY I'm sure you're frettin', da, whether it is or no.
>
> JUNO With all our churches an' religions, the worl's not a bit the bether.

BOYLE (*with a commanding gesture*) Tay! (p. 36)

The possibility of Mary's escaping from the world of her parents, suggested in the initial stage directions, is eliminated when this "Child o' Mary" (p. 62) discovers she will become another of the play's "mothers." The conflation of the two Marys is called to our attention when Johnny in his self-centredness turns on his pregnant sister, Mary flees, and *"the votive light flickers for a moment, and goes out."*[13] Johnny spurns the real Mary who might have helped him and cries to the illusory one: "Mother o' God, there's a shot I'm afther gettin'!" as the Irregulars come to take him away (p. 68).

By such juxtaposing of events and imagery O'Casey prompts the spectator to formulate a response to Juno's assertion that two mothers are better than a mother and a father. Armstrong calls this a "glowing declaration" and O'Riordan terms it "comforting."[14] But with Johnny Boyle's other two Mothers, Ireland and the Virgin Mary, still very much in control of the world he leaves behind, does the coming child have any better chance of survival than Johnny did? Will two "real" mothers make a difference? When last we see Johnny and Juno together she complains that she has "kep' th' home together for the past few years" and that she will "have to bear th' biggest part o' this throuble." Johnny replies: "You're to blame yourself for a gradle of it—givin' him his own way in everything, an' never assin' to check him, no matther what he done. Why didn't you look afther th' money? why . . ." (III, p. 64).[15] No direct answer is given here or elsewhere in the play. But the answer is there for the spectator to hear and see, especially in the play's triple climax and final tableau: Boyle and his like will prevail and the world remain in a state of chaos so long as boys refuse to become men, and mothers, whether real or symbolic, encourage by their very existence the worship of fantasies and the avoidance of reality.

Notes

1. Sean O'Casey, *Juno and the Paycock,* in *Three Plays* (London, 1969): III, p. 71. All quotations are from this edition.

2. William A. Armstrong, "The Integrity of *Juno and the Paycock,*" *Modern Drama* 17 (1974), 6, 8; Errol Durbach, "Peacocks and Mothers: Theme and Dramatic Metaphor in O'Casey's *Juno and the Paycock,*" *Modern Drama,* 15 (1972-73), 18; John O'Riordan, *A Guide to O'Casey's Plays: From the Plough to the Stars* (London, 1984), pp. 46, 59; James Simmons, *Sean O'Casey* (London, 1983), pp. 64, 73.

3. See Katharine Worth, "O'Casey's Dramatic Symbolism," *Modern Drama,* 4 (1961-62), 267: "Symbolism is, in fact, an intrinsic part of the dramatic process in O'Casey's plays, whether it functions in a fantastic or realistic context."

4. Gabriel Fallon, *Sean O'Casey: The Man I Knew* (London, 1965), p. 17.

5. In Durbach's perceptive discussion of the play he makes many of the points developed here.

6. There are two St. Anthonys: St. Anthony of Padua is the patron saint of protection against fire; St. Anthony Abbot or, "the great," is the father of monasticism whose fervor is signified by the flame. Whichever saint Johnny worships, O'Casey's implication is ironic.

7. See Durbach, 20.

8. See Durbach, 19: "Ireland as Mother, an over-idealised abstract Nationalism, is another of the play's informing metaphors."

9. See Durbach, 22.

10. Armstrong, 8; Heinz Kosok, *Sean O'Casey, The Dramatist,* trans., Kosok and Joseph T. Swann (Gerrards Cross, Bucks, 1985), p. 50; O'Riordan, p. 58.

11. Surely Juno's gushing over Bentham is meant to arouse our critical faculties. Simmons makes a related point: "As soon as the promise of money comes, Boyle confidently assumes the role of *pater familias* and Mrs. Boyle is his proud and subservient wife" (p. 56).

12. O'Casey tells us that Bentham is wearing a brown coat, brown knee breeches, and brown sweater, with a deep blue tie (I, p. 25). Again, several ironic allusions suggest themselves. A blue tie for the Theosophist hints obliquely at St. Anthony, whose flame Bentham checks on for Johnny. The pervasive brown attire is a reminder of Joyce's use of brown to signify the moral paralysis of *Dubliners* (published in 1914).

13. See Durbach, 20.

14. Armstrong, 8, O'Riordan, p. 48.

15. Simmons remarks that Johnny's assertion "seems true" (p. 56).

THE PLOUGH AND THE STARS

PRODUCTION REVIEWS

J. J. Hayes (review date 21 March 1926)

SOURCE: "Another by O'Casey," in *The New York Times,* Vol. LXXV, No. 24893, March 21, 1926, p. 2, section 8.

[*In the following review of the world premiere of* The Plough and the Stars, *Hayes assesses the play's mixed approach to comic and tragic themes, preferring its emotional motivation to its realistic presentation.*]

By comparison with what it was a decade ago, playwrighting has become almost a lost art in Ireland. First productions at the Abbey Theatre have become the exception rather than the rule and new plays are rarities. For this and other reasons, therefore, when it was announced that a play from the pen of Sean O'Casey would have its première on a Monday evening early in February there was a run on the box office and every seat in the house for that night, as well as for several following, was sold out almost before the ink on the advertisement was dry on the press.

The sensation caused by the same author's *The Shadow of a Gunman,* eclipsed as it was by that which obtained when his *Juno and the Paycock* was staged, together with the extraordinary reception given to the latter play in London, aroused considerable speculation as to what Sean O'Casey's next play would be like. It had been known for a long time that he was at work on a new play and rumor was very busy with regard to it.

When the curtain went up on Monday night on *The Plough and the Stars,* the Abbey Theatre was packed to the point of discomfort. Every seat was occupied and the aisles had their full quota of standees. The atmosphere was tense, and, in part, this was due to a report which had persisted for several days to the effect that the new play would evoke scenes of protest if not of violence. Dame Rumor was, however, not an honest woman of her word and nothing happened to mar the first performance of another remarkable O'Casey work. On the second night organized interruption was attempted by—as usual—a small group of overzealous women who claimed to be offended by the appearance of the Irish tricolor in a public house scene. The audience, however, did not rise to music and the interruptions soon subsided.

The first night audience waxed enthusiastic as scene after scene took place, and the fall of the curtain on each of the first three acts was the signal for outbursts of very emphatic approval. Feelings finally ran riot with the ending of the fourth and last act, and the ovation given to players and author surpassed anything of its kind that had ever previously taken place in the Abbey. Sean O'Casey has registered another high mark in the annals of Irish drama. In *The Plough and the Stars* he has gone back to 1915-16 for his story and his play obtains its name from the device on the flag of the Irish Citizen Army organized by the late James Connolly, the labor leader, who was executed for his part in the rising of Easter week, 1916.

Jack Clitheroe, a bricklayer, has resigned from the Citizens' Army, ostensibly to please his young wife, Nora, but it is suggested that the real cause of his withdrawal was disappointment at not having been made an officer. It is an evening in November, 1915, and a monster labor meeting is to take place that night in Dublin for the purpose of rallying the patriotic spirit of labor to militant activity. Everybody in the tenement house in which the Clitheroes dwell is going to the meeting with the exception of the Clitheroes themselves and Bessie Burgess, another tenant, who has a son at the front in the Dublin Fusiliers and who has no sympathy with Sinn Fein or its aims. To Jack Clitheroe suddenly comes a dispatch from General Connolly. It is addressed to Commandant Clitheroe and it informs him that he is to command a force which will later in the night make a practice attack on

Dublin Castle. Clitheroe questions the validity of the order as addressed to him, only to be informed that he was appointed to the rank two weeks previously and that a letter to that effect had been given to his wife for delivery to him. It transpires that Nora had burnt the letter and had concealed from her husband the fact of its receipt in the hope of keeping him out of the movement. Husband and wife have their first serious quarrel and the latter departs to assume his command.

Crushed and disappointed, Nora is left alone and a little girl in an advanced state of consumption comes in to keep her company, as a detachment of Dublin Fusiliers, en route to France, headed by a band playing "It's a Long Way to Tipperary," marches past on the street below. As the music dies away the consumptive turns to Nora and asks, "Is there nobody alive with a titther of sense," and the curtain falls on a magnificent and promising first act.

The author, however, reverts to the formless development which characterizes his previous plays and the acts that follow are a series of scenes reflecting the lives of the slum dwellers as they are severally and individually affected by the progress of events leading up to Easter Week, 1916. In the depicting of these scenes the author again reveals his extraordinary knowledge of the people among whom he lived until more or less recently, as well as his remarkable faculty for reproducing incidents which, obviously, he must have witnessed. One sees these tenement dwellers, their jealousies, their quarrels and enmities, their brawls, their weaknesses and their strong qualities. Everything is shown faithfully and pitilessly and back of it all one feels rather than sees the slow but sure development and growth of the movement which culminated in the outbreak that took Dublin by surprise on Easter Monday, 1916.

This movement is the background on which O'Casey has hung his play, and bit by bit the people of this little corner of Dublin slums are caught up by its tentacles until they are finally united in the common lot which is inevitably born of calamity or unusual crisis. Quarrels are forgotten, enmities are put aside as all combine, first, to share in the looting which grows out of the disorder prevailing in the city when established authority is challenged and put to rout, and, later, when Nora, prematurely confined as a result of her husband's participation in the rebellion and his refusal to yield to her pleadings, needs medical assistance and nursing. The death of the consumptive girl, occurring at the same time, also brings out the best that is in these slum dwellers.

The first three acts of the play are brimful of rapid changes from the humorous to the tragic, but the last act is the very quintessence of tragedy. The play ends with two Tommies calmly drinking tea at one side of the room, while on the other lies the dead body of the hated loyalist, Bessie Burgess, who had forgotten her contempt for Nora in order to nurse her in her illness and who, in attempting to draw her away from a window to which she had gone in her delirium, had been shot. Jack Clitheroe is dead, killed in the attack on O'Connell Street. His child is born dead and Nora is found, after the death of Bessie, cowering in a corner of the room and she is led away a hopeless lunatic. All the men found in the building, even though they are non-combatants, are rounded up and led away to internment. All is misery and tragedy and out of it comes clarion-like, the author's message of protest against a violence which is the child of patriotism as far as the men taking part are concerned but which, in the final analysis, is the scourge and torture of women. The little consumptive girl sums it all up at the end of the first act when she asks, "Is there nobody alive with a titther of sense?"

And yet one feels that in a month it will be all forgotten. New people will occupy the Clitheroe rooms and a new tenant will take Bessie Burgess's floor. In time they will become part of the tenement house life. New quarrels and enmities will develop, and brawls will have their natural place in the routine of slum life. The Communist, who talks incessantly of the rights of the proletariat, will continue to preach. Fluther Good will go on in his peculiar philosophic way, championing God and the Catholic Church by day against the Communist and consorting nightly with prostitutes Peter Flynn will boil with rage over the wrongs of Ireland and be ever ready to shoulder a gun as long as there is no prospect of his being called upon to do so, while Mrs. Gogan will, by the death of her child, add the details of that event and of the Funeral at night under military escort to her already voluminous store of morbid and gloomy chatter. It will all go on again until the Black and Tan tyranny unites them once more in common trouble. Tragedy and death will once, more visit the tenement house and the Minnie Powells will give up their lives for *The Shadow of a Gunman*.

The Plough and the Stars is strong stuff, and the author has not hesitated to make his characters use the language of their environment. Nothing is left to the imagination. One may not agree with all his theories, but many of them contain an element of truth. When Nora, after her wild rush through the streets of Dublin and among the barricades of Easter Monday, declares that it is not courage or patriotism that is behind the stand being made against machine guns and artillery but fear, the fear of showing fear, one feels that it is in part a terrible truth which at least applies to many of the rank and file of those who fought in the 1916 uprising. The author makes it clear that this theory did not hold good in the case of men like Jack Clitheroe, who was not only willing to but did actually throw wife, child and home aside for the privilege of leading men into battle against overwhelming odds and who gave his life for the cause he championed. Fear or the fear of showing fear does not prompt men to do these things.

The Plough and the Stars is not an artistic improvement on *Juno and the Paycock,* as far as technique and construction are concerned. It lacks even the thin thread of plot that holds the latter play together, but nevertheless it rivets attention from beginning to end. It is not a political play, and the politics of its period do not obtrude themselves into the action except in so far as they influence the lives of those concerned. Controversy does not appear and no speeches, political or otherwise, are made. At one period one hears the voice of a labor leader haranguing the crowd, but the sentiments expressed do not grate on anybody's susceptibilities. Again, as in his previous plays, the author blends tragedy and comedy almost in the same breath, but in the last act he abandons that method and paints stark tragic realism. The death scene of Bessie Burgess, in which she blasphemes, curses and prays indiscriminately, is terribly effective, and, while it might, in the hands of an indifferent actress, be made ridiculous the Abbey artist, Maureen Delaney, made it sink deep and terrible into the minds of the spectators. The presence of a coffin on the stage during the greater part of the final act had no part in the creating of the tragic atmosphere. It belonged. To many its presence was not noticeable, although it occupied a prominent place on the stage. The atmosphere was there, and it was the work of the author, superbly aided by the Abbey players. It was felt at once, and it deepened as the act progressed, even though nobody could faintly guess what was going to happen.

The plays of Sean O'Casey must be taken on their own merits. Three times he has now presented—and presented with telling effect—a more or less disconnected series of pictures. It is useless to take him to task for violating all the canons of dramatic law. He has succeeded by his sincerity and by the faithfulness of his characters of life. Sean O'Casey attempting to write according to the rules would be unconvincing and his efforts would be hopeless failures. He stands alone among dramatists because he is himself alone.

The Times (London) (review date 14 May 1926)

SOURCE: A review of *The Plough and the Stars,* in *The Times* (London), No. 44271, May 14, 1926, p. 4.

[*In the following review of the London debut of* The Plough and the Stars, *the critic describes the audience's differing responses to the comic and tragic aspects of the play.*]

There is a familiar kind of battle-picture which shows groups of civilians moving confusedly across a smoky background of war. This is the general design of Mr. O'Casey's new play. His background is the rebellion of Easter Week in Ireland; his detached study is of the dwellers in a Dublin tenement, caught up in a movement to which none of them gives purposeful support but which they share with the same swift alternation of violence and indifference that they bring to their personal quarrels. And how they quarrel! And how much they enjoy it! In this company a death or an insult is an opportunity for rhetoric, and what more can the heart of Celtic charwoman desire?

An English audience, which was not anxious to be critical on Wednesday night, had at the outset a welcome for every piece of grotesque extravagance, for Mr. O'Rourke's green uniform and Mr. Sydney Morgan's red tie, for Mr. Arthur Sinclair's carrot hair and slippery humour, and for each torrent of abuse that flowed from the lips of Miss Sara Allgood or Miss Maire O'Neill; but, when the play began to move towards tragedy, it became clear that into the foreground of Mr. O'Casey's battle-picture, from which he was now demanding pathos, there had drifted a stubborn group of comic figures, which not even flame-lit window-panes could fit for tragedy in the twinkling of an eye. A mad lady in her nightdress, who wandered about the room preparing tea for a Jack never to return, was unimpressive to the point of embarrassment. Still, recognizing that most of the acting was full of spirit and in gratitude for laughter when good humour was in the air, the audience was in no mood to be sparing of applause.

Oliver M. Sayler (review date 10 December 1927)

SOURCE: A review of *The Plough and the Stars,* in *The Saturday Review of Literature,* Vol. IV, No. 20, December 10, 1927, p. 427.

[*In the following review of the American premiere of* The Plough and the Stars, *Sayler addresses the emotional appeal of the play, noting that the production's general disregard for verisimilitude accented its humanistic concerns.*]

One of the most difficult tasks the theatre confronts in making dramatic literature oral and visual, in completing and fulfilling its latent promise as drama, is to bring to plausible life on the stage scenes of confusion and combat. Ever since Schiller marshalled the hosts of Wallenstein in his great trilogy, ever since Shakespeare set the legions of Roman civil strife chasing each other over the battlefield of Philippi in *Julius Caesar,* ever since Aristophanes sent the old men of Athens to a scalding bath at the hands of Lysistrata's conspirators on the Acropolis, the theatre's resources for giving plausibility and illusion to mass action in cross-section and microcosm have been strained to the breaking point. To this illusive and elusive end, the Greek stage invented and the Greek populace accepted conventions of which we have scant record. The Elizabethans, likewise, were content with symbolic stimuli to the imagination—a handful of soldiers with property swords serving as proxy for untold armies locked in mortal strife. In our own day, the two distinct and characteristic species of dramatic utterance—realism and expressionism—have shared the common trait of utilizing to the utmost the physical and mechanical as well as the human instruments of the theatre: the former, as in the Moscow Art Theatre's production of *The Family of Tiurbin,* for the sake of the representative illusion of life; the latter, as in Capek 's *R. U. R.,* Toller's *Man and the Masses,* and Kaiser's *Gas,* for the sake of the suggestive illusion of significant unreality.

Overstimulated by this craze for meticulous detail and yet never satisfied with what is at best an approximation, it is

with relief akin to that of escape from the pompous rigmarole of city traffic into open country that we encounter the bland indifference to the demands of external illusion displayed by the Irish Players in their production of Sean O'Casey's *The Plough and the Stars.* Paradoxically enough, the Irish gain this tranquil effect of wide spaces in the process of interpreting a series of high-strung scenes set not only in the streets and tenements of Dublin but in those streets and tenements as transformed into a shambles during the Easter Rebellion in 1916. This paradox resolves itself, however, the moment we stop to realize that in effectually reverting to the physical simplicity of the Elizabethans, these actors free themselves for the undisturbed pursuit of their true and natural task—acting.

In citing this paradox and its effect, I am not making excuses for a shabby, resourceless, and indigent scenic investiture for O'Casey's play. I realize full well that a masterly and prodigal regisseur could provide it with a nervous atmosphere of reality, drumming incessantly on all the senses. But I beg to doubt whether such an elaborate and provocative production could appeal so directly, so poignantly, to the emotions, especially if it sought to replace and conceal indifferent acting. I even suspect that superlative acting might be blurred and swamped by such a production. In other words, we have here an eloquent exhibit for the plaintiff in the immemorial case of the actor vs. stage settings.

In any event, the production of *The Plough and the Stars* by Arthur Sinclair and his associates is quite in keeping with the best traditions of Dublin's Abbey Theatre, from which they emerged to independent life some years ago. This group, fully entitled to the term, "Irish Players," since six of the leading members of the present company came to us direct from the Abbey on one or two previous visits, and two of them on both occasions, clings to both of the major tenets of the parent stage: the production of plays of sound literary merit dealing with Irish life and character, and their interpretation by means of naively simple, earnest, sincere acting. The Abbey never rocked the boat of its budget for the sake of stage settings.

In reading *The Plough and the Stars,* it is evident that O'Casey, too, honors these traditions. In this wise, dauntless, and human play that is both

Nor is the author pleading here for the rights of the subject peoples. He readily concedes that left to themselves they will make a mess of things. The comedy and tragedy, sometimes alternately, sometimes simultaneously, he has written, not for stage directors, scenic designers, electricians, or property men, but for actors. Beginning with that casual but ominous scene in the Clitheroes's parlor, on through the eccentric but increasingly intense dissensions in the public house adjoining the rostrum on the eve of revolution, through the snatches of fear, despair, and elation over plunder from stove-in shop windows after the storm breaks, to the bitter and tragic ironies of rebellion's ebb-tide, he has written winged words that live trebly when spoken, words that sublimate the mood of turmoil without the need of its physical counterpart. If it were not a matter of record that younger novices created these rôles at the première in Dublin, one might almost feel that, as Chekov did in Moscow, he had written for these particular players: for the comic genius of Arthur Sinclair, who knows as well as any man living how to bring a thought to birth on his face; for the volatile passions of Maire O'Neill; for the legendary dignity of Sara Allgood; for the suspicious irascibility of J. A. O'Rourke; and for the blunt geniality of Sydney Morgan—to name only those most familiar to us.

For those who would amplify a visit to the Irish Players by more than a reading of *The Plough and the Stars,* recent books contain no more illuminating glimpses of Dublin's Abbey and her dramatists than Padraic Colum's *The Road Round Ireland.* All that Colum says about O'Casey as author of **Juno and the Paycock** applies with even greater point and force to him as author of *The Plough and the Stars.* This episodic but cumulatively powerful drama of the metropolis does for the city worker and his tenements what Synge did for the peasant, his fields, his glens, and his roadsides. Both Synge and O'Casey have an instinctive ear for transcribing and crystallizing human speech, though the imagery of O'Casey's proletarians is necessarily cruder and less poetic than that of Synge's farmers and beggars. At one point, however, O'Casey all but merges with his great progenitor, for the reverberating periods of his drunken, voluble, but whole-souled fruit-vendor, Bessie Burgess, might have been written by Synge himself—a fact which is not so strange when we pause to realize that the fountain source of her speech is the same as that of the denizes of Synge's thatched cottages, the ritual of the church.

CRITICAL COMMENTARY

W. A. Armstrong (essay date 1961)

SOURCE: "The Sources and Themes of *The Plough and the Stars,*" in *Modern Drama,* Vol. 4, No. 3, December, 1961, pp 234-42.

[*In the following essay, Armstrong identifies specific sources for the main themes of* The Plough and the Stars, *drawing upon O'Casey's prose works to illuminate their significance.*]

Though Sean O'Casey did not fight in the Easter Rising of 1916, he helped to organise the Irish Citizen Army and was a shrewd and passionate observer of life in Dublin before, during, and after the most fateful week in the history of his native city. His autobiographical record of this period, *Drums Under the Windows* (1945), and his *The Story of the Irish Citizen Army* (1919) are important historical documents. They are also of much literary inter-

est because they reveal some of the sources of his tragedy, *The Plough and the Stars,* and elucidate some of its main themes.

In *The Story of the Irish Citizen Army,* O'Casey describes the origins of the Citizen Army and the Irish Volunteers, the two patriotic organisations which combined and fought the forces of the Crown during the Easter Rising. In 1912, the political leaders of Ulster organised the army known as the Ulster Volunteers as part of their opposition to the Bill for the institution of an Irish Parliament sponsored by the Liberal Party under H. H. Asquith and supported by John Redmond, leader of the Irish members of the Westminster parliament. In October, 1913, the Irish Transport and General Workers' Union formed the Irish Citizen Army. Not long afterwards, O'Casey became secretary of the Council in charge of this army. In November, 1913, another army, the National Volunteers, was inaugurated at a meeting in Dublin attended by representatives of such patriotic organisations as Sinn Féin, the Gaelic League, the Irish Republican Brotherhood, the Irish National Foresters, and the Gaelic Atheletic Association. In 1914, John Redmond's political party was allowed to have twenty-five representatives on the committee in control of the National Volunteers, but when Redmond spoke in favour of Irish participation in the First World War, the leaders of Sinn Féin denounced him and formed an army of their own, the Irish Volunteers. The Irish Volunteers marched under the green, white, and orange flag of the Sinn Féin organisation. The flag of the Citizen Army, as described in *Drums Under the Windows* (pp. 270-71), had a blue base on which was represented the formalised shape of a golden-brown Plough and the constellation of Stars which bears the same name. It thus symbolised the reality and the ideals of labour. The play for which it provided a title also portrays a relationship between the ideal and the real, but it is a tragic relationship. O'Casey's treatment of the militant patriotism of the Easter Rising is critical and ironical.

The patriotic ideal represented in *The Plough and the Stars* is that of a sacred war of national liberation. It is expounded in Act II[1] by the anonymous orator whose silhouette is seen through the windows of a public-house. The four passages declaimed by this orator are adapted from speeches by Padraic H. Pearse, who was a leader of Sinn Féin and the commander of the Irish Volunteers in the Easter Rising. The nature of O'Casey's borrowings and omissions is worth examining in some detail. The first speech by O'Casey's orator runs as follows:

> It is a glorious thing to see arms in the hands of Irishmen. *We must accustom ourselves to the thought of arms, we must accustom ourselves to the use of arms. . . . Bloodshed is a cleansing and sanctifying thing, and the nation that regards it as the final horror has lost its manhood. . . . There are many things more horrible than bloodshed, and slavery is one of them!*

The italicised sentences in this passage are all borrowed from a speech on "The Coming Revolution" which Pearse delivered in 1914.[2] Pearse, however, prefaced his description of bloodshed as "a cleansing and sanctifying thing" with the confession, "We may make mistakes in the beginning and shoot the wrong people. . . ." By omitting this admission of the possibility of errors and unnecessary killings, O'Casey makes his orator even more dogmatic in tone and oracular in attitude than Pearse. In his next speech, O'Casey's orator draws a lesson for patriots from the bloodshed of the World War then raging:

> Comrade soldiers of the Irish Volunteers and of the Citizen Army, we rejoice in this terrible war. *The old heart of the earth needed to be warmed with the red wine of the battlefield. . . . Such august homage was never offered to God as this: the homage of millions of lives given gladly for love of country.* And we must be ready to pour out the same red wine in the same glorious sacrifice, for without shedding of blood there is no redemption!

The italicised part of this passage is taken from a speech on "Peace and the Gael" delivered by Pearse in 1915.[3] In the sentence appended to his borrowing, O'Casey's orator far exceeds the fervours of Pearse when he introduces the idea that the blood given by patriots is comparable to the blood of Christ the Redeemer. In "Peace and the Gael," Pearse justified war in the following terms:

> *The last sixteen months have been the most glorious in the history of Europe. Heroism has come back to the earth.* On whichever side the men who rule the peoples have marshalled them, whether with England to uphold her tyranny of the seas, or with Germany to break that tyranny, the peoples themselves have gone into battle because to each the old voice that speaks out of the soil of a nation has spoken anew. . . . Belgium defending her soil is heroic, and so is Turkey with her back to Constantinople. . . . *War is a terrible thing, but war is not an evil thing.* It is the things that make war necessary that are evil. The tyrannies that wars break, the lying formulae that wars overthrow, the hypocrisies that wars strip naked, are evil. Many *people in Ireland dread war because they do not know it. Ireland has not known the exhilaration of war for over a hundred years. Yet who will say that she has known the blessings of peace? When war comes to Ireland, she must welcome it as she would welcome the Angel of God.*[4]

The italicised passages constitute the whole of the third speech of O'Casey's orator. By excluding Pearse's historical references, his explanatory remarks, and his rhetorical question, O'Casey again makes his speaker more dogmatic, aphoristic, and oracular. Similar conclusions can be drawn from O'Casey's adaptation of the following speech which Pearse delivered by the grave of the Irish patriot, J. O'Donovan Rossa, in July, 1915.

> *Our foes are strong* and wise and wary; *but, strong and* wise and wary *as they are, they cannot undo the miracles of God who ripens in the hearts of young men the seeds sown by the young men of a former generation.* . . . Rulers and Defenders of Realms had need to be wary if they would guard against such processes. . . . The Defenders of this Realm have worked well in secret and in the open. *They think that they have pacified Ireland.* They think that they have purchased half of us and intimidated the other half. *They think that they have foreseen everything, think that they have provided against everything; but the fools, the fools,*

the fools!—they have left us our Fenian dead, and while Ireland holds these graves, Ireland unfree shall never be at peace.[5]

The italicised passages constitute the whole of the final speech of O'Casey's orator. By omitting the references to the wariness of the rulers of Ireland and to the purchase of "half of us," O'Casey makes his orator so much the more confident about the outcome of the insurrection that he is advocating.

2

The religion of patriotism and the holiness of its wars expounded by O'Casey's orator have an intoxicating effect upon the four representatives of national organisations who appear in the second act of ***The Plough and the Stars***: Peter Flynn, an Irish National Forester, Langon, a lieutenant in the Irish Volunteers, and Clitheroe and Brennan, who are officers in the Citizen Army. In the words of the stage direction, Clitheroe, Brennan, and Langon enter *in a state of emotional excitement. Their faces are flushed and their eyes sparkle. . . . They have been mesmerised by the fervency of the speeches.* Flynn, too, is deeply stirred by the orator, burning "to dhraw me sword, an' wave an' wave it over me—." But the patriotism of these characters is not the pure and selfless emotion so glowingly praised by the orator; their love for their native land is adulterated by vanity and fear. These flaws in O'Casey's patriots were the cause of the riot which marred the fourth performance of the play at the Abbey Theatre on February 11, 1926.

The vanity of the patriots is especially apparent in their excessive love of picturesque regalia and military rank. In the first act, Flynn, an old labourer, is busy dressing himself to take part in a torchlight procession around places with patriotic associations, and the strenuous process of donning the accoutrements of an Irish National Forester is subjected to mock-heroic treatment. The ceremonial garb of a Forester consists of a frilled shirt, white breeches, top boots, a green coat with gold braid, a slouch hat with an ostrich plume, and a sword. These items of attire are exquisitely ridiculed by Fluther, Covey, and Mrs. Gogan. Flynn's frilled shirt is compared first to a woman's petticoat, then to a "Lord Mayor's nightdress"; his sword is "twiced too big for him"; and when he is fully dressed he is compared to "th' illegitimate son of an illegitimate child of a corporal in th' Mexican army." Nora Clitheroe makes his vanity seem like that of a small boy when she buckles his sword for him, puts his hat on his head, and hurries him out of the house.

Clitheroe, a bricklayer, and Brennan, a chicken butcher, are just as proud of their regalia as Flynn is of his. In his *The Story of the Irish Citizen Army*, O'Casey records how some of its members were equipped with "dark green uniforms and broad slouched hats of the same hue, most of which were jauntily turned up at one side, the leaf being fastened to the side with the ever-popular badge of the Red Hand."[6] Describing Clitheroe in the first act of the play, Fluther recalls how "you'd hardly ever see him without his gun, an' the Red Hand o' Liberty Hall in his hat," and how he was so cocksure of being made a captain that "he bought a Sam Browne belt, an' was always puttin' it on an' standin' at th' door showing it off, till th' man came an' put out th' street lamps on him." Clitheroe is jealous of Brennan's rank and uniform. In the same act, he sourly remarks that "tonight is the first chance that Brennan has got of showing himself off since they made a Captain of him—why, God only knows. It'll be a treat to see him swankin' it at th' head of the Citizen Army carryin' th' flag of the Plough and the Stars." In *The Story of the Irish Citizen Army*, O'Casey mentions that "the tallest man in the army was selected as banner bearer, and was always proud of his work,"[7] a remark which provides a commentary on Brennan's stature as well as his vanity.

As secretary of the Council of the Irish Citizen Army, O'Casey argued in vain against the use of uniforms. His colleagues, he remarks in *Drums Under the Windows*, "were immersed in the sweet illusion of fluttering banners, of natty uniforms, bugle-blow marches, with row on row of dead and dying foemen strewn over the Macgillicuddy's Reeks."[8] Favouring guerilla warfare, he poured scorn on the idea that if the citizen fighters wore uniforms they would be accorded the protection of International Law. "If we flaunt signs about of what we are, and what we do, we'll get it on the head and round the neck," he argued: "As for a uniform—that would be worst of all. We couldn't hope to hide ourselves anywhere clad in green and gold. Caught in a dangerous corner there would be a chance in your workaday clothes. You could slip among the throng, carelessly, with few the wiser."[9] The last act of the play illustrates the wisdom of this argument when Brennan is able to take refuge in the tenement after he has changed his uniform for civvies. "I'd never have got here," he admits, "only I managed to change me uniform for what I'm wearin'." He has also abandoned the flag that he once bore so proudly: "I seen the Plough and the Stars fallin' like a shot as th' roof crashed in."

In 1914, O'Casey withdrew from the Citizen Army and its Council. He was critical of the increasing collaboration between the Citizen Army and the Irish Volunteers, whose nationalistic principles were contrary, in some respects, to the Socialism in which he believed. At this time, O'Casey was an eager student of Darwin, Shaw, Marx, and Engels. In *Drums Under the Windows* he has described how he abandoned belief in the divine authorship of the Bible, the Garden of Eden, and Adam and Eve after reading Darwin's *Descent of Man*[10] and how he turned to "the new catechism of the *Communist Manifesto* with its great commandment of Workers of all lands, unite!"[11] Some of this reading went to the making of Covey, the Communist fitter in *The Plough and the Stars,* whose comments at times provide a Shavian counterpoint to the religious superstitions and nationalistic shibboleths of other characters in the play. In the first act, when Fluther suggests that Adam and Eve were the progenitors of mankind, Covey confronts him with "th' skeleton of th' man o' Java." In the following act, when the orator sets other characters talking about

freedom, Covey caustically rejoins, "Freedom! What's th' use o' freedom, if it's not economic freedom?" When the orator glorifies patriotic wars, he retorts, "There's only one war worth havin': th' war for th' economic emancipation of th' proletariat." For all the pointedness of some of his remarks, however, Covey is not designed as an embodiment of O'Casey's own ideals. He is as proud of his "big brain" as the patriots are of their uniforms, and Jenersky's *Thesis on the Origin, Development, and Consolidation of the Evolutionary Idea of the Proletariat* is as much a shibboleth with him as Holy Writ is with the religious or the speeches of Pearse with the nationalistic characters.

3

The positive values in **The Plough and the Stars** spring from human instincts and simple Christianity, not from patriotic or communistic doctrines. O'Casey began to apprehend these values when he was still a member of the Citizen Army. In *The Story of the Irish Citizen Army,* he reveals that even when he was being trained as a soldier at a camp set up in Croydon Park by the Citizen Army, there were times when the peace and harmony of the natural surroundings awoke within him feelings quite contrary to the military and patriotic ideals which he was voluntarily serving:

> The surrounding trees were swaying clumps of melody which sprang from the swelling throats of numerous finches and linnets, and, sometimes, one was forced to ask the question, was all the strife with which man's life was coloured a shining light or a gloomy shade?
>
> At times the stillness would be so strange that one would wonder if it were not death to again [*sic*] associate with man's noisy, selfish effort to explain and manifest human existence.
>
> Ah, this book of Nature is the best Bible from which to learn Charity towards all men and love towards all things. . . .
>
> Here, with one's head in the bosom of Nature, to what a small compass shrinks even the Constitution of the Irish Citizen Army. How horrible is a glistening, oily rifle to one of the tiny daisies, that cowers in a rosy sleep at my very feet, happy in itself, and giving to the world to which it has been born the fullest beauty and fragrance that its simple nature has to give.[12]

The ideal of outflowing "charity towards all men" finds expression in the play; so, too, does the feeling that militarism is at odds with the workings of nature. In the play, as in this autobiographical passage, trees, birds, and flowers are set in contrast to the callousness of the soldier's life, particularly in the episode in which Clitheroe sings his honeymoon song once again—

> Th' chestnut blooms gleam'd through th' glade, Nora,
>   A robin sang loud from a tree,
> When I first said I lov'd only you, Nora,
>   An' you said you lov'd only me!

—and immediately afterwards abandons his wife when he hears that he has been made a Commandant and is wanted for manoeuvres.

This episode also illustrates a basic and recurrent theme in the play: the way in which the vanity and excitements created by patriotism and war disrupt and destroy fundamental human relationships, particularly those between husband and wife, and those between mother and child. Just after Clitheroe leaves Nora, Mrs. Gogan goes out to enjoy the political meeting, leaving her consumptive daughter Mollser to her loneliness. In the second act, the excitements evoked by the meeting produce the episode in which Mrs. Gogan's baby is abandoned for a time on the floor of the public-house. In the following act, Mrs. Gogan deserts her baby and the enfeebled Mollser to loot shops, and Clitheroe ends his last meeting with his wife by thrusting her to the ground and departing with Brennan and Langon. These acts of desertion make manifest the moral inadequacy of the intoxicated patriotism which makes Clitheroe, Brennan, and Langon renounce filial and marital bonds so grandiloquently:

> CLITHEROE: You have a mother, Langon.
>
> LIEUT. LANGON: Ireland is greater than a mother.
>
> CAPT. BRENNAN: You have a wife, Clitheroe.
>
> CLITHEROE: Ireland is greater than a wife.

O'Casey questions the courage as well as the ethical principles of the patriots. When Nora risks her life to search for her husband during the insurrection, she discovers that it is fear, not bravery, that makes them fight: "I tell you they're afraid to say they're afraid!" Nora, Fluther, and Bessie Burgess exhibit a courage and charity which make them morally superior to any of the patriots in the play. Modelled on an unknown Dubliner whose chief characteristics were a fondness for drink and children,[13] Fluther is *l'homme moyen sensuel* of the play; he has no head for ideas and succumbs all too easily to the pleasures of liquor, boasting, whoring, and looting. But his instincts have not been perverted by doctrines; he defends the prostitute against Covey's puritanical insults, laughs at Flynn's regalia, rescues Nora from the barricades, and risks death again to make arrangements for the decent burial of Mollser and Nora's stillborn child.

One of the most remarkable passages in *The Story of the Irish Citizen Army* is highly relevant to the portrayal of Bessie Burgess in *The Plough and the Stars.* The finest person to die in the Rising, according to O'Casey, was Francis Sheehy-Skeffington. (Sheehy-Skeffington was a pacifist who had tried to dissuade the leaders of Sinn Féin from the use of force. During the Rising, he tried to organise his fellow-citizens to prevent the wanton looting of houses and shops. He was wrongfully arrested and was shot at Portobello Barracks.[14]) O'Casey describes him as a man "untarnished by worldly ambition," who was both "the living antithesis of the Easter Insurrection" and "the soul of revolt against man's inhumanity to man," thus linking Ireland with "the world's Humanity struggling for a higher life" and exemplifying "the perfect love that casteth out fear."[15] Correspondingly, in the world of the play the most heroic character is likewise an obscure non-

combatant, Bessie Burgess, who dies in the service of others, and, like Sheehy-Skeffington, has a charity which casts out fear. With her sharp temper and her face *hardened by toil, and a little coarsened by drink,* Bessie is no more idealised than Fluther, but the stress of events reveals the altruism and maternal strength of her nature. The first revelations of these characteristics occur in Act III and are the more impressive because they are silent and because they show her remedying some of those significant acts of desertion already described; she hands a mug of milk to Mollser and later comes down from the topmost tenement to carry Nora into the house after Clitheroe has abandoned her for the last time. Soon afterwards she braves the dangers of the battle in the streets to find a doctor for Nora, and watches over her for three nights after the birth of her child is followed by a condition close to madness. Bessie is mortally wounded by British bullets when she saves Nora's life by pushing her away from the window. The latter episode may derive from the occasion on which O'Casey's mother narrowly escaped death by a bullet when she stood near a window during the street fighting of Easter week.[16]

During the Easter Rising, O'Casey was imprisoned for a time in a granary. The molten glow of burning buildings shone through the shutters, but a group of his fellow-prisoners sat playing cards.[17] This experience helped to create a tragic image of the gamble of war and its waste of human potentialities in the last act of *The Plough and the Stars,* where Flynn, Covey, Fluther, and Brennan play cards beside the coffin which contains the bodies of Mollser and Nora's child. It is part of the dialectics of tragedy to show how the destruction of one set of human potentialities stimulates the development of another set. In *The Plough and the Stars* this development occurs when the bickerings between Nora, Mrs. Gogan, and Bessie Burgess give way to the reconciliation of these three characters in the last act, and when the intolerant Protestantism of some of Bessie's early diatribes gives way to her dying hymn of redemption:

> I do believe, I will believe
> That Jesus died for me
> That on th' cross He shed His blood
> From sin to set me free. . . .

This simple credo and the circumstances of Bessie Burgess's death expose the pretentiousness of the patriotic orator's declaration that "without shedding of blood there is no redemption." They also make us aware that she symbolises "the world's Humanity, struggling for a higher life" and is the agent of a greater redemption than the national liberation exalted by the orator.

Notes

1. Act II of *The Plough and the Stars* was probably drafted before any other part of the play. In *Inishfallen, Fare Thee Well* (London, 1949), O'Casey mentions (p. 128) that after *The Shadow of a Gunman* was produced at the Abbey Theatre, he submitted to its management "two one-act plays,

Cathleen Listens In and *The Cooing of Doves.*" The latter was "full of wild discussions and rows in a public-house." It was rejected "and later was used to form the second act of a later play." I infer that this "later play" was *The Plough and the Stars.*

2. *Collected Works of Padraic H. Pearse: Political Writings and Speeches* (Dublin, 1922), pp. 98-99.

3. *Ibid.,* p. 216.

4. *Ibid.,* pp. 216-17.

5. *Ibid.,* pp. 136-37.

6. *The Story of the Irish Citizen Army* (Dublin and London, 1919), p. 18.

7. *Ibid.,* p. 42.

8. *Drums Under the Windows* (London, 1945), p. 190.

9. *Ibid.,* p. 268.

10. *Ibid.,* pp. 94-95.

11. *Ibid.,* p. 289.

12. *The Story of the Irish Citizen Army,* p. 39.

13. *Inishfallen, Fare Thee Well,* p. 291.

14. See Dorothy Macardle, *The Irish Republic* (London, 1937), p. 189.

15. *The Story of the Irish Citizen Army,* p. 64.

16. *Drums Under the Windows,* p. 328.

17. *Ibid.,* p. 332.

Bernice Schrank (essay date 1985)

SOURCE: "'There's Nothin' Derogatory in th' Use o' th' Word': A Study in the Use of Language in *The Plough and the Stars,*" in *Irish University Review,* Vol. 15, No. 2, Autumn, 1985, pp. 169-88.

[In the following essay, Schrank analyzes the dramatic functions of language in The Plough and the Stars, *describing the effects of a developing political consciousness on the characters' discourse.]*

O'Casey's dramatic language is at once one of the most impressive aspects of his stagecraft and one of the least analysed. Impressionistic responses to O'Casey's language tend to alternate between nebulous enthusiasm for its Elizabethan lushness[1] and vague assertions about its 'ideological bloat and embarrassing bombast.'[2] Attempting a more precise description, David Krause emphasises the comic elements of dialogue[3] while Robert Hogan looks at such rhetorical devices as 'the personified adjective' and 'the derogatory epithet'.[4] Other critics focus on its dynamic qualities. For Raymond Williams, O'Casey's verbal flamboyance is 'the sound, really, of a long confusion and disintegration'.[5] For Ronald Ayling (using words borrowed from Williams), O'Casey's language is a "movement from dialogue to ritual incantation".[6] In a manner consistent with William's and Ayling's approach, I have previously examined the dramatic functions of language in *The Shadow of a Gunman*[7] and *Juno and the Paycock.*[8] In

this paper, I analyse the role of language in *The Plough and the Stars.*[9]

I argue that in this play circumstances press and shape the language the tenement dwellers use. While the lush verbal excesses of the characters in the first half of *The Plough* may be understood as partial compensation for the multiple impoverishments of the slum, their truncated language in the second half is a direct response to the accelerating political collapse. As the failure of the Rising impinges on the characters, Bessie cries after the retreating rebels, 'choke the chicken', Fluther drunkenly rages at an intimidating but invisible and unassailable enemy, and Nora, at the border of sanity, recalls happier times in wayward words. Anguished cries that provide a human accompaniment for the mechanical noise of guns and sirens, these speeches are startlingly surrealistic, effectively communicating to the audience the profound impact on the individual psyche of social disorder. But they also painfully record the deterioration of slum dwellers' usual methods of discourse.

For all that, the language of the slum dweller is protean, containing the possibilities for positive as well as negative development, dissolving and reforming in light of the unfolding events. As chaos overtakes these characters and their speeches shorten, some of their remarks assume a relevance, a concern for others and a dignity that was previously absent. This new wrinkle in their usage suggests that, having been shunted to the periphery of history before and during the Rising, they are beginning to fashion out of their recent experience and their verbal eccentricities a language of resistance to foreign occupation. Moderating the impression of total defeat with which the play ends, this new approach to language indicates that the slum dwellers may be starting to come of political age.

I

While critics commenting on O'Casey's manipulation of language in *The Plough* call attention to the verbal aggression of the Speaker, they usually emphasise the positive aspects of the other characters's speech. For instance, in his recent book *Sean O'Casey,* James Scrimgeour summarises this critical line by identifying the pronouncements of the Speaker as 'propaganda' and 'pseudo-poetry', and the speeches of many of the characters as 'authentic proletarian poetry'.[10] Although there is much to admire in the language of the slum dwellers, such a tidy dichotomy ignores how hostile the remarks of the characters are and how critical they are of each other's words. It disregards the fact that many of the rhetorical strategies of the Speaker, his use of repetition, alliteration, emotive words and phrases, and the imagery of blood sacrifice, do not distinguish him from the other characters, many of whom exploit the same devices in their speech. The dichotomy also fails to recognise that the contrast between the Speaker's rhetoric and that of the other characters is not always to the advantage of those characters. Whereas his speech demonstrates the discipline of purpose, theirs is often lazy and show-offy. Some of their funniest and fanci-est verbal creations—'upperosity', 'conspishous', 'mollycewels', 'dodgeries', 'compromization', 'malignified'—are used for display rather than for any precise meaning. Where the Speaker successfully recruits others to his point of view, the Covey, whose superficial socialism provides some insight into the deepest troubles of the slum, remains an isolated, inconsequential figure. As the only other ideologue in the play, he has the potential for offering a systematic critique of the Speaker's frenzied nationalism. Yet his attempts at argumentation always fail, his verbal repertoire is quickly exhausted and he retreats hastily from the give-and-take of the spoken word to the conversation-stopping references to the Jenersky text. While the Speaker illustrates the power of language in aid of what O'Casey presents as a destructive political cause, the Covey demonstrates the impotence of a positive social vision allied to a flawed and flabby rhetoric.

Examining various stylistic devices—exaggeration, al-literation, repetition, allusion—clarifies the strengths of the Speaker's rhetoric and the weaknesses of the other characters' speech. For example, the Speaker in the second act and the slum dwellers through most of the play exag-gerate. But whereas the politically motivated Speaker purposefully tries to make war attractive by asserting, among other things, that the 'last sixteen months have been the most glorious in the history of Europe' and that the fighting in Europe has brought heroism 'back to the earth',[11] the other characters use exaggeration to undermine each other and to gratify their own egos. Some of the most memorable lines in the first three acts exploit an insulting and dismissive sarcasm that depends on exaggeration for its humour and bite. The Covey for instance cuts Fluther down to size with a lengthy verbal sneer: 'When I hear some men talkin' I'm inclined to disbelieve that th' world's eight hundhred million years old, for its not long since th' fathers o' some o' them crawled out o' th' shel-therin' slime o' th' sea' (171). Later, Fluther denounces Peter for 'thryin' to out do th' haloes o' th' saints be lookin' as if he was wearin' around his head a flitherin' aroree boree allis' (200). Exaggeration for the purposes of deflating others is one of the tenement dwellers' favourite forms of verbal flamboyance. However, since these com-ments find fault without calling for any corrective action, they are esentially throwaway lines. To further the cause of rebellion, the Speaker's exaggeration excites admiration for and encourages emulation of war.

In addition, the characters favour alliteration and repeti-tion. Because these devices, like exaggeration, are elastic, allowing for seemingly infinite expansion, and because they frequently turn in on themselves, revealing less about the external world or personal experience than about their own possible permutations, these devices make it easy for characters like Peter and Mrs Gogan to abandon the demands of sense to the needs of rhythm and sound. While characters like Fluther and the Covey alliterate spectacu-larly, they do so only occasionally. Invariably, their al-literation marks a surrender to emotional frenzy in the

form of verbal excess. In Act I, after a vitriolic exchange, Peter lunges at the Covey with his sword and the Covey, approaching hysteria, explodes into denunciatory alliter-tion: 'It's a nice thing to have a lunatic like this lashin' around with a lethal weapon' (174). In Act II, although Fluther assures the other patrons of the pub that 'a thing like' the Covey cannot 'flutter a feather of Fluther', (209) his alliterative rage undercuts his ostensible indifference. Unlike Fluther and the Covey, Peter is a habitual alliter-ator. When he is angry, a state that he is often in, he bursts into an alliterative torrent that flows on until he is distracted or interrupted. He threatens the Covey with vi-sions of God 'rievin' an' roastin' [him], tearin' an' tor-mentin' [him], burnin' an' blastin'' him (174); he attacks the Covey for making him say 'things that sicken his soul with sin' (182); and he lambasts both the Covey and Fluther for being 'a pair o' picaroons, whisperin', concur-rin', concoctin' and conspirin' together to rendher' him 'unconscious' of life (253). Peter's manic language exploits alliterative rhyme without the influence of reason.

The only voice in the play to use alliteration consistently for calculated effect is the Speaker's. In his penultimate speech, for example, he comments that '[w]hen war comes to Ireland she must welcome it as she would welcome the Angel of God' (203). The Speaker's manipulation of the 'w' sound reinforces the link between 'war' and the repeated 'welcome', demonstrating that careful alliteration is a useful aid in the art of emotional persuasion. While the other characters fling their alliterating words around, the speaker produces his inflammatory impact by exercis-ing strict rhetorical control.

Along with alliteration, characters like Mrs Gogan and Fluther sprinkle their conversation with favoured words and phrases. While Mrs Gogan's variations on 'it is and it isn't' cluster at the beginning and Fluther's reliance on 'derogatory' and 'vice versa' are scattered through the play, both sorts of repetition excite laughter without conveying precise information. Their repetitions, in fact, imply an unwillingness to make distinctions, they indicate a mental fatigue and they create a semantic mush. They are amusing because they are imprecise yet familiar. However, the cumulative effect of these repetitions is not funny. O'Casey sugests that their language, having lost some of its creative unpredictability, may be in danger of surrendering to pure sound.

Five times in her exchange with Fluther at the start of the play, Mrs Gogan asserts and contradicts in the same breath and with the same rhetorical construction. When she describes Nora's looks to Fluther by saying 'there's pretti-ness an' prettiness in it' and when she comments on No-ra's greetings by noting 'there's politeness an' politeness in it' (164), Mrs Gogan uses a syntax of amorphous sug-gestion to express a wishy-washy censoriousness. When Fluther expresses concern about his state of health, Mrs Gogan hedges provocatively. All she is willing to venture is that thinking about death 'is, an' . . . isn't', in Fluther's word, 'creepy' (168).

Without further clarification, she goes on to generate even more anxiety by remarking obscurely, 'it's both bad an' good' (168). This cryptic yea- and nay-saying captures rhetorically Mrs Gogans unwillingness to morally and intellectually commit herself.

Like Mrs Gogan, Fluther depends on repetition to skirt intellectual or moral difficulties. When he tells Mrs Gogan that, although Peter appears 'dumb', 'when you get his goat, or he has a few jars up, he's vice versa' (167), or when he asserts that 'if we were without a tither o' courage for centuries, we're vice versa now' (195), Fluther sums up in 'vice versa' (and thus oversimplifies) all the complexities and contradictions of human nature. But when he assures Nora that no harm will come to Jack because 'in th' finish up it'll be vice versa', (221) he knowingly denies an unpalatable reality.

Fluther uses 'derogatory' for similar evasions. Thus Fluther details the discussion with the Covey about evolution and socialism in Act I by dismissing the speaker rather than addressing the ideas. 'It'd be a nice derogatory thing on me conscience, an' me dyin', to look back in rememberin' shame of talkin' to a word-weavin' . . . Socialist' (172). Like Mrs Gogan's 'it is an' it isn't', Fluther also uses 'derogatory' for the kind of assurances that reflect and create anxiety. Less overtly hostile than other contexts of this word, these usages are more insidiously debilitating. Choking with a cold in a slum environment congenial to tuberculosis, he insists that there is '[n]othing derogatory wrong with' him (168). 'Not wishin' to say anything derogatory' (164), he nevertheless informs Mrs Gogan that Jack has transferred his interest from his wife and home to the agitation in the streets outside. In spite of the danger inherent in Jack's participation in the Rising, Fluther offers Nora the same bland and false consolation using 'derogatory' ('nothin' derogatory'll happen to Mr. Clitheroe') (211) that he held out with 'vice versa'. As Peter and the Covey exchange murderous taunts and the Speaker incites the crowd to violence, Fluther comments with a smugness bordering on moral stupidity that '[t]here's nothin' derogatory in th' use o' th' word' (119). While Fluther repeatedly uses 'derogatory' to obscure problems, the circumstances of poverty and insurrection invariably suggest that these problems are real. Moreover, his reliance on 'derogatory' along with 'vice versa' to meet so many contingencies implies a sluggish habit of mind that prefers the superficial and the conventional to the analytic and the critical.

In contrast to Mrs Gogan's and Fluther's random repetitions, the Speaker repeats as he alliterates: to reinforce his ideas and to heighten their impact. While Mrs Gogan's and Fluther's repetitions are arbitrarily distributed throughout their speech, the Speaker's repetitions are part of a tight rhetorical structure that includes balanced phrasing arranged in order of increasing intensity. When the Speaker repeats 'accustom' and 'arms' in his first statement, '[w]e must accustom ourselves to the thought of arms, we must accustom ourselves to the sight of arms, we must accustom ourselves to the use of arms' (193), and when he repeats 'think' in his last, '[t]hey think they have pacified Ireland; think they have foreseen everything; think they have provided against everything' (213), his words have a momentum and a persuasive force that Mrs Gogan's and Fluther's lack. While Fluther does not convince either the audience or himself that Jack's participation in the Rising is of no consequence, the Speaker not only reinforces Clitheroe's, Langon's and Brennan's political commitment, he converts them to his rhetorical practices. Coming into the pub at the end of the second act, they alliterate and repeat in the same way as the Speaker does:

> *Lieut. Langon.* Th' time is rotten ripe for revolution.
>
> *Clitheroe.* Your have a mother, Langon.
>
> *Lieut. Langon.* Ireland is greater than a mother.
>
> *Capt. Brennan.* You have a wife, Clitheroe.
>
> *Clitheroe.* Ireland is greater than a wife.
>
> *Lieut. Langon.* The time for Ireland's battle is here.
>
> (213)

The resonating 'r' sound in Langon's first line echoes throughout the passage in 'mother', 'greater' and 'here', making his and Clitheroe's solemn incantation of 'Ireland' more emphatic. Langon, Brennan and Clitheroe not only accept the Sepaker's mesmerising nationalism, they incorporate into their speech his methods of structuring and articulating political views.

Besides exaggeration, alliteration and repetition, characters like Bessie and the Speaker cultivate a highly allusive style. From the first act to the third, Bessie enthusiastically appropriates the rhythms and language of the Old Testament to lend authority to her anger and her frustration. Taking Proverbs 19.29 as her text, she warns the retreating rebels that 'judgments are prepared for scorners an' sthripes for th' backs of fools' (220). Quoting Proverbs 7.11, she accuses Mrs Gogan of sexual licence, of being one 'whose feet abideth not in her own house' (202). Bessie's relatively long speech at the end of the first act is the best example of her oracular mode. Adapting biblical words, phrases and cadences ('arrow that flieth', 'sickness that wasteth'), Bessie denounces Nora for her superior airs. Bessie also denounces the Irish, 'th' lice' who are 'crawlin' about feedin' on th' fatness o' the land' (191), using the Great War as a cover for insurrectionary activities. She makes no distinction between Nora's social climbing, and Jack's and the others' paramilitary exercises, promising them all that 'they'll be scattered abroad, like th' dust in th' darkness' (191). Bessie takes malicious delight in the thesis that God is going to 'get them' because, instead of sacrificing their lives fighting for King and country in the European conflagration, they use polite verbal formulas (Nora) or plot rebellion (Jack).

Bessie's speech in Act I reworks Psalm 91.5-6. The Psalmist declares to the hearer that the believer 'shall not be afraid for the terror by night; nor the arrow that flieth by day'. Bessie not only reverses the timing of the arrow, which in her speech 'flieth be night', but the mood of the Psalm. Instead of comfort, Bessie's words are an undisguised threat. The Psalmist goes on to assure his listener that he or she has nothing to fear from 'the pestilence that walketh in darkness; nor the destruction that wasteth at noonday'. Bessie, in paraphrase, twists the Psalmist's meaning so that these words of support become promises of annihilation: 'But you'll not escape from . . . th' sickness that wasteth be day'. Bessie's perverse adaptation expresses an unfocused rage that can find no release save verbal aggression.

Whereas Bessie's words and phrases for the most part show the influence of the Old Testament, according to Vincent De Baun, the Speaker's linked references to 'red wine of the battlefields's, 'glorious sacrifice' 'shedding of blood' and 'redemption' (196), allude to 'the Catholic doctrines of Transubstantiation (changing of the wine in the Mass to the Blood of Christ); sacrifice (the essence of action in the Mass, as Christ's Body is offered to feed His people); and redemption through blood (the drama of the Crucifixion)'.[12] The Speaker, intent on persuasion, makes common cause with his audience, manipulating references to the dominant religion of Ireland to glorify and justify violence. Bessie uses biblical rhetoric to separate and elevate herself from her neighbours. Like Nora's affectation of a middle-class accent that Bessie bitterly resents, Bessie's own prophetic posturing is an equally futile attempt to establish superiority and distsance through language. Although Bessie and the Speaker both exploit religious allusions, their different intentions far more than their different religions determine their selection of material and their method of presentation.

Unlike the undisciplined effusions of the other characters, the rhetorical techniques the Speaker uses, whether he is exaggerating, repeating or alluding, are always subordinated to his political purposes. He is no more rational than the slum dwellers, but because his aims are clearly defined and his devices better controlled, he can recruit others to his point of view. Until late in the play, the language of the slum dwellers succeeds only in provocation and alienation.

II

The language of the slum dwellers, free of the confinements of exactitude, logic, social responsibility, and the Speaker's sense of political purpose, takes off in the directions of circumlocution, elaboration, digression, euphemism and free association. The politically motivated Speaker, however, heightens his persuasive power by relying on a verbal shorthand. Although these modes of discourse appear antithetical, they are in fact intimately related.

Mrs Gogan and Bessie Burgess best exemplify the tendency of the slum characters to use language surrealistically. Take, for example, the mad scene in Act III in which

Ginny and Bessie vie for possession of the pram. They exchange lush and lofty phrases to defend their own right to remove another neighbour's property. Neither will admit that she wants to loot and therefore needs a means of transporting stolen goods. Instead, Mrs Gogan sneeringly wonders how 'a lady-like singer o' hymns like [Bessie] would lower her thoughts from sky-thinkin' to sthretch out her arm in a sly-seekin' way to pinch anything dhriven asthray in th' confusion of th' battle' (228). Bessie assures Mrs Gogan 'that a passion for thievin' an' pinchin' would find her soul a foreign place to live in, an' that her present intention is quite th' lofty-hearted one of pickin' up anything shaken up an' scatthered about in th' loose confusion of a general plundher' (229). And with these elaborate verbal pirouettes, Mrs Gogan and Bessie Burgess take off with the pram to loot with the rest. Their words are clearly nothing more than a cover-up for what they think is a somewhat disreputable undertaking.

Mrs Gogan reserves her most bizarre elaborations for the subject of death. Her anxieties about her daughter Mollser's deteriorating health lead her not to any perception that social conditions ought to be changed so that tuberculosis might be eradicated from the slums, but to three long, convoluted, pointless and ghoulish digressions on the imagined deaths of Fluther and Nora. At first she worries excessively that Fluther might appear 'covered with bandages, splashed all over with th' red of his own blood' (216) so badly wounded that she would not have time to 'bring th' priest to hear th' last whisper of his final confession' (216). Next she claims to have envisioned Nora 'sthretched on her back in some hospital, moanin' with th' pain of a bullet in her vitals, an' nuns thryin' to get her to take a last look at th' crucifix' (217). Finally, she insists she has seen Fluther's corpse in a dream, his face so white it was 'gleamin' like a white wather-lily floatin' on th' top of a dark lake. Then a tiny whisper thrickled into me ear, sayin'' Isn't th' face very like the face o' Fluther?" (219). Thus, Mrs Gogan's verbal excesses dissipate potentially devastating social criticism in a stream of freely associated, obliquely relevant detail. By dwelling on the deaths of others, she tries to disguise her own deep fear of death. In refusing to acknowledge that deaths like Mollser's are preventable, she attenuates her social awareness. In using the verbal techniques of indirection and elaboration, she allows the conditions that cause Mollser's sickness and death to perpetuate themselves without adding the experience of her own suffering and loss to the verbal store of witness and opposition.

While the other characters are expansive in their use of language, the Speaker is terse and focussed. Using snippets from Padraic Pearse, his four oracular pronouncements in Act II are lean to the point of undernourishment. As William Amstrong demonstrates, O'Casey has edited and abbreviated Padraic Pearse's speeches to maximise their emotional effect.[13] The Speaker's persuasiveness rests in part on his hypnotic intensity and on his pruning away of irrelevancies.

But he is also able to maintain his narrow focus and dispense with intellectual difficulties because he tells his audience what they already know and say. The language of the Speaker and the language of the characters are more than interrelated by their exploitation of similar stylistic devices; they are interdependent. While the Speaker's overheated language in the second act stimulates the verbal barrage of the other characters in the pub, the intellectual and verbal preoccupations of slum dwellers render them susceptible to the Speaker's rhetorical manipulation. Fluther's image of th' speeches 'pattherin' on th' people's heads, like rain fallin' on th' corn' (195) accurately captures the reciprocity between uncritical audience and charismatic Speaker. In the immediate afterglow of the Speaker's words, Fluther, in his own inimitable style, is ready to do battle with Ireland's enemies past, present and future. When the Covey challenges Fluther's visceral nationalism, Fluther justifies himself not on the grounds of principle, but on the basis that what the Speaker says is consistent with what Fluther's mother preached. 'Fluther can remember th' time, an' him only a dawny chiselur, bein' taught at his mother's knee to be faithful to th' Shan Van Vok' (208). By trimming the diffuse and aggressive alliterations, exaggerations, repetitions and allusions preferred by many of the characters, and by bringing his rhetorical refinements to bear on matters over which a wide consensus exists, the Speaker is easily able to arouse his audience. The Speaker's verbal deftness is clearly menacing; the other characters' fatuous and funny discourse, because it encourages confusion, distorts reality, and leaves them vulnerable to the Speaker's appeal, is equally menacing.

III

Using the Covey's 'cuckoo' cry, O'Casey creates a verbal motif that overleaps the boundaries of realistic dramatic speech and speaks symbolically to the audience of the inherent madness in the verbal carry-on of both the slum dwellers and the Speaker. The Covey's use of 'cuckoo' in each of the first three acts is a particularly good example of the ways the slum dwellers exploit language and sound for emotive effect. In the second act, as the Covey exits from the pub he encounters Peter entering with Fluther and Mrs Gogan. From outside, the Covey thrusts a 'cuckoo-oo' at Peter, a word-noise that sends Peter into instantaneous and 'plaintive anger' (199). In an effort to calm Peter down, Fluther suggests that there is 'nothin' derogatory in th' use o' th' word "cuckoo"(199). But Peter argues correctly that it is 'not th' word; it's th' way he says it: he never says it straight out, but murmurs it with curious quiverin' ripples, like variations on a flute'(199). The audience already knows that Peter has accurately assessed the emotive, connotative and provocative force of words and even sounds, because they have already witnessed the Covey's manipulation of Peter's susceptibility to this particular word.

In the first act, as the verbal combat between the Covey and Peter degenerates into outright assault, the Covey dashes out of the room, *'slamming the door in the face of Peter'* (174), who stands outside battering it and denouncing the Covey. The Covey responds first with what Peter calls a 'divil-souled song o' provocation' (175), words that Peter rightly interprets as parodying his patriotic obsession. Next the Covey sends forth the highly inflammatory '[c]uckoo-oo' call (175), thereby undoing all of Peter's resolve to ignore his taunts. That an out-of-sight Covey, physically separated by a tangible barrier from Peter, can nevertheless make him frantic by a judicious selection of words and sounds dramatically illustrates the penetrating power of even apparently meaningless language. While the Covey's 'cuckoo-oo' in the first act anticipates the hostile encounter with Peter in the second, his repetition of this word in the third act allows for a retrospective reconsideration. When the Covey returns from a looting spree balancing a sack of flour and a ham on his head, Peter, seated outside the tenement, refuses to open the door for him. In a short while, someone else admits the Covey, and then, for the third time, the Covey, from behind a door, sends forth to Peter who is on the other side of the barrier, the taunting and irritating call, 'cuckoo-oo' (230). True to form, Peter rushes at the door, bellowing insults. The repetition of this basic situation reinforces Peter's point in the second act about the emotive power of words. It also demonstrates to the audience at a level beyond that of realistic speech how infantile this kind of verbal manipulation essentially is.

As a verbal motif the Covey's 'cuckoo' has further suggestive resonance. In Act II where the sophisticated rhetoric of the Speaker indicates a more dangerous talent for verbal manipulation, the emotive effect of the Speaker's words on the listeners is not far different from what the Covey more crudely accomplishes with Peter. Fluther and Peter rush in uncritically singing the praises of the Speaker. Although the Speaker engages their support while the Covey arouses Peter's opposition, the verbal efforts of both are pitched at the subliminal and irrational. Along with its first meaning of 'bird' and its second of a 'bird sound', 'cuckoo-oo' has a third, slang meaning of 'foolish' or 'crazy'. The word 'cuckoo-oo', used three times, the second time from the street outside the pub, breaching its walls and door as the Speaker's words do, provides its own telling commentary and judgement not only of Peter and the Covey, but of the verbal proceedings of all the tenement characters and of the Speaker. It emphasises the dangerous power and the incipient madness in the language used both within and without the pub, a language in both cases hostile to and destructive of reason.

IV

As the action in the second half of *The Plough* becomes more chaotic and threatening, the language of the slum dwellers reflects these changes. The enormity of events moderates the characters' normal verbal extravagance. Even when their more abbreviated later remarks resemble their earlier bombast, however, the Rising clarifies and emphasises the irresponsibility and insensitivity inherent in their previous utterance. The implications and permutations of Rosie's bawdy song that the aftermath of the Rising allows, show how changed conditions alter the verbal texture of the play. There is also an obvious relationship between the accelerating political collapse and the increasing coarseness of the characters' speech. The brutal reality of war transforms the superficially humorous verbal hostilities of the characters into the offensive crudities of the retreating rebels and the conquering British soldiers.

An examination of the resonances of Rosie's song illustrates how shifting circumstances expose unexpected nuances in seemingly straightforward statement. At the end of the second act, in a burst of playful anticipation, Rosie sings Fluther a lusty song of sexual gratification that comes as a welcome relief from the previous rounds of verbal jousting in the pub. Then, in a state of expectation and contentment, Rosie and Fluther experience the only affectionate moment in the entire act, going *out with their arms around each other'* (214). The patriotic remarks of Brennan, Langon and Clitheroe, moreover, spoken in a trance-like state immediately before Rosie's song, and the reductive language of Jack's military command that immediately follows Rosie's song, 'Dublin Battalion of the Irish Citizen Army, by th' right, quick march' (214), reinforce the positive aspect of Rosie's appeal. Rosie's recruitment of Fluther for a night of love seems, in this context, to be an attractive alternative to the Speaker's recruitment of Clitheroe, Brennan and Langon for military action.

But like so much else in *The Plough,* Rosie's song is not without ironic implication. The confirmation of its positive and procreative impulses is the arrival in the fourth line of 'a bright bouncing boy' (214). But such a blessing forces the hearer to consider that in a slum world in which milk for the dying Mollser is a luxury, a child 'bawlin' for butther an' bread' (214) would be a financial disaster for a streetwalker who cannot buy herself proper clothing, who has trouble attracting customers and who owes the Barman 'for three already' (207). Further, although bawdy and colloquial, Rosie's song nevertheless recalls an earlier, more conventional love song, Jack's sentimental serenade to Nora in Act I. Despite its promise of love, however, boredom has already begun to undermine the Clitheroe marriage and Jack leaps at the chance to renew his relationship with the Irish Citizen Army when Brennan arrives at the completion of the song. Far from an alternative to the political turmoil, Jack's relationship with Nora encourages him to seek his excitement in paramilitary exercises. Seen from the context of the Clitheroe marriage, Rosie and Fluther's departure to bed at the end of her song, for all its high spirits and harmony, is merely a temporary withdrawal from the political unrest, not an answer to it. Making love in *The Plough* is a compromised private option, not a realistic public policy. As Rosie and Fluther exit from the pub, they leave the Speaker, Brennan, Langon and Clitheroe in full possession of the stage of history.

In the aftermath of the Rising, the ironic reverberations of Rosie's song are even less happy. Rosie appears only in the second act; in the rest of the play, Nora, the only other sexually active female character, functions as Rosie's surrogate. Although Nora is less sexually assertive than Rosie, she conceives and eventually loses the child that Rosie celebrates in her song, she uses words, clothing and body language for sexual purposes, she advocates the virtues of personal satisfaction and she attempts to lock out politics. Yet the hope and fulfillment in Rosie's song take the form of Nora's obsessive egocentricity in Act III and her madness in Act IV. Before the Rising, Rosie can retreat from political involvement and appear sane. But after the Rising, Nora's refusal to acknowledge a radically altered reality is the first indication of her mental collapse. When Nora encounters Jack accompanied by Brennan and a wounded and dying Langon, she ignores Langon and insists that Jack abandon his comrades to remain with her. While a desperate Langon begs Brennan and Clitheroe to bring him 'some place where [his] wound'll be looked afther' (233), Nora intones, 'come up to our home, Jack, my sweetheart, my lover, my husband' (233). Reminiscent of her plea in Act I, 'Jack, please, Jack, don't go out tonight' (189), when she tried to dissuade Jack from joining Brennan for paramilitary practice, Nora again appeals to Jack in her and Rosie's language of private fulfillment. Counterpointed by Langon's cries of pain, Nora's second appeal to Jack has none of the force of her first and none of the charm of Rosie's song. Furthermore, as Nora recedes into madness, she sings snatches of Jack's courting song, the same song he sang to her in Act I. Inasmuch as these snatches are from a love song, they relate to Rosie's song in Act II and, from this retrospective vantage point, introduce the possibility of latent madness in Rosie's refusal (so similar to Nora's in everything but context) to take political reality into account.

In much the same way, O'Casey plays Rosie's song off against Fluther's drunken rendition of 'for he's a jolly good fellow' (237)[14]. While Fluther sings wildly, shouts that '[t]h' whole city can topple home to hell' (237), and bangs on the door, Nora's moans are heard from within. Disregarding the immediate reality of Nora's suffering and the larger social collapse, Fluther continues to sing. Because Rosie's song is sung before the Rising, it is possible to locate its affirmation of life in its obliviousness to politics. Coming in the midst of the Rising, Fluther's song of self-congratulation, like Nora's preoccupation with her personal life, is wilful, irresponsible and morally unacceptable. By repeating similar songs and comments in different situations, O'Casey creates a density of implication that echoes backwards and forwards through the play. Fluther's song may be a degenerate form of Rosie's, but Rosie's joyful outburst, in its exclusion of social concerns, has the potential to become Fluther's much less admirable variation of the tune.

While changing circumstances impose new meanings on words, the characters' usage become cruder as the effects of the Rising are felt in the slum. The terse, callous language of the British soldiers in their encounters with the slum dwellers in the final act dehumanises the conquered and debases the conquerers. Referring to the coffin containing Mollser and the dead Clitheroe baby, Corporal Stoddart wants to know if it contains 'the stiff' (248). Irritated by the Covey's comments on socialism, he orders him to 'cheese it, Paddy, cheese it' (250). And Sergeant Tinley, outraged that a sniper has killed a British soldier, *'vindictively'* orders the male occupants out into the street in words that effortlessly accommodate the killing of non-combatants: 'Aht into the streets with you, and if a snioper sends another of our men west, you gow with 'im' (255). Like Sergeant Tinley, some of the retreating rebels express hostility toward the civilian population. Thus, Captain Brennan *'savagely'* (231) questions Clitheroe: 'Why did you fire over their heads? Why didn't you fire to kill? (231). When Clitheroe tries to moderate Brennan's anger by pointing out that the looters are Irish men and women, Brennan again responds *'savagely'*: 'If these slum lice gather at our heels again, plug one o' them, or I'll soon shock them with a shot or two meself' (232). Brennan's remark is staggering even to Clitheroe, his comrade in arms. His use of the phrase 'slum lice' is, moreover, the most brutal variation in the play of this particular animal image. In Act I, Bessie talks in a general way of her neighbours as 'lice . . . crawlin' about feedin' on th' fatness o' the land' (191) but her point lacks specific applicability. In Act II, Rosie, humiliated because the Covey calls her 'a prostitute' (210), lashes out at him with the abusive, '[y]ou louse, you louse, you' (210). Rosie's use of the animal image has a context that makes her choice of words understandable. In both Bessie's and Rosie's cases, the use of the image is an end in itself. With Brennan, the depersonalisation of the looters is a preliminary to shooting them. Although warfare has blunted his sensibilities and his language, his naked utterance encourages further verbal and physical brutality.

V

Despite the progresive deterioration of the characters' usage, the end of the play marks a recovery. The Rising does not immediately liberate Ireland, but it liberates or at least redirects the verbal energy of the slum dwellers. Bessie's exit lines in Act III announce the change. Remembering the Psalmist's promise that God 'shall cover thee with his feathers, and under his wings shalt thou trust; his truth shall be thy shield and buckler', Bessie goes off into the fighting to find a doctor for the ailing Nora, *'tightening her shawl around her, as if it were a shield'* (238). As she exits, she prays, 'Oh, God, be Thou my help in time o' throuble. An' shelter me safely in th' shadow of thy wings'. Her restrained rhetoric here is in stark contrast to her ravings at the end of Act I, although the source is still Psalm 91. The allusive habit that previously enlivened her conversation with bloody images of destruction now provides her with the necessary courage to speak and thereby to act positively. Throughout the fourth act, although exhausted, Bessie looks after Nora, sings songs to her and quietens the noise of Fluther, Peter and the Covey. Even in the curses of her death agony, she retains a dignity and stature, purchased with blood, that her early verbosity lacked.

Bessie's transformation is typical of the verbal metamorphosis that most of the other surviving characters undergo. Quieter in the fourth than in any previous act, what they say has greater clarity and cogency than before. The presence of the English soldiers, moreover, allows them to direct their anger and their verbal cuts at a tangible external enemy. The indefinite Mrs Gogan discovers in the last act a more straight forward mode of conversing, thanking Bessie for her attentions to Mollser, arranging for Bessie's burial, and accepting the burden of caring for Nora without her usual circumlocutions:

> *Nora (whimperingly).* Take me away, take me away; don't leave me here to be lookin' an' lookin' at it!
>
> *Mrs Gogan (going over to Nora and putting her arm around her).* Come on with me, dear, an' you can doss in poor Mollser's bed, till we gather some neighbours to come an' give th' last friendly touches to Bessie in th' lonely layin' out of her.
>
> (260)

With the exception of 'poor', 'friendly' and 'lonely', every word in Mrs Gogan's speech is strictly functional. Part of Mrs Gogan's growing verbal strength depends on the contrast between her clear plans and Nora's incoherence. But an equally significant part of her strength depends on the contrast between her previous verbal embroidery and her present directness and simplicity.

In the fourth act, the Covey and Fluther also display unexpected verbal strength using verbal strategies that previously demonstrated their intellectual slackness. Anxious to distance himself from the other slum dwellers, the Covey refers to the Jenersky text in the first two acts as evidence of his superior intelligence. In each of these acts, he cites the author and full title, 'Jenersky's *Thesis on Th' Origin, Development, an' Consolidation of th' Evolutionary Idea of th' Proletariat'*. The foreign name of the author and the finesounding nouns of the title contribute to the Covey's pleasure of utterance. In the first act, he denounces Peter for reading bits of the book and "hee-hee'in'" (177). In the second act, frightened by Rosie's sexual advances, he offers to leave a copy of the *Thesis* for her at the pub (197). In the last act, the Covey for the third time cites Jenersky, but because the discussion is political, the effect is less ridiculous than before. When Corporal Stoddart questions him about Mollser's death, the Covey assures him that she died of consumption, not sniper fire. The Covey goes on to lucidly explain 'that more die o' consumption that are killed in th' wars', and that 'it's all because of th' system we're livin' undher' (249). Then Corporal Stoddart admits that he, like the Covey, is a 'Sowcialist' (249), but that he has to do his 'dooty'. The Covey responds with ironic point that the 'only dooty of a Socialist is th' emancipation of th' workers' a paraphrase of a comment he has less appropriately put to the apolitical Rosie in the pub. The Covey's clear exposition of the economic causes of Mollser's death is his most powerful statement in the play. When the Covey recommends Jenersky's *Thesis* to Corporal Stoddart, it has a relevance to the conversation and an authority that his previous two references have lacked. Although the Covey's last citation admits the humorous implications of his previous references to the *Thesis* and provokes laughter, the Covey has the better of the exchange with Corporal Stoddart whose impatient dismissal of the Covey reflects his own comprehensive shallowness.

Like the Covey, Fluther in the last act reshapes his delinquent words into more meaningful speech. He responds to the defeat of the rebellion with quiet courage, sheltering Brennan against the advice of the others without resorting to histrionics. He simply deals him into the card game and briefly directs his performance: 'Thry to keep your hands from shakin', man' (248). Although the men are rounded up and interned by the English soldiers, Corporal Stoddart and Sergeant Tinley are completely deceived by Fluther's charade and take Brennan for a card player rather than for a rebel on the run. Stoddart goes so far as to suggest that Fluther take 'the cawds' (254) to the church. Fluther responds with a characteristic turn of phrase: 'Ah, I don't think we'd be doin' anything derogatory be playin' cards in a Protestan' Church' (254). In the context of Fluther's successful deception, his use of 'derogatory' does not convey his usual lazy amiability. Rather, his usage is complex and ambiguous. To the English soldiers, it is further evidence authenticating that all the men are merely card players. But to the slum dwellers, it continues the passive resistance to foreign occupation begun when Fluther first dealt cards to Brennan. 'To play cards' in the final act means to deceive the English. To find nothing 'derogatory' in playing cards suggests that Fluther and the others will continue their game, a very different game from the one that the English soldiers think they are playing. Fluther's final use of 'derogatory' is thus more circumscribed, more complex and more political than his previous usage.

VI

The characters in **The Plough** have a pliant language, elastic enough to be moulded into rhetorical forms antagonistic to their social and personal needs and yet capable of being reshaped into a discourse expressive of their discontents. At first their use of language is so undisciplined that it contributes to the unfolding chaos. But as events overtake them, the characters quieten down and eventually gain a more suitable eloquence.

Having witnessed the painful process by which the worst excesses of the slum dwellers' speech—its insensitivity and its escapism—are eliminated, it is surely ironic for the audience to discover these weaknesses in the speech and song of the English soldiers. While the Irish tenement dwellers take the first halting steps towards opposing the English occupation, the English soldiers, through their appallingly sentimental concluding words and song, express the kind of disregard for reality that Fluther and the other slum dwellers have abandoned.

Notes

1. J. D. Trewin, 'O'Casey the Elizabethan', *New Theatre* (London), III (1946), pp. 2-3.

2. Robert Brustein, *The Theatre of Revolt* (Boston and Toronto: Little Brown, 1964), p. viii.

3. David Krause, *Sean O'Casey: The Man and His Work*. An Enlarged Edition (New York: Macmillan, 1975), pp. 225-54.

4. Robert Hogan, 'The Haunted Inkbottle: A Preliminary Study of Rhetorical Devices in the Late Plays of Seán O'Casey', *James Joyce Quarterly,* VIII (1970), pp. 83-4.

5. Raymond Williams, *Drama from Ibsen to Brecht* (New York: Oxford University Press, 1968), p. 151.

6. Ronald Ayling, 'Patterns of Language and Ritual in Sean O'Casey Plays' in A. Feder and B. Schrank (editors), *Literature and Folk Culture: Ireland and Newfoundland* (St. John's, Newfoundland: Memorial University of Newfoundland, 1977), p. 56.

7. Bernice Schrank, 'You needn't say no more': Language and the Problems of Communication in Seán O'Casey's *The Shadow of a Gunman', Irish University Review* VIII (1978), pp. 23-37.

8. Bernice Schrank, 'Dialectical Configurations in *Juno and the Paycock', Twentieth Century Literature* XXI (1975), pp. 438-456.

9. For a discussion of the imagery of *The Plough,* consult Bernice Schrank, 'Little Ignorant Yahoo': The Theme of Human Limitation in O'Casey's *The Plough and the Stars', Etudes Irlandaises* VI (*Nouvelle Serie*) (1981), pp. 37-40.

10. James R. Scrimgeour, *Sean O'Casey* (Boston: Twayne, 1978), p. 106.

11. Sean O'Casey, 'The Plough and the Stars', *Collected Plays* I (London: Macmillan, 1963), p. 202. Further references appear in the text.

12. Vincent De Baun, 'Sean O'Casey and the Road to Expressionism', *Modern Drama* IV (1961), p. 256.

13. William A. Armstrong, 'Sources and Themes in *The Plough and The Stars', Modern Drama* IV (1961), pp. 234-42.

14. O'Casey emphasises Fluther's drunken insensitivity by the pun on 'good'. Fluther's last name is 'Good'; in this sense he is literally 'a jolly good [Good] fellow'.

THE SILVER TASSIE

PRODUCTION REVIEWS

The Times (London) (review date 12 October 1929)

SOURCE: A review of *The Silver Tassie,* in *The Times* (London), October 12, 1929, p. 8.

[*In the following review of the world premiere of* The Silver Tassie, *the critic comments on the success of O'Casey's experimental dramatic practices.*]

Many years may pass before Mr. O'Casey's art [in *The Silver Tassie*] ceases to produce confusion in the mind of an audience accustomed by long theatrical usage to consistency of mood. Hitherto it has commonly been demanded of a play that it be tragic, or that it be comic, or, if by profession a tragi-comedy, that the contrasted elements should remain distinct, the one appearing as a "relief" to the other. This theory Mr. O'Casey has definitely abandoned, and has substituted for it another, still very unfamiliar in the theatre, though having its now recognized counterpart in the novels of Mr. Aldous Huxley. We are no longer invited to give attention to one aspect of life and to consider it dominant for the time being. The unity of the work of art is no longer to depend upon the consistency of its material. Instead, as if some diamond were being rolled over and tossed in air before our eyes, we are so to observe its facets of tragedy, comedy, and open farce that their flashing becomes at last one flash and perhaps, by imaginative and symbolic transition, one spiritual light. Unity is to spring from diversity. The elements of drama are to be compounded—not separated, not mixed.

Mr. O'Casey's experimental practice of this theory is of absorbing interest, and it is no less interesting because he has not perfected it. And of even greater value is his attempt to break free from the bonds of naturalism by the bold use of verse. Anyone in this hsitory of a footballer who was maimed in the War may break into verse at any moment. A group of soldiers, resting at night from their labours, fall into a rhythmical chanting which has no relation with the matter or manner of naturalistic speech. Another group joins them, and all, falling upon their knees, send up a bitter prayer to a gun raised against the skyline. Above them, like a figure of Death itself, crouches the solitary figure of a man, chanting—and Mr. Leonard Shepherd does it magnificently—a terrible parody of the Valley of Dry Bones. The whole scene is almost a masterpiece. Mr. Augustus John's setting is its background. Mr. Raymond Massey's direction of the stage—his assembling of the soldiers in closely packed groups and his disposition of them so that they have continuously the quality of great sculpture—marks him as a producer who is also a poet.

Mr. O'Casey's attempt to make his play take wings from naturalistic earth succeeds; we move in a new plane of imagination. Yet the scene is not a masterpiece. The elements are not truly compounded. There appear two farcical figures of a Staff Wallah and a Visitor whose coming shatters the illusion and momentarily reduces Mr. O'Casey's irony to the level of a mean, silly, and irrelevant sneer. And more important and more disastrous is the discovery, which we begin to make as the scene advances, that the greater part of its effect springs from the setting, the leaning crucifix, the shadowy gun, the grouping of men, and the rhythm of language—the rhythm of language, not the substance of it. Though the use of poetry has lifted the play from earth to dream, the poetry itself has not force enough to sustain so great a suspense. The scene is filled with a kind of wonder. It is, in the theatre, a new

wonder; it is exciting and, at intervals, moving; but little proceeds from it. Mr. O'Casey has not been able to give a full answer to his own challenge.

The other acts are more limited in their range. They are not, as the second act is, a brilliant failure that might have been the core of a masterpiece. But in them also Mr. O'Casey is working at his proper experiment, twirling his diamond, leaping suddenly from a music-hall turn at a telephone to a transcendental dialogue between a blind man and a cripple, giving to a dance at a football club an extraordinary tragic significance, matching a poem with a waltz, wringing a new intensity from a scene in a hospital ward which does not hesitate to continue the broad and delightful fooling of Mr. Barry Fitzgerald and Mr. Sidney Morgan. This method of compression does not and cannot yield the full, naturalistic portraits that arise from drama of a different kind. Miss Beatrix Lehmann plays with a fierce concentration admirably directed; Miss Una O'Connor gives life to a shrewd, hard sketch; Mr. Charles Laughton passes with remarkable skill from footballer to poet, becoming at last a pursuing conscience in a wheeled chair; and there is a beautifully controlled study by Mr. Ian Hunter. But the method and not the drawing of character is the central interest of this play. It is rash; it is extravagant; it fails sometimes with a great stumbling failure. But it is a method with a future.

The Illustrated London News (review date 19 October 1929)

SOURCE: A review of *The Silver Tassie*, in *The Illustrated London News*, October 19, 1929, p. 696.

[*In the following review of the London production of* The Silver Tassie, *the critic admires the "deeply felt and so remorselessly expressed" sentiments of the play.*]

The "Tassie" which furnished the title of Mr. Sean O'Casey's new play [*The Silver Tassie*] is a silver challenge cup which Harry Heegan, in the full flush of his youth and strength, wins for the third time for his football team in the first act, and which, robbed of the use of his limbs by the war and of his sweet-heart by the comrade who has saved his life, he smashes in a jealous fury at curtain-fall. Bitterness and defeat, indeed, are the emotions which the young Irish playwright depicts with such remarkable power and insight in the successor to *Juno and the Paycock*. The more the pity, then, that his depiction of these emotions should so often take the form of a rather flamboyant expressionism. The whole of the second act, for instance, is devoted to an interlude in which soldiers on fatigue duty, crouched round a fire, chant in unison curses on their officers and on their own exposure to mud, cold, and rain. And, though it may be granted that this interlude represents very vividly some of the occasional moods of some of the men, it is obviously satire and burlesque rather than drama. Moreover, it holds up the simple and affecting story of Harry Heegan's tragedy, which is played out first in a hospital ward, where his sweetheart refuses to visit him, and then at a dance given by the football team, where she meets the poor cripple in his invalid chair and rejects him for his strong and healthy rival. The poignancy of both the humour and the pathos of the last two acts of *The Silver Tassie* is indeed very searching, and fully justifies Mr. O'Casey in calling his play a "tragi-comedy." Nothing quite so deeply felt and so remorselessly expressed has been seen on our stage for many a long day; and it is only fair to say that Mr. Charles Laughton, the actor who takes the part of Heegan, shares in the triumph of the author.

Charles Morgan (review date 3 November 1929)

SOURCE: "As London Sees O'Casey," in *The New York Times,* November 3, 1929, p. 4, section 9.

[*In the following review of* The Silver Tassie, *Morgan assesses the strengths and weaknesses of the dramatic techniques found in the London production, claiming that O'Casey's political prejudices hurt the aesthetic dimension of the play.*]

There is a defiant boldness in Mr. O'Casey's writing that compels attention. *Juno and the Paycock* and *The Plough and the Stars* made a deep impression even upon those who found them wanting as works of art. It was evident that here was one who possessed many of the qualities of a great dramatist—a view of life proper to himself; courage enough to depart from fashionable dramatic technique when his work required such a departure; a fiercely critical humor and an extraordinary power to perceive, and to reproduce in the theatre, the entanglement—even the coincidence—of tragedy, comedy and farce on the lives of men. For these reasons, the performance of his new play was a theatrical happening of some importance and was awaited with the more curiosity because *The Silver Tassie* [recently produced here by the Irish Theatre—Ed.], having been already published and widely discussed, was known to be technically experimental and to contain at least one act—the second—of which no one could certainly foretell the effect on the stage.

Before entering into any discussion of them, let me briefly summarize the four acts. In the first, we are introduced to Sylvester Heegan and Simon Norton, two conventionally comic Irishmen; to Susie Monican who, being thwarted in her love for Harry Heegan, has turned violently to religion and shouts continually of the wrath of God at moments as inappropriate as farcical contrivance can make them; to Teddy Foran, a soldier, who bullies his wife and breaks up the furniture and crockery on the floor above; to Jessie Taite, a pretty girl who has captured Harry; and finally to Harry Heegan, a famous local athelete, who has won the football cup (the Silver Tassie) for his club and is now riotously returning from leave to the trenches. The second

act is a symbol of war. The third has its scene, after the war, in a hospital; Teddy Foran is blind, Harry Heegan is a cripple in a wheeled chair; Jessie is evidently deserting him in favor of another soldier, Barney Bagnal, who saved Heegan's life; the religious Susie has become Nurse Monican, very severe on duty, very amorous in her asides with the hospital staff; and the two comic Irishmen, in adjacent beds, are still two comic Irishmen disputing in extremely entertaining music-hall back-chat about baths and other subjects beloved in the music halls.

The last act shows us the football club dance with Jessie in Barney's arms; with Harry Heegan, a fierce, embittered cripple, pursuing her in his wheeled chair; and with the comic Irishmen providing another music-hall turn at a telephone.

The first act is fairly plain sailing until, at the end, the soldiers going off to the war and the crowd bidding them farewell break away from the naturalism in which the play began and take up a wild, defiant chanting. Nor is the third act difficult, though the deliberate violence of its emotional contrasts produces in the hospital ward a kind of insane tension that is the mark of Mr. O'Casey's style. The fourth act, containing the football club dance, is in many ways the most successful of all. The interlude of the comic Irishmen, which is intended to produce an impression of intense realism by its extravagant irrelevance, is, I think, a failure. It is amusing, but it is too long and breaks up the act. But the rest of the scene, in which poetry and naturalistic prose are inextricably mingled and the chanted laments of the blind man and the cripple are heard against the chatter, the frivolous indifference and the would-be sensuous music of the dance, has an astonishing and bitter power. It has something of the quality of certain dream-scenes by Strindberg in which reality and symbol become one.

And the highly controversial second act is unforgettable. Here, in a night scene designed by Augustus John and on a stage grouped and arranged with an artist's eye by Raymond Massey, a group of soldiers, using a kind of free verse, grumble and lament and pray. The effect of the scene and of their chanted rhythm is to lift illusion clear of the naturalistic plane, and the act has power to produce a spiritual influence beyond its own boundaries. With so much to recommend it, it might have been a beautiful work of art. But three things stand in its way: First, that the poetry is not good enough to answer the challenge which the use of poetry implies; secondly, that the introduction of two characters—a visitor and a staff officer—are used for the purpose of caricature that breaks the illusion and reduce tragic irony to the level of ignorant spite; thirdly, that you are left at the end with an impression that, though his dramatic method is a brilliant experiment, Mr. O'Casey lacks the experience or the greatness and generosity of mind to write of war on a spiritual plane. The pamphleteer interferes with the artist; the anger of an enraged child makes impossible the tranquillity of passion. Mr. O'Casey is too often an agile rhetorician who has jumped on a tub to teach the great gods their business, and is inclined to foam and scream when they disregard him; he is too seldom an artist on his knees.

These are the flaws in his present work. They are present, not because he is not an artist, but because the violence of his prejudices on the particular subject of war has, in this instance, distorted his esthetic vision.

CRITICAL COMMENTARY

Ronald G. Rollins and Llewellyn Rabby (essay date 1979)

SOURCE: "*The Silver Tassie*: The Post-World-War-I Legacy," in *Modern Drama,* Vol. XXII, No. 1, June, 1979, pp. 125-36.

[*In the following essay, Rollins and Rabby situate the dramatic patterns and techniques of* The Silver Tassie *within the context of other contemporary plays that deal with the horror of war, showing how O'Casey's adaptations of the theme contribute to the originality of the work*]

> Things fall apart; the centre cannot hold;
> Mere anarchy is loosed upon the world, . . .

In the final months and in the years following World War I, that extended nightmare that shattered an established hierarchical social order that had provided stability and spiritual serenity for centuries of European men, a new mood of bewilderment, despair, and cynical alienation tormented millions of disenchanted people in the western world. And as is so often the case, it was the artists, especially the playwrights, who first gave voice to this new cry of hopelessness, frustration, and fear. Beginning with the plays of the German Expressionists, 1912-1916, a new generation of post-war playwrights exerted themselves to assess the full impact of the old order upon those who were left behind to contemplate the ruins and to lament the loss of friends and cherished values. Repeatedly these playwrights recoiled in anger and anguish from the new lines of force in an historical process that was separating man from ancient patterns of life that had been passed on from father to son, that was regimenting man almost out of existence, and that was driving God from His heaven.

Although geographically removed from this post-World-War-I vortex of shrill polemics and relentless technical experimentation, Sean O'Casey was very much a marching member of this new cadre of avant-garde playwrights. His isolated country, with its established Abbey Theatre and the Dublin Drama League, set up in 1918 to stage foreign plays, had been alerted to the manifold possibilities of this new, non-naturalistic drama with the production in Dublin in the 1920's of the plays of Pirandello, Strindberg, Benavente, Andreyev, Lenormand, Toller,

Kaiser, and O'Neill.[1] Here were exciting examples of the new drama that fused angular and grotesque scenic tableaux, chant and ritualized movement, song, mask, dance, intensified symbolic gesture, and emblematic figures into an often musical and vivid dramatic form that would externalize man's hidden world of thought and impulse that had been activated by powerful forces that threatened to cripple or erase him.

Recording the fanatical polemics and the hedonistic frivolity of those in different states of shock after World War I, these non-representational plays frequently fused or juxtaposed remnants of classical and Christian myths, myths that enabled the dramatist to measure the fragmenting present against an apparently stable past and to impose a ritualistic sequence upon the situation being exploited. Hence, these dramas of distortion, emerging out of the playwrights' despairing reservations about individual man's ability to alter Collective History, often manifested both a linear, cause-and-effect relationship, and an epiphanic dimension, a dimension accented by recurring symbols and by ritualistic, ballet-like movements specifically intended to objectify these crucial, intense moments of psychic turbulence which threatened modern man repeatedly experienced.[2]

O'Casey's *The Silver Tassie* (1929) is transparently a play belonging to this large category of post-World-War-I-Expressionistic plays, a ritualistic parable of calculated ironic contrasts in setting, dress, dialogue, and lighting, and a protest play designed to bring the horrible realities of war-the pandemonium and pain of the battlefield—back from the trenches to the hospitals, homes, and athletic clubs of a complacent and often mercenary society. A drama with geometrical configurations, *The Silver Tassie* is, in part, then, a work that turns inward upon itself, a self-conscious, subtle masterpiece that invites the reader-observer to discover the complex network of interlocking and overlapping patterns that constitute its design.

O'Casey explains the objective of his play with ceremonial patterns in a letter to this writer:

> I wished to show the face & unveil the soul of war. I wanted a war play without noise; without the interruptions of gunfire, content to show its results, as in the chant of the wounded and the maiming of Harry; to show it in its main spiritual phases; its minor impulses and its actual horror of destroying the golden bodies of the young; & of the Church's damned approval in the sardonic hymn to the gun; as true today as it was then. I never consciously adopted "expressionism," which I don't understand & never did. To me there are no "impressionistic," "expressionistic," "realistic" (social or otherwise) plays: there are very good plays and bad ones. Like your students, I think this play my best one; but the thought isn't important, for it may well be wrong.[3]

O'Casey is behaving in his characteristically candid and truthful manner when he vigorously asserts that he did not "consciously adopt" Expressionism in arranging *The Silver Tassie.* Indeed, O'Casey did not "consciously adopt" any particular dramatic method (nor slavishly mimic any particular playwright) during his long and productive career, and so his drama is finally more eclectic than imitative-a drama distinguished always by a skillful diversity of dramatic methods. Yet O'Casey, as a serious and systematic student of world theatre, was profoundly influenced by the plays which he read and saw in his native city in the 1920's, especially those of the German Expressionists Toller and Kaiser and the American O'Neill. Hence, he incorporates—perhaps more subconsciously than consciously—the vivid mélange of materials and methods of Expressionistic drama into *The Silver Tassie,* again demonstrating the truth of T. S. Eliot's contention that all art is collaboration. As David Krause explains: "Instead of telling the audience through exposition that war is hell, he [O'Casey] had found in the techniques of Expressionism a way of showing them a symbolic nightmare of that hell—a new method of developing the tortured figure that once herculean Harry has become in the last two acts."[4]

Harry Heegan is the twenty-three-year-old athlete whose youthful "golden body" is seriously injured by the mechanized madness of a European war gradually discovering the destructive potential of armored tanks, and his tragic life seems intentionally arranged to duplicate the familiar phases of a scapegoat's career.[5] Like other hero-victims before him, Heegan is first introduced as a man superior to other men, a lover of adventure, a gifted athlete who could perhaps win the decathlon, and a successful lover of attractive young women. Appropriately, he is honored for a time by his devoted followers. Act I of *The Silver Tassie* ends with a ceremonial procession of Heegan's friends and admirers singing his praises and enumerating his singular achievements in the just completed championship games, an ending which suggests a reduced replica of the ancient Olympic games.

Yet when he enters the larger "game" of trench and mechanized warfare in Europe in Act II, he does not win; he is wounded in battle and saved from death by his companion Barney Bagnal, who carries him to safety. Thus, when he returns in Act III and IV as a crippled remnant of a man—a painful reminder of the "horror" of war—he is shunned and quickly rejected by those in the mood for hedonistic frivolity. As scapegoat, Heegan, confined to his wheelchair with leg paralysis, is thus wheeled off into exile—into the limbo land of neglect—by the blinded Teddy Foran, another victim of the ugly game of war.

To trace the trajectory of Heegan's rise and fall, O'Casey creates a geometric drama, a self-conscious parable inviting us to detect the direct intersections, the different triangles, and the gradual modulations in four different settings made fascinating by their scenic stylization. Amazingly, all four scenes, with slight modifications, can be located in the Heegan household, the similar eating-sitting-sleeping room used so often in the Dublin trilogy. Manipulating his scenic properties with consummate skill,

O'Casey seems to be deliberately working to bring war into a typical home, using the same cluster of major symbols (the bright star, the cross, the altar), the same patterns of movement, and the same colors (especially red, orange, and black) in clothing and room fixtures to suggest that history is a predictable nightmare of recurring cycles: life flows, then ebbs, only to flow again with different participants. Thus, each act can almost be superimposed upon the other in this vivid parable drama.

Acts I and II—the former situated in the eating-sitting-sleeping room of the Heegan household, and the latter near a ruined monastery in the war zone somewhere in France—are, with some exceptions, strikingly similar, both assuming the dimensions of a church or cathedral where a sacrifice is imminent. Both utilize large windows at the back, with the window in the first act looking out on a quay, and the window in the second looking out on a long expanse of desolate denuded terrain disfigured by trenches, barbed wire, and stumps of trees. Visible through the first window is the center mast of a steamer with a gleaming white light at the top; visible through the second window is another cross formed by two broken pieces of masonry, one jutting from the left and another from the right. A white star glows above this wartime wasteland. Beneath and directly in front of the window in Act I is a stand with silver gilded legs and a gold gilded top; the stand is flanked by a dresser to the left and a bed to the right, an arrangement suggesting an altar and two pulpits. A purple velvet shield, to which are pinned a number of silver and gold medals, is draped across the stand; two small vases containing artificial flowers stand on the two sides of the shield, a balanced grouping that again evokes an altar tableau. Directly in front of the window in Act II is a massive, black howitzer gun, emblematic of the weapons responsible for the maiming—the "crucifixion"—of Heegan, an action adumbrated by the symbolic mast-cross, altar-stand, and purple color of Act I.[6] Significantly, the colors silver and gold are absent in this act because war, especially large-scale war fought by naive young men who have been caught in the diplomatic machinations of diplomats, is, in O'Casey's view, decidedly devoid of spiritual splendor.

Other particulars reinforce the complementary natures of the two acts, and remind us of the parallel patterns and intersecting lines and angles in both. In Act I, Mrs. Heegan stands viewing the street through the right rear window; a right front door also provides access to the street. Later, both the window and the door provide Mrs. Heegan and others with means of distraction and escape from a house agitated at times by tension and tumult. In Act II, a stained-glass window made eye-arresting by a figure of the Virgin replaces Mrs. Heegan and her window, while a life-sized crucifix is situated near the area of the front side-street exit. A shell has blasted one arm from the figure on the cross, and so the shattered Christ leans forward with the released arm outstretched towards the Virgin. In similar fashion, Harry Heegan, after having his legs immobilized, will later assume the attitude and posture of a suppliant before a crucifix-wearing Sister, a nun and mortal virgin. So do tormented and suffering men repeatedly seek solace from compassionate, maternal figures in their hours of greatest distress. Moreover, as the people in Act I "escaped" from domestic uproar through windows and doors, so too the soldiers seek escape from the red menace of war through different but similarly placed outlets in Act II. By linking Mrs. Heegan and her window with the Virgin and her window, O'Casey achieves a stunning ironic effect. In Act I, Mrs. Heegan and Mrs. Foran, two mothers and mother figures, do not show great concern or weep at the departure of their sons for the trenches of Europe; however, in Act II, the Virgin Mother stares aghast and "white-faced" at the murder of so many of her sons. Finally, the other passageway, the left bedroom door of Act I, becomes the Red Cross archway entrance in Act II, both entrances hinting at the peace and restoration that comes from security and restful sleep. Hence, the doors and the windows in these two related acts are deliberately placed in similar areas, a device that causes us to view the two settings as related and interlinked.

Still other similarities integrate the two acts. Sylvester Heegan and Simon Norton, two dockworkers, sit before a fire at middle left in Act I, reminiscing about Harry Heegan's past exploits with fists and feet, thereby identifying Heegan as a modern Ossian among the Avondales. In Act II, a group of soldiers, wet, cold, and sullen-faced, form a circle at near center around a brazier in which a fire is burning. Since war is an ugly, deadly, larger game devoid of glory, they sing no songs to honor an Achilles in their midst; rather, they give us litanies of their profound fear and despair. Moreover, in Act I, Sylvester and Simon must endure the doleful chanting—the "tambourine theology"—of Susie Monican, a religious fanatic who is momentarily obsessed with visions of man's innate depravity and the coming of the Last Judgment:

> Man walketh in a vain shadow, and disquieteth himself
> in vain:
> He heapeth up riches, and cannot tell who shall gather
> them.[7]

Later, in Act II, the soldiers must listen to the Croucher, a blood-and mud-spattered soldier situated on a ramp above the brazier, and he sounds much like Susie:

> And the hand of the Lord was upon me, and carried
> me out in the spirit of the Lord, and set me down in
> the midst of a valley.[8]

Whereas Susie chanted of last things, the Croucher intones dreamily of a valley of dry bones, a collection of bones which will not be knit and animated by divine intervention. With their gloomy utterances about the frailty of human life and their apocalyptic visions of last things, these two chanting figures are almost interchangeable.

As she bombards the two men with the name of her deity, Susie, polishing a Lee-Enfield rifle, stands near a table at corner left on which are placed a bottle of whiskey, a large

parcel of bread-and-meat sandwiches, and some copies of English illustrated magazines. Near the table is a red colored stand resembling an easel which holds a silver gilt-framed picture of Harry Heegan in a crimson, yellow and black football uniform. Susie's excessive concern with "everlastin" fire and the rifle, the hero's icon-like portrait, the colors of violence (red and yellow), and the whiskey and sandwiches—strong connotations of the Eucharist here—again convey sacrificial overtones; so with her utterances and her conduct, Susie reveals herself as an altar celebrant or acolyte, as a soothsayer who knows of the future time when the young hero will, indeed, be enclosed by the red fires of war.[9]

The interaction between Harry Heegan and Barney Bagnal also links the first two acts, the zigzagging relationship reminding one of a game of musical chairs. For example, in Act II, Barney, lashed to a gunwheel, replaces the picture and the sandwich table at left front. A soldier companion of Heegan, Barney is being punished for stealing a cock, hardly the kind of action one associates with a hero-to-be. Since Barney was an insignificant subordinate—one who swells a progress—in Heegan's drink-dance, processional celebration (an orgiastic ballet pregnant with hints of disaster), it is appropriate that he be tied to but one of the several wheels of a large gun, the destructive weapon that will cripple Heegan for the rest of his life.

Yet it is quite significant that Heegan disappears in Act II while Barney is given a prominent role in the action, for the process of transition from one hero to another is underway in this act. In Act I, Barney was a doer, a coat-carrier, for the dynamic Harry; it was Heegan who won the gleaming tassie (the Grail), the girl (Jessie Taite), and the glory (leading performer on the Avondale team). In Act II, however, Heegan is crippled but Barney emerges unhurt; Barney is ready to assume Heegan's former heroic role and the alliteration in the two names suggests that O'Casey may have had this transference in mind. By Act IV, Barney gains the Grail (twisted and bent), the girl (soiled and opportunistic), and the glory (medals to attest to his bravery in battle), thereby completing the character reversal pattern and strengthening the relationship among the four acts.

Fewer scenic similarities are present in Acts III and IV, yet some scenic continuity—scene linkage—is maintained. At the center rear in Act III, set in a hospital ward, is a large double door which opens onto a garden warmed by the rays of a setting September sun; at the center rear in Act IV, set in a room of the Avondale Football Club, is a wide, tall window which also opens onto a garden. Three wooden cross-pieces enabling weak patients to pull themselves into a sitting posture are attached to the beds at right rear in Act III; three black and red lanterns, with the center one four times the length of its width, form a corresponding illuminated cross at center front in Act IV. Situated before the large glass door in Act III is a white, glass-topped table on which rest medicines, drugs, and surgical instruments. Thus, the healing instruments of the surgeon have replaced the ugly, destructive howitzer of Act II. Also, one vase of flowers, placed at the corner of the table, survives from the two that were on the altar-stand in Act I. No table is placed before the rear, wide window in Act IV. Instead, a long table, covered with a green cloth and laden with bottles of wine and a dozen glasses, is situated at stage right. The concern for drinking and dancing has replaced the concern for healing, as music and vivid colors—vivid hats and colored streamers—have replaced the subdued mood and bleak austerity—the pervasive whiteness—of Act III. Significantly, the crucifix and the Virgin have disappeared because the dancing couples prefer passionate self-indulgence to prayerful self-denial.

The characters also assume positions and re-enact behavioral routines roughly analogous to those established in the first two acts. In Act III, Sylvester and Simon, in or near beds in the ward, again perform a choral function as they comment on hero Heegan-his crippled body and shattered dreams. In Act IV, they first stand outside in the garden near the large, rear window, smoking and observing the activity at the dance; later, they enter to sit before a fire to lament the reversal in fortunes of Heegan, whose anguish is increased with the arrival of Barney, who leads Jessie Taite to the wine table as the act begins. As Harry's gold and silver medals adorned the purple shield in Act I, so now war medals—one is ironically the Victoria Cross—are attached to Bagnal's waistcoat. Barney had carried Heegan to safety in battle, but he now assists in his psychic disintegration. Likewise, as Harry and Jessie drank from the silver tassie in Act I, so now Barney and Jessie drink from the wine glasses in this act.[10] Also, Susie Monican, clad now in attractive, provocative attire, enters in Act III again to lecture Simon and Sylvester; however, she now speaks no longer of sin and gloom but of sunshine, yellowing trees, and the active, joyful life. In Act IV, she translates her doctrine into reality by dancing with Surgeon Forby Maxwell; she has reversed completely her previous mode of thinking and acting. Finally, Mrs. Heegan no longer looks *out* of the window in Act IV; rather, she studies her embittered, crippled son through the doorway which is adorned with crimson and black curtains.

One new stage property—a Roll of Honor listing the names of the five members of the Avondale Club killed in battle—appears in Act IV at left back. A wreath of laurel tied with red and black ribbons rests underneath this Roll. As a symbolic tombstone and epitaph, the Roll should also include Harry Heegan's name, as he is "dead" in body and weakened in spirit. So the mobile others ignore the list of the dead to respond rhythmically to a gay fox trot; these lively dancers represent the "full life on the flow"; abandoned Heegan, attended now by a new companion and follower, the blind Teddy Foran, who has assumed Barney's former role, must be wheeled into the garden, a shattered hulk of a man whose life will ebb agonizingly away.

Thus, *The Silver Tassie* stands finally as a modern Passion-play, a geometric drama that juggles and joins numerous ancient ceremonial patterns with Joycean exactness and evocativeness to deplore human sacrifice on a massive scale. Expressing the post-World-War-I traumatic recoil from the ghastly mangling of men by machines, O'Casey repeats the same major concerns first introduced in the Expressionistic plays of Ernst Toller and Georg Kaiser, especially in *Man and the Masses* and *From Morn to Midnight*.[11] While joining with others in the emerging tradition of post-World-War-I non-naturalistic protest plays, O'Casey also manifested his very real individual talent, carefully devising a ritualistic parable, a drama of ironic reversals, chanted poetry, mythical constructs, and jagged but forceful illuminations designed, as he confessed, to "capture the spirit of war, and to show the Christian fighters as they maimed and slew each other before the face of the son of God."[12]

Notes

1. Harold Ferrar, *Denis Johnston's Irish Theatre* (Dublin, 1973), p. 10.

2. *Masters of Modern Drama*, edd. with intro. and notes by Haskell M. Block and Robert C. Shedd (New York, 1962), pp. 6-7.

3. Letter to this writer from O'Casey, March 24, 1960 (reproduced with this article).

4. David Krause, *Sean O'Casey: The Man and His Work* (New York, 1962), p. 15. Robert Hogan adds: "The play exists to condemn war by showing its effects on an individual, Heegan. The Expressionistic art is included to represent a condemnation of war indirectly and on an abstract moral basis. . . . And also, stylization, by stripping away the cluttering detail, presents the essence, the emotional-intellectual core of war." (*The Experiments of Sean O'Casey* [New York, 1960], pp. 65-66.)

5. For a discussion of rites of human sacrifice in various agrarian religions, rites that later focus on a scapegoat figure, see: Mircea Eliade, *Myth, Dreams and Mysteries* (New York, 1960), p. 187; and G. S. Kirk, *Myth: Its Meaning and Function in Ancient and Other Cultures* (Berkeley, 1970), p. 16 and p. 19.

6. Jack Lindsay, discussing O'Casey's use of the canonical hours of the breviary in *Within the Gates*, reminds us that purple is the traditional liturgical color for penitence and death. See *Sean O'Casey: Modern Judgements*, ed. Ronald Ayling (Nashville, 1970), p. 199. See also Jacqueline Doyle's "Liturgical Imagery in Sean O'Casey's *The Silver Tassie*," *Modern Drama*, 21 (March 1978), 29-38.

7. O'Casey, *Collected Plays*, II (New York, 1956), p. 7.

8. *Ibid.*, p. 36.

9. Winifred Smith views Susie Monican as a "priestess" who attends the altar in this "ironic Graeco-Christian passion play." See "The Dying God in Modern Theatre," *The Review of Religion*, 5 (March 1941), 267-75.

10. See Krause, pp. 157-58.

11. Maureen Malone argues that the play is a condemnation of an hypocritical society that slaughters masses of men in war for selfish ends. See *The Plays of Sean O'Casey* (Carbondale, Ill., 1969), pp. 52-3.

12. Letter to this writer from O'Casey, July 25, 1959.

COCK-A-DOODLE DANDY

PRODUCTION REVIEWS

Alan Brien (review date 11 September 1959)

SOURCE: "Weill Away," in *The Spectator*, Vol. 203, No. 6846, September 11, 1959, pp. 331-32.

[*In the following review of the London debut of* Cock-a-Doodle Dandy, *Brien faults the eloquence of O'Casey's dramatic language, which, in his opinion, detracts from the action and motivation of the play.*]

In *Cock-a-Doodle Dandy* O'Casey, too, is out to scare the cassock off the priesthood. But he seems oddly unsure what he will find underneath the fancy dress—less than a man or more than a demon? His bog village of Nyadnanave is a haunted battlefield where strange, supernatural powers wrestle for the souls of men. All the farcical byplay of old-fashioned pantomime—geysers of smoke, glowing whiskey bottles, acrobatic scenery, dancing animals, trick furniture—are weapons in an unholy comic war. Father Domineer (Patrick Magee) is God's angry, implacable, English-vowelled drill-sergeant. A monstrous, life-sized Cock (danced by Berto Pasuka) is the mascot of the poor and the passionate, the proud and pitiful. The troops are enrolled by sex rather than by class, rather as though O'Casey had transferred his propaganda allegiance from the Red Prussian to the White Goddess. All the women are good by light of nature. All the men are evil by darkness of doctrine. In the end, the Church wins and drives out of sacred Ireland the priestesses of love and passion and charity.

Staged by George Devine with tireless roust-about zest, the battle is almost always picturesque and comical. O'Casey, like a drunken wordsmith, has forced his gaudy rhetoric on everyone indiscriminately. The red-hot phrases pour endlessly out of his forge, pile up on the stage, and overflow into the auditorium, burning and branding wherever they touch. In the second act, when the women in cheap fancy dress with beckoning eyes and gurgling laughter, flaunting legs and swirling hair, encircle and ensnare the dull, frightened old men, the play blossoms beyond eloquent farce. Joan O'Hara, Etain O'Dell and Pauline Flanagan, with their vivid physical presence and their strange giggling cameraderie, suggest that O'Casey is going to reveal his alternative to the Church. But the mo-

ment passes. The smoke blows away. The houses cease their rock and roll. And O'Casey returns to his old-fashioned priest-teasing and kulak-baiting as though he had not noticed the flames of genius which sprouted from his silver old head.

The men are not nearly so well played as the women. Patrick Magee's priest has the right hysterical undertone to his aggressive fanaticism. J. G. Devlin creeps craftily inside the role of the shrivelled Tartuffe of the backwoods. But the rest are little more than competent—perhaps reflecting the indecision of the author about their roles rather than any lack of technique in the actors. There is one more important part played on one note of creaking incoherence by Wilfrid Lawson. This old sea captain may be meant to be an average sensual man caught between fear of the Church and love of Life. It is hard to be sure, so persistently does Mr. Lawson swallow O'Casey's words like a series of suppressed belches.

Most reviews of O'Casey contain the phrase '. . . but, of course, despite these weaknesses, his incomparable language,' etc. I feel that too often the language is the weakness. O'Casey is too eloquent. What his play needs is a few ideas plainly expressed and dramatically worked through. Words are the alcohol of the Irish—though, of course, so is alcohol. If only O'Casey would swear off the thesaurus for a few months he might be able to give birth to that masterpiece which has continually been threatened, but never delivered, since *Juno and the Paycock.* He might do worse than drop in on *The Thrie Estaites* to see how anti-clericalism could be turned into poetry in the days when it was dangerous to attempt it.

CRITICAL COMMENTARY

David Krause (essay date 1991)

SOURCE: An introduction in *Cock-A-Doodle Dandy by Sean O'Casey*, The Catholic University of America Press, 1991, pp. 1-32.

[*In the following excerpt, Krause describes the historical and religious contexts of* Cock-a-Doodle Dandy *in relation to the comedic themes expressed in the play.*]

> The ban on laughter stretches back to the day when man wore skins and defended himself with the stone hammer. Many enemies have always surrounded laughter, have tried to banish it from life; and many have perished on the high gallows tree because they laughed at those who had been given power over them. Hell-fire tried to burn it, and the weeping for sins committed did all that was possible to drown it; but laughter came safely through the ordeals of fire and water; came smiling through.[1]

Comedy is Sean O'Casey's primary dramatic strategy. Looking back over his career, he felt he had used laughter as a weapon against evil or folly. There are often dark or repressive forces at work in his plays, and, although he relies upon his comic vision to expose and deflate them, the destructive forces tend to prevail. It is the hard way of the world. Nevertheless, even in defeat, his comic characters linger on as a positive value, a symbol of the human determination to endure. "A laugh is a great natural stimulator," he wrote, "a pushful entry into life; and once we can laugh, we can live. It is a hilarious declaration made by man that life is worth living."[2]

Satiric and ironic laughter, touched off by knockabout comedy and wild fantasy, are his most potent weapons against the pompous and pretentious, against any repressive attitudes that have become too rigid or too sacred. And since sacred notions tend to be inviolable in devout Ireland, even when they have deviated or departed from religious or political ideals, the stage was well set for O'Casey's comic catharsis in 1949 when he wrote yet another controversial play, *Cock-a-doodle Dandy.* He thought it was his best work. Unfortunately, however, this dark comedy about Irish life at mid-century would not be performed professionally in the Republic of Ireland until 1977 at the Abbey Theatre, where he had achieved his early controversial triumphs. Although his native theatre depended upon regular revivals of his Dublin trilogy—*The Shadow of a Gunman* (1923), *Juno and the Paycock* (1924), *The Plough and the Stars* (1926)—for much of its audience and income, the manager and directors of the theatre were pointedly not interested in his later plays.

That Ireland was not ready for O'Casey in 1949, when he was in his seventieth year, only served to illustrate his critical theme, that the country had become a repressed theocracy where, in maid Marion's lament to Robin Adair at the conclusion of the play, "a whisper of love in this place bites away some of th' soul!"[3] Perhaps uneasy Ireland had never been fully ready for O'Casey. Even before he decided upon self-exile after 1926, he was, like so many Irish writers, an exile in his own land. With his irreverent comic thrusts he was from the beginning a marked man, full of Swiftian rage or what his friend Jim Larkin (the fiery labor leader of the 1913 General Strike, in which O'Casey took part) had called "divine discontent" over the repressed conditions of life in Ireland. Ironically, that very discontent often became the catalyst for many significant works of Irish literature.

In this respect O'Casey was no different from the alienated Yeats and Joyce; Yeats, the isolated poet who had written about malicious Dublin in "The People" in 1919:

> The daily spite of this unmannerly town
> Where who has served the most is most defamed.[4]

And the impious Joyce, who, in his "Gas from a Burner" in 1902, had struck the same note of scorn for Ireland's shameful treatment of her artists and leaders:

> This lovely land that always sent
> Her writers and artists into banishment

> And in a spirit of Irish fun
> Betrayed her own leaders, one by one.[5]

In an ironic reversal, the people who rioted in the Abbey Theatre in 1926 against *The Plough and the Stars* were convinced that O'Casey had betrayed Ireland. The open and hidden protests against most of his plays arose because he was thought to be disrespectful, even blasphemous, toward Kathleen ni Houlihan's two most sacred cows (or sows, as Joyce preferred to call them): Irish Catholicism and Nationalism. The cleverly irreverent Joyce had also aimed at these vulnerable targets in his 1902 blast:

> O Ireland my first and only love
> Where Christ and Caesar are hand in glove!
> O lovely land where the shamrock grows
> (Allow me, ladies, to blow my nose)

O'Casey obviously shared this comic irreverence, but contrary to what the outraged defenders of Kathleen ni Houlihan believed, his own nose-blow or lack of respect did not mean he was opposed to the religious and political faith of the majority of his countrymen and women. It was usually the reprehensible means, not the idealistic ends, that troubled him, and his characters. They were suspicious of abstract slogans of martyrdom. In *Juno,* for example, when Johnny Boyle, who lost an arm fighting for the I.R.A. in the Civil War, insists that he would sacrifice himself again for his country because "a principle's principle," his mother Juno replies quietly:

> Ah, you lost your best principle, me boy, when you lost your arm; them's the only sort o' principles that's any good to a workin' man.[6]

Therefore O'Casey stood for a democratic workers' republic for Ireland, not a nationalist theocracy. And he openly rejected, mocked in his plays, the intolerance of sectarian Protestants as well as Catholics. It was the fanatical or unthinking devotion to religious or political causes that provoked his comic profanations. He deflated what he felt were blatant departures from essential dogma and idealism, the blind acceptance of holy patriotism and puritanism, which so often obsessed many of the die-hard nationalists and Jansenist clergy.

O'Casey frequently and consistently disavowed any imputation of anti-Catholicism, claiming instead that he was anti-clerical. The distinction is commonly accepted in continental Europe, where many Catholics themselves oppose the influence of the clergy in political or secular affairs. In Ireland, however, that distinction was often regarded as spurious, and those who dared to criticize the clergy were typically accused of hostility to the Catholic faith. . . .

It was partly the injustice and savagery of his Dublin critics that contributed to his decision to leave Ireland in 1926; this theme of alienation and exile became the crucial issue in his two 1949 works, *Inishfallen, Fare Thee Well* and *Cock-a-doodle Dandy.* The begrudging and sneering malice of Dublin would have destroyed him if he had remained in that city where there were, from a literary point of view, too many dogs and too few bones; where, as Yeats believed and Goethe had said earlier, the pack of hounds would always bring down the noble stag.

At the end of *A Portrait,* Joyce's autobiographical Stephen Dedalus declares a manifesto justifying his alienation and exile from Ireland:

> I will tell you what I will do and what I will not do. I will not serve that in which I no longer believe whether it call itself my home, my fatherland or my church; and I will try to express myself in some mode of life or art as freely as I can and as wholly as I can, using for my defence the only arms I allow myself to use—silence, exile, and cunning.[7]

At the beginning of the final chapter of *Inishfallen,* O'Casey's autobiographical Sean O'Casside declares his parallel manifesto of alienation and exile from Ireland:

> It was time for Sean to go. He had had enough of it. He would be no more of an exile in another land than he was in his own. He was a voluntary and settled exile from every creed, from every party, and from every literary clique, fanning themselves into silence with unmitigated praise of each other in the most select corners of the city's highways and byebye-ways. He would stay no longer to view life through a stained-glass window, a Sinn Fein spy-glass, from a prie-dieu, or through the thigh bone of a hare.[8]

Nevertheless, Joyce and O'Casey, in spite of their shared declaration of *non serviam,* left Ireland only in order to be more Irish; in order to be able to write more freely, more critically and more comically, about life in that country which inspired their constant love and frustration. Yeats, who never went into exile but wisely left the country often for periodic and necessary escapes, made it an artistic triumvirate of loving and hating Irishmen when he said in his poem "Meditations in Time of Civil War" (1923) about Irishmen who were killing Irishmen in the name of freedom:

> We had fed the heart on fantasies,
> The heart's grown brutal from the fare;
> More substance in our enmities
> Than in our love.[9]

In spite of this bitter tone, anyone who reads the poetry of Yeats, the fiction of Joyce, or the drama of O'Casey will find as much substance in the love for as well as the enmities toward Ireland. And if in their symbolic as well as literal exile they all resorted to Celtic cunning, they never took refuge in silence, despite Joyce's claim. They never abandoned their best weapons: powerful and poetic words. Yeats as the grand myth-maker wrote many of the finest poems of the twentieth century; but Yeats the "founder" and protector of literary and theatrical organizations could be olympian in his wrath, and he defended his role as leader by proclaiming: "I was the spokesman because I was born arrogant and had learnt an artist's arrogance—'Not what you want but what we want.'"[10]

Joyce as the aloof artificer transformed his enmities into comedies, lyric and Homeric, in his epiphanizations of Dublin; but Joyce the exiled Irishman, who had assumed the persona of an isolated and betrayed artist in Trieste, once offered up this comic malediction in the form of a black prayer he sent to his brother Stanislaus in 1905:

> O. Vague Something behind everything.
>
> For the love of the Lord Christ change my curse-o'-God state of affairs.
>
> Give me for Christ's sake a pen and an ink-bottle and some peace of mind, and then, by the crucified Jaysus, if I don't sharpen that little pen and dip it into fermented ink and write tiny little sentences about the people who betrayed me, send me to hell. After all, there are many ways of betraying people. It wasn't only the Galilean suffered that. Whoever the hell you are, I inform you that this is a poor comedy you expect me to play and I'm damned to hell if I'll play it for you.[11]

In a similar dark mood, O'Casey assumed the persona of an isolated and betrayed Irishman in the wilderness of Chalfont St. Giles, Buckinghamshire, where he was living in 1931, before he later moved to Devon. In an attempt to be a peacemaker, Bernard Shaw's wife Charlotte had written urging him not to become involved in literary conflicts: "And oh! dear Sean, don't be too belligerent!" He replied with a flourish of controlled rage, calling upon God to damn him if ever he put aside his avenging sword and retreated from battle:

> God be my judge that I hate fighting. If I be damned for anything, I shall be damned for keeping the two-edged sword of thought tight in its scabbard when it should be searching the bowels of knaves and fools. I assure you, I shrink from battle, and never advance into a fight unless I am driven into it.[12]

Throughout a stormy career his fierce integrity often drove him into verbal battle and he never shrank from a challenge. So God never had cause to damn him on this account. Anyone who would understand O'Casey's controversial love-hate relationship with Ireland might consider how he used his two-edged sword of tragicomedy to search the bowels of knaves and fools in *Cock-a-doodle Dandy*; how he dramatized a Manichean struggle between the forces of repression and the forces of liberation.

The knaves and fools and their joyful opponents in *Cock-a-doodle Dandy* live in the Irish village of Nyadnanave, which means, in Gaelic, Nest of Saints and also includes the ironic pun, Nest of Knaves. The apocalyptic Cock and his rebellious young cohorts are the true saints, while the mean-spirited Father Domineer and his crawthumping crew are the pseudosaints. Since the priestly and political figures repress and exploit the young people in the town, these rigid authority figures become the objects of O'Casey's broad range of farcical satire. In his essay on the therapeutic nature of laughter, he described his comic purpose:

> Laughter tends to mock the pompous and the pretentious; all man's boastful gadding about, all his petty pomps, his hoary customs, his wornout creeds, changing the glitter of them into the dullest hue of lead. The

bigger the subject, the sharper the laugh. No one can escape it; not the grave judge in his robe and threatening wig; the parson and his saw; the general full of his sword and his medals; the palled prelate, tripping about, a blessing in one hand, a curse in the other; the politician carrying his magic wand of Wendy windy words; they all fear laughter, for the quiet laugh or the loud one upends them, strips them of pretense, and leaves them naked to enemy and friend.[13]

O'Casey here is moving in the recognizable tradition of comic exposure that goes back to Aristophanes and Plautus, Shakespeare and Jonson, Molière and Dickens. In the liberating comedy of all these writers, pompous and pretentious authorities who torment their people, in minor as well as major hypocrisies and deceits, are prime targets for scornful or subversive laughter. Sometimes the repressive figures are self-appointed guardians of morality, like the puritanical Malvolio in *Twelfth Night,* who is mocked and punished for his folly; his sanctimonious manner is exposed by Sir Toby's classic speech that anticipates the free spirit of O'Casey's play and rings the rallying cry for all comic Dionysians: "Dost thou think because thou art virtuous there will be no more cakes and ale?"

Even in lesser-known examples of impious comedy there are significant precursors of O'Casey's farcical laughter. For example, writing about the medieval dramatist, the Wakefield Master, E. K. Chambers calls his most extravagant work, *The Second Shepherds' Play* (c. 1475), "an astonishing parody of the Nativity itself," where a stolen sheep is hidden under a peasant woman's skirt for a pretended pregnancy to fool the authorities with a spoof of the sacred birth. And Chambers adds: "There is no tenderness about him, and no impulse to devotion. He is a realist, even more than his contemporary York, a satirist with a hard outlook upon a hard age, in which wrong triumphs over right, but he is saved by an abundant sense of humour."[14] Chambers could well have been describing O'Casey (and his impious Cock) as the satirist with a hard and realistic outlook on a hard time when wrong was triumphing over right, but with the saving grace of an abundant humor.

Another striking parallel can be found in the modern revival of Sir David Lyndsay's *Ane Satyre of the Thrie Estates* (1540), which was directed at the Edinburgh Festival in 1948 by Tyrone Guthrie, who was later to direct the world premiere of O'Casey's next dark comedy, ***The Bishop's Bonfire,*** in Dublin in 1955. The following comment from a review of Guthrie's production of the Lyndsay play might easily have referred to O'Casey's *Cock,* which was a work-in-progress in 1948: "*The Three Estates* is half morality and half political satire and wholly a piece of angry, inspired knockabout. It preceded the Scottish Reformation by some twenty years and so angered the clergy that they ordered the manuscript to be burned by the public executioner."[15] O'Casey apparently knew the Lyndsay play and praised its irreverent comedy in his essay "The Power of Laughter" when he insisted that God must have a fine sense of humor, referring to "David Lyndsay, the Scottish poet of the sixteenth century, who saw

God near breaking his sides laughing at a rogue of an old woman who got past the indignant St. Peter by the use of her ready and tricky tongue."[16]

Since there was no likelihood of a Reformation in Catholic Ireland, ***Cock-a-doodle Dandy*** was simply ignored by the Irish for twenty-eight years. Nineteen years earlier, however, in 1930, an irate mob of nationalists performed the public executioner's function by burning reels of the film version of ***Juno and the Paycock*** in a Limerick street. A riot in the Abbey Theatre in 1926 against ***The Plough and the Stars*** had been provoked by Irish nationalists, some of whom still condemn it today, for presenting an ironic and tragicomic view of the 1916 Easter Rising. O'Casey was not against the Rising; he was for the innocent victims of military warfare. And by the 1940s he believed there were still many innocent victims—of psychological warfare and of religious and cultural repression. He felt that modern Ireland needed a reformation and liberalization, and he was almost alone in taking this heretical stand. Although he was roundly castigated for his "anti-Irish" attitude over the years and was warned by the Irish drama reviewers that his later plays were gross exaggerations, that he was "out of touch" with life in Ireland, at least two courageous writers, Sean O'Faolain and Frank O'Connor, agreed with him. They probably disagreed with him, and with each other, on all other matters, but they did agree about the dangerous conditions of religious repression and cultural deprivation. If they didn't incur the violent abuse that was hurled at O'Casey—they did receive some of it—probably it was because they protested but remained in Ireland, whereas he was living in England and writing, in the popular view, as an outsider, an exiled renegade who couldn't be believed or trusted.

In 1940 O'Faolain exposed the cultural wasteland of literary Dublin in terms that were much more invidious than anything O'Casey had said or would say in the future. After quoting Shaw's view of Dublin life in his Preface to *Immaturity*—"A certain flippant, futile derision and belittlement that confuses the noble and serious with the base and ludicrous seems to me peculiar to Dublin"— O'Faolain objected that "Shaw is too kind"; he went on to condemn the backbiting "rats" of Dublin in these merciless terms: "No sooner does any man attempt, or achieve, here, anything fine than the rats begin to emerge from the sewers, bringing with them a skunk-like stench of envy and hatred, worse than the drip of a broken drain."[17] These were the same destructive rats, he added, who opposed Yeats: "Yeats had to fight or ignore just the same kind of thing, and a great part of his hauteur, and aloofness, and self-imposed remoteness, was a defence against it and the mark of his contempt for it. The tragedy of Yeats was that he was too arrogant—he was driven into arrogance—ever to be accepted as a national poet. It was Dublin that drove him into that aloofness."[18] It could also be said that the envy and hatred of malicious Dublin had driven Joyce and O'Casey into arrogance, exile, and cunning. Joyce was not the national novelist, O'Casey was not the national dramatist.

Some years later in 1951 O'Faolain became involved in a bitter controversy with the bishop of Galway, who, sounding something like O'Casey's Father Domineer, had launched an attack against such "venomous and rancorous" periodicals as the *Irish Times* and *The Bell* for criticizing the clergy. The devout O'Faolain replied that he was neither venomous nor anti-Catholic if he sometimes felt duty bound to criticize repressive clerical behavior; that, according to His Lordship, clerical Ireland was not a country for writers, not even Catholic writers:

> Could a Graham Greene live here? A Mauriac, a Bernanos, a Peguy, a Mounier, a Pierre Emmanuel? Think of the things that Bernanos said about the Church in his Brazilian Diary! Which, by the way, was partially published in the Jesuit periodical *The Month*—in England. Can one imagine it appearing in *The Irish Monthly*? Or think of *Les Grandes Cimitières sous la lune!* The thing is patent. Writers need a generous atmosphere to grow in. His Lordship is certainly helping to create it! I'm afraid all His Lordship wants is abject compliance.[19]

Could an O'Casey live there? Clerical Ireland at mid-century was not ready for writers. In 1942 Frank O'Connor exposed the political and religious wasteland, the conditions of vulgarity, greed, and censorship that characterized Ireland in the 1930s and 40s when he wrote: "Every year that has passed, particularly since de Valera's rise to power, has strengthened the grip of the gombeen man, of the religious secret societies like the Knights of Columbanus, of the illiterate censorship. . . . The significant fact about it is that there is no idealistic opposition which would enable us to measure the extent of the damage."[20] O'Casey was there in 1949 measuring the damage with idealism and comedy in his new play, which clerical Ireland conveniently ignored. And it was precisely those three factors that O'Connor identified which stood out as the main enemies of the people in the *Cock*: the materialistic and exploiting local gombeen men, like Michael Marthraun and Sailor Mahan; these two also as members of the secret Knights of Columbanus and their terrorizing vigilantism, whipped up by Jansenist priests like Father Domineer and superstitious old frauds like Shanaar; and the Censorship of Publications Act, which not only banned important works of literature, many by Irish writers, but created a sterile atmosphere of cultural isolation throughout the country. And apart from the official censorship, every devout librarian and cautious bookseller in the land became an unofficial censor.

Why had O'Connor and O'Casey associated those three factors of economic, religious, and political pressure with de Valera's Ireland? Dev was a highly principled and honorable leader, but with his old-fashioned and myopic view of Ireland as an agricultural and Gaelic little island protected from the corrupt world outside, he did little to prevent those pressure groups from dominating and tyrannizing the country. He actually aided and encouraged them. As if to confirm O'Connor's accusation, in 1943 de Valera as Taoiseach (prime minister) made his famous speech to the Irish people on St. Patrick's Day, defining his pipe dream of an idyllic land of frugal and happy peasants:

> That Ireland which we dreamed of would be the home of a people who valued material wealth only as a basis of right living, of a people who were satisfied with frugal comfort and devoted their leisure to the things of the spirit; a land whose countryside would be bright with cosy homesteads, whose fields and villages would be joyous with the sounds of industry, the romping of sturdy children, the contests of athletic youths, the laughter of maidens; whose firesides would be the forums of the wisdom of serene old age.[21]

This well-meaning but unrealistic call for a retreat into an innocent and nonexistent past was unrelated to the practical problems of survival in modern Ireland, particularly peasant survival at a time when people were leaving the unproductive life on the land, when emigration to England and elsewhere was rising at an alarming rate. Ironically, only a year before Dev's speech, Patrick Kavanagh had published *The Great Hunger,* his great anti-pastoral poem which presents a withering portrait of the hardship and sterility of Irish peasant life, a tragic vision that makes a mockery of Dev's sentimental dream. Kavanagh's anti-heroic Maguire finds life too painfully frugal and without a single redeeming comfort. In a recent study of modern Ireland, Terence Brown makes this pointed observation: "Kavanagh's poem is an outraged cry of anger, an eloquently bleak riposte from the heart of the rural world to all those polemicists, writers and demagogues who in de Valera's Ireland sought to venerate the countryman's life from the study or political platform."[22] Throughout his career Kavanagh tried to balance his anger with a positive faith in an unrepressed Ireland, and more recently the poet Brendan Kennelly, in assessing Kavanagh's life, might have been describing the O'Casey of the *Cock* when he wrote: "Kavanagh is a believer. He believed in Kavanagh's God—not the Irish God of fear, mindless religiosity, money and respectability, but a gay, creative God who appreciates man's laughter and listens to the infinite echoes of 'love's terrible need.'"[23]

Again one hears O'Casey's warning about that Irish "fear," that "mindless religiosity," that worship of "money and respectability," all of them opposed by the Cock's spirit of gaiety, laughter, and love. Terence Brown attributes that overriding fear to constant pressure by Irish Vigilance Societies—the Dominican Order's Irish Vigilance Association and the Catholic Truth Society—which led to the passing of the Censorship of Publications Act of 1929: "It might reasonably have been feared that such bodies, in a country where the mass of the population was encouraged by the Church to observe a peculiarly repressive sexual code, would press for a censorship policy expressing not literary and aesthetic but strict Catholic moral values." It was this anti-literary and rigidly moralistic censorship that largely inspired O'Casey's play and that led to Sean O'Faolain's lament about "the difficulties of writing in a country where the policeman and the priest are in a perpetual glow of satisfaction."

In his own unique and comically fantastic beast fable, O'Casey tried to wipe that intimidating glow of satisfaction away from the policeman and priest in the symbolic village of Nyadnanave. It was appropriate that he dedicated his mythic extravaganza to that master of comic fantasy, James Stephens, "the jesting poet with a radiant star in's coxcomb." Unfortunately, the ailing Stephens, who was the same age as O'Casey, was to die in 1950, and O'Casey had to carry on without that radiant star for fourteen more years. . . .

> Red bird of March, begin to crow!
> Up with the neck and clap the wing,
> Red cock, and crow![24]

In the special introduction he wrote for a production of his play, O'Casey invoked the red cock from Yeats's play *The Dreaming of the Bones,* a cock that symbolizes the dawn of a dark day in Irish history. The day will eventually darken at the end of O'Casey's comedy, but first his own enchanted cock emerges as "the joyful, active spirit of life as it weaves a way through the Irish scene."[25] The merry and mischievous cock, who also has "the look of a cynical jester," is a dancing emblem of the liberated imagination, "the comic imagination as in *The Frogs;* the sad imagination as in *The Dream Play.*"[26] Then O'Casey expands the vital imagination beyond the plays of Aristophanes and Strindberg: "Blake thought imagination to be the soul; Shaw thought it to be the Holy Ghost, and, perhaps, they weren't far out; for it is the most beautiful part of life whether it be on its knees in prayer or gallivanting about with a girl."[27]

It is typical of O'Casey to relate the imagination finally to ordinary human activities—like those Joycean epiphanies—but since common needs like prayer and love have lost their vitality in the repressed atmosphere of Nyadnanave, the Dandy Cock must seize the day and lead the merry dance toward liberation. O'Casey had often shown an affinity for the common creatures of the beast-fable tradition, and he turned to them as his instinctive emblems of commitment, perhaps because they lacked the calculated deceit of human beings. In his first book of essays he had adopted the persona of a "flying wasp,"[28] who acts as an alert gadfly to sting the slumbering conscience of the theatrical world; and in his second collection, he became the "green crow,"[29] whose sharp caw-caw helps to keep the family of man and woman awake to the infinite possibilities of a better and richer life.

Now his human-sized comic Cock will dance and show the way, and its awakening "cock-a-doodle-doo" will rever-berate with uninhibited exuberance and launch the celebration of what might have been another brave new dawn; but that will change utterly at the end of the play. In his fantastic appearances the Cock suggests the bird-like Ariel of air and fire whose magical tricks served an exiled Prospero, and now an exiled O'Casey, as this bright little song announces the bold chanticleer in *The Tempest* (I, ii):

> Hark, hark! I hear
> The strain of the strutting chanticleer
> Cry, Cock-a-diddle-dow.

Then the cohorts of the Cock, led by Robin Adair, the trusty Messenger, with his beloved Marion the maid, add

implications of the folk tradition of the outlaw Robin Hood to the merriment, taking from the rich bog owner and giving to the poor peasants. Robin also assumes the mantle of a Robin Goodfellow or Puck, who with the Cock shows what fools these puritanical mortals are in Nyadnanave. Only the Cock and Robin and the three young women are touched by O'Casey's version of the Holy Ghost.

When the opposing forces, the frightened puritans, go forth to fight the shape-changing Cock, they identify him as a dangerous bird in various tongues: "Gallus" (Latin), "Le Coq" (French), "Kyleloch" (Gaelic). Old Shanaar, that "Latin-lustrous oul' cod of a prayer-blower," also tries to spout his "killakee" or bog-Latin at the "cockalorum," a slang term referring to any playfully strutting or cocky young fellow, but here invoked as an expression of abuse aimed at an evil spirit. O'Casey is relying upon the superstitious Irish tales in which devils are supposed to have taken possession of human beings and made them commit acts of violence, like those horrors fabricated by Shanaar, where only a priest like Father Domineer, armed with a barrage of bog-Latin, as well as bell, book, and candle, can exorcize the "demonological disturbances." There is something satirically reminiscent of Chaucer in these exorcizing episodes. Furthermore, the Oxford English Dictionary records some comic "cockalorum" references in eighteenth- and nineteenth-century folk literature that suggest that in the playful popular imagination, the cock can indeed be associated with a merry but harmless demon, as in the "Witches' Frolic," a singing and leapfrog dancing folk game with the lines,

> Now away! and away without delay,
> Hey Cockalorum, my Broomstick gay!

O'Casey's dancing Cock is devilishly clever as he leaps about as if he were riding a magic broomstick, and he knows the women are his allies. From the start, Marthraun is convinced that his young daughter Loreleen, recently returned from "pagan" England, is possessed by the devil, and so are the other women, due to their association with the "demon" Cock. If the women are truly possessed, however, it is by a natural desire for freedom and love, which are denied by the nay-saying Nyadnanaves. The three young women, Loreleen, Marthraun's second wife Lorna, and Marion, are in no mood to submit to threats, for they spring from an honorable tradition of strong-willed and sexually alert Irish women: the passionate Deirdre of Celtic mythology; the love-starved peasant girls of Brian Merriman's eighteenth-century *Midnight Court;* and in modern times, Joyce's earthy and sensual Molly Bloom and Yeats's sexually rebellious Crazy Jane. Nevertheless, in spite of the Cock's comic subversion in their behalf, the women of Nyadnanave will have to lose their fight in the end, because O'Casey refused to oversimplify or sweeten their unhappy fate. And, perhaps, because he believed that in 1949, Jansenist Ireland was not ready for liberated women—or men.

Led by the thou-shalt-not warnings of Father Domineer, the less-than-valiant Knights of Columbanus gain a hollow victory at the final curtain since they have been thoroughly discredited. The despairing women have gone away in symbolic exile, soon to be followed by Robin Adair; the paralyzed Julia has come back from Lourdes without a cure; Sailor Mahan has been rebuked for his compassion in trying to help the beaten Loreleen; Marthraun is left with the prospect of a lonely and barren life; and this narrow little world now belongs to a hard priest and his trio of grotesque crawthumpers, Shanaar and One-Eyed Larry and the Bellman. Absurdly, these three villainous clowns have won, though there is no longer any impulse toward laughter, even at their expense, in this place that "bites away some of the soul."

Wild laughter, however, consistently provides the sustaining energy of this dark comedy. First of all, the play is characterized by one of O'Casey's patented comic trademarks, the knockabout flytings between Marthraun and Mahan, those ridiculously fierce and cowardly lions, those devious word fighters, whose roar is reminiscent of those arguing "butties" Boyle and Joxer in *Juno,* Fluther and the Covey, the Covey and Uncle Peter in *The Plough;* and all of whom owe their boisterous clowning to the Plautine and Shakespearean braggart-warrior and parasite-slave duets. What O'Casey adds to this richly farcical tradition is a double view of his knock-about clowns, whose lively camaraderie is tainted but not quite destroyed by their blatant selfishness and culpability. They entertain us hugely even though we distrust them, particularly someone like the greedy and hypocritically pious Marthraun. The more attractive and salty Sailor Mahan may share in the greed, but he is wise enough to be skeptical about the crawthumpers, and his heart is in the right place during the mock battle between good and evil.

Even the outright comic villains are drawn with such strikingly colorful strokes that the religious quackery of old Shanaar, for example, creates a spectacle of hilarious confusion. The humbug-ridden Shanaar is not clever enough to be duplicitous, but with his supernatural tales, pseudo piety and exorcizing bog-Latin, he emerges as one of O'Casey's most entertainingly satirized clowns. A remarkable portrait of flam-boyant religious folly, his similarly exposed counterparts can readily be found in the works of Jonson, Molière and Dickens.

Continuing to stir the pot with comic chaos, O'Casey brings on the pompous and equivocating Porter, a bemused petty official who in various disguises appears in many of the pastoral comedies. With much verbal sidestepping he tries to explain the bullet holes in Marthraun's new tall hat, for the local police in their frantic hunt for the "demon" Cock are spraying the countryside with rifle shot. This accident calls for aid from the bumbling Dogberry of a Police Sergeant, who adds further confusion with his roundabout tale of how the hat was hit because "there was the demonizing Cock changin' himself into a silken glossified tall hat!"

In this burlesque treatment of the tall hat, O'Casey aimed his satire at the stilted masquerade of the new bourgeois Irish politicians. As the local councillor, manipulating entrepreneur, and Knight of Columbanus, Marthraun needs his formal hat for an audience with the tall-hatted president of Ireland. Himself a proud wearer of the workingman's cloth cap, O'Casey, paraphrasing Yeats in a satiric way, says "the terrible beauty of the tall-hat is born to Ireland."[30] He sees men like Marthraun, the Catholic bourgeois capitalist, as the new power in the country—the "devalerian" aristocracy of the tall hat. He echoes Joyce's warning that "Christ and Caesar are hand in glove" when he notes the alliance between the "purple biretta" of the Church and the "tall-hat" of the politicians: "A Terrible Beauty Is Borneo."

To mock this alliance of church and state, and to ridicule the puritanical apes of Nyadnanave who represent it, the Cock resorts to magic tricks, taking the shape of a tall hat or a beautiful woman. He makes whiskey bottles go dry or glow red hot; he imitates cuckoos and corncrakes; he makes chairs and flagpoles and houses collapse; he creates a powerful wind that blows off men's trousers; he brings down thunder and lightning; he casts all sorts of mischievous spells on holy objects, and on the men who oppose the vital way of life he represents. These merry pranks provoke a series of counterattacks, abetted by the absurd Shanaar and the petty villainy of One-Eyed Larry and the Bellman, those comic toadies of Father Domineer.

Except for the ailing Julia, Father Domineer is the only non-comic character in the play. As a one-dimensional symbol of authority and repression, he is the most transparent and least interesting person in Nyadnanave. A cardboard figure, there is no complexity or consciousness of cruelty in him, and his enraged killing of the lorry driver at the end of the second scene seems too sudden, too extreme. O'Casey apparently created him out of anger rather than artistry. Although he insisted that he had based Domineer on what he had read about an actual case of a parish priest in an Irish town who had struck and accidentally killed a man,[31] a newspaper account was in this instance not an adequate source for a successful characterization.

When Robert Lewis was originally planning to produce the play in 1950, he told O'Casey that the scene of the killing "bothered" him and should be softened: ". . . it is not necessary to have Domineer actually strike the lorry driver. He can instead, in his anger viciously grab the driver by the arm and pull him to him in the scuffle, the driver can lose his foothold and fall to the ground, striking his head severely and the rest follow precisely as you have written it."[32] O'Casey replied that he had written the scene exactly as it had occurred in life, but he agreed with Lewis's suggestion that it should be played "less brutally."[33]

When Tomas MacAnna finally produced the play at the Abbey Theatre in 1977, he decided to omit the episode of the killing entirely, not only because it was too brutal but because he believed "it didn't have anything to do with the rest of the play."[34] Since it was an extremely rare and untypical occurrence, Ireland, with some justification, was not ready to see a priest kill a man, even accidentally, on an Irish stage. This objection should be understandable in a country where several centuries earlier priests had been forbidden by British authorities to say Mass in public, had been hounded and driven underground, and in some instances had been brutally slain. Furthermore, even without the killing, Father Domineer condemns himself sufficiently by his savage treatment of Loreleen; his virulent attacks against innocent dancing and all forms of joy and free expression; his ruthless censorship and the destruction of a copy of Joyce's *Ulysses* and a book about Voltaire; and finally by his overall severe and unchristian behavior.

Nevertheless, O'Casey did have another valid target in mind, in Father Domineer's hysterical exorcism activities in the third scene, when he resorts to bell, book, and candle, bog-Latin, and vindictive ranting to purge the house of its evil influences. After Frank Carney's *The Righteous Are Bold* opened at the Abbey Theatre on 29 July 1946 and ran to packed houses for an unprecedented sixteen weeks, O'Casey, along with only a few enlightened reviewers in *The Bell* and the *Irish Times,* felt a dangerous concession had been made to sensational religiosity, which had corrupted the National Theatre and would thereafter make it difficult to attract audiences to good plays. O'Casey often mentioned this unfortunate situation in his letters. Carney's play is about a young Irish girl who is possessed by devils, which cause her to have mad fits and smash holy statues, until the evil spirits are exorcized by a priest. O'Casey called it bad religion as well as bad drama, "a travesty of the Catholic Faith and little more than 'pietistic hokum.'"[35] It should be apparent, therefore, that he intended the chaotic exorcism episode in the third scene to be a scathing parody of Carney's play and the Irish susceptibility for such religious claptrap.[36]

In the years ahead O'Casey must have felt the need to dramatize the sharp distinction between what he believed to be the genuine practice of the Catholic faith and the misleading Jansenist version fostered by some of the Irish clergy, for he created two attractive and noble young priests in his last two full-length plays, **The Bishop's Bonfire** (1955) and **The Drums of Father Ned** (1960). Again the setting is rural Ireland and in the first play, Father Boheroe, the local curate, urges his parishoners to practice their faith with abiding love and tolerance; much to the displeasure of his stiff-necked superior, the canon, he tells them that "merriment may be a way of worship." It is the O'Casey credo. Father Ned never appears in **The Drums,** but as its guiding spirit he is often heard off-stage beating his drum for a festival to celebrate the love of God and man and woman in one of O'Casey's brightest and happiest comedies.

Ironically and predictably, perhaps, unhappy situations arose around both plays. When Tyrone Guthrie directed Cyril Cusack's world premiere production of **The Bishop's Bonfire** in Dublin in 1955, the visiting London critics were on the whole pleased by what they saw, but the Dublin critics were unamused. As a typical example, the review in de Valera's *Irish Press* called it "a grievous disappointment," protesting that O'Casey was "completely out of touch with modern Irish life and thought."[37] Thereafter, however, as a curious illustration of how life sometimes illustrates art, Irish politicans and priests continued the dispute as if they were determined to act like characters in an O'Casey play and thereby prove how closely he really was in touch with Irish life.

First, the Irish Customs authorities, with an obvious prod from their political bosses but without any explanation, mysteriously banned O'Casey's *Green Crow* in 1956, the collection of essays and stories in which, among many other divertisements, he defended himself from attack by his Irish critics. After a year of this "unofficial" censorship, again without any explanation, the book was finally released for sale in Ireland in 1957. Then, as if not wanting to be left out of the censor-O'Casey-shenanigans, in 1958 the archbishop of Dublin played his role by "unofficially" banning **The Drums of Father Ned.** Although the play had been accepted for the Dublin Theatre Festival, along with a dramatization of Joyce's *Ulysses* and three mime plays by Samuel Beckett, the archbishop, who had of course not read O'Casey's light-hearted and pro-clerical comedy, refused to open the Festival with the traditional Mass. It was His Lordship's way of saying, indirectly, that a play by O'Casey was not acceptable. Frightened by this unmistakable sign of displeasure in a high place, all interested parties promptly found reasons for retiring from the theatre project. In devious ways the O'Casey and Joyce plays were dropped, and Beckett withdrew his plays in protest. It seemed as if Ireland were determined to act out an epilogue on censorship for **Cock-a-doodle Dandy.**

In 1949 O'Casey's play had predicted that Ireland was becoming emotionally and culturally repressed as a result of clerical and political domination. Almost thirty years later, in 1978, John Healy, the respected columnist and political reporter of the *Irish Times,* looking back over modern Irish history, indicated how prophetic O'Casey had been: "The 50s were not a great time in Dublin. It was the era when 'Catholic Mother of Ten' set the moral tone of the country. We blacklisted international performers on the say so of Tail Gunner Joe McCarthy—we picketed Eastern bloc footballers and Catholicism nearly choked the life out of Christianity."[38]

O'Casey's quarrel with the country he loved came down to this crucial point: he believed that Irish "Catholicism [had] nearly choked the life out of Christianity." With merry and dark laughter, he had dramatized precisely this tragic possibility in the **Cock.** He concluded his essay on laughter with this appropriate prayer:

> Let us pray: Oh, Lord, give us a sense of humor with courage to manifest it forth, so that we may laugh to shame the pomps, the vanities, the sense of self-importance of the Big Fellows that the world sometimes sends among us, and who try to take our peace away. Amen.[39]

Notes

1. Sean O'Casey, "The Power of Laughter: Weapon Against Evil," in *The Green Crow* (New York: Braziller, 1956), 227. Originally published in *Saturday Night* (Toronto) [Vol. 69, No.1], 3 October 1953.

2. Ibid., 226.

3. See Marion's speech, scene III, p. 115.

4. W. B. Yeats, *The Poems: A New Edition,* ed. Richard J. Finneran (New York: Macmillan, 1983), 150.

5. *The Critical Writings of James Joyce,* ed. Ellsworth Mason and Richard Ellmann (London: Faber and Faber, 1959), 243.

6. Sean O'Casey, *Collected Plays,* Vol. I (London: Macmillan, 1949), 31.

7. James Joyce, *A Portrait,* 246-47.

8. Sean O'Casey, *Inishfallen, Fare Thee Well* (New York: Macmillan, 1949), 370. See also Yeats's "The Collar-bone of a Hare," *The Poems,* 136.

9. W. B. Yeats, *The Poems,* 205.

10. W. B. Yeats, *On the Boiler* (1939), in *Selected Prose* (London: Macmillan, 1964), 261.

11. Herbert Gorman, *James Joyce* (London: John Lane, The Bodley Head, 1941), 144.

12. *Letters* I (New York: Macmillan, 1975), 433.

13. *The Green Crow,* 227.

14. E. K. Chambers, "Medieval Drama," *English Literature at the Close of the Middle Ages* (New York: Oxford University Press, 1945), 37.

15. *The Times* (London), 26 August 1948.

16. *The Green Crow,* 230.

17. Sean O'Faolain, *An Irish Journey* (London: Longmans, Green, 1940), 299.

18. Ibid., 299.

19. Sean O'Faolain, "The Bishop of Galway and 'The Bell,'" *The Bell,* September 1951.

20. Frank O'Connor, "The Future of Irish Literature," *Horizon,* January 1942.

21. *Irish Press,* 18 March 1943.

22. Terence Brown, *Ireland: A Social and Cultural History, 1922-79* (London: Fontana, 1981), 187.

23. Brendan Kennelly, "Patrick's Pilgrimage," *Irish Times,* 27 January 1979.

24. Sean O'Casey, "Cockadoodle Doo" (1958), in *Blasts and Benedictions,* ed. Ronald Ayling (London: Macmillan, 1967), 144. Probably working from memory, O'Casey used a slight variation of these lines from Yeats's *Dreaming of the Bones* (1919), *Collected Plays* (New York: Macmillan, 1953), 279. The article "Cockadoodle Doo" was first published as "O'Casey's Credo" in the *New York Times,* 9 November 1958, intended as an introduction to the New York premiere of the *Cock* in an off-Broadway production at the Carnegie Hall Playhouse on 12 November 1958, directed by Philip Burton.

25. Ibid., 144.

26. Ibid., 143.

27. Ibid., 143.

28. Sean O'Casey, *The Flying Wasp* (London: Macmillan, 1937) "A Laughing Look-over of What Has Been Said About the Things of the Theatre By the English Dramatic Critics, With Many Merry and Amusing Comments Thereon, With Some Shrewd Remarks By the Author on the Wise, Delicious, and Dignified Tendencies in the Theatre of Today."

29. Sean O'Casey, *The Green Crow* (1956), invokes the spirit of Chaucer's "The Parliament of Foules" and adds: "Some Latin writer once said, 'If a crow would feed in quiet, it would have more meat.' A thing this Green Crow could never do: it had always, and has still, to speak and speak while it seeks and finds its food, and so has had less meat than it might have had if only it had kept its big beak shut." (Foreword, xiv)

30. See the chapter "A Terrible Beauty is Borneo," in *Inishfallen,* 200-222.

31. For an account of the killing, see *Letters* II, 504.

32. Ibid., 728.

33. Ibid., 730.

34. MacAnna made this comment in 1977 to Robert Lowery, editor of the *Irish Literary Supplement.* MacAnna's production of the play opened at the Abbey Theatre on 11 August 1977.

35. *Letters* II, 414, 514.

36. For an illuminating discussion of the connection between the Carney and O'Casey plays, see Christopher Murray's "Two More Allusions in *Cock-a-doodle Dandy,*" *Sean O'Casey Review* 4 (Fall 1977).

37. O'Casey quotes this passage in his defense of his play, "Bonfire under a Black Sun," in *The Green Crow,* 131.

38. John Healy, "News Focus," *Irish Times,* 28 June 1978.

39. *The Green Crow,* 232.

FURTHER READING

Ayling, Robert. "Sean O'Casey and the Abbey Theatre, Dublin." In *Sean O'Casey: Centenary Essays,* edited by David Krause and Robert G. Lowery, pp. 13-40. Gerrards Cross, England: Colin Smythe, 1980.

   Attributes the enthusiastic popular reception of O'Casey's early plays to his artistic collaboration with the directorate at the Abbey Theatre.

———. "'Two Words for Women': A Reassessment of O'Casey's Heroines." In *Woman in Irish Legend, Life and Literature,* edited by S. F. Gallagher, pp. 91-114. Gerrards Cross, England: Colin Smythe, 1983.

Reviews the critical tradition with respect to O'Casey's treatment of women in his work, whom he portrays as life-enhancing agents who bear his anti-war message.

Benstock, Bernard. "The O'Casey Touch." In *Sean O'Casey,* pp. 89-121. Lewisburg, PA: Bucknell University Press, 1970.

Analyzes various dramatic techniques and aspects of stagecraft in O'Casey's later plays, beginning with *The Silver Tassie.*

———. *Paycocks and Others: Sean O'Casey's World.* New York: Harper and Row, 1976, 318 p.

Identifies general traits of typical characters that populate O'Casey's plays.

Greaves, C. Desmond. *Sean O'Casey, Politics & Art.* London: Lawrence and Wishart, 1979, 206 p.

Investigates the evolution of O'Casey's politics in terms of corresponding changes in his attitudes about dramatic art.

Hamburger, Miak. "Anti-Illusionism and the Use of Song in the Early Plays of Sean O'Casey." In *O'Casey Annual No. 2,* edited by Robert G. Lowery, pp. 3-26. London: Macmillan, 1983.

Examines the role of songs as formal devices that generate a distancing effect and compromise conventional dramatic unity.

Höhne, Horst. "Brecht vs. O'Casey, or Brecht & O'Casey?" In *O'Casey Annual No. 3,* edited by Robert G. Lowery, pp. 1-32. London: Macmillan, 1984.

Contrasts the dramatic technique and themes of two plays by Brecht with those of *Purple Dust* and *Red Roses for Me,* investigating the political and artistic implications of each play.

Hogan, Robert. "The Experiments of Sean O'Casey." In *The Experiments of Sean O'Casey,* pp. 3-15. New York: St. Martin's Press, 1960.

Refutes the mainstream opinion that O'Casey's dramatic technique gradually declined by analyzing the evolution of the perceived formlessness of the plays that followed *Cock-a-Doodle Dandy.*

———. "In Sean O'Casey's 'Golden Days.'" *Dublin Magazine* V, Nos. 3-4 (Autumn/Winter 1966): 80-93.

Traces the influence of sixteenth- and seventeenth-century pastoral dramatic conventions on O'Casey's dramaturgy, identifying this tradition as the unifying device in his later plays.

———. "O'Casey's Dramatic Apprenticeship." *Modern Drama* 4, No. 3 (December 1961): 243-53.

Discusses the dramatic methods of *Kathleen Listens In* and *Nannies Night Out* as indications of O'Casey's tendencies toward the fantastic in his mature productions.

Holladay, William "Song as Aesthetic Manipulation in Sean O'Casey's Dublin Trilogy." In *From the Bard to Broadway,* pp. 125-38. Lanham, MD: University Press America, 1987.

Demonstrates that O'Casey manipulates the audience's emotional response to the plot conflicts of the Dublin trilogy by contrasting the comic and heroic codes found in popular songs of contemporary melodrama.

Jones, Nesta, compiler. *File on O'Casey.* London: Methuen, 1987, 96 p.

Primary and secondary bibliographies, including plot summaries, initial reviews and major revivals, and samples of critical responses to each play.

Kaufman, Michael W. "O'Casey's Structural Designs in *Juno and the Paycock.*" *Quarterly Journal of Speech* 58, No. 2 (April 1972): 191-98.

Assesses the dramatic significance of the concluding scenes in *Juno* by focusing on the play's general thematic dialectic between reality and illusion.

Kleiman, Carol. "O'Casey's 'Homemade' Expressionism: His Debt to Toller." In *Sean O'Casey's Bridge of Vision: Four Essays on Structure and Perspective.* Toronto: University of Toronto Press, 1982.

Traces the influence of German Expressionist dramatist Toller in O'Casey's expressionist techniques, emphasizing the latter's difference in terms of his sympathies with the absurd.

Krause, David. "The Ironic Victory of Defeat in Irish Comedy." In *O'Casey Annual No. 1,* edited by Robert G. Lowery, pp. 33-63. London: Macmillan, 1982.

Draws parallels between the dramatic representations of the comedic theme in the plays of Synge, Yeats, Shaw, and O'Casey.

———. "Master of Knockabout: The Work Revisited." In *Sean O'Casey, the Man and his Work,* enlarged, pp. 302-25. New York: Macmillan Publishing, 1975.

Evaluates O'Casey's dramaturgy in terms of the antic comedy tradition of modern drama.

———. "The Paradox of Ideological Formalism: Art vs. Ideology." *Massachusetts Review* XXVIII, No. 3 (Autumn 1987): 516- 24.

Comments on the tension between literary and political impulses within the context of O'Casey's dramatic aesthetics and artistic ideology.

———. "The Risen O'Casey: Some Marxist and Irish Ironies." In *O'Casey Annual No. 3,* edited by Robert G. Lowery, pp. 134-68. London: Macmillan, 1984.

Reviews selected Marxist interpretations of O'Casey's plays to demonstrate differences between his artistic representation of Irish laborers and the proletariat as depicted in mainline communist ideology.

Lowery, Robert G. *A Whirlwind in Dublin, The Plough and the Stars Riots.* Westport, CT: Greenwood Press, 1984, 121 p.

Describes historical circumstances surrounding the riots as documented in selected journal and newspaper accounts as well as letters and memoirs of the main participants, beginning with an account of the dire financial situation of the Abbey Theatre before O'Casey arrived.

Malone, Maureen. "The Last Word." In *The Plays of Sean O'Casey,* pp. 150-60. Carbondale: Southern Illinois University Press, 1970.

Outlines general themes of O'Casey's last plays, beginning with *Behind the Green Curtains.*

Maroldo, William J. "Insurrection as Enthymeme in O'Casey's Dublin Trilogy." In *O'Casey Annual No. 2,* edited by Robert G. Lowery, pp. 88-113. London: Macmillan, 1983.

Discusses the rhetorical characteristics and the dramatic implications of "rebellion" as the fundamental premise informing the Dublin trilogy.

Mikhail, E. H. and John O'Riordan, eds. *The Sting and the Twinkle: Conversations with Sean O'Casey.* London: Macmillan, 1974, 184 p.

Contains mostly previously published interviews with O'Casey as well as personal and professional recollections of the dramatist, dating mainly from 1925 to 1964.

Mitchell, Jack. *The Essential O'Casey: A Study of Twelve Major Plays of Sean O'Casey.* New York: International Publishers, 1980, 346 p.

Assesses O'Casey's dramatic artistry and technique through Marxist readings of twelve plays.

Ó hAodha, Micheál. *The O'Casey Enigma.* Dublin: Mercier Press, 1980, 126 p.

Reassesses the significance of O'Casey's dramatic achievement in a socialist context.

O'Riordan, John. *A Guide to O'Casey's Plays, from the Plough to the Stars.* London: Macmillan, 419 p.

Comprehensive, chronological study of O'Casey's dramatic works, highlighting each play's theoretical orientation, plot and character summaries, staging issues, production history, and critical reception.

Rollins, Ronald G. "Dramatic Symbolism in Sean O'Casey's Dublin Trilogy." *Philological Papers* 15, No. 12 (June 1966): 49-58.

Explains the symbolic significance of such theatrical devices as costumes, props, and lighting in the Dublin trilogy.

———. "Form and Content in Sean O'Casey's Dublin Trilogy" *Modern Drama* 8, No. 1 (February 1986): 419-425.

Correlates the thematic violence of the Dublin trilogy with elements of naturalistic dramaturgy.

———. "Pervasive Patterns in *The Silver Tassie.*" *Elre-Ireland* VI, No. 4 (Winter 1971): 29-37.

Locates the structural unity of the play in its parallel patterns, ironic reversals, repetitive rhythms, and serial juxtapositions.

———. *Sean O'Casey's Drama: Verisimilitude and Vision.* University: University of Alabama Press, 1979, 139 p.

Studies mythopoetical influences on the dramatic structure and style of selected plays, including *The Plow and the Stars*, *The Silver Tassie*, *Within the Gates*, *Purple Dust*, *Cock-a-Doodle Dandy*, and *The Drums of Father Ned.*

Schrank, Bernice. "Anatomizing an Insurrection: Sean O'Casey's *The Plough and the Stars.*" *Modern Drama* XXIX, No. 2 (June 1986): 216-28.

Explores the ways by which the characters' attitudes toward history and death contribute to the radical social disintegration in the play, underscoring its essentially pessimistic outlook.

———. "Between Anarchy and Incarceration: The Struggle for Freedom in Sean O'Casey's *The Plough and the Stars.*" *Literatur in Wissenschaft und Unterricht* XVIII, No. 3 (1985): 213-38.

Examines O'Casey's use of windows and doors as well as a games motif in *The Plough and the Stars* to illustrate a dialectical relation between personal and political concerns.

———. *Sean O'Casey, A Research and Production Sourcebook.* Westport, CT: Greenwood Press, 1996, 298 p.

Comprehensive annotated primary and secondary bibliography, including play synopses, overviews of critical reactions to specific stagings and texts, production histories with cast lists, and archival sources.

———. "'You needn't say no more': Language and the Problems of Communication in Sean O'Casey's *The Shadow of a Gunman.*" *Irish University Review* 8, No. 1 (Spring 1978): 23-38.

Analyzes various uses of language that contribute to the play's chaotic vision.

Scrimgeour, James R. *Sean O'Casey.* Boston: Twayne Publishers, 1978, 186 p.

Biographical critical analysis of O'Casey's autobiographies and major plays, concentrating on character development techniques.

Styan, J. L. "Conflicts in Dublin: the Irish Dramatic Movement." In *Modern Drama in Theory and Practice, Volume 1, Realism and Naturalism,* pp. 91-109. Cambridge: Cambridge University Press, 1981.

Chronicles the contributions of the Irish Dramatic Movement to theatrical naturalism in terms of contemporary production values and aesthetic principles, using *The Plough and the Stars* and Synge's *Playboy of the Western World* as exemplars.

————. "Expressionism in Ireland: The Later O'Casey." In *Modern Drama in Theory and Practice, Volume 111, Expressionism and Epic Theatre,* pp. 121-28. Cambridge: Cambridge University Press, 1981.

> Chronicles O'Casey's expressionistic experiments in *The Silver Tassie* and other "colored" plays with respect to contemporary production values and aesthetic principles.

Waters, Maureen "The Paycocks of Sean O'Casey." In *The Comic Irishman,* pp. 149-61. Albany: State University of New York Press, 1984.

> Investigates O'Casey's satiric use of Irish stereotypes that motivate his plays.

Watt, Stephen. "O'Casey's Negotiations with the Popular." In *Joyce, O'Casey, and the Irish Popular Theater,* pp. 143-87. Syracuse, NY: Syracuse University Press, 1991.

> Examines the formal and allusive means O'Casey used in his plays to demythologize prevalent attitudes in Irish popular culture, emphasizing the ideological significance of his covert subversion of Irish stereotypes.

Williams, Raymond. "Sean O'Casey." In *Drama from Ibsen to Brecht,* pp. 147-53. London: Chatto and Windus, 1968.

> Provides a thematic overview of O'Casey's plays in relation to his evolving dramatic viewpoint.

Additional coverage of O'Casey's life and career is contained in the following sources published by the Gale Group: *Concise Dictionary of British Literary Biography, 1914-1945*; *Contemporary Literary Criticism,* Vols. 1, 5, 9, 11, 15, 88; *DISCovering Authors: British*; *DISCovering Authors: Canadian*; *DISCovering Authors: Dramatist Module, Most-Studied Authors Module*; *Dictionary of Literary Biography,* Vols. 10; and *Major 20th-Century Writers.*

Friedrich Schiller
1759-1805

German dramatist, poet, historian, philosopher, and essayist.

INTRODUCTION

One of the towering figures in German literature, Schiller was a universal genius whose dramatic writings, poetry, philosophy, and historical works give eloquent voice to the themes of justice and human freedom. His early plays, which reflect his affinity with the *Sturm und Drang* movement, feature the passionate struggles of revolutionaries as they seek to overthrow corruption and tyranny. The later works, characterized by more realistic and Classical subjects and forms, move from the external events that shape the choices and actions of his characters to their inner struggles, as the playwright shows how humans may rise above corruption and attain dignity through nonviolent means. As a dramatist of ideas, Schiller is concerned, especially in his later plays, to put on stage those notions which he believes can be morally instructive to his audience. He portrays, especially in his later plays, characters who, after deliberation and sometimes anguish, overcome their desires to make moral choices based on their reason. However, he does this not merely with polemics but appeals to the senses and emotions of his audience, portraying with high drama the tragic conflict that is central to human experience. Although Schiller is no longer widely read in the English-speaking world, he is revered as a national treasure in Germany, and is regarded, along with his contemporary Johann Wolfgang von Goethe, as one of the pillars of German literary achievement.

BIOGRAPHICAL INFORMATION

Schiller was born in Marbach, Württemberg, the son of an officer and surgeon in the army of the Duke Karl Eugen. At age seven he was enrolled in the Latin School at Ludwigsburg, to prepare for a career in the clergy. However, at age fourteen, at the insistence of the Duke, Schiller was placed in the elite Karlsschule, a military academy, where he would eventually study medicine. Schiller distinguished himself in his technical studies at the rigidly disciplined academy, but found the environment oppressive. He secretly studied literature, including the works of William Shakespeare, and clandestinely began writing his first play. After graduating in 1780, he was assigned a post as a military surgeon in Stuttgart. The following year he completed and self-published his first play, *Die Räuber,* which drew the attention of Wolfgang von Delberg, direc-

tor of the Mannheim National Theater. After having to rewrite portions of the manuscript to pass the censors, Schiller saw his work performed at Mannheim to enthusiastic audiences. However, the play caused considerable controversy because of its revolutionary tone and ecstatic poetry, and the Duke forbade his officer to publish anything further except medical research. Schiller thereupon fled Stuttgart and moved to Mannheim, where he lived for a time on the aid of friends. His health had always been poor, and it was further undermined by the the stress of his exile and his financial difficulties.

In Mannheim, he entered into a contract with von Delberg to write plays for the theater, but it was an uneasy relationship and Schiller found himself continuing to live off the kindness friends and was constantly in debt. His second play, *Die Verschwörung des Fiesko zu Genua* received only lukewarm reviews, but the production of *Kabale und Liebe* in 1784 was a resounding success, and established the young writer as one of the masters of German drama. In 1785 Schiller broke with von Dalberg and moved to Leipzig on the invitation of his friend Christian Gottfried

Köner. In Leipzig he edited the theatrical magazine *Die Rheinische Thalia,* published poetry, and completed his third play, *Don Karlos.*

For the next ten years Schiller wrote no plays, concentrating instead on historial and philosophical works. In 1787 he moved to Weimar, where he would meet the great poet and dramatist Johann Wolfgang von Goethe; the two writers formed a strong personal friendship and literary and intellectual alliance that lasted until Schiller's death. It was at Goethe's recommendation that Schiller was appointed Professor of History at the University of Jena in 1789. Having gained some measure of financial security, in 1790 he married Charlotte von Lengefeld. While at the university he devoted much time to studying philosophy, particularly the writings of the German idealist Immanuel Kant. He published prodigiously at this time, producing works of history and major aesthetic treatises based on Kant's philosophy.

1798 marked the beginning of Schiller's second great period of dramatic composition. In 1799 he completed his *Wallenstein* trilogy, which was staged by Goethe the following year. Schiller's health by this time was in serious decline, most likely due to tuberculosis. But he continued to write and produce plays at the rate of one or more per year: from 1800 to 1804 he wrote and saw the production of *Maria Stuart, Die Jungfrau von Orleans, Die Braut von Messina,* and *Wilhelm Tell.* He was working on another play, *Demetrius,* when he died of pneumonia in 1805.

MAJOR WORKS

Schiller's eleven major dramatic works span two distinct literary periods. His three earliest plays belong to the period of *Sturm und Drang,* the earliest dramatic manifestation of the romantic movement that was to sweep Europe. *Die Räuber,* which established his reputation, is a bombastic, sweeping tale of a rebel who, with his band of thieves, attempts to overthrow a corrupt political order. His second play, *Fiesko,* which deals with a struggle for power in the republic of Genoa, also involves a revolution, but this time the revolutionary becomes more corrupt than the system he endeavors to destroy. In *Kabale und Liebe,* a story of a pair of lovers who are forced apart because of social barriers, a despotic court not only thwarts romance but forces young German recruits to be sent to fight in America on behalf of the English. All these early plays feature passionate struggles of heroes who pursue freedom and justice in hypocritical societies, but also point out that reaction against tyranny can itself assume the form of oppression.

Don Karlos is seen by most critics as a "transitional" play. It is the first play written in verse, and in many ways anticipates the style of Schiller's later Classical works, but has as its theme the plea for freedom that marks his early efforts. The play, set in sixteenth-century Spain, about the attempt of the heir apparent Don Carlos to assume responsibilty and power from his father, treats political themes with considerable complexity and introduces philosophical ideas that were to figure prominently in the later dramas.

Schiller's later, Classical, plays were written after his ten-year immersion in historical and philosophical study, and they embody his newly developed aesthethic theories— including the idea that tragedy should be an instrument for humans' moral perfection. In his writings on aesthetics, Schiller distinguishes between "naive" works of art, which are the outpourings of genius, and "sentimental" works, which have goals. A naive work of art is moral, while a sentimental work has a moral. His particular brand of classicism, he claimed, was concerned with universal balance, and in his plays he depicts a movement toward this harmony as the soul triumphs over desire. In the trilogy of plays, *Wallensteins Lager, Die Piccolomini,* and *Wallensteins Tod,* which depict the downfall of a general suspected of treason during a brief period during the Thirty Years' War, the sentimental qualities of the title character are contrasted to the naive qualities of the young officer who idolizes him. The plays also marks a shift in Schiller's socio-political ideas, as he rejects the notion that freedom can be attained through revolution and seeks to show rather how individual and spiritual freedom may be achieved through moral self-discovery.

The theme of inner victory through moral regeneration is played out in the plays composed during Schiller's last years. In *Maria Stuart* and *Die Jungfrau von Orleans,* in which Schiller depicts the lives of the historical figures Mary, Queen of Scots and Joan of Arc, we see how each heroine rises above the corruption of Church and government to attain her own sense of moral victory and spiritual freedom. *Die Braut von Messina,* which is constructed along the lines of a Greek tragedy and concerns two brothers who are fated to fall in love with their sister, explores the tension between predestination and free will. Schiller's last finished work, *Wilhelm Tell,* also concerns the moral autonomy of the main character, the legendary Swiss hero who shoots an apple from his own son's head, but recalls too the theme of revolution that was a concern in the earlier dramas.

CRITICAL RECEPTION

Schiller's reputation as a boldly original thinker and artist was established with his controversial but highly successful first play, *Die Räuber.* By the age of twenty-four, with the production of *Kabale und Liebe,* he was recognized as one of the great masters of German drama. During his lifetime he was lauded as one of the figures who raised the stature of German literature, which hitherto had been overshadowed by the achievements of artists in England, France, and Italy. His plays were often met with standing ovations, and audiences and critics alike thrilled at his ability to portray with immediacy and complexity the sufferings and triumph of the human spirit. After his death he became a national icon, with monuments erected in his honor, and his works were and continue to be part of the

German literary curriculum. Thinkers such as Carl Gustav Jung, Friederich Nietzche, Friederich Hegel, and Karl Marx were indebted to the ideas he set forth in this philosophical and aesthetical works. The attention paid to his works by German literary critics can be compared to that accorded to Shakespeare in the English-speaking world. In the nineteenth century, British critics such as Thomas Carlyle and the American poet William Cullen Bryant admired his taste and feeling and his concern for human freedom. Schiller's name is not a familiar one among English-speaking readers today, however, and he does not enjoy the same recognition as does his great contemporary Goethe, for example. Contemporary critics have suggested that Schiller's dramas are less accessible to modern readers due to their flamboyant, sometimes bombastic language. However, most agree that there are to be found in the plays themes and concerns—political and individual freedom, the complexity of human endeavor, the struggle between the rational and sensual aspects of the self—that are of remarkably contemporary concern. Twentieth-century commentators writing in English tend to stress the philosophical underpinnings of the plays; the political themes; the impact of Schiller's historical study on his dramatic practice; the shift in concern in the later plays from external to internal events; and the dramas' rootedness in human life.

PRINCIPAL WORKS

Plays

Die Raüber: Ein Schauspiel [*The Robbers*] 1781

Die Verschwörung des Fiesko zu Genua: Ein republikanisches Trauerspiel [*Fiesco; or, The Genoese Conspiracy*] 1783

Kabale und Liebe: Ein bügerliches Trauerspiel in fünf Aufzügen [*Intrigue and Love: A Tragedy in Five Acts*] 1784

Don Karlos, Infant von Spanien [*Don Carlos, Infant of Spain*] 1798

Wallensteins Lager [*The Camp of Wallenstein*] 1800

Die Piccolomini [*The Piccolominis*] 1800

Wallensteins Tod [*The Death of Wallenstein*] 1800

Maria Stuart: Ein Trauerspiel [*Mary Stuart: A Tragedy*] 1801

Die Jungfrau von Orleans: Ein romantische Tragödie [*The Maid of Orleans: A Romantic Tragedy*] 1802

Die Braut von Messina, oder feindlichen Brüder: Ein Trauerspiel mit Chören [*The Bride of Messina*] 1803

Wilhelm Tell: Ein Schuspiel [*William Tell*] 1804

Demetrius (fragment) 1815

Other Major Works

Anthologie auf das Jahr 1782 (poetry) 1782

An die Freude ein Rundgesang für freye Männer. Mit Muzik (poetry) 1786

Der Geisterseher: Eine interessante Geschichte aus den Papieren des Grafen von O*** herausgegeben aus Herrn Schillers Thalia [*The Ghost-Seer*] (essay) 1788

Geschichte des Abfalls des vereinigten Niederlande von der Spanischen Regierung: Erster Theil enthaltend die Geschichte der Rebellionen bis zur Utrechtischen Verbindung [*History of the Defection of the United Netherlands from the Spanish Empire*] 1788

Historischer Calender für das Jahr 1791-1793: Geschichte des Dreißigjärhigen Kriegs [*History of the Thirty Years' War*] 1791

Über Naive Und Sentimentalische Dichtung [*On Naive and Sentimental Poetry*] (essays)

Friedrich v. Schiller Sämtliche Werke, 12 vols. [*Collected Works*] (drama, poetry, essays) 1812

The Philosophical And Aesthetic Letters And Essays 1845

AUTHOR COMMENTARY

Friedrich Schiller (lecture date 1784)

SOURCE: "The Stage Considered as a Moral Institution," in *Friedrich Schiller: An Anthology for our Time,* New York: Frederick Ungar, 1959, pp. 263-83.

[*In the following essay, which was first delivered as a lecture in 1784, Schiller asserts that theater serves a crucial moral function in society, and sets out in detail its sphere of influence and range of effects on human life, calling it "a school of practical wisdom, a guide through social life, an infallible key to the most secret passages of the soul."*]

The stage owes its origin to the irresistible attraction of things new and extraordinary, to man's desire for passionate experience, as Sulzer has observed. Exhausted by the higher efforts of the mind, wearied by the monotonous and frequently depressing duties of his profession, satiated with sensuality, man must have felt an emptiness in his nature that was at odds with his desire for constant activity. Human nature, incapable either of remaining forever in an animal state or of devoting itself exclusively to the more subtle work of the intellect, demanded a middle condition which would unite these two contradictory extremes; a condition that would ease the hard tension between them and produce a gentle harmony, thereby facilitating the mutual transition from one to the other. This function is performed by the aesthetic sense or the appreciation of beauty.

Since it must be the first aim of the wise legislator, when faced with two effects, to choose the higher, he will not be content merely to have disarmed the impulses of his people. He will also endeavor, if possible, to use these tendencies as instruments for higher plans and convert them into sources of happiness. To this end he selected the stage as the best means of opening an endless sphere to the spirit thristing for action, of feeding all spiritual powers without straining any, and of combining the cultivation of the mind and the emotions with the noblest entertainment.

The man who first made the statement that *religion* is the strongest pillar of the state; that without religion law itself would be deprived of its force, has, perhaps, unknowingly supplied the stage with its noblest defense. The very inadequacy and unreliability of political laws that make religion indispensable to the state also determine the moral influence of the stage. This man meant to imply that, while laws revolve around negative duties, religion extends her demands to positive acts. Laws merely impede actions that might cause the disintegration of society. Religion prescribes actions that tend to consolidate the structure of society. Laws control only the external manifestations of the will; actions alone are subject to them. Religion extends her jurisdiction to the remotest corners of the heart and traces thought to its deepest source. Laws are smooth and flexible, as changeable as mood and passion. The bonds of religion are stern and eternal.

Even if we assume, as indeed we cannot, that religion possesses this great power over every human heart, will it, or can it bring to perfection all of human culture? On the whole, religion (I am separating here the political aspect from the divine) acts mainly on the sensual part of the people. It probably has an infallible effect only by way of the senses. It loses its power if we take this away. And how does the stage achieve its effect? Religion ceases to be anything for most men if we remove its images, its problems, if we destroy its pictures of heaven and hell. And yet they are only fantasy pictures, riddles without a solution, terrifying phantoms and distant allurements.

What strength religion and law can gain when they are allied with the stage, where reality can be viewed as living presence, where vice and virtue, happiness and misery, folly and wisdom pass in review before man in thousands of true and concrete pictures, where Providence solves her riddles, ties her knots before our eyes; where the human heart, on the rack of passion, confesses its subtlest stirrings; where every mask is dropped, every painted cheek is faded, and truth, like Rhadamanthus, sits incorruptibly in judgment.

The jurisdiction of the stage begins where the domain of secular law comes to an end. When justice is blinded by gold and revels in the wages of vice; when the crimes of the mighty scorn her impotence and the dread of human power has tied the hands of legal authority, then the stage takes up the sword and the scales and drags vice before a dreadful tribunal. The entire realm of fantasy and history, the past and the future are at its beck and call. Bold criminals, who have long since turned to dust, are summoned to appear before us by the all-powerful voice of poetry and to reenact their shameful lives for the instruc-

tion of a horrified posterity. Like impotent shadow figures in a concave mirror, they unfold before our eyes the terrors of their own century, and we heap imprecations upon their memory in an ecstasy of horror. Even when morality is no longer taught, even when there is no longer any faith in religion, even when law has ceased to exist, we will still shudder at the sight of Medea as she staggers down the palace steps, the murder of her children having taken place. Humanity will tremble with wholesome horror and each man will secretly congratulate himself on his own good conscience when he sees that frightful sleepwalker, Lady Macbeth, washing her hands and hears her challenge all the perfumes of Arabia to obliterate the loathsome smell of murder. As surely as a visual representation has a more powerful effect than a dead text or a cold narrative, so the stage exercises a more profound and lasting influence than morality and law.

Here, however, the stage merely assists human justice. A still wider field is open to it. A thousand vices that are tolerated by justice are punished in the theater. A thousand virtues ignored by human law are recommended on the stage. Here it serves as a companion to wisdom and religion. It draws its teachings and examples from this pure source and clothes stern duty in a charming and alluring garb. What glorious emotions, resolutions, passions well up in our souls, and with what godlike ideals it challenges our ambitions! When gracious Augustus, magnanimous like his gods, holds out his hand to the traitor Cinna who already imagines he sees the death sentence on his lips, and says: "Let us be friends, Cinna,"—who among us, at this moment, would not gladly clasp the hand of his mortal enemy in order to emulate the divine Roman? When Franz von Sickingen, on his way to punish a prince and to fight for alien rights, happens to look back and see the smoke rising from the castle occupied by his helpless wife and children, continues on his journey to keep his word— then, how great man rises before me, how small and contemptible the dread power of insuperable destiny!

Vice, as reflected in the mirror of the stage, is made as hideous as virtue is made desirable. When the helpless, childish Lear, out in a stormy night, knocks in vain on his daughters' door; when, his white hair streaming in the wind, he describes the unnatural conduct of his daughter Regan to the raging elements; when at last he pours out his unbearable suffering in the words: "I gave you everything!": how abominable ingratitude seems to us, how solemnly we promise respect and filial love!

But the sphere of influence of the stage extends still farther. The theater continues to work for our development even in those areas where religion and law will not stoop to follow human sentiments. The happiness of society is as much disturbed by folly as by crime and vice. Experience as old as the world teaches us that in the web of human events, the heaviest weights are often suspended by the most delicate threads; and in tracing actions to their source, we have to smile ten times before revolting in horror once. My list of criminals grows shorter every day of my life, but my list of fools becomes more complete and longer. If the moral guilt of one class of people stems from one and the same source; if the appalling extremes of vice that have stigmatized it are merely altered forms, higher degrees of a quality which in the end provokes only smiles and sympathy, why should not nature have adopted the same course in the case of the other class? I know of only one method of guarding man against depravity, and that is to guard his heart against weaknesses.

We can expect the stage to serve this function to a considerable degree. It is the stage that holds the mirror up to the great class of fools and shames the manifold forms of their folly with wholesome ridicule. The effect it produced before by means of terror and pity, it achieves here (and perhaps more speedily and infallibly) by wit and satire. If we were to judge comedy and tragedy on the basis of their effectiveness, experience would probably decide in favor of the former. Loathing may torture a man's conscience, but he suffers more keenly when his pride is wounded by derision and contempt. Our cowardice causes us to recoil from what is frightening, but this very cowardice exposes us to the sting of satire. Law and conscience often protect us from crime and vice; the ludicrous demands a peculiarly fine perception which we exercise nowhere more than in front of the stage. We may allow a friend to attack our morals and our emotions, but we find it hard to forgive him a single laugh at our expense. Our transgressions may tolerate a mentor and judge, our bad habits hardly a witness. The stage alone is permitted to ridicule our weaknesses because it spares our sensibilities and does not care to know who is the guilty fool. Without blushing we can see our own mask reflected in its mirror and are secretly grateful for the gentle rebuke.

But the stage's broad scope by no means comes to an end here. The stage, more than any other public institution, is a school of practical wisdom, a guide through social life, an infallible key to the most secret passages of the human soul. Self-love and a callous conscience, admittedly, often neutralize its effect. A thousand vices brazenly persist despite its castigations. A thousand good feelings meet with no response from the cold heart of the spectator. I myself am of the opinion that perhaps Molière's Harpagon has never reformed a single usurer, that the suicide of Beverley has saved very few of his brothers from the abominable addiction to gambling, that Karl Moor's unfortunate brigands' story will not make the highroads safer for travelers. But even if we set limits to *this effect* of the stage, even if we are so unjust as to discount it altogether, is not what remains of its influence still vast enough? Even if the stage neither augments nor diminishes the total number of vices, has it not acquainted us with them? We have to live with these profligates and fools. We must either avoid them or put up with them, undermine their influence or succumb to it. But now they no longer surprise us. We are prepared for their assaults. The stage has revealed to us the secret of finding them out and rendering them harmless. It is the stage that has lifted the mask from the hypocrite's face and exposed the net in

which cunning and cabal have entangled us. It has dragged deception and falsehood from their labyrinthine dens and made them show their horrid countenances to the light of day. The dying Sarah may not frighten a single debauchee. All the pictures of the dreadful fate in store for the seducer may not quench his fire. The artful actress herself may be contriving to prevent her artistry from having this effect. Nevertheless we can be thankful that his snares have been revealed to unsuspecting innocence, and that it has been taught by the stage to mistrust his promises and tremble at his vows of love.

The stage not only makes us aware of men and human character, but also of the grim power of destiny, and teaches us the great art of bearing it. In the web of life chance and design play an equal role. The latter we can direct, to the former we must submit blindly. We have already gained much if an inevitable fate does not find us wholly unprepared, if our courage and our prudence have already been exercised in similar circumstances and if our hearts have been steeled for the blow. The stage presents us with many varied scenes of human woe. It involves us artificially in the troubles of strangers and rewards us for the momentary pain with pleasurable tears and a magnificent increase of courage and experience. It escorts us with the forsaken Ariadne through the echoing passages of Naxos. It descends with us to Ugolino's tower of starvation. In its company we ascend the steps of the frightful scaffold and witness the solemn hour of death. What we have experienced in our souls only as a vague presentiment, we hear on the stage loudly and incontrovertibly corroborated by nature taken by surprise. In the Tower dungeon the queen withdraws her favor from the deceived favorite. In the face of death, the treacherous sophistry of the frightened Moor deserts him. Eternity releases a dead man in order to reveal secrets which cannot be known to the living. The confident villain loses his last ghastly refuge because even the tomb can speak.

But the stage not only familiarizes us with the fate of mankind, it also teaches us to be more just toward the unfortunate and to judge him more leniently; for it is only when we know the full measure of his suffering that we are permitted to pronounce sentence upon him. No crime is more dishonorable than that of a thief, but, even as we condemn him, can we refrain from shedding a tear of compassion for Eduard Ruhberg when we have shared with him the dreadful agony that drives him to commit the deed? Suicide is usually regarded as a crime; but when Mariana, overwhelmed by the threats of an irate father, by her unhappy love and by the terrifying prospect of the convent walls, drains the poisoned cup, who would be the first to condemn this victim of an infamous maxim? Humanity and tolerance are becoming the ruling principles of our age. Their rays have penetrated to our courts of justice and even to the hearts of our princes. How great a share in this divine work belongs to our theaters? Is it not the theater that makes man known to man and discloses the secret mechanism that controls his conduct?

One noteworthy class of men has more cause to be grateful to the stage than any other. It is only here that the great of the world hear what they rarely if ever hear elsewhere: the truth. Here they see what they scarcely ever see: man.

While man's moral development has greatly benefited, and in a variety of ways, from the higher order of drama, his intellectual enlightenment is no less indebted to it. It is in this higher realm that the great mind, the warm-hearted patriot uses it to the best advantage.

Surveying the human race as a whole, comparing nations with nations, centuries with centuries, he sees how the majority of people are chained like slaves to prejudice and opinion which forever deter them from finding happiness, and that the pure rays of truth illumine only a few isolated minds which had perhaps expended their entire lives in order to purchase their little gain. How can a wise legislator enable his people to share in these benefits?

The stage is the common channel in which from the thinking, better part of the people the light of wisdom flows down, diffusing from there in milder rays through the entire state. More correct ideas, purified principles and feelings flow from thence through all the vein of all the people. The mists of barbarism, of gloomy superstition disappear. Night yields to victorious light.

Among the many magnificent fruits of the better stage, I would like to single out two. How universal has the tolerance of religious sects become in recent years! Even before Nathan the Jew and Saladin the Saracen shamed us and preached the divine doctrine that submission to the will of God is not dependent upon our misconceptions of Him; even before Joseph II battled with the dreadful hydra of pious hatred, the stage was engaged in planting the seeds of humanity and gentleness in our hearts. The shocking pictures of heathenish, priestly fanaticism taught us to avoid religious hatred. In this frightful mirror Christianity cleansed itself of its stains.

Errors in *education* might be combated in the stage with equal success. We are still awaiting the play that will deal with this significant subject. Because of its effects, no subject is of more importance to the state than this, and yet no institution is so at the mercy of the illusions and caprices of the citizenry as education. The stage alone could pass in review the unfortunate victims of careless education in a series of moving, upsetting pictures. Our fathers might learn to abandon their foolish maxims; our mothers might learn to love more wisely. The best-hearted teachers are led astray by false ideas. It is still worse when they pride themselves on a certain method and systematically ruin the tender young plant in philanthropinums and hothouses.

Likewise the chiefs and guardians of the state—if they knew how to do it—could use the stage to correct and enlighten popular opinion of government and the governing class. The legislating power might speak to those subject to it in foreign symbols, might defend its actions before they had time to utter a complaint, might silence their doubts without appearing to do so. Even industry and inventiveness might draw inspiration from the stage if the poets thought it worth while to be patriotic and if princes would condescend to hear them.

I cannot possibly overlook the great influence that a good permanent theater would exercise on the spirit of a nation. By national spirit I mean opinions and tendencies which are common to the people of one nation and differ from those of other nationalities. Only the stage can produce this accord to so great a degree because it takes all human knowledge as its province, exhausts all situations of life, and sheds light into every corner of the human heart; because it unites all sorts and conditions of people and commands the most popular road to the heart and understanding.

If a single characteristic predominated in all of our plays; if all of our poets were in accord and were to form a firm alliance to work for this end; if their work were governed by strict selection; if they were to devote their paintbrushes to national subjects; in a word, if we were to see the establishment of a national theater: then we would become a nation. What linked the Greek states so firmly together? What drew the people so irresistibly to the stage? It was the patriotic subjects of their plays. It was the Greek spirit, the great and consuming interest in the republic and in a better humanity that pervaded them.

The stage has another merit which I especially delight in mentioning, because the stage now seems to have won its case against its persecutors. The influence upon morals and enlightenment that we have so far claimed for it has been doubted. But even its enemies have admitted that it is to be preferred to all other luxuries and forms of public entertainment. Its services in this respect, however, are more important than is usually conceded.

Human nature cannot bear the constant, unrelenting grind of business. Sensual delight dies with gratification. Man, surfeited with animal pleasures, weary of long exertion, tormented by an unceasing desire for activity, thirsts for better and finer amusement. If he does not find it, he will plunge headlong into debauchery which hastens his ruin and destroys the peace of society. Bacchanalian carousings, the ruinous games of chance, a thousand revelries hatched by idleness become inevitable unless the legislator knows how to guide these tendencies in his people. The businessman is in danger of becoming a miserable hypochondriac in return for a life he has generously devoted to the state. The scholar is likely to sink into dull pedantry, the common man becomes a brute.

The stage is an institution where pleasure is combined with instruction, rest with exertion, amusement with culture. Not a single faculty is strained to the detriment of another, no pleasure is enjoyed at the expense of the whole. When grief gnaws at our hearts, when melancholy poisons our solitary hours, when the world and business have become repulsive to us, when our souls are oppressed by a thousand burdens and the drudgery of our profession threatens to deaden our sensibilities, the stage welcomes us to her bosom. In the dreams of this artificial world, we can forget the real one. We find ourselves once more. Our feeling reawakens. Wholesome passions stir our slumbering nature and the blood begins to circulate in our veins with renewed vigor. Here the unhappy man dispels his sorrow in weeping over that of another. The happy become more sober and the overconfident more cautious. The sensitive weakling learns to stand up to the tough demands of manhood. The unfeeling brute experiences human feeling for the first time.

And finally, what a triumph for you, oh nature—nature so often trampled underfoot, who has just as often risen again—when men from all corners of the earth and every walk of life, having shed their shackles of affectation and fashion, torn away from the insistent pressure of fate, united by the all-embracing bond of brotherly sympathy, resolved in one human race again, oblivious of themselves and of the world, come closer to their divine origin. Each enjoys the raptures of all, which are reflected on him from a hundred eyes in heightened beauty and intensity, and in his breast there is room for only one sensation: the awareness that he is a human being.

OVERVIEWS AND GENERAL STUDIES

William Witte (essay date 1949)

SOURCE: "Ideal Freedom," in *Schiller,* Basil Blackwell, 1949, pp. 165-86.

[*In the following essay, Witte argues that* Maria Stuart, Die Jungfrau von Orleans, *and* Die Braut von Messina *embody and illustrate Schiller's idea of the tragically sublime: the triumph of the moral self over the human being's material existence, emotional impulses, and physical nature, or the victory of spiritual freedom over the bondage of the flesh.*]

The years that remained to Schiller after the completion of *Wallenstein* were devoted almost entirely to the drama. After the self-imposed discipline of historical study and philosophical reflection, after the tardy growth of *Wallenstein,* the tempo of his dramatic production suddenly increased in a spectacular way: from now on, plays poured from his pen at the remarkable rate of one a year. This spate of creative work came at a time when Schiller was once again in close contact with the practical affairs of the stage; having moved to Weimar in December, 1799, he was able to assist Goethe in the management of the Weimar Court Theatre. With patient enthusiasm the two friends pursued their aims, seeking to improve the actors'

performances (and the taste of the public) by insisting on careful rehearsal, proper delivery, and a uniform style of acting in a well-balanced ensemble. In order to add good plays to the repertoire, Schiller busied himself with translations whenever illness or weariness forced him to interrupt his own work; among other things he provided a German version of *Macbeth* (1800)—remarkably unShakespearean, it is true, with its transformation of the witches and the porter scene, yet remarkably effective—a charming adaptation of Gozzi's *Commedia Turandot* (1801), and an excellent rendering of Racine's *Phèdre* in German blank verse (1805), composed (in less than a month) when already the shadow of death was upon him.

Schiller had given hard and earnest thought to the thorny problem of tragedy during the years that preceded his return to the drama. Having formulated his conclusions in various theoretical writings, he now felt the urge to translate critical theory into dramatic practice. Considered from this point of view, *Maria Stuart, Die Jungfrau von Orleans,* and *Die Braut von Messina* reveal a marked affinity, though they are very dissimilar in other respects. These three plays embody and illustrate Schiller's idea of the tragically sublime—the triumph of man's higher moral self over the limitations of his material existence, over his emotional impulses, and over the sufferings of his physical nature: a vindication of spiritual freedom, if need be at the cost of self-immolation. When the happy equilibrium of duty and desire which characterizes the 'virtuoso'[1] becomes impossible, when natural instincts conflict irreconcilably with moral obligation, and 'moral grace' is no longer sufficient to cope with a supreme crisis, then the man who wants to keep his soul inviolate must entrench himself in the citadel of his moral freedom.

> 'Fälle können eintreten, wo das Schicksal alle Außenwerke ersteigt, auf die er seine Sicherheit gründete, und ihm nichts weiter übrig bleibt, als sich in die heilige Freiheit der Geister zu flüchten. . . .'[2]

In doing so he rises to that sublime dignity which surrounds the tragic hero. Such a situation, culminating in a victory of the spirit over the flesh, provides the tragic poet with a fit theme. It is a spectacle that exalts and inspires, despite the dark and harrowing elements in it, for it carries the welcome assurance that man is not wholly determined by his physical nature and its material conditions; plucking inward triumph from outward failure, he proves that he is not just an unprofitable servant: with part of his being at least he belongs to a higher, ultimate order of things. The fate that threatens the hero may be not only hard but positively unjust by any ordinary standards of justice; the nexus between his actions and their consequences may be obscure; common sense may refuse to hold him responsible for the outcome and to interpret the tragic issue as a judgment on his frailties. But the hero, resolutely shouldering the tragic burden, rises superior even to a malign fate: by accepting the consequences of his deeds, unforeseeable and unmerited though they may appear, by willing his own destruction, he ceases to be a mere victim of hostile circumstance, and stands forth as a shining example of man's unconquerable mind. The fiery ordeal makes a new man of him; he emerges from it spiritually regenerate. As he meets the strain of a great crisis, his hidden strength is revealed; and while we sorrow over his anguish, we rejoice to witness his moral rebirth. The feeling with which we are left at the end is one of serenity after deep emotion. Like the chorus in Milton's tragedy we are dismissed, if not with any dogmatic assurances regarding the unsearchable dispose of highest wisdom, at any rate with peace and consolation, 'And calm of mind all passion spent'.

While the moral emphasis in all this is unmistakable, it is equally clear that Schiller does not think of tragedy 'as a divine law court, in which the dooms are proportioned to the mistakes of head or heart'³ Nothing is further from his mind than the suggestion that tragedy should exhibit a consistent and rational moral order, readily intelligible to our finite judgment, a world in which everyone is served according to his deserts, excluding all the hazards, the accidents, the moral perplexities that form so prominent a feature of our common human experience. There is no question of any such balancing of moral accounts, with an interim dividend on virtue, as was practised by the playwrights whom he ridicules in *Shakespeares Schatten.* Gundolf, it is true, asserts that Schiller's drama is founded on moral valuations and that it postulates a moral order as its ultimate system of reference; but if this claim is to be upheld, it must be interpreted in rather a special sense. It cannot be taken to mean that Schiller seeks to justify the tragic hero's suffering in terms of reason, thus obscuring or mitigating the tragic fact. What it does mean is that Schiller invites us to admire the sublime greatness of soul which, even in face of physical annihilation, attests its belief in the primacy of spiritual values by a supreme act of faith, and thus saves the spectacle of tragic suffering from being merely depressing. Schiller knows better than to press tragedy into the service of any religious or philosophic doctrine. But without seeking to extract from it any proof of a transcendental cosmic harmony, he is aware of what has been called the paradox of tragedy—the challenging and mysterious fact that 'its conclusions are not contained within its premises, that it radiates light from darkness, destroys hope and harbours it; that do what disaster may with these heroes they gain the more upon us . . . when Nature has vanquished and cast them out they continue to reign in our affections, in a kingdom inaccessible to Fortune, uncircumscribed by time and with a relish of remoter duration'.⁴

Maria Stuart exemplifies this conception of tragedy most clearly and, on the whole, most satisfyingly. Once again Schiller wrought his design from historical material, employing the same method as before in the imaginative re-creation of historic events. Having first made a fairly careful study of the period, he then proceeded to treat the data of history with the full freedom of the artist, suppressing what did not suit him, rearranging or inventing incidents (for example, the meeting of the two queens), and taking all manner of liberties with chronology and geography.⁵ As for the interpretation of his heroine's

character, he could not have asked for greater latitude, seeing that Mary Queen of Scots has to this day remained an enigmatic figure, a puzzle and a challenge to successive generations of historians. Saint or sinner, ambitious schemer or helpless victim, passionate lover, sensualist, or frigidly consenting party? The mystery seems to deepen with every new attempt to solve it. From such conflicting readings, Schiller was able to choose what fitted in with his purpose. He makes Mary a woman of great beauty and vitality in whom quick-witted discernment is at times blinded by the emotional impulses of a passionate nature; a queen who, throughout the long years of her captivity, remains proudly conscious of her royal blood. Her moral regeneration forms the main theme of the play. Using the analytic technique which he had studied and admired in the *Oedipus* of Sophocles, Schiller contrived to concentrate the whole action within the space of three days—the last three days of the heroine's life. All the events that lead up to the final crisis belong to the past. Mary's youth at the court of France, her brief French marriage which left her, in her own phrase, the widow of the greatest king in Christendom, her entrance upon her Scottish heritage, her marriage to Darnley, the Rizzio episode, her association with Bothwell and the murder at the Kirk-o' Field, the last defeat at Langside, her flight to England, her long, increasingly strait imprisonment, and her trial—all these are called to mind by the skillful and effective use of reminiscence, pleading, and altercation. The art of dramatic exposition, perfected in **Wallenstein,** is now applied with conscious virtuosity; and the prisoner at Fortheringhay, 'the Daughter of Debate,' though passive and powerless herself, is shown as the fulcrum of political forces in the outside world.

The concentration and spiritualization of the action, as well as the deliberately symmetrical architecture of the play, suggest a certain affinity with French tragedy; so does the quasi-forensic technique, the careful marshalling of the arguments for and against the execution of the death sentence (for example, in I, 7, and in II, 3-4). Although Schiller's attitude towards French drama always remained highly critical, with whole-hearted censure much more readily forthcoming than occasional qualified praise,⁶ the influence of the Weimar circle kept his interest in it alive. Both Goethe and Humboldt insisted on the positive merits of the French style of dramatic composition, its clarity, its harmony of design, and its perfect control. In spite of his aversion to the stiffness and dry artificiality which he found in many French plays, Schiller endeavoured to assimilate their good qualities; nowhere more so than in **Maria Stuart,** which of all his plays is the one most closely akin, in spirit and in technique, to the *tragédie classique.* It is not surprising to find Mme de Staël singling it out as 'de toutes les tragédies allemandes la plus pathétique et la mieux conçue'.

The decisive emphasis falls on the inward struggle. Mary is under sentence of death for her alleged complicity in Babington's plot against the life of Elizabeth; she has been tried by a tribunal composed of the first peers of the realm, and found guilty. Elizabeth has every reason to desire the death of her royal cousin: even behind prison walls, Mary acts as a focus of Catholic disaffection in the country, supported by the powerful forces of Roman Catholicism abroad. Moreover, Mary regards herself as the rightful heir to the throne of England; and the mere existence of a pretender whose claims are based on an unspotted lineage constitutes a permanent threat, because it perpetuates the doubts that exist in men's minds about the legitimacy of Elizabeth's succession. In addition to these political considerations, there is a strong personal motive: the jealous antipathy of a sexually frustrated older woman against a younger one who had never cherished any ambition to go down to posterity as a virgin queen. Nevertheless, Elizabeth hesitates to sign the death-warrant. Though she would like to see Mary dead, she shrinks from the odium of sanctioning the execution of her unfortunate rival. Her chief councillors offer conflicting advice. Talbot's generous humanity and incorruptible sense of justice prompt him to plead for Mary; Cecil, on the other hand, insists that only Mary's death can safeguard the peace and unity of the realm. While Elizabeth hesitates, others are active in Mary's behalf. Mortimer, a fanatical young partisan of Mary's cause, and desperately in love with Mary herself, is plotting to liberate her by a daring *coup de main*. At the same time, the Earl of Leicester, Elizabeth's favourite of many years' standing, and formerly a candidate for Mary's hand, endeavours, for reasons of his own, to bring about a gradual reconciliation between the two queens. Both plans miscarry. Leicester persuades Elizabeth to meet Mary, but the meeting ends disastrously. Mary humbles herself in vain; Elizabeth merely gloats over her stricken enemy's misfortune. When at last Mary realizes that no self-abasement will avail, her imperious, passionate spirit reasserts itself, and the interview ends in a violent quarrel. Grief and long-nourished resentment put deadly venom into Mary's taunts; she emerges victorious from the battle of words. For a few brief moments at the end of this emotional scene Schiller shows us the prisoner at Fotheringhay transformed into her former self, proud, rash, and tempestuously beautiful—Mary Stuart as she was during the stormy years of her Scottish reign.

Soon after the fatal meeting of the two queens, Mortimer's plot is foiled by the premature action of one of his accomplices, who makes an unsuccessful attempt on Elizabeth's life as she is returning to London. Mary's fate is sealed; after what has happened, she cannot hope for mercy from Elizabeth, while the new plot against the sovereign adds weight to Cecil's arguments. Elizabeth signs the warrant, and the sentence is carried out; the discovery that it was based on false evidence comes too late to stay the execution. Elizabeth tries to put the blame on Cecil and on her secretary Davidson; but Talbot's refusal to hold office any longer and Leicester's flight show that she cannot escape responsibility.

From the first rising of the curtain the heroine's death looms ahead. All attempts to avert it prove futile and serve only to accelerate the catastrophe. Being the kind of woman she is, placed in the circumstances in which we find her, Mary cannot be saved; inexorably the pressure of events impels her towards her doom. This sense of fatality which is present from the first does not, however, preclude suspense; nor can it be validly objected that the tragic ending, being prescribed by history, is in any case a foregone conclusion. Knowledge of how things turn out in the end is clearly not incompatible with suspense—otherwise no one could feel suspense when seeing *Lear* or *Othello* for the second time. As for the issue being, as it were, prejudged by history, there is no reason to assume that Schiller would have allowed the historian in him to stand in the way of the playwright: witness, for instance, the entirely unhistorical ending of *Die Jungfrau von Orleans*.

Hostile forces clash in the play: Mary's sympathizers oppose her enemies, and behind these contending parties we sense a vaster struggle—the rising power of Protestant England asserting itself against the Roman Catholic world. The essential conflict, however, is fought out, not between external forces, but in the mind of the heroine. The question at issue is whether she is to reconcile herself to the fate which she cannot hope to avert, or whether she is to meet her death defiantly, insisting on her rights, railing against fate, and denouncing the infamy of her enemies. The decision is rendered more difficult by the fact that Mary is innocent of the particular crime of which she stands accused and for which she is sent to the scaffold. In a strictly juridical sense, the case against her is not proven, and her execution is, as Hettner has pointed out, a miscarriage of justice. Unjust though the tribunal's sentence may be from an objectively legal point of view, however, Mary eventually comes to accept it as a necessary expiation—not of the crime for which she was tried and which she never committed, but of the sins of bygone days. By this act of deliberate self-abnegation, Mary lays the ghosts of her past; and, her conscience cleared, she rises superior to her temporal judges. Whatever crimes and follies she may have been guilty of in her time—when the hand of death is upon her, she knows herself to be once again every inch a great queen:

> —den Menschen adelt, Den tiefstgesunkenen,
>
> das letzte Schicksal.
>
> Die Krone fühl' ich wieder auf dem Haupt,
>
> Den würd'gen Stolz in meiner edeln Seele![7]

Schiller does not hesitate to introduce the ritual of a Catholic sacrament in order to give visible expression to the heroine's change of heart: as she prepares to receive the wages of sin, Mary at the same time receives absolution and the promise of grace from one who, according to her faith, holds the keys of the kingdom of heaven.

It has been said that this sublimation comes too late to be fully convincing. The historical Mary was a prisoner in England from her arrival in 1568 until her death in 1587. Schiller has shortened the period of her captivity in his play, thus making his two queens much younger than their middle-aged prototypes in history. But even on Schiller's own showing, about seven years are assumed to have elapsed between the murder of Darnley and Mary's execution: years during which, though troubled by pangs of conscience, she continues to cherish worldly ambitions, hoping for a return to freedom and power. This time-lag between her crime and its expiation is held to impair the sense of inevitability which is essential for a fully tragic effect.[8] Plainly such a criticism is founded on the assumption that tragedy should vindicate the rationality of events, exhibiting a clearly traceable causal connection between guilt and just retribution. There is no reason to think, however, that Schiller believed in so simple a formula. Schiller's tragedy is not exclusively concerned with the question of the heroine's moral responsibility; another aspect, no less important, is the way she meets the calamity that befalls her—a calamity rendered inevitable by the pressure of hostile circumstances as well as by her own conduct. It is the final ordeal that reveals her true mettle; snared in an evil time, she acts with a dignity that turns defeat into triumph. She is no longer blinded by her old passions; suddenly she sees her whole life in a new perspective, and what might have appeared unjust and meaningless from a less exalted standpoint falls into place as part of the pattern when viewed *sub specie aeternitatis*. This change of outlook cannot be other than sudden:

> Man löst sich nicht allmählich von dem Leben!
>
> Mit einem Mal, schnell, augenblicklich muß
>
> Der Tausch geschehen zwischen Zeitlichem
>
> Und Ewigem . . .[9]

If it be argued that the strong sense of guilt which brings about the final change of heart is incompatible with Mary's cherishing all kinds of worldly hopes during her imprisonment, the answer is that such criticism underrates the capacity of the human heart for harbouring contradictory impulses.

While the essence of the tragedy is to be found in the inward crisis, the external conflict between Mary and Elizabeth provides the play with its main structural principle; its scenes are evenly and symmetrically divided between Elizabeth's court and Mary's prison (an arrangement which combines with the severe concentration of the action to give the work its appearance of classical regularity), and the characters of the two queens tend to overshadow the male roles. Nevertheless, the men are more than mere foils. Burleigh is a carefully drawn portrait of a patriotic statesman, far-seeing, realistic, resourceful, who thinks in terms of political necessity, setting aside moral scruples if need be. Mortimer (modelled on Babington) is a clever study of a mentally and morally unstable person, with a convert's zeal and the desperate bravery of the fanatic. His fierce sensuality (which seems to have shocked some of Schiller's contemporaries) serves an important dramatic purpose: at a crucial moment, it conjures up the daemon of reckless passion which ruled Mary's past, and which would lie in wait for her again should she regain her freedom:

> MORTIMER. Der ist ein Rasender, der nicht das Glück
>
> Festhält in unauflöslicher Umarmung,
>
> Wenn es ein Gott in seine Hand gegeben.
>
> Ich will dich retten, kost' es tausend Leben,
>
> Ich rette dich, ich will es—doch so wahr
>
> Gott lebt! ich schwör's, ich will dich auch besitzen.
>
> MARIA. O will kein Gott, kein Engel mich beschützen!
>
> Furchtbares Schicksal! Grimmig schleuderst du
>
> Von einem Schrecknis mich dem andern zu.
>
> Bin ich geboren, nur die Wut zu wecken?
>
> Verschwört sich Hass und Liebe, mich zu schrecken?[10]

The portrayal of Leicester, on the other hand, is rather less convincing. His double-dealing and his ineffectual opportunism somehow tend to blur the outline of his character from a dramatic point of view. Some traits (his gift of flattery, for instance, and his proud bearing) are taken from history; but on the whole Schiller's Leicester is only the pale shadow of the historical Robert Dudley as he emerges from the pages of his latest biographer[11]—the first courtier of his age, known throughout Europe as 'the Great Lord', and invested by a loving sovereign with a title previously borne only by princes of the blood, regardless of the fact that he was 'noble onely in two descents, and both of them stained with the Block', and moreover, 'fleshed in conspiracy against the Royall bloud of King *Henries* children in his tender yeares'.[12] One does not quite believe that Schiller's Leicester could have long maintained his position as Elizabeth's undisputed favourite—except in so far as Schiller's Elizabeth, too, falls far below her historical counterpart. It suited Schiller's dramatic purpose to emphasize the unlovable features in Elizabeth's nature: the vanity and coquetry which she had inherited from her mother, her capriciousness, her cynicism. But there is hardly any trace in his portrait either of Good Queen Bess or of Gloriana.

In *Maria Stuart,* as in *Wallenstein,* Schiller had viewed the principal character with deliberate detachment. In his next play we find a different kind of approach; his personal interest in his heroine becomes a dominant factor. Fascinated by the story of Joan of Arc, a story of divinely inspired genius in a world shattered by war, he decides to shelve his plans for a tragedy on the subject of Perkin Warbeck, and very shortly after the completion of *Maria Stuart* his letters show him busily at work on *Die Jungfrau von Orleans.*

> 'Dieses Stück [as he told Göschen later on] floss *aus dem Herzen* und *zu dem Herzen* sollte es auch sprechen.[13]

He sounds the same note of enthusiasm in the poem *Das Mädchen von Orleans,* originally entitled *Voltaires Pucelle und die Jungfrau von Orleans.* In Voltaire's scurrilous epic, which had been enjoying a tremendous vogue, Joan of Arc's name had been dragged through the mire; and while Schiller has to admit that many readers derive amusement from *La Pucelle,* he feels that the world is the poorer for Voltaire's irreverent mockery:

> Dem Herzen will er seine Schätze rauben,
>
> Den Wahn bekriegt er und verletzt den Glauben.[14]

But the Muse of dramatic poetry will wipe out the Voltairean stigma; by a sympathetic and idealizing portrayal, she will restore Joan to her rightful place among the immortals:

> Mit einer Glorie hat sie dich umgeben—
>
> Dich schuf das Herz! Du wirst unsterblich leben.[15]

Schiller's warm sympathy with his heroine influenced his dramatic technique. In his desire to unfold the whole of her story before our eyes, he abandons the compactness of *Maria Stuart* in favour of a broader, more discursive manner. In both plays the heroine pits the power of her soul against untoward events, and, conquering, achieves spiritual purification. But whereas in **Maria Stuart** we have only the last phase, everything that precedes it being dealt with by means of an expository *tour de force,* in **Die Jungfrau von Orleans** Schiller leads up to the crisis in more leisurely fashion, presenting all the antecedent facts on the stage. In five acts and a Prologue he follows the heroine's whole career, from the time when, at her native village of Domrémy in Lorraine, celestial visions and voices bid the humble peasant girl go forth and bring succour and victory to her hard-pressed king. We witness the main stages in the accomplishment of her mission. We see her arriving at Charles VII's court at a moment when the French cause seems lost, inspiring everyone with fresh confidence by her prophetic fervour and by the tidings of her first success. We see her in battle, spreading terror and confusion in the ranks of the English. We see her bringing about a reconciliation between the French leaders and Duke Philip of Burgundy (an event which, in historical fact, did not happen until long after Joan's death).[16] We see her yielding, for a brief but fateful moment, to an impulse of love, and thus, in her own eyes, forfeiting her virgin purity and becoming unworthy of her exalted mission. We see her at the king's consecration in Reims, outwardly at the height of her fame, but inwardly rent and tortured by an intense feeling of guilt which prevents her from repudiating the accusations of witchcraft hurled at her by her old father, and melodramatically punctuated by claps of thunder. (When Schiller writes to Goethe

> 'Der Schluß des vorlezten Acts ist sehr theatralisch und der donnernde *Deus ex machina* wird seine Wirkung nicht verfehlen'[17]

one feels that one would like to be able to construe his comment in a Pickwickian sense.) We see her suddenly deserted by all those who had previously acclaimed her, an outcast, shunned even by the poorest of the poor, and eventually a prisoner in enemy hands. We see her stoically suffering afflictions which she regards as having been sent to purge her of her guilt; and the ordeal proves her to possess qualities of character which 'demonstrate her claim to the role of a prophetess'.[18] Her old powers return as she regains her inner security of heart; in the end we see her, after a decisive victory on the battlefield, passing away in an ecstatic vision of eternal bliss.

The historical Joan of Arc was found guilty of heresy and black magic by a tribunal of her enemies, and the 'fell banning hag', 'Pucelle, that witch, that damned sorceress',[19] was burned to death in the market place of Rouen in May, 1431, protesting her innocence to the end, in spite of the formal abjuration which her judges had wrung from her. As usual, Schiller has no hesitation in departing from historical fact to suit the requirements of his plot. In this case the ending of his play may be said to anticipate, by implication, not only the reopening of her case which, twenty-five years later, led to a revision of the original judgment and to her rehabilitation in the eyes of the world, but her canonization as well, although this did not take place until 1920.

It has often been remarked that in his later plays Schiller strove to combine elements of the Shakespearean type of drama with those features which he had come to admire in the Greek tragedians and, to a lesser extent, in the French *tragédie classique*—their restraint, their harmony of design, their simplicity, their use of a deliberately stylized poetic diction, their emphasis on the universally significant. There was a time when such a synthesis would have appeared to Schiller as a contradiction in terms. At that earlier stage of his development, Shakespeare had appealed to him primarily as a naturalist, with his sense of arresting detail, his freedom of construction, and his individualizing technique, placing the accent on character. The writings of Lessing and Herder, however, as well as his own reflection and experience, led Schiller to realize that not a few of the qualities which impressed him in classical drama were to be found in Shakespeare too. Later on, therefore, he sees no contradiction in presenting Shakespeare in the guise of Hercules (cf. the poem *Shakespeares Schatten*), or in linking his name with the Greek dramatists as the guiding stars of the German tragic Muse (in the poem on Goethe's adaptation of Voltaire's *Mahomet*).

Schiller's endeavour to steer by these two stars in his later plays resulted in a kind of zigzag course. In **Maria Stuart** and **Die Braut von Messina,** the emphasis is on the classical side, whereas **Die Jungfrau von Orleans, Tell,** and **Demetrius** are more Shakespearean in technique. The subtitle 'Eine romantische Tragödie', which Schiller chose for **Die Jungfrau von Orleans,** is intended to stress this affinity, although its significance does not end there. It refers, in addition, to the use of motifs frequently found in literature of the romantic kind: Catholic symbolism, for example; the influence of supernatural agencies; the conventions of mediaeval chivalry; nostalgic echoes of the minstrels' song, such as the Dauphin's description—in I, 2—of 'good King René' and of his endeavour to revive the spirit of the old *amour courtois.* (It is interesting to note that in this instance Schiller's Dauphin displays a more sympathetic, more 'romantic' attitude than Scott's young Arthur de Vere in his encounter with the King of the Troubadours.[20]) In a sense it may be said, therefore, that in *Die Jungfrau von Orleans* Schiller 'pays his tribute to the new Romantic movement'.[21] At the same time it should be remembered that as regards the appreciation of mediaeval Catholicism, the author of the essays on the times of the Crusades and on the events preceding the reign of Frederick Barbarossa[22] hardly needed any guidance from the Romantic school. Nor does he stand indebted to the Romantics in his handling of the supernatural, though in this respect he would have gained by modelling himself on them. Here, as elsewhere, Schiller shows himself lacking in that sense of the eerie, the demonic, the elemental, which Shakespeare and Goethe possessed in such marked degree and which some of the Romantic poets knew how to cultivate. No scene in the whole play is less convincing than that of the spectral black knight who issues ambiguous words of warning just before Joan's encounter with Lionel (III, 9). It is a scene in which everything depends on atmosphere; to make it succeed, the poet would have had to create a feeling of strangeness, of mystery, a half-light in which haunting fears take on visible shape. 'The earth hath bubbles, as the water has,' but Schiller's black knight is not of them, though he is meant to be. There can be no doubt whither he is vanished as he disappears through his trapdoor—nor does anyone feel disposed to exclaim, 'Would he had stayed!'

The supernatural element is, in point of fact, the crux of the play in more ways than one. As she appears in the Prologue and in the first three acts, Joan has no will of her own; in a kind of emotional trance she carries out the commands of a higher power. Her encounter with Lionel finally breaks the spell. She feels that she has betrayed her mission and, weighed down by her sense of guilt, she accepts the afflictions that follow as a means towards her moral regeneration. Joan's own attitude towards her lapse and its consequences is thus made perfectly clear; but can we share it? It is difficult to hold her responsible for the half-conscious stirring of a natural sex impulse over which she has no control; and there remains the uncomfortable feeling that the divinity which singled her out as its blind instrument, raising her out of her accustomed sphere, transforming the simple shepherdess into a conquering national heroine, abandons her to an unmerited fate, withholding its guidance when she is most in need of it.

It might be argued that Joan's heavenly voices are simply projections of her own inner consciousness, externalized manifestations of the powers of her soul which respond to her country's need; and that her vow of complete chastity, in thought as well as in deed, is bound up, in her own mind, with the success of a mission that demands a completely dedicated life. Viewed in that light, the story of Joan is seen as the tragedy of genius—genius battling against inertia and selfishness, carrying a sceptical world with it for a time, but overthrown in the end by ingratitude and distrust. Joan, who intuitively understands the signs of the times, appears as a herald of Protestant and nationalist ideals as opposed to scholastic dogma and feudalism. A vivid imagination being a frequent attribute of genius, it is not at all surprising that Joan should have clothed her desire for action in the imagery of her religion, visualizing it in the shape of blessed saints who came to lay a divinely appointed task upon her. Shaw has demonstrated that such an interpretation, on strictly psychological lines, can be made dramatically effective; his heroine, a sane and shrewd country girl of extraordinary strength of mind and hardihood of body, 'a born boss,' may or may not be like the historical Joan, but her personality and her achievements certainly lose none of their glory by being thus divested of their legendary halo.

The fact remains, however, that Schiller did not choose to treat the subject in that way. He makes no attempt to account for the miraculous in terms of human psychology, as Shaw does;[23] in *Die Jungfrau von Orleans* a miracle is not simply (in the words of Shaw's Archbishop) 'an event which creates faith', but, in the words of the dictionary definition, 'a marvellous event due to some supernatural agency'. The supernatural element is not used symbolically as an expression of Joan's faith in her mission; it is represented as having independent and objective existence, a force intervening from outside: witness Joan's inexplicable foreknowledge of the Dauphin's prayer and of Salisbury's death (I, 10 and 11), her invincibility in battle (II, 6), and the superhuman feat she performs when she bursts her chains and escapes from her prison in order to turn the rout of the French into victory (V, 11-12).[24]

This direct and active participation of divine Providence in the events of the play impairs the dramatic effect by confusing the tragic issue. To show where the weakness of the plot lies, it is not enough to point out the absence of any real guilt on the heroine's part: as has been remarked before, there is room in the world of Schiller's tragedy for the unaccountable hazards in human affairs. The reason why the play leaves us unsatisfied and rather ill at ease is that Schiller wants to have it both ways. He introduces an all-wise, all-powerful, and beneficent divinity, not merely as an object of faith, but as an active participant; having thus introduced it, he makes it act in a manner that is out of character, capriciously degrading Joan after having exalted her, and restoring her just as arbitrarily. Like Samson, whose example she invokes in her last desperate prayer, Joan is a chosen vessel suddenly cast aside; and if Samson's fall was too grievous for the trespass or omission', then Joan's ordeal is even more so, inasmuch as her passing regard for Lionel is hardly to be compared with Samson's wayward amorousness. Thus some of the reflections which the chorus in *Samson Agonistes* address to an inscrutable deity apply with peculiar force to Schiller's heroine:

> God of our Fathers, what is man!
>
> That thou towards him with hand so various,
>
> Or might I say contrarious,

Temperst thy providence through his short course . . .

Nor do I name of men the common rout,

That wandring loose about

Grow up and perish, as the summer flie,

Heads without name no more rememberd,

But such as thou hast solemnly elected,

With gifts and graces eminently adorn'd

To some great work, thy glory,

And peoples safety, which in part they effect:

Yet toward these thus dignifi'd, thou oft

Amidst their highth of noon,

Changest thy countenance, and thy hand with no regard

Of highest favours past

From thee on 'them, or them to thee of service.

. . . . .

In most of his plays Schiller uses characters and incidents from history, suitably adapted to his purpose, to give dramatic expression to his beliefs, his ideas, his experiences, and his sense of values. In *Die Braut von Messina,* however, he abandoned that procedure and relied entirely on his own imagination to provide him with the kind of story he wanted. That story takes up a theme which he had treated before, in his first play: the theme of the hostile brothers who are in love with the same woman. Twenty years had passed since *Die Räuber* had set the contemporary world by the ears; and although *Die Braut von Messina* caused much controversy too, it does not conjure up the perturbed spirits of Karl and Franz Moor. Not that the problem of human freedom had lost its perennial fascination for Schiller; but (as Goethe explained to Eckermann)

> 'die Idee von Freiheit . . . nahm eine andere Gestalt an, so wie Schiller in seiner Kultur weiterging und selbst ein anderer wurde. In seiner Jugend war es die physische Freiheit, die ihm zu schaffen machte, und die in seine Dichtungen überging; in seinem spätern Leben die ideelle.'[25]

In falling back upon a familiar Storm-and-Stress type of subject, Schiller—the mature Schiller who, according to another remark of Goethe's, seemed to grow week by week in wisdom and judgment[26]—had no intention of retracing his steps; indeed it might well be said that no two plays of Schiller's are more completely opposed than *Die Räuber* and *Die Braut von Messina.* In emphatic contrast with the unrestrained naturalism of *Die Räuber,* *Die Braut von Messina* is the most severely stylized of Schiller's plays—'a domestic drama in a royal house,' presented as a tragedy in the grand and simple antique manner, in which

> 'das Interesse nicht sowohl in den handelnden Personen, als in der Handlung liegt, so wie im *Oedipus* des Sophocles.'[27]

The comparison with *Oedipus,* as well as the implied reference to the celebrated passage in the *Poetics* where Aristo-

tle speaks of the plot as the soul of tragedy, both bear witness to the classical orientation of the play. So do numerous other passages in Schiller's correspondence. He comments with satisfaction on the 'Aeschylean' quality of his new tragedy; on other occasions he speaks of having engaged in 'a little contest with the ancient tragedians', and wonders whether he, too, might have won an Olympic prize had he been born as a contemporary of Sophocles.[28] The affinity with *Oedipus,* suggested in the first place by the technique of retrospective analysis, is further enhanced by the main features of the plot: the ancestral curse which rests upon a proud and noble family; the infant who was to be exposed and whose life is spared; incestuous love; the murder of a near relation; and, finally, a sinister prophecy, the fulfilment of which is hastened by the protagonists' efforts to prevent it from coming true.

There could be no question, however, of a mere imitation of classical models, least of all of the *Oedipus,* the classical fate tragedy *par excellence.* Schiller certainly wanted to recapture the imaginative effect of the Sophoclean play, the feeling of solemnity and awe that broods over it; but he knew very well that he could not produce this effect with the means used by the Greek poet. The idea of an ineluctable outward Fate, familiar to the ancients as part of their mythology, is repugnant to modern feeling which, in spite of all merely logical arguments to the contrary, insists on believing in the freedom of the will. Therefore, the tragic outcome had to be brought about, not by the unalterable decree of some external agency, but through the characters themselves. Still, Schiller takes care to show how those characters have become what they are through heredity and environment. Once again we witness only the last phases of a story which has its beginnings in an earlier generation; all the events on the stage are like windows opening on long vistas of time. Unlike *Oedipus, Die Braut von Messina* is not all analysis, not just the gradual discovery of what happened long ago and what is therefore immutable. There is action in Schiller's play; important things happen before our eyes. Yet these things are (or, at any rate, are meant to be) merely the last links in a chain of causation stretching far back into the past.

The scene is laid in mediaeval Sicily, where the races and religions of the West meet and mingle with those of the East. Although Christianity has become the dominant religion, the pagan mythology of the Greeks survives, blended with elements of Mohammedan fatalism and remnants of primitive superstition. A changing succession of conquerors have left their imprint on the island's chequered history; as a result the life of the people lacks political as well as religious stability.[29] There is something feverish and oppressive, something truly volcanic about the world of this play—a world in which the radiant beauty of the South is overhung by the ever-present threat of sudden, unpredictable disaster, and therefore an appropriate setting for a drama of passion, violence, and blood-guilt. The very first scene plunges us into this atmosphere of uncertain apprehensiveness. The ruling Prince of Messina, a hard, ruthless autocrat of Norman descent, has died; the bitter enmity that divides his two sons, Don Manuel and Don Cesar, threatens to disrupt the state. In order to put an end to the war of rival factions, the widowed princess, Isabella, has persuaded her sons to call a truce and to agree to a parley in her presence. In the past the two young princes had stubbornly refused to accept their mother's mediation, but now their hearts are softened by a new experience: they are both in love. Consequently they prove more amenable to Isabella's entreaties; their meeting ends in a complete, unfeigned reconciliation. Isabella is overjoyed at the prospect of welcoming her sons' brides to their new home, where all the members of her family will henceforth live peaceably together. At this happy moment she discloses a secret which she had kept for many years: Don Manuel and Don Cesar are shortly to meet a sister of whose existence they had not been aware. When, in the early years of her married life, Isabella had given birth to a daughter, the old prince had ordered the infant to be killed, because a dream had warned him that she would cause the death of his sons and thus bring his dynasty to utter ruin. Isabella, however, accepting a more hopeful-sounding interpretation of a dream of her own, had contrived to save the child's life and had had her brought up in the seclusion of a nearby nunnery, in complete ignorance of her parentage. The mother's joy and pride are shortlived. Don Cesar, on finding the woman he loves in Don Manuel's arms, stabs his brother in a fit of jealous rage; and the full horror of the situation is revealed when it becomes clear that that woman—the woman with whom both brothers had fallen in love—was none other than their long-lost sister Beatrice. When he realizes the heinousness of his deed, Don Cesar resolves to take his own life. Isabella, in the first mad paroxysm of grief over Manuel's death, disowns and curses her younger son; but it is not long before she repents and tries to dissuade Don Cesar from his purpose. But although Beatrice joins her mother in pleading with him, Don Cesar remains firm. Being the highest in the land, he cannot be called to account by anybody; and as he cannot live with the stigma of his crime upon him, he must execute his own sentence, exorcising, by a free sacrifice, the ancient curse upon his house.

> Nicht auf der Welt lebt, wer mich richtend strafen kann,
>
> Drum muß ich selber an mir selber es vollziehn.
> . . . . .
> Den alten Fluch des Hauses lös' ich sterbend auf,
>
> Der freie Tod nur bricht die Kette des Geschicks.[30]

Although such paraphernalia of the fate tragedy as dreams and prophecies are freely employed, Schiller obviously does not intend to present the events of the play as being preordained by some remote and superpersonal agency, acting independently of the dramatis personae. It is true that the element of fate is emphasized repeatedly. When Isabella, in her grief at Don Manuel's death, pours scorn on ambiguous oracles and lying auguries, on the hollow shams of astrology and divination, her sons' followers affirm their belief in prophecies and inescapable destiny in

accents of complete conviction. But apart from the fact that the views expressed by a character in a play need not represent the author's own, the exposition shows Schiller endeavouring to motivate the conduct of his protagonists in terms of character, heredity, and background. The superstitious fears of the old prince and his ruthless cruelty, Isabella's and Manuel's secretive ways, Don Cesar's lack of self-control—all these factors contribute to the tragic outcome.

Unfortunately, however, they are not in themselves enough to precipitate the catastrophe. At several points where a revelation of the true facts seems practically inevitable, Schiller has to resort to very questionable artifices in order to avoid a premature dénouement. In II, 2,[31] Beatrice, struck dumb by Don Cesar's unexpected appearance, has to remain speechless throughout, because a single word from her would explain the whole situation. In II, 6, Isabella withholds information which she should be only too anxious to give. In the same scene, Don Manuel has to fall into a kind of trance, and subsequently has to be removed from the stage, just when his presence and his undivided attention would have cleared up everything. Such deliberate manipulation defeats its own ends. The playwright falls between two stools: he loses the effect, grand though depressing, of inescapable destiny, and, on the other hand, the character tragedy is vitiated by the intrusion of blind chance. Instead of reminding us of Goethe's dictum

> 'Unser Leben ist wie das Ganze, in dem wir enthalten sind, auf eine unbegreifliche Weise aus Freiheit und Notwendigkeit zusammengesetzt',[32]

he creates a feeling of bewilderment, and even irritation, by wavering between two points of view.

It is not until the end that Don Cesar's tragedy comes clearly into focus. The scenes after Don Manuel's death owe nothing to the idea of fate; Don Cesar's bearing in those final scenes exemplifies once again Schiller's conception of the tragically sublime. A life of long drawn-out penance is impossible for a man of Don Cesar's temperament. By his act of voluntary self-immolation, he rises superior to the evil that encompasses him, while at the same time remaining true to himself.

> DON CESAR. Nein, Bruder! Nicht dein Opfer will ich dir
>
> Entziehen—deine Stimme aus dem Sarg
>
> Ruft mächt'ger dringend als der Mutter Tränen
>
> Und mächt'ger als der Liebe Flehn—Ich halte
>
> In meinen Armen, was das ird'sche Leben
>
> Zu einem Los der Götter machen kann—
>
> Doch ich, der Mörder, sollte glücklich sein,
>
> Und deine heil'ge Unschuld ungerächet
>
> Im tiefen Grabe liegen—das verhüte
>
> Der allgerechte Lenker unsrer Tage,
>
> Daß solche Teilung sei in seiner Welt—

—Die Tränen sah ich, die auch mir geflossen,

Befriedigt ist mein Herz, ich folge dir.[33]

Once more—for the last time—*Die Braut von Messina* reveals the dual aspect of Schiller's tragedy: pessimistic inasmuch as it recognizes the tragic fact—suffering, both deserved and undeserved, crime, cruelty, evil in all its forms; optimistic in that it asserts its faith in the powers and the nobility of the human soul.

Schiller's desire to recapture something of the spirit, the atmosphere, and the style of Greek tragedy prompted him to revive in his play one of the most characteristic features of ancient drama: the chorus. Unlike its classical models, however, his chorus is divided into two groups, formed by the followers of Don Cesar and Don Manuel. This arrangement helps to justify its twofold role. Part of the time its function is that of an ideal spectator who discusses the happenings in the play with calm detachment; at other times its two groups assume the character of active partisans, reflecting the moods and passions of their leaders. In his prefatory essay *Über den Gebrauch des Chors in der Tragödie*, Schiller describes the introduction of the chorus as an open declaration of war on all naturalism in dramatic art. It serves to remind the audience that the world of high tragedy is an ideal and symbolic world of the imagination, not a copy of everyday experience. If suitably handled, it helps to raise the poetic level of the whole work; above all, its reflective comments provide that element of repose which is essential to the enjoyment of great art.

No feature of this problematic play has been more adversely criticized, in spite of Schiller's attempts to meet the objections of actors and producers by assigning the choric parts to a number of individual speakers. He was being over-confident when he wrote to Körner

'. . . sie sollen mir das Stück spielen, ohne nur zu wissen, daß sie den Chor der alten Tragödie auf die Bühne gebracht haben';[34]

and although he maintained that a dozen plays of this type would suffice to popularize the *genre*,[35] he did not repeat the experiment. Before long we find him admitting that **Die Braut von Messina** is lacking in popular appeal,[36] and that plays in the Greek manner present an awkward problem on the modern stage.[37] But however dubious a dramatic asset his chorus may be, no one can deny that he made it the vehicle of some of his noblest poetry. The great choric speeches, with their varied metrical structure, realize the ambition which Schiller expresses in his preface: they clothe the hard outlines of the action in a rich garment of lyrical beauty; reflecting on things past and things to come, enforcing the lessons of wisdom, the chorus moves with godlike steps among the great issues of human life.

Notes

1. Cf. Part II, ch. 3 (The Legacy of Shaftesbury), *s.f.*

2. 'Cases may arise when Fate takes all the outworks on which a man relied for his safety, and when nothing remains for him but to take refuge in the sacred freedom of the spirit. . . .' (*Über das Erhabene*)

3. W. Macneile Dixon, *Tragedy* (London, 1938), p. 138.

4. Ibid., p. 145.

5. J. G. Robertson quotes the view that *Maria Stuart* is 'the least veracious of all Schiller's historical dramas (*Schiller after a Century,* p. 112). It is difficult to see, however, in what sense it can be said to be less 'veracious' than *Die Jung frau von Orleans*.

6. Cf., for instance, his letter to Goethe of May 31, 1799, and his poem on Goethe's adaptation of Voltaire's *Mahomet* for the German stage (*An Goethe, als er den Mahomet von Voltaire auf die Bühne brachte*). In view of such utterances—and the examples could easily be multiplied—it seems a trifle fanciful to speak of Schiller's Latin outlook upon life, his Latin attitude towards nature, motive, and character' (J. G. Robertson, *Schiller after a Century,* p. 131). Even if one makes full allowances for the self-evident fact that a man's professed convictions need not square with his practice, the statement that 'he led German tragedy back to the Canossa of French classicism' (ibid., p. 125), picturesque though it may be, remains none the less misleading.

7. The most degraded criminal's ennobled

   By his last sufferings, when he meets his fate;

   I feel again the crown upon my brow,

   And noble pride possess my swelling soul!

   (Adapted from the translation by Joseph Mellish; cf. *The Works of Frederick Schiller,* vol. 3, Bohn's Standard Library, London, 1847, p. 312)

8. L. Bellermann, *Schillers Dramen,* II, pp. 198 ff.

9. Not by degrees can we relinquish life;

   Quick, sudden, in the twinkling of an eye

   The separation must be made, the change

   From temporal, to eternal life . . .

   (Translation by J. Mellish)

   These lines echo a passage in the essay *Über das Erhabene*.

   10. MORITMER. He is a madman who neglects to hold

   His bliss in never-ending close embrace

   When Providence has placed it in his grasp.

   I will deliver you, and though it cost

   A thousand lives, I do it: but I swear,

   As God's in Heaven, I will possess you too!

   MARY. Oh, will no God, no angel shelter me?

   Dread destiny! thou throw'st me, in thy wrath,

   From one tremendous terror to the other!

Was I then born to waken nought but frenzy?

Do hate and love conspire alike to fright me?

(Adapted from the translation by J. Mellish)

11. Milton Waldman, *Elizabeth and Leicester;* 2nd ed., London and Glasgow, 1945.

12. *Copie of a Leter Wryten by a Master of Arte of Cambridge to his friend in London,* popularly known as *Leycester's Commonwealth,* and doubtfully attributed to one Robert Parsons; reprint, edited by F. J. Burgoyne, London, 1904; pp. 22 and 35.

13. 'This play came *from my heart,* and was meant to speak *to the heart.*' (February 10, 1802)

14. 'He seeks to rob the heart of man of its treasure; in his fight against superstition, he strikes at faith.'

15. 'She has surrounded thee with glory—The heart created thee: thou art immortal.'

16. To translate the duke's sudden change of heart and allegiance into terms of drama was a difficult undertaking, and it cannot be said that Schiller has been wholly successful. The corresponding scene in the First Part of *Henry VI* (III, 3) is even less convincing—'turn, and turn again,' as Joan rightly remarks.

17. 'The conclusion of the last Act but one is very theatrical, and the thundering *deus ex machina* will not fail of his effect.' (April 3, 1801)

18. Cf. Letter to Goethe, April 3, 1801.

19. Cf. *I Henry VI,* Act V, Scene 3, and Act III, Scene 2.

20. Cf. *Anne of Geierstein,* chaps. 29 and 30.

21. J. G. Robertson, *A History of German Literature,* p. 388.

22. *Universalhistorische Übersicht der vornehmsten an den Kreuzzügen teilnehmenden Nationen* and *Universalhistorische Übersicht der merkwürdigsten Staatsbegebenheiten aus den Zeiten Kaiser Friedrichs I.* These essays appeared in the *Allgemeine Sammlung historischer Memoires* which Schiller edited from 1790 till 1793.

23. For example, in the scene where Joan, on arriving at court, picks out the Dauphin from among his courtiers; cf. *Saint Joan,* Scene 2, and Schiller's totally different treatment in *Die Jungfrau von Orleans,* I, 10.

24. From the actors' and the producer's point of view, Scene 11 presents almost insuperable difficulties.

    With Joan's passionate prayer for divine intervention in this scene, cf. *Judges* xvi. 28 and *Acts* xii. 5-7.

25. 'The idea of freedom assumed a different form as Schiller advanced in his own development and became a different man. In his youth it was physical freedom that preoccupied him

and that found its way into his works; in later life it was spiritual freedom.' (January 18, 1827)

26. *Gespräche mit Goethe,* January 18, 1825.

27. '. . . as in the *Oedipus* of Sophocles, the interest lies not so much in the characters as in the plot.' (Letter to Körner, May 13, 1801)

28. Cf. Letters to Körner, September 9, 1802; to Iffland, April 22, 1803; and to W. von Humboldt, February 17, 1803.

29. Cf. the graphic account of these conditions in Schiller's *Universalhistorische Übersicht der merkwürdigsten Staatsbegebenheiten aus den Zeiten Kaiser Friedrichs I.*

30. No judge lives on this earth to punish me,
    Hence I myself must wield the avenging sword.
    Dying, I exorcise the ancient curse;
    Death self-imposed alone can break the chain of fate.

31. The division into acts and scenes derives from the stage copies; in the published version Schiller dispensed with it, in deference to the practice of the ancients.

32. 'Our lives, like the universe to which we belong, are mysteriously composed of freedom and necessity.' (*Dichtung und Wahrheit,* Part III, Book 11)

33. DON CESAR. I will not rob thee, brother!

The sacrifice is thine:—Hark! from the tomb,

Mightier than mother's tears, or sister's love,

Thy voice resistless cries:—my arms enfold

What could bring heavenly joy to earthly life—

But, having killed thee, shall I live in bliss,

While in the tomb thy sainted innocence

Sleeps unavenged? Thou Ruler of our days,

All-just, all-wise, let not thy world behold

Such rank injustice! No—I saw her tears

Flowing for me: I too was dear to her—

I am content, and now I follow thee!

(Adapted from the translation by A. Lodge in *The Works of Frederick Schiller,* vol. 3, Bohn's Standard Library, London, 1847, p. 516)

34. '. . . they are to perform the play without even realizing that they have been introducing the chorus of ancient tragedy.' (February 6, 1803)

35. Cf. Letter to Iffland, April 22, 1803.

36. Cf. Letter to Körner, October 16, 1803.

37. Cf. Letter to Goethe, February 8, 1804.

E. L. Stahl (essay date 1954)

SOURCE: "Necessity and Freedom," in *Friedrich Schiller's Drama: Theory and Practice,* The Clarendon Press, 1954, pp. 126-54.

[*In the following essay, Stahl discusses Schiller's last plays,* Die Braut von Messina, Wilhelm Tell, *and the fragment* Demetrius, *and finds in them several new features—notably the exploration of the tension between necessity and free will, the external rather than the internal compulsion of characters, and tragic action based on the transformation of the hero's character—that indicate a shift in style and emphasis in Schiller's dramatic works and a development in his notion of tragedy.*]

The new features of Schiller's last plays are striking enough to make us question once more how far his theory of tragedy may assist in the interpretation of his creative work. Whereas the theory is unthinkable without the notion of a single hero, neither *Die Braut von Messina* nor *Wilhelm Tell* possesses an individual protagonist. Moreover, these dramas portray human beings acting under compulsion far more strongly than the earlier plays. The tragic problem no longer appears to hinge on the interaction of character and circumstance; it seems to embrace a wider question involving the relation between necessity and free will in wholegroups of characters as well as individual persons.

Here *Über das Erhabene*, first written between 1793 and 1795 and probably rewritten before publication in 1801, gives an indication of the movement of Schiller's thought. He identifies nature with fate and glorifies the triumph of the human will over 'savage and destructive nature'.[1] This view of nature is in striking contrast to the opinions he expressed in *Über naive und sentimentalische Dichtung* and it should warn us that his conception of fate is not the normal one. He includes in the concept of fate or necessity the notions of injustice and tyranny which we should assign primarily to the realm of social responsibility,[2] so that the opposition he envisages in the conflict between the human will and nature may be said to represent a collision between rational and irrational forces. This view is also suggested by his inclusion of sensuous impulses and instincts in the idea of fate. As far as he was concerned it was immaterial whether the irrational force operated in the human or nonhuman world, for he believed that the supremacy of the will could and should manifest itself in combat with both worlds. We must bear in mind his conception of the struggle between fate and free will when we examine Don Cesar's motives for committing suicide in *Die Braut von Messina* and Tell's motives for killing Geßler, and ask ourselves whether these are sublime actions in Schiller's original sense.

Soon after he had completed *Die Jungfrau von Orleans* he wrote to Körner that he felt 'a keen desire to try my hand at writing a simple tragedy in the strictest Greek style' and mentioned a plot which was entirely his own invention.[3] He invented the story of *Die Braut von Messina* in order to treat his material 'nach der strengsten griechischen Form' without adhering too closely to the Greek idea of fate. He also chose the setting of the play with deliberate care: the action takes place after the Norman conquest of Sicily. As he pointed out in another letter to Körner, this choice of time and place enabled him to give his work a composite mythological character:

> Das Ideenkostüm, das ich mir erlaubte, hat dadurch seine Rechtfertigung, daß die Handlung nach Messina versetzt ist, wo sich Christentum, griechische Mythologie und Mohamedanismus wirklich begegnet und vermischt haben. . . . Die Vermischung dieser drei Mythologien, die sonst den Charakter aufheben würde, wird also hier selbst zum Charakter.[4]

He did not wish to offer a direct imitation of Greek tragedy. While the influence of Sophocles is again unmistakable—in his letter to Körner he mentions *Oedipus* as his model—the invention of a legend not derived from Greek sources, and the fusion of the fate theme with that of the incestuous love of two brothers for their sister, give the drama an individual stamp. Its modern features were no less obvious to Schiller's contemporaries than its Greek characteristics,[5] for a view similar to Herder's idea of fate underlies the presentation of the tragic complications: 'Nur also durch Menschen-charaktere wirke das Schicksal, doch so, daß jene unter der Gewalt dieses wirken.'[6] The decisive factor in the action of *Die Braut von Messina* is not an inscrutable supernatural power, but the behaviour of the principal characters, and in the last resort Isabella's responsibility is shared by her deceased husband and their three children.

Throughout the tragedy the reigning family is described as 'the alien race', and Isabella herself recognizes that the inhabitants of the city bear a deep hatred towards her and her family:

> Wie könnten sie's von Herzen mit euch meinen,
>
> Den Fremdlingen, dem eingedrungnen Stamm,
>
> Der aus dem eignen Erbe sie vertrieben,
>
> Sich über sie der Herrschaft angemaßt?[7]

Yet Schiller does not motivate the tragedy from this circumstance.[8] It is not the fact that the deceased Prince has been a foreign usurper per that brings about the downfall of his race. The disaster is caused by conditions prevailing within the family rather than by political opposition. The Prince's despotic rule over his children is the primary cause of the tragedy. In her first speech to the elders of Messina, Isabella describes his tyrannical nature, and later the chorus gives an account of his original guilt:

> Auch ein Raub war's, wie wir alle wissen,
>
> Der des alten Fürsten eheliches Gemahl
>
> In ein frevelnd Ehebett gerissen,
>
> Denn sie war des Vaters Wahl.
>
> Und der Ahnherr schüttete im Zorne
>
> Grauenvoller Flüche schrecklichen Samen
>
> Auf das sündige Ehebett aus. . . .
>
> Ja, es hat nicht gut begonnen,
>
> Glaubt mir, und es endet nicht gut,

Denn gebßt wird unter der Sonnen

Jede Tat der verblendeten Wut.

Es ist kein Zufall und blindes Los,

Daß die Brüder sich wütend selbst zerstören,

Denn verflucht ward der Mutter Schoß,

Sie sollte den Haß und den Streit gebären.[9]

If there is a supernatural power dominating the Prince's family, it is Nemesis rather than chance: the sins of the father are visited upon the children.

The Prince's intemperate character is the first, but not the only, cause of the tragic entanglements depicted in the play. When Don Manuel refuses to reveal the name of his bride, Isabella recognizes his secretiveness as an inherited trait:

Des Vaters eignen Sinn und Geist erkenn' ich

In meinem erstgebornen Sohn! Der liebte

Von jeher, sich verborgen in sich selbst

Zu spinnen und den Ratschluß zu bewahren

Im unzugangbar fest verschlossenen Gemüt![10]

This failing taints all the members of the family. The father is not its sole begetter, for the children inherit it from their mother as well.[11] Isabella's actions are just as surreptitious as those of her husband when she secretly consults the monk about her dream and conceals Beatrice in a convent, and she bears much of the blame for the situation that arises because she unnecessarily delays the discovery of her secret. The magnitude of her guilt is recognized by Don Cesar when he lays his fearful curse on her.

The difference between Sophocles and Schiller becomes clear when we consider this point. In *Oedipus Rex* the tragedy is not caused by the operation of an hereditary curse, nor is the secret intentionally devised by any of the characters, as is the case in **Die Braut von Messina**. Here all the characters are under a curse and by their acts of concealment as well as their intemperate conduct they bring about the catastrophe. Only through their inability to curb their passions are the oracles fulfilled whereby the sister both unites her brothers and encompasses their destruction.

Isabella's guilt lies in her secretive and dominating bearing. She 'clings to a position resting on the force of fear and power alone'.[12] An even more serious flaw is her total lack of moral sense: her attitude to the outside world is animated by hatred and arrogance. This is true of her relationship not only with the citizens of Messina but also with the gods. She never admits that her husband's guilt and her own are the real cause of her family's misfortune. Twice she uses the image of pouring lava to describe the deadly feud of her sons, only to profess her ignorance of its origin:

Hier ist das Mein und Dein,

Die Rache von der Schuld nicht mehr zu sondern.

—Wer möchte noch das alte Bette finden

Des Schwefelstroms, der glühend sich ergoß?[13]

Lacking humility she attributes her unhappiness to a *Verhängnis*, a *Schicksal*, a *tückisch Wesen* or *neid'scher Dämon*. This attitude culminates in her defiance of the gods:

Was kümmert's mich noch, ob die Götter sich

Als Lügner zeigen, oder sich als wahr

Bestätigen? Mir haben sie das Ärgste

Getan—Trotz biet' ich ihnen, mich noch härter

Zu treffen, als sie trafen—Wer für nichts mehr

Zu zittern hat, der fürchtet sie nicht mehr.[14]

It is difficult to believe that Schiller intended us to feel admiration or pity for Isabella when she exclaims these passionate and rebellious words. A comparison between her behaviour and that of Johanna in the fourth act of **Die Jungfrau von Orleans** suggests that it was not his purpose to portray Isabella as a sublime character.

We come to a similar conclusion when we consider Don Cesar. His death is the only instance we have in Schiller's dramas of self-immolation which is an act of outright suicide, and in this respect it differs even from Posa's self-sacrifice. Is it also an example of *das Erhabene der Handlung* dictated by *Reue* and *Buße*? True, when the chorus reminds him that the wrath of heaven may be ransomed by 'fromme Büßung', Cesar replies:

Bußfert'ge Sühne, weiß ich, nimmt der Himmel an,

Doch nur mit Blute büßt sich ab der blut'ge Mord.

Later he declares that the curse upon his family can only be redeemed by an act of free will:

Den alten Fluch des Hauses lös' ich sterbend auf,

Der freie Tod nur bricht die Kette des Geschicks.[15]

These sentiments may be called sublime in Schiller's sense: by committing suicide Don Cesar vindicates the principle of freedom. Yet his suicide is also dictated by a passionate urge:

Mich laß dem Geist gehorchen, der mich furchtbar treibt,

Denn in das Innre kann kein Glücklicher mir schaun.[16]

He explains this impulse in his reply to Isabella's plea that a life of penance would bring him peace and forgiveness:

Lebe, wer's kann, ein Leben der Zerknirschung,

Mit strengen Bußkasteiungen allmählich

Abschöpfend eine ew'ge Schuld—Ich kann

Nicht leben, Mutter, mit gebrochnem Herzen.

Aufblicken muß ich freudig zu den Frohen

Und in den Äther greifen über mir

Mit freiem Geist—Der Neid vergiftete mein Leben,

Da wir noch deine Liebe gleich geteilt.

Denkst du, daß ich den Vorzug werde tragen,

Den ihm dein Schmerz gegeben über mich?[17]

Don Cesar's motives for committing suicide, like those of Posa for courting death, compound idealism with egotism: his resolve to kill himself is an emotional rather than a moral decision.

One cannot say that Schiller abandoned his ideal of sublimity when he wrote **Die Braut von Messina,** but in Isabella and Don Cesar he portrayed the defeat of that ideal through the supremacy of passion. While arousing sympathy for them he did not wish to excite admiration in equal measure. The distinctive feature of the play is its emphasis on the emotional behaviour of its leading characters, the rational and reflective tones being assigned in the main to the chorus. Not even in **Die Räuber** or **Don Carlos** do we find conduct so consistently motivated from the irrational springs of human nature. Schiller uses the influence of heredity in **Die Braut von Messina** as nowhere else in his dramatic work. What strikes one in some of his earlier dramas is the decisive, yet unaccountable, difference in the character of members belonging to the same family, such as the brothers in **Die Räuber** and father and son in **Kabale und Liebe** or **Don Carlos.** In **Die Braut von Messina** the children take after their parents: they obey 'the voice of nature, the power of blood'.[18] The power which drives them to their doom is not merely an external force; their fate is in their blood. It would be absurd to claim **Die Braut von Messina** as a forerunner of *Ghosts,* for Schiller's conception of heredity derives from the doctrine of original sin rather than from biological theory. Yet it is remarkable that behind the statuesque form of his most severely classical play he revealed a source of life lying deeper than the mainsprings he had hitherto recognized.

That he wished to accentuate this aspect may be inferred from the importance he gave to the contrast between the destructive power of human passion and the idyllic landscape of Messina, just as he had stressed the beauty of Sicily in his *Universalhistorische Übersicht* when he opposed the bounty of nature in the island to the devastating passions of its conquerors.[19] In this respect the idea of fate in **Die Braut von Messina** is narrower than in *Über das Erhabene,* where Schiller describes the destructive power of nature in order to assert the high value of man's sublime conquest of nature:

> Wer bestaunt nicht lieber den wunderbaren Kampf zwischen Fruchtbarkeit und Zerstörung in Siziliens Fluren . . . Niemand wird leugnen, daß in Bataviens Triften für den physischen Menschen besser gesorgt ist als unter dem tückischen Krater des Vesuv. . . . Aber der Mensch hat noch ein Bedürfnis mehr, als zu leben und sich wohl sein zu lassen. . . .[20]

Significantly, it is left to Isabella in **Die Braut von Messina** to dwell on nature's destructiveness without asserting the ideal of sublimity. The chorus, on the other hand, remarks on the contrast between human and inanimate nature which underlies the tragic developments of the drama:

> Wohl dem! Selig muß ich ihn preisen,
>
> Der in der Stille der ländlichen Flur,
>
> Fern von des Lebens verworrenen Kreisen,
>
> Kindlich liegt an der Brust der Natur.[21]

In one of his letters to Körner, Schiller states that he intended the chorus to serve two different functions. It stands outside the action and speaks directly to the audience; it also participates in the action with Don Manuel and Don Cesar. In the first instance it is meant to represent a 'forum of justice', in the second an embodiment of popular superstition and zeal.[22] By giving his chorus an active as well as a passive role, Schiller intentionally departed from the practice observable in the best-known Greek dramas: he also gave point to the idealistic nature of his play. Moreover, by frankly conceding this feature of the work in the brilliantly written preface, *Über den Gebrauch des Chors in der Tragödie,* he gave the best defence of his artistic purpose.

Here he states his opinion that the introduction of the chorus in Greek tragedy was a natural development reflecting the normal Greek method of conducting public affairs in the open air, whereas in northern countries assemblies take place behind closed doors. This observation leads him to offer a significant explanation of the poet's function in modern times: 'Der Dichter muß die Paläste wieder auftun, er muß die Gerichte unter freien Himmel herausführen, er muß die Götter wieder aufstellen. . . .'[23] The Preface is his last public affirmation of his aesthetic creed entailing the rejection of naturalism in poetry and dramatic art. He recognizes the introduction of the chorus as a valid means of achieving his idealistic aims:

> Die Einführung des Chors wäre der letzte, der entscheidende Schritt—und wenn derselbe auch nur dazu diente, dem Naturalism in der Kunst offen und ehrlich den Krieg zu erklären, so sollte er uns eine lebendige Mauer sein, die die Tragödie um sich herumzieht, um sich von der wirklichen Welt rein abzuschließen und sich ihren idealen Boden, ihre poetische Freiheit zu bewahren.[24]

In his earlier plays he had used crowds to a different end: the robbers in **Die Räuber** and the soldiers in **Wallensteins Lager** are partisans; they act solely as foils to the enterprises of the heroes. **Die Braut von Messina** is Schiller's only tragedy in which the crowds are also 'ideal spectators' and commentators upon the actions of the principal characters, thus partly expressing the author's own judgements and feelings. In this way he was able to import into tragedy a subjective element which is, as he recognized in agreement with Goethe, not necessarily incompatible with the objective presentation demanded by the genre.[25] And since this subjectivism manifests itself in the expression of states of mind as well as ideas, a lyric strain pervades his choric odes. He envisaged a musical setting for these odes[26] and used all the resources of the lyricist's art at his command—intricate patterns of rhythm and rhyme, supple and suggestive word-formations and numerous refrains of phrases, lines, and stanzas—to promote this end. The choric songs of *Die Braut von Messina* are among the best lyric poetry he wrote. The growth of a lyric strain in his dramas since *Maria Stuart* has been noticed, and here *Die Braut von Messina* represents his best achievement, to be equalled only by *Demetrius*.

Wilhelm Tell is the final product of Schiller's development in a different way. The compulsion on the principal figure is entirely external. This profoundly affects the moral issue. When we consider Schiller's presentation of guilt and moral responsibility in the dramas written after he worked out his theory of tragedy, we note a gradual shift of emphasis. Maria Stuart's culpability can still be clearly defined: in *Die Jungfrau von Orleans* we have to ask ourselves to what extent the heroine is responsible for her transgression. Johanna incurs guilt although she is, at least partly, ruled by a power beyond her own control. The problem of her responsibility is much more complex than that which confronts us when we consider the crimes of Schiller's earlier heroes, and the same is to a large extent true of Don Cesar. The tragic problem in these later plays may be stated in the terms which Herder used to describe the issue implicit in the Greek tragedians' conception of necessity: 'Hier war die Frage nicht: Warum solche Schicksale die Menschen treffen? Sondern, wenn und weil sie sie treffen, wie sind sie anzusehen, wie zu ertragen?'[27] The crux is not merely the origin of guilt, but the moral demand consequent on the visitation of guilt, and here Schiller's idea of sublime conduct still holds good. We have also seen that he altered the Greek conception of necessity by imputing a human origin to fated calamities, although he dealt with this side of the tragic actions more summarily than in his earlier plays. For this reason it is also true to say that in *Die Jungfrau von Orleans* and *Die Braut von Messina* he still presents a moral issue, though he does not treat the problem of responsibility as resulting from a premeditated act of guilt.

By contrast, such a tragic problem is of secondary importance in *Wilhelm Tell.* True, the *Schauspiel* contains hidden depths of tragedy.[28] When Schiller began to write it he remarked in a letter to Wilhelm von Wolzogen that he planned *eine große Tragödie.*[29] But the finished work is not a tragedy: it is his only dramatic composition to avoid a tragic issue. In this respect it resembles Goethe's *Iphigenie,* on which Schiller passed a severe judgement: 'Jede Wirkung, die ich von diesem Stücke teils an mir selbst, teils an andern erfahren, ist, generisch poetisch, nicht tragisch gewesen, und so wird es immer sein, wenn eine Tragödie, auf epische Art, verfehlt wird.'[30]

The remark may be applied to *Wilhelm Tell* with more justice. Schiller undertook to dramatize the revolt of the Swiss cantons at Goethe's suggestion when the latter abandoned his plan to write an epic on the subject. Goet-

he's choice of genre was clearly the right one, if it is true that a national war is a theme that lends itself more readily to epic than dramatic treatment. The story of Tell offered potential material for a tragedy only if his aims and methods could be made to conflict with those of his fellow countrymen or if he was made to perform a deed which either he or his compatriots should subsequently disavow. Neither of these contingencies arises in Schiller's play. Although his Tell refuses to make common cause with the confederates of the Rütli and goes his own way, there is no question of a real conflict between them or within Tell himself. The much criticized 'Parricida scene' in Act V shows the total absence of such a conflict in Tell: far from revolting against his own assassination of Geßler, he utterly denies that he has done wrong, and the last scene of the play proves beyond doubt that he also enjoys the acclamation of his fellow countrymen. He has no need to exhibit moral sublimity, since in Schiller's presentation he has not committed a crime demanding expiation by means of *Reue und Verzweiflung.*[31]

When Schiller considered writing *eine große Tragödie* he may have had in mind a conflict like that mentioned by Tschudi in *Chronicon Helveticum,* where Tell's independent action arouses the displeasure of the confederates. On the other hand he may have contemplated a struggle similar to that in *Die Jungfrau von Orleans.* There is some evidence for believing that the latter was his original intention. On 17 March 1802 he wrote to Körner:

> Du wirst mich fragen, warum ich denn den Warbeck habe liegen lassen; ich habe viel über das Stück gedacht, und werde es auch unfehlbar mit Success ausführen. Aber ein anderes Sujet hat sich gefunden, das mich jetzt ungleich stärker anzieht, und welches ich getrost auf die Jungrau von Orleans kann folgen lassen.[32]

In other letters written at about the same time he calls his material 'accursed' and the problem he set himself 'an infernal task' because he found it difficult to treat a specific and localized event in such a way as to give it general validity.[33] When he began the work his mind was ruled by the idealistic principles he had hitherto followed in composing his tragedies: he was preoccupied with the invention of a moral crisis not vouchsafed by history but essential to his conception of tragedy. In the first stages of writing *Wilhelm Tell* his aims were thus not very different from those he followed when he invented the heroine's guilt in *Die Jungfrau von Orleans.*

A change occurred when he decided to produce a *Schauspiel* dealing with the liberation of the Swiss Cantons as the principal theme, rather than a tragedy embodying the idea of sublimity. The change appears to have taken place towards the end of 1803. His final decision to write a *Volksstück* explains why *Wilhelm Tell* became such a singular work among his dramas. It owes its instantaneous and lasting appeal to his success in carrying through this design. Yet his idealistic principle remained inviolate despite the concessions he made to popular taste, as may be seen when we examine his reasons for dividing the dramatic action into two parts and separating the Tell-Geßler episode from the main plot. Although the play is one of his most effective stage productions, its lack of unity is an obvious flaw which is first discovered in the motivation of Tell's absence from the Rütli meeting.

In Act I, Scene 3, Tell is exhorted to make common cause with the representatives of the Cantons, but he refuses to take part in their deliberations:

> Ich kann nicht lange prüfen oder wählen;
>
> Bedürft ihr meiner zu bestimmter Tat,
>
> Dann ruft den Tell, es soll an mir nicht fehlen.[34]

Subsequently he kills Geßler without having been called upon by the confederates and without reference to their resolutions. In one important respect his independent action is contrary to the policy they have adopted in obedience to Stauffacher's exhortation:

> Bezähme jeder die gerechte Wut
>
> Und spare für das Ganze seine Rache:
>
> Denn Raub begeht am allgemeinen Gut,
>
> Wer selbst sich hilft in seiner eignen Sache.[35]

The uprising of the Swiss is a bloodless revolt. Its incentive is not strictly revolutionary but conservative. The rebels do not wish to inaugurate a new order: they try to preserve the ancient rights which their Austrian rulers threaten to take away.

In another respect, however, Tell's deed accords with the policy of the *Rütlibund*. It is inspired not by vengeance but by the necessity to ward off further danger.[36] In his crucial monologue beginning 'Durch diese hohle Gasse muß er kommen' he ponders the danger threatening his family rather than the wrong Geßler has already done to him, and in his encounter with Johann von Schwaben he rejects the comparison of Parricida's crime with his own deed.[37]

It is noticeable that neither in his monologue nor in this scene does Tell mention the national cause, although he reassures Hedwig, in the second scene of the last act, that he has defended his family as well as saved the country from tyranny by killing Geßler. When he kills Geßler the national idea is far from his mind. Schiller made it quite clear that the assassination was not inspired by patriotic motives and he stressed the point in a letter to Iffland which also contains some interesting information about his method of writing the play. Iffland had requested him to send in each act as soon as it was completed, and Schiller replied that he could not do that, since he did not compose each act separately:

> Gerne wollte ich Ihnen das Stück aktenweise zuschicken, aber es entsteht nicht aktenweise, sondern die Sache erfordert, daß ich gewisse Handlungen, die zusammen gehören, durch alle fünf Akte durchführe, und dann erst zu andern übergehe. So z. B. steht der

> Tell selbst ziemlich für sich in dem Stück, seine Sache ist eine Privatsache, und bleibt es, bis sie am Schluß mit der öffentlichen Sache zusammengreift.[38]

From all we know about Schiller's method of writing his other plays, as for instance when we consider the evidence of the scenarios he made for **Don Carlos** and for **Demetrius,** this piecemeal procedure was not his customary manner. In **Wilhelm Tell** it was dictated by his resolve to keep the two actions of the play as widely separate as possible. Was he justified in claiming that Tell's private cause coincides with the public cause at the end of the play? It surely comes as a surprise to hear Tell acclaimed the country's saviour and to see him accept the homage of the assembled people in the final scenes. The closing tableau, from which the freedom-loving Bertha and the former renegade Rudenz are not missing, is an effective dramatic device: it is also Schiller's belated attempt to establish a unity which the play, in effect, does not possess. The coherence of the original conception was destroyed when he changed the *große Tragödie* into a *Schauspiel* and made the national theme its dramatic pivot, without either reducing Tell's importance in the work as a whole or raising him to the position of national leader.

In many ways Schiller closely followed the accounts of the Swiss revolt in his principal sources, Etterlin's and Tschudi's chronicles; he borrowed a large number of incidents, references, words and phrases from them. In one respect, however, he departed from his authorities. They bring out the fact that, although Tell was present at the Rütli meeting and took the same oath as the other conspirators, his later actions were contrary to his oath and aroused the disapproval of his fellow men. Tschudi also makes it clear that the murder of Geßler did not influence the course of the national revolt. Similarly, in Johannes von Müller's *Geschichte Schweizerischer Eidgenossenschaft* (1786-8) Tell's deed is presented as a mere episode. He is a member of the *Bund,* but, although he kills Geßler for patriotic reasons, the war is fought without his active participation and he does not assist in the counsels of those who promote it.[39]

The complete detachment of Tell from the *Bund* is Schiller's innovation. He had good reasons for making such an absolute separation, although it involved him in serious technical difficulties. When we consider why he gave Tell a dominating role without also making him the real hero of his play, we must take his political views into account, particularly his judgement of the French Revolution. Their relevance may be seen from the dedicatory poem accompanying the presentation copy he sent to Erzkanzler von Dalberg in 1804. Here he distinguishes between the just and the unjust use of violence in the fight for freedom. In *Briefe über die ästhetische Erziehung des Menschen* he similarly condemned the employment of physical force to bring about social and political change and relied on aesthetic education as the only safe means of redressing the balance of right and wrong in society. But he condoned the use of violence as a purely defensive measure, provided that it did not exceed humane limits, for instance

. . . wenn ein Volk, das fromm die Herden weidet,

Sich selbst genug nicht fremden Guts begehrt,

Den Zwang abwirft, den es unwürdig leidet,

Doch selbst im Zorn die Menschlichkeit noch ehrt.
. . .[40]

This view led him to idealize the rising of the Swiss and characterize it as a limited resistance movement. He presented it as a bloodless war led by rightminded *Biedermänner* like Stauffacher and Walther Fürst, not as a revolt of the infuriated lower orders, and eliminated its social aspect, the battle of the peasantry against their aristocratic masters. The romantic Bertha-Rudenz episode, an invention on Schiller's part, serves to obscure this side of the popular movement in the interest of portraying the Swiss as a compact and harmonious nation. Nothing could be more at variance with historical fact than the last line of the play. The liberation of the serfs was not the magnanimous deed of a socially minded aristocracy, but the achievement of the peasants after a long and arduous struggle. These facts are only important in so far as they help to explain Schiller's presentation of the material.

His characterization of the Swiss owes much to Johannes von Müller, who stressed the humanitarian nature of the popular revolt. The two writers held the same political views and Schiller accepted the Swiss historian's account of the uprising as being based on the people's historic rights. He did not, however, accept von Müller's justification of Geßler's murder. For Schiller it could not be justified on political grounds but only as a defensive act in a *Privatsache* revealing 'das Notwendige und Rechtliche der Selbsthilfe in einem streng bestimmten Fall'.[41] Thus Schiller's Tell is not faced with a tragic dilemma. His monologue in Act IV, Scene 3, differs from the monologues of Fiesco and Wallenstein at similarly decisive moments in that he does not consider the rights and wrongs of his projected deed, nor has he any cause to do so. He is not aware of any conflict between duty and inclination because such a conflict does not arise. He obeys the moral law; he does not transgress it. Moral necessity impels him and he freely chooses to submit to its compulsion. He follows the dictates of reason, not passion, and thus, unlike Maria Stuart or Johanna d'Arc, he has no need to achieve either *das Erhabene der Fassung* or *das Erhabene der Handlung*, although he exemplifies an untragic form of sublimity by his willing performance of an arduous task:

> Diese Sinnesart aber, welche die Moral unter dem Begriff der Resignation in die Notwendigkeit und die Religion unter dem Begriff der Ergebung in den göttlichen Ratschluß lehrt, erfordert, wenn sie ein Werk der freien Wahl und Überlegung sein soll, schon eine größere Klarheit des Denkens und eine höhere Energie des Willens, als dem Menschen im handelnden Leben eigen zu sein pflegt.[42]

In Wilhelm Tell Schiller created his only non-tragic sublime hero. By separating the Geßler action from the main plot he presented both the national uprising and the assassination as morally justifiable. He could not allow

Tell to participate in the deliberations on the Rütli or figure in the organized revolt, since the revolt would have been prejudiced by being directly linked to the killing of the Landvogt. The national victory had to be won by storming and burning the castles without bloodshed. Walther Fürst praises his followers for having gained their victory in this irreproachable way:

> Wohl Euch, daß Ihr den reinen Sieg
> Mit Blute nicht geschändet.[43]

In the same scene Stauffacher proclaims Tell the founder of Swiss freedom. The contradiction is not resolved. Iffland had urged Schiller to complete the work as quickly as possible and he was the first to recognize that the conclusion lacked sound motivation.

Again, it was Iffland who called Schiller's attention to the theatrical qualities inherent in the material, and the author did not fail to show his dramaturgic skill in the grouping and movement of masses on the stage and the employment of tension and surprise. In this respect the work is a masterpiece. Thus during the apple-shooting scene our attention is diverted from Tell by the skilfully prepared intervention of Rudenz and Bertha whereby the effectiveness of Tell's success is heightened. Similarly, Geßler's assassination is ingeniously handled: our expectations are successively aroused, retarded, intensified, and finally fulfilled. Such masterly scenes assured the play instantaneous applause.

It was hailed as a masterpiece of realistic stagecraft. Yet unqualified realism was not what Schiller aimed at producing, in spite of his frequent use of Swiss idioms in the peasants' homely speech. He did not wish to make the peasants true to life. The word *Biedermann* occurs frequently and is an apt description. It fits Schiller's Swiss citizens very well and here Tell is the true representative of his people, an exemplar of idealized middle-class virtues.[44] All the characters indulge in the habit of expressing themselves in aphorisms, and none more consistently, and even tediously, than Tell. His speech abounds in maxims, apophthegms, generalizations, and their theme is usually the dignity and the duty of man. Schiller brings out this moralizing bent from the beginning and thus we have no cause to be surprised when this side of his character asserts itself in his meeting with Johannes von Schwaben. Some critics discern a development in Tell from the peace-loving citizen at the beginning of the play to the unwilling criminal at the end. This is reading too much into the work. In truth Wilhelm Tell remains throughout a model of propriety. Schiller's last *Schauspiel* is also his only authentic tribute to bourgeois virtue in dramatic form.

In this respect the play is more closely allied to poems like *Der Spaziergang* and *Das Lied von der Glocke* than to his other dramatic work. When he had completed *Der Spaziergang* in 1795 he wrote to Wilhelm von Humboldt that he was planning to write an idyllic poem in the reflective style, a pendant to the elegiac poem he had just finished:

Ich will eine Idylle schreiben, wie ich hier eine Elegie schrieb. Alle meine poetischen Kräfte spannen sich zu dieser Energie noch an. . . . In der sentimentalischen Dichtkunst (und aus dieser heraus kann ich nicht) ist die Idylle das höchste, aber auch das schwierigste Problem.[45]

His plan did not mature, but we may look upon *Wilhelm Tell* as the fulfilment of his long-cherished desire.[46] There can be little doubt that he intentionally competed with Goethe when he undertook to dramatize the story of Tell. His profound admiration for his friend did not exclude a sense of rivalry. 'He has aroused in me a peculiar mixture of hate and love' he had written in 1789.[47] When their acquaintance ripened into friendship, Schiller's 'hatred' mellowed into a keen awareness of the fundamental differences between their natures and their art. This is clearly shown in *Über naive und sentimentalische Dichtung*. The section on idyllic poetry evinces his desire to rival Goethe's achievement. He exhorts the reflective poet to vie with and even surpass the 'naïve' writer by relinquishing pastoral subjects and depicting perfection in higher forms of social and cultural life:

> Er mache sich die Aufgabe einer Idylle, welche jene Hirtenunschuld auch in Subjekten der Kultur und unter allen Bedingungen des rüstigsten feurigsten Lebens, des ausgebreitetsten Denkens, der raffiniertesten Kunst, der höchsten gesellschaftlichen Verfeinerung ausführt, welche, mit einem Wort, den Menschen, der nun einmal nicht mehr nach Arkadien zurück kann, bis nach Elysium führt.[48]

'Der Begriff dieser Idylle', Schiller continues, 'ist der Begriff eines völlig aufgelösten Kampfes sowohl in dem einzelnen Mensch en als in der Gesellschaft, einer freien Vereinigung der Neigungen mit dem Gesetze, einer zur höchsten sittlichen Würde hinaufgeläuterten Natur. . . .'[49] The story of Wilhelm Tell and the Swiss uprising offered him an opportunity to portray such an 'idyllic' ideal of harmony in the individual and in society. Despite its singular position in the body of his dramatic work, *Wilhelm Tell* represents a culmination of his poetic development.

However important one may consider the difference between *Wilhelm Tell* and his other dramas, there is little justification for believing that it denotes a radical change in his outlook. His decision to write a *Schauspiel* does not mean that he resolved a tragic problem inherent in his earlier plays, if we mean by that a tragic problem of a personal kind such as the one that troubled Heinrich von Kleist. Problems of this kind did not exist for Schiller: they were ruled out by his adherence to the doctrine of harmony. The new task he set himself in *Wilhelm Tell* was no more than technical, namely to write a drama in the 'idyllic' manner.

In a different way the composition of *Demetrius* marks the execution of a project of some years' standing without denoting, as far as we can judge from the evidence at our disposal a decisive turn in the author's development.[50] There are several new features in this fragmentary work

and they are not lacking in significance, but there does not appear to be any fundamental difference between *Demetrius* and the dramas that immediately preceded it: Schiller again explores the relation between necessity and free will.

The beginnings are closely linked with his plan for a tragedy on Perkin Warbeck which he first formed in 1799. On 20 August of that year he wrote to Goethe outlining his views on the difference between a comic and a tragic treatment of the subject. In the former case the contrast between the pretender's claims and his inability to play the desired part would form the centre of interest; in the latter case the claims would seem to be substantiated by the pretender's capacity to act the chosen role. The tragedy would consist in the fact that he was being exploited by those who supported him, not in the fact that he was incompetent or that he was defeated by his enemies:

> Was die Behandlung des erwähnten Stoffs betrifft, so müßte man, däucht mir, das Gegenteil von dem tun, was der Komödiendichter daraus machen würde. Dieser würde durch den Kontrast des Betrügers mit seiner großen Rolle und seine Inkompetenz zu derselben das Lächerliche hervorbringen. In der Tragödie müßte er als zu seiner Rolle geboren erscheinen und er müßte sie sich so sehr zu eigen machen, daß mit denen, die ihn zu ihrem Werkzeug gebrauchen und als ihr Geschöpf behandeln wollten, interessante Kämpfe entstünden. Die Katastrophe müßte durch seine Anhänger und Beschützer, nicht durch seine Feinde . . . herbeigeführt werden.[51]

This passage is interesting for several reasons. It shows how little justified one is in seeking a purely personal bias behind Schiller's idea of tragedy: this thesis is disproved by his readiness to contemplate treating the same subject in a comic and a tragic manner. The passage also specifies his conception of the inward nature of tragic conflicts by his prescription that the catastrophe should be brought about through the hero's friends rather than his enemies.

Schiller soon found that he was unable to write the kind of tragedy he had in mind because the story of Perkin Warbeck was devoid of dramatic action and ended inconclusively. Instead he chose the history of Dmitri which commended itself for the 'greatness of its subject and scope'.[52] It offered him what the story of the English pretender lacked: Dmitri did become Czar of Russia, whereas Warbeck's whole enterprise miscarried. Dmitri's success, attended by an awareness that his claims were false, presented itself as the climax of a tragic action:

> Der am höchsten hervorragende Punkt oder der Gipfel der Handlung ist der Einzug des falschen Demetrius als wirklicher Czar zu Moskau, mit dem Bewußtsein, daß er ein Betrüger. Auf diese Partie fällt das höchste Licht der Darstellung. Bis dahin ist alles Streben und Hoffnung; von da an beginnt die Furcht und das Unglück.[53]

Schiller thus conceived the action as a development from innocence to consciousness of guilt in the hero himself. One of the main problems was to motivate the pretender's claim to the throne, and here Schiller decided to make his hero a victim of deceit, the tool of a vindictive enemy of the ruling Czar: 'Hauptsächlich ist zu erfinden, wie Demetrius für den Zaarowitz erkannt wird, ohne selbst zu betrügen, und wie auch er getäuscht wird. Jemand muß schlechterdings sein, der diesen Betrug absichtlich schmiedet, und die Absicht muß klar und begreiflich sein.'[54] The invention of such a *fabricator doli* kept him busy for a long time, and he finally decided in favour of 'a vengeful and intriguing priest whom Boris [the ruling Czar] has mortally offended'.[55] The heritage of the *Sturm und Drang* is evinced once more.

Demetrius manifests the continuity and the development of Schiller's tragic themes in another way. He described the drama as *das Gegenstück* of **Die Jungfrau von Orleans**—an apt description, since he was again portraying an inner conflict arising from an external struggle. Both Johanna and Demetrius have a mission, but whereas the former violates the terms of her vocation, the latter is tragic because his quest is a false one and he fails to give it up when his true origin is revealed to him. Dramatically, his guilt is more intimately linked to his enterprise, although he is, to begin with, a victim of circumstance. In Schiller's words Demetrius 'first appears in a state of happy innocence, for the real tragedy lies in the fact that the circumstances finally plunge him into guilt and crime'.[56] It is, however, significant that his claims are disproved before he ascends the throne, so that he still has a chance to give up his undertaking. This he fails to do; he is a tragic figure not merely because he is a victim of the priest's intrigue, but also, and perhaps predominantly, because he does not summon, or even possess, the moral strength to renounce his false pretensions while there is time. Like Wallenstein he succumbs to temptation without recovering his moral integrity by achieving sublimity. His tragedy, however, is not as ambiguous as Wallenstein's, for his enterprise is not tainted by selfish desires at the outset, nor is it backed up by a belief in astrology or a similar realist creed.

Demetrius may also be compared with **Die Verschwörung des Fiesco zu Genua.**[57] Both dramas deal with the theme of usurpation. But Schiller had moved far since writing his second tragedy. According to his *Studienheft,* one of his principal interests in his last and incomplete work was the hero's change of character resulting from his change of fortune, the 'Glücks- und Sinneswechsel des Demetrius' or, in a similar phrase, 'Demetrius Glückswechsel und Charakterwechsel'.[58] This conception opened up new possibilities of treating one of his abiding tragic themes. In his earlier dramas he had shown how the misfortunes of his heroes were caused by an inherent weakness of character. Their tragedy was occasioned by their natural predispositions no less than the situations in which they found themselves. Schiller had adhered to the psychological views of those eighteenth-century thinkers who regarded human beings as fixed entities and ruled out the notion of change.[59] Now, at the end of his life, he envisaged a tragic action based upon a radical transformation of the hero's character:

> Der falsche Demetrius glaubt an sich selbst bis auf den Augenblick wo er in Moskau soll einziehen. Hier wird er an sich irre, einer entdeckt ihm seine wahre Geburt und dies bringt eine schnelle unglückselige Veränderung im Charakter des Betrogenen hervor.[60]

The motivation of Fiesco's lust for power must be sought in himself: he is the sole instigator of prevarication and deceit. Demetrius' case is different. He is not predisposed to tyranny because he has been slowly corrupted by a like craving: a sudden change is wrought in him from without by the unexpected revelation of the truth.[61]

When Schiller abandoned the Warbeck plan in favour of Demetrius, he had come to realize the greater tragic potentiality of usurpation based on deceit over mere ambition. He also felt that the Russian story offered a larger number of splendid dramatic situations which encouraged the application of a special technique. In the introductory note to his *Szenar* for the play he observed that the material required the construction of a rapidly moving action: there should be no reversion to earlier events, and continuous progress must only be arrested at the peak of each episode. To fulfil these demands he elected to compose acts and scenes that were to be self-contained and complete in themselves to an unusual degree:

> Weil die Handlung groß und reichhaltig ist, und eine Welt von Begebenheiten in sich begreift, so muß mit einem kühnen Machtschritt auf den höchsten und bedeutungsvollsten Momenten hingeschritten werden. Jede Bewegung muß die Handlung um ein merkliches weiter bringen. . . . Was dahinten gelassen wird, bleibt dahinten liegen, der gegenwärtige Moment verdrängt den vergangenen. . . . Jeder Moment aber, wo die Handlung verweilt, ist ein bestimmtes, ausgeführtes Gemälde, hat seine eigene vollständige Exposition und ist ein für sich vollendetes Ganze.[62]

The two acts which he had almost completed when he died prove his ability to write a drama in this new style. The action is still a continuous series of events—*eine fortlaufende Handlung*—but it no longer begins with a single situation representing the starting-point of tragic analysis. The scene in the Polish Diet is a most impressive opening: it does not contain the seeds of the whole plot, nor does the second act develop organically from it. Each of the acts has its own exposition and climax. The contrast between the bustling Krakau Reichstag and the tranquil scene at Marfa's convent is no less impressive.

Schiller's choice of theme and style in **Demetrius,** his interpretation of the tragedy inherent in the material, the technique he chose for its treatment, the quality of his verse—particularly the pure lyric strains in the opening scene of the second act—all these features suggest that the drama might well have become a crowning achievement. They suggest that the ambiguities and inconsistencies of some of his later plays are by no means proof of failing craftsmanship. It is characteristic of Schiller that he was engaged in continuous literary activity during the last months of his life despite the most debilitating physical ailments. They stimulated that activity rather than impeded it. When he died at the age of forty-six he was at the height of his creative power.

Notes

1. Works, xii. 278.

2. We recall Schiller's examples of *das böse Verhängnis*: 'die pathetischen Gemälde der mit dem Schicksal ringenden Menschheit, der unaufhaltsamen Flucht des Glücks, der betrogenen Sicherheit, der triumphierenden Ungerechtigkeit und der unterliegenden Unschuld, welche die Geschichte in reichem Maß aufstellt und die tragische Kunst nachahmend vor unsre Augen bringt' (ibid., p. 280).

3. Letters, vi. 277.

4. 'The costume of ideas which I permitted myself to use may be justified because the action is placed in Messina where Christianity, Greek mythology, and Mohammedanism really met and mingled. . . . The mixture of these three mythologies would ordinarily obliterate distinctive character: here it becomes characteristic.' Letters, vii. 24. Cf. Schiller's description of Sicily after the Norman conquest in *Universalhistorische Übersicht* (*Works*, xiii, esp. pp. 146 ff.).

5. Cf. Buttmann, *Die Schicksalsidee in Schillers Braut von Messina*, pp. 60 *passim*. The incest motif frequently occurs in conjunction with the idea of fate in German literature at the end of the eighteenth century, for instance in *Wilhelm Meisters Lehrjahre*, and in many works by Romantic writers.

6. 'Fate should operate only through human characters, but in such a way that the latter should only act under the sway of the former.' *Adrastea, Viertes Stück*, 1801.

7. 'How can they mean well with you, the aliens, the tribe of invaders who drove them from their heritage and assumed dominion over them?' *Works*, vii. 17.

8. Hegel advanced the view that the conflicts are caused by a contention for the 'Recht zur Thronfolge' (*Die Idee und das Ideal*, loc. cit., p. 288).

9. 'And as we all know, the old Prince's rightful spouse was forced by rape into a sinful marriage bed, for she was his father's choice. And the ancestor in his wrath poured out fearful seeds of dire curses on the sinful bed. . . . Yes, it has not begun well and believe me it cannot end well, for every deed of deluded rage will be avenged under the sun. It is not a coincidence and blind chance that the brothers are destroying each other, for the mother's womb was cursed and she was destined to give birth to hatred and strife.' *Works*, vii. 41.

10. 'I recognize the father's own spirit and character in my firstborn. He always loved to ruminate in secret and to keep his counsel in his own inaccessibly barred mind.' *Works*, vii. 58.

11. Cf. Carruth, *Fate and Guilt in Schiller's 'Die Braut von Messina'*, p. 110: 'Secretiveness is the keynote and the very atmosphere of the whole drama.' Cf. also p. 112. In an Appendix (pp. 114-24) the author lists 100 instances of the use of words denoting concealment.

12. Appelbaum, *Goethe's Iphigenie and Schiller's Braut von Messina*, p. 58.

13. 'What is mine and thine, revenge and guilt, cannot be disentangled here any longer. Who is going to find the old bed of the lava stream that poured forth red hot?' *Works*, vii. 19. Cf. ibid., p. 61.

14. 'What do I now care whether the gods show themselves as liars or prove to be true? They have done their worst for me. I defy them to strike me harder than they have done. He who has nothing more to tremble for does not fear them any longer.' Ibid., p. 107.

15. 'I know that contrite penitence is acceptable to heaven, but a bloody murder can only be expiated with blood.'

    'By my death I dissolve the ancient curse on our house; only a freely chosen death can break the chain of destiny.' *Works*, vii. 112.

16. 'Let me obey the spirit that fearfully impels me, for no happy man can see what goes on within me.' Ibid., p. 113.

17. 'Let him who can, live a life of contrition and bit by bit skim off a never-ending guilt with austere mortification. I cannot live, my mother, with a broken heart. I must look up joyfully to the blessed ones and with a free spirit reach for the heights above me. Envy poisoned my life while we were still equally sharing your love. Do you think that I can endure the advantage which your suffering has given him over me?' Ibid., pp. 115 f.

18. Ibid., p. 67.

19. Works, xiii. 149.

20. 'Who would not rather gaze in wonder at the remarkable struggle between fertility and destruction in the fields of Sicily . . . None will deny that man is better provided for in the pastures of Batavia than under the treacherous crater of Vesuvius. . . . But man needs more than just to live and have a pleasant time.' *Works*, xii. 275.

21. 'Happy is he, and I call him blessed, who leans like a child in pastoral fields on nature's breast, far from the turbulent round of life.' *Work*, vii. 109 f.

22. Letters, vii. 24.

23. 'The poet must reopen the palaces, he must lead the tribunals into the open air, he must raise up the statues of the gods.' *Work*, xvi. 124.

24. 'The introduction of the chorus would be the last, the decisive measure, and if it served no other purpose than to declare open and honest war on naturalism in art, it could become a living wall with which tragedy surrounds itself in order to be completely isolated from the real world and safeguard its ideal sphere, its poetic freedom.' Ibid., p. 123.

25. Cf. the remarks on the mime in *Über epische und dramatische Dichtung*. They can be more readily applied to *Die Braut von Messina* than to Schiller's other tragedies.

26. Cf. Schiller's letter to Zelter on 28 Feb. 1803 and his view that poetry becomes musical 'je nachdem

sie, wie die Tonkunst, bloß einen bestimmten Zustand des Gemüts hervorbringt, ohne dazu eines bestimmten Gegenstandes nötig zu haben . . . ohne die Einbildungskraft durch ein bestimmtes Objekt zu beherrschen' (Works, xii. 209). Cf. also the review of Matthisson's poetry.

27. 'Here the question was not why men are assailed by such dire events but, if and when they are assailed by them, what should one think of them, how endure them?' *Adrastea, Viertes Stück,* 1801.

28. Cf. Moore, *A New Reading of Wilhelm Tell,* pp. 278 *passim.*

29. Letters, vii. 69.

30. 'All the impressions I have experienced from this work or observed in others have been poetic in a generic, not a tragic sense. This will always be the case when a tragedy fails because of its epic quality.' *Letters,* v. 311.

31. Cf. Schiller's defence of the 'Parricida scene' in his letter to Iffland (*Letters,* vii. 138).

32. 'You will ask me why I have laid Warbeck aside. I have thought a great deal about the play and shall certainly complete it successfully. But another subject has turned up which now attracts me much more and which will be a worthy successor to *Die Jungfrau von Orleans.*' *Letters,* vi. 369.

33. Ibid. vi. 415 and vii. 74.

34. 'I cannot tarry to probe and choose; if you have need of me for a definite task, call upon Tell; I shall not fail you.' *Works,* vii. 148. Cf. also Tell's reply to Hedwig when she surmises that he has joined the confederates (ibid., p. 194).

35. 'Let each restrain his righteous wrath and save his revenge for the general account. Whoever acts alone on his own behalf, is guilty of harm to the common good.' Ibid., p. 191.

36. Cf. Stauffacher's other exhortation:

Sprecht nicht von Rache. Nicht Geschehnes rächen,

Gedrohtem Übel wollen wir begegnen. (Ibid., p. 172.)

37. Ibid., p. 278.

38. 'I would gladly send you the play act by act, but it is not proceeding act by act; the subject requires that I should carry certain actions that belong together through all five acts and only then pass on to others. Thus Tell practically stands alone in the play. His affair is a private affair and remains so until at the end it merges with the common cause. *Letters,* vii. 98.

39. Cf. Kettner, *Schillers Wilhelm Tell,* pp. 9-14.

40. '. . . when a people which grazes its herds piously and with self-sufficiency, covets no alien property, throws off the yoke it unworthily suffers, yet even in its wrath respects humanity.' *Works,* ii. 88.

41. Cf. Buchwald, loc. cit., p. 474.

42. 'If this sentiment, which ethics teaches us under the heading of resigning ourselves to the inevitable, and religion under the heading of submitting to God's will, is to become a work of free choice and deliberation, much greater clarity of thought and much higher energy of will are required than human beings usually possess in ordinary life.' *Über das Erhabene* (*Works,* xii. 266).

43. 'Hail to you that you have not profaned our immaculate victory with bloodshed!' *Works,* vii. 264.

44. Cf. Hegel's report (*Die Idee und das Ideal,* loc. cit., p. 367) that 80 to 100 Swiss who attended the first performance of *Wilhelm Tell* in Jena on 17 Mar. 1804 were 'gar nicht befriedigt und meinten, das seien doch nicht die echten Schweizer'.

45. 'I wish to write an idyll to compare with the elegy I have just written. All my poetic powers are screwed up to this one task. . . . In the realm of sentimental poetry, from which I cannot escape, once and for all, the idyll is the highest as well as the most difficult problem.' *Letters,* iv. 337.

46. It should be remembered that for Schiller the term *Idylle* denoted an attitude of mind (*Empfindungsweise*) in the poet, as well as a poetic genre (*Gedichtart*) embodying that attitude, and that tragedy, like the epic and the novel, could be written in the idyllic, and likewise in the satirical or the elegiac, manner: 'Wer daher noch fragen könnte, zu welcher von den drei Gattungen (sc. Satire, Idylle, Elegie) ich die Epopöe, den Roman, das Trauerspiel u. a. m. zähle, der würde mich ganz und gar nicht verstanden haben. Denn der Begriff dieser letztern, als einzelner Gedichtarten, wird entweder gar nicht oder doch nicht allein durch die Empfindungsweise bestimmt; vielmehr weiß man, daß solche in mehr als einer Empfindungsweise, folglich auch in mehrern der von mir aufgestellten Dichtungsarten können ausgeführt werden' (*Works,* xii. 222).

47. *Letters,* ii. 218.

48. 'Let him undertake to write an idyll which will portray the same pastoral innocence in civilized beings and in all circumstances representing the most vigorous energetic life, the most embracing thought, the subtlest artifice, the utmost social refinement and which, in a word, since we can never return to Arcadia, will lead us forward to Elysium.' *Works,* xii. 228.

49. Cf. above, p. 69.

50. A view held by Fricke, Deubel, Gumbel.

51. 'As far as the treatment of this subject is concerned one would, I believe, have to do the opposite of what the writer of a comedy would make of it. The latter would arouse laughter by contrasting the pretender's great role with his lack of competence for it. In a tragedy he would have to seem born to assume this role and he would have to appropriate it so completely that interesting conflicts would arise with those who wish to use him as their tool and treat him as their creature. The catastrophe would have to be brought about by his adherents and protectors, not his enemies.' *Letters,* vi. 74. Mr. T. S. Eliot has a high opinion of Ford's *Perkin Warbeck* and commends the author for his performance of a task similar to that which Schiller had in mind. Cf. *Selected Essays,* p. 200.

52. *Schillers Demetrius,* ed. Kettner, pp. 115 f.

53. 'The most outstanding point or summit of the action is reached when the false Demetrius enters Moscow as actual Czar, though aware of the fact that he is a deceiver. The highest light of portrayal falls on this part. Previously all is hope and striving; now fear and misfortune begin.' Ibid., p. 114.

54. 'The principal invention concerns the way in which Demetrius comes to be recognized as Czarewitch without himself practising deceit and how he too is duped. There will have to be somebody who intentionally forges this deceit, and his intention must be clear and intelligible.' Ibid., p. 206.

55. Ibid., p. 214.

56. Ibid., p. 205, n. 2.

57. Schiller first came to know the story of Dmitri when he was writing this drama in 1782. Cf. ibid., p. xvi.

58. Ibid., pp. 115 and 84.

59. Cf. Dessoir, *Geschichte der neueren deutschen Psychologie;* Schmid, *Schillers Gestaltungsweise,* pp. 157 *passim.* It should, however, be noted that Schiller described change of character in the hero of *Der Verbrecher aus verlorener Ehre. Works,* xi. 191 ff.

60. 'The false Demetrius believes in himself until he is about to enter Moscow. Here he loses faith in himself; somebody reveals his true birth to him and this brings about a rapid and disastrous change in the character of the deceived man.' Kettner, loc. cit., p. 206. Kettner is not justified in saying that Demetrius shows a tyrannical *Herrschernatur* from the beginning. Schiller frequently stresses his initial innocence.

61. This point may be explained by reference to one of Coleridge's remarks: 'A flash of lightning has turned at once the polarity of the compass needle: and so, perhaps, now and then, but as rarely, a violent motive may revolutionize a man's opinions and professions. But more frequently his honesty dies away imperceptibly from evening into twilight, and from twilight to utter darkness. He turns hypocrite so gradually, and by such tiny atoms of motion, that by the time he has arrived at a given point, he forgets his own hypocrisy in the imperceptible degrees of his conversion' (*Table Talk and Omniana,* p. 341). Schiller's Demetrius may be cited as an example of the former, Fiesco of the latter process. Cf. also Schiller's account of the influence of 'material ideas' on the constitution of character, as quoted above, pp. 20 f.

62. 'Since the action is important and abundant and contains a wealth of incident, in the highest and most significant moments one must advance with bold and commanding steps. Every movement must advance the action palpably. . . . What is left behind is left behind for ever and the present moment supplants the last one. . . . But every moment on which the action dwells is a clear and detailed picture, containing its own exposition and forming a complete and independent whole.' Kettner, loc. cit., p. 114.

Oskar Seidlin (essay date 1960)

SOURCE: "Schiller: Poet of Politics," in *A Schiller Symposium: In Observance of the Bicentenary of Schiller's Birth,* University of Texas Department of Germanic Languages, 1960, pp. 31-48.

[*In the following essay, Seidlin asserts that the "complexities and perplexities of political man" is one of Schiller's most persistent themes, and claims that in his works the dramatist brings to life the ironies and paradoxes of political action—for example, that political ideals, however lofty, must be bound up with humans' particular desires and ambitions in order to be put into practice, but in being so bound lose their purity as ideals.*]

A Quarter of a century ago, when darkness descended upon Schiller's native country, a darkness that was to engulf all of mankind in the shortest possible time, a theater in Hamburg produced one of Schiller's great dramatic works, **Don Carlos.** It is the play which culminates in the stirring climax of its third act, the confrontation scene between King Philip of Spain and the Marquis Posa, the powerful verbal and intellectual battle between the rigid and autocratic monarch, contemptuous of mankind and gloomily convinced that only harsh and tyrannical suppression can preserve peace and order in his vast empire, and the young, enthusiastic advocate of revolutionary principles, who demands for his fellow citizens the untrammeled right to happiness, the possibility of unhampered self-development and self-realization of every individual. The scene rises to its pitch with Marquis Posa's brave challenge flung into the king's face: "Sire, give us all freedom of thought!" When this line, one of the most famous in all German dramatic literature, resounded from the Hamburg stage in the early years of Hitler's terror, the audience under the friendly protection of darkness burst out, night after night, into tumultuous applause. So dangerous and embarrassing to the new rulers proved a single verse of the greatest German playwright, who by then had been dead for fully a hundred and thirty years, that the management of the theater was forced to cut out the scandalous line. But the audience, knowing their classic well enough even if it was fed to them in an emasculated version, reacted quick-wittedly: from that evening on they interrupted the performance by thunderous applause at the moment when Marquis Posa should have uttered his famous plea on the stage—and did not. After these incidents the play was withdrawn from the repertoire altogether.

This is a touching and heart-warming story: people, at a time of national calamity and shame, turn to one of their great writers to find strength and direction in his words, protest with him and through him against a vicious political system which debased the noble thoughts that he, through his works, had bequeathed to his nation as a precious heritage. A touching, a heart-warming spectacle, and yet at the same time one that puts us somewhat ill-at-ease. Is he really a poet, so we must ask, whose creation can so easily release a stark political demonstration, even if we happen to be in complete agreement with this demonstration? Is he really a great dramatist, who speaks so directly to our political emotions, who turns the stage into a pulpit from which we are preached at, admonished and exhorted, nobly and loftily to be sure, but preached at nonetheless? Certainly we will not underrate or malign the need and importance of a programmatic appeal to our highest ideals, the inspiration and edification which we derive from the teachings of a great and venerable mentor; but very much aware of the borderline that has to be drawn between the word of wisdom and the word of poetry, we cannot help asking the anxious question: Uplifting as all of that may be, is it really and primarily art?

The question becomes more pressing when our minds shift from this scene in the Hamburg theater to the year 1859, to the celebrations on the occasion of Schiller's hundredth anniversary. It is surely no exaggeration to state that never before—and never since—in the history of Western civilization has a writer been so passionately and fervently honoured in his own country—and by the German population of this country, too—as was Schiller in 1859. Again, a touching, a heart-warming spectacle: a man of letters who, though beset by incessant illness and poverty during a short life of barely forty-six years, had produced a body of uncompromisingly serious plays, of sophisticated esthetic and philosophical essays, of high-flown poems and ambitious historical writings, assumes fifty-four years after his premature death the status of a popular hero, and is accorded the accolades of veneration which a nation generally reserves for the powerful and mighty, for its founding fathers and those who in moments of great historical decisions have established and saved its identity. Recalling the festivities of the year 1859, the torchlight parades of students and intellectuals in innumerable cities, the mass meetings of whole populations, the unveiling of dozens of monuments, the endless oratory reverberating through modest citizens' clubs no less than through huge assembly halls, we ask: Was ever a poet so honored? But upon looking over the list of famous speakers, upon reading their words of praise and adulation, we realize that it was hardly the poet Friedrich Schiller who was thus honored. As in the Hamburg theater, it was one stormy political demonstration which in 1859 swept over Germany under the guise of the centenary celebration of a great writer. A little more than ten years earlier, in 1848, the burning hopes of the German population for a fatherland united in the spirit of enlightened liberalism and constitutional government had died under the fusillades and deceitful machinations of the old regime. So dreadful was the shock, so thorough the blood-letting, that Germany lay numb for a whole decade. But then, in 1859, the muted voice of the German people rose again, and when it shouted the name of Friedrich Schiller, it actually bewailed the shattered dreams of a whole generation; it protested against a superannuated political and social order, and pledged to offer resistance and give new battle.

Was this the way, is this a way to honor a poet? Was it honorable of Robert Blum, the fiery tribune of radical republicanism, to ransack Schiller's works in search of stirring political slogans and to weave three such passages, lifted from three different plays—the famous line of Marquis Posa was certainly not missing—into one sentence, and by doing so make Schiller the crown witness of revolutionary convictions which impregnated the air a century ago? Becoming that popular, being transferred so enthusiastically from the pantheon to the market place, is a mixed blessing for a poet. As with no other man of letters before him, the nineteenth century transfigured and transformed Schiller into a political poet, political in the widest sense, meaning that he spoke on and for matters of the *polis,* the public life, warning and advising, chiding and guiding, judging and condemning—an orator and pamphleteer more than a poet. How easy it was to quote him, for he had an eminently quotable maxim for every noble purpose; how usable he was to every schoolmaster and dignitary who, facing solemn crowds, needed something edifying, lofty, and inspiring. The reaction became inevitable, inevitable the questions, whether Schiller was a poet at all, whether his place was in the *agora* rather than on Mount Parnassus, on a glorified soap-box rather than in the theater. And Friedrich Nietzsche, disrespectful iconoclast that he was, denigrated Schiller neatly and devastatingly by calling the poet simply "that tedious and brassy trumpet player of moralism."

This is brutal, and it is utterly wrong; wrong because it confuses with his true image the crudely glossy lacquer which posterity has generously spread over Friedrich Schiller's features. The nineteenth century—and in this respect the nineteenth century is by no means over—was mistaken in forcing Schiller into a posture which was that of a tribune of the people rather than that of a poet. Yet underneath the spurious overlay there exists a genuine and fundamental level upon which Schiller and politics meet. Though he was not a political poet, he was perhaps the greatest poet of politics. With a fervor unequalled, a passion unabated, his plays ask decisive and basic questions: What and where is man's place in this vital and fateful game called politics? How does he master it and how does it master him? In which sort of relationship does the private human being, his moral, emotional, and divine essence, stand to the *zoon politikon,* the political animal, which man, equally essentially, is? Someone as obsessed with these questions as was Schiller is not a political poet who furnishes us with slogans, with marching orders and banners to be waved on the shifting battleground of ideologies, but one who, through memorable figures and configurations, elucidates for us our human existence, our existence as humans, its complexities and paradoxes, its defeats and triumphs, its condition and possible consequences. And this, indeed, is the poet's task.

After he outgrew the fervor and furor of his youthful subjectivism, starting with ***Don Carlos,*** Schiller used decisive moments in Western European history as the subject matter of his plays: the breaking away of the Netherlands from Spain in ***Don Carlos,*** the Thirty Years' War in the ***Wallenstein*** trilogy, the rise of Britain to a world power in *Mary Stuart,* the liberation of France from England's yoke in *The Maid of Orleans,* and the foundation of Swiss democracy in *William Tell.* Yet he did not write dramatic chronicles in the manner of Shakespeare, nor give us a gallery of historical individuals, brave or cowardly, heroic or mean. Instead he traced again and again man's fateful involvement in history, in that process which we determine while being determined by it, which uses us as its pawns by mobilizing in us our freedom to act.

This dialectic interplay of determining power and freedom of action, the friction and tension between our moral obligations and the dictates of the necessities which the historical moment imposes upon us, in short, the problems of political man, have been Schiller's most persistent themes. We may as readily and enthusiastically as did that audience in the Hamburg theater applaud Marquis Posa's plea for political freedom, for the right of every individual to full expression; but if we do nothing but this, we have missed the human condition and the human tragedy which Schiller's *Don Carlos* probes. For Marquis Posa's ringing line: "Sire, give us all freedom of thought" is only a station in a series of arguments in which not this or that political ideology, not this or that form of government is being discussed and presented, but politics as such, its field and orbit, its function and aim. In the long speech that follows, Marquis Posa demands of the king: "Restore to man his lost nobility!" Now this, we must admit, is strange. Nobility, so we would think, is a value of the inner man, a private, a personal value, something untouchable, whose loss or preservation does not lie within the public domain, cannot be jeopardized or secured by the head of state, be he ever so enlightened, tolerant and liberal. Since the dawn of Christianity political theories have again and again started from Christ's saying: "Give unto Caesar what is Caesar's, and unto God what is God's," a clear separation between the powers that govern the public and the private existence of man, his outer and inner obligations, duties and rights. The most effective revolutionary attacks against various forms of tyranny were derived from the very conviction that Caesar had encroached upon a field that was God's, had demanded loyalties that were the prerogatives of the Highest. Yet Posa argues in the opposite direction: Caesar is to restore the lost nobility of mankind, the world is to be remade into paradise, the breach between this world and the other healed forever, and politics proclaimed as the field in which man in his totality, his truth and eternal essence will rule supreme. Politics, as Posa sees it, is no longer a carefully worked calculation which determines the distribution and balance of obligations and rights, the amount of freedom or freedoms which the citizen should enjoy, but is the very medium on which his total existence depends, not only his position and status within the machinery of the state, but the value, the inner verity of his being man. No less than his nobility, the visible activation of his moral essence is here proclaimed as the starting point and ultimate aim of politics.

Marquis Posa's famous plea, then, so heavily taxed and over-taxed by every freedom-loving speech-maker as a program point of an enlightened liberal political platform, is not only that. Within its context it serves to define politics as the very climate in which man as man, as a moral and spiritual being, can and must fulfill himself. But at this point, after the basic foundation has been laid, Schiller, the great dialectician of politics, begins his probings. So far Marquis Posa has been a private citizen, unwilling to assume any political responsibilities at King Philip's court, traveling about the empire as a mentor and friend to those who share his advanced political philosophy, a living link between men who dream of and prepare a better future, and, above all, the source of inspiration of Don Carlos, the crown-prince, who one day, guided by Posa and Posa's principles, will usher in a new and brighter world. But now, more or less against his will, he becomes involved on the plane of action. The king, shivering in the cold isolation of his loneliness, surrounded by the sterile servility of his selfish courtiers, is struck and overwhelmed by meeting a free man, who speaks his bold mind freely, asking no favors, despising the shrewd game of the manipulation of power. Suddenly Posa, the idealistic dreamer of a better world, the theoretician not only of a new politics but of politics as the medium which can restore mankind's lost nobility, has become from one moment to the next the king's most powerful seal-bearer, the unchallenged master over the fate and future of his country. Schiller's question and ours is: What will he do with this unparalleled power?

The outcome tells the whole story. Marquis Posa, champion of a new, happy life growing from what he called the lethal stillness of a churchyard that was Philip's Spain, is shot to death; the successor to the throne, Don Carlos, in whom Posa implanted the high ideals of progressive, freedom-loving government, is arrested and turned over to the executioner at the very moment when he sets out to flee to the Netherlanders to lead their rebellion and topple the Spanish system of suppression; the Duke of Alba, the most sinister and blood-thirsty of the king's hangmen, marches north with his troops, his knapsack filled with death sentences which are to break the Hollanders' spirit and will to resistance; King Philip himself, who in spite or because of his rigidity and misanthropic distrust, had been longing for a gentle human voice to help and guide him, now delivers himself and his power unreservedly to the merciless grip of the Inquisition, and when he asks the Grand Inquisitor the pathetic question: "For whom have I planted and collected?", receives and meekly accepts the brutal answer: "For the graves and worms rather than for liberty." What an ending after such high hopes, what a harvest of shambles and devastation growing from seeds that were meant to transform a barren field into a paradisiac garden!

What Schiller here presents is not only an accidental historical disaster, the pessimistically gloomy tableau of noble dreams destroyed and great expectations foiled. The dreadful outcome is, after all, the direct consequence of

Marquis Posa's involvement in the political game, of his active participation in the battle of power and passions raging at the Spanish court. We are witness to a truly vital process of politics, to the tragic dilemma that arises when an ideal, be it ever so benevolent and noble, enters upon the plane of reality, is drawn into the orbit of pressures and counter-pressures, distorted and ruined by the very forces which it mobilizes in the course of its attempted realization. Has Schiller, when telling the hapless story of the defeated idealist Marquis Posa, not indeed touched upon a basic problem of politics *per se,* a problem which the twentieth century has only too brutally exhibited: the disastrous and destructive effects of a political principle which, good in itself—meant as a panacea for all the social ills of mankind—is twisted by the currents which it unleashes into its very opposite, into a harbinger of darkness blacker than the one which it was to dispel. The true tragedy of politics, of man in the political arena, is here revealed: the noble ideal, man's highest hope is being ground to shreds by the inexorable maelstrom of uncontrollable forces; good itself has turned into an instrument of evil and destruction.

Yet Schiller's **Don Carlos** is more than a probing into the dialectic ambiguity of political ideologies. The play presents not only the havoc which the ideal can work when transferred from the realm of pure thought to the realm of concrete realities. More decisive, more tragic still is the moral *impasse,* the dubious road onto which the idealist is forced in pursuit of his ideal. Nothing could be purer than the flame that burns in Marquis Posa, nothing nobler than his intentions. And yet, how questionable the means, how frightening the detours that the realization of this idea prescribes to him! The one who had proclaimed the securing of man's totality as the very justification of politics, and as its purpose the free display of man's nobility, has donned, since he entered the plane of politics, an impenetrable mask, has become so divided within himself that every action he commits is calculated to conceal his true objectives. His friendship with the king, who had turned to him because he saw in him the only genuine human being in his whole entourage, free, unselfish, unpurposeful and therefore worthy of complete trust, is nothing but a subterfuge, a betrayal that is to promote his revolutionary aims. And his betrayal of Don Carlos—at least what seems to everybody, including the prince himself, a betrayal—is nothing but a subterfuge which is to save the beloved friend from grave impending danger. Treason under the cloak of friendship, friendship under the cloak of treason—what a disturbing twilight in the champion of a new world who was fighting for everybody's freedom of thought, which is in the last analysis nothing else but the individual's right to be himself, to accept as the guiding light of his life nothing but his own inner truth, the authenticity of his being. But, when Marquis Posa has laid down his life for his ideal, where was his authenticity?

Don Carlos, mourning at the bier of his friend and mentor, is convinced that he died for him, and taunts the king, who has tried in vain to gain Posa's heart and support:

> Mine was he, mine,
>
> While you were boasting loud of his esteem,
>
> While he, his nimble tricky eloquence
>
> Was playing with your proud, majestic mind. . . .
>
> You showered him with tokens of your favor;
>
> He died for me. Your friendship and your heart
>
> You urged upon him. And yet your crown
>
> Was but a plaything in his hands.
>
> He threw it down—and died for me.

But did he really? Or is not perhaps King Philip closer to the truth when he arrives at a very different answer:

> For whom then did he sacrifice himself?
>
> For Karl, that boy and son of mine? Oh never!
>
> I don't believe it. A Posa does not die
>
> For a mere youth. The meagre flame of friendship
>
> Does not fill a Posa's heart. That beat
>
> For all mankind. His passion was
>
> The world at large, with all its future generations.

Yet if this is the right answer, then Posa did not love the prince because he was Don Carlos; he loved Don Carlos because he was the prince, the future ruler who, under his tutelage, would usher in the new millenium. But what about man's nobility, if the human being, the closest friend is degraded to a tool, a tool, to be sure, that is to serve the loftiest purpose, but a tool nevertheless? Is the political idealist—and this is Schiller's most penetrating question in **Don Carlos**—who fights so bravely and passionately for humanity, not himself a human failure? Obsessed by the legitimate demands of mankind as a whole, he becomes blind to the legitimate demands of individual man. Infatuated by an abstract idea a noble, a grand idea, he plays havoc with man's dignity, which consists of one fact, and one fact alone: that every human being is, and must be treated as, an end in himself and not a means for a purpose, no matter how lofty—this is the very dignity for which Marquis Posa had spoken up so movingly and eloquently in his first encounter with the king.

How silly it was to call a poet who offered such trenchant insights into the complexities and perplexities of political man, into the ironies and paradoxes of political action, a "brassy trumpet player of moralism!" The duplicity of man—duplicity in the twofold meaning of the word—his position at the intersection of moral law and the inexorable force of circumstances, the tragic dilemma which results from the unavoidable intertwining of his emotional life with the demands of practical and responsible action in the world—this, and not any easy and starry-eyed proclamation of ethical conduct, was Schiller's vital concern. But were Schiller preoccupied only with the banal truth that man's subjective drives and motivations color his ideological aims and objectives, promote or obstruct them, deflect or pervert them, we might dismiss the poet as inconsequential. But here again, his glance probes much more deeply. He realizes that these objectives are essentially and fundamentally intertwined with the individual's personal and private life, that they can be translated into actions only when they enter the living tissue of man's total existence and form with the energies of his emotional being an amalgam in which alone they can become effective. Ideas and ideals which have not penetrated into the subsoil where passions rest are sterile and dead. If we want to make them realities, we can do so only by feeding them with our life-blood, by what in modern terms would be called a total commitment. And yet here arises another paradox in the existence of political man which Schiller has elucidated in his drama. If the political ideal, which as an ideal is an absolute and objective postulate, must in order to become effective necessarily enter into the tangle of man's impulses and drives, then its purity is automatically lost. The deed which he commits for the sake and in the service of the ideal becomes indistinguishable from the deed which his own often petty interest forces upon him. This insoluble dilemma—and it is truly insoluble—Schiller has made transparent in his most powerful evocations of political man, in those historical figures who are called upon to act as the servants of a great historical mission and yet are surrounded by the dubious light of selfishness and hypocrisy. Only by asserting themselves, their own personal needs and desires can they hope to assert the ideal which they pursue: Wallenstein in the great trilogy, and Queen Elizabeth of England in *Mary Stuart.*

Seeing in Wallenstein and in Elizabeth nothing but hypocrites, evil schemers for the sake of their own power, means again to miss Schiller's essential point. Is it thankless to ask which of the many faces that Wallenstein presents to the viewer is the true one. We have to realize that for him, as a political man, all of them are true and depend on each other even if at first glance they may seem exclusive. The great general of the imperial army, the idol of his soldiers, wants to reassure himself by a written declaration of the unreserved loyalty of his officers so that they will follow him blindly wherever he leads them, even against the emperor, even into the camp of the enemy, the Swedes. Schiller presents a clear case of treason, a preparation of mutiny against the supreme overlord, motivated by the boundless ambition of a man who wants to be not only his ruler's mightiest sword but, if need be, the ruler himself. And yet, is it really only Wallenstein's thirst for unlimited power that leads him onto the road of clandestine conspiracy and, finally, to open rebellion? It is, and it is not. He does not simply feign when he casts himself—again not quite without ulterior motives—in the rôle of a harbinger of peace, who after sixteen years of the bloodiest holocaust wants to put an end to the immeasurable misery of war. But he knows that this ideal—and it is a noble ideal, after all—can be realized only by cutting through the religious intolerance and the entangled dynastic interests which dominate the emperor and his house, the house of Hapsburg, by uprooting old hatreds and old loyalties which, the longer they last, drive the

course of history ever more deeply into a hopeless stalemate and an unbending rut. If this be treason, and it surely is, then treason there must be.

From this summary of Wallenstein's deeds and motivations one might conclude that Schiller raises mainly the question of the legitimacy of certain means to achieve certain ends, a question which is, indeed, one of Schiller's vital concerns. It is a vital question for a poet who, as hardly any other, has been the merciless anatomist and dissector of political man. But Schiller goes one decisive step further, or rather he goes one step back by asking the even more disturbing question: how do we, how can we, when on the stage of politics, decide at all upon the means we are to employ, be they good or foul? In order to arrive at any decision that is to inspire and guide an act we must be free agents, independent of alien authority, not subject to the pressures which pure hazard or the necessity of the moment may exert upon us. Now Wallenstein's craving for power appears in a somewhat different light. It is not simply a selfish desire for self-aggrandizement, but the inevitable corollary of the make-up of a man who is basically political. If he acts, responsibly and fruitfully, he must be in complete command, must be able to exclude interference that could hamper his plans and deeds, must eliminate the unforeseen that could thwart the action in the very process of its realization. In short, a political man, and the greater and truer he is the more so, must of necessity strive for omnipotence and omniscience, a striving as monstrous as it is pathetically futile.

It is for this reason that Schiller's Wallenstein, the great man of action, appears so strangely inactive during much of the play, so hesitant and evasive, so resistant to those who want him to commit himself to a definite course. It is this which Wallenstein is unwilling to do, because committing himself means to relinquish some part of his freedom, to start a chain of events which may not be controllable and calculable at every point, to be, perhaps, drawn against his will into a constellation and a development in which he becomes the slave of a situation instead of being its master. It is in the *Wallenstein* trilogy that Schiller drives the problem of political man to its last and extreme consequence, to the point where the man of action can no longer act, because in order to act freely—and only if he acts freely can he make history instead of being made by it—he must be able to choose freely, to keep all avenues open so that at no time will the direction of his course be dictated to him. Seen in this light, the freedom to act, which is the premise upon which the existence of political man rests, is transmuted into a freedom from action. Therefore, Wallenstein waits until the constellation and his calculations become unbeatable.

And yet, what Schiller presents in *Wallenstein* is the fateful irony which is likely to beset all politics. In order to act decisively and infallibly—and this is the aim of all purposeful action—Wallenstein has again and again postponed his decision. But he has postponed it just a minute too long. He who has hesitated for many precious months in order to be able to act as a free agent is now forced by the weight of circumstances to decide upon a course which he wanted to keep open only as a last and ultimate possibility. Was he really determined to commit treason, to lead his troops to the Swedes, the enemy he had been fighting so brilliantly for years? Just by trying to be uncommitted, to stand above the situation so that he could be its complete master, he has fastened the noose around his neck and has no other choice but to battle for his very life under the most unfavorable of circumstances. In the great monologue at the beginning of the last part of the trilogy, one of the most powerful poetic passages that Schiller ever wrote, Wallenstein asks himself the question:

> Must I commit the deed because
>
> Just in my thoughts I toyed with it?

Yes, he must. Because even thoughts have a momentum of their own and create a reality which, from one moment to the next, changes the stage upon which political man acts. While taking the first step he is still free, but the second is already prescribed. And who can tell which is the first step? Such is the irony of politics that when Wallenstein finally takes his first step, he has actually taken his last. Every plan, every bit of strategy has created conditions which now prove overwhelming, which force him from a strong position to a precarious one, from a precarious position to a shattered one, from a shattered position to a lost one, until finally his doom is sealed.

It may seem like a hopelessly gloomy picture that Schiller in his **Wallenstein** trilogy draws of man acting on the political plane. But at this point Schiller, the great dialectician, takes over again. Indeed, the ironic and tragic fate of Wallenstein, the master tactician and politician, is merciless and unrelieved. He who tried to insure for himself such complete freedom of action that he could move in any direction which would seem advantageous at a given moment is now fighting with his back against the wall, losing one support after the other, yielding inch by inch, until his last stronghold, the fortress of Eger, becomes a doorless trap where he finds an ignoble end at the hands of hired assassins. But it is this very downfall that Schiller surrounds with the halo of human greatness. The reckless scheme has now turned into a wild, pathetic gamble. The powerful schemer who acknowledged no other authority than his own unbridled will has become a plaything of forces he cannot control. The dream of scepter and crown has faded into the illusory hope of sheer survival. And yet, now the moment has come when Wallenstein can act— because he must. Now he reaches the status of full superiority and, a man alone, relying only on his inner strength, he goes down in defeat with an austere uprightness which lends him the majesty that he never possessed in the days of his power and exaltation. The man of political action who is fully committed, committed with his entire existence and personality, achieves in the face of radical insecurity and extreme exposure an amount of freedom which no strategic shrewdness and calculation could give him, and while utterly failing in his objectives

and ambitions, becomes witness to man's nobility which no success could have granted.

Indeed, success will not grant it. In **Mary Stuart,** his next tragedy, Schiller has given an almost complementary image of political man. At the end of the play, Elizabeth has vanquished her deadly rival, the hapless queen of the Scots. Her rule is now, and will in all the future be, secure and unchallenged, England saved from the threat of civil war. Yet, what might seem the moment of her complete victory is in truth the moment of her utter defeat. The picture over which the last curtain falls tells the whole story: Elizabeth, deserted by those who were close to her heart, holds herself painfully and forcibly upright, a human wreck whose hollowness is more exposed than concealed by the strained regal posture. No other poet has, I think, made us witness so closely the bitter and inexorable tragedy of political man, his defeated triumphs and triumphant defeats as Schiller did in the fate of Queen Elizabeth of England. Hers is the richest and most complex portrait of man as a political being, of his hopeless involvements, of the rôle which he is called upon to enact on the stage of history, and of the usurious price he has to pay for his acting and actions.

Again, the task Elizabeth has to fulfill is not only an inevitable necessity, but a truly noble mission. She feels destined to bring peace to her country which, after the death of her reckless father, has been shaken by religious strife and unrest, by the undermining of governmental authority and civil security, by the permanent threat from powers abroad, from France and Spain, whose might and ruthless exploitation of England's internal tensions conspire to bring the heretic island to her knees. All these dangers have one name, the name of Mary Stuart, "the scourge of my life," as Elizabeth calls her. Mary, without an active guilt and against her will, has become the very center of all destructive forces: as a Catholic, the idol of the religious opposition; as a former queen of France and Scotland, a permanent invitation to the foreign enemy to meddle in England's affairs; as the direct descendant of Henry VII, the first Tudor, a living reminder of Elizabeth's disorderly birth and disputable claim to the throne. This woman, the innocent source of all disturbances, is now a prisoner in an English citadel, her life completely at Elizabeth's mercy.

Still, with all this, Elizabeth's hands are tied; not only because of the divergent drives and counterdrives she has to consider, and even less because of the moral and legal problems which Mary's execution, a plain act of violence, would raise. How simple it would be if a clear demarkation line could be drawn between what is ethically right and justifiable and those impure motivations that are the consequence of petty personal interests or of the cold demands of statecraft, between actions morally obnoxious but politically necessary and motivations, personally perhaps pure but politically ineffectual. It is the impenetrable twilight shrouding the feelings and dealing of political man, the inseparable compound of values, energies, and impulses that fascinate Schiller and make the character of Elizabeth as baffling as it is symptomatic. The vast field of ambiguities upon which political man moves is here outlined, the pitfalls of political action laid bare. If Elizabeth sends Mary to the block, does she do so because the welfare of her country demands of her this extreme and cruel decision? She does and she does not; because when signing the death warrant, she will at the same time give vent to her personal idiosyncracies, her jealousy of a rival whose beauty and youthful charm show up her own unloveliness. But apart from this interference of the petty and all-too-human, is there any way at all to distinguish between the postulates of morality and of political action? Killing Mary is, and Elizabeth knows it, an act of gross injustice that the public good, the unity of the country seems to require unequivocally at this historical moment. But what if this dismisssal and overriding of the dictates of morality for the sake of politics turn out to be the very means which jeopardize the desired end? Elizabeth's power rests on the approval and consent of her people, who are now clamoring for Mary's death. But will not the bloody verdict, once pronounced and executed, cause a shudder of disgust to run through these same people and open up a schism between queen and nation, the very schism Elizabeth wanted to prevent by sacrificing the voice of her conscience to the harsh interests of state? What if the question of morality which had to abdicate before the demands of politics becomes itself a political question creating a new political situation?

Of these perplexities Elizabeth herself is eminently aware. In the great monologue spoken before she finally signs the fateful death warrant, she penetrates to the very bottom of the political dilemma:

> Why have I practiced justice all my life
>
> And shunned tyrannic arbitrariness, so that
>
> For this, my first and inescapable
>
> Despotic act, I weakened my own hands?
>
> The pattern which I set now damns me . . .
>
> Yet was it, after all, my own free choice
>
> To practice justice? Necessity,
>
> All powerful and governing the will
>
> Even of kings, has forced this virtue upon me.

How insoluble the paradox that confronts political man! Justice, which Elizabeth, a free moral agent and a responsible ruler, had chosen as the foundation stone upon which the edifice of her government was to rest, has turned into a strait-jacket which paralyzes her at the very moment when the existence of her state is at stake. Her own past—and a noble past it is—blocks the way into the future; and even this past, the rule of justice which she thought to have created by a free decision of her moral being, is now revealed as nothing but a response to a combination of circumstances that left her no other choice but to be just. Is there a way through the labyrinth, through the hopeless maze of duplicities, imperious necessities, high objectives, and unscrupulous means in which Elizabeth, in which political man, is lost?

Schiller's answer to this question seems to be given in the character of Mary Stuart, as in his **Wallenstein** trilogy it was given in the youthfully idealistic figure of Max Piccolomini. Though in physical bondage, a helpless object whose fate is determined by forces and constellations she cannot control, Mary represents man in his freedom, in the veracity of his being, not innocent—Schiller takes great pains not to absolve her from the criminal complicities with which history charges Scotland's queen—but truthful, showing her genuine face and refusing to hide behind the screen of deviousness, opportunism, and disingenuous representation in which Elizabeth is a master. It is from this vantage point that, in her dispute with Lord Burleigh, Elizabeth's prime minister, she challenges her regal rival:

> And what she really is
>
> She ought to dare appear,

a demand not for specific human qualities and virtues, not for this or that principle of action, but a demand for human authenticity, for the courage of one's own convictions and deeds, for the acceptance and frank display of one's own distinct and distinguishable individuality.

This, we may be inclined to argue, is a shirking of the issue. For is it not Schiller himself, the poet of politics, who has made us so acutely aware of the complexities of political man, the paradoxes of political action, the dissimulations that are part and parcel of the great game, and the dubious stratagems which even a noble intention needs on its road to realization? But all this, the very matrix of politics, which Schiller has so lucidly exposed in his dramatic works, is challenged by Mary Stuart's uncompromising insistence on human authenticity, an insistence which does not solve the perplexing problem that politics raises, but simply ignores and overrides it. Mary Stuart's voice, her very existence, represents, we might say, the attitude of apolitical, even of anti-political man. She can easily display this attitude, since she has withdrawn from the stage of politics and is no longer faced with the harsh needs and decisions which the operation and preservation of the body politic exact. To put it quite cynically: she can well afford to insist on man's inner freedom, on his authenticity, on his exemplary submission to the highest and eternal moral values, because all that is left to her is to die, and to die nobly. But is dying nobly, the extreme sacrifice by which we liberate ourselves from the burden of our earthly existence, an answer to the burning question of how to live in and with the world, how to act responsibly so that this world will bear the imprint of our existence as humans?

Surely it is not an answer, and Schiller did not offer it as an answer, since being a poet and not a soap-box orator his concern is with the essence and condition of this creature called man, and not with solutions that might easily be applied. And being a poet of politics and not a political poet, he had to show and insist on the limits and limitations of politics, lest man, all of man, be transformed into a nefarious political automaton. Just because Schiller saw, and presented more sharply and unflinchingly than any other poet, man's fateful and inescapable involvement in politics, the unrelievable pressures to which we are subject, the vulnerability of even our highest ideals when they enter the web of overpowering historical forces, as they must—for this very reason he insisted sharply and unflinchingly on the preservation of a realm of freedom, the only realm in which man, as a self-determining being subject only to immutable moral law, can fathom his own dignity. Not sharing the shallow smugness of the optimist, he knew only too well that no political formula and no political form could ever open up this field of freedom. He realized that it was and would remain a postulate that forever has to be raised, even if, or perhaps just because, it can never be fulfilled. Should our age, which is at the point of succumbing to the all-domineering demands of total politics, should a humanity, threatened by the fate of being paralyzed by suprapersonal powers and the inexorable pressures of state interests, should we not remember, commemorate, and listen to a poet who, profoundly aware of the commitments we cannot escape, of the entanglements and ambiguities we cannot avoid, proclaimed again and again the fight for man's inner freedom, a fight always at the brink of defeat and death but never to be abandoned? Each of Schiller's works is permeated by the spirit of the great scene in *Don Carlos:* man, proud and jealous of his independence and uniqueness, challenging forever the political power with the words: "Restore to man his lost nobility!" Defending this nobility and insisting upon it in the face of inevitable encroachments and threats was Schiller's mission as a poet of politics, just as he himself pronounced this guardianship the supreme mission of any artist. In one of his philosophical poems, which he entitled "The Artists," he addressed his fellows:

Man's dignity is laid into your hands.

Do guard it well!

It falls with you! With you it will rise high!

With him, with Friedrich Schiller, it rose to heights of which we must never lose sight.

G. A. Wells (essay date 1965)

SOURCE: "Poetry and Politics: An Aspect of Schiller's Diction," in *German Life and Letters,* Vol. 18, No. 2, January 1965, pp. 101-10.

[*In the following essay, Wells claims that Schiller deliberately employs poetical language and a declamatory style in his plays when dealing with facts he considers prosaic, and particularly when he presents legal and political details.*]

When Schiller was writing **Wallenstein** he was consciously trying to avoid both the declamatory style of his **Don Carlos** and also the dullness which he felt was inherent in a subject full of political detail and intrigue. He was trying to steer clear of 'beide Abwege, das Prosaische und das Rhetorische' (to Goethe, October 2nd, 1797). By rhetoric he means, among other things, a certain diffuseness—what E. T. A. Hoffmann called 'eine gewisse Schwatzhaftigkeit, eine gewisse Prägnanz, in der jede einzelne Strophe immer die zehn folgenden zu gebären scheint'. Hoffmann wrote this with both **Don Carlos** and **Wallenstein** in mind.[1] The tendency is one that Schiller never altogether eliminated. In **Demetrius,** his last work, we find the hero making a point he needs for his argument in one line, which then 'gives birth' to two more:

In der Gefangenschaft wardst du geboren, (341)

In einem Kerker kamest du zur Welt,

Dein erster Blick fiel auf Gefängnismauern.

Once Schiller began putting his prose draft of **Wallenstein** into blank verse he found it swelled alarmingly, and in a letter to Goethe he gave three reasons to excuse this diffuseness. First, the exposition contains so many details that it must necessarily be extensive, while the development of the action is exciting enough to preclude boredom; second, his contact with Goethe has infected him with the latter's 'epic spirit'. Schiller said in another letter that Goethe's plays do not move in a straight line, every scene presupposing the action of the previous one and itself leading into the next; that instead of following such a 'strenge gerade Linie', Goethe 'will sich überall mit einer freieren Gemütlichkeit äussern' (December 12th, 1797). And third, that this 'epic' treatment of the Wallenstein material was 'vielleicht das einzige Mittel, diesem prosaischen Stoff eine poetische Natur zu geben' (December 1st, 1797). The statement presupposes that some subject-matter or themes are in themselves 'poetic', others not. The same is implied when Schiller expresses his regret that no compiler has taken the trouble 'in alten Büchern nach poetischen Stoffen auszugehen' and 'das Punctum saliens an einer an sich unscheinbaren Geschichte zu entdecken' (to Goethe, December 15th, 1797). He feels that his productivity in play-writing is reduced because he cannot turn to a handbook of this kind. It is obvious that 'poetic' in this context means what is likely to be effective or moving on the stage. And Schiller has often indicated what material he thinks will fall into this category. The story must show the characters feeling emotions which we can understand and share. Thus when a man is angry, jealous, in love, or anxious to do his duty, he is in the grip of emotions which everyone has felt at some time or other, and so all can sympathize with his situation and be moved. On the other hand, political intrigue is, in this sense, unpoetic, and can only be made poetic if it is not the details of the intrigue that are stressed but the emotions of the hero, and furthermore only if these are of a kind we can share and sympathize with. Thus Schiller writes in his preface to **Fiesco:**

Wenn es wahr ist, dass nur Empfindung Empfindung weckt, so müsste, däucht mich, der politische Held in eben dem Grade kein Subjekt für die Bühne sein, in welchem er den Menschen hintenansetzen muss, um der politische Held zu sein. Es stand . . . bei mir . . . die kalte unfruchtbare Staatsaktion aus dem menschlichen Herzen herauszuspinnen und eben dadurch an das menschliche Herz wieder anzuknüpfen.

And while writing **Wallenstein** he noted that 'poetic' characters have the function of representing and enunciating 'das Allgemeine der Menschheit', i.e that in any man which is common to all men (to Goethe, August 24th, 1798).

Schiller, then, considers that the material for Wallenstein is unpoetic, yet can be made poetic by the 'epic spirit' or long-winded manner in which he has treated it. We see from this statement how difficult it was for him to avoid 'beide Abwege, das Prosaische und das Rhetorische', for he feels he needs the diffuseness inherent in 'das Rhetorische' to avoid being prosaic. He comes back to this argument in the letter to Goethe of August 24th, 1798. where he recognizes that lengthy declamation is unnatural and that brevity would be 'der Natur handelnder Charaktere gemässer'. He answers the objection by saying that drama needs to be unlike real life in certain ways. He adds a further justification:

Eine kürzere und lakonischere Behandlung würde nicht nur viel zu arm und trocken ausfallen: sie würde auch viel zu sehr realistisch, hart und in heftigen Situationen unausstehlich werden, da hingegen eine breitere und vollere Behandlungsweise immer eine gewisse Ruhe und Gemütlichkeit, auch in den gewaltsamsten Zuständen, die man schildert, hervorbringt.

Here, then, he repeats his earlier statement that 'epic' breadth takes the prosiness out of his material, and adds that, precisely because such diffuseness is unlike real life, it tones down the harsh realism of the subject-matter.

If crude or prosaic detail can be given poetic dignity by being presented in a diffuse, declamatory way, it might follow that where the subject-matter is not objectionable or dull, diffuse representation is unnecessary or even undesirable. And this is in fact Schiller's view, formulated in a letter to Goethe of November 4th, 1797:

Es scheint, dass ein Teil des poetischen Interesse in dem Antagonism zwischen dem Inhalt und der Darstellung liegt: ist der Inhalt sehr poetisch-bedeutend, so kann eine magre Darstellung und eine bis zum Gemeinen gehende Einfalt des Ausdruckes ihm recht wohl anstehen, da im Gegenteil ein unpoetischer gemeiner Inhalt, wie er in einem grössern Ganzen oft nötig wird, durch einen belebten und reichen Ausdruck poetische Dignität erhält.

The 'grösseres Ganzes' that Schiller has in mind is his **Wallenstein;** the exposition is very detailed and long and the hero does not take the decisive step until Act I, Scene 7 of the third play of the trilogy. The implication is that tedium can be avoided by 'ein belebter und reicher Ausdruck'. The epithets imply profusion of imagery and other devices to achieve elevated diction; and a certain

diffuseness is surely also implied by the contrast with 'eine magre Darstellung'.

Now if Schiller were incapable of writing tersely, we should be entitled to reject his theorizings on the advantages of diffuseness as mere rationalizations. But we see how very concise he can be from the summing-up speeches which inform a character of a situation already clear to the others and the audience. For example, at the beginning of **Tell,** Baumgarten explains in sixty lines of dialogue why he wishes to be put across the lake. Tell then arrives and has to be told who it is who is asking for what sort of help and why. He is told in a speech which condenses the sixty lines into six:

's ist ein Alzeller Mann: er hat sein' Ehr' (128)

Verteidigt und den Wolfenschiess erschlagen,

Des Königs Burgvogt, der auf Rossberg sass.

Des Landvogts Reiter sind ihm auf den Fersen.

Er fleht den Schiffer um die Überfahrt;

Der fürcht't sich vor dem Sturm und will nicht fahren.

The same condensation can be seen when Wallenstein's wife is told of a complicated situation which has already been enacted to the audience:

Empört hat sich der Herzog, zu dem Feind

Hat er sich schlagen wollen, die Armee

Hat ihn verlassen, und es ist misslungen.

(*Tod,* ll. 1783-5)

Schiller, then, can be terse, and there is no reason to doubt his statement that his diffuseness was sometimes a deliberate method of dealing with certain difficulties in his subject-matter. If he carries out his own theory, we shall expect him to, as it were, switch on a certain diffuseness when presenting matters which he considers dull and uninteresting.

We can find such details both in **Die Piccolomini** and in **Maria Stuart.** They are on the whole absent from **Wallensteins Tod** and, as Goethe saw, the powerful effect of this play is partly due to the fact that in it 'alles aufhört politisch zu sein und bloss menschlich wird' (to Schiller, March 18th, 1799), i.e. the problems discussed are of general human interest, such as: is a man obliged to keep his word under all circumstances? What shall he do when faced with a choice between duty and inclination? These ethical issues which concern all men at all times Goethe contrasted with the political fabric of **Die Piccolomini;** the spectator has difficulty in finding his way out of 'einem gewissen künstlichen, und hie und da willkürlich scheinenden Gewebe' (to Schiller, March 9th, 1799). If we seek an example of a long recital of political details, the obvious one is the speech by Buttler (Act I, Scene 2) which provokes from Questenberg the famous reply: 'Was ist der langen Rede kurzer Sinn?' Buttler takes thirty lines to make three points: (i) that the Kaiser has an enormous number of troops in Germany, (ii) that they are all commanded by Wallenstein's captains, and (iii) that they are not fighting for patriotic reasons but are united only by their devotion to Wallenstein. The way this final point is stated shows the style in which the whole is written:

Fremdlinge stehn sie da auf diesem Boden; 223

Der Dienst allein ist ihnen Haus und Heimat.

Sie treibt der Eifer nicht fürs Vaterland,

Denn Tausende, wie mich, gebar die Fremde.

Nicht für den Kaiser, wohl die Hälfte kam

Aus fremdem Dienst feldflüchtig uns herüber,

Gleichgültig unterm Doppeladler fechtend 229

Wie unterm Löwen und den Lilien.

Doch alle führt an gleich gewalt' gem Zügel

Ein Einziger, durch gleiche Lieb' und Furcht

Zu einem Volke sie zusammenbindend.

Und wie des Blitzes Funke sicher, schnell,

Geleitet an der Wetterstange, läuft, 235

Herrscht sein Befehl vom letzten fernen Posten,

Der an die Dünen branden hört den Belt,

Der in der Etsch fruchtbare Thäler sieht,

Bis zu der Wache, die ihr Schilderhaus

Hat aufgerichtet an der Kaiserburg. 240

Of these eighteen lines, 229-30 and 234-40 are superfluous in the sense that the ideas are fully and completely expressed without them. Thus the imagery of 231-3 makes Wallenstein's power perfectly clear. The simile of the lightning which follows and the specification of some of the outposts do, however, add a little poetry to statements which might otherwise 'zu arm und trocken ausfallen.' The picturesque details of the surf and the fruitful valleys certainly contrast with the factual matters of the opening lines.

A good many of the political facts in *Maria Stuart* are given in Act I, Scene 7. Schiller wrote to Goethe (April 26th, 1799) that he hoped to begin the play with the sentence against Maria and pass over all these political issues leading up to it. But this hope was not fully realized, and six weeks later (July 12th) he wrote again, saying that an account of her trial was necessary after all, and that he hoped he had overcome the 'tendency to dullness' inherent in such legal niceties. The reason why he could not avoid giving them is not far to seek. His Maria is not guilty of the crime for which she is executed, and so he has to make clear the official charge against her and begin to establish her innocence of it. In this scene she gives five reasons why her trial was invalid: her judges were not her peers, as they ought to have been according to English law; they were also clearly mere tools of the crown, for since the days of Henry VIII the English Lords have been prepared to change their faith with every new accession,

proving that they are not independent of their sovereign's whim; third, they were Protestants and therefore biased against her; fourth, they were English and bore the traditional English hatred for all that is Scottish; and fifth, the scribes who testified against her were not confronted with her as English law requires. Burleigh is not able to answer any of these objections, and Paulet, who as we see from the opening scenes is not exactly biased in her favour, admits, when challenged, that she is right and goes on to complain privately to Burleigh that 'Unziemlichkeiten' have occurred in her trial. The point of all this is clearly to show her innocence of the official charge against her.[2]

Schiller, then, could not avoid including much legal detail which he feared would be dull. My question is how he sets about avoiding dullness, and my theory is that he does so by applying his own principle of switching on a declamatory style. Thus, one of Maria's objections is, as we saw,

Dass vor Gericht kein Britte gegen den Schotten, (807)

Kein Schotte gegen jenen zeugen darf.

The next eleven lines bring a poetical elaboration of this prosaic point. Nature has flung these two impassioned peoples on a narrow board in the ocean, divided it unequally between them, and bade them fight for its possession. Only the narrow bed of the Tweed separates their tempestuous spirits, and often its waves are coloured by the blood of the combatants, who stand glowering at each other, their hands on their swords, on opposite banks. Here we have the 'belebter und reicher Ausdruck' that Schiller deemed appropriate to prosaic subject-matter.

The same technique is visible in the way the probability and importance of Elisabeth's marriage to the Duke of Anjou are communicated to us in Act II, Scene 1. Instead of just saying how the religious problem involved has been settled and how important it is that Elisabeth should have a child to prevent the throne from passing back to Catholic control (Maria being the next legitimate claimant), Schiller introduces these matters with an account of a (significantly fictitious) tournament, at which 'das Verlangen' (the French knights) made an assault on 'die keusche Festung der Schönheit' (defended by Elisabeth's knights). Here, then, a political matter of some importance to the plot is introduced not with images or elevated diction but with what one might almost call an allegory (reminiscent of the moral allegories of the pre-Elizabethan stage) which certainly involves treating the whole subject at greater length.

Schiller cannot, of course, always present legal and political details in this way. In Act I, Scene 6 Mortimer's plot to save Maria is compressed into seven factual lines (634-40), and only another seven (518-24) are needed to state a crucial factor in the political background, namely that from the Catholic point of view Elisabeth has no right to her throne, being the child of a marriage contracted without papal sanction. In this scene Schiller has to draw Mortimer's character in full; it is his first substantial appearance, and when we next see him (in Act II) he begins to act decisively in accordance with his character. Hence there are some really long speeches in this scene devoted to character-drawing, and this may well be Schiller's reason for not lengthening it even more by lengthy treatment of political details. For instance, in the first really long speech of the whole play, Mortimer denotes the religion in which he was brought up as 'streng', 'finster' and 'dumpf', and his own temperament and behaviour as 'heiss' and 'schnell'. He refers also to his 'unbezwingliche Begierde'. Thus these opening nine lines (409-17) tell us that he is a young hot-head, temperamentally inclined to react against puritanical constraints. His impulsiveness is of importance to the action. To give but one example, it leads him to take the initiative in frank speaking in the scene between him and Leicester (Act II, Scene 8). The elderly courtier whose motto is 'ich kann der Vorsicht nicht zu viel gebrauchen' (1749) would never have done this, and reproaches Mortimer for his rash plans (1868). Mortimer's speech in Act I continues for another thirty-two lines which bring out his susceptibility to the sensuous pageantry of Catholicism (418-50). A pilgrimage to Rome is described, the arrival in the impressive city, the effect of the ritual of the papal mass on the youth accustomed only to 'the word of God' recited in a joyless, undecorated kirk. This long description serves to show that he is a 'Sinnenmensch'. He prefers the physical and the concrete to the abstract. Catholicism appeals to him because he wants something concrete and tangible. This is reiterated when he says of the Cardinal who instructed him:

Er zeigte mir, dass grübelnde Vernunft (477)

Den Menschen ewig in der Irre leitet,

Dass seine Augen sehen müssen, was

Das Herz soll glauben, dass ein sichtbar Haupt

Der Kirche not tut . . .

Paulet states the puritan attitude in the first scene of the play, where he says that Mary has her Bible and can do without decorations such as jewellery or mirrors. Mortimer shows how completely he has abandoned this standpoint when he rejects the Bible in favour of the sensuous Catholic ritual:

Hass schwur ich nun dem engen dumpfen Buch, (457)

Mit frischem Kranz die Schläfe mir zu schmücken,

Mich fröhlich an die Fröhlichen zu schliessen.

Mortimer's character as a 'Sinnenmensch' is, of course, of great importance to the action. He wants to rescue Maria in order to marry and possess her, and it is the violence of his behaviour towards her in Act III, Scene 6 that sobers her after she has gloated over her triumph at humiliating Elisabeth at the interview. Almost everything he says there refers to violence. He talks of the universe collapsing, of himself being ripped to pieces at Tyburn, of murdering Elisabeth and his uncle, of fighting to the death with Le-

icester, and of tearing Maria from her chamber. Her reaction is to feel that life is not worth living if her supporters are going to treat her as roughly as do her enemies. As Schiller said, 'ihr Schicksal ist nur heftige Passionen zu erfahren und zu entzünden' (to Goethe, June 18th, 1799). And Maria herself asks despairingly: 'Bin ich geboren, nur die Wut zu wecken?' (2552).

Thus Mortimer's long speech in Act I brings out traits in his character which need to be made clear if we are to find the action of the whole play at all convincing. It is interesting to note how tersely Schiller makes him repeat to Leicester in Act II what he stated at such great length in Act I. When Leicester asks how he has come to take Maria's side, Mortimer replies:

Das kann ich Euch mit wenigem erklären. (1741)

Ich habe meinen Glauben abgeschworen

Zu Rom und steh' im Bündnis mit den Guisen.

Ein Brief des Erzbischofs zu Reims hat mich

Beglaubigt bei der Königin von Schottland.

Schiller does not, then, adopt an expansive and poetic style only when narrating matters which he fears might otherwise appear dull. Indeed, his very enthusiasm for some ideas can sometimes lead him to express them at great length. It was long ago noted that 'man hat ihm zum schweren Vorwurf gemacht, dass er der Versuchung nicht widerstand, einen schönen Gedanken auf den glänzenden Wellen seiner Beredsamkeit dahinströmen zu lassen, wenn auch mitunter die Handlung zu schnellerem Fortgang trieb'.[3] Some of Max Piccolomini's speeches are a good example. Schiller confessed that he felt much more drawn to Max than to the other characters (to Goethe, November 28th, 1796), and in *Die Piccolomini*, lines 534 ff. we find him talking for 25 lines in praise of peace. He imagines the homeward procession of the colours, the gaily decorated troops, the welcoming crowds and ringing bells. The blossoms with which the troops bedeck their helmets he calls their last and final theft from the fields; and he contrasts the voluntary opening of the gates to admit the joyous throng with the previous blasting open of the walls. He goes on to imagine the bewilderment of the soldier who finds his home surroundings so different after the long campaign:

Mit breiten Ästen

Deckt ihn der Baum bei seiner Wiederkehr,

Der sich zur Gerte bog, als er gegangen,

Und schamhaft tritt als Jungfrau ihm entgegen,

Die er einst an der Amme Brust verliess.

Now all this is by no means an irrelevant digression. Now that he is in love with Thekla he wants the war to be over so that he can marry and settle down. Octavio realizes the implications at once, and sees that he will have to inform his son of Wallenstein's treachery straightway, before the lad becomes so committed to Thekla that he will not be able to keep faith with his Kaiser. So the disclosures Max makes in this speech precipitate the conflict between father and son so essential to this play, from which it even derives its title. Nevertheless, we cannot avoid the impression that Max's ideas and emotions could have been communicated more succinctly, and that Schiller's diffuseness here is due to his sympathy with them. Other examples occur in Act III, Scene 4 where Max defends (at considerable length) Wallenstein's faith in the stars, saying that such belief is altogether becoming for 'ein liebend Herz':

> Die Fabel ist der Liebe Heimatwelt;
>
> Gern wohnt sie unter Feen, Talismanen,
>
> Glaubt gern an Götter, weil sie göttlich ist.

He is, of course, thinking of the emotional needs of his own 'liebend Herz', and continues to do so in his next speech, where he is also only ostensibly talking about Wallenstein. After saying that Wallenstein will bring peace to the world and then retire to his estates, Max spends fifteen lines (1662-76) painting an idyllic picture of such a life of peaceful retirement—thinking surely of his own life with Thekla, as is indicated by Gräfin Terzky's interruption. She pulls him back to the grim reality of the present, reminding him that Thekla is not yet his and must be won before he puts his weapons aside.

Practically the whole of this third act of **Die Piccolomini** deals with the relationship between Thekla and Max, and Schiller described it as 'der poetisch wichtigste Teil' of the whole (to Goethe, November 9th, 1798). He said too that these love scenes are in complete contrast to the political intrigue which constitutes the rest of the play (to Goethe, December 12th, 1797). They serve to put the point of view of the idealists. Max is conscious of the gulf which separates Thekla and himself from the other characters who are all realists:

> Betrug ist überall und Heuchelschein
>
> Und Mord und Gift und Meineid und Verrat;
>
> Der einzig reine Ort ist unsere Liebe.
>
> *(Tod, ll. 1218-20)*

Max is an entirely fictitious character, and Thekla is in effect also fictitious, since the daughter of the historical Wallenstein was only nine years of age when he was murdered. Schiller has invented them to pass judgement on the realists and has created special scenes for Max to do so on Wallenstein (*Tod,* Act II, Scene 2) and Octavio (Act II, Scene 7). Idealism is Schiller's own standpoint, and it seems that Max's lengthy speeches come straight from Schiller's heart.

My point, then, is not that Schiller is always diffuse when talking politics, nor that he is never diffuse about anything else, but that some of the long legal and political speeches are as they are because he is deliberately applying his own theory on how to sustain interest. It has long been appreciated that he chose the highly artificial form of rhymed verse for **Wallensteins Lager** to tone down the extreme realism of the subject-matter. Life in Wallenstein's army is not very edifying, and the rhymed verse 'destroys illusion', as Schiller puts it in the prologue, so that we know we are witnessing a poetic fiction and not a slice of life:

> Und wenn die Muse heut,
>
> Ihr altes deutsches Recht, des Reimes Spiel,
>
> Bescheiden wieder fordert—tadelt's nicht!
>
> Ja, danket ihr's, dass sie das düstre Bild
>
> Der Wahrheit in das heitre Reich der Kunst
>
> Hinüberspielt, die Täuschung, die sie schafft,
>
> Aufrichtig selbst zerstört und ihren Schein
>
> Der Wahrheit nicht betrüglich unterschiebt;
>
> Ernst ist das Leben, heiter ist die Kunst.

The humour in the **Lager** also serves to tone down the unpalatable subject-matter, and this again has often been noted. But the fact that Schiller deliberately employs a certain type of poetical diction when dealing with details that he thinks dull rather than unpalatable has tended to be overlooked, doubtless because the style employed in such passages is the rhetorical one he uses for different reasons elsewhere. The relevant examples have therefore been noted, if at all, as examples of 'Schiller's rhetoric', and their special significance overlooked.

But there is a wider question raised by all this, namely, what is poetry? How does it differ from prose? I think I have given evidence enough that in Schiller's view poetry often means long-winded and repetitive speeches, adorned with so-called 'poetical' epithets, similes, allegories and the like. This is of course the conception of poetry passed on to eighteenth-century writers by Opitz who (in his *Buch von der deutschen Poeterei* of 1624) said that in tragic and epic poetry 'man muss ansehnliche, volle und heftige Reden vorbringen und ein Ding nicht nur bloss nennen, sondern mit prächtigen hohen Worten umschreiben'. But Schiller, although he often thinks diffuse declamation, colour and richness appropriate, certainly does not equate poetry with them, for he thought that some subjects are poetic in themselves and should be treated tersely (see above, p. 103). So according to him, one can be poetical and brief. I have tried to show above that when he says some story or situation is poetical he means it is effective in that it stimulates a strong emotion, in particular sympathy with the person whose situation is portrayed. I think what he has in mind is that some situations in themselves produce this reaction in the audience: it does not depend upon the words used and may even occur if no words at all are uttered. The situation on the stage at the beginning of Act V of **Maria Stuart,** which is indicated not by spoken words but by long stage directions, would be a case in point. Modern producers tend (understandably enough) to cut those parts of his plays where the 'poetry' depends on long-winded repetitions. But there are many passages where the poetry is not of this kind, where it is the situation and the ideas and emotions springing from it that are—just as much as the words—poetical, and it is to this type of poetry that Schiller owes his permanent place in the repertory.

Notes

1. *Nachricht von den neuesten Schicksalen des Hundes Berganza,* in *Phantasiestücke, Werke,* ed. v. Maassen, München, 1912, vol. I, p. 171

2. I cannot agree with Professor Stahl, who seizes on Maria's objection that her judges were not her peers, and takes it as evidence that 'her pride is as strong as ever', that she bears Elisabeth a 'grievance' for having her tried by lesser men, and that when Mortimer reveals his plan to her, 'she accepts him as . . . an instrument to take vengeance on Elisabeth' (*Schiller's Drama,* Oxford, 1954, p. 111). Maria's concern at this stage is not with vengeance but with justice, and her complaint that her judges were not her peers is part of her argument that her trial did not fulfil the requirements of the law.

3. Goldbeck and Rudolph, *Schiller-Lexikon,* Berlin, 1869, art. Sprache.

G. A. Wells (essay date 1973)

SOURCE: "Villainy and Guilt in Schiller's *Wallenstein* and *Maria Stuart,*" in *Deutung und Bedeuntung: Studies in German and Comparative Literature Presented to Karl Werner Maurer,* edited by Brigitte Schuldermann, Victor G. Doerksen, Robert J. Glendinning, and Evelyn Scherabon Firchow, Mouton and Co., 1973, pp. 100-17.

[*In the following essay, Wells discusses the problem of how we are to understand the guilt and villainy of the heroes and antagonists in* Wallenstein *and* Maria Stuart, *and notes that Schiller places less and less emphasis on villainy as a source of tragic catastrophe in his later works.*]

Schiller believed that the effect of tragedy is greatest when both the hero and his opponent have an arguable moral case.[1] This paper sets out to ascertain to what extent he succeeded in *Wallenstein* and *Maria Stuart* in fulfilling this requirement. Scholars still disagree concerning the apportionment of guilt between hero (or heroine) and antagonist in these two plays—a remarkable state of affairs in view of the fact that Schiller was concerned to present characters actuated by ideas and emotions intelligible to all people at all times.[2] Many writers have, like Walter Scott, gone to great lengths to present their characters in local dress, speaking the proper dialect and harbouring the correct superstitions. Schiller had no desire to follow this practice of introducing such features which can only be understood by those who know the time and place, and in any case he lacked the historical knowledge to do so. In his later, as in the very first of his historical plays, his aim was "die kalte unfruchtbare Staatsaktion aus

dem menschlichen Herzen herauszuspinnen und eben dadurch an das menschliche Herz wieder anzuknüpfen".[3]

Schiller's Wallenstein has been held to be a hero who gets no more than his deserts.[4] His treatment of Buttler has been instanced as one of the chief grounds for withholding sympathy. In his *Geschichte des dreißigjährigen Krieges,* Schiller records that Wallenstein urged Illo "in Wien den Grafentitel zu suchen", but wrote in secret to the court that the application should not be granted. Now the dramatist did not need this anecdote to motivate the treason of a soldier of fortune, as is the Illo of his play, but utilized it in connection with Buttler; for such an honest man could not be represented as forsaking his emperor without strong provocation, and provocation of this kind had the advantage to the dramatist that it touches Buttler at his most sensitive spot (his consciousness of his lowly origin). And so we find that in *Wallensteins Tod* (II, 6) Buttler becomes convinced that Wallenstein, while pretending to support his application for elevation to the aristocracy, had in fact written to Vienna advising the court to castigate him for his arrogance. Hebbel asked concerning this whole incident: "Wallensteins schändlicher Betrug, . . . wie verträgt er sich mit der Würde eines tragischenCharakters?"[5] Hebbel did not deny that the deception was perpetrated, but W. F. Mainland has argued that "if we are to suppose Wallenstein guilty of the fraud, we may have to fix the notion of his amoral character beyond the normal limits acceptable even to us".[6] Let us study the details.

Mainland is certainly right to say that Wallenstein's own admission that he has behaved badly to Buttler (*Tod,* ll. 1448-50) has no reference to any deceitful letter writing. The context shows that he is here reproaching himself for having listened to a "Stimme . . . im Herzen" warning him against Buttler, who—and this is one of the many ironical elements in the play—has transpired to be his staunchest supporter. Wallenstein himself thus says nothing from which we could infer that he is the author of the incriminating letter which Octavio shows to Buttler in II, 6. Mainland further notes that, in that scene, we are not permitted to hear the text of the letter, and so "have no opportunity of trying to judge from its phrasing whether Wallenstein can possibly have composed it" (32-33). But in fact we could hardly infer much from its phrasing, as Wallenstein's style is anything but uniform. H. B. Garland states, in his recent close study of style in Schiller's plays, that Wallenstein's "way of speaking" shows him to be "the most mobile character in the play", "chameleon-like".[7] To give the text of the letter would have retarded the dialogue to no purpose, and so Schiller makes Octavio provide a summary of the contents (ll. 1141-43) while Buttler reads them. Buttler accepts the letter as genuine presumably because he recognizes Wallenstein's seal or hand, with which he is familiar.[8] Mainland notes that his reading of the letter "is completed during the speaking of six lines of text" and "can therefore at best be only cursory" (34). But Schiller is not an exponent of 'Sekundenstil' and so would not prolong a stage event because the same event in real life would require more time. It is obvious that Buttler aligned himself with Wallenstein only because the court had offended him so grievously. When he agreed (*Piccolomini,* IV, 4) to pledge his general unconditional support, he added that six months previously he would never have thus broken faith with his emperor (ll. 1971-74). The astute Wallenstein must have known this, and it is natural to suppose that he ensured—by writing the letter which Octavio later produces—that the court did alienate him.

Schiller has not recorded his own interpretation, but Goethe (who may be presumed to have been aware of his friend's intentions) says in his review of the play that Octavio "überführt ihn [Buttler] durch Vorzeigung authentischer Dokumente".[9] Mainland says that because Goethe here refers in the plural to the showing of one letter, "we should be justified in refusing to consider the passage altogether" (45). But it is more reasonable to suppose that Goethe, writing from his memory of a stage performance, thought that Octavio handed Buttler *some papers* instead of *a paper.*

If Wallenstein did not write the letter, the obvious alternative is that Octavio forged it; and some will agree with G. Storz "daß letzlich unsicher und offen bleibt, wer denn nun in Wahrheit Buttler irregeführt hat—Wallenstein oder Octavio."[10] But Mainland is unwilling to believe either Wallenstein or Octavio guilty of such fraud (39), and he concludes that Schiller may have deliberately left the origin of the letter obscure. "Such intention", he says, "would assort very well with the central theme of the play—the 'Doppelsinn des Lebens'". When Wallenstein says (*Tod,* l. 161): "mich verklagt der Doppelsinn des Lebens", he is voicing his awareness that even those of his actions which, he would claim, were inspired by pure motives, can be interpreted as determined by selfish ones. Mainland, however, seems to link the "Doppelsinn des Lebens" with the principle that great works of literature characteristically display a certain ambiguity.[11] But to suggest that Schiller gives no adequate account of the origin of a document which turns Buttler against Wallenstein, and which therefore leads indirectly to the hero's death, is tantamount to assuming that the dramatist has dropped all serious concern with motivation.

L. Bellermann long ago showed that Wallenstein's trickery of Buttler is not an isolated incident which depresses an otherwise morally acceptable character, but accords perfectly with his practice of treating everyone as a means to his own ends.[12] He expressly seeks (*Tod,* III, 18) to win Max from the emperor with the words: "Mir angehören, mir gehorchen, das / Ist deine Ehre, dein Naturgesetz." In spite of his egoism, we can admire Wallenstein for his fearlessness and strength of character in adversity.[13] And I have argued elsewhere that our basis for sympathy with him is our recognition that he is under considerable pressure to act as he does, that he is not entirely to blame for the difficult situation facing him in *Die Piccolomini,* and that not wholly impure motives have led him into a situation in which he must either inflict or suffer violence.[14]

While critics have made attempts to elevate Wallenstein, there has been a tendency to achieve the same end by blackening his antagonist. J. Müller, for instance, says that Octavio, "der geschmeidige Höfling", deceives Wallenstein "aus Ehrgeiz" (135). And E. L. Stahl suggests that Octavio "combines loyalty to his emperor with an unmistakable desire to further his own ends".[15] Some other critics have gone only so far as to claim that Octavio's purity or otherwise of motive is (as has been said of the origin of the letter shown to Buttler!) an open question. Thus F. W. Kaufmann holds that "bei Octavio . . . wird es nie ganz klar, ob die Kaisertreue oder der persönliche Vorteil vorwiegt, den er von seinen Intrigen im Dienst des Kaisers erwartet".[16] Max at first suspects his father of pursuing his own advantage but goes on to embrace him, and Schiller's purpose here is surely not to suggest that Max has been duped, but that both father and son have an arguable moral case. Our feelings towards the conflict between father and son, which forms the culmination of the second of the three plays, would not correspond to its importance in the action if we were to suppose that it was resolved by trickery. Octavio is no opportunist, but acts from stolid loyalty to his emperor. As he sees it, Wallenstein's "böse Tat" has left him only underhand methods of preventing civil war (*Piccolomini,* ll. 2364-68, 2452-60). W. Wittkowski has cogently argued that any further stress on Octavio's rectitude would have had the effect of lowering Wallenstein in our estimation and that, for this reason, Schiller is even concerned—through the mouth of Max—to show Octavio in a worse light than he deserves.[17] On Octavio's integrity external evidence is important, for Schiller in three letters absolves him from villainy, and is thus concerned in this play to implement his own principle that maximum effectiveness is achieved when both he who causes and he who suffers disaster become objects of our sympathy.[18] Octavio does rise as a result of Wallenstein's fall, but this is very different from saying that he engineered it in order to profit from it. The effectiveness of the final curtain of the trilogy depends largely on our realizing that Gordon's "Blick des Vorwurfs" as he hands the Emperor's letter to "dem *Fürsten* Piccolomini" is unjust; that Octavio, broken-hearted that he has lost his son, has now to accept the ascription of his actions to the basest of motives.[19] Here, indeed, is the "Doppelsinn des Lebens", in the sense in which Wallenstein used the phrase! Octavio's reaction to Gordon's taunt, although but a gesture, is more eloquent than words. We know what he must feel from our knowledge of the whole situation. In realistic drama generally we may to some extent have our emotions excited by the language used, but it is primarily the events and situations depicted which have this effect. Words are, of course, often needed to explain the significance of the events. But often the most effective words are those which state most briefly and at the same time most clearly what the situation is. We are much less impressed by what a character says he feels than by what we judge from the situation he must feel. He may rant as much as he likes, but if we see no reason in his situation to justify so much excitement, we shall not be excited or if our emotions are aroused it will be emotions of a very different kind.

Turning now to *Maria Stuart,* we find similar problems, in that there is disagreement as to whether Schiller's Elisabeth may justly be called villainous, and as to the extent and nature of Maria's guilt. To explain the issues involved I must briefly review the historical facts that Schiller found before him. Elizabeth reigned over many committed Catholics, from whose standpoint she had no right to her throne, being the child of a marriage contracted without papal sanction. It could hardly be disputed that, on her death, Mary Stuart (granddaughter of the eldest sister of Elizabeth's father) would be her rightful successor, although she naturally refused to recognize this formally, being well aware that more people worship the rising than the setting sun. English Catholics therefore knew that to assassinate her would automatically bring a Catholic monarch to the throne. Elizabeth and her Protestant advisors thus had a cogent motive for having Mary killed, even had she been innocent of political aspiration. In actual fact Mary was not without political ambition. After the death of Mary Tudor she had openly asserted her claim to the English throne by quartering her arms with the three lions of England. It was later stipulated—in the Treaty of Edinburgh (1560)—that she should abstain from using the arms and title of the kingdoms of England and Ireland, but she never ratified this treaty.[20]

Schiller's Maria had, in her youth, claimed to be rightful queen of England (ll. 1290-91; 1534-37; 2336-37). It is implied in Act I that she has not abandoned this claim, for Paulet says she could go free if only she were to ratify the Treaty of Edinburgh (ll. 105-09), and from Leicester we learn (ll. 1416-17) "Daß sie dies Reich in Anspruch nimmt, daß dich [Elisabeth] / Die Guisen nicht als Königin erkennen . . ."s (ll. 1416-17). Although Maria sees in this claim the source of all her suffering (ll. 534-35), she thus still affirms it and even speaks of revenge (l. 592). This affirmation, however inexpedient, is no crime, for a Catholic must necessarily regard Elisabeth as a usurper. In some passages Schiller implies that, like the historical Mary, Maria will be satisfied if her claim is acknowledged to the extent that she be declared Elisabeth's rightful successor. Thus she tells Burleigh that she had cherished the hope (fulfilled in history by her son) of uniting England and Scotland peacefully under one sceptre (ll. 829-31). At the interview with Elisabeth she states that all would have been well if only she had been declared Elisabeth's heir (ll. 2365-69). Later in this interview, as part of her attempt to humble herself, she waives all her rights—present and future—to the English throne (ll. 2378-79), only to re-assert them with maximum vehemence when Elisabeth has provoked her beyond endurance (ll. 2447-51). Maria's total renunciation of all her political claims is no more historically true than the interview during which it occurs, but is nevertheless quite intelligible as a desperate bid to win life and freedom by humbling herself before her rival.

Schiller's heroine is executed for conspiring with Babington against Elisabeth's life, but unlike the historical Mary, she was not in fact involved in any plot against Elisabeth. In the play her trial for conspiracy is represented as having been little more than a farce. But why, we ask, has she refrained from conspiracy? Ought not a usurper to be forcibly deposed? Maria's answer is that she personally has done nothing to foment a Catholic rising (ll. 839-43) because it would sully her to be a party to any plan involving Elisabeth's murder (l. 954). She does however admit, and even stress, that she has appealed to France and Spain to free her from English captivity, and that any prisoner wrongfully detained would have a perfect right to do likewise (ll. 946-51; 3727-28). Her hope is that Leicester will free her, and Kennedy does not contradict Paulet when he alleges that the queen is trying to bribe the gardener, presumably to take her letter to Leicester. In the upshot she is able to give it to Mortimer for delivery, but how little she cares for plots of violence is clear from her attempt to dissuade him from trying to rescue her by force (l. 650).

Mainland has noted that Elisabeth's assassination might well be "a possible result of her [Maria's] plea for help among the foreign powers" (82) and that although she "has vigorously denied the intention of assassination, she has cherished designs which might have had that end". Thus the attempt on Elisabeth's life reported in Act III does have the blessing of the French ambassador (ll. 638-40), if not of his government. I do not, however, agree with Mainland that Maria's behaviour makes her politically guilty and justifies the sentence of death passed on her. This view, as Kaufmann has said in criticism of Mainland, "geht . . . entschieden zu weit" (93). As is stressed by Burleigh, her very existence may lead to a Catholic attempt on Elisabeth's life; and if her appeal to the Catholic powers to free her increases the danger to Elisabeth, the latter can meet it by liberating, rather than executing, her rival. If Schiller had wished to make his heroine politically guilty he would hardly have made Burleigh's statement of the legal case against her so feeble that even Paulet, who has just called her vain and lascivious (ll. 40, 45) is forced to take her side, complaining as he does of the trial's "Unziemlichkeiten" (l. 985). Nor would Schiller have deviated from the historical facts in making the scribes who testified against her retract their evidence in Act V. He has freed Maria from political guilt and burdened her with a deep consciousness of personal sin. The historical Mary did plot with Babington to overthrow Elizabeth, but never admitted complicity in Darnley's murder. Schiller's heroine does not plot with Babington, but freely admits that she allowed Darnley to be killed.

Mainland is anxious to burden Maria with some political guilt so that we do not sympathize with her at the expense of her rival. For the same reason he also tries to elevate Elisabeth's character, as he has done with Wallenstein. Although it is certainly in accordance with Schiller's theory of tragedy that plays are more effective if disaster is contrived without villainy, the text does not bear out Mainland's charitable view of Elisabeth.

When Elisabeth receives Maria's letter requesting an interview, she weeps in sympathy with the queen, who, formerly so proud and powerful, is now so helpless and humble (ll. 1528-30). She then says that she will find means of reconciling clemency—which in this context means granting the interview—with necessity (ll. 1568-70). What she has in mind emerges when, immediately afterwards, she hints to Mortimer that she will be glad to have Maria murdered. She takes him into her confidence presumably because she knows that he alone will have opportunity to do the deed, now that Paulet has refused either to do it himself or to admit an assassin to his castle. Maria's murder will enable Elisabeth "den Schein [zu] retten" (l. 1598), to avoid the impropriety of sending a queen and a relative to the scaffold. Once she feels confident that Mortimer will carry out her commission, she will gladly grant Maria an interview in order to obtain a reputation for clemency—"sich den Schein der Gnade vor der Welt zu geben", as Leicester puts it (ll. 1900-01; cf. ll. 2048-50), and also in order to humiliate Maria (ll. 2830-31). In view of these facts it is surprising that both Mainland and Garland take her tears over Maria's letter as a genuine expression of compassion.[21] Later she unashamedly declares that she will have crocodile tears enough to bewail the death of her rival (ll. 3899-900). Her charge to Mortimer could be excused by the exigencies of her situation if it were not accompanied by hypocritical readiness to grant the interview. Schiller's designation "königliche Heuchlerin" (to Goethe, July 30, 1799) is indeed just, although Mainland rejects this explicit testimony on the ground that Schiller "was not [in] the mood [to] write with delicate precision" when he penned it (63).

Elisabeth is represented as about to marry, against her will, so that the nation will be assured of a Protestant successor. She hints to Leicester that, had she followed her heart instead of political necessity, she would have married him (ll. 1967-71). Yet she concludes her interview with Mortimer by promising her favours to him if he will kill Maria. Mainland thinks (74) that there can be "no doubt" that she is promising him marriage, but Mortimer himself is not sure that this is what she really means (ll. 1643-44) and, as usual, she avoids any clear and definite committal. She offers him "die engsten Bande, die zärtesten" (ll. 1630-31). Bellermann has noted how repulsive this is. Even if she intends to make him only a favourite, without sexual privileges, "so bleibt es doch ein sehr niedriger Zug, daß eine Frau so etwas ohne Liebe, nur zur Gewinnung eines äußeren Zweckes sprechen kann" (215). There is certainly no suggestion that she loves Mortimer, whom she here meets for the first time.

Schiller has retained and even augmented all that is unattractive in the character of the historical Elizabeth, whereas he has elevated that of the historical Mary. The result is that we cannot extend our sympathy equally to his two queens. Storz contrasts this with the situation in ***Wallen-***

stein, where "weder Wallenstein noch Octavio dürfte völlig recht haben, keiner durchaus im Unrecht sein" (332-33). Maria's final words in Act I urge Elisabeth to show herself as she really is (l. 974). This, as we rapidly learn, is what she will never do, for she is above all concerned to save appearance, and evades responsibility whenever she can. Thus in order to appear element she deliberately gives Leicester a cue to suggest the interview with Maria (ll. 1995-99; 2023), although she will not expressly commit herself to granting it. It is to take place as if by chance, and if anything goes amiss it is to be Leicester's fault, not hers (ll. 2065-66). Paulet sees through her and warns Mortimer that, if he lends her his hand, she will later disown him (l. 1676). This condemnation from such a scrupulously honest character is highly revealing, and its justice later becomes apparent when she behaves in this very way towards Davison.[22] If she ever reveals her own mind it is surely in her soliloquy (IV, 10) where, now that Mortimer has failed her, she is faced with the situation she has from the first striven to avoid, namely of having to assume the responsibility if Maria is to die. It is typical of Schiller's technique to sustain interest in Act IV by making a character take a decision crucial for the action of the play, and to show the workings of this character's mind by means of deliberation in a monologue. Mainland concedes (65) that at the end of this monologue "all she hears is her own voice . . . vibrant with anger against a hated rival"[23] I do not wish to deny that she is in a difficult situation, nor that there are unselfish reasons why she should have Maria killed. The attack on her life after the interview gives incontrovertible evidence that the very existence of her rival exposes her to murderous attacks from Catholics who know that her death will bring a Catholic queen to the throne (cf. Burleigh's words, ll. 1255-65; 3101-06; 3170-80). But she is represented as being influenced at least as much by malice as by the considerations of political expediency which weigh so heavily upon Burleigh. Political and personal considerations thus combine to motivate her signature of the warrant. At the beginning of Act IV it is discovered that the French ambassador was implicated in the attempt on her life, and so he is dismissed and the negotiations for her marriage with the Dauphin are abruptly terminated. We also learn that while Maria was in the castle grounds Paulet discovered and seized a second letter which she had begun to write to Leicester, urging him to keep his word and free her. Elisabeth thus has evidence that Maria has deprived her not only of her "Bräutigam", but even of her "Geliebten" (ll. 3234-35). The political and the personal elements seem inextricably entwined.

If our sympathies lie with Maria and not Elisabeth, we must be able to understand the development her character undergoes. Some have objected that there is no development, only an arbitrary alternation of moods. Otto Ludwig, for instance, complained that her fury in Act III is irreconcilable with her calm self-control in Acts I and V and has been contrived only because the plot demands a situation "wo sie sich in ihr Verderben schilt"[24] Ludwig even discerns a third Maria, a "Pensionsmädchen" of III, 1 who bubbles with delight in the castle grounds and is neither the resigned, self-controlled woman of Acts I and V nor the vindictive, sharp-tongued creature of III, 4. A dramatist who creates complex characters is almost certain to be charged with such inconsistency, if only because so many have followed Dryden in holding that character, although it cannot be supposed to consist of one particular virtue, vice or passion, must be shown in drama by making one quality predominant over all the rest.[25] Such is the easiest course for the dramatist, and it also simplifies the audience's task; for it is a common tendency to group men into classes, and if we can suppose that most of a man's actions are prompted by one particular passion, his whole behaviour becomes more predictable. However, in his later plays, Schiller disdains such methods.

In Act I Maria is a close prisoner, left with but a single servant. Schiller intended these severe circumstances to create an atmosphere of gloom from the first. He wrote (to Goethe, June 18, 1799) "daß man die Katastrophe gleich in den ersten Scenen sieht, und indem die Hand-lung des Stückes sich davon wegzubegeben scheint, ihr immer näher und näher geführt wird".[26] Furthermore in "Über das Pa-thetische" he says that the dramatist must place his hero in an unpleasant situation in order to show that he has the strength of character not to be dispirited. Maria's painful circumstances therefore make her composure the more commendable. It is Kennedy who complains about them, just as in the final Act it is her attendants, not Maria herself, who show signs of distress. Again, that she accepts her severe imprisonment calmly in Act I shows that she is no longer the irresponsible creature of her youth. Her situation thus strikes the note of tragedy from the first and shows both her strength and her change of character. This latter is stressed in scene 4 which acquaints us with her sense of guilt concerning her earlier relationships with Darnley and Bothwell. Schiller shows that she has discarded her earlier "Flattersinn" (l. 270) and "Leicht-sinn" (l. 362) by giving Kennedy long speeches, pleading extenuating circumstances in excuse of Maria's youthful crimes, whereas Maria brushes these pleas aside, reiterat-ing her guilt five times in short speeches of two lines each in reply. Her present moral earnestness is, then, clear from her behaviour. But her past character is not revealed exclusively by Kennedy's report, for Schiller had learned, perhaps from Lessing, that assurances from other people about what a person's character is will not ring true if they remain unsubstantiated by his own behaviour.[27]

Maria in Act I is penitent and resigned, and yet we are to believe that she was formerly a creature of fire and pas-sion. Schiller makes this credible by showing that she is still capable of passionate outbursts. We can well believe that the Maria we see in the interview with Elisabeth is capable of the behaviour reported of her earlier career.[28]

In I, 6 Mortimer offers Maria the prospect of freedom and his portrayal of the Catholic pageantry he experienced in Italy makes her painfully conscious of her deprivation (ll. 451-54). When we next see her, the pull of life upon her—

"der süße Trieb des Lebens" as it is later called (l. 3395)—is even stronger, for she is enjoying the freedom of the castle grounds in the belief that this new liberty is a preliminary to release (ll. 2119-22). The altered rhythm of her speech shows how completely she has abandoned the resigned attitude of Act I. Schiller, then, does not, as Lud-wig alleges, make her fall out of character in this lyrical monologue, but shows us that the prospect of freedom can kindle her zest for life. When she is told to prepare to face Elisabeth her mood is thus very different from that in which she had appealed for the interview, and she now feels burning resentment for what she has suffered from her rival (ll. 2177-87). She tries to conquer this mood with a dignified and humble appeal until Elisabeth goads her beyond endurance. Her final accusation that the throne is "durch einen Bastard entweiht" represents the truth for all Catholics, and that she has not descended to mere waspish-ness is also indicated by the stage-direction (after l. 2420) "von Zorn glühend, doch mit einer edlen Würde". However, when Elisabeth retires speechless, Maria does gloat over her triumph of revenge (ll. 2455-59) and is particularly gratified because Leicester witnessed it (l. 2464). I agree with Stahl that "her exultation is no less spiteful than Elisabeth's had been" and "represents the nadir of her spiritual development" (112). But how does she pass from this state to the noble and dignified attitude that characterizes her in Act V? She begins to recover her moral ascendency immediately after the interview when Mortimer's violent approaches show that he is determined to rescue and possess her, whatever her wishes. He speaks of murdering Elisabeth and Paulet, of fighting to the death with Leicester and of tearing Maria from her chamber. She is appalled and cries despairingly: "Bin ich geboren, nur die Wut zu wecken?" (l. 2532). Schiller wrote to Goethe (June 18, 1799) that her fate is "nur heftige Passionen zu erfahren und zu entzünden"—the lust of her supporters and the hate of her adversaries. She seems to feel that her life is worthless if it can be preserved only by terrible bloodshed (l. 2527), and in this sense we may say with B. von Wiese that her experiences drive her to abandon life.[29] Even so, the noise during the ensuing night, which she interprets as Mortimer's attempt to free her, awakens her desire to live and be free. The prospect of liberty produces this reaction quite instinctively in the captive (ll. 3395-96). Only when all hope of life is gone and she is told she must suffer does she attain to final composure, and this is quite plausible, for an action or attitude is not, as a rule, determined by a single motive. Motives often conflict, some impelling to and some deterring from a certain ac-tion, and the actual behaviour will depend on which are the stronger. This may well vary at different times, thus leading to actions which, to a superficial view, are inconsistent. So it is with Maria. On the one hand she is passionate and wilful, as we saw at the interview; on the other her moral consciousness drives her to atone for sins. When her situation suggests that she will be freed, her desire to live becomes so strong that it obliterates her penitence and resignation. This latter attitude is, on the other hand, strengthened by a situation that promises no release, as in Acts I and V, and also when she is forced to the conclusion (as she is by Mortimer in Act III) that she can be saved only at an appalling price of bloodshed and grief. Furthermore, in Act IV Leicester, to deflect suspicion from himself, counsels her execution and even agrees to help carry out the sentence. Such behaviour from the man she loved and trusted sickens her as much as did Mortimer's ferocious advances, again with the effect of weakening her hold on life. Mortimer's death and Paulet's grief also cannot fail to bring home to her that her life means bloodshed and misery for others. All these factors strengthen her moral determination to atone, which has been a prominent trait of her character throughout the play.

Mortimer's character is a striking parallel to Maria's. Both are capable of passionate wilfulness and also of high-flown idealism, and with both the prospect of success stimulates the first tendency, and imminent death the latter. Thus when he was confident that he would rescue and possess Maria, Mortimer cried: "Ist Leben doch des Lebens höchstes Gut!" (l. 2578). But when Leicester has him arrested, he says: "Das Leben ist das einz'ge Gut des Schlechten" (l. 2805). As with Maria, the deterioration of the situation brings out the moral fibre of his character.

There are a number of reasons why critics have been perplexed by Maria's development, apart from the obvious one that a complex character is likely to be accused of inconsistency. There is another obvious factor, namely that we do not witness the actual change. As A. Beck has noted: "wir sehen die Verwandelte, nicht die Verwandlung."[30] The question when exactly in the interval between Acts III and V this transformation occurs has, H. Koopmann has told us, rarely been asked and has not been given a uniform answer.[31] According to Kennedy, the change in Maria came suddenly, when, after the noises in the night, her cell opened to admit—not rescuers, but Paulet with the news that she must suffer on the scaffold then being erected. Kennedy says:

> Man löst sich nicht allmählich von dem Leben!
>
> Mit *einem* Mal, schnell, augenblicklich muß
>
> Der Tausch geschehen zwischen Zeitlichem
>
> Und Ewigem, und Gott gewährte meiner Lady
>
> In diesem Augenblick, der Erde Hoffnung
>
> Zurückzustoßen mit entschloßner Seele.
>
> (ll. 3402-7)

Claude David and others have linked this passage with the following extract from "Über das Erhabene":

> Das Erhabene verschafft uns . . . einen Ausgang aus der sinnlichen Welt . . . Nicht allmählich (denn es gibt von der Abhängigkeit keinen Übergang zur Freiheit), sondern plötzlich und *durch eine Erschütterung* reißt es den selbständigen Geist aus dem Netze los.[32]

My argument is that the shock of learning the truth about her situation can produce such a sudden effect in Maria

only because it is able to weaken the one and strengthen the other of two contrary tendencies which are both strongly developed in her character. The passage in the essay illuminates the play by stressing the efficacy of shock, but the reference to 'free-will' has thoroughly obscured the importance of the conflict of tendencies in the heroine, and suggested that her final composure is an arbitrary and unmotivated development. Bruford, for instance, has said that Schiller, because "influenced by Kant's conception of freedom as 'indeterminacy', liked incalculable characters, of whom no one could say what on earth they would or would not do" (324).

Let us see how Schiller conceives free-will. At the beginning of his "Über das Pathetische" he refers to the state of mind in which a strong urge or emotion deflects one from duty as "ein Zustand des Affekts", and declares that tragedy depicts moral independence from these natural promptings. Such independence is possible for man because he possesses "die Vernunft", a faculty which without reference to experience reveals to him absolute moral truths which are eternally valid.[33] Schiller thus speaks of 'reason' and of 'feelings' as alternative springs of behaviour. One man is prompted by his reason, another by his feelings. Faculty-psychology of this kind had been prominent in European philosophy since Descartes had sharply distinguished reason from the passions, attributing the former to an immaterial soul and the latter to the body. Such normal concomitants of emotion as acceleration of the heartbeat and trembling of the limbs suggested to him that emotions are a function of the body. But the calm unfolding of reflection seems to be without any effect on the body. Another reason why thought could be plausibly attributed to an immaterial soul is that thinking lacks material characteristics: it has neither weight, solidity, nor shape. Schiller's sharp distinction between reason and the passions was prompted also by the observation that a man may be under the influence of an emotion (e.g. fear), yet fail to betray it by any action or movement. Such behaviour may be rational (directed towards a rational end), and this suggested to Schiller that it is accomplished by a faculty of reason which is independent of all emotion. Now a modern psychologist would prefer to say that the control is due to some antagonistic emotion (such as pride, or desire or fear of something else). On this view, the so-called conflict between reason and passion, when it occurs, is really between one passion and another.[34] The "reason" is merely the imagination which presents in turn the different memories of the consequences of the actions to which the opposed passions prompt; and the appearance of free-will arises when the two contrary passions are both so strongly developed that the individual recognizes both as 'flesh of his flesh', and so infers that the slightest occurrence—a mere fiat of the will—can give one or the other a preponderance.[35] Critics have tried to apply to Schiller's play his theory that a person may suddenly cease acting from passion, and act instead from reason. Thus Beck argues that Maria's final development is a switch from the influence of 'Sinnlichkeit' to a condition where "der selbständige Geist" rules her, and she suddenly ceases to be "ein physisches Wesen" (319-320). This suggests an entirely arbitrary development of the kind which, we saw, Bruford declares to be normal among Schiller's characters; whereas my argument is that Schiller shows a profounder knowledge of human motivation in his play than in his abstract theory.

Maria, then, is finally dominated by the will to atone, and declares: "Gott würdigt mich, durch diesen unverdienten Tod / Die frühe schwere Blutschuld abzubüßen" (ll. 3735-36). As Aristotle had required (*Poetics,* 13), the hero is neither completely blameless, nor does he simply get his deserts. Schiller himself declared "eine ganz engelreine Heldin" to be "untragisch" and justly claimed that he had shown wherein Maria's guilt consists at the very beginning: "im Verfolg des Stücks verringere sich dann immer mehr ihr Vergehen, und zuletzt stehe sie fast makellos da, statt daß es eine unziemliche Wirkung tun werde . . . wenn erst nach und nach ihr Vergehen an den Tag komme."[36] One of Paulet's functions in the play is to convey her final 'Makellosigkeit'. His uncompromising honesty and virtue are not only essential to the plot—they underlie his refusal to murder her or have her murdered, and so force the responsibility upon Elisabeth; they also contribute to the pathos of the final scenes, where even so stern a judge as he shows admiration of Maria as he gives her his hand and urges Burleigh to grant her final request (ll. 3793, 3815). Approbation of the heroine from a figure of recognized honesty is here used to the same effect to which Hebbel was later to put it in making Titus finally declare of Marianne: "sie hat recht". Nevertheless, Schiller's concern to enlist our sympathy for his heroine in the final Act has seemed to some—including Hebbel—grossly overdone. Hebbel commented: "Daß selbst ein Mann wie Schiller auf feuchte Schnupftücher speculirte, ist entsetzlich. Und was thut er anders im fünften Akt!"[37] Hebbel characteristically attempted the more difficult task of compelling sympathy with characters whose behaviour is in many ways repellent.

From *Wallenstein* through *Maria Stuart* to *Die Jungfrau von Orleans* the link between the hero's character and his death becomes progressively weaker. Wallenstein's death is a consequence of the treason to which his character impelled him; Maria's is largely a consequence of a political situation not connected with her character. Although she accepts death as an opportunity to atone for personal sin, the reason why she must die is that Elisabeth has signed the warrant. Elisabeth was led to do so partly, it is true, because of the wilfulness in Maria's character that had provoked her at the interview (and had been itself provoked by Elisabeth's own malice), but this motive could never have sufficed had it not been supplemented by others deriving from the political situation. Johanna's fortuitous death in battle follows neither from her character nor from the antecedents portrayed in the play. No one else is even aware of the sense in which she has betrayed her mission and how her final behaviour rectifies this lapse. Perhaps the difficulty that critics have found in interpreting *Maria Stuart* is due to its middle position in this develop-

ment. *Wallenstein* must be interpreted from the political situation portrayed; in *Die Jungfrau,* on the other hand, the heroine's mental conflict is so independent of the historical and political situation that it is known only to her. In *Maria Stuart* both the political situation and also personal desires and motives which have nothing to do with it are important determinants, and critics have not found it easy to balance them. L. A. Rhoades noted, as long ago as 1894, that "various critics, and notably Hettner", have censured Schiller "for not making the plot of his drama turn upon the conflict of historic forces".[38] My discussion of more recent criticism has shown that it is still not fully appreciated how precisely such forces, together with other and quite different ones, contribute to the outcome of the play.

With *Die Jungfrau von Orleans* villainy and malice have been eliminated from the plot. Johanna's father, whose action brings about her disgrace and banishment, is actuated by the highest motives. In this play evil resides not in the characters but in the spirits which—so Johanna's opponents suppose—possess and rule her. The heroine certainly does possess supernatural powers. She picks out the king she has never seen, knows the substance of his private prayers, and snaps the heavy iron chains that fetter her. The interest is, however, centred not so much on such miracles as on the beliefs of the characters concerning divine and demoniacal possession. Johanna thinks she is inspired by the Virgin Mary herself, but her father from the first is convinced that she has sold her soul to the devil, and in Act IV he forces a crisis by persuading others that he is right. I have elsewhere argued that in Schiller's next play, *Die Braut von Messina,* the evil again lies not in the characters but in supernatural forces which this time are not figments of the imagination.[39] As Körner commented in a letter to Schiller (February 28, 1803) on this play: "Schauderhaft ist besonders die Entstehung des grössten Unglücks aus löblichen Handlungen." We see, then, that Schiller's later plays go far towards implementing his view that villainy is undesirable as a cause of tragic catastrophe.

Notes

1. "Über die tragische Kunst", *Schillers Sämtliche Werke,* ed. E. von der Hellen, Säkularausgabe (Stuttgart and Berlin, n.d.), XI, 163-64.

2. "Über Bürgers Gedichte", *Schillers Sämtliche Werke,* Säkularausgabe, XVI, 230f., 254; cf. to Goethe, August 24, 1798: "Alle poetischen Personen sind symbolische Wesen . . . als poetische Gestalten haben sie immer das Allgemeine der Menschheit darzustellen und auszusprechen."

3. Preface to "Fiesco", *Schillers Sämtliche Werke,* Säkularausgabe, XVI, 42.

4. W. H. Bruford shows how widespread this opinion has been. *Theatre Drama and Audience in Goethe's Germany* (London, 1950), 322-23.

5. Tagebuch No. 4307 (October 11, 1847).

6. *Schiller and the Changing Past* (London, 1957), 36. Further references to Mainland will be to this volume.

7. *Schiller the Dramatic Writer: A Study of Style in the Plays* (Oxford, 1969), 157.

8. He read, so he says, (*Tod*, l. 1134) the version of the letter which Wallenstein promised he would dispatch to Vienna. Mainland reminds us of Wallenstein's words "ich geb' nichts Schriftliches von mir" (*Piccolomini*, l. 854) but concedes that the context shows that this may refer only to "matters of strategy and dangerous negotiations with the enemies of the Empire" (38).

9. *Goethes Werke,* Weimar Ausgabe (Weimar, 1901), XL, 62.

10. *Der Dichter Friedrich Schiller* (Stuttgart, 1959), 288.

11. "The machinations of ambiguity", says Empson, "are among the very roots of poetry" (*Seven Types of Ambiguity* [London, 1930], 3). But ambiguity occurs in all language, and a word or phrase does not have any more associations when it occurs in verse than when it occurs in prose.

12. *Schillers Dramen,* 2nd ed. (Berlin, 1898), II, 92ff.

13. The effectiveness of these factors has repeatedly been stressed, e.g. by J. Müller, *Das Edle in der Freiheit* (Leipzig, 1959), 135.

14. "Astrology in Schiller's *Wallenstein*", *JEGP,* 68 (1969), 100-15.

15. *Schiller's Drama* (Oxford, 1954), 94.

16. "Schuldverwicklung in Schillers Dramen", in *Schiller, 1759/1959: Commemorative American Studies,* ed. J. R. Frey, Illinois Studies in Lang. and Lit., 46 (Urbana, 1959), 88.

17. "Octavio Piccolomini", *JDSG,* 5 (1961), 34, 42, 44.

18. The letters are quoted by Benno von Wiese, *Schiller* (Stuttgart, 1959), 641-42. M. Schunicht follows von Wiese in using this evidence to rebut the suggestion that Octavio is a villainous intriguer ("Intrigen und Intriganten in Schillers Dramen". *ZDP,* 82 [1963], 287).

19. Cf. H. Singer, "Dem Fürsten Piccolomini", *Euphorion,* 53 (1959), 301.

20. See W. Witte's account in his introduction to the text: *Schiller, Maria Stuart* (London, 1965), XXI.

21. See Garland's *Schiller* (London, 1949), 216. Stahl, *Schiller's Drama,* 114, alleges a deterioration and "violent change" in her character between the scene in which she receives Maria's letter (II, 4) and the interview with Mortimer "at the end of the second Act". In actual fact her commission to Mortimer follows immediately (II, 5), giving neither time nor occasion for a change in her character, whereas the Act continues with four further scenes. Even in the council scene (II, 3)—she scorns Shrewsbury when he suggests clemency.

22. She pretends (l. 3963) that she gave him the signed warrant "in Verwahrung", whereas earlier she had answered his question: "Du willst, daß ich ihn länger noch bewahre?" with: "Auf Eure Gefahr! Ihr haftet für die Folgen" (l. 3303).

23. She had dismissed her lords at the end of IV, 9 saying she would seek divine rather than human counsel concerning Maria. Bellermann notes (II, 210): "Geradezu ergreifend wirkt, nach diesem salbungsvollen Eingang, der unvermittelte gewaltsame Ausbruch ihres wahren Gefühls, sobald sie allein ist."

24. "Shakespeare-Studien", in *Ausgewählte Werke,* ed. W. Greiner (Leipzig, n.d.), II, 594.

25. "The grounds of criticism in tragedy", prefixed to *Troilus and Cressida, 1679,* in *Of Dramatic Poetry and Other Critical Essays,* ed. G. Watson (London, 1962), I, 249-50.

26. An obvious example is the interview between the queens which is requested by Maria to lower the tension and reduce her danger, but which in fact has the opposite effect; cf. A. Cüppers, *Schillers 'Maria Stuart' in ihrem Verhältnis zur Geschichte* (Münster, 1906), 19.

27. *Hamburgische Dramaturgie,* 9. Stück.

28. Bellermann, *Schillers Dramen,* 196-97. The effectiveness of this method of character portrayal is vouched for by its adoption by a dramatist so critical of Schiller as was Büchner. The hero of *Dantons Tod* is cynical and inactive, but we do not have to rely exclusively on hearsay for our knowledge that he was formerly an energetic idealist. When on trial for his life in Act III, he is goaded by the hypocrisy of his accusers into a stirring denunciation of them. Here, the former fiery idealist shows through the disillusioned cynic he has become.

29. "Die unfaßbare Dämonie menschlicher Geistesfreiheit entzündet sich in der tragischen Hölle des Verbrechens, der Schuld und des Leidens und treibt den Menschen Maria an die Grenze des Daseins, wo der Sprung in den Abgrund des Ewigen möglich wird" (*Die deutsche Tragödie von Lessing bis Hebbel* [Hamburg, 1948], I, 297).

30. "Maria Stuart", in *Das deutsche Drama: Interpretationen,* ed. B. von Wiese (Düsseldorf, 1958), I, 317.

31. *Schiller,* Sammlung Metzler (Stuttgart, 1966), II, 53.

32. "Über das Erhabene", *Schillers Sämtliche Werke,* Säkularausgabe, XII, 272 (my italics); David, "Le Personnage de la reine Elizabeth dans la *Maria Stuart* de Schiller", *Deutsche Beiträge zur geistigen Überlieferung,* 4 (1961), 20, 22.

33. Schiller also believes that "die Vernunft" supplies a metaphysical idea of beauty, with the aid of which we can tell whether what we are accustomed to call beautiful is justly so called (*Über die ästhetische Erziehung des Menschen,* letter X). Like many aestheticians he is anxious to believe that the principles of beauty are not merely the effect of certain animal propensities which vary with the race and the individual, but are something eternal and indefeasible.

34. In some passages in his *Über die ästhetische Erziehung des Menschen* Schiller does show awareness that reason alone cannot determine action, that man will only act if impelled by some drive or tendency. And so he invents a "Formtrieb", which is

an urge to posit ("behaupten") the "Person", which he in turn defines as that in man which may be called "reine Intelligenz" or "vernünftige Natur" (letter XI). Such an urge is not an intelligible psychological tendency and deserves the scorn with which Nicolai treated it (*Beschreibung einer Reise durch Deutschland und die Schweiz* [Berlin, 1796], XI, 272).

35. See, for instance, E. Rignano, *The Psychology of Reasoning,* trans. W. A. Holl (London, 1923), 24.

36. *Schillers Gespräche* in *Schillers Werke,* ed. L. Blumenthal and B. von Wiese, Nationalausgabe (Weimar, 1967), XLII, 294.

37. Tagebuch No. 3994 (February 27, 1847).

38. *Maria Stuart,* ed. Heath (1894), XIII.

39. "Fate-tragedy and *Die Braut von Messina*", *JEGP,* 64 (1965), 191-212.

Lesley Sharpe (essay date 1996)

SOURCE: "Introduction," in *Don Carlos and Mary Stuart,* Oxford University Press, 1996, pp. vii-xxvi.

[*In the following essay, Sharpe presents a critical overview of the historical dramas* Don Carlos *and* Mary Stuart, *and maintains that the hope evident in* Don Carlos *disappears in the later play and is replaced by a bleaker vision of human integrity in the world of action.*]

At first sight *Don Carlos* and *Mary Stuart,* with *Wallenstein* Friedrich Schiller's greatest historical dramas, are striking in their similarity. Both are blank-verse plays, set against the background of religious strife in sixteenth-century Europe. Both explore the private emotions of the great and powerful as they confront the insoluble dilemmas of the political world. Both also display the hallmarks of Schiller's style and technique—swift-moving action, great set-piece encounters, impassioned rhetorical speeches, strongly contrasting characters, an unabashed theatricality. In both plays the historical setting is used not as a backdrop for a costume drama but to provide an opportunity to explore problems of Schiller's own age. The later eighteenth century was also a time of violent upheaval and ideological conflict, of the clash of tradition with experiment. His plays are concerned with freedom and tyranny, the relation of power and responsibility, of ends and means in political life and with the challenge facing those called to act upon the stage of history to preserve humanity and integrity.

On closer inspection the dissimilarities between the plays are striking and significant. *Mary Stuart* is a compact, lucidly organized, and highly stylized play with an action that moves swiftly and inexorably towards the tragic conclusion, in spite of the best efforts of most of the characters to avert it. Formally it stands within the European tradition of high tragedy and shows Schiller's concern to meet the challenge of the classical and neo-

classical tradition. It is a play that, despite its clear departures from historical fact, is nevertheless based on a real political dilemma of the sixteenth century and firmly rooted in historical source study. *Don Carlos* is clearly a more youthful work and, for all its brilliant and moving moments, lacks this lucidity. It is based on a historical novel, while attested historical events provide only the background. It has a complex intrigue and confusing shifts of emphasis—is it mainly a dramatization of thwarted love, of kingly isolation, or of the idealist destroyed? The compositional shortcomings of the play reveal it as a work of transition, the final phase of Schiller's apprenticeship. After he completed the play in 1787 he wrote no more plays for over a decade, a silence indicative of the creative crisis the play had provoked in him. Only after lengthy deliberation on the nature of drama did he return to work as a playwright with his masterpiece, *Wallenstein. Mary Stuart* (1800) was the second play to be written after this long interval and thus is separated from *Don Carlos* by some thirteen years. In spite of its flaws *Don Carlos* is a rich and fascinating play for two reasons. First, it shows Schiller in the process of finding his own idiom as a dramatist. In it he moves away from the self-consciously radical tone and experimental style of his previous three dramas, all written in prose, towards deeper engagement with historical issues and the serenity and stylization characteristic of his later work. Secondly, along with Lessing's *Nathan the Wise* (1779) and Goethe's *Iphigenia on Tauris* (1787), it is one of the great literary expressions of the German Enlightenment (*Aufklärung*). All three works (all, incidentally, written in blank verse) carry the conviction that human beings, however cynical, weak, or foolish they may have been, however burdened by the guilt and wrongs of the past, can nevertheless find the courage to break free and choose a new way. In the case of *Don Carlos* that new way remains only a distant hope. . . .

Schiller's starting-point for *Don Carlos* was not historical source study but a work of French fiction, the Abbé de Saint-Réal's *Dom Carlos. Nouvelle historique* (1672), which had been brought to Schiller's attention by Dalberg. The historical Carlos, Philip II's only son and heir, was weak and slightly deformed from birth. In his late teens he developed signs of mental instability and was later rumoured to be intending to flee Spain. This, coupled with increasing paranoia and eccentricity, led to his being virtually confined to his quarters, where he died in not wholly unmysterious circumstances at the age of 23. Saint-Réal builds his fiction on the unfounded rumour that Carlos and Elizabeth of Valois, Philip's third wife, who as children had been betrothed for a time, were secretly in love. Carlos's fall is the result of court intrigues, in particular on the part of the King's adviser Ruy Gomez and his wife Princess Eboli. The Marquis Posa, a secret friend of Carlos, carries letters between Carlos and Elizabeth and is assassinated as Philip's suspicions fall on him. Carlos, who intended to flee to the Netherlands for safety (the political dimension is not exploited), is handed over to the Inquisition. Elizabeth is poisoned on Philip's orders.

The complex genesis of **Don Carlos** has caused critics to diverge considerably in their assessment of the relative importance of love and politics in the plot. Some see a distinct shift from family drama (influenced by Diderot's theory of the *drame bourgeois*) to political play, as though the work fell into two halves. Others argue that the work remains throughout a family drama with the political elements imperfectly grafted on. Yet others strongly emphasize the clear continuities in theme and plot—as Schiller himself had done in his defence of the play in his *Letters on 'Don Carlos'* (1788)—arguing in some cases that the play changes less in theme than in dramatic technique, moving from a more expansive and static type of portraiture to a more dynamic interaction of plot and character. The first two approaches tend to understate the extent to which a political element was always present in Schiller's conception of the material. From the start he wanted to make more of this project than a romantic historical costume drama. His letters from the Bauerbach period suggest he intended to use the play to denounce religious bigotry and state persecution through his depiction of the Inquisition. From the first version of the play onwards, the unhappy royal family reflects the greater unhappiness of a state dominated by the Inquisition. But any argument supporting the unity of **Don Carlos** has to take account of the fact that Schiller himself in the *Letters on 'Don Carlos'* admits to a loss of interest in the figure of Carlos. His Bauerbach letters testify to his passionate identification with the unhappy prince and this is still clearly reflected in the early scenes of the play. However, wider reading in the course of composition gave Schiller a profounder grasp of historical context and made him probe the nature of tyranny and the problem of action within the political world. The result is that Carlos, who is essentially a passive character, is increasingly overshadowed by Philip and Posa. The romantic involvement between Carlos and Elizabeth, though still central to the play's complex intrigue, does lose prominence to the political theme. Though Schiller managers to bring all the threads together at the end, we are left with a sense of unevenness.

As in Schiller's earliest plan, it is the Catholic Church, embodied in the final scenes by the Cardinal Inquisitor, that is the driving force behind the repressive Spanish government. This allows him to make all the main characters—Carlos, Posa, Elizabeth, and Philip—ultimately its victims. For most of the play we identify Philip with this cruel and cynical system. Yet in spite of this, Philip is arguably the great triumph of characterization of the play and the figure who most holds the audience's attention. The other characters, Carlos and Posa, for example, we feel we can read clearly. Philip keeps us in suspense. When announcing the serialization of his play Schiller wrote: 'If this tragedy is to move people it must do so, as I see it, through the situation and character of King Philip.' In the *Thalia* scenes Philip still comes across as something of a stage villain. In the completed play, however, Schiller does succeed not only in showing us Philip's fears, his disappointments, and his isolation, but in making us feel them too. Proud of his self-sufficiency in Act Two, Philip rejects his son's attempt at reconciliation. Later he sees in Posa the kind of valorous, confident, urbane, yet passionate young man he would like as a son. In the audience scene (III.x), which parallels and contrasts with the audience between Philip and Carlos in Act Two, Posa can find the needs of the human being beneath the imperious exterior ('By God, | He reaches to my soul'). We should find any true change of heart on Philip's part dramatically unconvincing. Not only history but Schiller's recognition of the weight of the Church, Philip's habits of mind, and his cynicism dictate that he will not change. But Posa makes him feel for a brief moment as if he actually could remake the world with a stroke of his pen. We do not see Philip weep over Posa's betrayal but we feel the momentary pathos more keenly by witnessing the dismay and astonishment of his courtiers at the report of such an unambiguous display of emotion. Though we recoil in horror at his desire to destroy all that remains of Posa's vision, Philip himself is revealed to be the unhappy pawn of the Inquisition, chastised by the fanatical blind Cardinal Inquisitor for having forgotten for a moment that for kings human beings are simply numbers.

The most controversial figure in the play is the Marquis Posa, educator of the Prince and, briefly, confidant of the King. Posa's role was expanded in the course of the play's development. Though it is a structural flaw in the drama that Posa's increasing prominence pushes Carlos into the background, that prominence comes about by a turn of events that strikes us as being utterly plausible. Posa has held himself aloof from the court and thus seems to threaten none of the courtiers, who can therefore speak generously of him. His aloofness is a strategy to give him independence of action, and it is this impression of independence that attracts Philip. Here at last is a man who will give him the truth about Carlos and Elizabeth without trying to gain some advantage for himself. Instead Philip is given quite a different kind of truth by Posa, while the truth about Carlos and Elizabeth is exactly what Posa will never tell him. The fact that Posa can say so much to Philip before being silenced is an indication of the former's urbanity and diplomatic skill. The passionate personal appeal by Carlos to Philip in Act Two falls on deaf ears. Philip is impressed by the man who can do without him and who has the courage to put himself at risk to plead a cause that brings him no personal gain. Posa is judicious in his responses, waiting for Philip to prompt him into saying more, while Philip is refreshed as well as taken aback by his confidence and his honesty. Posa presents Philip to himself not as a wilful tyrant but as the victim himself of the system he has inherited. His subjects have surrendered their self-determination. They have made Philip a god. But where does a god find solace and human fellowship? Posa reveals Philip's position as that of the false god who enslaves rather than of the true God who gives freedom to nature to act according to its inherent laws. The play's persistent appeal to nature through its imagery of sowing, planting, blossoming, and withering is given full political expression in Posa's argument.

Posa is, of course, an anachronism. No sixteenth-century Spanish grandee could speak in such terms and Schiller was well aware of the fact. Woven into Posa's arguments are Schiller's knowledge of the political philosophy of his time. It is one of the vital debates of the Revolutionary age, Schiller's own age, which is being enacted. In it we detect the impact on German intellectuals of the American War of Independence and hear echoes of the German natural law tradition, of Rousseau's faith in natural sentiments, and of Montesquieu's famous characterization in *De l'esprit des lois* of the different types of government.[1] Posa stresses how Philip's rule is based on fear, for Montesquieu the specific characteristic of a despotism, and leads only to the peace of the graveyard. But Posa's vision cannot be reduced to a single political doctrine, nor is the discussion merely a rehearsal of political argument. This scene is a turning-point of the play. Posa puts himself in extreme danger by revealing even this much of his mind to the King. He does so out of commitment to the cause of the Netherlands and in order by any means possible to slow the momentum of the intrigue against Carlos. Yet in winning the confidence of the King he is bound to disappoint him. Carlos, too, loses faith in his friend's loyalty, delivering himself a second time into the power of Eboli, whereupon Posa precipitates himself into the desperate attempt to throw suspicion on himself.

Posa would seem to be a wholly positive figure and spokesman for the playwright himself. This was certainly how he was viewed when the play first appeared and for one and a half centuries after. By the middle of the nineteenth century Schiller had become a cultural icon. The German liberals of the 1848 Revolution often borrowed quotations from *Don Carlos* in their speeches or saw their struggle as akin to that of Posa with Philip. The play has always had great resonance in situations of oppression. During the early years of the Third Reich in Germany audiences regularly applauded loud and long when Posa uttered his plea for freedom of thought, and such occurrences were taken by the regime as a form of protest. In 1946, when that regime had been overthrown, the play that seemed so to epitomize the noblest tradition of German thought was staged in no fewer than twenty-one theatres. Yet since the 1950s Schiller's plays have been universally recognized as more complex and ambiguous in their presentation of political change than may at first appear. Posa in particular has been seen as a manipulator, exploiting Carlos and abusing the King's confidence. He has been accused of insensitivity to Carlos's suffering and of indifference to the pain he causes the King. At the very least, it is claimed, he leaves devastation behind him after his death. Schiller has been seen as presenting in Posa the flawed idealist, who betrays actual human beings while proclaiming a love for humanity in the abstract. Posa certainly does play a very dangerous game and it is one of the triumphs of the play as a dramatic experience that we feel the bitterness of Philip's disappointment. Yet Posa is trying to save not just the Netherlands, arguably a distant and precarious goal, but also his friend, who is in the gravest danger, created in part through his own folly.

Posa does the most he can to save him by sacrificing his own life. Schiller is not presenting the idealist as a flawed character; he is, however, exploring the gulf between political ends and means, a gulf that opens up for Posa in the audience scene.

Schiller looks at the history of the sixteenth century as a man of the Enlightenment. In the struggle for freedom of religion he sees the beginning of the struggle for a more tolerant and humane society. In *Don Carlos,* though the representatives of that new way of thinking are doomed, the movement of history is on their side. Philip himself is aware that his empire is waning, and Schiller brings forward the defeat of the Spanish Armada by twenty years in order to signal this incipient decline. Posa speaks with the assurance of one who knows the future, accusing Philip of trying to put his hand into the spokes of a wheel that must turn. His argument for liberal government on the grounds that nature is free within its own laws is reinforced by the natural imagery of the play. Posa himself says to Philip: 'You want your garden to flower eternally / But the seed you sow is death.' These images are further supported by an underlying implication that the Spanish court itself is based on an artificiality that is contrary to nature. The Queen may not see her daughter except at the appointed hour. She enjoys the more natural setting of Aranjuez, while the woman who epitomizes the corruption of the court, Eboli, longs to return to Madrid. The representative of cruelty and repression, the Cardinal Inquisitor, calls on Philip to suppress the voice of nature and deliver up his son. Though the representatives of a better future are destroyed, the implication is that the course of history will vindicate them. The tragedy is thus set within a framework of guarded hope.

Don Carlos provoked a creative crisis in Schiller. He believed his greatest achievements would be in the field of drama and yet *Don Carlos* was over-long and over-complicated, its theatrical viability also impaired. In 1787, having moved to Weimar, he first met his future ally, Johann Wolfgang Goethe, who already enjoyed a towering reputation as a writer. Goethe's neo-classical verse drama *Iphigenia on Tauris* had just appeared. Schiller's unfinished review of it reveals through his admiration of the work how urgently he wished to be able to write a drama that would have the same formal perfection. For the next ten years he devoted himself to historiography, aesthetics, and dramatic theory, returning to drama with *Wallenstein*, which was completed in 1799. Of these activities his work as a historiographer tends to be taken least seriously, though in fact it was an important stage in the clarification of his ideas. Given the comparative backwardness of German historiography at the time, his accounts, influenced stylistically by his reading of French and British historiographers such as Voltaire, Condorcet, Hume, and Gibbon, are both readable and stimulating, even if he relied on published sources. He made good use of the reading he had done in connection with *Don Carlos* to write the first part of a *History of the Revolt of the United Netherlands from Spanish Rule* (1788). Although the work was not completed it was sufficiently admired to secure its author a Chair of History at the University of Jena. Schiller's financial problems were far from over (there was little money attached to the post), but this appointment gave him a position within society and the opportunity to marry. His bride was Charlotte von Lengefeld and they were married on 22 February 1790 and subsequently had four children.

Schiller's historiographical writing shows his move away from Enlightenment optimism towards a more sober depiction of the struggle for domination in Europe. His second major work was his *History of the Thirty Years' War* (1791), a continuation therefore of his interest in the long period of religious strife in the sixteenth and seventeenth centuries. The confident introduction to the *History of the Revolt of the Netherlands* claims that the work will demonstrate how united effort in the good cause can win through. Yet in the process of writing he loses confidence in this analysis and comes to regard the people of the Netherlands and their leaders in a more critical light. This appreciation of the greater complexities of the period may help to account for Schiller's failure to finish the work. The *History of the Thirty Years' War* is an admirable work of synthesis, written without any expectation of finding a thread of progress. Though the two most fascinating figures of the war, the Swedish King Gustavus Adolphus and the Imperial General Wallenstein, are for a time made into hero and villain respectively, Schiller reverses his assessment of both, aware of the bias in his sources and the partiality of his own judgement.

After concentrating on historiography, Schiller turned to dramatic theory (discussed later in connection with *Mary Stuart*) and aesthetics. He had always had a lively interest in philosophy from the time of his medical studies. His friend Körner had long impressed upon him the importance of the work of Immanuel Kant. The occasion for detailed study arose in 1792 while he was recovering from a serious illness which nearly cost him his life and left him a permanent invalid until his death in 1805. He was concerned to develop an aesthetics that would make art central to what it is to be fully human. Taking up from Kant's *Critique of Judgement* the suggestion that the aesthetic provides a bridge between the phenomenal realm of nature and the noumenal realm of the ethical, Schiller developed a transcendental aesthetics in which the beautiful is the means of reuniting the sensuous and the spiritual in human beings and thus of re-creating their lost inner harmony. These deliberations were given added impetus by the shock delivered to German intellectuals by the course taken by the French Revolution. His comments on the initial phase of the Revolution are sparse, though in 1791 he was made an Honorary Citizen of France on the strength of *The Robbers.* By 1793, however, he was, like many of his compatriots, appalled by the bloodshed. His best-known work of aesthetics, *Letters on the Aesthetic Education of Man* (1794), is an attempt to analyse where enlightenment had failed and to propose that through art human beings find a way to reconcile reason and impulse.

Far from being peripheral to a revolutionary age, art is the means by which we may progress towards a humane civil society. This treatise was followed by a major work of poetics, *On Naïve and Sentimental Poetry* (1795), in which Schiller addresses the question of different kinds of poetic consciousness and the inadequacy of traditional genre definitions to account for their literary products. These essays, both classic statements on the nature of modernity—the divided self and the fragmentation of society brought by the division of labour—have been immensely influential, and cultural commentators from Hegel to C. G. Jung, to Sir Herbert Read, and Herbert Marcuse have taken up their analyses.

On Naïve and Sentimental Poetry was shaped in part by Schiller's growing friendship with Goethe, which began in 1794 and continued to his death. Though for some years aloof, Goethe was eventually won over by Schiller's acute mind and by the recognition that they both treated art with the same high seriousness. They were also both committed to the creation of a literature that drew on the best traditions of European writing and, while incorporating elements of realism, moved towards the universal and symbolic. While Schiller never had Goethe's deep affinity with the art of the Ancients, he constantly used the myth of Greek perfection and wholeness as a starting-point for his elaboration of the modern writer's dilemma: how to bring into harmony the constraints of form and a subjective vision that constantly reached for the infinite. This striving for form and this belief in the universal applicability of notions of beauty separate Goethe and Schiller from the subjectivity of their younger Romantic contemporaries, writers such as August Wilhelm and Friedrich Schlegel, Ludwig Tieck and Novalis. Weimar Classicism—the work of Goethe and Schiller from the late 1780s through the decade of their collaboration—incorporates the legacy of the Enlightenment, that of the classical tradition, and elements of Romanticism. Though sometimes embattled by both their rationalist and Romantic critics, the two men drew out the best in each other's creativity. Schiller encouraged Goethe to take up work again on his *Faust,* an incomplete version of which had been published as *Faust: A Fragment* in 1790. He also proved an invaluable collaborator in the work of the Weimar theatre, of which Goethe was the Director, providing not only his own plays but adapting several others, including Goethe's *Egmont* and *Iphigenia,* Racine's *Phaedra,* and Shakespeare's *Macbeth.*

After *On Naïve and Sentimental Poetry* Schiller declared himself ready to shut up the philosophical shop and return to creative writing. He had already begun to write his series of great reflective poems. After the long break from drama his first project, *Wallenstein* (1799), took some three years to complete. There followed four more plays, *Mary Stuart* (1800), *The Maid of Orleans* (1801), *The Bride of Messina* (1803), and *William Tell* (1804), in rapid succession up to his death on 9 May 1805. His final, unfinished drama, *Demetrius,* was on his desk when he died. It was as though he had recaptured the power of rapid composition and was using it in his race to realize his potential and range as a dramatist before death overtook him. On reading in his letters about his physical struggle with ill health one senses that he kept himself going by sheer will power. Yet his creative writing is full of vigour and energy, a testimony to his extraordinary mental resilience and intellectual commitment. The later dramas, like the earlier ones, are very diverse. Schiller was constantly driven on to the next experiment, though always writing in verse and insisting on the essentially symbolic character of the plays. Increasingly he experimented with a more open form of drama and with the inclusion of operatic elements. In *Wallenstein* and ***Mary Stuart,*** however, he felt he needed to render account to the traditions of European high tragedy.

In the ten-year dramatic silence he had, in addition to putting down his thoughts on the theory of tragedy, translated Euripides, read Aristotle's *Poetics* and renewed his acquaintance with Shakespeare. In ***Wallenstein,*** though its genesis was as protracted as that of ***Don Carlos,*** the result is a perfectly lucid action, a vast panorama compressed into a plot that never loses momentum or clear direction. Yet he did not succeed in reducing his vast material to the scope of one five-act play but had to compromise by splitting it into three parts. In ***Mary Stuart*** he came closer to realizing his ambition to create a drama that rivalled the economy as well as the clarity of classical drama. The unities of time, place, and action are not slavishly adhered to but approached in spirit through the careful symmetry and compression of the plot. Mary is attended by a small retinue, chiefly her nurse Hannah. Elizabeth's court is presented with economy of means; Burleigh, Shrewsbury, and Leicester are those on whom she relies. Leicester and Mortimer provide the link between these two centres of action. Schiller spotted early on the dramatic possibilities in beginning the action after Mary's trial. To Goethe he wrote: '[The material] already has the important advantage that the action is concentrated in a dynamic moment and, balanced between hope and fear, must rush to its conclusion.' Hope is introduced in the form of Mortimer, Leicester, and the prospect of a meeting of the queens, but far from averting disaster these factors merely speed it up. The result is the sense of inevitability associated with great tragedy. A little later Schiller wrote, again to Goethe: 'Already in the process of writing I am beginning to be increasingly convinced of the truly *tragic* quality of my material. In particular this is because one can see the catastrophe immediately in the first scenes, and while the action of the play seems to be moving away from it, it is actually being brought nearer and nearer.'

Given Schiller's concern with dramatic form and his obvious departures from historical fact, one might be tempted to see the play as making as free with history as ***Don Carlos*** did. The queens are much younger than their historical counterparts. Schiller suggested that on stage Mary should appear about 25 and Elizabeth 30, whereas in fact Mary was 45 and Elizabeth 53 at the time of the execution. The meeting of the queens, the figure of Mortimer, the assas-

sination attempt, and the romantic involvement of Mary and Leicester are all invented. Schiller chose to make his Mary guilty of complicity in the plot to murder Darnley but innocent of involvement in the Babington Plot—both matters of historical dispute—so that he could make her accept her death as an atonement for her earlier guilt. Yet many details of the historical situation are faithfully retained and given dramatic importance: the circumstances of Mary's trial; the details of her past life before her flight to England; the fact that she did not sign the Treaty of Edinburgh; Elizabeth's scapegoating of Davison after the execution. Schiller made a careful study of sources before beginning work, prominent among them being William Robertson's *History of Scotland,* which had been translated into German in 1762. Mary's final words in the play, for example, are given in several of these accounts. In spite of his freedom with history Schiller was impressed by the insoluble political dilemma posed by the Scottish Queen and his drama succeeds in conveying the intractability of the problem she posed, her continuing political importance to Catholic Europe as well as to English Catholics, and Elizabeth's struggle to maintain stability in turbulent times. By placing this insoluble problem at the heart of the drama and by constructing a closely integrated action, Schiller creates a world where decision and action swiftly draw their consequences after them. Yet those consequences are unpredictable and the only refuge from them is in duplicity or disguise. The framework of hope that relieved the tragedy of ***Don Carlos*** has disappeared and has been replaced by a much bleaker vision of the narrow scope for retaining integrity and humanity in the world of action.

Mary and Elizabeth seem at first sight to be conceived as polar opposites. Schiller frequently created pairs of contrasting figures, a favourite technique since his first play, ***The Robbers.*** Mary is accused, isolated, a queen without a throne or a country, condemned to suffer passively, the victim of a judicial murder. Elizabeth is powerful, outwardly confident, supported by loyal subjects and experienced counsellors, about to enter into a marriage that will forge a lasting alliance with France. Mary is Catholic and Elizabeth Protestant. Beyond this religious difference there is a gulf between them in their conception of their role and position. Mary belongs to a long tradition of monarchy as well as of religion. The Catholic Church, though not portrayed so negatively as it was in ***Don Carlos,*** is still clearly regarded as the power behind the throne in Catholic Europe and associated with tyranny, repression, and double-dealing. In her monologue Elizabeth recalls the arbitrary tyranny of her predecessor and half-sister Mary I. The French ambassador Aubespine is implicated in Mortimer's plot, even while negotiations for Elizabeth's French marriage are in progress. Mary's own record as a ruling monarch is morally shameful, but she considers herself no less a queen, for in her own eyes she is still God's anointed. Elizabeth finds herself in an experimental situation. Her legitimacy is in doubt. Her country needs stability and to consolidate her position she has to provide just and consistent government. Difficult though this way may be, it is presented as the better way, if only Elizabeth can live up to it. Though her life has contained reprehensible acts, her religion nevertheless provides Mary with a framework for moral evaluation and with the means of coming to terms with her unjust execution. Elizabeth tries to behave justly but less from a sense of moral conviction than from a sense of necessity. When she dismisses her counsellors in Act Four so that she can seek the counsel of a higher judge we know that this is simply a formula; in her monologue she takes counsel only with herself, and her calm tone in dismissing her counsellors is immediately followed when she is alone by rage and frustration. At the end of the play Mary would seem to have found freedom from the guilt that tormented her and she dies, mourned by her faithful retinue and in receipt of the sacrament administered by a priest of her own Church. Elizabeth by the end is alone, deceived by Mortimer and Leicester, forsaken by Shrewsbury, and unwilling to acknowledge her debt to the banished Burleigh.

Yet Schiller's polar opposites reveal deeper similarities. By embedding his presentation of the two queens within a situation of irreconcilable political conflict, Schiller can explore through these similarities the complexities of the political world. Elizabeth strives for freedom, no less than Mary. For her, freedom is to be released from slavery to the will of the people, whose fickleness she despises. Her refuge is in ambiguous appearances as the only way to wriggle out of the consequences of her actions. Elizabeth's show of confidence and prudence in public is quickly revealed as covering fear and insecurity. And if Elizabeth is weaker than she at first appears Mary is stronger. Through the power of the Catholic monarchies of Europe she remains a key political figure, and though she is revealed as the pawn of the Catholic Church she can still strike at the very heart of Elizabeth's court. The assassination attempt in Act Four, as well as fuelling the post-quarrel crisis, shows that Mary is a threat to Elizabeth's life.

Most obviously, both Mary and Elizabeth are women exerting influence within a man's world, an aspect of the play that has received increasing attention in criticism and performances in recent years. The sexual rivalry between them is used by Schiller to increase the tension of their meeting and of the decision over the signing of the death warrant. But Schiller is not implying that women allow their feelings to dominate their decisions but rather shows how both women are trapped within traditional expectations. Mary's beauty has always made her the object of men's passionate desire. Her reputation has gone before her to England, and Paulet bemoans the day that brought this 'Helen' to trouble its peace. The Church exploits her beauty. It is a portrait of her that first captivates Mortimer, and the Cardinal of Lorraine soon capitalizes on that incipient passion to win him for Mary's cause. Mortimer wants not only to free her but to possess her, and he reminds her of her past amours. And Mary is complicit in this process. She has a reputation for receptivity to love and though she exclaims with indignation to Elizabeth that she is better

than the world thinks her to be, she delivers herself up into the hands of two men who prove fatal to her.

Elizabeth has tried to break free of the traditional shackles of the expectations of a female. This is less a denial of her femininity than a wish to avoid being restricted by those expectations attached to her sex. She is aware of the great responsibility she carries for the stability of her country and has devoted herself to it. She resists marriage to the French Duke of Anjou, believing she has ruled 'like a man and a king' and that where a woman fulfils the highest tasks she should be allowed to be exempt from the duties of nature. The present of her ring to Bellièvre is not only an example of her vacillation, it also suggests her unwillingness to allow her very body to be invaded for state purposes, her biological function forced back on her in spite of her efforts to transcend it. But though imperious in manner and contemptuous of men's weaknesses, Elizabeth longs nevertheless for their approbation. Her vanity requires that she be thought desirable as a woman as well as dutiful as a monarch. We do not sympathize greatly with him, but Leicester bemoans the years he has spent as a slave to her whims, and while it is probably not the main reason why she agrees to meet Mary, the satisfaction of triumphing over her rival in the presence of Leicester plays a supporting role.

The meeting of the queens is at the centre of the action. Schiller was fully aware of the difficulties of handling such a scene but shows his skill in the way he lays bare the reasons why both parties desire it and why their hopes are bound to be frustrated. Mary knows that in spite of the support she enjoys both in England and abroad the way to freedom lies in persuading Elizabeth to grant it: 'neither guile nor violence can save me, / Only the will of Queen Elizabeth can set me free.' She aims to appeal directly to her as a kinswoman and move her to compassion. Burleigh vigorously opposes the meeting when Paulet brings Elizabeth Mary's letter, no doubt fearing that Elizabeth might weaken but also giving a prudent and logical reason:

> She is condemned to death! The axe is raised!
>
> To speak to someone under such a sentence
>
> Would compromise the standing of the monarch!
>
> The implication of the royal presence
>
> Is mercy—once the interview had happened
>
> The sentence would be inapplicable.

Mary may wish to move Elizabeth as though their dynastic quarrel could be settled by the exercise of humanity and compassion. Burleigh, however, is alive to the ceremonial importance of such a meeting. Elizabeth cannot meet Mary unless it is to pardon her. By meeting her the world would be given a signal that pardon was not far off. This is also the reason why Leicester tries to gain Elizabeth's agreement to a meeting, as he says to Mortimer: 'It would bind her. / An execution after such a meeting, / As Burleigh says, would be against tradition.' Although flattery and her own curiosity play a part in her eventual consent to the meeting, it would be quite wrong to think that these are Elizabeth's primary motives. She has already, as she believes, won Mortimer's services to assassinate Mary. Now she can give the appearance to the world of considering mercy in the knowledge that Mary will be murdered before any hard decision will be required of her. Thus she will have disposed of Mary and rescued appearances. The meeting is thus foredoomed because Elizabeth does not come to it with any intention of pardoning Mary, whereas Mary assumes that the humiliation she has undergone in the course of the meeting must be the preliminary to the act of mercy she expects:

> Sister, finish now,
>
> Say what you came to say, for that you came
>
> Simply to mock me, I will not believe.
>
> Speak the word, tell me, 'Mary you are free'

But Elizabeth, spurred on by Leicester's ill-judged flattery earlier and by the added piquancy of his presence, goes too far in grinding her rival into the dust and Mary, also aware of her prospective lover's presence, retaliates. Once she has called Elizabeth a bastard to her face, challenging her right to the throne and activating all of Elizabeth's deepest insecurities, Elizabeth cannot maintain a pretence of wanting to pardon her.

It is in her monologue (IV. x), when Elizabeth signs the death warrant, that she adds the final words to the disastrous meeting. The people, whom she despises but on whose favour she depends, clamour for the death of Mary. But will they still applaud her after the deed is done? Her avoidance of the arbitrary exercise of power and her respect for the law now make it impossible to commit a manifest injustice. Her own example has tied her hands. Isolated from Europe and threatened by powerful enemies, betrayed by those closest to her, Elizabeth is overcome by rage and humiliation. 'Am I a bastard in your eyes?' She addresses Mary directly, taking up the quarrel where it broke off. Enraged and frustrated though she is, it is still the political threat that is uppermost in her mind: 'When there are no more Queens than I, the bed I Where I began will be an honoured one!'

Much critical controversy surrounds the treatment and significance of Mary's death. Mary comes to terms with being the victim of a judicial murder by regarding it as God's sign that she may atone for her complicity in Darnley's murder. The ability to accept her punishment allows her to triumph over the injustice and the humiliation of the execution. Thus the spectacle of her composure and dignity mediates to the audience a sympathetic experience of the indestructibility of the human spirit. To this experience of transcendence Schiller assigned the term 'sublime'. More than any other of his plays *Mary Stuart* has been interpreted as a demonstration of Schiller's theory of tragedy as he developed it during his philosophical phase in the early 1790s, in his essay *On Tragic Pity* (*Über das Pathetische*) in particular. The sublime was a phenomenon

that fascinated numerous writers in the later decades of the eighteenth century. They recognized the existence of an aesthetic response of admiration and awe mixed with pain or terror, such as that occasioned by raging seas or deep ravines. It was a response distinct from the serenity and unalloyed delight associated with the beautiful. In his *Critique of Judgement* Kant interpreted the sublime in the light of his fundamental epistemological distinction between the phenomenal and the noumenal realms, the realm of nature and the realm of freedom. Human beings belong to the one by virtue of being physical creatures and to the other by virtue of being moral beings. When witnessing a scene of overwhelming natural power, human beings are at first terrified by their knowledge that nature can crush them but then exhilarated by the realization that within mankind is a moral dimension that transcends nature. Schiller saw the possibility of making this approach to the sublime fruitful in a theory of tragedy, which is an art form traditionally associated with the mixed response of pain and pleasure. In so doing he could demonstrate the interdependence of the moral and the aesthetic in the tragic response, without subordinating the aesthetic to the moral. The sublime response is mediated to the audience by the spectacle of the suffering of the tragic figure and his or her inner freedom, shown in resistance to being defeated by that suffering. Resistance could be active, as when someone freely chooses to die to uphold the right, or passive, when the suffering is stoically accepted. Though Schiller's essays on tragedy are couched in the language of Kantian philosophy, he can be seen as finding a new idiom in which to make intelligible to his contemporaries Aristotle's notion of catharsis. The play does not teach us a moral lesson but rather mediates an experience that reminds us that we are autonomous moral beings.

Mary Stuart has often been interpreted as if it were an exact demonstration of that theory. The problem with seeing any work of art as a demonstration of a theory is that with truly great art the theory never seems equal to the complexity of the work. Great emphasis on Mary's final moral freedom tends to reduce the scope of the work almost irretrievably. Most of the outer action of the play, particularly the scenes at Elizabeth's court, becomes secondary to this spiritual victory. The rich pattern of comparisons and contrasts between the two worlds of the play is lost, Elizabeth becomes the villain, and the world of politics stands condemned as morally tainted. Yet it is clear that even Mary's death has its own ambiguity. She knows it is her final appearance on the public stage and she can be seen as being determined to use it for maximum impact. Even her avowed innocence in the confession scene of plotting against Elizabeth can be put in doubt when one thinks of her association with Mortimer. She may not have wanted her rival to be assassinated but she has put herself in the hands of those who vow to free her by whatever means. On the other hand, she is about to die and she undoubtedly arouses pity and admiration for her ability to invest her death with the meaning that gives her the strength to face it. The play as moral triumph and the play as political tragedy need not be mutually exclusive. Schiller was as concerned with the art of living as with the art of dying, and it is not to detract from his portrayal of the possibility of transcendence to recognize his fascination with the ambiguities of the political world. It allows us to reserve a little sympathy for Elizabeth as she stands alone at the end, knowing she has failed the test of her humanity.

Notes

1. For detailed commentary on the political echoes in this scene see *Schillers Werke, Nationalausgabe,* vii/ll, ed. Paul Böckmann and Gerhard Kluge, and *Schiller. Sämtliche Werke, Berliner Ausgabe,* iii, ed. Hans-Günther Thalheim and Regine Otto, as well as Allan Blunden's article listed in the Select Bibliography.

F. J. Lamport (essay date 1998)

SOURCE: "Schiller and the "European Community": "Universal History" in Theory and Practice," in *The Modern Language Review* Vol. 93, No 2, April 1998, pp. 428-40.

[*In the following essay, Lamport argues that Schiller's interest in history and his study of people in action on the historical stage contributed to his fuller treatment of the complex relationship of character and event in his dramatic works.*]

'Die europäische Staatengesellschaft scheint in eine große Familie verwandelt. Die Hausgenossen können einander anfeinden, aber hoffentlich nicht mehr zerfleischer.' So declared Schiller, Professor of Philosophy in the University of Jena, in his inaugural lecture, 'Was heißt und zu welchem Ende studiert man Universal-geschichte?',[1] delivered on 21 May 1789, eight weeks before the storming of the Bastille and six months before his thirtieth birthday. The young Schiller had already made the acquaintance of Universal History as a student at the Karlsschule: his medical dissertation *Über den Zusammenhang der tierischen Natur des Menschen mit seiner geistigen* quotes from Schlözer's *Universalhistorie* (*SW,* v, 304) and it is in terms derived from Schlözer that Schiller speaks in the inaugural lecture of the brute facts of history as an 'Aggregat von Bruchstücken' that it is the task of 'der philosophische Verstand' to turn into a 'System' (*SW,* IV, 763). In the intervening years he had also read Kant's essays in the *Berlinische Monatsschrift,* being especially impressed, as he wrote to Körner on 29 August 1787, with the *Idee zu einer allgemeinen Geschichte in weltbürgerlicher Absicht.* The idea of universal human progress now provided the 'Leitfaden *a priori*', as Kant had there called it,[2] with which, Schiller tells us, the philosophical spirit 'bringt einen vernünftigen Zweck in den Gang der Welt und ein teleologisches Prinzip in die *Weltgeschichte*' (*SW,* IV, 764). The task of the Universal Historian is to look back and discover in the dark ages of the past the workings of those

forces that have come or are coming to fruition in the present, in 'unser *menschliches* Jahrhundert' (*SW,* IV, 766).

Meanwhile, Schiller's interest had been aroused in the concrete particulars of history in the course of his work on **Fiesco** and in particular on **Don Carlos,** the work whose dramatic shaping had caused him so much difficulty and led to a profound dissatisfaction with his work as a playwright. 'Täglich wird mir die *Geschichte* teurer', he wrote to Körner on 15 April 1786, 'ich wollte, daß ich zehen Jahre hintereinander nichts als Geschichte studiert hätte.' In the political and religious conflicts of the sixteenth century he discovered the 'Morgendämmerung der Wahrheit', as he wrote in the *Briefe über Don Carlos* (*SW,* II, 228), the origins of modern enlightened Europe, and to expound these and related conflicts according to the principles of Universal History was the task he set himself in the series of historical works he was to produce between 1788 and 1793, the *Geschichte des Abfalls der vereinigten Niederlande von der spanischen Regierung,* the lectures delivered at Jena, his editorial contributions to the *Sammlung historischer Memoires* (especially the essays on the Crusades and on the French wars of religion), and the *Geschichte des Dreißigjährigen Kriegs.* From the chaos of this (as Schiller hoped) final great struggle, the international order of modern Europe had at last appeared: 'Europa ging ununterdrückt und frei aus diesem fürchterlichen Krieg, in welchem es sich zum erstenmal als eine zusammenhängende Staatengesellschaft erkannt hatte' (*SW,* IV, 366), and the dispositions of the Peace of Westphalia of 1648 could still be described by Schiller, writing the final pages of his history in September 1792, as 'unverletzlich' and 'heilig', as 'dieses [. . .] teure und dauernde Werk der Staatskunst' (*SW,* IV, 745).

But even as he wrote this, history appeared to be taking a different turn. The Jacobin government in Paris unleashed the Terror and executed the King. New wars began, not merely dynastic and territorial disputes between the 'Hausgenossen' but once again, as in 1618-48, ideological confrontations between profoundly different conceptions of European order. General Bonaparte, ostensibly in the service of the Directory, began to make war and peace, to redraw frontiers, to destroy states and create them at his own imperious (if not yet Imperial) whim. By the time Schiller, now returned to playwriting, completed his **Wallenstein** trilogy 'an des Jahrhunderts ernstem Ende' (Prologue to **Wallenstein,** l. 61), the 'alte feste Form' was visibly disintegrating (ll. 70-1), even if Schiller did not live to see the humiliation of Jena and the formal dissolution of the Reich in 1806. With the dismemberment of the old 'europäische Staatengesellschaft', so too the promise of universal historical progress seemed to be abrogated, and the study of history could no longer perform the civilizing task envisaged for it in the 'Antrittsvorlesung'. Only art could now reveal to man, beyond the storms of history, his potential for true humanity and so 'das Individuum unvermerkt in die Gattung hinüber[führen]' (compare *SW,* IV, 765). History, for the author of *Über das Erhabene,* shows only 'der Konflikt der Naturkräfte untereinander selbst und mit der Freiheit des Menschen' (*SW*, v, 803). In this grim spectacle, rather than in the programmatic optimism of the 'Antrittsvorlesung', Schiller appears to give, in Theodor Schieder's words, 'das Fazit seiner eigenen Geschichtschreibung'.[3]

The appearance of a volume of essays under the title *Schiller als Historiker*[4] reminds us, however, that there is still a good deal of controversy among scholars as to the intrinsic significance and originality of Schiller's historical writings, their place in his intellectual development and in the contemporary debates on the meaning of history from Schlözer through Herder and Kant to Fichte and beyond, and their relevance for the interpretation of his plays. Schiller's 'historical period' was relatively brief, though it did produce some substantial (and highly readable) pieces of prose writing, but it occupies a crucial stage of his career. It has often been regarded, as Lesley Sharpe observes, as 'something of a diversion from poetry';[5] it was certainly a diversion from dramatic work, or a substitute for it, at a time when as a result of the difficulties experienced in completing *Don Carlos* Schiller felt that he had reached a dead end in his playwriting and had to make a completely fresh start: 'So ein Machwerk wie der Carlos ekelte mich nunmehr an', as he wrote to Körner on 4 September 1794. Those difficulties concerned the proper relationship of character and action in the dramatic context. Schiller had discovered that given the choice of a complex historical situation as a dramatic subject, it was not good enough simply to create characters and leave the action more or less to take care of itself, as he had thought when embarking on *Don Carlos.* 'Der Charakter eines feurigen, großen und empfindenden Jünglings, der zugleich der Erbe einiger Kronen ist,—einer Königin, die durch den Zwang ihrer Empfindung bei allen Vorteilen ihres Schicksals verunglückt,—eines eifersüchtigen Vaters und Gemahls—eines grausamen heuchlerischen Inquisitors, und barbarischen Herzogs von Alba u.s.f. sollten mir, dächte ich, nicht wohl mißlingen': so he had written to Reinwald on 27 March 1783, but it had proved otherwise, at any rate in Schiller's own subsequent estimation. The study of men in action on the stage of history led him to a fuller and truer understanding of the complex relationships of character and event, of 'the individual agent and the moment of history',[6] from which the mature dramatist could only profit.

What, though, of the concerns of the Universal Historian? In his contribution to *Schiller als Historiker,* Manfred Riedel argues that the plays from *Die Verschwörung des Fiesco* to *Demetrius,* taken together, do in fact add up to a dramatic panorama of the emergence of the 'europäische Staatengesellschaft': Italy, Spain and the Netherlands, the Empire, England, France, Switzerland, and Russia; Beatrix Langner suggests that even the apparently ahistorical or suprahistorical *Braut von Messina* can be read on a symbolic level as a 'Familiengemälde des alten politischen Europa',[7] in which the 'Hausgenossen', symbolic incarnations of successive manifestations of the 'Reichsidee'. Roman (Cesar), Byzantine (Manuel), Hohenstaufen (Beatrice),

and Habsburg (Isabella), do indeed, contrary to the hopes expressed in the 'Antrittsvorlesung', 'einander zerfleischen'. Be this as it may, it is certainly the case that the three great historical dramas marking the centre and the summit of Schiller's career as a playwright, **Don Carlos, Wallenstein,** and **Maria Stuart,** are all closely related in subject-matter to his major historiographical works (the events of **Maria Stuart** are of course contemporaneous with, and closely linked to, those portrayed in the *Abfall der Niederlande* and the *Geschichte der französischen Unruhen*). They deal precisely with the religio-political struggles of the sixteenth and seventeenth centuries, from which the 'europäische Staatengesellschaft' of Schiller's day had emerged, and they do so, despite their high artistic stylization, in an essentially realistic manner. That is, they treat these conflicts in purely human terms, without resort to the visions, oracles, and other mythical or legendary elements that characterize the plays that follow them, as well as in a more 'classical' and less operatic or overtly decorative manner. Whether or not they convey, directly or by implication, any notion of universal historical progress, is however by no means so clear.

Anyone attempting to interpret the plays in relation to Schiller's philosophy of history or his political vision of Europe, or anything else extraneous to the texts themselves, must proceed with caution. Schiller the playwright and Schiller the historical writer are pursuing different goals; they are shaping their material according to different generic considerations, and often seem to invite different or even contradictory judgements on the same character or course of action. Schiller's notoriously cavalier treatment of historical fact in his plays, from *Fiesco* all the way to *Die Jungfrau von Orleans,* also makes it more than usually problematic to invoke our (or Schiller's audience's) knowledge of the actual course of history beyond (and in particular subsequent to) the events depicted in the play. As Lessing observed (*Hamburgische Dramaturgie,* No. 34), 'Dem Genie ist es vergönnt, tausend Dinge nicht zu wissen, die jeder Schulknabe weiß': any interpretation that appeals to 'things that every schoolboy knows' must be corroborated from within the dramatic text.

It has also frequently been observed that not even the historiographical works live up to the idealistic 'universalgeschichtlich' programme set out in their opening pages. In one of the very first contemporary reviews of the *Abfall der Niederlande,* Johannes von Müller wondered, in the light of Schiller's depiction of events, 'ob man noch an die vorhergedachten theoretischen und kritischen Fragen denken soll'.[8] Schieder comments on the 'ständige Spannung zwischen geschichtsphilosophischer Axiomatik und geschichtlicher Empirie' (p. 62) that characterizes this work and to some extent all Schiller's historical writing, though significantly modified (p. 68) in the *Geschichte des dreißigjährigen Kriegs.* He also notes as a characteristic feature of Schiller's historiography 'das Nebeneinander verschiedener Bewertungskategorien bei geschichtlichen Persönlichkeiten: einer solchen des politischen Kalküls und einer der ethischen Struktur' (Schieder,

p. 64). Similar ambiguities lie at the heart of the three great historical dramas.

The incommensurability of historical or political judgment (or any kind of judgement as to the appropriateness of means to ends) on the one hand, and of 'pure' moral judgement on the other, is an essential feature of the *tragedy* of history: a tragedy the optimism of the Universal Historian seeks to sublimate or to transcend (or at worst, simply to ignore). It is, indeed, the crux of the personal tragedy of Marquis Posa in **Don Carlos,** of Wallenstein, and (if we allow her to be a tragic character) of Elisabeth in **Maria Stuart.** It is by no means clear that we can, as Manfred Riedel argues, 'mit Schiller den Unterschied zwischen der *eingebildeten Größe* des heroischen, zum Scheitern verurteilten Schwärmertums, und dem *weltgeschichtlich Großen* genauer angeben' (Riedel, p. 38). It is more the case, for both the historian and the dramatist, that as Friedrich Sengle observed of Wallenstein, 'Die geschichtliche Tat [. . .] ist ein undurchdringliches Gemisch von Größe und Verbrechen'.⁹ Riedel follows Schiller's moral condemnation of Posa in the *Briefe über Don Carlos* as a 'Schwärmer' who abandons himself to the 'gefahrlichen Leitung universeller Vernunftideen, die er sich künstlich erschaffen hat' (*SW,* II, 262) and sees in this a condemnation of the 'universalistischer Moralismus der Aufklärung' as a whole (Riedel, p. 37). But when, in his monologue before the great audience scene, Posa reflects upon his unexpected summons before the King and resolves to seize the opportunity with which fate, or chance, or Providence has presented him—

> Ein Zufall nur? Vielleicht auch mehr—Und was
>
> Ist Zufall anders als der rohe Stein,
>
> Der Leben annimmt unter Bildners Hand?
>
> Den Zufall gibt die Vorsehung—zum Zwecke
>
> Muß ihn der Mensch gestalten . . .
>
> (l. 2960)

—he is using the very same image Schiller himself uses in the introduction to the *Abfall der Niederlande,* apparently suggesting that men are historically or even morally obliged to seize such opportunities, not to let them slip, whatever the outcome may be:

> Aber das Unternehmen selbst darf uns darum nicht kleiner erscheinen, weil es anders ausschlug, als es gedacht worden war. Der Mensch verarbeitet, glättet und bildet den rohen Stein, den die Zeiten herbeitragen; ihm gehört der Augenblick und der Punkt, aber die Weltgeschichte rollt der Zufall. (*SW,* IV, 44-5)¹⁰

Posa seizes an opportunity to bring his ideals nearer to fruition, which it would be irresponsible of him to let slip. He thereby finds himself trapped into playing the fatal role of double agent, through which he ultimately brings about his own death and the destruction of Carlos and the Queen, but he can nevertheless be seen as accepting an objective challenge of history. The deviousness with which Posa pursues his aims is not so very different from the Machiavellian tactics of Oranien that earn Schiller's apparent approval in the *Abfall der Niederlande.*¹¹ And Posa's prophecy to the King that 'Sanftere | Jahrhunderte verdrängen Philipps Zeiten' (ll. 3148-49), echoed later by Lerma's assurance to Carlos that 'schönre Zeiten werden kommen' (l. 4937), directly anticipates the language of the 'Antrittsvorle-sung' and would naturally have been understood by the play's first audiences as a prophecy which in their own 'menschliches Jahrhundert' had been seen to be fulfilled.¹² If Schiller really intended to condemn Posa, as the *Briefe über Don Carlos* undoubtedly suggest, then playwright and historian are speaking with different voices. But perhaps it is rather the author of the *Briefe,* standing now, as he puts it himself, 'gleichsam in der Mitte zwischen dem Künstler und seinem Betrachter' (*SW,* II, 226), too clearly aware of the faults of both work and character as he now sees them and at the same time overanxious to defend himself against the general verdict that the presentation of Posa is 'zu idealisch' (*SW,* II, 227), who fails to take full account of the historical perspective that the play itself implies.

In the case of Elisabeth in **Maria Stuart,** historian and playwright do appear to speak with different voices. In Schiller's translation of Mercier's *Philipp der Zweite, König von Spanien,* Elisabeth is characterized as the champion of Protestant freedom, motivated by 'Liebe zum wahren Ruhme, Toleranz und Standhaftigkeit' (*SW,* IV, 15), and in the *Abfall der Niederlande* she is celebrated as the creator of the English nation: 'Erst auf ihren schöpferischen Ruf sollte dieser Staat aus einer demütigen Dunkelheit steigen und die lebendige Kraft, womit er seinen Nebenbuhler endlich darnieder ringt, von der fehlerhaften Politik dieses letztern empfangen' (*SW,* IV, 77). The defeat of the Spanish Armada is also hymned by Schiller in the poem 'Die unüberwindliche Flotte' (*SW,* I, 145-46), and is reported by Medina Sidonia in **Don Carlos** (III, 6-7), providing further evidence within the text of that play (and, of course, deliberately and anachronistically introduced into it, for the 'real' date of the main action, that leading to the imprisonment and presumed death of Prince Carlos, is 1568) that the tide of history is indeed flowing against Philipp's Spain and all that it stands for. But in **Maria Stuart,** Elisabeth, albeit loved by the people, we are told, as the guarantor of their new-found liberties, is shown as acting from very different and far more questionable motives, and the execution of Mary is shown as a relapse into tyranny, proving the new order no better in this respect than the *ancien régime* it has replaced. Here the prophecy the play seems to endorse is not Burleigh's 'Gewähr auch dieses, und der heutge Tag | Hat Englands Wohl auf immerdar gegründet' (ll. 1252-53), but rather Shrewsbury's fear that the execution will 'deines Volkes Herzen von dir wenden' (l. 3120), whatever the historical record may say. If Elisabeth is a tragic figure, then it is because she *fails* to rise to the challenge of shaping a better future for her people: as in the case of the French revolutionaries, as evoked by Schiller in the *Briefe über* *die ästhetische Erziehung des Menschen,* 'der freigebige Augenblick findet ein unempfängliches Geschlecht' (*SW*, v, 579-80).[13]

Peter Pfaff interprets the end of the play as an apotheosis of Elisabeth: 'In der moralisch kompromittierten Königin triumphiert die Staatsraison, *der England eine glanzvolle Epoche dankt.*'[14] But the last words invoke a historical perspective the play itself seems rather to close off. In the play, and especially in the final Act, all the emphasis is on Mary's moral triumph and Elisabeth's moral failure: her refusal to accept responsibility for her actions, her scapegoating of Davison and Burleigh, and her desertion both by the loyal Shrewsbury, lamenting that 'Ich habe deinen edlern Teil | Nicht retten können' (ll. 4028-29), and by the less than admirable Leicester, shamed at last into giving up his course of selfish double-dealing and committing himself to the juster cause, or so it would seem here, of Elisabeth's enemies. The defection of Shrewsbury and Leicester is totally unhistorical, an invention surely intended by Schiller to cast an unfavourable light on Elisabeth.

There is also further evidence that by the turn of the century, Schiller's view of England and her historical destiny had changed considerably from that of the 1780s. In 'Die unüberwindliche Flotte' England is lauded as 'glückselge Insel', 'der Unterdrückung letzter Felsendamm', 'der Freiheit Paradies' (*SW*, I, 145-46). But in the poem 'Der Antritt des neuen Jahrhunderts' of 1801, she is portrayed in precisely opposite and highly unflattering terms, as a greedy colonial power intent, alongside France, on world domination:

Zwo gewaltge Nationen ringen

Um der Welt alleinigen Besitz,

Aller Länder Freiheit zu verschlingen,

Schwingen sie den Dreizack und den Blitz . . .

Seine Handelsflotten streckt der Brite

Gierig wie Polypenarmen aus,

Und das Reich der freien Amphitrite

Will er schließen wie sein eignes Haus.

Zu des Südpols nie erblickten Sternen

Dringt sein rastlos ungehemmter Lauf,

Alle Inseln spürt er, alle fernen

Küsten—nur das Paradies nicht auf.

(*SW*, I,459)[15]

Pfaff similarly sees Schiller as vindicating Wallenstein's treason against the Emperor: 'Mag der Generalissimus seinen Kaiser verraten [. . .] so kann er allein, bei gegebener Konstellation der Mächtigen, den Krieg beenden' (p. 409). Certainly the play itself invites speculation on this possibility. Max Piccolomini's eulogy of Wallenstein to Questenberg in the first Act of *Die Piccolomini* (hereafter *Picc.*) culminates in the assertion that he, Wallenstein, is working for peace and for 'Europas großem Besten', the

Imperial party for a continuation of the war (*Picc.*, ll. 561-77). Max's first scene with Thekla ends with a similar encomium (ll. 1654-57). Octavio himself ironically confirms that Wallenstein is working for peace, though at a price (ll. 2333-38), and Buttler, as the tragedy draws to its close, informs us that the citizens of Eger are rallying to Wallenstein's support because 'Sie sehn im Herzog einen Friedensfürsten | Und einen Stifter neuer goldner Zeit' (*Tod*, ll. 3217-18). But quite apart from the fact that the text also offers much to support a quite different interpretation of Wallenstein's motives and intentions, the possibility remains, despite Pfaff's indicative, a highly speculative one. It is not certain what *might* have happened *if* Wallenstein *had* acted differently. His failure to seize the moment 'eh die Glücks- | Gestalt mir wieder wegflieht überm Haupt' (*Tod*, ll. 33-4: when he speaks these words it is, of course, already too late) may represent a culpable failure to rise to the challenge of history, though it should be noted that those most strongly urging him to act are the play's most brutal political realists, Illo and the Countess, whose selfish power-seeking is unclouded by any hint of pacific intent. What is certain is that (to adopt Pfaff's terms) in the morally compromised figure of Octavio, who stands centre-stage at the end of the drama, as does Elisabeth at the end of **Maria Stuart**, we see a triumph of 'Staatsraison' (the 'Staatskunst' excoriated by Max in *Picc.*, l. 2632), which results not in a 'glanzvolle Epoche' but in another fourteen years' prolongation of the war. Of this historical fact Schiller has explicitly reminded his audience in the Prologue to the trilogy:

In jenes Krieges Mitte stellt euch jetzt

Der Dichter. Sechzehn Jahre der Verwüstung,

Des Raubs, des Elends sind dahingeflohn,

In trüben Massen gäret noch die Welt,

Und keine Friedenshoffnung strahlt von fern.

(*Prolog*, l. 79)

The Prologue also reminds the audience that they are expected to be familiar with the hero of the drama ('Ihr kennet ihn' (l. 94)), thus explicitly opening up the perspective of extra-textual historical knowledge that the conclusion of **Maria Stuart** seems to deny.

R. Marleyn rather oddly asserts that 'the fall of Wallenstein must entail the fall of the Habsburg power (the actual historical outcome is, of course, irrelevant to the dramatic situation)'.[16] The immediate dramatic outcome represents, surely, a *victory* for the Habsburg power, and, as in this case Schiller plainly expects his audience to know, the prolongation of the war. What of the longer term? As has already been mentioned, Schiller the Universal Historian has seen the horros of the Thirty Years' War as in some sense justified, in the eyes of the 'Weltbürger', by the emergence of a 'zusammenhängende Staatengesellschaft' (*SW*, IV, 366) and by the 'unter dem Namen des Westfälischen berühmten, unverletzlichen und heiligen Frieden' (*SW*, IV, 745) to which it eventually led. Even in 1792 this might have seemed an unduly optimistic verdict; six years later, in the Prologue to **Wallenstein,** Schiller recognizes that the old order is falling to pieces.[17] Yet here, too, he asserts a similar kind of 'dialectical' optimism, urging his audience to draw some kind of positive conclusion from the gloomy spectacle he is about to present to them:

Noch einmal laßt des Dichters Phantasie

Die düstre Zeit an euch vorüberführen,

Und blicket froher in die Gegenwart

Und in der Zukunft hoffnungsreiche Ferne.

(l. 75)

Are we then to see, in the bitter triumph of Octavio's 'Staatskunst' with which the tragedy continues, the working of some kind of 'teleologisches Prinzip' (*SW,* IV, 764), some kind of 'List der Vernunft'? Hegel, with his famous characterization of the end of **Wallenstein** as the 'Sieg des Nichts',[18] seemed not to think so. Or are we to see it as a vindication of those 'alten, engen, Ordnungen' that at an early stage of the drama (*Picc.,* ll. 463-79) Octavio not uneloquently defends? In **Don Carlos,** whatever we may think of Posa's character or his actions, Philipp's tyrannical government, described in the *Briefe* as 'geistliche[r], politische[r] und häusliche[r] Despotismus' (*SW,* II, 255), is unequivocally condemned. In both **Wallenstein** and **Maria Stuart** Schiller seems to be suggesting that the familiar devils of the *ancien régime* might be preferable to the unknown demons of revolutionary liberation. As Jens-F. Dwars argues, 'Als Zeitgenosse der Französischen Revolution verteidigt Schiller aus Furcht vor der Anarchie dieselbe Ordnung, deren innerer Zerfall er ästhetisch unabweisbar gestaltet.'[19] In Schiller's eyes, if the 'europäische Staatengesellschaft' were to survive, it could only be by some cautious reform of the old order, rather than by the arbitrary dispositions of such as General Bonaparte, or of any charismatic leader promising millennial renewal. And if in 'Deutsche Größe' Schiller seems to envisage a specific historical 'mission' for Germany in leading Europe forward to a brighter future beyond the political confusions of the 1790s, 'Der Antritt des neuen Jahrhunderts' ends on a note of complete resignation and withdrawal: 'Freiheit ist nur in dem Reich der Träume, | Und das Schöne blüht nur im Gesang' (*SW,* I, 459). No doubt Schiller was reluctant to give up all hope of real historical progress, but the evidence seemed to point strongly against it.

In the thirteen eventful years between the completion of **Don Carlos** and that of **Maria Stuart** Schiller has plainly become, at all events, much less unambiguously hostile towards the *ancien régime.* He has also become much more ambivalent in his portrayal of the *ancien régime*'s spiritual arm, the Roman Catholic Church. As W. M. Simon says: 'Over and over again Schiller makes the point that tyranny and the Roman Catholic church were inseparable allies, indeed that the Church was the evil genius behind many tyrants and acts of tyranny.'[20] But in the last Act of **Maria Stuart,** Mary's Catholic religion is presented in quite a different light, and the end of **Die jungfrau von Orleans** is, if not as Shaw claimed 'drowned

in a witch's caldron of raging romance',[21] then at all events suffused with a rosy glow (see Schiller's stage direction!) of Catholic Mariolatry and martyr symbolism in which Schiller's earlier fierce opposition to the Roman Church and all its works is quite forgotten. Are we to see these Catholicizing elements in a purely symbolic light, or do they indicate a change in his view of the historical and political role of the Church?

Growing up in arch-Protestant Württemberg, the young Schiller imbibed Protestantism with his mother's milk, and for a Württemberger the association of the Catholic Church, and in particular the Inquisition, with political tyranny was reinforced by the fact that since the accession of the convert Karl Alexander in 1734 the arch-Protestant duchy had been ruled by Catholic dukes, eager to introduce absolutist rule. In **Die Räuber,** Schiller's most directly political criticisms are actually voiced in scenes involving religious figures. The Catholic Church is represented by the Pater, the corrupt and hypocritical agent of a corrupt and tyrannical authority, who comes to confront Karl in the closing scene of Act II. It was, Karl tells him, a 'Pfaff[e] Ihres Gelichters [. . .] , den ich mit eigener Hand erwürgte, als er auf offener Kanzel geweint hatte, dass die Inquisition so in Zerfall käme' (*SW,* I, 552). Protestantism is contrastingly embodied in Pastor Moser, the voice of conscience and true religion, who triumphs over the evil Franz in Act V. It is usually claimed that Moser's name is a tribute to the pastor of Lorch, who was Schiller's first teacher, but it may well also be intended to suggest that of Johann Jakob Moser, the Swabian jurist whose opposition to the absolutist ambitions of Duke Karl Eugen earned him five years' imprisonment without trial (1759-64, a year or two after the action of the play is set). Moser's rebukes to Franz also have a strongly political flavour: 'Ich will an Eurem Bette stehn, wenn ihr sterbet—ich möchte so gar gern einen Tyrannen sehn dahinfahren [. . .] . Ihr habt das Leben von Tausenden an der Spitze Eures Fingers, und von diesen Tausenden habt ihr neunhundertneunundneunzig elend gemacht' (*SW,* I, 604-05).[22] In **Don Carlos** the Catholic Church ispainted in the blackest of hues.[23] It is Domingo, the *Domini canis,* 'des Königs lustge[r] Beichtiger's, as Carlos ironically describes him (l. 67), who speaks the play's very opening words, whose mastery of political intrigue surprises even his ally Alba (ll. 2069-72) and whose unclerical or all-too-clerical innuendoes horrify the King (l. 2740), and it is the terrifying figure of the aged but unyielding Inquisitor who dominates the closing scenes and is shown to be the real power behind the throne. In **Wallenstein** the Church also plays a significant if less directly active role. In the **Lager** it is the Kapuziner who introduces a violently discordant, hostile note into the chorus of praise for the hero (and who, incidentally, first mentions Wallenstein by name (**Lager,** l. 620)); it is also a Capuchin who obstructs Isolani's mission to obtain remounts for the troops (**Picc.,** ll. 166-79). In the banquet scene the Kellermeister praises both the religious and the civil liberties of the Bohemians, represented on the coronation goblet by the allegorical figure of 'die Wahlfreiheit der böhmschen Kron' (l. 2073) bearing the hat of liberty, the communion chalice, and the Letter of Majesty, riding triumphant 'übern Krummstab [. . .] und Bischofsmützen' (l. 2068). Max describes Octavio's report of Wallenstein's intended treachery as a 'Pfaffenmärchen' (l. 2320), just as Schiller himself, in his summing-up of Wallenstein's career at the end of Book IV of the *Geschichte des Dreissigjährigen Kriegs,*tells us that Wallenstein owed both his dismissal at Regensburg and his reputation as a traitor, during his life and after it, to 'Mönchsintrigen' and 'mönchische Künste' (*SW,* IV, 688). Wallenstein himself was a Catholic convert (which seems to be adduced (*Tod,* ll. 2563-66) as a sign of mental imbalance!) but proclaims to the Burgomaster of Eger his hatred of the Jesuits and his tolerance, or indifference, in religious matters (ll. 2597-600). But it is only a gentle rebuke that Wallenstein utters to Seni when the astrologer (a comic, but in these final scenes not unsympathetic figure) comes to warn him for the last time against the alliance with the Swedes, with 'diesen Heiden [. . .] , | Die Krieg mit unsrer heilgen Kirche führen' (ll. 3618-19).[24]

In *Maria Stuart* Catholicism plays a much more prominent but also a much more ambivalent role; indeed, it could be said to play two quite different ones. From a realistic point of view, the Church is shown, exactly as in the earlier plays, as closely allied to the forces of the *ancien régime,* supporting as it does Mary's claim to the throne by right of hereditary legitimacy. It is also deeply involved in political intrigue, encouraging plots and conspiracies against Elisabeth. It is, as Elisabeth herself says, the Cardinal de Guise, 'der stolze, | Herrschwütge Priester' (ll. 2333-34), rather than Mary herself, who is the originator of Mary's claim to the throne of England, and it is also the priests, the Cardinal and Bishop Lesley, who convert Mortimer to Mary's cause, as Mortimer tells her in Act I, Scene 6. The Catholic party are not only the enemies of Elisabeth and of Protestant England: they are also, through encouraging Mary's claim to the throne and engaging Mortimer, the 'keckentschlossner Schwärmer' (l. 2976), to their cause, doubly if indirectly responsible for Mary's death. But side by side with (and at the end of the play effectively supplanting) this realistic picture of the Catholic Church at its deadly work of political intrigue, the most solemn Catholic ritual is used to symbolize the transcendence of the material, historical, and political realm and theachievement of true spiritual freedom. Mary receives the Eucharist from Melvil in both kinds, enjoying by papal dispensation the privilege for which the Kellermeister in *Wallenstein* tells us his ancestors fought under Prokop and Ziska (*Picc.,* ll. 2103-04). In historical fact Mary sought, but was denied the comfort of her own religion in death (see Act I, 180-89), and Melvil, though a loyal follower of Mary, was actually a Protestant. It is this deliberate and symbolic, rather than realistic, deployment of Catholic religious motifs that seems to move the play (decisively, in the view of many critics) away from the presentation of history and politics into the realm of private suffering and private moral transcendence, the 'Darstellung des moralischen Widerstandes gegen das Leiden' that is, according to Schiller in *Über das Pathetische* (*SW,* v, 515), the business

of pure tragic art. But if Mary's moral triumph suggests, as it evidently does to Leicester, the justice of her political cause, then we cannot rule out the interpretation that on a realistic level too, Schiller would appear to have become considerably more sympathetic to the role of the Catholic religion as the ideological guarantor of the principle of legitimate monarchy. It is certainly difficult to imagine anything, not even the end of *Die Jungfrau von Orleans,* more different from the tableau of tyrannical Catholic monarchy that ends *Don Carlos.*

Though in 1788 he had appeared to distance himself altogether from Christianity in 'Die Götter Griechenlands', in the 'Antrittsvorlesung' Schiller still addresses himself specifically to 'protestantische Christen' (*SW,* IV, 759). In the *Abfall der Niederlande,* he sets out his programme as the champion of religious and political liberty, and insists on the intimate connection between tyranny and Catholicism embodied in Charles V ('Karl der Fünfte, der bei dieser grossen Glaubenstrennung die Partie genommen hatte, die ein Despot nicht verfehlen kann' (*SW,* IV, 67)) and even more plainly in his son Philip II. But he is at the same time careful to distinguish between monarchical legitimacy, the principle of which he does not challenge, and religious bigotry: 'Zum Unglück für die verbesserte Religion war die politische Gerechtigkeit auf der Seite ihres Verfolgers' (*SW,* IV, 67). A similar distinction is drawn in the case of Ferdinand II in the *Geschichte des Dreissigjährigen Kriegs.*[25] In the historiographical works, Schiller also dissociates himself explicitly from the more revolutionary manifestations of Protestantism amongst the people, and spares no details in his depiction of the horrors perpetrated by the iconoclasts in the Netherlands (*Abfall der Niederlande,* Book 4), or of the 'Rache des Hugenottenpöbels' (*SW,* IV, 956) in the French wars of religion.[26] By the time of the appearance of the *Geschichte des Dreissigjährigen Kriegs* the execution of Louis XVI by the 'elenden Schinderknechte' of the Revolution (to Körner, 8 February 1793) had confirmed Schiller's monarchical loyalties and made him more suspicious than ever of thecrimes committed (to quote Madame Roland) in the name of liberty. In the opening pages of the *Geschichte des Dreissigjährigen Kriegs* he can still present the Reformation as the point of origin of the modern family of nations: 'Und so musste es durch einen seltsamen Gang der Dinge die *Kirchentrennung* sein, was die Staaten unter sich zu einer engen *Vereinigung* führte' (*SW,* IV, 366). Even in 'Deutsche Grösse' Germany's historic mission is still specifically associated with Protestantism (*SW,* I, 475-76). But by the time of completing *Maria Stuart* he seems at least to be flirting with the Catholicizing nostalgia of a Novalis for the 'schöne glänzende Zeiten, wo Europa ein christliches Land war, wo *Eine* Christenheit diesen menschlich gestalteten Weltteil bewohnte',[27] and he was to give this Romantic nostalgia free reign in his 'romantische Tragödie' *Die Jungfrau von Orleans.* In *Maria Stuart* he is still sufficient of a historical as well as a dramatic realist to know that this will not do. He knows that the Catholic party is seeking to place on the throne of England a Queen who has so abused her hereditary privileges that she has been deposed and expelled by her own people (ll. 99-100). He is still historical and political idealist enough to hope that one day a truly educated, enlightened, and civilized humanity will prove itself worthy of the 'freigebiger Augenblick' of history and create a 'Staat der Freiheit', but he knows that this is still a very long way off. The events of the years following 1789 had shown him that the social, political, and ideological conflicts necessary to create the 'europäische Staatengesellschaft' were far from being fully played out.

In Schiller's next two plays, both the vision of the Universal Historian and the concrete concern with that formative period of European history have largely disappeared. The subject-matter both of **Die Jungfrau von Orleans** and of **Wilhelm Tell** incorporates highly topical political themes: the legitimacy of hereditary government (a thorough analysis of the plays from **Wallenstein** onwards in terms of Weber's theory of 'Herrschaftslegitimierung' still remains to be written), and the cause of national liberation from alien rule (though this theme is present in **Die Braut von Messina** at best by implication). But neither could be said to present a realistic analysis of historical forces, and the high degree of artistic stylization employed, whether 'romantisch' or pseudo-Greek, suggests that Schiller's aim here was 'den Stoff durch die Form zu vertilgen' (see *SW*, v, 639), and that the banner placed in Johanna's hand at the end of **Die Jungfrau von Orleans** is not so much the banner of national liberation as the 'Fahne der Wahrheit und Schönheit', under which, in the preface to *Die Horen* in 1794, Schiller had promised to heal political divisions and unite humanity in true (that is, ideal, aesthetic) freedom. The real concern of both plays is not so much history as 'Poesie jenseits der Geschichte' (Oellers, *Friedrich Schiller*, pp. 228-29).²⁸ **Wilhelm Tell** and **Demetrius,** however, seem to move back towards a more realistic assessment of human motives and human actions on the stage of history. (Joan of Arc is a real historical figure and Tell a figure of legend, but in Schiller's treatment sober history and romantic legend seem to have changed places.) Both plays seem deeply sceptical of any universal historical progress. In **Wilhelm Tell,** though the vision is not entirely backward-looking (the dying Attinghausen promises that 'Aus diesem Haupte, wo der Apfel lag, | Wird euch die *neue bessre* Freiheit grünen' (ll. 2423-24, my italics), and the liberation of the serfs anachronistically proclaimed by Rudenz in the play's last line had at last been accomplished in Schiller's own 'menschliches Jahrhundert', by Joseph II in 1782), the fundamental political ethos of the play is not only conservative but anti-universalist. It seems to be the good fortune of the Swiss (or to have been, for at the time Schiller wrote, their traditional liberties had been extinguished in the name of new 'republican' ones by General Bonaparte) *not* to have been caught up in any grand current of Universal History, but rather to be allowed to live at peace in their Alpine backwater. If there is any meaning in history, then it is to be found in the particular, almost fortuitous, triumph of a just cause at a particular moment, without this necessarily being seen to validate any 'tele-

ologisches Prinzip'.²⁹ **Demetrius** presents an altogether grimmer picture: the 'ewige Wiederkehr des Gleichen' invoked at the end of the scenario, where 'gleichsam das Alte von neuem beginnt' (*SW*, III, 76) is only partly alleviated by the promise of the return of just and legitimate government under the Romanovs. Since Schiller's day, the Swiss have regained, and still jealously guard, their traditional liberties, Russian history continues to proceed through revolutionary cycles to a still uncertain future, and both Switzerland and Russia remain on the margins of the 'europäische Staatengesellschaft', as Schiller knew it and as we know it today.

Notes

1. *Sämtliche Werke,* ed. by Gerhard Fricke and Herbert G. Göpfert, 3rd edn, 5 vols (Munich: Hanser, 1962), IV, 749-67 (p. 757). All quotations and references according to this edition (*SW*). References to verse plays are by line numbers.

2. Kant, *Werke,* ed. by Wilhelm Weischedel, 10 vols (Wiesbaden: Insel Verlag, 1956-60), IX, 49.

3. Theodor Schieder, 'Schiller als Historiker', in der *Begegnungen mit der Geschichte* (Göttingen: Vandenhoeck & Ruprecht, 1962), pp. 56-79 (p. 62). See also Gerhard Fricke, 'Schiller und die geschichtliche Welt', in *Studien und Interpretationen* (Frankfurt a.M.: Menck, 1956), pp. 95-118, esp. pp. 102-03; Hans-Dietrich Dahnke, 'Zum Verhältnis von historischer und poetischer Wahrheit in Schillers Konzeptionsbildung und Dramenpraxis', in *Friedrich Schiller: Angebot und Diskurs. Zugänge, Dichtung, Zeitgenossenschaft,* ed. by Helmut Brandt (Berlin and Weimar: Aufbau Verlag, 1987), pp. 264-81, esp. pp. 274-75.

4. Ed. by Otto Dann, Norbert Oellers, and Ernst Osterkamp (Stuttgart and Weimar: Böhlau, 1995): see my review, pp. 569-70 here.

5. *Friedrich Schiller: Drama, Thought and Politics* (Cambridge: Cambridge University Press, 1991), p. 109.

6. Sharpe, p. 109; see also her earlier study, *Schiller and the Historical Character: Presentation and Interpretation in the Historiogrpahical Works and in the Historical Dramas* (Oxford: Oxford University Press, 1982).

7. Manfred Riedel, 'Geschichte und Gegenwart. Europa in Schillers Konzept der Universalgeschichte', *Schiller als Historiker,* pp. 29-58. Beatrix Langner, 'Der Name der Blume. Schillers Trauerspiel *Die Braut von Messina* als Dramaturgie der geschichtlichen Vernunft', *Schiller als Historiker,* pp. 219 42 (p. 241).

8. Quoted by Michael Gottlob, 'Schiller und Johannes Müller', *Schiller als Historiker,* pp. 309-33 (p. 310).

9. Friedrich Sengle, *Das historische Drama in Deutschland,* 2nd edn (Stuttgart: Metzler, 1969), p. 56.

10. Compare also *SW,* IV, 36: 'Noch fehlte die letzte vollendende Hand [that of William the Silent]—der erleuchtete unternehmende Geist, der diesen großen politischen Augenblick haschte und die Geburt des

Zufalls zum Plan der Weisheit erzöge.' On the role of chance in *Wallenstein,* see Norbert Oellers, 'Das Zufällige ist das Notwendige. Bemerkungen zu Schillers *Wallenstein*', in *Friedrich Schiller: Zur Modernität eines Klassikers* (Frankfurt a.M. and Leipzig: Insel Verlag, 1966), pp. 232-46.

11. For a further discussion of Posa and Oranien, see Ernst Osterkamp, 'Die Seele des historischen Subjekts. Historische Portraitkunst in Schillers *Geschichte des Abfalls der Vereinigten Niederlande von der Spanischen Regierung*', in *Schiller als Historiker,* pp. 157-78.

12. See Wolfgang Düsing, '"Das kühne Traumbild eines neuen Staates." Die Utopie in Schillers *Don Karlos* [*sic*]', in *Geschichtlichkeit und Gegenwart. Festschrift für Hans Dietrich Irmscher zum 65. Geburtstag,* ed. by Hans Esselborn and Werner Keller, Kölner germanistische Studien, 34 (Cologne, Weimar, and Vienna: Böhlau, 1994), pp. 194-208, esp. p. 197, pp. 203-06.

13. See my article, 'Krise und Legitimitätsanspruch: *Maria Stuart* als Geschichtstragödie', *Zeitschrift für deutsche Philologie,* 109 (1990), Sonderheft, 134-45.

14. 'König René oder die Geschichte', in *Schiller und die höfische Welt,* ed. by Achim Aurnhammer, Klaus Manger, and Friedrich Strack (Tübingen: Niemeyer, 1990), pp. 407-21 (p. 409: my italics).

15. Compare also the similar formulations in the unfinished 'Deutsche Größe' of 1797 (*SW*,I, 473-78), and the echo in *Demetrius,* ll. 925-93 (*SW*,III, 38). (In the latter case, it is rather 'des Nordpols nie erblickte Sterne' which attract British maritime adventure!)

16. R. Marleyn, '*Wallenstein* and the Structure of Schiller's Tragedies', *Germanic Review,* 32 (1957), 186-99 (p. 189).

17. Karl-Heinz Hahn, while noting Schiller's concentration, in both his historiography and his major historical dramas, on the 'Herausbildung des europäischen Staatensystems' (and, of course, on the 'advancement of the bourgeoisie') in the sixteenth and seventeenth centuries, observes that the dispositions of 1648 had in effect already been destroyed by the Seven Years' War and the consequent emergence of the Austro-Prussian duopoly within the Empire ('Schiller und die Geschichte', *Weimarer Beiträge,* 16 (1970), 39-69, esp. pp. 45-47).

18. G. W. F. Hegel, 'Uber "Wallenstein"', in *Schiller: Zeitgenosse aller Epochen. Dokumente zur Wirkungsgeschichte Schillers in Deutschland,* ed. by Norbert Oellers, Teil I: *1782-1859* (Wirkungen der Literatur, Band 2/:) (Frankfurt a.M.: Athenäum, 1970), p. 87).

19. Jens-F. Dwars, 'Dichtung im Epochenumbruch. Schillers *Wallenstein* im Wandel von Alltag und Offentlichkeit', *Jahrbuch der Deutschen Schillergesellschaft,* 35 (1991), 150-79 (p. 176). Wolfgang Wittkowski argues that while recognizing the price in personal integrity that has to be paid, Schiller nevertheless fully endorses Octavio's 'Höfische Intrige für die gute Sache': see his article thus entitled, in *Schiller und die höfische Welt,* pp. 378-97.

20. W. M. Simon, Inaugural Lecture, 'Friedrich Schiller (1759-1805): The Poet as Historian' (Keele: University of Keele, 1966), p. 7.

21. G. B. Shaw, *Saint Foan,* preface, in *The Bodley Head Bernard Shaw: Collected Plays with their Prefaces,* 7 vols, ed. by Dan H. Laurence (London: Bodley Head, 1970-74), VI, 40.

22. Compare Hans-Günther Thalheim, 'Der württembergische Pietismus im Erfahrungshorizont des frühen Schiller', *Weimarer Beiträge,* 31 (1985), 1823-48, esp. pp. 1832-35.

23. Schiller's heavily biased presentation of Philip II and the Spanish church is criticized by Bärbel Becker-Cantarino, 'Die "Schwarze Legende". Ideal und Ideologie in Schillers *Don Carlos*', *Fahrbuch des Freien Deutschen Hochstifts,* 1975, 153-73. See also the fuller but very superficial account in Herbert Koch, *Schiller und Spanien,* Münchener romanistische Arbeiten, 31 (Munich: Hueber, 1973), pp. 28-73.

24. Helmut Koopmann stresses the anti-clerical elements in *Wallenstein,* beginning with the Kapuziner scene ('Die Tragödie der verhinderten Selbstbestimung', in *Freiheitssonne und Revolutionsgewitter* (Tübingen: Niemeyer, 1989), pp. 13-58, esp. pp. 41-43). Koopmann argues that in both *Don Carlos* and *Wallenstein* the Church represents a 'gegenaufklärerisch[e] Macht' (p. 41), opposed above all to man's spiritual and intellectual, rather than political, emancipation.

25. See Karl Pestalozzi, 'Ferdinand II in Schillers *Geschichte des Dreissigjährigen Kriegs:* Die Rechtfertigung eines Üblen', in *Schiller als Historiker,* pp. 179-90.

26. See Werner Kohlschmidt, 'Schiller und die Reformation', in *Dichter, Tradition und Zeitgeist* (Bern and Munich: Francke, 1965), pp. 68-77. Kohlschmidt denies Schiller any understanding of the specifically religious or spiritual issues involved. For a different view, see Koopmann (n. 24) and Gerhard Fricke, *Der religiöse Sinn der Klassik Schillers* (Munich: Kaiser, 1927).

27. Novalis, 'Die Christenheit oder Europa', in *Werke,* ed. by G. Schulz, Studienausgabe (Munich: Beck, 1969), p. 499. Schiller had met Novalis on a number of occasions, and may well have been aware of the contents of the essay, though it was not published until 1827: compare Langner (n. 7), pp. 232-33 and n. 60. For a vision of the European Community for our own times, strongly reminiscent of that of Novalis, see Nicholas Boyle, 'The End of Individualism?', *Guardian,* 15 October 1991.

28. For a contrary view of *Die Braut von Messina* as embodying a 'Thematisierung des triadischen Geschichtsverlaufs', see Rolf-Peter Carl, 'Sophokles und Shakespeare? Zur deutschen Tragödie um 1800', in *Deutsche Literatur zur Zeit der Klassik,* ed. by Karl Otto Conrady (Stuttgart: Reclam, 1977), pp. 296-318 (p. 304).

29. See my article, 'The Silence of Wilhelm Tell', *MLR,* 76 (1981), 857-68, esp. p. 862; also Norbert Oellers, 'Idylle und Politik. Französische Revolution,

ästhetische Erziehung und die Freiheit der Urkantone', in *Friedrich Schiller*, pp. 289-312, esp. pp. 309-11 (originally in *Friedrich Schiller, Kunst, Humanität und Politik in der späten Aufklärung*, ed. by Wolfgang Wittkowski (Tübingen: Niemeyer, 1982), pp. 114-33): R. C. Ockenden, 'Wilhelm Tell as Political Drama', *Oxford German Studies*, 18/19 (1989-90), 23-44.

DIE RÄUBER

CRITICAL COMMENTARY

Alan C. Leidner (essay date 1988)

SOURCE: "Karl Moor's Charisma," in *Friedrich von Schiller and the Drama of Human Existence*, edited by Alexej Ugrinsky, Greenwood Press, 1988, pp. 57-61.

[*In the following essay, Leidner notes that* Die Räuber, *Schiller's hugely successful first play, was and is so popular because of the charisma of the protagonist, Karl Moor, and because of the emotional ritual created in a work where the audience takes vicarious pleasure in identifying with a murderer.*]

When Friedrich von Schiller, a twenty-two year old cadet at the Hohe Karlsschule in Stuttgart, went A.W.O.L. to attend the first performance of *Die Räuber* (1781), he could hardly have been disappointed with the response. "No play," wrote one reviewer, "has ever had such an effect in the German theatre"[1]; and another: "The theatre was like a madhouse, full of rolling eyes, clenched fists, stomping feet, and hoarse cries!"[2] There were, of course, also negative reactions, but his first drama was a sensation, and further productions—as well as imitations—in the 1780s testified to the fact that the work had hit a responsive chord with the German public. Surprisingly, the theme for *Die Räuber* was not very different from a number of other plays of the previous decade, often with violent protagonists who, like Schiller's Karl Moor, wildly expressed their frustrations with society. What, then, made *Die Räuber* so different from the storm and stress of Leisewitz, Klinger, and other dramatists of the 1770s whose work more often than not overwhelmed, rather than entertained audiences? I propose that the answer to this question lies in Schiller's sensitivity to the kind of group dynamics that, given Germany's social and political underdevelopment, was needed to improve the German theatre, and that his key innovation was to give his hero, Karl Moor, *charisma*. While theories of charismatic leadership do not catch up to Schiller until our own century, the principle of social unification through charisma is a neglected tradition of German classical humanism with its origins in Winckelmann's theories of Greek sculpture.

By the second half of the eighteenth century, Germany's centuries-old problem of political disunity had developed into the more subtle one of national identity. Among literary genres, drama suffered most acutely from this state of affairs, and it was drama that was in most need of attention. Certainly every dramatist must, by definition, deal in rituals that celebrate a culture, but the German dramatist had first to come to terms with his country's weak national self-image. He was faced with, above and beyond the usual demands of his craft, the task of creating a German public out of thin air. Given these facts. it is not hard to see why so many dramas of the 1770s failed to inspire the general public. Storm and stress faithfully reflected its public's dissatisfactions with the age and, in figures like Goethe's Götz, Leisewitz's Guido, Klinger's Guelfo, and Wagner's Evchen, tended to depict frustration without pointing the way toward psychological release. But Schiller, more than any other German dramatist before him, was aware that the tensions reflected by storm and stress were rooted in the social and political helplessness of the middle class and, especially, in Germany's lack of a healthy national identity. In his 1784 essay, "Die Schaubühne als moralische Anstalt betrachtet" ("The Theatre as a Moral Institution"), he proposed that a public and its theatre might simultaneously improve each other: "When we have a national theater, he argues, "then we will also have a nation."[3] He is, moreover, aware that Germany's lack of a closely-knit community with a unified and positive self-image was not just an intellectual, but also an emotional, problem.

> "When a thousand burdens press on our soul and threaten to dampen our emotional susceptibilities," he wrote, the stage welcomes us: in this artificial world we can dream the real world away; we are given ourselves again; our sensitivity awakens, healing passions shake our slumbering selves, and our blood is made to flow more vigorously. (8, p. 106)

The right kind of drama, in Schiller's opinion, holds the promise to "give us ourselves" as it liberates us from tensions that have been inhibiting our self-realization.

Contemporary theories of catharsis suggest, in fact, that Schiller's association of self-realization with discharge of tension may have been perfectly accurate. Although there has never been a consensus on what Aristotle meant by *katharsis,* in its most common interpretation—the one made popular by Freud's brother-in-law Bernays—it is a beneficial release of emotion that had formerly been impossible due to an inability to respond to a difficult situation. The specific beneficial effects of emotional discharge are equally controversial, but one twentieth-century school of cathartic therapy has advanced a theory of catharsis with fascinating implications for explaining the attraction of drama like *Die Räuber.* These psychologists—including T. J. Scheff, Percival Symonds, Michael Nichols, and Melvin Zax—maintain that catharsis is the most efficient approach to problems associated with a community's identity. Scheff writes: "The feelings of relief from tension, increased clarity of thought, and heightened fellow-feeling which follow collective catharsis give rise to extremely powerful forces of cohesion and group solidarity"[4]; and Nichols and Zax: "Aristotle's concept of catharsis is not simply a passive intellectual exercise. The shock of emotional arousal helps to rearrange perceptions and so leads to a modification of the audience's self-concept and world-view."[5] Emotional discharge, writes Percival Symonds, cures nothing in and of itself, but the dissolution of tension that it brings about can lead to "a change in the perception of the self" and, subsequently, "greater self-acceptance."[6] People, write Nichols and Zax, need only to be given "permission to experience their feelings" (p. 59) and, given the right conditions, there will follow a release of tension, an unburdening of frustrations, and a chance to take a new look at themselves.

When Schiller speculates on the self-realization that the right kind of theatre can make possible, he is not theorizing in a vacuum; he is, of course, thinking of the function that drama was able to perform in France, where the writer, with a developed and settled society to work with, could be a flatterer of his nation's established ideals. The French theatregoer could feel himself part of an exclusive "ingroup" whose members felt cultivated enough to appreciate and understand things that would leave the uninitiated cold. France woed the possibility of such socially invigorating group dynamics largely to the aristocracy, who had actively nurtured an indigenous French culture. But how different was the situation in eighteenth-century Germany, where the only aristocratic house in a position to unify the country had no interest in native German culture. The typical Prussian aristocrat's self-image and cultural values did not derive from German society and its traditions, but, rather, from his identification with other European nobility. The young Prussian nobleman completed his education by travelling to foreign courts in an attempt to shed as much of his Germanness as possible, then returned to rule a people with whom he was determined not to identify. Ironically, the only unity that the upper classes were in a position to contribute to Germany was the inadvertent one of providing a negative foil for middle-class virtue. Nonetheless, while a drama like Lessing's *Emilia Galotti* (1772) could begin to tap one source of pride by contrasting the unprincipled German aristocrat to the "good" bourgeois, its effect on German national self-consciousness was only a beginning. *Emilia Galotti* was not yet an emotionally liberating ritual that would allow its German public to "clear the air" as it reconsidered its view of itself. Decentralized Germany, without a well-knit social fabric and a corps of flattering writers, had not yet discovered an invigorating ingroup ritual that could make it feel like a nation.

Schiller, Germany's most avid proponent of the notion that art can mold society, triggered *Die Räuber*'s liberating catharsis of self-realization by causing Karl Moor to be perceived as a charismatic leader, a role which, according to modern social psychology, always involves coaxing a particularly depressed collectivity into accepting constructive self-flattery. In the original Greek, *kharisma* refers to the grace, or favor, which a God can bestow on a human,

and in the New Testament it is used to denote the gift of God's grace. But in the eighteenth century, charisma was becoming recognized more for its socializing properties. When, in 1764, Johann Winckelmann praised his favorite Greek sculpture—the so-called Beautiful Style which he ascribes to the Alexandrian Age—he claims that the qualities distinguishing it from earlier sculpture were its "grace" and the impression that it was a "gift of god."[7] The *Apollo Belvedere,* his favorite example of the Beautiful Style, possessed a "more than common soul" that made it "lead us willingly along with it" (5, p. 215). It is clear from Winckelmann's description of his first encounter with the *Apollo Belvedere* that he sees in his favorite sculpture a human stance or pose that can inspire, admonish, and coax spectators to take pride in the ideals it represents while building their sense of dignity: "In the presence of this miracle of art I forget all else, and I myself take a lofty position for the purpose of looking upon it in a worthy manner. My breast seems to enlarge and swell with reverence."[8]

In modern usage, charisma has come to denote a special quality of leadership. Irvine Schiffer writes that a charismatic individual does not "carve out his own public image from ingredients of his own personality"; rather, society projects such an image onto a suitable person.[9] A society searches for the charismatic individual, writes Schiffer, just as it would search for its own sense of self: when we search for the charismatic leader, we are on a "quest for identity." (p. 21) His success provides us with a "short-cut to an identity, a quick solution to the agonizing problems of maturation." (p. 51) While Schiller cannot provide his society with an actual leader, he can create a protagonist to provide it with a form of relief from its own problems of identity—and perhaps even hint at directions his public may someday be able to take in order to build a unified community. So that he may win over his audience, Karl is given qualities that no other raging anti-hero of storm and stress ever possessed: vision, imagination, and "great plans." (II. iii) The robbers, who immediately recognize Karl's charisma, recruit him for his ability to pull them together into an effective group with a positive self-image. By giving convincing expression to their righteous indignation, he makes the actions of misfits poignantly appropriate, makes outsiders feel like insiders, and makes crime feel divinely inspired. "Without Moor," exclaims Roller, "we are body without soul" (I. ii). And Schweizer, who has been given the honor of avenging Karl's father, declares: "Today you have made me proud for the first time" (IV. v). Karl's charisma, which inspires the band despite its criminal violence, infects *Die Räuber*'s audience as well, a group to whom Schiller appeals as to a public reaching out for a better understanding of itself. Karl, after all, is a spirited hero who successfully turns an impeccable but rudely disappointed moral life into a battle cry, who dares to act vigorously on behalf of the vital, if invisible, principles of his religious background. Schiller's audience, on whom history had not bestowed a social and political tradition with which it could proudly identify, was still in possession of a vital moral heritage, and here was just the hero to bring it into relief. Karl leads Schiller's public to live vicariously a role denied to it by a religious tradition that tended to capitulate in the vainglorious affairs of the worldly life in order to be masters of the inner life. Identifying with this robber captain, the audience is flattered into envisioning that it constitutes a special in-group capable of appreciating Karl's point of view. What I am suggesting, then, is that Schiller's first play is a moral fantasy that allowed an otherwise respectable middle-class audience to luxuriate in its capacity to appreciate the acts of a horribly violent man. And in giving the public an opportunity for vicarious criminality, it also let them discharage their frustrations with a society that had—along with other political inequities—let the needs of national identity go unanswered.

Through the magic of its protagonist's charisma, *Die Räuber* offers an audience—or, rather, this special audience whose strengths are not social but religious—a standard around which it can rally, and for which it can be flattered. But a dicussion of Karl Moor's charisma is not complete without mentioning its inauthentic side. We remember that the process that makes this play's spectators feel like a society is analogous to the same process Karl uses to infuse pride into a band of murderers. Irvine Schiffer finds in all followers of charismatic leaders unacknowledged complicity in a scheme that helps the group avert attention from their worst shortcomings. In order better to flatter us for our stengths, in other words, charisma draws attention away from our weaknesses. As a "victory for our jeopardized self-esteem," charisma is therefore also "an uplift from the depression and helplessness that would infiltrate our awareness, expose our limitations, and force us into a recognition of all those failures that we find most difficult to reconcile" (Schiffer 50). For both the robbers and Schiller's first auditors, an inspiring sense of social unity was built on a comfortable self-deception made possible by the "grace" of charismatic flattery. As it succumbed to the pleasurable sensation of a communal life in the theatre, Schiller's spectators let themselves be blinded to the contradiction inherent in accepting a multiple murderer as a hero—and in the belief that their vicarious indulgence in anti-social behavior constituted a viable social foundation.

Still, Schiller's achievement was remarkable. Despite the sharp discontinuity between the communal feeling inspired by Karl's charimsa and the sad realities of German life, *Die Räuber* is, in the last analysis, the work of a master dramatist who knew how to create an appropriate emotional ritual for his audience. After a decade of dramatists whose rebellious heroes had realistically reflected a non-society's own frustrations, here was a writer to provide a release by inviting his public to project on a hero the invigorating flattery of Winckelmann's *Apollo Belvedere*. "Strangers," states one account of *Die Räuber*'s premiere, "fell, sobbing, into each others' arms." (Buchwald, p. 352) The sense of community that he successfully created in the theatre—however brief and by whatever means it had been purchased—was Schiller's gift to a nation searching for itself.

Notes

1. Julius W. Braun, *Schiller und Goethe im Urtheile ihrer Zeitgenossen,* vol. 1 (Leipzig: Schlicke, 1882), p. 23. Translations are my own.

2. Reinhard Buchwald, *Schiller,* vol. 1 (Leipzig: Insel, 1937), p. 352.

3. Friedrich Schiller, *Gesammelte Werke,* vol. 8 (Berlin: Aufbau, 1955), p. 105.

4. T. J. Scheff, *Catharsis in Healing, Ritual and Drama* (Berkeley: University of California Press, 1973), p. 53.

5. Michael P. Nichols and Melvin Zax, *Catharsis in Psychotherapy* (New York: Gardiner Press, 1971), p. 59.

6. Percival Symonds, "A Comprehensive Theory of Psychotherapy." *American Journal of Orthopsychiatry* 24 (1954), pp. 707-08.

7. J. J. Winckelmann, *Johann Winckelmanns sämtliche Werke,* vol. 5, edited by Joseph Eiselein (Osnabrück: Zeller, 1965), p. 221.

8. J. J. Winckelmann, *History of Ancient Art,* vol. 2, translated by G. Henry Lodge (Boston: Osgood, 1880), p. 313.

9. Irvine Schiffer, *Charisma: A Psychoanalytic Look at Mass Society* (Toronto: University of Toronto Press, 1973), p. 19.

WALLENSTEIN

CRITICAL COMMENTARY

Robin Harrison (essay date 1995)

SOURCE: "'Wer die Wahl hat, hat die Qual': Philosophy and Poetry in Schiller's Wallenstein", in *Publications of the English Goethe Society* Vol. 65, 1995, pp. 136-60.

[*In the following essay, Harrison explores the central theme of* Wallenstein, *"the agony of choice between the demands of the senses and those of reason," which he notes is central to Schiller's vision of life.*]

Popular proverbs express in a concise and memorable form a commonplace fact of experience. 'Wer die Wahl hat, hat die Qual' is a fine example. With its alliteration and assonance it pleases the ear, and it describes an experience so widespread that it needs no illustration. But it states a truth which can be applied not just to a wide range of particular situations in life, but also to life as a whole. It is the pain of being simultaneously drawn in opposite directions that Goethe's Faust expresses in the lines:

Zwei Seelen wohnen, ach! in meiner Brust,

Die eine will sich von der andern trennen.

(Faust I, 1112 f.; HA, III, 41)

And it is the agony of choice, seen as the dilemma of human life itself, that is, I wish to suggest, the central theme of Schiller's **Wallenstein.**

But let me begin at the beginning. In his 1994 Bithell Memorial Lecture, Professor T. J. Reed urged on us, most persuasively, the importance of studying the genesis of a work if we are to understand it fully, quoting in support of his thesis Goethe's remark: 'Natur- und Kunstwerke lernt man nicht kennen wenn sie fertig sind; man muß sie im Entstehen aufhaschen, um sie einigermaßen zu begreifen' (letter to Zelter, 4 August 1803; *Briefe,* HA, II, 454). Not surprisingly, he mentioned **Wallenstein** as illustrating the genetic complexity so frequently found in German literature, and it is to this complex genesis that I wish to turn first, in the belief that it can help us to grasp the drama's ultimate significance. For **Wallenstein** is a supreme example of the phenomenon which Professor Reed was describing, a work which 'grows towards coherent meaning and form', one in which, excitingly, 'the writer's mind and skills are stretched by unforeseen demands far beyond the bounds of any prior literary intention'.[1]

The genesis of **Wallenstein** extends over almost an entire decade. On 12 January 1791 Schiller wrote to Körner that he had at last found a subject, a historical one, for a tragedy; but it was only on 20 April 1799 that **Wallensteins Tod** was first performed. It is, however, significant that for over five years Schiller made no progress with his plan, even though he regularly returned to it. Initially it was his work as a historian on the very material which had provided the subject that prevented him from starting work on the play. On the positive side, this allowed him to continue developing his ideas. Thus, something over a year after his first mention of the plan, he raises, in the concluding paragraph of Book IV of his *Geschichte des Dreißigjährigen Kriegs,* the possibility of a much more favourable interpretation of Wallenstein's motives than he has given so far. It may well have been this paragraph that revived his enthusiasm for the drama: 'Ich bin jetzt voll Ungeduld, etwas poetisches vor die Hand zu nehmen, besonders jückt mir die Feder nach dem Wallenstein' (letter to Körner, 25 May 1792; NA, XXVI, 141). But the need to press ahead with the *History,* to which he was at the time devoting six hours a day, left no time for drama. And there was also a deeper problem: theory was starting to get in the way of practice. For the knowledge of the 'rules' which he has acquired has made his creativity self-conscious, so that his imagination has lost its freedom. His hope is that his philosophizing about theory will restore to him a freedom in which theory has become second nature.

Not surprisingly, therefore, when, four months later, the *History* was completed, Schiller shied away from his dramatic project: he is afraid of tackling any large-scale work and therefore doubts whether **Wallenstein** will

receive his immediate attention (letter to Körner, 21 September 1792). And it certaily didn't. He devoted himself instead to his philosophical writings. 1793 was a year of essays and letters, and it was only in January 1794 that he interrupted his studies to resume work on the plan for the drama. Eight weeks later he is in almost over-confident mood as he reports that the plan is slowly maturing and that, once it is ready, the execution will take him only three weeks (letter to Körner, 17 March 1794). But for whatever reason—perhaps the distraction of his more active social life in Stuttgart, where he had moved two days earlier—he made no further progress. There followed a period in which he gave priority to his study of Kant, and when after six months he writes about **Wallenstein** again his confidence has evaporated.

The problem was partly caused by the fact that he was now trying to work on two fronts at once, writing his essay *Über das Naive* at the same time as thinking about the **Wallenstein** plan, with the result that the two different sorts of activity interfered with each other: he increasingly feels that he lacks poetic inspiration, which, perversely, comes to him, if at all, only when he wants to philosophize. In addition, he is discouraged by his previous plays, declaring that a 'Machwerk' such as **Don Carlos** would disgust him now; and, claiming that in poetic matters he has become a completely new man, he sees the way ahead as leading into unfamiliar territory. Small wonder that he hesitates to proceed out of fear of the result being a disaster (letter to Körner, 4 September 1794). Instead, he turned to fulfilling his promise to the Herzog von Augustenburg to recreate from his drafts the letters to the Duke which had been destroyed by fire. The resulting letters, *Über die ästhetische Erziehung des Menschen,* preoccupied him from September 1794 to June 1795. During the second half of 1795 he completed *Über das Naive* and then supplemented it with *Die sentimentalischen Dichter,* before combining the two essays in **Über naive und sentimentalische Dichtung** in January 1796.

Throughout this period **Wallenstein** remained submerged. But an important change was taking place in Schiller: his poetic inspiration was beginning to return. Four days after completing the *Aesthetic Letters,* he wrote his first poem for nearly seven years, 'Poesie des Lebens' (letter to Goethe, 12 June 1795); and once the blockage was breached, a flood of other poems followed, as the pages of the *Musen-Almanach für das Jahr 1796* testify. It was this resurgence of poetic creativity that prepared the way for the resurfacing of **Wallenstein.** The decision to proceed with it, rather than with *Die Malteser,* was taken in a conversation with Goethe on 16 March 1796, a decision announced to Körner five days later (21 March 1796) in a letter which reads like a recantation of the one written eighteen months earlier. There he speaks of apprehension, here of pleasure and confidence, there of the danger of failure, here of taking the risk. For while still admitting that he can make little use of his old manner, he now feels confident enough to attempt the new one.

There can be little doubt that the Schiller who is now actually embarking on **Wallenstein** is a somewhat different Schiller from the one whose pen was itching to get started four years earlier. In the intervening years he had completed the whole series of major philosophical writings for which his hesitation to tackle **Wallenstein** made room. And it is difficult to believe that, once he had clarified his ideas and once his suppressed creativity began to assert itself again, his creative work was not enriched by the views he had developed on art and human nature. Philosophy may have excluded poetry, but there was no reason why poetry should not embrace philosophy.

This is not to claim that Schiller abandoned his interest in the question of the historical Wallenstein's motivation which seems to have first inspired his enthusiasm to get on with the play. It is, rather, to argue that he would not have chosen to proceed with it four years later if he had not felt that the subject had the potential to absorb some of his later, and wider, preoccupations. Indeed, this is just what he suggests in a letter to Wilhelm von Humboldt also written five days after the decision to proceed with **Wallenstein,** days which he spent reviewing the ideas for it which he had written down at various times: 'Groß war freilich dieser Fund nicht, aber auch nicht ganz unwichtig, und ich finde doch, daß schon dieses, was ich bereits darüber gedacht habe, die Keime zu einem höhern und ächtern dramatischen Interesse enthält, als ich je einem Stück habe geben können' (21 March 1796; NA, xxviii, 203). He has no intention of discarding his earlier ideas, but they hardly seem sufficient in themselves; their value lies primarily in their containing the seeds out of which a play of greater interest and significance could grow. His task is: 'eine so dürre Staatsaction in eine menschliche Handlung umzuschaffen' (letter to Körner, 10 July 1797; NA, xxix, 99).

The suggestion that Schiller's philosophical writings played a part in his thinking about **Wallenstein** finds corroboration in the same letter to Humboldt, where he writes not just that he has received remarkable confirmation of some of the ideas on realism and idealism contained in his recent essay *Über naive und sentimentalische Dichtung,* but even that he will be happy to be guided by these ideas in his poetic composition. He sees the character of Wallenstein as incorporating in the highest degree what he said about realism in the essay: 'Er hat nichts Edles, er erscheint in keinem einzelnen LebensAkt groß, er hat wenig Würde und dergleichen.' Moreover, just as in the essay he sees the morality of the realist's character as residing not in any single action, but rather in the sum of his whole life, so that to do him justice one must judge him by his life as a whole, so in the letter he asserts: 'Wallenstein ist ein Charakter, der—als ächt realistisch—nur im Ganzen aber nie im Einzelnen interessieren kann' (NA, xxviii, 204).

The essay thus contributes to the breadth of Schiller's handling of his material: 'Vordem legte ich das ganze Gewicht in die Mehrheit des Einzelnen; jetzt wird alles auf die Totalität berechnet.' At the same time, it clarified for him the way he must portray Wallenstein himself, for, responding to Wallenstein's realism, he sets out to exchange the 'schöne Idealität' with which he depicted Posa and Carlos for 'die bloße Wahrheit' (NA, xxviii, 203 f.). His hope is by purely realistic means to create in Wallenstein a dramatically great character who incorporates a genuine life principle. In doing so he is exchanging the 'sentimental' for the 'naiv' mode and thus, as he himself admits, entering Goethe's territory. But he is confident that, as a result of his association with Goethe as well as his study of classical literature and his own greater maturity, he has now acquired a much greater degree of realism. He even believes that Goethe himself will be pleased with him, for he writes that he is succeeding in remaining detached from his material and objective in its presentation, treating Wallenstein as well as most of the supporting figures 'mit der reinen Liebe des Künstlers' (28 November 1796; NA, xxix, 15).

But though he was happy about the spirit in which he was working, he was having considerable problems with the dramatic action. The content has virtually nothing to offer, he complains. Driven by the base motives of revenge and ambition, Wallenstein does not even achieve the poetic greatness which the success of his scheming would bestow; and it is he, rather than fate, that bears the main responsibility for his misfortune. Moreover, it seems impossible to contain the material within the framework of a tragedy: the political events are too diffuse, and the army, on which Wallenstein's power rests, too vast. Hence, Schiller concludes, he can create a satisfactory tragedy only by finding a successful form and achieving an artistic treatment of the action (letters to Goethe and Körner, 28 November 1796).

Two months later these difficulties have plunged him into a deep crisis, and whereas he had had no hesitation in acknowledging his debt to Goethe for his new realistic approach in general, he is now positively glad that Goethe is not there, since he knows that the solutions to these specific artistic problems must be entirely his own (letters to Goethe, 24 January and 7 February 1797). A further two months on, however, he is beginning to see the way forward more clearly: lateral thinking has come to the rescue, for he is now approaching the drama in the light of a totally new view of the nature of the poetic, modelled on Greek tragedy.

As he drafts a detailed scenario of his whole play to obtain a visual overview of the main elements and the links between them, and at the same time considers the Greeks' treatment of tragedy, he concludes that the essence of art lies in the invention of a *poetic* plot (letter to Goethe, 4 April 1797, my italics). The modern poet, he argues, is in his attempt to imitate reality too concerned with the fortuitous and the secondary, which have no significance; what he aspires to is, by contrast, a plot concentrating on the essence of the situation. Three days later he finds support for this view in the way in which, in *Julius Caesar,*

Shakespeare boldly selects a few figures to represent the Roman crowd (letter to Goethe, 7 April 1797). Applying the same technique to solve the artistic problem posed by Wallenstein's army, he was able, two months after this letter (18 June 1797), to send Körner the first version of *Wallensteins Lager.* The play was at last truly under way, even if Schiller now had to interrupt work on it for nearly three months to devote himself to preparing the next number of the *Musenalmanach,* the famous 'Balladenalmanach'. But the break seems to have done him good, for on returning to the drama he expresses his confidence that through its poetic organization the material has been transformed into a tragic action: past events converge in, and later ones issue from, the 'pregnant moment', and the tragic impression is heightened by the fact that Wallenstein's downfall is now caused less by his own actions than by the momentum of events which he cannot control (letter to Goethe, 2 October 1797).

In line with his move away from the imitation of reality and the new emphasis on the poetic character of the plot, Schiller now also modified the 'naiv' manner which he had adopted in his eagerness to avoid the subjective idealism of his earlier work. In the previous year he had already admitted to a certain dryness of style, though at that stage he preferred to be in danger of the extreme of sobriety rather than that of intoxication (letter to Körner, 28 November 1796). He now feels that, in his anxiety to remain as close as possible to his subject, he has indeed gone too far in that direction and that particularly such a subject, in itself somewhat dry, needs poetic liberality. He thus aspires to a truly pure *poetic* atmosphere which avoids the extremes of the prosaic and the rhetorical (letter to Goethe, 2 October 1797, Schiller's italics). And it was but the logical consequence of this shift from a prosaic to a poetic treatment that, one month later, he began to recast the prose of *Wallenstein* in verse. He can hardly understand how he ever wanted it otherwise, he wrote to Körner: 'es ist unmöglich ein Gedicht in Prosa zu schreiben' (20 November 1797; NA, xxix, 158).

But Schiller's new view of art affected not just the selection and organization of his material, but also his view of its significance, which he now sees as symbolic. When, writing to Goethe, he rejects the modern poet's concern to reproduce reality, he justifies this rejection by asserting that such an approach, in attempting to imitate a real case, is in danger of missing the deeper, absolute truth which constitutes the poetic. This truth does not, however, exist independently of the real case, as he illustrates from his reading of Sophocles. How completely is Deianira, in the *Trachiniae,* the wife of Heracles, he exclaims, how individual, 'und doch wie tief menschlich, wie ewig wahr und allgemein'! Similarly, in the *Philoctetes* everything which could be is taken from the particular situation, 'und bey dieser Eigenthümlichkeit des Falles ruht doch alles wieder auf dem ewigen Grund der menschlichen Natur' (4 April 1797; NA, xxix, 56). Thus the particular, without losing any of its particularity, contains within it the general.

Truth is, for Schiller, in this context not the objective view of the 'naiv' poet but the universal truth about human nature.

The relevance of these ideas to *Wallenstein* is confirmed by the letter in which, three days later (7 April 1797), Schiller wrote to Körner of the important consequences for his play of the deeper insight into the nature of art which he has gained from his reading of Shakespeare and Sophocles. This has not shaken the foundations of his drama, which he believes to be genuine and solid, but he realizes that he must make some revisions to his original view of it. The most difficult task will still be the poetic execution of such a difficult plan. On the other hand, he remains grateful for the historical nature of his material. Indeed, he believes that it would be best for him always to choose historical material, since in balancing the particular and the general, the real and the ideal, he is better able to idealize the real than vice versa, while the resistant specificity of the material curbs his imagination (letter to Goethe, 5 January 1798).

The change from prose to verse was the natural result of Schiller's poetic treatment of his material; its effect was to enhance the poetic character of the drama, not only by demanding a more poetic treatment of some motifs, but also by reinforcing its symbolic nature. For he feels that the uniformity with which the verse treats all characters and situations, despite their differences, compels both poet and reader to look for universal human truth, 'etwas Allgemeines, rein menschliches' (letter to Goethe, 24 November 1797; NA, xxix, 160). He also comes to regard the expansion resulting from the leisureliness of the verse as entirely appropriate to poetic drama (letter to Goethe, 1 December 1797). For he not only sees a diffuseness in the expression of opinions in Greek tragedy as pointing to a higher poetic law which demands, in this very respect, a departure from reality; he also sees this diffuseness as justified by his view 'daß alle poetische Personen symbolische Wesen sind, daß sie, als poetische Gestalten, immer das allgemeine der Menschheit darzustellen und auszusprechen haben' (letter to Goethe, 24 August 1798; NA, xxix, 266).

As Schiller increasingly gave weight to the symbolic aspect of his drama, he became ever more concerned to emphasize the gap between art and reality. When he originally saw the solution to his crisis as lying in the invention of a poetic plot, he wrote of the danger of coming too close to reality; now he sees it as the poet's duty not only positively to distance himself from reality in an open and honest way, but also to draw attention to the fact that he is doing so. The link with the concluding lines of the Prologue, written to introduce the performance, less than seven weeks later, of *Wallensteins Lager,* is unmistakable: the audience is to thank the Muse for resorting to rhyme, for thereby she 'plays' the sombre picture of truth over into the serene realm of art and, rather than deceitfully substituting its semblance for truth, herself honestly destroys the illusion she creates. But these lines not only seem to grow out of Schiller's letter; they echo, often word for word, his characterization of 'Schein' in the *Aesthetic Letters*—semblance, which, as the essence of art, is to be distinguished from, and not substituted for, truth; which is aesthetic only inasmuch as it is honest, i.e. expressly renounces all claim to reality; and enjoyment of which opens the way to the aesthetic freedom conferred by the play-drive. Indeed, in the final line of the Prologue Schiller encapsulates the whole aesthetic credo of the *Letters*: 'Ernst ist das Leben, heiter ist die Kunst'.[2] *Wallenstein* has clearly become associated in Schiller's mind with the ideas in the most important of his philosophical essays.

Schiller's conception of *Wallenstein* has undergone a remarkable metamorphosis. The 'Staatsaction' has grown into a poetic drama—poetic in its rejection of the close imitation of reality, in the organization of its material, and finally in its transformation into verse; and this poetic drama has in turn taken on symbolic significance as the truth portrayed has been widened beyond that of the particular situation to embrace a universal truth about human nature. During this process Schiller was influenced by the example of Goethe and by his reading of Greek tragedy, but he also drew on the two major philosophical works he wrote in the eighteen months prior to his final decision to proceed with *Wallenstein.* He himself writes expressly of the significance for the drama of the ideas he had expressed on the character of the realist in *Über naive und sentimentalische Dichtung;* but it is also apparent that he came to see the play's rejection of realism in terms of the view of art which he had developed in the *Aesthetic Letters.*

However poetic and symbolic *Wallenstein* may grow to be, it still remains a powerful historical drama in which, developing the view he sketched at the end of Book IV of the *History*, Schiller offers an alternative interpretation of Wallenstein's actions to that provided by historians biased in favour of the Catholic cause. Admittedly, the picture he paints there leaves the way open for an even more favourable interpretation than that presented in the drama, for he argues that the treasonable intentions and the designs on the Bohemian throne imputed to Wallenstein do not have any basis in proven fact but are merely plausible suppositions, and in view of the lack of any documentary evidence for his motives suggests that Wallenstein did nothing which could not have had an innocent origin, in particular his earnest desire for peace. In the play, by contrast, he does present Wallenstein as actually contemplating treason, but his motives, even if somewhat ambiguous, are basically honourable. He does, it is true, aim at the Bohemian throne, driven as he is by the ambition which has consumed him since his dismissal at Regensburg and which manifests itself least attractively in his determination that Thekla shall not throw herself away on Max but marry one of Europe's monarchs. But this throne will only be his if he succeeds in bringing about the peace which Europe so desperately needs after fifteen years of war, and, as even Octavio admits, it is primarily to force the Emperor to accept a peace which Vienna does not want that Wallenstein is negotiating with the enemy.

At the same time, these negotiations are prompted by Wallenstein's need to protect himself against an Emperor who, fearing his power and no longer trusting him, is trying first to weaken and then to replace him. And, in both the *History* and the drama, it is ultimately this need that actually drives him to treason, so that the court itself is seen as being partly responsible. 'So fiel Wallenstein, nicht weil er Rebell war, sondern er rebellirte, weil er fiel', as the *History* puts it (NA, XVIII, 329). 'O! sie zwingen mich, sie stoßen / Gewaltsam, wider meinen Willen, mich hinein', Wallenstein himself complains when told that there is talk in Vienna of a second dismissal (*Picc.*, II. 2, 701 f.). This view is shared by Max, who protests to his father:

> Ihr werdet ihn durch eure Staatskunst noch
>
> Zu einem Schritte treiben—Ja, ihr könntet ihn,
>
> Weil ihr ihn schuldig *wollt,* noch schuldig *machen.*
>
> (***Picc.,*** v. 3, 2633 ff.)

And this is indeed what happens. For the court pounces on the evidence of Wallenstein's negotiations with the enemy which is provided by the capture of Sesin, and Wallenstein, knowing that, even though he has not actually committed himself, he is now a traitor in their eyes, accepts that he has no choice but to break with the Emperor and ally himself with the Swedes.

But, as we have seen, in the process of developing his ideas, Schiller came to give Wallenstein a wider significance, seeing him not just as a particular historical figure but also as representing a general human type, the realist. Certainly, in the completed drama he corresponds to this type to the extent that he has worldly aims. On the other hand, there are reasons for suggesting that this view of him represents no more than a further stage in the growth of the play. For example, Schiller's claim, in the letter to Humboldt, that Wallenstein embodies to the highest degree the notion of realism developed in his essay because, among other characteristics, he shows little dignity, is hardly borne out by the completed work, for once he has taken the fateful decision to rebel, he increasingly lives up to the resolve: 'Wir handeln, wie wir müssen. / So laß uns das Notwendige mit Würde, / Mit festem Schritte tun' (*Ws Tod,* II. 2, 833 ff.). Indeed, the dignity which he preserves in misfortune helps to create the sense of Wallenstein's greatness which makes his murder so tragic.

A more important reason for suggesting that Schiller's view of Wallenstein as a realist represents only a stage in the growth of the drama is the fact that it does not take us to the heart of the completed work. For this centres, not on our judgement of Wallenstein as either a historical figure or a particular type, but on the agony caused him as a human being by the need for choice as he finds himself compelled to break with the Emperor if he is not to surrender his power and abandon his ambition—'die Qual der Wahl'. 'Die Wahl ist's, was ihm schwer wird', Illo tells Terzky (*Picc.,* III.I, 1369); and it is the agony which the choice caused him that Wallenstein recalls in his final words:

Ich denke einen langen Schlaf zu tun,

Denn dieser letzten Tage Qual war groß.

(*Ws Tod,* v. 5, 3677 f.)

Wallenstein has put himself in a position to make a move: his armies are assembled at Pilsen, and he has brought his wife and daughter there to prevent their being used as hostages. To make sure of the support of his generals he instructs Illo to get them, by whatever means, to sign a pledge of unconditional loyalty to him. He, by contrast, carefully avoids committing himself, for he puts nothing in writing in his negotiations with the enemy. And despite these preparations he firmly resists Illo's eloquent plea to him to take the decision to act before this uniquely favourable moment passes. With the news of the capture of Sesin, however, the situation changes totally, though Wallenstein continues to postpone his final choice for as long as he can: he refuses to bow to pressure from Wrangel, tells Terzky and Illo that he shrinks from the curse which treachery, as the ultimate crime, will bring, and finally comes to his reluctant decision only when persuaded by Gräfin Terzky that his relationship with the Emperor is based not on duty and justice but on power and opportunity.

What Wallenstein finds so difficult to grasp is that because he considered the deed he now seems compelled to do it.

Wie? Sollt ichs nun im Ernst erfüllen müssen,

Weil ich zu frei gescherzt mit dem Gedanken?

he asks Illo, provoking the response:

Wenns nur dein Spiel gewesen, glaube mir,

Du wirsts in schwerem Ernste büßen müssen.

(*Ws Tod,* I. 3, 112 ff.)

And then, reflecting on his situation in the subsequent great monologue, 'die Achse des Stücks', as Goethe called it ('Die Piccolomini'; JA, xxxvi, 180), he summarizes his attitude in four lines, the last two of which acquire special significance from the fact that they form the exact centre of the first and most important section of the speech:

Beim großen Gott des Himmels! Es war nicht

Mein Ernst, beschloßne Sache war es nie.

In dem Gedanken bloß gefiel ich mir;

Die Freiheit reizte mich und das Vermögen.

(*Ws Tod,* I. 4, 146 ff.)

Wallenstein has good reasons for being so reluctant to act, as he explains in the rest of the monologue. He knows that, once the thought has become deed, it will belong to powers no one can control; moreover, it will be no battle of equals, for he will be challenging an authority reinforced by the hallowing power of tradition. Hence the need to choose, with the help of the planets, the right moment to act—though even now, when the planets suggest that it

has arrived, he still hesitates. But Wallenstein's hesitation comes not simply from such fears; it also comes from his reluctance to abandon a position which he actually enjoys. It is not just, as he tells Terzky, that he takes a vindictive pleasure in his power to harm the Emperor, should he wish to do so (*Picc.,* II. 5, 866 ff.); as the key lines of his monologue reveal, he delights in the sense of freedom and potential conferred by his having the capacity to turn against the Emperor without his being compelled to do so.

A clue to the deeper significance of this delight is provided by the recurring contrast in the passages I have quoted between 'Ernst' and 'Spiel' (or 'Scherz'). The question, in terms of the plot, is whether Wallenstein has the serious intention of linking up with the enemy or is merely playing with the idea. But the contrast is also central to the *Aesthetic Letters:* 'Mit dem Angenehmen, mit dem Guten, mit dem Vollkommenen ist es dem Menschen *nur* ernst, aber mit der Schönheit spielt er' (Letter 15; NA, xx, 358). We have already seen that, with the contrast in the Prologue between life as 'ernst' and art as 'Spiel', Schiller links *Wallensteins Lager*—and by implication the drama as a whole—with the aesthetic theory of the *Letters,* and the recurrence of this contrast within the drama itself provides strong evidence for the notion that in the action he is drawing on the analysis of human nature on which that aesthetic theory is based.

Seen in this light, the symbolic nature of Wallenstein's situation becomes clear: the choice confronting him is the ultimate choice between the demands of reason and those of the senses, as this is presented in the *Aesthetic Letters.* In so far as he is bound by his duty to the Emperor, he is, as a rational being, subject to the constraint of the form-drive, with its universally valid moral principles; in so far as he is driven by his personal ambition and the need to safeguard his position, he is, as a sensuous being, subject to the constraint of the sense-drive, i.e. his own individual desires and his attachment to life itself.

However, being equally strong, these two demands hold each other in balance, so that Wallenstein has a sense of not being coerced by either of them, but rather of having his options completely open. His situation is reminiscent of the condition of play as this is depicted in the *Aesthetic Letters:* when sense-drive and form-drive, each wholly 'earnest' in its demands, exercise equal constraint on the psyche, the two constraints cancel each other out and give way to the freedom of the play-drive (Letter 15; NA, xx, 355 ff.). The same pattern of thought recurs in the next, and for Schiller most important, section of the *Letters,* in the notion of the aesthetic condition—aesthetic in the sense that it involves not just the senses, intellect or will, but the totality of our powers. This comes about when one determination is balanced by another, the result being a middle disposition in which the psyche is subject to neither physical nor moral constraint and yet is active in both spheres. Combining an absence of determination with a state of unlimited determinability, the aesthetic condition confers total freedom: the individual is not only free from all constraint; because he has had restored to him his total capacity ('das ganze Vermögen') he has the freedom to make of himself what he will (Letters 20-21; NA, xx, 373 ff.).³

Both play and the aesthetic condition are seen in the *Letters* as ideal states since they represent the wholeness of perfect humanity. Play, in the strict sense, is the expression of the complete humanity to which we can only aspire: 'Der Mensch . . . *ist nur da ganz Mensch, wo er spielt*' (Letter 15; NA, xx, 359); but Schiller goes on to associate the play-drive with aesthetic freedom and to describe the capacity granted to us in the aesthetic condition as the highest of all bounties, as the gift of humanity itself. And the experience of such humanity is not as exceptional as it might seem, for, he argues, although we lose it every time we enter into a determinate condition, it must be restored to us as we pass from one condition into an opposite one. Some people, because of the speed with which they make this transition—from sensation to thought, for example— are hardly, if at all, aware of the aesthetic mode through which they necessarily pass. Others, by contrast, find enjoyment more in the feeling of *total capacity* ('das Gefühl *des ganzen Vermögens*') than in any *single* action (Schiller's italics). Such people, Schiller comments, are destined for wholeness and great roles (Letter 21; NA, xx, 378).⁴

We can now understand the meaning of the association of Wallenstein with 'Spiel' in contrast with 'Ernst' and his declaration, in that key line of his monologue, 'Die Freiheit reizte mich und das Vermögen'.⁵ Delighting in his sense of freedom and capacity, he seems to be one of those who enjoy the wholeness conferred by the aesthetic mode and thus to embody a Schillerian ideal. On the other hand, this impression is undermined by the fact that, seen without its philosophical overtones, Wallenstein's 'Spiel' is presented in a negative light. For he does not just play with the idea of joining the enemy; he also plays with people.

In his concern to avoid committing himself he certainly plays with the Swedes, so that Graf Thurn concludes that he is not in earnest (*Picc.*, II. 5, 819) and Wrangel fears that his offer could turn out to be 'nur falsches Spiel' (*Ws Tod,* I. 5, 339). He also plays with his own generals, as Terzky complains when he is reproved by Wallenstein for suggesting he knows his commander's intentions: 'So hast du stets dein Spiel mit uns getrieben!' (*Picc.*, II. 5, 871). But Wallenstein's 'Spiel' involves not just dissemblance but also hypocritical exploitation designed to strengthen his position. He was always a great calculator, Buttler tells Gordon, moving people like pieces in a board game to suit his purpose:

> Nicht Anstand nahm er, andrer Ehr und Würde
>
> Und guten Ruf zu würfeln und zu spielen.
>
> > (*Ws Tod*, IV. 8, 2857 f.)

Buttler is in a position to know, having learned from Octavio how Wallenstein, in order to alienate him from the

Emperor, advised against granting the petition for the title of Graf which he had himself encouraged Buttler to submit: 'Man hat mit Euch ein schändlich Spiel getrieben' (*Ws Tod,* II. 6, 1139). And in the action of the play itself Wallenstein is, as the Gräfin recognizes, indulging in a similar 'Spiel' in using Thekla to bind Max to him (*Picc.*, III. 2, 1398).⁶

By showing the effect which Wallenstein's 'Spiel' has on others, Schiller suggests that there is a flaw in his attempt to preserve the sense of wholeness which comes from his feeling of total capacity. The possibility of such a flaw is acknowledged in the *Aesthetic Letters,* where Schiller includes a proviso in his suggestion that those who enjoy this feeling are destined for wholeness and great roles: they must combine this capacity with a sense of reality. This is what Wallenstein fails to do, for he does not realize that the aesthetic condition must be seen as a preparation for action, not as a substitute for it. Every other condition, according to Schiller, arises out of a previous one and is terminated by a subsequent one; the aesthetic condition, by contrast, is a whole in itself: 'Hier allein fühlen wir uns wie aus der Zeit gerissen' (Letter 22; NA, xx, 379).⁷ To seek to prolong the aesthetic condition is, therefore, to ignore the reality of time, and this is precisely what Wallenstein does when, claiming to be waiting for 'die rechte Sternenstunde', he declares, 'Die Zeit ist noch nicht da' (*Picc.*, II. 6, 994, 958).⁸ He should, rather, have heeded Illo's warning:

> Das Heer ist dein; jetzt für den Augenblick
>
> Ists dein; doch zittre vor der langsamen,
>
> Der stillen Macht der Zeit.
>
> > (*Ws Tod*, I. 3, 82 ff.)

For Illo's prediction is fulfilled: given time, Wallenstein's enemies secretly undermine his reputation and cunningly lure away his supporters, one by one.⁹

Wallenstein is thus not just a historical figure. Nor is he just a realist—far from it, for in Schiller's typology in *Über naive und sentimentalische Dichtung,* the realist sees man 'niemals in seinem reinen Vermögen, immer nur in einem bestimmten, und eben darum begrenzten Wirken' (NA, xx, 499). He is, above all, a symbolic figure who believes that he can with impunity delight in the sense of wholeness which comes from constantly postponing choice. But to do so is to disregard the limitations of the human condition, the fact that in a temporal world we cannot simultaneously follow two mutually exclusive courses of action, but must choose between them. As the opening of 'Das Ideal und das Leben' makes clear, only the gods, existing outside time, enjoy the freedom of complete wholeness; man, living within time, cannot ultimately avoid the choice between the demands of the senses and those of morality, however anxious he may be about the outcome:

> Zwischen Sinnenglück und Seelenfrieden

Bleibt dem Menschen nur die bange Wahl.

(NA, II. 1, 396)

In emphasizing the agony of his choice the play does indeed, as the Prologue announces, portray, in Wallenstein, 'den Menschen in des Lebens Drang' (108). But once it becomes clear to him that the court is irrevocably intent on his destruction, all his doubts are dispelled. It may seem that in the actual choice he then makes—not 'Seelenfrieden', the path of duty, but 'Sinnenglück', at best the fulfilment of his ambitions, at worst simply survival—he is opting for the baser alternative. But that is not the point; in making any choice he is accepting his human limitations.[10] As a result, all his old greatness is revived and, healed of his 'Zweifelsqualen', he confidently accepts the necessity now imposed on him:

Notwendigkeit ist da, der Zweifel flieht,

Jetzt fecht ich für mein Haupt und für mein Leben.

(**Ws Tod**, III. 10, 1741, 1747 f.)

Max, being a creation of Schiller's imagination (the historical Octavio had no son), has, strictly speaking, no part in the actual historical drama. He was introduced by Schiller, partly perhaps to give himself a figure for whom he could feel affection as a relief from his purely objective portrayal of Wallenstein, but more importantly to add a new dimension to the drama. For the love Max shares with Thekla, characterized by 'ihr ruhiges Bestehen auf sich und ihre Freiheit von allen Zwecken', contrasts with the rest of the action, 'welche ein unruhiges planvolles Streben nach einem Zwecke ist' (letter to Goethe, 12 December 1797; NA, XXIX, 166); it thus completes a certain human circle, making the play a small universe (letter to Körner, 8 January 1798).

This contrast is echoed in the drama itself when Thekla warns Max, 'Trau niemand hier als mir. Ich sah es gleich, / Sie haben einen Zweck' (*Picc.,* III. 5, 1685 f.) and tells him that they must rely on their hearts. It is clearly reminiscent of Schiller's contrast between idealist and realist in *Über naive und sentimentalische Dichtung,* according to which the former's actions are guided by absolutes, the latter's by 'äußre Ursachen' and 'äußre Zwecke' (NA, XX, 494). But however great the difference in spirit between the poetically most important part of the drama, as Schiller described the love strand, and the rest of the 'Staatsaction' (letter to Goethe, 9 November 1798), its function is not simply to provide a different moral standard by which to judge Wallenstein's actions. Indeed, the essence of Max's situation is not so much that he idealistically responds to the moral imperative as that he is destroyed by the agonizing choice with which he is presented. He may be a contrast figure to Wallenstein, but he also shares the same human dilemma; the difference between them is that, whereas Wallenstein ultimately accepts the inevitability of choice, Max is incapable of doing so.

Hitherto in his life Max has been spared all inner conflict and, ruled entirely by the dictates of his heart, has been able to follow both the emotions which attach him to Wallenstein and the instinctive moral sense which binds him to the Emperor. However, Wallenstein's confirmation of his treasonable plans marks the end of the harmony Max has enjoyed, as Wallenstein himself makes clear in words which suggest the end of that unity between form-drive and sense-drive which constitutes the play-drive, as the two drives separate and oppose each other:

Sanft wiegte dich bis heute dein Geschick,

Du konntest spielend deine Pflichten üben,

Jedwedem schönen Trieb Genüge tun,

Mit ungeteiltem Herzen immer handeln.

So kanns nicht ferner bleiben. Feindlich scheiden

Die Wege sich. Mit Pflichten streiten Pflichten.

Du mußt Partei ergreifen in dem Krieg,

Der zwischen deinem Freund und deinem Kaiser

Sich jetzt entzündet.

(**Ws Tod**, II. 2, 719 ff.)

Max can only lament his loss of wholeness as he feels torn apart by the equally strong demands of senses and soul, affection and duty:

O! welchen Riß erregst du mir im Herzen!

· · · · ·

Die Sinne sind in deinen Banden noch,

Hat gleich die Seele blutend sich befreit!

(**Ws Tod**, II. 2, 736 ff.)

Nevertheless, it initially seems that Max will follow the call of duty, despite the pain it costs him; he tells Octavio that he only needs to take his leave of Thekla before leading the Pappenheimer out of Pilsen, dying if necessary in the attempt; and assuring Thekla that he *must* leave her, he begs her to acknowledge that he has no choice. But when Wallenstein implores him as 'das Kind des Hauses' not to leave, Max has to struggle to stick to his resolve: 'in *heftigem Kampf* O Gott! Wie kann ich anders? Muß ich nicht? / Mein Eid—die Pflicht—' (**Ws Tod,** III. 18, 2160, 2176 f.). And his resolve is further undermined as Wallenstein claims that by the law of nature Max is his:

Auf *mich* bist du gepflanzt, ich bin dein Kaiser,

Mir angehören, mir gehorchen, *das*

Ist deine Ehre, dein Naturgesetz.

(**Ws Tod**, III. 18, 2183 ff.)

Thus, anticipating Faust's words, Max confesses to Thekla that, although he came convinced of the right action, he now no longer knows:

es erheben

Zwei Stimmen streitend sich in meiner Brust,

In mir ist Nacht, ich weiß das Rechte nicht zu wählen.

(*Ws Tod*, III. 21, 2279 ff.)

In his agony Max turns to Thekla for her decision. He is now ready to stay with Wallenstein if she can then still love him, but he does not question her verdict: 'Folge deinem ersten / Gefühl. . . . Geh und erfülle deine Pflicht' (*Ws Tod*, III. 21, 2338 ff.). However, he only half does her bidding. He leaves Wallenstein and thus fulfils his duty to the extent that he is not disloyal to the Emperor; but he does not go so far as to transfer his allegiance. For in leading the Pappenheimer in the attack on the Swedish camp he is not so much courageously pursuing victory over the Emperor's enemy as despairingly seeking his own death. If military considerations had been uppermost in his mind, he would not have left the infantry so far behind as he led the cavalry charge of the Pappenheimer, with the result that, unsupported, they became trapped between the Swedish cavalry and pikemen, and in this hopeless situation he would hardly have rejected the summons to honourable surrender. As it is, his call to them to attempt to break out is suicidal, and it is appropriate that he dies, not at the hands of the enemy, but beneath the hooves of his own horses—'man sagt, er wollte sterben' (*Ws Tod,* IV. 10, 3072).

Deprived of the wholeness which he had enjoyed, Max is totally disorientated in the world of conflicting demands which he now inhabits, for he can no longer rely on his heart. When first confronted with the news of Wallenstein's treasonable plans he refused to believe his father: 'Dein Urteil kann sich irren, nicht mein Herz' (*Picc.*, v. 1, 2547). Now he is forced to admit, 'Zu viel vertraut ich auf das eigne Herz' (*Ws Tod*, III. 21, 2283), for he is unable to choose between the two courses of action demanded with equal force by his heart, since to give priority to either his love of Wallenstein or his duty to the Emperor would do violence to an equally important part of his being.

Such a choice between the demands of the senses and those of reason is the ultimate dilemma of human life, so that the only alternative is death. Max's death thus symbolizes the inevitable demise of wholeness which is man's fate, and it is this loss that is the subject of the final lines of Thekla's lament:

—Da kommt das Schicksal—Roh und kalt

Faßt es des Freundes zärtliche Gestalt

Und wirft ihn unter den Hufschlag seiner Pferde—

—Das ist das Los des Schönen auf der Erde!

(*Ws Tod*, IV. 12, 3177 ff.)

It is the tragedy of life that the unity of feeling and reason, which is the essence of complete humanity and is symbolized by the union of life and form in beauty, ineluctably gives way to the potentially agonizing choice between their demands.

The figure of Octavio is based on the historical general who, blindly trusted by Wallenstein, intrigued against him;

and in the drama it is he who exploiting such trust, plays the leading part in bringing about Wallenstein's downfall. But what Schiller focuses on is the choice which this role involves. Whereas Max seeks to preserve the primal purity which precedes the need to choose, Octavio knows that this is not possible:

Mein bester Sohn! Es ist nicht immer möglich,

Im Leben sich so kinderrein zu halten,

Wie's uns die Stimme lehrt im Innersten.

(*Picc.*, v. 1, 2447 ff.)

And he acts accordingly, for although he admits that it would be better if one could always follow one's heart (for him merely the seat of the emotions), he disregards its voice as, without any misgiving, he sacrifices his friend in order to fulfil his duty to the Emperor.

The choice Octavio has been presented with is the same as that facing Max, even if in his case the demands of feeling do not seem as powerful as those of duty, for the simple reason that he has already rejected them. But the repulsion he now feels for Wallenstein should not be allowed to obscure the warmth of their relationship in the past. They had always been friends and comrades-in-arms, as Octavio himself admits; for thirty years, according to Wallenstein, they had shared camp-bed, drink and food. And Octavio's former affection for Wallenstein is evident from the concern he showed as, in response to his dream, he asked his 'Bruder' not to ride into battle on his usual horse, but to take the one he would provide: 'Tus mir zu Lieb' (*Ws Tod*, II. 3, 938).

Octavio's interpretation of his duty leads him not simply to abandon Wallenstein for the Emperor, but to deceive his friend. He may try to exonerate himself by arguing that he has not hypocritically sought Wallenstein's confidence, but merely hidden his own true attitude. However, we can only endorse Wallenstein's own condemnation of Octavio's exploitation of the childlike trust he had placed in him ever since fate, as he believed, revealed him to be the most loyal of his followers: 'Das war kein Heldenstück, Octavio!' (*Ws Tod,* III. 9, 1681). Certainly, Max, so sensitive to the claims of both friendship and duty, cannot excuse his father's deceit.

Schiller still defended Octavio as 'ein ziemlich rechtlicher Mann, nach dem Weltbegriff': 'Die Schändlichkeit, die er begeht, sehen wir auf jedem Welttheater von Personen wiederholt, die, so wie er, von Recht und Pflicht strenge Begriffe haben. Er wählt zwar ein schlechtes Mittel, aber er verfolgt einen guten Zweck' (letter to Böttiger, 1 March 1799; NA, xxx, 33). Yet while drawing attention to the moral rightness of Octavio's conduct, Schiller also suggests the narrowness of such a code, and it is here that his fault lies. Of the three major characters, he is the only one who does not suffer from 'die Qual der Wahl'. If, therefore, in opting so painlessly for the path of duty, he evades the central dilemma of human life, he also reveals the loss involved in surrendering so unreservedly to the demands of morality. His choice makes him, in every sense, a poorer human being, for he not only betrays his friend, he also renounces any aspiration to the wholeness of complete humanity.

In the final two Acts of the drama Wallenstein, confident that a new flood will succeed the ebb in his fortunes, has shed all indecision. But the theme of the agony of choice persists in a lower key in the figure of Gordon—appropriately enough, since it was only with reluctance that the historical Gordon became involved in Wallenstein's death.

Gordon is totally torn between head and heart. He cannot help agreeing with Buttler that, if Wallenstein has betrayed the Emperor, he cannot be saved, indeed that he must die in order to prevent his being joined by the Swedes. But he resents being chosen by fate as the instrument of Wallenstein's downfall, for they had been pages together, and it was Wallenstein who gave him the command of Eger.

> O Gott! Was sein muß, seh ich klar wie Ihr,
>
> Doch anders schlägt das Herz in meiner Brust,

he tells Buttler (*Ws Tod,* IV. 6, 2738 f.). And recalling Wallenstein's greatness, he begs him: 'O wenn das Herz euch warnt, folgt seinem Triebe!' (*Ws Tod,* IV. 8, 2882). He even considers attempting to rescue Wallenstein, but then, recalling his oath to the Emperor, shrinks from responsibility for the possible consequences and prefers to leave the outcome to heaven.

At the last minute, however, Gordon does act: putting his life at stake, he impulsively throws himself in the path of the assassins. It is a futile gesture, for Buttler simply thrusts him aside. But his surrender to his emotions endears him to us more than Octavio's adherence to the path of duty recommends him, for at this tragic moment Gordon acts on our, the audience's, behalf. And our identification with him proves justified, for his plea that within an hour there could be a decisive change in the situation is vindicated as he rushes in to announce that the sound of trumpets which has accelerated Wallenstein's death came not from the Swedes, but from Octavio's escort.

Gordon may be, as Schiller wrote to Iffland, 'ein gutherziger fühlender Mann von Jahren, der weit mehr Schwäche als Charakter hat'; still, Schiller wanted a good actor for the part: 'Er muß aber in guten Händen seyn, denn er nimmt an den wichtigsten Scenen teil, und spricht die Empfindung, ich möchte sagen, die Moral des Stücks aus' (24 December 1798; NA, xxx, 18). He had in mind, perhaps, Gordon's words:

> O was ist Menschengröße!
>
> Ich sagt es oft: das kann nicht glücklich enden,
>
> Zum Fallstrick ward ihm seine Größ und Macht.
>
> . . . . .
>
> Der stolze Geist verlernte sich zu beugen.

> O schad um solchen Mann!
>
> (*Ws Tod,* IV. 2, 2480 ff.)

Certainly, Wallenstein is presented in the Prologue as the victim of his own unrestrained ambition, and Schiller's wish to have on the title-page a vignette of Nemesis, 'eine interessante und bedeutende Verzierung' (letter to Goethe, 1 December 1797; NA XXIX, 163), suggests that he saw his downfall in terms of the Greek notion of divine retribution on human immoderation. Our overwhelming feeling, moreover, as the drama draws to a close is indeed a sense of the tragic fall of a great man who strove too high. But if Gordon expresses the most obvious moral of the historical drama, what is the wider moral of its symbolic dimension?

The hubris of which Wallenstein is guilty is not just an excess of ambition; it is, more fundamentally, the metaphysical presumption of attempting to rise above the limitations of the human condition by ignoring the reality of time. It is his consequent failure to commit himself to action as he revels in his sense of freedom and capacity that is the immediate cause of his downfall, so that the figure of Nemesis is doubly appropriate. [11] The wider moral is embodied not just in Wallenstein, but in all three major figures, each of whom represents a different attitude to the central dilemma of life. It is in the choice confronting Max that we see this dilemma at its starkest. For him there can be no right decision: he cannot ignore his duty, but he cannot turn against Wallenstein either. Yet life demands that he make a choice. He cannot, and so must accept the only alternative, death. Octavio has no problem in turning against Wallenstein in order to do his duty. He does the 'right' thing, but it makes him a poorer human being, for, in contrast with Schiller's earlier Kantian stance, it is not simply morality that is at stake. Wallenstein, by contrast, tries to avoid making the choice between loyalty to the Emperor and his own designs; he is forced to do so, but by then it is too late. [12]

What is needed, we are driven to conclude, is a balance, precarious though it may be: we must seek to preserve our wholeness, as Wallenstein does, but not at the cost of refusing to commit ourselves to action; we must choose, as does Octavio, but without the sacrifice of wholeness which he too readily accepts. Ironically, it is Gordon who comes closest to this ideal, even if only in a very pale form. Torn between his duty and his feelings, he seeks to avoid any decision; but faced with the actual threat to Wallenstein's life, he acts.

It is just such a balance that characterizes the relationship between the *Aesthetic Letters* and **Wallenstein.** The former offers us the possibility of achieving a state of capacity which restores to us the wholeness of ideal humanity; the latter depicts the reality of the choice which we have to make as we participate in life. The two works thus express complementary aspects of a single view of the human condition, the optimism of the philosopher being transposed into the tragic vision of the poet. Philosophy, for so long an obstacle to Schiller's poetic creativity, has borne rich fruit in his dramatic masterpiece.

Schiller himself took the moral of **Wallenstein** to heart: he did not wish to prolong the freedom from determination and the resulting condition of mere capacity granted him by the completion of **Wallensteins Tod.** Two days later he was complaining to Goethe: 'Mir dünkt als wenn ich bestimmungslos im luftleeren Raume hienge.' Rather than delighting in his new freedom, he is afraid he will never be able to produce anything again and is longing to concentrate on a new subject: 'Habe ich wieder eine Bestimmung, so werde ich dieser Unruhe los seyn' (19 March 1799; NA, xxx, 38 f.). Five and a half weeks later he has already begun studying as material for a new play the reign of Elizabeth and the trial of Mary Stuart: 'Ein paar tragische Hauptmotive haben sich mir gleich dargeboten und mir großen Glauben an diesen Stoff gegeben' (letter to Goethe, 26 April 1799; NA, xxx, 45). One of these tragic motifs was no doubt—it certainly is in the completed play—the choice confronting Elisabeth between the necessity of getting rid of Maria in order to safeguard her own life and the moral obligation to spare her:

> die verhaßte Wahl[. . .,] in ewger Furcht
>
> Auf meinem Thron zu zittern, oder grausam
>
> Die Königin, die eigne Blutsverwandte
>
> Dem Beil zu unterwerfen.
>
> (*Maria Stuart*, I. 8, 1034 ff.; NA, ix, 39)

The agony of the choice between the demands of the senses and those of reason, which I have argued is the central theme of **Wallenstein**, is so central to Schiller's vision of life that he continues to explore it in **Maria Stuart:** 'Wer die Wahl hat, hat die Qual.' [13]

Notes

[*] Quotations from **Wallenstein** are from *Schillers Werke, Nationalausgabe*, Volume VIII, edited by Hermann Schneider and Lieselotte Blumenthal, Weimar, 1949. The abbreviation NA is used to refer to other volumes of the Nationalausgabe.

1. *Genesis: Some Episodes in Literary Creation,* Bithell Memorial Lecture, Institute of Germanic Studies, University of London, 1995, pp. 8, 18. Compare William Witte, *Schiller,* Oxford, 1949, p. 152: 'The genesis of *Wallenstein* [. . .] shows how a work of art, in taking shape, tends to become a law unto itself, acquiring a momentum, a life, a will of its own, overriding the intentions of its begeter and taking him where he had not dreamt of going.'

2. See the article on 'Schein, Erscheinung, Täuschung' in Friedrich Schiller, *On the Aesthetic Education of Man,* edited and translated by Elizabeth M. Wilkinson and L. A. Willoughby, Oxford, 1967, 1982[2], pp. 327 ff.

3. A link between Wallenstein's desire for freedom and the notion of 'Spiel' was made as long ago as 1937 by Reinhard Buchwald: 'Wir wissen ja [. . .] , daß der Mensch nur dann Mensch sei, wenn er spiele.

Jedoch Wallenstein wird der Spieler am falschen Orte' (*Schiller,* Volume II: *Der Weg zur Vollendung,* first published Leipzig, 1937, second edition Wiesbaden, 1954, pp. 356 f.). Since then, two studies have offered detailed interpretations of the figure of Wallenstein in terms of the ideas of the *Aesthetic Letters:* Oskar Seidlin, 'Wallenstein: Sein und Zeit', in I'*on Goethe zu Thomas Mann. Zwölf Versuche,* Göttingen, 1963, pp. 120-35, and Ilse Graham, 'Wallenstein's poodle: an essay in elusion and commitment', Chapter 6 of *Schiller's Drama. Talent and Integrity.* London, 1974, pp. 121-45. The importance of Seidlin's study lies, from my point of view, in its emphasis on the theme of time: he sees Wallenstein as wanting to escape from the passage of time so that he can act with complete freedom and thus as stepping from the historical into the aesthetic sphere, the timeless realm of purpose-free 'Spiel' (pp. 122 ff.). The importance of Graham's study, on the other hand, lies in the connection she makes between Wallenstein's attitude and the aesthetic condition: she regards his failure to act decisively as due to his desire for 'the freedom of possibility' and his clinging to 'a dream of totality of being' (p. 126). Neither Seidlin nor Graham discuss the link between the drama and the *Aesthetic Letters* which I see as created by the actual nature of the choice confronting not only Wallenstein but also the other major figures—even though Graham notes that each of the courses of action open to Wallenstein rules out the other, leaving him in a state of total indeterminacy, and even refers to the image of the pair of equally weighted scales used by Schiller to illustrate the aesthetic condition.

4. Wilkinson and Willoughby comment that 'though Schiller is here thinking primarily of the stage of the World, the word "role" inevitably calls up the theatre' (p. 264).

5. Compare Wolfgang Binder, 'Die Begriffe "naiv" und "sentimentalisch" in Schillers Drama', *JDSG,* IV (1960), 155: 'Das Wort *"Die Freiheit reizte mich und das Vermögen"* führt [. . .] auf den Begriff des ästhetischen Zustandes, der [. . .] als totales Vermögen ohne Fixierung verstanden wird.'

6. Seidlin argues that Wallenstein's 'Spiel', since it is not disinterested, inevitably becomes calculation: as 'Würfler' and 'Spieler' he can only be a 'Falsch-Spieler' and as such is prefigured by the peasant caught with the loaded dice in *Wallensteins Lager* (pp. 129 ff.). For Graham it becomes play-acting as he seeks to protect 'his inner self from corroding contact with reality' (pp. 126, 131). It is merely this role-playing and the wearing of masks that the majority of critics see as its significance, e.g. Benno von Wiese, *Friedrich Schiller,* Stuttgart, 1959, p. 650; Lesley Sharpe, *Schiller and the Historical Character. Presentation and Interpretation in the Historiographical Works and in the Historical Dramas,* Oxford, 1982, pp. 97 f.; F. J. Lamport, 'The Charismatic Hero: Goethe, Schiller, and the Tragedy of Character', *PEGS,* LVIII (1987-88), 72 f.

7. Seidlin notes that at his first mention of it in the *Aesthetic Letters* (Letter 14) Schiller sees the

'Spieltrieb' as being 'dahin gerichtet [. . .] , die Zeit *in der Zeit* aufzuheben' (p. 130).

8. For Seidlin, Wallenstein's 'Spiel' is in itself culpable since he believes that, in wishing to escape from the restrictions of time, Wallenstein is in fact hoping to manipulate it and thus direct the course of history (pp. 124 ff.; see also Buchwald, p. 357). By contrast, I see his 'Spiel' as an attempt to escape from time as well as from history and thus, with Graham, regard his fault as lying not in his adopting this stance but rather in his reluctance to abandon it: 'He [. . .] continues to play when play is out of season. To remain whole, he remains indeterminate when decisive action is demanded' (p. 126).

9. As Lesley Sharpe observes, the drama is, from the first word of *Die Piccolomini* ('Spät'), 'governed by the ever-accelerating passing of time' (*Friedrich Schiller. Drama, Thought and Politics*, Oxford, 1991, p. 224). Schiller saw this increasing pace of events, with Wallenstein powerless to halt it, as making circumstances rather than character responsible for Wallenstein's downfall and hence as increasing the tragic impression (Letter to Goethe, 2 October 1797), but it also emphasizes that there can be no escape from the reality of time.

10. Seidlin believes, as I do, that Wallenstein rises to greatness and human dignity only when, realizing that he can no longer postpone action, he gives up the dream of 'play' outside time and accepts his exposure to the forces of history (p. 133). For Graham, the 'enrichment and liberation which transform his whole being' take place much later, when he 'comes to accept his doing and its consequences as his own', as he does in acknowledging his responsibility for Max's death (pp. 143 ff.).

11. For von Wiese the drama is, above all, a tragedy of nemesis, which he sees as lying in the historical forces which Wallenstein, in his attempt to direct the course of history, unleashes through his own action (pp. 649 ff., 675). However, what proves fatal is not so much the action he finally takes as his failure to take it until it is too late. I therefore agree rather with T. J. Reed that it is Wallenstein's 'planning and temporizing' that generates 'ample nemesis', even if I regard this as representing more than 'a minimum of hubris' (*Schiller*, Oxford, 1991, p. 83).

12. Sharpe rightly concludes that 'the clash of moral and political attitudes goes far beyond the simple contrast of realism and idealism to be an exploration of the insolubility of the dilemmas confronting all parties' (*Friedrich Schiller*, 1991, p. 239). For her, however, Wallenstein's dilemma lies in the problem posed by the anxiety which, despite his belief in his special destmy, he feels about the incalculability of events (p. 229) rather than, as I have argued, in the dilemma of the choice with which he, and the other major characters, are confronted.

13. See my article, 'Ideal Perfection and the Human Condition: Morality and Necessity in Schiller's *Maria Stuart*', *OGS*, xx-xxi (1991-92), 46-68.

WILHELM TELL

CRITICAL COMMENTARY

F. J. Lamport (essay date 1981)

SOURCE: "The Silence of Wilhelm Tell," in *The Modern Language Review*, Vol. 76, No. 4, Summer 1983, pp. 857-68.

[*In the following essay, Lamport argues that Tell, a simple and humble man, undergoes a profound change after his confrontation with and triumph over Gessler: he moves out of his simple world and gains historical significance, and he finds a new eloquence as result of the important moral decision he makes in silence.*]

Schiller's **Wilhelm Tell** seems at first sight a fairly simple play. The action is, of course, a complex one, with four separate strands (the conspiracy of Stauffacher and his associates; the love of Rudenz for Berta; the assassination of the Emperor by Duke John; and Tell's ordeal and the killing of Gessler), but these all converge in a single point, all are gathered together to assert a single, simple meaning—the defence by the Swiss of their traditional liberties, their successful rebellion against Habsburg tyranny. A tale of epic simplicity, with an appropriately epic quality in the telling—indeed, Schiller has taken over the main lines of his story very largely from the epic chronicler of Swiss history, Ägidius Tschudi. It is customary to point out Schiller's divergences from Tschudi, but it is remarkable how much of Schiller's play is taken directly from this source: sometimes whole scenes or sequences of action, sometimes phrases reproduced verbatim; sometimes, admittedly, only a hint—as when Tschudi tells us that among the local nobility, sympathetic to the people's cause, there was an 'Edelknecht von Rudentz ob dem Kernwald . . . dem gedacht Er ouch der Sachen noch nit | bis über etwas Zits'.[1] The episode of Bertha and Rudenz as we have it in the play is almost entirely the product of Schiller's imagination, but the rest is all in the chronicle—Baumgarten and Stauffacher, Walther Fürst and Melchthal, the meeting on the Rütli, Attinghausen and the nobility, Duke John, Gessler, his hat and his apple, and Tell.

Tell himself is admirably suited to be the hero of this simple story, because he is a simple man. He is a man of action, not words: as he tells Gessler, in Tschudi's account, 'wär ich witzig | so hieß ich nit der Tell'.[2] He is a strong, silent man, characterized, at any rate in the first half of the play, by what have been aptly called 'self-coined proverbs',[3] utterances which have the appearance of being the tips of vast icebergs of accumulated rustic wisdom. But in their insistence that to every problem, however new and complex it may appear, there is a ready-made and simple answer, they mark him as a man of limited insight. It is of course entirely consistent that such a man has no time for the deliberations of politicians. He is, indeed, unwilling to commit himself to any sort of collective action, being reluctant or even unable to face the surrender of total autonomy and independence which such commitment would involve. He remains outside social life and its complexities, preferring the simplicity of the solitary huntsman's calling:

> Zum Hirten hat Natur mich nicht gebildet,
>
> Rastlos muß ich ein flüchtig Ziel verfolgen,
>
> Dann erst genieß ich meines Lebens recht,
>
> Wenn ich mirs jeden Tag aufs neu erbeute.
>
> (III.I, ll. 1486-89)

Indeed his attachment to solitude is not without a tinge of misanthropic suspicion:

> Ja, wohl ists besser, Kind, die Gletscherberge
>
> Im Rücken haben als die bösen Menschen.
>
> (ll. 1812-13)

And this adds up to a perfectly plausible, realistic characterization of a recognizable human type—perhaps a distinctively rustic type of simple man.

Half-way through the play this simple man is violently confronted with a problem so complex and unprecedented that there cannot possibly be any simple, readymade answer. There is no proverbial way out: Tell is reduced to total, agonized silence in which he has to make up his mind for himself unaided. The quality of this silence is eloquently conveyed in Schiller's stage direction: 'Tell steht in fürchterlichem Kampf, mit den Händen zuckend, und die rollenden Augen bald auf den Landvogt, bald zum Himmel gerichtet.—Plötzlich greift er in seinen Köcher, nimmt einen zweiten Pfeil heraus und steckt ihn in seinen Goller. Der Landvogt bemerkt alle diese Bewegungen' (stage direction after line 1989). The last sentence of this description, if it is not simply superfluous (Gessler himself subsequently tells us that he was watching Tell's actions closely), I take to imply that this little pantomine lasts some time: Schiller wants an appreciable silent pause at this point. But eventually, encouraged by his little boy ('Vater, schieß zu, ich fürcht mich nicht'), Tell makes up his mind, cries 'Es muß!' and, characteristically enough, while others (in this case Rudenz) are talking, acts.

In the later part of the play, however, a change appears to have come over Tell, or at any rate a change comes over his linguistic behaviour. In three of the four scenes in which he appears he is, by his previous standards, almost unrecognizably eloquent. He is given a longish narration (to the fisherman and boy in IV.I), a very long introspective monologue (in IV. 3—the longest soliloquy in Schiller's mature dramatic work) and a scene of intense argument in which he rises to considerable heights of rhetorical passion (V. 2, the famous, or notorious, Parricida scene). This newfound eloquence of Tell's has encountered objections on grounds of linguistic and psychological implausibility; but these objections seem to me to be unfounded. It is surely perfectly plausible that as the shock of that terrible silent

moment of decision wears off, our simple hero should have to struggle to come to terms with the complexity of his new situation. And when the struggle is over, Tell is probably grateful that in the last scene he is not required to say anything: the just cause is victorious, the people cheer, the music plays, Berta and Rudenz are betrothed, and Tell is again silent.

This simple tale and its simple hero have however been subjected to a number of complex interpretations. The starting-point of these seems to be the fact that the play is untypical of its author in that it has a happy ending. Various attempts have been made to explain this, to relate **Wilhelm Tell** to some other more general or more familiar Schillerian pattern. They fall into two groups, which one could call, very roughly, a positive and a negative group. The positive group sees Tell as an ideal figure, who is able to conquer or reconcile those historical forces which defeat Schiller's other, tragic, protagonists. The play represents an ideal state, a paradigm making clear the meaning of the historical process, affirming a historical teleology; Tell himself is not a simple but a complex figure, an examplar of 'aesthetic man', superior in harmony and psychic organization to the other characters.[4] The negative group sees Tell not as the conqueror or reconciler but as the *victim* of historical forces, just (or almost) as much as Schiller's tragic heroes: a near-tragic, or perhaps tragi-comic, figure at the mercy both of events and of the interpretation and appropriation of events by others, politicians like Stauffacher, men more sophisticated than he. This process of appropriation, this writing of history, we are asked to view ironically or even satirically; the simple Tell becomes an ambiguous figure, and his self-justification after killing Gessler is seen as specious or even pharisaical. This view of the play seems to be confined to the English-speaking world, but has at all events found favour on both sides of the Atlantic.[5]

Both schools of interpretation naturally claim support from the text of the play and from Schiller's other writings—his aesthetic essays and his correspondence. They even, in their different ways, claim support from Tell's silences. Thus Ilse Graham draws attention to the silence in which Tell takes his decision to obey Gessler's command, and argues that what we see in this silent moment is the self-control of Tell's instinctual nature, the harmony of his inner drives, the complete permeation of his nature by his spirit, in a word the manifestation of aesthetic totality (Graham, p. 208). I do not recognize in Professor Graham's interpretation the 'fürchterlicher Kampf', the 'zuckende Hände' and 'rollende Augen' of Schiller's stage direction; but in fact she is not really talking about Tell's demeanour but about that of his little boy, claiming that from this and from this alone we can measure the true significance of Tell's act. This is to my mind a strangely selective reading. On the other hand, the proponents of the ironic or quasi-tragic view of the play lay great stress on the fact that Tell says nothing in the last scene: 'his silence . . . is eloquent', they say,[6] seemingly inferring from it that Tell's peace of mind is shattered; that his attempt at self-justification, which with the monologue seemed to have succeeded, has been undermined by the confrontation with Parricida; that he can hardly bear the acclamation of his countrymen, feeling it to be based on something other than the truth. This is again a selective view; after all, the last scene is only ten lines long, and those ten lines are largely given to Berta, with responses from 'Alle' and from Rudenz—the Berta—Rudenz strand of the action being the only one still requiring to be concluded and tied in with the whole, and all the other principal characters having by now had their say. And if what is going on in Tell's mind at that earlier moment of crisis can all too readily be imagined—one might well be rendered speechless in such a situation—Tell's final silence may well be nothing more than a literal enactment of the familiar rhetorical *captatio*, 'Friends, I really do not know what to say'.

As we have said, however, what is at issue here is not simply a matter of psychology, but touches upon the vision of human life and, in particular, of human history which is presented in this play. Professor Mainland complains of 'the habit of seeing Schiller's play as some sort of stage-version of the old Swiss story' (Mainland, p. liv); but on his own showing no less than any other, the play is clearly, whatever else it may be, *some* sort of stage version of the old story, that is, *some* kind as Herbert Lindenberger's useful book[7] reminds us, there are many) of history play. It seems appropriate, therefore, to consider Tell's action, his silent crisis and his final—grateful, puzzled, shattered?—silence against the background of Schiller's treatment of history in the works of his maturity.

In his inaugural lecture of 1789, *Was heißt und zu welchem Ende studiert man Universalgeschichte?,* Schiller appears to be taking up the challenge or invitation issued by Kant a few years previously in his *Idee zu einer allgemeinen Geschichte in weltbürgerlicher Absicht,* namely to write a universal history on teleological principles. Indeed he had already, as dramatist and historiographer, if not as 'philosophischer Kopf',[8] produced two essays on these lines: the play **Don Carlos** and the *Geschichte des Abfalls der vereinigten Niederlande. Don Carlos* reads most convincingly, I think, as a play whose tragedy is set off or illuminated by an ultimate historical optimism: by its dramatic action, its language, its imagery,[9] it endorses the ideals of liberty proclaimed by Marquis Posa, endorses his attempt to advance the transformation of those ideals into reality (though Schiller is under no illusions whatever about the difficulties and dangers attendant upon any such attempt) and assures us, or at any rate suggests very strongly, that despite the tragedy we witness those ideals will ultimately triumph, and that therefore (in some sense) their champions, Posa and Carlos, will not have died in vain. This is very much the kind of teleological interpretation of history which Kant had in mind: a particular negative instance is subsumed into a larger positive pattern. And the *Abfall der Niederlande* sets out to present a part of the same complex of historical material, the stirrings of rebellion against the authoritarian rule of Philip II, as a 'schönes Denkmal bürgerlicher Stärke',[10] and as the first

chapter of a story of liberation running on, by implication, to Schiller's own day and progressively (as Kant had envisaged) into the future. Indeed Schiller's vision seems more optimistic than Kant's, because whereas Kant sees progress brought about by conflict, competition and 'Ungeselligkeit', and man's conscious or deliberate efforts as of little or no efficacy or even value, Schiller appears to attach more positive significance to man's idealism, aware though he is of its problematic side.

However, the events of 1789, and more particularly of the subsequent course of the Revolution, and their effects on the polity of Europe, seemed increasingly to deny the possibility of attaching any meaning to history. The events of the contemporary world seemed more and more to suggest a radical dualism between the realm of nature, causality, action, and history, and that of reason, morality, and human freedom. Kantian moral philosophy accepts and affirms this dualism, driving the individual moral conscience ruthlessly back into itself and making effective action in the real world virtually impossible. Nothing is good, we are told, but the 'guter Wille', and 'Der gute Wille ist nicht durch das, was er bewirkt, oder ausrichtet, nicht durch seine Tauglichkeit zu Erreichung irgend eines vorgesetzten Zweckes, sondern allein durch das Wollen, d.i. an sich, gut'.[11] Faced with a radically corrupt world, Kant strives to preserve the purity of the moral conscience by prescribing for it laws of maximum generality and abstraction, which admit of no exception, no accommodation to particular circumstances. This rigorism is epitomized in *Über ein vermeintes Recht, aus Menschenliebe zu lügen* (1797): if you do what is right, no one can blame you whatever the result, whereas if you do wrong, even with the best of intentions, you can be held morally or indeed legally responsible for any resulting evil—while, it appears, not being able to claim credit for any resulting good. This leads to a complete discontinuity of the moral life: true moral action is completely severed from any consequences. And the political conclusions are drawn in *Über den Gemeinspruch: Das mag in der Theorie gut sein, taugt aber nicht für die Praxis* (1793) and reiterated in the *Rechtslehre* (1797): although in theory the subject has rights which the ruler ought to respect, in practice the subject has no means of securing them, because resistance to the ruler, even to the most extreme and unnatural tyranny, is totally condemned. Anyone who as much as attempts such resistance is regarded as 'einer, der sein *Vaterland umzubringen* versucht (parricida)'.[12] Again the universal law is asserted independent of any circumstantial modification; the general is completely divorced from the particular, morality (the doctrine of what *should* be) from politics, the art of the possible. In *Über den Gemeinspruch . . .* Kant argues that no rebellion could ever have been thought to be justified 'wenn man zu allererst gefragt hätte, was Rechtens ist (wo die Prinzipien a priori feststehen, und kein Empiriker darin pfuschen kann)' (Kant, *Wke.,* VI, 159).

Schiller's later work bears eloquent testimony to the influence (to use a convenient shorthand term) which such ideas had upon him. In **Wallenstein** and the plays which succeeded it, history is portrayed as a battleground of conflicting forces—ambitious individuals, powers temporal and (ostensibly) spiritual—of none of which Schiller seems to approve; '[die] Schönen auf der Erde' can preserve their own moral purity only by voluntarily encompassing their own destruction. This is the 'Konflikt der Naturkräfte untereinander selbst und mit der Freiheit der Menschen'[13] which resists any philosophical schematization. Yet Schiller is never quite as radical as Kant. In *Über Anmut und Würde* he explicitly criticizes the rigorism of Kant's presentation of the moral law (*SW*, v, 465), and in **Über naive und sentimentalische Dichtung** he correctly identifies the paradox of this moral rigorism, in observing that the idealist, who claims to judge everything by absolute moral standards, cannot in fact give his life any moral continuity; though in theory he always submits the particular case to the general law, in practice his life falls apart into a series of discrete, particular moral acts (*SW*, v, 772 f.). In all his speculative writings Schiller is concerned to establish some kind of mediation between the realms of 'Natur' and 'Freiheit', between the 'physical' and 'moral' aspects of man's existence; and in his concepts of 'aesthetic education' and the 'aesthetic state' Schiller appears to believe that he has, at least in potential, found it. But while Schiller the philosopher is concerned to build this bridge at the general level, Schiller the playwright, and indeed Schiller the historiographer, is exploring the interaction of the two realms in particular instances. Although the *Abfall der Niederlande* did start off with some such 'Leitfaden a priori', as Kant proposes in the *Idee . . .* (*Wke.*, vi, 49), as it goes on Schiller finds himself more and more discovering that history is actually the story of human beings coping, to the best of their imperfect but not utterly contemptible abilities, with the demands of particular historical situations. And in the plays, although the historical teleology which informs **Don Carlos** has vanished, and although the *a priori* demands of his Kant-influenced moral philosophy on the one hand, and of the tragic genre and its conventional requirements on the other, tend to produce irreconcilable conflicts, Schiller's balanced presentation leads one to believe that while reserving his admiration for characters who fulfill his theoretical standards of 'sublimity' by choosing to leave this world behind them, he feels at least as much pity for those who try to survive in it, and would gladly welcome compromise if it showed itself to be possible. In the end it is not the 'philosophischer Kopf', but rather the practitioner of a 'bloß *empirisch* abgefaßte Historie' as Kant rather patronizingly calls it (*Wke.*, vi, 49), who is able to discover a positive meaning in history, not as a whole but in particular historical events and the reaction of particular human beings to them. **Wilhelm Tell** is the record of a particular moment in history when a just cause was enabled to triumph by a somewhat fortuitous combination of purposeful and principled action, opportunism and sheer good luck. The beneficiaries interpret this as providential, but we do not have to; nor however do we have to regard them as dishonest manipulators. The combination of circumstances which the play depicts seems to me unique

to the extent that it forbids the drawing of any general conclusions, at any rate of a prescriptive kind—it does not offer any general formula for the justification of rebellion or tyrannicide. In this sense it is not paradigmatic or exemplary. But nor do I think it very appropriate or helpful to describe it as 'ironic' or 'tragi-comic' or even 'satirical'.[14] If Schiller does not insinuate generally optimistic conclusions, still less does he invite general reactions of such a negative kind. **Wilhelm Tell** is a work of powerful positive affirmation; yet that affirmation is strictly limited to the 'streng bestimmter Fall' (compare below, p. 866) which it describes. It is neither optimistic nor pessimistic, neither comic nor tragic nor ironic nor satirical, but, despite a high degree of artistic stylization in its manner, soberly realistic in its vision.

If this is accepted, then it seems to me we must accept that the eponymous hero of the play is to be taken as a real human being. Proponents of the 'exemplary' view of the play tend to deny this. Fritz Martini, in particular, 'doth protest too much' that we must not consider Tell in terms of realistic psychology.[15] Tell is of course, or has become, a legendary figure, and already in the eighteenth century doubts had been cast upon his historical authenticity. But Schiller seems to have been concerned to combat these doubts; as K. A. Böttiger reports, he told people in Weimar that his intention was 'durch die Entwicklung von Tells harmlos, einfach handelnden Character, der nicht einmal an der Verschwörung teilnahm, und durch die psychologische Motivierung der Hauptszene beim Apfelschuß die unbestreitbare Wahrheit des Ganzen ins vollste Licht zu setzen und so dem böslich angefochtenen Schatten Tells die rühmlichste Ehrenerklärung, das wohlgefälligste Sühn- und Totenopfer darzubringen'.[16]

Tell is then for Schiller a real human being. He partakes of two human types who recur throughout Schiller's later drama. First, he is a simple ordinary person who is summoned, by some mysterious historical force or collocation of circumstances, to play a major role in history. Second, he is a man who has lived a life of instinctive harmony, wholeness and self-confidence, but is brought up short by a traumatic shock which forces him to take stock of his situation in a way to which he has not hitherto been accustomed. Both Johanna, in **Die Jungfrau von Orleans,** and Demetrius have their historical 'missions', but are forced into doubt and crisis—Johanna by the encounter with the Black Knight, Demetrius by the discovery that he is an impostor. But for Tell the summons of history and the traumatic shock come at the same moment, namely with Gessler's order in III. 3.

As I have said, Tell is a simple man, whose proverbial wisdom reduces life to a corresponding and therefore manageable simplicity. He likes to deal with everything and everybody in isolation, one thing and one person at a time: he will always help an individual human being, or a lamb (l. 440), without asking questions or without thought of the possible consequences, but he will not engage in collective or premeditated or even consecutive action. He lives, as he himself says (ll. 1487 ff.), from hand to mouth. He is suspicious of getting involved with other human beings: 'Besser ists, Ihr fallt in Gottes Hand, | Als in der Menschen' (ll. 157 f.). And yet, oddly, but I think not inconsistently with his essential simplicity, he will not put two and two together and draw conclusions about other people's intentions with regard to himself. He goes to Altdorf in spite of his wife's warnings: he ought to realize, as she says, that the Landvogt will have it in for him, but he does not make connexions in that kind of way. And when he gets to Altdorf he fails to salute the hat, although he was present in Act II when the proclamation was read out, and so ought to know perfectly well what will happen; and though it looks like provocation, I think we are to believe him when he claims it was done 'Aus Unbedacht, nicht aus Verachtung' (ll. 1869 f.). He simply fails to make any connexion between the proclamation read out in I. 3 and the situation he is in in III. 3: he deals with every situation in isolation, as it comes. He is rather like that other unpolitical hero, Egmont, who insists on living for the moment and refuses to calculate and prognosticate like the chess-player Orange; another great solitary—Egmont the horseman, Tell the huntsman with his crossbow. But of course, unlike Egmont, Tells gets a second chance; once Egmont has got off his horse in the palace yard under Alba's watchful eye, his fate is sealed, but Tell gets his crossbow back in the storm and does not fail with his second 'Meisterschuß' (l. 2649).

But I am overleaping the crucial moment, the summons of history, the traumatic shock to which Tell is subjected when Gessler orders him to shoot the apple from Walter's head, when Tell is converted from his previous belief that 'Die Schlange sticht nicht ungereizt' (l. 429) and his naïve failure to see his own action as in any way provocative, to the realization that 'Es kann der Frömmste nicht im Frieden bleiben | Wenn es dem bösen Nachbar nicht gefällt' (ll. 2682 f.). In silence Tell has to cope with this destruction of the patterns and assumptions upon which his life has been unthinkingly built. In that moment of silence are incapsulated, as it were, all the agonizings and self-analyses which occupy Wallenstein from his dismissal at Regensburg to the moment when 'Notwendigkeit ist da, der Zweifel flieht' (*Tod,* III. 10); all the doubt and self-accusation which torture Johanna from her traumatic encounter with the Black Knight, through her self-imposed silence until the second meeting with Lionel (v. 9). Tell has to go through all that in one moment. No wonder that it cannot be put into words; but no wonder either that his decision, once taken, is subjected—not to doubt, but to (however uncharacteristically) eloquent self-appraisal and self-justification. Tell has undergone a profound change; it is not really a matter of 'the real Tell' emerging from behind his protective screen (see Garland, p. 272). And when one finds D. B. Richards, for example, calling the Tell of the later scenes a 'prating Pharisee' (Richards, p. 472), one can only say, as Tell says to Stauffacher (l. 2089), 'Bezwinge sich, wer meinen Schmerz gefühlt!'.

I should like to draw attention to two features of Tell's decision which are perhaps obvious but which seem to me

to have received insufficient comment. First, Tell decides not to defy Gessler but to *obey* him: to obey a tyrannical, unnatural command whose gratuitous sadism is emphasized by the fact that no-one is more surprised by Tell's compliance with it than Gessler himself—'Er hat geschossen? Wie? der Rasende!' (l. 2033). This is very remarkable: not just the carrying-out of it, but the decision itself. It is, one might say, a Kantian decision: a decision in full conformity with Kant's moral and, indeed, political philosophy, in accordance with the maxim that 'alle Obrigkeit ist von Gott' and that 'wenn der Regent auch den Gesetzen zuwider verführe . . . so darf der Untertan dieser Ungerechtigkeit zwar *Beschwerden* (gravamina) aber keinen Widerstand entgegensetzen'.[17] In Kant's view, as Hans Reiss has neatly summarized it, 'obedience to the powers that be, even if they were unjust, showed a greater respect for human dignity and freedom than disobedience' (Reiss, p. 190). It is, I think, this aspect of Tell's action which makes it so uniquely appropriate for symbolic appropriation by the conspirators (and by their successors in the writing of patriotic history, such as Tschudi and, in Schiller's own day, Johannes von Müller)—and which makes it 'memorable history' in the precise sense of Messrs Sellar and Yeatman. Tell's almost superhuman act of obedience becomes symbolically the supreme act of defiance:[18] Wilhelm Tell, we all know, was the man who secured Swiss liberties—not by killing Gessler, but by shooting an apple off his little boy's head. This version of the history is already present in Schiller's play: in Attinghausen's dying speech (ll. 2423 f.), in Stauffacher's words, 'Das Größte hat *er* [Tell] getan, das Härteste *erduldet*' (ll. 3083 f.), and even more explicitly in the exchange which opens the next scene, v. 2:

> HEDWIG: Heut kommt der Vater, Kinder, liebe Kinder!
>
> Er lebt, ist frei, und wir sind frei und alles!
>
> Und euer Vater ists, der's Land gerettet.
>
> WALTER: Und ich bin auch dabei gewesen, Mutter!
>
> Mich muß man auch mit nennen. Vaters Pfeil
>
> Ging mir am Leben hart vorbei, und ich
>
> Hab nicht gezittert.
>
> (ll. 3087-93)

In a way the story ought to end there, like that of Lady Godiva: but unlike Earl Leofric, Gessler is unrelenting.

And now Schiller departs from Kant. For he seems to suggest that by his obedience to Gessler's command in the first instance, Tell has, as it were, earned the right subsequently to exact revenge:

> Wer sich des Kindes Haupt zum Ziele setzte,
>
> Der kann auch treffen in das Herz des Feinds.
>
> (l. 2575 f.)

And here we come to the other aspect of Tell's decision to which I wish to draw attention, for it marks the crucial change in Tell's personality and in the nature of his engagement with the world. For the first time in his life, Tell, who has previously 'rastlos ein flüchtig Ziel verfolgt' and 'sich das Leben jeden Tag aufs neu erbeutet' (see l. 1487 ff.), decides to do *two* things, one consequent upon the other: to obey Gessler, *and then* to shoot him. We *see* him take this twofold decision in the first silence, that moment of 'fürchterlicher Kampf' when he takes out the second arrow.[19] It is not possible, nor even perhaps desirable, to analyse into its separate components the very subtle blend of motives which lead Tell to make the decision he does—the blend of 'Notwehr' and 'Rache', the blend of private and political considerations.[20] Tell's own subsequent attempts to do so *are* perhaps not entirely convincing, for the various factors are inseparably interwined. What is important is that with that decision Tell steps into the world of history, the world of connected actions and consequences. He realizes that his action is a political one: and he realizes that the call has come of which he spoke earlier to Hedwig ('Ich war nicht mit dabei [i.e. on the Rütli]—doch werd' ich mich Dem Lande nicht entziehen, wenn es ruft'; ll. 1519 f.), though it has come, not from the conspirators, but from the moral challenge of Gessler. The people cry out, as Tell is arrested, 'Mit Euch geht unser letzter Trost dahin!' (l. 2092); and though Tell's reply to Stauffacher suggests the same withdrawal into the private realm with which he had rebuffed Stauffacher's political overtures in II. 3, when we next see him Tell has for the fisherman in IV. 1 a very different message. After ascertaining that the fisherman was present at the gathering on the Rütli, he tells him to reassure the confederates:

> Sie sollen wacker sein und gutes Muts,
>
> Der Tell sei *frei* und seines Armes mächtig,
>
> Bald werden sie ein Weitres von mir hören.
>
> (ll. 2296-98)

The old asocial Tell is gone: the huntsman Tell has one more appearance to make and one more only, for he knows that the second 'Meisterschuß' which he has vowed (l. 2649; compare l. 2042) will be his last. After it, Tell's crossbow will be seen no more. If the crossbow is, as Ilse Graham maintains, the symbol of Tell's self-regulative economy' and of his 'psychic span and power',[21] are these things gone? Tell certainly is not the same man at the end of the play as he was at the beginning.

There are still some lessons which Tell has to learn, and which it seems to be the function of the Parricida scene to teach him. First of these is that if you choose to act—or indeed, like Tell, are forced to act—a part on the stage of history, you are forced to submit to the judgement of history. 'Die Weltgeschichte ist das Weltgericht', Schiller had written in 'Resignation'; not in any proto-Hegelian sense, but rather in a Kantian one, of a complete separation of moral and historical judgement. Moral acts are right or wrong; but according to Kant the moral character of an action is totally dependent upon the intention informing it, and intentions are inscrutable, being wrapped in the silence

in which decisions are normally taken. Historical actions are therefore judged, as Kant says, by the worldly standards of success or failure: 'Auch ist kaum zu bezweifeln, daß, wenn jene Empörungen, wodurch die Schweiz, die Vereinigten Niederlande, oder auch Großbritannien ihre itzige für so glücklich gepriesene Verfassung errungen haben, mißlungen wären, die Leser der Geschichte derselben in der Hinrichtung ihrer itzt so erhobenen Urheber nichts als verdiente Strafe großer Staatsverbrecher sehen würden'.[22] And the proponents of the 'ironical' view of the play seem to impute to it a meaning not very different from that sentence, in which Kant voices a cynicism about the efforts of honest men to cope with the demands of history, of a kind to which rigorous moralists are all too prone. Tell's attempted moral justification of his action in the Parricida scene (his 'desperate insistence on seeing the confrontation as a moral issue' (McKay, p. 111)) only goes to show how needful, or perhaps impossible, of such justification the action is. Schiller of course made quite other claims for the scene in defending it against Iffland, who first voiced the since often-repeated objection that the appearance of Parricida was unnecessary and that l'ell 'übe sich zu hart'. Schiller replied that the scene was the 'Schlußstein des Ganzen' and expressed the 'Hauptidee des ganzen Stücks . . . nämlich "das Notwendige und Rechtliche der Selbsthilfe in einem streng bestimmten Fall"',[23] The ironical view of the play apparently requires us to suppose either that the real meaning of the Parricida scene runs contrary to Schiller's conscious and declared intention, or that Schiller was for some reason deliberately withholding the real meaning from Iffland; neither of which suppositions seems to me satisfactory.

Iffland thought that Parricida got a rough deal in this scene—'was mit ihm vorgeht, gab mir Mißgefühl'. He evidently thought that the two deeds were after all very similar, and that Tell therefore had not the right to lecture Parricida so severely. Parricida claims that the deeds are similar in nature and effect:

> Ihr erschlugt
>
> Den Landvogt, der Euch Böses tat—Auch ich
>
> Hab einen Feind erschlagen, der mir Recht
>
> Versagte—Er war Euer Feind wie meiner—
>
> Ich hab das Land von ihm befreit.
>
> (ll. 3151-55)

Schiller on the other hand insists, like his hero, that they are 'ganz unähnlich' in respect of *motive*—the least apparent factor to the public eye, but the crucial one in moral judgement. Parricida no doubt thinks that it is a mere irony of history that he and his deed are reviled while Tell and his are acclaimed; but Schiller surely does not. Though he has abandoned any idea of a teleology in history, he does think that on this particular occasion ('in [diesem] streng bestimmten Fall') those who won actually deserved to, and if they had lost then we should *not* simply, as Kant averred, be thinking of them as 'Staatsverbrecher'. He thinks that this particular rebellion was justified not merely historically, by its success (and after all, in 1798 history had apparently reversed its verdict!),[24] but also morally— whereas the French Revolution was not.[25] It was therefore necessary to draw as sharp a distinction as possible between two actions which in a purely historical sense appeared very similar. But this does mean that although Schiller vindicates Tell, and vindicates the Swiss in their acclamation of Tell as national saviour, he does not intend to vindicate rebellion in general, and it is therefore appropriate that the Parricida scene should have, as it undoubtedly does have, a dampening effect on the apotheosis of freedom with which the play concludes. If the Parricida scene is omitted, the play becomes a much more unqualified endorsement of rebellion and tyrannicide; and this of course is what usually happens when the play is performed in Switzerland, and transformed from a dramatic examination of a particular historical incident with universal overtones into a simple nationalistic celebration.[26]

Just how much of this Tell is aware of, and how much of it contributes to his final silence, is very doubtful. One sobering reflection on the historical process definitely presents itself to his mind: the fact that history can raise up the humble (himself) and cast down the mighty (Duke John):

> Gott des Himmels!
>
> So jung, von solchem adeligem Stamm,
>
> Der Enkel Rudolfs, meines Herrn und Kaisers,
>
> Als Morder flüchtig, hier an meiner Schwelle,
>
> Des armen Mannes, flehend und verzweifeland—
>
> (ll. 3190-94)

But I think this is a reflection prompted by humility rather than arrogance. And this humility is another lesson which Tell learns in the course of the scene, as he is forced to reflect upon the complexity of the world which he has entered. After the murder of Gessler, Tell had leapt forth triumphant from his ambush crying 'Du kennst den Schützen, suche keinen andern!' (l. 2792). Back home, to Hedwig's awed 'Diese Hand—O Gott!', he answers, *'herzlich und mutig'* [stage direction], 'Hat Euch verteidigt und das Land gerettet' (ll. 3142 f.). But perhaps even if this is true, Tell himself is not the man to say it. Stauffacher may say it—but Stauffacher also acknowledges that in real rather than symbolic terms it is Parricida's deed which is the decisive one ('Gefallen ist der Freiheit größter Feind', l. 3019). Tell may claim moral credit for doing the right thing in the circumstances, but he cannot legitimately claim the (so to speak) historical credit for the consequences of that moral action—and that is Kantian enough, except for that vital qualification, 'the right thing *in the circumstances'*. And if Tell does appear self-righteous, even pharisaical, in his opening exchanges with Parricida, he very soon takes on a different tone. 'Und doch erbarmt mich deiner—Gott des Himmels!' And, 'Was Ihr auch Gräßliches | Verübt—Ihr seid ein Mensch—Ich bin es auch' (l. 3223 f.).[27] Schiller's Tell is, I repeat, a human be-

ing. He is not an idealized figure, not a tragic hero in the traditional or indeed the usual Schillerian sense. Schiller grants him his triumph; but Schiller introduces Parricida—to justify Tell, yes, but also to whisper in his ear, as the slave whispered in the honorand's ear at a Roman triumph, 'Remember you are only a man'. To the acclamation with which he is received, the only appropriate response is the silence of gratitude and humility.

Notes

1. Quoted in Schiller, *Wilhelm Tell,* Rowohlts Klassiker (Reinbek, 1967), p. 130.

2. Quoted in *Wilhelm Tell* (Rowohlts Klassiker edition), p. 130.

3. H. B. Garland, *Schiller the Dramatic Writer* (Oxford, 1969), p. 271.

4. Most recently G. Ueding, in *Schillers Dramen: Neue Interpretationen,* edited by W. Hinderer (Stuttgart, 1979), pp. 271-93; see also F. Martini, 'Wilhelm Tell, der ästhetische Staat und der ästhetische Mensch', *DU,* 12 (1960), 90-118; I. Graham, *Schiller's Drama: Talent and Integrity* (London, 1974), pp. 195-215; G. Kaiser, *Von Arkadien nach Elysium: Schiller-Studien* (Göttingen, 1978), pp. 167-205.

5. W. F. Mainland, Introduction to Schiller, *Wilhelm Tell* (London, 1968); G. W. McKay, 'Three Scenes from *Wilhelm Tell',* in *The Discontinuous Tradition: Studies in German Literature in Honour of Ernest Ludwig Stahl,* edited by P. F. Ganz (Oxford, 1970), pp. 99-112; D. B. Richards, 'Tell in the Dock: Forensic Rhetoric in the Monologue and Parricida-scene in *Wilhelm Tell', GQ,* 48 (1975), 472-86; F. G. Ryder, 'Schiller's Tell and the Cause of Freedom', *GQ,* 48 (1975), 487-504.

6. McKay, p. 112; compare Mainland, p. lxvi.

7. H. Lindenberger, *Historical Drama: The Relation of Literature and Reality* (Chicago and London, 1975).

8. Schiller, *Sämtliche Werke,* edited by G. Fricke, H. G. Göpfert, and H. Stubenrauch, 5 volumes (Munich, 1958-59), IV, 750 (*Was heißt . . .*); compare Kant, *Werke,* edited by W. Weischedel, 6 volumes (Wiesbaden, 1956-60), VI, 50 (*Idee zu einer allgemeinen Geschichte . . .*). Further references to the works of Schiller and Kant are to these editions, which are abbreviated to *SW* and *Wke.* respectively.

9. Compare F. M. Fowler, 'The Dramatic Image: Observations on the Drama with Examples from Schiller and Lessing', in *Tradition and Creation: Essays in Honour of Elizabeth Mary Wilkinson,* edited by C. P. Magill and others (Leeds, 1978), pp. 63-96 (especially pp. 69-71).

10. Schiller, *SW,* IV, 34 (*Abfall der Niederlande,* Einleitung).

11. Kant, *Wke.,* IV, 19 (*Grundlegung der Metaphysik der Sitten,* i).

12. Kant, *Wke.,* IV, 439-40 (*Metaphysik der Sitten: Rechtslehre*). Compare H. S. Reiss, 'Kant and the Right of Rebellion', *Journal of the History of Ideas,* 17 (1956), 179-92.

13. Schiller, *SW*, v, 803 (*Über das Erhabene*).

14. Compare especially Mainland, op. cit.

15. Martini, pp. 96, 104, 110, 112 and footnote. Compare also Kaiser, p. 192.

16. Quoted in *Dichter über ihre Dichtungen: Friedrich Schiller,* edited by Bodo Lecke (Munich, 1969), II, 516.

17. Kant, *Wke.,* IV, 438 (*Rechtslehre*).

18. It conforms also to Schiller's definition of a morally sublime act, an 'Erhabenes der Handlung' of the type in which the person 'aus Achtung für irgend eine Pflicht', in this case obedience to legitimate authority, 'das Leiden erwählt'—aims at his own child, with the possibility of killing him. See Schiller, *SW*, v, 528 (*Über das Pathetische*).

19. The inconsistency between Tell's subsequent explanations—in l. 2060, in which the killing of Gessler is a *conditional* decision, and in l. 2579 ff., in which it appears as an *absolute* one—seems to me unimportant: the point is that the two 'Meisterschüsse' are perceived by Tell as connected, in some way or other. It is quite clear that Tell's first excuse to Gessler—'Herr, das ist also bräuchlich bei den Schützen' (l. 2051)—is not true: this is demonstrated by the stage direction 'verlegen' (ibid.), and we have *seen* the second arrow taken 'plötzlich', after 'fürchterlichem Kampfe' (stage direction to line 1989).

20. It is, notably, no discredit to Tell's political act that it is done partly if not wholly for private, that is, non-ideological reasons. Compare Margaret C. Ives, 'In tyrannos! Rebellion and Regicide in Schiller's *Wilhelm Tell* and Jozsef Katona's *Bánk Bán',* GLL, 30 (1976-77), 269-82.

21. Graham, p. 213. On the disapperance of Tell's crossbow, see Mainland, p. lxvii f.

22. Kant, *Wke.,* VI, 158 (*Über den Gemeinspruch. . . .*

23. See Iffland's letter to Schiller, 7 April 1804, and Schiller's reply, quoted in *Wilhel Tell* (Rowohlts Klassiker edition), pp. 171 ff. (especially p. 179).

24. Compare Schiller's sardonic comment to Wilhelm von Wolzogen (27 October 1803), '. . . jetzt besonders ist von der schweizerischen Freiheit desto mehr die Rede, weil sie aus der Welt verschwunden ist', and the even more bitter irony in the suggestion to Cotta (27 June 1804) that the play bear the dedication 'zum fünten Jubeliahr der schweizerischen Freiheit'.

25. Compare the poem 'Wenn rohe Kräfte . . .', Schiller, *SW*, I, 462.

26. H. G. Thalheim, in 'Notwendigkeit und Rechtlichkeit der Selbsthilfe in Schiller's *Wilhelm Tell', Goethe* (Neue Folge des Jahrbuchs der Goethe-Gesellschaft), 18 (1956), 216-57, argues persuasively that Schiller in this play, and in the Parricida scene above all, is seeking to counter Kant's anti-revolutionary argument on its own ground.

27. Note, incidentally, that Tell, having previously slipped from the formal to the familiar mode of address for his expression of moral revulsion at Parricida's deed, has now reverted to the polite form.

FURTHER READING

Criticism

Blunden, Alan G. "Nature and Politics in Schiller's *Don Carlos.*" *Educational Theater Journal* 27 (August 1975): 504-07.
> Notes the importance of the organic metaphors underlying the political themes in the play.

Garland, H. B. *Schiller.* New York: Medill McBridge, 1950. 280 p.
> General introduction emphasizing "the human character of the writer which is the foundation of the literary works"; includes detailed analyses of individual plays.

Graf, Günter. "Criticism of Power: A Strategic Device in *Kabald und Liebe.*" In *Friedrich von Schiller and the Drama of Human Existence,* edited by Alexej Ugrinsky, Westport, CT: Greenwood Press, 1988, pp. 43-8.
> Examines Schiller's poetical adaptation of his criticism of power as exemplified in *Kabald und Liebe.*

Graham, Ilse. "The Structure of the Personality in Schiller's Tragic Poetry."*Schiller: Bicentary Lectures,* edited by F. Norman. London: University of London Institute of Germanic Studies, 1960. pp. 104-44.
> Considers Schiller's work as rooted deeply in the reality of human life.

Graham, Ilse. *Schiller's Drama: Talent and Integrity.* London: Methuen, 1974. 406 p.
> Comprehensive survey of the plays, containing readings of individual dramas and discussions of special issues raised by the plays as whole; emphasizes the "thematic, artistic, and aesthetic idiosyncrasies which constitute the poet's signature."

Hibberd, J. L. "The Patterns of Imagery in Schiller's *Die Braut von Messina.*" *Germanic Languages and Literature* 20 (1967): 306-15.
> Interprets the patterns of imagery in light of Schiller's insistence of the primacy of form in ideal art in his writings on aesthetics.

Linn, Rolf N. "Wallenstein's Innocence." *The Germanic Review* 34, No. 3 (October 1959): 200-08.
> Considers and interpretation that Wallenstein is innocent of treason.

Mainland, William F. *Schiller and the Changing Past.* London: William Heinemann, Ltd., 1957, 207 p.

Assessment of Schiller's dramatic treatment of history; includes discussions of the early play *Fiesco* and the later dramas.

Mann, Thomas. "On Schiller." In *Last Essays.* New York: Alfred A. Knopf, 1959, pp. 3-95.
Survey of Schiller's life and art by one of the most respected German novelists of the twentieth century.

Martinson, Steven D. *Harmonious Tensions: The Writings of Friedrich Schiller.* Cranbury, NJ: Associated University Presses, 1996, 448 p.
Investigates the thematics, form, and function of Schiller's writings in the light of the writer's mutidisciplinary activities; includes a comprehensive list of secondary sources.

Miller, R. D. *Interpreting Schiller: A Study of Four Plays.* Harrogate: The Duchy Press, 1986. 146 p.
Analyses of *Wilhelm Tell, Die Jungfrau von Orleans, Don Karlos,* and *Wallenstein.*

Miller, R. D. *A Study of Schiller's "Jungfrau von Orleans."* Harrogate: The Duchy Press, 1995 105 p.
Detailed study of the play, with chapters covering the prologue and each of the five acts.

Passage, Charles E. *Friedrich Schiller.* New York: Frederick Ungar Publishing, 1975, 205 p.
Study of Schiller's drama for the non-specialist; offers character studies, thematic interpretations, and historical background for each of the major plays.

Proudhoe, John. "Schiller's Major Plays: His Theory and Practice." In *The Theatre of Goethe and Schiller.* London: Basil Blackwell, 1973. 218 p.
Concise discussions of the action and themes of the major plays and Schiller's theory of tragedy.

Sharpe, Lesley. *Schiller and the Historical Character: Presentation and Interpretation in the Historiographical Works and in the Historical Dramas.* Oxford: Oxford University Press, 1982, 211 p.

Explores the impact of historical study on Schiller's dramatic practice.

Sharpe, Lesley. *Friedrich Schiller: Drama, Thought and Politics.* Cambridge: Cambridge University Press, 1991, 389 p.
Traces Schiller's development as a poet, dramatist, and thinker, and provides detailed discussions of his major works.

Simons, John D. *Friedrich Schiller.* Boston: Twayne Publishers, 1981. 163 p.
General overview of Schiller's life and work geared toward the nonspecialist, covering aesthetics, poetry, and drama; includes two chapters on Schiller's plays from the early and middle and classical periods.

Stahl, E. L. "The Genesis of Schiller's Theory of Tragedy." In *German Studies Presented to H. G. Fiedler by Pupils, Colleagues, and Friends.* Freeport, NY: Libraries Press, 1969, pp. 403-23.
Notes the stages of development in Schiller's conception of tragedy, and claims that the dramatist's theory in its final form is a synthesis of elements from the dramatist Gottfried Lessing and the philosopher Immanuel Kant.

Utz, Peter. "Schiller's Dramaturgy of the Senses: The Eye, the Ear, and the Heart." In *Friedrich von Schiller and the Drama of Human Existence,* edited by Alexej Ugrinsky, Westport, CT: Greenwood Press, 1988, pp. 13-19.
Maintains that Schiller makes dramatic use of his theory of sensual perception, and says that his plays, notably *Wallenstein,* consciously appeal to the eyes and ears as well as the emotions of the audience.

Wells, G. A. "Astrology in Schiller's *Wallenstein.*" *Journal of English and German Philology* 68, No. 1 (January 1969): 100-15.
Discusses the significance of the stars and the force of circumstance that leads to the Wallenstein's downfall.

How to Use This Index

> **Calvino, Italo**
> 1923-1985 .... **CLC 5, 8, 11, 22, 33, 39,**
> **73; SSC 3**

list all author entries in the following Gale Literary Criticism series:

BLC = *Black Literature Criticism*
CLC = *Contemporary Literary Criticism*
CLR = *Children's Literature Review*
CMLC = *Classical and Medieval Literature Criticism*
DA = *DISCovering Authors*
DAB = *DISCovering Authors: British*
DAC = *DISCovering Authors: Canadian*
DAM = *DISCovering Authors: Modules*
    DRAM: Dramatists Module; MST: Most-Studied Authors Module;
    MULT: Multicultural Authors Module; NOV: Novelists Module;
    POET: Poets Module; POP: Popular Fiction and Genre Authors Module
DC = *Drama Criticism*
HLC = *Hispanic Literature Criticism*
LC = *Literature Criticism from 1400 to 1800*
NNAL = *Native North American Literature*
NCLC = *Nineteenth-Century Literature Criticism*
PC = *Poetry Criticism*
SSC = *Short Story Criticism*
TCLC = *Twentieth-Century Literary Criticism*
WLC = *World Literature Criticism, 1500 to the Present*

The cross-references

> See also CANR 23; CA 85-88;
> obituary CA116

list all author entries in the following Gale biographical and literary sources:

AAYA = *Authors & Artists for Young Adults*
AITN = *Authors in the News*
BEST = *Bestsellers*
BW = *Black Writers*
CA = *Contemporary Authors*
CAAS = *Contemporary Authors Autobiography Series*
CABS = *Contemporary Authors Bibliographical Series*
CANR = *Contemporary Authors New Revision Series*
CAP = *Contemporary Authors Permanent Series*
CDALB = *Concise Dictionary of American Literary Biography*
CDBLB = *Concise Dictionary of British Literary Biography*
DLB = *Dictionary of Literary Biography*
DLBD = *Dictionary of Literary Biography Documentary Series*
DLBY = *Dictionary of Literary Biography Yearbook*
HW = *Hispanic Writers*
JRDA = *Junior DISCovering Authors*
MAICYA = *Major Authors and Illustrators for Children and Young Adults*
MTCW = *Major 20th-Century Writers*
SAAS = *Something about the Author Autobiography Series*
SATA = *Something about the Author*
YABC = *Yesterday's Authors of Books for Children*

Literary Criticism Series
Cumulative Author Index

Anderson, Jessica (Margaret) Queale 1916-
CLC 37
See also CA 9-12R; CANR 4, 62

Anderson, Jon (Victor) 1940- . **CLC 9; DAM POET**
See also CA 25-28R; CANR 20

Anderson, Lindsay (Gordon) 1923-1994
.... **CLC 20**
See also CA 125; 128; 146; CANR 77

Anderson, Maxwell 1888-1959 .... **TCLC 2; DAM DRAM**
See also CA 105; 152; DLB 7; MTCW 2

Anderson, Poul (William) 1926- .... **CLC 15**
See also AAYA 5; CA 1-4R, 181; CAAE 181; CAAS 2; CANR 2, 15, 34, 64; CLR 58; DLB 8; INT CANR-15; MTCW 1, 2; SATA 90; SATA-Brief 39; SATA-Essay 106

Anderson, Robert (Woodruff) 1917-
.... **CLC 23; DAM DRAM**
See also AITN 1; CA 21-24R; CANR 32; DLB 7

Anderson, Sherwood 1876-1941 ..... **TCLC 1, 10, 24; DA; DAB; DAC; DAM MST, NOV; SSC 1; WLC**
See also AAYA 30; CA 104; 121; CANR 61; CDALB 1917-1929; DA3; DLB 4, 9, 86; DLBD 1; MTCW 1, 2

Andier, Pierre
See Desnos, Robert

Andouard
See Giraudoux, (Hippolyte) Jean

Andrade, Carlos Drummond de ...... **CLC 18**
See also Drummond de Andrade, Carlos

Andrade, Mario de 1893-1945 .... **TCLC 43**

Andreae, Johann V(alentin) 1586-1654
.... **LC 32**
See also DLB 164

Andreas-Salome, Lou 1861-1937 ... **TCLC 56**
See also CA 178; DLB 66

Andress, Lesley
See Sanders, Lawrence

Andrewes, Lancelot 1555-1626 .... **LC 5**
See also DLB 151, 172

Andrews, Cicily Fairfield
See West, Rebecca

Andrews, Elton V.
See Pohl, Frederik

Andreyev, Leonid (Nikolaevich) 1871-1919 **TCLC 3**
See also CA 104

Andric, Ivo 1892-1975 .... **CLC 8; SSC 36**
See also CA 81-84; 57-60; CANR 43, 60; DLB 147; MTCW 1

Androvar
See Prado (Calvo), Pedro

Angelique, Pierre
See Bataille, Georges

Angell, Roger 1920- .... **CLC 26**
See also CA 57-60; CANR 13, 44, 70; DLB 171, 185

Angelou, Maya 1928- .... **CLC 12, 35, 64, 77; BLC 1; DA; DAB; DAC; DAM MST, MULT, POET, POP; WLCS**
See also AAYA 7, 20; BW 2, 3; CA 65-68; CANR 19, 42, 65; CDALBS; CLR 53; DA3; DLB 38; MTCW 1, 2; SATA 49

Anna Comnena 1083-1153 .... **CMLC 25**

Annensky, Innokenty (Fyodorovich) 1856-1909 .... **TCLC 14**
See also CA 110; 155

Annunzio, Gabriele d'
See D'Annunzio, Gabriele

Anodos
See Coleridge, Mary E(lizabeth)

Anon, Charles Robert
See Pessoa, Fernando (Antonio Nogueira)

Anouilh, Jean (Marie Lucien Pierre) 1910-1987 .... **CLC 1, 3, 8, 13, 40, 50;**

DAM DRAM; DC 8
See also CA 17-20R; 123; CANR 32; MTCW 1, 2

Anthony, Florence
See Ai

Anthony, John
See Ciardi, John (Anthony)

Anthony, Peter
See Shaffer, Anthony (Joshua); Shaffer, Peter (Levin)

Anthony, Piers 1934- .... **CLC 35; DAM POP**
See also AAYA 11; CA 21-24R; CANR 28, 56, 73; DLB 8; MTCW 1, 2; SAAS 22; SATA 84

Anthony, Susan B(rownell) 1916-1991
.... **TCLC 84**
See also CA 89-92; 134

Antoine, Marc
See Proust, (Valentin-Louis-George-Eugene-) Marcel

Antoninus, Brother
See Everson, William (Oliver)

Antonioni, Michelangelo 1912- .... **CLC 20**
See also CA 73-76; CANR 45, 77

Antschel, Paul 1920-1970
See Celan, Paul
See also CA 85-88; CANR 33, 61; MTCW 1

Anwar, Chairil 1922-1949 .... **TCLC 22**
See also CA 121

Anzaldua, Gloria 1942-
See also CA 175; DLB 122; HLCS 1

Apess, William 1798-1839(?) .... **NCLC 73; DAM MULT**
See also DLB 175; NNAL

Apollinaire, Guillaume 1880-1918 .. **TCLC 3, 8, 51; DAM POET; PC 7**
See also Kostrowitzki, Wilhelm Apollinaris de CA 152; MTCW 1

Appelfeld, Aharon 1932- .... **CLC 23, 47**
See also CA 112; 133; CANR 86

Apple, Max (Isaac) 1941- .... **CLC 9, 33**
See also CA 81-84; CANR 19, 54; DLB 130

Appleman, Philip (Dean) 1926- .... **CLC 51**
See also CA 13-16R; CAAS 18; CANR 6, 29, 56

Appleton, Lawrence
See Lovecraft, H(oward) P(hillips)

Apteryx
See Eliot, T(homas) S(tearns)

Apuleius, (Lucius Madaurensis) 125(?)-175(?) .... **CMLC 1**
See also DLB 211

Aquin, Hubert 1929-1977 .... **CLC 15**
See also CA 105; DLB 53

Aquinas, Thomas 1224(?)-1274 ..... **CMLC 33**
See also DLB 115

Aragon, Louis 1897-1982 .. **CLC 3, 22; DAM NOV, POET**
See also CA 69-72; 108; CANR 28, 71; DLB 72; MTCW 1, 2

Arany, Janos 1817-1882 .... **NCLC 34**

Aranyos, Kakay
See Mikszath, Kalman

Arbuthnot, John 1667-1735 .... **LC 1**
See also DLB 101

Archer, Herbert Winslow
See Mencken, H(enry) L(ouis)

Archer, Jeffrey (Howard) 1940- ...... **CLC 28; DAM POP**
See also AAYA 16; BEST 89:3; CA 77-80; CANR 22, 52; DA3; INT CANR-22

Archer, Jules 1915- .... **CLC 12**
See also CA 9-12R; CANR 6, 69; SAAS 5; SATA 4, 85

Archer, Lee
See Ellison, Harlan (Jay)

Arden, John 1930- .... **CLC 6, 13, 15; DAM DRAM**
See also CA 13-16R; CAAS 4; CANR 31, 65, 67; DLB 13; MTCW 1

Arenas, Reinaldo 1943-1990 . **CLC 41; DAM MULT; HLC 1**
See also CA 124; 128; 133; CANR 73; DLB 145; HW 1; MTCW 1

Arendt, Hannah 1906-1975 .... **CLC 66, 98**
See also CA 17-20R; 61-64; CANR 26, 60; MTCW 1, 2

Aretino, Pietro 1492-1556 .... **LC 12**

Arghezi, Tudor 1880-1967 .... **CLC 80**
See also Theodorescu, Ion N. CA 167

Arguedas, Jose Maria 1911-1969 .... **CLC 10, 18; HLCS 1**
See also CA 89-92; CANR 73; DLB 113; HW 1

Argueta, Manlio 1936- .... **CLC 31**
See also CA 131; CANR 73; DLB 145; HW 1

Arias, Ron(ald Francis) 1941-
See also CA 131; CANR 81; DAM MULT; DLB 82; HLC 1; HW 1, 2; MTCW 2

Ariosto, Ludovico 1474-1533 .... **LC 6**

Aristides
See Epstein, Joseph

Aristophanes 450B.C.-385B.C. .... **CMLC 4; DA; DAB; DAC; DAM DRAM, MST; DC 2; WLCS**
See also DA3; DLB 176

Aristotle 384B.C.-322B.C. .... **CMLC 31; DA; DAB; DAC; DAM MST; WLCS**
See also DA3; DLB 176

Arlt, Roberto (Godofredo Christophersen) 1900-1942 .... **TCLC 29; DAM MULT; HLC 1**
See also CA 123; 131; CANR 67; HW 1, 2

Armah, Ayi Kwei 1939- . **CLC 5, 33; BLC 1; DAM MULT, POET**
See also BW 1; CA 61-64; CANR 21, 64; DLB 117; MTCW 1

Armatrading, Joan 1950- .... **CLC 17**
See also CA 114

Arnette, Robert
See Silverberg, Robert

Arnim, Achim von (Ludwig Joachim von Arnim) 1781-1831 ..... **NCLC 5; SSC 29**
See also DLB 90

Arnim, Bettina von 1785-1859 .... **NCLC 38**
See also DLB 90

Arnold, Matthew 1822-1888 ..... **NCLC 6, 29; DA; DAB; DAC; DAM MST, POET; PC 5; WLC**
See also CDBLB 1832-1890; DLB 32, 57

Arnold, Thomas 1795-1842 .... **NCLC 18**
See also DLB 55

Arnow, Harriette (Louisa) Simpson 1908-1986 .... **CLC 2, 7, 18**
See also CA 9-12R; 118; CANR 14; DLB 6; MTCW 1, 2; SATA 42; SATA-Obit 47

Arouet, Francois-Marie
See Voltaire

Arp, Hans
See Arp, Jean

Arp, Jean 1887-1966 .... **CLC 5**
See also CA 81-84; 25-28R; CANR 42, 77

Arrabal
See Arrabal, Fernando

Arrabal, Fernando 1932- ... **CLC 2, 9, 18, 58**
See also CA 9-12R; CANR 15

Arreola, Juan Jose 1918- .... **SSC 38; DAM MULT; HLC 1**
See also CA 113; 131; CANR 81; DLB 113; HW 1, 2

Arrick, Fran .... **CLC 30**
See also Gaberman, Judie Angell

Baxter, George Owen
See Faust, Frederick (Schiller)
Baxter, James K(eir) 1926-1972 .... **CLC 14**
See also CA 77-80
Baxter, John
See Hunt, E(verette) Howard, (Jr.)
Bayer, Sylvia
See Glassco, John
Baynton, Barbara 1857-1929 .... **TCLC 57**
Beagle, Peter S(oyer) 1939- .... **CLC 7, 104**
See also CA 9-12R; CANR 4, 51, 73; DA3;
DLBY 80; INT CANR-4; MTCW 1;
SATA 60
Bean, Normal
See Burroughs, Edgar Rice
Beard, Charles A(ustin) 1874-1948 . **TCLC 15**
See also CA 115; DLB 17; SATA 18
Beardsley, Aubrey 1872-1898 .... **NCLC 6**
Beattie, Ann 1947- ..... **CLC 8, 13, 18, 40, 63;
DAM NOV, POP; SSC 11**
See also BEST 90:2; CA 81-84; CANR 53,
73; DA3; DLBY 82; MTCW 1, 2
Beattie, James 1735-1803 .... **NCLC 25**
See also DLB 109
Beauchamp, Kathleen Mansfield 1888-1923
See Mansfield, Katherine
See also CA 104; 134; DA; DAC; DAM
MST; DA3; MTCW 2
Beaumarchais, Pierre-Augustin Caron de
1732-1799 .... **DC 4**
See also DAM DRAM
Beaumont, Francis 1584(?)-1616 . **LC 33; DC
6**
See also CDBLB Before 1660; DLB 58, 121
**Beauvoir, Simone (Lucie Ernestine Marie
Bertrand) de** 1908-1986 .... **CLC 1, 2, 4,
8, 14, 31, 44, 50, 71, 124; DA; DAB;
DAC; DAM MST, NOV; SSC 35; WLC**
See also CA 9-12R; 118; CANR 28, 61;
DA3; DLB 72; DLBY 86; MTCW 1, 2
Becker, Carl (Lotus) 1873-1945 ..... **TCLC 63**
See also CA 157; DLB 17
Becker, Jurek 1937-1997 .... **CLC 7, 19**
See also CA 85-88; 157; CANR 60; DLB
75
Becker, Walter 1950- .... **CLC 26**
Beckett, Samuel (Barclay) 1906-1989
. **CLC 1, 2, 3, 4, 6, 9, 10, 11, 14, 18, 29,
57, 59, 83; DA; DAB; DAC; DAM
DRAM, MST, NOV; SSC 16; WLC**
See also CA 5-8R; 130; CANR 33, 61; CD-
BLB 1945-1960; DA3; DLB 13, 15;
DLBY 90; MTCW 1, 2
Beckford, William 1760-1844 .... **NCLC 16**
See also DLB 39
Beckman, Gunnel 1910- .... **CLC 26**
See also CA 33-36R; CANR 15; CLR 25;
MAICYA; SAAS 9; SATA 6
Becque, Henri 1837-1899 .... **NCLC 3**
See also DLB 192
Becquer, Gustavo Adolfo 1836-1870
See also DAM MULT; HLCS 1
Beddoes, Thomas Lovell 1803-1849 . **NCLC 3**
See also DLB 96
Bede c. 673-735 .... **CMLC 20**
See also DLB 146
Bedford, Donald F.
See Fearing, Kenneth (Flexner)
Beecher, Catharine Esther 1800-1878
.... **NCLC 30**
See also DLB 1
Beecher, John 1904-1980 .... **CLC 6**
See also AITN 1; CA 5-8R; 105; CANR 8
Beer, Johann 1655-1700 .... **LC 5**
See also DLB 168
Beer, Patricia 1924-1999 .... **CLC 58**
See also CA 61-64; 183; CANR 13, 46;
DLB 40

Beerbohm, Max
See Beerbohm, (Henry) Max(imilian)
Beerbohm, (Henry) Max(imilian) 1872-1956
TCLC 1, 24
See also CA 104; 154; CANR 79; DLB 34,
100
Beer-Hofmann, Richard 1866-1945
.... **TCLC 60**
See also CA 160; DLB 81
Begiebing, Robert J(ohn) 1946- .... **CLC 70**
See also CA 122; CANR 40, 88
Behan, Brendan 1923-1964 ...... **CLC 1, 8, 11,
15, 79; DAM DRAM**
See also CA 73-76; CANR 33; CDBLB
1945-1960; DLB 13; MTCW 1, 2
Behn, Aphra 1640(?)-1689 . **LC 1, 30, 42; DA;
DAB; DAC; DAM DRAM, MST, NOV,
POET; DC 4; PC 13; WLC**
See also DA3; DLB 39, 80, 131
Behrman, S(amuel) N(athaniel) 1893-1973
CLC 40
See also CA 13-16; 45-48; CAP 1; DLB 7,
44
Belasco, David 1853-1931 .... **TCLC 3**
See also CA 104; 168; DLB 7
Belcheva, Elisaveta 1893- .... **CLC 10**
See also Bagryana, Elisaveta
Beldone, Phil "Cheech"
See Ellison, Harlan (Jay)
Beleno
See Azuela, Mariano
Belinski, Vissarion Grigoryevich 1811-1848
NCLC 5
See also DLB 198
Belitt, Ben 1911- .... **CLC 22**
See also CA 13-16R; CAAS 4; CANR 7,
77; DLB 5
Bell, Gertrude (Margaret Lowthian)
1868-1926 .... **TCLC 67**
See also CA 167; DLB 174
Bell, J. Freeman
See Zangwill, Israel
Bell, James Madison 1826-1902 ... **TCLC 43;
BLC 1; DAM MULT**
See also BW 1; CA 122; 124; DLB 50
Bell, Madison Smartt 1957- ...... **CLC 41, 102**
See also CA 111, 183; CAAE 183; CANR
28, 54, 73; MTCW 1
Bell, Marvin (Hartley) 1937- ...... **CLC 8, 31;
DAM POET**
See also CA 21-24R; CAAS 14; CANR 59;
DLB 5; MTCW 1
Bell, W. L. D.
See Mencken, H(enry) L(ouis)
Bellamy, Atwood C.
See Mencken, H(enry) L(ouis)
Bellamy, Edward 1850-1898 .... **NCLC 4**
See also DLB 12
Belli, Gioconda 1949-
See also CA 152; HLCS 1
Bellin, Edward J.
See Kuttner, Henry
**Belloc, (Joseph) Hilaire (Pierre Sebastien
Rene Swanton)** 1870- .... **TCLC 7, 18;
DAM POET; PC 24**
See also CA 106; 152; DLB 19, 100, 141,
174; MTCW 1; SATA 112; YABC 1
Belloc, Joseph Peter Rene Hilaire
See Belloc, (Joseph) Hilaire (Pierre Sebas-
tien Rene Swanton)
Belloc, Joseph Pierre Hilaire
See Belloc, (Joseph) Hilaire (Pierre Sebas-
tien Rene Swanton)
Belloc, M. A.
See Lowndes, Marie Adelaide (Belloc)
Bellow, Saul 1915- . **CLC 1, 2, 3, 6, 8, 10, 13,
15, 25, 33, 34, 63, 79; DA; DAB; DAC;
DAM MST, NOV, POP; SSC 14; WLC**

See also AITN 2; BEST 89:3; CA 5-8R;
CABS 1; CANR 29, 53; CDALB 1941-
1968; DA3; DLB 2, 28; DLBD 3; DLBY
82; MTCW 1, 2
Belser, Reimond Karel Maria de 1929-
See Ruyslinck, Ward
See also CA 152
Bely, Andrey .... **TCLC 7; PC 11**
See also Bugayev, Boris Nikolayevich
MTCW 1
Belyi, Andrei
See Bugayev, Boris Nikolayevich
Benary, Margot
See Benary-Isbert, Margot
Benary-Isbert, Margot 1889-1979 .... **CLC 12**
See also CA 5-8R; 89-92; CANR 4, 72;
CLR 12; MAICYA; SATA 2; SATA-Obit
21
Benavente (y Martinez), Jacinto 1866-1954
**TCLC 3; DAM DRAM, MULT; HLCS
1**
See also CA 106; 131; CANR 81; HW 1, 2;
MTCW 1, 2
Benchley, Peter (Bradford) 1940- . **CLC 4, 8;
DAM NOV, POP**
See also AAYA 14; AITN 2; CA 17-20R;
CANR 12, 35, 66; MTCW 1, 2; SATA 3,
89
Benchley, Robert (Charles) 1889-1945
.... **TCLC 1, 55**
See also CA 105; 153; DLB 11
Benda, Julien 1867-1956 .... **TCLC 60**
See also CA 120; 154
Benedict, Ruth (Fulton) 1887-1948 . **TCLC 60**
See also CA 158
Benedict, Saint c. 480-c. 547 .... **CMLC 29**
Benedikt, Michael 1935- .... **CLC 4, 14**
See also CA 13-16R; CANR 7; DLB 5
Benet, Juan 1927- .... **CLC 28**
See also CA 143
Benet, Stephen Vincent 1898-1943 . **TCLC 7;
DAM POET; SSC 10**
See also CA 104; 152; DA3; DLB 4, 48,
102; DLBY 97; MTCW 1; YABC 1
Benet, William Rose 1886-1950 .... **TCLC 28;
DAM POET**
See also CA 118; 152; DLB 45
Benford, Gregory (Albert) 1941- ..... **CLC 52**
See also CA 69-72, 175; CAAE 175; CAAS
27; CANR 12, 24, 49; DLBY 82
Bengtsson, Frans (Gunnar) 1894-1954
.... **TCLC 48**
See also CA 170
Benjamin, David
See Slavitt, David R(ytman)
Benjamin, Lois
See Gould, Lois
Benjamin, Walter 1892-1940 .... **TCLC 39**
See also CA 164
Benn, Gottfried 1886-1956 .... **TCLC 3**
See also CA 106; 153; DLB 56
Bennett, Alan 1934- .... **CLC 45, 77; DAB;
DAM MST**
See also CA 103; CANR 35, 55; MTCW 1,
2
Bennett, (Enoch) Arnold 1867-1931
.... **TCLC 5, 20**
See also CA 106; 155; CDBLB 1890-1914;
DLB 10, 34, 98, 135; MTCW 2
Bennett, Elizabeth
See Mitchell, Margaret (Munnerlyn)
Bennett, George Harold 1930-
See Bennett, Hal
See also BW 1; CA 97-100; CANR 87
Bennett, Hal .... **CLC 5**
See also Bennett, George Harold DLB 33
Bennett, Jay 1912- .... **CLC 35**

See also BW 2, 3; CA 65-68; CANR 24, 43, 81; DA3; MTCW 1, 2

Chabon, Michael 1963- .... **CLC 55**
See also CA 139; CANR 57

Chabrol, Claude 1930- .... **CLC 16**
See also CA 110

Challans, Mary 1905-1983
See Renault, Mary
See also CA 81-84; 111; CANR 74; DA3; MTCW 2; SATA 23; SATA-Obit 36

Challis, George
See Faust, Frederick (Schiller)

Chambers, Aidan 1934- .... **CLC 35**
See also AAYA 27; CA 25-28R; CANR 12, 31, 58; JRDA; MAICYA; SAAS 12; SATA 1, 69, 108

Chambers, James 1948-
See Cliff, Jimmy
See also CA 124

Chambers, Jessie
See Lawrence, D(avid) H(erbert Richards)

Chambers, Robert W(illiam) 1865-1933
TCLC 41
See also CA 165; DLB 202; SATA 107

Chamisso, Adelbert von 1781-1838
.... **NCLC 82**
See also DLB 90

Chandler, Raymond (Thornton) 1888-1959
TCLC 1, 7; SSC 23
See also AAYA 25; CA 104; 129; CANR 60; CDALB 1929-1941; DA3; DLBD 6; MTCW 1, 2

Chang, Eileen 1920-1995 .... **SSC 28**
See also CA 166

Chang, Jung 1952- .... **CLC 71**
See also CA 142

Chang Ai-Ling
See Chang, Eileen

Channing, William Ellery 1780-1842
.... **NCLC 17**
See also DLB 1, 59

Chao, Patricia 1955- .... **CLC 119**
See also CA 163

Chaplin, Charles Spencer 1889-1977
.... **CLC 16**
See also Chaplin, Charlie CA 81-84; 73-76

Chaplin, Charlie
See Chaplin, Charles Spencer
See also DLB 44

Chapman, George 1559(?)-1634 .... **LC 22; DAM DRAM**
See also DLB 62, 121

Chapman, Graham 1941-1989 .... **CLC 21**
See also Monty Python CA 116; 129; CANR 35

Chapman, John Jay 1862-1933 .... **TCLC 7**
See also CA 104

Chapman, Lee
See Bradley, Marion Zimmer

Chapman, Walker
See Silverberg, Robert

Chappell, Fred (Davis) 1936- ..... **CLC 40, 78**
See also CA 5-8R; CAAS 4; CANR 8, 33, 67; DLB 6, 105

Char, Rene(-Emile) 1907-1988 .... **CLC 9, 11, 14, 55; DAM POET**
See also CA 13-16R; 124; CANR 32; MTCW 1, 2

Charby, Jay
See Ellison, Harlan (Jay)

Chardin, Pierre Teilhard de
See Teilhard de Chardin, (Marie Joseph) Pierre

Charlemagne 742-814 .... **CMLC 37**

Charles I 1600-1649 .... **LC 13**

Charriere, Isabelle de 1740-1805 .. **NCLC 66**

Charyn, Jerome 1937- .... **CLC 5, 8, 18**

See also CA 5-8R; CAAS 1; CANR 7, 61; DLB 83; MTCW 1

Chase, Mary (Coyle) 1907-1981 .... **DC 1**
See also CA 77-80; 105; SATA 17; SATA-Obit 29

Chase, Mary Ellen 1887-1973 .... **CLC 2**
See also CA 13-16; 41-44R; CAP 1; SATA 10

Chase, Nicholas
See Hyde, Anthony

Chateaubriand, François Rene de 1768-1848
NCLC 3
See also DLB 119

Chatterje, Sarat Chandra 1876-1936(?)
See Chatterji, Saratchandra
See also CA 109

Chatterji, Bankim Chandra 1838-1894
NCLC 19

Chatterji, Saratchandra .... **TCLC 13**
See also Chatterje, Sarat Chandra

Chatterton, Thomas 1752-1770 ..... **LC 3, 54; DAM POET**
See also DLB 109

Chatwin, (Charles) Bruce 1940-1989
.... **CLC 28, 57, 59; DAM POP**
See also AAYA 4; BEST 90:1; CA 85-88; 127; DLB 194, 204

Chaucer, Daniel
See Ford, Ford Madox

Chaucer, Geoffrey 1340(?)-1400 .. **LC 17, 56; DA; DAB; DAC; DAM MST, POET; PC 19; WLCS**
See also CDBLB Before 1660; DA3; DLB 146

Chavez, Denise (Elia) 1948-
See also CA 131; CANR 56, 81; DAM MULT; DLB 122; HLC 1; HW 1, 2; MTCW 2

Chaviaras, Strates 1935-
See Haviaras, Stratis
See also CA 105

Chayefsky, Paddy .... **CLC 23**
See also Chayefsky, Sidney DLB 7, 44; DLBY 81

Chayefsky, Sidney 1923-1981
See Chayefsky, Paddy
See also CA 9-12R; 104; CANR 18; DAM DRAM

Chedid, Andree 1920- .... **CLC 47**
See also CA 145

Cheever, John 1912-1982 ..... **CLC 3, 7, 8, 11, 15, 25, 64; DA; DAB; DAC; DAM MST, NOV, POP; SSC 1, 38; WLC**
See also CA 5-8R; 106; CABS 1; CANR 5, 27, 76; CDALB 1941-1968; DA3; DLB 2, 102; DLBY 80, 82; INT CANR-5; MTCW 1, 2

Cheever, Susan 1943- .... **CLC 18, 48**
See also CA 103; CANR 27, 51; DLBY 82; INT CANR-27

Chekhonte, Antosha
See Chekhov, Anton (Pavlovich)

Chekhov, Anton (Pavlovich) 1860-1904
TCLC 3, 10, 31, 55, 96; DA; DAB; DAC; DAM DRAM, MST; DC 9; SSC 2, 28; WLC
See also CA 104; 124; DA3; SATA 90

Chernyshevsky, Nikolay Gavrilovich 1828-1889 .... **NCLC 1**

Cherry, Carolyn Janice 1942-
See Cherryh, C. J.
See also CA 65-68; CANR 10

Cherryh, C. J. .... **CLC 35**
See also Cherry, Carolyn Janice AAYA 24; DLBY 80; SATA 93

Chesnutt, Charles W(addell) 1858-1932
TCLC 5, 39; BLC 1; DAM MULT; SSC 7

See also BW 1, 3; CA 106; 125; CANR 76; DLB 12, 50, 78; MTCW 1, 2

Chester, Alfred 1929(?)-1971 .... **CLC 49**
See also CA 33-36R; DLB 130

Chesterton, G(ilbert) K(eith) 1874-1936
TCLC 1, 6, 64; DAM NOV, POET; PC 28; SSC 1
See also CA 104; 132; CANR 73; CDBLB 1914-1945; DLB 10, 19, 34, 70, 98, 149, 178; MTCW 1, 2; SATA 27

Chiang, Pin-chin 1904-1986
See Ding Ling
See also CA 118

Ch'ien Chung-shu 1910- .... **CLC 22**
See also CA 130; CANR 73; MTCW 1, 2

Child, L. Maria
See Child, Lydia Maria

Child, Lydia Maria 1802-1880 .. **NCLC 6, 73**
See also DLB 1, 74; SATA 67

Child, Mrs.
See Child, Lydia Maria

Child, Philip 1898-1978 .... **CLC 19, 68**
See also CA 13-14; CAP 1; SATA 47

Childers, (Robert) Erskine 1870-1922
.... **TCLC 65**
See also CA 113; 153; DLB 70

Childress, Alice 1920-1994 .. **CLC 12, 15, 86, 96; BLC 1; DAM DRAM, MULT, NOV; DC 4**
See also AAYA 8; BW 2, 3; CA 45-48; 146; CANR 3, 27, 50, 74; CLR 14; DA3; DLB 7, 38; JRDA; MAICYA; MTCW 1, 2; SATA 7, 48, 81

Chin, Frank (Chew, Jr.) 1940- .... **DC 7**
See also CA 33-36R; CANR 71; DAM MULT; DLB 206

Chislett, (Margaret) Anne 1943- ...... **CLC 34**
See also CA 151

Chitty, Thomas Willes 1926- .... **CLC 11**
See also Hinde, Thomas CA 5-8R

Chivers, Thomas Holley 1809-1858
.... **NCLC 49**
See also DLB 3

Choi, Susan .... **CLC 119**

Chomette, Rene Lucien 1898-1981
See Clair, Rene
See also CA 103

Chopin, Kate .. **TCLC 5, 14; DA; DAB; SSC 8; WLCS**
See also Chopin, Katherine CDALB 1865-1917; DLB 12, 78

Chopin, Katherine 1851-1904
See Chopin, Kate
See also CA 104; 122; DAC; DAM MST, NOV; DA3

Chretien de Troyes c. 12th cent. - . **CMLC 10**
See also DLB 208

Christie
See Ichikawa, Kon

Christie, Agatha (Mary Clarissa) 1890-1976
CLC 1, 6, 8, 12, 39, 48, 110; DAB; DAC; DAM NOV
See also AAYA 9; AITN 1, 2; CA 17-20R; 61-64; CANR 10, 37; CDBLB 1914-1945; DA3; DLB 13, 77; MTCW 1, 2; SATA 36

Christie, (Ann) Philippa
See Pearce, Philippa
See also CA 5-8R; CANR 4

Christine de Pizan 1365(?)-1431(?) .... **LC 9**
See also DLB 208

Chubb, Elmer
See Masters, Edgar Lee

Chulkov, Mikhail Dmitrievich 1743-1792
.... **LC 2**
See also DLB 150

Churchill, Caryl 1938- .... **CLC 31, 55; DC 5**
See also CA 102; CANR 22, 46; DLB 13; MTCW 1

Churchill, Charles 1731-1764 .... **LC 3**

Collins, Hunt
See Hunter, Evan
Collins, Linda 1931- .... CLC 44
See also CA 125
Collins, (William) Wilkie 1824-1889
.... NCLC 1, 18
See also CDBLB 1832-1890; DLB 18, 70, 159
Collins, William 1721-1759 . LC 4, 40; DAM POET
See also DLB 109
Collodi, Carlo 1826-1890 .... NCLC 54
See also Lorenzini, Carlo CLR 5
Colman, George 1732-1794
See Glassco, John
Colt, Winchester Remington
See Hubbard, L(afayette) Ron(ald)
Colter, Cyrus 1910- .... CLC 58
See also BW 1; CA 65-68; CANR 10, 66; DLB 33
Colton, James
See Hansen, Joseph
Colum, Padraic 1881-1972 .... CLC 28
See also CA 73-76; 33-36R; CANR 35; CLR 36; MAICYA; MTCW 1; SATA 15
Colvin, James
See Moorcock, Michael (John)
Colwin, Laurie (E.) 1944-1992 .... CLC 5, 13, 23, 84
See also CA 89-92; 139; CANR 20, 46; DLBY 80; MTCW 1
Comfort, Alex(ander) 1920- .... CLC 7; DAM POP
See also CA 1-4R; CANR 1, 45; MTCW 1
Comfort, Montgomery
See Campbell, (John) Ramsey
Compton-Burnett, I(vy) 1884(?)-1969
.... CLC 1, 3, 10, 15, 34; DAM NOV
See also CA 1-4R; 25-28R; CANR 4; DLB 36; MTCW 1
Comstock, Anthony 1844-1915 ...... TCLC 13
See also CA 110; 169
Comte, Auguste 1798-1857 .... NCLC 54
Conan Doyle, Arthur
See Doyle, Arthur Conan
Conde (Abellan), Carmen 1901-
See also CA 177; DLB 108; HLCS 1; HW 2
Conde, Maryse 1937- .... CLC 52, 92; BLCS; DAM MULT
See also Boucolon, Maryse BW 2; MTCW 1
Condillac, Etienne Bonnot de 1714-1780
.... LC 26
Condon, Richard (Thomas) 1915-1996
... CLC 4, 6, 8, 10, 45, 100; DAM NOV
See also BEST 90:3; CA 1-4R; 151; CAAS 1; CANR 2, 23; INT CANR-23; MTCW 1, 2
Confucius 551B.C.-479B.C. .. CMLC 19; DA; DAB; DAC; DAM MST; WLCS
See also DA3
Congreve, William 1670-1729 . LC 5, 21; DA; DAB; DAC; DAM DRAM, MST, POET; DC 2; WLC
See also CDBLB 1660-1789; DLB 39, 84
Connell, Evan S(helby), Jr. 1924- . CLC 4, 6, 45; DAM NOV
See also AAYA 7; CA 1-4R; CAAS 2; CANR 2, 39, 76; DLB 2; DLBY 81; MTCW 1, 2
Connelly, Marc(us Cook) 1890-1980 . CLC 7
See also CA 85-88; 102; CANR 30; DLB 7; DLBY 80; SATA-Obit 25
Connor, Ralph .... TCLC 31
See also Gordon, Charles William DLB 92
Conrad, Joseph 1857-1924 .... TCLC 1, 6, 13, 25, 43, 57; DA; DAB; DAC; DAM MST, NOV; SSC 9; WLC

See also AAYA 26; CA 104; 131; CANR 60; CDBLB 1890-1914; DA3; DLB 10, 34, 98, 156; MTCW 1, 2; SATA 27
Conrad, Robert Arnold
See Hart, Moss
Conroy, Pat
See Conroy, (Donald) Pat(rick)
See also MTCW 2
Conroy, (Donald) Pat(rick) 1945- ... CLC 30, 74; DAM NOV, POP
See also Conroy, Pat AAYA 8; AITN 1; CA 85-88; CANR 24, 53; DA3; DLB 6; MTCW 1
Constant (de Rebecque), (Henri) Benjamin 1767-1830 .... NCLC 6
See also DLB 119
Conybeare, Charles Augustus
See Eliot, T(homas) S(tearns)
Cook, Michael 1933- .... CLC 58
See also CA 93-96; CANR 68; DLB 53
Cook, Robin 1940- .... CLC 14; DAM POP
See also AAYA 32; BEST 90:2; CA 108; 111; CANR 41; DA3; INT 111
Cook, Roy
See Silverberg, Robert
Cooke, Elizabeth 1948- .... CLC 55
See also CA 129
Cooke, John Esten 1830-1886 .... NCLC 5
See also DLB 3
Cooke, John Estes
See Baum, L(yman) Frank
Cooke, M. E.
See Creasey, John
Cooke, Margaret
See Creasey, John
Cook-Lynn, Elizabeth 1930- . CLC 93; DAM MULT
See also CA 133; DLB 175; NNAL
Cooney, Ray .... CLC 62
Cooper, Douglas 1960- .... CLC 86
Cooper, Henry St. John
See Creasey, John
Cooper, J(oan) California (?)- .... CLC 56; DAM MULT
See also AAYA 12; BW 1; CA 125; CANR 55; DLB 212
Cooper, James Fenimore 1789-1851
.... NCLC 1, 27, 54
See also AAYA 22; CDALB 1640-1865; DA3; DLB 3; SATA 19
Coover, Robert (Lowell) 1932- ...... CLC 3, 7, 15, 32, 46, 87; DAM NOV; SSC 15
See also CA 45-48; CANR 3, 37, 58; DLB 2; DLBY 81; MTCW 1, 2
Copeland, Stewart (Armstrong) 1952-
.... CLC 26
Copernicus, Nicolaus 1473-1543 .... LC 45
Coppard, A(lfred) E(dgar) 1878-1957
.... TCLC 5; SSC 21
See also CA 114; 167; DLB 162; YABC 1
Coppee, Francois 1842-1908 .... TCLC 25
See also CA 170
Coppola, Francis Ford 1939- ... CLC 16, 126
See also CA 77-80; CANR 40, 78; DLB 44
Corbiere, Tristan 1845-1875 .... NCLC 43
Corcoran, Barbara 1911- .... CLC 17
See also AAYA 14; CA 21-24R; CAAS 2; CANR 11, 28, 48; CLR 50; DLB 52; JRDA; SAAS 20; SATA 3, 77
Cordelier, Maurice
See Giraudoux, (Hippolyte) Jean
Corelli, Marie 1855-1924 .... TCLC 51
See also Mackay, Mary DLB 34, 156
Corman, Cid 1924- .... CLC 9
See also Corman, Sidney CAAS 2; DLB 5, 193

Corman, Sidney 1924-
See Corman, Cid
See also CA 85-88; CANR 44; DAM POET
Cormier, Robert (Edmund) 1925- ... CLC 12, 30; DA; DAB; DAC; DAM MST, NOV
See also AAYA 3, 19; CA 1-4R; CANR 5, 23, 76; CDALB 1968-1988; CLR 12, 55; DLB 52; INT CANR-23; JRDA; MAICYA; MTCW 1, 2; SATA 10, 45, 83
Corn, Alfred (DeWitt III) 1943- .... CLC 33
See also CA 179; CAAE 179; CAAS 25; CANR 44; DLB 120; DLBY 80
Corneille, Pierre 1606-1684 ..... LC 28; DAB; DAM MST
Cornwell, David (John Moore) 1931-
.... CLC 9, 15; DAM POP
See also le Carre, John CA 5-8R; CANR 13, 33, 59; DA3; MTCW 1, 2
Corso, (Nunzio) Gregory 1930- .... CLC 1, 11
See also CA 5-8R; CANR 41, 76; DA3; DLB 5, 16; MTCW 1, 2
Cortazar, Julio 1914-1984 ... CLC 2, 3, 5, 10, 13, 15, 33, 34, 92; DAM MULT, NOV; HLC 1; SSC 7
See also CA 21-24R; CANR 12, 32, 81; DA3; DLB 113; HW 1, 2; MTCW 1, 2
CORTES, HERNAN 1484-1547 .... LC 31
Corvinus, Jakob
See Raabe, Wilhelm (Karl)
Corwin, Cecil
See Kornbluth, C(yril) M.
Cosic, Dobrica 1921- .... CLC 14
See also CA 122; 138; DLB 181
Costain, Thomas B(ertram) 1885-1965
.... CLC 30
See also CA 5-8R; 25-28R; DLB 9
Costantini, Humberto 1924(?)-1987 . CLC 49
See also CA 131; 122; HW 1
Costello, Elvis 1955- .... CLC 21
Costenoble, Philostene
See Ghelderode, Michel de
Cotes, Cecil V.
See Duncan, Sara Jeannette
Cotter, Joseph Seamon Sr. 1861-1949
.... TCLC 28; BLC 1; DAM MULT
See also BW 1; CA 124; DLB 50
Couch, Arthur Thomas Quiller
See Quiller-Couch, SirArthur (Thomas)
Coulton, James
See Hansen, Joseph
Couperus, Louis (Marie Anne) 1863-1923
TCLC 15
See also CA 115
Coupland, Douglas 1961- ..... CLC 85; DAC; DAM POP
See also CA 142; CANR 57
Court, Wesli
See Turco, Lewis (Putnam)
Courtenay, Bryce 1933- .... CLC 59
See also CA 138
Courtney, Robert
See Ellison, Harlan (Jay)
Cousteau, Jacques-Yves 1910-1997 .. CLC 30
See also CA 65-68; 159; CANR 15, 67; MTCW 1; SATA 38, 98
Coventry, Francis 1725-1754 .... LC 46
Cowan, Peter (Walkinshaw) 1914- .... SSC 28
See also CA 21-24R; CANR 9, 25, 50, 83
Coward, Noel (Peirce) 1899-1973 . CLC 1, 9, 29, 51; DAM DRAM
See also AITN 1; CA 17-18; 41-44R; CANR 35; CAP 2; CDBLB 1914-1945; DA3; DLB 10; MTCW 1, 2
Cowley, Abraham 1618-1667 .... LC 43
See also DLB 131, 151
Cowley, Malcolm 1898-1989 .... CLC 39
See also CA 5-8R; 128; CANR 3, 55; DLB 4, 48; DLBY 81, 89; MTCW 1, 2

Dodgson, Charles Lutwidge 1832-1898
See Carroll, Lewis
See also CLR 2; DA; DAB; DAC; DAM
MST, NOV, POET; DA3; MAICYA;
SATA 100; YABC 2

Dodson, Owen (Vincent) 1914-1983 . **CLC 79;
BLC 1; DAM MULT**
See also BW 1; CA 65-68; 110; CANR 24;
DLB 76

Doeblin, Alfred 1878-1957 .... **TCLC 13**
See also Doblin, Alfred CA 110; 141; DLB
66

Doerr, Harriet 1910- .... **CLC 34**
See also CA 117; 122; CANR 47; INT 122

Domecq, H(onorio Bustos)
See Bioy Casares, Adolfo

Domecq, H(onorio) Bustos
See Bioy Casares, Adolfo; Borges, Jorge
Luis

Domini, Rey
See Lorde, Audre (Geraldine)

Dominique
See Proust, (Valentin-Louis-George-
Eugene-) Marcel

Don, A
See Stephen, SirLeslie

Donaldson, Stephen R. 1947- . **CLC 46; DAM
POP**
See also CA 89-92; CANR 13, 55; INT
CANR-13

Donleavy, J(ames) P(atrick) 1926- .... **CLC 1,
4, 6, 10, 45**
See also AITN 2; CA 9-12R; CANR 24, 49,
62, 80; DLB 6, 173; INT CANR-24;
MTCW 1, 2

Donne, John 1572-1631 .... **LC 10, 24; DA;
DAB; DAC; DAM MST, POET; PC 1;
WLC**
See also CDBLB Before 1660; DLB 121,
151

Donnell, David 1939(?)- .... **CLC 34**

Donoghue, P. S.
See Hunt, E(verette) Howard, (Jr.)

Donoso (Yanez), Jose 1924-1996 ... **CLC 4, 8,
11, 32, 99; DAM MULT; HLC 1; SSC
34**
See also CA 81-84; 155; CANR 32, 73;
DLB 113; HW 1, 2; MTCW 1, 2

Donovan, John 1928-1992 .... **CLC 35**
See also AAYA 20; CA 97-100; 137; CLR
3; MAICYA; SATA 72; SATA-Brief 29

Don Roberto
See Cunninghame Graham, Robert
(Gallnigad) Bontine

Doolittle, Hilda 1886-1961 . **CLC 3, 8, 14, 31,
34, 73; DA; DAC; DAM MST, POET;
PC 5; WLC**
See also H. D. CA 97-100; CANR 35; DLB
4, 45; MTCW 1, 2

Dorfman, Ariel 1942- ...... **CLC 48, 77; DAM
MULT; HLC 1**
See also CA 124; 130; CANR 67, 70; HW
1, 2; INT 130

Dorn, Edward (Merton) 1929- ... **CLC 10, 18**
See also CA 93-96; CANR 42, 79; DLB 5;
INT 93-96

Dorris, Michael (Anthony) 1945-1997
.... **CLC 109; DAM MULT, NOV**
See also AAYA 20; BEST 90:1; CA 102;
157; CANR 19, 46, 75; CLR 58; DA3;
DLB 175; MTCW 2; NNAL; SATA 75;
SATA-Obit 94

Dorris, Michael A.
See Dorris, Michael (Anthony)

Dorsan, Luc
See Simenon, Georges (Jacques Christian)

Dorsange, Jean
See Simenon, Georges (Jacques Christian)

Dos Passos, John (Roderigo) 1896-1970
..... **CLC 1, 4, 8, 11, 15, 25, 34, 82; DA;
DAB; DAC; DAM MST, NOV; WLC**
See also CA 1-4R; 29-32R; CANR 3;
CDALB 1929-1941; DA3; DLB 4, 9;
DLBD 1, 15; DLBY 96; MTCW 1, 2

Dossage, Jean
See Simenon, Georges (Jacques Christian)

Dostoevsky, Fedor Mikhailovich 1821-1881
**NCLC 2, 7, 21, 33, 43; DA; DAB; DAC;
DAM MST, NOV; SSC 2, 33; WLC**
See also DA3

Doughty, Charles M(ontagu) 1843-1926
TCLC 27
See also CA 115; 178; DLB 19, 57, 174

Douglas, Ellen .... **CLC 73**
See also Haxton, Josephine Ayres; William-
son, Ellen Douglas

Douglas, Gavin 1475(?)-1522 .... **LC 20**
See also DLB 132

Douglas, George
See Brown, George Douglas

Douglas, Keith (Castellain) 1920-1944
.... **TCLC 40**
See also CA 160; DLB 27

Douglas, Leonard
See Bradbury, Ray (Douglas)

Douglas, Michael
See Crichton, (John) Michael

Douglas, (George) Norman 1868-1952
.... **TCLC 68**
See also CA 119; 157; DLB 34, 195

Douglas, William
See Brown, George Douglas

Douglass, Frederick 1817(?)-1895 .. **NCLC 7,
55; BLC 1; DA; DAC; DAM MST,
MULT; WLC**
See also CDALB 1640-1865; DA3; DLB 1,
43, 50, 79; SATA 29

Dourado, (Waldomiro Freitas) Autran 1926-
CLC 23, 60
See also CA 25-28R; 179; CANR 34, 81;
DLB 145; HW 2

Dourado, Waldomiro Autran 1926-
See Dourado, (Waldomiro Freitas) Autran
See also CA 179

Dove, Rita (Frances) 1952- .... **CLC 50, 81;
BLCS; DAM MULT, POET; PC 6**
See also BW 2; CA 109; CAAS 19; CANR
27, 42, 68, 76; CDALBS; DA3; DLB 120;
MTCW 1

Doveglion
See Villa, Jose Garcia

Dowell, Coleman 1925-1985 .... **CLC 60**
See also CA 25-28R; 117; CANR 10; DLB
130

Dowson, Ernest (Christopher) 1867-1900
TCLC 4
See also CA 105; 150; DLB 19, 135

Doyle, A. Conan
See Doyle, Arthur Conan

Doyle, Arthur Conan 1859-1930 .... **TCLC 7;
DA; DAB; DAC; DAM MST, NOV;
SSC 12; WLC**
See also AAYA 14; CA 104; 122; CDBLB
1890-1914; DA3; DLB 18, 70, 156, 178;
MTCW 1, 2; SATA 24

Doyle, Conan
See Doyle, Arthur Conan

Doyle, John
See Graves, Robert (von Ranke)

Doyle, Roddy 1958(?)- .... **CLC 81**
See also AAYA 14; CA 143; CANR 73;
DA3; DLB 194

Doyle, Sir A. Conan
See Doyle, Arthur Conan

Doyle, Sir Arthur Conan
See Doyle, Arthur Conan

Dr. A
See Asimov, Isaac; Silverstein, Alvin

Drabble, Margaret 1939- . **CLC 2, 3, 5, 8, 10,
22, 53, 129; DAB; DAC; DAM MST,
NOV, POP**
See also CA 13-16R; CANR 18, 35, 63;
CDBLB 1960 to Present; DA3; DLB 14,
155; MTCW 1, 2; SATA 48

Drapier, M. B.
See Swift, Jonathan

Drayham, James
See Mencken, H(enry) L(ouis)

Drayton, Michael 1563-1631 ..... **LC 8; DAM
POET**
See also DLB 121

Dreadstone, Carl
See Campbell, (John) Ramsey

Dreiser, Theodore (Herman Albert)
1871-1945 .... **TCLC 10, 18, 35, 83; DA;
DAC; DAM MST, NOV; SSC 30; WLC**
See also CA 106; 132; CDALB 1865-1917;
DA3; DLB 9, 12, 102, 137; DLBD 1;
MTCW 1, 2

Drexler, Rosalyn 1926- .... **CLC 2, 6**
See also CA 81-84; CANR 68

Dreyer, Carl Theodor 1889-1968 ...... **CLC 16**
See also CA 116

Drieu la Rochelle, Pierre(-Eugene)
1893-1945 .... **TCLC 21**
See also CA 117; DLB 72

Drinkwater, John 1882-1937 .... **TCLC 57**
See also CA 109; 149; DLB 10, 19, 149

Drop Shot
See Cable, George Washington

Droste-Hulshoff, Annette Freiin von
1797-1848 .... **NCLC 3**
See also DLB 133

Drummond, Walter
See Silverberg, Robert

Drummond, William Henry 1854-1907
.... **TCLC 25**
See also CA 160; DLB 92

Drummond de Andrade, Carlos 1902-1987
CLC 18
See also Andrade, Carlos Drummond de CA
132; 123

Drury, Allen (Stuart) 1918-1998 .... **CLC 37**
See also CA 57-60; 170; CANR 18, 52; INT
CANR-18

Dryden, John 1631-1700 .... **LC 3, 21; DA;
DAB; DAC; DAM DRAM, MST,
POET; DC 3; PC 25; WLC**
See also CDBLB 1660-1789; DLB 80, 101,
131

Duberman, Martin (Bauml) 1930- ..... **CLC 8**
See also CA 1-4R; CANR 2, 63

Dubie, Norman (Evans) 1945- .... **CLC 36**
See also CA 69-72; CANR 12; DLB 120

Du Bois, W(illiam) E(dward) B(urghardt)
1868-1963 ... **CLC 1, 2, 13, 64, 96; BLC
1; DA; DAC; DAM MST, MULT, NOV;
WLC**
See also BW 1, 3; CA 85-88; CANR 34,
82; CDALB 1865-1917; DA3; DLB 47,
50, 91; MTCW 1, 2; SATA 42

Dubus, Andre 1936-1999 ..... **CLC 13, 36, 97;
SSC 15**
See also CA 21-24R; 177; CANR 17; DLB
130; INT CANR-17

Duca Minimo
See D'Annunzio, Gabriele

Ducharme, Rejean 1941- .... **CLC 74**
See also CA 165; DLB 60

Duclos, Charles Pinot 1704-1772 .... **LC 1**

Dudek, Louis 1918- .... **CLC 11, 19**
See also CA 45-48; CAAS 14; CANR 1;
DLB 88

Duerrenmatt, Friedrich 1921-1990 ... **CLC 1,
4, 8, 11, 15, 43, 102; DAM DRAM**

Esterbrook, Tom
See Hubbard, L(afayette) Ron(ald)
Estleman, Loren D. 1952- ..... **CLC 48; DAM NOV, POP**
See also AAYA 27; CA 85-88; CANR 27, 74; DA3; INT CANR-27; MTCW 1, 2
Euclid 306B.C.-283B.C. .... **CMLC 25**
Eugenides, Jeffrey 1960(?)- .... **CLC 81**
See also CA 144
Euripides c. 485B.C.-406B.C. ...... **CMLC 23; DA; DAB; DAC; DAM DRAM, MST; DC 4; WLCS**
See also DA3; DLB 176
Evan, Evin
See Faust, Frederick (Schiller)
Evans, Caradoc 1878-1945 .... **TCLC 85**
Evans, Evan
See Faust, Frederick (Schiller)
Evans, Marian
See Eliot, George
Evans, Mary Ann
See Eliot, George
Evarts, Esther
See Benson, Sally
Everett, Percival L. 1956- .... **CLC 57**
See also BW 2; CA 129
Everson, R(onald) G(ilmour) 1903- . **CLC 27**
See also CA 17-20R; DLB 88
Everson, William (Oliver) 1912-1994 . **CLC 1, 5, 14**
See also CA 9-12R; 145; CANR 20; DLB 212; MTCW 1
Evtushenko, Evgenii Aleksandrovich
See Yevtushenko, Yevgeny (Alexandrovich)
Ewart, Gavin (Buchanan) 1916-1995
.... **CLC 13, 46**
See also CA 89-92; 150; CANR 17, 46; DLB 40; MTCW 1
Ewers, Hanns Heinz 1871-1943 ..... **TCLC 12**
See also CA 109; 149
Ewing, Frederick R.
See Sturgeon, Theodore (Hamilton)
Exley, Frederick (Earl) 1929-1992 .... **CLC 6, 11**
See also AITN 2; CA 81-84; 138; DLB 143; DLBY 81
Eynhardt, Guillermo
See Quiroga, Horacio (Sylvestre)
Ezekiel, Nissim 1924- .... **CLC 61**
See also CA 61-64
Ezekiel, Tish O'Dowd 1943- .... **CLC 34**
See also CA 129
Fadeyev, A.
See Bulgya, Alexander Alexandrovich
Fadeyev, Alexander .... **TCLC 53**
See also Bulgya, Alexander Alexandrovich
Fagen, Donald 1948- .... **CLC 26**
Fainzilberg, Ilya Arnoldovich 1897-1937
See Ilf, Ilya
See also CA 120; 165
Fair, Ronald L. 1932- .... **CLC 18**
See also BW 1; CA 69-72; CANR 25; DLB 33
Fairbairn, Roger
See Carr, John Dickson
Fairbairns, Zoe (Ann) 1948- .... **CLC 32**
See also CA 103; CANR 21, 85
Falco, Gian
See Papini, Giovanni
Falconer, James
See Kirkup, James
Falconer, Kenneth
See Kornbluth, C(yril) M.
Falkland, Samuel
See Heijermans, Herman
Fallaci, Oriana 1930- .... **CLC 11, 110**
See also CA 77-80; CANR 15, 58; MTCW 1

Faludy, George 1913- .... **CLC 42**
See also CA 21-24R
Faludy, Gyoergy
See Faludy, George
Fanon, Frantz 1925-1961 ... **CLC 74; BLC 2; DAM MULT**
See also BW 1; CA 116; 89-92
Fanshawe, Ann 1625-1680 .... **LC 11**
Fante, John (Thomas) 1911-1983 ..... **CLC 60**
See also CA 69-72; 109; CANR 23; DLB 130; DLBY 83
Farah, Nuruddin 1945- ...... **CLC 53; BLC 2; DAM MULT**
See also BW 2, 3; CA 106; CANR 81; DLB 125
Fargue, Leon-Paul 1876(?)-1947 .... **TCLC 11**
See also CA 109
Farigoule, Louis
See Romains, Jules
Farina, Richard 1936(?)-1966 .... **CLC 9**
See also CA 81-84; 25-28R
Farley, Walter (Lorimer) 1915-1989 . **CLC 17**
See also CA 17-20R; CANR 8, 29, 84; DLB 22; JRDA; MAICYA; SATA 2, 43
Farmer, Philip Jose 1918- .... **CLC 1, 19**
See also AAYA 28; CA 1-4R; CANR 4, 35; DLB 8; MTCW 1; SATA 93
Farquhar, George 1677-1707 ... **LC 21; DAM DRAM**
See also DLB 84
Farrell, J(ames) G(ordon) 1935-1979 . **CLC 6**
See also CA 73-76; 89-92; CANR 36; DLB 14; MTCW 1
Farrell, James T(homas) 1904-1979 . **CLC 1, 4, 8, 11, 66; SSC 28**
See also CA 5-8R; 89-92; CANR 9, 61; DLB 4, 9, 86; DLBD 2; MTCW 1, 2
Farren, Richard J.
See Betjeman, John
Farren, Richard M.
See Betjeman, John
Fassbinder, Rainer Werner 1946-1982
.... **CLC 20**
See also CA 93-96; 106; CANR 31
Fast, Howard (Melvin) 1914- . **CLC 23; DAM NOV**
See also AAYA 16; CA 1-4R, 181; CAAE 181; CAAS 18; CANR 1, 33, 54, 75; DLB 9; INT CANR-33; MTCW 1; SATA 7; SATA-Essay 107
Faulcon, Robert
See Holdstock, Robert P.
Faulkner, William (Cuthbert) 1897-1962
CLC 1, 3, 6, 8, 9, 11, 14, 18, 28, 52, 68; DA; DAB; DAC; DAM MST, NOV; SSC 1, 35; WLC
See also AAYA 7; CA 81-84; CANR 33; CDALB 1929-1941; DA3; DLB 9, 11, 44, 102; DLBD 2; DLBY 86, 97; MTCW 1, 2
Fauset, Jessie Redmon 1884(?)-1961
.... **CLC 19, 54; BLC 2; DAM MULT**
See also BW 1; CA 109; CANR 83; DLB 51
Faust, Frederick (Schiller) 1892-1944(?)
TCLC 49; DAM POP
See also CA 108; 152
Faust, Irvin 1924- .... **CLC 8**
See also CA 33-36R; CANR 28, 67; DLB 2, 28; DLBY 80
Fawkes, Guy
See Benchley, Robert (Charles)
Fearing, Kenneth (Flexner) 1902-1961
.... **CLC 51**
See also CA 93-96; CANR 59; DLB 9
Fecamps, Elise
See Creasey, John
Federman, Raymond 1928- .... **CLC 6, 47**
See also CA 17-20R; CAAS 8; CANR 10, 43, 83; DLBY 80

Federspiel, J(uerg) F. 1931- .... **CLC 42**
See also CA 146
Feiffer, Jules (Ralph) 1929- ..... **CLC 2, 8, 64; DAM DRAM**
See also AAYA 3; CA 17-20R; CANR 30, 59; DLB 7, 44; INT CANR-30; MTCW 1; SATA 8, 61, 111
Feige, Hermann Albert Otto Maximilian
See Traven, B.
Feinberg, David B. 1956-1994 .... **CLC 59**
See also CA 135; 147
Feinstein, Elaine 1930- .... **CLC 36**
See also CA 69-72; CAAS 1; CANR 31, 68; DLB 14, 40; MTCW 1
Feldman, Irving (Mordecai) 1928- ..... **CLC 7**
See also CA 1-4R; CANR 1; DLB 169
Felix-Tchicaya, Gerald
See Tchicaya, Gerald Felix
Fellini, Federico 1920-1993 .... **CLC 16, 85**
See also CA 65-68; 143; CANR 33
Felsen, Henry Gregor 1916-1995 ..... **CLC 17**
See also CA 1-4R; 180; CANR 1; SAAS 2; SATA 1
Fenno, Jack
See Calisher, Hortense
Fenollosa, Ernest (Francisco) 1853-1908
TCLC 91
Fenton, James Martin 1949- .... **CLC 32**
See also CA 102; DLB 40
Ferber, Edna 1887-1968 .... **CLC 18, 93**
See also AITN 1; CA 5-8R; 25-28R; CANR 68; DLB 9, 28, 86; MTCW 1, 2; SATA 7
Ferguson, Helen
See Kavan, Anna
Ferguson, Samuel 1810-1886 .... **NCLC 33**
See also DLB 32
Fergusson, Robert 1750-1774 .... **LC 29**
See also DLB 109
Ferling, Lawrence
See Ferlinghetti, Lawrence (Monsanto)
Ferlinghetti, Lawrence (Monsanto) 1919(?)-
CLC 2, 6, 10, 27, 111; DAM POET; PC 1
See also CA 5-8R; CANR 3, 41, 73; CDALB 1941-1968; DA3; DLB 5, 16; MTCW 1, 2
Fernandez, Vicente Garcia Huidobro
See Huidobro Fernandez, Vicente Garcia
Ferre, Rosario 1942- .... **SSC 36; HLCS 1**
See also CA 131; CANR 55, 81; DLB 145; HW 1, 2; MTCW 1
Ferrer, Gabriel (Francisco Victor) Miro
See Miro (Ferrer), Gabriel (Francisco Victor)
Ferrier, Susan (Edmonstone) 1782-1854
NCLC 8
See also DLB 116
Ferrigno, Robert 1948(?)- .... **CLC 65**
See also CA 140
Ferron, Jacques 1921-1985 .... **CLC 94; DAC**
See also CA 117; 129; DLB 60
Feuchtwanger, Lion 1884-1958 .... **TCLC 3**
See also CA 104; DLB 66
Feuillet, Octave 1821-1890 .... **NCLC 45**
See also DLB 192
Feydeau, Georges (Leon Jules Marie)
1862-1921 .... **TCLC 22; DAM DRAM**
See also CA 113; 152; CANR 84; DLB 192
Fichte, Johann Gottlieb 1762-1814 . **NCLC 62**
See also DLB 90
Ficino, Marsilio 1433-1499 .... **LC 12**
Fiedeler, Hans
See Doeblin, Alfred
Fiedler, Leslie A(aron) 1917- .. **CLC 4, 13, 24**
See also CA 9-12R; CANR 7, 63; DLB 28, 67; MTCW 1, 2
Field, Andrew 1938- .... **CLC 44**
See also CA 97-100; CANR 25

Field, Eugene 1850-1895 .... **NCLC 3**
See also DLB 23, 42, 140; DLBD 13; MAI-
CYA; SATA 16
Field, Gans T.
See Wellman, Manly Wade
Field, Michael 1915-1971 .... **TCLC 43**
See also CA 29-32R
Field, Peter
See Hobson, Laura Z(ametkin)
Fielding, Henry 1707-1754 ..... **LC 1, 46; DA;
DAB; DAC; DAM DRAM, MST, NOV;
WLC**
See also CDBLB 1660-1789; DA3; DLB
39, 84, 101
Fielding, Sarah 1710-1768 .... **LC 1, 44**
See also DLB 39
Fields, W. C. 1880-1946 .... **TCLC 80**
See also DLB 44
Fierstein, Harvey (Forbes) 1954- .... **CLC 33;
DAM DRAM, POP**
See also CA 123; 129; DA3
Figes, Eva 1932- .... **CLC 31**
See also CA 53-56; CANR 4, 44, 83; DLB
14
Finch, Anne 1661-1720 .... **LC 3; PC 21**
See also DLB 95
Finch, Robert (Duer Claydon) 1900-
.... **CLC 18**
See also CA 57-60; CANR 9, 24, 49; DLB
88
Findley, Timothy 1930- . **CLC 27, 102; DAC;
DAM MST**
See also CA 25-28R; CANR 12, 42, 69;
DLB 53
Fink, William
See Mencken, H(enry) L(ouis)
Firbank, Louis 1942-
See Reed, Lou
See also CA 117
Firbank, (Arthur Annesley) Ronald
1886-1926 .... **TCLC 1**
See also CA 104; 177; DLB 36
Fisher, Dorothy (Frances) Canfield
1879-1958 .... **TCLC 87**
See also CA 114; 136; CANR 80; DLB 9,
102; MAICYA; YABC 1
Fisher, M(ary) F(rances) K(ennedy)
1908-1992 .... **CLC 76, 87**
See also CA 77-80; 138; CANR 44; MTCW
1
Fisher, Roy 1930- .... **CLC 25**
See also CA 81-84; CAAS 10; CANR 16;
DLB 40
Fisher, Rudolph 1897-1934 .. **TCLC 11; BLC
2; DAM MULT; SSC 25**
See also BW 1, 3; CA 107; 124; CANR 80;
DLB 51, 102
Fisher, Vardis (Alvero) 1895-1968 ...... **CLC 7**
See also CA 5-8R; 25-28R; CANR 68; DLB
9, 206
Fiske, Tarleton
See Bloch, Robert (Albert)
Fitch, Clarke
See Sinclair, Upton (Beall)
Fitch, John IV
See Cormier, Robert (Edmund)
Fitzgerald, Captain Hugh
See Baum, L(yman) Frank
FitzGerald, Edward 1809-1883 .... **NCLC 9**
See also DLB 32
Fitzgerald, F(rancis) Scott (Key) 1896-1940
**TCLC 1, 6, 14, 28, 55; DA; DAB; DAC;
DAM MST, NOV; SSC 6, 31; WLC**
See also AAYA 24; AITN 1; CA 110; 123;
CDALB 1917-1929; DA3; DLB 4, 9, 86;
DLBD 1, 15, 16; DLBY 81, 96; MTCW
1, 2
Fitzgerald, Penelope 1916- ... **CLC 19, 51, 61**

See also CA 85-88; CAAS 10; CANR 56,
86; DLB 14, 194; MTCW 2
Fitzgerald, Robert (Stuart) 1910-1985
.... **CLC 39**
See also CA 1-4R; 114; CANR 1; DLBY
80
FitzGerald, Robert D(avid) 1902-1987
.... **CLC 19**
See also CA 17-20R
Fitzgerald, Zelda (Sayre) 1900-1948
.... **TCLC 52**
See also CA 117; 126; DLBY 84
Flanagan, Thomas (James Bonner) 1923-
CLC 25, 52
See also CA 108; CANR 55; DLBY 80; INT
108; MTCW 2
Flaubert, Gustave 1821-1880 .... **NCLC 2, 10,
19, 62, 66; DA; DAB; DAC; DAM MST,
NOV; SSC 11; WLC**
See also DA3; DLB 119
Flecker, Herman Elroy
See Flecker, (Herman) James Elroy
Flecker, (Herman) James Elroy 1884-1915
TCLC 43
See also CA 109; 150; DLB 10, 19
Fleming, Ian (Lancaster) 1908-1964 . **CLC 3,
30; DAM POP**
See also AAYA 26; CA 5-8R; CANR 59;
CDBLB 1945-1960; DA3; DLB 87, 201;
MTCW 1, 2; SATA 9
Fleming, Thomas (James) 1927- ...... **CLC 37**
See also CA 5-8R; CANR 10; INT CANR-
10; SATA 8
Fletcher, John 1579-1625 .... **LC 33; DC 6**
See also CDBLB Before 1660; DLB 58
Fletcher, John Gould 1886-1950 .... **TCLC 35**
See also CA 107; 167; DLB 4, 45
Fleur, Paul
See Pohl, Frederik
Flooglebuckle, Al
See Spiegelman, Art
Flying Officer X
See Bates, H(erbert) E(rnest)
Fo, Dario 1926- . **CLC 32, 109; DAM DRAM;
DC 10**
See also CA 116; 128; CANR 68; DA3;
DLBY 97; MTCW 1, 2
Fogarty, Jonathan Titulescu Esq.
See Farrell, James T(homas)
Follett, Ken(neth Martin) 1949- ..... **CLC 18;
DAM NOV, POP**
See also AAYA 6; BEST 89:4; CA 81-84;
CANR 13, 33, 54; DA3; DLB 87; DLBY
81; INT CANR-33; MTCW 1
Fontane, Theodor 1819-1898 .... **NCLC 26**
See also DLB 129
Foote, Horton 1916- .... **CLC 51, 91; DAM
DRAM**
See also CA 73-76; CANR 34, 51; DA3;
DLB 26; INT CANR-34
Foote, Shelby 1916- ..... **CLC 75; DAM NOV,
POP**
See also CA 5-8R; CANR 3, 45, 74; DA3;
DLB 2, 17; MTCW 2
Forbes, Esther 1891-1967 .... **CLC 12**
See also AAYA 17; CA 13-14; 25-28R; CAP
1; CLR 27; DLB 22; JRDA; MAICYA;
SATA 2, 100
Forche, Carolyn (Louise) 1950- . **CLC 25, 83,
86; DAM POET; PC 10**
See also CA 109; 117; CANR 50, 74; DA3;
DLB 5, 193; INT 117; MTCW 1
Ford, Elbur
See Hibbert, Eleanor Alice Burford
Ford, Ford Madox 1873-1939 ... **TCLC 1, 15,
39, 57; DAM NOV**
See also CA 104; 132; CANR 74; CDBLB
1914-1945; DA3; DLB 162; MTCW 1, 2
Ford, Henry 1863-1947 .... **TCLC 73**

See also CA 115; 148
Ford, John 1586-(?) .... **DC 8**
See also CDBLB Before 1660; DAM
DRAM; DA3; DLB 58
Ford, John 1895-1973 .... **CLC 16**
See also CA 45-48
Ford, Richard 1944- .... **CLC 46, 99**
See also CA 69-72; CANR 11, 47, 86;
MTCW 1
Ford, Webster
See Masters, Edgar Lee
Foreman, Richard 1937- .... **CLC 50**
See also CA 65-68; CANR 32, 63
Forester, C(ecil) S(cott) 1899-1966 ... **CLC 35**
See also CA 73-76; 25-28R; CANR 83;
DLB 191; SATA 13
Forez
See Mauriac, Francois (Charles)
Forman, James Douglas 1932- .... **CLC 21**
See also AAYA 17; CA 9-12R; CANR 4,
19, 42; JRDA; MAICYA; SATA 8, 70
Fornes, Maria Irene 1930- . **CLC 39, 61; DC
10; HLCS 1**
See also CA 25-28R; CANR 28, 81; DLB
7; HW 1, 2; INT CANR-28; MTCW 1
Forrest, Leon (Richard) 1937-1997 .. **CLC 4;
BLCS**
See also BW 2; CA 89-92; 162; CAAS 7;
CANR 25, 52, 87; DLB 33
Forster, E(dward) M(organ) 1879-1970
..... **CLC 1, 2, 3, 4, 9, 10, 13, 15, 22, 45,
77; DA; DAB; DAC; DAM MST, NOV;
SSC 27; WLC**
See also AAYA 2; CA 13-14; 25-28R;
CANR 45; CAP 1; CDBLB 1914-1945;
DA3; DLB 34, 98, 162, 178, 195; DLBD
10; MTCW 1, 2; SATA 57
Forster, John 1812-1876 .... **NCLC 11**
See also DLB 144, 184
Forsyth, Frederick 1938- .... **CLC 2, 5, 36;
DAM NOV, POP**
See also BEST 89:4; CA 85-88; CANR 38,
62; DLB 87; MTCW 1, 2
Forten, Charlotte L. .... **TCLC 16; BLC 2**
See also Grimke, Charlotte L(ottie) Forten
DLB 50
Foscolo, Ugo 1778-1827 .... **NCLC 8**
Fosse, Bob .... **CLC 20**
See also Fosse, Robert Louis
Fosse, Robert Louis 1927-1987
See Fosse, Bob
See also CA 110; 123
Foster, Stephen Collins 1826-1864 . **NCLC 26**
Foucault, Michel 1926-1984 . **CLC 31, 34, 69**
See also CA 105; 113; CANR 34; MTCW
1, 2
**Fouque, Friedrich (Heinrich Karl) de la
Motte** 1777-1843 .... **NCLC 2**
See also DLB 90
Fourier, Charles 1772-1837 .... **NCLC 51**
Fournier, Pierre 1916- .... **CLC 11**
See also Gascar, Pierre CA 89-92; CANR
16, 40
Fowles, John (Philip) 1926- .. **CLC 1, 2, 3, 4,
6, 9, 10, 15, 33, 87; DAB; DAC; DAM
MST; SSC 33**
See also CA 5-8R; CANR 25, 71; CDBLB
1960 to Present; DA3; DLB 14, 139, 207;
MTCW 1, 2; SATA 22
Fox, Paula 1923- .... **CLC 2, 8, 121**
See also AAYA 3; CA 73-76; CANR 20,
36, 62; CLR 1, 44; DLB 52; JRDA; MAI-
CYA; MTCW 1; SATA 17, 60
Fox, William Price (Jr.) 1926- .... **CLC 22**
See also CA 17-20R; CAAS 19; CANR 11;
DLB 2; DLBY 81
Foxe, John 1516(?)-1587 .... **LC 14**
See also DLB 132

Gallup, Ralph
    See Whitemore, Hugh (John)
Galsworthy, John 1867-1933 .... **TCLC 1, 45;**
    DA; DAB; DAC; DAM DRAM, MST,
    NOV; SSC 22; WLC
    See also CA 104; 141; CANR 75; CDBLB
    1890-1914; DA3; DLB 10, 34, 98, 162;
    DLBD 16; MTCW 1
Galt, John 1779-1839 .... **NCLC 1**
    See also DLB 99, 116, 159
Galvin, James 1951- .... **CLC 38**
    See also CA 108; CANR 26
Gamboa, Federico 1864-1939 .... **TCLC 36**
    See also CA 167; HW 2
Gandhi, M. K.
    See Gandhi, Mohandas Karamchand
Gandhi, Mahatma
    See Gandhi, Mohandas Karamchand
Gandhi, Mohandas Karamchand 1869-1948
    TCLC 59; DAM MULT
    See also CA 121; 132; DA3; MTCW 1, 2
Gann, Ernest Kellogg 1910-1991 ..... **CLC 23**
    See also AITN 1; CA 1-4R; 136; CANR 1,
    83
Garber, Eric 1943(?)-
    See Holleran, Andrew
Garcia, Cristina 1958- .... **CLC 76**
    See also CA 141; CANR 73; HW 2
Garcia Lorca, Federico 1898-1936 . **TCLC 1,**
    7, 49; DA; DAB; DAC; DAM DRAM,
    MST, MULT, POET; DC 2; HLC 2; PC
    3; WLC
    See also CA 104; 131; CANR 81; DA3;
    DLB 108; HW 1, 2; MTCW 1, 2
Garcia Marquez, Gabriel (Jose) 1928-
    ...... **CLC 2, 3, 8, 10, 15, 27, 47, 55, 68;**
    DA; DAB; DAC; DAM MST, MULT,
    NOV, POP; HLC 1; SSC 8; WLC
    See also AAYA 3; BEST 89:1, 90:4; CA 33-
    36R; CANR 10, 28, 50, 75, 82; DA3;
    DLB 113; HW 1, 2; MTCW 1, 2
Garcilaso de la Vega, El Inca 1503-1536
    See also HLCS 1
Gard, Janice
    See Latham, Jean Lee
Gard, Roger Martin du
    See Martin du Gard, Roger
Gardam, Jane 1928- .... **CLC 43**
    See also CA 49-52; CANR 2, 18, 33, 54;
    CLR 12; DLB 14, 161; MAICYA; MTCW
    1; SAAS 9; SATA 39, 76; SATA-Brief 28
Gardner, Herb(ert) 1934- .... **CLC 44**
    See also CA 149
Gardner, John (Champlin), Jr. 1933-1982
    CLC 2, 3, 5, 7, 8, 10, 18, 28, 34; DAM
    NOV, POP; SSC 7
    See also AITN 1; CA 65-68; 107; CANR
    33, 73; CDALBS; DA3; DLB 2; DLBY
    82; MTCW 1; SATA 40; SATA-Obit 31
Gardner, John (Edmund) 1926- ...... **CLC 30;**
    DAM POP
    See also CA 103; CANR 15, 69; MTCW 1
Gardner, Miriam
    See Bradley, Marion Zimmer
Gardner, Noel
    See Kuttner, Henry
Gardons, S. S.
    See Snodgrass, W(illiam) D(e Witt)
Garfield, Leon 1921-1996 .... **CLC 12**
    See also AAYA 8; CA 17-20R; 152; CANR
    38, 41, 78; CLR 21; DLB 161; JRDA;
    MAICYA; SATA 1, 32, 76; SATA-Obit 90
Garland, (Hannibal) Hamlin 1860-1940
    TCLC 3; SSC 18
    See also CA 104; DLB 12, 71, 78, 186
Garneau, (Hector de) Saint-Denys 1912-1943
    TCLC 13
    See also CA 111; DLB 88

Garner, Alan 1934- ..... **CLC 17; DAB; DAM**
    POP
    See also AAYA 18; CA 73-76, 178; CAAE
    178; CANR 15, 64; CLR 20; DLB 161;
    MAICYA; MTCW 1, 2; SATA 18, 69;
    SATA-Essay 108
Garner, Hugh 1913-1979 .... **CLC 13**
    See also CA 69-72; CANR 31; DLB 68
Garnett, David 1892-1981 .... **CLC 3**
    See also CA 5-8R; 103; CANR 17, 79; DLB
    34; MTCW 2
Garos, Stephanie
    See Katz, Steve
Garrett, George (Palmer) 1929- .. **CLC 3, 11,**
    51; SSC 30
    See also CA 1-4R; CAAS 5; CANR 1, 42,
    67; DLB 2, 5, 130, 152; DLBY 83
Garrick, David 1717-1779 .... **LC 15; DAM**
    DRAM
    See also DLB 84
Garrigue, Jean 1914-1972 .... **CLC 2, 8**
    See also CA 5-8R; 37-40R; CANR 20
Garrison, Frederick
    See Sinclair, Upton (Beall)
Garro, Elena 1920(?)-1998
    See also CA 131; 169; DLB 145; HLCS 1;
    HW 1
Garth, Will
    See Hamilton, Edmond; Kuttner, Henry
Garvey, Marcus (Moziah, Jr.) 1887-1940
    TCLC 41; BLC 2; DAM MULT
    See also BW 1; CA 120; 124; CANR 79
Gary, Romain .... **CLC 25**
    See also Kacew, Romain DLB 83
Gascar, Pierre .... **CLC 11**
    See also Fournier, Pierre
Gascoyne, David (Emery) 1916- .... **CLC 45**
    See also CA 65-68; CANR 10, 28, 54; DLB
    20; MTCW 1
Gaskell, Elizabeth Cleghorn 1810-1865
    NCLC 70; DAB; DAM MST; SSC 25
    See also CDBLB 1832-1890; DLB 21, 144,
    159
Gass, William H(oward) 1924- . **CLC 1, 2, 8,**
    11, 15, 39; SSC 12
    See also CA 17-20R; CANR 30, 71; DLB
    2; MTCW 1, 2
Gassendi, Pierre 1592-1655 .... **LC 54**
Gasset, Jose Ortega y
    See Ortega y Gasset, Jose
Gates, Henry Louis, Jr. 1950- .... **CLC 65;**
    BLCS; DAM MULT
    See also BW 2, 3; CA 109; CANR 25, 53,
    75; DA3; DLB 67; MTCW 1
Gautier, Theophile 1811-1872 .. **NCLC 1, 59;**
    DAM POET; PC 18; SSC 20
    See also DLB 119
Gawsworth, John
    See Bates, H(erbert) E(rnest)
Gay, John 1685-1732 .. **LC 49; DAM DRAM**
    See also DLB 84, 95
Gay, Oliver
    See Gogarty, Oliver St. John
Gaye, Marvin (Penze) 1939-1984 ..... **CLC 26**
    See also CA 112
Gebler, Carlo (Ernest) 1954- .... **CLC 39**
    See also CA 119; 133
Gee, Maggie (Mary) 1948- .... **CLC 57**
    See also CA 130; DLB 207
Gee, Maurice (Gough) 1931- .... **CLC 29**
    See also CA 97-100; CANR 67; CLR 56;
    SATA 46, 101
Gelbart, Larry (Simon) 1923- .... **CLC 21, 61**
    See also CA 73-76; CANR 45
Gelber, Jack 1932- .... **CLC 1, 6, 14, 79**
    See also CA 1-4R; CANR 2; DLB 7
Gellhorn, Martha (Ellis) 1908-1998 . **CLC 14,**
    60

See also CA 77-80; 164; CANR 44; DLBY
    82, 98
Genet, Jean 1910-1986 .. **CLC 1, 2, 5, 10, 14,**
    44, 46; DAM DRAM
    See also CA 13-16R; CANR 18; DA3; DLB
    72; DLBY 86; MTCW 1, 2
Gent, Peter 1942- .... **CLC 29**
    See also AITN 1; CA 89-92; DLBY 82
Gentile, Giovanni 1875-1944 .... **TCLC 96**
    See also CA 119
Gentlewoman in New England, A
    See Bradstreet, Anne
Gentlewoman in Those Parts, A
    See Bradstreet, Anne
George, Jean Craighead 1919- .... **CLC 35**
    See also AAYA 8; CA 5-8R; CANR 25;
    CLR 1; DLB 52; JRDA; MAICYA; SATA
    2, 68
George, Stefan (Anton) 1868-1933 . **TCLC 2,**
    14
    See also CA 104
Georges, Georges Martin
    See Simenon, Georges (Jacques Christian)
Gerhardi, William Alexander
    See Gerhardie, William Alexander
Gerhardie, William Alexander 1895-1977
    CLC 5
    See also CA 25-28R; 73-76; CANR 18;
    DLB 36
Gerstler, Amy 1956- .... **CLC 70**
    See also CA 146
Gertler, T. .... **CLC 34**
    See also CA 116; 121; INT 121
Ghalib .... **NCLC 39, 78**
    See also Ghalib, Hsadullah Khan
Ghalib, Hsadullah Khan 1797-1869
    See Ghalib
    See also DAM POET
Ghelderode, Michel de 1898-1962 ..... **CLC 6,**
    11; DAM DRAM
    See also CA 85-88; CANR 40, 77
Ghiselin, Brewster 1903- .... **CLC 23**
    See also CA 13-16R; CAAS 10; CANR 13
Ghose, Aurabinda 1872-1950 .... **TCLC 63**
    See also CA 163
Ghose, Zulfikar 1935- .... **CLC 42**
    See also CA 65-68; CANR 67
Ghosh, Amitav 1956- .... **CLC 44**
    See also CA 147; CANR 80
Giacosa, Giuseppe 1847-1906 .... **TCLC 7**
    See also CA 104
Gibb, Lee
    See Waterhouse, Keith (Spencer)
Gibbon, Lewis Grassic .... **TCLC 4**
    See also Mitchell, James Leslie
Gibbons, Kaye 1960- .... **CLC 50, 88; DAM**
    POP
    See also CA 151; CANR 75; DA3; MTCW
    1
Gibran, Kahlil 1883-1931 . **TCLC 1, 9; DAM**
    POET, POP; PC 9
    See also CA 104; 150; DA3; MTCW 2
Gibran, Khalil
    See Gibran, Kahlil
Gibson, William 1914- .. **CLC 23; DA; DAB;**
    DAC; DAM DRAM, MST
    See also CA 9-12R; CANR 9, 42, 75; DLB
    7; MTCW 1; SATA 66
Gibson, William (Ford) 1948- ... **CLC 39, 63;**
    DAM POP
    See also AAYA 12; CA 126; 133; CANR
    52; DA3; MTCW 1
Gide, Andre (Paul Guillaume) 1869-1951
    TCLC 5, 12, 36; DA; DAB; DAC; DAM
    MST, NOV; SSC 13; WLC
    See also CA 104; 124; DA3; DLB 65;
    MTCW 1, 2
Gifford, Barry (Colby) 1946- .... **CLC 34**

See also CA 65-68; CANR 9, 30, 40
Gilbert, Frank
See De Voto, Bernard (Augustine)
Gilbert, W(illiam) S(chwenck) 1836-1911
TCLC 3; DAM DRAM, POET
See also CA 104; 173; SATA 36
Gilbreth, Frank B., Jr. 1911- .... **CLC 17**
See also CA 9-12R; SATA 2
Gilchrist, Ellen 1935- ...... **CLC 34, 48; DAM**
POP; SSC 14
See also CA 113; 116; CANR 41, 61; DLB
130; MTCW 1, 2
Giles, Molly 1942- .... **CLC 39**
See also CA 126
Gill, Eric 1882-1940 .... **TCLC 85**
Gill, Patrick
See Creasey, John
Gilliam, Terry (Vance) 1940- .... **CLC 21**
See also Monty Python AAYA 19; CA 108;
113; CANR 35; INT 113
Gillian, Jerry
See Gilliam, Terry (Vance)
Gilliatt, Penelope (Ann Douglass) 1932-1993
CLC 2, 10, 13, 53
See also AITN 2; CA 13-16R; 141; CANR
49; DLB 14
Gilman, Charlotte (Anna) Perkins (Stetson)
1860-1935 .... **TCLC 9, 37; SSC 13**
See also CA 106; 150; MTCW 1
Gilmour, David 1949- .... **CLC 35**
See also CA 138, 147
Gilpin, William 1724-1804 .... **NCLC 30**
Gilray, J. D.
See Mencken, H(enry) L(ouis)
Gilroy, Frank D(aniel) 1925- .... **CLC 2**
See also CA 81-84; CANR 32, 64, 86; DLB
7
Gilstrap, John 1957(?)- .... **CLC 99**
See also CA 160
Ginsberg, Allen 1926-1997 . CLC 1, 2, 3, 4, 6,
13, 36, 69, 109; DA; DAB; DAC; DAM
MST, POET; PC 4; WLC
See also AITN 1; CA 1-4R; 157; CANR 2,
41, 63; CDALB 1941-1968; DA3; DLB
5, 16, 169; MTCW 1, 2
Ginzburg, Natalia 1916-1991 . CLC 5, 11, 54,
70
See also CA 85-88; 135; CANR 33; DLB
177; MTCW 1, 2
Giono, Jean 1895-1970 .... **CLC 4, 11**
See also CA 45-48; 29-32R; CANR 2, 35;
DLB 72; MTCW 1
Giovanni, Nikki 1943- . CLC 2, 4, 19, 64, 117;
BLC 2; DA; DAB; DAC; DAM MST,
MULT, POET; PC 19; WLCS
See also AAYA 22; AITN 1; BW 2, 3; CA
29-32R; CAAS 6; CANR 18, 41, 60;
CDALBS; CLR 6; DA3; DLB 5, 41; INT
CANR-18; MAICYA; MTCW 1, 2; SATA
24, 107
Giovene, Andrea 1904- .... **CLC 7**
See also CA 85-88
Gippius, Zinaida (Nikolayevna) 1869-1945
See Hippius, Zinaida
See also CA 106
Giraudoux, (Hippolyte) Jean 1882-1944
TCLC 2, 7; DAM DRAM
See also CA 104; DLB 65
Gironella, Jose Maria 1917- .... **CLC 11**
See also CA 101
Gissing, George (Robert) 1857-1903
.... **TCLC 3, 24, 47; SSC 37**
See also CA 105; 167; DLB 18, 135, 184
Giurlani, Aldo
See Palazzeschi, Aldo
Gladkov, Fyodor (Vasilyevich) 1883-1958
TCLC 27
See also CA 170
Glanville, Brian (Lester) 1931- .... **CLC 6**

See also CA 5-8R; CAAS 9; CANR 3, 70;
DLB 15, 139; SATA 42
Glasgow, Ellen (Anderson Gholson)
1873-1945 .... **TCLC 2, 7; SSC 34**
See also CA 104; 164; DLB 9, 12; MTCW
2
Glaspell, Susan 1882(?)-1948 . TCLC 55; DC
10
See also CA 110; 154; DLB 7, 9, 78; YABC
2
Glassco, John 1909-1981 .... **CLC 9**
See also CA 13-16R; 102; CANR 15; DLB
68
Glasscock, Amnesia
See Steinbeck, John (Ernst)
Glasser, Ronald J. 1940(?)- .... **CLC 37**
Glassman, Joyce
See Johnson, Joyce
Glendinning, Victoria 1937- .... **CLC 50**
See also CA 120; 127; CANR 59; DLB 155
Glissant, Edouard 1928- . CLC 10, 68; DAM
MULT
See also CA 153
Gloag, Julian 1930- .... **CLC 40**
See also AITN 1; CA 65-68; CANR 10, 70
Glowacki, Aleksander
See Prus, Boleslaw
Gluck, Louise (Elisabeth) 1943- .. CLC 7, 22,
44, 81; DAM POET; PC 16
See also CA 33-36R; CANR 40, 69; DA3;
DLB 5; MTCW 2
Glyn, Elinor 1864-1943 .... **TCLC 72**
See also DLB 153
Gobineau, Joseph Arthur (Comte) de
1816-1882 .... **NCLC 17**
See also DLB 123
Godard, Jean-Luc 1930- .... **CLC 20**
See also CA 93-96
Godden, (Margaret) Rumer 1907-1998
.... **CLC 53**
See also AAYA 6; CA 5-8R; 172; CANR 4,
27, 36, 55, 80; CLR 20; DLB 161; MAI-
CYA; SAAS 12; SATA 3, 36; SATA-Obit
109
Godoy Alcayaga, Lucila 1889-1957
See Mistral, Gabriela
See also BW 2; CA 104; 131; CANR 81;
DAM MULT; HW 1, 2; MTCW 1, 2
Godwin, Gail (Kathleen) 1937- ..... **CLC 5, 8,**
22, 31, 69, 125; DAM POP
See also CA 29-32R; CANR 15, 43, 69;
DA3; DLB 6; INT CANR-15; MTCW 1,
2
Godwin, William 1756-1836 .... **NCLC 14**
See also CDBLB 1789-1832; DLB 39, 104,
142, 158, 163
Goebbels, Josef
See Goebbels, (Paul) Joseph
Goebbels, (Paul) Joseph 1897-1945
.... **TCLC 68**
See also CA 115; 148
Goebbels, Joseph Paul
See Goebbels, (Paul) Joseph
Goethe, Johann Wolfgang von 1749-1832
NCLC 4, 22, 34; DA; DAB; DAC; DAM
DRAM, MST, POET; PC 5; SSC 38;
WLC
See also DA3; DLB 94
Gogarty, Oliver St. John 1878-1957
.... **TCLC 15**
See also CA 109; 150; DLB 15, 19
Gogol, Nikolai (Vasilyevich) 1809-1852
NCLC 5, 15, 31; DA; DAB; DAC; DAM
DRAM, MST; DC 1; SSC 4, 29; WLC
See also DLB 198
Goines, Donald 1937(?)-1974 . CLC 80; BLC
2; DAM MULT, POP
See also AITN 1; BW 1, 3; CA 124; 114;
CANR 82; DA3; DLB 33

Gold, Herbert 1924- .... **CLC 4, 7, 14, 42**
See also CA 9-12R; CANR 17, 45; DLB 2;
DLBY 81
Goldbarth, Albert 1948- .... **CLC 5, 38**
See also CA 53-56; CANR 6, 40; DLB 120
Goldberg, Anatol 1910-1982 .... **CLC 34**
See also CA 131; 117
Goldemberg, Isaac 1945- .... **CLC 52**
See also CA 69-72; CAAS 12; CANR 11,
32; HW 1
Golding, William (Gerald) 1911-1993
. **CLC 1, 2, 3, 8, 10, 17, 27, 58, 81; DA;**
DAB; DAC; DAM MST, NOV; WLC
See also AAYA 5; CA 5-8R; 141; CANR
13, 33, 54; CDBLB 1945-1960; DA3;
DLB 15, 100; MTCW 1, 2
Goldman, Emma 1869-1940 .... **TCLC 13**
See also CA 110; 150
Goldman, Francisco 1954- .... **CLC 76**
See also CA 162
Goldman, William (W.) 1931- ...... **CLC 1, 48**
See also CA 9-12R; CANR 29, 69; DLB 44
Goldmann, Lucien 1913-1970 .... **CLC 24**
See also CA 25-28; CAP 2
Goldoni, Carlo 1707-1793 .... **LC 4; DAM**
DRAM
Goldsberry, Steven 1949- .... **CLC 34**
See also CA 131
Goldsmith, Oliver 1728-1774 . LC 2, 48; DA;
DAB; DAC; DAM DRAM, MST, NOV,
POET; DC 8; WLC
See also CDBLB 1660-1789; DLB 39, 89,
104, 109, 142; SATA 26
Goldsmith, Peter
See Priestley, J(ohn) B(oynton)
Gombrowicz, Witold 1904-1969 .... CLC 4, 7,
11, 49; DAM DRAM
See also CA 19-20; 25-28R; CAP 2
Gomez de la Serna, Ramon 1888-1963
.... **CLC 9**
See also CA 153; 116; CANR 79; HW 1, 2
Goncharov, Ivan Alexandrovich 1812-1891
NCLC 1, 63
Goncourt, Edmond (Louis Antoine Huot) de
1822-1896 .... **NCLC 7**
See also DLB 123
Goncourt, Jules (Alfred Huot) de 1830-1870
NCLC 7
See also DLB 123
Gontier, Fernande 19(?)- .... **CLC 50**
Gonzalez Martinez, Enrique 1871-1952
TCLC 72
See also CA 166; CANR 81; HW 1, 2
Goodman, Paul 1911-1972 ..... **CLC 1, 2, 4, 7**
See also CA 19-20; 37-40R; CANR 34;
CAP 2; DLB 130; MTCW 1
Gordimer, Nadine 1923- ...... **CLC 3, 5, 7, 10,**
18, 33, 51, 70; DA; DAB; DAC; DAM
MST, NOV; SSC 17; WLCS
See also CA 5-8R; CANR 3, 28, 56, 88;
DA3; INT CANR-28; MTCW 1, 2
Gordon, Adam Lindsay 1833-1870 . NCLC 21
Gordon, Caroline 1895-1981 . CLC 6, 13, 29,
83; SSC 15
See also CA 11-12; 103; CANR 36; CAP 1;
DLB 4, 9, 102; DLBD 17; DLBY 81;
MTCW 1, 2
Gordon, Charles William 1860-1937
See Connor, Ralph
See also CA 109
Gordon, Mary (Catherine) 1949- .... **CLC 13,**
22, 128
See also CA 102; CANR 44; DLB 6; DLBY
81; INT 102; MTCW 1
Gordon, N. J.
See Bosman, Herman Charles
Gordon, Sol 1923- .... **CLC 26**
See also CA 53-56; CANR 4; SATA 11
Gordone, Charles 1925-1995 .... **CLC 1, 4;**

DAM DRAM; DC 8
See also BW 1, 3; CA 93-96, 180; 150;
CAAE 180; CANR 55; DLB 7; INT 93-
96; MTCW 1

Gore, Catherine 1800-1861 .... **NCLC 65**
See also DLB 116

Gorenko, Anna Andreevna
See Akhmatova, Anna

Gorky, Maxim 1868-1936 ..... **TCLC 8; DAB;**
SSC 28; WLC
See also Peshkov, Alexei Maximovich
MTCW 2

Goryan, Sirak
See Saroyan, William

Gosse, Edmund (William) 1849-1928
.... **TCLC 28**
See also CA 117; DLB 57, 144, 184

Gotlieb, Phyllis Fay (Bloom) 1926- .. **CLC 18**
See also CA 13-16R; CANR 7; DLB 88

Gottesman, S. D.
See Kornbluth, C(yril) M.; Pohl, Frederik

Gottfried von Strassburg fl. c. 1210-
.... **CMLC 10**
See also DLB 138

Gould, Lois .... **CLC 4, 10**
See also CA 77-80; CANR 29; MTCW 1

Gourmont, Remy (-Marie-Charles) de
1858-1915 .... **TCLC 17**
See also CA 109; 150; MTCW 2

Govier, Katherine 1948- .... **CLC 51**
See also CA 101; CANR 18, 40

Goyen, (Charles) William 1915-1983 . **CLC 5,**
8, 14, 40
See also AITN 2; CA 5-8R; 110; CANR 6,
71; DLB 2; DLBY 83; INT CANR-6

Goytisolo, Juan 1931- . **CLC 5, 10, 23; DAM**
MULT; HLC 1
See also CA 85-88; CANR 32, 61; HW 1,
2; MTCW 1, 2

Gozzano, Guido 1883-1916 .... **PC 10**
See also CA 154; DLB 114

Gozzi, (Conte) Carlo 1720-1806 .... **NCLC 23**

Grabbe, Christian Dietrich 1801-1836
.... **NCLC 2**
See also DLB 133

Grace, Patricia Frances 1937- .... **CLC 56**
See also CA 176

Gracian y Morales, Baltasar 1601-1658
.... **LC 15**

Gracq, Julien .... **CLC 11, 48**
See also Poirier, Louis DLB 83

Grade, Chaim 1910-1982 .... **CLC 10**
See also CA 93-96; 107

Graduate of Oxford, A
See Ruskin, John

Grafton, Garth
See Duncan, Sara Jeannette

Graham, John
See Phillips, David Graham

Graham, Jorie 1951- .... **CLC 48, 118**
See also CA 111; CANR 63; DLB 120

Graham, R(obert) B(ontine) Cunninghame
See Cunninghame Graham, Robert
(Gallnigad) Bontine
See also DLB 98, 135, 174

Graham, Robert
See Haldeman, Joe (William)

Graham, Tom
See Lewis, (Harry) Sinclair

Graham, W(illiam) S(ydney) 1918-1986
.... **CLC 29**
See also CA 73-76; 118; DLB 20

Graham, Winston (Mawdsley) 1910-
.... **CLC 23**
See also CA 49-52; CANR 2, 22, 45, 66;
DLB 77

Grahame, Kenneth 1859-1932 ...... **TCLC 64;**
DAB

See also CA 108; 136; CANR 80; CLR 5;
DA3; DLB 34, 141, 178; MAICYA;
MTCW 2; SATA 100; YABC 1

Granovsky, Timofei Nikolaevich 1813-1855
NCLC 75
See also DLB 198

Grant, Skeeter
See Spiegelman, Art

Granville-Barker, Harley 1877-1946
.... **TCLC 2; DAM DRAM**
See also Barker, Harley Granville CA 104

Grass, Guenter (Wilhelm) 1927- ... **CLC 1, 2,**
4, 6, 11, 15, 22, 32, 49, 88; DA; DAB;
DAC; DAM MST, NOV; WLC
See also CA 13-16R; CANR 20, 75; DA3;
DLB 75, 124; MTCW 1, 2

Gratton, Thomas
See Hulme, T(homas) E(rnest)

Grau, Shirley Ann 1929- . **CLC 4, 9; SSC 15**
See also CA 89-92; CANR 22, 69; DLB 2;
INT CANR-22; MTCW 1

Gravel, Fern
See Hall, James Norman

Graver, Elizabeth 1964- .... **CLC 70**
See also CA 135; CANR 71

Graves, Richard Perceval 1945- .... **CLC 44**
See also CA 65-68; CANR 9, 26, 51

Graves, Robert (von Ranke) 1895-1985
.... **CLC 1, 2, 6, 11, 39, 44, 45; DAB;**
DAC; DAM MST, POET; PC 6
See also CA 5-8R; 117; CANR 5, 36; CD-
BLB 1914-1945; DA3; DLB 20, 100, 191;
DLBD 18; DLBY 85; MTCW 1, 2; SATA
45

Graves, Valerie
See Bradley, Marion Zimmer

Gray, Alasdair (James) 1934- .... **CLC 41**
See also CA 126; CANR 47, 69; DLB 194;
INT 126; MTCW 1, 2

Gray, Amlin 1946- .... **CLC 29**
See also CA 138

Gray, Francine du Plessix 1930- ..... **CLC 22;**
DAM NOV
See also BEST 90:3; CA 61-64; CAAS 2;
CANR 11, 33, 75, 81; INT CANR-11;
MTCW 1, 2

Gray, John (Henry) 1866-1934 ...... **TCLC 19**
See also CA 119; 162

Gray, Simon (James Holliday) 1936- . **CLC 9,**
14, 36
See also AITN 1; CA 21-24R; CAAS 3;
CANR 32, 69; DLB 13; MTCW 1

Gray, Spalding 1941- ..... **CLC 49, 112; DAM**
POP; DC 7
See also CA 128; CANR 74; MTCW 2

Gray, Thomas 1716-1771 .... **LC 4, 40; DA;**
DAB; DAC; DAM MST; PC 2; WLC
See also CDBLB 1660-1789; DA3; DLB
109

Grayson, David
See Baker, Ray Stannard

Grayson, Richard (A.) 1951- .... **CLC 38**
See also CA 85-88; CANR 14, 31, 57

Greeley, Andrew M(oran) 1928- ..... **CLC 28;**
DAM POP
See also CA 5-8R; CAAS 7; CANR 7, 43,
69; DA3; MTCW 1, 2

Green, Anna Katharine 1846-1935 . **TCLC 63**
See also CA 112; 159; DLB 202

Green, Brian
See Card, Orson Scott

Green, Hannah
See Greenberg, Joanne (Goldenberg)

Green, Hannah 1927(?)-1996 .... **CLC 3**
See also CA 73-76; CANR 59

Green, Henry 1905-1973 .... **CLC 2, 13, 97**
See also Yorke, Henry Vincent CA 175;
DLB 15

Green, Julian (Hartridge) 1900-1998
See Green, Julien
See also CA 21-24R; 169; CANR 33, 87;
DLB 4, 72; MTCW 1

Green, Julien .... **CLC 3, 11, 77**
See also Green, Julian (Hartridge) MTCW
2

Green, Paul (Eliot) 1894-1981 .... **CLC 25;**
DAM DRAM
See also AITN 1; CA 5-8R; 103; CANR 3;
DLB 7, 9; DLBY 81

Greenberg, Ivan 1908-1973
See Rahv, Philip
See also CA 85-88

Greenberg, Joanne (Goldenberg) 1932-
.... **CLC 7, 30**
See also AAYA 12; CA 5-8R; CANR 14,
32, 69; SATA 25

Greenberg, Richard 1959(?)- .... **CLC 57**
See also CA 138

Greene, Bette 1934- .... **CLC 30**
See also AAYA 7; CA 53-56; CANR 4; CLR
2; JRDA; MAICYA; SAAS 16; SATA 8,
102

Greene, Gael .... **CLC 8**
See also CA 13-16R; CANR 10

Greene, Graham (Henry) 1904-1991 . **CLC 1,**
3, 6, 9, 14, 18, 27, 37, 70, 72, 125; DA;
DAB; DAC; DAM MST, NOV; SSC 29;
WLC
See also AITN 2; CA 13-16R; 133; CANR
35, 61; CDBLB 1945-1960; DA3; DLB
13, 15, 77, 100, 162, 201, 204; DLBY 91;
MTCW 1, 2; SATA 20

Greene, Robert 1558-1592 .... **LC 41**
See also DLB 62, 167

Greer, Richard
See Silverberg, Robert

Gregor, Arthur 1923- .... **CLC 9**
See also CA 25-28R; CAAS 10; CANR 11;
SATA 36

Gregor, Lee
See Pohl, Frederik

Gregory, Isabella Augusta (Persse)
1852-1932 .... **TCLC 1**
See also CA 104; 184; DLB 10

Gregory, J. Dennis
See Williams, John A(lfred)

Grendon, Stephen
See Derleth, August (William)

Grenville, Kate 1950- .... **CLC 61**
See also CA 118; CANR 53

Grenville, Pelham
See Wodehouse, P(elham) G(renville)

Greve, Felix Paul (Berthold Friedrich)
1879-1948
See Grove, Frederick Philip
See also CA 104; 141, 175; CANR 79;
DAC; DAM MST

Grey, Zane 1872-1939 . **TCLC 6; DAM POP**
See also CA 104; 132; DA3; DLB 212;
MTCW 1, 2

Grieg, (Johan) Nordahl (Brun) 1902-1943
TCLC 10
See also CA 107

Grieve, C(hristopher) M(urray) 1892-1978
CLC 11, 19; DAM POET
See also MacDiarmid, Hugh; Pteleon CA
5-8R; 85-88; CANR 33; MTCW 1

Griffin, Gerald 1803-1840 .... **NCLC 7**
See also DLB 159

Griffin, John Howard 1920-1980 ..... **CLC 68**
See also AITN 1; CA 1-4R; 101; CANR 2

Griffin, Peter 1942- .... **CLC 39**
See also CA 136

Griffith, D(avid Lewelyn) W(ark)
1875(?)-1948 .... **TCLC 68**
See also CA 119; 150; CANR 80

Griffith, Lawrence
See Griffith, D(avid Lewelyn) W(ark)
Griffiths, Trevor 1935- .... **CLC 13, 52**
See also CA 97-100; CANR 45; DLB 13
Griggs, Sutton Elbert 1872-1930(?)
.... **TCLC 77**
See also CA 123; DLB 50
Grigson, Geoffrey (Edward Harvey)
1905-1985 .... **CLC 7, 39**
See also CA 25-28R; 118; CANR 20, 33;
DLB 27; MTCW 1, 2
Grillparzer, Franz 1791-1872 . **NCLC 1; SSC 37**
See also DLB 133
Grimble, Reverend Charles James
See Eliot, T(homas) S(tearns)
Grimke, Charlotte L(ottie) Forten
1837(?)-1914
See Forten, Charlotte L.
See also BW 1; CA 117; 124; DAM MULT,
POET
Grimm, Jacob Ludwig Karl 1785-1863
NCLC 3, 77; SSC 36
See also DLB 90; MAICYA; SATA 22
Grimm, Wilhelm Karl 1786-1859 .. **NCLC 3, 77; SSC 36**
See also DLB 90; MAICYA; SATA 22
**Grimmelshausen, Johann Jakob Christoffel
von** 1621-1676 .... **LC 6**
See also DLB 168
Grindel, Eugene 1895-1952
See Eluard, Paul
See also CA 104
Grisham, John 1955- .... **CLC 84; DAM POP**
See also AAYA 14; CA 138; CANR 47, 69;
DA3; MTCW 2
Grossman, David 1954- .... **CLC 67**
See also CA 138
Grossman, Vasily (Semenovich) 1905-1964
CLC 41
See also CA 124; 130; MTCW 1
Grove, Frederick Philip .... **TCLC 4**
See also Greve, Felix Paul (Berthold
Friedrich) DLB 92
Grubb
See Crumb, R(obert)
Grumbach, Doris (Isaac) 1918- . **CLC 13, 22, 64**
See also CA 5-8R; CAAS 2; CANR 9, 42,
70; INT CANR-9; MTCW 2
Grundtvig, Nicolai Frederik Severin
1783-1872 .... **NCLC 1**
Grunge
See Crumb, R(obert)
Grunwald, Lisa 1959- .... **CLC 44**
See also CA 120
Guare, John 1938- . **CLC 8, 14, 29, 67; DAM
DRAM**
See also CA 73-76; CANR 21, 69; DLB 7;
MTCW 1, 2
Gudjonsson, Halldor Kiljan 1902-1998
See Laxness, Halldor
See also CA 103; 164
Guenter, Erich
See Eich, Guenter
Guest, Barbara 1920- .... **CLC 34**
See also CA 25-28R; CANR 11, 44, 84;
DLB 5, 193
Guest, Edgar A(lbert) 1881-1959 ... **TCLC 95**
See also CA 112; 168
Guest, Judith (Ann) 1936- . **CLC 8, 30; DAM
NOV, POP**
See also AAYA 7; CA 77-80; CANR 15,
75; DA3; INT CANR-15; MTCW 1, 2
Guevara, Che .... **CLC 87; HLC 1**
See also Guevara (Serna), Ernesto
Guevara (Serna), Ernesto 1928-1967
.... **CLC 87; DAM MULT; HLC 1**

See also Guevara, Che CA 127; 111; CANR
56; HW 1
Guicciardini, Francesco 1483-1540 ..... **LC 49**
Guild, Nicholas M. 1944- .... **CLC 33**
See also CA 93-96
Guillemin, Jacques
See Sartre, Jean-Paul
Guillen, Jorge 1893-1984 .... **CLC 11; DAM
MULT, POET; HLCS 1**
See also CA 89-92; 112; DLB 108; HW 1
Guillen, Nicolas (Cristobal) 1902-1989
.... **CLC 48, 79; BLC 2; DAM MST,
MULT, POET; HLC 1; PC 23**
See also BW 2; CA 116; 125; 129; CANR
84; HW 1
Guillevic, (Eugene) 1907- .... **CLC 33**
See also CA 93-96
Guillois
See Desnos, Robert
Guillois, Valentin
See Desnos, Robert
Guimaraes Rosa, Joao 1908-1967
See also CA 175; HLCS 2
Guiney, Louise Imogen 1861-1920 . **TCLC 41**
See also CA 160; DLB 54
Guiraldes, Ricardo (Guillermo) 1886-1927
TCLC 39
See also CA 131; HW 1; MTCW 1
Gumilev, Nikolai (Stepanovich) 1886-1921
TCLC 60
See also CA 165
Gunesekera, Romesh 1954- .... **CLC 91**
See also CA 159
Gunn, Bill .... **CLC 5**
See also Gunn, William Harrison DLB 38
Gunn, Thom(son William) 1929- . **CLC 3, 6,
18, 32, 81; DAM POET; PC 26**
See also CA 17-20R; CANR 9, 33; CDBLB
1960 to Present; DLB 27; INT CANR-33;
MTCW 1
Gunn, William Harrison 1934(?)-1989
See Gunn, Bill
See also AITN 1; BW 1, 3; CA 13-16R;
128; CANR 12, 25, 76
Gunnars, Kristjana 1948- .... **CLC 69**
See also CA 113; DLB 60
Gurdjieff, G(eorgei) I(vanovich)
1877(?)-1949 .... **TCLC 71**
See also CA 157
Gurganus, Allan 1947- . **CLC 70; DAM POP**
See also BEST 90:1; CA 135
Gurney, A(lbert) R(amsdell), Jr. 1930-
.... **CLC 32, 50, 54; DAM DRAM**
See also CA 77-80; CANR 32, 64
Gurney, Ivor (Bertie) 1890-1937 ... **TCLC 33**
See also CA 167
Gurney, Peter
See Gurney, A(lbert) R(amsdell), Jr.
Guro, Elena 1877-1913 .... **TCLC 56**
Gustafson, James M(oody) 1925- ... **CLC 100**
See also CA 25-28R; CANR 37
Gustafson, Ralph (Barker) 1909- ..... **CLC 36**
See also CA 21-24R; CANR 8, 45, 84; DLB
88
Gut, Gom
See Simenon, Georges (Jacques Christian)
Guterson, David 1956- .... **CLC 91**
See also CA 132; CANR 73; MTCW 2
Guthrie, A(lfred) B(ertram), Jr. 1901-1991
CLC 23
See also CA 57-60; 134; CANR 24; DLB
212; SATA 62; SATA-Obit 67
Guthrie, Isobel
See Grieve, C(hristopher) M(urray)
Guthrie, Woodrow Wilson 1912-1967
See Guthrie, Woody
See also CA 113; 93-96
Guthrie, Woody .... **CLC 35**

See also Guthrie, Woodrow Wilson
Gutierrez Najera, Manuel 1859-1895
See also HLCS 2
Guy, Rosa (Cuthbert) 1928- .... **CLC 26**
See also AAYA 4; BW 2; CA 17-20R;
CANR 14, 34, 83; CLR 13; DLB 33;
JRDA; MAICYA; SATA 14, 62
Gwendolyn
See Bennett, (Enoch) Arnold
H. D. .... **CLC 3, 8, 14, 31, 34, 73; PC 5**
See also Doolittle, Hilda
H. de V.
See Buchan, John
Haavikko, Paavo Juhani 1931- .. **CLC 18, 34**
See also CA 106
Habbema, Koos
See Heijermans, Herman
Habermas, Juergen 1929- .... **CLC 104**
See also CA 109; CANR 85
Habermas, Jurgen
See Habermas, Juergen
Hacker, Marilyn 1942- . **CLC 5, 9, 23, 72, 91;
DAM POET**
See also CA 77-80; CANR 68; DLB 120
Haeckel, Ernst Heinrich (Philipp August)
1834-1919 .... **TCLC 83**
See also CA 157
Hafiz c. 1326-1389 .... **CMLC 34**
Hafiz c. 1326-1389(?) .... **CMLC 34**
Haggard, H(enry) Rider 1856-1925
.... **TCLC 11**
See also CA 108; 148; DLB 70, 156, 174,
178; MTCW 2; SATA 16
Hagiosy, L.
See Larbaud, Valery (Nicolas)
Hagiwara Sakutaro 1886-1942 ..... **TCLC 60;
PC 18**
Haig, Fenil
See Ford, Ford Madox
Haig-Brown, Roderick (Langmere)
1908-1976 .... **CLC 21**
See also CA 5-8R; 69-72; CANR 4, 38, 83;
CLR 31; DLB 88; MAICYA; SATA 12
Hailey, Arthur 1920- ..... **CLC 5; DAM NOV,
POP**
See also AITN 2; BEST 90:3; CA 1-4R;
CANR 2, 36, 75; DLB 88; DLBY 82;
MTCW 1, 2
Hailey, Elizabeth Forsythe 1938- ..... **CLC 40**
See also CA 93-96; CAAS 1; CANR 15,
48; INT CANR-15
Haines, John (Meade) 1924- .... **CLC 58**
See also CA 17-20R; CANR 13, 34; DLB
212
Hakluyt, Richard 1552-1616 .... **LC 31**
Haldeman, Joe (William) 1943- .... **CLC 61**
See also Graham, Robert CA 53-56; 179;
CAAE 179; CAAS 25; CANR 6, 70, 72;
DLB 8; INT CANR-6
Hale, Sarah Josepha (Buell) 1788-1879
NCLC 75
See also DLB 1, 42, 73
Haley, Alex(ander Murray Palmer)
1921-1992 . **CLC 8, 12, 76; BLC 2; DA;
DAB; DAC; DAM MST, MULT, POP**
See also AAYA 26; BW 2, 3; CA 77-80;
136; CANR 61; CDALBS; DA3; DLB 38;
MTCW 1, 2
Haliburton, Thomas Chandler 1796-1865
NCLC 15
See also DLB 11, 99
Hall, Donald (Andrew, Jr.) 1928- ...... **CLC 1,
13, 37, 59; DAM POET**
See also CA 5-8R; CAAS 7; CANR 2, 44,
64; DLB 5; MTCW 1; SATA 23, 97
Hall, Frederic Sauser
See Sauser-Hall, Frederic

Hall, James
  See Kuttner, Henry
Hall, James Norman 1887-1951 ..... **TCLC 23**
  See also CA 123; 173; SATA 21
Hall, Radclyffe
  See Hall, (Marguerite) Radclyffe
  See also MTCW 2
Hall, (Marguerite) Radclyffe 1886-1943
  TCLC 12
  See also CA 110; 150; CANR 83; DLB 191
Hall, Rodney 1935- .... **CLC 51**
  See also CA 109; CANR 69
Halleck, Fitz-Greene 1790-1867 .... **NCLC 47**
  See also DLB 3
Halliday, Michael
  See Creasey, John
Halpern, Daniel 1945- .... **CLC 14**
  See also CA 33-36R
Hamburger, Michael (Peter Leopold) 1924-
  CLC 5, 14
  See also CA 5-8R; CAAS 4; CANR 2, 47;
  DLB 27
Hamill, Pete 1935- .... **CLC 10**
  See also CA 25-28R; CANR 18, 71
Hamilton, Alexander 1755(?)-1804 . **NCLC 49**
  See also DLB 37
Hamilton, Clive
  See Lewis, C(live) S(taples)
Hamilton, Edmond 1904-1977 .... **CLC 1**
  See also CA 1-4R; CANR 3, 84; DLB 8
Hamilton, Eugene (Jacob) Lee
  See Lee-Hamilton, Eugene (Jacob)
Hamilton, Franklin
  See Silverberg, Robert
Hamilton, Gail
  See Corcoran, Barbara
Hamilton, Mollie
  See Kaye, M(ary) M(argaret)
Hamilton, (Anthony Walter) Patrick
  1904-1962 .... **CLC 51**
  See also CA 176; 113; DLB 191
Hamilton, Virginia 1936- ...... **CLC 26; DAM
  MULT**
  See also AAYA 2, 21; BW 2, 3; CA 25-28R;
  CANR 20, 37, 73; CLR 1, 11, 40; DLB
  33, 52; INT CANR-20; JRDA; MAICYA;
  MTCW 1, 2; SATA 4, 56, 79
Hammett, (Samuel) Dashiell 1894-1961
  .... **CLC 3, 5, 10, 19, 47; SSC 17**
  See also AITN 1; CA 81-84; CANR 42;
  CDALB 1929-1941; DA3; DLBD 6;
  DLBY 96; MTCW 1, 2
Hammon, Jupiter 1711(?)-1800(?) . **NCLC 5;
  BLC 2; DAM MULT, POET; PC 16**
  See also DLB 31, 50
Hammond, Keith
  See Kuttner, Henry
Hamner, Earl (Henry), Jr. 1923- ...... **CLC 12**
  See also AITN 2; CA 73-76; DLB 6
Hampton, Christopher (James) 1946-
  .... **CLC 4**
  See also CA 25-28R; DLB 13; MTCW 1
Hamsun, Knut .... **TCLC 2, 14, 49**
  See also Pedersen, Knut
Handke, Peter 1942- ... **CLC 5, 8, 10, 15, 38;
  DAM DRAM, NOV**
  See also CA 77-80; CANR 33, 75; DLB 85,
  124; MTCW 1, 2
Handy, W(illiam) C(hristopher) 1873-1958
  TCLC 97
  See also BW 3; CA 121; 167
Hanley, James 1901-1985 ..... **CLC 3, 5, 8, 13**
  See also CA 73-76; 117; CANR 36; DLB
  191; MTCW 1
Hannah, Barry 1942- .... **CLC 23, 38, 90**
  See also CA 108; 110; CANR 43, 68; DLB
  6; INT 110; MTCW 1

Hannon, Ezra
  See Hunter, Evan
Hansberry, Lorraine (Vivian) 1930-1965
  **CLC 17, 62; BLC 2; DA; DAB; DAC;
  DAM DRAM, MST, MULT; DC 2**
  See also AAYA 25; BW 1, 3; CA 109; 25-
  28R; CABS 3; CANR 58; CDALB 1941-
  1968; DA3; DLB 7, 38; MTCW 1, 2
Hansen, Joseph 1923- .... **CLC 38**
  See also CA 29-32R; CAAS 17; CANR 16,
  44, 66; INT CANR-16
Hansen, Martin A(lfred) 1909-1955
  .... **TCLC 32**
  See also CA 167
Hanson, Kenneth O(stlin) 1922- .... **CLC 13**
  See also CA 53-56; CANR 7
Hardwick, Elizabeth (Bruce) 1916- . **CLC 13;
  DAM NOV**
  See also CA 5-8R; CANR 3, 32, 70; DA3;
  DLB 6; MTCW 1, 2
Hardy, Thomas 1840-1928 .. **TCLC 4, 10, 18,
  32, 48, 53, 72; DA; DAB; DAC; DAM
  MST, NOV, POET; PC 8; SSC 2; WLC**
  See also CA 104; 123; CDBLB 1890-1914;
  DA3; DLB 18, 19, 135; MTCW 1, 2
Hare, David 1947- .... **CLC 29, 58**
  See also CA 97-100; CANR 39; DLB 13;
  MTCW 1
Harewood, John
  See Van Druten, John (William)
Harford, Henry
  See Hudson, W(illiam) H(enry)
Hargrave, Leonie
  See Disch, Thomas M(ichael)
Harjo, Joy 1951- . **CLC 83; DAM MULT; PC
  27**
  See also CA 114; CANR 35, 67; DLB 120,
  175; MTCW 2; NNAL
Harlan, Louis R(udolph) 1922- .... **CLC 34**
  See also CA 21-24R; CANR 25, 55, 80
Harling, Robert 1951(?)- .... **CLC 53**
  See also CA 147
Harmon, William (Ruth) 1938- .... **CLC 38**
  See also CA 33-36R; CANR 14, 32, 35;
  SATA 65
Harper, F. E. W.
  See Harper, Frances Ellen Watkins
Harper, Frances E. W.
  See Harper, Frances Ellen Watkins
Harper, Frances E. Watkins
  See Harper, Frances Ellen Watkins
Harper, Frances Ellen
  See Harper, Frances Ellen Watkins
Harper, Frances Ellen Watkins 1825-1911
  **TCLC 14; BLC 2; DAM MULT, POET;
  PC 21**
  See also BW 1, 3; CA 111; 125; CANR 79;
  DLB 50
Harper, Michael S(teven) 1938- ... **CLC 7, 22**
  See also BW 1; CA 33-36R; CANR 24;
  DLB 41
Harper, Mrs. F. E. W.
  See Harper, Frances Ellen Watkins
Harris, Christie (Lucy) Irwin 1907- . **CLC 12**
  See also CA 5-8R; CANR 6, 83; CLR 47;
  DLB 88; JRDA; MAICYA; SAAS 10;
  SATA 6, 74
Harris, Frank 1856-1931 .... **TCLC 24**
  See also CA 109; 150; CANR 80; DLB 156,
  197
Harris, George Washington 1814-1869
  .... **NCLC 23**
  See also DLB 3, 11
Harris, Joel Chandler 1848-1908 ... **TCLC 2;
  SSC 19**
  See also CA 104; 137; CANR 80; CLR 49;
  DLB 11, 23, 42, 78, 91; MAICYA; SATA
  100; YABC 1

**Harris, John (Wyndham Parkes Lucas)
  Beynon** 1903-1969
  See Wyndham, John
  See also CA 102; 89-92; CANR 84
Harris, MacDonald .... **CLC 9**
  See Heiney, Donald (William)
Harris, Mark 1922- .... **CLC 19**
  See also CA 5-8R; CAAS 3; CANR 2, 55,
  83; DLB 2; DLBY 80
Harris, (Theodore) Wilson 1921- ..... **CLC 25**
  See also CA 65-68; CAAS 16;
  CANR 11, 27, 69; DLB 117; MTCW 1
Harrison, Elizabeth Cavanna 1909-
  See Cavanna, Betty
  See also CA 9-12R; CANR 6, 27, 85
Harrison, Harry (Max) 1925- .... **CLC 42**
  See also CA 1-4R; CANR 5, 21, 84; DLB
  8; SATA 4
Harrison, James (Thomas) 1937- ...... **CLC 6,
  14, 33, 66; SSC 19**
  See also CA 13-16R; CANR 8, 51, 79;
  DLBY 82; INT CANR-8
Harrison, Jim
  See Harrison, James (Thomas)
Harrison, Kathryn 1961- .... **CLC 70**
  See also CA 144; CANR 68
Harrison, Tony 1937- .... **CLC 43, 129**
  See also CA 65-68; CANR 44; DLB 40;
  MTCW 1
Harriss, Will(ard Irvin) 1922- .... **CLC 34**
  See also CA 111
Harson, Sley
  See Ellison, Harlan (Jay)
Hart, Ellis
  See Ellison, Harlan (Jay)
Hart, Josephine 1942(?)- .... **CLC 70; DAM
  POP**
  See also CA 138; CANR 70
Hart, Moss 1904-1961 .... **CLC 66; DAM
  DRAM**
  See also CA 109; 89-92; CANR 84; DLB 7
Harte, (Francis) Bret(t) 1836(?)-1902
  ... **TCLC 1, 25; DA; DAC; DAM MST;
  SSC 8; WLC**
  See also CA 104; 140; CANR 80; CDALB
  1865-1917; DA3; DLB 12, 64, 74, 79,
  186; SATA 26
Hartley, L(eslie) P(oles) 1895-1972 ... **CLC 2,
  22**
  See also CA 45-48; 37-40R; CANR 33;
  DLB 15, 139; MTCW 1, 2
Hartman, Geoffrey H. 1929- .... **CLC 27**
  See also CA 117; 125; CANR 79; DLB 67
Hartmann, Eduard von 1842-1906 . **TCLC 97**
Hartmann, Sadakichi 1867-1944 ... **TCLC 73**
  See also CA 157; DLB 54
Hartmann von Aue c. 1160-c. 1205
  .... **CMLC 15**
  See also DLB 138
Hartmann von Aue 1170-1210 ...... **CMLC 15**
Haruf, Kent 1943- .... **CLC 34**
  See also CA 149
Harwood, Ronald 1934- .... **CLC 32; DAM
  DRAM, MST**
  See also CA 1-4R; CANR 4, 55; DLB 13
Hasegawa Tatsunosuke
  See Futabatei, Shimei
Hasek, Jaroslav (Matej Frantisek)
  1883-1923 .... **TCLC 4**
  See also CA 104; 129; MTCW 1, 2
Hass, Robert 1941- ... **CLC 18, 39, 99; PC 16**
  See also CA 111; CANR 30, 50, 71; DLB
  105, 206; SATA 94
Hastings, Hudson
  See Kuttner, Henry
Hastings, Selina .... **CLC 44**
Hathorne, John 1641-1717 .... **LC 38**

See also CA 1-4R; CANR 5, 20; DLB 88

Johnston, Jennifer 1930- .... **CLC 7**
    See also CA 85-88; DLB 14

Joinville, Jean de 1224(?)-1317 ..... **CMLC 38**

Jolley, (Monica) Elizabeth 1923- ..... **CLC 46; SSC 19**
    See also CA 127; CAAS 13; CANR 59

Jones, Arthur Llewellyn 1863-1947
    See Machen, Arthur
    See also CA 104; 179

Jones, D(ouglas) G(ordon) 1929- ..... **CLC 10**
    See also CA 29-32R; CANR 13; DLB 53

Jones, David (Michael) 1895-1974 . **CLC 2, 4, 7, 13, 42**
    See also CA 9-12R; 53-56; CANR 28; CD-BLB 1945-1960; DLB 20, 100; MTCW 1

Jones, David Robert 1947-
    See Bowie, David
    See also CA 103

Jones, Diana Wynne 1934- .... **CLC 26**
    See also AAYA 12; CA 49-52; CANR 4, 26, 56; CLR 23; DLB 161; JRDA; MAI-CYA; SAAS 7; SATA 9, 70, 108

Jones, Edward P. 1950- .... **CLC 76**
    See also BW 2, 3; CA 142; CANR 79

Jones, Gayl 1949- .. **CLC 6, 9; BLC 2; DAM MULT**
    See also BW 2, 3; CA 77-80; CANR 27, 66; DA3; DLB 33; MTCW 1, 2

Jones, James 1921-1977 ...... **CLC 1, 3, 10, 39**
    See also AITN 1, 2; CA 1-4R; 69-72; CANR 6; DLB 2, 143; DLBD 17; DLBY 98; MTCW 1

Jones, John J.
    See Lovecraft, H(oward) P(hillips)

Jones, LeRoi .... **CLC 1, 2, 3, 5, 10, 14**
    See also Baraka, Amiri MTCW 2

Jones, Louis B. 1953- .... **CLC 65**
    See also CA 141; CANR 73

Jones, Madison (Percy, Jr.) 1925- ...... **CLC 4**
    See also CA 13-16R; CAAS 11; CANR 7, 54, 83; DLB 152

Jones, Mervyn 1922- .... **CLC 10, 52**
    See also CA 45-48; CAAS 5; CANR 1; MTCW 1

Jones, Mick 1956(?)- .... **CLC 30**

Jones, Nettie (Pearl) 1941- .... **CLC 34**
    See also BW 2; CA 137; CAAS 20; CANR 88

Jones, Preston 1936-1979 .... **CLC 10**
    See also CA 73-76; 89-92; DLB 7

Jones, Robert F(rancis) 1934- .... **CLC 7**
    See also CA 49-52; CANR 2, 61

Jones, Rod 1953- .... **CLC 50**
    See also CA 128

Jones, Terence Graham Parry 1942-
    .... **CLC 21**
    See also Jones, Terry; Monty Python CA 112; 116; CANR 35; INT 116

Jones, Terry
    See Jones, Terence Graham Parry
    See also SATA 67; SATA-Brief 51

Jones, Thom (Douglas) 1945(?)- .... **CLC 81**
    See also CA 157; CANR 88

Jong, Erica 1942- . **CLC 4, 6, 8, 18, 83; DAM NOV, POP**
    See also AITN 1; BEST 90:2; CA 73-76; CANR 26, 52, 75; DA3; DLB 2, 5, 28, 152; INT CANR-26; MTCW 1, 2

Jonson, Ben(jamin) 1572(?)-1637 .. **LC 6, 33; DA; DAB; DAC; DAM DRAM, MST, POET; DC 4; PC 17; WLC**
    See also CDBLB Before 1660; DLB 62, 121

Jordan, June 1936- .... **CLC 5, 11, 23, 114; BLCS; DAM MULT, POET**
    See also AAYA 2; BW 2, 3; CA 33-36R; CANR 25, 70; CLR 10; DLB 38; MAI-CYA; MTCW 1; SATA 4

Jordan, Neil (Patrick) 1950- .... **CLC 110**

See also CA 124; 130; CANR 54; INT 130

Jordan, Pat(rick M.) 1941- .... **CLC 37**
    See also CA 33-36R

Jorgensen, Ivar
    See Ellison, Harlan (Jay)

Jorgenson, Ivar
    See Silverberg, Robert

Josephus, Flavius c. 37-100 .... **CMLC 13**

Josiah Allen's Wife
    See Holley, Marietta

Josipovici, Gabriel (David) 1940- . **CLC 6, 43**
    See also CA 37-40R; CAAS 8; CANR 47, 84; DLB 14

Joubert, Joseph 1754-1824 .... **NCLC 9**

Jouve, Pierre Jean 1887-1976 .... **CLC 47**
    See also CA 65-68

Jovine, Francesco 1902-1950 .... **TCLC 79**

Joyce, James (Augustine Aloysius)
    1882-1941 .. **TCLC 3, 8, 16, 35, 52; DA; DAB; DAC; DAM MST, NOV, POET; PC 22; SSC 3, 26; WLC**
    See also CA 104; 126; CDBLB 1914-1945; DA3; DLB 10, 19, 36, 162; MTCW 1, 2

Jozsef, Attila 1905-1937 .... **TCLC 22**
    See also CA 116

Juana Ines de la Cruz 1651(?)-1695 .... **LC 5; HLCS 1; PC 24**

Judd, Cyril
    See Kornbluth, C(yril) M.; Pohl, Frederik

Juenger, Ernst 1895-1998 .... **CLC 125**
    See also CA 101; 167; CANR 21, 47; DLB 56

Julian of Norwich 1342(?)-1416(?) . **LC 6, 52**
    See also DLB 146

Junger, Ernst
    See Juenger, Ernst

Junger, Sebastian 1962- .... **CLC 109**
    See also AAYA 28; CA 165

Juniper, Alex
    See Hospital, Janette Turner

Junius
    See Luxemburg, Rosa

Just, Ward (Swift) 1935- .... **CLC 4, 27**
    See also CA 25-28R; CANR 32, 87; INT CANR-32

Justice, Donald (Rodney) 1925- .. **CLC 6, 19, 102; DAM POET**
    See also CA 5-8R; CANR 26, 54, 74; DLBY 83; INT CANR-26; MTCW 2

Juvenal c. 60-c. 13 .... **CMLC 8**
    See also Juvenalis, Decimus Junius DLB 211

Juvenalis, Decimus Junius 55(?)-c. 127(?)
    See Juvenal

Juvenis
    See Bourne, Randolph S(illiman)

Kacew, Romain 1914-1980
    See Gary, Romain
    See also CA 108; 102

Kadare, Ismail 1936- .... **CLC 52**
    See also CA 161

Kadohata, Cynthia .... **CLC 59, 122**
    See also CA 140

Kafka, Franz 1883-1924 . **TCLC 2, 6, 13, 29, 47, 53; DA; DAB; DAC; DAM MST, NOV; SSC 5, 29, 35; WLC**
    See also AAYA 31; CA 105; 126; DA3; DLB 81; MTCW 1, 2

Kahanovitsch, Pinkhes
    See Der Nister

Kahn, Roger 1927- .... **CLC 30**
    See also CA 25-28R; CANR 44, 69; DLB 171; SATA 37

Kain, Saul
    See Sassoon, Siegfried (Lorraine)

Kaiser, Georg 1878-1945 .... **TCLC 9**
    See also CA 106; DLB 124

Kaletski, Alexander 1946- .... **CLC 39**

See also CA 118; 143

Kalidasa fl. c. 400- .... **CMLC 9; PC 22**

Kallman, Chester (Simon) 1921-1975 . **CLC 2**
    See also CA 45-48; 53-56; CANR 3

Kaminsky, Melvin 1926-
    See Brooks, Mel
    See also CA 65-68; CANR 16

Kaminsky, Stuart M(elvin) 1934- ..... **CLC 59**
    See also CA 73-76; CANR 29, 53

Kandinsky, Wassily 1866-1944 .... **TCLC 92**
    See also CA 118; 155

Kane, Francis
    See Robbins, Harold

Kane, Paul
    See Simon, Paul (Frederick)

Kanin, Garson 1912-1999 .... **CLC 22**
    See also AITN 1; CA 5-8R; 177; CANR 7, 78; DLB 7

Kaniuk, Yoram 1930- .... **CLC 19**
    See also CA 134

Kant, Immanuel 1724-1804 ..... **NCLC 27, 67**
    See also DLB 94

Kantor, MacKinlay 1904-1977 .... **CLC 7**
    See also CA 61-64; 73-76; CANR 60, 63; DLB 9, 102; MTCW 2

Kaplan, David Michael 1946- .... **CLC 50**

Kaplan, James 1951- .... **CLC 59**
    See also CA 135

Karageorge, Michael
    See Anderson, Poul (William)

Karamzin, Nikolai Mikhailovich 1766-1826
    NCLC 3
    See also DLB 150

Karapanou, Margarita 1946- .... **CLC 13**
    See also CA 101

Karinthy, Frigyes 1887-1938 .... **TCLC 47**
    See also CA 170

Karl, Frederick R(obert) 1927- .... **CLC 34**
    See also CA 5-8R; CANR 3, 44

Kastel, Warren
    See Silverberg, Robert

Kataev, Evgeny Petrovich 1903-1942
    See Petrov, Evgeny
    See also CA 120

Kataphusin
    See Ruskin, John

Katz, Steve 1935- .... **CLC 47**
    See also CA 25-28R; CAAS 14, 64; CANR 12; DLBY 83

Kauffman, Janet 1945- .... **CLC 42**
    See also CA 117; CANR 43, 84; DLBY 86

Kaufman, Bob (Garnell) 1925-1986 . **CLC 49**
    See also BW 1; CA 41-44R; 118; CANR 22; DLB 16, 41

Kaufman, George S. 1889-1961 ...... **CLC 38; DAM DRAM**
    See also CA 108; 93-96; DLB 7; INT 108; MTCW 2

Kaufman, Sue .... **CLC 3, 8**
    See also Barondess, Sue K(aufman)

Kavafis, Konstantinos Petrou 1863-1933
    See Cavafy, C(onstantine) P(eter)
    See also CA 104

Kavan, Anna 1901-1968 .... **CLC 5, 13, 82**
    See also CA 5-8R; CANR 6, 57; MTCW 1

Kavanagh, Dan
    See Barnes, Julian (Patrick)

Kavanagh, Julie 1952- .... **CLC 119**
    See also CA 163

Kavanagh, Patrick (Joseph) 1904-1967
    .... **CLC 22**
    See also CA 123; 25-28R; DLB 15, 20; MTCW 1

Kawabata, Yasunari 1899-1972 . **CLC 2, 5, 9, 18, 107; DAM MULT; SSC 17**
    See also CA 93-96; 33-36R; CANR 88; DLB 180; MTCW 2

Kaye, M(ary) M(argaret) 1909- .... **CLC 28**

Kinnell, Galway 1927- ..... **CLC 1, 2, 3, 5, 13, 29, 129; PC 26**
See also CA 9-12R; CANR 10, 34, 66; DLB 5; DLBY 87; INT CANR-34; MTCW 1, 2

Kinsella, Thomas 1928- .... **CLC 4, 19**
See also CA 17-20R; CANR 15; DLB 27; MTCW 1, 2

Kinsella, W(illiam) P(atrick) 1935- . **CLC 27, 43; DAC; DAM NOV, POP**
See also AAYA 7; CA 97-100; CAAS 7; CANR 21, 35, 66, 75; INT CANR-21; MTCW 1, 2

Kinsey, Alfred C(harles) 1894-1956
.... **TCLC 91**
See also CA 115; 170; MTCW 2

Kipling, (Joseph) Rudyard 1865-1936
... **TCLC 8, 17; DA; DAB; DAC; DAM MST, POET; PC 3; SSC 5; WLC**
See also AAYA 32; CA 105; 120; CANR 33; CDBLB 1890-1914; CLR 39; DA3; DLB 19, 34, 141, 156; MAICYA; MTCW 1, 2; SATA 100; YABC 2

Kirkland, Caroline M. 1801-1864 . **NCLC 85**
See also DLB 3, 73, 74; DLBD 13

Kirkup, James 1918- .... **CLC 1**
See also CA 1-4R; CAAS 4; CANR 2; DLB 27; SATA 12

Kirkwood, James 1930(?)-1989 .... **CLC 9**
See also AITN 2; CA 1-4R; 128; CANR 6, 40

Kirshner, Sidney
See Kingsley, Sidney

Kis, Danilo 1935-1989 .... **CLC 57**
See also CA 109; 118; 129; CANR 61; DLB 181; MTCW 1

Kivi, Aleksis 1834-1872 .... **NCLC 30**

Kizer, Carolyn (Ashley) 1925- ... **CLC 15, 39, 80; DAM POET**
See also CA 65-68; CAAS 5; CANR 24, 70; DLB 5, 169; MTCW 2

Klabund 1890-1928 .... **TCLC 44**
See also CA 162; DLB 66

Klappert, Peter 1942- .... **CLC 57**
See also CA 33-36R; DLB 5

Klein, A(braham) M(oses) 1909-1972
.... **CLC 19; DAB; DAC; DAM MST**
See also CA 101; 37-40R; DLB 68

Klein, Norma 1938-1989 .... **CLC 30**
See also AAYA 2; CA 41-44R; 128; CANR 15, 37; CLR 2, 19; INT CANR-15; JRDA; MAICYA; SAAS 1; SATA 7, 57

Klein, T(heodore) E(ibon) D(onald) 1947-
.... **CLC 34**
See also CA 119; CANR 44, 75

Kleist, Heinrich von 1777-1811 . **NCLC 2, 37; DAM DRAM; SSC 22**
See also DLB 90

Klima, Ivan 1931- .... **CLC 56; DAM NOV**
See also CA 25-28R; CANR 17, 50

Klimentov, Andrei Platonovich 1899-1951
See Platonov, Andrei
See also CA 108

Klinger, Friedrich Maximilian von
1752-1831 .... **NCLC 1**
See also DLB 94

Klingsor the Magician
See Hartmann, Sadakichi

Klopstock, Friedrich Gottlieb 1724-1803
NCLC 11
See also DLB 97

Knapp, Caroline 1959- .... **CLC 99**
See also CA 154

Knebel, Fletcher 1911-1993 .... **CLC 14**
See also AITN 1; CA 1-4R; 140; CAAS 3; CANR 1, 36; SATA 36; SATA-Obit 75

Knickerbocker, Diedrich
See Irving, Washington

Knight, Etheridge 1931-1991 . **CLC 40; BLC 2; DAM POET; PC 14**

See also BW 1, 3; CA 21-24R; 133; CANR 23, 82; DLB 41; MTCW 2

Knight, Sarah Kemble 1666-1727 .... **LC 7**
See also DLB 24, 200

Knister, Raymond 1899-1932 .... **TCLC 56**
See also DLB 68

Knowles, John 1926- . **CLC 1, 4, 10, 26; DA; DAC; DAM MST, NOV**
See also AAYA 10; CA 17-20R; CANR 40, 74, 76; CDALB 1968-1988; DLB 6; MTCW 1, 2; SATA 8, 89

Knox, Calvin M.
See Silverberg, Robert

Knox, John c. 1505-1572 .... **LC 37**
See also DLB 132

Knye, Cassandra
See Disch, Thomas M(ichael)

Koch, C(hristopher) J(ohn) 1932- .... **CLC 42**
See also CA 127; CANR 84

Koch, Christopher
See Koch, C(hristopher) J(ohn)

Koch, Kenneth 1925- .... **CLC 5, 8, 44; DAM POET**
See also CA 1-4R; CANR 6, 36, 57; DLB 5; INT CANR-36; MTCW 2; SATA 65

Kochanowski, Jan 1530-1584 .... **LC 10**

Kock, Charles Paul de 1794-1871 . **NCLC 16**

Koda Rohan 1867-
See Koda Shigeyuki

Koda Shigeyuki 1867-1947 .... **TCLC 22**
See also CA 121; 183; DLB 180

Koestler, Arthur 1905-1983 ... **CLC 1, 3, 6, 8, 15, 33**
See also CA 1-4R; 109; CANR 1, 33; CD-BLB 1945-1960; DLBY 83; MTCW 1, 2

Kogawa, Joy Nozomi 1935- ..... **CLC 78, 129; DAC; DAM MST, MULT**
See also CA 101; CANR 19, 62; MTCW 2; SATA 99

Kohout, Pavel 1928- .... **CLC 13**
See also CA 45-48; CANR 3

Koizumi, Yakumo
See Hearn, (Patricio) Lafcadio (Tessima Carlos)

Kolmar, Gertrud 1894-1943 .... **TCLC 40**
See also CA 167

Komunyakaa, Yusef 1947- .... **CLC 86, 94; BLCS**
See also CA 147; CANR 83; DLB 120

Konrad, George
See Konrad, Gyoergy

Konrad, Gyoergy 1933- .... **CLC 4, 10, 73**
See also CA 85-88

Konwicki, Tadeusz 1926- . **CLC 8, 28, 54, 117**
See also CA 101; CAAS 9; CANR 39, 59; MTCW 1

Koontz, Dean R(ay) 1945- .... **CLC 78; DAM NOV, POP**
See also AAYA 9, 31; BEST 89:3, 90:2; CA 108; CANR 19, 36, 52; DA3; MTCW 1; SATA 92

Kopernik, Mikolaj
See Copernicus, Nicolaus

Kopit, Arthur (Lee) 1937- ..... **CLC 1, 18, 33; DAM DRAM**
See also AITN 1; CA 81-84; CABS 3; DLB 7; MTCW 1

Kops, Bernard 1926- .... **CLC 4**
See also CA 5-8R; CANR 84; DLB 13

Kornbluth, C(yril) M. 1923-1958 .... **TCLC 8**
See also CA 105; 160; DLB 8

Korolenko, V. G.
See Korolenko, Vladimir Galaktionovich

Korolenko, Vladimir
See Korolenko, Vladimir Galaktionovich

Korolenko, Vladimir G.
See Korolenko, Vladimir Galaktionovich

Korolenko, Vladimir Galaktionovich
1853-1921 .... **TCLC 22**
See also CA 121

Korzybski, Alfred (Habdank Skarbek)
1879-1950 .... **TCLC 61**
See also CA 123; 160

Kosinski, Jerzy (Nikodem) 1933-1991
.... **CLC 1, 2, 3, 6, 10, 15, 53, 70; DAM NOV**
See also CA 17-20R; 134; CANR 9, 46; DA3; DLB 2; DLBY 82; MTCW 1, 2

Kostelanetz, Richard (Cory) 1940- .. **CLC 28**
See also CA 13-16R; CAAS 8; CANR 38, 77

Kostrowitzki, Wilhelm Apollinaris de
1880-1918
See Apollinaire, Guillaume
See also CA 104

Kotlowitz, Robert 1924- .... **CLC 4**
See also CA 33-36R; CANR 36

Kotzebue, August (Friedrich Ferdinand) von
1761-1819 .... **NCLC 25**
See also DLB 94

Kotzwinkle, William 1938- ..... **CLC 5, 14, 35**
See also CA 45-48; CANR 3, 44, 84; CLR 6; DLB 173; MAICYA; SATA 24, 70

Kowna, Stancy
See Szymborska, Wislawa

Kozol, Jonathan 1936- .... **CLC 17**
See also CA 61-64; CANR 16, 45

Kozoll, Michael 1940(?)- .... **CLC 35**

Kramer, Kathryn 19(?)- .... **CLC 34**

Kramer, Larry 1935- .. **CLC 42; DAM POP; DC 8**
See also CA 124; 126; CANR 60

Krasicki, Ignacy 1735-1801 .... **NCLC 8**

Krasinski, Zygmunt 1812-1859 .... **NCLC 4**

Kraus, Karl 1874-1936 .... **TCLC 5**
See also CA 104; DLB 118

Kreve (Mickevicius), Vincas 1882-1954
TCLC 27
See also CA 170

Kristeva, Julia 1941- .... **CLC 77**
See also CA 154

Kristofferson, Kris 1936- .... **CLC 26**
See also CA 104

Krizanc, John 1956- .... **CLC 57**

Krleza, Miroslav 1893-1981 .... **CLC 8, 114**
See also CA 97-100; 105; CANR 50; DLB 147

Kroetsch, Robert 1927- .... **CLC 5, 23, 57; DAC; DAM POET**
See also CA 17-20R; CANR 8, 38; DLB 53; MTCW 1

Kroetz, Franz
See Kroetz, Franz Xaver

Kroetz, Franz Xaver 1946- .... **CLC 41**
See also CA 130

Kroker, Arthur (W.) 1945- .... **CLC 77**
See also CA 161

Kropotkin, Peter (Alekseieevich) 1842-1921
TCLC 36
See also CA 119

Krotkov, Yuri 1917- .... **CLC 19**
See also CA 102

Krumb
See Crumb, R(obert)

Krumgold, Joseph (Quincy) 1908-1980
.... **CLC 12**
See also CA 9-12R; 101; CANR 7; MAI-CYA; SATA 1, 48; SATA-Obit 23

Krumwitz
See Crumb, R(obert)

Krutch, Joseph Wood 1893-1970 ..... **CLC 24**
See also CA 1-4R; 25-28R; CANR 4; DLB 63, 206

Krutzch, Gus
See Eliot, T(homas) S(tearns)

See also CA 21-24R; 162; CAAS 22; CANR
9, 47; DLB 48; DLBY 96, 97

Laurence, (Jean) Margaret (Wemyss)
1926-1987 . **CLC 3, 6, 13, 50, 62; DAC;
DAM MST; SSC 7**
See also CA 5-8R; 121; CANR 33; DLB
53; MTCW 1, 2; SATA-Obit 50

Laurent, Antoine 1952- .... **CLC 50**

Lauscher, Hermann
See Hesse, Hermann

Lautreamont, Comte de 1846-1870
.... **NCLC 12; SSC 14**

Laverty, Donald
See Blish, James (Benjamin)

Lavin, Mary 1912-1996 . **CLC 4, 18, 99; SSC
4**
See also CA 9-12R; 151; CANR 33; DLB
15; MTCW 1

Lavond, Paul Dennis
See Kornbluth, C(yril) M.; Pohl, Frederik

Lawler, Raymond Evenor 1922- .... **CLC 58**
See also CA 103

Lawrence, D(avid) H(erbert Richards)
1885-1930 .... **TCLC 2, 9, 16, 33, 48, 61,
93; DA; DAB; DAC; DAM MST, NOV,
POET; SSC 4, 19; WLC**
See also CA 104; 121; CDBLB 1914-1945;
DA3; DLB 10, 19, 36, 98, 162, 195;
MTCW 1, 2

Lawrence, T(homas) E(dward) 1888-1935
TCLC 18
See also Dale, Colin CA 115; 167; DLB
195

Lawrence of Arabia
See Lawrence, T(homas) E(dward)

Lawson, Henry (Archibald Hertzberg)
1867-1922 .... **TCLC 27; SSC 18**
See also CA 120; 181

Lawton, Dennis
See Faust, Frederick (Schiller)

Laxness, Halldor .... **CLC 25**
See also Gudjonsson, Halldor Kiljan

Layamon fl. c. 1200- .... **CMLC 10**
See also DLB 146

Laye, Camara 1928-1980 ... **CLC 4, 38; BLC
2; DAM MULT**
See also BW 1; CA 85-88; 97-100; CANR
25; MTCW 1, 2

Layton, Irving (Peter) 1912- .... **CLC 2, 15;
DAC; DAM MST, POET**
See also CA 1-4R; CANR 2, 33, 43, 66;
DLB 88; MTCW 1, 2

Lazarus, Emma 1849-1887 .... **NCLC 8**

Lazarus, Felix
See Cable, George Washington

Lazarus, Henry
See Slavitt, David R(ytman)

Lea, Joan
See Neufeld, John (Arthur)

Leacock, Stephen (Butler) 1869-1944
.... **TCLC 2; DAC; DAM MST**
See also CA 104; 141; CANR 80; DLB 92;
MTCW 2

Lear, Edward 1812-1888 .... **NCLC 3**
See also CLR 1; DLB 32, 163, 166; MAI-
CYA; SATA 18, 100

Lear, Norman (Milton) 1922- .... **CLC 12**
See also CA 73-76

Leautaud, Paul 1872-1956 .... **TCLC 83**
See also DLB 65

Leavis, F(rank) R(aymond) 1895-1978
.... **CLC 24**
See also CA 21-24R; 77-80; CANR 44;
MTCW 1, 2

Leavitt, David 1961- ..... **CLC 34; DAM POP**
See also CA 116; 122; CANR 50, 62; DA3;
DLB 130; INT 122; MTCW 2

Leblanc, Maurice (Marie Emile) 1864-1941
TCLC 49

See also CA 110

Lebowitz, Fran(ces Ann) 1951(?)- ... **CLC 11,
36**
See also CA 81-84; CANR 14, 60, 70; INT
CANR-14; MTCW 1

Lebrecht, Peter
See Tieck, (Johann) Ludwig

le Carre, John .... **CLC 3, 5, 9, 15, 28**
See also Cornwell, David (John Moore)
BEST 89:4; CDBLB 1960 to Present;
DLB 87; MTCW 2

Le Clezio, J(ean) M(arie) G(ustave) 1940-
CLC 31
See also CA 116; 128; DLB 83

Leconte de Lisle, Charles-Marie-Rene
1818-1894 .... **NCLC 29**

Le Coq, Monsieur
See Simenon, Georges (Jacques Christian)

Leduc, Violette 1907-1972 .... **CLC 22**
See also CA 13-14; 33-36R; CANR 69;
CAP 1

Ledwidge, Francis 1887(?)-1917 .... **TCLC 23**
See also CA 123; DLB 20

Lee, Andrea 1953- ... **CLC 36; BLC 2; DAM
MULT**
See also BW 1, 3; CA 125; CANR 82

Lee, Andrew
See Auchincloss, Louis (Stanton)

Lee, Chang-rae 1965- .... **CLC 91**
See also CA 148

Lee, Don L. .... **CLC 2**
See also Madhubuti, Haki R.

Lee, George W(ashington) 1894-1976
.... **CLC 52; BLC 2; DAM MULT**
See also BW 1; CA 125; CANR 83; DLB
51

Lee, (Nelle) Harper 1926- . **CLC 12, 60; DA;
DAB; DAC; DAM MST, NOV; WLC**
See also AAYA 13; CA 13-16R; CANR 51;
CDALB 1941-1968; DA3; DLB 6;
MTCW 1, 2; SATA 11

Lee, Helen Elaine 1959(?)- .... **CLC 86**
See also CA 148

Lee, Julian
See Latham, Jean Lee

Lee, Larry
See Lee, Lawrence

Lee, Laurie 1914-1997 . **CLC 90; DAB; DAM
POP**
See also CA 77-80; 158; CANR 33, 73;
DLB 27; MTCW 1

Lee, Lawrence 1941-1990 .... **CLC 34**
See also CA 131; CANR 43

Lee, Li-Young 1957- .... **PC 24**
See also CA 153; DLB 165

Lee, Manfred B(ennington) 1905-1971
.... **CLC 11**
See also Queen, Ellery CA 1-4R; 29-32R;
CANR 2; DLB 137

Lee, Shelton Jackson 1957(?)- .... **CLC 105;
BLCS; DAM MULT**
See also Lee, Spike BW 2, 3; CA 125;
CANR 42

Lee, Spike
See Lee, Shelton Jackson
See also AAYA 4, 29

Lee, Stan 1922- .... **CLC 17**
See also AAYA 5; CA 108; 111; INT 111

Lee, Tanith 1947- .... **CLC 46**
See also AAYA 15; CA 37-40R; CANR 53;
SATA 8, 88

Lee, Vernon .... **TCLC 5; SSC 33**
See also Paget, Violet DLB 57, 153, 156,
174, 178

Lee, William
See Burroughs, William S(eward)

Lee, Willy
See Burroughs, William S(eward)

Lee-Hamilton, Eugene (Jacob) 1845-1907
TCLC 22
See also CA 117

Leet, Judith 1935- .... **CLC 11**

Le Fanu, Joseph Sheridan 1814-1873
.... **NCLC 9, 58; DAM POP; SSC 14**
See also DA3; DLB 21, 70, 159, 178

Leffland, Ella 1931- .... **CLC 19**
See also CA 29-32R; CANR 35, 78, 82;
DLBY 84; INT CANR-35; SATA 65

Leger, Alexis
See Leger, (Marie-Rene Auguste) Alexis
Saint-Leger

**Leger, (Marie-Rene Auguste) Alexis
Saint-Leger** 1887-1975 .. **CLC 4, 11, 46;
DAM POET; PC 23**
See also CA 13-16R; 61-64; CANR 43;
MTCW 1

Leger, Saintleger
See Leger, (Marie-Rene Auguste) Alexis
Saint-Leger

Le Guin, Ursula K(roeber) 1929- ..... **CLC 8,
13, 22, 45, 71; DAB; DAC; DAM MST,
POP; SSC 12**
See also AAYA 9, 27; AITN 1; CA 21-24R;
CANR 9, 32, 52, 74; CDALB 1968-1988;
CLR 3, 28; DA3; DLB 8, 52; INT CANR-
32; JRDA; MAICYA; MTCW 1, 2; SATA
4, 52, 99

Lehmann, Rosamond (Nina) 1901-1990
.... **CLC 5**
See also CA 77-80; 131; CANR 8, 73; DLB
15; MTCW 2

Leiber, Fritz (Reuter, Jr.) 1910-1992 . **CLC 25**
See also CA 45-48; 139; CANR 2, 40, 86;
DLB 8; MTCW 1, 2; SATA 45; SATA-
Obit 73

Leibniz, Gottfried Wilhelm von 1646-1716
LC 35
See also DLB 168

Leimbach, Martha 1963-
See Leimbach, Marti
See also CA 130

Leimbach, Marti .... **CLC 65**
See also Leimbach, Martha

Leino, Eino .... **TCLC 24**
See also Loennbohm, Armas Eino Leopold

Leiris, Michel (Julien) 1901-1990 ..... **CLC 61**
See also CA 119; 128; 132

Leithauser, Brad 1953- .... **CLC 27**
See also CA 107; CANR 27, 81; DLB 120

Lelchuk, Alan 1938- .... **CLC 5**
See also CA 45-48; CAAS 20; CANR 1, 70

Lem, Stanislaw 1921- .... **CLC 8, 15, 40**
See also CA 105; CAAS 1; CANR 32;
MTCW 1

Lemann, Nancy 1956- .... **CLC 39**
See also CA 118; 136

Lemonnier, (Antoine Louis) Camille
1844-1913 .... **TCLC 22**
See also CA 121

Lenau, Nikolaus 1802-1850 .... **NCLC 16**

L'Engle, Madeleine (Camp Franklin) 1918-
CLC 12; DAM POP
See also AAYA 28; AITN 2; CA 1-4R;
CANR 3, 21, 39, 66; CLR 1, 14, 57; DA3;
DLB 52; JRDA; MAICYA; MTCW 1, 2;
SAAS 15; SATA 1, 27, 75

Lengyel, Jozsef 1896-1975 .... **CLC 7**
See also CA 85-88; 57-60; CANR 71

Lenin 1870-1924
See Lenin, V. I.
See also CA 121; 168

Lenin, V. I. .... **TCLC 67**
See also Lenin

Lennon, John (Ono) 1940-1980 .. **CLC 12, 35**
See also CA 102

Lennox, Charlotte Ramsay 1729(?)-1804
NCLC 23

See also DLB 39

Lentricchia, Frank (Jr.) 1940- .... **CLC 34**
See also CA 25-28R; CANR 19

Lenz, Siegfried 1926- .... **CLC 27; SSC 33**
See also CA 89-92; CANR 80; DLB 75

Leonard, Elmore (John, Jr.) 1925- . **CLC 28, 34, 71, 120; DAM POP**
See also AAYA 22; AITN 1; BEST 89:1, 90:4; CA 81-84; CANR 12, 28, 53, 76; DA3; DLB 173; INT CANR-28; MTCW 1, 2

Leonard, Hugh .... **CLC 19**
See also Byrne, John Keyes DLB 13

Leonov, Leonid (Maximovich) 1899-1994
CLC 92; DAM NOV
See also CA 129; CANR 74, 76; MTCW 1, 2

Leopardi, (Conte) Giacomo 1798-1837
.... **NCLC 22**

Le Reveler
See Artaud, Antonin (Marie Joseph)

Lerman, Eleanor 1952- .... **CLC 9**
See also CA 85-88; CANR 69

Lerman, Rhoda 1936- .... **CLC 56**
See also CA 49-52; CANR 70

Lermontov, Mikhail Yuryevich 1814-1841
NCLC 47; PC 18
See also DLB 205

Leroux, Gaston 1868-1927 .... **TCLC 25**
See also CA 108; 136; CANR 69; SATA 65

Lesage, Alain-Rene 1668-1747 .... **LC 2, 28**

Leskov, Nikolai (Semyonovich) 1831-1895
NCLC 25; SSC 34

Lessing, Doris (May) 1919- ... **CLC 1, 2, 3, 6, 10, 15, 22, 40, 94; DA; DAB; DAC; DAM MST, NOV; SSC 6; WLCS**
See also CA 9-12R; CAAS 14; CANR 33, 54, 76; CDBLB 1960 to Present; DA3; DLB 15, 139; DLBY 85; MTCW 1, 2

Lessing, Gotthold Ephraim 1729-1781 . **LC 8**
See also DLB 97

Lester, Richard 1932- .... **CLC 20**

Lever, Charles (James) 1806-1872 . **NCLC 23**
See also DLB 21

Leverson, Ada 1865(?)-1936(?) .... **TCLC 18**
See also Elaine CA 117; DLB 153

Levertov, Denise 1923-1997 .. **CLC 1, 2, 3, 5, 8, 15, 28, 66; DAM POET; PC 11**
See also CA 1-4R, 178; 163; CAAE 178; CAAS 19; CANR 3, 29, 50; CDALBS; DLB 5, 165; INT CANR-29; MTCW 1, 2

Levi, Jonathan .... **CLC 76**

Levi, Peter (Chad Tigar) 1931- .... **CLC 41**
See also CA 5-8R; CANR 34, 80; DLB 40

Levi, Primo 1919-1987 . **CLC 37, 50; SSC 12**
See also CA 13-16R; 122; CANR 12, 33, 61, 70; DLB 177; MTCW 1, 2

Levin, Ira 1929- .... **CLC 3, 6; DAM POP**
See also CA 21-24R; CANR 17, 44, 74; DA3; MTCW 1, 2; SATA 66

Levin, Meyer 1905-1981 . **CLC 7; DAM POP**
See also AITN 1; CA 9-12R; 104; CANR 15; DLB 9, 28; DLBY 81; SATA 21; SATA-Obit 27

Levine, Norman 1924- .... **CLC 54**
See also CA 73-76; CAAS 23; CANR 14, 70; DLB 88

Levine, Philip 1928- .. **CLC 2, 4, 5, 9, 14, 33, 118; DAM POET; PC 22**
See also CA 9-12R; CANR 9, 37, 52; DLB 5

Levinson, Deirdre 1931- .... **CLC 49**
See also CA 73-76; CANR 70

Levi-Strauss, Claude 1908- .... **CLC 38**
See also CA 1-4R; CANR 6, 32, 57; MTCW 1, 2

Levitin, Sonia (Wolff) 1934- .... **CLC 17**

See also AAYA 13; CA 29-32R; CANR 14, 32, 79; CLR 53; JRDA; MAICYA; SAAS 2; SATA 4, 68

Levon, O. U.
See Kesey, Ken (Elton)

Levy, Amy 1861-1889 .... **NCLC 59**
See also DLB 156

Lewes, George Henry 1817-1878 ... **NCLC 25**
See also DLB 55, 144

Lewis, Alun 1915-1944 .... **TCLC 3**
See also CA 104; DLB 20, 162

Lewis, C. Day
See Day Lewis, C(ecil)

Lewis, C(live) S(taples) 1898-1963 .... **CLC 1, 3, 6, 14, 27, 124; DA; DAB; DAC; DAM MST, NOV, POP; WLC**
See also AAYA 3; CA 81-84; CANR 33, 71; CDBLB 1945-1960; CLR 3, 27; DA3; DLB 15, 100, 160; JRDA; MAICYA; MTCW 1, 2; SATA 13, 100

Lewis, Janet 1899-1998 .... **CLC 41**
See also Winters, Janet Lewis CA 9-12R; 172; CANR 29, 63; CAP 1; DLBY 87

Lewis, Matthew Gregory 1775-1818
.... **NCLC 11, 62**
See also DLB 39, 158, 178

Lewis, (Harry) Sinclair 1885-1951 . **TCLC 4, 13, 23, 39; DA; DAB; DAC; DAM MST, NOV; WLC**
See also CA 104; 133; CDALB 1917-1929; DA3; DLB 9, 102; DLBD 1; MTCW 1, 2

Lewis, (Percy) Wyndham 1882(?)-1957
TCLC 2, 9; SSC 34
See also CA 104; 157; DLB 15; MTCW 2

Lewisohn, Ludwig 1883-1955 .... **TCLC 19**
See also CA 107; DLB 4, 9, 28, 102

Lewton, Val 1904-1951 .... **TCLC 76**

Leyner, Mark 1956- .... **CLC 92**
See also CA 110; CANR 28, 53; DA3; MTCW 2

Lezama Lima, Jose 1910-1976 .... **CLC 4, 10, 101; DAM MULT; HLCS 2**
See also CA 77-80; CANR 71; DLB 113; HW 1, 2

L'Heureux, John (Clarke) 1934- ...... **CLC 52**
See also CA 13-16R; CANR 23, 45, 88

Liddell, C. H.
See Kuttner, Henry

Lie, Jonas (Lauritz Idemil) 1833-1908(?)
TCLC 5
See also CA 115

Lieber, Joel 1937-1971 .... **CLC 6**
See also CA 73-76; 29-32R

Lieber, Stanley Martin
See Lee, Stan

Lieberman, Laurence (James) 1935- . **CLC 4, 36**
See also CA 17-20R; CANR 8, 36

Lieh Tzu fl. 7th cent. B.C.-5th cent. B.C.
CMLC 27

Lieksman, Anders
See Haavikko, Paavo Juhani

Li Fei-kan 1904-
See Pa Chin
See also CA 105

Lifton, Robert Jay 1926- .... **CLC 67**
See also CA 17-20R; CANR 27, 78; INT CANR-27; SATA 66

Lightfoot, Gordon 1938- .... **CLC 26**
See also CA 109

Lightman, Alan P(aige) 1948- .... **CLC 81**
See also CA 141; CANR 63

Ligotti, Thomas (Robert) 1953- ...... **CLC 44; SSC 16**
See also CA 123; CANR 49

Li Ho 791-817 .... **PC 13**

Liliencron, (Friedrich Adolf Axel) Detlev von 1844-1909 .... **TCLC 18**

See also CA 117

Lilly, William 1602-1681 .... **LC 27**

Lima, Jose Lezama
See Lezama Lima, Jose

Lima Barreto, Afonso Henrique de 1881-1922 .... **TCLC 23**
See also CA 117; 181

Limonov, Edward 1944- .... **CLC 67**
See also CA 137

Lin, Frank
See Atherton, Gertrude (Franklin Horn)

Lincoln, Abraham 1809-1865 .... **NCLC 18**

Lind, Jakov .... **CLC 1, 2, 4, 27, 82**
See also Landwirth, Heinz CAAS 4

Lindbergh, Anne (Spencer) Morrow 1906-
CLC 82; DAM NOV
See also CA 17-20R; CANR 16, 73; MTCW 1, 2; SATA 33

Lindsay, David 1878-1945 .... **TCLC 15**
See also CA 113

Lindsay, (Nicholas) Vachel 1879-1931
.... **TCLC 17; DA; DAC; DAM MST, POET; PC 23; WLC**
See also CA 114; 135; CANR 79; CDALB 1865-1917; DA3; DLB 54; SATA 40

Linke-Poot
See Doeblin, Alfred

Linney, Romulus 1930- .... **CLC 51**
See also CA 1-4R; CANR 40, 44, 79

Linton, Eliza Lynn 1822-1898 .... **NCLC 41**
See also DLB 18

Li Po 701-763 .... **CMLC 2; PC 29**

Lipsius, Justus 1547-1606 .... **LC 16**

Lipsyte, Robert (Michael) 1938- ..... **CLC 21; DA; DAC; DAM MST, NOV**
See also AAYA 7; CA 17-20R; CANR 8, 57; CLR 23; JRDA; MAICYA; SATA 5, 68, 113

Lish, Gordon (Jay) 1934- ... **CLC 45; SSC 18**
See also CA 113; 117; CANR 79; DLB 130; INT 117

Lispector, Clarice 1925(?)-1977 .... **CLC 43; HLCS 2; SSC 34**
See also CA 139; 116; CANR 71; DLB 113; HW 2

Littell, Robert 1935(?)- .... **CLC 42**
See also CA 109; 112; CANR 64

Little, Malcolm 1925-1965
See Malcolm X
See also BW 1, 3; CA 125; 111; CANR 82; DA; DAB; DAC; DAM MST, MULT; DA3; MTCW 1, 2

Littlewit, Humphrey Gent.
See Lovecraft, H(oward) P(hillips)

Litwos
See Sienkiewicz, Henryk (Adam Alexander Pius)

Liu, E 1857-1909 .... **TCLC 15**
See also CA 115

Lively, Penelope (Margaret) 1933- .. **CLC 32, 50; DAM NOV**
See also CA 41-44R; CANR 29, 67, 79; CLR 7; DLB 14, 161, 207; JRDA; MAICYA; MTCW 1, 2; SATA 7, 60, 101

Livesay, Dorothy (Kathleen) 1909- ... **CLC 4, 15, 79; DAM MST, POET**
See also AITN 2; CA 25-28R; CAAS 8; CANR 36, 67; DLB 68; MTCW 1

Livy c. 59B.C.-c. 17 .... **CMLC 11**
See also DLB 211

Lizardi, Jose Joaquin Fernandez de 1776-1827 .... **NCLC 30**

Llewellyn, Richard
See Llewellyn Lloyd, Richard Dafydd Vivian
See also DLB 15

Llewellyn Lloyd, Richard Dafydd Vivian 1906-1983 .... **CLC 7, 80**

See also Llewellyn, Richard CA 53-56; 111; CANR 7, 71; SATA 11; SATA-Obit 37
Llosa, (Jorge) Mario (Pedro) Vargas
See Vargas Llosa, (Jorge) Mario (Pedro)
Lloyd, Manda
See Mander, (Mary) Jane
Lloyd Webber, Andrew 1948-
See Webber, Andrew Lloyd
See also AAYA 1; CA 116; 149; DAM DRAM; SATA 56
Llull, Ramon c. 1235-c. 1316 .... **CMLC 12**
Lobb, Ebenezer
See Upward, Allen
Locke, Alain (Le Roy) 1886-1954 . **TCLC 43; BLCS**
See also BW 1, 3; CA 106; 124; CANR 79; DLB 51
Locke, John 1632-1704 .... **LC 7, 35**
See also DLB 101
Locke-Elliott, Sumner
See Elliott, Sumner Locke
Lockhart, John Gibson 1794-1854 .. **NCLC 6**
See also DLB 110, 116, 144
Lodge, David (John) 1935- ... **CLC 36; DAM POP**
See also BEST 90:1; CA 17-20R; CANR 19, 53; DLB 14, 194; INT CANR-19; MTCW 1, 2
Lodge, Thomas 1558-1625 .... **LC 41**
Lodge, Thomas 1558-1625 .... **LC 41**
See also DLB 172
Loennbohm, Armas Eino Leopold 1878-1926
See Leino, Eino
See also CA 123
Loewinsohn, Ron(ald William) 1937-
.... **CLC 52**
See also CA 25-28R; CANR 71
Logan, Jake
See Smith, Martin Cruz
Logan, John (Burton) 1923-1987 .... **CLC 5**
See also CA 77-80; 124; CANR 45; DLB 5
Lo Kuan-chung 1330(?)-1400(?) .... **LC 12**
Lombard, Nap
See Johnson, Pamela Hansford
London, Jack . **TCLC 9, 15, 39; SSC 4; WLC**
See also London, John Griffith AAYA 13; AITN 2; CDALB 1865-1917; DLB 8, 12, 78, 212; SATA 18
London, John Griffith 1876-1916
See London, Jack
See also CA 110; 119; CANR 73; DA; DAB; DAC; DAM MST, NOV; DA3; JRDA; MAICYA; MTCW 1, 2
Long, Emmett
See Leonard, Elmore (John, Jr.)
Longbaugh, Harry
See Goldman, William (W.)
Longfellow, Henry Wadsworth 1807-1882
NCLC 2, 45; DA; DAB; DAC; DAM MST, POET; WLCS
See also CDALB 1640-1865; DA3; DLB 1, 59; SATA 19
Longinus c. 1st cent. - .... **CMLC 27**
See also DLB 176
Longley, Michael 1939- .... **CLC 29**
See also CA 102; DLB 40
Longus fl. c. 2nd cent. - .... **CMLC 7**
Longway, A. Hugh
See Lang, Andrew
Lonnrot, Elias 1802-1884 .... **NCLC 53**
Lopate, Phillip 1943- .... **CLC 29**
See also CA 97-100; CANR 88; DLBY 80; INT 97-100
Lopez Portillo (y Pacheco), Jose 1920-
.... **CLC 46**
See also CA 129; HW 1
Lopez y Fuentes, Gregorio 1897(?)-1966
.... **CLC 32**

See also CA 131; HW 1
Lorca, Federico Garcia
See Garcia Lorca, Federico
Lord, Bette Bao 1938- .... **CLC 23**
See also BEST 90:3; CA 107; CANR 41, 79; INT 107; SATA 58
Lord Auch
See Bataille, Georges
Lord Byron
See Byron, George Gordon (Noel)
Lorde, Audre (Geraldine) 1934-1992
...... **CLC 18, 71; BLC 2; DAM MULT, POET; PC 12**
See also BW 1, 3; CA 25-28R; 142; CANR 16, 26, 46, 82; DA3; DLB 41; MTCW 1, 2
Lord Houghton
See Milnes, Richard Monckton
Lord Jeffrey
See Jeffrey, Francis
Lorenzini, Carlo 1826-1890
See Collodi, Carlo
See also MAICYA; SATA 29, 100
Lorenzo, Heberto Padilla
See Padilla (Lorenzo), Heberto
Loris
See Hofmannsthal, Hugo von
Loti, Pierre .... **TCLC 11**
See also Viaud, (Louis Marie) Julien DLB 123
Lou, Henri
See Andreas-Salome, Lou
Louie, David Wong 1954- .... **CLC 70**
See also CA 139
Louis, Father M.
See Merton, Thomas
Lovecraft, H(oward) P(hillips) 1890-1937
TCLC 4, 22; DAM POP; SSC 3
See also AAYA 14; CA 104; 133; DA3; MTCW 1, 2
Lovelace, Earl 1935- .... **CLC 51**
See also BW 2; CA 77-80; CANR 41, 72; DLB 125; MTCW 1
Lovelace, Richard 1618-1657 .... **LC 24**
See also DLB 131
Lowell, Amy 1874-1925 .... **TCLC 1, 8; DAM POET; PC 13**
See also CA 104; 151; DLB 54, 140; MTCW 2
Lowell, James Russell 1819-1891 .... **NCLC 2**
See also CDALB 1640-1865; DLB 1, 11, 64, 79, 189
Lowell, Robert (Traill Spence, Jr.)
1917-1977 .... **CLC 1, 2, 3, 4, 5, 8, 9, 11, 15, 37, 124; DA; DAB; DAC; DAM MST, NOV; PC 3; WLC**
See also CA 9-12R; 73-76; CABS 2; CANR 26, 60; CDALBS; DA3; DLB 5, 169; MTCW 1, 2
Lowenthal, Michael (Francis) 1969-
.... **CLC 119**
See also CA 150
Lowndes, Marie Adelaide (Belloc) 1868-1947
TCLC 12
See also CA 107; DLB 70
Lowry, (Clarence) Malcolm 1909-1957
.... **TCLC 6, 40; SSC 31**
See also CA 105; 131; CANR 62; CDBLB 1945-1960; DLB 15; MTCW 1, 2
Lowry, Mina Gertrude 1882-1966
See Loy, Mina
See also CA 113
Loxsmith, John
See Brunner, John (Kilian Houston)
Loy, Mina ...... **CLC 28; DAM POET; PC 16**
See also Lowry, Mina Gertrude DLB 4, 54
Loyson-Bridet
See Schwob, Marcel (Mayer Andre)
Lucan 39-65 .... **CMLC 33**

See also DLB 211
Lucas, Craig 1951- .... **CLC 64**
See also CA 137; CANR 71
Lucas, E(dward) V(errall) 1868-1938
.... **TCLC 73**
See also CA 176; DLB 98, 149, 153; SATA 20
Lucas, George 1944- .... **CLC 16**
See also AAYA 1, 23; CA 77-80; CANR 30; SATA 56
Lucas, Hans
See Godard, Jean-Luc
Lucas, Victoria
See Plath, Sylvia
Lucian c. 120-c. 180 .... **CMLC 32**
See also DLB 176
Ludlam, Charles 1943-1987 .... **CLC 46, 50**
See also CA 85-88; 122; CANR 72, 86
Ludlum, Robert 1927- .... **CLC 22, 43; DAM NOV, POP**
See also AAYA 10; BEST 89:1, 90:3; CA 33-36R; CANR 25, 41, 68; DA3; DLBY 82; MTCW 1, 2
Ludwig, Ken .... **CLC 60**
Ludwig, Otto 1813-1865 .... **NCLC 4**
See also DLB 129
Lugones, Leopoldo 1874-1938 ...... **TCLC 15; HLCS 2**
See also CA 116; 131; HW 1
Lu Hsun 1881-1936 .... **TCLC 3; SSC 20**
See also Shu-Jen, Chou
Lukacs, George .... **CLC 24**
See also Lukacs, Gyorgy (Szegeny von)
Lukacs, Gyorgy (Szegeny von) 1885-1971
See Lukacs, George
See also CA 101; 29-32R; CANR 62; MTCW 2
Luke, Peter (Ambrose Cyprian) 1919-1995
CLC 38
See also CA 81-84; 147; CANR 72; DLB 13
Lunar, Dennis
See Mungo, Raymond
Lurie, Alison 1926- .... **CLC 4, 5, 18, 39**
See also CA 1-4R; CANR 2, 17, 50, 88; DLB 2; MTCW 1; SATA 46, 112
Lustig, Arnost 1926- .... **CLC 56**
See also AAYA 3; CA 69-72; CANR 47; SATA 56
Luther, Martin 1483-1546 .... **LC 9, 37**
See also DLB 179
Luxemburg, Rosa 1870(?)-1919 ..... **TCLC 63**
See also CA 118
Luzi, Mario 1914- .... **CLC 13**
See also CA 61-64; CANR 9, 70; DLB 128
Lyly, John 1554(?)-1606 .... **LC 41; DAM DRAM; DC 7**
See also DLB 62, 167
L'Ymagier
See Gourmont, Remy (-Marie-Charles) de
Lynch, B. Suarez
See Bioy Casares, Adolfo; Borges, Jorge Luis
Lynch, B. Suarez
See Bioy Casares, Adolfo
Lynch, David (K.) 1946- .... **CLC 66**
See also CA 124; 129
Lynch, James
See Andreyev, Leonid (Nikolaevich)
Lynch Davis, B.
See Bioy Casares, Adolfo; Borges, Jorge Luis
Lyndsay, Sir David 1490-1555 .... **LC 20**
Lynn, Kenneth S(chuyler) 1923- ...... **CLC 50**
See also CA 1-4R; CANR 3, 27, 65
Lynx
See West, Rebecca

See also AAYA 3; CA 81-84; CABS 3;
    CANR 15, 41, 67, 72; DA3; DLB 7;
    MTCW 1, 2
Mamoulian, Rouben (Zachary) 1897-1987
    CLC 16
    See also CA 25-28R; 124; CANR 85
Mandelstam, Osip (Emilievich)
    1891(?)-1938(?) .... **TCLC 2, 6; PC 14**
    See also CA 104; 150; MTCW 2
Mander, (Mary) Jane 1877-1949 ... **TCLC 31**
    See also CA 162
Mandeville, John fl. 1350- .... **CMLC 19**
    See also DLB 146
Mandiargues, Andre Pieyre de .... **CLC 41**
    See also Pieyre de Mandiargues, Andre
    DLB 83
Mandrake, Ethel Belle
    See Thurman, Wallace (Henry)
Mangan, James Clarence 1803-1849
    .... **NCLC 27**
Maniere, J.-E.
    See Giraudoux, (Hippolyte) Jean
Mankiewicz, Herman (Jacob) 1897-1953
    TCLC 85
    See also CA 120; 169; DLB 26
Manley, (Mary) Delariviere 1672(?)-1724
    .... **LC 1, 42**
    See also DLB 39, 80
Mann, Abel
    See Creasey, John
Mann, Emily 1952- .... **DC 7**
    See also CA 130; CANR 55
Mann, (Luiz) Heinrich 1871-1950 ... **TCLC 9**
    See also CA 106; 164, 181; DLB 66, 118
Mann, (Paul) Thomas 1875-1955 ... **TCLC 2,
    8, 14, 21, 35, 44, 60; DA; DAB; DAC;
    DAM MST, NOV; SSC 5; WLC**
    See also CA 104; 128; DA3; DLB 66;
    MTCW 1, 2
Mannheim, Karl 1893-1947 .... **TCLC 65**
Manning, David
    See Faust, Frederick (Schiller)
Manning, Frederic 1887(?)-1935 ... **TCLC 25**
    See also CA 124
Manning, Olivia 1915-1980 .... **CLC 5, 19**
    See also CA 5-8R; 101; CANR 29; MTCW
    1
Mano, D. Keith 1942- .... **CLC 2, 10**
    See also CA 25-28R; CAAS 6; CANR 26,
    57; DLB 6
Mansfield, Katherine . **TCLC 2, 8, 39; DAB;
    SSC 9, 23, 38; WLC**
    See also Beauchamp, Kathleen Mansfield
    DLB 162
Manso, Peter 1940- .... **CLC 39**
    See also CA 29-32R; CANR 44
Mantecon, Juan Jimenez
    See Jimenez (Mantecon), Juan Ramon
Manton, Peter
    See Creasey, John
Man Without a Spleen, A
    See Chekhov, Anton (Pavlovich)
Manzoni, Alessandro 1785-1873 .... **NCLC 29**
Map, Walter 1140-1209 .... **CMLC 32**
Mapu, Abraham (ben Jekutiel) 1808-1867
    NCLC 18
Mara, Sally
    See Queneau, Raymond
Marat, Jean Paul 1743-1793 .... **LC 10**
Marcel, Gabriel Honore 1889-1973 . **CLC 15**
    See also CA 102; 45-48; MTCW 1, 2
March, William 1893-1954 .... **TCLC 96**
Marchbanks, Samuel
    See Davies, (William) Robertson
Marchi, Giacomo
    See Bassani, Giorgio
Margulies, Donald .... **CLC 76**

Marie de France c. 12th cent. - ..... **CMLC 8;
    PC 22**
    See also DLB 208
Marie de l'Incarnation 1599-1672 ...... **LC 10**
Marier, Captain Victor
    See Griffith, D(avid Lewelyn) W(ark)
Mariner, Scott
    See Pohl, Frederik
Marinetti, Filippo Tommaso 1876-1944
    TCLC 10
    See also CA 107; DLB 114
Marivaux, Pierre Carlet de Chamblain de
    1688-1763 .... **LC 4; DC 7**
Markandaya, Kamala .... **CLC 8, 38**
    See also Taylor, Kamala (Purnaiya)
Markfield, Wallace 1926- .... **CLC 8**
    See also CA 69-72; CAAS 3; DLB 2, 28
Markham, Edwin 1852-1940 .... **TCLC 47**
    See also CA 160; DLB 54, 186
Markham, Robert
    See Amis, Kingsley (William)
Marks, J
    See Highwater, Jamake (Mamake)
Marks-Highwater, J
    See Highwater, Jamake (Mamake)
Markson, David M(errill) 1927- .... **CLC 67**
    See also CA 49-52; CANR 1
Marley, Bob .... **CLC 17**
    See also Marley, Robert Nesta
Marley, Robert Nesta 1945-1981
    See Marley, Bob
    See also CA 107; 103
Marlowe, Christopher 1564-1593 . **LC 22, 47;
    DA; DAB; DAC; DAM DRAM, MST;
    DC 1; WLC**
    See also CDBLB Before 1660; DA3; DLB
    62
Marlowe, Stephen 1928-
    See Queen, Ellery
    See also CA 13-16R; CANR 6, 55
Marmontel, Jean-Francois 1723-1799 .. **LC 2**
Marquand, John P(hillips) 1893-1960
    .... **CLC 2, 10**
    See also CA 85-88; CANR 73; DLB 9, 102;
    MTCW 2
Marques, Rene 1919-1979 ..... **CLC 96; DAM
    MULT; HLC 2**
    See also CA 97-100; 85-88; CANR 78;
    DLB 113; HW 1, 2
Marquez, Gabriel (Jose) Garcia
    See Garcia Marquez, Gabriel (Jose)
Marquis, Don(ald Robert Perry) 1878-1937
    TCLC 7
    See also CA 104; 166; DLB 11, 25
Marric, J. J.
    See Creasey, John
Marryat, Frederick 1792-1848 .... **NCLC 3**
    See also DLB 21, 163
Marsden, James
    See Creasey, John
Marsh, Edward 1872-1953 .... **TCLC 99**
Marsh, (Edith) Ngaio 1899-1982 . **CLC 7, 53;
    DAM POP**
    See also CA 9-12R; CANR 6, 58; DLB 77;
    MTCW 1, 2
Marshall, Garry 1934- .... **CLC 17**
    See also AAYA 3; CA 111; SATA 60
Marshall, Paule 1929- .. **CLC 27, 72; BLC 3;
    DAM MULT; SSC 3**
    See also BW 2, 3; CA 77-80; CANR 25,
    73; DA3; DLB 157; MTCW 1, 2
Marshallik
    See Zangwill, Israel
Marsten, Richard
    See Hunter, Evan
Marston, John 1576-1634 .... **LC 33; DAM
    DRAM**
    See also DLB 58, 172

Martha, Henry
    See Harris, Mark
Marti (y Perez), Jose (Julian) 1853-1895
    NCLC 63; DAM MULT; HLC 2
    See also HW 2
Martial c. 40-c. 104 .... **CMLC 35; PC 10**
    See also DLB 211
Martin, Ken
    See Hubbard, L(afayette) Ron(ald)
Martin, Richard
    See Creasey, John
Martin, Steve 1945- .... **CLC 30**
    See also CA 97-100; CANR 30; MTCW 1
Martin, Valerie 1948- .... **CLC 89**
    See also BEST 90:2; CA 85-88; CANR 49
Martin, Violet Florence 1862-1915 . **TCLC 51**
Martin, Webber
    See Silverberg, Robert
Martindale, Patrick Victor
    See White, Patrick (Victor Martindale)
Martin du Gard, Roger 1881-1958 . **TCLC 24**
    See also CA 118; DLB 65
Martineau, Harriet 1802-1876 .... **NCLC 26**
    See also DLB 21, 55, 159, 163, 166, 190;
    YABC 2
Martines, Julia
    See O'Faolain, Julia
Martinez, Enrique Gonzalez
    See Gonzalez Martinez, Enrique
Martinez, Jacinto Benavente y
    See Benavente (y Martinez), Jacinto
Martinez Ruiz, Jose 1873-1967
    See Azorin; Ruiz, Jose Martinez
    See also CA 93-96; HW 1
Martinez Sierra, Gregorio 1881-1947
    .... **TCLC 6**
    See also CA 115
Martinez Sierra, Maria (de la O'LeJarraga)
    1874-1974 .... **TCLC 6**
    See also CA 115
Martinsen, Martin
    See Follett, Ken(neth Martin)
Martinson, Harry (Edmund) 1904-1978
    .... **CLC 14**
    See also CA 77-80; CANR 34
Marut, Ret
    See Traven, B.
Marut, Robert
    See Traven, B.
Marvell, Andrew 1621-1678 .. **LC 4, 43; DA;
    DAB; DAC; DAM MST, POET; PC 10;
    WLC**
    See also CDBLB 1660-1789; DLB 131
Marx, Karl (Heinrich) 1818-1883 . **NCLC 17**
    See also DLB 129
Masaoka Shiki .... **TCLC 18**
    See also Masaoka Tsunenori
Masaoka Tsunenori 1867-1902
    See Masaoka Shiki
    See also CA 117
Masefield, John (Edward) 1878-1967
    .... **CLC 11, 47; DAM POET**
    See also CA 19-20; 25-28R; CANR 33;
    CAP 2; CDBLB 1890-1914; DLB 10, 19,
    153, 160; MTCW 1, 2; SATA 19
Maso, Carole 19(?)- .... **CLC 44**
    See also CA 170
Mason, Bobbie Ann 1940- ... **CLC 28, 43, 82;
    SSC 4**
    See also AAYA 5; CA 53-56; CANR 11, 31,
    58, 83; CDALBS; DA3; DLB 173; DLBY
    87; INT CANR-31; MTCW 1, 2
Mason, Ernst
    See Pohl, Frederik
Mason, Lee W.
    See Malzberg, Barry N(athaniel)
Mason, Nick 1945- .... **CLC 35**

Mason, Tally
See Derleth, August (William)

Mass, William
See Gibson, William

Master Lao
See Lao Tzu

Masters, Edgar Lee 1868-1950 . **TCLC 2, 25; DA; DAC; DAM MST, POET; PC 1; WLCS**
See also CA 104; 133; CDALB 1865-1917; DLB 54; MTCW 1, 2

Masters, Hilary 1928- .... **CLC 48**
See also CA 25-28R; CANR 13, 47

Mastrosimone, William 19(?)- .... **CLC 36**

Mathe, Albert
See Camus, Albert

Mather, Cotton 1663-1728 .... **LC 38**
See also CDALB 1640-1865; DLB 24, 30, 140

Mather, Increase 1639-1723 .... **LC 38**
See also DLB 24

Matheson, Richard Burton 1926- .... **CLC 37**
See also AAYA 31; CA 97-100; CANR 88; DLB 8, 44; INT 97-100

Mathews, Harry 1930- .... **CLC 6, 52**
See also CA 21-24R; CAAS 6; CANR 18, 40

Mathews, John Joseph 1894-1979 .. **CLC 84; DAM MULT**
See also CA 19-20; 142; CANR 45; CAP 2; DLB 175; NNAL

Mathias, Roland (Glyn) 1915- .... **CLC 45**
See also CA 97-100; CANR 19, 41; DLB 27

Matsuo Basho 1644-1694 .... **PC 3**
See also DAM POET

Mattheson, Rodney
See Creasey, John

Matthews, (James) Brander 1852-1929
.... **TCLC 95**
See also DLB 71, 78; DLBD 13

Matthews, Greg 1949- .... **CLC 45**
See also CA 135

Matthews, William (Procter, III) 1942-1997
CLC 40
See also CA 29-32R; 162; CAAS 18; CANR 12, 57; DLB 5

Matthias, John (Edward) 1941- .... **CLC 9**
See also CA 33-36R; CANR 56

Matthiessen, F. O. 1902-1950 .... **TCLC 100**
See also DLB 63

Matthiessen, Peter 1927- ... **CLC 5, 7, 11, 32, 64; DAM NOV**
See also AAYA 6; BEST 90:4; CA 9-12R; CANR 21, 50, 73; DA3; DLB 6, 173; MTCW 1, 2; SATA 27

Maturin, Charles Robert 1780(?)-1824
.... **NCLC 6**
See also DLB 178

Matute (Ausejo), Ana Maria 1925- .. **CLC 11**
See also CA 89-92; MTCW 1

Maugham, W. S.
See Maugham, W(illiam) Somerset

Maugham, W(illiam) Somerset 1874-1965
CLC 1, 11, 15, 67, 93; DA; DAB; DAC; DAM DRAM, MST, NOV; SSC 8; WLC
See also CA 5-8R; 25-28R; CANR 40; CD-BLB 1914-1945; DA3; DLB 10, 36, 77, 100, 162, 195; MTCW 1, 2; SATA 54

Maugham, William Somerset
See Maugham, W(illiam) Somerset

Maupassant, (Henri Rene Albert) Guy de 1850-1893 . **NCLC 1, 42, 83; DA; DAB; DAC; DAM MST; SSC 1; WLC**
See also DA3; DLB 123

Maupin, Armistead 1944- ..... **CLC 95; DAM POP**
See also CA 125; 130; CANR 58; DA3; INT 130; MTCW 2

Maurhut, Richard
See Traven, B.

Mauriac, Claude 1914-1996 .... **CLC 9**
See also CA 89-92; 152; DLB 83

Mauriac, Francois (Charles) 1885-1970
.... **CLC 4, 9, 56; SSC 24**
See also CA 25-28; CAP 2; DLB 65; MTCW 1, 2

Mavor, Osborne Henry 1888-1951
See Bridie, James
See also CA 104

Maxwell, William (Keepers, Jr.) 1908-
.... **CLC 19**
See also CA 93-96; CANR 54; DLBY 80; INT 93-96

May, Elaine 1932- .... **CLC 16**
See also CA 124; 142; DLB 44

Mayakovski, Vladimir (Vladimirovich) 1893-1930 .... **TCLC 4, 18**
See also CA 104; 158; MTCW 2

Mayhew, Henry 1812-1887 .... **NCLC 31**
See also DLB 18, 55, 190

Mayle, Peter 1939(?)- .... **CLC 89**
See also CA 139; CANR 64

Maynard, Joyce 1953- .... **CLC 23**
See also CA 111; 129; CANR 64

Mayne, William (James Carter) 1928-
.... **CLC 12**
See also AAYA 20; CA 9-12R; CANR 37, 80; CLR 25; JRDA; MAICYA; SAAS 11; SATA 6, 68

Mayo, Jim
See L'Amour, Louis (Dearborn)

Maysles, Albert 1926- .... **CLC 16**
See also CA 29-32R

Maysles, David 1932- .... **CLC 16**

Mazer, Norma Fox 1931- .... **CLC 26**
See also AAYA 5; CA 69-72; CANR 12, 32, 66; CLR 23; JRDA; MAICYA; SAAS 1; SATA 24, 67, 105

Mazzini, Guiseppe 1805-1872 .... **NCLC 34**

McAlmon, Robert (Menzies) 1895-1956
TCLC 97
See also CA 107; 168; DLB 4, 45; DLBD 15

McAuley, James Phillip 1917-1976 .. **CLC 45**
See also CA 97-100

McBain, Ed
See Hunter, Evan

McBrien, William Augustine 1930- .. **CLC 44**
See also CA 107

McCaffrey, Anne (Inez) 1926- .... **CLC 17; DAM NOV, POP**
See also AAYA 6; AITN 2; BEST 89:2; CA 25-28R; CANR 15, 35, 55; CLR 49; DA3; DLB 8; JRDA; MAICYA; MTCW 1, 2; SAAS 11; SATA 8, 70

McCall, Nathan 1955(?)- .... **CLC 86**
See also BW 3; CA 146; CANR 88

McCann, Arthur
See Campbell, John W(ood, Jr.)

McCann, Edson
See Pohl, Frederik

McCarthy, Charles, Jr. 1933-
See McCarthy, Cormac
See also CANR 42, 69; DAM POP; DA3; MTCW 2

McCarthy, Cormac 1933- ...... **CLC 4, 57, 59, 101**
See also McCarthy, Charles, Jr. DLB 6, 143; MTCW 2

McCarthy, Mary (Therese) 1912-1989
..... **CLC 1, 3, 5, 14, 24, 39, 59; SSC 24**
See also CA 5-8R; 129; CANR 16, 50, 64; DA3; DLB 2; DLBY 81; INT CANR-16; MTCW 1, 2

McCartney, (James) Paul 1942- . **CLC 12, 35**
See also CA 146

McCauley, Stephen (D.) 1955- .... **CLC 50**

See also CA 141

McClure, Michael (Thomas) 1932- ... **CLC 6, 10**
See also CA 21-24R; CANR 17, 46, 77; DLB 16

McCorkle, Jill (Collins) 1958- .... **CLC 51**
See also CA 121; DLBY 87

McCourt, Frank 1930- .... **CLC 109**
See also CA 157

McCourt, James 1941- .... **CLC 5**
See also CA 57-60

McCourt, Malachy 1932- .... **CLC 119**

McCoy, Horace (Stanley) 1897-1955
.... **TCLC 28**
See also CA 108; 155; DLB 9

McCrae, John 1872-1918 .... **TCLC 12**
See also CA 109; DLB 92

McCreigh, James
See Pohl, Frederik

McCullers, (Lula) Carson (Smith) 1917-1967
CLC 1, 4, 10, 12, 48, 100; DA; DAB; DAC; DAM MST, NOV; SSC 9, 24; WLC
See also AAYA 21; CA 5-8R; 25-28R; CABS 1, 3; CANR 18; CDALB 1941-1968; DA3; DLB 2, 7, 173; MTCW 1, 2; SATA 27

McCulloch, John Tyler
See Burroughs, Edgar Rice

McCullough, Colleen 1938(?)- . **CLC 27, 107; DAM NOV, POP**
See also CA 81-84; CANR 17, 46, 67; DA3; MTCW 1, 2

McDermott, Alice 1953- .... **CLC 90**
See also CA 109; CANR 40

McElroy, Joseph 1930- .... **CLC 5, 47**
See also CA 17-20R

McEwan, Ian (Russell) 1948- .... **CLC 13, 66; DAM NOV**
See also BEST 90:4; CA 61-64; CANR 14, 41, 69, 87; DLB 14, 194; MTCW 1, 2

McFadden, David 1940- .... **CLC 48**
See also CA 104; DLB 60; INT 104

McFarland, Dennis 1950- .... **CLC 65**
See also CA 165

McGahern, John 1934- ... **CLC 5, 9, 48; SSC 17**
See also CA 17-20R; CANR 29, 68; DLB 14; MTCW 1

McGinley, Patrick (Anthony) 1937- . **CLC 41**
See also CA 120; 127; CANR 56; INT 127

McGinley, Phyllis 1905-1978 .... **CLC 14**
See also CA 9-12R; 77-80; CANR 19; DLB 11, 48; SATA 2, 44; SATA-Obit 24

McGinniss, Joe 1942- .... **CLC 32**
See also AITN 2; BEST 89:2; CA 25-28R; CANR 26, 70; DLB 185; INT CANR-26

McGivern, Maureen Daly
See Daly, Maureen

McGrath, Patrick 1950- .... **CLC 55**
See also CA 136; CANR 65

McGrath, Thomas (Matthew) 1916-1990
CLC 28, 59; DAM POET
See also CA 9-12R; 132; CANR 6, 33; MTCW 1; SATA 41; SATA-Obit 66

McGuane, Thomas (Francis III) 1939-
.... **CLC 3, 7, 18, 45, 127**
See also AITN 2; CA 49-52; CANR 5, 24, 49; DLB 2, 212; DLBY 80; INT CANR-24; MTCW 1

McGuckian, Medbh 1950- .... **CLC 48; DAM POET; PC 27**
See also CA 143; DLB 40

McHale, Tom 1942(?)-1982 .... **CLC 3, 5**
See also AITN 1; CA 77-80; 106

McIlvanney, William 1936- .... **CLC 42**
See also CA 25-28R; CANR 61; DLB 14, 207

McIlwraith, Maureen Mollie Hunter
See Hunter, Mollie
See also SATA 2

McInerney, Jay 1955- .... **CLC 34, 112; DAM POP**
See also AAYA 18; CA 116; 123; CANR 45, 68; DA3; INT 123; MTCW 2

McIntyre, Vonda N(eel) 1948- .... **CLC 18**
See also CA 81-84; CANR 17, 34, 69; MTCW 1

McKay, Claude . **TCLC 7, 41; BLC 3; DAB; PC 2**
See also McKay, Festus Claudius DLB 4, 45, 51, 117

McKay, Festus Claudius 1889-1948
See McKay, Claude
See also BW 1, 3; CA 104; 124; CANR 73; DA; DAC; DAM MST, MULT, NOV, POET; MTCW 1, 2; WLC

McKuen, Rod 1933- .... **CLC 1, 3**
See also AITN 1; CA 41-44R; CANR 40

McLoughlin, R. B.
See Mencken, H(enry) L(ouis)

McLuhan, (Herbert) Marshall 1911-1980 **CLC 37, 83**
See also CA 9-12R; 102; CANR 12, 34, 61; DLB 88; INT CANR-12; MTCW 1, 2

McMillan, Terry (L.) 1951- .... **CLC 50, 61, 112; BLCS; DAM MULT, NOV, POP**
See also AAYA 21; BW 2, 3; CA 140; CANR 60; DA3; MTCW 2

McMurtry, Larry (Jeff) 1936- .. **CLC 2, 3, 7, 11, 27, 44, 127; DAM NOV, POP**
See also AAYA 15; AITN 2; BEST 89:2; CA 5-8R; CANR 19, 43, 64; CDALB 1968-1988; DA3; DLB 2, 143; DLBY 80, 87; MTCW 1, 2

McNally, T. M. 1961- .... **CLC 82**

McNally, Terrence 1939- ... **CLC 4, 7, 41, 91; DAM DRAM**
See also CA 45-48; CANR 2, 56; DA3; DLB 7; MTCW 2

McNamer, Deirdre 1950- .... **CLC 70**

McNeal, Tom .... **CLC 119**

McNeile, Herman Cyril 1888-1937
See Sapper
See also CA 184; DLB 77

McNickle, (William) D'Arcy 1904-1977
.... **CLC 89; DAM MULT**
See also CA 9-12R; 85-88; CANR 5, 45; DLB 175, 212; NNAL; SATA-Obit 22

McPhee, John (Angus) 1931- .... **CLC 36**
See also BEST 90:1; CA 65-68; CANR 20, 46, 64, 69; DLB 185; MTCW 1, 2

McPherson, James Alan 1943- .. **CLC 19, 77; BLCS**
See also BW 1, 3; CA 25-28R; CAAS 17; CANR 24, 74; DLB 38; MTCW 1, 2

McPherson, William (Alexander) 1933-
.... **CLC 34**
See also CA 69-72; CANR 28; INT CANR-28

Mead, George Herbert 1873-1958 . **TCLC 89**

Mead, Margaret 1901-1978 .... **CLC 37**
See also AITN 1; CA 1-4R; 81-84; CANR 4; DA3; MTCW 1, 2; SATA-Obit 20

Meaker, Marijane (Agnes) 1927-
See Kerr, M. E.
See also CA 107; CANR 37, 63; INT 107; JRDA; MAICYA; MTCW 1; SATA 20, 61, 99; SATA-Essay 111

Medoff, Mark (Howard) 1940- ... **CLC 6, 23; DAM DRAM**
See also AITN 1; CA 53-56; CANR 5; DLB 7; INT CANR-5

Medvedev, P. N.
See Bakhtin, Mikhail Mikhailovich

Meged, Aharon
See Megged, Aharon

Meged, Aron
See Megged, Aharon

Megged, Aharon 1920- .... **CLC 9**
See also CA 49-52; CAAS 13; CANR 1

Mehta, Ved (Parkash) 1934- .... **CLC 37**
See also CA 1-4R; CANR 2, 23, 69; MTCW 1

Melanter
See Blackmore, R(ichard) D(oddridge)

Melies, Georges 1861-1938 .... **TCLC 81**

Melikow, Loris
See Hofmannsthal, Hugo von

Melmoth, Sebastian
See Wilde, Oscar

Meltzer, Milton 1915- .... **CLC 26**
See also AAYA 8; CA 13-16R; CANR 38; CLR 13; DLB 61; JRDA; MAICYA; SAAS 1; SATA 1, 50, 80

Melville, Herman 1819-1891 ..... **NCLC 3, 12, 29, 45, 49; DA; DAB; DAC; DAM MST, NOV; SSC 1, 17; WLC**
See also AAYA 25; CDALB 1640-1865; DA3; DLB 3, 74; SATA 59

Menander c. 342B.C.-c. 292B.C. ... **CMLC 9; DAM DRAM; DC 3**
See also DLB 176

Menchu, Rigoberta 1959-
See also HLCS 2

Menchu, Rigoberta 1959-
See also CA 175; HLCS 2

Mencken, H(enry) L(ouis) 1880-1956
.... **TCLC 13**
See also CA 105; 125; CDALB 1917-1929; DLB 11, 29, 63, 137; MTCW 1, 2

Mendelsohn, Jane 1965(?)- .... **CLC 99**
See also CA 154

Mercer, David 1928-1980 .... **CLC 5; DAM DRAM**
See also CA 9-12R; 102; CANR 23; DLB 13; MTCW 1

Merchant, Paul
See Ellison, Harlan (Jay)

Meredith, George 1828-1909 .. **TCLC 17, 43; DAM POET**
See also CA 117; 153; CANR 80; CDBLB 1832-1890; DLB 18, 35, 57, 159

Meredith, William (Morris) 1919- .... **CLC 4, 13, 22, 55; DAM POET; PC 28**
See also CA 9-12R; CAAS 14; CANR 6, 40; DLB 5

Merezhkovsky, Dmitry Sergeyevich
1865-1941 .... **TCLC 29**
See also CA 169

Merimee, Prosper 1803-1870 ... **NCLC 6, 65; SSC 7**
See also DLB 119, 192

Merkin, Daphne 1954- .... **CLC 44**
See also CA 123

Merlin, Arthur
See Blish, James (Benjamin)

Merrill, James (Ingram) 1926-1995 .. **CLC 2, 3, 6, 8, 13, 18, 34, 91; DAM POET; PC 28**
See also CA 13-16R; 147; CANR 10, 49, 63; DA3; DLB 5, 165; DLBY 85; INT CANR-10; MTCW 1, 2

Merriman, Alex
See Silverberg, Robert

Merriman, Brian 1747-1805 .... **NCLC 70**

Merritt, E. B.
See Waddington, Miriam

Merton, Thomas 1915-1968 ..... **CLC 1, 3, 11, 34, 83; PC 10**
See also CA 5-8R; 25-28R; CANR 22, 53; DA3; DLB 48; DLBY 81; MTCW 1, 2

Merwin, W(illiam) S(tanley) 1927- ... **CLC 1, 2, 3, 5, 8, 13, 18, 45, 88; DAM POET**
See also CA 13-16R; CANR 15, 51; DA3; DLB 5, 169; INT CANR-15; MTCW 1, 2

Metcalf, John 1938- .... **CLC 37**
See also CA 113; DLB 60

Metcalf, Suzanne
See Baum, L(yman) Frank

Mew, Charlotte (Mary) 1870-1928 .. **TCLC 8**
See also CA 105; DLB 19, 135

Mewshaw, Michael 1943- .... **CLC 9**
See also CA 53-56; CANR 7, 47; DLBY 80

Meyer, Conrad Ferdinand 1825-1905
.... **NCLC 81**
See also DLB 129

Meyer, June
See Jordan, June

Meyer, Lynn
See Slavitt, David R(ytman)

Meyer-Meyrink, Gustav 1868-1932
See Meyrink, Gustav
See also CA 117

Meyers, Jeffrey 1939- .... **CLC 39**
See also CA 73-76; CANR 54; DLB 111

Meynell, Alice (Christina Gertrude Thompson) 1847-1922 .... **TCLC 6**
See also CA 104; 177; DLB 19, 98

Meyrink, Gustav .... **TCLC 21**
See also Meyer-Meyrink, Gustav DLB 81

Michaels, Leonard 1933- .... **CLC 6, 25; SSC 16**
See also CA 61-64; CANR 21, 62; DLB 130; MTCW 1

Michaux, Henri 1899-1984 .... **CLC 8, 19**
See also CA 85-88; 114

Micheaux, Oscar (Devereaux) 1884-1951 **TCLC 76**
See also BW 3; CA 174; DLB 50

Michelangelo 1475-1564 .... **LC 12**

Michelet, Jules 1798-1874 .... **NCLC 31**

Michels, Robert 1876-1936 .... **TCLC 88**

Michener, James A(lbert) 1907(?)-1997
. **CLC 1, 5, 11, 29, 60, 109; DAM NOV, POP**
See also AAYA 27; AITN 1; BEST 90:1; CA 5-8R; 161; CANR 21, 45, 68; DA3; DLB 6; MTCW 1, 2

Mickiewicz, Adam 1798-1855 .... **NCLC 3**

Middleton, Christopher 1926- .... **CLC 13**
See also CA 13-16R; CANR 29, 54; DLB 40

Middleton, Richard (Barham) 1882-1911 **TCLC 56**
See also DLB 156

Middleton, Stanley 1919- .... **CLC 7, 38**
See also CA 25-28R; CAAS 23; CANR 21, 46, 81; DLB 14

Middleton, Thomas 1580-1627 . **LC 33; DAM DRAM, MST; DC 5**
See also DLB 58

Migueis, Jose Rodrigues 1901- .... **CLC 10**

Mikszath, Kalman 1847-1910 .... **TCLC 31**
See also CA 170

Miles, Jack .... **CLC 100**

Miles, Josephine (Louise) 1911-1985 . **CLC 1, 2, 14, 34, 39; DAM POET**
See also CA 1-4R; 116; CANR 2, 55; DLB 48

Militant
See Sandburg, Carl (August)

Mill, John Stuart 1806-1873 .... **NCLC 11, 58**
See also CDBLB 1832-1890; DLB 55, 190

Millar, Kenneth 1915-1983 ... **CLC 14; DAM POP**
See also Macdonald, Ross CA 9-12R; 110; CANR 16, 63; DA3; DLB 2; DLBD 6; DLBY 83; MTCW 1, 2

Millay, E. Vincent
See Millay, Edna St. Vincent

Millay, Edna St. Vincent 1892-1950
... **TCLC 4, 49; DA; DAB; DAC; DAM MST, POET; PC 6; WLCS**

See also CA 109; CANR 55, 84; DLB 81, 124; MTCW 2

Muske, Carol 1945- .... **CLC 90**
See also Muske-Dukes, Carol (Anne)

Muske-Dukes, Carol (Anne) 1945-
See Muske, Carol
See also CA 65-68; CANR 32, 70

Musset, (Louis Charles) Alfred de 1810-1857 **NCLC 7**
See also DLB 192

Mussolini, Benito (Amilcare Andrea) 1883-1945 .... **TCLC 96**
See also CA 116

My Brother's Brother
See Chekhov, Anton (Pavlovich)

Myers, L(eopold) H(amilton) 1881-1944 **TCLC 59**
See also CA 157; DLB 15

Myers, Walter Dean 1937- . **CLC 35; BLC 3; DAM MULT, NOV**
See also AAYA 4, 23; BW 2; CA 33-36R; CANR 20, 42, 67; CLR 4, 16, 35; DLB 33; INT CANR-20; JRDA; MAICYA; MTCW 2; SAAS 2; SATA 41, 71, 109; SATA-Brief 27

Myers, Walter M.
See Myers, Walter Dean

Myles, Symon
See Follett, Ken(neth Martin)

Nabokov, Vladimir (Vladimirovich) 1899-1977 . **CLC 1, 2, 3, 6, 8, 11, 15, 23, 44, 46, 64; DA; DAB; DAC; DAM MST, NOV; SSC 11; WLC**
See also CA 5-8R; 69-72; CANR 20; CDALB 1941-1968; DLB 2; DLBD 3; DLBY 80, 91; MTCW 1, 2

Naevius c. 265B.C.-201B.C. .... **CMLC 37**
See also DLB 211

Nagai Kafu 1879-1959 .... **TCLC 51**
See also Nagai Sokichi DLB 180

Nagai Sokichi 1879-1959
See Nagai Kafu
See also CA 117

Nagy, Laszlo 1925-1978 .... **CLC 7**
See also CA 129; 112

Naidu, Sarojini 1879-1943 .... **TCLC 80**

Naipaul, Shiva(dhar Srinivasa) 1945-1985 **CLC 32, 39; DAM NOV**
See also CA 110; 112; 116; CANR 33; DA3; DLB 157; DLBY 85; MTCW 1, 2

Naipaul, V(idiadhar) S(urajprasad) 1932- **CLC 4, 7, 9, 13, 18, 37, 105; DAB; DAC; DAM MST, NOV; SSC 38**
See also CA 1-4R; CANR 1, 33, 51; CD-BLB 1960 to Present; DA3; DLB 125, 204, 206; DLBY 85; MTCW 1, 2

Nakos, Lilika 1899(?)- .... **CLC 29**

Narayan, R(asipuram) K(rishnaswami) 1906- . **CLC 7, 28, 47, 121; DAM NOV; SSC 25**
See also CA 81-84; CANR 33, 61; DA3; MTCW 1, 2; SATA 62

Nash, (Frediric) Ogden 1902-1971 . **CLC 23; DAM POET; PC 21**
See also CA 13-14; 29-32R; CANR 34, 61; CAP 1; DLB 11; MAICYA; MTCW 1, 2; SATA 2, 46

Nashe, Thomas 1567-1601(?) .... **LC 41**
See also DLB 167

Nashe, Thomas 1567-1601 .... **LC 41**

Nathan, Daniel
See Dannay, Frederic

Nathan, George Jean 1882-1958 .... **TCLC 18**
See also Hatteras, Owen CA 114; 169; DLB 137

Natsume, Kinnosuke 1867-1916
See Natsume, Soseki
See also CA 104

Natsume, Soseki 1867-1916 .... **TCLC 2, 10**

See also Natsume, Kinnosuke DLB 180

Natti, (Mary) Lee 1919-
See Kingman, Lee
See also CA 5-8R; CANR 2

Naylor, Gloria 1950- .... **CLC 28, 52; BLC 3; DA; DAC; DAM MST, MULT, NOV, POP; WLCS**
See also AAYA 6; BW 2, 3; CA 107; CANR 27, 51, 74; DA3; DLB 173; MTCW 1, 2

Neihardt, John Gneisenau 1881-1973
.... **CLC 32**
See also CA 13-14; CANR 65; CAP 1; DLB 9, 54

Nekrasov, Nikolai Alekseevich 1821-1878 **NCLC 11**

Nelligan, Emile 1879-1941 .... **TCLC 14**
See also CA 114; DLB 92

Nelson, Willie 1933- .... **CLC 17**
See also CA 107

Nemerov, Howard (Stanley) 1920-1991 .. **CLC 2, 6, 9, 36; DAM POET; PC 24**
See also CA 1-4R; 134; CABS 2; CANR 1, 27, 53; DLB 5, 6; DLBY 83; INT CANR-27; MTCW 1, 2

Neruda, Pablo 1904-1973 .. **CLC 1, 2, 5, 7, 9, 28, 62; DA; DAB; DAC; DAM MST, MULT, POET; HLC 2; PC 4; WLC**
See also CA 19-20; 45-48; CAP 2; DA3; HW 1; MTCW 1, 2

Nerval, Gerard de 1808-1855 ... **NCLC 1, 67; PC 13; SSC 18**

Nervo, (Jose) Amado (Ruiz de) 1870-1919 **TCLC 11; HLCS 2**
See also CA 109; 131; HW 1

Nessi, Pio Baroja y
See Baroja (y Nessi), Pio

Nestroy, Johann 1801-1862 .... **NCLC 42**
See also DLB 133

Netterville, Luke
See O'Grady, Standish (James)

Neufeld, John (Arthur) 1938- .... **CLC 17**
See also AAYA 11; CA 25-28R; CANR 11, 37, 56; CLR 52; MAICYA; SAAS 3; SATA 6, 81

Neumann, Alfred 1895-1952 .... **TCLC 100**
See also CA 183; DLB 56

Neville, Emily Cheney 1919- .... **CLC 12**
See also CA 5-8R; CANR 3, 37, 85; JRDA; MAICYA; SAAS 2; SATA 1

Newbound, Bernard Slade 1930-
See Slade, Bernard
See also CA 81-84; CANR 49; DAM DRAM

Newby, P(ercy) H(oward) 1918-1997 . **CLC 2, 13; DAM NOV**
See also CA 5-8R; 161; CANR 32, 67; DLB 15; MTCW 1

Newlove, Donald 1928- .... **CLC 6**
See also CA 29-32R; CANR 25

Newlove, John (Herbert) 1938- .... **CLC 14**
See also CA 21-24R; CANR 9, 25

Newman, Charles 1938- .... **CLC 2, 8**
See also CA 21-24R; CANR 84

Newman, Edwin (Harold) 1919- ...... **CLC 14**
See also AITN 1; CA 69-72; CANR 5

Newman, John Henry 1801-1890 .. **NCLC 38**
See also DLB 18, 32, 55

Newton, (Sir)Isaac 1642-1727 .... **LC 35, 52**

Newton, Suzanne 1936- .... **CLC 35**
See also CA 41-44R; CANR 14; JRDA; SATA 5, 77

Nexo, Martin Andersen 1869-1954 . **TCLC 43**

Nezval, Vitezslav 1900-1958 .... **TCLC 44**
See also CA 123

Ng, Fae Myenne 1957(?)- .... **CLC 81**
See also CA 146

Ngema, Mbongeni 1955- .... **CLC 57**
See also BW 2; CA 143; CANR 84

Ngugi, James T(hiong'o) .... **CLC 3, 7, 13**
See also Ngugi wa Thiong'o

Ngugi wa Thiong'o 1938- .. **CLC 36; BLC 3; DAM MULT, NOV**
See also Ngugi, James T(hiong'o) BW 2; CA 81-84; CANR 27, 58; DLB 125; MTCW 1, 2

Nichol, B(arrie) P(hillip) 1944-1988 . **CLC 18**
See also CA 53-56; DLB 53; SATA 66

Nichols, John (Treadwell) 1940- .... **CLC 38**
See also CA 9-12R; CAAS 2; CANR 6, 70; DLBY 82

Nichols, Leigh
See Koontz, Dean R(ay)

Nichols, Peter (Richard) 1927- .... **CLC 5, 36, 65**
See also CA 104; CANR 33, 86; DLB 13; MTCW 1

Nicolas, F. R. E.
See Freeling, Nicolas

Niedecker, Lorine 1903-1970 ..... **CLC 10, 42; DAM POET**
See also CA 25-28; CAP 2; DLB 48

Nietzsche, Friedrich (Wilhelm) 1844-1900 **TCLC 10, 18, 55**
See also CA 107; 121; DLB 129

Nievo, Ippolito 1831-1861 .... **NCLC 22**

Nightingale, Anne Redmon 1943-
See Redmon, Anne
See also CA 103

Nightingale, Florence 1820-1910 ... **TCLC 85**
See also DLB 166

Nik. T. O.
See Annensky, Innokenty (Fyodorovich)

Nin, Anais 1903-1977 ..... **CLC 1, 4, 8, 11, 14, 60, 127; DAM NOV, POP; SSC 10**
See also AITN 2; CA 13-16R; 69-72; CANR 22, 53; DLB 2, 4, 152; MTCW 1, 2

Nishida, Kitaro 1870-1945 .... **TCLC 83**

Nishiwaki, Junzaburo 1894-1982 .... **PC 15**
See also CA 107

Nissenson, Hugh 1933- .... **CLC 4, 9**
See also CA 17-20R; CANR 27; DLB 28

Niven, Larry .... **CLC 8**
See also Niven, Laurence Van Cott AAYA 27; DLB 8

Niven, Laurence Van Cott 1938-
See Niven, Larry
See also CA 21-24R; CAAS 12; CANR 14, 44, 66; DAM POP; MTCW 1, 2; SATA 95

Nixon, Agnes Eckhardt 1927- .... **CLC 21**
See also CA 110

Nizan, Paul 1905-1940 .... **TCLC 40**
See also CA 161; DLB 72

Nkosi, Lewis 1936- ... **CLC 45; BLC 3; DAM MULT**
See also BW 1, 3; CA 65-68; CANR 27, 81; DLB 157

Nodier, (Jean) Charles (Emmanuel) 1780-1844 .... **NCLC 19**
See also DLB 119

Noguchi, Yone 1875-1947 .... **TCLC 80**

Nolan, Christopher 1965- .... **CLC 58**
See also CA 111; CANR 88

Noon, Jeff 1957- .... **CLC 91**
See also CA 148; CANR 83

Norden, Charles
See Durrell, Lawrence (George)

Nordhoff, Charles (Bernard) 1887-1947 **TCLC 23**
See also CA 108; DLB 9; SATA 23

Norfolk, Lawrence 1963- .... **CLC 76**
See also CA 144; CANR 85

Norman, Marsha 1947- .... **CLC 28; DAM DRAM; DC 8**

Pasquini
See Silone, Ignazio

Pastan, Linda (Olenik) 1932- . **CLC 27; DAM POET**
See also CA 61-64; CANR 18, 40, 61; DLB 5

Pasternak, Boris (Leonidovich) 1890-1960 **CLC 7, 10, 18, 63; DA; DAB; DAC; DAM MST, NOV, POET; PC 6; SSC 31; WLC**
See also CA 127; 116; DA3; MTCW 1, 2

Patchen, Kenneth 1911-1972 .. **CLC 1, 2, 18; DAM POET**
See also CA 1-4R; 33-36R; CANR 3, 35; DLB 16, 48; MTCW 1

Pater, Walter (Horatio) 1839-1894 .. **NCLC 7**
See also CDBLB 1832-1890; DLB 57, 156

Paterson, A(ndrew) B(arton) 1864-1941 **TCLC 32**
See also CA 155; SATA 97

Paterson, Katherine (Womeldorf) 1932-
.... **CLC 12, 30**
See also AAYA 1, 31; CA 21-24R; CANR 28, 59; CLR 7, 50; DLB 52; JRDA; MAICYA; MTCW 1; SATA 13, 53, 92

Patmore, Coventry Kersey Dighton
1823-1896 .... **NCLC 9**
See also DLB 35, 98

Paton, Alan (Stewart) 1903-1988 . **CLC 4, 10, 25, 55, 106; DA; DAB; DAC; DAM MST, NOV; WLC**
See also AAYA 26; CA 13-16; 125; CANR 22; CAP 1; DA3; DLBD 17; MTCW 1, 2; SATA 11; SATA-Obit 56

Paton Walsh, Gillian 1937-
See Walsh, Jill Paton
See also AAYA 11; CANR 38, 83; DLB 161; JRDA; MAICYA; SAAS 3; SATA 4, 72, 109

Patton, George S. 1885-1945 .... **TCLC 79**

Paulding, James Kirke 1778-1860 ... **NCLC 2**
See also DLB 3, 59, 74

Paulin, Thomas Neilson 1949-
See Paulin, Tom
See also CA 123; 128

Paulin, Tom .... **CLC 37**
See also Paulin, Thomas Neilson DLB 40

Pausanias c. 1st cent. - .... **CMLC 36**

Paustovsky, Konstantin (Georgievich)
1892-1968 .... **CLC 40**
See also CA 93-96; 25-28R

Pavese, Cesare 1908-1950 .. **TCLC 3; PC 13; SSC 19**
See also CA 104; 169; DLB 128, 177

Pavic, Milorad 1929- .... **CLC 60**
See also CA 136; DLB 181

Pavlov, Ivan Petrovich 1849-1936 . **TCLC 91**
See also CA 118; 180

Payne, Alan
See Jakes, John (William)

Paz, Gil
See Lugones, Leopoldo

Paz, Octavio 1914-1998 . **CLC 3, 4, 6, 10, 19, 51, 65, 119; DA; DAB; DAC; DAM MST, MULT, POET; HLC 2; PC 1; WLC**
See also CA 73-76; 165; CANR 32, 65; DA3; DLBY 90, 98; HW 1, 2; MTCW 1, 2

p'Bitek, Okot 1931-1982 .... **CLC 96; BLC 3; DAM MULT**
See also BW 2, 3; CA 124; 107; CANR 82; DLB 125; MTCW 1, 2

Peacock, Molly 1947- .... **CLC 60**
See also CA 103; CAAS 21; CANR 52, 84; DLB 120

Peacock, Thomas Love 1785-1866 . **NCLC 22**
See also DLB 96, 116

Peake, Mervyn 1911-1968 .... **CLC 7, 54**
See also CA 5-8R; 25-28R; CANR 3; DLB 15, 160; MTCW 1; SATA 23

Pearce, Philippa .... **CLC 21**
See also Christie, (Ann) Philippa CLR 9; DLB 161; MAICYA; SATA 1, 67

Pearl, Eric
See Elman, Richard (Martin)

Pearson, T(homas) R(eid) 1956- ...... **CLC 39**
See also CA 120; 130; INT 130

Peck, Dale 1967- .... **CLC 81**
See also CA 146; CANR 72

Peck, John 1941- .... **CLC 3**
See also CA 49-52; CANR 3

Peck, Richard (Wayne) 1934- .... **CLC 21**
See also AAYA 1, 24; CA 85-88; CANR 19, 38; CLR 15; INT CANR-19; JRDA; MAICYA; SAAS 2; SATA 18, 55, 97; SATA-Essay 110

Peck, Robert Newton 1928- .... **CLC 17; DA; DAC; DAM MST**
See also AAYA 3; CA 81-84, 182; CAAE 182; CANR 31, 63; CLR 45; JRDA; MAICYA; SAAS 1; SATA 21, 62, 111; SATA-Essay 108

Peckinpah, (David) Sam(uel) 1925-1984
.... **CLC 20**
See also CA 109; 114; CANR 82

Pedersen, Knut 1859-1952
See Hamsun, Knut
See also CA 104; 119; CANR 63; MTCW 1, 2

Peeslake, Gaffer
See Durrell, Lawrence (George)

Peguy, Charles Pierre 1873-1914 ... **TCLC 10**
See also CA 107

Peirce, Charles Sanders 1839-1914
.... **TCLC 81**

Pellicer, Carlos 1900(?)-1977
See also CA 153; 69-72; HLCS 2; HW 1

Pena, Ramon del Valle y
See Valle-Inclan, Ramon (Maria) del

Pendennis, Arthur Esquir
See Thackeray, William Makepeace

Penn, William 1644-1718 .... **LC 25**
See also DLB 24

PEPECE
See Prado (Calvo), Pedro

Pepys, Samuel 1633-1703 . **LC 11; DA; DAB; DAC; DAM MST; WLC**
See also CDBLB 1660-1789; DA3; DLB 101

Percy, Walker 1916-1990 . **CLC 2, 3, 6, 8, 14, 18, 47, 65; DAM NOV, POP**
See also CA 1-4R; 131; CANR 1, 23, 64; DA3; DLB 2; DLBY 80, 90; MTCW 1, 2

Percy, William Alexander 1885-1942
.... **TCLC 84**
See also CA 163; MTCW 2

Perec, Georges 1936-1982 .... **CLC 56, 116**
See also CA 141; DLB 83

Pereda (y Sanchez de Porrua), Jose Maria de 1833-1906 .... **TCLC 16**
See also CA 117

Pereda y Porrua, Jose Maria de
See Pereda (y Sanchez de Porrua), Jose Maria de

Peregoy, George Weems
See Mencken, H(enry) L(ouis)

Perelman, S(idney) J(oseph) 1904-1979
.... **CLC 3, 5, 9, 15, 23, 44, 49; DAM DRAM; SSC 32**
See also AITN 1, 2; CA 73-76; 89-92; CANR 18; DLB 11, 44; MTCW 1, 2

Peret, Benjamin 1899-1959 .... **TCLC 20**
See also CA 117

Peretz, Isaac Loeb 1851(?)-1915 ... **TCLC 16; SSC 26**
See also CA 109

Peretz, Yitzkhok Leibush
See Peretz, Isaac Loeb

Perez Galdos, Benito 1843-1920 ... **TCLC 27; HLCS 2**
See also CA 125; 153; HW 1

Peri Rossi, Cristina 1941-
See also CA 131; CANR 59, 81; DLB 145; HLCS 2; HW 1, 2

Perrault, Charles 1628-1703 ..... **LC 3, 52, 56**
See also MAICYA; SATA 25

Perry, Anne 1938- .... **CLC 126**
See also CA 101; CANR 22, 50, 84

Perry, Brighton
See Sherwood, Robert E(mmet)

Perse, St.-John
See Leger, (Marie-Rene Auguste) Alexis Saint-Leger

Perutz, Leo(pold) 1882-1957 .... **TCLC 60**
See also CA 147; DLB 81

Peseenz, Tulio F.
See Lopez y Fuentes, Gregorio

Pesetsky, Bette 1932- .... **CLC 28**
See also CA 133; DLB 130

Peshkov, Alexei Maximovich 1868-1936
See Gorky, Maxim
See also CA 105; 141; CANR 83; DA; DAC; DAM DRAM, MST, NOV; MTCW 2

Pessoa, Fernando (Antonio Nogueira)
1888-1935 .... **TCLC 27; DAM MULT; HLC 2; PC 20**
See also CA 125; 183

Peterkin, Julia Mood 1880-1961 ...... **CLC 31**
See also CA 102; DLB 9

Peters, Joan K(aren) 1945- .... **CLC 39**
See also CA 158

Peters, Robert L(ouis) 1924- .... **CLC 7**
See also CA 13-16R; CAAS 8; DLB 105

Petofi, Sandor 1823-1849 .... **NCLC 21**

Petrakis, Harry Mark 1923- .... **CLC 3**
See also CA 9-12R; CANR 4, 30, 85

Petrarch 1304-1374 .... **CMLC 20; DAM POET; PC 8**
See also DA3

Petronius c. 20-66 .... **CMLC 34**
See also DLB 211

Petrov, Evgeny .... **TCLC 21**
See also Kataev, Evgeny Petrovich

Petry, Ann (Lane) 1908-1997 ... **CLC 1, 7, 18**
See also BW 1, 3; CA 5-8R; 157; CAAS 6; CANR 4, 46; CLR 12; DLB 76; JRDA; MAICYA; MTCW 1; SATA 5; SATA-Obit 94

Petursson, Halligrimur 1614-1674 .... **LC 8**

Peychinovich
See Vazov, Ivan (Minchov)

Phaedrus c. 18B.C.-c. 50 .... **CMLC 25**
See also DLB 211

Philips, Katherine 1632-1664 .... **LC 30**
See also DLB 131

Philipson, Morris H. 1926- .... **CLC 53**
See also CA 1-4R; CANR 4

Phillips, Caryl 1958- . **CLC 96; BLCS; DAM MULT**
See also BW 2; CA 141; CANR 63; DA3; DLB 157; MTCW 2

Phillips, David Graham 1867-1911 . **TCLC 44**
See also CA 108; 176; DLB 9, 12

Phillips, Jack
See Sandburg, Carl (August)

Phillips, Jayne Anne 1952- . **CLC 15, 33; SSC 16**
See also CA 101; CANR 24, 50; DLBY 80; INT CANR-24; MTCW 1, 2

Phillips, Richard
See Dick, Philip K(indred)

Phillips, Robert (Schaeffer) 1938- .... **CLC 28**

Powell, Adam Clayton, Jr. 1908-1972
.... **CLC 89; BLC 3; DAM MULT**
See also BW 1, 3; CA 102; 33-36R; CANR 86

Powell, Anthony (Dymoke) 1905- . **CLC 1, 3, 7, 9, 10, 31**
See also CA 1-4R; CANR 1, 32, 62; CD-BLB 1945-1960; DLB 15; MTCW 1, 2

Powell, Dawn 1897-1965 .... **CLC 66**
See also CA 5-8R; DLBY 97

Powell, Padgett 1952- .... **CLC 34**
See also CA 126; CANR 63

Power, Susan 1961- .... **CLC 91**

Powers, J(ames) F(arl) 1917-1999 . **CLC 1, 4, 8, 57; SSC 4**
See also CA 1-4R; 181; CANR 2, 61; DLB 130; MTCW 1

Powers, John J(ames) 1945-
See Powers, John R.
See also CA 69-72

Powers, John R. .... **CLC 66**
See also Powers, John J(ames)

Powers, Richard (S.) 1957- .... **CLC 93**
See also CA 148; CANR 80

Pownall, David 1938- .... **CLC 10**
See also CA 89-92; 180; CAAS 18; CANR 49; DLB 14

Powys, John Cowper 1872-1963 ... **CLC 7, 9, 15, 46, 125**
See also CA 85-88; DLB 15; MTCW 1, 2

Powys, T(heodore) F(rancis) 1875-1953 **TCLC 9**
See also CA 106; DLB 36, 162

Prado (Calvo), Pedro 1886-1952 ... **TCLC 75**
See also CA 131; HW 1

Prager, Emily 1952- .... **CLC 56**

Pratt, E(dwin) J(ohn) 1883(?)-1964 . **CLC 19; DAC; DAM POET**
See also CA 141; 93-96; CANR 77; DLB 92

Premchand .... **TCLC 21**
See also Srivastava, Dhanpat Rai

Preussler, Otfried 1923- .... **CLC 17**
See also CA 77-80; SATA 24

Prevert, Jacques (Henri Marie) 1900-1977 **CLC 15**
See also CA 77-80; 69-72; CANR 29, 61; MTCW 1; SATA-Obit 30

Prevost, Abbe (Antoine Francois) 1697-1763 **LC 1**

Price, (Edward) Reynolds 1933- ... **CLC 3, 6, 13, 43, 50, 63; DAM NOV; SSC 22**
See also CA 1-4R; CANR 1, 37, 57, 87; DLB 2; INT CANR-37

Price, Richard 1949- .... **CLC 6, 12**
See also CA 49-52; CANR 3; DLBY 81

Prichard, Katharine Susannah 1883-1969 **CLC 46**
See also CA 11-12; CANR 33; CAP 1; MTCW 1; SATA 66

Priestley, J(ohn) B(oynton) 1894-1984
... **CLC 2, 5, 9, 34; DAM DRAM, NOV**
See also CA 9-12R; 113; CANR 33; CD-BLB 1914-1945; DA3; DLB 10, 34, 77, 100, 139; DLBY 84; MTCW 1, 2

Prince 1958(?)- .... **CLC 35**

Prince, F(rank) T(empleton) 1912- .. **CLC 22**
See also CA 101; CANR 43, 79; DLB 20

Prince Kropotkin
See Kropotkin, Peter (Aleksieevich)

Prior, Matthew 1664-1721 .... **LC 4**
See also DLB 95

Prishvin, Mikhail 1873-1954 .... **TCLC 75**

Pritchard, William H(arrison) 1932-
.... **CLC 34**
See also CA 65-68; CANR 23; DLB 111

Pritchett, V(ictor) S(awdon) 1900-1997
.... **CLC 5, 13, 15, 41; DAM NOV; SSC 14**
See also CA 61-64; 157; CANR 31, 63; DA3; DLB 15, 139; MTCW 1, 2

Private 19022
See Manning, Frederic

Probst, Mark 1925- .... **CLC 59**
See also CA 130

Prokosch, Frederic 1908-1989 ...... **CLC 4, 48**
See also CA 73-76; 128; CANR 82; DLB 48; MTCW 2

Propertius, Sextus c. 50B.C.-c. 16B.C.
.... **CMLC 32**
See also DLB 211

Prophet, The
See Dreiser, Theodore (Herman Albert)

Prose, Francine 1947- .... **CLC 45**
See also CA 109; 112; CANR 46; SATA 101

Proudhon
See Cunha, Euclides (Rodrigues Pimenta) da

Proulx, Annie
See Proulx, E(dna) Annie

Proulx, E(dna) Annie 1935- .. **CLC 81; DAM POP**
See also CA 145; CANR 65; DA3; MTCW 2

Proust, (Valentin-Louis-George-Eugene-) Marcel 1871-1922 .... **TCLC 7, 13, 33; DA; DAB; DAC; DAM MST, NOV; WLC**
See also CA 104; 120; DA3; DLB 65; MTCW 1, 2

Prowler, Harley
See Masters, Edgar Lee

Prus, Boleslaw 1845-1912 .... **TCLC 48**

Pryor, Richard (Franklin Lenox Thomas) 1940- .... **CLC 26**
See also CA 122; 152

Przybyszewski, Stanislaw 1868-1927
.... **TCLC 36**
See also CA 160; DLB 66

Pteleon
See Grieve, C(hristopher) M(urray)
See also DAM POET

Puckett, Lute
See Masters, Edgar Lee

Puig, Manuel 1932-1990 .... **CLC 3, 5, 10, 28, 65; DAM MULT; HLC 2**
See also CA 45-48; CANR 2, 32, 63; DA3; DLB 113; HW 1, 2; MTCW 1, 2

Pulitzer, Joseph 1847-1911 .... **TCLC 76**
See also CA 114; DLB 23

Purdy, A(lfred) W(ellington) 1918- ... **CLC 3, 6, 14, 50; DAC; DAM MST, POET**
See also CA 81-84; CAAS 17; CANR 42, 66; DLB 88

Purdy, James (Amos) 1923- .... **CLC 2, 4, 10, 28, 52**
See also CA 33-36R; CAAS 1; CANR 19, 51; DLB 2; INT CANR-19; MTCW 1

Pure, Simon
See Swinnerton, Frank Arthur

Pushkin, Alexander (Sergeyevich) 1799-1837
NCLC 3, 27, 83; DA; DAB; DAC; DAM DRAM, MST, POET; PC 10; SSC 27; WLC
See also DA3; DLB 205; SATA 61

P'u Sung-ling 1640-1715 .... **LC 49; SSC 31**

Putnam, Arthur Lee
See Alger, Horatio Jr., Jr.

Puzo, Mario 1920-1999 . **CLC 1, 2, 6, 36, 107; DAM NOV, POP**
See also CA 65-68; CANR 4, 42, 65; DA3; DLB 6; MTCW 1, 2

Pygge, Edward
See Barnes, Julian (Patrick)

Pyle, Ernest Taylor 1900-1945
See Pyle, Ernie
See also CA 115; 160

Pyle, Ernie 1900-1945 .... **TCLC 75**
See also Pyle, Ernest Taylor DLB 29; MTCW 2

Pyle, Howard 1853-1911 .... **TCLC 81**
See also CA 109; 137; CLR 22; DLB 42, 188; DLBD 13; MAICYA; SATA 16, 100

Pym, Barbara (Mary Crampton) 1913-1980
CLC 13, 19, 37, 111
See also CA 13-14; 97-100; CANR 13, 34; CAP 1; DLB 14, 207; DLBY 87; MTCW 1, 2

Pynchon, Thomas (Ruggles, Jr.) 1937-
. **CLC 2, 3, 6, 9, 11, 18, 33, 62, 72; DA; DAB; DAC; DAM MST, NOV, POP; SSC 14; WLC**
See also BEST 90:2; CA 17-20R; CANR 22, 46, 73; DA3; DLB 2, 173; MTCW 1, 2

Pythagoras c. 570B.C.-c. 500B.C. . **CMLC 22**
See also DLB 176

Q
See Quiller-Couch, SirArthur (Thomas)

Qian Zhongshu
See Ch'ien Chung-shu

Qroll
See Dagerman, Stig (Halvard)

Quarrington, Paul (Lewis) 1953- ..... **CLC 65**
See also CA 129; CANR 62

Quasimodo, Salvatore 1901-1968 ..... **CLC 10**
See also CA 13-16; 25-28R; CAP 1; DLB 114; MTCW 1

Quay, Stephen 1947- .... **CLC 95**

Quay, Timothy 1947- .... **CLC 95**

Queen, Ellery .... **CLC 3, 11**
See also Dannay, Frederic; Davidson, Avram (James); Lee, Manfred B(ennington); Marlowe, Stephen; Sturgeon, Theodore (Hamilton); Vance, John Holbrook

Queen, Ellery, Jr.
See Dannay, Frederic; Lee, Manfred B(ennington)

Queneau, Raymond 1903-1976 ..... **CLC 2, 5, 10, 42**
See also CA 77-80; 69-72; CANR 32; DLB 72; MTCW 1, 2

Quevedo, Francisco de 1580-1645 .... **LC 23**

Quiller-Couch, SirArthur (Thomas)
1863-1944 .... **TCLC 53**
See also CA 118; 166; DLB 135, 153, 190

Quin, Ann (Marie) 1936-1973 .... **CLC 6**
See also CA 9-12R; 45-48; DLB 14

Quinn, Martin
See Smith, Martin Cruz

Quinn, Peter 1947- .... **CLC 91**

Quinn, Simon
See Smith, Martin Cruz

Quintana, Leroy V. 1944-
See also CA 131; CANR 65; DAM MULT; DLB 82; HLC 2; HW 1

Quiroga, Horacio (Sylvestre) 1878-1937
TCLC 20; DAM MULT; HLC 2
See also CA 117; 131; HW 1; MTCW 1

Quoirez, Francoise 1935- .... **CLC 9**
See also Sagan, Francoise CA 49-52; CANR 6, 39, 73; MTCW 1, 2

Raabe, Wilhelm (Karl) 1831-1910 . **TCLC 45**
See also CA 167; DLB 129

Rabe, David (William) 1940- .. **CLC 4, 8, 33; DAM DRAM**
See also CA 85-88; CABS 3; CANR 59; DLB 7

Rabelais, Francois 1483-1553 ...... **LC 5; DA; DAB; DAC; DAM MST; WLC**

See also CA 122; 136; 167
Rhine, Richard
See Silverstein, Alvin
Rhodes, Eugene Manlove 1869-1934
.... **TCLC 53**
Rhodius, Apollonius c. 3rd cent. B.C.-
.... **CMLC 28**
See also DLB 176
R'hoone
See Balzac, Honore de
Rhys, Jean 1890(?)-1979 ...... **CLC 2, 4, 6, 14, 19, 51, 124; DAM NOV; SSC 21**
See also CA 25-28R; 85-88; CANR 35, 62; CDBLB 1945-1960; DA3; DLB 36, 117, 162; MTCW 1, 2
Ribeiro, Darcy 1922-1997 .... **CLC 34**
See also CA 33-36R; 156
Ribeiro, Joao Ubaldo (Osorio Pimentel) 1941- .... **CLC 10, 67**
See also CA 81-84
Ribman, Ronald (Burt) 1932- .... **CLC 7**
See also CA 21-24R; CANR 46, 80
Ricci, Nino 1959- .... **CLC 70**
See also CA 137
Rice, Anne 1941- .. **CLC 41, 128; DAM POP**
See also AAYA 9; BEST 89:2; CA 65-68; CANR 12, 36, 53, 74; DA3; MTCW 2
Rice, Elmer (Leopold) 1892-1967 ...... **CLC 7, 49; DAM DRAM**
See also CA 21-22; 25-28R; CAP 2; DLB 4, 7; MTCW 1, 2
Rice, Tim(othy Miles Bindon) 1944- . **CLC 21**
See also CA 103; CANR 46
Rich, Adrienne (Cecile) 1929- ... **CLC 3, 6, 7, 11, 18, 36, 73, 76, 125; DAM POET; PC 5**
See also CA 9-12R; CANR 20, 53, 74; CDALBS; DA3; DLB 5, 67; MTCW 1, 2
Rich, Barbara
See Graves, Robert (von Ranke)
Rich, Robert
See Trumbo, Dalton
Richard, Keith .... **CLC 17**
See also Richards, Keith
Richards, David Adams 1950- .... **CLC 59; DAC**
See also CA 93-96; CANR 60; DLB 53
Richards, I(vor) A(rmstrong) 1893-1979
.... **CLC 14, 24**
See also CA 41-44R; 89-92; CANR 34, 74; DLB 27; MTCW 2
Richards, Keith 1943-
See Richard, Keith
See also CA 107; CANR 77
Richardson, Anne
See Roiphe, Anne (Richardson)
Richardson, Dorothy Miller 1873-1957
.... **TCLC 3**
See also CA 104; DLB 36
Richardson, Ethel Florence (Lindesay) 1870-1946
See Richardson, Henry Handel
See also CA 105
Richardson, Henry Handel .... **TCLC 4**
See also Richardson, Ethel Florence (Lindesay) DLB 197
Richardson, John 1796-1852 .... **NCLC 55; DAC**
See also DLB 99
Richardson, Samuel 1689-1761 ...... **LC 1, 44; DA; DAB; DAC; DAM MST, NOV; WLC**
See also CDBLB 1660-1789; DLB 39
Richler, Mordecai 1931- . **CLC 3, 5, 9, 13, 18, 46, 70; DAC; DAM MST, NOV**
See also AITN 1; CA 65-68; CANR 31, 62; CLR 17; DLB 53; MAICYA; MTCW 1, 2; SATA 44, 98; SATA-Brief 27

Richter, Conrad (Michael) 1890-1968
.... **CLC 30**
See also AAYA 21; CA 5-8R; 25-28R; CANR 23; DLB 9, 212; MTCW 1, 2; SATA 3
Ricostranza, Tom
See Ellis, Trey
Riddell, Charlotte 1832-1906 .... **TCLC 40**
See also CA 165; DLB 156
Ridge, John Rollin 1827-1867 ...... **NCLC 82; DAM MULT**
See also CA 144; DLB 175; NNAL
Ridgway, Keith 1965- .... **CLC 119**
See also CA 172
Riding, Laura .... **CLC 3, 7**
See also Jackson, Laura (Riding)
Riefenstahl, Berta Helene Amalia 1902-
See Riefenstahl, Leni
See also CA 108
Riefenstahl, Leni .... **CLC 16**
See also Riefenstahl, Berta Helene Amalia
Riffe, Ernest
See Bergman, (Ernst) Ingmar
Riggs, (Rolla) Lynn 1899-1954 ..... **TCLC 56; DAM MULT**
See also CA 144; DLB 175; NNAL
Riis, Jacob A(ugust) 1849-1914 ..... **TCLC 80**
See also CA 113; 168; DLB 23
Riley, James Whitcomb 1849-1916
.... **TCLC 51; DAM POET**
See also CA 118; 137; MAICYA; SATA 17
Riley, Tex
See Creasey, John
Rilke, Rainer Maria 1875-1926 .. **TCLC 1, 6, 19; DAM POET; PC 2**
See also CA 104; 132; CANR 62; DA3; DLB 81; MTCW 1, 2
Rimbaud, (Jean Nicolas) Arthur 1854-1891
NCLC 4, 35, 82; DA; DAB; DAC; DAM MST, POET; PC 3; WLC
See also DA3
Rinehart, Mary Roberts 1876-1958
.... **TCLC 52**
See also CA 108; 166
Ringmaster, The
See Mencken, H(enry) L(ouis)
Ringwood, Gwen(dolyn Margaret) Pharis 1910-1984 .... **CLC 48**
See also CA 148; 112; DLB 88
Rio, Michel 19(?)- .... **CLC 43**
Ritsos, Giannes
See Ritsos, Yannis
Ritsos, Yannis 1909-1990 .... **CLC 6, 13, 31**
See also CA 77-80; 133; CANR 39, 61; MTCW 1
Ritter, Erika 1948(?)- .... **CLC 52**
Rivera, Jose Eustasio 1889-1928 ... **TCLC 35**
See also CA 162; HW 1, 2
Rivera, Tomas 1935-1984
See also CA 49-52; CANR 32; DLB 82; HLCS 2; HW 1
Rivers, Conrad Kent 1933-1968 .... **CLC 1**
See also BW 1; CA 85-88; DLB 41
Rivers, Elfrida
See Bradley, Marion Zimmer
Riverside, John
See Heinlein, Robert A(nson)
Rizal, Jose 1861-1896 .... **NCLC 27**
Roa Bastos, Augusto (Antonio) 1917-
.... **CLC 45; DAM MULT; HLC 2**
See also CA 131; DLB 113; HW 1
Robbe-Grillet, Alain 1922- .... **CLC 1, 2, 4, 6, 8, 10, 14, 43, 128**
See also CA 9-12R; CANR 33, 65; DLB 83; MTCW 1, 2
Robbins, Harold 1916-1997 .... **CLC 5; DAM NOV**

See also CA 73-76; 162; CANR 26, 54; DA3; MTCW 1, 2
Robbins, Thomas Eugene 1936-
See Robbins, Tom
See also CA 81-84; CANR 29, 59; DAM NOV, POP; DA3; MTCW 1, 2
Robbins, Tom .... **CLC 9, 32, 64**
See also Robbins, Thomas Eugene AAYA 32; BEST 90:3; DLBY 80; MTCW 2
Robbins, Trina 1938- .... **CLC 21**
See also CA 128
Roberts, Charles G(eorge) D(ouglas) 1860-1943 .... **TCLC 8**
See also CA 105; CLR 33; DLB 92; SATA 88; SATA-Brief 29
Roberts, Elizabeth Madox 1886-1941
.... **TCLC 68**
See also CA 111; 166; DLB 9, 54, 102; SATA 33; SATA-Brief 27
Roberts, Kate 1891-1985 .... **CLC 15**
See also CA 107; 116
Roberts, Keith (John Kingston) 1935-
.... **CLC 14**
See also CA 25-28R; CANR 46
Roberts, Kenneth (Lewis) 1885-1957
.... **TCLC 23**
See also CA 109; DLB 9
Roberts, Michele (B.) 1949- .... **CLC 48**
See also CA 115; CANR 58
Robertson, Ellis
See Ellison, Harlan (Jay); Silverberg, Robert
Robertson, Thomas William 1829-1871
NCLC 35; DAM DRAM
Robeson, Kenneth
See Dent, Lester
Robinson, Edwin Arlington 1869-1935
.... **TCLC 5; DA; DAC; DAM MST, POET; PC 1**
See also CA 104; 133; CDALB 1865-1917; DLB 54; MTCW 1, 2
Robinson, Henry Crabb 1775-1867
.... **NCLC 15**
See also DLB 107
Robinson, Jill 1936- .... **CLC 10**
See also CA 102; INT 102
Robinson, Kim Stanley 1952- .... **CLC 34**
See also AAYA 26; CA 126; SATA 109
Robinson, Lloyd
See Silverberg, Robert
Robinson, Marilynne 1944- .... **CLC 25**
See also CA 116; CANR 80; DLB 206
Robinson, Smokey .... **CLC 21**
See also Robinson, William, Jr.
Robinson, William, Jr. 1940-
See Robinson, Smokey
See also CA 116
Robison, Mary 1949- .... **CLC 42, 98**
See also CA 113; 116; CANR 87; DLB 130; INT 116
Rod, Edouard 1857-1910 .... **TCLC 52**
Roddenberry, Eugene Wesley 1921-1991
See Roddenberry, Gene
See also CA 110; 135; CANR 37; SATA 45; SATA-Obit 69
Roddenberry, Gene .... **CLC 17**
See also Roddenberry, Eugene Wesley AAYA 5; SATA-Obit 69
Rodgers, Mary 1931- .... **CLC 12**
See also CA 49-52; CANR 8, 55; CLR 20; INT CANR-8; JRDA; MAICYA; SATA 8
Rodgers, W(illiam) R(obert) 1909-1969
.... **CLC 7**
See also CA 85-88; DLB 20
Rodman, Eric
See Silverberg, Robert
Rodman, Howard 1920(?)-1985 .... **CLC 65**
See also CA 118

Author Index

Seghers, Anna .... **CLC 7**
See also Radvanyi, Netty DLB 69
Seidel, Frederick (Lewis) 1936- .... **CLC 18**
See also CA 13-16R; CANR 8; DLBY 84
Seifert, Jaroslav 1901-1986 .. **CLC 34, 44, 93**
See also CA 127; MTCW 1, 2
Sei Shonagon c. 966-1017(?) .... **CMLC 6**
Séjour, Victor 1817-1874 .... **DC 10**
See also DLB 50
Sejour Marcou et Ferrand, Juan Victor
See S
Selby, Hubert, Jr. 1928- . **CLC 1, 2, 4, 8; SSC 20**
See also CA 13-16R; CANR 33, 85; DLB 2
Selzer, Richard 1928- .... **CLC 74**
See also CA 65-68; CANR 14
Sembene, Ousmane
See Ousmane, Sembene
Senancour, Etienne Pivert de 1770-1846 **NCLC 16**
See also DLB 119
Sender, Ramon (Jose) 1902-1982 ...... **CLC 8; DAM MULT; HLC 2**
See also CA 5-8R; 105; CANR 8; HW 1; MTCW 1
Seneca, Lucius Annaeus c. 1-c. 65 . **CMLC 6; DAM DRAM; DC 5**
See also DLB 211
Senghor, Leopold Sedar 1906- .... **CLC 54; BLC 3; DAM MULT, POET; PC 25**
See also BW 2; CA 116; 125; CANR 47, 74; MTCW 1, 2
Senna, Danzy 1970- .... **CLC 119**
See also CA 169
Serling, (Edward) Rod(man) 1924-1975 .... **CLC 30**
See also AAYA 14; AITN 1; CA 162; 57-60; DLB 26
Serna, Ramon Gomez de la
See Gomez de la Serna, Ramon
Serpieres
See Guillevic, (Eugene)
Service, Robert
See Service, Robert W(illiam)
See also DAB; DLB 92
Service, Robert W(illiam) 1874(?)-1958 **TCLC 15; DA; DAC; DAM MST, POET; WLC**
See also Service, Robert CA 115; 140; CANR 84; SATA 20
Seth, Vikram 1952- .... **CLC 43, 90; DAM MULT**
See also CA 121; 127; CANR 50, 74; DA3; DLB 120; INT 127; MTCW 2
Seton, Cynthia Propper 1926-1982 .. **CLC 27**
See also CA 5-8R; 108; CANR 7
Seton, Ernest (Evan) Thompson 1860-1946 **TCLC 31**
See also CA 109; CLR 59; DLB 92; DLBD 13; JRDA; SATA 18
Seton-Thompson, Ernest
See Seton, Ernest (Evan) Thompson
Settle, Mary Lee 1918- .... **CLC 19, 61**
See also CA 89-92; CAAS 1; CANR 44, 87; DLB 6; INT 89-92
Seuphor, Michel
See Arp, Jean
Sevigne, Marie (de Rabutin-Chantal) Marquise de 1626-1696 .... **LC 11**
Sewall, Samuel 1652-1730 .... **LC 38**
See also DLB 24
Sexton, Anne (Harvey) 1928-1974 . **CLC 2, 4, 6, 8, 10, 15, 53; DA; DAB; DAC; DAM MST, POET; PC 2; WLC**
See also CA 1-4R; 53-56; CABS 2; CANR 3, 36; CDALB 1941-1968; DA3; DLB 5, 169; MTCW 1, 2; SATA 10
Shaara, Jeff 1952- .... **CLC 119**
See also CA 163

Shaara, Michael (Joseph, Jr.) 1929-1988 .... **CLC 15; DAM POP**
See also AITN 1; CA 102; 125; CANR 52, 85; DLBY 83
Shackleton, C. C.
See Aldiss, Brian W(ilson)
Shacochis, Bob .... **CLC 39**
See also Shacochis, Robert G.
Shacochis, Robert G. 1951-
See Shacochis, Bob
See also CA 119; 124; INT 124
Shaffer, Anthony (Joshua) 1926- ..... **CLC 19; DAM DRAM**
See also CA 110; 116; DLB 13
Shaffer, Peter (Levin) 1926- .. **CLC 5, 14, 18, 37, 60; DAB; DAM DRAM, MST; DC 7**
See also CA 25-28R; CANR 25, 47, 74; CDBLB 1960 to Present; DA3; DLB 13; MTCW 1, 2
Shakey, Bernard
See Young, Neil
Shalamov, Varlam (Tikhonovich) 1907(?)-1982 .... **CLC 18**
See also CA 129; 105
Shamlu, Ahmad 1925- .... **CLC 10**
Shammas, Anton 1951- .... **CLC 55**
Shange, Ntozake 1948- .... **CLC 8, 25, 38, 74, 126; BLC 3; DAM DRAM, MULT; DC 3**
See also AAYA 9; BW 2; CA 85-88; CABS 3; CANR 27, 48, 74; DA3; DLB 38; MTCW 1, 2
Shanley, John Patrick 1950- .... **CLC 75**
See also CA 128; 133; CANR 83
Shapcott, Thomas W(illiam) 1935- .. **CLC 38**
See also CA 69-72; CANR 49, 83
Shapiro, Jane .... **CLC 76**
Shapiro, Karl (Jay) 1913- . **CLC 4, 8, 15, 53; PC 25**
See also CA 1-4R; CAAS 6; CANR 1, 36, 66; DLB 48; MTCW 1, 2
Sharp, William 1855-1905 .... **TCLC 39**
See also CA 160; DLB 156
Sharpe, Thomas Ridley 1928-
See Sharpe, Tom
See also CA 114; 122; CANR 85; INT 122
Sharpe, Tom .... **CLC 36**
See also Sharpe, Thomas Ridley DLB 14
Shaw, Bernard .... **TCLC 45**
See also Shaw, George Bernard BW 1; MTCW 2
Shaw, G. Bernard
See Shaw, George Bernard
Shaw, George Bernard 1856-1950 .. **TCLC 3, 9, 21; DA; DAB; DAC; DAM DRAM, MST; WLC**
See also Shaw, Bernard CA 104; 128; CD-BLB 1914-1945; DA3; DLB 10, 57, 190; MTCW 1, 2
Shaw, Henry Wheeler 1818-1885 .. **NCLC 15**
See also DLB 11
Shaw, Irwin 1913-1984 . **CLC 7, 23, 34; DAM DRAM, POP**
See also AITN 1; CA 13-16R; 112; CANR 21; CDALB 1941-1968; DLB 6, 102; DLBY 84; MTCW 1, 21
Shaw, Robert 1927-1978 .... **CLC 5**
See also AITN 1; CA 1-4R; 81-84; CANR 4; DLB 13, 14
Shaw, T. E.
See Lawrence, T(homas) E(dward)
Shawn, Wallace 1943- .... **CLC 41**
See also CA 112
Shea, Lisa 1953- .... **CLC 86**
See also CA 147
Sheed, Wilfrid (John Joseph) 1930- . **CLC 2, 4, 10, 53**
See also CA 65-68; CANR 30, 66; DLB 6; MTCW 1, 2

Sheldon, Alice Hastings Bradley 1915(?)-1987
See Tiptree, James, Jr.
See also CA 108; 122; CANR 34; INT 108; MTCW 1
Sheldon, John
See Bloch, Robert (Albert)
Shelley, Mary Wollstonecraft (Godwin) 1797-1851 ..... **NCLC 14, 59; DA; DAB; DAC; DAM MST, NOV; WLC**
See also AAYA 20; CDBLB 1789-1832; DA3; DLB 110, 116, 159, 178; SATA 29
Shelley, Percy Bysshe 1792-1822 .. **NCLC 18; DA; DAB; DAC; DAM MST, POET; PC 14; WLC**
See also CDBLB 1789-1832; DA3; DLB 96, 110, 158
Shepard, Jim 1956- .... **CLC 36**
See also CA 137; CANR 59; SATA 90
Shepard, Lucius 1947- .... **CLC 34**
See also CA 128; 141; CANR 81
Shepard, Sam 1943- .... **CLC 4, 6, 17, 34, 41, 44; DAM DRAM; DC 5**
See also AAYA 1; CA 69-72; CABS 3; CANR 22; DA3; DLB 7, 212; MTCW 1, 2
Shepherd, Michael
See Ludlum, Robert
Sherburne, Zoa (Lillian Morin) 1912-1995 **CLC 30**
See also AAYA 13; CA 1-4R; 176; CANR 3, 37; MAICYA; SAAS 18; SATA 3
Sheridan, Frances 1724-1766 .... **LC 7**
See also DLB 39, 84
Sheridan, Richard Brinsley 1751-1816 .... **NCLC 5; DA; DAB; DAC; DAM DRAM, MST; DC 1; WLC**
See also CDBLB 1660-1789; DLB 89
Sherman, Jonathan Marc .... **CLC 55**
Sherman, Martin 1941(?)- .... **CLC 19**
See also CA 116; 123; CANR 86
Sherwin, Judith Johnson 1940-
See Johnson, Judith (Emlyn)
See also CANR 85
Sherwood, Frances 1940- .... **CLC 81**
See also CA 146
Sherwood, Robert E(mmet) 1896-1955 .... **TCLC 3; DAM DRAM**
See also CA 104; 153; CANR 86; DLB 7, 26
Shestov, Lev 1866-1938 .... **TCLC 56**
Shevchenko, Taras 1814-1861 .... **NCLC 54**
Shiel, M(atthew) P(hipps) 1865-1947 .... **TCLC 8**
See also Holmes, Gordon CA 106; 160; DLB 153; MTCW 2
Shields, Carol 1935- .... **CLC 91, 113; DAC**
See also CA 81-84; CANR 51, 74; DA3; MTCW 2
Shields, David 1956- .... **CLC 97**
See also CA 124; CANR 48
Shiga, Naoya 1883-1971 ..... **CLC 33; SSC 23**
See also CA 101; 33-36R; DLB 180
Shikibu, Murasaki c. 978-c. 1014 ... **CMLC 1**
Shilts, Randy 1951-1994 .... **CLC 85**
See also AAYA 19; CA 115; 127; 144; CANR 45; DA3; INT 127; MTCW 2
Shimazaki, Haruki 1872-1943
See Shimazaki Toson
See also CA 105; 134; CANR 84
Shimazaki Toson 1872-1943 .... **TCLC 5**
See also Shimazaki, Haruki DLB 180
Sholokhov, Mikhail (Aleksandrovich) 1905-1984 .... **CLC 7, 15**
See also CA 101; 112; MTCW 1, 2; SATA-Obit 36
Shone, Patric
See Hanley, James
Shreve, Susan Richards 1939- .... **CLC 23**

See also CA 81-84; CANR 36; DLB 13, 14, 207; MTCW 1

Storm, Hyemeyohsts 1935- ..... **CLC 3; DAM MULT**
See also CA 81-84; CANR 45; NNAL

Storm, Theodor 1817-1888 .... **SSC 27**

Storm, (Hans) Theodor (Woldsen) 1817-1888
NCLC 1; SSC 27
See also DLB 129

Storni, Alfonsina 1892-1938 . **TCLC 5; DAM MULT; HLC 2**
See also CA 104; 131; HW 1

Stoughton, William 1631-1701 .... **LC 38**
See also DLB 24

Stout, Rex (Todhunter) 1886-1975 ..... **CLC 3**
See also AITN 2; CA 61-64; CANR 71

Stow, (Julian) Randolph 1935- ... **CLC 23, 48**
See also CA 13-16R; CANR 33; MTCW 1

Stowe, Harriet (Elizabeth) Beecher
1811-1896 .... **NCLC 3, 50; DA; DAB; DAC; DAM MST, NOV; WLC**
See also CDALB 1865-1917; DA3; DLB 1, 12, 42, 74, 189; JRDA; MAICYA; YABC 1

Strabo c. 64B.C.-c. 25 .... **CMLC 37**
See also DLB 176

Strachey, (Giles) Lytton 1880-1932 . **TCLC 12**
See also CA 110; 178; DLB 149; DLBD 10; MTCW 2

Strand, Mark 1934- .... **CLC 6, 18, 41, 71; DAM POET**
See also CA 21-24R; CANR 40, 65; DLB 5; SATA 41

Straub, Peter (Francis) 1943- . **CLC 28, 107; DAM POP**
See also BEST 89:1; CA 85-88; CANR 28, 65; DLBY 84; MTCW 1, 2

Strauss, Botho 1944- .... **CLC 22**
See also CA 157; DLB 124

Streatfeild, (Mary) Noel 1895(?)-1986
.... **CLC 21**
See also CA 81-84; 120; CANR 31; CLR 17; DLB 160; MAICYA; SATA 20; SATA-Obit 48

Stribling, T(homas) S(igismund) 1881-1965
CLC 23
See also CA 107; DLB 9

Strindberg, (Johan) August 1849-1912
... **TCLC 1, 8, 21, 47; DA; DAB; DAC; DAM DRAM, MST; WLC**
See also CA 104; 135; DA3; MTCW 2

Stringer, Arthur 1874-1950 .... **TCLC 37**
See also CA 161; DLB 92

Stringer, David
See Roberts, Keith (John Kingston)

Stroheim, Erich von 1885-1957 ..... **TCLC 71**

Strugatskii, Arkadii (Natanovich) 1925-1991
CLC 27
See also CA 106; 135

Strugatskii, Boris (Natanovich) 1933-
.... **CLC 27**
See also CA 106

Strummer, Joe 1953(?)- .... **CLC 30**

Strunk, William, Jr. 1869-1946 ...... **TCLC 92**
See also CA 118; 164

Stryk, Lucien 1924- .... **PC 27**
See also CA 13-16R; CANR 10, 28, 55

Stuart, Don A.
See Campbell, John W(ood, Jr.)

Stuart, Ian
See MacLean, Alistair (Stuart)

Stuart, Jesse (Hilton) 1906-1984 ... **CLC 1, 8, 11, 14, 34; SSC 31**
See also CA 5-8R; 112; CANR 31; DLB 9, 48, 102; DLBY 84; SATA 2; SATA-Obit 36

Sturgeon, Theodore (Hamilton) 1918-1985
CLC 22, 39

See also Queen, Ellery CA 81-84; 116; CANR 32; DLB 8; DLBY 85; MTCW 1, 2

Sturges, Preston 1898-1959 .... **TCLC 48**
See also CA 114; 149; DLB 26

Styron, William 1925- .... **CLC 1, 3, 5, 11, 15, 60; DAM NOV, POP; SSC 25**
See also BEST 90:4; CA 5-8R; CANR 6, 33, 74; CDALB 1968-1988; DA3; DLB 2, 143; DLBY 80; INT CANR-6; MTCW 1, 2

Su, Chien 1884-1918
See Su Man-shu
See also CA 123

Suarez Lynch, B.
See Bioy Casares, Adolfo; Borges, Jorge Luis

Suassuna, Ariano Vilar 1927-
See also CA 178; HLCS 1; HW 2

Suckow, Ruth 1892-1960 .... **SSC 18**
See also CA 113; DLB 9, 102

Sudermann, Hermann 1857-1928 .. **TCLC 15**
See also CA 107; DLB 118

Sue, Eugene 1804-1857 .... **NCLC 1**
See also DLB 119

Sueskind, Patrick 1949- .... **CLC 44**
See also Suskind, Patrick

Sukenick, Ronald 1932- .... **CLC 3, 4, 6, 48**
See also CA 25-28R; CAAS 8; CANR 32; DLB 173; DLBY 81

Suknaski, Andrew 1942- .... **CLC 19**
See also CA 101; DLB 53

Sullivan, Vernon
See Vian, Boris

Sully Prudhomme 1839-1907 .... **TCLC 31**

Su Man-shu .... **TCLC 24**
See also Su, Chien

Summerforest, Ivy B.
See Kirkup, James

Summers, Andrew James 1942- .... **CLC 26**

Summers, Andy
See Summers, Andrew James

Summers, Hollis (Spurgeon, Jr.) 1916-
.... **CLC 10**
See also CA 5-8R; CANR 3; DLB 6

Summers, (Alphonsus Joseph-Mary Augustus) Montague 1880-1948
.... **TCLC 16**
See also CA 118; 163

Sumner, Gordon Matthew .... **CLC 26**
See also Sting

Surtees, Robert Smith 1803-1864 .. **NCLC 14**
See also DLB 21

Susann, Jacqueline 1921-1974 .... **CLC 3**
See also AITN 1; CA 65-68; 53-56; MTCW 1, 2

Su Shih 1036-1101 .... **CMLC 15**

Suskind, Patrick
See Sueskind, Patrick
See also CA 145

Sutcliff, Rosemary 1920-1992 .... **CLC 26; DAB; DAC; DAM MST, POP**
See also AAYA 10; CA 5-8R; 139; CANR 37; CLR 1, 37; JRDA; MAICYA; SATA 6, 44, 78; SATA-Obit 73

Sutro, Alfred 1863-1933 .... **TCLC 6**
See also CA 105; DLB 10

Sutton, Henry
See Slavitt, David R(ytman)

Svevo, Italo 1861-1928 . **TCLC 2, 35; SSC 25**
See also Schmitz, Aron Hector

Swados, Elizabeth (A.) 1951- .... **CLC 12**
See also CA 97-100; CANR 49; INT 97-100

Swados, Harvey 1920-1972 .... **CLC 5**
See also CA 5-8R; 37-40R; CANR 6; DLB 2

Swan, Gladys 1934- .... **CLC 69**

See also CA 101; CANR 17, 39

Swanson, Logan
See Matheson, Richard Burton

Swarthout, Glendon (Fred) 1918-1992
.... **CLC 35**
See also CA 1-4R; 139; CANR 1, 47; SATA 26

Sweet, Sarah C.
See Jewett, (Theodora) Sarah Orne

Swenson, May 1919-1989 ...... **CLC 4, 14, 61, 106; DA; DAB; DAC; DAM MST, POET; PC 14**
See also CA 5-8R; 130; CANR 36, 61; DLB 5; MTCW 1, 2; SATA 15

Swift, Augustus
See Lovecraft, H(oward) P(hillips)

Swift, Graham (Colin) 1949- ...... **CLC 41, 88**
See also CA 117; 122; CANR 46, 71; DLB 194; MTCW 2

Swift, Jonathan 1667-1745 ..... **LC 1, 42; DA; DAB; DAC; DAM MST, NOV, POET; PC 9; WLC**
See also CDBLB 1660-1789; CLR 53; DA3; DLB 39, 95, 101; SATA 19

Swinburne, Algernon Charles 1837-1909
TCLC 8, 36; DA; DAB; DAC; DAM MST, POET; PC 24; WLC
See also CA 105; 140; CDBLB 1832-1890; DA3; DLB 35, 57

Swinfen, Ann .... **CLC 34**

Swinnerton, Frank Arthur 1884-1982
.... **CLC 31**
See also CA 108; DLB 34

Swithen, John
See King, Stephen (Edwin)

Sylvia
See Ashton-Warner, Sylvia (Constance)

Symmes, Robert Edward
See Duncan, Robert (Edward)

Symonds, John Addington 1840-1893
.... **NCLC 34**
See also DLB 57, 144

Symons, Arthur 1865-1945 .... **TCLC 11**
See also CA 107; DLB 19, 57, 149

Symons, Julian (Gustave) 1912-1994 . **CLC 2, 14, 32**
See also CA 49-52; 147; CAAS 3; CANR 3, 33, 59; DLB 87, 155; DLBY 92; MTCW 1

Synge, (Edmund) J(ohn) M(illington)
1871-1909 . **TCLC 6, 37; DAM DRAM; DC 2**
See also CA 104; 141; CDBLB 1890-1914; DLB 10, 19

Syruc, J.
See Milosz, Czeslaw

Szirtes, George 1948- .... **CLC 46**
See also CA 109; CANR 27, 61

Szymborska, Wislawa 1923- .... **CLC 99**
See also CA 154; DA3; DLBY 96; MTCW 2

T. O., Nik
See Annensky, Innokenty (Fyodorovich)

Tabori, George 1914- .... **CLC 19**
See also CA 49-52; CANR 4, 69

Tagore, Rabindranath 1861-1941 ... **TCLC 3, 53; DAM DRAM, POET; PC 8**
See also CA 104; 120; DA3; MTCW 1, 2

Taine, Hippolyte Adolphe 1828-1893
.... **NCLC 15**

Talese, Gay 1932- .... **CLC 37**
See also AITN 1; CA 1-4R; CANR 9, 58; DLB 185; INT CANR-9; MTCW 1, 2

Tallent, Elizabeth (Ann) 1954- .... **CLC 45**
See also CA 117; CANR 72; DLB 130

Tally, Ted 1952- .... **CLC 42**
See also CA 120; 124; INT 124

Talvik, Heiti 1904-1947 .... **TCLC 87**

Thomson, James 1700-1748 ... **LC 16, 29, 40; DAM POET**
   See also DLB 95
Thomson, James 1834-1882 .... **NCLC 18; DAM POET**
   See also DLB 35
Thoreau, Henry David 1817-1862 .. **NCLC 7, 21, 61; DA; DAB; DAC; DAM MST; WLC**
   See also CDALB 1640-1865; DA3; DLB 1
Thornton, Hall
   See Silverberg, Robert
Thucydides c. 455B.C.-399B.C. ..... **CMLC 17**
   See also DLB 176
Thumboo, Edwin 1933- .... **PC 29**
Thurber, James (Grover) 1894-1961 . **CLC 5, 11, 25, 125; DA; DAB; DAC; DAM DRAM, MST, NOV; SSC 1**
   See also CA 73-76; CANR 17, 39; CDALB 1929-1941; DA3; DLB 4, 11, 22, 102; MAICYA; MTCW 1, 2; SATA 13
Thurman, Wallace (Henry) 1902-1934
   .... **TCLC 6; BLC 3; DAM MULT**
   See also BW 1, 3; CA 104; 124; CANR 81; DLB 51
Tibullus, Albius c. 54B.C.-c. 19B.C.
   .... **CMLC 36**
   See also DLB 211
Ticheburn, Cheviot
   See Ainsworth, William Harrison
Tieck, (Johann) Ludwig 1773-1853 . **NCLC 5, 46; SSC 31**
   See also DLB 90
Tiger, Derry
   See Ellison, Harlan (Jay)
Tilghman, Christopher 1948(?)- .... **CLC 65**
   See also CA 159
Tillinghast, Richard (Williford) 1940-
   .... **CLC 29**
   See also CA 29-32R; CAAS 23; CANR 26, 51
Timrod, Henry 1828-1867 .... **NCLC 25**
   See also DLB 3
Tindall, Gillian (Elizabeth) 1938- ...... **CLC 7**
   See also CA 21-24R; CANR 11, 65
Tiptree, James, Jr. .... **CLC 48, 50**
   See also Sheldon, Alice Hastings Bradley DLB 8
Titmarsh, Michael Angelo
   See Thackeray, William Makepeace
Tocqueville, Alexis (Charles Henri Maurice Clerel, Comte) de 1805-1859 . **NCLC 7, 63**
Tolkien, J(ohn) R(onald) R(euel) 1892-1973 **CLC 1, 2, 3, 8, 12, 38; DA; DAB; DAC; DAM MST, NOV, POP; WLC**
   See also AAYA 10; AITN 1; CA 17-18; 45-48; CANR 36; CAP 2; CDBLB 1914-1945; CLR 56; DA3; DLB 15, 160; JRDA; MAICYA; MTCW 1, 2; SATA 2, 32, 100; SATA-Obit 24
Toller, Ernst 1893-1939 .... **TCLC 10**
   See also CA 107; DLB 124
Tolson, M. B.
   See Tolson, Melvin B(eaunorus)
Tolson, Melvin B(eaunorus) 1898(?)-1966 **CLC 36, 105; BLC 3; DAM MULT, POET**
   See also BW 1, 3; CA 124; 89-92; CANR 80; DLB 48, 76
Tolstoi, Aleksei Nikolaevich
   See Tolstoy, Alexey Nikolaevich
Tolstoy, Alexey Nikolaevich 1882-1945
   .... **TCLC 18**
   See also CA 107; 158
Tolstoy, Count Leo
   See Tolstoy, Leo (Nikolaevich)
Tolstoy, Leo (Nikolaevich) 1828-1910
   . **TCLC 4, 11, 17, 28, 44, 79; DA; DAB;**

DAC; DAM MST, NOV; SSC 9, 30; WLC
   See also CA 104; 123; DA3; SATA 26
Tomasi di Lampedusa, Giuseppe 1896-1957
   See Lampedusa, Giuseppe (Tomasi) di
   See also CA 111
Tomlin, Lily .... **CLC 17**
   See also Tomlin, Mary Jean
Tomlin, Mary Jean 1939(?)-
   See Tomlin, Lily
   See also CA 117
Tomlinson, (Alfred) Charles 1927- .... **CLC 2, 4, 6, 13, 45; DAM POET; PC 17**
   See also CA 5-8R; CANR 33; DLB 40
Tomlinson, H(enry) M(ajor) 1873-1958
   TCLC 71
   See also CA 118; 161; DLB 36, 100, 195
Tonson, Jacob
   See Bennett, (Enoch) Arnold
Toole, John Kennedy 1937-1969 . **CLC 19, 64**
   See also CA 104; DLBY 81; MTCW 2
Toomer, Jean 1894-1967 .... **CLC 1, 4, 13, 22; BLC 3; DAM MULT; PC 7; SSC 1; WLCS**
   See also BW 1; CA 85-88; CDALB 1917-1929; DA3; DLB 45, 51; MTCW 1, 2
Torley, Luke
   See Blish, James (Benjamin)
Tornimparte, Alessandra
   See Ginzburg, Natalia
Torre, Raoul della
   See Mencken, H(enry) L(ouis)
Torrence, Ridgely 1874-1950 .... **TCLC 97**
   See also DLB 54
Torrey, E(dwin) Fuller 1937- .... **CLC 34**
   See also CA 119; CANR 71
Torsvan, Ben Traven
   See Traven, B.
Torsvan, Benno Traven
   See Traven, B.
Torsvan, Berick Traven
   See Traven, B.
Torsvan, Berwick Traven
   See Traven, B.
Torsvan, Bruno Traven
   See Traven, B.
Torsvan, Traven
   See Traven, B.
Tournier, Michel (Edouard) 1924- .... **CLC 6, 23, 36, 95**
   See also CA 49-52; CANR 3, 36, 74; DLB 83; MTCW 1, 2; SATA 23
Tournimparte, Alessandra
   See Ginzburg, Natalia
Towers, Ivar
   See Kornbluth, C(yril) M.
Towne, Robert (Burton) 1936(?)- ..... **CLC 87**
   See also CA 108; DLB 44
Townsend, Sue .... **CLC 61**
   See also Townsend, Susan Elaine AAYA 28; SATA 55, 93; SATA-Brief 48
Townsend, Susan Elaine 1946-
   See Townsend, Sue
   See also CA 119; 127; CANR 65; DAB; DAC; DAM MST
Townshend, Peter (Dennis Blandford) 1945-
   CLC 17, 42
   See also CA 107
Tozzi, Federigo 1883-1920 .... **TCLC 31**
   See also CA 160
Traill, Catharine Parr 1802-1899 .. **NCLC 31**
   See also DLB 99
Trakl, Georg 1887-1914 .... **TCLC 5; PC 20**
   See also CA 104; 165; MTCW 2
Transtroemer, Tomas (Goesta) 1931-
   .... **CLC 52, 65; DAM POET**
   See also CA 117; 129; CAAS 17

Transtromer, Tomas Gosta
   See Transtroemer, Tomas (Goesta)
Traven, B. (?)-1969 .... **CLC 8, 11**
   See also CA 19-20; 25-28R; CAP 2; DLB 9, 56; MTCW 1
Treitel, Jonathan 1959- .... **CLC 70**
Trelawny, Edward John 1792-1881
   .... **NCLC 85**
   See also DLB 110, 116, 144
Tremain, Rose 1943- .... **CLC 42**
   See also CA 97-100; CANR 44; DLB 14
Tremblay, Michel 1942- . **CLC 29, 102; DAC; DAM MST**
   See also CA 116; 128; DLB 60; MTCW 1, 2
Trevanian .... **CLC 29**
   See also Whitaker, Rod(ney)
Trevor, Glen
   See Hilton, James
Trevor, William 1928- .. **CLC 7, 9, 14, 25, 71, 116; SSC 21**
   See also Cox, William Trevor DLB 14, 139; MTCW 2
Trifonov, Yuri (Valentinovich) 1925-1981
   CLC 45
   See also CA 126; 103; MTCW 1
Trilling, Diana (Rubin) 1905-1996 . **CLC 129**
   See also CA 5-8R; 154; CANR 10, 46; INT CANR-10; MTCW 1
Trilling, Lionel 1905-1975 .... **CLC 9, 11, 24**
   See also CA 9-12R; 61-64; CANR 10; DLB 28, 63; INT CANR-10; MTCW 1, 2
Trimball, W. H.
   See Mencken, H(enry) L(ouis)
Tristan
   See Gomez de la Serna, Ramon
Tristram
   See Housman, A(lfred) E(dward)
Trogdon, William (Lewis) 1939-
   See Heat-Moon, William Least
   See also CA 115; 119; CANR 47; INT 119
Trollope, Anthony 1815-1882 ... **NCLC 6, 33; DA; DAB; DAC; DAM MST, NOV; SSC 28; WLC**
   See also CDBLB 1832-1890; DA3; DLB 21, 57, 159; SATA 22
Trollope, Frances 1779-1863 .... **NCLC 30**
   See also DLB 21, 166
Trotsky, Leon 1879-1940 .... **TCLC 22**
   See also CA 118; 167
Trotter (Cockburn), Catharine 1679-1749
   .... **LC 8**
   See also DLB 84
Trotter, Wilfred 1872-1939 .... **TCLC 99**
Trout, Kilgore
   See Farmer, Philip Jose
Trow, George W. S. 1943- .... **CLC 52**
   See also CA 126
Troyat, Henri 1911- .... **CLC 23**
   See also CA 45-48; CANR 2, 33, 67; MTCW 1
Trudeau, G(arretson) B(eekman) 1948-
   See Trudeau, Garry B.
   See also CA 81-84; CANR 31; SATA 35
Trudeau, Garry B. .... **CLC 12**
   See also Trudeau, G(arretson) B(eekman) AAYA 10; AITN 2
Truffaut, Francois 1932-1984 ... **CLC 20, 101**
   See also CA 81-84; 113; CANR 34
Trumbo, Dalton 1905-1976 .... **CLC 19**
   See also CA 21-24R; 69-72; CANR 10; DLB 26
Trumbull, John 1750-1831 .... **NCLC 30**
   See also DLB 31
Trundlett, Helen B.
   See Eliot, T(homas) S(tearns)
Tryon, Thomas 1926-1991 . **CLC 3, 11; DAM POP**

Weiss, Theodore (Russell) 1916- ... **CLC 3, 8, 14**
See also CA 9-12R; CAAS 2; CANR 46; DLB 5

Welch, (Maurice) Denton 1915-1948
.... **TCLC 22**
See also CA 121; 148

Welch, James 1940- ..... **CLC 6, 14, 52; DAM MULT, POP**
See also CA 85-88; CANR 42, 66; DLB 175; NNAL

Weldon, Fay 1931- . **CLC 6, 9, 11, 19, 36, 59, 122; DAM POP**
See also CA 21-24R; CANR 16, 46, 63; CDBLB 1960 to Present; DLB 14, 194; INT CANR-16; MTCW 1, 2

Wellek, Rene 1903-1995 .... **CLC 28**
See also CA 5-8R; 150; CAAS 7; CANR 8; DLB 63; INT CANR-8

Weller, Michael 1942- .... **CLC 10, 53**
See also CA 85-88

Weller, Paul 1958- .... **CLC 26**

Wellershoff, Dieter 1925- .... **CLC 46**
See also CA 89-92; CANR 16, 37

Welles, (George) Orson 1915-1985 .. **CLC 20, 80**
See also CA 93-96; 117

Wellman, John McDowell 1945-
See Wellman, Mac
See also CA 166

Wellman, Mac 1945- .... **CLC 65**
See also Wellman, John McDowell; Wellman, John McDowell

Wellman, Manly Wade 1903-1986 ... **CLC 49**
See also CA 1-4R; 118; CANR 6, 16, 44; SATA 6; SATA-Obit 47

Wells, Carolyn 1869(?)-1942 .... **TCLC 35**
See also CA 113; DLB 11

Wells, H(erbert) G(eorge) 1866-1946
.... **TCLC 6, 12, 19; DA; DAB; DAC; DAM MST, NOV; SSC 6; WLC**
See also AAYA 18; CA 110; 121; CDBLB 1914-1945; DA3; DLB 34, 70, 156, 178; MTCW 1, 2; SATA 20

Wells, Rosemary 1943- .... **CLC 12**
See also AAYA 13; CA 85-88; CANR 48; CLR 16; MAICYA; SAAS 1; SATA 18, 69

Welty, Eudora 1909- ...... **CLC 1, 2, 5, 14, 22, 33, 105; DA; DAB; DAC; DAM MST, NOV; SSC 1, 27; WLC**
See also CA 9-12R; CABS 1; CANR 32, 65; CDALB 1941-1968; DA3; DLB 2, 102, 143; DLBD 12; DLBY 87; MTCW 1, 2

Wen I-to 1899-1946 .... **TCLC 28**

Wentworth, Robert
See Hamilton, Edmond

Werfel, Franz (Viktor) 1890-1945 ... **TCLC 8**
See also CA 104; 161; DLB 81, 124

Wergeland, Henrik Arnold 1808-1845
.... **NCLC 5**

Wersba, Barbara 1932- .... **CLC 30**
See also AAYA 2, 30; CA 29-32R, 182; CAAE 182; CANR 16, 38; CLR 3; DLB 52; JRDA; MAICYA; SAAS 2; SATA 1, 58; SATA-Essay 103

Wertmueller, Lina 1928- .... **CLC 16**
See also CA 97-100; CANR 39, 78

Wescott, Glenway 1901-1987 .. **CLC 13; SSC 35**
See also CA 13-16R; 121; CANR 23, 70; DLB 4, 9, 102

Wesker, Arnold 1932- ... **CLC 3, 5, 42; DAB; DAM DRAM**
See also CA 1-4R; CAAS 7; CANR 1, 33; CDBLB 1960 to Present; DLB 13; MTCW 1

Wesley, Richard (Errol) 1945- .... **CLC 7**

See also BW 1; CA 57-60; CANR 27; DLB 38

Wessel, Johan Herman 1742-1785 .... **LC 7**

West, Anthony (Panther) 1914-1987 . **CLC 50**
See also CA 45-48; 124; CANR 3, 19; DLB 15

West, C. P.
See Wodehouse, P(elham) G(renville)

West, (Mary) Jessamyn 1902-1984 ... **CLC 7, 17**
See also CA 9-12R; 112; CANR 27; DLB 6; DLBY 84; MTCW 1, 2; SATA-Obit 37

West, Morris L(anglo) 1916- .... **CLC 6, 33**
See also CA 5-8R; CANR 24, 49, 64; MTCW 1, 2

West, Nathanael 1903-1940 . **TCLC 1, 14, 44; SSC 16**
See also CA 104; 125; CDALB 1929-1941; DA3; DLB 4, 9, 28; MTCW 1, 2

West, Owen
See Koontz, Dean R(ay)

West, Paul 1930- .... **CLC 7, 14, 96**
See also CA 13-16R; CAAS 7; CANR 22, 53, 76; DLB 14; INT CANR-22; MTCW 2

West, Rebecca 1892-1983 ... **CLC 7, 9, 31, 50**
See also CA 5-8R; 109; CANR 19; DLB 36; DLBY 83; MTCW 1, 2

Westall, Robert (Atkinson) 1929-1993
.... **CLC 17**
See also AAYA 12; CA 69-72; 141; CANR 18, 68; CLR 13; JRDA; MAICYA; SAAS 2; SATA 23, 69; SATA-Obit 75

Westermarck, Edward 1862-1939 . **TCLC 87**

Westlake, Donald E(dwin) 1933- . **CLC 7, 33; DAM POP**
See also CA 17-20R; CAAS 13; CANR 16, 44, 65; INT CANR-16; MTCW 2

Westmacott, Mary
See Christie, Agatha (Mary Clarissa)

Weston, Allen
See Norton, Andre

Wetcheek, J. L.
See Feuchtwanger, Lion

Wetering, Janwillem van de
See van de Wetering, Janwillem

Wetherald, Agnes Ethelwyn 1857-1940
.... **TCLC 81**
See also DLB 99

Wetherell, Elizabeth
See Warner, Susan (Bogert)

Whale, James 1889-1957 .... **TCLC 63**

Whalen, Philip 1923- .... **CLC 6, 29**
See also CA 9-12R; CANR 5, 39; DLB 16

Wharton, Edith (Newbold Jones) 1862-1937
TCLC 3, 9, 27, 53; DA; DAB; DAC; DAM MST, NOV; SSC 6; WLC
See also AAYA 25; CA 104; 132; CDALB 1865-1917; DA3; DLB 4, 9, 12, 78, 189; DLBD 13; MTCW 1, 2

Wharton, James
See Mencken, H(enry) L(ouis)

Wharton, William (a pseudonym) .. **CLC 18, 37**
See also CA 93-96; DLBY 80; INT 93-96

Wheatley (Peters), Phillis 1754(?)-1784
..... **LC 3, 50; BLC 3; DA; DAC; DAM MST, MULT, POET; PC 3; WLC**
See also CDALB 1640-1865; DA3; DLB 31, 50

Wheelock, John Hall 1886-1978 .... **CLC 14**
See also CA 13-16R; 77-80; CANR 14; DLB 45

White, E(lwyn) B(rooks) 1899-1985 . **CLC 10, 34, 39; DAM POP**
See also AITN 2; CA 13-16R; 116; CANR 16, 37; CDALBS; CLR 1, 21; DA3; DLB 11, 22; MAICYA; MTCW 1, 2; SATA 2, 29, 100; SATA-Obit 44

White, Edmund (Valentine III) 1940-
.... **CLC 27, 110; DAM POP**
See also AAYA 7; CA 45-48; CANR 3, 19, 36, 62; DA3; MTCW 1, 2

White, Patrick (Victor Martindale) 1912-1990 . **CLC 3, 4, 5, 7, 9, 18, 65, 69**
See also CA 81-84; 132; CANR 43; MTCW 1

White, Phyllis Dorothy James 1920-
See James, P. D.
See also CA 21-24R; CANR 17, 43, 65; DAM POP; DA3; MTCW 1, 2

White, T(erence) H(anbury) 1906-1964
.... **CLC 30**
See also AAYA 22; CA 73-76; CANR 37; DLB 160; JRDA; MAICYA; SATA 12

White, Terence de Vere 1912-1994 ... **CLC 49**
See also CA 49-52; 145; CANR 3

White, Walter
See White, Walter F(rancis)
See also BLC; DAM MULT

White, Walter F(rancis) 1893-1955
.... **TCLC 15**
See also White, Walter BW 1; CA 115; 124; DLB 51

White, William Hale 1831-1913
See Rutherford, Mark
See also CA 121

Whitehead, Alfred North 1861-1947
.... **TCLC 97**
See also CA 117; 165; DLB 100

Whitehead, E(dward) A(nthony) 1933-
.... **CLC 5**
See also CA 65-68; CANR 58

Whitemore, Hugh (John) 1936- .... **CLC 37**
See also CA 132; CANR 77; INT 132

Whitman, Sarah Helen (Power) 1803-1878
NCLC 19
See also DLB 1

Whitman, Walt(er) 1819-1892 .. **NCLC 4, 31, 81; DA; DAB; DAC; DAM MST, POET; PC 3; WLC**
See also CDALB 1640-1865; DA3; DLB 3, 64; SATA 20

Whitney, Phyllis A(yame) 1903- ...... **CLC 42; DAM POP**
See also AITN 2; BEST 90:3; CA 1-4R; CANR 3, 25, 38, 60; CLR 59; DA3; JRDA; MAICYA; MTCW 2; SATA 1, 30

Whittemore, (Edward) Reed (Jr.) 1919-
.... **CLC 4**
See also CA 9-12R; CAAS 8; CANR 4; DLB 5

Whittier, John Greenleaf 1807-1892
.... **NCLC 8, 59**
See also DLB 1

Whittlebot, Hernia
See Coward, Noel (Peirce)

Wicker, Thomas Grey 1926-
See Wicker, Tom
See also CA 65-68; CANR 21, 46

Wicker, Tom .... **CLC 7**
See also Wicker, Thomas Grey

Wideman, John Edgar 1941- . **CLC 5, 34, 36, 67, 122; BLC 3; DAM MULT**
See also BW 2, 3; CA 85-88; CANR 14, 42, 67; DLB 33, 143; MTCW 2

Wiebe, Rudy (Henry) 1934- .. **CLC 6, 11, 14; DAC; DAM MST**
See also CA 37-40R; CANR 42, 67; DLB 60

Wieland, Christoph Martin 1733-1813
.... **NCLC 17**
See also DLB 97

Wiene, Robert 1881-1938 .... **TCLC 56**

Wieners, John 1934- .... **CLC 7**
See also CA 13-16R; DLB 16

Wiesel, Elie(zer) 1928- .... **CLC 3, 5, 11, 37;**

DC Cumulative Nationality Index

ALGERIAN

Camus, Albert **2**

AMERICAN

Albee, Edward (Franklin III) **11**
Baldwin, James (Arthur) **1**
Baraka, Amiri **6**
Brown, William Wells **1**
Bullins, Ed **6**
Chase, Mary (Coyle) **1**
Childress, Alice **4**
Chin, Frank (Chew Jr.) **7**
Elder, Lonne III **8**
Fornes, Maria Irene **10**
Fuller, Charles (H. Jr.) **1**
Glaspell, Susan **10**
Gordone, Charles **8**
Gray, Spalding **7**
Hansberry, Lorraine (Vivian) **2**
Hellman, Lillian (Florence) **1**
Henley, Beth **6**
Hughes, (James) Langston **3**
Hurston, Zora Neale **12**
Hwang, David Henry **4**
Kennedy, Adrienne (Lita) **5**
Kramer, Larry **8**
Kushner, Tony **10**
Mamet, David (Alan) **4**
Mann, Emily **7**
Miller, Arthur **1**
Norman, Marsha **8**
Odets, Clifford **6**
Shange, Ntozake **3**
Shepard, Sam **5**
Sheridan, Richard Brinsley **1**
Valdez, Luis (Miguel) **10**
Wasserstein, Wendy **4**
Wilder, Thornton (Niven) **1**
Williams, Tennessee **4**
Wilson, August **2**
Zindel, Paul **5**

AUSTRIAN

Hofmannsthal, Hugo von **4**

BARBADIAN

Kennedy, Adrienne (Lita) **5**

CUBAN

Fornes, Maria Irene **10**

CZECH

Capek, Karel **1**
Havel, Vaclav **6**

ENGLISH

Beaumont, Francis **6**
Behn, Aphra **4**
Churchill, Caryl **5**
Congreve, William **2**
Dekker, Thomas **12**
Dryden, John **3**
Fletcher, John **6**
Jonson, Ben(jamin) **4**
Kyd, Thomas **3**
Lyly, John **7**
Marlowe, Christopher **1**
Middleton, Thomas **5**
Orton, Joe **3**
Shaffer, Peter (Levin) **7**
Stoppard, Tom **6**
Webster, John **2**

FRENCH

Anouilh, Jean (Marie Lucien Pierre) **8**
Beaumarchais, Pierre-Augustin Caron de **4**
Camus, Albert **2**
Dumas, Alexandre (fils) **1**
Ionesco, Eugene **12**
Marivaux, Pierre Carlet de Chamblain de **7**
Perrault, Charles **12**
Rostand, Edmond (Eugene Alexis) **10**
Sartre, Jean-Paul **3**
Scribe, (Augustin) Eugene **5**

GERMAN

Brecht, (Eugen) Bertolt (Friedrich) **3**
Schiller, Friedrich **12**

GREEK

Aeschylus **8**
Aristophanes **2**
Euripides **4**
Menander **3**
Sophocles **1**

IRISH

Friel, Brian **8**
Goldsmith, Oliver **8**
O'Casey, Sean **12**
Synge, (Edmund) J(ohn) M(illington) **2**

ITALIAN

Fo, Dario **10**
Pirandello, Luigi **5**

JAPANESE

Mishima, Yukio **1**
Zeami **7**

NIGERIAN

Clark, John Pepper **5**
Soyinka, Wole **2**

NORWEGIAN

Ibsen, Henrik (Johan) **2**

ROMAN

Seneca, Lucius Annaeus **5**
Terence **7**

ROMANIAN

Ionesco, Eugene **12**

RUSSIAN

Chekhov, Anton (Pavlovich) **9**
Gogol, Nikolai (Vasilyevich) **1**
Turgenev, Ivan **7**

SOUTH AFRICAN

Fugard, (Harold) Athol **3**

SPANISH

Calderon de la Barca, Pedro **3**
Garcia Lorca, Federico **2**

ST. LUCIAN

Walcott, Derek (Alton) **7**

DC Cumulative Title Index

Title Index

Title Index

Title Index

ISBN 0-7876-3140-X

90000

9 780787 631406